FOR REFERENCE
Do Not Take
From This Room

Contemporary
Literary Criticism

Guide to Gale Literary Criticism Series

For criticism on	Consult these Gale series
Authors now living or who died after December 31, 1959	*CONTEMPORARY LITERARY CRITICISM (CLC)*
Authors who died between 1900 and 1959	*TWENTIETH-CENTURY LITERARY CRITICISM (TCLC)*
Authors who died between 1800 and 1899	*NINETEENTH-CENTURY LITERATURE CRITICISM (NCLC)*
Authors who died between 1400 and 1799	*LITERATURE CRITICISM FROM 1400 TO 1800 (LC)* *SHAKESPEAREAN CRITICISM (SC)*
Authors who died before 1400	*CLASSICAL AND MEDIEVAL LITERATURE CRITICISM (CMLC)*
Black writers of the past two hundred years	*BLACK LITERATURE CRITICISM (BLC)*
Authors of books for children and young adults	*CHILDREN'S LITERATURE REVIEW (CLR)*
Dramatists	*DRAMA CRITICISM (DC)*
Hispanic writers of the late nineteenth and twentieth centuries	*HISPANIC LITERATURE CRITICISM (HLC)*
Poets	*POETRY CRITICISM (PC)*
Short story writers	*SHORT STORY CRITICISM (SSC)*
Major authors from the Renaissance to the present	*WORLD LITERATURE CRITICISM, 1500 TO THE PRESENT (WLC)*

ISSN 0091-3421

Volume 83

Contemporary Literary Criticism

Excerpts from Criticism of the Works
of Today's Novelists, Poets, Playwrights,
Short Story Writers, Scriptwriters, and
Other Creative Writers

James P. Draper
EDITOR

Jennifer Brostrom
Brigham Narins
ASSOCIATE EDITORS, CLC

Jeffery Chapman
Nancy Dziedzic
Jennifer Gariepy
Christopher Giroux
Kelly Hill
Drew Kalasky
Marie Lazzari
Thomas Ligotti
Jennifer Mast
Sean René Pollock
Brian St. Germain
Lynn Spampinato
Janet Witalec
ASSOCIATE EDITORS

 Gale Research Inc. • *DETROIT* • *WASHINGTON, D.C.* • *LONDON*

STAFF

James P. Draper, *Editor*

Jennifer Brostrom, Jeffery Chapman, Nancy Dziedzic, Jennifer Gariepy, Christopher Giroux, Kelly Hill, Drew Kalasky,
Marie Lazzari, Thomas Ligotti, Jennifer Mast, Brigham Narins, Sean René Pollock, Brian St. Germain,
Lynn M. Spampinato, Janet Witalec, *Associate Editors*

Martha Bommarito, *Assistant Editor*

Jeanne A. Gough, *Permissions & Production Manager*
Linda M. Pugliese, *Production Supervisor*
Donna Craft, Paul Lewon, Maureen A. Puhl, Camille P. Robinson, Sheila Walencewicz, *Editorial Associates*

Sandra C. Davis, *Permissions Supervisor (Text)*
Maria L. Franklin, Josephine M. Keene, Michele Lonoconus, Shalice Shah, Kimberly F. Smilay, *Permissions Associates*
Jennifer A. Arnold, Brandy C. Merritt, *Permissions Assistants*

Margaret A. Chamberlain, *Permissions Supervisor (Pictures)*
Pamela A. Hayes, Arlene Johnson, Keith Reed, Barbara A. Wallace, *Permissions Associates*
Susan Brohman, *Permissions Assistant*

Victoria B. Cariappa, *Research Manager*
Frank Vincent Castronova, Andrew Guy Malonis, Mary Beth McElmeel,
Donna Melnychenko, Tamara C. Nott, Norma Sawaya, Tracie A. Richardson, *Research Associates*
Melissa E. Brown, Maria E. Bryson, Eva M. Felts, Shirley Gates, Michele McRobert, Michele P. Pica, Amy T. Roy,
Laurel D. Sprague, Amy B. Wieczorek, *Research Assistants*

Mary Beth Trimper, *Production Director*
Deborah Milliken, *Production Assistant*

Cynthia Baldwin, *Product Design Manager*
Barbara J. Yarrow, *Graphic Services Supervisor*
Todd Nessel, *Macintosh Artist*
Willie F. Mathis, *Camera Operator*

Library of Congress Catalog Card Number 76-38938
ISBN 0-8103-4991-4
ISSN 0091-3421

Printed in the United States of America
Published simultaneously in the United Kingdom
by Gale Research International Limited
(An affiliated company of Gale Research Inc.)
10 9 8 7 6 5 4 3 2 1

I(T)P™

The trademark **ITP** is used under license.

Contents

Preface vii

Acknowledgments xi

Preface

A Comprehensive Information Source on Contemporary Literature

Named "one of the twenty-five most distinguished reference titles published during the past twenty-five years" by *Reference Quarterly*, the *Contemporary Literary Criticism (CLC)* series provides readers with critical commentary and general information on more than 2,000 authors now living or who died after December 31, 1959. Previous to the publication of the first volume of *CLC* in 1973, there was no ongoing digest monitoring scholarly and popular sources of critical opinion and explication of modern literature. *CLC*, therefore, has fulfilled an essential need, particularly since the complexity and variety of contemporary literature makes the function of criticism especially important to today's reader.

Scope of the Series

CLC presents significant passages from published criticism of works by creative writers. Since many of the authors covered by *CLC* inspire continual critical commentary, writers are often represented in more than one volume. There is, of course, no duplication of reprinted criticism.

Authors are selected for inclusion for a variety of reasons, among them the publication or dramatic production of a critically acclaimed new work, the reception of a major literary award, revival of interest in past writings, or the adaptation of a literary work to film or television.

Attention is also given to several other groups of writers—authors of considerable public interest—about whose work criticism is often difficult to locate. These include mystery and science fiction writers, literary and social critics, foreign writers, and authors who represent particular ethnic groups within the United States.

Format of the Book

Each *CLC* volume contains about 500 individual excerpts taken from hundreds of book review periodicals, general magazines, scholarly journals, monographs, and books. Entries include critical evaluations spanning from the beginning of an author's career to the most current commentary. Interviews, feature articles, and other published writings that offer insight into the author's works are also presented. Students, teachers, librarians, and researchers will find that the generous excerpts and supplementary material in *CLC* provide them with vital information required to write a term paper, analyze a poem, or lead a book discussion group. In addition, complete bibliographical citations note the original source and all of the information necessary for a term paper footnote or bibliography.

Features

A *CLC* author entry consists of the following elements:

- The **Author Heading** cites the author's name in the form under which the author has most commonly published, followed by birth date, and death date when applicable. Uncertainty as to a birth or death date is indicated by a question mark.

■ A **Portrait** of the author is included when available.

■ A brief **Biographical and Critical Introduction** to the author and his or her work precedes the excerpted criticism. The first line of the introduction provides the author's full name, pseudonyms (if applicable), nationality, and a listing of genres in which the author has written. Previous volumes of *CLC* in which the author has been featured are also listed in the introduction.

■ A list of **Principal Works** notes the most important works by the author.

■ The **Excerpted Criticism** represents various kinds of critical writing, ranging in form from the brief review to the scholarly exegesis. Essays are selected by the editors to reflect the spectrum of opinion about a specific work or about an author's literary career in general. The excerpts are presented chronologically, adding a useful perspective to the entry. All titles by the author featured in the entry are printed in boldface type, which enables the reader to easily identify the works being discussed. Publication information (such as publisher names and book prices) and parenthetical numerical references (such as footnotes or page and line references to specific editions of a work) have been deleted at the editor's discretion to provide smoother reading of the text.

■ Critical essays are prefaced by **Explanatory Notes** as an additional aid to readers. These notes may provide several types of valuable information, including: the reputation of the critic, the importance of the work of criticism, the commentator's approach to the author's work, the purpose of the criticism, and changes in critical trends regarding the author.

■ A complete **Bibliographical Citation** designed to help the user find the original essay or book follows each excerpt.

■ A concise **Further Reading** section appears at the end of entries on authors for whom a significant amount of criticism exists in addition to the pieces reprinted in *CLC*. Cross-references to other useful sources published by Gale Research in which the author has appeared are also included: *Children's Literature Review, Contemporary Authors, Something about the Author, Dictionary of Literary Biography, Drama Criticism, Poetry Criticism, Short Story Criticism, Contemporary Authors Autobiography Series,* and *Something about the Author Autobiography Series.*

Other Features

CLC also includes the following features:

■ An **Acknowledgments** section lists the copyright holders who have granted permission to reprint material in this volume of *CLC*. It does not, however, list every book or periodical reprinted or consulted during the preparation of the volume.

■ A **Cumulative Author Index** lists all the authors who have appeared in the various literary criticism series published by Gale Research, with cross-references to Gale's biographical and autobiographical series. A full listing of the series referenced there appears on the first page of the indexes of this volume. Readers will welcome this cumulated author index as a useful tool for locating an author within the various series. The index, which lists birth and death dates when available, will be particularly valuable for those authors who are identified with a certain period but whose death dates cause them to be placed in another, or for those authors whose careers span two periods. For example, Ernest Hemingway is found in *CLC*, yet a writer often associated with him, F. Scott Fitzgerald, is found in *Twentieth-Century Literary Criticism.*

■ A **Cumulative Nationality Index** alphabetically lists all authors featured in *CLC* by nationality, followed by numbers corresponding to the volumes in which the authors appear.

■ A **Title Index** alphabetically lists all titles reviewed in the current volume of *CLC*. Listings are followed by the author's name and the corresponding page numbers where the titles are discussed. English translations of foreign titles and variations of titles are cross-referenced to the title under which a work was originally published. Titles of novels, novellas, dramas, films, record albums, and poetry, short story, and essay collections are printed in italics, while all individual poems, short stories, essays, and songs are printed in roman type within quotation marks; when published separately (e.g., T. S. Eliot's poem *The Waste Land*), the titles of long poems are printed in italics.

■ In response to numerous suggestions from librarians, Gale has also produced a **Special Paperbound Edition** of the *CLC* title index. This annual cumulation, which alphabetically lists all titles reviewed in the series, is available to all customers and is published with the first volume of *CLC* issued in each calendar year. Additional copies of the index are available upon request. Librarians and patrons will welcome this separate index: it saves shelf space, is easy to use, and is recyclable upon receipt of the following year's cumulation.

Citing *Contemporary Literary Criticism*

When writing papers, students who quote directly from any volume in the Literary Criticism Series may use the following general forms to footnote reprinted criticism. The first example pertains to material drawn from periodicals, the second to material reprinted in books:

[1]Anne Tyler, "Manic Monologue," *The New Republic* 200 (April 17, 1989), 44-6; excerpted and reprinted in *Contemporary Literary Criticism,* Vol. 58, ed. Roger Matuz (Detroit: Gale Research Inc., 1990), p. 325.

[2]Patrick Reilly, *The Literature of Guilt: From 'Gulliver' to Golding* (University of Iowa Press, 1988); excerpted and reprinted in *Contemporary Literary Criticism,* Vol. 58, ed. Roger Matuz (Detroit: Gale Research Inc., 1990), pp. 206-12.

Suggestions Are Welcome

The editor hopes that readers will find *CLC* a useful reference tool and welcomes comments about the work. Send comments and suggestions to: Editor, *Contemporary Literary Criticism,* Gale Research Inc., Penobscot Building, Detroit, MI 48226-4094.

Acknowledgments

The editors wish to thank the copyright holders of the excerpted criticism included in this volume, the permissions managers of many book and magazine publishing companies for assisting us in securing reprint rights, and Anthony Bogucki for assistance with copyright research. We are also grateful to the staffs of the Detroit Public Library, the Library of Congress, the University of Detroit Mercy Library, Wayne State University Purdy/Kresge Library Complex, and the University of Michigan Libraries for making their resources available to us. Following is a list of the copyright holders who have granted us permission to reprint material in this volume of *CLC*. Every effort has been made to trace copyright, but if omissions have been made, please let us know.

COPYRIGHTED EXCERPTS IN *CLC*, VOLUME 83, WERE REPRINTED FROM THE FOLLOWING PERIODICALS:

The American Book Review, v. 11, January/February, 1990. © 1990 by *The American Book Review*. Reprinted by permission of the publisher.—*The American Poetry Review*, v. 10, July-August, 1981 for "El Salvador: An Aide Memoire" by Carolyn Forché; v. 12, January-February, 1983 for "War as Parable and War as Fact: Herbert and Forché" by Larry Levis. Copyright © 1981, 1983 by World Poetry, Inc. Both reprinted by permission of the respective authors.—*Book Week—The Washington Post*, July 9, 1967. © 1967, *The Washington Post*. © 1994, The Washington Post Writers Group. Reprinted by permission of The Washington Post Writers Group—*Books in Canada*, v. 17, April, 1988 for "Village Scribe" by Brian Fawcett. Reprinted by permission of the author.—*The Centennial Review*, v. XXX, Spring, 1986 for "Politicizing the Modern: Carolyn Forché in El Salvador and America" by Michael Greer. © 1986 by The Centennial Review. Reprinted by permission of the publisher and the author.—*CLIO*, v. 14, Spring, 1985 for "Bakhtin's Truths of Laughter" by Robert Anchor. © 1985 by Robert H. Canary and Henry Kozicki. Reprinted by permission of the author.—*Commentary*, v. 39, April, 1965 for "Unworldly Wisdom" by Daniel J. Callahan; v. 83, April, 1987 for "Señor Borges's Portico" by Joseph Epstein. Copyright © 1965, 1987 by the American Jewish Committee. All rights reserved. Both reprinted by permission of the publisher and the respective authors.—*Commonweal*, v. CXV, December 2, 1988. Copyright © 1988 Commonweal Foundation. Reprinted by permission of Commonweal Foundation.—*The Commonweal*, v. XLII, June 22, 1945. Copyright 1945, renewed 1973 Commonweal Publishing Co., Inc. Reprinted by permission of the Commonweal Foundation./ v. LXII, May 13, 1955; v. LXIV, April 13, 1956. Copyright © 1955, renewed 1983; copyright © 1956, renewed 1984 Commonweal Publishing Co., Inc. Both reprinted by permission of Commonweal Foundation.—*Comparative Criticism*, v. 2, 1980 for "Between Marxism and Formalism: The Stylistics of Mikhail Bakhtin" by Ann Shukman. Reprinted by permission of the publisher and the author.—*Critical Inquiry*, v. 10, December, 1983 for "Shouts on the Street: Bakhtin's Anti-Linguistics" by Susan Stewart. © 1983 by The University of Chicago. Reprinted by permission of the publisher and the author.—*Encounter*, vs. LVIII & LIX, June-July, 1982 for "In the Labyrinth: The Borges Phenomenon" by James Neilson. © 1982 by the author./v. XXVIII, June, 1967 for an interview with Marshall McLuhan by G.E. Stearn. © 1967 by the author. Reprinted by permission of the Literary Estate of Marshall McLuhan.—*The Georgia Review*, v. XLI, Summer, 1987. Copyright, 1987, by the University of Georgia. Reprinted by permission of the publisher.—*The Hudson Review*, v. XLIII, Autumn, 1990. Copyright © 1990 by The Hudson Review, Inc. Reprinted by permission of the publisher.—*Interpretation: A Journal of Bible & Theology*, v. XXIV, January, 1970. Copyright 1970 Interpretation. Reprinted by permission of the publisher.—*International Journal of Women's Studies*, v. 1, May-June, 1978 for " 'Fear of Flying': Developing the Feminist Novel" by Joan Reardon. Copyright © Eden Press, 1978. Reprinted by permission of the author.—*The Journal of American History*, v. 78, June, 1991. Copyright Organization of American Historians, 1991. Reprinted by permission of the publisher.—*The Kenyon Review*, n.s. v. XIII, Spring, 1991 for "Solitaires and Storytellers, Magicians and Pagans: Five Poets in the World" by Leslie Ullman; v. XV, Summer, 1993 for an interview with Joy Harjo by Marilyn Kallet. Copyright 1991, 1993 by Kenyon College. All rights reserved. Both reprinted by permission of the respective authors.—*Maclean's Magazine*, v. 103, February 19, 1990. © 1990 by *Maclean's Magazine*. Reprinted by permission of the publisher.—*Modern Drama*, v. 10, February 1968 for

COPYRIGHTED EXCERPTS IN *CLC,* VOLUME 83, WERE REPRINTED FROM THE FOLLOWING BOOKS:

in *Pasó por Aquí: Critical Essays on the New Mexican Literary Tradition, 1542-1988.* Edited by Erlinda Gonzales-Berry. University of New Mexico Press, 1989. © 1989 by the University of New Mexico Press. All rights reserved. Reprinted by permission of the publisher.—Todorov, Tzvetan. From "Bakhtin's Theory of the Utterance," translated by Claudine Frank, in *Semiotics Themes.* Edited by Richard T. De George. University of Kansas Publications, 1981. Copyright 1981 Center for Humanistic Studies: University of Kansas, 1981. Reprinted by permission of the publisher.—Todorov, Tzvetan. From *Literature and Its Theorists: A Personal View of Twentieth-Century Criticism.* Translated by Catherine Porter. Cornell, 1987. Translation copyright © 1987 by Cornell University. All rights reserved. Used by permission of the publisher, Cornell University Press.—Ulibarri, Sabine R. From *Mi Abuela Fumaba Puros y Otros Cuentos de Tierra Amarilla/My Grandma Smoked Cigars and Other Stories.* Quinto Sol Publications, Inc., 1977. Copyright © 1977 by Sabine R. Ulibarri. All rights reserved.—Woodcock, George. From *The World of Canadian Writing: Critiques & Recollections.* Douglas & McIntyre, 1980. Copyright © 1980 by George Woodcock. All rights reserved. Reprinted by permission of the author.

PHOTOGRAPHS AND ILLUSTRATIONS APPEARING IN *CLC*, VOLUME 83, WERE RECEIVED FROM THE FOLLOWING SOURCES:

Mikhail Bakhtin

1895-1975

(Full name Mikhail Mikhailovich Bakhtin; also transliterated as Bachtin and Baxtin; also published under the names P. N. Medvedev and V. N. Voloshinov) Russian critic, essayist, and literary theorist.

The following entry provides an overview of Bakhtin's career.

INTRODUCTION

One of the most significant literary theorists of the twentieth century, Bakhtin is noted for his studies of the relationship between language, popular culture, and the history of the novel as a literary genre. Claiming that language is an evolving entity whose form and meaning are constantly molded by history and culture, Bakhtin rejected rigid systems of thought that could not account for what he termed "heteroglossia": the polyphony of languages and perspectives that make up modern society and are reflected in its art—most strikingly for Bakhtin in the novel.

Biographical Information

Born in Orel, south of Moscow, Russia, Bakhtin grew up in Vilnius, Lithuania and the Russian port city Odessa. He attended Novorossia University and later transferred to Petersburg University, from which he graduated in 1918. Bakhtin began writing in Petrograd during the postrevolutionary regime of Joseph Stalin, publishing his early works, *Formal'nyj metod v literaturovedenii* (1928; *The Formal Method in Literary Scholarship*), *Freidizm: Kriticheskii ocherk* (1927; *Freudianism: A Marxist Critique*), and *Marksizm i filosofija jazyka* (1929; *Marxism and the Philosophy of Language*) under the names of his students Pavel Nikolaevich Medvedev and V. N. Voloshinov to avoid the censorship and possible exile or execution common to intellectuals during the Stalinist administration. Despite his precautions, Bakhtin fell into disfavor with the government and was arrested in 1929. Due to his poor health, he was exiled to the Russian territory Kazakh rather than sent to prison camp. Before leaving, however, Bakhtin published *Problemy tvorčestva Dostoevskogo* (1929; *Problems of Dostoevsky's Poetics*) under his own name; the book was immediately suppressed by the government. Bakhtin lived in Kazakh from 1929 to 1936, preparing his dissertation on the works of François Rabelais. Completed in 1940, *Tvorčestva Fransua Rable i narodnaja kul'tura srednevekov'ja i Renessansa* (*Rabelais and His World*) was suppressed by officials until 1965. Bakhtin taught at the Mordovian Teachers' Training College until the beginning of World War II, when he took time off to work on another manuscript. He returned to the college after the war, where he remained until his retirement in 1961. In the 1960s and early 1970s, Bakhtin's reputation outside the Soviet Union grew with the publication of *Vo-*

prosy literatury i estetiki (*The Dialogic Imagination*) in 1973, and with the increasing academic interest in deconstructionist and structuralist theory. He died in Moscow in 1975.

Major Works

Bakhtin is credited with introducing several seminal concepts to the field of literary theory. Contemporary critics comment that in the earliest works Bakhtin's ideas proved to be precursors to much modern structuralist and poststructuralist theory. In *The Formal Method in Literary Scholarship*, Bakhtin criticized Russian Formalism's essentialist approach to literature, positing instead a sociological materialist method of study. *Marxism and the Philosophy of Language* outlines Bakhtin's sociohistorical theory of language, criticizing Ferdinand de Saussure's biophysiological linguistics. *Freudianism: A Marxist Critique* evaluates Freudian psychoanalysis from a Marxist materialist perspective. In his later works, Bakhtin expanded upon his sociohistorical focus—which he would eventually term "heteroglossia"— applying it to literature as well as linguistics. *Problems of Dostoevsky's Poetics* presents the ideas of polyphony and dialogism. Contending that Dostoevsky created a new kind of novel by giving each of his characters an individual voice unmarked by his own beliefs and opinions, Bakhtin believed that Dostoevsky's work proved that authors could escape their own reality in order to create another. The various voices of the novel together form what Bakhtin termed "dialogism"—the democratic and polyphonic intermingling of "high" and "low" forms of language and culture that reflects the heteroglot society at large. The concept of dialogism appears in most of Bakhtin's works and forms the basis of many of his literary and cultural theories. In *Rabelais and His World*, Bakhtin examined medieval and Renaissance European culture through an analysis of François Rabelais's *Gargantua and Pantagruel*. Using the concepts of carnival and the culture of laughter—both of which helped the underclasses in medieval and Renaissance times to parody official languages and established notions of high culture, as in, according to Bakhtin, Rabelais's free display of the human body—Bakhtin asserted that the carnival liberated and empowered those in the lower strata of society. The collection of essays entitled *The Dialogic Imagination* outlines Bakhtin's theory of the novel and includes much of his language theory, particularly in the essay "Discourse in the Novel."

Critical Reception

After decades of suppression in Soviet Russia, Bakhtinian theory emerged in the West in the early 1960s as a major force in modern linguistics. Characterized by an aversion to the more systematized theories of such thinkers as Ferdinand de Saussure and Roman Jakobson, Bakhtin's concepts favored contextual openness and dialogue. Tzvetan Todorov and other critics have perceived this as evidence of an inherent lack of structure and therefore a major flaw in Bakhtin's work. Other critics such as Michael Holquist contend that Bakhtin's approach, while less structured than others, is not without order and reflects his conception of the novel: Bakhtin's "concept of language stands in relation to others . . . much as the novel stands in opposition to other, more formalized genres. That is, the novel—as Bakhtin more than anyone has taught us to see—does not lack its organizing principles, but they are of a different order from those regulating sonnets or odes." Controversy has also surrounded Bakhtin's theory of the carnival. Many scholars believe that the carnival primarily served not as a form of liberation and empowerment for the lower classes—as Bakhtin asserted—but as a practical method supported by the upper classes for defusing the frustrations of the underclasses, thus squelching real revolutionary fervor. Nonetheless, many critics have praised Bakhtin's attempts to "democratize" literature and theory, maintaining that his depiction of literature as a product and reflection of popular rather than high or elite culture is emblematic of humanistic social ideals. Stanley Aronowitz has written: "Bakhtin is the social theorist of difference, who, unlike Derrida and Foucault, gives top billing to historical agents and agency. For Bakhtin, there are no privileged protagonists, no final solutions, only a panoply of divergent voices which somehow make their own music."

PRINCIPAL WORKS

Freidizm: Kriticheskii ocherk [as V. N. Voloshinov] (criticism) 1927
  [*Freudianism: A Marxist Critique* 1976]
Formal'nyj metod v literaturovedenii [as P. N. Medvedev] (criticism) 1928
  [*The Formal Method in Literary Scholarship* 1978]
Marksizm i filosofija jazyka [as V. N. Voloshinov] (criticism) 1929
  [*Marxism and the Philosophy of Language* 1973]
Problemy tvorčestva Dostoevskogo (criticism) 1929
  [*Problems of Dostoevsky's Poetics,* 1973]
Tvorčestva Fransua Rable i narodnaja kul'tura srednevekov'ja i Renessansa (criticism) 1965
  [*Rabelais and His World,* 1968]
Voprosy literatury i estetiki (essays) 1973
  [*The Dialogic Imagination,* 1981]

CRITICISM

Ann Shukman   (essay date 1980)

[*In the following excerpt, Shukman surveys Bakhtin's major works and disputes the assumption that works published under the names Medvedev and Voloshinov are solely attributable to Bakhtin, due primarily to what she considers drastic stylistic differences between the three scholars.*]

Outstanding among scholars who survived the decimation of the Leningrad intelligentsia in the late twenties and thirties is the literary historian, theorist and philosopher, Mikhail Mikhailovich Bakhtin. By the time of his death at the age of eighty in 1975, Bakhtin's reputation as an original thinker in the semiotic-structuralist manner was rapidly growing, both abroad and in his native land. Eulogies from, among others, Julie Kristeva (1970) and the Soviet semiotician Vyacheslav Vsevolodovich Ivanov (1973) spoke of Bakhtin as a man before his time by virtue of his ideas on the notion of text, on the communicative functions of language, and on the binary structures of culture. As a literary scholar his work was already widely known through his studies of Dostoevsky (1929/1972) and Rabelais (1965). The year of his death saw the publication in the Soviet Union of an important collection of papers, for the most part previously unpublished, **Questions of Literature and Aesthetics** (1975). These papers . . . concentrate for the most part on problems of the novel and of discourse in the novel, topics that have been central for Bakhtin's literary studies since the 1920s. There is also an English translation of the volume, **The Dialogic Imagination,** edited by Professor J. M. Holquist.

For a major thinker so close to us in time much about Bakhtin still remains unknown: the circumstances of his leaving Leningrad in 1929 immediately after the publication of the book on Dostoevsky, of the six years spent in remote Kustanai, of the loss in the early days of the war of a major work on the European novel; it is not clear why the publication of the study on Rabelais was delayed for twenty years, nor how he came to live and work in Saransk. Finally, and most importantly, there still remains the problem of the Bakhtin canon. When in 1973 Ivanov published his long and appreciative study of Bakhtin's contribution to semiotic thinking, he made the claim that Bakhtin was in fact the author of, or at least very largely responsible for, the books known as V. N. Voloshinov's *Freudianism* (1927) and *Marxism and the Philosophy of Language* (1929) and P. N. Medvedev's *The Formal Method in Literary Scholarship* (1928), as well as several papers published under Voloshinov's and Medvedev's names. Voloshinov and Medvedev, both established scholars in their own right who perished in the thirties (Voloshinov disappeared in 1934, Medvedev was 'illegally repressed' in 1938), were, according to Ivanov, close associates and pupils of Bakhtin. Bakhtin, possibly because of the onset of what was to become chronic osteomyelitis, seems to have had no established employment in Leningrad in the twenties, though he was associated with the State Institute for the History of the Arts, and with the State Publishing House. Voloshinov and Medvedev, both evidently enthusiastic Marxists, could, so the argument goes, have lent their names and status to get Bakhtin's work published. The main source of information on Bakhtin's life to date merely notes the friendship and scholarly associations among the three men, which dated back to the early twenties when all three were in Vitebsk. Bakhtin himself during his lifetime neither denied nor confirmed Ivanov's claims publicly. The question is no doubt more complex than Ivanov gave his readers to understand, and until the publication of more of Bakhtin's archive the question remains an open one. . . .

Problems of Dostoevsky's Poetics (1929/1972) is Bakhtin's best-known work and the first to be widely translated. As a profound and original reading of Dostoevsky's fictional writings and an epoch-making investigation of types of discourse in the novel, the book is still essential reading for anyone concerned with the theory of the novel, or with Dostoevsky studies. Julia Kristeva's preface to one of the two French versions (1970) claims Bakhtin as a pioneer thinker in the theory of the anti-representational text, and of language as a self-creating process. Although Bakhtin's theory of the novel is based on discourse rather than on represented world, for him behind each 'voice' that makes up the plural novel-text is a 'consciousness' which is an ultimate reality; and Kristeva's epistemological void is alien to Bakhtin's personalism, steeped as it is in Western humanist values.

Problems of Dostoevsky's Poetics is the cornerstone of Bakhtin's later thinking and, although his ideas were added to, modified, and rephrased, the essential is already here. The book is divided into five substantial chapters. The first considers previous Dostoevsky criticism and puts forward the notion of the 'polyphonic' text. It was Dostoevsky's genius, according to Bakhtin, to be the first writer to come to a new manner of artistic thinking that presented human consciousness in all its fullness and thereby broke out of the shackles of 'monologic' artistic thinking:

> The originality of Dostoevsky lies not in the fact that he monologically proclaimed the value of the personality (others had done this before him), but in that he was able to see the personality objectively-artistically, and to show it as another, someone else's, personality, without making it lyrical, without fusing his voice with its, and at the same time not reducing it to a reified psychic reality.

The polyphonic work is constructed on the principles of dialogue, so that there is no one dominant voice, but a plurality of voices (consciousnesses) of equal validity, among which the author's may be one.

The second chapter discusses characterization in Dostoevsky's works and authorial attitudes to character. The Dostoevskian character, Bakhtin suggests, is presented through his own self-awareness: all the fixed objective qualities of the character, his social position, his personal characteristics, his environment, even his appearance, are presented through the character's own reflections. In novels before Dostoevsky's the self-awareness of the character was usually one element only in the construction of the character. In Dostoevsky's works the author does not 're-serve anything for himself', the character lives himself in endless ideological confrontations and discussions with himself and with others. The third chapter, 'The Idea in Dostoevsky', discusses the treatment of ideological material in the novels and how it is essentially bound up with characterization.

The fourth chapter looks at Dostoevsky's works from the perspective of classical and West European literature and suggests that the novels belong to the genre of Menippean satire and 'carnival' literature. In later works, discussed below, Bakhtin looks to these sources as the originators of the genre of the novel as a whole, and these ideas are the basis for his study of Rabelais.

The final chapter entitled 'The Word in Dostoevsky' is the key section for the understanding of Bakhtin's theory of discourse in the novel. By 'word' (*slovo*) Bakhtin means 'language in its concrete and living totality' as against the abstract and systematized language studied in linguistics. This is language in its essentially dialogic functioning, the 'discourse' of actual communication. One of the central notions running through *Problems of Dostoevsky's Poetics* is that of *dialogue,* understood in the widest sense as the continuous flow of verbal communication in which man thinks, enters into social relations, and out of which he builds his literature and ideologies. 'For dialogic relationships are . . . an almost universal phenomenon that permeates all human speech and all relationships and manifestations of human life, in general everything that has sense and meaning'. Closely connected with the notion of dialogue is the notion of *consciousness.* The ultimate reality that lies beneath all human activity is the individual personality and its self-awareness in consciousness. Consciousness is itself dialogic, is in dialogic relationships with other consciousnesses, and can be revealed only through dialogue.

For there to be dialogue (or polyphony) there must be awareness of the 'other's' voice, the 'you' which is neither

'I' nor 'he'. A key concept in Bakhtin's thinking about language is the opposition 'own voice'/'other's voice'. This concept can be neatly expressed in Russian (*svoi:* 'own'/*chuzhoi:* 'other's') but translates more clumsily into English where *chuzhoi* has been variously rendered as 'someone else's', 'another's', even 'alien', or 'reported' (as in the English version of Voloshinov 1929). Bakhtin's typology of prose discourse distinguishes three main types, of which the third type, two-voice discourse, the most important type for the novel, is based on the own/other's distinction.

1. Discourse focused directly on to its referent which expresses the speaker's ultimate meaning.

2. 'Object discourse' (the speech of a represented character).

3. Discourse that focuses on 'another's discourse' (*chuzoe slovo*) or 'two-voice' discourse. This, the largest category, is further subdivided into:

(a) Unidirectional two-voice discourse (for example, first-person narrative, narrative by a narrator, stylization);

(b) Multidirectional two-voice discourse (this group includes all kinds of parody, and any reporting of another person's speech with a change of accent);

(c) The active type (or, reflected 'other's discourse')—this group includes: hidden internal polemic, polemically coloured autobiography, any discourse 'that glances round at another's discourse'; it includes also any replique in dialogue, as well as hidden dialogue.

Bakhtin points out that these schematic categories are in no way mutually exclusive, and in reality merge into one another, but a study of discourse 'from the point of view of its relationship to another's discourse has, it seems to us, exceptionally important significance for the understanding of literary prose' a view which many literary scholars today would agree with.

Bakhtin's ideas in **Problems of Dostoevsky's Poetics** give rise to at least two major objections, both of which Bakhtin was to some extent aware of and on which he commented. Firstly, if the polyphonic text is the open-ended self-revelation of a plurality of voices, then what gives the text its unity and actual finiteness? Bakhtin does no more than point to this problem in the Preface; but the problem is a real one and, being unresolved, leaves Bakhtin's theory a theory of discourse *in* the novel rather than a theory *of* the novel. The second objection is perhaps a weightier one: can one have any theory of literature, or theory of an aspect of literature, that ignores, as Bakhtin does, the boundary between fiction and life? The Dostoevskian character, we are told, 'rebels' against his literary embodiment, enters into 'free' dialogic relationships with the authorial voice. But this kind of 'life' of the character, his parity with the author, is in reality a fiction and an illusion, the 'own' and the 'other's' voice being both in fact the product of an author. Against this, Bakhtin argues as follows:

> On this point we should forestall a possible misunderstanding. It might seem that the independence of the hero contradicts the fact that he is wholly given merely as an aspect of the work of literature and consequently is wholly, from beginning to end, created by the author. In fact this contradiction does not exist. We are arguing for the freedom of the hero within the bounds of the artistic intention, and in this sense, the freedom of the hero is just as much created as the unfreedom of the object- [i. e. reified] hero.

For, Bakhtin then argues, to create is not the same as to invent. Creation 'is bound both by its own laws and by the laws of the material with which it is working'; creation, in fact, 'merely reveals that which is given in the object itself'. These remarks should probably be interpreted to mean that art is a search for truth, and that truth is truth whether it is within the fictional world or without. One is left with the feeling that what **Problems of Dostoevsky's Poetics** is ultimately about is a philosophy of man rather than a theory of literature. It is interesting to note in this connection how far Bakhtin is from the Formalist position: for them the starting point was the notion of *literariness,* the qualities which mark off literature from non-literature.

These objections apart, **Problems of Dostoevsky's Poetics** is a seminal work: it not only laid the foundation for many of the key ideas in Bakhtin's later thinking, but it opened up a totally new way of considering the novel. In his subsequent writings on the novel Bakhtin moved on from the idea of the polyphony of the Dostoevskian novel to a view of the essential polyphony (or 'polyglottism'—*mnogoyazychie* was his later term) of all novels as compared with other genres. His investigations into the prehistory of the European novel led him to explore the binary nature of human culture and to give profound significance to the formative role of unofficial, 'carnival' or 'laughter' culture. He developed some original notions about the time structures of literature, and of the novel as compared with other genres, seeing the novel as essentially open-ended, concerned with the flow of time, and with contact with contemporaneity, as against the epic, for instance, whose time was distanced and closed. Through all his works is the underlying notion of man and of human values, as the hub of all literary activity.

The years spent before the war in remote regions far from the main centres of Russian cultural life were fruitful ones for Bakhtin. By the mid thirties he had completed **'The Word in the Novel'** (1935), a book-length study of the stylistics of the novel. . . . This work, like most of Bakhtin's work from this period, was published only in 1975. It begins with a criticism of contemporary stylistics which, Bakhtin argues, has so far been unable to deal with the novel as such. This is because stylistics has been 'deaf to dialogue'. The second chapter explores the differences between the word in poetry and the word in the novel: unlike the essentially polyglot nature of novel-discourse, poetry-discourse is characterized by its unitary and incontrovertible nature:

> The world of poetry, however many contradictions and hopeless conflicts are revealed in it by the poet, is always illumined by unitary and incontrovertible discourse. Contradictions, conflicts and doubts remain in the object, in the

thought and experiences, i.e. in the material, but not in the language. In poetry the word about doubt must be a word without doubt.

Subsequent chapters discuss polyglottism in the novel, the 'speaking man' in the novel, and the development of the European novel.

In 1937-8, Bakhtin completed a large work on the European novel of education of which only a section, **'Forms of Time and of Chronotopos in the Novel',** survives (1938). This study, to which Bakhtin added concluding remarks in 1973, is a masterly survey of the representation of time and space in the novel. Bakhtin argues that the *chronotopos* (lit. the time-space) has important genre-defining significance for literature: 'One can say directly that it is the chronotopos which determines genre and subtypes of genre. . . The chronotopos as a form-content category also determines (to a considerable extent) the image of man in literature. This image is always essentially chronotopic'. Bakhtin follows these ideas through in considerations of the Greek novel; the works of Apuleius and Petronius; biography and autobiography in ancient literature; historical inversion and the chronotopos in folklore; the books of chivalry; the functions of the rogue, buffoon and fool in the novel; the chronotopos in Rabelais and its roots in folklore; the idyllic chronotopos. The concluding remarks briefly survey the eighteenth- and nineteenth-century novel. This study must be classed as one of Bakhtin's finest works. As with the notion of dialogue in *Problems of Dostoevsky's Poetics,* so here with the notion of the chronotopos, what could have been a mere technical device becomes the starting point for a rich investigation into the nature of man in literature and the function of literature in human culture.

By 1937 Bakhtin had returned from exile and was settled near Moscow at Kimry, and by 1940 he had completed his doctoral dissertation on Rabelais (this was not defended until 1946, when it was awarded not a doctor's but merely a *kandidat*'s degree; it was published only in 1965). At this period, Bakhtin gave two lectures to the Institute of World Literature in Moscow, eventually published (in 1975) under the titles **'From the Prehistory of the Novel-Word'** (1940) and **'The Epic and the Novel'** (1941). . . . These two papers admirably summarize Bakhtin's thinking about the novel. The first paper is in two parts, the first discussing the interplay of languages in the novel, and the second considering the origins of the novel which, Bakhtin argues, arises from two factors—laughter and polyglottism (*mnogoyazychie*). Bakhtin surveys the currents of parody and travesty in classical and medieval literature, which led to the great novels of the Renaissance period. He concludes:

> At the end of the middle ages and at the time of the Renaissance parodic-travestying discourse burst all barriers. It burst into all the strict and closed direct genres . . . Finally there appeared the great novel of the age of the Renaissance, the novels of Rabelais and Cervantes. It is precisely in these two works that the novel-discourse which had been prepared by all the forms discussed above and also by the heritage of antiquity revealed its capabilities and played its titanic

role in the formation of the new literary-linguistic consciousness.

In **'The Epic and the Novel'** Bakhtin summarizes the principal differences between epic and novel. The novel, he says, is the 'sole genre in process of becoming, because it reflects more profoundly, more essentially, more sensitively and more quickly the becoming of reality itself'. The novel is distinguished by its 'three-dimensionality' which is bound up with the polyglot consciousness that is realized in it. The novel has radically different time-coordinates from those of other genres, by virtue of its central concern with the present and the process of becoming, and its images are radically different as befits its concern with contact with passing life. The epic world, on the other hand, 'is completed [*zavershen*] through and through not only as a real event of the distant past, but also in its purport and its values: it cannot be altered or reinterpreted or revalued . . . This is what determines the absolute epic distance'. Bakhtin goes on to discuss the role of memory and cultural values in the formation and preservation of literature, the opposition of official and unofficial literature, the role of carnival literature in the origin of the novel, and the particular importance of the Socratic dialogue and Menippean satire in this process, and he ends up with a discussion of the image of man in the novel.

In Bakhtin's study of Rabelais (1965) we find the fullest exposition of his ideas on the role of unofficial art, of the 'carnival' in culture. Carnival laughter is universal, everyone can and does laugh at everyone and everything including the sacred. This is laughter 'at the world'. But it is ambivalent laughter: 'It is merry and exultant and yet at the same time mocking and ridiculing. It negates and affirms, buries and resurrects'. All cultures have had their unofficial, carnival side, but in the Renaissance the laughter-culture came into the open: 'The Renaissance was, so to speak, the direct carnivalization of consciousness, world-outlook and literature'. Bakhtin's approach to Rabelais, unlike that of previous Rabelais scholars, was to show that his work stems from these traditions of popular 'laughter-culture', and he examined in detail how various forms of popular, unofficial art are reflected in Rabelais' work.

It is witness to Bakhtin's stature that in the darkest years of Soviet history and of his own personal life he could conclude this magnum opus with the words:

> We repeat, every act of world history has been accompanied by a chorus of laughter. But not in every age has the laughing chorus had a coryphaeus like Rabelais. And although he was the coryphaeus of the popular chorus only in the age of the Renaissance, he revealed the original and difficult language of the laughing people with such clarity and fullness that his work sheds light on the popular laughter-culture of other ages as well.

To turn now to the works whose authorship is disputed, these are discussed here in what seems to the present writer to be the descending order of Bakhtin's involvement. Voloshinov's *Marxism and the Philosophy of Language* is in many respects nearest to the rest of the Bakhtin canon. It applies the notion of dialogue to a general theory of language, starting from the premise that 'speech inter-action is the basic reality of language'. The book is divided into three sections. There is first an important, though sketchily worked out, semiotic theory. For Voloshinov there can be no sign without ideology (by this he means that no sign is without cultural significance or value), and conversely no ideology (scientific knowledge, literature, religion, ethics, etc.) that is not expressed in signs and sign systems. Signs, besides being ideological, are also material and social. Consciousness too is linguistic and hence sign-bound. These views show affinity with the ideas of C. S. Peirce (for instance, 'Man—a Sign'), with which Voloshinov was evidently not familiar, and with those of Ernst Cassirer (*Philosophie der symbolischen Formen*), with which he evidently was. For all three thinkers, man's mental activities are sign-creating and sign-bound. The particular originality in Voloshinov's thinking is the emphasis on the materiality and social nature of the sign.

The second part of the book, devoted to the philosophy of language, is a powerful criticism of current linguistic theories which Voloshinov treats under two main headings: 'individualistic subjectivism' (von Humboldt, Wundt, Vossler and Croce), and 'abstract objectivism' (Saussure and the Geneva school, whose origins may be found in the ideas of Descartes and Leibniz). Against these trends Voloshinov proposes a theory of language based on the *utterance* which is taken as 'a point in the continuous process of speech communication'. His is a sociological approach to language, which sees language as inextricably bound up with ideology, meaning as context-bound, and all essential language activity, even the process of understanding, as dialogic.

The third part of the book, which is of particular interest to literary scholars, is an application of these ideas to an area of syntax: the forms of direct, indirect and free indirect speech. The analysis uses the 'own/other's' opposition and is concerned with the various ways by which a second interlocutor's words are reported by a first interlocutor. This extensive and penetrating study of the two-voice discourse in literature complements and elaborates on the typology Bakhtin outlined in *Problems of Dostoevsky's Poetics.* Although in some respects superseded by more recent studies, Voloshinov's study remains a classic pioneering work. A recent elaboration of its ideas in the Soviet Union is Boris Uspensky's *Poetika Kompozitsii* (1970).

If *Marxism and the Philosophy of Language* is to be ascribed at least in part to Bakhtin, then at a rough guess one might ascribe the Marxism to Volshinov and the philosophy of language to Bakhtin. The emphasized materialism of the first part sounds like an intrusion of another's voice into Bakhtin's own discourse and it is hard to agree with the translator of the French version that 'There can, of course, be no question of doubting Bakhtin's Marxist convictions; the book is Marxist through and through . . .'. A sociological approach need not necessarily be a Marxist one, and an extension of Bakhtin's theory of consciousness based on dialogue into a sociological theory of language based on dialogue was a natural and logical one. Bakhtin's evidently deeply held personalist understanding of man would not necessarily commit him either to adopt or to reject any one particular doctrine: for the essential Bakhtin seems to have been a man of extraordinarily open mentality to whom all dogmatism was alien.

Another work that appeared under the authorship of Voloshinov is a slender volume on Freud (1927). This too has been ascribed to Bakhtin, but here the evidence would seem to be more slender. A fairly superficial reading of Freud's main ideas with certain notable omissions (as Neal Bruss points out in his excellent commentary), the book's main interest probably lies in the extension of the theory of discourse and the criticism of Freudianism for its neglect of linguistics, a criticism that sounds rather hollow today. The main thrust of Voloshinov's criticism is directed against Freud's ignoring the social reality of human discourse, the fact that 'self-consciousness in the final analysis always leads us to class consciousness . . . Here we have the objective roots of even the most personal and intimate reactions'. This is a fairly pedestrian work and one which it is hard to ascribe to the pen of Bakhtin.

Another alleged contender for inclusion in the Bakhtin canon is P. N. Medvedev's *The Formal Method in Literary Scholarship* (1928). This is an extraordinarily uneven work. It starts (Part One) with a cogently argued programme for a Marxist theory of literature, one which would get away from the crude content/form approach and look at the work of literature as an ideological unit of form and content in which the structures of socio-economic life are refracted. It argues against an oversimplified reflectionist theory of literature. The book then goes on in Part Two to an erudite and sophisticated account of Formalism in West European (mostly German) art scholarship, and an overview of the Russian Formalist movement. The rest of the book (Parts Three and Four), however, shows a marked change of tone as specific items of Formalist thinking are brought under review. The selection here is biased in the extreme: attention is focused almost exclusively on the earliest, *Opoyaz* works; Tynyanov, one of the most brilliant of the Formalist theorists, gets scant mention; Jakobson hardly figures at all. Those topics that are chosen for discussion are criticized in a naive and clumsy way: the plot/story (*fabula/syuzhet*) opposition is treated in a crudely reflectionist way; Shklovsky's fruitful ideas on the laws of plot-construction (elaborated by Vladimir Propp in his *Morphology of the Folktale,* published in the same year as Medvedev's book) are dismissed in a scant two pages. It is perhaps unfair to operate with hindsight, but from Medvedev's clumsy polemic it would in no way be possible to envisage the enormously fruitful heritage of Russian Formalism in modern structuralist and semiotic thinking. It is hard to resist the impression that two hands were involved in this book, and if one of them was Bakhtin's then the temptation to ascribe Part Two to him is overwhelming, and if Part One also then the presentation of Bakhtin as non-Marxist will have to be revised. If he is really responsible for the whole book, then he must also be the author of the pre-run (1925) and the re-hash (1934), neither of which has so far been ascribed to Bakhtin.

The problem further arises of how to fit in Bakhtin's own

earlier critique of Formalism, written in 1924 and published only in 1975. In this work, Bakhtin criticized the Formalists on three main counts: for their ignoring of aesthetic considerations, for their isolation of literature from the totality of culture and cultural values; and for their overemphasis on material, especially language material. This early work shows the main line of Bakhtin's thinking:

> Artistically-creating form gives form above all to man, and to the world only as to the world of man . . . As a result, the relationship of form to content in the unity of the aesthetic object has a special *personal* character, while the aesthetic object is a kind of special realized event of action and reaction of the creator and the content.

This work is a plea for a fuller understanding of the work of literature as the bearer of aesthetic and personal values. It shares with Medvedev (1928) a criticism of the overemphasis on language (and the use of linguistics in literary criticism), but it differs from Medvedev in not having a sociological approach, still less a Marxist one.

The canonic face of Bakhtin was always turned against two tendencies in contemporary linguistic and literary scholarships: against any kind of monologic tendency, that is, any attempt to make language or literature into a static, reified, object; and against all attempts to deprive language and literature of their rightful burden of ideology and values. In place of these tendencies Bakhtin offered a conception of language and literature that emphasized process and open-endedness, that saw language and literature as inseparable from cultural values, and dialogue, in the widest sense, as the natural medium for man's cultural life. It is Bakhtin's too long neglected genius that he put forward these new conceptions, and offered a methodology for their application.

Ann Shukman, "Between Marxism and Formalism: The Stylistics of Mikhail Bakhtin," in Comparative Criticism, *Vol. 2, 1980, pp. 221-34.*

Tzvetan Todorov   (essay date 1981)

[*A Bulgarian-born French critic, Todorov is a significant scholar in structuralist and post-structuralist theory. His writings include* Littérature et signification *(1967);* Introduction à la littérature fantastique *(1970; translated and published as* The Fantastic: A Structural Approach to a Literary Genre, *1973); and* Théories du symbole *(1977). In the essay below, Todorov explores Bakhtin's theory of the utterance as rooted in social context.*]

Bakhtin formulates his theory of the utterance on two occasions: once during the late twenties, in the texts signed by Medvedev and especially by Voloshinov; and in several works published at the end of the fifties, some thirty years later. I will present these two syntheses separately, although there is no great difference between them (in fact, the only changes involve accentuations of various aspects of the utterance).

The first general formulations concerning the utterance are already to be found in *Freudism* (1927); one page of *The Formal Method in Literary Studies* (1928) evokes

this problem from a similar viewpoint, with an insistence on the social rather than the individual nature of the utterance; but Bakhtin introduces here a new notion, which is not reiterated in subsequent writings: that of a discursive strategy.

> Discursive strategy plays a particularly significant role in daily verbal communication by determining its form as well as its organization. It gives form to everyday utterances by establishing both the style and the genre of the verbal expression. Strategy is to be understood here in a broad sense: politeness represents but one of its moments. This strategy can pursue different directions, moving, as it were, between two poles—the compliment and the insult. The strategy is determined by the set of all social interrelations between the speakers, by their ideological horizons, and finally by the concrete situation of the discussion. Whatever may be its particular nature, such a strategy determines our every utterance. There is no discourse without strategical consciousness.

In *Marxism and the Philosophy of Language* (1929), Bakhtin accomplishes a major step by forsaking his general theories to propose instead a detailed description of the utterance: this will constitute Chapter 3 of the second part, entitled "Verbal Interaction."

One may recall the criticism which Bakhtin voiced about the "individualist subjectivism" school (Vossler and his disciples): although superior to that of Saussure insofar as it does not ignore the utterance, yet it mistakenly believes that this utterance is individual.

> Any moment of the expression-utterance one may observe will invariably be determined by the real conditions of the speech-act, primarily by the *nearest social situation. Verbal communication will never be understood or explained without a reference to its link with the concrete situation.*

In other words, the difference between an utterance and a proposition (or a sentence), a unity of language, is that the former is necessarily produced within a particular context which is always social. This sociality has a dual origin: first of all, the utterance is addressed to someone (this implies the existence of a micro-society comprising two people, the speaker and the addressee); secondly, the speaker himself is always a social being to begin with. These are two primary elements of the speech-act context which we need to consider in our interpretations of an utterance.

> Let us first observe the role of the addressee. The utterance is established between two socially organized people: should there be no real interlocutor, then he is presupposed, in a certain sense, as a normal representative of the social group to which the speaker belongs. *The discourse is oriented towards the interlocutor,* towards what the interlocutor *is.*

Instead of the individual interlocutor we can thus imagine a certain type of addressee or, in other words, a certain horizon of reception; a notion we shall again encounter in an article published the following year (1930):

From the daily primitive utterance to the achieved poetic utterance, each one invariably comprises, as a necessary ingredient, an "implied" extra-verbal horizon. We can analyze this living and concrete horizon in terms of three components: *spatial, semantic,* and *of values.* The *value horizon* assumes the most important role in the organization of a literary work, especially in its formal aspects. [V. Voloshinov, "O granizakh poetiki i lingvistiki," in *V bor'be za marksizm v literaturnoi nauke,* 1930]

As we shall see, Bakhtin later returns to this question of values (although the suggestions formulated above will not be pursued).

The sociality of the speaker is equally important, albeit less evident. After taking certain precautions (acts of acoustical phonation and perception are indeed individual but they do not concern the essential aspect of language: its significance; a biological and individual "I-experience" does indeed exist, however, unlike the "we-experience," it remains inaccessible), Bakhtin states that the expression of an individual is not individual in the least.

> There can exist no experience beyond its incarnation in signs. This immediately precludes the possible principle of any qualitative difference between interior and exterior. (. . .) Expression is not organized by experience, but on the contrary, experience is organized by expression which, for the first time, imbues this experience with form and direction. Aside from material expression, there is no such thing as experience. Moreover, expression precedes experience; it is the cradle of experience.

A footnote to the last sentence declares that this "assertion was in fact originally drawn from certain statements of Engels" which are to be found in *Ludwig Feuerbach;* beyond this, we can perhaps perceive a more distant and common source in the work of Humboldt (the inspiration for "individualist subjectivism"): an experience is preformed by the possibilities of its expression. Once we have located the formative traces of an expression at the very core of the expressible, then whatever its sources may be, there can no longer exist any sphere which is entirely devoid of sociality (since words and other linguistic forms do not belong to the individual).

> Only the inarticulate animal cry is truly organized within an individual physiological system. (. . .) But even the most primitive human utterance, produced by the individual organism, is already organized in external terms, through the inorganic conditions of a social milieu which shapes its content, significance, and meaning. The very howls of an infant are "oriented" towards its mother.

We might formulate this observation by saying that every utterance can be perceived as part of a dialogue, in the general sense of the word; only in his subsequent writings will Bakhtin define this more specifically (as a dialogue between discourses).

> Verbal interaction is the fundamental reality of language; and dialogue, in its narrow sense, is a

single form, though clearly the most important one, of verbal interaction. But dialogue can be interpreted in a much broader manner, as referring not only to the direct verbal communication which is voiced between interlocutors, but also encompassing every form of verbal communication.

As a first important consequence of this new framework, we must radically distinguish between meaning in language from meaning in discourse or, to use the terminology adopted by Bakhtin at the time, to distinguish meaning from *theme.* In and of itself, this distinction is nothing very new; however, it will quickly become so, due to the increasing importance Bakhtin attaches to the theme. Indeed, the standard oppositions of that period between current and occasional meaning, between fundamental and marginal meaning, or between denotation and connotation, are equally fallacious in that they favor the first term, while in fact discursive meaning, or theme, is never marginal.

Thus we will strictly reserve the term "meaning" for language ("langue"); meaning is recorded by dictionaries, and any one meaning is always identical to itself (since it is merely potential): in other words, like all other linguistic elements, it can be repeated.

> Meaning in opposition to theme, will represent those moments of an utterance which *can be repeated* and yet *remain identical to themselves.* Meaning actually signifies nothing except for the potentiality, the possibility of meaning within a concrete theme.

In contrast, the theme—like the utterance as a whole—is unique and cannot be repeated, since it arises from the interaction of meaning with the equally unique context of the speech-act.

> Let us call the significance of an entire utterance its *theme.* (. . .) In fact, like the utterance itself, the theme is individual and cannot be repeated. It is an expression of the concrete historical situation which engendered the utterance. (. . .) It must then follow that the theme of an utterance is not only determined by the linguistic forms which compose it—words, morphological and syntactical forms, sounds, and intonation—but also by the extra-verbal aspects of the situation. And if we should lose these aspects, we will not be able to understand the utterance, as if we had lost the most important words themselves.

One essential feature of a theme, and therefore of an utterance, is that it is endowed with *values* (in the broad sense of the term). Vice versa, meaning, and therefore language, do not share this relation with the world of values:

> Only an utterance can be beautiful, just as only an utterance can be sincere, delusive, courageous, or timid, etc. These value determinations are linked to the organization of utterances and literary works insofar as they involve the functions assumed by the latter within the unity of social existence and, above all, within the concrete unity of an ideological horizon.

The idea of an evaluative dimension in the utterance is further pursued by the article already referred to, **"On the Boundaries Between Poetics and Linguistics."** Bakhtin investigates the possible formal embodiments of this value judgment; and first considers the use of non-linguistic means.

> Let us say that any evaluation which is incarnated through the (verbal) material is an *expression of values*. The human body itself will provide the original raw material for such an expression of values: *gesture* (the signifying movement of the body) and *voice* (outside of articulated language).

Within language itself, phonetic means are naturally to be distinguished from semantic means; and somewhat more remarkably, these are classified according to a dichotomy between selection and combination; this division is familiar today, but was unpublished at the time (although one may seek its origin in the work of Kruszewski).

> We must distinguish two forms of *value expression* [in poetic creation]: 1) *phonic* and 2) *structural* [tektonicheskuju], whose functions can be separated into two groups: first, *elective* (selective), and secondly, *compositional* (organizational). The elective functions of the social evaluation emerge through the choice of lexical material (lexicology), the choice of epithets, metaphors, and other tropes (the entire range of poetical semantics), and finally, through the choice of a "content." In this way, most stylistics and certain elements of thematics belong to the elective group.
>
> The compositional functions of the evaluation determine the level and hierarchical positioning of each verbal element in the work as a whole; they also determine its general structure. This involves all problems of poetic syntax, of composition in its literal sense, and finally of *genre*.

In the first book signed by Bakhtin himself, which is devoted to the work of Dostoevsky, the utterance will assume a new dimension, whose importance will steadily increase: every utterance can be linked to preceding utterances, thereby giving rise to intertextual relations. In this first edition, Bakhtin does not concern himself with general theories but rather with a typology of the utterance, thus he merely states:

> No member of the verbal community will ever discover any words in language which are totally neutral, devoid of another's aspiration and evaluations, or free of another's voice. No, a word is apprehended through the voice of another which will remain forever imbedded within it. A word reaches one context in terms of another context, penetrated by the intentions of another; its own intentionality encounters a word which is already inhabited. (In the second edition of the work, 1963, the instances of "intention" will disappear to be replaced by *osmyslenie*, interpretation, and *mysl'*, thought.)

In a previously cited article, signed by Voloshinov, these contentions, as well as several others, are paraphrased with one curious variation: "intonation" here replaces "intention":

For the poet, language is permeated with living intonations; it is entirely contaminated by social considerations and by the embryonic phases of social orientations. The creative process must continually struggle with such elements; it is from among their midst that one must choose one linguistic form or another, one expression or another, etc. . . . An artist never receives any word in a linguistically virginal form; it has already been 'impregnated' by the practical circumstances and poetic contexts in which it is encountered. (. . .)

This is why the work of a poet, like that of any artist, can only accomplish certain transvaluations, or certain displacements of intonation; these will be perceived by the artist as well as his public through the perspective of previous evaluations and intonations.

Let us now turn to the second synthesis which appears in the notes written during the fifties, and published after Bakhtin's death, under the title **"The Problem of the Text"**; the "Methodological Remarks" of the second edition *Dostoevsky* presents a summary of these issues. The frame of reference is no longer sociology, as it was thirty years earlier, but now involves translinguistics, the new discipline Bakhtin intends to found, whose primary object will be the utterance. Three factors are immediately set forth to distinguish an utterance from a sentence: an utterance has a speaker and an object, moreover it partakes in a dialogue with previous utterances.

> The utterance is determined not only by its relation to the object and the speaking subject—the author (and by its relations to language as a system of potential possibilities, or givens) but, most importantly from our perspective, it is directly determined by other utterances within the framework of a certain field of communication. In simpler terms: purely linguistic relations (that is to say the object of linguistics), comprise the relations between one sign and another, or several others (in other words all systematic or linear relations between signs). The relations an utterance may have with reality, the real speaking subject, and other real utterances, that is to say, those relations which render the utterance true, false, or beautiful, etc., can never become an object of linguistics.

We must make a slight digression at this point concerning the speaking subject, the speaker. He is viewed as a constituent element of a speech-act and thus of an utterance; at the same time, one refers to the image of the author which is deduced from the utterance; and one naturally tends to project the second onto the first. However, a clear distinction between the two must be maintained. An author produces an entire utterance which does comprise the "image of the author" but he himself is a producer and never a product, *natura naturans* instead of *natura naturata*.

> Even if an author-creator could create the most truthful autobiography of confession, he would still remain excluded from the universe he has portrayed simply insofar as he has produced it. If I should recount (or write) an event I have just

experienced, then the mere act of narrating (or writing) this event will place me outside the time-space in which it has occurred. It is impossible to be absolutely identified with one-self, to reconcile one's veritable "I" with the "I" of his narration, just as it is inconceivable to lift oneself up by his own hair. However realistic and authentic a represented universe may be, yet it can never be chronotopically identical to the real representing universe in which the author-creator of the representation is located. For this reason, it seems to me that the term "author's image" is quite unfortunate: what has become an image of the work and thereby entered its chronotope, is a product, not a producer. "The author's image," when perceived as the image of the author-creator, is a *contradictio in adjecto;* each image represents something which has been produced and cannot be a producer.

Let us return to the general scheme of the utterance. We have seen that language ("langue"), the speaker, the object, and other utterances are all to be taken into consideration; we must not forget the addressee.

> Discourse (like any sign in general) is inter-individual. All that is said or expressed exists outside the "soul" of the speaker; it does not belong to him. Discourse cannot be attributed to the speaker alone. He clearly holds inalienable rights over the discourse, but the auditor has certain rights as well, as do those, whose voices reverberate in the words chosen by the author (since there are no words which do not belong to somebody). Discourse is a drama with a cast of three characters (not a duet, but a trio). It is performed outside the author, and one may not introject it (introjection) back into him.

Meaning, a property of language, will be opposed here to significance; this more familiar term replaces *theme* and links the utterance to the world of values which language does not know.

> Isolated signs, and linguistic or textual systems (insofar as they represent a unity of signs) can never be true, false, or beautiful, etc. Only an utterance can be exact (or inexact), beautiful, just, etc.

We can summarize the preceding observations by reconstituting a *communication model* according to Bakhtin, and by comparing it with the currently more familiar model which Roman Jakobson has presented in his article "Linguistics and Poetics."

Bakhtin
object
speaker utterance auditor
intertext
language

Jakobson
context
addresser message addressee
contact
code

Two kinds of differences are immediately apparent. Jakob-

son isolates "contact" as an independent factor. This is absent from the Bakhtinian model, yet the relation to other utterances (which I have designated here as the "intertext") is absent from Jakobson's schema. There are then a series of differences which would seem to involve minor questions or terminology. Jakobson uses rather general terms (semiotic as well as linguistic) and they reveal the influence of his frequent associations with communication engineers. "Context" and "object" both correspond to that which other language theorists would call the "referent."

But after a more careful scrutiny, it is clear that the differences are much more important, and that the terminological discrepancies betray a deeply-rooted opposition. Jakobson sets forth these notions as a description of "the constitutive factors in any speech event, in any act of verbal communication." While for Bakhtin, there exist two radically distinct events, so distinct that they necessitate the use of two independent disciplines, linguistics and translinguistics. In linguistics, words and grammar rules provide the initial basis for the formation of sentences; in translinguistics, one starts off with sentences and the speech-act context eventually to obtain utterances. From Bakhtin's point of view, any attempt to formulate a proposal concerning "any speech event," that is to say, of language as well as discourse, would be futile. In the very schema I have drawn above, the "language" factor is not to be considered on a par with the others.

Moreover, it is no accident that Bakhtin says "utterance" instead of "message," "language" rather than "code," etc.: he quite deliberately rejects the use of engineering language to speak of verbal communication. This language could all too easily lead us to perceive a linguistic exchange in terms of telegraphic work: in order to transmit a certain content, one telegrapher first encodes it with a key and then broadcasts it; once contact has been made, the other uses the same key to decode the message and recover the initial content. This image does not correspond to discursive reality: in fact, prior to the speech-act, the speaker and the addressee literally do not exist as such; it is only the discursive process which thus defines them in relation to each other. For this reason, language is not to be considered as a code; for this reason as well, Bakhtin cannot possibly isolate one "contact" factor amidst the others: the entire utterance is contact, but in a stronger sense of the word than the "contact" of radiotelegraphy or electric work.

It is quite curious to find a page in the book signed by Medvedev which criticized the Jakobsonian model of language, thirty years before it was actually formulated; however one must note that the critique was written as a reply to certain theories of the Formalist group—to which Jakobson belonged.

> That which is transmitted cannot be separated from the forms, the means, and the concrete conditions of the transmission; whereas the Formalist interpretations tacitly presuppose an entirely predetermined and immutable communication, as well as an equally immutable transmission. This might be explained schematically in the following manner: let us take two members of Society, A (the author), and B (the read-

er); for the time being, the social relations between them are unchangeable and immutable; we also have a prepared message X, which A must simply deliver to B. In this prepared message X, the "what" ("content") is distinct from the "how" ("form"), since literary discourse is characterized by the "set toward the expression" ("how") [this is a quotation from the first published text of Jakobson].

(. . .)

The schema set forth above is completely wrong. In actual fact, the relations between A and B are in a state of continual formation and transformation; they are further modified during the very process of communication itself. There is no prepared message X; it is established by the communicative process between A and B. Moreover, it is not transmitted from one to the other but is built between them like an ideological bridge through the process of their interaction.

Thus, in 1928, we can discern a rather precise prefiguration of certain recent French language theories which are sometimes based on the work of Benveniste (for example those of Oswald Ducrot or François Flahault).

As we now turn from the model of the particular utterance to the set of utterances constituting the verbal life of a community, we should note the fact which would appear to be most striking in the eyes of Bakhtin: there exists a large, but nonetheless limited, number of utterance or discourse *types*. One must indeed beware of two possible extremes: first, to recognize the diversity of languages and ignore that of utterances; secondly, to consider this variety as being individual and therefore limitless. Besides which, Bakhtin accentuates difference rather than plurality (one need not attempt to conceive of any common denominator which would reconcile various discourses; the argument here runs counter to the idea of unification). To designate this irreducible diversity of discursive types, Bakhtin introduces a neologism, *raznorechie,* which I translate (literally but in Greek) as *heterology;* this term is flanked by two parallel neologisms, *raznojazychie,* heteroglossy, or diversity of languages, and *raznogolosie,* heterophony, or diversity of voices (individual).

We will recall that every utterance is oriented towards a social horizon which comprises semantic and value elements. The number of these verbal and ideological horizons is quite high but not unlimited; and every utterance necessarily falls within one or several of the discursive types determined by a horizon.

There are no longer any words or forms in language which are neutral and belong to no one: it appears that language has been pillaged, pierced through and through by intentions, and accentuated. For a consciousness which exists within language, it is not an abstract system of normative forms but a concrete heterological opinion of the world. Each word evokes a profession, a genre, a trend, a party, a particular work, a particular man, a generation, an age, a day and an hour. Each word evokes a context and the contexts within which it has experienced an intense social life; every word and every form is in-

habited by intentions. Contextual harmonies found in a word (of the genre, of the trend, of the particular individual) are inevitable.

Through the preceding enumerations we can already see that the stratification of language in discourse is not restricted to one dimension. In the course of the most detailed study which he devoted to heterology (in **"Discourse in the Novel,"** text of 1934-35), Bakhtin discerns up to five types of stratification: genres, profession, social levels, ages and regions (dialects *strictu sensu*). Let us merely note that social class does not play a different role from that of profession or age group: it is simply one diversifying factor among several others.

In a certain sense, heterology is inherent to society; it is engendered spontaneously by social diversification. But just as the unique state attempts to contain this social diversity by means of its laws, so do the authorities fight the diversity of discourse by aspiring to a common language (or rather idiom).

The category of common language is a theoretical expression of the historical processes of unification and centralization—an expression of the centripetal forces in language. A common language is not a given; in actual fact it is always ordered, and opposes genuine heterology at every instant throughout the life of a language. Yet at the same time, this common language is perfectly real when seen as a force which overcomes this heterology, constrains it within certain limitations, assures a maximum mutual comprehension, and is crystallized in the real, albeit relative, unity of literary and spoken (everyday) language, which is the "proper language."

Bakhtin will refer, as one can see, to this tendency towards unification as a "centripetal force" and by the same token, to heterology as a "centrifugal force." Different types of discourse themselves favor one force over the other for varying reasons. For example, the novel (or what Bakhtin defines as such) reinforces heterology, while poetry does not; for heterology is linked to the representation of language, which is a characteristic feature of the novel.

While the principal sorts of poetic genres develop within the flow of the centripetal unifying and centralizing forces which inform verbal and ideological existence, the novel, as well as other related genres of literary prose, emerged historically within the flow of decentralizing, centrifugal forces.

Therefore, the high periods of the novel correspond to those which witnessed a weakening of centralized power.

The embryonic forms of novelistic prose appear in the heteroglossic and heterological world of the Hellenistic epoch, in imperial Rome, also in the decomposition and decadence of the verbal and ideological centralism of the medieval church. Similarly, the period of fruition of the modern novel is always tied to a general decomposition of verbal and ideological systems, to a process of reinforcement and intensification which opposes linguistic heterology in the literary dialect but also outside it!

On the other hand, as Bakhtin remarks, the different theories or philosophies of language are always born in the wake of unifying movements; this moreover explains their helplessness when confronted by heterology. Thus, for example, the sad fate of stylistics when it tackles the novel: a "Ptolemaic" discipline cannot account for a "Galilean" genre.

> Traditional stylistics ignores the kind of combination whereby languages and styles merge in a superior unity; it has no means of approaching the particular social dialogue of languages within a novel. This is why stylistic analysis is not oriented towards the novel seen as a whole but only towards one or the other of its subordinate stylistic aspects. The specialist bypasses the distinctive characteristic of the novelistic genre; he transforms the object of his study, and instead of the novelistic style he in fact analyses something completely different. He transposes an orchestrated symphonic theme in the place of a piano.

Bakhtin enumerates several other examples of such helplessness in the face of heterology:

> The poetics of Aristotle, the poetics of Augustine, Medieval religious poetics of the common language of truth, the Cartesian poetics of Neo-Classicism, the abstract grammatical universalism of Leibniz (the idea of universal grammar), the concrete ideologism of Humboldt—whatever may be the distinguishing nuances—these all express the same centripetal forces of sociolinguistic and ideological existence; they all serve the same objective: the centralization and unification of European languages.

The rather surprising name in this roster is Humboldt, a distant source of inspiration for Bakhtin, as we know, and an advocate of linguistic diversity, that of languages as well as that of individuals (language expressing a national spirit, the utterance—an individual one). However, Humboldt forgets a crucial gap between these two: social diversity. Beyond the unicity of Classicism and the Romantic infinite variety, Bakhtin seeks a third path: that of typology.

Tzvetan Todorov, "Bakhtin's Theory of the Utterance," translated by Claudine Frank, in Semiotic Themes, *edited by Richard T. De George, University of Kansas Publications, 1981, pp. 165-78.*

Anthony Wall   (essay date Fall 1984)

[*In the following essay, Wall discusses the importance of fictional characters to Bakhtin's theory of the novel, examining the notion that "heteroglossia," or "other-voicedness," is the defining characteristic of the genre.*]

The present essay explores the nature of characters and narrators in the writings of Mikhail Bakhtin and his circle. Our project is a hazardous one because Bakhtin's texts do not provide us with a systematic discussion of this problem. As a consequence, it must be understood that the passages we have selected for discussion are taken out of a variety of contexts in his essays. As well, they come from all of his various intellectual periods. We have tried to systematize the concept of character in a series of texts where no such system exists, and we can only hope that ours is the position that Bakhtin would have espoused.

In order to understand his concept of character we must first discard all notions of language as *langue* and think of it rather as *parole,* that is, as a pure product of interpersonal contacts. Bakhtin's conception of character is so original that we feel compelled to define it first by saying what it is not, before being able to explain what it is.

When we try to make sense of Bakhtin, it is advisable to approach his texts with a particular question in mind and to let them answer. In Bakhtin's eyes, this is the way that Dostoevsky, his favorite author, treated the characters of his novels. Once created, they seemed to speak for themselves. The responses obtained from any interview with Bakhtin's texts contain just as many questions as they do answers. Consulting Bakhtin does not simply consist of looking up "character" or "hero" in an index at the back of his books, for Bakhtin does not provide us with indices. It can never be like feeding a question into a computer, because no separate piece of data in the hypothetical printout would be a logical extension of the others. Bakhtin-data qualify and/or contradict each other when used to answer a single question or a series of questions.

Narrative works of literature are often regarded as monologues emanating from a position of power. Bakhtin's view of narrative, however, as language composed of special sorts of dialogue radically changes the way in which we see characters. They are the sources of dialogue in the text. His view does not lead us to reject the concept of character altogether, unlike that of others who dismiss the very notion of "character and everything it implies in terms of illusion and complicity with classical meaning and the appropriating economy that such a reasoning supports" [Hélène Cixous, "The Character of Character," *New Literary History* 5 (1974)]. It is important to clarify Bakhtin's conception of character for the simple reason that it occupies a central role in his overall theory of novelistic discourse.

An early article by Bakhtin entitled **"The Author and the Hero in Aesthetic Activity,"** written between 1922-1924, hints at the new direction of this concept. The article deals with the differing perspectives available to narrators and characters and with the relationship between them. Bakhtin gives examples of the hero's domination of the author, of the author's domination of the hero, and of the hero as his own author.

An important consequence of Bakhtin's view of dialogic discourse in the novel is present in the current rejection among narratologists of the "assumption that a narrative is necessarily a discourse by the narrator" [Ann Banfield, "The Formal Coherence of Represented Speech and Thought," *PTL* 3 (1978)]. This outlook appears to be shared by writers from very different backgrounds such as Julia Kristeva and Hans Robert Jauss. The novel is more than a dialogue between an author and a reader: it is an exchange amongst dialogic positions within the text itself.

Seen against contemporary theory of the concept of character, Bakhtin's proposals occupy an intermediary position. Traditionally, characters are seen as remnants of a writer's past, as mere appendages to his thought. They are presented as incarnations of certain opinions in his intellectual development or of a representative of a social group in his mind. They have been seen as objects of a central monopolistic vision or even as signs of some hidden personality. In opposition to such conceptions, French structuralists sought to free the idea of character from this psychological aura and to promote him primarily as a structuring element of the story. Theorists of the Greimassian school have further reduced characters to the status of products of the plot, or rather of the intrinsic structure and logic of narrative in general. Some modern trends in structuralist criticism do try to combine structural and "human" elements of character in a way that is foreign to the view we take to be Bakhtin's. Fernando Ferrara, for example, sees the "social personality" of characters as the "essential nucleus" of a middle structure situated between deep structure, social norms and values, and the surface structure of the text.

Many other features commonly found in a variety of views about character are completely lacking in Bakhtin's writings. For example, he does not see character as a "cluster of appurtenances": characters for Bakhtin are not products of their environment, that is, objects in themselves. They are seen as voice sources in the text. Furthermore, Bakhtin is not interested in finding out whom each character is supposed to represent in reality. Nor does he attempt to discuss in detail an onomastic theory of individual characters' names. This, too, would reduce characters to a mere appendage to a foregone conclusion.

For Bakhtin, a character is not a simple filter of the author's intentions or desires, nor a mere paper entity devoid of all real significance. Character is not a psychologically based entity nor a simple product of textual structures. Our objective here will be to pinpoint the middle ground that the Bakhtinian character occupies, first by ridding the concept of the psychological aura one might be tempted to attribute to him. In this way we can at least hope to find Bakhtin's original view of what constitutes the novelistic character.

In this study of his writings on character, we shall use the following five theoretical questions as guideposts for our analysis:

1) the concept of the separate character-individual

2) unfinishedness

3) character as a point of convergence

4) the question of hierarchy

5) the question of identification.

The polemical text, *Freudianism. A Marxist Critique* (1927), signed by Voloshinov, attacks the very heart of the traditional notion of character. The author refuses to grant the existence of an isolated psychological consciousness in human beings, of the independent, psychological entity upon which we normally base our image of human beings in literary texts. For Bakhtin, the idea of a subjective, isolable consciousness in a human being, and thus in the literary character, is nothing less than a false notion. The nature of literary character that we seek to define will have to be based elsewhere than in the psychological uniqueness of a separate entity.

We see a development of this position in *Rabelais and His World* (written largely in 1940). As the author notes, characters in ancient literature and especially in Rabelais' works cannot be conceived as something based on a split between inner and outer factors. Novelistic characters were originally universal figures, very often born in carnivalized works where the boundaries between exterior (spectators) and interior (actors) were neatly swept away.

In this regard, it is very easy to make an analysis of personalized narrators and characters based on a false premise. As we can discern in reading *Problems of Dostoevsky's Poetics* (1929), the consciousness of that which we call a character is never a self-contained entity, but rather, like the living ideas that characters incarnate, it is in constant interaction with everything that surrounds it. "In Dostoevsky's works the consciousness is never self-sufficient; it always finds itself in an intense relationship with another consciousness." "The principle category of Dostoevsky's artistic vision is not evolution, but *coexistence* and *interaction*. He saw and conceived his world chiefly in space, not in time."

Because of this constant interaction, the boundaries that set off each character are by definition fuzzy and forever moving. In one untranslated essay **("On thePhilosophical Bases of the Humanities"** [1941]) Bakhtin posits the basic difficulty of knowing others from inside of one's self, an unknowability because each individual has a different perspective and purview. Each individual is unknowable to every other individual precisely because of the different set of experiences, contacts, and range of vision that each individual possesses. In the same respect, the individual is equally unknowable to himself because, given his unique but limited field of vision, there are certain aspects of himself he cannot see. Bakhtin wrote in 1970 that

> a person can never really see and interpret as a whole his own outward appearance; mirrors and photographs cannot help him here; only other persons can see and comprehend his outward appearance precisely because they occupy a different spatial plane and because of the fact that they are *not the same.*

But even if he is separate, the individual is nonetheless unisolable, because if we were able to isolate a single individual, that is, to assign him precise boundaries, this would be to presuppose a thorough knowledge of the outer limits of what constitutes an individual. The same can be said of the novelistic character. We cannot determine for a single character specific bounds which unequivocally delimit him from all other elements of the text. Because he has no perfectly isolable body or psychological entity, the character is in constant interaction with other characters, each of which posits the image of a current passing through the whole of the text, currents which have countless possibilities of confluence and branching apart.

It could also be said that characters are in constant contact with an unending generation of ideologemes in and outside of the work. [In an endnote, Wall explains the term "ideologeme" by quoting Bakhtin from *The Dialogic Imagination:* "Every word/discourse betrays the ideology of its speaker; great novelistic heroes are those with the most coherent and individuated ideologies. Every speaker, therefore, is an ideologue, and every utterance an ideologeme."] The most important of these ideologemes is the very institution of literature which, being formulated by social discourse, in itself without beginning or end, is also a living receptacle of other ideological forms.

The novelistic character must therefore be envisaged against the dialogic background of anonymous social discourse. In this context, the speech of characters, alongside of narrators and "inserted genres," must be seen as those components of the novel which allow heteroglossia to enter the text. [In an endnote, Wall explains the term "heteroglossia" by quoting Bakhtin from *The Dialogic Imagination:* "At any given time, in any given place, there will be a set of conditions—social, historical, meteorological, physiological—that will insure that a word uttered in that place and at that time will have a meaning different than it would have under any other conditions; all utterances are heteroglot in that they are functions of a matrix of forces practically impossible to recoup, and therefore impossible to resolve. Heteroglossia is that which a systematic linguistics must always suppress."] Heteroglossia enters through their discourse. Discourse is in itself to be viewed as a polyphonic conveyor of otherness. Each separate line contains other languages in it, and each character who expresses his field of vision through speech speaks a language which contains the language of others. Social discourse is an unending ebb and tide, and the character who transmits it is therefore a product of unfinishedness.

We now see the unfinished nature of Dostoevsky's creations due to the fact that they are so self-aware, and as a result, undefinable. No matter how the narrator wishes to depict them, they are aware of his commentaries and can easily prove him wrong.

> A loophole is the retention for oneself of the possibility to alter the final, ultimate sense of one's word. If the word leaves this loophole open, then that fact must be inevitably reflected in its structure. This possible other sense, i.e. the open loophole, accompanies the word like a shadow. According to its sense, the word with a loophole must be the last word, and it presents itself as such, but in fact it is only the next-to-last word, and is followed by only a conditional, not a final, period.

If it is true that a work of art as a whole can achieve a certain "aesthetic" completeness, characters by contrast are always unfinished. Characters are carriers of social discourse and as such cannot be finished. Furthermore, they enter into the ever changing dialogic world of the reader. The character is twice under dialogic influence. He is un-

finished because unisolable, and unfinished because of the social discourse of which he is composed and in which he must participate.

In the essay **"Epic and Novel"** (1941), character is defined through the retention of his potential capacity, by his power of "incongruity with himself." This is the power to be more than a mere function. As we have seen in Bakhtin's book on Dostoevsky, this aptitude of the character is translated by his constant need to keep in reserve the "last word."

Early texts signed by Voloshinov are particularly useful for understanding Bakhtin's later statements on character. In **"Discourse in Life and Discourse in Art"** (1926), for example, the word "hero" is used almost as a metaphor for content:

> any locution actually said aloud or written down for intelligible communication (i.e. anything but words merely reposing in a dictionary) is the expression and product of the social interaction of three participants: the speaker (author), the listener (reader), and the topic (the who or what) of speech (the hero).

If we bear in mind this equalizing metaphor of character seen as a special kind of literary content, we can interpret other statements in which characters are viewed as incarnations of ideas in their capacity as novelistic events or as ethical subjects who bear the weight of evaluating contemplation. In his study of Dostoevsky's poetics, Bakhtin states that that Russian novelist elaborates in aesthetic terms a "sociology of the consciousness"; that is, we can picture character as the point of intersection of a specific but unspecifiable set of voices in the text. These voices come from that underlying verbal interaction that literary discourse is particularly apt at capturing. Indeed, the ideas expounded in the book *Marxism and the Philosophy of Language* (1929) enable us to understand that this special "content" to which character was earlier assimilated is this same coming together of social voices in literary form. Any possible individuality attributable to a personage "can only be completely discovered and defined in this process of interaction." Character is no static, abstract entity but rather an active ingredient in the event of novelistic discourse.

Being active means a character is more than a point of convergence. He is essentially the literary incarnation of a field of vision. He is constituted by a specific purview made up of certain points of view, but is also constituent of others. In the essay **"Discourse in the Novel"** (1934-1935), Bakhtin speaks of "character zones," zones of influence which infiltrate, as it were, other zones. A character is both a point of convergence and a point of emanation for social voices in the text.

And since characters form an integral and active ingredient in the workings of the novelistic text, and since they are not abstract entities but rather products of "objective" social forces, they are necessarily sensitive to important structural variants of a particular genre (psychological novel, adventure novel, *Bildungsroman,* etc.) and to different genres (novel, epic, drama, tragedy, etc.). A character is always determined by the particular text in which he participates.

The problem one faces in trying to present the novelistic character in Bakhtin's theory lies in the level of abstraction we must reach for. We should remember that for Bakhtin, however, character "in general," that is *in abstracto*, does not exist. He is always part and parcel of a specific aesthetic object serving the communication between a novelist and a reader, and of a specific relationship between narrator and narratee within the text itself.

This point leads us to examine the relationship between narrators, narratees, and characters, as well as those distinguishing features that allow us to differentiate between heroes and minor characters.

Bakhtin states in his essay **"Forms of Time and Chronotope in the Novel"** (1937-1938) that the problem of the personalized narrator is a problem of modern literature. The narrator came into being primarily as a vehicle that allowed the author to see through the eyes of someone else, to speak in the language of someone else. More often than not, this was the foreign language of someone who did not understand, the language of the fool. The infiltration of otherness in literary discourse is the essential trait which distinguishes the novel from other literary genres.

In the monologic novel, it is the narrator and/or the main character who speak most directly the language of the author. Yet this is only one possibility of novelistic discourse. Characters can also be the organizational center of the novel. In the polyphonic novel, the narrator comes into the line of vision of the self-aware characters. Characters are the narrator's equals. And we can imagine works where characters get out of the control of the narrator, such as Diderot's *Jacques le fataliste*. Depending on the type of insertion afforded someone else's voice, the narrator can submit himself to the character's word, be equal to it, or dominate it.

It is precisely the development of silent, personal reading which historically would have permitted the evolution of the novel as a genre capable of accommodating so many voices in a single line. The fact is that silent reading actualizes no single voice in particular but leaves all the possibilities equally open. The reversibility of the traditional schema that depicts the narrator in control of the speech of characters is that contribution of Bakhtin's poetics which enables us to view characters as currents or zones of influence which pervade every nook and cranny of novelistic discourse. In this sense, narrators are seen to exist on the same plane as other characters. Each character is present in secret ways which only a careful reading can bring forth and detect.

Therefore, it cannot be said that a narrator necessarily dominates the characters in a novel. As Bakhtin notes, even the social status of the main character can impose upon the narrator various linguistic positions. In this regard, the social rank of the hero can also influence the range of genres open to the author:

> The basic stylistic tone of an utterance is therefore determined above all by who is talked about and what his relation is to the speaker—whether he is higher or lower or equal to him on the scale of the social hierarchy. . . . The most important stylistic components of the heroic epic, the tragedy, the ode, and so forth are determined precisely by the hierarchical status of the object of the utterance with respect to the speaker.

If we assume that the narrator can be subjected to the influence of certain characters, then we must ask what becomes of the author in respect to his creations. We must remember that the author always looms behind the entire dialogic interplay of the novel. He is situated not *in* the various language planes present in the voices of characters, but rather at their point of divergence. Consequently, we must not consider characters' languages to be simple extensions of the author, for this would be just as gauche, says Bakhtin, as taking characters' grammar mistakes and saying the author has bad grammar. Bakhtin argues that we must rid ourselves of the notion that all literary characters are mere incarnations of the author's sole volition. The good novelist manages to create a literary facsimile of that social dialogue which constitutes human language. It is only the poor novelist who cannot produce a viable literary image of social dialogue. Therefore, we must not search for the style of the novelist in the sum of all the stylistic, semantic and syntactic variants in his text, because the unified style of a novelist is something that does not exist. The novel contains *styles*. Furthermore, what would be his own personal style becomes inevitably lost in the general interaction of the characters' and narrators' styles. The most important feature of Bakhtin's conception of character is that it allows for, but does not require the full potential of the character to be exposed vis-à-vis narrators.

The character, as a result, once created, lives on in the text not through the power of his creator but solely by virtue of the life given to him by each new reading. We can see character as a sort of latent force in the very pages of a closed text, a force that is ignited with the reader's participation. He is reborn each time, since we can view the novel in its incarnations of fictive entities communicating amongst one another as the "process of communication *in statu nascendi*" [Floyd Merrel, "Communication and Paradox in Carlos Fuentes' *The Death of Artemio Cruz*: Toward a Semiotics of Character," *Semiotics* 18 (1976)].

In treating briefly the second question of the hierarchical distinctions between heroes and minor characters, one must concede that this distinction remains on the whole undeveloped in Bakhtin's texts. In ***Rabelais and his World,*** for example, he often speaks of "heroization" without ever defining the term. He does nevertheless briefly touch on the matter when he says that in the monologic novel it is the hero who transmits the author's point of view. Elsewhere he states that it is the hero who can surpass his mere structural and social role in the novel, whereas the minor character remains a mere function. We are certainly far from a comprehensive set of criteria for defining the term hero.

It could be nonetheless argued that the wherewithal is provided in Bakhtin's texts to develop such a theory. Minor characters, as distinguished from major characters, would be those whose number of constitutive voices could be easily counted. For the major character, such an exercise would be futile because of his complexity. It is precisely the major character who must contain, as Jauss writes, the "power to surpass all our expectations" [Hans Robert Jauss, "Levels of Identification of Hero and Audience," *New Literary History* 5 (1974)]. Being of uncertain boundaries, the character's voices can be heard where we least expect to find them. He can take on voices that we least expected to hear. We could never count and give the origin of all his voices, and this point tends to confer a negative definition of what would be the hero in Bakhtinian terms.

Still, in this context, we can understand J. Kristeva's claim that Bakhtin's *Problems of Dostoevsky's Poetics* presents us with an early sketch of a theory of the subject. We can compare Kristeva's claim to what H. Cixous has written about the concept of character:

> So long as we take to be the representation of a true subject that which is only a mask, so long as we ignore the fact that the "subject" is an effect of the unconscious and that it never stops producing the unconscious—which is unanalyzable, uncharacterizable, we will remain prisoners of the monotonous machination that turns every "character" into a marionette. ["The Character of Character," *New Literary History* 5 (1974)]

It is, however, difficult to ascertain if it is a would-be theory of the subject that prompts Bakhtin not to discuss in greater detail the distinction between hero and minor characters or whether it is a linguistically induced oversight brought on by the frequent use of the Russian term "geroj," which can be used generically to cover the general idea of literary character but which more often than not is used to convey the signified of its English cognate. Thus Bakhtin can semantically slide from one concept to the other as if both had been dealt with extensively. Philippe Hamon, in his article "Pour un statut sémiologique du personnage," notices the same problem of a confusion of the terms "hero" and "character" in Tomashevsky's writings but does not mention the idiomatic peculiarity of Russian itself.

Whatever the reason for the lack of a thorough discussion of the hero/minor character distinction, whether it be a simple oversight, a conscious refusal, or neither, it is this theoretical hole that keeps Bakhtin from analyzing the phenomenon of the *reader's* identification with characters and specifically with the hero. Indeed, the reader's perception of a hero in connection with a valued set of social givens is what permits this phenomenon to occur.

Any quick reading of Bakhtin's *Problems of Dostoevsky's Poetics* readily convinces us that Bakhtin viewed the novelistic character as more than just a paper entity, more than the mere sum of all the passages of a novel referring to the same fictive individual. The literary character attains a special status in the novel over and above that afforded to other linguistic entities of a text precisely because readers happen to be human beings who identify with human figures more readily than with trees, rocks, and the weather, even if all of these elements are fictional entities. We can still question the validity of showing sim-

plistic characters, mirror images of a simplistic view of what constitutes a human being, without rejecting outright the concept of character. In the polyphonic novel the hero is complicated enough to capture the reader's imagination and to lead him into new unexplored grounds beyond, perhaps, the reaches of manipulative ideology.

On the other hand, it would be difficult to contend that Bakhtin chose to ignore the problem of the reader's identification because it is not specific to the novel, whose superiority to other literary genres he wished to demonstrate. The nature of the novelistic hero requires a special kind of understanding by every potential reader, but this question remains nevertheless absent in Bakhtin's writings.

He does provide some bases for such a discussion. We understand that any such discussion must take into account the dialogic background of the reader. This, we have seen, is a major factor in the unfinishedness of a character and consequently in his capacity to speak to successive generations. The presentification of literature in general carried out by the novel genre is responsible not only for the possibility of dialogic relations between author and characters, but also between reader and characters. In *Problems of Dostoevsky's Poetics,* Bakhtin hints that gauging the variance in distance between reader and author and among reader, author, and characters can be a determinant factor in mapping out various modes of satiric and parodic literature, to name but two instances.

The pursuit of the question of the reader's identification with characters in the text could also lead to valuable insights into problems such as the ways in which the culture industry can manipulate its consuming public. It is always important to explore the means by which an author can move a reader through literature, and it is essential to determine what role character plays in this theatre, through his, and not just the author's, relationship with the reader.

Finally, the often latent importance of the role characters play in Bakhtin's theoretical concepts can be seen in the many metaphors where the idea of hero or character is employed. To give but two brief examples, in *Marxism and the Philosophy of Language,* haphazard thoughts unanchored in social contact are compared to "novels without heroes"; in the article **"Epic and Novel,"** Bakhtin speaks of the novel as having become the "leading hero in the drama of literary development." These metaphors underscore what has already been said concerning the positive and active roles that the concept of character fulfills in Bakhtin's thought.

A thorough study of these metaphors would show that this concept of character was ingrained in Bakhtin's writings on literature; were he in fact to be developing a theory of the subject, this theory would not entail a dismissal of the notion of character, but rather a remodelling of it to suit his conception of the novel. The problem of a polyphonic novel presupposes the existence of characters who function not as simple human mannequins but as interdependent sets of voices in the text.

To arrive at our schematic picture of how Bakhtin viewed the concept of character, it was necessary to paste together passages scattered about in different contexts of Bakhtin's multifarious interests. This is a dangerous approach because we may have assumed a constant line of thought throughout his writings. There is no one single Bakhtin, and we have tried to recognize this aspect of his theoretical texts by letting pertinent passages cross one another dialogically, as it were, in answer to the questions put to them in our study.

The picture sketched in such a manner cannot be a systematic program of how to analyze character à la Bakhtin. Such a system does not exist. As always, Bakhtin's writings, when carefully considered, can lead us to rethink certain literary concepts and prompt us toward new directions. The research of Ann Banfield, for example, is one possible direction in which Bakhtin's "theory" of character could lead us. A study of character in Bakhtinian terms has to concentrate on developing devices for listening for the voices of each character in the most unexpected instances, and this rather than attempting to assign him defined limits through a study of his physical appearance, personality traits, social origins, domicile and such. For Bakhtin, a novelistic character is an unclosed set of intonations, harmonies and overtones that we can assign to one more or less personalized figure of the text, a set of voices actualized in a different manner with each separate reading of the text.

A thorough look at character can lead us in this way to the very essence of dialogue in the novel. Through a study of Bakhtin's conception of characters, we see more clearly how one theoretician managed to throw aside the yoke of a single master's dogmatic voice which has always hampered anyone wishing to use the path of dialogue as a means of reaching for something true.

Anthony Wall, "Characters in Bakhtin's Theory," in Studies in Twentieth Century Literature, *Vol. 9, No. 1, Fall, 1984, pp. 41-56.*

Robert Anchor   (essay date Spring 1985)

[*Anchor is an American historian and translator. In the following essay, he examines Bakhtin's interpretation of the carnival as a liberating experience in popular culture and shows the important role it plays in his theory of the novel.*]

Mikhail M. Bakhtin is best known for his visionary conception of carnival—the carnivalesque, "carnival consciousness," "the culture of laughter"—as a model for the regeneration of time and the world and the emancipation of the human spirit: "This carnival spirit offers the chance to have a new outlook on the world, to realize the relative nature of all that exists, and to enter a completely new order of things" [Bakhtin, ***Rabelais and His World,*** trans. Helen Iswolsky, 1968]. Bakhtin elaborated this model most fully in his best known work, ***Rabelais and His World,*** written largely in 1940, though not published until 1965, partly at least because of its anti-Stalinist implications. But the role of the carnival spirit and its revolutionary potential—its power "to consecrate inventive freedom, and to permit the combination of a variety of different elements and their rapprochement, to liberate from the prevailing point of view of the world, from conventions and established truths, from clichés, from all that is hum-

drum and universally accepted," —this conception of the carnival spirit is fundamental to all of Bakhtin's work, dating back to the 1920s, and clearly goes beyond cultural history in the usual sense, as a relatively specialized mode of cultural analysis in the tradition of, say, Burckhardt, Huizinga, and Friedell. What Bakhtin aimed for (and produced) was a richly textured, historically and aesthetically informed model which would transform cultural *analysis* into cultural *critique* from the standpoint of the utopian potential to be found in the diverse manifestations of the carnival spirit, a spirit Bakhtin regarded as itself universal.

For Bakhtin, carnivalization—always a source of liberation, destruction, and renewal—flourished in premodern times as a *social practice,* nurtured by a rich and pervasive folkloric culture. It began to deteriorate in the seventeenth century with the triumph of absolute monarchy and the birth of a new official "serious" culture which excluded the general population and its culture of the "marketplace." The carnival spirit survives in modern times (in both capitalist and socialist societies) principally in the realm of literature, specifically in the novel. For the novel, as Bakhtin tried to show in his radical reinterpretation of its history and distinctive aesthetic properties, is unique among literary forms in being an *anti*genre that is as old as literature itself, that alone has the capacity for constant self-renewal, and that, in the carnival spirit which informs it, thrives on travestying and parodying all "systems"—political, epistemological, and cultural—and pointing up the arbitrariness of all norms and rules, *including* its own. For Bakhtin, the novel is not merely one literary form among many, but the very image of culture in general, the genre of Becoming. To understand the novel, then, as the parodic genre *par excellence,* the genre that *historicizes* by disclosing the conditions that engender claims of unconditionality, is to understand what carnival was as a social practice that once provided people with an actual experience of life without hierarchy in opposition to the fixed categories and humdrum institutions and rhythms of official culture.

The purpose of this essay is to present a coherent account of the main lines of Bakhtin's thought, especially the relationship between his conception of carnival and his ideas concerning language and literature. This task is complicated by the fact that Bakhtin's writings themselves are carnivalistic in nature, often deliberately playful and inconsistent. His zestful wealth of surprising allusion gives to many a passage in his works something of the colorful, carnivalesque aura he looked for in all great literature. Gary Saul Morson scarcely exaggerates when he says: "Ideas are often toys for him; he is extravagant in his expression of them, and he could have used a good editor" ["The Heresiarch of Meta," *PTL* 3 (1978)]. Indeed, some of Bakhtin's arguments—for example, that Dostoevsky is linked to the "underworld naturalism" of the Menippea of Petronius and Apuleius, or that Rabelais was more of a populist than a humanist—have the appearance of a scholarly trapeze act. But, then, Bakhtin always maintained that words cannot be conceived apart from the voices which speak them, that every word, therefore, raises the question of authority, and that *all* language (including his own) necessarily engages in contest and struggle. Given the realities of life and literature in Stalinist Russia, it is not surprising that Bakhtin (like many other Russian intellectuals) resorted to an Aesopian language of indirection and circumlocution to question the authority of that totalitarian regime, as well as to deceive the censorship and circumvent its vigilance. What is surprising is that Bakhtin succeeded in creating from such a situation a critical vision of society and culture in which the utopian dimension reveals itself as a transfiguration of historical phenomena that still manages to preserve a viable connection with the requirements of institutionally structured life.

Bakhtin's conception of carnival (the totality of all the various festivals, rituals, and forms of a carnival type) is grounded in an anthropology—an intuition of the individual as existentially free, unique, and unpredictable, hence impossible to understand, except within his own point of view, and equally impossible to categorize or define in any fixed and immutable fashion. This intuition is basic to Bakhtin's analysis of the origins and history of the novel and its indebtedness to the most ancient forms of folk humor (in which mockery of authority, both divine and human, was fused with rejoicing), and basic also to his insight into carnival as the vital link between life and literature. In *Problems of Dostoevsky's Poetics* (1929), Bakhtin writes:

> The carnival forms, transposed into the language of literature become *powerful means* of artistically comprehending life, they become a special language, the words and forms of which possess an extraordinary capacity for *symbolic* generalization, i. e., *generalization in depth.* Many of the essential sides, or, more precisely strata of life, and profound ones at that, can be discovered, comprehended and expressed only with the help of this language.

Unlike many other leading literary scholars of his generation (e.g., Curtius, Auerbach, and Spitzer), Bakhtin sought the novel's progenitors not only in the literary hierarchy it parodies, but also in the extraliterary forms of folk humor which, like the novel itself, are suffused with a sense of "jolly relativity," a consciousness of the historicity of all social and literary forms. The novel was born when the three principal kinds of folk humor—ritual spectacles like carnival pageants, comic verbal compositions, and genres of billingsgate—fused and entered the literary tradition they so often parody, a tradition fathered by Rabelais and Rabelaisian in spirit.

The link Bakhtin established between carnival and the novel is that both challenge the instrumentality of society by challenging the way in which words, objects, and actions signify in ceremony and serious discourse. Carnival, with its peculiar logic of the "inside out" and "turnabout," was an enactment of the world turned upside down, a period of institutionalized disorder, a set of rituals of reversal which sent time flowing backwards and temporarily suspended the rules regulating what was permitted and forbidden in speech and conduct. Carnival converted the town or city into a theater without walls, transformed the streets and squares into a stage, and abolished all distinctions between actors and spectators. The defining feature

of Bakhtin's utopian conception of carnival is in fact this vision of society as a community of equals, a realm of pure spontaneity and freedom, a rite of universal participation whose essentially affirmative character is guaranteed by its universality.

> Carnival is not a spectacle seen by the people; they live in it, and everyone participates because its very idea embraces all the people. While carnival lasts, there is no life outside it. During carnival time life is subject only to its laws, that is, the laws of its own freedom. It has a universal spirit; it is a special condition of the world, or of the world's revival and renewal, in which all take part.

To the "serious" culture of the Middle Ages, which banished laughter from all its spheres, carnival juxtaposed its "feast of fools" and other ritual inversions of the official world and its canons. Carnival crowned and uncrowned mock kings and clergymen, celebrated obscene versions of religious ceremonies, and wore clothing inside out and upside down. Carnival provided an occasion for social protest, but also for social control that often erupted into violence through which members of the upper classes eliminated opponents of the lower classes. Carnival masks, costumes, and grotesque distortions of the body served to destabilize fixed identities and role differentiations. Contemporaries aptly described carnival as "a time of 'madness', in which Folly was king." The festive popular images epitomized in carnival—preserved in engravings and pamphlets in which mice eat cats, wolves tend sheep, children spank parents, carts precede horses, rabbits trap hunters, geese roast cooks, and the like—signified a parodic inversion of the official world with its intricate network of social definitions and claims to immutable authority that, Bakhtin believed, "reveal[s] the deepest meaning of the historic process."

Bakhtin's incorporation of these inversions and transformations of carnival was crucial to his conception of the ambiguous complexity of the novel and its capacity to discover, comprehend, and express deep strata of life accessible only to the language of carnivalization. The defining characteristic of Bakhtin's theory of the novel may be stated in terms of its relationship to time, to the historical process. The novel is the only genre that continues to develop, that is never completed. The novel is ever novel, ever contemporary, hence ever inconclusive and open-ended. Unlike every other literary genre, the novel conceives itself as of the present moment, and is ever aware of its location within the flux of history. In his essay, **"Epic and Novel"** (1941), Bakhtin writes: "From the very beginning the novel was structured not in the distanced image of the absolute past but in the zone of direct contact with inconclusive present-day reality." The novelistic perception of the world is deeply and self-consciously relativistic; it regards all assertions of timeless norms and canons as time-bound and thus ephemeral. In the novel, conventions are always just that, never more than arbitrary, ever given to change, transitory codifications of hierarchy. Born of parodies of linguistic and social norms—its predecessors include the "serio-comical" genres of antiquity (Socratic dialogues, Menippean satire, and dialogues of the Lucianic type) and medieval parodic grammars and monkish travesties of religious rituals—the novel emerged as the literary expression of the world in process, a macaronic mixture of linguistic forms, the old and the new, the dying and the procreating, beginnings and ends.

The polar opposite of the novel in this respect is the epic in which "the tradition of the past is sacred. There is as yet no consciousness of the possible relativity of the past." The epic past is an "absolute past"—closed, complete, retrospective, walled off from all subsequent times, above all the times of the epic narrators themselves. The epic hero, like the absolute past to which he belongs, is finished and complete, entirely externalized, "hopelessly ready-made." He views himself exactly as his society views him and as he anticipates his descendants will view him because he assumes they will hold the same views and values held by him and his contemporaries. No steady succession of times connects the epic past and its heroes with the present, or even with the past as experienced in the present. On the contrary, the epic past resists the possibility of approach, familiarization, or reevaluation; it is always opposed in principle to any merely transitory, future-oriented past. In the epic absolute past, only what comes "first" is good, and all the really good things— "beginnings," "founders," "ancestors"—occur *only* in this past, which is the sole source and beginning of everything good for all later times as well. The epic absolute past, then, is not simply one temporal category among many but a "monochronic and valorized" category, one that is normative and conclusive, remote and immutable.

Epic gives way to the novel when laughter is invoked to deprive the epic past of its distanced and sacrosanct character, and to bring the past into familiar proximity to the present. To be comical, Bakhtin argues, an object or image must be close at hand, where it can be divested of the fear and piety it inspires at a distance; where it can be examined, questioned, judged, ridiculed, and finally forgotten, so that creativity may be renewed. In the comic world, in contrast to the epic, "there is nothing for memory and tradition to do"; laughter delivers the object or image into the hands of "free experimental fantasy." Comedy thus contemporizes the past, makes the past accessible to the present, transforms it into a relative and relevant past. But Bakhtin also distinguished clearly between modernizing the past, which distorts its uniqueness, and contemporizing the past, which requires "an authentic profile of the past, an authentic language from another time." A parody can only be funny after all if we know what is being parodied. If a parody violates a former code, then that code must always be implictly there and *recognizable* in the parody itself. In other words, parody is as much a reassertion and revitalization of the code it travesties as it is the violation of that code. Parody, then, produces its unique comic effect not by "modernizing" the past, but by abolishing the temporal distance between the two codes and juxtaposing the present code to the past one within the same temporal frame—that is, by carnivalizing the temporal dimension itself. "Novel" and "epic" are, for Bakhtin, not genres in the usual sense, but rather stages in the development of genres; he might have said that every genre begins as a novel and ends as an epic.

The language of comedy transposed into the language of the novel thus produces a radically new temporal model of the world in which "there is no first word (no ideal word) and the final word has not yet been spoken." By destroying the distancing plane, the novel challenges the hierarchy of times with its linear, monological ideology. Through contact with the ever uncompleted present, time and the world become genuinely historical for the first time. Persons and events lose their finished and remote quality; and past, present, and future merge into a single, indivisible, ever-unfolding temporal continuum. Thus, for the novelist, personality is always in the making, never exhausted by the plot, never defined or definable once and for all. Unlike the epic hero, who is always equal to himself and to others' expectations of him, the novel's hero exists in a continual process of flux and redefinition, ever eluding finality. The novel's hero, like the novel itself, dwells in the zone of incompleteness; what both preserve through time is their openness to time, i. e., their contemporaneity. Depicting the present in all its inconclusiveness, the novel itself is ever inconclusive, ever at one with Becoming. In this inconclusive context, all the semantic and ideological stability of the past is lost; its sense and significance are constantly renewed and transformed as the context continues to unfold.

Thus, from the very beginning, as Bakhtin tried to show in the essays that make up *The Dialogic Imagination,* the novel developed as a literary form that had at its core a new way of conceptualizing time in which the hierarchization of temporalities played no role. As the literary form of Becoming, as the only literary form that brings the past into direct contact with developing reality, the novel could never be merely one genre among others or have a canon of its own. On the contrary, the novel not only parodies the other literary genres, it also parodies its own forms whenever they threaten to ossify. The novel seeks paradox and is at home in the interstices of human experience. But the novel does not simply play on its own definitions and the definitions of other genres, it also questions the literary frame itself, probes the boundaries of literature as a whole and its relationship to life outside literature. For the novel knows the boundaries of literature as simply another social convention, as arbitrary and historical as any other. In the presence of the novel, all other genres necessarily change. Bakhtin conceived the history of literature in fact as a constant struggle between the novel and the other genres, a struggle in which the novel compels them to acknowledge and abdicate their claims to unconditionality and to establish contact with the indeterminate present. By the "novelization" of the other genres Bakhtin did not mean their imitation of the novel, but rather their liberation from everything that would congeal them, and the novel itself, into stylized forms fated to outlive themselves. "Novel," in other words, is what Bakhtin called all those forces at work within a given literary system which reveal the limits, the artificial constraints of that system.

It is not surprising that Bakhtin sought and found the origins of the novel and novelistic discourse in just those transitional periods—between the classical and Hellenistic, and between the Middle Ages and the Renaissance—when past and present confronted and interpenetrated each other in carnivalistic fashion. In the Hellenistic period, Bakhtin argues, the carnivalization of culture produced prenovelistic works, like the Menippean satire, which parodied the absolute past of the classical age, with its "hopelessly ready-made" heroes and unitary language, in a style that is hybrid, multi-voiced, dialogic (or polyphonic)—a style in which there is a constant interaction among conflicting linguistic and ideological meanings and different time-frames. The ancient parodic travestying forms contributed to later novelistic discourses by creating a distance between language and reality that allowed for multiple meanings within the same text, thus subverting the architectonic myth implicit in the classical literary consciousness, and in every subsequent monologic consciousness, of an absolute identity or fusion of words with a particular ideological meaning.

Bakhtin suggests that late medieval man also lived simultaneously in two worlds, defined by a series of oppositions: sacred/profane, virtue/vice, official/unofficial, social hierarchy/utopian equality, Latin/vernacular, classical-normative/carnival-grotesque. In the literature of the waning Middle Ages, as in Hellenistic parody, the tendency was toward "a laughing double" for every serious form. The playing off of one (comic) version of the world against another (serious) version, epitomized in carnival, highlighted the importance of the border zone where seeming opposites collided or coexisted in ambiguous and often tensely charged relationships, as in the macaronic verse of the *Carmina Burana*. Carnival rituals and literature conveyed simultaneous messages about food and sex, religion and politics. Indeed, the outstanding characteristic of medieval carnival is that it was polysemous, meaning different things to different people within the same cultural context. Pagan meanings were juxtaposed to Christian ones, modifying both but obliterating neither; and the result, Bakhtin suggested, must be read and understood as a palimpsest. Just this carnivalization of culture, this interaction of incongruous linguistic and ideological perspectives within the same text produced the novel in the Renaissance.

By the end of the Middle Ages, the boundary line separating the official cult and ecclesiastical ideology from the culture of laughter was in dissolution. The lower genres began to penetrate the higher levels of literature, and laughter began to enter into all spheres of ideological life. This process was completed during the Renaissance and found its highest expression in Cervantes, Shakespeare, Grimmelshausen, but especially in Rabelais in whom the destruction of the old world-view and the creation of a new one are indissolubly interwoven. The medieval rogues, clowns, fools—those "life's maskers" who claim the right to be "other" in this world, "the right not to make common cause with any single one of the categories that life makes available;" and who, through their wholly theatricalized beings, reassert "the public nature of the human figure"—became the progenitors of the modern novel's heroes, those marginal figures who elude social definition and finality, who ever test and contest the conditions of their existence. The novel as a distinctive literary form was born when medieval culture, with its dualism and eschatological conception of history (the creation of the world, the fall from grace, the first expulsion, redemption, the second exile, and the final judgment—concepts in which the time of this world is devalued and subsumed to extratemporal categories), gave way to a "generative" time: a time measured by creative acts, constant birth and rebirth; a time in which death is not decisive in the larger socio-historical scheme of things; a time "maximally tensed toward the future." Rooted in the genres of folk humor and carnival narrative, and reflecting its parodic and metacultural origins, the novel depicts moments of maximum indeterminacy that call all fixed forms and structures into question. Standing outside and defying cultural hierarchies, the novel and its heroes become agents of a sociolinguistic universe that "defamiliarizes" existing conditions by playing off one mode of arrangement or perspective against another, revealing in the process possibilities for historical transformation.

For Bakhtin, then, literary structure is not something that exists unto itself, which can be discovered by the static segmentation and analysis of individual texts. His view of the novel as the site on which contesting and contested discourses of different periods, groups, or classes engage one another as sociolinguistic forces implied, rather, that literature—indeed, culture in general—must be understood as a system of signification that dialogically manifests itself and its multiple meanings in all their historical specificity and social valence. Bakhtin was one of the first in fact to propose a model for interpreting not only phenomena like carnival and carnival narrative, but for interpreting any sign system, be it literary or nonliterary, verbal or nonverbal. This original conception of culture ("high" and "low" alike) as the symbolic exchange of language, circumscribed and permeated by a specific historical environment, was the outcome of Bakhtin's novel attempt to solve what was in his time, and still is, the key problem confronting literary theory: to square the formalist conception of the autonomy of literature with the obvious fact of literature's interaction with other social phenomena.

Or, to rephrase the question in light of the vigorous debate Saussure's synchronic model stirred among Russian literary scholars of the 1920s: how can one speak of literary *history,* of the process of *becoming,* of *inter*textuality, if what is meant is simply a sequence of self-referential linguistic structures? On the one hand, Bakhtin agreed with Saussure and the Russian formalists in placing language at the center of literary theory and in positing a sharp and categorical distinction between the world as a source of representation and the world as represented in literature. When text is confused with context, words with the things they stand for, Bakhtin warned, the result is some form of naive naturalism, mimesis, reflection theory or psychologism, all of which in various ways obscure the differences between what is aesthetic and what is social in literature. On the other hand, Bakhtin joined with Marxist scholars (notably P. N. Medvedev and V. N. Voloshinov, with whom, or under whose names Bakhtin published some of his own work) in criticizing the formalist conception of language as an ahistorical system that posits a radical disjunction between the aesthetic and the social. Viewing both models as themselves contesting discourses confronting each other dialogically as it were, Bakhtin sought to synthesize elements of each to produce a theory of literature that would neither conceal nor exaggerate the boundary line between the aesthetic and the social, expressing his own position by an organic metaphor suggesting symbiosis:

> However forcefully the real and the represented world resist fusion, however immutable the presence of that categorical boundary line between them, they are nevertheless indissolubly tied up with each other and find themselves in continual mutual interaction; uninterrupted exchange goes on between them, similar to the uninterrupted exchange of matter between living organisms and the environment that surrounds them. As long as the organic lives, it resists a fusion with the environment, but if it is torn out of its environment, it dies.

Reacting against the "abstract objectivism" of Saussurean linguistics (the idea of language as a system of conventional, arbitrary signs of a fundamentally rational nature), Bakhtin and the members of his circle emphasized the speech aspect of language. Not the sentence, but the *utterance*—which differs from the linguist's sentence not in length or substance, but in its contextuality, its "historicity"—stands at the center of Bakhtin's conception of language. For Bakhtin, there is no such thing as a "general language" that is spoken by a general voice, that may be divorced from a specific speech act, which is charged with particular overtones. Living discourse, unlike a dictionary, is always in flux and in rebellion against its own rules. The recurring motifs in *The Formal Method in Literary Scholarship* (1928), *Marxism and the Philosophy of Language* (1929), and the works published under Bakhtin's own name—"the concrete life of the word," "the living word," and "the word within the word"—bespeak an emphasis on the here and now, on the intensely immediate exchange between living people in actual historical and social encounters. Language, when it *means,* is somebody talking to somebody else, even when that someone else is one's own inner self. To understand an utterance, therefore, means to formulate a reply to it (even if not to make it overtly), to evaluate it, to determine its meaning within a particular context. Understanding is thus itself dialogue. It follows, moreover, that "meaning" does not belong alone either to the speaker or the listener, but to the interaction between the two.

> In point of fact, *the word is a two-sided act.* It is determined equally by *whose* word it is and *for whom* it is meant. As word, it is precisely *the product of the reciprocal relationship between speaker and listener, addresser and addressee.* . . . I give myself, verbal shape from another's point of view, ultimately, from the point of view of the community to which I belong. A word is a bridge thrown between myself and another. If one end of the bridge depends on me, then the other depends on my addressee. A word is territory shared. . . .

The French linguist, Emile Benveniste, would later verify Bakhtin's insistence on the impossibility of isolating language from discourse, or discourse from subjectivity, through his analysis of linguistic components he claimed can only have meaning in actual discursive situations. In "Subjectivity in Language" (1958), Benveniste argues, for example, that the pronouns "I" and "you" lack the standardized and conventional significance of other linguistic terms. "I" always implies a speaker to whom it refers, and "you" always implies a listener whom the speaker addresses. These roles are endlessly reversible, as are the signifiers which depend upon them; the person who functions as a speaker one moment functions as a listener the next. These pronouns are also only intermittently activated, and thus have only a periodic meaning. In the intervals between speech utterances, they cease to mean anything at all.

> There is no concept "I" that incorporates all the *I*'s that are uttered at every moment in the mouths of speakers, in the sense that there is a concept "tree" to which all the individual uses of *tree* refer. . . . We are in the presence of a class of words, the "personal pronouns," that escape the status of all the other signs of language. Then what does *I* refer to? To something very peculiar which is exclusively linguistic: *I* refers to the act of individual discourse in which it is pronounced, and by this it designates the speaker. It is a term that cannot be identified except in what we have called elsewhere an instance of discourse and that has only a momentary reference. . . . It is in the instance of discourse in which *I* designates the speaker that the speaker proclaims himself as the "subject." And so it is literally true that the basis of subjectivity is in the exercise of language. [Benveniste, *Problems in General Linguistics,* trans. Mary E. Meek, 1971]

Benveniste notes that language also contains other elements whose status is equally dependent upon discourse, and equally marked by subjectivity—words, that is, which take on meaning only in relation to a subject. Verb forms imply a similar conceptualization of time, one keyed to the moment in which discourse occurs. Benveniste shows in "The Nature of Pronouns" (1956) that "the 'verb form' is an inextricable part of the individual instance of discourse: it is always and necessarily activated by the act of discourse and in dependence on that act." And in "Subjectivity in Language," he asserts that "language is marked so deeply by the expression of subjectivity that one might ask if it could still function and be called language if it were constructed otherwise."

Another Bakhtinian insight that informs Benveniste's theory is that subjectivity is entirely relational; it only comes into play through the principle of difference, by the opposition of the "other" or the "you" to the "I." In other words, subjectivity is not an essence but a set of relationships. Moreover, it can only be induced by discourse, by the activation of a signifying system which precedes the individual, and which determines his or her cultural identity. Benveniste (following Lacan) demonstrates that, in ordinary conversational situations, the speaking subject automatically links the pronouns "I" and "you" to the mental images by means of which it recognizes both itself and the person it addresses, and it identifies with the former of these. In "Language in Freudian Theory" (1956), Benveniste describes discourse in precisely these terms:

> All through Freudian analysis it can be seen that the subject makes use of the act of speech and discourse in order to "represent himself" to himself as he wishes to see himself and as he calls upon the "other" to see him. His discourse is appeal and recourse: a sometimes vehement solicitation of the other through the discourse in which he figures himself desperately, and an often mendacious recourse to the other in order to individualize himself in his own eyes. Through the sole fact of addressing another, the one who is speaking of himself installs the other in himself and thereby apprehends himself, confronts himself, and establishes himself as he aspires to be, and finally historicizes himself in this incomplete or falsified history. . . . The subject's language (*langue*) provides the instrument of a discourse in which his personality is released and creates itself, reaches out to the other and makes itself be recognized by him.

For Benveniste, then, as for Bakhtin, language is emphatically *not* a unitary, coherent system, separable from ideological and cultural flux. Because "the word" (i. e., the utterance as distinct from the sentence) is shared territory, the same set of words can differ in meaning in different verbal interactions. And because even the simplest communication act is never uniform, never transparent, never ahistorical, no amount of analysis of language as a synchronic "system" is sufficient to explain how words *can* (as Alice marveled) mean so many different things. The formalist idea of an utterance as simply a collocation of linguistic features Bakhtin would regard as a fundamental misconception of verbal exchange. For him, an utterance is shaped from within by the speaker's expectations of the listener's responses. And these expectations are in turn a product of all the speaker knows, or thinks he knows, about the listener (the attitudes of his social group, his personal history, the nature of his ties with the speaker) and the occasion and purpose of the utterance. Thus, we can understand the meaning of a speech act, Bakhtin and his group would argue, only when we succeed in connecting it to the linguistic and extralinguistic context in which it occurs, to the unstated social premises on which it depends. It would be impossible, for example, to recognize irony, parody, or stylization without reference to the context of another utterance, since they all rely for their meaning on something outside themselves. As Voloshinov put it, "the whole utterance is, after all, defined by its boundaries, and these boundaries run along the line of contact between a given utterance and the extraverbal and verbal (i. e., made up of other utterances) milieu."

In other words, no communication can be understood on the level at which it occurs because it is only at still higher orders of contextualization that the communicative system comes to be defined. This means that global patternings of meanings which are immanent in the organization of a cultural system at all levels can never be entirely reduced to a unique, determinate meaning in some local situation of occurrence or realization. At the higher levels of semiotic organization these discursive formations con-

stitute an entire culture. The multiple conflicting "voices" in dialogic discourse form the basis of a social process in which identity, status, and ideology among various social groups may generate conflict and change within the sociolinguistic system itself. This can happen because a cultural system comprises an ordered system of codes which determine both the distribution of meanings in society *as well as* ownership and access to the means of production of social meanings. Hence the ever-present possibility of *mis*understanding.

Thus, Bakhtin could claim that language is the most sensitive barometer of social and historical change. The synchronic and diachronic dimensions of language, he argued against the formalists, can never be separated, even for purposes of analysis, because "whatever a word might mean, it is first of all materially present, as a thing uttered, written, printed, whispered, or thought" [*The Formal Method in Literary Scholarship: A Critical Introduction to Sociological Poetics*]. At any given time, language consists of a multitude of jargons, dialects, and discourses of regional and social subgroups, all more or less successful, depending upon their social scope and ideological authority. Language, in other words, is always languages, defined by "multi-speechedness," "heteroglot from top to bottom," ever in motion. To a synchronic view of language, however, change must appear as but an irrational force distorting the logical purity of language. There is no development, only inexplicable disruption. "What interests the mathematically minded rationalists is not the relationship of the sign to the actual reality it reflects nor to the individual who is its originator, but the *relationship of sign to sign within a closed system* already accepted and authorized." Once an analysis excludes the utterance and its necessary socio-historical context, change can only be described in terms of the altering of the components of a sentence—which is something like describing the history of philosophy as a random succession of ideas. As Bakhtin saw it, language is a dynamic process in which an endless contest between *langue* and *parole,* between canonization and innovation, is fought out at every level.

> Language is not a neutral medium that passes freely and easily into the private property of the speaker's intentions; it is populated—over-populated—with the intentions of others. Expropriating it, forcing it to submit to one's own intentions and accents, is a difficult and complicated process. . . . Consciousness finds itself inevitably facing the necessity of *having to choose a language*.

Literary language is also a jargon like any other, used in a particular milieu and in a specific speaker-listener relationship. The very existence (not to mention the primacy) of literary language in some cultures but not in others is itself a salient *social* fact about it, and social changes that affect everyday language will eventually affect literary language as well. It is only by conceiving language itself as not merely permeated by ideological values, but also as constituted out of the social interaction in which those values are born, live, and die that we can begin to understand a literary text as part of a social process. As Medvedev and Bakhtin tried to show in *The Formal Method In Literary*

Scholarship, the literary work participates in the larger economy of material and ideological production. "Literary history is concerned with the concrete life of the literary work in the unity of the generating literary environment, the literary environment in the generating ideological environment, and the latter, finally, in the generating socio-economic environment which permeates it."

To put it another way, the life cycles of literary forms do not run their course within a closed aesthetic space, independent of what goes on in the world outside literature. Literary forms have no predictable life-span, and mere frequency of use has nothing to do with their durability or obsolescence. Literary forms become obsolete when they no longer tell, or are thought to tell, the truth about the world, and there is no predicting how long it may take for this perceived failing to overtake a particular form. But changes of this kind, when they occur, always bear the traces of a material history and culture antecedent to the change itself. As Bakhtin wrote in **"Discourse in the Novel"** (1934-35):

> When discourse is torn from reality, it is fatal for the word itself as well: words grow sickly, lose semantic depth and flexibility, the capacity to expand and renew their meanings in new living contexts—they essentially die as discourse, for the signifying word lives beyond itself, that is, it lives by means of directing its purpose outward.

The final point here—that consciousness is linguistically (and through language socio-historically) determined—forms the central argument of ***Freudianism: A Marxist Critique*** (1927). Here Voloshinov and Bakhtin reject Freud's distinction between the conscious and unconscious in favor of the view that the unconscious is simply a variant of the conscious, differing from it ideologically but not ontologically. What Freud called the unconscious (the realm of repressed drives and desires), Voloshinov and Bakhtin rename the "unofficial conscious" as distinct from the ordinary "official conscious" whose ideologies may be shared openly with others. The language of the unofficial conscious is "inner speech"; the language of the official conscious, "outward speech." But both (as Lacan and Benveniste would argue) operate according to the same general rules governing all verbal behavior. Inner speech is essentially the same as outward speech, differing from it only in the matter it addresses. Both are socio-historically determined. The structure of every utterance, internal or external, is social, as is every experience it expresses.

> *The verbal component of behavior is determined in all the fundamentals and essentials of its content by objective social factors.* . . . Therefore, nothing verbal in human behavior (inner and outward speech equally) can under any circumstances be reckoned to the account of the individual subject in isolation; the verbal is not his property but the property of his social group (his social milieu).

Far from being private, inner speech is the most sensitive and immediate register of social change. Although both variants of consciousness are ideological through and through, ideology has a different status in each. The primary difference consists in the greater stability of the official conscious whose ideologies are shared by the group as a whole. At this level, "inner speech comes easily to order and freely turns into outward speech or, in any case, has no fear of becoming outward speech. . . . In a healthy community and in a socially healthy personality . . . there is no discrepancy between the official and unofficial conscious." But once an ideology ceases to be shared by the group as a whole, as happens when it no longer expresses the group's real socioeconomic interests, a gap develops between the two levels of consciousness which disrupts their internal dialogue and stifles inner speech. And the greater the gap between them, the more difficult it becomes for the motives of inner speech to find verbal expression, and the more apt they are to turn into a "foreign body" in the psyche and to become *"asocial."* This doesn't mean, however, that every motive in contradiction with the official ideology is doomed to become asocial and lose contact with verbal communication; a "censored" motive might well engage in a struggle with the official ideology.

> If such a motive *is founded on the economic being of the whole group,* if it is not merely the motive of a déclassé loner, then it has a chance for a future and perhaps even a victorious future. . . . Only, at first a motive of this sort will develop within a small social milieu and will depart into the underground—not the psychological underground of repressed complexes, but the salutary political underground. That is exactly how a *revolutionary ideology* in all spheres of culture comes about.

The master text of Voloshinov's and Bakhtin's political underground is *Notes From Underground,* in which the narrator's tortured soul and "anti-social" tendencies bespeak the disintegration of the official ideology (and through it, his own disintegration), against which he rants in the name of the rights of repressed consciousness—the right to be "other" in this world, to be unique and unpredictable, to throw everything into question, including oneself. "We are oppressed at being men—men with a real individual body and blood, we are ashamed of it, we think it a disgrace and try to contrive to be some sort of impossible generalized man." In contrast to Lukács, for example, Bakhtin argues that the hero interests Dostoevsky in the *Notes,* and throughout his writings, not as a typical (or atypical) manifestation of a fixed and stable external reality, nor as a profile composed of objective features which, taken together, constitute his identity. What is important to Dostoevsky is not how his hero appears in the world, but first and foremost how the world appears to his hero, and how the hero appears to himself. In a Dostoevsky novel, the rules governing the psyche coexist on the same level as the rules governing the state. Dostoevsky politicizes his heroes, in other words, by giving their inner speech the same weight and status as the outward speech they contest, thereby undermining its stability and ideological authority. The hero's voice in a Dostoevsky novel is only one, albeit the central one, in a chorus of voices in which any "authoritative" discourse can in fact be made to appear relative. In thus revising Freud's conscious/unconscious dichotomy and insinuating it into his interpretation of Dostoevsky, Bakhtin was in a sense, as Michael Holquist suggests [in "The Politics of Representation"], giving voice to his own dilemma, the dilemma of a Dostoevskyan underground man "sending out transcoded messages from the catacombs"—one being that "in the history of literary language, there is a struggle constantly being waged to overcome the official line . . . a struggle against various kinds and degrees of authority."

It is in Dostoevsky, and in Dostoevsky alone, that Bakhtin finds the polyphonic ideal fully realized: the ideal of the coexistence, interaction, and interdependence of several different, relatively autonomous consciousnesses that express simultaneously the various contents of the world within the unity of a single text. "What Dostoevsky's characters *say* constitutes an arena of never-ending struggle with others' words, in all realms of life and creative activity. . . . the life experience of the characters and their discourse may be resolved as far as plot is concerned, but internally they remain incomplete and unresolved." This greatest of all literary contrapuntalists genuinely surrenders to his characters and allows them to speak in ways other than his own. Heroes are no longer reduced to the dominating consciousness of the author, as they are in monologic narrative (in Tolstoy, for example, with whom Bakhtin often compares Dostoevsky), and secondary characters are no longer encompassed by and reduced to their usefulness to heroes—or to the author. Dostoevsky's characters are, in short, respected as full subjects, shown as consciousnesses which can never be fully defined or exhausted, rather than as objects fully known, once and for all, in their roles—and then discarded as expendable.

Bakhtin shared with Dostoevsky a view of the individual as comprehensible only within his own point of view (his "confessional self-utterance"), hence impossible to define or categorize in any permanent and immutable fashion. This view—indeed, all the significant aspects of Bakhtin's thought—is apparent in **Problems of Dostoevsky's Poetics,** the only one of his writings of the 1920s he published under his own name. This work, which may be read as Bakhtin's own confessional self-utterance, clearly rests on a vision of the world as essentially a network of subjects who are themselves social in essence, not private or autonomous individuals in the Western sense. Bakhtin expressed this vision always in terms of the "multivoicedness" or "multi-centeredness" of the world as we experience it. We come into consciousness speaking a language already permeated by many voices—a social, not a private or unitary language. From the very beginning we are "polyglot," already in process of mastering a variety of social dialects derived from parents, teachers, clan, class, religion, and region. We grow in consciousness by assimilating more voices, then by learning which to accept as "internally persuasive." In this way, we achieve a kind of individuality, one which recognizes and respects the fact that each of us is a "we," not just an "I." Polyphony, the interaction of many voices which finds its supreme literary expression in the novel, is thus both a fact of life and a value to be pursued endlessly against the suffocating forces of regimentation and conformity.

It is largely from Bakhtin's writings, especially his books

on Dostoevsky and Rabelais, that we have learned to apply terms like "carnivalization" to the dissolution of hierarchy in all spheres of life, and it is a major part of his legacy to have taught us about the liberating energy of the carnivalesque and carnival laughter. "There is no standpoint counterposed to laughter. Laughter is 'the only positive hero' " [**"The Art of the word and The Culture of Folk Humor (Rabelais and Gogol),"** *Semiotics and Structuralism*]. Bakhtin's unshakable faith in the transcendent power of laughter permeates his lavish descriptions of the carnivalesque, descriptions which clearly celebrate a tradition whose full realization he found in Rabelais, and whose renaissance he discovered in Dostoevsky. It is characteristic of Bakhtin that the carnival-grotesque serves, in some respects, as his model of the "normal" in that it embodies both the conventional *and* the unexpected, the established *and* the creative. This model enabled him to see how traditional literary forms are abolished or transformed through parody as part of the complex interaction of social forces within particular periods of upheaval and transition; how the novel may be said to characterize literature as a whole; and how language systems are revitalized by creolization and restricted by stabilization. The most important part of Bakhtin's legacy, however, is not his immensely fruitful struggle with worn-out words and literary

---

Ken Hirschkop on the sociological implications of Bakhtin's theories:

The ease with which *everyone* can endorse the central elements of the Bakhtinian programme indicates that the hard work has not really begun. What is this 'dialogism' that so many celebrate as liberating and democratic: what are its actual cultural forms, its social or political preconditions, its participants, methods and goals? When we first meet this concept in Bakhtin's work it describes a certain relation between distinct 'voices' in a narrative text, in which each takes its shape as a conscious reaction to the ideological position of the other; but even then it is a metaphor for a broader principle of discourse. 'Heteroglossia', when first mentioned, is a description of stylistic and generic stratification and conflict within the confines of a national vernacular. But what are the consequences of this stratification? Do all such divisions have political significance? Is it a recipe for social diversity or the establishment of warring interest groups? 'Carnivalesque' works, in Bakhtin's parlance, use motifs, themes and generic forms drawn from a tradition of subversive medieval popular culture, a tradition linked to a very specific festive practice and to the significance of the body in medieval and Renaissance culture. How can these practices be translated into the very different kinds of popular culture one finds in modern capitalist societies? These are all questions which the Bakhtin circle left unanswered, but they pose in particularly acute form the problem of how to establish a democratic culture and language in modern societies.

Ken Hirschkop in his introduction to Bakhtin and Cultural Theory, *Manchester University Press, 1989.*

forms, but rather his struggle—often resourceful, cunning, and oblique—with the forces of stagnation and finalization, with the determinism of being, whether in the fixed forms of unitary discourse, genre conventions in literature, or in the rigidity of thought patterns. In other words, Bakhtin might have said that he wished to be read as a novel, not an epic.

Robert Anchor, "Bakhtin's Truths of Laughter," in CLIO, *Vol. 14, No. 3, Spring, 1985, pp. 237-57.*

Susan Stewart　(essay date 1986)

[*In the essay below, which was originally published in 1983, Stewart analyzes how Bakhtin's linguistic theories reject the abstract conception of language in favor of a purely social, "practical" one.*]

During the period of the New Economic Policy, as Lenin sought, rather abashedly, to approach communism via a new form of "state capitalism," and as the concrete mode of peasant existence was being transformed into the abstractions of industrial labor, the contradictions between synchrony and diachrony, between "sincerity" and "irony," between insistences simultaneously upon meaning and "multivocality" were in full flower. The work of the Bakhtin school may be located within this milieu of contradiction. It is clear that Mikhail Bakhtin's project was not a linguistics but, to use his word, a "metalinguistics," an attempt to avoid an essentialist view of language and to see, within a social and historical frame, the creation and uses of both language and the term "language." [In an endnote, Stewart directs the reader to Gary Saul Morson's essay, "The Heresiarch of *Meta*," *PTL* 3, (October 1978): 407-27, for more information on this.] As Bakhtin wrote in *Problems of Dostoevsky's Poetics:*

> The point is not the mere presence of several linguistic styles, social dialects, etc., a presence which is measured by purely linguistic criteria; the point is the *dialogical angle* at which they (the styles, dialects, etc.) are juxtaposed and counterposed in the work. But that dialogic angle cannot be measured by means of purely linguistic criteria, because dialogic relationships, although they belong to the province of the *word,* fall outside the province of its purely linguistic study.

> Dialogical relationships (including the dialogical relationships of the speaker to his own word) are a matter for metalinguistics. [In an endnote Stewart explains that she follows "the current practice of attributing the works of the Bakhtin school to Bakhtin himself."]

In short, only through metalinguistics could one account for the history and social life of language.

It is important to remember, however, that Bakhtin's meta-position is not so much a move toward transcendence as it is a battle stance, a polemical insistence upon situating theories of language within the constraints of their particular social and historical periods. M. A. K. Halliday has noted that some forms of speech, such as thieves' jargon and tinkers' argot, are shaped in direct op-

position to the speech of the dominant class of their times; he calls these forms of speech "anti-languages" ["Anti-Languages," *American Anthropologist* 78 (September 1976): 170-83]. Analogously, Bakhtin's linguistics is an *anti-linguistics,* a systematic questioning and inverting of the basic premises and arguments of traditional linguistic theory. It follows that recent attempts to "appropriate" Bakhtin's theories of language into the tradition he rejects are largely misguided. Erasing not only Bakhtin's sense of the radically *un*systematic nature of the linguistic world but also the conflicting, anarchic nature of his very texts, semioticians and structuralists have let him speak only by silencing him.

Nowhere does this problem of appropriation emerge more clearly than in examining Bakhtin's critique of language. Indeed, even using the term "language" skews the position that Bakhtin took toward verbal behavior. In **Marxism and the Philosophy of Language,** his critique of "abstract objectivist" theories is directed to the following points: that such theories stabilize language at the expense of its real mutability and the creativity of its users; that such theories assume language to be outside of contextualization and consequently outside of history; and that such theories tend to hypostatize their own categories. [In an endnote, Stewart directs the reader to **Marxism and the Philosophy of Language**, p. 77, and **Freudianism: A Marxist Critique** for more on this.] Ferdinand de Saussure had written in the *Cours de linguistique générale:*

> In separating language from speaking we are at the same time separating: (1) what is social from what is individual; and (2) what is essential from what is accessory and more or less accidental.

> Language is not a function of the speaker; it is a product that is passively assimilated by the individual. It never requires premeditation, and reflection enters in only for the purpose of classification. . . .

> Speaking, on the contrary, is an individual act. It is willful and intellectual.

No position could be more the antithesis of Bakhtin's. Saussure is interested in language as an abstract and ready-made system; Bakhtin is interested only in the dynamics of living speech. Where Saussure sees passive assimilation, Bakhtin sees a process of struggle and contradiction. And whereas Saussure dichotomizes the individual and the social, Bakhtin assumes that the individual is constituted by the social, that consciousness is a matter of dialogue and juxtaposition with a social Other.

In **"Discourse in the Novel"** Bakhtin writes: "A passive understanding of linguistic meaning is no understanding at all, it is only the abstract aspect of meaning." For Bakhtin such an abstraction from the concrete utterance would be a dead end, reifying its own categories of the linguistic norm and producing a model with no capability of discussing linguistic—and thereby, for Bakhtin, social—change. If Bakhtin has until recently lacked his true inheritors, Saussure has not, and the major heirlooms of Saussurian linguistics—*langue* vs. *parole,* the arbitrary nature of the sign, and, more indirectly, the distinction between poetic and ordinary language—reappear in transformational grammar, in the old (and the new) stylistics, and even, surprisingly, in quasi-Marxist theories of language such as Julia Kristeva's.

The transformational grammarian's devoted outlining of abstract syntactical structures and the stylistician's almost magical rendering of phonetic and morphological structures into thematic structures stand in direct contrast to Bakhtin's object of study. [In an endnote, Stewart writes: "For an attempt to link syntactic to larger social transformations, see Rosalind Coward and John Ellis, *Language and Materialism: Developments in Semiology and the Theory of the Subject* (London, 1977), pp. 127-30. This attempt seems at best metaphorical and at worst strangely skewed: without a corresponding theory of language use in context, the linkage involves a confusion of levels of analysis."] When Bakhtin discusses "problems of syntax," he has in mind the utterance as it occurs in context, in lived social time. Hence that object of study has rather fluid, generically determined boundaries, ranging from utterances consisting of a single word to utterances consisting of the entire text of a literary work. In *The Formal Method in Literary Scholarship,* he writes:

> It is the whole utterance as speech performance that is directed at the theme, not the separate word, sentence, or period. It is the whole utterance and its forms, which cannot be reduced to any linguistic forms, which control the theme. The theme of the work is the theme of the whole utterance as a definite sociohistorical act. Consequently, it is inseparable from the total situation of the utterance to the same extent that it is inseparable from linguistic elements.

The critique of abstraction in Bakhtin's work is a profound and relentless one. At every point he proclaims that the model of pure linguistic form arose from neoclassical philosophies and from the study of dead languages, that only in its living reality, shaped and articulated by social evaluation, does the word exist. He insists upon contextualizing even the notion of abstraction itself, suggesting that the tradition of normative linguistics from Aristotle and Saint Augustine through the Indo-Europeanists served the needs of sociopolitical and cultural centralization. These "centripetal forces," he contends, can be perceived only against the backdrop of the very "heteroglossia" they sought to deny. We see a rejection in his work not only of a distinction between "language" and "speech" but also of a distinction between synchrony and diachrony. Bakhtin traces these dichotomies to Cartesian rationalism and Leibniz's conception of a universal grammar. Because it denies the actual creativity of language use, Bakhtin rejects the systematizing impulse of such linguistic thought: "Formal, systematic thought about language is incompatible with living, historical understanding of language. From the system's point of view, history always seems merely a series of accidental [*sic*] transgressions." [In an endnote, Stewart writes: "It is thus puzzling when Krystyna Pomorska, in her foreword to Bakhtin's *Rabelais and His World,* insists repeatedly that Bakhtin is a structuralist. Although Roman Jakobson and Jurij Tynjanov wrote in their 'Problems in the Study of Literature and Language' that 'every system necessarily exists as an evolution while, on the other hand, evolution is inescapably of a systematic nature' (quoted in Titunik, 'The Formal Method and the Sociological Method [M. M. Baxtin, P. N. Medvedev, V. N. Vološinov] in Russian Theory and Study of Literature,' appendix 2, *Marxism and the Philosophy of Language,* p. 187), this is hardly a mirror of Bakhtin's rejection of the distinction between synchrony and diachrony. In a later essay, 'Mixail Baxtin [Mikhail Bakhtin] and His Verbal Universe,' Pomorska writes that Bakhtin is a 'real semiotician,' and she goes on to explain that, in his rejection of an autonomous function for literature, he prefigures the Tartu school's semiotics. She also writes that, in addition to the Einsteinian revolution and Husserlian philosophy, 'the other source, more obvious for Baxtin than, say, for Jakobson or Tynjanov, is classical Marxist dialectics' (*PTL* 3 [April 1978]: 381, 384-85)."]

Not only does such systematization lead to a denial of history—it also results in a vision of speech as a series of "accidental transgressions," a vision we find most prevalent in Noam Chomsky's distinction between competence and performance. There is perhaps no clearer description of linguistic alienation than Chomsky's position on this point: "Any interesting generative grammar will be dealing, for the most part, with mental processes that are far beyond the level of actual or even potential consciousness; furthermore, it is quite apparent that a speaker's reports and viewpoints about his behavior and competence may be in error" [*Aspects of the Theory of Syntax,* 1965]. The social and political consequences of such an abstract linguistics are brought out in Bakhtin's own observations on the concept of error: "Only in abnormal and special cases do we apply the criterion of correctness to an utterance (for instance, in language instruction). Normally, the criterion of linguistic correctness is submerged by a purely ideological [i. e., thematic] criterion." Rather than assume a transcendent grammar to which actual speech performance can be only imperfectly compared, Bakhtin looks at the social articulation and uses of diversity. The consequences of the Cartesian position become clearer when we look at its current application in state policy. In such domains as the exclusion of bi- (and multi-) lingual education, language requirements attached to immigration restrictions, tensions between nonstandard and standard "dialects" (these terms themselves the necessary fictions by which a transcendent "standard" is created), and the language of state apparatuses in general, the Cartesian position functions to reinforce state institutions and to trivialize change and everyday linguistic creativity. To silence the diversity of the powerful "unsaids" of actual speech in favor of an opaque and universal form of language is to strip language of its ideological significance—a stripping that is itself strongly and univocally ideological. [In an endnote, Stewart writes: "For a sociolinguistic critique of transformational grammar, see Dell Hymes, *Foundations in Sociolinguistics: An Ethnographic Approach* (Philadelphia, 1974), particularly pp. 119-24, where Herderian and Cartesian linguistics are contrasted; and William Labov, *Sociolinguistic Patterns* (Philadelphia, 1972), p. 200. In a suggestive essay, Henri Gobard has traced some of the sociological functions of abstract languages, particularly the effect of a multinational English upon vernacular French:

see Gobard, *L'Alienation linguistique: Analyse tetraglossique* (Paris, 1976)."]

His careful attention to actual social behavior also prohibits Bakhtin from accepting any facile distinction between ordinary and poetic language. Such distinctions tend to trivialize both everyday speech acts—by making them automatic or indistinguishable—and "poetic" utterances—by making them parasitic. Most important, theories of poetic language trivialize the activities of speakers by assuming an essentialist, rather than a social, definition of genre. [In an endnote, the critic writes: "See Stanley E. Fish, 'How Ordinary Is Ordinary Language?', *New Literary History*, Vol. 5, Autumn, 1973, pp. 41-54; and Mary Louise Pratt, 'The Poetic Language Fallacy,' *Toward a Speech Act Theory of Literary Discourse*, pp. 3-37."] A critique of the concept of poetic language forms a major part of **The Formal Method:** "If the poetic construction had been placed in a complex, many-sided relationship with science, with rhetoric, with the fields of real practical life, instead of being declared the bare converse of a fabricated practical language, then formalism as we know it would not have existed." In this study, Bakhtin not only objects to the formalist concept of the autonomy of poetic language but also, in a characteristic move, attempts to show the sources and purposes of this formalist position in futurist poetics.

Although we find in Bakhtin an early critic of the linguistics of abstract objectivism, we do not find a neat precursor of contemporary social theories of language. Whereas such studies as William Labov's on the social implications of sound-change vindicate Bakhtin's rejection of a purely "linguistic" conception of phonology, the majority of sociolinguistic studies tends, no less problematically, to emphasize context in a highly abstract way—that is, without a corresponding discussion of the location of the utterance in history and social life. [In an endnote, the critic adds: "See Labov, *Sociolinguistic Patterns and Language in the Inner City: Studies in the Black English Vernacular.*"] In other words, as the abstract objectivists tend to hypostatize grammar, the sociolinguists often tend to hypostatize rules for speech behavior. They do not seem to realize that such rules are not simply located *behind* the historical processes of social life but are also *emergent in* them. Hence there is a tendency to want to *name* the situation, to close off its boundaries, particularly in speech-act theory. Consider, for instance, John Searle's original formulation of his philosophy of speech acts [in *Speech Acts: An Essay in the Philosophy of Language*]: "The form this hypothesis will take is that the semantic structure of a language may be regarded as a conventional realization of a series of sets of underlying constitutive rules, and that speech acts are acts characteristically performed by uttering expressions in accordance with these sets of constitutive rules."

Similarly, although the sociolinguistic study of styles of speaking goes beyond such a static concept of situation by contrasting the "referential" and "social" aspects of discourse, it does not present a model of the historical transformation of social values and ideologies. The emphasis on rule-governed behavior in current social studies of language again tends toward a focus on "form" at the expense of ideological strategy and a focus on "system" at the expense of social creativity. As a result, such studies search for a grammar of situation; and so, their Romantic humanism notwithstanding, they recapitulate many of the methodological pitfalls of the abstract objectivists.

Bakhtin's positions on verbal interaction thus overlap—but also go beyond—the aims of both sociolinguistics and speech-act theory. The difference is that his primary concern is not so much with how things *work* as with how things *change*. In contrast to Searle's atemporality, Bakhtin presents a theory of the sequential order of change: "This is the order that the actual generative process of language follows: *social intercourse is generated* (stemming from the basis); *in it verbal communication and interaction are generated; and in the latter, forms of speech performances are generated; finally, this generative process is reflected in the change of language forms.*" Like Searle and John Austin, Bakhtin is concerned with identifying what he calls the "little behavioral genres" of speech situations—question, exclamation, command, request, the light and casual causerie of the drawing room. But Bakhtin is even more interested in the relationships between those genres and their contexts in the rest of social life: "The behavioral genre fits everywhere into the channel of social intercourse assigned to it and functions as an ideological reflection of its type, structure, goal, and social composition," particularly as history changes the ideological functions of such contexts. Searle specifies the "happiness conditions" of successful speech acts; Bakhtin is the master of what we might call "unhappiness conditions," those circumstances in which the utterance stands in tension or conflict with the utterances of others. For utterances are always preceded by alien utterances which face them in the form of an addressee or social Other and which surround them with an always significant silence. Whereas linguistic theory must be grateful to sociolinguistics for specifying the profound uses of silence, it must be grateful to Bakhtin for articulating the powerful force of the silenc*ed* in language use. [In an endnote, the critic adds: "See, for example, K. H. Basso, 'To Give Up on Words': Silence in Western Apache Culture, in *Language and Social Context: Selected Readings*, pp. 67-86."]

Thus, Bakhtin presents us with a "generative" linguistics, but that linguistics is accounted for in a *social* sense. The "rules" it seeks are conventions of genre, conventions of voice, character, idea, temporality, and closure which will be modified by the ongoing transformations of social life. Because it emphasizes the social, it is directly opposed to those contemporary theories of language, such as Chomsky's, that ultimately locate transformation in biological evolutionary processes. And although Bakhtin presents an investigation of utterances in context, his concern with dialogue, with conflict, and, especially, with the cumulative forces of history acting upon each speech situation distinguishes his work from contemporary sociolinguistic theories. Finally, although many careful comparisons have been made between Bakhtin's semiotics and contemporary semiotic theory, Bakhtin's position on the sign differs from traditional semiotics in several crucial ways. [In an endnote, the critic adds: "See Matejka, 'On the First Russian Prolegomena to Semiotics,' appendix 1, *MPL*, pp.

161-74; Viach Vs. Ivanox, 'The Significance of M. M. Bakhtin's Ideas on Sign, Utterance, and Dialogue for Modern Semiotics (1),' *Soviet Studies in Literature* 11 Spring-Summer, 1975, pp. 186-243; and Tzvetan Todorov, *Mikhail Bakhtine et la théorie de l'histoire littéraire.*"]

The powerful critique of "language" offered in **Marxism and the Philosophy of Language** is supplemented throughout the rest of his works by an equally powerful critique of the concept of the sign. The Saussurian theory of the referent naively assumes a univocality of meaning, and Charles Sanders Peirce's theory of iconicity assumes an actual physical referent to which the sign-vehicle corresponds. In contrast, Bakhtin clearly distinguishes between the mechanistic and pragmatic functions of signals and the cultural and "polyvocal" functions of signs: "The process of understanding is on no account to be confused with the process of recognition. These are thoroughly different processes. Only a sign can be understood; what is recognized is a signal." For Bakhtin, the material life of the sign does not arise out of the world of physical objects; rather, it arises out of the actual material practices of everyday social life. And, unlike Saussure, Bakhtin does not see the sign as a part of an abstract system resulting from the structure of psychological perception. Instead, he looks for the ontology of the sign in the "practical business of living speech." Here again we see Bakhtin's rebellion against system. The semiotic character of culture is the result of concrete and dynamic historical processes, processes of tension and conflict inseparable from the basis of social and economic life.

Bakhtin's critique of the univocal sign is perhaps most fully developed in his study of Dostoevsky and in his early essay, **"Discourse in Life and Discourse in Art."** In the works of Dostoevsky, Bakhtin both found and created the aesthetic correspondent to his theories of thought and language:

> The idea, as *seen* by Dostoevsky the artist, is not a subjective individual-psychological formulation with a "permanent residence" in a person's head; no, the idea is interindividual and intersubjective. The sphere of its existence is not the individual consciousness, but the dialogical intercourse *between* consciousnesses. The idea is a *living event* which is played out in the point where two or more consciousnesses meet dialogically. In this respect the idea resembles the *word,* with which it forms a dialogical unity. Like the word, the idea wants to be heard, understood, and "answered" by other voices from other positions. Like the word, the idea is by nature dialogical, the monolog being merely the conventional form of its expression which arose from the soil of the ideological monologism of modern times.

The idea and the word are here conceptualized as "arenas of conflict," and this conflict arises not simply, as sociolinguistics suggests, out of the tension between the referent and the physical context of utterances but rather from bringing all past experience with the word to bear upon the present situation. For example, Bakhtin sees the works of Dostoevsky as integrating the aphoristic thinking of the Enlightenment and Romanticism into locations of contrast and conflict. And those locations invite the social value judgments of readers who are themselves implicated in the text.

In **"Discourse in Life and Discourse in Art,"** these aspects of polyvalence are worked into a sociological theory of literature. Bakhtin outlines the ways in which the relations between the author's, hero's (character's), and reader's voices intersect within the constraints of genre. "The interrelationship of author and hero, never, after all, actually is an intimate relationship of two; all the while form makes provision for the third participant—the listener—who exerts crucial influence on all the other factors of the work." It is out of these contrasting and collaborating positions that satire, parody, and irony arise as forms depicting conflicting social value judgments.

We might contrast this approach to literature with modern speech-act theories that assume, in Mary Louise Pratt's term, that literary works are "verbal displays." Such theories often neglect the specific effects that the literary work uses to create distancing and irony. [In an endnote, the critic adds: "Pratt presents a convincing argument regarding the ways in which narrative literary works should not be separated formally from narratives of everyday life. But her assumptions of the linearity and univocality of both types of narrative preclude consideration of the ways in which face-to-face narratives most often are constructed collaboratively and, hence, reveal conflicting social value judgments just as literary works do."] In other words, speech-act theories of literature often assume the same systematic and transparent univocality we find in speech-act theories of language. But Bakhtin's literary theory assumes that the problems of dialogue and multivocality that are found in face-to-face communication will be compounded by the specific effects used within the structure of the literary genre. Because the literary work relies on a common ideological purview of both author and reader and, at the same time, cannot rely upon an apparent "extraverbal" context, the work is a complex presentation of display *and* concealment, of the over- and under-articulated. This presentation is further complicated by the history of generic conventions. Bakhtin writes: "We might say that *a poetic work is a powerful condenser of unarticulated social evaluations*—each word is saturated with them. *It is these social evaluations that organize form as their direct expression.* "

Bakhtin's concerted opening up of the word may be characterized as having distinguishable, if interwoven, formal and semantic levels. We have seen how his position takes a stance against both abstract objectivism and Romanticism, but we also might consider the influence of Bakhtin's historical work on the development of his theory. In the introduction to **Rabelais and His World,** Bakhtin writes that the function of the "carnival-grotesque" is "to consecrate inventive freedom, to permit the combination of a variety of different elements and their rapprochement, to liberate from the prevailing point of view of the world, from conventions and established truths, from clichés, from all that is humdrum and universally accepted." It is characteristic of Bakhtin that, in several ways, the carnival-grotesque serves as a model of the normal. For carnival contains both the conventional and the unexpected, the established and the creative. He also focuses on the transitional linguistic forms of the Hellenic period, the late Middle Ages, and the Renaissance—that is, on loci of change. Here and in his discussion of the prehistory of the novel, he is interested in how traditional forms are parodied, or "carnivalized," as part of the complex interaction of social forces within particular historical periods of upheaval and transformation. He consequently paid great attention to the creolized language of the marketplace and street while he formed an image of language as mediating between conventionality and creativity.

For Bakhtin, language is mutable, reversible, antihierarchical, contaminable, and powerfully regenerative. It is always meeting—has always been meeting—what is strange, foreign, other:

> Linguistics, itself the product of [the] foreign word, is far from any proper understanding of the role played by the foreign word in the history of language and linguistic consciousness. On the contrary, Indo-European studies have fashioned categories of understanding for the history of language of a kind that preclude proper evaluation of the role of [the] alien word. Meanwhile, that role, to all appearances, is enormous.

At language's point of origin, Bakhtin assumes ambivalence, multivocality, conflict, incorporation, and transformation. Not the least profound implication of this position might be that the model which linguistics has assumed, whereby stable languages eventually become creolized, has been moving backward; instead, we might assume creolization at the point of origin and view stabilization of the linguistic system not as the normal but as the restricted case.

Semantically, Bakhtin's dialogic conception of the word can be seen not only as a contribution to linguistic theory but also as a contribution to the theory of ideology. For although Bakhtin continually erases the abstract concept of language, he just as continually reformulates the concept of ideology. Indeed, it might be more appropriate to place Bakhtin among theorists of ideology rather than among theorists of linguistics and semiotics. To understand the radicalism of Bakhtin's theory of ideology, we must first turn to his own outline of the subject.

Alongside the rejection of transcendence implicit in Bakhtin's critique of abstraction and system is a corresponding rejection of "individual" consciousness. His critique of Freud suffers from the naiveté of his rather knee-jerk reaction to Freud's early published writings; yet that critique substantially predicts Jacques Lacan's reformulation of Freudianism in light of linguistic theory, particularly the translation of the unconscious into a form of language. In place of the concept of the unconscious, which Bakhtin viewed as unanalyzable so long as it remained neither physiological nor verbal, Bakhtin advances the concept of inner speech: through inner speech, all consciousness is social in its formulation. Accordingly, Bakhtin sees inner speech and outer, articulated speech as having ideological status. Inner speech is no less subjected to social evalua-

tion than outer speech, because of the intrinsically social history and nature of the word:

> The complex apparatus of verbal reactions functions in all its fundamental aspects also when the subject says nothing about his experiences but only undergoes them "in himself," since, if he is conscious of them, a process of *inner* ("covert") speech occurs (we do, after all, think and feel and desire with the help of words; without inner speech we would not become conscious of anything in ourselves). This process of inner speech is just as material as is outward speech.

To be sure, Bakhtin recognizes that "the formation of verbal connections (the establishment of connections among visual, motor, and other kinds of reactions over the course of interindividual communication, upon which the formation of verbal reactions depends) proceeds with special difficulty and delay in certain areas of life (for example, the sexual)," but he nevertheless does not explore in any depth the tensions between the unarticulated and articulated in those cases. In his work, little distinction is made between the nature of inner and outer speech, and he sometimes describes inner speech as a mere practice ground for what will or may later be articulated. This theoretical lack might be attributed to Bakhtin's apparent adherence in *Freudianism: A Marxist Critique* to a rather mechanistic behavioral psychology. He does write, however, that both inner and outer speech form a type of behavioral ideology that "is in certain respects more sensitive, more responsive, more excitable and livelier than an ideology that has undergone formulation and become 'official'."

Thus we begin to receive an outline of constraints that could distinguish between the qualities of inner and outer speech. His sensitivity to those varying constraints was most likely responsible for a major contribution in his discussion of Freud: Bakhtin stresses the shaping power of the specific dialogic situation of the psychoanalytic interview. Going beyond Freud's own individual-centered notions of transference, Bakhtin explains that the interview situation is a highly complex one and must be understood in light of the social dynamic between doctor and patient, and not—or not only—in terms of the patient's individual psyche. [In an endnote, the critic writes: "See Vološinov, *Fr*, pp. 78-79; Cf. Gregory Bateson, 'The Message "This Is Play," ' in *Group Processes: Transactions of the Second Congress of the Josiah Macy, Jr., Foundation*, pp. 145-242; and Ray L. Birdwhistell, 'Contribution of Linguistic-Kinesic Studies to the Understanding of Schizophrenia,' in *Schizophrenia: An Integrated Approach*, pp. 99-123."]

Bakhtin's insistence upon the primary place of the social, the "already said," in the formation of consciousness is at the heart of his struggle against the "bourgeois ideology" of individualism. In *Marxism and the Philosophy of Language*, we see a critique of Herderian linguistics, with all its Romantic assumptions about the individual soul. In the work of Wilhelm von Humboldt, Karl Vossler, and their followers, Bakhtin points out that a reformulation of this bourgeois philosophy appears in the theory that laws of linguistic creativity are laws of individual psychology. Bakhtin argues that such a position strips language of its ideological content and neglects the intrinsically social nature of linguistic change. In his book *Freudianism,* he pursues his attack on the abstract concept of the individual by criticizing Freud's asocial and tautological notion of self-consciousness. Here Bakhtin writes:

> In becoming aware of myself, I attempt to look at myself, as it were, through the eyes of another person, another representative of my social group, my class. Thus, *self-consciousness,* in the final analysis, always leads us to *class consciousness,* the reflection and specification of which it is in all its fundamental and essential respects. Here we have the *objective roots* of even the most personal and intimate reactions.

According to Bakhtin, all social, antisocial, and warring impulses within consciousness are reflections of social, antisocial, and warring impulses within the mutually experienced world of lived reality. When a class is in decline, we may expect to see manifestations of its decay in the behavior of its individual members.

In *Freudianism* and the essay on discourse in life and art, the critique of individualism is mirrored within an aesthetic theory. Bakhtin criticizes theories of art that place the significance of the artwork within the psyche of either the creator or the contemplator: "We might say that such a thing is similar to the attempt to analyze the individual psyche of a proletarian in order thereby to disclose the objective production relations that determine his position in society." Instead, Bakhtin places the work in the interaction between these two positions and concludes that artistic value arises only in the dynamics of such social communication. Similarly, in *Problems of Dostoevsky's Poetics,* Bakhtin situates the subject within sociality and argues that identity is produced by speech, particularly through the contradictions of narrative. Using Dostoevsky as an example, Bakhtin observes that each of that novelist's heroes is *the man of an idea,* an idea that is itself a construct of contradiction and dialogue:

> Only the unfinalizable and inexhaustible "man in man" can become the man of an idea, whose image is combined with the image of a full-valued idea. This is the first condition of the representation of the idea in Dostoevsky.
>
> But this condition contains, as it were, its inverse as well. We can say that in Dostoevsky's works man overcomes his "thingness" (*veshchnost'*) and becomes "man in man" only by entering the pure and unfinalized sphere of the idea, i. e., only by becoming the selfless man of an idea. Such are all of Dostoevsky's leading characters, i. e. all of the participants in the great dialog.

Here we find a radical departure from traditional Marxist aesthetics, in fact, the inverse of Marx's position in *The German Ideology* where he writes: "We do not set out from what men say, imagine, conceive, nor from men as narrated, thought of, imagined, conceived, in order to arrive at men in the flesh. We set out from real, active men, and on the basis of their real life-process we demonstrate the development of the ideological reflexes and echoes of this life-process." Rather than assume the "real" man at the point of beginning for ideology, Bakhtin would say that it is precisely within narrative, and within ideological

structures, that the concept of the individual subject, of the "real" man is born. And the conclusion to *The Formal Method* makes clear that such ideological structures are themselves constituted by and through speech.

Bakhtin's concept of ideology differs significantly from the early reflectionist theories of Marx. In *Capital,* Marx writes:

> The religious world is but the reflex of the real world. And for a society based upon the production of commodities, in which the producers in general enter into social relations with one another by treating their products as commodities and values, whereby they reduce their individual private labour to the standard of homogeneous human labour—for such a society, Christianity with its *cultus* of abstract man, more especially in its bourgeois developments, Protestantism, Deism, etc., is the most fitting form of religion.

Marx's theory is deferred and utopian in its outlook: ideology represents the false consciousness produced under class society; after the revolution of the proletariat, the slippage between this false consciousness and the real world will be healed and an actual relation to reality lived. This notion of ideology as false consciousness also lies behind Louis Althusser's distinction between ideology and science and Georg Lukács' attempt in *History and Class Consciousness* to identify truth with proximity to proletarian consciousness. Similarly, in Lucien Goldmann's distinction between a limited ideology and an embracing world view, we see a kind of "monologic" vision of ideology.

By contrast, Bakhtin asserts that ideology is manifested and created in the practical material activity of speech behavior: hence his notion of "behavioral ideology." As in his theory of linguistics, Bakhtin rejects the abstract concept in favor of the material and dynamic relation. The dialogic nature of the sign, its inner and outer form, allows the intersection of sign with sign, idea with idea, at the same time that it ensures continual upheaval and change in signifying practices as they occur in concrete historical contexts. Thus, ideology is not only the product of social life but is also both productive and reproductive of lived social relations. Furthermore, although in Bakhtin's theory of ideology the socioeconomic base is seen as determining, it is not a base that locks ideology into a static and transcendent form. Rather, ideology is seen as an arena of conflict: one's speech both reveals *and produces* one's position in class society, in such a way, moreover, as to set into dialogue the relations among classes. Consider this passage from Bakhtin's *Marxism:*

> Existence reflected in sign is not merely reflected but *refracted.* How is this refraction of existence in the ideological sign determined? By an intersecting of differently oriented social interests within one and the same sign community, i.e., . . . with the community, which is the totality of users of the same set of signs for ideological communication. Thus various different classes will use one and the same language. As a result, differently oriented accents intersect in every

ideological sign. Sign becomes an arena of class struggle.

Once he moves the materiality of language away from essence into the domain of practice, Bakhtin can present the cacophony of voices present in any utterance, can reject a notion of speech community based on phonology in favor of a much more useful one based on interest and on what might be termed "positionality," the place of the subject within the social structure, a place where subject and structure are mutually articulated. [In an endnote, the critic notes that in *The Formal Method,* Bakhtin writes: "We think and conceptualize in utterances, complexes complete in themselves. As we know, the utterance cannot be understood as a linguistic whole, and its forms are not syntactic forms. These integral, materially expressed inner acts of man's orientation in reality and the forms of these acts are very important. One might say that human consciousness possesses a series of inner genres for seeing and conceptualizing reality. A given consciousness is richer or poorer in genres, depending on its ideological environment."] What Bakhtin's theory of ideology offers is a model of ideological production. In this model, ideology is not assumed to be either a foggy lens or a mirroring cloud. It is, rather, assumed to be an ongoing product and producer of social practices. The semantic transition from reflection to refraction marks a movement from repetition to production.

Most radically, Bakhtin is unwilling to limit the place of ideology to a particular or narrow sphere of social life. Instead, he concludes that "all of these things [ideological phenomena] in their totality comprise the ideological environment, which forms a solid ring around man. And man's consciousness lives and develops in this environment. Human consciousness does not come into contact with existence directly, but through the medium of the surrounding ideological world." This is a considerable departure from traditional Marxist positions, which either locate the real in the supposedly direct purview of science or in the deferred idealism of revolution. [In an endnote, the critic adds: "In the recent work of Terry Eagleton we find a similar position, one which sees science, no less than ideology, as the product of concrete social practices." See Eagleton, "Ideology, Fiction, Narrative," *Social Text,* Vol. 1, Winter, 1979.] In contrast, Bakhtin concludes that both science and ideology are products whose absolute "reality"—if it existed at all—could be apprehended only by a transcendent consciousness, a consciousness that would itself be, ironically, an ideological construct. Bakhtin's movement away from a reflectionist theory can perhaps be traced to his familiarity with the carnival mode, where refraction and inversion considerably complicate a traditional functionalist model.

To understand how ideological practice is performed, we cannot begin with a model of the utterance as the spontaneous production of an individual consciousness. Rather, the utterance must be seen as bearing within itself a complex and contradictory set of historical elements. In this sense, Bakhtin observes, *all* speech is reported speech, for all speech carries with it a history of use and interpretation by which it achieves both identity and difference. It is within this rather remarkable capacity for making present

the past that speech acquires its social meaning. Hence for Bakhtin the proper study of ideology would begin with an examination of ideological form, with the study of genre, and not in any autonomous or transcendent sense of genre or form but in the sense that form presents a location of tension between the past and the present. Bakhtin begins by distinguishing ideological objects both from instruments of production (which are consumed by their function) and from consumer goods (which, in existing for individual use, are not available for social evaluation). The specificity of ideological objects lies in their "concrete material reality" and "social meaning."

In *The Formal Method,* Bakhtin insists that literary form is unique in that it refracts the generating socioeconomic reality in ways particular to its own history and at the same time "reflects and refracts the reflections and refractions of other ideological spheres." Thus, literature serves as a type of super superstructure, in part because of the levels of representation involved in literary production. Here we might contrast the various possibilities of slippage offered by this model to the currently fashionable notion, offered by newer Marxist critics, of the absences in ideological discourse. [In an endnote, the critic adds: see Coward and Ellis, *Language and Materialism;* Pierre Macherey, *A Theory of Literary Production;* and Eagleton, *Criticism and Ideology: A Study in Marxist Literary Theory.*] Bakhtin offers a much more positivist outlook than this deconstructionist one, for he believes that the utterance will carry within it a set of articulate silences and that the common ideological purview of author and reader will work toward the discernment of patterns in the unsaid. Thus, his theory is not necessarily burdened with a nostalgia for full presence: here the contradictions, ambivalences, and silences of the text are seen as part of its essentially dialogic nature.

According to Bakhtin, the reason that literature is the most ideological of all ideological spheres may be discovered in the structure of genre. He criticizes the formalists for ending their theory with a consideration of genre; genre, he observes, should be the first topic of poetics. The importance of genre lies in its two major capacities: conceptualization and "finalization." A genre's conceptualization has both inward and outward focus: the artist does not merely represent reality; he or she must use existing means of representation in tension with the subject at hand. This process is analogous to the dual nature of the utterance, its orientation simultaneously toward its past contexts and its present context. "A particular aspect of reality can only be understood in connection with the particular means of representing it." Genre's production of perception is not simply a matter of physical orientation; it is also a matter of ideology: "Every significant genre is a complex system of means and methods for the conscious control and finalization of reality." According to Bakhtin, nonideological domains are "open work;" not subject to an ultimate closure; but one goal of works of art is precisely to offer closure, a "finalization" that accounts for their ideological power and their capacity to produce consciousness. In the particular finalization of genre, we see a continual tension between tradition and situation. [In an endnote, the critic adds: "For a discussion of the tension between genre and performance, and between tradition and situation, in folkloric performances, see Hymes, 'Folklore's Nature and the Sun's Myth,' *Journal of American Folklore* Vol. 88 October-December, 1975, pp. 345-69.''] As Terry Eagleton suggests in *Criticism and Ideology,* "A power-loom, for one thing, is not altered by its products . . . in the way that a literary convention is transformed by what it textually works." Analogously, Bakhtin writes that "the goal of the artistic structure of every historical genre is to merge the distances of space and time with the contemporary by the force of all-penetrating social evaluation." It is perhaps because of this purported goal that Bakhtin himself seemed to prefer the novel, which he viewed as a meta-genre incorporating at once all domains of ideology and all other literary genres. Finally, we must emphasize that Bakhtin's model of genre rests upon his insistence that literary evolution is not the result of device reacting against device, as Viktor Shklovsky believed, but rather of ideological, and ultimately socioeconomic, changes.

We see, then, that Bakhtin's work, in its radical rejection of abstraction, system, and the ideology of bourgeois individualism, forms an arena for a powerful struggle between linguistics and speech, theory and history. His theories' capacities for negation and critique are apparent whether we contrast them to the linguistic theories of his time or of ours. Moreover, this capacity for dialogue, contradiction, and complexity also exists in his work's inner speech—in its allusions to, or silences in the presence of, its own social context. In *The Formal Method,* at the culmination of Bakhtin's presentation of multivalence, we find as a dominant motif an insistence not only on meaning but also on meaningful*ness.* Bakhtin cannot accept the futurist model of perpetual and content-less motion: he continually rejects the futurists, and their influence on formalism, as nihilistic, even hedonistic, perhaps reminding us of Trotsky's position in *Literature and Revolution.* In *Rabelais and His World,* Bakhtin describes a historical period in which the language of the body was transformed by the rise of capitalism into an alien form of discourse. Bakhtin himself lived in a period when a similar drama was being enacted in the transformations of the peasantry by the industrial state. And yet we never find in his work a discussion of the effects of industrial practice or mechanical reproduction on ideological thought. If we look for a pattern of absences in these texts, we may gradually limn the image of the futurist machine and its totalitarian capacity for the negation of dialogue.

Susan Stewart, "Shouts on the Street: Bakhtin's Anti-Linguistics," in Bakhtin: Essays and Dialogues on His Work, *edited by Gary Saul Morson, The University of Chicago Press, 1986, pp. 41-57.*

Richard Jackson   (essay date Summer 1987)

[*In the essay below, Jackson presents an overview of Bakhtin's texts and themes.*]

Two citations from *Problems of Dostoevsky's Poetics* by Mikhail Bakhtin (1895-1975) are enough to suggest the difficulty involved in coming to any terms (in that phrase's

sense of a unifying label and a temporal enclosure) with this increasingly important Russian writer. The first citation comes from his third chapter, "The Idea in Dostoevsky": "It is quite possible to imagine and postulate a unified truth that requires a plurality of consciousness, one that is, so to speak, by its very nature *full of event potential* and is born at a point of contact among various consciousnesses." Later, in talking about catharsis, he says: "Nothing conclusive has yet taken place in the world, the ultimate word of the world and about the world has not yet been spoken, the world is open and free, everything is still in the future and will always be in the future." What marks this pluralistic approach where nothing is conclusive, according to Katerina Clark and Michael Holquist, is "variety, nonrecurrence, and discorrespondence," a self that "never coincides with itself," an open, subversive, "carnivalistic" view of literature and the world. In Bakhtin's texts, *laughter* becomes a crucial "weapon" (military metaphors abound in his style), and *polyphony, dialogism, intertext, utterance,* and *heteroglossia* become the crucial code words. Each refers, in various contexts, to the ways in which characters and authors interchange language, the way each speaks in the voice of the other and at the same time undercuts the other. Here, process, not product, is the aim, and expressions such as *difference, decentering,* and other buzz words of deconstruction are "always already" deployed—that is, present implicitly in the text they are used to describe. What we are faced with, then, is a world of vague origins and indeterminate ends. According to Bakhtin, "The novel begins by presuming a verbal and semantic decentering of the ideological world, a certain linguistic homelessness of literary consciousness, which no longer possesses a sacrosanct and unitary linguistic medium for containing ideological thought" (*Dialogic Imagination*). In other words, the novel sets us adrift in a world we must half invent by entering into a dialogue with it.

Bakhtin's position in contemporary thought is not so much that of a direct influence on authors, though several acknowledge their debt to him, but that his texts, unavailable so long to English and American readers, help to describe and redefine what has been happening in Western thought during the past few decades. In our own time the poet Richard Howard admits the influence of Bakhtin's dialogic sense of character upon his own dialogues and monologues; Stephen Dobyns and Derek Walcott seem to use Bakhtin's notion of the dialectic relation between self and society; John Ashbery's and A. R. Ammons' use of the idea of the linguistic process of imagination can be better defined in Bakhtin's terms than in the deconstructive terms often used to describe their work; the play between reality and fiction in works by John Irving and Tim O'Brien can be better understood by Bakhtin's description of Dostoevsky's use of character; and the surrealistic texts of James Tate, Charles Simic (who we know has read Bakhtin), and others owe something to the idea of literature as carnivalistic. The influence here is as pervasive as it is (in most cases) nonspecific; but just this sort of influence, as we shall see below, is in strict keeping with Bakhtin's own work.

The difficulty of entering into a dialogue with Bakhtin's

texts is precisely the above-mentioned "plurality of consciousness" (note the singular), which even encompasses the immediate problem of authorship: both *Freudianism* and *Marxism and the Philosophy of Language* (published under the name of Voloshinov) as well as *The Formal Method in Literary Studies* (published under the name of Medvedev) are disputed texts, as are a number of essays. Tzvetan Todorov, from convincing internal evidence, suggests that these books are probably not by Bakhtin, but influenced by him. The short, choppy sentences and sections of *Formal Method,* for example, are opposed to the looser, more rambling style of unquestioned texts. A "Bakhtin Circle" of critics, writers, and other artists existed in the 1920's and '30's in a way that can only be defined as a single, pluralistic consciousness—and Bakhtin himself, Todorov points out, disdained the idea of simple authorship and favored the medium of the public-meeting forum, a Socratic form of debate. Yet Bakhtin admitted to these disputed texts later on, after Voloshinov and Medvedev had died, and the political constraints of the times may have prompted Bakhtin to authorship under other names. Bakhtin was arrested in 1929, and many Marxist references in all the texts are nods to the censor, though Bakhtin has a distinctly socialist stance.

The question of what constitutes authorship is central to Bakhtin because it relates to his underlying concern with the nature of the self. Does authorship mean providing new ideas in an "idiosyncratic vocabulary," or the translation of those ideas and words into a more public format, or the actual preparation of a manuscript? "There are no pure texts, nor can there be," Bakhtin writes (quoted in Clark and Holquist). For Bakhtin, the self is never finished—and his habits of writing in an illegible pencil script, of leaving texts unfinished and projects abandoned in notebooks in the manner of Coleridge, underscore this. The self exists for Bakhtin as a "dialogic" relationship, that is, as a "set of responses to the world." These responses are given in language, through "utterances" (including nonverbal associations, the "force" of language) that by definition take the "other" into account. Each utterance changes as the "boundaries" of the speaker and listener do; it is expressive, not just denotative; it is always addressed to someone; it has an evolving relation to past and future utterances so that its meaning cannot be fixed. In other words, the utterance is based upon the possibility of a response and the fact that such utterance itself is always already a response. Utterance is thus always point of view. This is why, for Bakhtin, "a word's meaning never coincides with the word itself," but with the larger and more evasive movement of the dialogue: the self.

The self, then, is known "from other selves. I cannot see the self that is my own, so I must try to perceive it in other's eyes." This bifocal or dialogic self is always futural; every "I" has a "thou" and includes the "thou." What characterizes this relationship between self and other is "answerability": the inclusion of dialectic viewpoints in any statement or judgment, the notion that being means "being with." The early and continuing influence upon Bakhtin here is Kant's notion of a dialectic between mind and world. However, for Bakhtin the result is not a transcendental synthesis, but rather an ongoing, historical

process, a series of provisional syntheses. He also relies on Einstein's notion of "simultaneity"—in the universe we can't determine simultaneity as fact, and "there is thus no actual simultaneity: there are only systems of reference by which two different events can be brought into a conceptual unity." There is only dialogism.

These notions of the self as open and under revision, when applied to authorship, are precisely what attract Bakhtin to Dostoevsky and mark the uniqueness, indeed the greatness, of his treatment of that author. For Bakhtin, the author exists somewhere between a character and a person, and in this respect is an invisible "I." In *Problems of Dostoevsky's Poetics* Bakhtin focuses upon the polyphonic point of view of the narrator. As opposed to Tolstoy, whose procedure is to have all characters speak through the narrator's controlling point of view, Dostoevsky allows his characters to speak for themselves, usually undercutting each other as well as the narrator both in theme and style. The result is heteroglossia (multiple language types and levels) as opposed to Tolstoy's monoglossia. The real "hero interests Dostoevsky as a *particular point of view on the world* and on oneself, as the position enabling a person to interpret and evaluate his own self and his surrounding reality" (*Problems.*) Thus the hero "is not an objectified image but an autonomous discourse, *pure voice;* we do not see him, we hear him." So, Bakhtin notes, "Dostoevsky—to speak paradoxically—thought not in thoughts but in points of view, consciousnesses, voices. He tried to perceive and formulate each thought in such a way that a whole person was expressed and began to sound it." Dostoevsky's fundamental technique is a "transferral of words from one mouth to another, where content remains the same although the tone and ultimate meaning are changed," a form that Bakhtin calls the "double voice." This voice can sound through various embedded forms existing like Chinese boxes, one inside another—with, say, the narrator revealing a character revealing another character's perspective. Parody, rejoinder, dialogue, and folk forms are all deployed. Raskolnikov, for instance, can allow various languages to enter his "inner speech" as a way of evaluating points of view—just as Dostoevsky himself can. It is important to spend time describing this bifocal voice because it is something that also marks the critical procedure of Bakhtin himself. He never does a close reading of a novel; rather he focuses on specific characters as perspectives, citing them amply, letting them speak for themselves. His structure is usually fragmented, a sort of unending dialogue that evades monologic closure. For Bakhtin, the critic does not bring meaning, only further questions.

A good example of the way Bakhtin reads dialogically occurs in his essay **"Discourse in the Novel"** in *The Dialogic Imagination.* Here he closely analyzes passages from (among others) Dickens' *Little Dorrit,* showing how Dickens adopts into his own style the styles of various characters, thus producing a sort of "refracted" or indirect quotation, what Bakhtin calls a "hybrid construction." Dickens' "entire text is, in fact, everywhere dotted with quotation marks that serve to separate out little islands of scattered direct speech and purely authorial speech, washed by heteroglot waves from all sides. But it would have been impossible actually to insert such marks, since, as we have seen, one and the same word often figures both as the speech of the author and as the speech of another—and at the same time." For Bakhtin, every novel is a "hybrid," consciously formulated. In his Dostoevsky book, Bakhtin identifies "authorial" and "reported" speech—the first is direct speech, the second is speech within speech (the other's perspective given by syntax, diction, grammar, etc. affecting the hypothetically "pure" authorial speech). The author resides at the boundary of these two, in a way characterized either by linear structures (where the boundaries are clear) or reported structures (where the boundaries blur). Dickens and Dostoevsky are, for Bakhtin, examples of the second, more sophisticated form.

Bakhtin's other essays in **Dialogic Imagination** examine the problems of genre. **"Epic and Novel"** traces the development of the closed Greek system, the monologic epic, to more open systems in the modern dialogic novel. The central essay, **"Forms of Time and Chronotope in the Novel,"** analyzes the development of the novel from its beginnings in epic through the use of "chronotopes." The chronotope is a unit of analysis that focuses on the structure of thinking as it reflects the social-linguistic forces of a culture. (The term itself reflects the time/space categories of Kant and Einstein.) Bakhtin sees, for example, a development from "adventure time" (abstract, fragmented sequences in early stories) to "everyday time" (more individual units according to place and person, linked, and with more sophisticated use of point of view) to "biographical time" (where the characters, places, and moments are fully individualized and dialectically related). This historical process is called "novelization"—a term that can be used to talk about the lyric, drama, or any other sort of text. A novelized text is one that exhibits dialogic forces—heteroglossia, multiple viewpoints. The traditional lyric voice does not interest Bakhtin because it is a monoglossic, unified, pure voice. The problems of genre definition he implicitly poses (how do we fit in, say, Williams' *Paterson,* Pound's *Cantos,* Stevens, Ashbery?) do not become so insurmountable if we keep in mind that novelization is, like dialogism, a process, not a static category. In fact, these concepts provide a better way to analyze such poets, and indeed to view the developments in contemporary poetry, than do other methodologies.

Perhaps the most Bakhtinian author Bakhtin analyzes is Rabelais. *Gargantua and Pantagruel* is essentially marked, according to Bakhtin, by clashes in language reflecting different histories, the grotesque use of the body as an intertext for the temporality of the physical world, and the use of the "carnival" atmosphere as an intertext of evolving ideologies. Bakhtin's concern in **Rabelais and His World** is thus always with history: "all the symbols of the carnival idiom are filled with this pathos of change and renewal, with the sense of the gay relativity of prevailing truths and authorities." Laughter, in this context, becomes a way of laughing with time, a way to perceive sanely the transience of our existence, to topple the structures of an official society which tries to assert the constancy of its laws. So too, "Popular festive forms look into the future. They present the victory of all the people's material abundance, freedom, equality, brotherhood." Analyzing

Rabelais' use of the marketplace, the carnival, and colloquial language and images—all of which developed out of Menippean satire—Bakhtin finds the birth of the modern novel. Language, as always, is the main determinant for Bakhtin. He notes, for instance, in high "medieval Latin, which levels all things, the markers of time were almost entirely effaced," but in Rabelais' vernacular (with all its "low" associations), a progressive, optimistic process of renewal—and revolution—can begin.

Most of what we have been examining constitutes, sometimes in earlier forms, the basis of Bakhtin's dismissal of the Russian Formalists in **The Formal Method in Literary Scholarship,** a work that could also be read as a valuable critique of American New Criticism. According to Bakhtin, the Formalists ignored history and attempted to present a single, monoglossic vision that preserved a simple truth for each text. The Formalists felt they could see a static world of poetic values objectively, rigidly, accurately; Bakhtin laughs at their "pathetic references to 'the facts themselves'." Behind Formalism is a set of value assumptions, evolving within the language of philosophy, culture, and criticism, that allows the world to be divided between the pure and eternal poetic language and the historical, pragmatic language that changes in time—as well as between subject and object, form and content. Thus, Bakhtin notes, the Formalists "brought along the features of poetic language and the devices they had used to study it. Their conception of the constructive functions of the elements of the poetic work was predetermined by their characterization of the elements of poetic language. The poetic construction had to illustrate the theory of poetic language already developed." The writer—critic or novelist—cannot escape the dialogue that language already has with him or her, because that dialogue is inherent in the value systems the writer inherits *from* that language.

Another problem Bakhtin sees with Formalism is its exclusive focus on the text itself, to the abandonment of the author and the reader—both of whom "participate equally in the creation of the represented world in the text" (**Dialogic Imagination.**). Bakhtin avoids, however, the simple subjectivism of much contemporary reader-response criticism because of the dialogism of his stance, just as he avoids the pseudo-objectivism of the Formalists. For him, text, author, and reader make up an "archetonic" structure, an evolving "situation." What Bakhtin tries to avoid is "turning active and generating problems into ready theses, statements, and philosophical, political, religious, etc. conclusions."

It is interesting, in the light of these various contexts of Bakhtin's thought, to note the distinctions between the study by Todorov [*Mikhail Bakhtin: The Dialogic Principle*] and that by Clark and Holquist [*Mikhail Bakhtin*]. Todorov provides a succinct account of Bakhtin's "system" in a schematic and closed way; Clark and Holquist opt for a narrative that preserves much of the openness that Bakhtin himself valued. The approach of Clark and Holquist allows more of the richness and historical development of Bakhtin's ideas to emerge. Theirs is a brilliant study, a full picture of Bakhtin, his circle, the dialogic forces in his life, texts, and times.

What all the recent activity in Bakhtin studies suggests is that this very important thinker—or interlocutor—may finally claim the central position he deserves as one of the key writers of the century. Of course, he is not served by the sort of simplified view of, say, a Denis Donoghue, who takes several pages in a recent issue of *Raritan* (Fall 1985) to convince himself that all of Bakhtin can be reduced to the struggle between "monologic" and "dialogic." Donoghue wants to place Bakhtin within the context of his own either/or war between "secure" conservatives and wild radicals. But Bakhtin's work is rich both in its metaphors for points of view and in its play among such points of view. He does not, as Donoghue claims, merely echo Auerbach or C. L. Barber, unless one wants to reduce the arguments of those writers to bottom lines and college trot notes. After all, it is *process* that is so important to Bakhtin. He stands as a corrective to the oversimplifications offered by New Critics and as a more constructive deconstructionist—one who attempts, through dialogue, to build bridges (however provisional) across the "differences" he sees at least as clearly as the deconstructionists themselves.

Richard Jackson, "The Dialogic Self," in The Georgia Review, *Vol. XLI, No. 2, Summer, 1987, pp. 415-20.*

Bakhtin on the epic tradition:

It is impossible to achieve greatness in one's own time. Greatness always makes itself known only to descendents, for whom such a quality is always located in the past (it turns into a distanced image); it has become an object of memory and not a living object that one can see and touch. In the genre of the "memorial," the poet constructs his image in the future and distanced plane of his descendents (cf. the inscriptions of oriental despots, and of Augustus). In the world of memory, a phenomenon exists in its own peculiar context, with its own special rules, subject to conditions quite different from those we meet in the world we see with our own eyes, the world of practice and familiar contact. The epic past is a special form for perceiving people and events in art. In general the act of artistic perception and representation is almost completely obscured by this form. Artistic representation here is representation *sub specie aeternitatis*. One may, and in fact one must, memorialize with artistic language only that which is worthy of being remembered, that which should be preserved in the memory of descendents; an image is created for descendents, and this image is projected on to their sublime and distant horizon. Contemporaneity for its own sake (that is to say, a contemporaneity that makes no claim on future memory) is molded in clay; contemporaneity for the future (for descendents) is molded in marble or bronze.

Mikhail Bakhtin, in his "Epic and Novel," in The Dialogic Imagination, *1981.*

Caryl Emerson (essay date Winter 1988)

[*An American critic and educator, Emerson is the translator and editor, with Michael Holquist, of* The Dialogic Imagination: Four Essays by M. M. Bakhtin *(1981) and* Speech Genres and Other Late Essays by Bakhtin *(1987), as well as the author, with Gary Saul Morson, of* Mikhail Bakhtin: Creation of a Prosaics *(1990). Here, she explores problems in the application of Bakhtin's theories.*]

Baxtin Studies have come of age. For evidence of this one should look not at the exploding number of references, nor at the extraordinary seepage of his name into unlikely disciplines, nor even at the frequency of old themes now being newly reworked under the labels "dialogic" or "carnivalesque." Signs of maturity are registered, rather, in the *nature* of the dialogue. In the past two years, several "stabilizing" events have occurred.

A major biography has appeared in English (Clark and Holquist). A Festschrift in Baxtin's honor has been compiled by his former students in Saransk (S. S. Konkin), and the Soviet Academy of Sciences has published a summarizing account of Baxtin scholarship in the West (Maxlin). Half a dozen professional journals . . . have sponsored forums or special issues on Baxtin. In the Soviet Union, the concepts of dialogism and chronotope have been progressively refined—most creatively by the scholars of the Tartu School, who devoted an entire issue of *Trudy po znakovym sistemam* (17 [1984]) to the structure of dialogue as a semiotic mechanism. In 1986, large chunks of the remaining archival material from the early 1920s were published in the Soviet press. In a recent review essay of the latest Soviet anthology of Baxtin's writings, Sergej Averincev claims that Baxtin has achieved the status of "classic"—and thus merits a thoroughly researched, multi-volume academy edition of his works, not another one-volume *sbornik*.

The task is thus no longer one of maiden translation or primary explication, but considerably more difficult. We must now ask: Has the body of Baxtin's writing been articulate and forceful enough to stimulate a genuine countervoice—as opposed to the mere backlash predictable in the wake of any cult figure? Do Baxtin's core theoretical ideas survive when they are *applied*, or does continued work with them only bring into focus their paradoxical, perhaps even fatally flawed sides?

It is this most recent stage that I would like to address in this essay. "Problems with Baxtin's Poetics" are, of course, everywhere: his astonishing *logos*-centrism (that is, his presumption that if you can't talk about an experience, you didn't have it), his often naive personification of genres, his reluctance to analyze artistic wholes, his narrow and unsympathetic definition of the lyric, his idealization of carnival, and the general imprecision of his terms. Some of these problems, to be sure, become less problematic as more of the archive becomes available. Among the recently published material, for example, is an ingenious analysis of Puškin's lyric "Dlja beregov otčiznoj dal'noj"—an analysis that demonstrates Baxtin's thorough appreciation of the complexity and multi-voicedness of lyrical form. But large, troublesome areas remain.

A good starting point might be the title of this essay. For

the problems, clearly, are not only with Baxtin's poetics, but with the very way he uses the word "poetics." Baxtin does not, of course, have in mind the traditional neoclassical model, that is, poetics understood as a fixed hierarchy of genres or aesthetic norms. But even more radically, he does not have in mind a poetics exclusively of *art.*

Here we might compare Baxtin with his Russian Formalist compatriots. For the Formalists, the very concept of a "poetics" implied the relative autonomy of art from life. Baxtin, in contrast, aggressively combines the two. Thus he has little use for notions of "poetic language," for what the Formalists called "literariness," or for the purely aesthetic function. But we should note that Baxtin combines life and art in a very special way.

First, he situates the separation of art and life historically, that is, as something that may or may not be true at any given time or place, and always as a matter of degree. To use his terminology, the separation of life and art is not given, *dan,* but posited, *zadan.* And then, Baxtin does not presume that in the many and energetic efforts of aesthetes to keep art and life apart, art has been the only side to benefit. In his first published essay, a six-paragraph fragment entitled **"Art and Responsibility"** dating from 1919, Baxtin concludes that the whole fraught question of the art-life boundary has in fact worked to the mutual convenience of *both* sides. "Both art and life desire to lighten their respective burdens," Baxtin writes, "for it is, after all, easier to create without answering to life, and easier to live not reckoning with art." Then there follows one of Baxtin's more elusive and provocative formulations: "Art and life are not one, but they must become united in me, in the unity of my responsibility."

We might say, therefore, that two realms confront one another in each individual: the ethical and the aesthetic. Where they meet is what we call the "I." This special sense of the "I" as a threshold concept—or, better, as a boundary phenomenon—has its counterpart, of course, in Baxtin's model of the utterance: not a slice of system, and not an individual speech act, but a unique exchange between or among people. The ethical-aesthetic boundary is also analogous to Baxtin's larger concept of the self as a social entity. The *self* is a special relation among the voices that inhabit us; as Baxtin would say, the socium lives within us. But it is important to emphasize that this socium is not an undifferentiated mass; the social always partakes of the accents and intonations of each individual speaker. The social self, therefore, is not the generalized self, the self that can be reduced (as in certain facile Marxist or Formalist models) to economic class or psychological reflex. As it is with self and society, so it is with life and art. The two are separate and irreducible, but the pattern of their responses to each other determines the shape of the self. Expanding this scenario into a theory of art, Baxtin claims that such patterns of ethical-aesthetic interaction shape the inner form of the artwork itself.

The process is discussed in the early manuscripts, where Baxtin takes to task the Formalist idea of the *device* as art's marker and guarantor of the creative act. The aesthetic project, Baxtin insists, begins not with the device but with the creation of a second consciousness in addition to the author. What makes any work aesthetic is the degree to which this second consciousness can follow its *own* laws—in the presence of that primary force, the author, who strives to surmount it. In this struggle, aesthetic *form* belongs to the author, ethical *content* to the hero.

Elsewhere in the manuscripts, Baxtin illustrates this "struggle" through an analysis of lyrical and dramatic texts. Every poem—or for that matter every aesthetic event—is, Baxtin claims, a "reaction to a reaction." The primary reaction belongs to the protagonist and is therefore ethical: the hero reacts from within a world that is real to him, with gestures that (from his point of view) have real consequences. The secondary reaction is aesthetic: the author, from his outside point of view, shapes the events of that created world. In highly structured metric poetry, such a "reaction to a reaction" sets up rich countercurrents, which Baxtin investigates in terms of the protagonist's "realistic intonation" and the author's "formal rhythm." Since all these variables must of necessity be expressed externally on the same verbal plane, they will struggle for dominance. The more subtle and well-crafted this struggle between ethical "real-life" acts and the author's aesthetic shaping of them, the more satisfying the artwork.

What follows from this radical inter-penetrability, even inter-responsibility, of life and art is one of the peculiar constants of Baxtin's universe: the presumption that literary or aesthetic categories must have their real-life ethical counterparts. Thus a problem in the poetics of art will always have its analogous problem in a poetics of life. From this set of *parallel* problems with Baxtin's poetics I hope to map out two major troubling areas.

The first troubling area is that cluster of concepts all designating one or another kind of multiplicity or openness: those unlovely, overworked words—dialogism, unfinalizability, polyphony, heteroglossia. What all these terms share is a commitment to a special sort of change, change that is neither systematic nor systemic. In this Baxtin again differs from the Russian Formalists, whose theories of literary history were largely predicated on the evolution of literary, and nonliterary, *systems.* For Baxtin, most change is of a different order.

Here we must return to Baxtin's early, as yet untranslated writing before 1925. For it is a peculiar lopsidedness of Baxtin's received image in the West that the so-called "Baxtin School canon" (which includes the work authored by Vološinov and Medvedev) begins only in 1926, *after* Baxtin had discovered language as a central metaphor, and after he had targeted Saussurian concepts of language as his principal foe. Before this time, the central concept for Baxtin was not *slovo* (the word) but *postupok* (the act). What was to become, in the late 1920s, a juxtaposition of responsible utterance versus system is cast in the early writings as life versus theory, as the act versus any abstraction of the act. In these early manuscripts, published as **"K filosofii postupka" ("Toward a philosophy of the act")**, Baxtin makes a passionate plea—very much in the spirit of Gercen and Tolstoj—against abstraction as the chief enemy of personal responsibility. As soon, Baxtin writes, as the content of any cognitive act (thought as well as deed) is torn away from its concrete embodiment, an independent logic begins to govern it, it begins to develop spontaneously (*samoproizvol'no*) and we are at the mercy of its logic. We cease to exist actively in our own act. What is only *posited* in life suddenly appears as *given*. And as a result, we lose all that is "absolutely new, creating, impending in the act, all that by which it lives."

In these early writings, Baxtin directly addresses what he considers to be a shortcoming of Kantian ethics. Our individual will is indeed creatively active, Baxtin asserts, but our will "does not in any way generate a norm or a general position." Laws and norms of all sorts—and here Baxtin has the categorical imperative in mind—cannot be productively active first principles in the real world of events. "It is a sad misunderstanding, the legacy of rationalism," Baxtin writes, "that truth [*pravda*] can only be the sort of truth [*istina*] that coalesces out of generalized moments; that the truth of a position is [taken to be] precisely what is repeatable and permanent in it." In fact, Baxtin claims, language as such—permeated by intonation, emotion, intention—is not capable of expressing the logically abstract moment. Thus any act or word which does not arise responsibly out of its own nonreproducible context and author, any act which is the product of abstraction or of some "immanent law of development," can invade our lives as a "terrifying and destructive force." Baxtin dismisses as unlikely the dangers at the opposite extreme—that is, the possibility that an act, thus stripped of any ethical system, might become arbitrary or irrational. In fact, he would dismiss the very opposition between objectivity (supposedly systematic and rational) and subjectivity (the presumed realm of the individual and the arbitrary). Such a dichotomy is itself a fiction, Baxtin insists, a "rationalist prejudice." "The act, in its integral wholeness, is more than rational, it is *responsible.*"

Fifty years later, near the end of his life, Baxtin reaffirmed this optimistic role for the asystemically creative personal act. He jotted down in his note-book that cultural phenomena can be approached in two ways. First, he wrote, there is "the study of culture (or some area of it) at the level of system and [then] at the higher level of organic unity: open, becoming, unresolved and unpredetermined, capable of death and renewal, transcending itself, that is, exceeding its own boundaries." In art and in life, "unfinalizability" seems to mean for Baxtin that at any point in the development of a word, a culture, a person or a text there is a multiplicity of possibilities which are *not* implicit or inscribed in earlier stages. Thus the world can genuinely surprise us, and we can surprise the world. Each of those terms—dialogism, polyphony, heteroglossia—presupposes not just change, but *unpredictable* change.

One could say, then, that Baxtin's fundamental value is newness, creativity, what he himself called (in one of his awkward neologisms) *sjurpriznost'*, "surprisingness." It should be stressed, however, that "surprisingness" is never generated by chaos, nor is it the product of some aleatory principle. Surprise, as Baxtin sees it, is saturated with responsibility. This point is worth stressing, because the image of Baxtin in current literary theory is somewhat askew. Due to the extraordinary popularity of the essays

from the 1930s translated as **The Dialogic Imagination**—and due to some misplaced emphases on the part of Baxtin's early interpreters, including myself—the dominant image is now that of the "libertarian Baxtin," the apostle of freedom who rejoices, Bakunin-like, in the undoing of rules, in centrifugal energy, in carnival clowning, in novels as loopholes, and in sly denials of authorship. To be sure, a strain of utopian anarchism has always been strong in Russian thought, which is no stranger to the wedding of millenarian fantasies with holy foolishness. But Baxtin in fact insulates himself against that sort of thought better than it at first appears. Judging him not only by the essays of his best-known middle period but by the evolution of his work as a whole, Baxtin is, if anything, an apostle of *constraints.*

Thus he does not advocate the sort of novelty that makes a self-conscious "cult of the new," or that claims to make a fresh start by canceling out all previous movements or norms. Baxtin's aesthetic does not necessarily privilege modernism or modernity. On the contrary, Baxtin rarely mentions the modern novel, and he saw Futurism—and other forms of radical experimentation in art—as largely *spurious* attempts at novelty, spurious to the extent that they denied the past and diminished the presence of the responsible individual in the aesthetic act. What Baxtin seems to have sought was newness that did not stress the autonomy of the present or the future, but that addressed the past in unanticipated, productive ways—and invited similar approaches to itself.

Let us first consider how this idea of unpredictable, but response-laden, change works in Baxtin's poetics of literary art. Here, of course, it would be truer to say "poetics of the novel"—or even better, *prosaics* of the novel—for the novel embodied for Baxtin the essential open principle. No friend of New-Critical, structuralist, or neo-Aristotelian notions of closure and autonomy, Baxtin was forever on the lookout for genuine baggy monsters to staff his eccentric pantheon of master-novels. In this pantheon, true novelists are those like Dostoevskij, who somehow manage to locate themselves *among* their characters and not above them, and who appear to grant their characters in art the same cunning mix of freedom and necessity that we all know in life. The novel, Baxtin intimates, is the only art form of true potentiality.

This "freedom in openness" that supposedly characterizes polyphonic works has been, perhaps, the most troublesome aspect of Baxtin's theory of the novel. Baxtin, at any rate, thought so: as he wrote his literary executor Vadim Kožinov in July 1961, "more than any other thing, the position of the author in the polyphonic novel has given rise to objections and misunderstandings" (cited by Averincev and Bočarov). And well it might. Polyphony has been misunderstood as many things: as authorlessness (that is, as an *abdication* of the author), or as relativism (that is, as the *indifference* of the author), or as a disdain for the finished whole of an artwork. It has even been taken to mean—by (among others) Rene Wellek and, more recently, Joseph Frank—as the failure of an author to establish any responsible point of view.

A careful reading of Baxtin's texts absolves him, I believe, from most of these charges. He specifically states that polyphonic authors are neither absent nor passive: they are profoundly active, but active in a way different from monophonic authors. As regards the problem of relativism, Baxtin was equally explicit. In the Dostoevskij book he wrote, with perhaps regrettable understatement, that "we see no special need to point out that the polyphonic approach has nothing in common with relativism (or with dogmatism) . . . both . . . equally exclude all argumentation, all authentic dialogue, by making it either unnecessary (relativism) or impossible (dogmatism)." What makes relativism and dogmatism twin sins for Baxtin is that both shut off the possibility of new, meaningful exchange. For one must be capable of *some* commitment in order to propose the new and suspicious of total commitment which denies the possibility of the new. The alternative to both relativism and dogmatism is the situation Baxtin elaborates in his **"K filosofii postupka":** a world in which one makes committed statements, but recognizes them as provisional.

We might sum up the polyphonic position in this way. Because an artistic work is decentered and the authority in it is provisional does not mean that it ceases to embody value, or that it celebrates the impossibility of meaning, or that it begins to "play." On the contrary, Baxtin and his circle repeatedly insist on the necessity of concrete meaning and value in every utterance. The final chapter of Vološinov's **Marxism and the Philosophy of Language** ends on an impassioned plea for "the revival of the ideological word . . . the word with its theme intact, permeated with confident social value judgments, the word that really *means* and takes responsibility for what it says." Baxtin assumes that words and values are historical, social, and therefore conditional. But to admit this much is not to endorse ethical relativism, for that would release individuals from the obligation to assign value. In like manner, authors do not relinquish an "authorial point of view" when they choose to design works in which the truth of a situation is to be found *among* speakers, rather than embedded within a single speaker. But such authors do, of course, reconceive the structure of truth.

Charges of authorlessness and relativism, then, cannot really be sustained against the polyphonic novel. But the final problem with Baxtin's concept of aesthetic "openness" is not so easy to dismiss. This is Baxtin's reluctance to deal with the whole of a work of art, and especially with the whole of novels. This reluctance is all the more unfortunate, because one of the few things that aestheticians of almost all persuasions agree upon is the primacy of *unity* in an artwork—be it a unity of structure, or more loosely a unity of effect, or even (as in some modern works) a unity in the calculated failure to achieve unity. Baxtin admits that the issue is important, but endlessly defers dealing with it. None of his work sounds like a New-Critical reading, or even like its post-structuralist inversion.

It is possible, of course, that Baxtin declined to analyze individual novels rigorously because the claims he made for their "polyphonic" authors—and for Dostoevskij in particular—are very overstated. And he might have been urged toward overstatement because of that parallel set of

poetics we must always keep in mind. Baxtin appears to seek in novels only what he can transpose into a philosophy of living.

Let us move, then, to the other side of the chart, to the poetics of life. The problem of *human* closure, that is, of the properly finalized life, is discussed by Baxtin at length in his early manuscripts. There he makes it clear that "finalizability" is both necessary and desirable—as long as it is not the act of a single isolated consciousness. Closure, Baxtin assures us, is something we can never will from within our *own* life. Our own inner consciousness always knows how partial and open-ended our every act and utterance really is; we appear whole to others, but not to ourselves. Thus the only whole gift we can give others is our death, because only after death can the other's "aestheticizing" of our personality begin.

Death, as Baxtin conceives of it, can be an aestheticizing agent because it makes wholes possible; thus it is always in the past or the future, never in the present, which can only anticipate or remember it. From our living present, we can only describe *someone else's* death. Tolstoy's Ivan Il'ič notwithstanding, we can never take a stance of closure with respect to our own selves.

Baxtin's reluctance to engage the artistic whole in novels might well have something to do with his tendency to link it with death, that is, with the way in which lives are given closure. Here a contrast with Georg Lukács might be helpful. In his *Soul and Form* and *Theory of the Novel*, Lukács argues that aesthetic form functions as a sort of compensation for the fragmentation and alienation of modern life. The modern novelist's task, he claims, is to impose form on a world otherwise devoid of necessary value. The price we pay for taking pleasure in this form is the knowledge that any world thus portrayed must be eternally a fiction. For Baxtin, in contrast, the novel's task lies in a representation of the openness of development, in an unfolding of potentials that are precisely unforeseen, as yet unformed, and can therefore mimic real experience. And thus—while Baxtin and Lukács agree that the novel is the genre best suited to depicting man's struggle in a world without a priori forms—Lukács expects novelists to bestow form on their novels and novelistic characters to bestow form on their lives. The novelists Baxtin celebrates are much less likely to redeem humankind through bestowed meaning. That, perhaps, is the task of readers, who close down the text in their own ways and in so doing liberate an author from captivity to his own epoch. Baxtin links the baggy, open-ended novel with redemption not because he cares any less about truth but because he is persuaded that only real death, not real life, has the sort of meaning that can be redeemed through wholeness.

To appreciate the analogies Baxtin intends here between life and art, we must remember that for Baxtin authorship is an everyday activity. Nothing could be further from Baxtin's poetics than the insistence—shared in different ways by Romantics, New Critics, and Formalists—that authorship is something special. On the contrary, it is the very business of living. We author others at each encounter with them, and are in turn "authored" by those who interact with us.

Here we should note a crucial distinction Baxtin draws between inner and outer self. The inner self is always open, potential, hopeful, not-yet-concrete; this Baxtin calls the "I-for-myself." This inner "I" always knows that whatever it does is provisional; any act could, and should, have been better and different. The outer self, in contrast, is the personality *others* perceive and help bring into being. This so-called "I-for-others" is always to some extent closed, finalized, and identified with completed deeds—because that is the only self others can see. Both of these "I"s are socially constituted; one, however, is relatively open, the other relatively closed. And they are absolutely indispensable to each other: we could not go on living if we felt that what we have been so far for others is all we can become. Thus Baxtin can write in his final notes that genuine creative existence, a true quest for one's own word, is always "a striving to depart from one's own words—with which nothing essential can be said." In this scheme of things, we literally do not know what we have said, or who we are, until others respond to us.

This privileging of the *outside perspective* is a constant feature of Baxtin's approach to the world, and provides the necessary constraint on his too-easily-sung hymn to freedom. "Insideness," one's "I-for-myself," might indeed be free, but freedom in that raw state cannot contribute anything significant to understanding. Genuine freedom and understanding lie not on the inside but on the outside. This is true even for so interior a form as autobiography. When we tell the story of our own lives, Baxtin insists, what speaks in us most often is not direct experience or memory but a narrator with someone else's values and intonations, "the valuable other *in me*," as Baxtin puts it. "I-for-myself," he says, "is not capable of telling any stories."

Thus even autobiographical value—our own self's sense of itself—is composite, with a unity that is only posited. As heroes of our own ongoing life we want to *live*, to keep options open. But as authors of our own biography we strive to assign value, to consummate and shape; we see here traces of the struggle between inner (ethical) and outer (aesthetic) pressures that define any creative act. Thus Baxtin can conclude that even one's own biography is bestowed: "I receive it as a gift from others and for others."

This continual presence of the *embodied other* in all acts of identity is, according to Baxtin, the one guarantee that genuine authorship will continue to occur. At the end of his early essay on authors and their heroes, Baxtin devotes a special section to the "Problem of the Author." There he delineates possible causes for a crisis in authorship and style. Three major misunderstandings, he claims, can trigger a crisis in authorship. The first occurs whenever aesthetic movements endorse a "cult of the artist." Authors during such a time (Baxtin has Romanticism in mind, and doubtless Symbolism as well) are unwilling to "humble themselves to the status of toilers," and they resist defining their place in existence "among others and alongside others." This resistance to the cult of the artist was, of course, also part of the Formalist ethos, which proclaimed the poet a craftsman, not a seer. But Baxtin goes further.

From the later perspective of the Dostoevskij book we see that Baxtin already poses, in this early essay, a homology between art and life: how polyphonic authors place themselves among their own created characters—as participants in an event, not as masters of it—is also the ideal model for poets functioning in society.

The second crisis (indeed related to the first) occurs whenever authors lose faith in their right to be *outside* another. In such instances the author insists that life can be viewed correctly only from within; the act of understanding then comes to mean entering an object and judging the world through *its* eyes. Both God and religion become interiorized and psychologized, and one's creative energies "withdraw from the boundaries, thereby leaving them to the mercy of arbitrary fate." Such a shrinking of the "I" happens, not surprisingly, when life begins to "fear boundaries and strives to dissolve them, having lost faith in the essentialness or benevolence of the force shaping it from without." When the "I" of an author ceases to be a boundary phenomenon, it ceases to be altogether.

The third type of authorship-crisis is more conventional, and draws Baxtin's poetics firmly back into the aesthetic sphere. Authors may find themselves paralyzed, Baxtin intimates, when their position of outsideness becomes too purely, too "painfully ethical." Such an ethical imperative, which summons consciousness to action and judgment in the world, acts to *de*stabilize the boundary separating human beings and their art. Aesthetic authorship is threatened when there is "no confident, calm, unshakable and rich position of outsideness."

We see, therefore, that Baxtin's dictum on "art and life uniting *in me*" in no sense sanctions an erasing of boundaries between the two spheres, nor does it "reduce" art to life. What such union makes possible, rather, is an awareness of parallel challenges in the ethical and the aesthetic realm. Through aesthetic authoring we can—in Baxtin's wonderfully suggestive phrase—"exit into the unity of the event," that is, abandon the open, but sterile, I-for-myself and allow ourselves to be defined in interaction with others.

Here the problems begin in earnest, on both sides of Baxtin's poetics. We recall that dialogue and unfinalizability in a poetics of art raise compositional problems: can authorial intention in fact be encoded in "open heroes" and "open plots," and do not such concepts misrepresent the control an author exercises over the shape of the text? In a poetics of life, analogously, this endless deferment of one's self to the other for finalization raises moral and ethical questions. What, ultimately, can we call our identity? Since the very concept of responsibility assumes that there is a self to be responsible, how do we define personal morality?

All the ready ways out of this dilemma prove equally problematic. If, for example, it is truly up to others to complete us, then what we must do is seek *not* to remain ourselves (which in any case would be an impossibility, if not a contradiction in terms); we must instead seek the key to our freedom in permitting ourselves to be finalized by more than one person, perhaps even by as many people as possible. An analogue suggests itself in Baxtin's theory of "speech genres." In that essay, Baxtin argues that "individuality" as we know it is not a function of radical originality but depends, rather, upon our ability to assimilate the many conventional templates made available by our particular culture and time. It follows that we are flexible and rich in our individuality to the extent that we have mastered—and can therefore choose among and recombine—the speech or behavioral genres that others recognize and share. In the same way, one might argue, we must have many outside "finalizers" to express our multiple selves and our multiple potentialities for self.

But in this scenario of ever-expanding otherness, what does it mean to be "true to oneself"? What continuities does the multiple self know, and—more importantly—how does it express its responsibility? Baxtin clearly had these questions on his mind all his life. In his final notes he remarked, with what must have been a certain fatal weariness, "Are there genres of pure *self*-expression. . . . Do there exist genres without an addressee?" But still one feels a certain uneasiness at the casualness with which Baxtin dismisses—or declines to engage—what is genuinely problematic in this issue.

For him, the presence of the other and of the other's *response* is so indispensable to human being that other considerations—and perhaps even moral ones—are shunted aside. As Baxtin concludes in his late essay on the role of the text in the human sciences ["**Problem of the Text**"]:

> For the word (and consequently for a human being) there is nothing more terrible than a *lack of response*. Even a word that is known to be false is not absolutely false, and always presupposes an instance that would understand and justify it, even if in the form: "anyone *in my position* would have lied, too."

Lies, it seems, are better than nothing. And for some, this is a troubling form of tolerance. The moral dilemma here is the one confronting all socially-based theories of self: the possibility that the others who shape the self may be wrong.

Baxtin suggests that *any* finalization has value, because it completes us from a point of view fundamentally inaccessible to us and thus enriches our sense of self. But surely this makes light of the politics involved. If, as Baxtin insists, the worst human state (what he calls absolute death or non-being) is "the state of being unheard, unrecognized, unremembered," then do we ever have an inner, ethical right to *non*-response? Do we have a right to say: "Don't touch me, I don't want to be finalized by you," or, in more familiar language, "You are to blame, for making me see myself that way"? Within Baxtin's ethical universe, there appear to be few legitimate options for being left alone.

Baxtin does provide a loophole, to be sure—the same loophole he claims that Dostoevskij provided for the Underground Man. He reserves for the self an infinite supply of additional words to counter any outside verdict, positive as well as negative. But in Baxtin's scenario even these inner words—which save us from the trap of definition

and final judgment—must in turn be finalized from without in order to achieve any stability of definition, any biographical validity. Baxtin is fully aware of the implications of this progression. "As something possessed by otherness," he wrote in the 1920s, "biographical value is precarious. The biographically valuable life hangs by a thread, for it cannot be definitely grounded internally. . . . [Thus] biographical life . . . is always enveloped by a naive faith, its atmosphere is warm. Biography is deeply trustful, but naively so (without crises); it presupposes a kind, gentle activity situated outside it and encompassing it, but this is not the activity of the author, who is in need of such activity right alongside the hero."

Baxtin's implied potential other lives forever on friendly boundaries and continuums. This is a major difference, as has been pointed out, between Baxtin's model and the discontinuous stratifications and incompatible discourses of Foucault; Baxtin's other always works to define us in ways we can live with. The self is presumed resilient or vigorous enough to incorporate, or counter, any definition the other might thrust upon it—and the other, as a rule, rises up to meet the self from a warm and trustful atmosphere. Baxtin characterizes this ideal otherness succinctly in his final notes, where he writes: "Benevolent demarcation and only then cooperation. . . . The more demarcation the better, but benevolent demarcation. Without border disputes. Cooperation."

This leads me to the second major troubling area in Baxtin's poetics, what we might call its presumption of "benevolence" or "benignness." Just as in Baxtin's scheme of things an openness to others can never really be threatening, so Baxtin seems to assume that dialogue just naturally optimizes itself for its participants. Is it not equally plausible that making dialogue happen takes a lot of inner work, work that is not social in its essence but more like moving rocks in a field you want to plow, or a struggle against terror? This idea is beginning to be developed in some provocative "revisionist" criticism against the Baxtinian model. One of the most persuasive is Aaron Fogel's *Coercion to Speak*, a study of Joseph Conrad from an anti-dialogic perspective. What Fogel suggests is that dialogue is not the normal human relation at all; that most human speech is forced, under constraint, and that Conrad is a master at portraying this truth in novelistic form. The exemplar here is the wretched Razumov in *Under Western Eyes*, who comes home one evening to a dialogue he never chose to enter and spends the rest of his life trying to regain control over his own, lost word. With that "Russian" novel of Conrad's in mind—so obviously modeled on Dostoevskij—we might rethink Baxtin's **Problems of Dostoevsky's Poetics.**

It has often been noted that Baxtin's book on Dostoevskij affords spiritual inspiration to the reader but is not, at many crucial points, true to the spirit of Dostoevskij. Most of us would agree that many characters and scenes in Dostoevskij's novels are genuinely pathological; so, often enough, is Dostoevskij himself. In Baxtin's reading, however, both the man and his work somehow come out therapeutic. Even the tortured moves of the Underground Man ultimately come to represent a celebration of unrealized potential, the right to postpone forever the final word. A similar tender warmth envelopes Baxtin's discussion of the Idiot, Prince Myškin. Baxtin appropriately places Nastasja Filippovna, the infernal heroine, in a "carnival hell," but Myškin he places in a "carnival heaven"—because the Prince strives so mightily to finalize others benevolently, to release them from their most desperate selves and even to deny the existence of those negative selves. But surely this ignores a crucial paradox in Dostoevskij's novel. When the Prince exclaims to Rogožin, "Parfen! I don't believe it!" or to Nastasja Filippovna that he knew "she was really not that sort of woman," he monologizes his fellow characters—and this move they will inevitably resist. Myškin's stubborn reductive benevolence is itself a central factor impelling the novel's heroes to their destruction.

Readers of Baxtin's book on Rabelais (and the other texts on carnival) might experience a similar discomfort—a sense that the dark side has somehow evaporated. In those works, Baxtin rejoices in the open orifices and robust laughter of the Renaissance body. To be grotesque is to be forever available for fundamental change. But openness and laughter—and this is the important point—do not necessarily affirm any new or significant value. Sometimes the most they can document is the potential for survival, and sometimes they signify the purest desperation. Yet Baxtin refuses to admit nihilism, absurdity, or pain into his Rabelaisian poetics of the body. Such bodies always embody positive and concrete meaning.

The noncontinuity between these two corporealities—the individual mortal body and the regenerating folkloric body—is also felt, in somewhat altered form, beneath Baxtin's remarkably benign construct for cultures of laughter. Historians of carnival have been quick to point out that real-life carnival can be both conservative and repressive, and can function as a societal safety valve that domesticates conflict by sanctioning victimization. Critics have also noted that Baxtin projects a rather eccentric image of the people's appetites: he tends to consign all formal and elevated aspects of carnival life—and of noncarnival life as well—to the "official spheres" of culture, while ascribing to the folk a passion solely for life's mocking and open forms.

There are also complications in Baxtin's model when cultural boundaries are crossed. Its image of the common people might indeed reflect the Rabelaisian carnival experience. But it is—as Lotman and Uspenskij have pointed out—quite foreign to medieval *Russian* culture. There the guffaw was not open or ambivalent, it was the laugh of Satan.

Only occasionally in the Rabelais book does Baxtin let it be known that real carnival—or, for that matter, the real Rabelais—is not his primary concern. Drawing on the work of the Soviet Renaissance scholar Leonid Pinskij, Baxtin reveals his underlying agenda, the connection between laughter and truth. The purpose of carnival laughter in literature is to work a change on readers: to liberate them from fear, and thus free them to create. Laughter purifies the world by making it possible to *see*. And this, according to Baxtin, is the paradoxical truth of Rabelaisian

negation. Neither affirmation nor denial are fixed points; what matters is the *movement* from a negative to a positive pole. That liminal moment, so familiar to us from Formalist concepts of *ostranenie* but used here to such different purpose, is where all genuine learning takes place.

Here, I suggest, we glimpse Baxtin's version of a world in a state of grace. In that world, learning is always possible because value is already there, presumed to exist in a myriad of concrete forms always on the brink of transformation and nourished by a basically benign environment. Baxtin is a Heraclitian pantheist. He presumes no conflict *in principle* between an organism and its surroundings, just as he presumes no conflict in principle between self and society. This "benevolent environment" for life is much more than a nod to evolutionary biology. Baxtin connects essential benevolence with consciousness itself. As he discusses the issue in his early essay on authors and their heroes:

> A certain degree of warmth is necessary in the value-laden atmosphere surrounding me in order for self-consciousness and self-utterance to be realized, in order for life to begin. . . . One lives and becomes conscious neither within a guarantee, nor within a wilderness. . . . One can only live in faith.

A faith so constituted is an attitude, a search for higher authority, and precisely as a search it is always open to redefinition. In fact, Baxtin would probably argue that ultimate value exists largely in order to *make striving meaningful*. Since genuine seeking (like true dialogue) can only take place between embodied subjects, each of whom possesses the power to change the other, higher authority is never abstract or impersonal. Here Baxtin resembles his great contemporary in exile, Nikolaj Berdjaev, for whom Godmanhood was intimate and reciprocal—and in whose Christian, personalist socialism man could be redeemed from the Fall not by asceticism, and not by mere obedience, but only by creativity.

This brings me to my final and most general point about Baxtin's "benevolence." The celebration of an ability to create something new is but one example of Baxtin's extraordinary privileging of the immediate future. He has little interest in distant or abstract futures, in the conventional utopia; when he says that "everything is still in the future and will always be in the future" he means the cutting edge of the present, tied with innumerable strands to *now*. But this stance carries within it an inevitable tension. Baxtin both insists upon the reality of events in the present, and at the same time wants to make it possible for closure not to happen—for events not to add up, stick, or cripple future action. Events *can* be laughed away. The future is important not as the sum of past events, but as the realm of newly-arranged value. In contrast to some American post-structuralists, Baxtin draws his primary data not from the category of "always already" but rather from the category of "always about to be." The "always already" component in Russian formalist criticism—its reliance on recombining old forms, its negative thrust, its equation of aesthetic experience with subtraction of meaning, and the absence in it of a genuinely constructive, creative impulse—was in fact the master complaint that the Baxtin

Circle lodged against the Formal Method. True freedom is freedom of creative judgment. But there is little here of the "judgmental": what matters in the act of judging is not condemnation, not catching-in-the-act or any other such legal category. What matters about judging is its potential transformative power.

We might illustrate Baxtin's ideas by applying them to the concluding chapters of *The Brothers Karamazov.* Dmitrij is indeed a man unjustly finalized by others. The court that finds him guilty of murder is a caricature; its judges and jurors cannot even reconstruct the outer event. But the *act* of being judged brings about a transformation in the accused and makes possible a new self. As Baxtin jotted down in his final notes, one's inner freedom "cannot change existence, as it were, materially (nor can it want to)—it can change only the *sense* of existence . . . This is the freedom of the witness and the judge. It is expressed in the *word.*"

Here we recognize in Baxtin's poetics a reinterpretation, from a dialogic perspective, of stoicism. And this is intriguing because for Baxtin—unlike the Stoics—self is always social.

This powerful, open role for the future makes Baxtin's world remarkably free of bitterness, and singularly incapable of comprehending texts of true rage. Winston Smith, after all, lived in a world where he was all too free to "change the sense of existence" and reassess the significance of facts. It is one of the inspiring ironies of Baxtin's life that his work—all produced under Soviet conditions and much of it under Stalinist conditions—seems so little poisoned by the realities that Orwell confronted in *1984.* This benevolence of Baxtin's is the most appealing and perhaps the most troublesome aspect of his poetics; as in the most challenging of Christ's parables, the capacity to affirm seems closely tied to a tolerance of injustice.

Where does this leave us as critics of Baxtin's legacy? We might consider first his poetics of literary art. In this realm it is clear that dialogue, heteroglossia and polyphony should not be invoked as strict technical terms for analyzing the structural whole of a literary work. They are rather like *functions* which can govern select patches of certain novels—rarely the whole of a novel, and not all novels. There are, nevertheless, genuine differences between dialogically and monologically inspired works. A dialogic work invites a certain sort of response. It may be more loosely constructed; its ending may not be planned in advance, and therefore the significance of any particular incident in it cannot be guaranteed. The work can be designed so that at each moment of reading the openness of each act is paramount—thus the act itself potentiates many patterns, but need not conform to any single one. By such criteria, Tolstoj is perhaps more thoroughly polyphonic than Dostoevskij.

As part of a poetics of life, "benign openness" offers a slightly different mix of benefits and dangers.

Here one must ask: is Baxtin's huge privileging of the future, his insistence on the creative potential of the next response and the capacity of response to transfigure event, really compatible with *responsibility* for events? Can we—as Baxtin put it in that 1919 essay—answer for art with our life, if we endlessly defer the meaning of that life as we wait for the next response to it to come in? At what point does one stand still and take stock in one's own voice? Read Baxtin carefully, and he will tell you: never. When you stand still you are dead, and *others* take stock of your life. To be conscious is to always have an exit—or at least to be always looking for an exit. In contrast to this benign scenario, we might consider an alternative vision, the perhaps apocryphal story of Dostoevskij's final thesis at the Engineering School in Petersburg where he was a student in the 1840s: a fortress designed with no windows and no doors.

One final way of viewing the problematics of openness might be to consider the ambiguities in the Russian abstract noun *otvetstvennost'.* Its root is *otvet,* the word for "answer" or "response," and the conventional English equivalent for *otvetstvennost'* is "responsibility." But Baxtin plays with the word, using it in contexts that suggest not only responsibility but also "answerability," that is, an openness to new answers, responsive listening. Between this privileging of the future where everything is open, and a recognition that action cannot be undone and must be answered *for,* lies the challenge of combining, if possible, the responsively new and the morally responsible. For Baxtin, the supreme value in life is the potential for creativity. But much in his own model makes the pursuit of this value problematic.

Some of these problems are inevitable, given Baxtin's priorities and the cast of his mind; they are the blindnesses, as it were, that must accompany his insights. Other problems can be traced to a "fetishization" of certain highly visible and marketable sides of Baxtin—especially the carnivalesque—to the exclusion of more "conservative" concerns arguably more central to his thought. And yet a third set of problems with Baxtin's poetics can actually be eased by a consideration of the ethical position Baxtin mapped out for art in his early manuscripts. This position underwent considerable—and often surprising—change throughout Baxtin's life, re-emerging in his final years as central to his vision of the human sciences. Several ideas suggested by these earliest and latest writings might serve to summarize the problems raised in this essay.

First, Baxtin was not just offering a new poetics, he was undoing the very idea of a poetics. For he seems to have associated impersonal systems of all sorts with the mode of thinking proper to a "poetics" of the aesthetic world: initially an Aristotelian poetics of closed wholes and well-shaped plots, but soon Formalist, then Structuralist, and—had he lived to hear of it—quite certainly deconstructionist. "[I have] a different understanding of specification," he wrote near the end of his life, in response to the methodologies of formalism and structuralism. For Baxtin, the *specific* in the human sciences was always found in the nongeneralizable human context and not in a code, or, as he put it, in *depth* rather than *precision.* The realization that no two living contexts could ever repeat themselves sufficiently to create a genuinely applicable code—a fact that guaranteed, not undermined, the authenticity of meaning and value—is the first step toward understanding Baxtin's ideas on wholeness and unity.

As Gary Saul Morson and I will argue in our forthcoming study of Baxtin, such an idea of specification is less poetic than it is *prosaic*. This is prosaic in both senses of the term: both prose-like as opposed to poetical, and ordinary, that is, pertaining to and celebrating the mass of unmarked everyday decisions that require work of us precisely because we cannot ground them in general norms, principles, or the drama of clean-cut openings and closings. Baxtin is a singer of middle spaces. A "prosaic" approach to his work, therefore, might shed some light on what many consider to be the most problematic sides of Baxtinian poetics: its insistence on decentering and "openness" in the novel, and its presumption that this openness is essentially benign.

A quote from the early manuscripts will illustrate "prosaics" with a difficult but crucial Russian phrase. "We live," Baxtin writes, "in a world of exitless reality, not of random potential." Note that for Baxtin this "exitlessness" is a very good thing. Random potential, mere possibility, always splits me off from the world; it is, as Baxtin says, the "unbridled play of empty objectivity," an "infinity of cognition" that no one has yet signed.

The positive term in that little sentence, then, is "exitless reality," *bezysxodnaja dejstvitel'nost'*, the world you cannot get out of and cannot help answering for. This is not, significantly, the no-exit of *no* meaning but the no-exit of unlimited meaning. And in this context, doublevoicedness, loophole, carnival—all those terms of freeing-up and letting-go—do *not* mean "getting out of it," escaping meaning, but simply getting out of one thing into something else, getting a second chance at it that will again bind you and bind your act. Polyphony is the tie that binds, not releases, and polyphonic bonds are infinitely more complex and delimiting than those in a monologic text.

For this reason one could argue that the weakest, least consistent, and most dangerous category in Baxtin's arsenal is the concept of "carnival." Properly placed in his world, carnival is valuable solely as a mechanism for laughing at system, not for laughing at individual answerability for acts. For a prosaic world must begin with personal responsibility. What is important is *not* the holiday (with its masks, its extraordinary inversions and suspensions of personality) but rather the ordinary, unrepeatable, radically individual everyday event, events of the sort that novels are made of. What is also not important—what is even fraudulent—are all systems that would claim to classify those events and rank them according to impersonal hierarchies. Few contemporary -isms, from Marxism to post-structuralism, would wish to claim such freedom from system.

More helpful here than any dialogue with twentieth-century theoretical trends might be Baxtin's debt to the Orthodox, Slavophile strain in Russian romanticism. Much in the Baxtinian dualistic universe recalls mid-nineteenth-century debates between Westernizers and Slavophiles. The world is a battleground between material and moral freedom. On one side (the West) there is mere

external unity, logic, system, coercion—that is, centripetal forces. The other side (Orthodoxy) has access to *cel'noe bytie*, "integral existence," which alone makes faith possible. From that stable position the self can reach out in a voluntary, centrifugal gesture and never fear difference.

For both Baxtin and these early Slavophiles, politics is a distortion and a burden. Their implied communities are outside political parties, and perhaps even outside history itself. If indeed, as Baxtin claims, there can be no human unit of less than two consciousnesses, then the *upper* limit seems also to be of cozy, chamber-room dimensions: not humanity, not a state or institution, but people we can see, touch, and alter by our everyday authoring. Under these conditions, individuality is not suppressed in collectivity but is, in Konstantin Aksakov's celebrated phrase, "most free in a chorus." To the extent that this miraculous balance is achieved in life and in art, Baxtin's poetics ceases to be problematic.

Caryl Emerson, "Problems with Baxtin's Poetics," in Slavic and East-European Journal, *n. s. Vol. 32, No. 4, Winter, 1988, pp. 503-25.*

Paul de Man   (essay date 1989)

[*A Belgian-born American literary theorist, critic, and educator, de Man was a pioneer in establishing the theoretical movement known as "deconstruction," which he promoted in such works as* Blindness and Insight: Essays in the Rhetoric of Contemporary Criticism *(1971),* Allegories of Reading: Figural Language in Rousseau, Nietzsche, Rilke, and Proust *(1979), and* The Resistance to Theory *(1986). The discovery in 1987 of anti-Semitic, pro-Nazi articles written by de Man for a collaborationist newspaper in Belgium in the early 1940s complicated the controversy already surrounding deconstruction, with some critics noting what they considered the biased, political nature of the movement. In the essay below, originally published in 1983, de Man analyzes Bakhtin's notion of dialogism and criticizes the ways in which it has been employed by subsequent thinkers.*]

The set of problems that surrounds the relationship between fiction and reality in the novel recurs in many forms to organize contemporary theories of narration as well as of the relationship between narrative, discursive, and poetic language. Much is at stake, stylistically, philosophically, and historically, in these discussions whose importance, not only in the realm of theory but also in the practical sphere of ethics and politics, is superseded only by their difficulty. The higher the stakes the harder the game. Such situations, conducive to obsession and to fatigue, are prone to generate legitimate admiration with regard to predecessors who have somehow managed to sustain the ordeal of these difficulties and to bequeath to us some of the skills and strategies gained in the course of this experience. Literary theory, and especially theory of narrative, a rather barren area of endeavor constantly threatened by the tedium of its techniques as well as by the magnitude of the issues, offers poor soil for the heroes and the hero worship that it rather desperately needs. So when a possible candidate for such a status comes along, he is likely to be very well received, especially if he is safely and posthumously out of reach. Such belated "receptions," for being rare, are all the more intense in the field of literary theory. A fairly recent example is, of course, the case of Walter Benjamin. More recent, and more intense still, is that of Mikhail Bakhtin, who was recently heralded, by his highly competent and clear-eyed introducers, as "le plus important penseur soviètique dans le domaine des sciences humaines et le plus grand théoricien de la littérature au 20 siècle" ("the most important Soviet thinker in the area of the human sciences and the greatest literary theorist of the twentieth century") and "as one of the leading thinkers of the 20th century." In both cases, this entirely justified admiration is focused on Bakhtin's contribution to the theory of the novel, not only in the relatively well-known books on Rabelais and Dostoevsky but in more theoretical studies such as the essay entitled **"Discourse in the Novel"** which dates from 1934-35. This essay is singled out by both Todorov and Holquist as the major theoretical statement. And, within the theory of the novel, it is the concept of dialogism, rather than related but other Bakhtinian terms such as chronotopes, refraction, heteroglossia, or the carnivalesque, that receives major attention, as is apparent from the titles of the two books: *Le principe dialogique* (1981) and *The Dialogic Imagination* (1981).

The last thing I wish to do here is to dispute or dispel this enthusiasm. There is no merit whatever to the facile and always cheaply available gesture that protects mediocrity by exposing the blindness that is part of any dedication and of the admiration it inspires. The attentive and critical reading of Bakhtin's work has barely begun, at least in the West, and since I ignore the Russian language, it is not an enterprise in which I can responsibly hope to take part. My question therefore does not address the significance of Bakhtin, or of Voloshinov/Bakhtin or of Medvedev/Bakhtin, as a theoretician or as a thinker, but the much more narrow question of why the notion of dialogism can be so enthusiastically received by theoreticians of very diverse persuasion and made to appear as a valid way out of many of the quandaries that have plagued us for so long. Or, to put it in the terms of this issue: how does dialogism, as developed in Bakhtin and his group, cope with and indeed seem to overcome the ever-recurring question of the status of fact, meaning, and fiction in the novel?

Dialogism can mean, and indeed has meant, many things to many critics, sometimes without reference to Bakhtin. . . . It can, first of all, simply mean double-talk, the necessary obliqueness of any persecuted speech that cannot, at the risk of survival, openly say what it means to say: there is ample evidence, from what is known of Bakhtin's biography, that this meaning is entirely relevant in his case. The readers of oppressed thinkers, in the words of a major theoretician of the discourse of persecution, "are to be led step by step from the popular view [. . .] to the truth which is merely and purely theoretical, guided by certain obtrusively enigmatic features in the presentation of the popular teaching—obscurity of the plan, contradictions, pseudonyms, inexact repetitions of earlier statements, strange expressions, etc." This quotation from Leo Strauss's *Persecution and the Art of Writing* fits the

case of Bakhtin very well. Strauss could have added another salient feature: the circulation of more or less clandestine class or seminar notes by initiated disciples or, even more symptomatic, the rumored (and often confirmed) existence of unpublished manuscripts made available only to an enterprising or privileged researcher and which will decisively seal one mode of interpretation at the expense of all rival modes—at least until one of the rivals will, in his turn, discover the real or imaginary countermanuscript on which to base his counterclaim. What in the context of our topic interests us primarily in this situation is that it is bound to engender a community tied together by the common task of decrypting the repressed message hidden in the public utterance. As the sole detainers of an esoteric knowledge, this community is bound to be small, self-selective, and likely to consider itself as a chosen elite. To the extent, however, that the process of understanding becomes constitutively linked to the elaboration and the life of a society, fact and fiction are brought together by the mediation of shared communal labor. The possibility of this mediation is built within the production of the text itself: since it does not mean to say what it actually says, it is a fiction, but a fiction that, in the hands of the right community of readers, will become fact.

For Leo Strauss, the model of persecution applies predominantly to philosophical rather than to literary texts; Bakhtin's stress on the novel adds a potentially libertarian and revolutionary dimension. "Im Sklaven fängt die Prosa an": it is in the slave, says Hegel, that prose begins and he says this in the section of the *Aesthetics* that deal precisely with fables as the ancestors of the novel. Like Strauss's philosopher, Bakhtin's novelist is persecuted per definition and carries within himself the image of his liberation. But this image exists not, as is still the case in Lukács, in the form of a nostalgia for the presumably unified world of the epic; the novelist does not set out to take the place of his master, the epic poet, but to set him free from the restricting coercions of his single-minded, monological vision. Bakhtin's novel definitely belongs to what Northrop Frye calls the low-mimetic modes: it is ideologically prosaic, anti-romance, anti-epical, and anti-mythical; its multivoicedness or heteroglossia postulates distinct and antagonistic class structures as well as the celebratory crossing of social barriers. The dialogism of a revolutionary community reconciles fact and fiction in a manner that is not essentially distinct from the persecutory model, except for the introduction of a temporal dimension: the freedom that is being celebrated is not utopian, yet it is not actualized in the immediacy of the textual invention. It is projected in a metatextual future as the prolepsis of a no longer fictional freedom. The scheme is bound to exercise a powerful attraction on a type of literary criticism that stems from a rebellion against the constraints of transcendental and monological systems such as institutional religions. An author and a concept—dialogism—that can be made to accommodate the textual model of Leo Strauss as well as of some disciples of Gilles Deleuze shows, to say the least, remarkable scope.

In Bakhtin's writings, the notion of dialogism is also systematically developed, not only, as in **"Discourse in the Novel"** or in the Rabelais book, in dialectical exchange with the persecutory power of monistic discourses, but in a prolonged and complex discussion of formalism. As is well known, the topic figures prominently in the pseudonymous books *Marxism and the Philosophy of Language* (Voloshinov) and *The Formal Method in Literary Scholarship* (Medvedev). Very summarily put, it is possible to think of dialogism as a still formal method by which to conquer or to sublate formalism itself. Dialogism is here still a descriptive and metalinguistic term that says something about language rather than about the world. Bakhtin is consistent in his assertion that the dialogical relationship is intra-linguistic, between what he calls two heterogeneous "voices," as in a musical score. It is, in his terms, the image of a *language* (rather than the *image* of a language) and not of a society or of an interpersonal relationship. Therefore, as becomes evident in examples taken from Dickens and Turgenev, it is possible to analyze descriptively dialogical structures in actual texts, in a manner that is by no means unusual to "formalist" practitioners of an American style of close reading. On the other hand, dialogism also functions, throughout the work and especially in the Dostoevsky book, as a principle of radical otherness or, to use again Bakhtin's own terminology, as a principle of *exotopy:* far from aspiring to the *telos* of a synthesis or a resolution, as could be said to be the case in dialectical systems, the function of dialogism is to sustain and think through the radical exteriority or heterogeneity of one voice with regard to any other, including that of the novelist himself. She or he is not, in this regard, in any privileged situation with respect to his characters. The self-reflexive, autotelic, or, if you wish, narcissistic structure of form, as a definitional description enclosed within specific borderlines, is hereby replaced by an *assertion* of the otherness of the other, preliminary to even the possibility of a *recognition* of his otherness. Rather than having to do with class structures, as in the societal models of **"Discourse in the Novel,"** exotopy has to do with relationships between distinct cultural and ideological units. It would apply to conflicts between nations or religions rather than between classes. In this perspective, dialogism is no longer a formal and descriptive principle, nor does it pertain particularly to language: heteroglossia (multivariedness between discourses) is a special case of exotopy (otherness as such) and the formal study of literary texts becomes important because it leads from intralinguistic to intracultural relationships. At that point, the binary opposition between fiction and fact is no longer relevant: in any differential system, it is the assertion of the space *between* the entities that matters. Binaries, to the extent that they allow and invite synthesis, are therefore the most misleading of differential structures. Novelists like Dostoevsky or, one might surmise, Balzac reveal their exotopy when they simply ignore such strongly suggestive oppositions as those between author and character: Dostoevsky's or Balzac's characters are not voices of authorial identity or identification (not: *Madame Bovary, c'est moi*) but voices of radical alterity, not because they are fictions and the author isn't, but because their otherness *is* their reality. The reality principle coincides with the principle of otherness. Bakhtin at times conveys the impression that one can accede from dialogism as a metalinguistic (i.e., formal) structure to dialogism as a recognition of exotopy. The

itinerary beyond form by ways of formal analysis is particularly attractive to someone skilled in the formal analysis of structural semiotics or structural stylistics but grown impatient with the inability to break out of the formal shell and to address, at long last, questions that appear no longer to be merely linguistic. Todorov is, of course, himself a case in point.

It is also by ways of exotopy that, finally, a larger philosophical claim can be made for Bakhtin not just as a technician of literary discourse but as a thinker or metaphysician whose name can be considered next to those of Husserl, Heidegger, or, as Todorov aptly suggests, Levinas. The radical experience of voiced otherness as a way to a regained proximity can indeed be found as a dominant theme in Levinas and to have at least a submerged existence in Heidegger. One can think of the lines in Hölderlin's poem *Mnemosyne, "Seit ein Gespräch wir sind / Und hören können von einander"* as a common ground. Whether the passage from otherness to the recognition of the other—the passage, in other words, from dialogism to dialogue—can be said to take place in Bakhtin as more than a desire, remains a question for Bakhtin interpretation to consider in the proper critical spirit. This renders premature any more specific consideration of how this recognition is to occur: as a religious transcendentalism which would allow one to read "God" wherever Bakhtin says "society," as a Heideggerian disclosure of ontological truth in the otherness of language or as a secular but messianic ideologism that would bear a superficial, and perhaps misleading, resemblance to the position attributed to Walter Benjamin. To adjudicate hastily between these various options would be unthinkable; what can be observed is that, in each case, dialogism appears as a provisional stage under way toward a more absolute claim, a claim that is not necessarily monological but that points, at any rate, well beyond the limited confines of literary theory. Whether such an extension of Bakhtin's range is sound and legitimate also remains to be established. But that it is a possibility is made clear by the tone, even more than by the substance, of what is being written about him in Western Europe and in the United States.

One sees that it would be possible to line up an impressive list of contemporary theorists of very diverse persuasion, all of which would have a legitimate claim on Bakhtin's dialogism as congenial or even essential to their enterprise: the list could include analytical philosophers, formalist semioticians grown weary with their science, narratologists, technicians of reader reception, religious phenomenologists, Heideggerian critical ontologists, defenders of permanent revolution, disciples of Leo Strauss—and one could easily play the game of extending still further this list of unlikely bedfellows. If one then would be curious to know what they have in common, at least negatively, one should perhaps ask who, if anyone, would have reason to find it difficult or even impossible to enlist Bakhtin's version of dialogism among his methodological tools or skills. Such as, for example, a literary theoretician or critic concerned with tropological displacements of logic, with a rhetoric of cognition as well as of persuasion. Bakhtin has very astute things to say about tropes but, if one is willing to suspend for a moment the potential dialogical otherness of these statements, he seems, on the whole, to consider that the discourse of tropes is not dialogical, does not account for dialogism, and remains, by and large, on the near side of the theories of narrative that dialogism allows one to elaborate. Bakhtin frequently asserts the separation of trope from dialogism, for instance in the passage on the distinction between discourse in poetry and in prose, as stated in terms of refraction, in **"Discourse"** or in the later, even more dogmatically explicit passage in the same text, on the distinction between the tropological polysemy of poetry and the dialogism of prose. Here Bakhtin unambiguously asserts that "no matter how one understands the interrelationship of meanings in a poetic symbol (or trope), this relationship is never of the dialogical sort; it is impossible under any conditions or at any time to imagine a trope (say, a metaphor) being unfolded into the two exchanges of a dialogue, that is, two meanings parceled out between two separate voices." These passages are among the richest in the canon of Bakhtin's works, but this implies that they are also among the most contradictory and, for that reason, monologically aberrant. More than any other, they reveal the metaphysical *impensé* of Bakhtin's thought, the dogmatic foundations that make the dialogical ideology so attractive and so diverse. This is not the time and the place for a detailed analysis of the passages in question. But lest you suspect me of being evasive, let me state the direction that such a reading would take—while adding, as a matter of course, that at the moment when I appropriate these passages as the ground of my own admiration for the revealingly aberrant character of Bakhtin's writings, I have included myself in the odd list of Bakhtin admirers from which I first pretended to be excluded; this, however, in no way disposes of the negative thrust of the proposed argument. One would have to point out (1) that, for Bakhtin, the trope is an intentional structure directed toward an object and, as such, a pure *episteme* and not a fact of language; this in fact excludes tropes from literary discourse, poetic as well as prosaic, and locates them, perhaps surprisingly, in the field of epistemology; (2) that the opposition between trope as object-directed and dialogism as social-oriented discourse sets up a binary opposition between object and society that is itself tropological in the worst possible sense, namely as a reification; (3) and more revealing for us, that as the analysis of dialogical refraction develops, Bakhtin has to reintroduce the categorical foundations of a precritical phenomenalism in which there is no room for exotopy, for otherness, in any shape or degree. When it is said, for example, that "the heteroglot voices [. . .] create the background necessary for [the author's] own voice," we recognize the foreground-background model derived from Husserl's theories of perception and here uncritically assimilating the structure of language to the structure of a secure perception: from that moment on, the figure of refraction and of the light ray becomes coercive as the only possible trope for trope, and we are within a reflective system of *mise en abŷme* that is anything but dialogical. It is therefore not at all surprising that, still in the same passage, Bakhtin modulates irrevocably from dialogism to a conception of dialogue as question and answer of which it can then be said that "the speaker breaks through the alien conceptual horizon of the listener, constructs his own utterance on

alien territory against his, the listener's, apperceptive background." Again, there is no trace of dialogism left in such a gesture of dialectical imperialism that is an inevitable part of any hermeneutic system of question and answer. The ideologies of otherness and of hermeneutic understanding are not compatible, and therefore their relationship is not a dialogical but simply a contradictory one. It is not a foregone conclusion whether Bakhtin's discourse is itself dialogical or simply contradictory.

Let me turn, in conclusion, to a text which can, I think, be said to be dialogical, which also happens to be a dialogue and a dialogue about the novel at that. Rousseau's prefatory post-face to *La Nouvelle Héloise,* sometimes entitled *Dialogue on the Novel,* combines two modes of dialogue. First a hermeneutic mode in which author and reader are engaged in a sequence of questions and answers, a set of who's and what's for the purpose of determining whether the contents of the novel are fact or fiction: Who is Julie? Did she exist? The outcome of this hermeneutic quest is utterly inconclusive: the hermeneutics of reference are undecidable. But, in case you worry about the legitimacy of the present performance, the decision of undecidability is itself entirely rational and legitimate: although another session on fact and fiction within the novel in next year's MLA is not going to get any further than we got today, such a continuation is entirely legitimate and, in fact, inevitable. The formal expression of this certainty is manifest in the symmetry of the question and answer patterns which would allow one, within the orbit of such a question, to substitute author for reader without any loss of consistency: the unreadability of the referent is just as challenging, and for the same reasons, for the one as for the other, and their complicity in the hermeneutic quest is manifest.

On the other hand, the text also stages something very different: a battle of wits between author and reader in which they try to outdo each other, parrying, feinting, and setting traps in a sequence of attacks and defenses somewhat like a fencing match, or like the seduction which is being carried on in the exchange of letters that make up the first part of Rousseau's novel. In this exchange, the question is no longer a question of who or what: it would be naive to ask who wins the match since in this model, Rousseau, as author, controls the moves of each of the antagonists. And it would be equally naive to ask over what one is fighting: one fights over whether or not there is a question, which means that one is at least twice removed from any possibility of an answer as to what, in this fight, is at stake. All the interest focuses on *how* one fights (or seduces), on the how, the *poetics* of writing and of reading rather than the hermeneutics. The author wants to know what all authors always want to know: Did you read my book? Did you read it to the end? Do you think people will want to buy it? Will it sell in Paris? All of which amounts to wondering if he put it together right—questions all belonging to the realm of empirical poetics (how to write a book that will achieve fame) rather than hermeneutics (what is the truth of the text). This puts him at an obvious disadvantage in the ensuing battle in which the urbane reader can constantly play on the vulnerability of his position and make him look foolish: the smart reader always outwits an author who depends on him from the moment he has opened a dialogue that is never entirely gratuitous, that is always a battle for mastery. Yet, at the end of Rousseau's text, the character designated by *R,* and who is the author, refuses the substitution offered to him:

> N. . . . I advise you, however, to switch parts. Pretend that I am the one who urges you on to publish this collection of letters and that you are the one who resists. You give yourself the objections and I'll rebut them. It will sound more humble and make a better impression.
>
> R. Will it also be in conformity with what you find to be praiseworthy in my character?
>
> N. No, I was setting you a trap. Leave things as they are.

One of the ways in which this tricky passage has to be read is as the refusal, in terms of poetics, to grant the substitutive symmetry implied in a hermeneutics. Rousseau does

---

Wayne C. Booth on Bakhtin's interpretation of the carnival:

Bawdy, scatological laughter is for Bakhtin a great progressive force, the expression of an ideology that opposes the official and authoritarian languages that dominate our surfaces. Bakhtin sees Rabelais' period and his work as the last full expression of a folk wisdom that could enjoy a harmonious dialogue between the "lower" body and the "higher" and more official "spirit": the "voice" of the body transforms monologue into chorus. Carnival laughter, the intrusion of everything forbidden or slanderous or joyfully blasphemous into the purified domains of officialdom, expressed a complex sense that the material body was not unequivocally base: every death contains within it the meaning of rebirth, every birth comes from the same region of the body as does the excremental. And the excremental is itself a source of regeneration—it manures life just as the dogs' urine in Panurge's trick becomes the source of a well-known modern creek.

Rabelais in this view represents a possibility that the world later lost, the possibility for what Bakhtin calls "grotesque realism." When Rabelais and his predecessors made sexual and scatological jokes, they were not serving a sniggering laughter that divorced spirit from body, seeing the latter as merely dirty. References to the lower body were not simply naughty or degrading: they were used to produce a regenerative, an affirmative, a healing—finally a politically progressive—laughter. When the natural forces of joyful celebration of the lower body reached their peak, in time of carnival, mankind was healed with a laughter that was lost when, in later centuries, the body, and especially the lower body, came to be viewed as entirely negative and shameful.

Wayne C. Booth, in his "Freedom of Interpretation: Bakhtin and the Challenge of Feminist Criticism," Critical Inquiry, *September 1982.*

---

not have the least intention to relinquish to his reader the benefit in fame or money of the 70,000 copies which, at the time of writing the so-called preface, he knew his novel had already sold, in Paris as well as in the provinces. *Rira bien qui rira le dernier.* This success of his poetics is in no way compatible, however, with the rules of his hermeneutics. The relationship between poetics and hermeneutics, like that between R the author and N the reader, is dialogical to the precise extent that the one cannot be substituted for the other, despite the fact that the nondialogical discourse of question and answer fully justifies the substitution. What one has to admire Bakhtin for (that is, want to be in his place in having written what he wrote), as all his present readers, including myself, do, is his hope that, by starting out, as he does, in a poetics of novelistic discourse one may gain access to the power of a hermeneutics. The apparent question of the relationship between fact and fiction in the novel hides the more fundamental question of the compatibility between the descriptive discourse of poetics and the normative discourse of hermeneutics. Such compatibility can only be achieved at the expense of dialogism. To imitate or to apply Bakhtin, to read him by engaging him in a dialogue, betrays what is most valid in his work.

Paul de Man, "Dialogue and Dialogism," in Rethinking Bakhtin: Extensions and Challenges, *edited by Gary Saul Morson and Caryl Emerson, Northwestern University Press, 1989, pp. 105-14.*

Michael Holquist   (essay date 1990)

[*Holquist is an American critic, educator, and translator whose works include* Dostoevsky and the Novel: The Wages of Biography *(1977) and the biography* Mikhail Bakhtin *(1985, with Katerina Clark). In the following excerpt from his book* Dialogism: Bakhtin and His World, *Holquist traces fundamental issues in Bakhtin's theories of language and society.*]

Mikhail Bakhtin made important contributions to several different areas of thought, each with its own history, its own language, and its own shared assumptions. As a result, literary scholars have perceived him as doing one sort of thing, linguists another, and anthropologists yet another. We lack a comprehensive term that is able to encompass Bakhtin's activity in all its variety, a shortcoming he himself remarked when as an old man he sought to bring together the various strands of his life's work. At that time he wrote:

> our analysis must be called philosophical mainly because of what it is not: it is not a linguistic, philological, literary or any other particular kind of analysis. . . . On the other hand, a positive feature of our study is this: [it moves] in spheres that are liminal, i. e., on the borders of all the aforementioned disciplines, at their junctures and points of intersection.

But if we accept even so privative a sense of "philosophy" as a way to describe the sort of thing Bakhtin does, the question remains: what kind of philosophy is it?

Stated at the highest level of (quite hair-raising) abstraction, what can only uneasily be called "Bakhtin's philosophy" is a pragmatically oriented theory of knowledge; more particularly, it is one of several modern epistemologies that seek to grasp human behavior through the use humans make of language. Bakhtin's distinctive place among these is specified by the dialogic concept of language he proposes as fundamental. For this reason, the term used in [*Dialogism: Bakhtin and His World*] to refer to the interconnected set of concerns that dominate Bakhtin's thinking is "dialogism," a term, I hasten to add, never used by Bakhtin himself. There can be no theoretical excuse for spawning yet another "ism," but the history of Bakhtin's reception seems to suggest that if we are to continue to think about his work in a way that is useful, some synthetic means must be found for categorizing the different ways he meditated on dialogue. That is, some way must be found to conceive his varied activity as a unity, without losing sight of the dynamic heterogeneity of his achievement. Before looking at any of Bakhtin's particular works, it will be useful to have some sense of the ideas that permeate them all. This [essay] will seek, then, to lay out in a general way some of the ideas considered by Bakhtin at the beginning of his career, and which—with different shifts of emphasis and new accretions of significance—he never ceased to hold.

Dialogue is an obvious master key to the assumptions that guided Bakhtin's work throughout his whole career: dialogue is present in one way or another throughout the notebooks he kept from his youth to his death at the age of 80. Most of these are lost, some remain in the form of communications so self-directed they are now almost impossible to decipher or understand, while others eventually took on the more public and comprehensible form of published books. But early or late, no matter what the topic of the moment, regardless of the name under which he wrote or the degree of shared communication he presumed, all Bakhtin's writings are animated and controlled by the principle of dialogue. It is becoming increasingly evident that Bakhtin's lifelong meditation on dialogue does not have a place solely in the history of literary theory, capacious as the borders of that subject have recently become. It is now clear that dialogism is also implicated in the history of modern thinking about thinking.

In this it is far from unique: the work of many other recent thinkers, especially in France, combines literary criticism, even literary production, with concerns that are essentially philosophical. But the *kind* of literature and the *kind* of philosophy that are woven together in the writings of a Sartre or a Derrida constitute genres significantly different from those that characterize dialogism. Rousseau, Hegel, Nietzsche, and Heidegger, the philosophers recently "discovered" by students of literature, represent, not surprisingly, the *literary* aspect of philosophy. They are lyrical thinkers, some of whom set out consciously to poeticize metaphysics.

Bakhtin is working out of a very different philosophical tradition, one that is little known, even among many Anglo-American professors of philosophy. The men who constitute a dialogizing background for Bakhtin differ from most thinkers now in fashion in so far as they were,

in their own day, very much in the mainstream of academic philosophy. They held chairs in the important German universities and sought to make metaphysics even more systematic than had Hegel (most were, in fact, militantly *anti*-Hegelian, as was Bakhtin himself). Systematic metaphysics is now out of fashion and the names by which philosophy was defined in the latter half of the nineteenth century are for the most part forgotten. It is difficult for most of us now to conceive the passion excited in their time by such men as Hermann Cohen or Richard Avenarius. And if we take the trouble to look into their books, it becomes even harder, for they are written in the forbidding language of German technical philosophy in one of its more complex phases. And there are very few translations. I mention this tradition (emphatically) not to scare anyone away from a deeper involvement in Bakhtin's philosophical roots, but only to make it clear that such an involvement requires the extra effort always required to go beyond the categories and concepts (and translations) currently in fashion.

Dialogism, let it be clear from the outset, is itself not a systematic philosophy. But the specific way in which it refuses to be systematic can only be gauged against the failure of all nineteenth-century metaphysical systems to cope with new challenges raised by the natural and mathematical sciences. The most spectacular of these failures was the increasingly obvious irrelevance of Hegelianism (right *or* left) to the new scientific discoveries. As a result, from the 1860s on, more and more attention was paid to Kant: by the 1890s Neo-Kantianism in one form or another had become the dominant school of philosophy in Germany—and Russia.

There are many reasons why the rallying cry "Back to Kant!" proved so successful, but chief among them was a compatibility between Kant's work and developments in the realm of science outside philosophy. Kant himself had taught scientific subjects for many years before he published his first critique and became known as a philosopher. And the first critique was aimed precisely at the kind of pure reason divorced from experience that would bring Hegel's Absolute Spirit into disrepute in the later nineteenth century, an age when empiricism and experiment were yielding such obvious scientific benefits. In the fields of physics, mathematics, and physiology, such men as Ernst Mach and Wilhelm von Helmholtz were explicitly committed to working out the larger implications of Kant's speculative epistemology not in the philosopher's study, but in the scientist's laboratory, as they charted new paths in physics and physiology.

Dialogism's immediate philosophical antecedents are to be found in attempts made by various Neo-Kantians to overcome the gap between "matter" and "spirit." After the death of Hegel, this gap became increasingly apparent in the growing hostility between science and philosophy. Dialogism, then, is part of a major tendency in European thought to reconceptualize epistemology the better to accord with the new versions of mind and the revolutionary models of the world that began to emerge in the natural sciences in the nineteenth century. It is an attempt to frame a theory of knowledge for an age when relativity dominates physics and cosmology and thus when *non-coincidence* of one kind or another—of sign to its referent, of the subject to itself—raises troubling new questions about the very existence of mind.

Bakhtin begins by accepting Kant's argument that there is an unbridgeable gap between mind and world (but as we shall see, he differs from Kant in assuming that therefore there are things *in themselves;* there may be things outside mind, but they are nevertheless not in themselves). The non-identity of mind and world is the conceptual rock on which dialogism is founded and the source of all the other levels of non-concurring identity which Bakhtin sees shaping the world and our place in it. Bakhtin's thought is a meditation on how we know, a meditation based on *dialogue* precisely because, unlike many other theories of knowing, the site of knowledge it posits is never unitary. I use the admittedly cumbersome term "meditation on knowledge" here, because from his very earliest work Bakhtin is highly critical of what he calls "epistemologism," a tendency pervading all nineteenth- and early twentieth-century philosophy. A theory of knowledge devolves into mere epistemologism when there is posited "a unitary and unique consciousness . . . any determinateness must be derived from itself [thus it] cannot have another consciousness outside itself . . . any unity is its own unity."

In dialogism, the very capacity to have consciousness is based on *otherness.* This otherness is not merely a dialectical alienation on its way to a sublation that will endow it with a unifying identity in higher consciousness. On the contrary: in dialogism consciousness *is* otherness. More accurately, it is the differential relation between a center and all that is not that center. Now, a caution is in order here. Serious questions have recently been raised about the validity of any discourse that invokes the concept of center, as in various versions of what has come to be called "logocentrism." "Center" has often been used as a name for the unreflective assumption of ontological privilege, the sort of mystification sometimes attacked as the "illusion of presence." It is important from the outset, then, that "center" in Bakhtin's thought be understood for what it is: a *relative* rather than an absolute term, and, as such, one with no claim to absolute privilege, least of all one with transcendent ambitions.

This last point is particularly important, for certain of the terms crucial to Bakhtin's thought, such as "self" and "other," have so often been used as masked claims to privilege. Before we further specify the roles played by these protagonists in Bakhtinian scenarios, the simple yet all-important fact should be stressed again that they always enact a drama *containing more than one actor.*

Self and other are terms that sound vaguely atavistic in an age remarkable for its celebration of all that is extra- and impersonal. We are frequently told that not only God has died, but so has the subject. And perhaps no subject is quite so moribund as the particular kind that once was honored as author. It has even been argued with self-immolating eloquence that man (or at least Man) himself has died in history. All these deaths are melodramatic ways of formulating an end to the same thing: the old conviction that the individual subject is the seat of certainty, whether the subject so conceived was named God, the soul, the author, or—my self. Bakhtin, too, is suspicious of untrammeled subjectivity's claims; he perhaps least of all is mystified by them. And he attacks such claims at their root, in the self itself, which is why for him "self" can never be a self-sufficient construct.

It cannot be stressed enough that for him "self" is dialogic, a *relation.* And because it is so fundamental a relation, dialogue can help us understand how other relationships work, even (or especially) those that preoccupy the sometimes stern, sometimes playful new Stoics who most dwell on the death of the subject: relationships such as signifier/signified, text/context, system/history, rhetoric/language, and speaking/writing. . . . [We must recognize] that for Bakhtin the key to understanding all such artificially isolated dualisms is the dialogue between self and other.

Whatever else it is, self/other is a relation of simultaneity. No matter how conceived, simultaneity deals with ratios of same and different in space and time, which is why Bakhtin was always so concerned with space/time. Bakhtin's thought was greatly influenced by the new concepts of time and space that were being proposed by revolutionary physicists after the collapse of the old Newtonian cosmos. In Newton's mechanics it was possible for physical processes to propagate at *infinite* velocity through space. This meant that if one and the same action emanates from one body and reaches another body at the same instant, the process is purely spatial for it has occupied zero time. In Newton's universe, the sum of instants occurring simultaneously over all of space add up to a time that is absolute in the sense that it is a flux of simultaneous instants embracing the whole of the universe. It was, in other words, a dream of unity in *physics* that could serve as the proper setting for a dream of unity in Newton's *theology,* and which could later underwrite in *philosophy* the absolute oneness of consciousness in Hegelian dialectic. Dialogue, by contrast, knows no sublation. Bakhtin insists on differences that cannot be overcome: separateness and simultaneity are basic conditions of existence. Thus the physics proper to such a universe are post-Newtonian. Bakhtin grew up amidst battles that raged over the concepts of space and time among such "empiriocritics" as Mach, his Russian followers (primarily Bogdanov) and his Russian opponents (such as Lenin). Of these scientists and philosophers, the most helpful in grasping Bakhtin's thought is Einstein. Although there can be no question of immediate influence, dialogism is a version of relativity.

Einstein invented a number of just-so stories, or "thought experiments," as a way to elide physical limits on experimentation. Although not directly related, these experiments in some ways correspond to Bakhtin's attempts to use the situation of dialogue as a means for getting around traditional limitations of ideas of the subject. Both resort to what might be called a "philosophical optics," a conceptual means for seeing processes invisible to any other lens. More particularly, both resort to experiments with *seeing* in order to meditate on the necessity of the other. Einstein invented several situations (typically involving people looking at moving objects such as trains) that involve problems in perception raised by the speed of light. For instance, if light travels at a certain velocity in one system and at the same velocity in another system moving without acceleration relative to the first, it is impossible to detect the first system's movement by optical means, no matter how refined: the observer's ability to see motion depends on one body changing its position *vis-à-vis* other bodies. Motion, we have come to accept, has only a relative meaning. Stated differently, one body's motion has meaning only in relation to another body; or—since it is a relation that is mutual—has meaning only in *dialogue* with another body.

Dialogism argues that all meaning is relative in the sense that it comes about only as a result of the relation between two bodies occupying *simultaneous but different* space, where bodies may be thought of as ranging from the immediacy of our physical bodies, to political bodies and to bodies of ideas in general (ideologies). In Bakhtin's thought experiments, as in Einstein's, the position of the observer is fundamental. If motion is to have meaning, not only must there be two different bodies in a relation with each other, but there must as well be someone to grasp the nature of such a relation: the non-centeredness of the bodies themselves requires the center constituted by an observer. But unlike the passive stick figures who are positioned at a point equidistant between two railway trains in the cartoons often used to illustrate Einsteinian motion, Bakhtin's observer is also, simultaneously, an *active participant* in the relation of simultaneity. Conceiving being dialogically means that reality is always experienced, not just perceived, and further that it is experienced from a particular position. Bakhtin conceives that position in kinetic terms as a situation, an event, the event of being a self.

The self, moreover, is an event with a structure. Perhaps predictably for so attentive a student of Kant and post-Newtonian mechanics as Bakhtin, that structure is organized around the categories of space and time. They articulate what has been called the "law of placement" in dialogism, which says everything is perceived from a unique position in existence; its corollary is that the meaning of whatever is observed is shaped by the place from which it is perceived. Bakhtin explicates this law with a just-so story that uses seeing as a means for grasping what is essentially a non-visual situation. He begins with a simple datum from experience; not an observer looking at trains, but an observer looking at another observer. You can see things behind my back that I cannot see, and I can see things behind your back that are denied to your vision. We are both doing essentially the same thing, but from different places: although we are in the same event, that event is different for each of us. Our places are different not only because our bodies occupy different positions in exterior, physical space, but also because we regard the world and each other from different centers in cognitive time/space.

What is cognitive time/space? It is the arena in which all perception unfolds. Dialogism, like relativity, takes it for granted that nothing can be perceived except against the perspective of something else: dialogism's master assumption is that there is no figure without a ground. The mind is structured so that the world is always perceived according to this contrast. More specifically, what sets a figure off from its dialogizing background is the opposition between a time and a space that one consciousness uses to model its own limits (the I-for-myself) and the quite different temporal and spatial categories employed by the same consciousness to model the limits of other persons and things (the not-I-in-me)—and (this is crucial) vice versa.

At a very basic level, then, dialogism is the name not just for a dualism, but for a necessary *multiplicity* in human perception. This multiplicity manifests itself as a series of distinctions between categories appropriate to the perceiver on the one hand and categories appropriate to whatever is being perceived on the other. This way of conceiving things is not, as it might first appear to be, one more binarism, for in addition to these poles dialogism enlists the additional factors of situation and relation that make any specific instance of them more than a mere opposition of categories.

For the perceivers, their own time is forever open and unfinished; their own space is always the center of perception, the point around which things arrange themselves as a horizon whose meaning is determined by wherever they have their place in it. By contrast, the time in which we model others is perceived as closed and finished. Moreover, the space in which others are seen is never a significance-charged surrounding, but a neutral environment, i.e. the homogenizing context of the rest of the world. From the perspective of a self, the other is simply *in* the world, along with everyone and everything else. The contrast between spatial and temporal categories that are appropriate to me and the very different categories I employ to give shape to the other must not be misinterpreted as yet another Romantic claim for primacy of the absolute subject: self for Bakhtin is a cognitive necessity, not a mystified privilege.

We will see this—and the intimate relation dialogism bears to language—if we understand that cognitive time/space is ordered very much as time and space categories are deployed in speech. It has long been recognized that the formal means for expressing subjectivity occupy a unique place in any language. "I" is a word that has no referent in the way "tree," for instance, nominates a class of flora; if "I" is to perform its task as a *pro*-noun, must not be a noun, i. e. it must not refer to anything as other words do. For its task is to indicate the person uttering the present instance of the discourse containing "I," a person who is always changing and different. "I" must not refer to anything in particular if it is to be able to mean everybody in general. In Jakobson's suggestive phrase, "I" is a "shifter" because it moves the center of discourse from one speaking subject to another: its emptiness is the no man's land in which subjects can exchange the lease they hold on all of language by virtue of saying "I." When a particular person utters that word, he or she fills "I" with meaning by providing the central point needed to calibrate all further time and space discriminations: "I" is the invisible ground of all other indices in language, the benchmark to which all its spatial operations are referred, and the Greenwich mean by which all its time distinctions are calibrated. "I" marks the point between "now" and "then," as well as between "here" and "there." The difference between all these markers is manifested by the relation each of them bears either to the proximity of the speaker's horizon (here and now), or to the distance of the other's environment (there and then). As the linguist Émile Benveniste has remarked [in *Problems in General Linguistics*, trans. Mary Elizabeth Mary, 1971], "Language itself reveals the profound difference between these two planes." The gate of the "I" is located at the center not only of one's own existence, but of language as well.

This is so because there is an intimate connection between the project of language and the project of selfhood: they both exist in order to mean. The word Bakhtin uses for "project," (*zadanie*) is another twist on the central distinction between something that is "given" (*dan*) and something that presents itself in the nature of a task, as something that must be "conceived" (*zadan.*) The situatedness of the self is a multiple phenomenon: it has been given the task of *not* being merely given. It must stand out in existence because it is dominated by a "drive to meaning," where meaning is understood as something still in the process of creation, something still bending toward the future as opposed to that which is already completed.

It should be added in passing that brute chronological indicators are no guarantee of whether a thing has meaning in this sense or not, for events initiated in the most distant past, as measured by the clock, may still be fresh and unfinished in cognitive time/space. Dialogism's drive to meaning should not be confused with the Hegelian impulse toward a single state of higher consciousness in the future. In Bakhtin there is no *one* meaning being striven for: the world is a vast congeries of contesting meanings, a heteroglossia so varied that no single term capable of unifying its diversifying energies is possible.

Since Bakhtin sees the world as activity, it will come as no surprise that he defines existence as an event. But it will perhaps seem contradictory that his term for existence is "the unique and unified event of being" (*edinstvennoe i edinoe sobytie bytija*), a phrase that recurs with obsessive regularity in Bakhtin's early work, and a formulation so important for understanding Bakhtin that each word requires some glossing.

The activity of the world comes to each of us as a series of events that uniquely occur in the site I, and only I, occupy in the world. If I slash my finger with a knife, an "other" may be intellectually aware that I am in pain, and may even deeply empathize with me. But the pain itself happens to me; it is addressed to where "I" am, not to the other (pre-positions, like pro-nouns, grammatically instance the unique placedness of subjects). One way in which the uniqueness of my place in life may be judged is by the uniqueness of the death that will be mine. However, this uniqueness—in what only appears to be a paradox—is *shared*. We shall all die, but you cannot die in my place, any more than you can live fromthat site. And of course the reverse is also true: I cannot be in the unique place you occupy in the event of existence.

Nevertheless, the event of existence is "unified"; for although it occurs in sites that are unique, those sites are never complete in themselves. They are never in any sense of the word *alone.* They need others to provide the stability demanded by the structure of perception if what occurs is to have meaning. In order that the event of existence be more than a random happening, it must have meaning, and to do that it must be perceptible as a stable figure-against the ground of the flux and indeterminacy of everything else. This unification occurs as the result of an *event,* the action of me fulfilling my task (*zadanie*), i. e. by making the slice of existence that is merely given (*dan*) to me something that is conceived (*zadan*). I perform this transformation by imposing time/space categories appropriate to the other on what is happening. Remember that those categories differ from self-categories precisely in their ability to consummate, to finish off, what is being perceived, to complete it in time and to assign it a space.

The word "event" as it occurs in the formulation above is particularly complex. The Russian word used, *sobytie,* is the normal word Russians would use in most contexts to mean what we call in English an "event." But as Bakhtin uses it, certain aspects of the word long-forgotten in its everyday usage, are brought to the fore. The most important of these emerges from the fact that in Bakhtin's philosophical writings the word is almost never used alone, but always in conjunction with the word "being." He insists on being as an *event.*

The obligatory grouping of these two words in this way is a syntactic doubling that points to the mutuality of their meaning. It points as well to the etymological relations of the two words. In Russian, "event" is a word having both a root and a stem; it is formed from the word for being-*bytie*-with the addition of the prefix implying sharedness, "so-, co-," (or, as we should say in English, "co-" as in co-operate or co-habit), giving *sobytie,* event as co-being. "Being" for Bakhtin then is, not just an event, but an event that is shared. Being is a simultaneity; it is always *co-being.*

[Sergi] Karcevskij, too, meditates on simultaneity [in "The asymmetric dualism of the linguistic Sign," in *The Prague School: Selected Writings 1929—1946,* ed. Peter Steiner, 1982]: "the simultaneous presence of these two possibilities is indispensable for any act of comprehension." Like Bakhtin—and in marked contrast to the French reading of the asymmetry of the sign that finds its most radical extreme in Derrida's differ*a*nce—Karcevskij recognized that "opposition pure and simple necessarily leads to chaos and cannot serve as the basis of a *system.* True differentiation presupposes a simultaneous resemblance and difference." In other words, it presupposes a center and a non-center.

What Karcevskij is saying about language is essentially what Bakhtin is saying about reality as such: the self (the perceiver) and the other (the perceived) exist not as separate entities, but as "relations between two coordinates . . . each serving to differentiate the other." The coordinates proposed by Bakhtin for modeling this simultaneity are the two sets of time/space categories inherent in each of its poles: self and other (Bakhtin speaks of them as two interacting legal codes). The interaction of the binaries resemblance/difference, and figure/ground, both have at their heart the master distinction of self/other. In cognition, even more than in the physical world, two bodies cannot occupy the same space at the same time. As subject, I must not share the time/space of an object. Using self and other as basic categories does not obliterate the split between subject and object, but it complicates that distinction in ways that make it productive.

The other is in the realm of completedness, whereas I experience time as open and always as yet *un*-completed, and I am always at the *center* of space. This condition has certain virtues; in a world filled with the determining energies of impersonal social force, it is a potential source of freedom, the ground of other liberties from constraint of the sort Bakhtin celebrates in carnival. . . . In common with everything else, however, this openness exists in tension with its dialogic partner, closure. The unfinished nature of self is not mere subjective license: like any border, it is also a limit. The very immediacy which defines my being as a self is the same condition that insures I cannot *perceive* my self: one way to grasp how far removed the self is from any privilege is to be aware that *like anything else,* its perception requires temporal categories that are less fluid and spatial categories that are more comprehensive than are provided by the manner in which my "I" is fated to live the event of being. For all their comparative openness, indeed *because* of it, self-categories cannot do what categories of the other can. Seeing requires a certain outsideness to what is seen, a certain stasis. "In the realm of culture, outsideness is the most powerful factor in understanding," precisely because it permits the finalized quality needed for the whole of a culture to be seen. . . . But as the primal activity that marks being as an *ongoing* event, the self "*itself*" cannot abide even the most minimal degree of fixity.

When I look at you, I see your whole body, and I see it as having a definite place in the total configuration of a whole landscape. I see you as occupying a certain position *vis-à-vis* other persons and objects in the landscape (you are *one* other among *many* others). Moreover, you not only have definite physical characteristics, specific social standing, and so on, but I see you as having a definite character as well. I imagine you as being good or bad at your trade, a good or bad husband, wife, parent, as being more or less close to dying, and a number of other things that sum you up as a (more or less definitely) consummated whole. If we imagine self and other in painterly terms, the former would be non-figurative and the latter extremely hard-edged. And yet I must have some way of forming myself into a subject having something like the particularity of the other. My "I" must have contours that are specific enough to provide a meaningful addressee: for if existence is shared, it will manifest itself as the condition of being addressed (*obrashchënnost'*, or *addressivnost'*). Existence is not only an event, it is an utterance. The event of existence has the nature of dialogue in this sense; there is no word directed to no one.

It is here we approach the ineluctable association of dialogism and authorship. In order to see this connection, let

us go back for a moment to the peculiarity of the first person pronoun. Remember other nouns are signs in so far as their material sound, such as the locution "tree" when we actually pronounce it, evokes the fixed notion of a particular sort of object (some kind of natural growth, let us say). In the signifier "tree" we see a signified tree. Most nouns work something like this, but not the pronoun for the self, for what "I" refers to cannot be seen, at least in the same way that the word "tree" enables us to see a tree.

In order for my specific subjectivity to fill the general slot of the first person pronoun, that word must be empty: "I" is a word that can mean nothing in general, for the reference it names can never be visualized in its consummated wholeness. But this invisibility (which, as we shall see, is akin to the invisibility of the unconscious) is not mysterious. It is a general token of absence that can be filled in any *particular* utterance. It is invisible only at the level of *system.* At the level of performance, in the event of an utterance, the meaning of "I" can always be seen. It can be said, then, that the pronoun "I" marks the point of articulation between the pre-existing, repeatable system of language and my unique, unrepeatable existence as a particular person in a specific social and historical situation.

Existence, like language, is a shared event. It is always a border incident on the gradient both joining and separating the immediate reality of my own living particularity (a uniqueness that presents itself as only for me) with the reality of the system that precedes me in existence (that is always-already-there) and which is intertwined with everyone and everything else. Through the medium of the first person pronoun each speaker appropriates a whole language to himself. Much as Peter Pan's shadow is sewn to his body, "I" is the needle that stitches the abstraction of language to the particularity of lived experience. And much the same structure insures that in all aspects of life dialogue can take place between the chaotic and particular centrifugal forces of subjectivity and the rule-driven, generalizing centripetal forces of extra-personal system.

The single word "I" is exploited in language very much as the single eye of the fates is used in Greek mythology. The three old women all pass around the same organ. If they did not share their eye they could not see. In order to have her own vision, each must use the means by which the others see. In dialogism this sharedness is indeed the nature of fate for us all. For in order to see our selves, we must appropriate the vision of others. Restated in its crudest version, the Bakhtinian just-so story of subjectivity is the tale of how I get my self from the other: it is only the other's categories that will let me be an object for my own perception. I see my self as I conceive others might see it. In order to forge a self, I must do so from *outside.* In other words, *I author myself.*

Even in this brutalized rendition it will be apparent that things cannot be so simple, and in the event (of being) they are not. First, because the act of creating a self is not free: we *must,* we *all* must, create ourselves, for the self is not given (*dan*) to any one of us. Or, as Bakhtin puts it, "we have no alibi in existence." This lack of choice extends to the materials available for creation, for they are always provided by the other. I cannot choose to model my self as, let us say, a Martian might see me if I have not had experience of Martians. I may, of course, *imagine* what Martians might be like, and then seek to appropriate their image of me as my own. But even an imaginary Martian will be made up of details provided from previous experience, for in existence that is shared, there can be nothing absolute, including nothing absolutely new.

The self, then, may be conceived as a multiple phenomenon of essentially three elements (it is—at least—a triad, not a duality): a center, a not-center, and the relation between them. Until now we have been discussing the first two elements, the center (or I-for-itself) and the not-center (the-not-I-in-me) in terms of the time/space categories appropriate to each. In taking up the third item, the relation that center and not-center bear to each other, we will have to keep in mind one or two new terms that are crucial to Bakhtin's undertaking. Dialogism is a form of architectonics, the general science of ordering parts into a whole. In other words, architectonics is the science of relations. A relation is something that always entails ratio and proportion. In addition, Bakhtin emphasizes that a relation is never static, but always in the process of being made or unmade.

In so far as a relation involves the *construction of ratios,* it is aesthetic in much the same way that a statue or a building may be judged in terms of how its parts have been constructed with respect to each other. Relation, it will be helpful to remember, is also a *telling,* a narrative, an aspect of the word's meaning that Bakhtin will not ignore as he takes the somewhat unusual step of treating the relation of the self to the other as a problem in *aesthetics.*

By choosing aesthetic categories to discuss questions in epistemology, Bakhtin is drawing attention to the importance in dialogism of authoring. Sharing existence as an event means among other things that we are—we cannot choose *not* to be—in dialogue, not only with other human beings, but also with the natural and cultural configurations we lump together as "the world." The world addresses us and we are alive and human to the degree that we are answerable, i. e. to the degree that we can respond to addressivity. We are responsible in the sense that we are *compelled* to respond, we cannot choose but give the world an answer. Each one of us occupies a place in existence that is uniquely ours; but far from being a privilege, far from having what Bakhtin calls an *alibi* in existence, the uniqueness of the place I occupy in existence is, in the deepest sense of the word, an answerability: in that place only am I addressed by the world, since only I am in it. Moreover, we must keep on forming responses as long as we are alive.

I am always answerable *for* the response that is generated *from* the unique place I occupy in existence. My responses begin to have a pattern; the dialogue I have with existence begins to assume the form of a text, a kind of book. A book, moreover, that belongs to a genre. In antiquity, too, the world was often conceived as a book, the text of *libri naturae.* Bakhtin conceives existence as the kind of book we call a novel, or more accurately as many novels (the radically manifold world proposed by Bakhtin looks much like Borges' Library of Babel), for all of us write our own

such text, a text that is then called our life. Bakhtin uses the literary genre of the novel as an allegory for representing existence as the condition of authoring.

The author of a novel may unfold several different plots, but each will be merely one version of a more encompassing story: the narrative of how an author (as a dialogic, non-psychological self) constructs a relation with his heroes (as others). Authors are somehow both inside and outside their work. In literary texts, interaction between author and heroes is what constructs the relation that gives deepest coherence to the other meanings of relation, not least relation understood as a telling.

The particular corner (really an angle of refraction) in apperception where such authoring can take place—the self 's workshop, as it were—Bakhtin calls *unenakhodimost',* or "outsideness" (sometimes rendered into English—from French rather than from Russian—as "exotopy"). The term, as always in dialogism, is not only spatial, but temporal: it is only from a position outside something that it can be perceived in categories that complete it in time and fix it in space. In order to be perceived as a whole, as something finished, a person or object must be shaped in the time/space categories of the other, and that is possible only when the person or object is perceived from the position of outsideness. An event cannot be wholly known, cannot be seen, from inside its own unfolding as an event. As Bergson, an important source of ideas for Bakhtin, puts it: "in so far as my body is the center of *action* [or what Bakhtin calls a deed], it cannot give birth to a representation." [Henri Bergson, *Matters and Memory,* trans. Nancy Margaret Paul and W. Scott Palmer, 1911].

In a dialogue that takes place between two different persons (one self/other constellation to another self/other constellation) in physical space, the medium of exchange is, of course, natural language. In such exchanges it is words that fix (if only very fleetingly) meanings. They can do so because syntax, grammar, and the sound laws governing phonology provide a relatively stable armature for marking distinctions in the unstable flux of life outside language. Words can segment experience into meaningful patterns because their essence is so radically differential: they exist only to register differences. As Saussure, summing up his argument at a crucial point [in *Course in General Linguistics,* trans. Wade Baskin, 1966], says: "Everything that has been said up to this point boils down to this: in language there are only differences." Bakhtin insists that language is *also a matter of sameness,* but he would certainly agree that "language is only a system of pure values."

And so, argues Bakhtin, is *the self.* Once again quoting Saussure to gloss Bakhtin, we may say that for the units of existence we call "selves," as for the units of language we call "words," "Their most precise characteristic is in being what the others are not." While the self/other distinction does not operate as a complete algorithm of natural language, it does share with language the three fundamental features of function, means, and purpose. The function of each is to provide a mechanism for differentiating; each uses values to distinguish particular differences, and the purpose of doing so in each case is to give order to (what otherwise would be) the chaos of lived experience.

Let us return, then, to the example of two people regarding each other, each attempting to make sense out of the existence each shares with the other. We may now describe the dialogue of radical self/other distinctions unfolding within their cognitive space in linguistic terms. This dialogue takes place much as dialogues in natural language do: by using particular values to specify otherwise unmarked differences.

In our imagined encounter, the first person will see the second, the "other," through the relation of difference that divides all phenomena either into categories of self or categories of the other, never both. But once the distinction is made that defines the second person as one who must be perceived through the lens of the other, distinctions of a secondary order will follow that fill in the other's general outline with shades of particular differences (the progression from primary to secondary differentiation is, of course, logical, not chronological). These shadings will be made with colors drawn from the palette of specific values that obtain in the event of existence as it manifests itself in a particular time and a particular place. The first person will see the second, then, in terms much too detailed to be frozen into the sort of abstract account that a hapless expositor is condemned to provide as an example. But the terms could reasonably be expected to include such things as how physical appearance is judged (is long hair, or curly hair, or blonde hair, or perhaps no hair a good or bad thing? is being round in the tummy to be "portly" or is it to be "fat"?), also manner of speaking ("common," "stilted," "natural"), politics, relation to the major theory dominating a particular discipline at the moment, and so on. The other is always perceived in terms that are specified socially and historically, and for all the abstraction of our discussion so far, dialogism's primary thrust is always in the direction of historical and social specificity.

The only perspective from which values of such specificity and completeness may be brought to bear on the other is from the position of "outsideness." The first person succeeds in attaining the position needed to perceive the second from outside. But will he or she be able to achieve that extreme degree of outsideness toward the second which Bakhtin calls "transgredience"? Transgredience (*transgradientsvo*) is reached when the *whole* existence of others is seen from outside not only their own knowledge that they are being perceived by somebody else, but from beyond their awareness that such an other even exists. It is a cardinal assumption of dialogism that every human subject is not only highly conscious, but that his or her cognitive space is coordinated by the same I/other distinctions that organize my own: there is in fact no way "I" can be completely transgredient to another *living* subject, nor can he or she be completely transgredient to me.

We touch here on two other important concerns of dialogism: authority as authorship; and authority as power. Transgredience is a topic that bears on the specificity of art within a general aesthetic; and it also bears on the question of power in the state. As we shall see, transgredience,

when it is used well, results in art; when used badly, it results in totalitarianism.

Although, then, dialogism is primarily an epistemology, it is not just a theory of knowledge. Rather, it is in its essence a hybrid: dialogism exploits the nature of language as a modeling system for the nature of existence, and thus is deeply involved with linguistics; dialogism sees social and ethical values as the means by which the fundamental I/other split articulates itself in specific situations and is thus a version of axiology; and in so far as the act of perception is understood as the patterning of a relation, it is a general aesthetic, or it is an architectonics, a science of building.

Use of the term architectonics betrays once again Bakhtin's debt to Kant, who used it not only in its technical sense (as a way to refer to any systematization of knowledge), but to emphasize the active, constructive role of mind in perception. By using the same word, Bakhtin also seeks to foreground these aspects; but in addition he wants to draw a line between the kind of authoring we all must do all the time, and the kind of authoring some persons do some of the time, the results of which we then call art. Architectonics involves us all; but the branch of architectonics involving artists is aesthetics proper.

What is the difference between the two? It is the ability of the artist in his or her text to treat other human subjects from the vantage point of transgredience, a privilege denied the rest of us who author only in lived experience (and denied to artists too, when they are not being artists). The author of a novel, for instance, can manipulate the other not only as an other, but as a *self*. This is, in fact, what the very greatest writers have always done, but the paradigmatic example is provided by Dostoevsky, who so successfully permits his characters to have the status of an "I" standing over against the claims of his own authorial other that Bakhtin felt compelled to coin the special term "polyphony" to describe it. Lesser authors treat their heroes as mere others, a relation that can be crafted in architectonics, and which does not therefore require the aesthetic privilege of art for its achievement: it is what we all do anyway. And then there are those authors who treat their characters not only as others, but as having the otherness of mere things, lacking any subjectivity. They exploit their transgredience of their characters much as scientists exploit theirs toward laboratory rats. This is formulaic pseudo-art, in which all possible initiative within the text is sacrificed to a formula pre-existing the text. If in western movies of a certain kind the "hero" ends up kissing a horse instead of a girl, or if in Stalinist fiction the boy always gets a tractor instead of a girl, we feel no violation, because we understand that neither the cowboy nor the collective farmer has any reserve of subjectivity: they are, themselves, effectively, only horses or tractors anyway.

This formulaic art makes explicit the connection of transgredience to power. For not only is snuffing out the "I" of other subjects bad aesthetics, it is bad politics. Dialogically conceived, authorship is a form of governance, for both are implicated in the architectonics of responsibility, each is a way to adjudicate center/non-center relations between subjects. Totalitarian government always seeks the (utopian) condition of absolute monologue: the *Gleichschaltung* which was attempted in Germany during the 1930s to "Nazify" trade unions, universities, publishing houses, professional associations, and so on had as its aim the suppression of all otherness in the state so that its creator alone might flourish. Dialogism has rightly been perceived by certain thinkers on the left as a useful correlative to Marxism, for it argues that sharing is not only an ethical or economic mandate, but a condition built into the structure of human perception, and thus a condition inherent in the very fact of being human. But by the same token dialogism differs from the pseudo-Marxism of regimes that use "Communism" as a license for totalitarian government. For as the ultimate critique of any claim to monologue, it is intransigently pluralist.

We have looked at several versions of self/other relations. In so doing certain fundamentals have emerged, not least of which is that dialogism is able to make claims in many different areas because it is basically a theory of knowledge, an architectonics of perception. Dialogism argues that we make sense of existence by defining our specific place in it, an operation performed in cognitive time and space, the basic categories of perception. Important as these categories are, they themselves are shaped by the even more fundamental set of self and other. We perceive the world through the time/space of the self *and* through the time/space of the other. The difference between the two is a relation of otherness that can be gauged by differing positions of outsideness that are enacted as varying degrees of transgredience. Up until this point we have discussed such relations almost exclusively in terms of the other. We must now address the difficult question of how the self achieves the outsideness it needs to perceive itself.

So as always to be an open site where the event of existence can have its occurrence, the self must never stop in time or be fixed in space. Since, however, being finished in time and being specifically located in space are conditions necessary for being "seen" in perception, the self is by definition invisible to itself. In the wake of a still-potent Romanticism, it is necessary to repeat that there is nothing mysterious about this invisibility, for it is merely structural. The self's non-referentiality can be understood by analogy with the non-referentiality of "I" as the first person pronoun in natural language. If each is to perform its function of indicating a unique place that must be shared by *everybody* (which is what the self marks in existence, and what the "I" marks in language), then they must both refer to nothing—or at least not refer to anything in the same manner other signs refer.

But the self is like a sign in so far as it has no absolute meaning in itself: it, too (or rather, it most of all), is relative, dependent for its existence on the other. A conventional sign is not a unitary thing, but rather a differential relation between two aspects, a signifier and a signified. In this triad it is the relation that is absolute, not the elements it yokes together, for neither of the two elements exists in itself; neither has any meaning on its own, without the simultaneous presence of the other. Nor is the "self" a unitary thing; rather, it consists in a relation, the relation be-

tween self and other. A traditional metaphor representing the unity of the linguistic sign's two elements is the unity shared by the recto and verso sides of the same sheet of paper. But in so far as the self is an *activity,* such a static means of conceiving it will not do: Bakhtin's metaphor for the unity of the two elements constituting the relation of self and other is *dialogue,* the simultaneous unity of differences in the event of utterance.

One of Bakhtin's simple illustrations will help us overcome the complexity of this last formulation. If we return for a moment to the situation of two people facing each other, we remember that although they share an external space and time (they are physically simultaneous), inside his or her own head each sees something the other does not. Let us envisage you and me confronting each other. There are certain things we both perceive, such as the table between us. But there are other things in the same encounter we do not both perceive. The simplest way to state the difference between us is to say that you see things about me (such as, at the most elementary level, my forehead) and the world (such as the wall behind my back) which are out of my sight. The fact that I cannot see such things does not mean they do not exist; we are so arranged that I simply cannot see them. But it is equally the case that I see things you are unable to see, such as your forehead, and the wall behind your back. In addition to the things we see jointly, there are aspects of our situation each of us can see only on our own, i. e. only from the unique place each of us occupies in the situation.

The aspect of the situation that you see, but I do not, is what Bakhtin calls your "surplus of seeing"; those things I see but you cannot constitute my "surplus of seeing." You know I have a surplus, and I know you have one as well. By adding the surplus that has been "given" to you to the surplus that has been "given" to me I can build up an image that includes the whole of me and the room, including those things I cannot physically see: in other words, I am able to "conceive" or construct a whole out of the different situations we are in together. I author a unified version of the event of our joint existence from my unique place in it by means of combining the things I see which are different from (in addition to) those you see, and the things you see which are different from (in addition to) that difference.

Such acts of combination are a rudimentary form of "narrativity," or the ability to put myself into scenarios of the kind I see others enacting. I never see others as frozen in the immediacy of the isolated present moment. The present is not a static moment, but a mass of different combinations of past and present relations. To say I perceive them as a whole means that I see them surrounded by their whole lives, within the context of a complete narrative having a beginning that precedes our encounter and an end that follows it. I see others as bathed in the light of their whole biography.

My "I-for-itself" lacks such a consummated biography: because the self's own time is constantly open, it resists such framing limits. Within my own consciousness my "I" has no beginning and no end. The only way I know of my birth is through accounts I have of it from others; and I shall never know my death, because my "self" will be alive only so long as I have consciousness—what is called "my" death will not be known by me, but once again only by others. In order to remain a constantly potential site of being, my self must be able to conduct its work as sheer capability, a flux of sheer becoming. If this energy is to be given specific contours, it must be shaped not only in values, but in story. Stories are the means by which values are made coherent in particular situations. And this narrativity, this possibility of conceiving my beginning and end as a whole life, is always enacted in the time/space of the other: I may see my death, but not in the category of my "I." For my "I," death occurs only for others, even when the death in question is my own.

Since Bakhtin places so much emphasis on otherness, and on otherness defined precisely as other *values,* community plays an enormous role in his thought. Dialogism is, among other things, an exercise in social theory. Although frequently overlooked by those who tear "carnival" out of its larger Bakhtinian context, extrapersonal social force is accorded so much weight in dialogism that it almost (but not quite) begins to verge on determinism. If my "I" is so ineluctably a product of the particular values dominating my community at the particular point in its history when I coexist with it, the question must arise, "Where is there any space, and what would the time be like, in which I might define myself against an otherness that is other from that which has been 'given' to me?"

In answering this question it will be helpful to remember that dialogue is not, as is sometimes thought, a dyadic, much less a binary, phenomenon. Dialogue is a manifold phenomenon, but for schematic purposes it can be reduced to a minimum of three elements having a structure very much like the triadic construction of the linguistic sign: a dialogue is composed of an utterance, a reply, and a relation between the two. It is the relation that is most important of the three, for without it the other two would have no meaning. They would be isolated, and the most primary of Bakhtinian a prioris is that nothing is anything in itself.

The tripartite nature of dialogue bears within it the seeds of hope: in so far as my "I" is dialogic, it insures that my existence is not a lonely event but part of a larger whole. The thirdness of dialogue frees my existence from the very circumscribed meaning it has in the limited configuration of self/other relations available in the immediate time and particular place of my life. For in later times, and in other places, there will always be other configurations of such relations, and in conjunction with *that* other, my self will be differently understood. This degree of thirdness outside the present event insures the possibility of whatever transgredience I can achieve toward myself.

At the heart of any dialogue is the conviction that what is exchanged has meaning. Poets who feel misunderstood in their lifetimes, martyrs for lost political causes, quite ordinary people caught in lives of quiet desperation—all have been correct to hope that outside the tyranny of the present there is a possible addressee who will understand them. This version of the significant other, this "super-addressee," is conceived in different ways at different times and by different persons: as God, as the future triumph of my version of the state, as a future reader.

As the need to posit a category such as "super-addressee" outside the present moment makes clear, conditions for creating meaning in the present moment are not always the best. A dialogic world is one in which I can never have my own way completely, and therefore I find myself plunged into constant interaction with others—and with myself. In sum, dialogism is based on the primacy of the social, and the assumption that all meaning is achieved by struggle. It is thus a stern philosophy. This fact should surprise no one, given dialogism's immediate sources in revolution, civil war, the terror of the purges, and exile. But the very otherness that makes it at times a version of Stoicism is also what insures that we are not alone. Dialogism is ultimately an epistemology founded on a loophole, for

> there is neither a first word nor a last word. The contexts of dialogue are without limit. They extend into the deepest past and the most distant future. Even meanings born in dialogues of the remotest past will never be finally grasped once and for all, for they will always be renewed in later dialogue. At any present moment of the di-

---

Bakhtin's definition of the novel:

The novel can be defined as a diversity of social speech types (sometimes even diversity of languages) and a diversity of individual voices, artistically organized. The internal stratification of any single national language into social dialects, characteristic group behavior, professional jargons, generic languages, languages of generations and age groups, tendentious languages, languages of the authorities, of various circles and of passing fashions, languages that serve the specific sociopolitical purposes of the day, even of the hour (each day has its own slogan, its own vocabulary, its own emphases)—this internal stratification present in every language at any given moment of its historical existence is the indispensable prerequisite for the novel as a genre. The novel orchestrates all its themes, the totality of the world of objects and ideas depicted and expressed in it, by means of the social diversity of speech types [*raznorečie*] and by the differing individual voices that flourish under such conditions. Authorial speech, the speeches of narrators, inserted genres, the speech of characters are merely those fundamental compositional unities with whose help heteroglossia [*raznorečie*] can enter the novel; each of them permits a multiplicity of social voices and a wide variety of their links and interrelationships (always more or less dialogized). These distinctive links and interrelationships between utterances and languages, this movement of the theme through different languages and speech types, its dispersion into the rivulets and droplets of social heteroglossia, its dialogization—this is the basic distinguishing feature of the stylistics of the novel.

Mikhail Bakhtin, in his "Discourse in the Novel," in The Dialogic Imagination, *1981.*

alogue there are great masses of forgotten meanings, but these will be recalled again at a given moment in the dialogue's later course when it will be given new life. For nothing is absolutely dead: every meaning will someday have its homecoming festival.

Michael Holquist, in his Dialogism: Bakhtin and His World, *Routledge, 1990, 204 p.*

Mikita Hoy   (essay date Summer 1992)

[*In the following essay, Hoy applies Bakhtin's model of textual dialogism and the carnivalesque to an analysis of contemporary popular culture.*]

Mikhail Bakhtin is acknowledged in increasingly wide circles as a sensitive observer of popular culture in its sociohistorical context. His acute study of the folkloric rituals of carnival—from the phallophors of epic Saturnalia, whose role was to joke and cavort obscenely, to the rogue comedians at turn-of-the-century country fairs—uncovers a vast and fertile dialogue of heteroglossia. Not only at the carnival but pervading all levels of language, Bakhtin identifies infinitely shifting heteroglottal strata made up of loosely bound generic wholes, subgeneric wholes, accents, systems, dialects, and constantly fragmented layers of language working together, or at battle, or at play. This dialogic scheme covers, in *The Dialogic Imagination* and *Rabelais and His World,* most epic drama and Russian and European nineteenth-century realist literature and invites its own extension into areas of recent Western popular culture.

Although Bakhtin insists that the novel is the key form of the time, his advantage over everyone else working on novel theory is his appreciation that the novel, rather than assimilating its language to form, shapes its form to languages and consequently appears as what Michael Holquist describes as a "supergenre," ingesting and engulfing all other genres. Therefore the range of texts composed of a series of different languages interpenetrating one another—Bakhtin's classification of "novelness"—must clearly be immense. In fact, rather than limiting the term *novel* to a narrow definition of a piece of textual fiction, Bakhtin uses it to name the interplay of heteroglottal strata at work within any given literary system in order to reveal the artificial limits and constraints of that system; for "novelization" as Bakhtin sees it is fundamentally opposed to the ordering into genres and canons that is characteristic of most literary systems.

Bakhtin's version of novelization does not permit generic monologue, but rather insists on an interplay of dialogues between what any given system will admit as literature, or "high culture," or art, or "good writing," and on the other hand all those texts excluded from these definitions as nonliterature, "low culture," popular culture, or subculture. *All* writing features this interplay, and therefore *all* kinds of language, even those which might not be classed as "higher literary forms" by the traditional critic, such as musical lyrics or advertisement logos, to Bakhtin represent important forms of novelization. That piece of textual fiction more conventionally described as the "novel" is

merely the most refined and distilled version of this definition, which spills over into other kinds of texts and novels in other times. As Bakhtin himself writes in *The Dialogic Imagination,* "texts continue to grow and develop even after the moment of their creation. . . . they are capable of being creatively transformed in different eras, far distant from the day and hour of their original birth."

Bakhtinian analysis of the novel represents then a theoretical system to which it is not only possible but critically essential to submit today's magazines, comedy, advertisements, popular music, art, and fashion, since in their continual interchange and deliberate fusion of high and low styles, politics, parody and pastiche, comic strip and literature, haut couture and street fashion, they constitute a singular shifting dialogism whose rich carnival of discourse lies open to Bakhtin's radical definition of "novelness," and their instances of language, say in rock lyrics or advertisements, are in this way very similar to the instances of language that Bakhtin finds in the novel.

It is vital however to realize that, according to Bakhtin, in any analysis of the social ideology of genres such as "high" and "low" styles, "politics," "parody," "pastiche," and so on, it is impossible to escape the fact that the author / artist / designer is Russian or Polish, Jewish or Catholic, male or female, old or young, formally educated or formally uneducated, and so on. Bakhtin finds it difficult to identify specific genres beyond "relatively stable *forms of construction of the whole*" in every discourse and utterance, from the literary and the rhetorical to the spontaneous and the everyday—hence his theory of "sociopolitical genre," or "generic wholes." Real "genres" as such do not actually *exist;* rather, they *play* at being all-encompassing and "total." Consequently, the very notion of a "unity" is false, since that supposed "unity" encompasses infinite strata of other, autonomous unities. Absolute, ideal extremes are illusory—it is possible to theorize and quantify only, according to Bakhtin, in terms of approximate "wholes" and the generalization of generic regularities.

Bakhtin's theory of heteroglossia rests upon his vision of language not as a static, communicable representation of the speaker's intention but as a system bearing the weight of centuries of intention, motivation, and implication. Language can never be molded into working for the speaker's unique purpose but can only be handed back and forth like printed books borrowed from a lending library. Since it is already composed of weighted uses, grammatical rules, and agreed conventional lexis, Bakhtin sees all language as negating the uniqueness of personal experience, and with it any possibility of maintaining a connection with value and intention, as does Sartre in *Being and Nothingness:* "the 'meaning' of my expressions always escapes me. I never know if I signify what I wish to signify. . . . As soon as I express myself, I can only guess at the meaning of what I express—i. e. the meaning of what I am."

Within every single word, within every single utterance, Bakhtin identifies a large and ancient collection of ideas, motives, and intentions utilized by centuries of speakers and writers. All language, according to Bakhtin, is prestratified into social dialects, characteristic group behavior, professional jargons, languages of generations and age-groups, tendentious languages, languages of authority, and, especially in recent media language, the discourse of various circles and passing fashions of the day, even of the hour.

Bakhtin finds himself unable to describe social forms and conventions (what most critics today would define as "genres") without reducing them to the obviously individualistic category of voices, and equally unable to imagine consistentdialogue among similar genres, or among works within a genre, except as a kind of loose, multiform "whole." Bakhtin reserves the term *genre* for obvious, widely accepted generic structures—epic, myth, poetry, or the space-time structures of youth, age, the beginning, the end, and so on. Essentially, *genre* in Bakhtin is something of a nonce-word. He seems ultimately to suggest that it is possible—indeed, necessary—to reduce *all* forms, narratives, structures, and so on, to their own "ideological languages." Nevertheless, he keeps the terms *genre* and *generic wholes* to identify and theorize widely accepted forms, partly in order to enable reference to wider literary and narrative traditions than his consistent return to sociological and ideological theory would generate.

But as Ken Hirschkop points out [in "Introduction: Bakhtin and Cultural Theory," in *Bakhtin and Cultural Theory,* 1989], even the meanings of words like *dialogism* and *carnival* are "a sedimentation of past uses, current and past social conflicts, the changing forms of ideological life; in short, these terms are themselves dialogical." Yet this does not mean that the schema at play in even the most basic language-unit are too densely interwoven ever to comprehend: "Such is the fleeting language of a day, of an epoch, a social group, a genre, a school and so forth," writes Bakhtin, that "[i]t is possible to give a concrete and detailed analysis of any utterance, once having exposed it as a contradiction-ridden, tension-filled unity of . . . embattled tendencies in the life of language."

In recent popular culture, nowhere is the influence of heteroglossia more obvious and immediate than in so-called style magazines like *Arena, i.d.,* and *The Face. Arena* is a fairly new magazine, on sale mainly in England, the United States, Germany, and Italy, published and edited in England by Nick Logan, and specializing in "exclusive" interviews with film and rock stars, upmarket articles on sport and fashion, and pieces on politics and architecture. The market for *Q* has similar international aspirations; this is also a relatively new publication which aims to be "the modern guide to music and more," focusing mainly on rock interviews and reviews. *i.d.* has been around for rather longer; it is marketed over most of Europe as well as the United States, Japan, and Australia but focuses mainly on British music, fashion, film, television, and so on.

Such forms of what Bakhtin would class as heteroglottal novelization consistently obliterate the distinctions, on the written page and, it is suggested, in youth society, between high-artistic-noncommercial and mass-pop-consumerist, between street and Parisian fashions, art and advertising, pop and nonpop, poetry and lyrics, comic-strip and literature, the marginal and the mainstream. It is impossible to tell fashion shots from advertisement photographs, virtually impossible to distinguish between articles and commercials. The prose is a fusion of colloquial Americanisms, technical jargon, black street rap, quasi-academic analysis, and fashionable puns. In this extract from *The Face,* Jim McClellan reviews a Percy Adlon film, *Rosalie Goes Shopping:*

> A comic fantasy about the consumer credit trap and the personal computer, it stars Marianne Sagebrecht as a German housewife . . . determined to live life the shop-till-you-drop postmodern American way. Hubbie Brad Davis's wages can't even pay the interest on all those afternoons at the mall, so she starts double-dealing with a vast deck of credit cards and number-crunching on her personal computer. Trouble is, her crimes don't feel wrong. *Rosalie* ends up nearly saying something about the hyperconformist consumer and the double standards of the debt economy. Pity about the soundtrack, though.

Here the dialogue consists of a fusion of British middle-class colloquialisms ("Hubbie") and ellipsis ("Pity about . . ."), fairly respectable economic textbook language ("the consumer credit trap," "the double standards of the debt economy"), the language of nontabloid, ostensibly apolitical British journalism ("A comic fantasy, it stars Marianne Sagebrecht as a German housewife"), tabloid language ("shop-till-you-drop"), American language—or, at least, the Americanisms commonly used by British journalists ("Trouble is . . . ," "number-crunching") and a parody of current critical sociological and literary discourse ("postmodern American way," "the hyperconformist consumer").

Each stratification of discourse inevitably incorporates various motives, leanings, intentions—unconscious, prereflective ideologies that are often defined as political. Bakhtin himself, in a string of dialogues from 1934 onwards, moves on to define dialogism as "the unmasking of social languages." So while Jim McClellan's film review—as a form of heteroglottal "novelization"—constitutes an interweaving of leftist economics, anticapitalism, anticonsumerism, fashionable British anti-Americanism (although the utilization of American colloquialisms suggests, on another level, a certain subcurrent of pro-American sentiment), what these strata most clearly convey is the discourse of the white, Western, middle-class, male, formally educated intellectual. Hirschkop develops this idea of conflicting ideologies into straight political tendencies: "If each language is a voice, then society is a welter of intersecting groups and different ideologies, more or less the version of society on offer from liberalism. And yet things are in a way even worse than that. For each point of view is described as an *interested* point of view: it embodies not just a perspective but a set of values or desires."

By an *interested* point of view, however, it seems more likely that Bakhtin is suggesting a subconscious, preexistent, unthinking ideological worldview rather than the active political aims Hirschkop suggests in his use of evaluative terms like *worse.* In **"Discourse in the Novel,"** a similar point is made: "all languages of heteroglossia, whatever the principle underlying them and making each unique, are specific points of view on the world, forms for conceptualizing the world in words, specific world views, each characterized by its own objects, meanings and values."

The main point about heteroglossia is that all language has a sideways glance, and yet in Jim McClellan's film review, the sideways glance seems to be partly directed at itself. This kind of language is self-referential, self-regarding—aware, in a way, of its own shifting dialogism. The result of this self-parody, which in youth style magazines such as the self-confessedly superficial *The Face* seems almost inevitable, is that the language loses much of its primary intention (here, the film review) and develops instead into a game of words, a kind of linguistic solitaire. This is the kind of discourse that "lives, as it were, beyond itself, in a living impulse [*napravlennost*] toward the object" [**"Discourse in the Novel"**]. Ann Jefferson writes [in "Bodymatters: Self and other in Bakhtin, Sartre and Barthes," *Bakhtin and Cultural Theory*]: "Looking (at yourself) while you leap is a highly dangerous thing to do, and on the figurative plain the effects of such self-regarding attitudes can be just as devastating, because they empty acts of their substance and purpose, and *action* is, significantly, turned into *play* or *gesture.*"

This kind of ironic, self-reflecting parody of the dialogism inherent in language is often the style of the traditional fool, who mocks others' uses of words by using them himself. Shakespeare's Fool in *King Lear,* for example, is introduced into the text partly for purposes of "making strange" (*ostranenie*) the world of conventional pathos by making Lear's dramatic, aristocratic language of suffering seem distant and unreal when it is cited beside similar meanings couched in the Fool's own folkloric, nursery riddles.

And this is precisely the relation between dialogism—both lived and textual—and the Bakhtinian notion of carnival. Carnival is the time when all social groups and classes join together in a wild Saturnalian celebration, which involves the fusion of each group's dialogical stratum into a parodic, ironic festival of language. According to Bakhtin, each level of heteroglossia is linked to the next by a common folkloric laughter, whose roots go back deep into preclass folklore and which destroys traditional connections and abolishes idealized strata, bringing out the crude, unmediated links between words and concepts that are normally kept very separate. Carnival, according to Bakhtin, represents "the disunification of what has traditionally been linked, and the bringing together of that which has been traditionally kept distant and disunified." Carnival, in the written text as well as in lived language, brings the everyday into sacred life in the form of ritualistic violations (*skvernoslovie'*), causing ritualistic laughter and clownishness. The slave and jester become substitutes for the ruler and god, various forms of ritualistic parody make their appearance, and "the passions" are mixed with laughter and gaiety. Bakhtinian carnival cavalierly suppresses hierarchies and distinctions, "recalling us to a common creatureliness" [Terry Eagleton, "Bakhtin,

Schopenhauer, Kundera," in *Bakhtin and Cultural Theory*].

So just as the court jester's ironic repetition of common language estranges that language and alienates it, so at the carnival does the riotous confusion of all varieties of discourse, both high and low, make strange the similar level of dialogism preexistent in language. Opposed to all those who are well-to-do in life, suggests Bakhtin, comes the language of the merry rogue—streetsongs, folksayings, anecdotes, a lively parody of the words of poets, scholars, monks, knights, and others. Like the interplay of genres and levels within the prose of popular style magazines such as *The Face,* the language of the merry rogue parodically reprocesses other people's discourse, but always in such a way as to rob them of their power, to "distance them from the mouth," as it were, by means of a roguish deception, to mock their language and thus turn what was direct discourse into light self-parody. "Falsehood is illuminated by ironic consciousness and in the mouth of the happy rogue parodies itself" [**"Discourse in the Novel"**].

In this respect, much of recent popular culture appears as *"permanent"* carnivalization (though "permanent" in the sense of "permanently" ephemeral, constantly changing). Style magazines consistently offer a wide range of interweaving discourses, languages, ontologies, and dialogues characteristic of the anticanonism Bakhtin defines as essential to the language of novelization, and the festival of heteroglossia that results is not a mere sideshow at a traveling carnival, but a "permanently" ephemeral, playful, self-referential, self-parodying component of postmodern popular culture. Bakhtin's idea of carnival, both lived and textual, as the self-regarding parody of different language styles and levels of dialogue, and his description of the stock-in-trade carnival jester who has to be able to mimic "birds and animals, . . . the speech, facial expressions and gesticulation of a slave, a peasant, a procurer, a scholastic pedant and a foreigner" [**"From the Prehistory of Novelistic Discourse," *The Dialogic Imagination***], are still relevant to mass culture's current and continuous taste for impersonation and parody, as testified by the viewing figures for stand-up comics keen on topical political subject matter, . . . and the popularity of the political caricatures on television programs like "Spitting Image."

Yet it would be unwise to empty Bakhtin's carnival theory of its political conflict—to reduce it to an eclectic blend of styles and languages, to see it as conflation rather than contention, as generalized indifference rather than the clash of highly interested standpoints. There is also much of the merry rogue in a number of popular musicians, notably in the punk movement where ritualistic violation and cultic indecency are all part of the act. Like the carnival jester, Lords of Misrule like Johnny Rotten and Sid Vicious celebrated a thoughtless deceit opposed to everything that is conventional and false—synthetic forms for the parodied exposure of others. As the harbinger of carnival, the punk, like the clown, is granted "the right *not* to understand, the right to confuse . . . the right to parody others while talking, the right not to be taken literally . . . the right to act life as a comedy and to treat others as actors, the right to rip off masks, the right to rage at others with a primeval (almost cultic) rage" ["**Forms of Time and of the Chronotope in the Novel,**" in *The Dialogic Imagination*].

In popular style magazines, this notion of the carnivalesque manifests itself as parody, pastiche, or irony ("that which cannot be put in words without betraying itself")—a type of folkloric laughter which, Bakhtin believes, works to bring "official," "sacred" things (politics, religion, business—although such areas can be separated only insofar as Bakhtin's theory of generic wholes will permit, since all borders, according to Bakhtin, have already been crossed and no "zone" is ever separate) to a place of maximal proximity where they can be turned inside out and closely examined from all angles. In *The Face* and *i.d.,* in fact, all representatives of the established canonical literary system and the old, official, sacred world (the royal family, politicians, businessmen, the upper classes, well-established media figures) are treated as absurd and ridiculous and laughed down in favor of the latest top model, alternative comedian, or cult musician, kings and queens for an issue precisely because of their hip, chic ephemerality (look at *The Face's* occasional features on the latest independent bands such as Ride or Lush—spotlighted usually because their refusal to sign up to any major record label virtually guarantees their status as flash-in-the-pan, up-to-the-minute underground fads, never likely to become mainstream acts).

At other times, this carnivalesque impulse will take the form of a mockery of academic prose and criticism. In such cases, the language of the author strives to overcome "literariness" and to get away from outmoded styles and period-bound language by fusing this very "literariness" with folk language and, creating a dialogue between the canonical literary system and the generic languages of various subcultures in what is defined by Bakhtin as heteroglottal novelization, thus making the language parody itself.

One important function of this spirited, self-conscious dialogism is to reduce all false sublimations back to their earthy, earthly roots. As in Menippean satire, the cruder, more bawdy, brawling, more obviously mocking forms of carnival bring everything down to a single level—like the wave of new American comedians epitomized by Andrew Dice Clay, whose "Comedy of Hate" consists in ritualistic abuse of audience members. Bakhtin points out that laughter is associated with folklore and the gross realities of life, possessing the capacity to strip the object of the false verbal and ideological husk that encloses it—a carnivalesque performance which realizes the theories of the textual and linguistic carnivalesque (embodied by, say, the style magazine).

Here it is important to distinguish between carnival as a vast mélange of styles, which lends itself well enough to postmodernism, and carnival as political animus. In other words, to graft Bakhtinian carnival onto postmodern culture without reservation brings the latter out as rather more subversive than much of it actually is. This second kind of political carnivalesque destroys epic distance and restores a "dynamic authenticity" ["**Epic and Novel,**" in *The Dialogic Imagination*] to man, allowing participants to investigate themselves freely, to study the disparity between their potential and their reality, in the text as well as on the street. Bakhtin talks about the performances of obscenely cavorting phallophors in religious processions, and *deikilists* (mimers) who both travestied national and local myths and mimicked the characteristically typical "languages" and speech mannerisms of foreign doctors, procurers, heterae, peasants, slaves, scholars, judges, and so on.

The Sex Pistols sing about "bodies" and one of their slogans declares "Fuck Forever." In fact, much of the punk movement's motivation centered around an impulse to disgust and appall by reducing the sublimations of serious artists and musicians to a celebration of what Bakhtin in "**Forms of Time and Chronotope in the Novel**" describes as the "series of the human body" (a space-time which, for Bakhtin, seems to replace conventional definitions of "genre"—in other words, an unbound "generic whole")—vomiting (the food series), wearing dustbin-liners held together with safety-pins (the human clothing series), "getting pissed" to "destroy" (the drink and drunkenness series), fucking forever (sexual series), sporting "Sid Lives" T-shirts (death series). "The pleasures of carnival," writes Ken Hirschkop, "are not the pleasures of mere talk but those of a discourse that has rediscovered its connection to the concrete"—thus, again, the fusion of textual carnivalesque with the carnivalesque in performance to form the heteroglottal "novelization" of texts and forms of language more usually excluded from the literary system.

Much of this political kind of carnivalization, of course, revolves around the destruction of images sacred in other, different, often opposing cultural levels and dialogues. Just as magazine and television advertisements through a process of ritual disembowelment use celebrated and highly revered pieces of music (popular or classical) and images (old masters, pieces of "high" art, and highly paid popular musicians and media figures) for what is considered to be the trivial process of selling, things held sacred in one language or discourse are inevitably parodied in another. Much of the Sex Pistols material is sacrilegious to other dialogues—their lyrics make parody out of the monarchy ("God Save the Queen"), the government ("Anarchy in the U.K."), the human body ("Bodies"), multinational corporations ("EMI"), and the holocaust ("Belsen was a Gas"). Malcolm McLaren's sale of "Sid Lives" T-shirts only a couple of weeks after Vicious's overdose smacks a great deal of Bakhtin's carnivalesque version of death, which he applies particularly to Rabelaisian burlesque ("in . . . the grotesque [clownish] portrayal of death, the image of death itself takes on humorous aspects: *death* is inseparable from *laughter*" ["**Forms of Time and of the Chronotope in the Novel**"]). Bakhtin's celebration of carnival is perhaps too undifferentiating, since (as some critics have pointed out) carnival actually involved a lot of violence and machismo.

That once-taboo topics like sex and death can be treated with such hilarity during the carnival is a signifier not just of the carnivalesque reduction of all cultural sublimations to their folkloric roots, but—even further—the desecration of all that a culture considers "sacred" or meaningful to nothing more than another of the merry rogue's clownish jests. Everything that has been built up to have significance and moment for mankind is rendered absurd: there is an emphasis in the carnivalesque on the healthy failure of the fool (the "man of the people") to understand accepted conventions and falsehoods (religion, the government, education, capitalism, advertising, even the pretensions of the music industry itself)—which exposes them for what they are. Here, again, there is little difference between textual and lived carnivalesque. The carnivalesque of this textual heteroglossia—the fusion of canonical and noncanonical literary and subliterary systems—is embodied in the performance of "real life." The punk and the skinhead "estrange" the discourse of mass-appeal, major-label, commercialized chart music by means of an uncomprehending stupidity (simplicity, naivety)—where the very aspect of not understanding, not *grasping* the conventions of a society, not comprehending lofty, meaning-charged lyrics, chords, words, labels, things, and events—remains vital.

But the key to popular culture today lies in the aesthetic (or, often, anti-aesthetic) avowal of superficiality, of vacancy, of *as little meaning as possible.* Texts like the magazine *The Face,* its very title heralding an uncompromising superficiality, are temples to ephemera, to the garish colors and images of a transient, drifting pop life. These magazines, like many television and cinema commercials, are not meant to be read or studied closely, but to be "cruised" through, looked at fleetingly with a vague sense of admiration and temptation, the same way you would look at a shop window or an advertisement offering seductive, brightly colored consumer goods in a plastic carnival where, like Rosalie in *Rosalie Goes Shopping,* you become a "hyperconformist consumer" in the "shop-till-you-drop postmodern American way" when "there is nowhere left to go but to the shops."

These forms of carnivalesque and examples of heteroglottal novelization in text (magazine, soap opera, pulp novel) as well as in reality (game show, rock concert, shopping spree) are characterized by a self-evident failure to "stand up" to philosophical literary theories, but of value for their capacity for "breaking down" into infinite layers of dialogical strata to reveal the limits and constraints of such definitions which restrict, for example, a variety of heteroglottal novelization from inclusion in a traditionally narrow literary canon. Like the anti-academic, anti-serious, anti-intelligent Saturnalian humor of the punk movement and its music, the popular postmodern text is joyously aware of the inadequacies of its own language. In its gleeful celebration of pop art, pop journalism, pop advertising, pop cinema, pop literature, pop feminism, and pop shopping, every dialogue in the style magazine is a joke at the expense of its own irrelevance, its own unimportance, its own meaninglessness, its own ephemerality.

Heteroglottal dialogues and systems of "novelness" like *The Face* recognize the emptiness of society, the plasticity of consumerism and, like the Sex Pistols singing about their own vacancy ("Pretty Vacant") or their manager Malcolm McLaren making a film entitled *The Great Rock and Roll Swindle* (and, incidentally, profiting financially from his rebellion), resolve that there is nothing left to do but to celebrate that very vacancy, to go shopping. Terry Eagleton points out that Bakhtin fails to stress the politically limited nature of carnival, which is after all *licensed* misrule, a contained and officially sanctioned rebellion, after which everything returns to normal.

Yet for Bakhtin, this ambivalent image of wise ignorance brings to mind the self-praise of the Socratic dialogue ("I am wiser than everyone, because I know that I know nothing"), and the image of Socrates ("a wise man of the most elevated sort," "wearing the popular mask of a bewildered fool [almost a *Margit*]") ["**Epic and Novel**"]. There is no sort of direct discourse, suggests Bakhtin—artistic, rhetorical, philosophical, everyday ("styles" rather than "genres"; Bakhtin describes the novel as a "stylistics of genre" and can never reconcile the idea of genre with the idea of style, redeeming *genre* as a term for describing "finished and resolved wholes" and *style* as designating the syntactic and lexical patterns of identifiable social voices)—that doesn't have "its own parodying and travestying double, its own comic-ironic *contre-partie.*"

In this light, popular culture appears as the reverse of "high" culture, its alter ego, where all pretensions to meaning, relevance, and aesthetic value are travestied by a parodic, mocking dialogue of vacancy, anti-aestheticism and plasticity. In **"From the Prehistory of Novelistic Discourse,"** Bakhtin observes that the most wise and revered figures in epic have their comic counterparts, and become themselves comic: "Odysseus . . . donned a clown's fool's cap (*pileus*) and harnessed his horse and ox to a plow, pretending to be mad in order to avoid participation in the war. . . . Hercules, who had conquered death in battle . . . descended into the nether world [to become] the monstrous glutton, the playboy, the drunk and scrapper, but especially Hercules the madman."

Popular culture, then—where pop art, music, fashion, and literature all parody their more serious counterparts and where monarchs and political leaders are mocked by figures like Johnny Rotten, the Lord of Misrule—becomes what Bakhtin describes as the Holiday of Fools or *"festa stultorum,* a form of *ludus* in which everything is reversed, even clothing; trousers were worn on the head, for instance, an operation that symbolically reflects in some measure the jongleurs, who are depicted in miniatures head-downward": a dialogue between what the given system will admit into its canons, and what it systematically rejects—forms of language embraced by Bakhtin in his universal definition of heteroglottal novelization.

Everything serious has to have a comic double, in text and in reality. Just as in the Saturnalia the clown is the double of the ruler, the slave the double of the master, similar comic doubles exist in all forms of literature and culture. And the funhouse of popular images, pictures, commercials, music, art, and literature displayed in current style magazines as in current popular culture represents, in the same way that the Lord of Misrule doubles the king, the parodic, self-referential, carnivalesque counterpart to all forms of "high" culture.

Perhaps neither phenomenon—carnival nor popular culture—is as unqualifiedly positive as it seems to be, since this systemic reversal or inversion figured by the carnivalesque can equally be interpreted as madness. There is a constant similarity between the polyglossia of the carnival, textual and nontextual, and the manifold layers and levels of discourse within the madman's psychological dialogism. Clair Wills, in her feminist interpretation of carnival, draws a parallel between the carnival itself, which disrupts by juxtaposing public indecency with official order, and women's texts considered hysteric even by avant-garde writers such as Julia Kristeva. Wills charts a connection between carnival, which fuses common and official types of discourse as well as many others in a polyglossia, and the hysteric's reliving of past history, family situations, and so on, in the present: "her capacity for turning things 'upside-down' is contained within the family. The. . . 'transgressive' nature of popular festive forms and hysterical discourse are connected not only in their similar relation to history, but also in their content. . . . Freud's descriptions of the hysteric call on popular festive imagery: 'it is striking how the broken fragments of carnival, terrifying and disconnected, glide through the discourse of the hysteric' " ["Upsetting the Public: Carnival, Hysteria and Women's Texts," in *Bakhtin and Cultural Theory*].

This kind of hysteria—a form of Bakhtin's heteroglottal novelization in its anticanonical dialogue between what the given system admits as the language of "literature" and what it rejects as subculture—manifests itself not only in the fusion of retrospective and up-to-the-minute language in style magazines and in popular culture in particular but, more clearly perhaps, in the continuous, repetitive, confused stream of discourse that comes from the radio deejay or rap artist. Wills views the discourse of the hysteric as "an attempt to open up the protests of the women of the past by seeing their similarity with the feminist protest of the present," just as Bakhtinian carnival brings together the crises of the past and present. "The crises of the past," writes Wills, "live on in a separate area of the psyche like the last vestiges of a small-town marketplace carnival." In *The Newly Born Woman*, Catherine Clément cites Marcel Mauss to describe people with a "dangerous symbiotic mobility" as afflicted with what she calls "madness, anomaly, perversion"—people whom Mauss labels "neurotics, ecstatics, outsiders, carnies, drifters, jugglers, acrobats."

This interpretation of carnival as insanity—where the fusing strands of each type of heteroglottal discourse represent the madman's reliving of past events, emotions, lives, and dialogues—bodes ill for recent popular culture. If the textual and nontextual heteroglossia of elements of today's popular cultural "novelness" and dialogues—television comedians, comedy shows, pop art, advertisements, films, and most of all magazines—is symptomatic of a carnivalesque madness, then that madness is accepted all over the Western world as popular culture. If the interplay between official, unofficial, academic, nonacademic, popular, parodic, journalistic, artistic, vulgar, colloquial, and plenty of other forms of textual and nontextual discourse is to be interpreted as symptomatic of the hysteric's revertive, transgressive reliving of past and other dialogues, then the

hysteria of popular culture is a part of everyday life. The furthest extent of this argument is perhaps best illustrated by the current debate over "fiction factory" television, where fake footage and false news reports have been aired as real news. In one instance, ABC staff members acted out a news story about a spy's alleged dealings with Soviet agents, but "forgot" to label the footage as a recreation. There is no distinction to be made any more between irony, pastiche, and fiction, on the one hand, and, on the other, the reality it imitates and mocks.

An article on the resurgent popularity of the T-shirt in *The Face* is accompanied by "artistic" photos of vague-looking models—and, a few pages later, a nine-page photographic fashion supplement features similar images of slightly puzzled, slightly aloof "art" characters. The models chosen are always young and beautiful, the writers affect a youthful idiom, the pop music featured is aimed at the young, and played by young musicians. The films and books reviewed are the latest hip releases, the outlandish clothes modeled could be worn only by the young, the advertisements (for new bank accounts, cosmetics, sound systems and stereos, cigarettes, drink, clothes, other style magazines) and notices (of forthcoming concerts, shows, new clubs, discos) are all aimed at an audience under thirty. *The Face* seems permanently suspended in its own dream of youth-time, where the interests and concerns of older and less chic generations (marriage, the family, jobs, health, finances, the home) are featured only parodically, as subjects for comedy, and are otherwise dismissed as of interest only to the readers of other, outmoded magazines like *Cosmopolitan* or *Vogue*.

This permanent existence in a vacuum of youth-time resembles a kind of generic whole which Bakhtin in his studies on the novel refers to as the *chronotope* (space-time: according to Bakhtin every entry into the sphere of meaning is accomplished only through the gates of the chronotope). In the novel, the chronotope can take a variety of forms—Bakhtin mentions chronotopes of the road, the threshold, the castle, the family idyll. *The Face* figures an eternal chronotope of youth, of youth adventure, the folkloric conception of the idealized *beginning*, youth idyll with its magic costumes and accoutrements—cosmetics, fashionable clothes, pop music, certain brands of cigarettes, and so on. The youth idyll presented by *The Face* is a characteristic of folkloric time charted against the background of the reader's own, contemporary perception of time. Bakhtin points out in **"Forms of Time and Chronotope in the Novel"** that our understanding of folkloric time is not a fact of primitive man's consciousness, but rather something that must be adduced from a study of objective material, since the chronotope is what determines the unity of every motif and idea in a text, as well as determining the logic by which these images unfold. The chronotope, then, is artificial—the youth idyll of the style magazine, for example, exhibits no teenage suicide, no young people who are not beautiful, no young classical artists or musicians, no youthful depression or psychological breakdown except when angst and neurosis are chic.

This filtering of moments in chronotope, Hirschkop believes, takes place not because all authors are necessarily prejudiced, but because "they must approach the object language with some task, project, or aim in mind if speech is to exhibit its ideological structure." The reasoning behind each motif of youth chronotope selected for a style magazine article, pop song, or advertisement, then, is connected to the capitalist nature of the market in which these texts are sold and the fact that they are almost universally produced as commercial, consumerist, money-making commodities.

And this is where any application of Bakhtinian analysis of the carnivalesque to textual practices encounters a stumbling block. So far in this essay I have been referring to carnivalesque practices in text and in reality as realizing similar effects. However, the textual carnival can never completely realize the dialogical struggle current in the social carnival. Although their effects and implications may be similar, it will never be possible completely to align the carnivalesque in text and the carnivalesque in performance, unless the solitary activity of reading is regarded as a kind of performance.

However joyous and festive they may appear, commodities of the textual carnivalesque—those artifacts which emphasize words and language rather than being and doing: the pop song, the advertisement, the magazine, the comic—are still no more than static studies, inevitably far distanced from the active, nontextual, participatory reality of being and doing which they attempt to achieve in print or on the screen. There is a vast difference between the text which promotes the carnivalesque in linguistic terms, and the actual carnival of being and doing itself (concert, festival, disco, club, shopping, and so on). Clair Wills is hasty to criticize the lack of connections between the textual carnival and the carnivalesque as a genuine social force. Similarly, Ann Jefferson agrees that authoring is by its very nature a decarnivalizing activity, since the authorial perspective and the demarcation between observer and participants are against the whole spirit of carnival.

So although Bakhtin's interpretation of what he refers to as "the novel"—defined by a proclivity to display different languages interpenetrating one another—allows examples of language outside the bounds of what traditional scholars would think of as strictly *literary* history, such as pop lyrics and advertising, to be studied as instances of the language use he finds in heteroglottal novelization, despite the linguistic heteroglossia of the style magazine and the dialogism of the advertisement, cinema film or pop record, no text can come closer to carnival than the levels of description, imitation, and representation. There will always be some kind of dichotomy between the carnivalesque discourses of the text and the social power of its actual equivalent—the festivals at Woodstock or Altamont, for example, a Sex Pistols gig or all-night disco, a consumer spree in a giant shopping mall, audience participation on a popular television game show, the realities of being and doing.

Nevertheless, it is important to remember Bakhtin's words: "great novelistic images continue to grow and develop even after the moment of their creation; they are capable of being creatively transformed in different eras, far distant from the day and hour of their original birth"

["**Discourse in the Novel**"]. Rather than simply subscribing to the cliche of "different times, different interpretations," Bakhtin is suggesting that the heteroglottal novelization of all language structures in all dialogic texts, irrespective of origin and original purpose, allows them to be given new relevance, new meaning, new interest as they are subjected, like the texts used in this study, to new readings and new analyses.

It is this independent, interdependent battle and play of different levels and layers of interested dialogue that gives every text a variety of meanings, interpretations, subtexts. This quality of inherent polyglossia means that texts produced for very direct and immediate purposes like the rebellion and outrageousness of a Sex Pistols lyric or the hyped-up, overexposed commercialism of magazines like *The Face* can, in other times and contexts, come to assume a radically different meaning. But their meaning is still a textual meaning, their dialogism a textual dialogism. In the place of the powerful, social polyglossia of the *real* carnival, all we can observe instead is the "lonely carnival of reading" [Jefferson, "Body Matters"].

Mikita Hoy, "Bakhtin and Popular Culture," in New Literary History, *Vol. 23, No. 3, Summer, 1992, pp. 765-82.*

FURTHER READING

Biography

Clark, Katerina, and Holquist, Michael. *Mikhail Bakhtin.* Cambridge: Harvard University Press, 1984, 398 p.
> Discusses Bakhtin's life and works.

Criticism

Bauer, Dale M., and McKinstry, Susan Jaret, eds. *Feminism, Bakhtin, and the Dialogic.* Albany: State University of New York Press, 1991, 259 p.
> Collection of essays that apply Bakhtinian theory to feminist literary analysis.

Booth, Wayne C. "Freedom of Interpretation: Bakhtin and the Challenge of Feminist Criticism." *Critical Inquiry* 9, No. 1 (September 1982): 45-76.
> Applies a feminist reading to Bakhtin's analysis of François Rabelais's *Gargantua and Pantagruel* in his *Rabelais and His World.*

Emerson, Caryl. "Russian Orthodoxy and the Early Bakhtin." *Religion and Literature* 22, Nos. 2-3 (Summer-Autumn 1990): 109-31.
> Asserts that Bakhtin's religious beliefs combined spiritual Russian Orthodoxy with academic Western European philosophy and assesses how those beliefs contributed to his cultural and literary theories.

Guéorguiéva-Dikranyan, Névéna. "Historicity and the Historical Novel in the Work of Bakhtin." *Critical Studies* 2, Nos. 1-2 (1990): 123-36.
> Examines Bakhtin's views on literary history through a discussion of the historical novel genre.

Hirschkop, Ken, and Shepherd, David. *Bakhtin and Cultural Theory*. Manchester, England: Manchester University Press, 1989, 224 p.

Collects essays examining Bakhtin's influence on contemporary cultural studies.

Holquist, Michael. Introduction to *The Dialogic Imagination: Four Essays by M. M. Bakhtin*, edited and translated by Michael Holquist and Caryl Emerson, pp. xv-xxxiv. Austin: University of Texas Press, 1981.

Provides a biographical sketch of Bakhtin and explications of the ideas presented in the essays that make up *The Dialogic Imagination*.

Lachmann, Renate. "Bakhtin and Carnival: Culture as Counter-Culture." *Cultural Critique* 11 (Winter 1989-1990): 115-52.

Discusses Bakhtin's concepts of the carnivalesque and folk culture, focusing on his book *Rabelais and His World*.

Lodge, David. *After Bakhtin: Essays on Fiction and Criticism*. New York: Routledge, 1990, 198 p.

Traces the development of Bakhtin's career and applies Bakhtinian theory to a variety of literary works.

Morson, Gary Saul. "Bakhtin, Genres, and Temporality." *New Literary History* 22, No. 4 (Autumn 1991): 1071-92.

Maintains that Bakhtin's devotion to the novel genre coincides with his aversion to totalizing conceptions of language and culture because of the novel's openness to polyphony, particularity, and the potentiality of time.

Patterson, David. *Literature and Spirit: Essays on Bakhtin and His Contemporaries*. Lexington: University Press of Kentucky, 1988, 166 p.

Collection of essays connecting Bakhtin with other critical and literary figures.

Rutland, Barry. "Bakhtinian Categories and the Discourse of Postmodernism." *Critical Studies* 2, Nos. 1-2 (1990): 123-36.

Discusses Bakhtin in terms of postmodernism as defined by Jean-François Lyotard in his *The Postmodern Condition*.

Shevtsova, Maria. "Dialogism in the Novel and Bakhtin's Theory of Culture." *New Literary History* 23, No. 3 (Summer 1992): 747-63.

Examines how Bakhtin's linguistic theory is derived from his cultural theory, which holds that language is a corporal entity originating in the speech of popular culture.

White, Allon. "Bakhtin, Sociolinguistics and Deconstruction." In *The Theory of Reading*, edited by Frank Gloversmith, pp. 123-46. New Jersey: Barnes and Noble, 1984.

Addresses how Bakhtin's ideas "prefigured both structuralist and deconstructionist views of the language of literature."

Zylko, Boguslaw. "The Author-Hero Relation in Bakhtin's Dialogical Poetics." *Critical Studies* 2, Nos. 1-2 (1990): 65-76.

Asserts that for Bakhtin, "the author sees and knows more than the hero, and this asymmetry is an essential condition of creativity, the real reservoir of all artistic possibilities."

Additional coverage of Bakhtin's life and career is contained in the following source published by Gale Research: *Contemporary Authors,* Vols. 113 and 128.

Roland Barthes

1915-1980

(Full name Roland Gerard Barthes) French theorist, critic, essayist, and autobiographer.

The following entry provides an overview of Barthes's career. For further information on his life and career, see *CLC*, Vol. 24.

INTRODUCTION

One of the seminal figures in the French intellectual movement known as Structuralism, Barthes was a fundamental influence on the practice of modern social and literary criticism. His most widely studied works are those in which he rigorously applied semiologic principles—derived from Ferdinand de Saussure's structural linguistics and influenced by Jean-Paul Sartre's approach to political engagement—to the practice of literary criticism and the analysis of modern cultural artifacts. Barthes's theoretical approach developed and changed over time, however, and his later works largely eschew systematic, scientific investigation for more meditative, belletristic considerations. While some commentators view this evolution negatively as an abandonment of his earlier aspirations toward a scientific theory of narrative and culture, most see it as a refinement of style and perspective.

Biographical Information

Barthes was born in Cherbourg, France, to middle-class Protestant parents. His father was killed in a naval battle in World War I, and Barthes was raised by his mother and maternal grandmother, first in Bayonne and then in Paris from the age of nine. In 1935 he began his studies at the Sorbonne, focusing on French, Greek, and Latin. A case of tuberculosis that Barthes suffered when he was nineteen left him ineligible for military service during World War II. He taught off and on for a number of years in Bayonne, Paris, Biarritz, and Bucharest, Romania, although a relapse of his TB in 1941 forced him to spend most of the next six years in sanatoriums. After being pronounced cured of tuberculosis in 1947, Barthes began publishing the essays that would later be collected in his first book, *Le degré zéro de l'écriture* (1953; *Writing Degree Zero*). From 1952 to 1959, while working as a teaching fellow at the Centre National de Recherche Scientifique, Barthes published the essays that were later compiled in his famous book, *Mythologies* (1957; *Mythologies*). In 1960 he joined the faculty at the École Practique des Hautes Études, serving as director of studies from 1962 until 1977 when he was elected to the chair of literary semiology at the Collège de France. From the 1960s on, Barthes's reputation as France's foremost literary theorist, social critic, and essayist was confirmed by such works as *Système de la mode* (1967; *The Fashion System*), *S/Z* (1970, *S/Z*), *Le plaisir du texte* (1973; *The Pleasure of the Text*), and *Frag-*

ments d'un discours amoureux (1977; *A Lover's Discourse*). Commentators have noted that Barthes came to assume the unofficial position—formerly occupied by Jean-Paul Sartre—of the leading French intellectual and preeminent Western thinker. Barthes remained at the Collège de France until his death in 1980 from injuries suffered during a traffic accident.

Major Works

Critic Bjørnar Olsen has distinguished four stages in Barthes's critical development. He labels Barthes's first three works—*Writing Degree Zero, Michelet* (1954; *Michelet*), and *Mythologies*—his "committed writings" in that they reflect the influence of the two dominant ideological systems of their time, Marxism and Sartrean existentialism. *Writing Degree Zero* examines the distinctions Barthes perceived between language, literary style, and *écriture*, the aspect of discourse in which the author's existential situation, or sociohistorical context, imbues writings with unintended meanings that are revealed through close structural analysis. In *Michelet* he demonstrated the significance of *écriture* in the writings of French historian Jules Michelet, analyzing linguistic characteristics and textual structure in order to reveal hidden connotations and meanings. Karl Marx's early writings provided a model for *Mythologies*, in which Barthes studied aspects of contemporary French culture—such as professional wrestling, strip-tease, travel guides, the advertising of soap and laundry detergent—to illuminate the ways in which bourgeois ideology is disseminated and made to seem natural. The second phase of Barthes's career according to Olsen encompasses his most rigorous semiological writings of the 1960s, works that marked the highpoint of Structuralism in France. In his 1964 essay "Eléments de sémiologie," published in English in book form as *Elements of Semiology*, Barthes elaborated on ideas from Saussure, Roman Jakobson, and other noted linguists to distinguish between language, which refers to the abstract set of rules and conventions governing verbal and written communication, and speech, which refers to individual instances of the actual use of language. In *The Fashion System* Barthes's method, according to Mason Cooley, was "to study and classify the captions under the photographs in a year's issues of two fashion magazines, examining the theoretical ramifications of such statements as 'Prints win at the races' and 'Slim piping is striking.' " Whereas *Elements of Semiology* laid out the blueprint for semiological analysis, *The Fashion System* demonstrated it. The third phase of Barthes's career—in which he popularized concepts formulated by French literary theorists Jacques Derrida and Julia Kristeva—signalled the general shift in Western critical thinking in the early 1970s from Structuralism to Post-Structuralism. While his previous writings championed the notion that a text's meaning inheres in the structure of its components and is therefore knowable and fixed, works such as *S/Z* and *The Pleasure of the Text* examine the ways in which texts present a plurality of shifting connotations that are open to numerous interpretations. *S/Z* is a painstakingly detailed, line-by-line analysis of the Honoré de Balzac novella *Sarrasine* in which Barthes detects five "codes"—specific kinds of references, meanings, and connotations—that, through their interplay, offer the reader a multiplicity of meanings. In *The Pleasure of the Text*, Barthes categorizes all literary works as either texts of pleasure or texts of bliss. He associates the former with classic literary works and those that emulate them, describing texts of pleasure as "readerly" texts in that they reward traditional forms of interpretation and refer to common areas of knowledge. Texts of bliss he associated with modernist works, describing them as "writerly" texts in that they require the reader to "complete" the text by filling in gaps and making intertextual connections in ways that mainstream literature does not. The final phase of Barthes's career—typified by such works as *Roland Barthes*, (1975; *Roland Barthes*), *A Lover's Discourse: Fragments*, and *Le chambre claire* (1980; *Camera Lucida*)—is frequently described as his "hedonist" period because his subjects are more purely aesthetic than earlier ones and his style is meditative and introspective. Referring to himself in the third person throughout his autobiography, *Roland Barthes*, Barthes comments on photographs from his childhood and expounds upon matters of personal intellectual interest, presenting a portrait of his mind rather than of his social, emotional, and professional life. The most popular book

Barthes ever wrote, *A Lover's Discourse: Fragments* was a bestseller in France and served as the basis for a play. The work grew out of a seminar he taught on "amorous discourse" in Johann Wolfgang von Goethe's novel *Die Leiden des jungen Werthers* (1774; *The Sorrows of Werther*) and uses monologues by a semi-autobiographical narrator to attempt to explain the meaning of love in a variety of contexts. In the first section of *Camera Lucida*, he analyzes news photographs and family snapshots and concludes that photography, though it can touch the emotions, is not an art because its close connection to reality fixes the interplay of connotations and thus leaves little room for interpretation. In the second part Barthes meditates on a photograph of his deceased mother and, writing movingly of his relationship with her, draws a connection between photography and death.

Critical Reception

Being at the forefront of "the new criticism" in France, Barthes's works of the late 1950s through the 1960s were frequently criticized by older, university-based academics and critics for being pseudoscientific and jargon-laden. In two essays later collected in *Essais critiques* (1964; *Critical Essays*)—"Les deux critiques" ("The Two Criticisms") and "Qu'est-ce que la critique?" ("What Is Criticism?") —Barthes distinguished between the kind of criticism practiced in universities; which he disparaged as boring, naively objective, and excessively reliant on author biographies for causal explanations; and the structuralist, ideologically aware criticism he espoused. The controversy sparked by these two essays came to a head when Barthes published *Sur Racine* (1963; *On Racine*). This structuralist and psychoanalytic reading of the French dramatist's works was attacked by noted Racine scholar Raymond Picard in an essay entitled "Nouvelle critique ou nouvelle imposture?" (meaning "New Criticism or New Fraud?"). Picard's main points were that Barthes's brand of criticism was subjective and did not take history into account. Outside of France, Barthes's works were accorded great critical acclaim and did much to establish Structuralism and, subsequently, Post-Structuralism in the United States. As his work began to focus on issues of pleasure and became increasingly autobiographical, Barthes was attacked by some commentators for abandoning his earlier Marxist and Structuralist agendas. However, his work, praised for its uniqueness and instructiveness, is generally regarded as among the most significant contributions to critical theory of the twentieth century, as much for the qualities of individual works as for the unique and instructive character of the oeuvre. As noted Marxist scholar Fredric Jameson noted, Barthes's work is "a veritable fever-chart of all the significant intellectual and critical tendencies since World War II."

PRINCIPAL WORKS

Le degré zéro de l'écriture (criticism) 1953
   [*Writing Degree Zero*, 1967]

Michelet (criticism) 1954
   [*Michelet*, 1987]
Mythologies (criticism) 1957
   [*Mythologies* (partial translation), 1972]
Sur Racine (criticism) 1963
   [*On Racine*, 1964]
"Eléments de sémiologie" (essay) 1964
   [*Elements of Semiology*, 1967]
Essais critiques (essays) 1964
   [*Critical Essays*, 1972]
La Tour Eiffel [with André Martin] (essay) 1964
   [**The Eiffel Tower, and Other Mythologies*, 1979]
Critique et vérité (criticism) 1966
   [*Criticism and Truth*, 1987]
Système de la mode (criticism) 1967
   [*The Fashion System*, 1983]
L'empire des signes (criticism) 1970
   [*Empire of Signs*, 1982]
S/Z (criticism) 1970
   [*S/Z*, 1974]
Sade, Fourier, Loyola (criticism) 1971
   [*Sade, Fourier, Loyola*, 1976]
†Le degré zéro de l'écriture, suivi de: Nouveaux essais critiques (essays) 1972
   [*New Critical Essays*, 1980]
Le plaisir du texte (nonfiction) 1973
   [*The Pleasure of the Text*, 1975]
Roland Barthes (autobiography) 1975
   [*Roland Barthes*, 1977]
Fragments d'un discours amoureux (nonfiction) 1977
   [*A Lover's Discourse: Fragments*, 1978]
‡Image—Music—Text (essays) 1977
Leçon inaugurale faite le vendredi 7 janvier 1977 (lecture) 1977
   [§"Inaugural Lecture, Collège de France," 1982]
Sollers écrivain (criticism) 1979
   [*Writer Sollers*, 1987]
Le chambre claire: Note sur la photographie (nonfiction) 1980
   [*Camera Lucida: Reflections on Photography*, 1981]
A Barthes Reader (essays) 1981
Le grain de la voix: Entretiens 1962-1980 (interviews) 1981
   [*The Grain of the Voice: Interviews, 1962-1980*, 1985]
Obvie et l'obtus (essays) 1982
   [*The Responsibility of Forms: Critical Essays on Music, Art, and Representation*, 1984]
Le bruissement de la langue (nonfiction) 1984
   [*The Rustle of Language*, 1986]
L'aventure sémiologique (criticism) 1985
   [*The Semiologic Adventure*, 1988]
Incidents (criticism) 1987
   [*Incidents*, 1992]

*This work includes translations of essays from the 1957 edition of *Mythologies* that were left out of the 1972 partial translation.

†A reprint of *Le degré zéro de l'écriture* along with eight essays written between 1961 and 1972.

‡The essays comprising this work were selected and translated by Stephen Heath.

§This translation is included in *A Barthes Reader*, edited with an introduction by Susan Sontag.

CRITICISM

Gérard Genette   (essay date 1964)

[*Genette is a distinguished French literary theorist, critic, and educator best known in the United States for his* Narrative Discourse: An Essay in Method *(1980), in which he analyzes Marcel Proust's* A la recherche du temps perdu *(1954;* Remembrance of Things Past) *and proposes general categories for the study of narration. In the following essay, first translated into English in 1982, he analyzes the approach to semiology Barthes delineated in such early works as* Writing Degree Zero, Critical Essays, *and* Mythologies.]

The work of Roland Barthes is apparently highly varied, both in its object (literature, clothes, cinema, painting, advertising, music, news items, etc.) and in its method and ideology. ***Le Degré zéro de l'Écriture*** (1953) seemed to extend into the domain of "form" the reflection begun by Sartre some years earlier on the social situation of literature and the responsibility of the writer before history—a reflection on the frontiers of existentialism and Marxism. His ***Michelet*** (1954), though offered as a simple, "precritical" reading, borrowed from Gaston Bachelard the idea of a substantial psychoanalysis and showed what a thematic study of the material imagination could bring to the understanding of a work regarded hitherto as essentially ideological. His work for the review *Théâtre populaire* and in the struggle waged around that review to introduce the work and theories of Bertolt Brecht into France brought him a reputation, in the next few years, of being an intransigent Marxist, although official Marxists never shared his interpretation of Brecht's theory; but, at the same time, and contradictorily, two articles on *Les Gommes* and *Le Voyeur* made him the official interpreter of Robbe-Grillet and the theoretician of the *nouveau roman,* which was widely regarded as a Formalist offensive and as an attempt to "disengage" literature. In 1956, ***Mythologies*** revealed a sarcastic observer of the petty-bourgeois ideology concealed in the most seemingly innocuous manifestations of contemporary social life; a new "critique of everyday life," clearly Marxist in inspiration, which marked an unequivocal political attitude. In 1960, there was a new metamorphosis, a commentary on Racine for the Club français du Livre (revised in 1963 as ***Sur Racine***), which seemed to effect a return to psychoanalysis, but this time closer to Freud than to Bachelard, though to the Freud of *Totem and Taboo,* an anthropologist in his own way: Racine's tragedies are interpreted in terms of the prohibition of incest and Oedipal conflict, "at the level of this ancient fable (that of the 'primal horde'), situated far beyond history or the human psyche." Lastly, the latest texts collected in ***Essais critiques*** (1964) seem to express a decisive conversion to structuralism, understood in its strictest form, and the abandonment of any responsibility towards meaning; literature and social life are now merely languages, which should be studied as pure formal systems, not for their content, but for their structure.

This many-sided image is obviously a superficial and even, as we will see, a highly unfaithful one. Not that the scope of Barthes' reflection is actually circumscribed, open as it is in principle to the most varied tendencies of modern thought. He himself admits that he has often dreamed "of a peaceful coexistence of critical languages or, perhaps, of a 'parametric' criticism which would modify its language to suit the work proposed to it," and, speaking of the fundamental "ideological principles" of contemporary criticism (existentialism, Marxism, psychoanalysis, structuralism), he declares: "For my part, in a certain sense I subscribe to each of them *at the same time.*" But this apparent eclecticism conceals a constant in his thought that was already at work in *Le Degré zéro,* and which has become ever more marked, more conscious, and more systematic. If criticism can claim allegiance to several ideologies at once, it is, Barthes hastens to add, because "ideological choice does not constitute the being of criticism and because 'truth' is not its sanction": its task is not to *uncover* the secret truth of the works of which it speaks, but to *cover* their language "as completely as possible," with its own language, to *adjust* as closely as possible the language of our period to that of the works of the past, "that is to say, to the formal system of logical constraints worked out by the author in accordance with his own period." This *friction* between literary language and critical language has the effect not of bringing out the "meaning" of a work, but of "reconstituting the rules and constraints governing the elaboration of this meaning," in other words, its technique of signification. If the work is a language and criticism a metalanguage, their relation is essentially formal, and criticism no longer has to concern itself with a message, but with a code, that is to say, a system the structure of which it is its task to uncover, "just as the linguist is not responsible for deciphering the sentence's meaning but for establishing the formal structure which permits this meaning to be transmitted." In consideration of which, out of the varied languages that criticism can *try* on the literary works of the past (or of the present) "would appear a general form, which would be the very intelligibility our age gives to things and which critical activity helps, dialectically, both to decipher and to constitute." The exemplary value of critical activity, then, derives clearly from this double semiological character: as a metalanguage (a discourse on literary language), it studies a system from the viewpoint of that metacriticism, or "criticism of criticisms," which is simply semiology in its most general form. Thus criticism helps both "to decipher and to constitute" the intelligible, since it is at the same time semantics and semanteme, subject and object, of the semiological activity.

These remarks lead us then to the central point of Barthes' thought: the problem of signification. *Homo significans:* man the sign-maker, "man's freedom to make things signify," "the strictly human process by which men give meaning to things," such is the essential object of his research. It is a traditional, even fundamental, orientation, since already *Le Degré zéro* studied the various ways in which the

writer, beyond all the explicit contents of his discourse must in addition—perhaps essentially—*signify Literature,* and this book was offered as a contribution to "a history of literary expression which is neither that of a particular language, nor that of the various styles, but simply that of the Signs of Literature," that is to say, of the signs by which literature draws attention to itself as literature, and *points out its mask.* It is an old question, then, but one that has continued to reflect upon itself and to define its terms.

As we know, it was the linguist Ferdinand de Saussure who first conceived of the idea of a general science of significations, of which linguistics would be no more than a particular case, "a science that studies the life of signs within society," which would show "what constitutes signs, what laws govern them," and which he proposed to call *semiology.* The natural languages (*langues*) being by far the most elaborate and best-known systems of signs, linguistics necessarily remains the irreplaceable model for all semiological research, but the domain of signs goes beyond that of articulated language. Indeed, there exist on the one hand signs outside language, which function so to speak beside it, such as those emblems or signals of all kinds that men have always used, from "primitive totemism" to the various sign-posts and symbols that modern civilization constantly proliferates before our eyes. Some of these signs have already constituted highly complex systems: one has only to think of the degree of elaboration once attained by the art of the coat-of-arms and its corresponding science of heraldry; the ability to constitute a system is precisely the characteristic of any set of signs, and it is this constitution that marks the passage from pure symbolism to the strictly semiological state, since a symbol becomes a sign only at the moment when it ceases to suggest of itself, and by virtue of an analogical or historical relationship (the Crescent, the emblem of Islam, the Cross, the symbol of Christianity) which it maintains with its "referent," in order to signify in an indirect way, mediatized by the relation of kinship and opposition that it maintains with other concurrent symbols; the Cross and the Crescent, taken in isolation, are two autonomous symbols, but the use of an Arab Red Crescent with a European Red Cross sets up a paradigmatic system in which red holds the place of a common root, and the opposition Cross/Crescent that of a distinctive inflection.

What we have, then, or at least it would seem so, is a series of *extralinguistic* semiological systems; but their social importance, and still more their autonomy in relation to articulated language appear to be highly questionable: "Until now semiology has had to concern itself only with codes of little interest, such as the highway code; as soon as one passes to systems possessing real social depth, one meets language once again." This is because nonlinguistic objects actually become signifiers only insofar as they are *duplicated* or *relayed* by language, as is clear enough in advertising or newspaper photography, which invariably accompany the visual image with a verbal commentary intended to confirm or to localize its virtual or floating significations, or again, in fashion writing, which gives objects (clothes, food, furniture, cars, etc.) their symbolic value by "speaking" of them, that is to say, by analyzing the signifying parts and naming the signifieds: the image might represent a man wearing a tweed jacket, standing in front of a country house, but the commentary will state more precisely "tweed jacket for the weekend," designating by name tweed as a sign and weekend as the meaning. "There is only meaning when it is named, and the world of signifieds is simply that of language." The extralinguistic domain rapidly gives way therefore (or is *absorbed* into) that other domain of semiology, which is the translinguistic, or metalinguistic order, and which embraces techniques of signification situated not beside, but above, or within, language. Semiology is thus brought back into the linguistic fold, which leads Barthes to reverse the Saussurian formula: semiology is no longer seen as an extension, but on the contrary as a specification of linguistics. However, it is not a question of assimilating the semiological fact to the linguistic fact, for language used in this way concerns semiology only as a *secondary* language, either because the verbal text is supposed to impose a signification on a nonverbal object, as in the case of the blurbs attached to press photographs or advertising images, or because it duplicates itself as it were in order to add to its own explicit, literal signification, or *denotation,* an additional power of *connotation,* which enriches it with one or several secondary meanings. Many pages of literature, as Valéry more or less remarks, mean nothing more than "I am a page of literature," a sentence which, however, is nowhere to be found in them; and Sartre rightly stresses that the meaning or intrinsic quality of a text is never after all directly designated by the words of this text, and that "the literary object, though realized *through* language, is never given *in* language."

This oblique language that suggests some unstated meaning is the language of *connotation,* of which literature is the domain *par excellence,* the study of which may avail itself of an illustrious, if sometimes decried precedent, that of Rhetoric. When a rhetorician of the classical period taught, for example, that the use of the word "sail" to designate a ship is a figure called synecdoche, and that this figure achieves its finest effect in an epic poem, he simply brought out, in his own way, the epic connotation implied in the use of this figure, and a treatise of rhetoric was a code of literary connotation, a collection of the means by which a poet could signify, over and above the explicit "content" of his poem, its quality of being epic, lyrical, bucolic, etc. Such is the case of those obscenities with which the prose of *Père Duchêne* is dotted, not to signify anything in the discourse, but to signal, obliquely, a whole historical situation: the precious figures of revolutionary rhetoric.

In fact it is the phenomena and techniques of connotation that, since *Le Degré zéro de l'écriture,* have particularly commanded Barthes' attention. Writing, we should remember, is that *responsibility for Form* which, between the Nature represented by the horizon of the language (imposed by time and place) and that other Nature determined by the vertical thrust of style (dictated by the depths of the body and psyche), manifests the writer's choice of a particular literary attitude, and therefore indicates a particular modality of literature; the writer chooses neither his language nor his style, but he is responsible for the methods of writing that indicate whether he is a novel-

ist or a poet, a classicist or a naturalist, bourgeois or populist, etc. All these facts of writing are means of connotation, since over and above their literal meaning, which is sometimes weak or negligible, they manifest an attitude, a choice, an intention.

This effect of super-signification may be represented by a simple schema, for which we will borrow from rhetoric once again its classic example: in the synecdoche *sail ship,* there is a signifying word, "sail," and an object (or concept) signified, the ship: that is the denotation; but since the word "sail" has been substituted for the literal word "ship," the relation (signification) that links the signifier to the signified constitutes a figure; this figure in turn clearly designates, in the rhetorical code, a poetic state of discourse: it functions then as the signifier of a new signified, poetry, on a second semantic plane, which is that of rhetorical connotation; the essence of connotation is in effect to establish itself above (or below) the primary signification, but in a dislocated way, using the primary meaning as a form to designate a secondary concept; hence the schema (which might be expressed more or less in some such formula as: *the semiological system in which the word "sail" may be used to designate a ship is a figure; the secondary semiological figure in which a figure, such as the use of the word "sail" to designate a ship, may be used to signify poetry, is rhetoric*). [In an endnote, Genette renders this Relationship as: "[(sail = ship) = poetry] = Rhetoric."]

Readers of *Mythologies* will recognize a similarity between this schema and the one used by Barthes to represent the dislocation of myths in relation to the semiological system onto which it is grafted. This is because we are dealing with an effect of the same order, and Barthes says quite rightly that *Le Degré zéro* "was, all told, nothing but a mythology of literary language" in which he defined · writing "as the signifier of the literary myth, that is, as a form which is already filled with meaning and which receives from the concept of Literature a new signification." From the point of view that concerns us here, what distinguishes *Mythologies* from *Le Degré zéro* is, on the one hand, an explicit recourse to the notion of semiological system and a clear view of the superimposition and dislocation of the two systems and, on the other hand, the application of this analysis to non-literary objects and even, in some cases, non-linguistic objects, such as the photograph of a black soldier saluting a French flag, which adds to this uncoded and purely denoted visual message a second connoted, ideological message, which is the justification of the French empire.

Thus a whole world is opened up to semiological analysis, a much vaster world than that of literature and one that still awaits its rhetoric: the world of *communication,* of which the press, the cinema, and advertising are the most obvious and best-known forms. But the field of signification does not stop there, for the language of connotation shows that man can endow with an additional meaning any object that has previously been provided either with a primary meaning (verbal statement, graphic or photographic image, film shot or sequence, etc.) or with a nonsignifying primary function, which may, for example, be some kind of use: "Food is to be eaten; but it also serves to *signify* (conditions, circumstances, tastes); food is therefore a signifying system and must one day be described as such." Similarly clothes are intended to be worn, a house to provide shelter, a car to move around, but clothes, houses, and cars are also signs, indications of a condition or personality, instruments or a "showing." Semiology thus becomes coextensive with a whole civilization and the world of objects becomes a universe of signs: "In a single day, how many really non-signifying fields do we cross? Very few, sometimes none." What we call history, or culture, is also that "shudder of an enormous machine which is humanity tirelessly undertaking to create meaning, without which it would no longer be human."

But it has to be realized that this signifying activity is always carried out, for Barthes, as an *addition of use* imposed on things, and therefore on occasion as a distortion or an abuse. For Barthes, signs are almost never, like ships' flags, roadsigns, or any other of the clarion calls with which semiology has traditionally concerned itself, signifiers deliberately invented for explicit, limited signifieds, in short the elements of a recognized and overt code. The systems that interest him are always, as he says of literary criticism, "semiologies that dare not speak their name," ashamed or unconscious codes, always marked by a certain bad faith. To decide that a red or a green lamp will signify "stop" or "go" is not in the least equivocal: I have created a sign that could not be clearer, I have abused nothing and nobody. To decide that a leather jacket "suggests sportiness" and therefore to turn leather into a sign of "sportiness," is something quite different: for leather exists outside this imposition of meaning, as a substance that one might like for profound reasons having to do with its feel, its consistency, its color, its texture; by turning it into a signifier, I obliterate these substantial qualities and substitute for them a social concept of doubtful authenticity; but, on the other hand, I confiscate to the benefit of this signifying link the perceptible properties of leather, which are always available as a reserve of natural justification: leather *is* sporty *because* it is supple, convenient, and so forth; I wear leather *because* I am sporty: what could be more natural? The semiological link is concealed beneath an apparently causal relation, and the naturalness of the sign *exculpates* the signified.

Barthesian semiology is, both in its origin and in its active principle, that of a man fascinated by the sign, a fascination that no doubt involves, as it does for Flaubert or Baudelaire, an element of repulsion, and which has the essentially ambiguous character of a passion.

—Gérard Genette

It is clear that semiological reflection has shifted here from the level of facts to that of values. There is for Barthes an axiology of the sign, and it is doubtless not excessive to see

in this system of preferences and rejections the deeper motive for his activity as a semiologist. Barthesian semiology is, both in its origin and in its active principle, that of a man fascinated by the sign, a fascination that no doubt involves, as it does for Flaubert or Baudelaire, an element of repulsion, and which has the essentially ambiguous character of a passion. Man makes rather too many signs, and these signs are not always very *healthy.* One of the texts collected in **Essais critiques** is entitled **"The Diseases of Costume."** It begins with this characteristic sentence: "I should like to sketch here not a history of an esthetic, but rather *a pathology or, if you prefer, an ethic* of costume. I shall propose a few very simple rules which may permit us to judge whether costume is *good or bad, healthy or sick."* The diseases of theatrical costume, which is obviously a sign, are three in number and all three turn out to be hypertrophies: hypertrophy of the historical function, archeological accuracy; hypertrophy of formal beauty, estheticism; hypertrophy of sumptuosity, money. In another text on the theater, Barthes reproaches traditional Racinian diction for its "hypertrophy of detailed significance" (signification parcellaire), a plethora of details that spread over the text like a film of greasy dirt and impair the clarity of the whole; the same criticism is leveled, with more violence, at the performance of a modern actress in the *Oresteia:* "a dramatic art of the intention, of the gesture and the glance heavy with meaning, of the *signified secret,* an art suitable for any scene of conjugal discord and bourgeois adultery, but which introduces into tragedy a cunning and, in a word, a vulgarity utterly anachronistic to it." It is an indiscretion comparable to that of the *rubato* dear to the romantic pianists, and which Barthes finds again in a particular interpretation of a Fauré song: "this pleonasm of intentions muffles both words and music, and chiefly their junction, which is the very object of the vocal art." All these redundant, *overfed* significations, like Michelet's "lacteous and sanguine" Englishwomen or the apoplectic burgomasters of Dutch painting, arouse a disapproval that is indissolubly of a logical, moral, and esthetic, but perhaps above all physical, order: it is nausea, that "immediate judgment of the body" which Barthes finds so easily in his Michelet, who judges history "at the tribunal of the flesh." The bad sign is bloated because it is redundant, and it is redundant because it wants to be *true,* that is, both a sign and a thing, like the costume for Chanticleer of 1910, made up of several pounds of real feathers "sewn one over the other." The good sign is arbitrary: it is the common word, the name "tree" or the verb "to run," which has value only through an express convention, and does not try to deceive by adding to this conventional value the oblique power of natural evocation. It is the flag in the Chinese theater, which on its own signifies a whole regiment, the masks and costumes of the *Commedia dell'arte,* or better still, the red gown of the Caliph in the *Thousand and One Nights,* which signifies "I am angry." The bad sign *par excellence* is the meaning-form which serves as signifier to the mythical concept, because it uses the natural character of the meaning surreptitiously in order to justify the secondary signification. The *naturalization* of culture, and therefore of history, is in Barthes' eyes, as we know, the major sin of petty-bourgeois ideology, and its denunciation the central theme of **Mythologies.**

Now the semiological instrument of this naturalization is the fraudulent motivation of the sign. When a Racinian actress utters the words "Je brûle" (I burn) in an obviously burning tone, when a singer interprets "tristesse affreuse" (terrible sadness) by terribly saddening the sounds of these two words, they commit a pleonasm and an imposture: they have to choose between the sentence and the cry, "between the intellectual sign and the visceral sign," which latter is really no longer a sign, but a direct manifestation of the signified, an *expression,* in the full sense of the term; but such effects are practically outside the reach of art, which must be accepted fully as a language. Now "if there is a 'health' of language, it is the arbitrariness of the sign which is its grounding. What is sickening in myth is its resort to a false nature, its superabundance of significant forms, as in those objects which decorate their usefulness with a natural appearance. The will to weigh the signification with the full guarantee of nature causes a kind of nausea: myth is too rich, and what is in excess is precisely its motivation." The health of an art, its virtue, its elegance, lies in its strict fidelity to the system of conventions on which it rests: "The exercise of a signifying system . . . has only one requirement, which will therefore be the esthetic requirement itself: rigor": this is the case of Brechtian dramaturgy, *cleansed* by the effect of distancing, which knows that "the responsibility of a dramatic art is not so much to express reality as to signify it"; it is the case with the sober acting of Helene Weigel, the literal performances of a Panzera or a Lipatti, the photographs of Agnès Varda, shot with "exemplary humility," the cathartic writing of Robbe-Grillet, determined *to kill the adjective* and to restore to the object its "essential thinness."

The *naturalization* of culture, and therefore of history, is in Barthes' eyes the major sin of petty-bourgeois ideology.

—*Gérard Genette*

Barthes does not see the semiological activity, then, as exclusively, or even essentially, belonging to the order of knowledge. For him, signs are never the neutral objects of disinterested knowledge, as Saussure conceived them when he contemplated the founding of a semiological science. The normative choice is never far behind analytical discourse, and this *ethical origin* that he recognizes in the work of the mythologist is to be found throughout his work. "Brechtian criticism will therefore be written by the spectator, the reader, the consumer, and not the exegete: it is a criticism of a *concerned* man." This attitude marks all Barthes' critical activity, which is constantly underpinned by the question: in what sense does this work concern us? This criticism is and is always intended to be profoundly and aggressively subjective, because every reading, "however impersonal it forces itself to be, is a projective test" into which the critic "puts all his 'profundity,' i. e., his choices, his pleasures, his resistances, his obsessions." It has nothing to do, we realize, with the intersubjective participation which animates criticism like that of Georges Poulet, and which always operates to the benefit of the "thought criticized," before which critical thought stands back and falls silent, its sole *raison d'être* being to recreate a space and a language for it. Barthesian criticism is not the resumption of one subject by another, of one speech by another: it is a dialogue, and a dialogue that is "egoistically shifted toward the present." Thus, paradoxically, this notorious representation of the "newest" new criticism is alone in honoring in his work the ancient meaning of the word "criticism," which designates a militant act of assessment and challenge. His literary criticism is certainly a semiology of literature; but his semiology, in turn, is not only a study of significations, but also, in the most vivid sense of the term, a critique of signs.

Noting in the final section of ***Mythologies*** the imposture involved in the ambiguity of the mythical sign, "this turnstile of form and meaning," Barthes adds that one can escape this imposture, stop this turnstile, only if one focuses on form and meaning separately, that is, by applying to the mythical object a semiological *analysis.* Semiology, then, is not only a tool of knowledge and criticism: it is also, for the man besieged by signs, the only possible recourse, the only defense. To analyse the sign, to distinguish between its constitutive elements, to place on one side the signifier, on the other the signified: this activity, which, for Saussure, was a simple technique, a methodological routine, becomes for Barthes something like the instrument of an ascesis and the beginnings of a salvation. The semiological discipline stops the vertigo of meaning and authorizes a liberating choice: for it is the privilege of the semiologist to turn away from the signified in order to devote himself to the study of the signifier, and therefore to an exclusive commerce with it. He has given himself as his "moral goal," as Barthes says of the critic, "not the decipherment of the work's meaning but the reconstruction of the rules and constraints of that meaning's elaboration": thus he avoids "good conscience" and "bad faith." His gaze stops at the frontier of meaning and does not cross it: like the linguist, he is concerned only with forms. But this prejudice in favor of forms is no mere methodological rule, it is an existential choice.

We have to remember that the forms in question are not sentences, words, phonemes—they are objects; and when the semiologist has operated the semiological reduction, the *epoché* of meaning on the object-form, he is presented with a matte object, cleansed of the varnish of dubious, abusive significations, with which social speech had covered it, restored to its essential freshness and solitude. Thus the formalist enterprise opens up, in an unexpected way, an adhesion to, a very profound conformity with, the reality of things. The paradox and difficulty of such a deviation have not escaped the author of ***Mythologies,*** who devotes the last page of that book to them: the mythologist wishes "to protect reality" against the "evaporation" with which it is threatened by the alienating speech of myth, but he fears he has himself contributed to its disappearance. The "goodness of wine" is a French myth, but at the same time wine is good and the mythologist is condemned to speak only of its mythical goodness. This abstention is regrettable, and Barthes recognizes that he has been unable to avoid it altogether: "Finding it painful constantly to work on the evaporation of reality, I have started to make it excessively dense, and to discover in it a surprising compactness which I savored with delight, and I have given a few examples of 'substantial psychoanalysis' about some mythical objects." All critical irony laid aside, he gives himself up for example to praising old wooden toys, the nostalgic associations of which are characteristic: "A sign which fills one with consternation is the gradual disappearance of wood, in spite of its being an ideal material because of its firmness and its softness, and the natural warmth of its touch. . . . It is a familiar and poetic substance, which does not sever the child from close contact with the tree, the table, the floor. . . . Wood makes essential objects, objects for all time." Material intimacy, access to the "essence of things" is here, as in Proust, a lost paradise, which he must try to recover, but by some indirect way. For Barthes, semiology plays the role of a *catharsis,* but this ascesis, which rejects the meaning added by history, is in its own way a return, or an attempted return, to reality. His method is almost the opposite of that of (modern) poetry, that language *without writing* by which man "confronts the world of objects without going through any of the forms of history or of social life": the semiological procedure seems to consist on the contrary in accepting the deviation as inevitable, in the belief that ideology and its rhetoric overlie the entire surface of reality, that the only way of obviating this is to confront them in order to traverse them, and therefore that the poetic project of an immediate speech is a sort of utopia. But the opposition of means must not conceal the kinship of ends: the semiologist as Barthes understands him is also in search of "the inalienable meaning of things," which he uncovers beneath their alienated meaning. The movement from the (ideological) signified to the (real) signifier is only apparently therefore an abandonment of meaning. It would be better to say that it leads from the ideological meaning, which is an (abusive) speech, to the poetic meaning, which is a silent presence. "Things must taste of what they are," Curnonsky demands. The rediscovery of this profound taste is perhaps the unacknowledged aim of the semiologist.

This explains the privilege accorded, and preserved throughout his work, to Literature. For Barthes, literature uses signs, following Kafka's lesson, not to name a meaning but to "deceive," that is to say, both to offer it and to suspend it. In the literary work, the transitive movement of the verbal message stops and is absorbed into a "pure spectacle." To the proliferation of meaning, literature opposes a resistance that is all the more effective in that its instruments are exclusively of a semantic order, and that all its works are composed of language. Far from turning away from that rather sickening technique which Barthes calls the "cooking up of meaning," literature is wholly and entirely committed to it, but in act, in order to free itself from it, preserving the significations, but diverting them from their signifying function. The literary work tends to turn itself into a monument of reticence and ambiguity, but it constructs this silent object, so to speak, with words, and this work of abolishing meaning is a typically semiological process, liable as such to an analysis of the same

order: literature is a rhetoric of silence. [In an endnote Genette observes: "We know that on certain jukeboxes one can get, for the same price as the latest tune, a period of silence equal to that of a record: it may in fact be a blank record specially made for this purpose. But whatever the means, the lesson of this invention is clear, namely, that in a civilization of noise silence must also be a *product,* that it is the fruit of a technology and a commercial object. There is no question of stopping the racket, which ought to be muffled as quickly as possible, but on occasion one is able, by paying the price, to get it to run silently. Likewise, in a civilization of meaning, though there is no longer any place for 'truly insignificant objects,' it is still possible to produce objects loaded with significations, but conceived in such a way that these significations cancel each other out, disperse, or are reabsorbed, like mechanical functions in Ashby's homeostat. No one is really able (or permitted) to be entirely silent, but the writer has the special, indispensable, indeed sacred function, of speaking 'in order to say nothing,' or to say *'What?'.''*] Its *art* consists entirely in making language, a vehicle of knowledge and rather hasty opinion, a locus of uncertainty and interrogation. It suggests that the world signifies, but "without saying *what*": it describes objects and people, relates events, and instead of imposing on them definite, fixed significations, as does social speech (and also, of course, "bad" literature), it leaves them, or rather restores to them, by a very subtle technique (which is still to be studied) of semantic evasion, that "shaky," ambiguous, uncertain meaning, which is their truth. Thus it *breathes new life into the world,* freeing it from the pressure of social meaning, which is a named meaning, and therefore a dead meaning, maintaining as long as possible that opening, that *uncertainty of signs,* which allows one to breathe. Thus literature is for the semiologist (the critic) a permanent temptation, an endless vocation postponed until later, experienced only in this dilatory mode: like the Proustian Narrator, the semiologist is a "writer postponed": he constantly intends to *write,* that is to say, to turn over the meaning of signs and to send language back to the silence that forms part of it; but the postponement is only apparent, for this intention to write, this "Moses-like gaze" on the work to come is already Literature.

Gérard Genette, "The Obverse of Signs," in his Figures of Literary Discourse, *translated by Alan Sheridan, Columbia University Press, 1982, pp. 27-44.*

Edward W. Said   (review date 30 July 1972)

[*Said is a Palestinian-born American critic and educator who has written extensively on culture and politics. In the following review, he offers praise for* Mythologies *and* Critical Essays *and examines the principal tenets of Barthes's early writings.*]

Roland Barthes is one of the very few literary critics in any language of whom it can be said that he has never written a bad or uninteresting page. . . .

Barthes is neither an academic critic, nor a reviewer, but strictly an occasional writer: he produces writing for prefaces, commemoratives, conferences, events, seminars, commissions from publishers, captions for pictures, descriptions of striking objects. Although his *Critical Essays* and *Mythologies* collect relatively early work—roughly from 1954 to the early sixties—they illustrate the beautiful generosity of Barthes's progressive interest in the meaning (his word is "signification") of practically everything around him, not only the books and paintings of high art, but also the slogans, trivia, toys, food and popular rituals (cruises, striptease, eating, wrestling matches) of contemporary life. How enjoyable it is for Barthes's readers to be able to choose as their favorite among his books perhaps the analysis of a Balzac story or a dazzling characterization of the Eiffel Tower.

Roland Barthes is one of the very few literary critics in any language of whom it can be said that he has never written a bad or uninteresting page.

—*Edward W. Said*

The clue to Barthes's genius is that he employs the method of a system, but never makes an unquestioning commitment to it. At least four of his books do little more than articulate sets of analytic rules for the study of verbal objects, yet I am convinced that no matter how useful these are to Barthes and to other critics, the rules are more valuable for the fact of their articulation than for what they enable one to do with them. The overcoming of a senseless "thereness" in things by a method that shows what put them there, and how and why they are there: this matters more than whether the method's rules are universally applicable. For Barthes, words and objects have in common the organized capacity to say something; at the same time, since they are signs, words and objects have the bad faith always to appear natural to their consumer, as if what they say is eternal, true, necessary, instead of arbitrary, made, contingent.

Mythologies finds Barthes revealing the fashioned systems of ideas that make it possible, for example, for "Einstein's brain" to stand for, be the myth of, "a genius so lacking in magic that one speaks about his thought as of a functional labour analogous to the mechanical making of sausages." Each of the little essays in the book wrenches a definition out of a common but constructed object, making the object speak its hidden, but ever-so-present, reservoir of manufactured sense. The epitome of bad faith is plastic, a shaped and "disgraced" thing, which in toys has replaced wood, a substance for which Barthes seems to have the greatest love:

> Wood is a familiar and poetic substance, which does not sever the child from close contact with the tree, the table, the floor. Wood does not wound or break down; it does not shatter, it wears out, it can last a long time, live with the child, alter little by little the relations between the object and the hand.

In bourgeois society, "whose disease is to think in essences," things are made to stand for values, much as words can be distorted into neologisms that stand for objects. In films a Roman always wears a fringe—hence, his Roman-ness; as for foam, which appears to lack usefulness, "its abundant, easy, almost infinite proliferation" in advertisements signifies the "luxurious" power of a detergent.

In instances of this sort Barthes's intelligent combativeness deciphers the numerous myths that arrest history and give it the appearance of an unchanging Nature. Because he is himself so exacting, and his admiration for the theater of Brecht so thorough, Barthes's tools in his discourse are the italic and the telling epithet, startling emphasis where a disguise had been intended, giving a name to things where what Barthes calls myth's "exnomination," its habit of identifying everything but itself, prevents a name. According to Barthes, myth is an alibi, it celebrates but does not act, it is a sort of depoliticized speech, it is always right-wing, it tends towards proverbs; a mythologist like Barthes is connected with the world by sarcasm, he is condemned to metalanguage, to semioclasm (the destruction, by explicit study, of myths-as-signs).

In *Critical Essays* Barthes's subject-matter is almost exclusively literary, yet his manner is no less semioclastic than it was in *Mythologies.* He gets hold of writers and books in brilliantly clever ways: Voltaire is treated as the last happy writer, Baudelaire and Balzac are discussed in terms of their plays, Tacitus as the writer who made death into a protocol, Kafka as a technique but not as Kafkaism.

Since our world is organized like a language, it follows for Barthes that literature is a particular type of language, but by no means a natural one. In nothing is Barthes's quiet aggressiveness so evident as in his attack upon the myths of humanism, of bourgeois high culture and academic literary criticism, with their reliance upon biography, taste and dogma in the misapprehension of literature as a sort of second-rate life. For him written language is made either by desacralized "authors," whose intention begins and ends in language, or by "writers," who use language to transact another bit of business (to give evidence, to explain, to instruct). Everything writers and authors say, however, involves a dislocation of language, a signification, which cannot be explained by sending us off to an elsewhere—the writer's biography, his "age" or a phoney history—that is comfortably static. Barthes's own program of criticism comes therefore to be based upon an understanding of how it is that the poetic imagination systematically deforms, rather than forms, images.

It is impossible in a short space to do any sort of justice to the enormously graceful complexity of Barthes's work in the second half of *Critical Essays.* His use of structural linguistics and of Marxism, for example, deforms these methods in ways that pay them a very high compliment, even as Barthes himself turns up illuminating readings of classic texts from La Bruyère to Proust. His criticism openly declares its alliance not with the cult of art, but with "the science of writing"—that is, the science of using verbal, spatial or aural objects to signify—represented by

Robbe-Grillet, Mondrian and Boulez. Unlike most Anglo-American critics Barthes is not shy of abstractions, and theory for him is a matter of ideological honesty, never of philosophical cant.

Above all, Barthes represents a unique even ascetic, seriousness. Since literature is language, all language is worthy of study *as language* (for instance, Proust's use of pronouns), all literary language can be interpreted and described and illustrated. Since quite apart from its origins, with which Barthes is not concerned, language takes place in history, then literary art "can and must intervene in history . . . it must contribute to the same goal as the sciences." Whether novelist or critic, every author is also a writer whose work "is not an 'homage' to the truth of the past or to the truth of 'others'—it is a construction of the intelligibility of our own time." That last phrase perfectly characterizes Barthes's work—its invigoration and its order.

Edward W. Said, in a review of "Critical Essays" and "Mythologies," in The New York Times Book Review, *July 30, 1972, pp. 5, 15.*

Paul de Man   (essay date 1972)

[*De Man was a Belgian-born American literary theorist, critic, and educator. His reputation as a pioneer in establishing the literary theory known as "deconstruction"— promoted in such works as* Blindness and Insight: Essays in the Rhetoric of Contemporary Criticism *(1971),* Allegories of Reading: Figural Language in Rousseau, Nietzsche, Rilke, and Proust *(1979), and* The Resistance to Theory *(1986)—was tainted by the discovery of anti-Semitic, pro-Nazi articles he wrote while working for a collaborationist newspaper in Belgium in the early 1940s. In the following essay, posthumously published in 1990, he examines the strengths and weaknesses of Barthes's theoretical positions.*]

Despite the refinements of modern means of communication, the relationship between Anglo-American and continental—especially French—literary criticism remains a star-crossed story, plagued by a variety of cultural gaps and time lags. The French have only just gotten around to translating an essay by Empson, and by the time American works of literary theory or literary criticism appear in Paris they often have lost much of their youthful freshness. There is more good will and curiosity in the other direction, yet here too a mixture of misguided enthusiasm and misplaced suspicion blurs the actual issues. Even some of the most enlightened of English and American critics keep considering their French counterparts with the same suspicion with which English-speaking tourists might approach the café au lait they are being served for breakfast in French Provincial hotels: they know they don't like it but aren't entirely certain whether they are being imposed upon or if, for lack of some ritualistic initiation, they are perhaps missing out on a good thing. Others are willing to swallow French culture whole, from breakfast coffee to Mont Saint Michel and Chartres, but since intellectual fashions change faster than culinary tastes, they may find themselves wearing a beret and drinking

Pernod at a moment when the French avant-garde has long since switched to a diet of cashmere sweaters and cold milk. The *Critical Essays* of Roland Barthes that have just become available in excellent English translations date from 1953 to 1963; *Mythologies* goes back to 1957 and appears in a regrettably abridged version. I cannot help speculating about all the things that could go wrong in the reception of texts that now combine a nostalgic with a genuine but out-of-phase revolutionary quality. Perhaps the most useful function for an American-based view of Roland Barthes may be to try to anticipate unwarranted dismissal as well as misplaced enthusiasm for the aspects of the work with which Barthes himself may no longer be so pleased. Barthes has been introduced to Americans as possibly "the most intelligent man of our time" [to paraphrase Susan Sontag] and any man needs and deserves protection from the expectations raised by such hyperbole.

For despite the emphasis on structure, code, sign, text, reading, intratextual relationships, etc., and despite the proliferation of a technical vocabulary primarily derived from structural linguistics, the actual innovations introduced by Roland Barthes in the analytic study of literary texts are relatively slight. Even in his more technical works, unfortunately not yet available in English, such as *S/Z* (the analysis of a brief narrative text by Balzac), and the various articles on narrative technique published in *Communications,* the contribution to practical criticism is not as extensive as the methodological apparatus would lead one to expect. The work of "pure" structuralists such as the linguist Greimas and his group or of some among Barthes's most gifted associates, such as Gérard Genette or Tzvetan Todorov, is more rigorous and more exhaustive than Barthes's—though it is only fair to point out here its avowed indebtedness to him. Hence the risk of disappointment or overhasty dismissal for the wrong reasons. Barthes is primarily a critic of literary ideology and, as such, his work is more essayistic and reflective than it is technical—perhaps most of all when the claim to methodological precision is most emphatically being stated. The close integration of methodology with ideology is an attractive characteristic of European intellectual life ever since structuralism became a public issue in the sixties— and, for better or worse, French writers on literature are still much closer to being public figures, committed to articulate positions, than their American counterparts. Barthes played an active part in the recent Battles of the Books and his work bears the traces of his involvements. It has to be read and understood as an intellectual adventure rather than as the scientifically motivated development of a methodology. He is at least as interested in the reasons for advocating certain technical devices as in their actual application; hence the polemical, proselytizing tone of many of his essays, hence also the many interviews, pamphlets, position papers, etc. His work should be read within the context of the particular situation within which it is written, that of the ideological demons underlying the practice of literary criticism in France. This situation is idiosyncratically French and cannot be transposed *tel quel* (*c'est le cas de le dire*) to the American situation. It does not follow however that the story of Barthes's intellectual itinerary is without direct interest for American readers.

American criticism is notoriously rich in technical instruments (but much poorer in understanding the rationale for their use); but it is frustrated, as well it might be, in its attempts to relate particular studies and findings to larger historical, semantic, and epistemological questions. That such difficulties exist is by no means a sign of weakness; it only becomes one if the very awareness of the larger context is lost or if the broader inferences of a method are misunderstood. Regardless of its regional peculiarities, the configuration of Barthes's enterprise is of wide enough significance to have paradigmatic value for all students of literature willing to put the premises of their craft into question.

Barthes is primarily a critic of literary ideology and, as such, his work is more essayistic and reflective than it is technical—perhaps most of all when the claim to methodological precision is most emphatically being stated.

—*Paul de Man*

A somewhat euphoric, slightly manic tone runs through Barthes's writings, tempered by considerable irony and discretion but unmistakably braced by the feeling of being on the threshold of major discoveries: "A new anthropology, with unsuspected watersheds of meaning is perhaps being born: the map of human *praxis* is being redrawn, and the form of this enormous modification (but not, of course, its content) cannot fail to remind us of the Renaissance." This statement dates from 1966, but one still finds similar trumpet blasts, only slightly muted, in recent utterances. It is the tone of a man liberated from a constraining past, who has "the earth . . . all before (him)," and who looks about "with a heart / Joyous, not scared at its own liberty." The exact nature of this liberation can best be stated in linguistic terms, in a formula justly borrowed from Barthes himself: it is the liberation of the signifier from the constraints of referential meaning. In all the traditional polarities used throughout the ages to describe the inherent tension that shapes literary language—polarities such as content/form, logos (that which is being said) and lexis (the manner of saying it), meaning/sign, message/code, *langue/parole, signifié/signifiant,* voice/writing (and the sequence could be continued)—the implicit valorization has always privileged the first terms and considered the second as an auxiliary, an adjunct in the service of the former. Language itself, as the sign of a presumably nonlinguistic "content" or "reality," is therefore devalorized as the vehicle or carrier of a meaning to which it refers and that lies outside it; in the polarity man/language, it seems commonsensical enough for us humans to privilege the first term over the second and to rate experience above utterance. Literature is said to "represent" or "express" or at most, "transform" an extralinguistic entity or event which it is the interpreter's (or

critic's) task to reach as a specific unit of meaning. Whatever the shadings used in describing the relationship (and they are infinite), it remains fundamentally best expressed by the metaphor of the *dependence* of language (literary or not) on something in whose *service* it operates. Language acquires dignity only to the extent that it can be said to resemble or to partake of the entity to which it refers. The Copernican revolution heralded by Barthes consists not in turning this model simply around (and thus claiming that, instead of being the slave of meaning, language would now become its master) but in asserting the autonomy of what the linguist Saussure was the first to call the signifier, i. e., the objective properties of the sign independent of their semantic function as code, such as, for example, the redness of a traffic sign as optical event, or the sound of a word as acoustic event. The possibility for the signifier to enter into systems of relationship with other signifiers despite the constraint of the underlying or, if one prefers, over-standing or transcendental, meaning proves that the relationship between sign or word and meaning is not simply one of dependence; it suggests that this metaphorical language of polarized hierarchies and power structures fails to do justice to the delicate complexity of these relationships. The science that sets out to describe the functions and the interrelationships of signifiers (including reference, one among others) is called semiology, the study of signs independent of their particular meanings, in contrast to *semantics,* which operates on the level of meaning itself. Barthes is one of the leading representatives of this science, not so much as its initiator—he is the first to acknowledge his debt to Saussure, Jakobson, Hjelmslev and others—but as one of its most effective advocates.

Why is it that ideas about language leading to the science of semiology acquired such a polemical vigor in the hands of Barthes? They had been around for quite a while, not only in the field of linguistics, but in various philosophies of language and in the formalist schools of literary criticism that dominated the scene in most countries—with the possible exception of France. It is true that the French have a way of taking hold, often belatedly, of other peoples' ideas and suddenly rediscovering them with so much original energy that they are positively re-born; this happened, in recent years, with Hegel, Heidegger, Freud, and Marx and is about to happen now with Nietzsche. In this case however there is more to it than mere Gallic energy. Barthes's deliberate excursion into the realm of ideology is typical of the development summarized under the catchall term of "structuralism" and of all his books, the early ***Mythologies*** is perhaps best suited to illustrate the process I am trying to describe.

Barthes is a born semiologist, endowed with an innate sense for the formal play of linguistic connotations, the kind of eye and mind that notices at once how an advertisement for a brand of spaghetti seduces the onlooker by combining, in the picture of the *red* tomatoes, the *white* spaghetti and the *green* peppers, the three colors of the house of Savoy and of the national Italian flag—thus allowing the potential consumer to taste all that makes Italy Italian in one single bite of canned pasta. He has used this gifted eye not only to scrutinize literature, but social and

> Barthes is a born semiologist, endowed
> with an innate sense for the formal play of
> linguistic connotations.
>
> —*Paul de Man*

cultural facts as well, treating them in the same manner in which a formalistically oriented critic would treat a literary text. *Mythologies,* a book that remains remarkably fresh although the facts it describes belong to the bygone era of pre-Gaullist France in the early fifties, undertakes precisely this kind of semiocritical sociology. The undisputed masters of the genre are Walter Benjamin and Theodor Adorno and, although Barthes was an early exponent of the work of Brecht in France, I doubt that he knew Benjamin or Adorno well when he wrote the *Mythologies.* The common ancestry is nevertheless apparent from reference, in the important concluding essay on history and myth, to Marx's *German Ideology,* the model text for all ideological demystifications.

Almost any of the *Mythologies* can be used to illustrate Barthes's main insight. Take, for instance, the opening essay on catch-as-catch-can wrestling as an example of the contrast between a referential, thematic reading and the free play of signifiers. The point is not that, in the world of catch-as-catch-can, all the fights are rigged; this would not make the event less referential but merely displace the referent from the theme "competition" to that of "deceit." What fascinates Barthes is that actors as well as spectators fully acquiesce to the deceit and that all pretense at open contest has been abandoned, thus voiding the event of content and of meaning. There only remains a series of gestures that can be highly skillful at simulating the drama of competition (the triumph of winning, the abjection of loss, or the drama of peripeteia or reversal) but that exist purely formally, independently of an outcome that is no longer part of the game. Catch is not a game but a *simulacrum,* a fiction; Barthes calls it a "myth."

Myths of this type abound in the fabric of any society. Their attraction is not due to their actual content but to the glitter of their surface, and this glitter in turn owes its brilliance to the gratuity, the lack of semantic responsibility, of the fictional sign. This play is far from innocent. It is in the nature of fictions to be more persuasive than facts, and especially persuasive in seeming more "real" than nature itself. Their order, their coherence, their symmetry is possible because they are accountable only to themselves, yet these are precisely the qualities wistfully associated with the world of nature and necessity. As a result, the most superfluous of gestures are most likely to become the hardest to do without. Their very artificiality endows them with a maximum of natural appeal. Fictions or myths are addictive because they substitute for natural needs by being more natural than the nature they displace. The particular shade of perversity and bad conscience associated with fiction stems from the complicity involved in partial awareness of this ambivalence coupled with an even

stronger desire to resist its exposure. It follows that fictions are the most saleable commodity manufactured by man; an adman's dream of perfect coincidence between description and promotion. Disinterested in themselves, they are the defenseless prey of any interest that wishes to make use of them. When they are thus being enlisted in the service of collective patterns of interest—including interests of the "highest" moral or metaphysical order—fictions become ideologies. One can see that any ideology would always have a vested interest in theories of language advocating the natural correspondence between sign and meaning, since they depend on the illusion of this correspondence for their effectiveness whereas theories that put into question the subservience, resemblance or potential identity between sign and meaning are always subversive, even if they remain strictly confined to linguistic phenomena. Barthes's *Mythologies* are fully aware of this; they bring the subversiveness into the open by exposing the structure of the social myths as well as their manipulation. The political results are clearly visible as *Mythologies* moves from the relatively innocent mystifications of catch-as-catch-can or the Tour de France to consumer goods (e.g., the Citroën DS, steak pommes frites or the singing style of the baritone Gérard Souzay, etc.) to reach finally the domain of the printed word and image as it appears in the movies or in *Paris-Match.* After having been the target of a heavy handed and vicious attack by Raymond Picard, a Sorbonne Professor of French literature whose field of specialization is the life of Racine, Barthes wrote perhaps his best *mythologie* in the first part of the counterattacking pamphlet entitled *Critique et vérité,* in which the ideological infrastructure of French academic criticism is revealed with masterful economy and without an ounce of personal spite.

The demystifying power of semiology is both a source of strength and a danger. It is impossible to be so completely right at the expense of others without some danger to oneself. The perfect convergence between Barthes's social criticism, including the criticism of academic traditionalism, and the means used in accomplishing this highly desirable aim engenders its own mystification, this time on the level of method rather than of substance. The very power of the instrument used creates an overconfidence that generates its own set of counter-questions. In this case, the questions have to do with the claim of having finally grounded the study of literature in foundations epistemologically strong enough to be called scientific. The heady tone alluded to earlier occurs whenever this claim appears on the horizon. It is accountable for some of his most powerful influence. Putting it into question nowise means a desire to turn the clock back—a foolish wish at best, for there can be no return from the demystifying power of semiological analysis. No literary study can avoid going through a severe semiocritical process and there is much to be said for going through these fires with as urbane, surefooted, and entertaining a guide as Roland Barthes. At stake is the status of structuralism, a methodological blueprint for scientific research that, like Rousseau's state of nature, "no longer exists, has perhaps never existed and will probably never come into being" but which we nevertheless cannot do without.

As in Barthes's social myths, the referential, representational effectiveness of literary language is greater than in actual communication because, like his catch-as-catch-can wrestlers, it is so utterly devoid of message. Literature overmeans, as we say of bombs that they overkill. This referential suggestiveness, which accounts for the fact that one responds with stronger emotion to a fictional narrative than to an actual event, is of course illusory and something for which a science of literature (whether we call it stylistics or literary semiology or whatever) should account without being taken in by it. The classical way of dealing with the question is to bypass it, as when Roman Jakobson rightfully asserts that, in literature, the language is autotelic, i.e., "focus[sed] on the message for its own sake" rather than on its content. By getting rid of all the mess and muddle of signification, the formula opens up a heretofore undiscovered world of scientific discourse, covering the entire field of literary syntax, grammar, phonology, prosody, and rhetoric. With the inevitable result, however, that the privileged adequation of sign to meaning that governs the world of fiction is taken as the ideal model towards which all semantic systems are assumed to tend. This model then begins to function as a regulatory norm by means of which all deviations and transformations of a given system are being evaluated. Literature becomes, to borrow a phrase from the title of Barthes's first book, a degree zero of semantic aberration. We know that it owes this privileged position to the bracketing of its referential function, dismissed as contingency or ideology, and not taken seriously as a semantic interference within the semiological structure.

The seduction of the literary model has undoubtedly worked on Barthes, as it has to on all writers endowed with literary sensitivity. Up through *Mythologies* it takes at times rather naive forms, as when, in the concluding essay of that book, literature is held up, in opposition to ideology, as a "transformation of the sign into meaning: its ideal would be . . . to reach, not the meaning of words, but the meaning of the things themselves." More technical versions of the same myth appear in various texts, as when, in an article on names in Proust (whose planned title for the concluding section of his novel is known to have been at some point, "The Age of Things") he speaks of literature as [that which "would be defined by a Cratylian consciousness of signs and the writer would be the mouthpiece of an age-old myth which decrees that language imitates ideas and that, contrary to the specifications of linguistic science, signs are motivated"]. Unqualified assent to such propositions would be an example of misplaced enthusiasm for the most debatable aspect of Barthes's enterprise.

In the manifesto *Critique et vérité* (1966) in which the vocabulary is more transformational than structural, closer to Chomsky than to Jakobson, the position is more complex but not essentially different. It now takes the form of a three-pronged, hierarchized approach to literature in which a distinction is made between literary science, literary criticism, and literary reading. The controlling authority of the first discipline, the only one to be free of the error of semantization and to lay claim to truth, is beyond question. "If one is willing to admit the textual nature of the literary work (and draw the proper conclusions from this knowledge), then a *certain type* of literary science becomes possible. . . . Its model will undoubtedly be linguistic. . . . Literary science will have for its object, not to explain why a certain meaning has to be accepted, nor even why it has been accepted (this being the task of the historians), but why it is acceptable. Not in terms of the philological rules of literary meaning, but in terms of the linguistic rules of symbolic meaning" [de Man's translation]. By emphatically drawing attention to its own methodological apparatus, *S/Z,* Barthes's most systematic piece of literary analysis to date, allows itself to be taken as a first exemplary move in the elaboration of such a science. The impact of this program on literary studies has been and will remain considerable. It will not do to dismiss the methodological claims as a hoax or as ironic window-dressing used by a writer of more traditional literary virtues. We cannot reassure ourselves by stressing the elegance, the sensitivity, the strongly personal, even confessional element that is part of Barthes's distinctive tone and that makes him into one of the "best" writers at work today in any genre, in the most traditional sense of this qualitative epithet. The theoretical challenge is genuine. It has to be taken all the more seriously since the particular quality of Barthes's writing is due to his desire to believe in its theoretical foundations and to repress doubts that would break its stability.

The unresolved question is whether the semantic, reference-oriented function of literature can be considered as contingent or whether it is a constitutive element of all literary language. The auto-telic, nonreferential aspect of literature stressed by Jakobson cannot seriously be contested, but the question remains why it is always again and systematically being overlooked, as if it were a threat that had to be repressed. The first quoted passage from *Critique et vérité* laying down the directives for the literary science of the future is a good example: one can see Barthes fluttering around the question like a moth around a flame, fascinated but backing away in self-defense. All theoretical findings about literature confirm that it can never be reduced to a specific meaning or set of meanings, yet it is always being interpreted reductively as if it were a statement or message. Barthes grants the existence of this pattern of error but denies that it is the object of literary science to account for it; this is said to be the task of historians, thus implying that the reasons for the pattern's existence are not linguistic but ideological. The further implication is that the negative labor of ideological demystification will eventually be able to prevent the distortion that superimposes upon literature a positive, assertive meaning foreign to its actual nature. Barthes has never renounced this hope; in a recent interview, despite many nuances and reservations, he still talks about "the ultimate transparency of social relationships" as the goal of the critical enterprise. Yet, in the meantime, his methodological postulates have begun to erode under the impact of the question which he delegated to other, more empirical disciplines.

That literature can be ideologically manipulated is obvious but doesn't suffice to prove that this distortion is not a particular aspect of a larger pattern of error. Sooner or later, any literary study, no matter how rigorously and legitimately formalistic it may be, must return to the problem of interpretation, no longer in the naive conviction of a priority of content over form, but as a consequence of the much more unsettling experience of being unable to cleanse its own discourse of aberrantly referential implications. The traditional concept of reading used by Barthes and based on the model of an encoding/decoding process becomes inoperative if the original master code remains out of reach of the operator, who then becomes unable to understand his own discourse. A science unable to read itself can no longer be called a science. The possibility of a scientific semiology is challenged by a problem that can no longer be accounted for in purely semiological terms.

This challenge reached Barthes from the somewhat unexpected quarters of philosophy, a discipline that earlier structuralists had dismissed in favor of the so-called sciences of man: psychology, anthropology, and linguistics considered as a social science. This dismissal proved to be premature, based as it was on an inadequate evaluation of the specifically philosophical ability to put the foundations of philosophy into question, in a self-destructive manner that no science could ever dare to emulate. The work of Michel Foucault and especially of Jacques Derrida—whose determining impact on literary theory is confirmed by the recently published book *La Dissémination*—thematizes the problem of linguistic delusion in a manner which semiological critics of Barthes's persuasion cannot afford to ignore, all the more since it reveals that the challenge had never ceased to be present in a philosophical and literary activity that structuralists tried to ignore. One thinks of certain recurrent misreadings of Rousseau's, Hegel's, and especially Nietzsche's (as well as Heidegger's) attitude towards literature and also of Barthes's cryptic remark during a recent discussion that "A criticism of Lautréamont, for example, is probably not possible," a remark that could be read as an abdication of semiology when it confronts the language of poetry.

Barthes's intellectual integrity is apparent in his reaction to this philosophical challenge. For the moment, it has taken the form of a retreat from the methodological optimism that still inspired *S/Z.* More recent theoretical papers (not other recent books such as *L'Empire des signes,* inspired by a trip to Japan, or *Sade, Fourier, Loyola,* in which the semiological euphoria is allowed to reign undisturbed) sketch out a much less ambitious program that sounds like a return to a pragmatic collecting of literary data, and are sharply aware of the inability of semiology to account for the stylistic tension between written and spoken language. One of these papers available in English translation invites us to embark on "the search for models, of patterns: sentence structures, syntagmatic clichés, divisions and *clausulae* of sentences; and what would inspire such work is the conviction that style is essentially a citational process, a body of formulae, a memory (almost in the cybernetic sense of the word), a cultural and not an expressive inheritance. . . . These models are only the depositories of culture (even if they seem very old). They are repetitions, not essential elements; citations, not expressions; stereotypes, not archetypes." Traces of the reading of Derrida, Gilles Deleuze, Foucault (and perhaps also of the Columbia-based stylist, Michael Riffaterre) are noticeable in these sentences. They cannot however represent a definitive position. The mind cannot remain at rest in a mere repertorization of its own recurrent aberrations; it is bound to systematize its own negative self-insight into categories that have at least the appearance of passion, novelty, and difference. There is every reason to suppose that Barthes's future work will participate in this development as he participated in the development that led up to it. The avant-garde review *Tel Quel,* whose attitude toward orthodox structuralism has always been healthily uncomplacent, recently devoted an entire issue to Roland Barthes, thus creating the misleading impression that they were trying to erect a monument of a man who is about as monumental as a Cheshire cat. I doubt that *Tel Quel* was trying to kick Barthes upstairs into some kind of Pantheon of unchanging forms; whoever assumes this to be possible would seriously misjudge the resilience of one of the most agile and resourceful minds in the field of literary and linguistic studies.

As far as American criticism is concerned, its reaction to Barthes is not yet clear. The recent translations are a useful but still inadequate first step in introducing his work into English. The *Critical Essays,* mostly prefaces written for commercial editions, stem from the period that precedes the development of semiology—roughly 1963—and are mostly interesting in showing Barthes's discontent with the prevailing methods of literary study during the fifties in France, and his delight at discovering the new perspective opened by his readings in linguistics. They create the somewhat misleading impression that his main interests are confined to the theater of Brecht and to the novels of Robbe-Grillet and they should certainly not be taken as a fair sample of his accomplishments. There is more semiological finesse to be gathered from the *Mythologies,* including several not included in this selection, than from the *Critical Essays.* How the availability of his more important theoretical books (*On Racine, Critique et vérité, S/Z,* various theoretical papers) might influence American criticism can be inferred from the reactions of some American specialists who are familiar with his work and show a fundamental resistance. In a recent essay entitled "On Defining Form," even as knowledgeable a scholar as Seymour Chatman, who has already done a good deal in bringing together continental and American studies of literature, takes Barthes to task for putting the referential function of literary language into question: "It is difficult to understand," he writes, "why one should deny that there are, ultimately, contents or *signifiés* referred to. . . . The content of a literary work is not the language but what the language stands for, its reference. . . . The language is a mediating form between the *literary* form (structure-texture) and the ultimate content." Barthes's point never was that literature had no referential function but that no "ultimate" referent could ever be reached and that therefore the rationality of the critical metalanguage is constantly threatened and problematic. I have suggested that Barthes was being all too hopeful in having believed, for a while, that the threat could be ignored or delegated to historians. At least, the scientific self-assurance thus gained is productive and has a negative validity, as far as it goes—and now that it seems to know its horizons, it remains a necessary fact of any critical education. To return to an unproblematic notion of signification is to take two steps backward, a step backward into a pseudo-science in a domain in which no science is possible, and a step backward into a pseudo-science that, unlike Barthes's semiology, is too remote from its object to be demystified by it. As long as the "libération du signifiant" is being resisted for the wrong reasons, Barthes's criticism will have little to teach American students of literature.

Paul de Man, "Roland Barthes and the Limits of Structuralism," in Yale French Studies, *No. 77, 1990, pp. 177-90.*

Frank Kermode   (review date 7 August 1977)

[*Kermode is an English critic and educator. In the following review, he praises the autobiography* Roland Barthes *and discusses the many paradoxes that define Barthes's literary career.*]

[**Roland Barthes**] is a sort of serious joke. It first appeared in a series called *x par lui-même*—for example, *Michelet by Himself,* to name the volume for which Barthes happens to have been responsible. So to ask a writer to do his own "par lui-même" was part compliment, part gag, and Barthes followed up by reviewing the book himself in the Quinzaine litteraire, under the heading " 'Barthes by Barthes' by Barthes." But the joke is serious because there is more to it than literary frivolity or once-off publicity value. Asking Barthes to do something so close to autobiography is no light challenge; for to anybody holding his views on writing (and this remains true however they change) autobiography ought to be anathema. Consequently the book is partly about the problem he must have in writing it and partly about other and related problems such as the difference between what, as a writer, he thinks ought to be done and what in fact he does.

Barthes is an extraordinary virtuoso though people who read him in English—a language, incidentally, in which he takes very little interest—may be skeptical about this remark. It remains true. Highly original, extremely fertile and inventive, he really does represent, in a peculiarly qualified way, a new kind of writing, and he continually discovers new ways of writing about writing. He is not a philosopher, not a linguist, not a poet, not a novelist and even not an essayist. His ideal "text" is not controlled by an author at all. He "dreams of a world which would be *exempt from meaning* (as one is from military service)," and the ideal text would also be without meaning and without style. Yet he is, and knows he is, a conscious stylist and heavy with meanings.

His work is therefore full of paradoxes (though the very idea of an author's Work is of course as intolerable, theoretically, as the idea of an author). That shelf of books constitutes a potent, old-fashioned, presiding personality, even as the books themselves disown the notion. Always looking for the totally unstructured text, he himself is always concerned to communicate. "I write classic," he admits. "I am on the side of structure . . . ." He is, of course, well aware—comfortably, I think, not painfully—of these contradictions. His prose, however brilliant, is somehow professorial. The voice of so many *avant-gardes*

is carefully modulated, full of the tones of the past. "At best," I once heard him say, "I am the *arrière-garde* of the *avant-garde.*" He admires texts most which are uncoded, free of inherited notions of structure—they offer more opportunities for perversity, fetishism, that orgasmic reading experience he calls *jouissance*. But he moves most easily among the "classic" texts which offer the duller, more continuous, more orderly rewards of simple *plaisir*.

To write an autobiography is to risk conformity with structural stereotypes, and he takes steps to avoid this. The book opens with a series of photographs, adorned with wry or gnomic comments: an "image-repertoire." The child Barthes: his town, his house, his garden, his parents, the father killed in 1916 before he was a year old; Barthes as student, as a heavier, older man; as left-handed. After that, apart from a brief chronology of his life, there is only a series of discontinuous passages of meditation and reflection, arranged in roughly alphabetical order. They are said to constitute a text which "in substance is . . . totally fictive." There are some allusions to his life, especially to the tuberculosis which plagued him till he was past 30. The most vivid of these is an account of how he disposed of a piece of his own rib, presented to him by the surgeons after a pneumothorax operation. But mostly he meditates on the shifts and contradictions of his own work.

He begins (against his will) to find patterns, consistencies. He is always at war with unreflecting public assumptions about the world, *Doxa* being his name for that enemy. And he sees his own strategy. "To free myself of it I postulate a paradox; then this paradox turns bad, becomes a new concretion, itself becomes a new *Doxa,* and I must seek further for a new paradox." He sees himself as starting from the stereotype, from the banal opinion he himself holds, and moving away from it by paradox; so his work is always dependent on the prevalence of the hated *Doxa.* Carrying out this process in the present book of fragments, he sees a danger—that in writing aphorisms or maxims he is creating the kind of lie that *Doxa* consists of, the lie of the "classical ideology": "actually it's always like that." Yet the assemblage of maxims, fragmentary, clashing, structureless, makes up a new thing. As it grows, it determines its own structure without his planning it: "it constructs for itself . . . a repertoire which is both finite and perpetual, like that of a language."

> **Most of Barthes's work, as he says, has been done under the influence of some great system—Marx, Sartre, Brecht, semiology. Now he thinks he has emerged from those shadows.**
>
> **—Frank Kermode**

Or so he hopes; there are constraints, but they leave him free. Most of his work, as he says, has been done under the influence of some great system—Marx, Sartre, Brecht, semiology. Now he thinks he has emerged from those shadows. He is free but feels his insecurity, and the danger that he will replace them by some "image-system" founded on psychological self-scrutiny. And he remembers the radical paradoxes of his writing practice: there should be no author, no manipulation of the reader; yet he manipulates his reader. There should be no style, yet his style is extremely personal; he comments upon his "etymological delirium," and indeed he has probably made up more new French words from Greek roots than any other Frenchman.

Barthes likes the story of the ship *Argo,* which over the years was entirely renewed, piece by piece, so that nothing of the original remained, though it was the same ship. This proves the superiority of the system over its constituent parts. Yet it is unavoidable that he should see *himself* as such a system; he remakes himself in book after book, yet is recognizably the same structure. Whole sections of his hull have been removed and replaced with material borrowed from, say Lacan; but it is the same ship, and the design is somehow still, in all its inventiveness, classical.

The privilege granted the reader of this book is to watch Barthes contemplating his own paradoxes, or contemplating himself contemplating them. It has to be read slowly. Some parts of it will rightly be judged to be dull, affected or obscure. On the whole it is very striking. But it is not the best testimony to the elegance and severity of Barthes's mind and the range of his intellectual achievement. The insights of *Mythologies,* the theoretical work in semiology, the work on textual analysis, the splendid . . . manifesto *Critique et Verité,* the dazzling meditations of *Pleasure of the Text*—these are the primary works. So it seems ignorant to claim, as somebody does on the book jacket, that this is Barthes's finest achievement. Nevertheless it is a remarkable book, out of the reach of any other living . . . critic? essayist? autobiographer? writer? Some or all of these: not the insubstantial ghost, the *scriptor,* with whom Barthes says he would like to replace them.

Frank Kermode, "Captured by Meanings," in The New York Times Book Review, *August 7, 1977, pp. 13, 28.*

Geoffrey H. Hartman   (essay date 4 February 1979)

[*Hartman is an American critic and educator. In the following essay, he discusses* Image—Music—Text, A Lover's Discourse, *and Barthes's attempt to construct a unique critical style out of "fictional and systematic forms of learning."*]

These are still the Banquet Years in France, though not everyone will savor the feast of books and essays produced there since 1945. One might have thought that Jean-Paul Sartre, Claude Lévi-Strauss and Maurice Merleau-Ponty had exhausted a certain vein. Philosophy and literature invaded each other's realm; science mingled with cultural criticism. Yet Jacques Derrida, Michel Foucault, Roland Barthes and others are still taking on linguistics, semiotics, structuralism, sociology and psychoanalysis. New and fantastic words appear on the scene to express this

mixture of disciplines: "economimesis," "anasematics," "mimology." It is a heady period of scribbledihobble.

Barthes is a fine pedagogical writer in whom toughness of intellect and a remarkable erudition have not killed readability and charm. He actually enjoys doing criticism.

—*Geoffrey H. Hartman*

There is a danger to literature in this Parisian plenty, for it loses part of its privilege. Literature is seen as one kind of "inscription" or sign system among others. Semiology, the study of signs, nourishes this tendency; and Roland Barthes, its most protean and engaging prophet, is as interested in the culture industry, fashion and popular art as in such classic writers as Racine and Balzac. He is himself rapidly becoming an institution, having received the accolade of the Modern Language Association and of Susan Sontag. Sixty thousand copies of the French version of *A Lover's Discourse* are said to have been sold in a little over a year. Ten of his books are now available in English and he's beginning to have a gurulike influence.

What lies behind his success? Quite simply, he's a fine pedagogical writer in whom toughness of intellect and a remarkable erudition have not killed readability and charm. He actually enjoys doing criticism. It does not seem to him a secondary or subordinated sort of work. We are allowed to see his mind thinking, tussling with metaphors, throwing off aphorisms, constructing and deconstructing systems. More of a scout than a pioneer, he brings essential news from the frontier; but his real importance, I think, might be in doubt were it not for his love of literature, constantly threatened but never overcome by ideological and scientific modes of thought. His passion for science stops short of wishing to substitute a more positive knowledge for what he has labeled "the pleasure of the text."

The dominant perspective of the 13 essays collected in *Image/Music/Text* is semiology. Barthes extends the "empire of signs" over film and photography, music criticism, biblical narrative, the Bunraku puppet theater, and writing and reading as historically situated activities. Several essays, like the early **"The Photographic Image"** and the famous **"Introduction to the Structural Analysis of Narrative"** are frankly didactic. They review and expand the domain of a certain terminology: interpretive codes, narrational systems, functions and indices, denotation and connotation. Yet those impatient with special terms will not mind too much, for where else do they get, under the same cover, Beethoven and *Goldfinger,* the Bible and *Double Bang à Bangkok?* Besides, as the insights come fast, the terminology has to show athletic prowess in ordering them.

Barthes is perhaps most interesting when he focuses on the fate of reading in a modern technological culture. What makes a reader active rather than passive, a producer rather than a consumer? We see that semiology can be a weapon as well as a science, for it helps Barthes to demystify the realism of media that penetrate life more deeply than we have time to observe. Any medium that, like photography, pretends to give a direct image of reality hides its encoded and manipulative character. Nowhere else, Barthes remarks, "does connotation assume so completely the 'objective' mask of denotation." His careful analysis, revealing the coded structure, builds a resistance to those who fabricate "reality."

If Barthes's interest in mental hygiene seems familiar, it is because of our acquaintance with the New Criticism, which attempted to preserve culture in the 1930's by stressing the intellectual probity of artifacts as compared to political messages. It overemphasized, however, the independence of literature from what Saussure, the founder of semiology, named "the life of signs within society." Barthes shares with Kenneth Burke a refusal to exalt art at the expense of other cultural activities, while still rejecting vulgar sociology. There is an oblique or even gratuitous element in all sign systems, which the thinker can extend but not purge. Barthes writes of "a kind of voluptuous pleasure in inserting, like a perfumed dream, into a sociological analysis, 'wild cherries, cinnamon, vanilla and sherry, Canadian tea, lavender, bananas.' "

"Unfortunately," Barthes adds, "I am condemned to assertion"; and he attributes the fault to the lack, in French, perhaps in all languages, of "a grammatical mode which would speak *lightly*" of important matters. Must every philosopher be high-serious in style? Is there not a teacherly frivolity? The scruple does Barthes honor, and of all recent French thinkers he has the least German philosophy in him, no Hegel or Heidegger to perplex the mind, no Teutonic straining. He is technical without being heavy, and a professional without ceasing to be an amateur. His precise yet fluent prose treats personal insight and systematic concepts with equal courtesy: as different vocabularies to be matched rather than as dialectical contradictions. This makes him hard to type intellectually. He is a man of roles rather than of allegiances (some affinity with Gide in this); what he is producing is not so much an *oeuvre* as a series of texts or at best a *Roman de Roland.*

Yet when he does enter the realm of theory, he is indeed assertive. "Writing is the destruction of every voice, of every point of origin," he proclaims in **"The Death of the Author,"** published close to the revolutionary turmoil of May 1968, and included in *Image/Music/Text.* This concept of writing, which he opposes to the idea of original genius, is elaborated into a theory—better, a vision—of literary history. Genius implies individuality. It is related to our image of the author as one who has a real and potent self that is the source of his creative talent. According to Barthes, however, writing always works against stability of self or any fixed meaning. As he puts it, literature "disseminates" (a fertility metaphor) rather than establishes truth. He introduces the word "scriptor" to make his point that, at least in the modern period, literature does not create something original and stable but rather a

"multi-dimensional space in which a variety of writings, none of them original, blend and clash."

To some extent this re-envisioning of author as scriptor returns us to a medieval notion of the anonymous scribal artist. To locate the scriptor only in the modern period is obviously a myth; but the important thing for Barthes is that through this notion of scriptor we come to reinterpret all art, not only modern works. He wants to purge from criticism the Romantic idea of a personal genius writing a personal book that only he was capable of producing. Barthes proposes a belated and desperate theory of impersonality.

Already a century ago, Matthew Arnold denounced the "French mania" for translating ideas into a revolutionary program. The Anglo-Saxon reserve in matters of theory has something to do with the assertiveness of theory. (Compare Barthes's propaganda for a radical change in our perception of past works of art with T. S. Eliot's laconic statement of 1919 that a new work of art changes the "order" of all existing works.) Where we confine ourselves to "practical criticism," Barthes summons us toward an "unknown *praxis,*" a form of reading that could match the blending and clashing energy of what he calls the disseminative text.

Like most French intellectuals, of course, Barthes is under constant ideological pressure, and especially that of responding to Marxism and allied forms of social critique. By his sponsorship of structuralism, and more recently of semiotics, as well as his special theory of impersonality, he seeks to reconstruct poetics in the midst of politics—a very broad poetics that includes narrative and symbol formation of all kinds. Gide could flaunt the gratuitousness by which art escapes social constraints; Barthes must justify it. He accepts the analogy of art to work or to a mode of production; also of writers to workers that produce meaning. But the obliquity of signs and the impersonal energy of literature show that art is productive precisely because it is plural and escapes ownership by any one person (even the author) or social group. If ownership is anywhere, it is with readers.

All art aspires to the condition of music, as Walter Pater said; and rarely has a translation caught, like Richard Howard's, the musical genius of its original. *A Lover's Discourse* is a Passion narrative or recitative broken curiously into dictionary headings: from *"s'abymer/*to be engulfed" to *"vouloir-saisir/*will-to-possess."

The dictionary form, a cool and unrhetorical mode of presentation, lets us know at once that there is nothing private or confessional here. More important, it suggests that the lover, too, is not an original genius but rather an exploiter of received ideas and stock phrases. The lover acts the part of the lover. Convention prescribes his role; the arts supply his feelings and words. His anguish is non-attainment, but in the sense that he cannot bypass convention to realize his desire by more direct means. He is forced to magnify sign or fetish, token or trace, the loved one's "absence," which is the only "presence." In short, his desire—even when realized—remains unreal. Barthes associates this pattern, enacted so many times since Petrarch, with semiotic process. The ego on love's stage is a passionate machine: a restless producer and consumer of signs.

Like most French intellectuals Barthes is under constant ideological pressure, and especially that of responding to Marxism and allied forms of social critique.

—Geoffrey H. Hartman

No distinction is made between a man's and a woman's discourse. Barthes remains a structuralist who will not give up his search for universals even if they prove to be as arbitrary as linguistic forms. Language rather than anatomy is fate. How much evasion is there in this slighting of sexual difference? The "dazzling" of love, as Stendhal calls it with a nice lapse into English, is diminished in my mind by Barthes's indifference to sexual difference.

Yet Barthes is profound in showing that while the unstable and voluble sign is love's very element, it achieves exceptional permanence in the structures we call texts. The writings of Plato, Proust, Balzac, Boehme, Winnicott, Lacan, Schubert, Goethe—and more! —feed a meditation that also embraces conventional exchanges ("I-love-you/So-do-I") and anonymous fragments of inner colloquy. All these orders of discourse blend into a single musical mélange. And though the word "discourse" (as in the title) seems odd—it suggests a highly analytic writing purged of figure and fable—Barthes is clearly seeking to invest analysis with a music of its own. The beast of "discourse" is to be made beautiful.

Hence only the pleasure of the text is felt in this text about pleasure. Here is how Barthes describes what goes on between lovers: "Nothing but signs, a frenzied activity of language: to institute, on each furtive occasion, the system (the paradigm) of demand and response." Is this how a lover would perceive or speak his passion? Surely Barthes's language is a stylized, uncolloquial product, made up of technical expressions and exegetical *pensées*. His erotics of semiotics approaches at times the diction of the *précieuses* ridiculed by Molière.

Yet Barthes persists in his folly, and succeeds. Not only does the influence of the fortuitous and the trivial emerge hauntingly in love, but by refusing the novelist's way of dealing with the power of trifles—the way, essentially, of "Romantic irony"—Barthes rethinks Racine, Valéry and the Neo-Classical tradition. The discretion and minimalism of signs is a "Classic" virtue, and what is signified recedes, as in periphrasis, until it approaches a second muteness. "With my language I can do everything," we read in *A Lover's Discourse,* "even and especially *say nothing.*"

Barthes, like Flaubert, writes that "nothing." Whether our language is veiled, as in the Classic manner, or exhibi-

tionistic as in the modern, we confront, says Barthes, "the *muck* of language: that region of hysteria where language is both *too much* and *too little.*" So Barthes's own style shuttles between too much and too little, between operatic and Classic.

In this book then, the "discourse of an Amateur," as Richard Blackmur called criticism, seeks to become "amorous discourse." Barthes as critic, semiotician, master of metalanguage, constructs an elegant confection out of his struggle with both fictional and systematic forms of learning. From these, by a recycling that literature is always meditating, he draws a new "primary" language. Jacques Derrida in *Glas* (1974) and Norman O. Brown in *Love's Body* (1966) accomplish, in very different ways, a similar feat. Is criticism finding its own style at last? Or recovering a formal possibility that is, in truth, very old? To make criticism creative, to reconcile learning with the language of love, inspired one of the first essays of the vernacular muse in the Renaissance, appropriately entitled by Dante "La Vita Nuova."

Geoffrey H. Hartman, "Signs and Symbols," in The New York Times Book Review, *February 4, 1979, pp. 12-13, 34-5.*

Susan Sontag   (essay date 15 May 1980)

[*Sontag is a distinguished American critic, essayist, and novelist. In the following essay, occasioned by Barthes's death, she reviews his life as a writer and singles out* A Lover's Discourse: Fragments *and* Roland Barthes *as "his most wonderful books."*]

Roland Barthes was sixty-four when he died last week [26 March 1980], but the career was younger than that age suggests, for he was thirty-seven when he published his first book. After the tardy start there were many books, many subjects. One felt that he could generate ideas about anything. Put him in front of a cigar box and he would have one, two, many ideas—a little essay. It was not a question of knowledge (he couldn't have known much about some of the subjects he wrote about) but of alertness, a fastidious transcription of what *could* be thought about something, once it swam into the stream of attention. There was always some fine net of classification into which the phenomenon could be tipped.

In his youth he acted a bit in a provincial avant-garde theater company, reviewed plays. And something of the theater, a profound love of appearances, colors his work when he began to exercise, at full strength, his vocation as a writer. His sense of ideas was dramaturgical: an idea was always in competition with another idea. Launching himself onto the inbred French intellectual stage, he took up arms against the traditional enemy: what Flaubert called "received ideas," and came to be known as the "bourgeois" mentality; what Marxists excoriated with the notion of false consciousness and Sartreians with bad faith; what Barthes, who had a degree in classics, was to label *doxa* (current opinion).

He started off in the postwar years, in the shadow of

> All Barthes's writings are polemical. But
> the deepest impulse of his temperament
> was not combative. It was celebratory.
>
> —*Susan Sontag*

Sartre's moralistic questions, with manifestos about what literature is (*Writing Degree Zero*) and witty portraits of the idols of the bourgeois tribe (the articles collected in *Mythologies*). All his writings are polemical. But the deepest impulse of his temperament was not combative. It was celebratory. His debunking forays, which presumed the readiness to be made indignant by inanity, obtuseness, hypocrisy—these gradually subsided. He was more interested in bestowing praise, sharing his passions. He was a taxonomist of jubilation, and of the mind's earnest play.

What fascinated him were mental classifications. Hence, his outrageous book *Sade, Fourier, Loyola,* which, juxtaposing the three as intrepid champions of fantasy, obsessed classifiers of their own obsessions, obliterates all the issues of substance which make them *not* comparable. He was not a modernist in his tastes (despite his tendentious sponsorship of such avatars of literary modernism in Paris as Robbe-Grillet and Philippe Sollers), but he was a modernist in his practice. That is, he was irresponsible, playful, formalist—making literature in the act of talking about it. What stimulated him in a work was what it defended, and its systems of outrage. He was conscientiously interested in the perverse (he held the old-fashioned view that it was liberating).

Everything he wrote was interesting—vivacious, rapid, dense, *pointed.* Most of his books are collections of essays. (Among the exceptions is an early polemical book on Racine. A book of uncharacteristic length and explicitness on the semiology of fashion advertising, which he wrote to pay his academic dues, had the stuff of several virtuoso essays.) He produced nothing that could be called juvenilia; the elegant, exacting voice was there from the beginning. But the rhythm accelerated in the last decade, with a new book appearing every year or two. The thought had greater velocity. In his recent books, the essay form itself had splintered—perforating the essayist's reticence about the "I." The writing took on the freedoms and risks of the notebook. In *S/Z,* he reinvented a Balzac novella in the form of a doggedly ingenious textual gloss. There were the dazzling Borgesian appendices to *Sade, Fourier, Loyola*; the para-fictional pyrotechnics of the exchanges between text and photographs, between text and semi-obscured references in his autobiographical writings; the celebrations of illusion in his last book, on photography, published two months ago.

He was especially sensitive to the fascination exerted by that poignant notation, the photograph. Of the photographs he chose for *Roland Barthes by Roland Barthes,* perhaps the most moving shows an oversized child, Barthes at ten, being carried by, clinging to, his young mother (he titled it "asking for love"). He had an amorous relation to reality—and to writing, which for him were the same. He wrote about everything; besieged with requests to write occasional pieces, he accepted as many as he could; he wanted to be, and was often, seduced by a subject. (His subject became, more and more, seduction.) Like all writers, he complained of being overworked, of acceding to too many requests, of falling behind—but he was in fact one of the most disciplined, surest, most appetitive writers I've known. He found the time to give many eloquent, intellectually inventive interviews.

As a reader he was meticulous but not voracious. Almost everything he read he wrote about, so one could surmise that if he didn't write about it, he probably hadn't read it. He was as uncosmopolitan as most French intellectuals have been (an exception was his beloved Gide). He knew no foreign language well and had read little foreign literature, even in translation. The only foreign literature that seems to have touched him was German: Brecht was an early, potent enthusiasm; recently the sorrow discreetly recounted in *A Lover's Discourse* had led him to *The Sorrows of Young Werther* and to lieder. He was not curious enough to let his reading interfere with his writing.

He enjoyed being famous, with an ingenuous ever-renewed pleasure: in France one saw him often on television in recent years, and *A Lover's Discourse* was a best seller. And yet he spoke of how eerie it was to find his name every time he leafed through a magazine or newspaper. His sense of privacy was expressed exhibitionistically. Writing about himself, he often used the third person, as if he treated himself as a fiction. The later work contains much fastidious self-revelation, but always in a speculative form (no anecdote about the self which does not come bearing an idea between its teeth), and dainty meditation on the personal; the last article he published was about keeping a journal. All his work is an immensely complex enterprise of self-description.

Nothing escaped the attention of this devout, ingenious student of himself: the food, colors, odors he fancied; how he read. Studious readers, he once observed in a lecture in Paris, fall into two groups: those who underline their books and those who don't. He said that he belonged to the second group: he never made a mark in the book about which he planned to write but transcribed key excerpts onto cards. I have forgotten the theory he then confected about this preference, so I shall improvise my own. I connect his aversion to marking up books with the fact that he drew, and that this drawing, which he pursued seriously, was a kind of writing. The visual art that attracted him came from language, was indeed a variant of writing; he wrote essays on Erté's alphabet formed with human figures, on the calligraphic painting of Réquichot, of Twombly. His preference recalls that dead metaphor, a "body" of work—one does not usually write on a body one loves.

His temperamental dislike for the moralistic became more overt in recent years. After several decades' worth of dutiful adherence to right-minded (that is, left-wing) stands, the aesthete came out of the closet in 1974 when with some close friends and literary allies, all Maoists of the moment,

> After several decades' worth of dutiful adherence to right-minded (that is, left-wing) stands, the aesthete came out of the closet in 1974. Barthes's work, along with that of Wilde and Valéry, gives being an aesthete a good name.
>
> *—Susan Sontag*

he went to China; in the scant three pages he wrote on his return, he said that he had been unimpressed by the moralizing and bored by the asexuality and the cultural uniformity. Barthes's work, along with that of Wilde and Valéry, gives being an aesthete a good name. Much of his recent writing is a celebration of the intelligence of the senses, and of the texts of sensation. Defending the senses, he never betrayed the mind. Barthes did not entertain any Romantic clichés about the opposition between sensual and mental alertness.

The work is about sadness overcome or denied. He had decided that everything could be treated as a system—a discourse, a set of classifications. Since everything was a system, everything could be overcome. But eventually he wearied of systems. His mind was too nimble, too ambitious, too drawn to risk. He seemed more anxious and vulnerable in recent years, as he became more productive than ever. He had always, as he observed about himself, "worked successively under the aegis of a great system (Marx, Sartre, Brecht, semiology, the Text). Today it seems to him that he writes more openly, more unprotectedly. . . ." He purged himself of the masters and master-ideas from which he drew sustenance ("In order to speak one must seek support from other texts," he explained), only to stand in the shadow of himself. He became his own Great Writer. He was in assiduous attendance at the sessions of a seven-day conference devoted to his work in 1977—commenting, mildly interjecting, enjoying himself. He published a review of his speculative book on himself (Barthes on Barthes on Barthes). He became the shepherd of the flock of himself.

Vague torments, a feeling of insecurity, were acknowledged—with the consoling implication that he was on the edge of a great adventure. When he was in New York a year and a half ago he avowed in public, with almost tremulous bravery, his intention to write a novel. Not the novel one might expect from the critic who made Robbe-Grillet seem for a while a central figure in contemporary letters; from the writer whose most wonderful books—**Roland Barthes by Roland Barthes** and **A Lover's Discourse**—are themselves triumphs of modernist fiction in that tradition inaugurated by Rilke's *The Notebooks of Malte Laurids Brigge,* which crossbreeds fiction, essayistic speculation, and autobiography, in a linear-notebook rather than a linear-narrative form. No, not a modernist novel, but a "real" one, he said. Like Proust.

Privately he spoke of his longing to climb down from the academic summit—he'd held a chair at the Collège de France since 1977—in order to devote himself to this novel, and of his anxiety (on the face of it, unwarranted) about material security should he resign his teaching position. The death of his mother two years ago was a great blow. He recalled that it was only after Proust's mother died that Proust was able to begin *A la Recherche du temps perdu.* It was characteristic that he hoped to find a source of strength in his devastating grief.

As sometimes he wrote about himself in the third person he usually spoke of himself as without age, and alluded to his future as if he were a much younger man, which in a way he was. He yearned for greatness, yet felt himself to be (as he says in **Roland Barthes by Roland Barthes**) always in danger of "*recession* toward the minor thing, the old thing he is when 'left to himself.' " There was something reminiscent of Henry James about his temperament and the indefatigable subtlety of his mind. The dramaturgy of ideas yielded to the dramaturgy of feeling; his deepest interests were in things almost ineffable. His ambition had something of the Jamesian pathos, as did his self-doubts. If he could have written a great novel, one imagines it more like late James than like Proust.

It was hard to tell his age. Rather, he seemed to have no age—appropriately, his life's chronology being askew. Though he spent much time with young people, he never affected anything of youth or its contemporary informalities. But he didn't seem to be old, though his movements were slow, his dress professorial. It was a body that knew how to rest: as Garcìa Marquez has observed, a writer must know how to rest. He was very industrious, yet also sybaritic. He had an intense but businesslike concern that he receive a regular ration of pleasure. He had been ill (tubercular) for many years when he was young, and one had the impression that he came into his body relatively late—as he did his mind, his productivity. He had sensual revelations abroad (Morocco, Japan); gradually, somewhat tardily he assumed the considerable sexual privileges that a man of his sexual tastes and great celebrity can command. There was something childlike about him, in the wistfulness, in the plump body and soft voice and beautiful skin, in the self-absorption. He liked to linger in cafés with students; he wanted to be taken to bars and discos—but, sexual transactions aside, his interest in you tended to be your interest in him. ("Ah, Susan. Toujours fidèle," were the words with which he greeted me, affectionately, when we last saw each other. I was, I am.)

He affirmed something childlike in his insistence, which he shared with Borges, that reading is a form of happiness, a form of joy. There was also something less than innocent about the claim, the hard edge of adult sexual clamorousness. With his boundless capacity for self-referring, he enrolled the invention of sense in the search for pleasure. The two were identified: reading as *jouissance* (the French word for joy that also means coming); the pleasure of the text. This too was typical. He was, as a voluptuary of the mind, a great reconciler. He had little feeling for the tragic. He was always finding the advantage of a disadvantage. Though he sounds many of the perennial themes of the modern culture critic, he was anything but catastrophe-minded. His work offers no visions of last judgments, civilization's doom, the inevitability of barbarism. It is not even elegiac. Old-fashioned in many of his tastes, he felt nostalgic for the decorum and the literacy of an older bourgeois order. But he found much that reconciled him to the modern.

He was extremely courteous, a bit unworldly, resilient—he detested violence. He had beautiful eyes, which are always sad eyes. There was something sad in all this talk about pleasure; *A Lover's Discourse* is a very sad book. But he had known ecstasy and wanted to celebrate it. He was a great lover of life (and denier of death); the purpose of his unwritten novel, he said, was to praise life, to express gratitude for being alive. In the serious business of pleasure, in the splendid play of his mind, there was always that undercurrent of pathos—now made more acute by his premature, mortifying death.

Susan Sontag, "Remembering Barthes," in her Under the Sign of Saturn, *Farrar, Straus and Giroux, Inc., 1980, pp. 169-80.*

Kaja Silverman   (essay date 1983)

[*Silverman is an American critic and educator best known for her books* The Subject of Semiotics *(1983) and* The Acoustic Mirror: The Female Voice in Psychoanalysis and the Cinema *(1988). In the following excerpt from the former work, which also includes a chapter-length analysis of* S/Z, *she examines Barthes's notion of connotation, showing how it evolved from an early formulation in* Mythologies *to its complex articulation in* S/Z.]

Because of the liveliness of his prose, and the sophistication of his textual interpretations, Barthes has probably done more than any other single theoretician to introduce recent semiotics to American readers.

Barthes has repeatedly returned to the issue of connotation. It constitutes a central theme in such diverse works as *Elements of Semiology, Writing Degree Zero,* "The Rhetoric of the Image," "The Photographic Image," *S/Z,* and perhaps most importantly *Mythologies,* a collection of essays devoted to aspects of French popular culture. The topic re-emerges with such insistence because Barthes invariably directs his attention to what are known as "second-order" signifying systems—systems which build on already existing ones. Literature is a prime example of a second-order signifying system since it builds upon language. Barthes describes these systems as "connotative," and in *Mythologies* he sharply distinguishes them from "denotative" or "first-order" signifying systems.

Barthes was not the first theoretician to propose the category of connotation as an indispensable one for semiotic analysis. The Danish linguist Louis Hjelmslev not only isolated the category much earlier, but in *Prolegomena to a Theory of Language* formulated the model with which Barthes works in *Mythologies.* [As Hjelmslev wrote in that work]:

> . . . it seems appropriate to view the connotators as content for which the denotative semiotics are expression, and to designate this content

and this expression as a *semiotic,* namely a con-notative semiotic. In other words, after the analysis of the denotative semiotic is completed, the connotative semiotic must be subjected to an analysis according to just the same procedure. . . .

> Thus a connotative semiotic is a semiotic that is not a language, and one whose expression plane is provided by the content plane and expression plane of a denotative semiotic. Thus it is a semiotic one plane of which (namely the expression plane) is a semiotic.

Hjelmslev here elaborates a signifying model within which the denotative signifier and the denotative signified join together to form the connotative signifier. In other words, the denotative sign, which in the case of language would be the unit formed by the sound image and the concept it evokes, or in the case of photography the unit formed by the photograph and the concept it elicits, becomes in its entirety the starting point for the connotative process. . . . The connotative sign consists of both parts of the denotative sign as well as the additional meaning or meanings which they have helped to generate.

Barthes appropriates Hjelmslev's model, but he also complicates it. He identifies connotation with the operation of ideology (also called "myth"). For Barthes ideology or myth consists of the deployment of signifiers for the purpose of expressing and surreptitiously justifying the dominant values of a given historical period. [In *Mythologies* he] cites as an example the full-page photographs of ornamental cookery in the French journal *Elle.* These photographs offer a falsification of food—poultry and fish which have been painstakingly glazed and coated, and either made to look like something else altogether, or reconstituted in imitation of their original condition. They evoke not merely the concept of "food," but those of "wealth," "art," and "inaccessibility." These photographs unabashedly affirm that expensive cuts of meat can never be anything but a dream for the majority of the people who read *Elle.* At the same time they articulate that dream for the working class, promoting desire for bourgeois products.

Similarly, the *Guide bleu,* most middle-class of French travel guides, perpetuates nineteenth-century values through its celebration of mountainous terrain (invariably characterized as "picturesque"), the tone of moral exaltation it adopts when speaking of certain kinds of art, and its presentation of native populaces in terms of types ("the Basque is an adventurous sailor, the Levantine a light-hearted gardener, the Catalan a clever tradesman and the Catabrian a sentimental highlander"). The reader of the *Guide bleu* comes away with a good deal more than an assortment of historical, geographical, artistic, and sociological facts; he or she imbibes with those facts (indeed *through* those facts) a host of ideological assumptions about history, geography, art, and sociology.

Perhaps the most illuminating of Barthes' various examples is a little allegory he tells about the imbrication of French journalism and French colonialism:

> I am at the barber's and a copy of *Paris-Match*

is offered to me. On the cover, a young Negro in a French uniform is saluting, with his eyes uplifted, probably fixed on a fold of the tricolor. All this is the *meaning* of the picture. But, whether naïvely or not, I see very well what it signifies to me: that France is a great Empire, that all her sons, without any color discrimination, faithfully serve under her flag, and that there is no better answer to the detractors of an alleged colonialism than the zeal shown by this Negro in serving his so-called oppressors. I am therefore faced with a greater semiological system: there is a signifier, itself already formed with a previous system (*a black soldier is giving the French salute*); there is a signified (it is here a purposeful mixture of Frenchness and militariness); finally, there is the presence of the signified through the signifier.

Barthes's scheme represents an improvement over Saussure's not only in that it accommodates connotation as well as denotation, but in that it accounts for motivated as well as unmotivated signifying relationships.

—*Kaja Silverman*

Within this formulation the photographic image of the black soldier saluting a French flag functions as the denotative signifier, while the concept of a black soldier saluting a French flag provides the denotative signified. The photographic image and its corresponding concept are then seen as conjoining to form the denotative sign. That sign becomes a signifier in a second signifying transaction, that of connotation. Thus the sign of the black soldier saluting a French flag constitutes in its entirety a signifier for such ideological signifieds as "nationalism" and "militarism."

Barthes's scheme represents an improvement over Saussure's not only in that it accommodates connotation as well as denotation, but in that it accounts for motivated as well as unmotivated signifying relationships. The relationship between glossy photographs of ornately prepared food and the concepts "wealth," "art," and "inaccessibility" is not arbitrary in the way that the relationship between the word "food" and the concept which it evokes is understood to be. There are points of similarity between each of the connotative signifieds and the connotative signifer (e. g. the cuts of meat which are shown are in fact very costly; they have been artificially fabricated; and they are photographed from a low angle, as if to emphasize their remoteness). An analogous argument could be made for the connotative operations of the *Guide bleu:* the first level of motivation in each of the racial stereotypes cited by Barthes is one of synecdoche—of taking the part for the whole. The *Guide bleu* assumes from certain instances of Levantine gardeners that all Levantines are gardeners. The attribution of lightheartedness to this group of gar-

deners suggests a number of closely related connotative signifieds, among which would be "contentedness with one's state in life," "lack of emotional complexity," and—by implication—"primitivism" and "cultural inferiority." Finally, the connotations "nationalism" and "militarism" are respectively motivated by the depiction within the *Paris-Match* photograph of a tricolor and a soldier. (It must of course be noted that in the instances of the *Elle* and *Paris-Match* photographs even the denotative sign is motivated; the denotative signifier enjoys what Peirce would call both an iconic and an indexical relationship with its denotative signified.)

Barthes's model also suggests that the relationship between a connotative signifier and a connotative signified can only be explained through reference to a larger social field, a social field which is structured in terms of class interests and values. Saussure does not exclude the category of culture from his argument, but it figures there merely as a collectivity which maintains a series of neutral and arbitrary linguistic conventions—conventions of syntax, grammar, and meaning. Barthes's very different notion of culture is not genuinely collective, but riven with contradictions. These contradictions are covered over and smoothed out by ideology or myth, which creates the world in the image of the dominant class. One of the major devices for transforming actual heterogeneity into apparent homogeneity is here seen to be connotation, which reduces all textual materials, all cultural artifacts, all signifying formations to a circumscribed group of privileged signifieds. Since ideology motivates the relationship between those materials, artifacts, and formations on the one hand, and a circumscribed group of privileged signifieds on the other, that relationship can no longer be perceived as either neutral or arbitrary.

There are of course certain problems with this model, some of which Barthes himself attempts to resolve in *S/Z* and elsewhere. One such problem is the assumption that whereas connotation necessarily involves an ideological coercion of the reader or viewer, denotation engages that reader or viewer at an ideologically innocent level. A careful reading of certain other theoreticians, like Louis Althusser, suggests that during the child's linguistic initiation, when he or she is ostensibly learning denotation rather than connotation, he or she is already positioned within ideology. Through the first words which the child learns, which generally include "want," "no," "mother," and "father," he or she enters the realm of negation, desire, and the family. From that point forward it becomes preposterous to posit any act of listening or speaking which would be free of ideology.

Another problem with this early formulation is its conflation of the terms "myth" and "ideology." Barthes suggests in *Mythologies* that ideology is a condition of false consciousness promoted through fictions sponsored by the dominant class, fictions which it is presumably possible to penetrate by means of a deconstructive analysis. This definition implies that there is a reality outside of ideology to which we would have direct access were it not for the myths of the ruling class. However, as Althusser observes in "Marxism and Humanism," we cannot step outside of ideology since it is only inside of it that we find our subjectivity and our social reality. As long as there is culture there will continue to be ideology. At the same time it is important to keep in mind that there is always a heterogeneity of conflicting ideologies concealed behind the dominant one. While it may not be possible to step outside of ideology altogether, it *is* possible to effect a rupture with one, and a rapprochement with another.

A third difficulty with the model advanced in **Mythologies** is that it associates connotation with a signifying operation which necessarily results in an impoverishment of meaning. The denotative signifier can be as small as the curl worn on the forehead of an American film actor to indicate "Romanness," or as extensive as a novel by Jules Verne. It is apparent that if a gesture or a photograph can open onto the same amount of meaning as an entire film, or a 500-page novel, connotation leads to a serious attrition. We are led to assume that each paragraph of the novel, or each image in the film, repeats essentially the same ideological message.

In *S/Z* Barthes also equates connotation with cultural inscription, but he formulates the equation quite differently. Culture is seen as imposing itself upon the text as insistently as before, but not so monolithically. *S/Z* suggests that ideological imperatives express themselves through a multiplicity of codes which "invade" the text in the form of key signifiers. Each of these signifiers represents a digression outside of the text to an established body of knowledge which it connotes; each one functions as an abbreviated version of the entire system (code) of which it is a part.

Barthes registers considerable ambivalence about these codes, and by implication about connotation. On the one hand, they concoct a "nauseating mixture of common opinions, a smothering layer of received ideas," but on the other hand, they provide access to whatever plurality of meaning the classic text affords. And within the context of *S/Z,* plurality carries the highest value.

S/Z also rethinks the relationship between connotation and denotation. Denotation is associated with closure and singularity. It becomes the enemy of free play, opposing even the limited plurality made possible by connotation. The very authenticity of denotation is called into question—it is charged with being an imposter, a metaphysical fiction which passes itself off as the "hearth, center, guardian, refuge, light of truth":

> . . . denotation is not the first meaning, but pretends to be so; under this illusion, it is ultimately no more than the *last* of the connotations (the one which seems both to establish and to close the reading), the superior myth by which the text pretends to return to the nature of language. . . .

I would like to note [that Barthes's notion of the ideal text] would be irreducible to the sorts of meanings Barthes discovers in *Elle* or the *Guide bleu*. It would consist of a "triumphant plural" of signifiers which would "float" above the signified, refusing to be in any way anchored down or constrained.

Kaja Silverman, "From Sign to Subject, A Short History," in her The Subject of Semiotics, *Oxford University Press, Inc., 1983, pp. 3-53.*

On Roland Barthes's contribution to contemporary thought:

Roland Barthes was central to the post-structuralist project, as he was to the semiological and structuralist projects preceding it. As a writer largely on the margin of the academic scene he played an important role in introducing the theoretical approaches of semiology and post-structuralism to a wider audience through an impressive number of articles and essays in newspapers and magazines. He was also a pioneer in applying these theories to cultural objects outside linguistics and literary texts, through his studies of the semiotics of food, photographs and fashion, the myths of mass culture, the 'rhetoric' of love, etc. He became famous for his demystification of the 'naturalness' and 'universality' with which newspapers, literature and common sense constantly dressed up a socially and historically determined reality. It is when history is denied, he says, that it is most unmistakably at work. By a radical integration of the reader in the production of the text, his literary criticism opposed the traditional notion of authors as producers and readers as consumers. He proclaimed 'the death of the author', and questioned the mimetic function of writing as a representation of reality or a 'dress to thought'.

Bjørnar Olsen, in his "Roland Barthes: From Sign to Text," in Reading Material Culture: Structuralism, Hermeneutics, and Post-Structuralism, *edited by Christopher Tilley, 1990.*

Tzvetan Todorov   (essay date 1984)

[*Todorov is an eminent Bulgarian-born French literary theorist, critic, and educator. In the following excerpt from a work first translated in 1987, he discusses the "fictional," or literary, aspects of Barthes's criticism.*]

A personal relationship linked me with Roland Barthes while he was alive, and it did not end with his death. I cannot claim even the illusion of impartiality if I am to speak of him. Not only will I be irresistibly tempted to suppress anything in him that does not suit me and to valorize the ways in which he is close to me, but I cannot find in myself the necessary strengths that would allow me to see him as a closed entity capable of being completely circumscribed, an object, as Genet had become for Sartre. So I shall not deal with Roland Barthes in the pages that follow, but with "my" Barthes.

I do not believe that this partiality prevents me from seeing all that derives, in his writings, from the "Romantic" syndrome and thus falls outside the scope of the present inquiry. I shall refer to these areas only briefly, for the record. His definition of literature, in particular, maintains two of the characteristics that the Romantics attributed to it, intransitivity and plurality of meanings. Barthes may have gotten the idea of intransitivity from Sartre, but he extended it to literature as a whole, instead of limiting it to poetry: "The literary act . . . is an absolutely intransitive act"; "for the author, *to write* is an intransitive verb" (*Critical Essays*); intransitivity is the basis for the opposition between writers and scribblers (poetry/prose for Sartre, already poetry/scribbling for Döblin). Ambiguity, plurality of meanings, infinite interpretations, these are modern commonplaces whose precise itinerary is hard to follow; for Barthes, this aspect of literature establishes the oppositions between readable and writable, between work and text (the second term is always the one valorized). "The Text is plural. This does not mean only that it has several meanings but that it fulfills the very plurality of meaning: an *irreducible* (and not just acceptable) plural" ("From Work to Text," in *The Rustle of Language*).

His view of criticism, as found for example in a short essay entitled **"What Is Criticism?"** (reprinted in *Critical Essays*), is likewise purely "Romantic." Spinoza wanted the question of truth to be abandoned entirely in favor of meaning. Barthes takes a step further in the same direction: the critic's task is "not the decipherment of the work's meaning but the reconstruction of the rules and constraints of that meaning's elaboration"; "the critic is not responsible for reconstructing the work's message but only its system"; the critical task is "purely formal": strange vows of poverty. As for truth, it is rejected in all senses. On the one hand, on the basis of an erroneous association of criticism and logic (erroneous since only the former has an empirical object), Barthes declares that criticism must settle for "validity" alone, internal coherence without reference to meaning. His explicit model for criticism is language; but although language taken as a whole is neither true nor false, each individual utterance may be one or the other. And so it is with criticism, for which the implicit model is not in fact language, but a game: a system of rules that lacks any meaning. On the other hand, supposing that the only truth with which literature itself has to deal is a truth of equivalence (Proust's Charlus is the Count of Montesquiou), he rejects this truth and considers it of no relevance to criticism. He is right, of course; but then literature has never aspired to this kind of truth, and Proust's novel is "true" in a completely different sense of the word (one which Spinoza may have had in mind when he speculated about the truth of the Bible). Barthes takes the current coexistence of diverse ideologies and viewpoints as a sufficient reason for criticism to give up speaking "in the name of 'true' principles" once and for all. Thus he combines a radical historicism (there is no general truth, there are only provisional ideologies) with a lack of interest in history: he knows that, in his case, critical dialogue "is egotistically shifted toward the present."

Finally, though Barthes is rarely concerned with more general principles, it comes as no surprise to find him defending not only relativism but individualism, and his defense is explicit, however questionable it may be in historical terms:

> For two hundred years, we have been conditioned by philosophical and political culture to valorize collectivity in general. All philosophies are philosophies of collectivity, of society, and individualism is frowned upon. . . . One should not be intimidated by this morality of the collective superego, so widespread in our society with its values of responsibility and political engagement. One should perhaps accept the scandal of individualist positions. [*The Grain of the Voice*]

Individualism, however, has not scandalized anyone for ages; it is even our "dominant ideology"! Just as Sade and Nietzsche, authors cherished by Barthes as well as Blanchot, have long since stopped appearing scandalous.

It suffices that he has formulated an idea for him to lose interest in it. Like a writer-for-hire, Barthes is concerned with finding the best formulation for each idea, but that does not lead him to espouse it.

—Tzvetan Todorov

We may as well admit it: this whole set of ideas is indeed present in Barthes's writings. But it is not only my feeling for Barthes as a person that convinces me they must not be overemphasized. There is also the status that ideas have in Barthes's discourse. Although within a given text one might take these passages as the expression of his thought, the set of texts as a whole reveals that this cannot be, since one sees Barthes constantly changing position: it suffices that he has formulated an idea for him to lose interest in it; and it becomes obvious that his constant shifts cannot be written off to frivolity but have to be attributed to a particular attitude toward ideas. Like a writer-for-hire, Barthes is concerned with finding the best formulation for each idea, but that does not lead him to espouse it. Moreover, he described himself reliably in his *Roland Barthes*: his writing is a "theft of language"; "in relation to the systems which surround him, what is he? Say an echo chamber: he reproduces the thoughts badly, he follows the words." And he adds the following sentence, which also appears on the jacket flap of his book: "All this must be considered as if spoken by a character in a novel—or rather by several characters."

The word "novel" is not here by chance. In fact the status of fiction is what these unespoused ideas call to mind: the author has his characters speak without identifying personally with what they are saying. Barthes's text differs from a novel in two ways. First, at the time its statements were uttered, its characters were invisible (readers had to wait for 1975, and *Roland Barthes,* in order to have it from Barthes himself that he did not believe in them; nothing in **"What Is Criticism?"** indicates that he does not adhere to what he is declaring, that it was merely a question of "thefts of language"). Second, rather than making everyday statements, his characters give voice to theoretical discourse, using the language of mastery for which the dimension of truth is what matters most. Barthes can thus say of himself: "For my part, I do not see myself as a critic, but rather as a novelist, one who crafts not novels, to be sure, but the 'novelesque' "; and in *Roland Barthes* he is still more specific: "Let the essay avow itself *almost* a novel: a novel without proper names." As utterances, the essay and the novel diverge; the one refers to the world of individuals, the other does not; but they are alike in the mode of their enunciation: in both cases there is discourse not assumed by its author—there is a fiction.

Barthes thus rejoins [writer-critics such as Maurice Blanchot and Jean-Paul Sartre], and he does so not only through the qualities of his style, but also because he brackets the truth value of criticism, and because he insists, on the contrary, on its fictional or poetic aspect (language ceases to be an instrument and becomes a problem). This is even, in his eyes, the distinctive feature of contemporary criticism: "If the new criticism has any reality, it lies here: . . . in the solitude of the critical act, which is henceforth declared to be an act of authentic writing, far from the alibis of science or institutions" (*Critique et vérité,* 1966). And it is certain that Barthes's books challenge the tradition of the genre through their very form: who could have predicted *S/Z, Roland Barthes,* or *A Lover's Discourse: Fragments*? Scandalizing some, delighting others, Barthes's texts were those of a writer drawn by the vicissitudes of destiny to pursue his career in the world of ideas and knowledge.

If he had really written novels, the entire originality of the gesture would clearly have disappeared. Toward the end of his life, Barthes was planning to write a "true" novel, with descriptions and proper names. But we have no assurance that the project could ever have been completed: Barthes explained that he was experiencing a "tenacious desire to paint those I love" (*Prétexte: Roland Barthes,* 1978), and that he was counting on novelistic writing to serve this end; but the very last text he completed bears a melancholy title: "On échoue toujours à parler de ce qu' on aime" (One always fails at talking about what one loves). However this may be, if he had written novels, Barthes would have been one more novelist among others, just as, when he does recount his own life, in *Camera lucida,* he becomes one more autobiographer or memoir writer among others (although one of the best): there is no formal invention. Barthes's originality depends upon an *almost,* it lies entirely in the transition between the two genres.

I do not share Barthes's attitude with respect to truth: literature already has a relationship with truth, and criticism has more than one. I subscribe, however, to the idea that the result of critical activity is a *book,* and that this fact is fundamental. Observation or the formulation of general laws may be nothing more than the utterance of a state of affairs; but the work of interpretation, although it depends upon knowledge, cannot be reduced to it. Interpretation is the (re)construction of a unique whole: whether a book of history, or ethnology, or literary criticism (not to mention all the mixed genres), this construction makes up a part of the very statement one is making about the object under analysis. Readers in the social sciences and humanities may well be justified when they forget the ideas but remember the books (although this choice of target is not entirely fair).

Barthes's challenge to this discourse of mastery has had a refreshing effect in the atmosphere of arrogance and one-upmanship that characterizes the intellectual community. But beyond this prophylactic and basically negative effect, we may legitimately wonder about the meaning of this rejection of discourse that has truth as its horizon. Is it anything but adherence to generalized relativism? Barthes himself sought in particular to see in it a reflection of the internal dispersion of the individual; it is a modern variant of Montaigne's adage: "Man is nothing but scraps and patches, through and through." We have seen Brecht valorize the presence of two voices in a single subject, whatever the nature of those voices may be. Barthes, who always greatly admired Brecht, does not fail to invoke him when he is attempting to explain this plurality in his own case: "I would be so happy if these words of Brecht could be applied to me: 'He thought in the heads of others; and in his own, others than he were thinking.' That is true thought" (*The Grain of the Voice*).

Recognizing others as oneself, recognizing the others in oneself, this is certainly a good point of departure for thought; but does it suffice? Is the other sufficiently defined by the eminently relative criterion of otherness? May I not also distinguish between the others that I approve of and those that I do not? If I think back over what I liked in Barthes, I do not find it in the statement that one heard, through his voice, the voices of others. I should be almost tempted to say the opposite: the best thing to be found in what was called "Barthes" (the life and the works) was Barthes himself. I see that he expressed a parallel idea: "Having reached this point in my life, at the end of a colloquium of which I was the pretext, I want to say that I have the impression, the feeling, and almost the certainty of having succeeded more in my friends than in my work" (*Prétexte*). I shall be told that that has nothing to do with literary criticism. It does, though, for Barthes wrote about literature, unceasingly; thus I can say that the texts I value most today are those in which he is most present, though we have still not crossed over into the personal genre: I am speaking of *Roland Barthes,* a book that is at once intimate and public, subjective and objective (a book of criticism), the text, once again, of a transition.

Since the public and the private areas must be distinguished, let me add this: up to the publication of *Roland Barthes,* in 1975, I see Barthes as adhering fully, in his writings, to the idea of the dispersion of the subject, of the inauthenticity of being. The task of turning this dispersed subject into the object of a book led him to change, though there was nothing spectacular about the change: "I'm taking more responsibility for myself as a subject," he said (*The Grain of the Voice*). In one of his courses, Barthes also said that one must choose between being a terrorist and being an egotist; it is this choice that accounts for the difference between the pre-1975 and post-1975 Barthes. What Barthes had been, until then, in his life and for his friends (a nonterrorist), he became also in his books; and he could write: "The playfulness of conflict, of jousting: I hate it. The French seem to love it: rugby, 'face-to-face,' round tables, bets, always stupid, etc." (*Prétexte*). But this kind of egotism has nothing in common with the kind that had been more or less deliberately displayed in his previous criticism: instead of offering a pure discourse in his books (a type of discourse that always remains an injunction), he came to propose a being, his own. Rather than suggest how man is, he left—with uneven results, to be sure—each individual the freedom to choose his own position with regard to the proffered discourse. The risks (and the corresponding rewards) in saying "this is the way I am" are much greater than those that come from saying "others are thinking in me."

By the same token, the others—the ones that exist materially, outside Barthes's consciousness—receive their due perhaps more justly than when they were all expected to agree to a complicity that was imposed upon them. This is what Barthes himself expresses when he attempts to understand his suffering over his mother's death: "What I have lost is not a Figure (the Mother), but a being" (*Camera lucida*). A human being is not the Other, nor the others; he or she is only himself, herself. To recognize the other's alterity (rather than continuing to say that "I" is an other or that the others are within me) is to recognize the other, period; it is to give up a little bit more of the egocentric illusion. So long as I take myself to be a pure echo chamber, the other exists only for me, undifferentiated; if "I assume myself as subject," I allow the other to do as much, thus I respect him. That is what I find, too, in the following passage in which Barthes describes his own evolution:

> Little by little, within myself, a growing desire for readability asserts itself. I want the texts I receive to be "readable," I want the texts I write to be the same. . . . I have a preposterous idea (preposterous in virtue of humanism): "No one will ever make it clear enough what love (for the other, for the reader) there is in the struggle with a sentence." [*Prétexte*]

This preposterous humanism is something new in Barthes's writing (whereas it had always been present in his conversation), and I value it highly. In it I see, above and beyond the nihilist clichés that Barthes shared with his era, a groping for a new transcendence, based not on the divine but on the social nature of humanity and the plurality of human beings. And I am moved to see that the last words of the very last interview he gave, a few days before his accidental death, dealt with this, even though somewhat awkwardly: "But despite everything, when one writes one scatters seeds, one can imagine that one disseminates a kind of seed and that, consequently, one returns to the general circulation of *semences*" (*The Grain of the Voice*).

Tzvetan Todorov, "Critics as Writers: Sartre, Blanchot, Barthes," in his Literature and Its Theorists: A Personal View of Twentieth-Century Criticism, *translated by Catherine Porter, Cornell, 1987, pp. 44-69.*

Colin MacCabe (essay date 1985)

[*MacCabe is an English critic and educator who has written extensively on literary and film theory. In the following excerpt, he examines* S/Z, *focusing on the five codes Barthes proposed for the study of narrative texts.*]

The written trace of a seminar held in the years 1968 and 1969, *S/Z* is the text which focuses, for me, the strengths and weaknesses of that period in an intellectual form.

It is Barthes's choice of a story to analyse which determines Balzac's place in the title of this paper ["Realism: Balzac and Barthes"] but it would be a mistake to think that Barthes's choice was aleatory. If the immediate occasion for the selection of Balzac's story *Sarrasine* was an article by Jean Reboul in *Cahiers pour l'analyse* and some fleeting comments of Bataille's, it is also the case that to analyse a story by Balzac is to engage with traditional Marxist definitions of the novel. Is it not Balzac that Engels praises as the most complete guide to the reality of France in the post-Napoleonic era? Is it not Balzac who functions for Lukács as one of the key figures in the elaboration of the crucial terms for the debate about realism?

> The question arises whether it is the unity of the external and internal worlds or the separation between them which is the social basis of the greatness of a novel; whether the modern novel reached its culminating point in Gide, Proust and Joyce or had already reached its peak much earlier, in the works of Balzac and Tolstoy; so that today only individual great artists struggling against the current—as for instance Thomas Mann—can reach the heights already long attained. [Lukács]

In this Marxist debate between ancient and modern, Barthes with his championing of *le nouveau roman* had already placed himself on the side of the modern. His earlier work, *Le Degré zéro de l'écriture* and *Mythologies* had, however, continued to accept the Marxist definition of 1848 as the watershed before which the bourgeoisie were able to express their universal aspirations with good conscience but, after which, the European-wide revolutions had made clear the class limitations of those universal ideals. Indeed, in many ways, *Mythologies* sought to explain the signifying mechanisms which enabled the bourgeoisie to transform the limiting features of their culture into irreducible facts of nature. These operations which Barthes termed *myth* ensured that the processes of signification were ignored in favour of a reality thereby produced as always already brute and always already given.

By the mid-sixties, however, Barthes oscillated between considering the operations of myth and the consequent denial of the processes of signification as the central feature of bourgeois culture, and a more radical view which analysed this occultation of the sign as fundamental to a western concern with representation which went back to the Greeks and which post-Renaissance Europe had merely accentuated. In challenging the very terms of representation, Barthes was taking issue not simply with Lukács's evaluation of ancient and modern but with his characterisation of the opposition in terms of the relation between internal and external worlds.

These concerns were illuminatingly set out in a short article entitled 'L' effet du réel' which Barthes published in *Communications* in 1968 and the composition of which was presumably contemporary with the beginning of the seminar which was to produce *S/Z*. The majority of the article is taken up with considering part of the description of Madame Aubain's room in *Un Coeur simple* when Flaubert writes that 'un vieux piano supportait, sous un baromètre, un tas pyramidal de boîtes et de cartons' ('Under a barometer stood an old piano loaded with a pyramid of boxes and cartons'). Barthes starts from the puzzle of how we are to account for the information that this description contains? For anyone concerned with the structural analysis of narrative such sentences seem simply redundant. They do not contribute to the narrative development and they cannot be integrated into a wider thematic function. If the piano might conceivably be analysed as an indicator of social function and the boxes and cartons as a sign of disorder within the *maison* Aubain, it is impossible to attach a signification to the barometer which appears like a stain of insignificance in the text. What is the significance, Barthes asks, of this insignificance? And it is to that question that the article addresses itself.

Description has long been a feature of western writing but it has always been governed by certain laws of genre. No such generic conventions govern the descriptions within the nineteenth-century text. Barthes refuses to accept the standard explanation that the laws of genre have been replaced by the features of reality itself. The examination of Flaubert's endless rewriting of the description of the town of Rouen in *Madame Bovary* reveals, for Barthes, that Flaubert has no concern with the reality of Rouen but, rather, with the reality of his own style. For Barthes the descriptions of Rouen are not governed by the narrative of the book but by the general function of representation which works on the basis of a double refusal. On the one hand representation refuses to accept the unlimited nature of the real, a nature which entails that no description can be brought to an end, while, on the other, it refuses to acknowledge the operations of fantasy in the description by supposedly grounding the writing in external conditions. The representation that is left after this double operation seems to resist meaning, to display its own insignificance. But this insignificance merely reduplicates the mythic opposition, which Barthes finds central to bourgeois culture, between the intelligible and the lived. And this brute concrete element of the lived, this barometer, exists within the novel as a guarantee that the intelligibility that the novel articulates is not in fact an articulation, for, like the barometer, it rests exterior to the text. Barthes contrasts this novelistic relation with the relation between the real and the *vraisemblable* in classical culture which defined intelligibility in terms of the *exclusion* of the real. Barthes continues: 'Par là-même, il y a rupture entre le vraisemblable ancien et le réalisme moderne; mais par là-même aussi, un nouveau vraisemblable naît, qui est précisément le réalisme (entendons par là tout discours qui accepte des énonciations créditées par le seul référent).' 'By that very fact there is a break between the old *vraisemblable* and modern realism but by that same fact a new *vraisemblable* is born which is, precisely, realism (let us understand by that term any discourse which accepts enunciations guaranteed by the referent alone.')

At a more technical level Barthes analyses the operation as the abolition of the signified so that the signifier is placed in direct relation to the referent in a movement which seems to escape all questions of meaning. But we should not think thereby that we escape meaning; what is in question in this whole operation is the production of a meaning, the absence of signification signifies direct contact with the real: 'car dans le moment même où ces détails sont réputés dénoter directement le réel, ils ne font rien d'autre, sans le dire, que le signifier.' ('Because in the very moment when these details are held to denote the real directly, they do nothing except, without admitting it, to signify it'.) [In an endnote MacCabe explains that "Barthes is evidently talking in terms of a second order of signification. At the level of language, the signifier *barometer* has its appropriate meaning. It is in so far as that linguistic sign is taken up by a literary discourse as a signifier that we can locate the absence of a signified. The relation between literary discourse and language may not, however, be quite as clear-cut as Barthes's analysis would seem to imply. . . . A further cavil might dispute the 'insignificance' of the barometer in terms of thematic functions."] Barthes's task in *S/Z,* which is implicitly set out in the article, is to unmask the operations of the realist text: to rework all questions of the referent in terms of the signified. The weakness of this position, which is not to say that it does not have strengths, can be briefly indicated by arguing that the setting of Rouen is an absolutely central feature of *Madame Bovary*—it is the juxtaposition of an adulterous love affair and a provincial town which made the book so shocking on its appearance. The historical point can be made theoretically by arguing that the passage to the referent always engages the signified and that Barthes's dream of a bracketing out of the referent presupposes a unity of language which does not apply when there is any question of specific practices of writing. . . .

Barthes analyses Balzac's story line by line fracturing the text into five codes in which each fragment participates and whose interweaving composes the text. The codes are not strict rules of paradigmatic and syntagmatic substitution and, in that, Barthes distances himself from those in the sixties who wished to produce a universal grammar of narrative. Much structural analysis of narrative before Barthes had attempted to read texts as instantiations of structures which existed independently of their textual realisation. Barthes, conscious of the dialectic between reader and text, refused to locate the codes immanently within the text but in the relation of reading. But if the codes are the result of the interests that the analyst brings to the text, they are not, therefore, to be located in some subjective voluntarism; it is not the analyst's choice any more than the author's consciousness or the text's identity that guarantee the codes, rather it is a particular set of operations:

> Je ne suis pas caché dans le texte, j'y suis seulement irrepérable: ma tâche est de mouvoir, de translater des systèmes dont le prospect ne s'arrête ni au texte ni à "moi", opératoirement, les sens que je trouve sont avérés, non par "moi" ou d'autres, mais par leur marque *systématique*: il n'y a pas d'autre *preuve* d'une lecture que la qualité et l'endurance de sa systématique; autrement dit: que son fonctionnement.
>
> (I am not hidden in the text, I am simply irrecov-

erable from it: my task is to move, to shift systems whose perspective ends neither at the text nor with me, the meanings I find are confirmed, not by me or by others but by their systematic mark: there is no other proof of a reading than the quality and endurance of its systematic; in other words: than its functioning.)

Barthes's comments indicate how the repetitions analysed in the text find their validity within a process of interpretation which is social. What is not allowed any determination in that functioning is the social practices which constitute the moment of the text's production.

The story itself starts with a description of a ball in fashionable Paris. The narrator who is describing the scene is drawn into the action when a mysterious aged figure appears in whom the narrator's partner becomes inordinately interested. The narrator wishes to seduce his partner and promises to tell her the story of this figure in exchange for the promise of an affair. It is this story which is the story of Sarrasine, a sculptor who goes to Rome and falls in love with a singer called Zambinella. What Sarrasine does not know is that women's roles in these operas are taken by castrated men. The story of Sarrasine is the story of this discovery and Sarrasine's subsequent death. The figure at the ball is this same Zambinella now very old. The story so horrifies the young woman that she renounces all thoughts of a sexual affair.

Barthes's five codes into which he analyses the text are as follows:

Proairetic code

This code is the code of actions and its name is derived from the term Aristotle uses in his analysis of actions: *proairesis.* It refers to the logic of actions that make up a text. Thus, in a famous example, when in a [James] Bond novel a phone rings there is an expectation that it will be answered. It is these sequences which can be endlessly expanded—'The phone rang. He hesitated for a moment and then answered'—which contribute in large part to the 'realism' of the text.

Hermeneutic code

This is the code which refers to the plot or the enigma—to the text's production of a mystery which it then resolves. In *Sarrasine* the fundamental enigma is the identity of the figure who appears at the ball—an identity revealed to us by the gradual unfolding of the text. It is this unfolding, across a series of delays and false expectations, which constantly invites the reader to read further.

Semic code

This is the code which collects together those parts of the text that might appear in a thematic reading. Thus, in *Sarrasine,* for example, the moon recurs in a variety of different contexts. In some ways this code would correspond to certain kinds of impressionistic literary critical readings.

The analysis of these three codes: the code of *actions,* the code of *enigmas* and the code of *themes* contributes much to our understanding of narratives. It serves, in some sense, as a particularly succinct and brilliant summary of

the previous decade's work on the structural analysis of narratives. But it is the other two codes which are both original and more problematic because they pose more clearly questions of the text's production and reception— on the one hand the systems of distribution, the standards of literacy, the forms of economic relations in which the text first appeared, and, on the other, those same forms in their contemporary operation with special emphasis on the forms of education and commerce which produce the text in the present in an active relation with its contemporary readers.

Cultural or Referential Code

This is the code which refers to the general area of cultural and historical knowledges; it ransacks a whole series of contemporary sciences and ideologies and weaves them into the text. The political and economic situation in France, the cultural and political milieu in Rome—the list proliferates endlessly. For Barthes this code can be fully understood in terms of the positioning of the reader in an already ordained position of knowledge. It is this code which, 150 years after the text's production, we often need to relearn but which would have been readily available to Balzac's audience. It must be emphasised that it is not a question of what Balzac's audience knew, but their understanding of the positions from which knowledge was to be produced. What is significant about the references is that they are understood as references to accepted knowledges. They thus figure a position of knowledge which is occupied by both text and reader.

Symbolic code

This is the most important and problematic of the codes not least because, in this case more than any other, code is a misleading word. The symbolic does not refer, as it does in its most common English meaning, to a set of symbols which represent other entities across a grid of interpretation. Instead it is understood (following Lévi-Strauss and Lacan) in terms of the whole field in which symbols are produced—*the very possibility of representing one thing by another.* The symbolic thus refers to the processes which render representation possible, most importantly and centrally in language. On this reading the symbolic is conceived as the articulation of a series of differences which inaugurate both identity and language. The world is rendered into identities by the very process of representation. The rendering of identities and the signifying practice of language are, on this account, *one and the same process.* The symbolic code is thus the space of the investigation of difference and signification. Centrally in the Balzac text, it is articulated around sexual difference and the problem of sexual difference posed by Zambinella. Both male and female s/he collapses difference and identity on the most crucial of sites: the body. Zambinella's very existence poses a threat to any possibility of representation and this threat runs through every level of the text where all the means of representation seem on the point of a vertiginous collapse: money, language, painting and indeed the text itself become unreliable and arbitrary as world and language, difference and signification are unravelled by a sexuality that cannot be determined in its identity.

In his opening remarks Barthes writes: 'il faut, à la fois, dégager le texte de son extérieur et de sa totalité.' ('It is necessary, at one and the same time, to disengage the text from its exterior and its totality'.) This comment refuses any reading in terms of either a sociology or a psychology and thus refuses the very terms of Lukács's definition of realism, which would try to locate texts in either external or internal worlds. For Barthes, the novel is only connotation, denotation is defined away until it is only the final connotation within the realist text, functioning as an alibi for the activities of language. Reality is no longer external or internal, social or psychological but linguistic and textual. In marking this displacement Barthes used a different theoretical vocabulary in the book than that employed in the earlier article. Whereas he had earlier talked of signifier, signified and referent, in *S/Z* denotation and connotation become the major focus of the early theoretical preliminaries. In both cases denotation and the referent have the same function: the illusory guarantor of the innocence of language; the disavowal of both the multiplicity of the real and the insistence of fantasy.

Colin MacCabe, "Realism: Balzac and Barthes," in his Tracking the Signifier, Theoretical Essays: Film, Linguistics, Literature, *University of Minnesota Press, 1985, pp. 131-50.*

Peter Fitting   (essay date Winter 1988)

[*In the following excerpt, Fitting examines* Mythologies, *showing that semiology and a desire to expose ideology inform the essays that comprise the book, and comments on changes in Barthes's thought later in his career.*]

> In a single day, how many really non-signifying fields do we cross? Very few, sometimes none. Here I am before the sea; it is true that it bears no message. But on the beach, what material for semiology! Pennants, slogans, signals, signboards, clothes, suntan even, which are so many messages to me.
>
>   *Mythologies*

To speak of Roland Barthes's *Mythologies* and their influence means going back for a moment to the Paris of the 1950s in which they were written. For this was not only the period of Existentialism, of Camus and particularly, in Barthes's case, of Sartre, but already the prelude to what was to be a methodological explosion in the human sciences.

At the time, the study of myth was a privileged site for the debates and intellectual upheavals now associated with structuralism, a debate which is summed up in Claude Levi-Strauss's questioning of traditional approaches and methods in his essay "The Structural Study of Myth," published in 1955. Already, before the structuralists, myth was a concept with different and contradictory meanings, from the pejorative designation of false beliefs, to those anthropological or historical perspectives which considered myths as the legends or traditional stories of a culture, stories which recounted events from that culture's past (which may or may not be considered "true") and which were seen as embodying and conveying aspects of that cul-

ture's worldview and identity. Although anthropologists had almost always been interested in the function of myth within a particular society—a concern which underlies Barthes's interest as well—Levi-Strauss's structural study challenged the ways that myth had been understood, and the methodology that was used to interpret them. Rather than considering myth as expressing—whether symbolically or literally—the beliefs and values of a culture, Levi-Strauss was interested in their "social function": not what the contents of a particular myth might mean, but how the myths of a particular culture could be understood as a mechanism for dealing with or "mediating" social contradictions. Moreover, the method Levi-Strauss developed for reading or interpreting myths was, in a move which came to typify Structuralism, grounded in Fernand de Saussure's description of language as a system of differences: myths were to be studied and understood as a corpus whose basic units of meaning lay in a series of binary oppositions.

This is the context in which Barthes wrote his *Mythologies* (a context which he later described as shaped by the triple influence of Brecht, Marx, and Sartre). The essays which would eventually be published as *Mythologies* began not as an organized project, but with an article on wrestling written in 1952 (in *L'Esprit*); which was followed a year later by what was to become a regular column—"The Mythology of the Month"—in the literary magazine, *Les Lettres Nouvelles,* from 1954 through 1956. This series of more than 50 short sketches was followed by a theoretical essay, **"Myth Today,"** which he wrote in 1957 as the conclusion for the book publication of the collected *Mythologies.* (The English translation of 28 of these "mythologies" appeared in 1972.)

Over three decades of an increasingly public career, in more than 20 books and hundreds of articles, Roland Barthes was to become the archetypal French intellectual of the generation following Sartre, someone whose writings may be seen as "a veritable fever-chart of all the significant intellectual and critical tendencies since World War II" [in Fredric Jameson's words]. Barthes's essays began with an interest in activities which were explicitly invested with myth, notably forms of spectacle in which individuals acted out symbolic roles which were larger than life—from wrestlers to film and theatre actors. But his interest quickly expanded to include any aspect of everyday life which was invested with what he considered a mythical signification and which, unlike the spectacle, tried to pass itself off as natural. In his attempts to discover and chart the full extent of the codes and conventions of the social mythology embedded in a heterogeneous range of phenomena, Barthes moved from the literary writers and their work to other art forms, sports, and public entertainments; through advertising campaigns, tourism (guide books, cruise ships), public figures, politics and language, to the press itself, and to some of the fundamental "icons" of French life like wine or steak and French fries.

Certain activities, like wrestling, with which he began, had not previously been looked at from such a sociological perspective (if sociology is what we call the application of anthropological methods to one's own society). It was simply taken for granted that the Tour de France bicycle race and wrestling were sports events, and that the spectator's pleasure lay in the vicarious experience of that competitive effort, not in his or her socially learned ability to decode such socially symbolic rituals. In the case of wrestling, which, because of television, is today an immensely popular sport in North America, the first question people not familiar with it ask is—"Is it real?" —a question which points to the essential ambiguity of this so-called "sport." In opposition to boxing, Barthes argued that wrestling was not a sport at all, but a form of spectacle, a highly coded and conventional theatrical event where the spectators have a clear idea of what the match's outcome will be, unlike other sports events. (Can you imagine betting on the outcome of a wrestling match?)

These essays began, then, as occasional sketches of the mythologies of daily life. It was only after he had "explored a number of current social phenomena that [Barthes] attempted to define contemporary myth in methodological fashion" [as he wrote in the preface to the 1957 edition of *Mythologies*], in the concluding theoretical essay, **"Myth Today,"** which has often been the focus for discussions of the book. In the 1970 preface to the paperback edition of *Mythologies* he explains that,

> This book has a double theoretical framework: on the one hand an ideological critique bearing on the language of so-called mass-culture; on the other, a first attempt to analyze semiologically the mechanics of this language. I had just read Saussure and as a result acquired the conviction that by treating 'collective representations' as sign-systems, one might hope to go further than the pious show of unmasking them and account in detail for the mystification which transforms petit-bourgeois culture into a universal nature.

Let us look then at the semiological mechanics of myth. Barthes begins with the provocative assertion that myth is "a type of speech," a statement that raised a fair amount of controversy because this description seemed to go against the views of almost everyone previously interested in myth. Barthes insisted that he was talking about myth today, and not about historical myths or the myths of other cultures; moreover he does examine the contents of various contemporary myths as well as their function. But by using a semiological model as a way of explaining the formal mechanics of myth he drew the criticism of sociologists and anthropologists who attacked his definition of myth and of linguists, who found fault with what they considered his rather loose applications of semiology. (Parenthetically I might add that his next two books were attempts to achieve a stricter semiological analysis. *Elements of Semiology* [1964] and *The Fashion System* [1967] were studies which a few years later he described as a "euphoric dream of scientificity" in which he no longer believed.)

Once he has defined myth as a form of communication, Barthes introduces the notion of primary and secondary levels of meaning and of the ways that a primary system acquires, beyond or "on top of " its denotative function, secondary or connotative meanings. This interest in meaning beyond denotation will take many turns and twists in Barthes's later career, but here that interest is specific to what he is calling myth. . . .

In human languages, words are the "signifiers," while the concepts they bear constitute the "signified," and the two are bound together in the linguistic sign. A *secondary* system is built on the first in the following way: the English phrase "my tailor is rich" perhaps tells us something on a first, denotative level about the economic status of tailors in Toronto. But for a French man or woman who has studied English, this phrase is familiar not for what it says about one's tailor, but as an example of English grammar; it reminds a French person of learning English, it *connotes* a particular situation which is not present in the first meaning of the phrase.

Barthes's first example of the way that a myth attaches itself to a denotative meaning is a visual one—the cover of a popular French magazine and the image of a black soldier saluting the French flag. Now remembering that this was written in 1957, and that France was still a colonial power (most noticeably in Algeria, where a war for independence was underway), Barthes points out that in this picture, the signifier is composed of the colours and shapes on the page, in whose arrangement we recognize the signified: a black soldier saluting the flag. The sign is the combination of those two terms, for the concept of a black soldier saluting a flag could be conveyed in other ways, as I am doing now by describing it in words. In the context of the 1950s, moreover, that sign becomes the signifier for a myth, for a French viewer would have no trouble reading that magazine cover on a second level for which the image of the black soldier had become the signifier for a second mythic meaning.

> Whether naïvely or not, I see very well what it signifies to me: that France is a great Empire, that all her sons, without any colour discrimination, faithfully serve under her flag, and that there is no better answer to the detractors of an alleged colonialism than the zeal shown by this Negro in serving his so-called oppressors.

Let me illustrate this by turning to Barthes's analysis of one of the icons of French life. In the essay **"Wine and Milk,"** he begins with the observation that, "Wine is felt by the French nation to be a possession which is its very own, just like its three hundred and sixty types of cheese or its culture." Although this example is in appearance less appropriate to the semiological analysis I have been describing, and too, apparently less political than the photograph of the black soldier, Barthes shows (through a rewriting of Marx's concept of "commodity fetishism" in Volume I of *Capital,* and through the concept of use and exchange value) that wine has both of these functions. In addition to a first level at which wine is a pleasurable or intoxicating drink, the myth of wine invests thinking about or actually consuming wine with an "integrative" social function: it serves to bind the French people together and to give them a sense of themselves as a nation:

> To believe in wine is a coercive collective act. A Frenchman who kept this myth at arm's length would expose himself to minor but definite prob-

lems of integration, the first of which, precisely, would be that of having to explain his attitude. . . . Knowing how to drink [wine] is a national technique which serves to qualify the Frenchman, to demonstrate at once his performance, his control and his sociability.

As this example suggests, there are any number of objects around us—from clothes and cars to restaurants and their fare—which, in addition to their first, utilitarian purpose, also function as signs. For if clothes serve first of all as warmth, or cars for transportation and food for nourishment, they also signify—a fact which is well understood by the advertising industry, which often explicitly refers to our choice of clothes or a car, our brand of cigarettes, or of beer and soft drinks, as a way of "making a statement."

In addition to the semiological pleasure of discovering collective meanings in the hitherto unexamined phenomena of daily life, these analyses also had a political focus for Barthes, as he explained in the 1957 Preface:

> The starting point of these reflections was usually a feeling of impatience at the sight of the 'naturalness' with which newspapers, art and common sense constantly dress up a reality which, even though it is the one we live in, is undoubtedly determined by history. In short, in the account given of our contemporary circumstances, I resented seeing Nature and History confused at every turn, and I wanted to track down, in the decorative display of what-goes-without-saying, the ideological abuse which, in my view, is hidden there.

Thus, in the conclusion to the essay on wine, Barthes argues that the myth of wine itself is not neutral:

> For . . . its production is deeply involved in French capitalism, whether it is that of the private distillers or that of the big settlers in Algeria who impose on the Muslims, on the very land of which they have been dispossessed, a crop of which they have no need, while they lack even bread. There are thus very engaging myths which are however not innocent. And the characteristic of our current alienation is precisely that wine cannot be an unalloyedly blissful substance, except if we wrongfully forget that it is also the product of an expropriation.

Thus, if the first stage in Barthes's myth analysis is the uncovering of a second level of meaning in an apparently innocent or "natural" phenomenon, the second stage lies in identifying the political or ideological function of this passing off of an historical phenomenon as a natural one.

To take an issue closer to us, let us look briefly at the essay **"Novels and Children,"** for surely one of the most powerful sources of contemporary myths lies in the equation of biology with destiny, as in the belief that the biological difference between men and women is in fact an indication of other differences, both mental and physical (a myth which may have something to do with the fact that only 18 per cent of university teachers in Ontario are women). In this essay, Barthes comments on a photograph of a number of French women writers in the women's magazine *Elle* in which the women in the picture were identified by three "ingredients": their name, the number of books they had written, and the number of children they had produced. In his analysis of the significance of this linking of women as producers of books and of children, he concludes that it is an important signal of the double standard which differentiates women from men in our society:

> Love, work, write, be business-women or women of letters, but always remember that man exists, and that you are not made like him; your order is free on condition that it depends on his; your freedom is a luxury, it is possible only if you first acknowledge the obligations of your nature. Write, if you want to . . . but don't forget on the other hand to produce children, for that is your destiny.

The importance of *Mythologies* 30 years later can be measured by the relative obscurity of semiology and ideology at the time, and their central position and influence today.

—*Peter Fitting*

In the preceding, I've tried to show the two theoretical currents informing the essays in *Mythologies*—semiology and ideology. The importance of Barthes's book 30 years later can be measured by the relative obscurity of these areas at the time, and their central position and influence today. While he certainly did not invent the concept of ideology (it was coined in the late eighteenth century by the French philosopher Destutt de Tracy, and it has been a crucial part of Marxist theory since the mid-nineteenth century), Barthes did—as he did with semiology—anticipate some of the major developments which were to follow. If, in each case, there were subsequent specialists who found fault with Barthes's theoretical elaboration of these concepts, he nonetheless helped to revive them and to define the terrain on which subsequent debates were conducted. This is particularly important in the case of ideology, not only because Barthes's name is much more often linked with semiology (he was named to the newly created Chair of Literary Semiology at the Collège de France in 1977), but also because his earlier, more politically committed views and contributions are often overlooked. In fact his analysis of contemporary myth anticipates many of the developments of the subsequent study of ideology, particularly those associated with the work of the French philosopher Louis Althusser. . . .

In *Mythologies* Barthes had been concerned, as we have seen, with the ways that myth is able to pass itself off as that which "goes-without-saying," as common sense. But later in his career he becomes increasingly suspicious of attempts to pin down the sign, to ascribe to it a single meaning. This led, in his later literary criticism, in *S/Z*

(1970) and in *The Pleasure of The Text* (1973), for instance, to the concept of "plurality" which reverses the earlier, implicit priority of denotation and the corrupting secondariness of connotation. [In *S/Z* he wrote]: "To interpret a text is not to give it . . . meaning, but on the contrary to appreciate what plural constitutes it." Connotation now becomes "the way into the polysemy of the classic text"; while denotation becomes a newer form of ideology, the way that a single meaning is imposed on the plurality of the real (or of the text).

Thus, attempts to impose a single reading of the text, to restrict and control meaning, lead him, in his **"Inaugural Lecture"** at the Collège de France (1977), to assert that all language is "fascist": for language, "[the language we speak and write] is neither reactionary nor progressive; it is quite simply fascist; for fascism does not prevent speech, it compels speech."

In the early texts, Barthes's first reply to Sartre's call for the commitment of the writer was the acknowledgment of an impasse, of the impossibility of writing along with the hope for historical change. But still Barthes continued to write, to pose writing as a form of action in the world. At the same time, another, more "textual" alternative to this dilemma has occurred to him, as can be seen in *Mythologies* when he suggests that "the best weapon against myth is perhaps to mythify it in its turn, and to produce an artificial myth. . . . Since myth robs language of something, why not rob myth?" In opposition to Sartre's call for a "littérature engagée" which ostensibly abandons formal questions in favour of a politicized "content," Barthes's attitude here sums up his own life-long hope for the possibilities of literature. Thus, even as he stated that language was "fascist" (in his 1977 speech), he went on to describe how literature might be able to undermine this authoritarian dimension of language:

> If we call freedom not only the capacity to escape power but also and especially the capacity to subjugate no one, then freedom can exist only outside language. Unfortunately, human language has no exterior: there is no exit. We can get out of it only at the price of the impossible: by mystical singularity, as described by Kierkegaard when he defines Abraham's sacrifice as an action unparalleled, void of speech, even interior speech, performed against the generality, the gregariousness, the morality of language; or again by the Nietzschean "yes to life," which is a kind of exultant shock administered to the servility of speech. . . . But for us, who are neither knights of faith nor supermen, the only remaining alternative is, if I may say so, to cheat with speech, to cheat speech. This salutary trickery, this evasion, this grand imposture which allows us to understand speech *outside the bounds of power,* in the splendor of a permanent revolution of language, I for one call *literature.*

Despite these brave words, the problem of co-optation remains: for even as Barthes tried to subvert the sign, this very subversion has itself become a part of the accepted order, where the most advanced and sophisticated critical tactics are but further rhetorical devices in the arsenal of

> **Barthes tried to subvert the sign. But this very subversion has itself become a part of the accepted order, where the most advanced and sophisticated critical tactics are but further rhetorical devices in the arsenal of capital, as television advertisements playfully intertextualize and deconstruct.**
>
> **—Peter Fitting**

capital, as television advertisements playfully intertextualize and deconstruct. Today's heightened awareness of the constructed nature of meaning—an awareness which *Mythologies* helped to develop—has led to a new phase or historical moment, now identified as the "Post-Modern." The recognition that we are surrounded by signs which we have made; that our social reality is not natural, but constructed and historical has led some to claim that there are no original meanings, but only an endless chain of signifiers, while the "referent," the reality from which the Sign takes its original meaning, does not exist. I cannot follow these implications any further here, but the uncovering of the underlying conventions of our social reality (a process which was to a large extent inaugurated, or at least popularized, by Barthes) has played a part in the gradual unraveling of traditional beliefs and certainties. . . .

However fashionable Barthes has become, he wrote from within a commitment to writing and literature, to criticism and theory which I do not want to see lost. However much others may try to reshape him to fit their own self-justifying fantasies of the intellectual as media star, Barthes did not give himself over to the *status quo* quite so quickly. "What I claim," he wrote in the last sentence of the 1957 Preface to *Mythologies,* "is to live to the full the contradiction of my time, which may well make sarcasm the condition of truth."

Peter Fitting, "To Read the World: Barthes's 'Mythologies' Thirty Years Later," in Queen's Quarterly, *Vol. 95, No. 4, Winter, 1988, pp. 857-71.*

Clara Claiborne Park   (essay date Autumn 1990)

[*Park is an American educator and essayist who has written widely on such diverse topics as English literature and the nature of mental illness, particularly autism. In the following essay, she describes the intellectual milieu in which Barthes was raised and educated—examining the French system of public education and the cultural importance of the French language to the French people—thereby attempting to account for much that appears unique, difficult, or idiosyncratic in not only Barthes's work but most contemporary French critical theory as well. Park concludes by praising Barthes "for his commitment to freedom, to multiplicity, and to delight, for his intelligence, and the generosity of his intentions."*]

When the Author died in France in 1968, it was Roland Barthes who with his essay **"La mort de l'auteur"** administered the *coup de grâce*. Jacques Derrida had already warned, in *Of Grammatology,* of the frivolity of thinking that " 'Descartes,' 'Leibniz,' 'Rousseau,' 'Hegel,' are names of authors," since they indicated "neither identities nor causes," but rather "the name of a problem." Michel Foucault would later record an "author-function" arising out of the "scission" between "the author" and "the actual writer." The subtext for all three shimmered in the Parisian spring, in the great year of academic revolution, when the students took to the streets and even the sacred *baccalauréat* felt the tremor. Barthes's way of putting it was somewhat more inspiriting than the transmogrification of authors into functions or problems: "We know now that a text is not a line of words releasing a single 'theological' meaning (the 'message' of the Author-God) but a multi-dimensional space, in which a variety of writings, none of them original, blend and clash." What Barthes was celebrating, in language permeated with the rhetoric of liberation, was release from the very idea of an origin; it was nothing less than that staple of the sixties, the death of God.

To be able to associate authors with God, you have to be French.

—*Clara Claiborne Park*

Barthes made sure his language told the story. The Author is "believed in"; his image is to be "desacralized," and with it his theological meaning. He is the God, "the origin, the authority, the Father" (as Barthes would write two years later), and not a very nice one. Literature is centered on him "tyrannically"; his "sway" is "powerful"; the new literature, now to be renamed *writing,* "liberates"; the Author is a myth it is "necessary to overthrow." Criticism, as Barthes would tell *L'Express* in 1970, could participate in "a kind of collective action." (Asked what it did, he answered, "It destroys.") The text, and the reader, are prisoners in the Bastille. With the erasure of the Author-God, the text, escaped from its Great Original, is revealed as an infinite regress of prior traces, of language, of ideas, of societal memories and assumptions. For "to give a text an Author is to impose a limit on that text, to furnish it with a final signified, to close the writing," and the reading with it. To dissolve the Author is to inaugurate that exhilaratingly "anti-theological activity," the conversion of literature to *écriture,* which "ceaselessly posits meaning ceaselessly to evaporate it." It is "an activity that is truly revolutionary since to refuse to fix meaning is, in the end, to refuse God and his hypostases—reason, science, law."

To the reader coming in late, and from over the water, the excitement may be somewhat hard to understand. Certainly revolutionaries of the word are easier to live with (and to embrace) than the other kind. But what is all the verbal shooting about? Is this Author-God, this Freudian

Father ("a somewhat decrepit deity," Barthes would later call him) anybody we know?

Sixty years ago, like many American children, I had a game of Authors. It was geared to seven-year-olds, about the simplest game there was to play, on a level with Go Fish—a pack of cards with four suits, headed by Henry Wadsworth Longfellow, John Greenleaf Whittier, Edgar Allan Poe, and Oliver Wendell Holmes. (Not Melville back then, not Whitman, not Dickinson or Thoreau—an early lesson in the temporality of canons.) From the cards we learned such truths as that Longfellow wrote *Evangeline* and Holmes *The Autocrat of the Breakfast Table.* Naturally, we did not learn to think of the Author as God, Father, or even (*Whittier?*) as an Authority. And even had we been English children, with a deck displaying Shelley, Keats, Tennyson, and Browning, we wouldn't have learned it either. To be able to associate authors with God, let alone with his institutional hypostases, you have to be French.

In 1635, in a book significantly entitled *De l'Esclaircissement des temps,* a portrait appeared of the powerful politician who the year before had founded the Académie Française, Armand Jean du Plessis, duc de Richelieu. From the Cardinal's head, as if prefiguring the Sun-King whose effulgence his policies prepared, shone forty rays of light. Each of those rays bore the name of an Academician—an Author.

Shall we try to imagine an analogous representation in an English-speaking context? No English prime minister has ever exercised Richelieu's absolute power. Had he done so, it remains inconceivable that the most sycophantic artist could ever have rayed forth from his head the names, say, of Milton, Dryden, Shadwell, and thirty-seven more, to Enlighten the Times with their harmonious and even brightness. Nor can we conceive of an English prime minister—still less an American president—concerning himself to create, as Richelieu did, an institution to regularize the national language, guard its purity, and impose upon its primary public literature, the drama, binding rules of literary practice. We are likely to imagine that a chief of state, even if he is not a cardinal, has more important things to do. But that too is to think an English-speaking thought. Long before Barthes, before Derrida, before Foucault, Richelieu had made the connection between Authors and Authority, between language and power. The relation of the dramatic Unities to monarchical unity, of literary Decorum to political and social conformity, was neither coincidental nor the expression of a vague French Zeitgeist, an Esprit des Temps. As David Kramer has recently shown [in an unpublished doctoral dissertation], the Academy and its projects were a deliberate response to the exigencies of an absolutism emerging from a century of fragmentation and religious war. The Rules, literary and linguistic, imposed by Richelieu's Academy expressed the absolute vision of what was to be Le Grand Siècle while helping to bring it into being.

It was Richelieu's Academy indeed. Perceiving their potential usefulness—or danger—he had by fiat institutionalized the cheerfully intellectual discussions of a group of literary friends, who were something less than enthusiastic to see their informal gatherings transmuted into an assembly of forty so-called Immortals. Some wished to decline the honor, but since Richelieu had forbidden unlicensed assemblies they thought better of it. "The Academy's statutes," Kramer reminds us, "were drawn up, not by a poet or a playwright, but by a *Conseiller d'Etat.*" The Immortals, when not raying directly from Richelieu's head, were in his pocket. He awarded pensions at will. "No one could be so much as proposed for election unless he was 'agréable au protecteur.'" All projects and decisions had to be likewise agreeable; many of them were directly suggested by the protector. The Academy's first and continuing project, the codification and purification of French, was initially undertaken so that the conquering tongue could be more readily learned by those whom the Cardinal's military campaigns were to subject to the glory of the crown. This was the original impetus for the great French Dictionary. Language was a means of control; French was to spread French *civilisation* abroad, as Latin had. It would equally set limits on what could be written—and thought—at home. We may, if we like, imagine a world in which Dr. Johnson composed his Dictionary not to make the money he told Boswell every sane man wrote for, but to enhance the glory of the Hanoverian monarchy. That done, we have to imagine him thinking of himself as one of forty immortals and not laughing. It isn't easy.

It was, then, more than the afflatus of the sixties that impelled Barthes to kill the Author, and rebel against "a language political in its origin" . . . "born at the moment when the upper classes wished . . . to convert the particularity of their writing into a universal language." Though there were contemporary reasons to proclaim liberation from the heavy rod of the Father-God, Barthes's sense of urgency, of need, of triumph was rooted deep in the historic soil of France. Only in France would it be possible to claim, as Barthes already had in **"Authors and Writers"** (1960), that "for the entire classical capitalist period, i.e. from the sixteenth to the nineteenth century . . . the uncontested owners of the language, and they alone, were authors"; that "no one else spoke." *No one else spoke.* The outrageousness of the hyperbole bespeaks its urgency. For when Barthes describes a "literary discourse subjected to rules of use, genre, and composition more or less immutable from Marot to Verlaine, from Montaigne to Gide," it is not hyperbole, but a truism of French literary history. "The certitudes of language . . . the imperatives of the structure of the genre"—these are not Barthes's own dismissive sarcasms, but the words of Professor Raymond Picard, a critic sufficiently infuriated by the originality of Barthes's criticism to call his "Nouvelle Critique" a "Nouvelle Imposture." Outside France, his essay *On Racine* wouldn't have raised an eyebrow. But in France those certitudes and imperatives *exist,* for everything from drama to orthography; one challenges them at one's peril. The walls of the prison house of language are far thicker in France.

What rayed forth from Richelieu's head was exactly that clarity later to be called Cartesian, the absolute and simple brightness of the "clear and distinct ideas" that Descartes thought he could find in his own mind and from them validate a universe; *la clarté cartésienne* was the visual mani-

festation of what Foucault calls "the great utopia of a perfectly transparent language." Barthes had already written, in ***Mythologies,*** of that "blissful clarity," how it "abolishes the complexity of human acts," giving them "the simplicity of essences," organizing "a world without contradictions because it is without depth, a world . . . wallowing in the evident." The myth was powerful enough, even in America, that an American graduate student could be told to read Kant in a French translation, because (*bien sûr,* this was forty years ago) it was impossible to be obscure in French. Clarity was the glory of that class monopoly, "the great French language," whose "lexicon and euphony," Barthes notes in **"Authors and Writers,"** could be "respectfully preserved" even through that "greatest paroxysm of French history," the Revolution. Though nineteenth-century authors might broaden, even transform that language, they were still its "acknowledged owners." Let us reactivate our English-speaking incredulity: it is quite simply inconceivable to us that authors, of all people, could even in imagination own a language. We speak and write a language that from its beginnings has been the product not of authority but of receptivity, of foreign influence and invasion, that from the time of its greatest poet, and in his person, has been defined by its rich intransigence, its falls into obscurity, its resistance to purity or purification. For us as for Shakespeare, language has been the product not of Authors, but of people talking.

But Barthes, with Derrida and Foucault and fifty million other Frenchmen, grew up within the secure structures of the great French language. There were forty Immortals in their youth, and there are forty Immortals today, three hundred and fifty years after Richelieu and two hundred years after that revolutionary paroxysm which nevertheless scarcely interrupted the Academy's guardianship over the integrity of French. Americans from time to time are made aware of the Immortals, as during the flap over the admission of the late Marguerite Yourcenar, and we are reminded that this is something that seems to matter—to matter less, presumably, than when three brilliant French minds were being formed by an educational system whose director was said to have claimed that he knew what page in what book every French schoolchild was turning on a given day, but still far more than we can readily imagine. The Quarante Immortels are still at work on their Dictionary. A centralized educational system still guarantees that a whole nation invests its emotions in the idea of an authoritative language. Summering in a country village, the astonished foreigner is lectured on what is and is not permissible French by the man who retails fish from door to door. Someone encountered in a train, asked to explain a word he has probably known all his life, defines it, then quickly adds, "But that's not French." It is, of course, *argot*—what we'd call slang, rich and self-renewing like any popular speech. When Victor Hugo introduced a few phrases of thieves' argot into *Les Misérables,* he appended thousands of words of justification. Authority is defined by power, and power is defined by its ability to forbid. That the vocabulary of classic French drama is confined to some 2500 words (2000, says Barthes, for Racine) as against Shakespeare's 25,000 is not just a quirk of literary history, still less of national character. It is the product of conscious decision. Though the vocabulary of permissible

French is of course very much larger today, it is still defined by exclusion.

Helen Vendler has described the "intellectual formation of a French child attracted to literature"—the *cahier* (the obligatory blot-free notebook), the *dictée,* the *manuel littéraire* enshrining every received idea of literary history—and has noted Barthes's own awareness of "how little he could escape from this training." Barthes, in *S/Z,* describes it considerably more abstractly: "a predetermination of messages, as in secondary-school education." But the structures of French civilization are formed long before its élite attends the lycée, which is what Barthes understands by secondary education. The certitudes and imperatives of French are encountered much earlier. Few of the children whose education Lawrence Wylie describes in his *Village in the Vaucluse* would ever reach secondary school. Yet in their elementary classroom the Cartesian light still shone, clear and sharp, mandating a dedication to abstract formulation, to analysis, to classification that readers of contemporary French theory will find eerily familiar. American amateurs of the School of Paris may compare Wylie's description with their own grade-school experience and ponder how it applies to their favorite authors—or texts—as these exemplify it at once in conformity and rebellion.

> In teaching morals, grammar, arithmetic, and science the teacher always follows the same method. She first introduces a principle or rule that each pupil is supposed to memorize so thoroughly that it can be repeated on any occasion without the slightest faltering. Then a concrete illustration or problem is presented and studied or solved in the light of the principle. More problems or examples are given until the children can recognize the abstract principle implicit in the concrete circumstance. . . . The principle itself is not questioned and is hardly discussed.

"Children," Wylie observes, "are not encouraged to formulate principles independently on the basis of an examination of concrete cases. They are given the impression that principles exist autonomously . . . always there: immutable and constant. One can only learn to recognize . . . and accept them." French education is not Baconian; its motion is not inductive but deductive. English-speaking readers may recall a flicker of surprise upon discovering that "empirical" is not, for French theorists, a word of praise.

In approaching a subject, "the children are first presented with a general framework which they are asked to memorize. . . . An isolated fact is unimportant in itself. It assumes importance only when one recognizes [the] relationship . . . of the part to the whole." Applied to literature, this ensures that "no attempt is made to understand or to appreciate the text which is presented to the class until it has been thoroughly . . . analyzed, . . . broken down into its logical divisions, and the author's purpose in each division . . . explained. . . . Thus a child comes to believe that every fact, every phenomenon . . . is an integral part of a larger unit," intelligible "only if their proper relationship is recognized." "To approach problems with these assumptions is to approach them sensibly, reasonably, logically, and therefore . . . correctly."

French of course, "is recognized as the most important subject taught. . . . Any other subject may be slighted or sacrificed in order to increase the time for drill" in the proper use of *la langue maternelle.* Wylie notes how hard it is for an Anglo-Saxon "to comprehend how essential this language study is to the French." Yet this is what we must comprehend if we are to appreciate the sense of free air breathed at last that pervades Barthes's *écriture.* Though so difficult a writing must severely, if regretfully, limit Equality and Fraternity, Liberty's banner floats triumphant, celebrating freedom from the Author/Father/God, from his "predetermined messages," his tyrannical intentions; from the imposed interpretation that wallows in the evident; from consistency; from logic. To rebel against the Author is to challenge Authority in a way neither imaginable nor necessary in an educational culture which valorizes the wayward and the polyphonic; which begs reluctant students to question principles they would much rather accept; and where no author (just ask one) has authority over language or anything else.

· · · · ·

Barthes opens *Le Plaisir du texte,* his celebration of the delight of reading, with imagining

> an individual . . . who would abolish within himself all barriers, all classes, all exclusions, not by syncretism but by simply getting rid of that old specter: *logical contradiction;* who would mix up all kinds of languages, even those thought incompatible; who would mutely endure all the accusations of illogicality, of infidelity; who would remain impassive in the face of Socratic irony (which works by leading the other to the supreme opprobrium: *to contradict oneself*) and of legal terrorism (how much penal evidence is founded on a psychology of consistency!). That man would be in our society the lowest of the low; the courts, the school, the asylum, ordinary conversation would make him a stranger: who endures contradiction without shame?

Any reader whose pleasure has been taken largely in texts written in English will recognize an accent, even in translation. From Chaucer to Sterne to Salman Rushdie, the glory of English has been the mixing up of languages thought incompatible. And only in French could "illogicality" be associated with "infidelity." The translator of the American edition was forced to render *infidélité* as "incongruity" lest he stymie the English-speaking reader in mid-sentence. *Infidelity?* To whom? To whom but the Author-God, with his "hierarchical sentence," his tyrannical meanings; with his hypostases of law, science, reason; with his fixation on logical consistency. God is *French.* That great rebel against the Rules, Victor Hugo, could still write with perfect naturalness in *Les Misérables* that "artistic peoples are logical peoples," since "the ideal is nothing but the culmination of logic, just as beauty is the apex of truth." No wonder Barthes complained, defending *Sur Racine,* that the *classes supérieures,* universalizing their own ideal of language, put forward "la 'logique' française" as "une logique absolue." The disclaiming quotes are, of course, Barthes's own.

Who endures contradiction without shame? Barthes's language vacillates here, as he likes it to do, with its initial suggestion that it's the representatives of school, court, and asylum who can't bear to be contradicted by Barthes's "counter-hero," the reader-writer taking his free pleasure. But "shame" takes us back to that *abjection* which I have translated as "the lowest of the low," to the shame of a Frenchman who has been caught out in a logical contradiction. *C'n'est pas logique!* Even the superficial tourist has heard it, in the racket of a train station or screamed on a playground: the continuing battle cry of Cartesian clarity.

Who, then, can endure the shame of logical contradiction? English shouts its answer. Emerson can endure it ("A foolish consistency is the hobgoblin of little minds"); Whitman can endure it ("Do I contradict myself? Very well then I contradict myself"); Blake can endure it; the metaphysicals can endure it. Shakespeare can endure it. Sir Philip Sidney, cosmopolite and aristocrat, his own French almost accentless, rejected a "mungrell Tragycomedie" that mingled kings and clowns. Shakespeare went right ahead, befouling the purity of tragedy with comic gravediggers who spoke the people's prose. Voltaire hated the gravediggers, though there were a lot of things he admired in Shakespeare; you don't come across such barbarities in Racine.

French intellectuals, of course, do not read Emerson or Whitman; they read Poe, who is *plus logique.* And they generally read in French. Barthes refers to "The Purloined Letter" in Mallarmé's translation. Though he does quote Blake (a single Proverb of Hell) he quotes in French, and his reference is not to *The Marriage of Heaven and Hell* but to a book (in translation) by Norman O. Brown. He seems unaware of the literature of modernism in English; there is an extraordinary passage in *Plaisir* in which he describes the experience of sitting in a bar, amusing himself by enumerating its "whole stereophony" of "music, conversations, noises of chairs, of glasses," the "little voices" which dissolve the hierarchical sentence into the "nonsentence." It is as if Joyce's "Sirens" had never been written—or translated. "Why," he asks, in his autobiography, "so little talent for foreign languages?" English at the lycée was "boring (*Queen Mab, David Copperfield, She Stoops to Conquer*)." The candor is characteristic and disarming; still, so comfortable an admission is unexpected from someone who feels so intensely the difference between one word and another, and emphasizes the distinction between denotation and connotation as if he had discovered it. Though he excoriated the "narcissisme linguistique" of the guardians of the "idiome sacré," French is for him "nothing more or less than the umbilical language." It is in French he writes, in French he reads (with occasional hints of German and Italian); it is to the readers and writers of *la langue maternelle* that he addresses his *écriture.*

So it is curious that it is not in France that his work has acquired its maximum power. There the liberation of the text from the structures of decorum, of consistency, of

logic could be felt as an exhilarating duty. Let its false and deceptive unity dissolve, its meanings float free, in "a paradise of words" a "happy Babel" in which "one may hear the grain of the gullet, the patina of consonants, the voluptuousness of vowels," and exult in the amorous perversity (his word) of an *écriture* that "granulates, . . . crackles, . . . caresses, . . . grates, . . . cuts,": and at last, joyously, "*comes.*" But how perverse is that perversity for readers whose experience of literature has been formed by the happy Babel of Chaucer, of Shakespeare, of Carroll and Lear and Joyce? What needs exploring is why these quintessentially French linguistic preoccupations have found so warm a welcome in an educational culture so different from, even antithetic to, that of France.

Although Barthes's valorization of ambiguity might have been news to the French Academy, the American academy had started amusing itself with seven types of ambiguity in 1930.

—Clara Claiborne Park

After all, it's been fifty years and more that English and American criticism has been preoccupied with language; with metaphors and metaphorical systems (Caroline Spurgeon got us started in 1930); with the referentiality of poetic statement (I. A. Richards and T. S. Eliot in the twenties); with the layered suggestiveness which makes words rejoice as they fend off all attempts at paraphrase. French students learn that their greatest playwright wrote the speeches out in prose to cast into alexandrines; in classical French "no word," wrote Barthes (*Writing Degree Zero*) "has a density by itself." Here few students who undergo Introduction to Literature escape an exercise expressly designed to raise their consciousness of verbal densities. The distinction between denotation and connotation has been a staple of freshman writing texts ever since this year's retirees can remember. The inseparability of content and form is a truism: as Cleanth Brooks wrote in 1938, in words destined to inform introductory literature courses in colleges, then high schools, all over America, "the experience that [the poet] 'communicates' is itself created by the organization of the symbols he uses," so that "the total poem is therefore the communication, and indistinguishable from it." The sentence, including its suspicion of communication, could be Barthes's own. As he would put it twenty-one years later, with characteristic abstraction, "signification [is] the union of what signifies and what is signified . . . neither form nor content, but the proceedings between them."

Barthes's Author-God emitted "messages" in 1968: Brooks and Robert Penn Warren had warned American teenagers to stop hunting them thirty years before. Barthes put the Author's intentionality in question; "the intentional fallacy" hit American criticism in 1946. Did New Critics direct us away from the poet to The Poem Itself? In 1963, so did Barthes, rejecting traditional criticism's interest in "coordinating the details of a work with the details of a life" in favor of an "immanent analysis" functioning "in a realm purely internal to the work," "a criticism which establishes itself within the work and posits its relation to the world only after having entirely described it from within."

Nor could it have surprised an English-speaker to have read that "the Word in poetry can never be untrue," shining as it does "with an infinite freedom," "preparing to radiate toward innumerable and uncertain connections." For how many years have we been telling each other that poetic language is inexhaustible? In French, however, ambiguity is not a positive value: my *Larousse de poche* defines it as "a defect of that which is equivocal." We may cheer, then, as Barthes in 1963 converts defect to virtue and tells the French establishment that "each time we write ambiguously enough to suspend meaning . . . writing releases a question . . . gives the world an energy . . . permits us to breathe." Indeed, breathing wasn't all that easy; Barthes would soon have to defend against professorial attack his "right" (imagine it!) to read in Racine's "literal discourse" "other senses which [he was still stepping gingerly] do not contradict it." But though his valorization of ambiguity might be news to the French Academy, the American academy had started amusing itself with seven types of ambiguity in 1930. Thrilling as it is to read of language as "an immense halo of implications" making "knowledge festive" with words "flung out as projections, explosions, vibrations, devices, flavors," readers whose language long before Hopkins embraced "all things counter, original, spare, strange," must take it as confirmation rather than battle cry.

Even deconstruction has a familiar ring. Excise the word "personal" from the following; guess the writer; guess the date: "That radical mode of romantic polysemism in which the latent personal significance of a narrative poem is found not merely to underlie, but to contradict and cancel the surface intention." In 1966, confronting Picard, Barthes was still leery of contradiction. In 1953, M. H. Abrams was as much at home with it as Blake had been in 1790.

Nor can Barthes's amorous embrace of the concrete, of the physical object seem radical, though it may surprise us as we persevere through aridities of abstraction which, while less extensive than those in Foucault and Derrida, are equally uninviting to the Anglo-American explorer. Empiricism informs English-speaking style as well as English-speaking epistemology. Freshman composition texts are as one in discouraging abstraction and enjoining specificity; like McGuffey before them, they do their best to get American students, in Wylie's words, "to formulate principles independently on the basis of an examination of concrete cases." Helen Vendler's examples of "compositional subjects of the sort set for French students— 'Arrogance,' 'Ease,' 'Coincidence' "—would appear, if at all, only to illustrate the kind of subject to avoid. Barthes too believes in concreteness. Outraged when Picard accuses him of "an inhuman abstraction," he insists that "the works of *la nouvelle critique* are very rarely abstract,

because they treat of substances and objects." Reversing the deductive method taught the French pupil, he "starts," he says "from a sensuous object, and then hopes to meet in his work with the possibility of finding an *abstraction* for it" (italics his). He complains of the classic taste that considers objects "trivial," incongruous when introduced "into a rational discourse"; he commits himself to the object in full physicality he likes to call erotic; his "body," he says, "cannot accommodate itself to *generality*, the generality that is in language." The language is a bit warm for a freshman text, but the message (you should excuse the expression) is wholly familiar.

American critics, intellectual historians, and pedagogues, however, are not among the prior traces which constitute the text called Roland Barthes, which is entirely truthful in saying in 1963 (**"What is Criticism?"**) that French criticism "owes little or nothing to Anglo-American criticism." (The Anglo-American texts Barthes does refer to address very different preoccupations: Bruno Bettelheim, D. W. Winnicott, Alan Watts, Norman O. Brown.) The relation of La Nouvelle Critique to The New Criticism is *post,* not *propter.*

Barthes on his reasons for writing:

Writing is creation, and to that extent it is also a form of procreation. Quite simply, it's a way of struggling, of dominating the feeling of death and complete annihilation. I'm not talking about a belief that as a writer one will be eternal after death, that's not it at all. But, despite everything, when one writes one scatters seeds, one can imagine that one disseminates a kind of seed and that, consequently, one returns to the general circulation of *semences.*

Roland Barthes, in his The Grain of the Voice: Interviews 1962-1980, *translated by Linda Coverdale, Hill and Wang, 1985.*

What, then, explains our fascination? There is, of course, a peculiar pleasure in re-encountering one's own *idées reçues,* especially when expressed with an elegant difficulty that lends them the dark glow of revelation. From New to Nouvelle was an easy transition, as the case of Hillis Miller shows. The transatlantic breezes started blowing just as the New began to seem old hat. Barthes was affirming, with supremely French intelligence, the pieties of English 101.

But of course there's more to it. In retrospect, the New Critics seem surprisingly modest. They might distrust "messages," but they were comfortable enough with meanings. They left epistemology alone; they had no aspirations to philosophy or psychology. Though they discouraged biographical approaches, though they directed attention from poet to speaker and novelist to narrator, though they might (some of them) bracket authorial intentions, they didn't meddle with the idea of the self. But if authorial selves are (in the words of Vincent Leitch) "fabrications . . . interpretations . . . effects of language, not causes," why should our own selves be any different? As Frank Lentricchia puts it, "the self is an intersubjective construct formed by cultural systems over which the individual person has no control." A heady idea, the dissolution of the self; if personal responsibility dissolves along with it, it's a well-known revolutionary maxim that you can't make an omelet without breaking eggs.

Because there is more to it than old wine in new bottles. There is true exhilaration about the dissolving of certainties, the breaking of tablets. "Damn braces: bless relaxes," said Blake, in the book he began in 1789. The New Critics had scarcely been revolutionaries, literary or philosophical, least of all political. Yet the familiarity of their ideas could pave the way to the Paris of '68. Though the shadow of the Author-God did not reach across the sea, though the guardians and structures of English possessed minimal power either to preserve or coerce, though these were French texts speaking to the French, still they had their message for American intellectuals living in a country whose imperial impositions were increasingly difficult to ignore or justify. They aimed at the Author, but their target was Power. We could imagine with them a grand international democracy of power-free language—or if that were an impossible dream, we could at least proclaim our awareness of the invisibly tyrannical habits of our discourse. In the disillusioned seventies and the shameful eighties, there were new, progressive uses for our old New Critical techniques. They could be applied to any writing. "Literature" was only a category, as artificial as any of those frozen seventeenth-century genres. Guilt of nationality, class, and gender could revivify a tired scrutiny. For there is a politics of language. Orwell had told us that in 1946, in his blunt, concrete, English way; thirty years after, we could examine the matter with new French subtlety.

And somewhere in the last paragraph irony gives way to appreciation. Barthes would have recognized the movement: of reversal, of the statement no sooner made than put in question, of contradiction not merely acknowledged but embraced. One may—I do—question the cost-free radicalism, so much easier than actual political engagement, of our American warriors of theory, called to no undertaking more heroic than the reading of these admittedly exigent texts and the acquisition of a *parole* which now, in universities all over the country, itself exerts the power to require, insist, and exclude. For academics who have joined the club, the return of grand theory has brought not risk but a bonanza of renewal, liberating them into a hermeneutic paradise of publication where the professional reader (not the hapless freshman, who retains the privilege of getting things wrong) is Adam, forever encountering beasts that invite him to name them anew. Critical theory, I'm told, is a game; you don't have to play it unless you enjoy it. But power games are rarely optional. Barthes, like Foucault, like Derrida, had something more radical in mind than the substitution of one linguistic tyranny for another.

For they were French. A true radicalism goes to the root; theirs attacked the root assumptions of an unusually restrictive socio-politico-linguistic culture. There was a her-

oism in their assault on *clarté,* their determination to validate a darkness all the richer by contrast with that vaunted *ésclaircissement,* to honor the category of what Foucault called "the unthought." It's even explicable, though it would have surprised, then appalled Orwell, that stylistic obscurity should join the other insignia of liberation, the *étandards sanglants* of the good fight they were fighting.

Their status as revolutionaries was helped, of course, by the unique history of the French seventeenth century, which permitted such a ready association of oppressive structures of literature with oppressive structures of economics and of class. A phrase like Barthes's "the entire classical capitalist period" won't work in England or America, neither of which has a classical tradition you could put in your eye. In France it is at least intelligible. With "capitalist" functioning as negative shorthand in literature as well as economics, Barthes could claim a radicalism just as genuine as Sartre's, and a lot more subtle. Though Susan Sontag admires Barthes, she calls him a dandy. That's not wholly fair. When he rejects political engagement for a different responsibility, the responsibility to his umbilical language, it is more than mere aestheticism. The radicalism was genuine, the status as outsider absolutely real. In his fragmentary autobiography, Barthes defines himself as his culture had defined him: religiously, sexually, and academically marginal. "Who does not feel how *natural* it is, in France, to be Catholic, married, and properly accredited with the right degrees?" He wasn't, he tells us, even right-handed. We should not forget that the game American insiders now play was originally an enterprise of risk.

Barthes meant it about power. His essays were *essais* in Montaigne's original sense, tentative, trials of ideas. In his last decade even these came to seem too domineering, too insistently coherent, too "classical"; better to relax, to group paragraphs under topic headings, in alphabetical order, open to the aleatory air. Thus *The Pleasure of the Text, Roland Barthes by Roland Barthes, A Lover's Discourse.* Aleatory was a favorite word. Perhaps, to do him justice, that's the way this essay should end, miming his progress from the impersonal to the personal, from the essay's assertive form—thesis, argument, conclusion—to something more wavering, more faithful to the moods of thought, its tenuous demands, how it's always escaping, from reader, from writer, yet can't escape its paradoxical consistency, its message, its loyalty to the values of a lifetime. The older you get, the more everything you write and do connects, yes, into a self. What Keats, who didn't get old, called soul-making. So:

Abstraction: How could he escape it? And though we may grumble for a more fraternal ratio of specific to general, we had better appreciate it. Abstraction, analysis, is just so much *harder* than concrete specificity, not just to read but to do. Anybody can learn to be specific, and most of our freshmen will. But try setting them to write on Arrogance, Coincidence, or Ease. To discuss an abstraction and produce anything but truisms you have really to think. In *A Lover's Discourse* Barthes produces eight pages (in ten short takes) of analysis of the "holophrase" I-love-you. Here's just a bit of it:

> *I-love-you* is active. It affirms itself as force—against . . . the thousand forces of the world, which are, all of them, disparaging forces (science, *doxa*, reality, reason, etc.). Or again: against language. Just as the *amen* is at the limit of language, without collusion with its system . . . so the proffering of love (*I-love-you*) stands at the limit of syntax, welcomes tautology (*I-love-you* means *I-love-you*), rejects the servility of the Sentence . . . is not a sign, but plays against the signs.

No wonder we're impressed. As Dr. Faustus said, "Sweet Analytics, 'tis thou hast ravish'd me." As well they might. But they don't always. "The actantial model" may "stand the test of a large number of narratives," but it's hard to keep our attention on "the regulated transformations (replacements, confusions, duplications, substitutions) . . . of an actantial typology" through page after page when the ratio of generalization to example is about 50 to 1.

Assertion: how nicely RB tries to avoid it, sure that it can't be done. "The work is always dogmatic"; the author's (his word) "silences, his regrets, his naivetés, his scruples, his fears, everything that would make the work fraternal— none of this can pass into the written object." The sentence is by nature assertive; "writing *declares*"; "there is no such thing as a generous language." Perhaps. But that's what he tried for.

Author: in **RB by RB,** RB reproduces without comment a secondary school exam question on a passage he had written twenty-four years and hundreds of thousands of words ago. He knows, who better, that he has become the Author. Style, he wrote then, is "a way of speaking, a lexicon . . . born of the body and the past of the writer . . . an autarchic language . . . its depths in the personal and secret mythology of the author." Do I contradict myself? Very well, I contain multitudes.

Boredom: has an entry to itself in **The Pleasure of the Text,** pervades his writing about literature/life. Who, he asks, reads a classic text without skipping? The word "nausea" too recurs, as in this from *S/Z*: "The referential codes have a kind of emetic virtue, they bring on nausea by the boredom, conformism, and disgust that establishes them." Master of a tradition that bores him, he sticks with it; he doesn't go foraging abroad, or open a backward window on Villon or Rabelais. What are you going to *do* with a story like *Sarrasine?* Forget it, we might say, but Barthes is *French;* the myth of the great French language is *his* myth, however he demythicizes; Balzac is *his* Author. Skipping is one solution; another is to read into, read around, read under—having already dissolved the Author, so the question of whether to credit him with all these new pluralizing riches needn't arise. Here's a technique that can work with any text one's read so many times one can no longer imagine what it might be to encounter freshly what it says. RB liberated, alas, not so much the reader as the professor.

Bourgeois: show them no mercy. Functions, like "capitalist," as a simple pejorative. Nobody is nicer, more generous than RB, yet he depersonalizes with a word. For him, Marx joins with Flaubert to evoke in mid-twentieth century M. Homais and the boredom of Yonville. The domain of the bourgeois is the domain of the "self-evident," of the "violence" of unexamined conventions, of those who are "content to utter *what is self-evident, what follows of itself: the 'natural' is,* in short, *the ultimate outrage.*" The emphasis, of course, his. Though he rejected stereotypes, including those of the left, he held on to this one.

Dilettante: What he was. In its fine, original sense. He did read skippingly, skim over the flowers, take what he could use, leave it behind when it came to bore him, committed not to philosophy but to pleasure. Unlike ourselves, who now take him so seriously.

Fragments: RB on himself, in his not very impersonal third-person: "His first, or nearly first text (1942) consists of fragments, . . . 'because incoherence is preferable to a distorting order.' Since then . . . he has never stopped writing in brief bursts . . . ." As in "Fragments d'un discours amoureux," which precisely does not equal "A lover's discourse."

Freedom: the primary, pervasive value. From the self-evident, from the classic, from the bourgeois, from what he called the *Doxa;* from Nature which is not nature but nurture; from the "binary prison" of conventional sexuality, text and sexuality released together. Released from what? Ah, there's the rub. "From meaning." To "achieve a state of infinite expansion," in a text of enjoyment, of *jouissance,* a text which "comes."

Grammar: Abstract by its very nature, who in English can write like this about it?

> Obsolete in spoken French, the preterite, which is the cornerstone of Narration, always signifies the presence of Art. . . . Its function is no longer that of a tense [but] to reduce reality to a point of time, and to abstract, from the depth of a multiplicity of experience, a pure verbal act. . . . It presupposes a world which is constructed, elaborated, self-sufficient, reduced to significant lines, and not one which has been sent sprawling before us, for us to take or leave. Behind the preterite there always lurks a demiurge, a God, or a reciter.

Can you get any more intelligent than this?

Logic: The mind can't entertain two ideas at once, wrote Descartes, because the pineal gland can't be in two places at the same time. *C'n'est pas logique.* Boileau's "Twelfth Satire" equated ambiguity and equivocation long before Larousse. Reason was the Goddess the Revolution installed in Notre Dame. In the French words of the *Internationale* it's Reason that announces the final conflict. It's Justice in the English version. Experiential versus cognitive, empirical versus rational.

Neologism: Professor Picard accused him of jargon. He loved neologisms: they too were insignia of liberty. Against *Doxa,* paradox; against stereotypes, "novation": escape from the limits of authorized French. Playing with roots. With Greek ("holophrase," "semiophysis," "semioclasty"). The petty bourgeois can't do it; their Larousse, unlike English dictionaries, gives no derivations. You have to go to Littré, Robert; derivations are the privilege of the educated, the signifiers of (don't say it) power.

Object: He believes in it, repudiates abstraction. Yet *il n'y a pas de hors-texte.* There being no outside to the text, the object is hard to get at. The text is our universe, and we live inside it like the Shropshire Lad, in a world we never made. But what for Derrida is a philosophical position is for Barthes the actuality of experience. He really does live in a universe of signs. It's not surprising that he wants us to join him there; language, he says somewhere, was his Nature. He likes to quote vivid descriptions; it's the physicality of objects that he admires in Michelet. Yet his own language rarely evokes direct physical experience. The scarf the lover of *A Lover's Discourse* selects for his beloved is merely a sign; we are not told its texture or color. What RB describes, so well that we examine them as never before, are not objects but texts, written but also visual, stills from *Ivan the Terrible,* the plates of the *Grande Encyclopédie:* signifying phrases of the world's language. Texts were for him Nature, took the place of the conventional Nature which excluded him and which he repudiated as one more of the masks of *clarté.* Language he can describe incomparably, the nuance of its structures, the susurrus of its words. It is the rustle of language that he hears, not the rustle of Julia's silks, or anybody else's. Vendler doubts, in the course of her fine appreciation, that he was interested enough in people to write the novel he intended, and indeed, even in the clearly personal *A Lover's Discourse* the beloved X seems as abstract as his designation. Through abstraction the brilliant intelligence can at once confess its pain and hold it at an ironic distance. So the examples are far more often taken from literature than from life: Proust, Goethe. When we do get a signifying object, the blue coat and yellow vest belong to Werther.

Obscurity: **RB by RB:** "He realizes then how obscure such statements, clear as they are to him, must be for many others." Language obscure enough, elliptical enough, must in its "dreadful freedom" sacrifice fraternity and equality to liberty. The reader is continually being tested: are you intelligent enough? Industrious enough? Not what RB envisaged in 1963 when he rejected an academic ideology "articulated around a technique difficult enough to constitute an instrument of selection," in favor of an "immanent criticism" which required, "in the work's presence, only a power of astonishment." Obscurity becomes protective clothing, thick enough, all too often, to convert what might otherwise be productive challenge into dismissible peevishness: that wasn't Barthes's intention, who claimed, growing older, "no power, a little knowledge, a little wisdom, and as much flavor as possible." The author's work escapes him; he told us that. And the academy does not deal in astonishment; he told us that too.

Power: Why so much when he claimed none? The young thrill, perhaps, of putting everything at risk, safe in the suspicion that everything deconstructed will come together again by pure bourgeois inertia?

Plural: Central to his lexicon, the word evokes the consistency of a life. Invoking *La Déesse Homosexualité* ("all she

permits to say, to do, to understand, to know"), he would speak of "cruising," in reading too. That too was liberty.

Received ideas: he had his own. Marxism afforded them; so did psychoanalysis. *Self-evident,* they *followed of themselves.*

Responsibility: "What we can ask of a writer is that he be responsible"—but not for his opinions, and not to truth, to which he "loses all claim." Yet Barthes continues: a writer's "true responsibility" is to "literature . . . as a Mosaic glance at the Promised Land of the real." For him, as for Orwell, writing was an ethical enterprise. But where Orwell warred against the abstraction that obfuscates the appalling cruelty of the actualities it is our duty to see feelingly, Barthes felt the characteristic French responsibility, not first to the real, but to language. Still, though you can desire the escape from meaning, try for it, you can't accomplish it. Language foils you, stubbornly referential. The reader foils you, always looking for a meaning, not really satisfied to think he's free to find his own, wanting at least to approximate yours. And saying the same thing over a lifetime's *écriture,* you foil yourself. You thought it was true, and necessary to be said. Which brings us back to responsibility—the old-fashioned kind.

Truth: "Literature has an effect of truth much more violent for me than that of religion." A sentence from his journal, his last published work; he had been reading of the death of old Prince Bolkonsky in *War and Peace* while his own mother was dying. Cagy still: an *effect.* Yet somehow *truth* made its way into the sentence. When push comes to shove, it's the Promised Land that seems real.

(Hand)Writing: Introducing **RB by RB:** "All this must be considered as if spoken by a character in a novel." Cagy again; hide-and-seek, RB's discreet charm. Yet he arranged for the words to appear not in print but in his own fine rapid cursive, most personal of signatures. On another page, notes made in bed show handwriting loosened but still his own. Of course he didn't type.

Zed: He called it "The letter of deviance" and made it his own. First the straight line of assertion, then the zigzag of "reversal, contradiction, reactive energy"; *but, on the other hand, yet.* In the end of **Mythologies,** for instance: one demystifies the bourgeois myth of "good French wine"—but thereby regretfully "cut[s] oneself off from those who are . . . warmed" by what is in fact good, condemned, however progressive one's politics, to a sociality one's intelligence must render merely theoretical. So too the Author zigzags back in **The Pleasure of the Text**; though "as an institution" he's dead, yet "lost in the midst of the text (not *behind* it, like a god from the machine) there's always the other, the author." For (emphasis again his) "*I desire* the author"—"*d'une certaine façon.*"

When the Author died in France in 1968 it seemed a local matter. But as the report spread and discipline after discipline faced the demands of grand theory, the game turns serious. The insouciant critic gives way to the sober philosopher; people get nervous. In 1989 the lead article in the journal of the American Historical Association called "authorial presence" a "dream"; invoked Barthes, and after him Foucault and Derrida; worried whether, the author absent, intellectual history could be written at all. The simplicity of the answer may perhaps startle; the writer confesses that "it is beginning to look as if *belief* in the author may be our best response" (italics his). "Writers from a variety of disciplines are now suggesting that, if we hope to make sense of any text, we must first attribute to it an author." He had to read an awful lot to get to that point; my grandmother called it going round your elbow to get to your thumb. Perhaps, after the years in the wilderness, the professors are again turning their eyes toward the Promised Land, joining the Common Reader, to whose common sense Dr. Johnson trusted because it was "uncorrupted with literary prejudices," "the refinements of subtilty," or "the dogmatism of learning."

"Of all the intellectual notables who have emerged since World War II in France," writes Susan Sontag, "Roland Barthes is the one whose work I am most certain will endure." If so, it is because he is the one whose writing can be read, at least intermittently, for pleasure. Pleasure of the text and pleasure of the author, no god and no authority, but a human being to be enjoyed, for his commitment to freedom, to multiplicity, and to delight, for his intelligence, and for the generosity of his intentions. He desired the author. So do we.

Clara Claiborne Park, "Author! Author! Reconstructing Roland Barthes," in The Hudson Review, *Vol. XLIII, No. 3, Autumn, 1990, pp. 377-98.*

FURTHER READING

Bibliography

Freedman, Sanford. *Roland Barthes: A Bibliographical Reader's Guide.* New York: Garland, 1983, 409 p.
    Extensive bibliography of primary and secondary sources.

Criticism

Brown, Andrew. *Roland Barthes: The Figures of Writing.* Oxford: Clarendon Press, 1992, 303 p.
    Detailed analysis of Barthes's works that attempts to "chart some of the difficulties inherent in reading Barthes."

Calvino, Italo. "In Memory of Roland Barthes." In his *The Uses of Literature: Essays*, pp. 300-06. San Diego: Harcourt Brace Jovanovich, 1986.
    Eulogizes Barthes and discusses his last book, *Camera Lucida: Reflections on Photography.*

Eco, Umberto. "Language, Power, Force." In his *Travels in Hyperreality: Essays*, pp. 239-55. San Diego: Harcourt Brace Jovanovich, 1986.
    Analyzes the conception of power put forth in Barthes's "Inaugural Lecture" at the Collège de France.

Haverkamp, Anselm. "The Memory of Pictures: Roland Barthes and Augustine on Photography." *Comparative Literature* 45, No. 3 (Summer 1993): 258-79.
    Focuses on *Camera Lucida: Reflections on Photography* and analyzes the nature of photographic representation and memory.

Jameson, Fredric. "Pleasure: A Political Issue." In his *The Ideologies of Theory: Essays 1971-1986. Volume 2: The Syntax of History*, pp. 61-74. Minneapolis: University of Minnesota Press, 1988.
    Discusses the issue of pleasure in literature and the arts, referring to ideas presented in Barthes's *The Pleasure of the Text.*

Johnson, Barbara. "The Critical Difference: BartheS/BalZac." In her *The Critical Difference: Essays in the Contemporary Rhetoric of Reading*, pp. 3-12. Baltimore: The Johns Hopkins University Press, 1980.
    Examines the concept of "textual difference"—a term from deconstructive literary theory—in relation to Barthes's work in *S/Z.*

Kristeva, Julia. "How Does One Speak to Literature?" In her *Desire in Language: A Semiotic Approach to Literature and Art*, pp. 92-123. New York: Columbia University Press, 1980.
    Discusses the philosophical assumptions and implications of Barthes's work as it relates to the practice of avant-garde literary criticism.

Kurzweil, Edith. "Roland Barthes: Literary Structuralism and Erotics." In her *The Age of Structuralism: Lévi-Strauss to Foucault*, pp. 165-91. New York: Columbia University Press, 1980.
    Critical overview of Barthes's career. Kurzweil places his work in the context of the French Structuralist movement.

Lavers, Annette. *Roland Barthes: Structuralism and After.* Cambridge: Harvard University Press, 1982, 300 p.
    Examines the various literary and semiotic theories Barthes put forth and provides introductions to Structuralism and semiology.

Lombardo, Patrizia. *The Three Paradoxes of Roland Barthes.* Athens: The University of Georgia Press, 1989, 165 p.
    Examines aspects of Barthes's work from the perspective of "the failure of Structuralism [and] Barthes's invalidation of the scientific dream of the 1960s and 1970s." Lombardo also finds that Barthes's work fluctuates "between a revolutionary position and a reactionary one, between the rhetoric of the new and the inclination toward the past."

Miller, D. A. *Bringing Out Roland Barthes.* Berkeley: University of California Press, 1992, 55 p.
    Contemplates homosexual themes in Barthes's work while examining Miller's own feelings about being gay.

Mortimer, Armine Kotin. *The Gentlest Law: Roland Barthes's "The Pleasure of the Text."* New York: Peter Lang Publishing, 1989, 254 p.
    Analyzes, section by section, *The Pleasure of the Text*, providing commentary and asides on the issues raised or implied by Barthes's text.

Olsen, Bjørnar. "Roland Barthes: From Sign to Text." In *Reading Material Culture: Structuralism, Hermeneutics and Post-Structuralism*, edited by Christopher Tilley, pp. 163-205. Oxford: Basil Blackwell, 1990.
    Reviews Barthes's work in detail and discusses ways in which it can be applied to the practice of archeology.

O'Neill, John. "Breaking the Signs: Roland Barthes and the Literary Body." In *The Structural Allegory: Reconstructive Encounters with the New French Thought*, edited by John Fekete, pp. 183-200. Minneapolis: University of Minnesota Press, 1984.

Examines the political ramifications of Barthes's work and discusses his transition from Structuralism to Post-Structuralism.

Schleifer, Ronald. "The Rhetoric of Textuality: Roland Barthes and the Discomfort of Writing." In his *Rhetoric and Death: The Language of Modernism and Postmodern Discourse Theory*, pp. 146-75. Urbana: University of Illinois Press, 1990.

Examines the notion of textuality as it relates to the literary theories Barthes advanced in his later writings.

Silverman, Kaja. "Re-Writing the Classic Text." In her *The Subject of Semiotics*, pp. 237-83. New York: Oxford University Press, 1983.

Chapter-length explication and analysis of *S/Z*.

Thody, Philip. *Roland Barthes: A Conservative Estimate*. Atlantic Highlands, N. J.: Humanities Press, 1977, 180 p.

Detailed introduction to Barthes's work, the history of semiology, and the French intellectual milieu of the twentieth century.

Ungar, Steven. *Roland Barthes: The Professor of Desire*. Lincoln: University of Nebraska Press, 1983, 206 p.

Examines Barthes's career and attempts to account for his changes of philosophy and critical approach.

Ungar, Steven, and McGraw, Betty R., eds. *Signs In Culture:*

Roland Barthes Today. Iowa City: University of Iowa Press, 1989, 164 p.

Collects essays by noted authors who examine the semiological theory implicit in Barthes's work.

Vendler, Helen. "The Medley Is the Message." *The New York Review of Books* XXXIII, No. 8 (8 May 1986): 44-50.

Reviews later works by Barthes, notably *The Rustle of Language* and *The Responsibility of Forms: Critical Essays on Music, Art, and Representation*, and assesses the development of his thought, concluding that a "mind like that of Barthes, attuned to the aesthetic, accepts its own transiency in the processional of historical belief and rejoices in its own capacity for incorporating, over its lifetime, more than a single truth."

Wiseman, Mary Bittner. *The Ecstasies of Roland Barthes*. London: Routledge, 1989, 204 p.

Analyzes various aspects of Barthes's early and late writings in an attempt "to spell out the radically rewritten concept of the human subject, the material subject, the agent, the patient, the person."

Wood, Michael. "Rules of the Game." *The New York Review of Books* XXIII, No. 3 (4 March 1976): 31-4.

Reviews *Empire of Signs*, *S/Z*, *Sade, Fourier, Loyola*, *The Pleasure of the Text*, and *Roland Barthes*, concluding that "Barthes's determination to make everything in a text mean something . . . keeps the form of a text alive without sacrificing its content. It reminds us that form *is* a content (and content is a content too, and the question is the kind of sense we can make of them together)."

Additional coverage of Barthes's life and career is contained in the following sources published by Gale Research: *Contemporary Authors*, Vols. 97-100 (rev. ed.), 130 [obituary]; *Contemporary Literary Criticism*, Vol. 24; and *Major 20th Century Writers*.

Endgame

Samuel Beckett

The following entry presents criticism on Beckett's play *Fin de partie* (1957; *Endgame*). For further information on Beckett's complete career, see *CLC*, Volumes 1, 2, 3, 4, 6, 9, 10, 11, 14, 18, 29, and 59. For discussion of *En attendant Godot* (1953; *Waiting for Godot*), see *CLC*, Volume 57.

INTRODUCTION

One of the most celebrated authors in twentieth-century literature, Beckett is especially recognized for his significant impact on contemporary drama. *Endgame*, his second full-length play, focuses on the interaction of Hamm and Clov, two enigmatic modern figures forced to confront the nothingness of their existence. Like *Waiting for Godot*, *Endgame* features black humor, economical and fragmented language, experimental techniques, and stark images of alienation and absurdity. Despite the comic aspects of its surface level repartee, *Endgame* has been characterized by many critics as bleak, terrifying, and nihilistic.

Plot and Major Characters

Endgame is a long one-act play set during a single day in a bare room with two windows—one looking out onto an ocean, the other land—and a door that leads to a kitchen. The setting, as in most absurdist drama, serves to emphasize the central absurdity of everyday existence. The principal characters are Hamm and Clov. Hamm, who is blind and confined to an armchair mounted on castors, has been described by Beckett as "a king in this chess game lost from the start. From the start, he knows he is making loud senseless moves. . . . He is only trying to delay the inevitable end." Clov, who cannot walk very well, waits on Hamm and Hamm's parents, Nagg and Nell, who are legless and confined to two trash cans from which their heads periodically appear and disappear. Mutual dependence and hatred informs the relationships between Hamm and the other characters; as the play begins, Hamm's supply of food and pain killer is dwindling. Clov verbally spars with Hamm, and occasionally peers out the windows with a telescope to assure Hamm that nothing else is alive. Nagg and Nell discuss the past, and Nagg tells a story about a tailor and some trousers. Hamm relates two versions of a "chronicle" about a man and his son, and responds cruelly to pleas from the other characters for sustenance and relief from suffering. Toward the end of the play, Hamm orders Clov to seal the lids of the trash cans; Nagg and Nell apparently die. Looking out the window, Clov reports seeing a small boy. Hamm tells Clov he no longer needs him and Clov prepares to leave. The play concludes with Clov waiting by the door and Hamm, as

he began the play, resting motionless in his chair with a bloody handkerchief over his face.

Major Themes

One of the most obvious themes of *Endgame* is the necessity of interdependence, even if the relationship is one of hate. Clov, for example, depends on Hamm for access to food since only Hamm knows how to open the larder, while Hamm relies on Clov to be his eyes and to move his chair. The play also focuses on confinement: Hamm is paralyzed, Nagg and Nell cannot leave their trash cans, and the action of the play occurs in a bare room, outside of which life apparently cannot survive. Generational conflict, particularly between father and son, also emerges as a prominent theme. Hamm twice tells a story about a father and son and seems to view parent-child relationships only in terms of power and resentment. Critics have argued that Hamm resents Nagg, his father, for not being kind to him when he was young, while Hamm resents Clov, his son, for being young at a time when his life is in decline. *Endgame* has also been interpreted as a depiction of humanity's denial of such life processes as death and procreation. Finally, the actors make numerous, explicit references throughout *Endgame* to their roles as characters in a play. For example, Hamm at one point states: "I'm warming up for my last soliloquy." At another point, Clov announces: "This is what we call making an exit." Critics contend that such references to the action of the play as a performance suggest that *Endgame* depicts humanity's penchant for self-dramatization, the act through which it assigns meaning to an otherwise meaningless universe.

Critical Reception

Critics often compare *Endgame* to Beckett's previous drama *Waiting for Godot*, noting, for instance, that characters in both plays are grouped in symmetrical pairs. However, *Endgame* is considered much bleaker and more perplexing than the latter play because it lacks the hope for redemption that informs *Waiting for Godot*. Speculation as to the significance of the play's setting, characters, and Hamm's and Nagg's narratives have generated diverse opinions. The metaphor governing the setting has been variously identified as a bomb shelter in the wake of a nuclear war, the interior of an individual's mind, and Noah's ark; Hamm and Clov have been supposed to represent James Joyce and Beckett, respectively; and interpretations of Hamm's chronicle range from an expression of guilt to the story of Hamm's adoption of Clov. Commentators have also focused on Beckett's numerous biblical allusions, his use of irony, and his attempt to "undo" cliches and idioms by having the characters respond to them on a literal level. Commenting on *Endgame* himself, Beckett identified the speech "nothing is funnier than unhappiness" as key to the play's interpretation and performance.

---

*PRINCIPAL WORKS

Whoroscope (poem) 1930
Proust (essay) 1931
More Pricks than Kicks (short stories) 1934
Murphy (novel) 1938
Malone meurt (novel) 1951
  [*Malone Dies*, 1956]
Molloy (novel) 1951
  [*Molloy*, 1955]
En attendant Godot (drama) 1953
  [*Waiting for Godot*, 1955]
L'innommable (novel) 1953
  [*The Unnamable*, 1958]
Watt (novel) 1953
Nouvelles et textes pour rien (short stories) 1955
  [*Stories and Texts for Nothing*, 1967]
†*Actes sans paroles I* (drama) 1957
All that Fall (drama) [first publication] 1957
†*Fin de Partie* (drama) 1957
  [*Endgame*, 1958]
Krapp's Last Tape (drama) 1958
Actes san paroles II (drama) 1960
Comment c'est (novel) 1961
  [*How It Is*, 1964]
Happy Days (drama) 1961

Comédie (drama) 1964
  [*Play*, 1964]
Imatination morte imaginez (drama) [first publication] 1965
  [*Imagination Dead Imagine*, 1965]
Va et vient (drama) 1966
  [*Come and Go*, 1968]
‡*Eh Joe, and Other Writings* (drama and screenplay) 1967
No's Knife: Collected Shorter Prose, 1945-1966 (dramas and short stories) 1967
Breath (drama) 1970
Le dépeupleur (drama) [first publication] 1970
  [*The Lost Ones*, 1972]
§*Mercier et Camier* (novel) 1970
  [*Mercier and Camier*, 1974]
§*Premier amour* (drama) [first publication] 1970
  [*First Love*, 1973]
Not I (drama) 1972
Ends and Odds (dramas and radio plays) 1976
Foot Falls (drama) 1976
That Time (drama) 1976
Companie (novel) 1979
  [*Company*, 1980]
A Piece of Monologue (drama) 1979
Ohio Impromptu (drama) 1981
Rockaby (drama) 1981
Texts for Nothing (drama) 1981
Mal vu mal dit (prose poem) 1981
  [*Ill Seen Ill Said*, 1982]
Westward Ho (novel) 1983
Stirrings Still (novella) 1989

---

*Beckett translated or cotranslated from the French all of the translations listed.

†These dramas were first performed together.

‡This work includes *Eh Joe*, *Act Without Words II*, and *Film*.

§These works were originally written in 1945.

CRITICISM

Robert Hatch (review date 15 February 1958)

[*In the excerpt below, Hatch presents a mixed assessment of* Endgame.]

> Use your head, can't you, use your head, you're on earth, there's no cure for that!

There is no bottom to the nihilism of Samuel Beckett, but each time, as he is going down forever, he finds a flicker of wit and kicks on for another few strokes. For a poet, total renunciation is probably impossible—he is forced to believe in his own poetry and from that he can rebuild a universe.

So **Endgame** (Cherry Lane) is not really the end; it merely approaches the end as the parallel lines approach infinity. However, it is much further along than **Waiting for**

Godot: it looks as though we might be extinguished at any minute—not with a bang and not with a whimper, but stuttering importantly like a rundown clock. The past ("accursed progenitor") is refuse. Ancient father and mother, they stand in ash cans on the stumps of their legs, having lost their shanks "in the Ardennes" . . . "on the road to Sedan"; which may suggest where and when Beckett thinks the end officially began. The lord of the present is blind and paralyzed, enthroned in his filth, sardonic and mawkish with the worn-out poses of an eternity of posing. The slave is truculent and spavined, but still slaving—out of habit, and perhaps because it is the only activity left on earth. It is something to be able to get around, however painfully.

There has been a disaster (at least we are now deep in a "shelter"), or perhaps it is just cosmic fatigue—the tides no longer flow, nothing moves, nothing grows, there is no sunlight "out there." Or *was* that a child, flashing just past the edge of the window? Impossible, absurd, ha ha! And yet if it were so, we could give up this silly game, this word play, this humiliating crawl to infinity. We could die without committing the treason of extermination. Beckett will not quite give up the hope he does not have:

> HAMM. The bastard! [God, that is] He doesn't exist!
>
> CLOV. Not yet.

"This is not much fun," says Hamm the master, and compared to *Waiting for Godot* it really isn't. The mad dialogue still rings like china, and shocks of wicked laughter still spill out of the surrounding gibberish:

> CLOV. Do you believe in the life to come?
>
> HAMM. Mine has always been that.

But when two of your four characters are stuck in ash cans (with the tops on a good part of the time) and a third is confined to a throne on casters, you must rely for action on the comings and goings of the one remaining on his feet (just barely on his feet). This degenerates fairly soon into a sorry pendulum of busyness. . . . *Endgame* is in one act and runs for about ninety minutes, but it seems a long evening.

The new parable lacks the playfulness, the lovable naughtiness of its predecessor. That was not all Bert Lahr's doing—Beckett kicked up his own heels. Now it is so much later in the day that defiance and gaiety are almost used up—the effect is powerful enough, but there is less theatre to it. And more poetry, perhaps. The characteristic staccato lines clash against one another like cymbals, the voices within voices are like the supporting and echoing choirs in an orchestra. It is the song of final dissolution by a minstrel-prophet with the logic of death in his mind and the conviction of life forever in his blood. The great drama of Beckett is always his inability to subdue himself.

Robert Hatch, in a review of "Endgame," in The Nation, *New York, Vol. 186, No. 7, February 15, 1958, pp. 145-46.*

Tom F. Driver　(review date 5 March 1958)

[*An American educator, theologian, and critic, Driver has written several books on modern drama. In the following excerpt, he considers* Endgame *less accomplished than* Waiting for Godot.]

Two years ago, Samuel Beckett's theatrical parable *Waiting for Godot* came to the attention of American audiences and moved many of us to wild enthusiasm. (The fact that many others were put off entirely by it only added to the fun.) Whatever Mr. Beckett may have intended in that play, actually he had written an enigma which teased one with the question whether it was worth it to wait for the appearance of an absolute that seemed perpetually slow in coming. The play was open-ended, somewhat like Frank Stockton's story "The Lady or the Tiger?" It left at least the possibility that the attitude of waiting is a part of salvation.

It was too much to hope that Mr. Beckett's next play would be as good. Any such hope is now disappointed with the arrival of *Endgame,* which, however, is not without its points.

Samuel Beckett's plays have no plot. Little or nothing happens in them. To write plays about a world in which there is no action is a neat trick, and surely the playwright deserves some sort of award for pulling if off at all. In *Waiting for Godot* the situation was partly relieved by the expectation that something *might* happen. The symbols Beckett used in that play were closely associated with Christian symbols, and therefore of themselves (not to mention the dialogue and form of the play) they engendered the notion that action might at any moment break into the thoroughly inactive situation.

In *Endgame,* on the other hand, there is no such possibility. The set is in a filthy courtyard, bricked in on every side. All the characters are on stage at the beginning: nobody comes and nobody goes. One of them speaks of going and even gets packed to leave; but it is impossible to imagine him anywhere else, and so he stays. The principal character is blind and sits in a wheelchair; he cannot stand. His menial is afflicted in the legs and cannot sit. The parents of the blind man have lost their legs and are kept in a couple of ash cans. Their son feeds them on dog biscuits.

Theatrically, the remarkable part of it is how such a play, if not dull, could turn out to be anything but horrifying. At the deepest level it *is* horrifying; but the playwright manages to keep the surface of it interesting, comic, and even sentimental. It will be hard for me to erase the memory of the sweet old couple, popping up from under their galvanized lids and reminiscing about the day their boat capsized in Lake Como. It made us children laugh and cry.

Beckett writes plays of the spirit, plays of man's relation to his hopes and to his neighbor. The form of *Endgame* and its tone suggest that the game is up. Mr. Beckett is tolling a little tinkly bell for the end of the world. Man has made such ugly use of his neighbor that the two are now inextricably bound together by iron chains of exploitation.

They suffer their mutual captivity by learning to find moments of love.

At times Mr. Beckett's anger at this condition flares out. Once, the blind man rolls his chair to the edge of the stage and cries to the audience: "Get out of here and love one another!" Yet the audience I was in made no stir. The playwright's irony is that even though we may begin to see the nature of our sickness it is too far advanced for cure.

Tom F. Driver, "Out in Left Field," in The Christian Century, *Vol. LXXV, March 5, 1958, pp. 282-83.*

Hugh Kenner   (essay date 1961)

[*Kenner is the foremost American critic and chronicler of literary Modernism. He is best known for* The Pound Era *(1971), an extensive study of the Modernist movement, and for his influential works on T. S. Eliot, James Joyce, Samuel Beckett, and Wyndham Lewis. In the following essay originally published in 1961 in his* Samuel Beckett: A Critical Study, *he interprets* Endgame *as a self-conscious performance designed to explore the boundaries of theatricalism.*]

The stage is a place to wait. The place itself waits, when no one is in it. When the curtain rises on *Endgame,* sheets drape all visible objects as in a furniture warehouse. Clov's first act is to uncurtain the two high windows and inspect the universe; his second is to remove the sheets and fold them carefully over his arm, disclosing two ash cans and a figure in an armchair. This is so plainly a metaphor for waking up that we fancy the stage, with its high peepholes, to be the inside of an immense skull. It is also a ritual for starting the play; Yeats arranged such a ritual for *At the Hawk's Well,* and specified a black cloth and a symbolic song. It is finally a removal from symbolic storage of the objects that will be needed during the course of the performance. When the theater is empty it is sensible to keep them covered against dust. So we are reminded at the outset that what we are to witness is a dusty dramatic exhibition, repeated and repeatable. The necessary objects include three additional players (two of them in ash cans). Since none of them will move from his station we can think of them after the performance as being kept permanently on stage, and covered with their dust cloths again until tomorrow night.

The rising of the curtain disclosed these sheeted forms; the removal of the sheets disclosed the protagonist and his ash cans; the next stage is for the protagonist to uncover his own face, which he does with a yawn, culminating this three-phase strip tease with the revelation of a very red face and black glasses. His name, we gather from the program, is Hamm, a name for an actor. He is also Hamlet, bounded in a nutshell, fancying himself king of infinite space, but troubled by bad dreams; he is also "a toppled Prospero," remarking partway through the play, with judicious pedantry, "our revels now are ended"; he is also the Hammer to which Clov, Nagg and Nell (Fr. *clou,* Ger. *Nagel,* Eng. *nail*) stand in passive relationship; by extension, a chess player ("Me—[*he yawns*]—to play"); but also (since Clov must wheel him about) himself a chessman, probably the imperiled King.

Nagg and Nell in their dustbins appear to be pawns; Clov, with his arbitrarily restricted movements ("I can't sit") and his equestrian background ("And your rounds? Always on foot?" "Sometimes on horse") resembles the Knight, and his perfectly cubical kitchen ("ten feet by ten feet by ten feet, nice dimensions, nice proportions") resembles a square on the chessboard translated into three dimensions. He moves back and forth, into it and out of it, coming to the succor of Hamm and then retreating. At the endgame's end the pawns are forever immobile and Clov is poised for a last departure from the board, the status quo forever menaced by an expected piece glimpsed through the window, and King Hamm abandoned in check:

> Old endgame lost of old, play and lose and have done with losing. . . . Since that's the way we're playing it, let's play it that way . . . and speak no more about it . . . speak no more.

Even if we had not the information that the author of this work has been known to spend hours playing chess with himself (a game at which you always lose), we should have been alerted to his long-standing interest in its strategy by the eleventh chapter of *Murphy,* where Murphy's first move against Mr. Endon, the standard P—K, is described as "the primary cause of all [his] subsequent difficulties." (The same might be said of getting born, an equally conventional opening.) Chess has several peculiarities which lend themselves to the metaphors of this jagged play. It is a game of leverage, in which the significance of a move may be out of all proportion to the local disturbance it effects ("A flea! This is awful! What a day!"). It is a game of silences, in which new situations are appraised: hence Beckett's most frequent stage direction, *"Pause."* It is a game of steady attrition; by the time we reach the endgame the board is nearly bare, as bare as Hamm's world where there are no more bicycle wheels, sugarplums, painkillers, or coffins, let alone people. And it is a game which by the successive removal of screening pieces constantly extends the range of lethal forces, until at the endgame peril from a key piece sweeps down whole ranks and files. The king is hobbled by the rule which allows him to move in any direction but only one square at a time; Hamm's circuit of the stage and return to center perhaps exhibits him patrolling the inner boundaries of the little nine-square territory he commands. To venture further will evidently expose him to check. ("Outside of here it's death.") His knight shuttles to and fro, his pawns are pinned. No threat is anticipated from the auditorium, which is presumably off the board; and a periodic reconnaissance downfield through the windows discloses nothing but desolation until very near the end. But on his last inspection of the field Clov is dismayed. Here the English text is inexplicably sketchy; in the French one we have,

> CLOV. Aïeaïeaïe!
>
> HAMM. C'est une feuille? Une fleur? Une toma—(*il bâille*)—te?
>
> CLOV. (*Regardant*) Je t'en foutrai des tomates! Quelqu'un! C'est quelqu'un!
>
> HAMM. Eh bien, va l'exterminer. (*Clov descend*

de l'escabeau) Quelqu'un! *(Vibrant)* Fais ton devoir!

In the subsequent interrogatory we learn the distance of this threat (fifteen meters or so), its state of rest or motion (motionless), its sex (presumably a boy), its occupation (sitting on the ground as if leaning on something). Hamm, perhaps thinking of the resurrected Jesus, murmurs "La pierre levée," then on reflection changes the image to constitute himself proprietor of the Promised Land: "Il regarde la maison sans doute, avec les yeux de Moïse mourant." It is doing, however, nothing of the kind; it is gazing at its navel. There is no use, Hamm decides, in running out to exterminate it: "If he exists he'll die there or he'll come here. And if he doesn't . . ." And a few seconds later he has conceded the game:

> It's the end, Clov, we've come to the end. I don't need you any more.

He sacrifices his last mobile piece, discards his staff and whistle, summons for the last time a resourceless Knight and an unanswering Pawn, and covers his face once more with the handkerchief: somehow in check.

Not that all this is likely to be yielded up with clarity by any conceivable performance. It represents however a structure which, however we glimpse it, serves to refrigerate the incidental passions of a play about, it would seem, the end of humanity. It is not for nothing that the place within which the frigid events are transacted is more than once called "the shelter," outside of which is death; nor that the human race is at present reduced to two disabled parents, a macabre blind son, and an acathisiac servant. Around this shelter the universe crumbles away like an immense dry biscuit: no more rugs, no more tide, no more coffins. We hear of particular deaths:

> CLOV. *(Harshly)* When old Mother Pegg asked you for oil for her lamp and you told her to get out to hell, you knew what was happening then, no? *(Pause)* You know what she died of, Mother Pegg? Of darkness.
>
> HAMM. *(Feebly)* I hadn't any.
>
> CLOV. *(As before)* Yes, you had.

We observe particular brutalities: Hamm, of his parents: "Have you bottled her?" "Yes." "Are they both bottled?" "Yes." "Screw down the lids." What has shrunken the formerly ample world is perhaps Hamm's withdrawal of love; the great skull-like setting suggests a solipsist's universe. "I was never there," he says. "Absent, always. It all happened without me. I don't know what's happened." He has been in "the shelter"; he has also been closed within himself. It is barely possible that the desolation is not universal:

> HAMM. Did you ever think of one thing?
>
> CLOV. Never.
>
> HAMM. That here we're down in a hole. *(Pause)* But beyond the hills? Eh? Perhaps it's still green. Eh? *(Pause)* Flora! Pomona! *(Ecstatically)* Ceres! *(Pause)* Perhaps you won't need to go very far.
>
> CLOV. I can't go very far. *(Pause)* I'll leave you.

As Hamm is both chessman and chess player, so it is conceivable that destruction is not screened off by the shelter but radiates from it for a certain distance. Zero, zero, words we hear so often in the dialogue, these are the Cartesian coordinates of the origin.

Bounded in a nutshell yet king of infinite space, Hamm articulates the racking ambiguity of the play by means of his dominance over its most persuasive metaphor, the play itself. If he is Prospero with staff and revels, if he is Richard III bloodsmeared and crying "My kingdom for a nightman!" if he is also perhaps Richard II, within whose hollow crown

> Keeps Death his court, and there the Antic sits,
> Scoffing his state and grinning at his pomp,
> Allowing him a breath, a little scene
> To monarchize, be feared, and kill with looks—

these roles do not exhaust his repertoire. He is (his name tells us) the generic Actor, a creature all circumference and no center. As master of the revels, he himself attends to the last unveiling of the opening ritual:

> *(Pause. Hamm stirs. He yawns under the handkerchief. He removes the handkerchief from his face. Very red face, black glasses.)*
> HAMM. Me—*(he yawns)*—to play. *(He holds the handkerchief spread out before him.)* Old stancher! (. . . *He clears his throat, joins the tips of his fingers.)* Can there be misery—*(he yawns)*—loftier than mine?

The play ended, he ceremoniously unfolds the handkerchief once more (five separate stage directions governing his tempo) and covers his face as it was in the beginning. "Old Stancher! *(Pause.)* You . . . remain." What remains, in the final brief tableau specified by the author, is the immobile figure with a bloodied Veronica's veil in place of a face: the actor having superintended his own Passion and translated himself into an ultimate abstraction of masked agony.

Between these termini he animates everything, ordering the coming and going of Clov and the capping and uncapping of the cans. When Clov asks, "What is there to keep me here?" he answers sharply, "The dialogue." A particularly futile bit of business with the spyglass and the steps elicits from him an aesthetic judgment, "This is deadly." When it is time for the introduction of the stuffed dog, he notes, "We're getting on," and a few minutes later, "Do you not think this has gone on long enough?" These, like comparable details in *Godot,* are sardonic authorizations for a disquiet that is certainly stirring in the auditorium. No one understands better than Beckett, nor exploits more boldly, the kind of fatalistic attention an audience trained on films is accustomed to place at the dramatist's disposal. The cinema has taught us to suppose that a dramatic presentation moves inexorably as the reels unwind or the studio clock creeps, until it has consumed precisely its allotted time which nothing, no restlessness in the pit, no sirens, no mass exodus can hurry. "Something is taking its course," that suffices us. Hence the vast leisure in which the minimal business of *Godot* and *Endgame* is transacted; hence (transposing into dramatic terms the author's characteristic pedantry of means) the occasional lingering over points of technique, secure in the knowledge that the clock-bound patience of a twentieth-century audience will expect no inner urgency, nothing in fact but the actual time events consume, to determine the pace of the exhibition. Clov asks, "Why this farce, day after day?" and it is sufficient for Hamm to reply, "Routine. One never knows." It is the answer of an actor in an age of films and long runs. In *Endgame* (which here differs radically from *Godot*) no one is supposed to be improvising; the script has been well committed to memory and well rehearsed. By this means doom is caused to penetrate the most intimate crevices of the play. "I'm tired of going on," says Clov late in the play, "very tired," and then, "Let's stop playing!" (if there is one thing that modern acting is not it is playing). In the final moments theatrical technique, under Hamm's sponsorship, rises into savage prominence.

> HAMM. . . . And me? Did anyone ever have pity on me?
>
> CLOV. (*Lowering the telescope, turning towards Hamm*) What? (*Pause*) Is it me you're referring to?
>
> HAMM. (*Angrily*) An aside, ape! Did you never hear an aside before? (*Pause*) I'm warming up for my last soliloquy.

Ten seconds later he glosses "More complications!" as a technical term: "Not an underplot, I trust." It is Clov who has the last word in this vein:

> HAMM. Clov! (*Clov halts, without turning*) Nothing. (*Clov moves on*) Clov! (*Clov halts, without turning*)
>
> CLOV. This is what we call making an exit.

By this reiterated stress on the actors as professional men, and so on the play as an occasion within which they operate, Beckett transforms Hamm's last soliloquy into a performance, his desolation into something prepared by the dramatic machine, his abandoning of gaff, dog, and whistle into a necessary discarding of props, and the terminal business with the handkerchief into, quite literally, a curtain speech. *Endgame* ends with an unexpected lightness, a death rather mimed than experienced; if it is "Hamm as stated, and Clov as stated, together as stated," the mode of statement has more salience than a paraphrase of the play's situation would lead one to expect.

The professionalism also saves the play from an essentially sentimental commitment to *simpliste* "destiny." Much of its gloomy power it derives from contact with such notions as T. H. Huxley's view of man as an irrelevance whom day by day an indifferent universe engages in chess. We do not belong here, runs a strain of Western thought which became especially articulate in France after the War; we belong nowhere; we are all surds, ab-surd. There is nothing on which to ground our right to exist, and we need not be especially surprised one day to find ourselves nearly extinct. (On such a despair Cartesian logic converges, as surely as the arithmetic of Pythagoras wedged itself fast in the irrationality of 2.) Whatever we do, then, since it can obtain no grip on our radically pointless situation, is *behavior* pure and simple; it is play acting, and may yield us the satisfaction, if satisfaction there be, of playing well,

of uttering our *cris du coeur* with style and some sense of timing. We do not trouble deaf heaven, for there is only the sky ("Rien," reports Clov, gazing through his telescope; and again, "Zéro.") We stir and thrill, at best, ourselves. From such a climate, miscalled existentialist, Beckett wrings every available *frisson* without quite delivering the play into its keeping; for its credibility is not a principle the play postulates but an idea the play contains, an idea of which it works out the moral and spiritual consequences. The despair in which he traffics is a conviction, not a philosophy. He will even set it spinning like a catharine wheel about a wild point of logic, as when he has Hamm require that God be prayed to in silence ("Where are your manners?") and then berate him ("The bastard!") for not existing.

The play contains whatever ideas we discern inside it; no idea contains the play. The play contains, moreover, two narrative intervals, performances within the performance. The first, Nagg's story about the trousers, is explicitly a recitation; Nell has heard it often, and so, probably, has the audience; it is a vaudeville standby. Nagg's performance, like a production of *King Lear*, whose story we know, must therefore be judged solely as a performance. Its quality, alas, discourages even him ("I tell this story worse and worse"), and Nell too is not amused, being occupied with thoughts of her own, about the sand at the bottom of Lake Como. The other is Hamm's huffe-snuffe narrative, also a recitation, since we are to gather that he has been composing it beforehand, in his head. This time we do not know the substance of the tale, but contemplate in diminishing perspective an actor who has memorized a script which enjoins him to imitate a man who has devised and memorized a script:

> The man came crawling towards me, on his belly. Pale, wonderfully pale and thin, he seemed on the point of—(*Pause. Normal tone.*) No, I've done that bit.

Later on he incorporates a few critical reflections: "Nicely put, that," or "There's English for you." This technician's narcissism somewhat disinfects the dreadful tale. All Hamm's satisfactions come from dramatic self-contemplation, and as he towers before us, devoid of mercy, it is to some ludicrous stage villain that he assimilates himself, there on the stage, striking a stage-Barabbas pose ("Sometimes I go about and poison wells"). It is to this that life as play-acting comes.

> In the end he asked me would I consent to take in the child as well—if he were still alive. (*Pause*) It was the moment I was waiting for. (*Pause*) Would I consent to take in the child. . . . (*Pause*) I can see him still, down on his knees, his hands flat on the ground, glaring at me with his mad eyes, in defiance of my wishes.

"It was the moment I was waiting for": the satisfaction this exudes isconsiderably less sadistic than dramatic, and the anticlimax into which the long performance immediately topples would try a creator's soul, not a maniac's:

> I'll soon have finished with this story. (*Pause*) Unless I bring in other characters. (*Pause*) But where would I find them? (*Pause*) Where would

I look for them? (*Pause. He whistles. Enter Clov.*)
Let us pray to God.

So the hooks go in. There is no denying what Beckett called in a letter to Alan Schneider "the power of the text to claw." It strikes, however, its unique precarious balance between rage and art, immobilizing all characters but one, rotating before us for ninety unbroken minutes the surfaces of Nothing, always designedly faltering on the brink of utter insignificance into which nevertheless we cannot but project so many awful significances: theater reduced to its elements in order that theatricalism may explore without mediation its own boundaries: a bleak unforgettable tour de force and probably its author's single most remarkable work.

Hugh Kenner, "Life in the Box," in Samuel Beckett's *"Endgame", edited by Harold Bloom, Chelsea House Publishers, 1988, pp. 41-48.*

Though I prefer *Waiting for Godot*, I consider *Endgame* a masterpiece. It is a complete theatre statement of a consummate poet's experience. Its writing is endowed with a marvelous musicality which, while mordant, is graced by subtle repetition and thematic variations.

—Harold Clurman, in a review of Endgame *in* The Nation, *26 February 1973*.

Martin Esslin   (essay date 1961)

[*Esslin, a prominent and sometimes controversial critic of contemporary theater, is perhaps best known for coining the term "theater of the absurd." His* The Theatre of the Absurd *(1961) is a major study of the avant-garde drama of the 1950s and early 1960s, including the works of Samuel Beckett, Eugene Ionesco, and Jean Genet. In the following excerpt from an essay originally published in that work, he critiques various interpretations of* Endgame *and discusses the significance of the small boy that Clov sees near the play's conclusion.*]

If *Waiting for Godot* shows its two heroes whiling away the time in a succession of desultory, and never-ending, games, Beckett's second play deals with an "endgame," the final game in the hour of death.

Waiting for Godot takes place on a terrifyingly empty open road, *Endgame* in a claustrophobic interior. *Waiting for Godot* consists of two symmetrical movements that balance each other; *Endgame* has only one act that shows the running down of a mechanism until it comes to a stop. Yet *Endgame*, like *Waiting for Godot*, groups its characters in symmetrical pairs.

In a bare room with two small windows, a blind old man, Hamm, sits in a wheelchair. Hamm is paralyzed, and can no longer stand. His servant, Clov, is unable to sit down. In two ash cans that stand by the wall are Hamm's legless parents, Nagg and Nell. The world outside is dead. Some great catastrophe, of which the four characters in the play are, or believe themselves to be, the sole survivors, has killed all living beings.

Hamm and Clov (ham actor and clown?) in some ways resemble Pozzo and Lucky. Hamm is the master, Clov the servant. Hamm is selfish, sensuous, domineering. Clov hates Hamm and wants to leave him, but he must obey his orders "Do this, do that, and I do it. I never refuse. Why?" Will Clov have the force to leave Hamm? That is the source of the dramatic tension of the play. If he leaves, Hamm must die, as Clov is the only one left who can feed him. But Clov also must die, as there is no else left in the world, and Hamm's store is the last remaining source of food. If Clov can muster the will power to leave, he will not only kill Hamm but commit suicide. He will thus succeed where Estragon and Vladimir have failed so often.

Hamm fancies himself as a writer—or, rather, as the spinner of a tale of which he composes a brief passage every day. It is a story about a catastrophe that caused the death of large numbers of people. On this particular day, the tale has reached an episode in which the father of a starving child asks Hamm for bread for his child. Finally the father begs Hamm to take in his child, should it still be alive when he gets back to his home. It appears that Clov might well be that very child. He was brought to Hamm when he was too small to remember. Hamm was a father to him, or, as he himself puts it, "But for me . . . no father. But for Hamm . . . no home." The situation in *Endgame* is the reverse of that in Joyce's *Ulysses,* where a father finds a substitute for a lost son. Here a foster son is trying to leave his foster father.

Clov has been trying to leave Hamm ever since he was born, or as he says, "Ever since I was whelped." Hamm is burdened with a great load of guilt. He might have saved large numbers of people who begged him for help. "The place was crawling with them!" One of the neighbors, old Mother Pegg, who was "bonny once, like a flower of the field" and perhaps Hamm's lover, was killed through his cruelty: "When old Mother Pegg asked you for oil for her lamp and you told her to get out to hell . . . you know what she died of, Mother Pegg? Of darkness." Now the supplies in Hamm's own household are running out: the sweets, the flour for the parents' pap, even Hamm's painkiller. The world is running down. "Something is taking its course."

Hamm is childish; he plays with a three-legged toy dog, and he is full of self-pity. Clov serves him as his eyes. At regular intervals he is asked to survey the outside world from the two tiny windows high up in the wall. The right-hand window looks out on land, the left-hand onto the sea. But even the tides have stopped.

Hamm is untidy. Clov is a fanatic of order.

Hamm's parents, in their dustbins, are grotesquely sentimental imbeciles. They lost their legs in an accident while cycling through the Ardennes on their tandem, on the road to Sedan. They remember the day they went rowing on Lake Como—the day after they became engaged—one April afternoon (cf. the love scene in a boat on a lake in *Krapp's Last Tape*), and Nagg, in the tones of an Edwardian raconteur, retells the funny story that made his bride laugh then and that he has since repeated *ad nauseam*.

Hamm hates his parents. Nell secretly urges Clov to desert Hamm. Nagg, having been awakened to listen to Hamm's tale, scolds him: "Whom did you call when you were a tiny boy, and were frightened in the dark? Your mother? No. Me." But he immediately reveals how selfishly he ignored these calls.

> We let you cry. Then we moved out of earshot, so that we might sleep in peace. . . . I hope the day will come when you'll really need to have me listen to you. . . . Yes, I hope I'll live till then, to hear you calling me like when you were a tiny little boy, and were frightened, in the dark, and I was your only hope.

As the end approaches, Hamm imagines what will happen when Clov leaves him. He confirms Nagg's forecast: "There I'll be in the old shelter, alone against the silence and . . . the stillness. . . . I'll have called my father and I'll have called my . . . my son," which indicates that he does indeed regard Clov as his son.

For a last time, Clov looks out of the windows with his telescope. He sees something unusual. "A small . . . boy!" But it is not entirely clear whether he has really seen this strange sign of continuing life, "a potential procreator." In some way, this is the turning point. Hamm says, "It's the end, Clov, we've come to the end. I don't need you any more." Perhaps he does not believe that Clov will really be able to leave him. But Clov has finally decided that he will go: "I open the door of the cell and go. I am so bowed I only see my feet, if I open my eyes, and between my legs a little trail of black dust. I say to myself that the earth is extinguished, though I never saw it lit. . . . It's easy going. . . . When I fall I'll weep for happiness." And as blind Hamm indulges in a last monologue of reminiscence and self-pity, Clov appears, dressed for departure in a Panama hat, tweed coat, raincoat over his arm, and listens to Hamm's speech, motionless. When the curtain falls, he is still there. It remains open whether he will really leave.

The final tableau of *Endgame* bears a curious resemblance to the ending of a little-known but highly significant play by the brilliant Russian dramatist and man of the theatre Nikolai Evreinov, which appeared in an English translation as early as 1915—*The Theatre of the Soul*. This one-act play is a monodrama that takes place *inside a human being* and shows the constituent parts of his ego, his emotional self and his rational self in conflict with each other. The man, Ivanov, is sitting in a café, debating with himself whether to run away with a night-club singer or go back to his wife. His emotional self urges him to leave, his rational self tries to persuade him of the advantages, moral and material, of staying with his wife. As they come to blows, a bullet pierces the heart that has been beating in the background. Ivanov has shot himself. The rational and emotional selves fall down dead. A third figure, who has been sleeping in the background, gets up. He is dressed in trav-

eling clothes and carries a suitcase. It is the immortal part of Ivanov that now has to move on.

While it is unlikely that Beckett knew this old and long-forgotten Russian play, the parallels are very striking. Evreinov's monodrama is a purely rational construction designed to present to a cabaret audience what was then the newest psychological trend. Beckett's play springs from genuine depths. Yet the suggestion that *Endgame* may also be a monodrama has much to be said for it. The enclosed space with the two tiny windows through which Clov observes the outside world; the dustbins that hold the suppressed and despised parents, and whose lids Clov is ordered to press down when they become obnoxious; Hamm, blind and emotional; Clov, performing the function of the senses for him—all these might well represent different aspects of a single personality, repressed memories in the subconscious mind, the emotional and the intellectual selves. Is Clov then the intellect, bound to serve the emotions, instincts, and appetites, and trying to free himself from such disorderly and tyrannical masters, yet doomed to die when its connection with the animal side of the personality is severed? Is the death of the outside world the gradual receding of the links to reality that takes place in the process of aging and dying? Is *Endgame* a monodrama depicting the dissolution of a personality in the hour of death?

It would be wrong to assume that these questions can be definitely answered. *Endgame* certainly was not planned as a sustained allegory of this type. But there are indications that there is an element of monodrama in the play. Hamm describes a memory that is strangely reminiscent of the situation in *Endgame*:

> I once knew a madman who thought the end of the world had come. He was a painter—an engraver. . . . I used to go and see him in the asylum. I'd take him by the hand and drag him to the window. Look! There! All that rising corn! And there! Look! The sails of the herring fleet! All that loveliness! . . . He'd snatch away his hand and go back into his corner. Appalled. All he had seen was ashes. . . . He alone had been spared. Forgotten. . . It appears the case is . . . was not so . . . so unusual.

Hamm's own world resembles the delusions of the mad painter. Moreover, what is the significance of the picture mentioned in the stage directions? "Hanging near door, its face to wall, a picture." Is that picture a memory? Is the story a lucid moment in the consciousness of that very painter whose dying hours we witness from behind the scenes of his mind?

Beckett's plays can be interpreted on many levels. *Endgame* may well be a monodrama on one level and a morality play about the death of a rich man on another. But the peculiar psychological reality of Beckett's characters has often been noticed. Pozzo and Lucky have been interpreted as body and mind; Vladimir and Estragon have been seen as so complementary that they might be the two halves of a single personality, the conscious and the subconscious mind. Each of these three pairs—Pozzo-Lucky; Vladimir-Estragon; Hamm-Clov—is linked by a relationship of mutual interdependence, wanting to leave each other, at war with each other, and yet dependent on each other. *"Nec tecum, nec sine te."* This is a frequent situation among people—married couples, for example—but it is also an image of the interrelatedness of the elements within a single personality, particularly if the personality is in conflict with itself.

In Beckett's first play, *Eleutheria,* the basic situation was, superficially, analogous to the relationship between Clov and Hamm. The young hero of that play wanted to leave his family; in the end he succeeded in getting away. In *Endgame,* however, that situation has been deepened into truly universal significance; it has been concentrated and immeasurably enriched precisely by having been freed from all elements of a naturalistic social setting and external plot. The process of contraction, which Beckett described as the essence of the artistic tendency in his essay on Proust, has here been carried out triumphantly. Instead of merely exploring a surface, a play like *Endgame* has become a shaft driven deep down into the core of being; that is why it exists on a multitude of levels, revealing new ones as it is more closely studied. What at first might have appeared as obscurity or lack of definition is later recognized as the very hallmark of the density of texture, the tremendous concentration of a work that springs from a truly creative imagination, as distinct from a merely imitative one.

The force of these considerations is brought out with particular clarity when we are confronted by an attempt to interpret a play like *Endgame* as a mere exercise in conscious or subconscious autobiography. In an extremely ingenious essay ["Joyce the Father, Beckett the Son," *The New Leader* (December 14, 1959)] Lionel Abel has worked out the thesis that in the characters of Hamm and Pozzo, Beckett may have portrayed his literary master, James Joyce, while Lucky and Clov stand for Beckett himself. *Endgame* then becomes an allegory of the relationship between the domineering, nearly blind Joyce and his adoring disciple, who felt himself crushed by his master's overpowering literary influence. Superficially the parallels are striking: Hamm is presented as being at work on an interminable story, Lucky is being made to perform a set piece of thinking, which, Mr. Abel argues, is in fact a parody of Joyce's style. Yet on closer reflection this theory surely becomes untenable; not because there may not be a certain amount of truth in it (every writer is bound to use elements of his own experience of life in his work) but because, far from illuminating the full content of a play like *Endgame,* such an interpretation reduces it to a trivial level. If *Endgame* really were nothing but a thinly disguised account of the literary, or even the human, relationship between two particular individuals, it could not possibly produce the impact it has had on audiences utterly ignorant of these particular, very private circumstances. Yet *Endgame* undoubtedly has a very deep and direct impact, which can spring only from its touching a chord in the minds of a very large number of human beings. The problems of the relationship between a literary master and his pupil would be very unlikely to elicit such a response; very few people in the audience would feel directly involved. Admittedly, a play that presented the conflict be-

tween Joyce and Beckett openly, or thinly disguised, might arouse the curiosity of audiences who are always eager for autobiographical revelations. But this is just what *Endgame* does *not* do. If it nevertheless arouses profound emotion in its audience, this can be due only to the fact that it is felt to deal with a conflict of a far more universal nature. Once that is seen, it becomes clear that while it is fascinating to argue about the aptness of such autobiographical elements, such a discussion leaves the central problem of understanding the play and exploring its many-layered meanings still to be tackled.

As a matter of fact, the parallels are by no means so close: Lucky's speech in *Waiting for Godot,* for example, is anything but a parody of Joyce's style. It is, if anything, a parody of philosophical jargon and scientific double-talk— the very opposite of what either Joyce or Beckett ever wanted to achieve in their writing. Pozzo, on the other hand, who would stand for Joyce, is utterly inartistic in his first persona, and becomes reflective in a melancholy vein only after he has gone blind. And if Pozzo is Joyce, what would be the significance of Lucky's dumbness, which comes at the same time as Pozzo's blindness? The novel that Hamm composes in *Endgame* is characterized by its attempt at scientific exactitude, and there is a clear suggestion that it is not a work of art at all, but a thinly disguised vehicle for the expression of Hamm's sense of guilt about his behavior at the time of the great mysterious calamity, when he refused to save his neighbors. Clov, on the other hand, is shown as totally uninterested in Hamm's "Work in Progress," so that Hamm has to bribe his senile father to listen to it—surely a situation as unlike that of Joyce and Beckett as can be imagined.

The experience expressed in Beckett's plays is of a far more profound and fundamental nature than mere autobiography. They reveal his experience of temporality and evanescence; his sense of the tragic difficulty of becoming aware of one's own self in the merciless process of renovation and destruction that occurs with change in time; of the difficulty of communication between human beings; of the unending quest for reality in a world in which everything is uncertain and the borderline between dream and reality is ever shifting; of the tragic nature of all love relationships and the self-deception of friendship (of which Beckett speaks in the essay on Proust), and so on. In *Endgame* we are also certainly confronted with a very powerful expression of the sense of deadness, of leaden heaviness and hopelessness, that is experienced in states of deep depression: the world outside goes dead for the victim of such states, but inside his mind there is ceaseless argument between parts of his personality that have become autonomous entities.

This is not to say that Beckett gives a clinical description of psychopathological states. His creative intuition explores the elements of experience and shows to what extent all human beings carry the seeds of such depression and disintegration within the deeper layers of their personality. If the prisoners of San Quentin responded to *Waiting for Godot,* it was because they were confronted with *their own experience* of time, waiting, hope, and despair; because they recognized the truth about *their own human re-*

lationships in the sadomasochistic interdependence of Pozzo and Lucky and in the bickering hate-love between Vladimir and Estragon. This is also the key to the wide success of Beckett's plays: to be confronted with concrete projections of the deepest fears and anxieties, which have been only vaguely experienced at a half-conscious level, constitutes a process of catharsis and liberation analogous to the therapeutic effect in psychoanalysis of confronting the subconscious contents of the mind. This is the moment of release from deadening habit, through facing up to the suffering of the reality of being, that Vladimir almost attains in **Waiting for Godot.** This also, probably, is the release that could occur if Clov had the courage to break his bondage to Hamm and venture out into the world, which may not, after all, be so dead as it appeared from within the claustrophobic confines of Hamm's realm. This, in fact, seems to be hinted at by the strange episode of the little boy whom Clov observes in the last stages of **Endgame.** Is this boy a symbol of life outside the closed circuit of withdrawal from reality?

It is significant that in the original, French version, this episode is dealt with in greater detail than in the later, English one. Again Beckett seems to have felt that he had been too explicit. And from an artistic point of view he is surely right; in his type of theatre the half-light of suggestion is more powerful than the overtly symbolical. But the comparison between the two versions is illuminating nevertheless. In the English version, Clov, after expressing surprise at what he has discovered, merely says:

> CLOV. (*Dismayed*). Looks like a small boy!
>
> HAMM. (*Sarcastic*). A small . . . boy!
>
> CLOV. I'll go and see. (*He gets down, drops the telescope, goes towards the door, turns*) I'll take the gaff. (*He looks for the gaff, sees it, picks it up, hastens towards the door*)
>
> HAMM. No!
> (*Clov halts*)
>
> CLOV. No? A potential procreator?
>
> HAMM. If he exists he'll die there or he'll come here. And if he doesn't . . . (*Pause*)

In the original, French version, Hamm shows far greater interest in the boy, and his attitude changes from open hostility to resignation.

> CLOV. There is someone there! Someone!
>
> HAMM. Well, go and exterminate him! (*Clov gets down from the stool*) Somebody! (*With trembling voice*) Do your duty! (*Clov rushes to the door*) No, don't bother. (*Clov stops*) What distance? (*Clov climbs back on the stool, looks through the telescope*)
>
> CLOV. Seventy . . . four meters.
>
> HAMM. Approaching? Receding?
>
> CLOV. (*continues to look*). Stationary.
>
> HAMM. Sex?
>
> CLOV. What does it matter? (*He opens the win-*

dow, leans out. Pause. He straightens, lowers the telescope, turns to Hamm, frightened.) Looks like a little boy.

> HAMM. Occupied with?
>
> CLOV. What?
>
> HAMM. (*Violently*). What is he doing?
>
> CLOV. (*Also*). I don't know what he's doing. What little boys used to do. (*He looks through the telescope. Pause. Puts it down, turns to Hamm.*) He seems to be sitting on the ground, with his back against something.
>
> HAMM. The lifted stone. (*Pause*) Your eyesight is getting better. (*Pause*) No doubt he is looking at the house with the eyes of Moses dying.
>
> CLOV. No.
>
> HAMM. What is he looking at?
>
> CLOV. (*Violently*). I don't know what he is looking at. (*He raises the telescope. Pause. Lowers the telescope, turns to Hamm.*) His navel. Or thereabouts. (*Pause*) Why this cross-examination?
>
> HAMM. Perhaps he is dead.

After this, the French text and the English version again coincide: Clov wants to tackle the newcomer with his gaff, Hamm stops him, and, after a brief moment of doubt as to whether Clov has told him the truth, realizes that the turning point has come:

> It's the end, Clov, we've come to the end. I don't need you any more.

The longer, more elaborate version of this episode clearly reveals the religious or quasi-religious symbolism of the little boy; the references to Moses and the lifted stone seem to hint that the first human being, the first sign of life discovered in the outside world since the great calamity when the earth went dead, is not, like Moses, dying within sight of the promised land, but, like Christ the moment after the resurrection, has been newly born into a new life, leaning, a babe, against the lifted stone. Moreover, like the Buddha, the little boy contemplates his navel. And his appearance convinces Hamm that the moment of parting, the final stage of the endgame, has come.

It may well be that the sighting of this little boy—undoubtedly a climactic event in the play—stands for redemption from the illusion and evanescence of time through the recognition, and acceptance, of a higher reality: the little boy contemplates his own navel; that is, he fixes his attention on the great emptiness of nirvana, nothingness, of which Democritus the Abderite has said, in one of Beckett's favorite quotations, "Nothing is more real than nothing."

There is a moment of illumination, shortly before he himself dies, in which Murphy, having played a *game of chess,* experiences a strange sensation:

> . . . and Murphy began to see nothing, that colorlessness which is such a rare post-natal treat, being the absence . . . not of *percipere* but of *percipi.* His other senses also found themselves

at peace, an unexpected pleasure. Not the numb peace of their own suspension, but the positive peace that comes when the somethings give way, or perhaps simply add up, to the Nothing, than which in the guffaw of the Abderite naught is more real. Time did not cease, that would be asking too much, but the wheels of rounds and pauses did, as Murphy with his head among the armies [i.e., of the chessmen] continued to suck in, through all the posterns of his withered soul, the accidentless One-and-Only conveniently called Nothing.

Does Hamm, who has shut himself off from the world and killed the rest of mankind by holding on to his material possessions—Hamm, blind, sensual, egocentric—then die when Clov, the rational part of the self, perceives the true reality of the illusoriness of the material world, the redemption and resurrection, the liberation from the wheels of time that lies in union with the "accidentless One-and-Only, conveniently called Nothing"? Or is the discovery of the little boy merely a symbol of the coming of death—union with nothingness in a different, more concrete sense? Or does the reappearance of life in the outside world indicate that the period of loss of contact with the world has come to an end, that the crisis has passed and that a disintegrating personality is about to find the way back to integration, "the solemn change towards merciless reality in Hamm and ruthless acceptance of freedom in Clov," as the Jungian analyst Dr. Metman puts it?

There is no need to try to pursue these alternatives any further; to decide in favor of one would only impair the stimulating coexistence of these and other possible implications. There is, however, an illuminating commentary on Beckett's views about the interrelation between material wants and a feeling of restlessness and futility in the short mime-play *Act Without Words,* which was performed with *Endgame* during its first run. The scene is a desert onto which a man is "flung backwards." Mysterious whistles draw his attention in various directions. A number of more or less desirable objects, notably a carafe of water, are dangled before him. He tries to get the water. It hangs too high. A number of cubes, obviously designed to make it easier for him to reach the water, descend from the flies. But however ingeniously he piles them on top of one another, the water always slides just outside his reach. In the end he sinks into complete immobility. The whistle sounds—but he no longer heeds it. The water is dangled in front of his face—but he does not move. Even the palm tree in the shade of which he has been sitting is whisked off into the flies. He remains immobile, looking at his hands.

Here again we find man flung onto the stage of life, at first obeying the call of a number of impulses, having his attention drawn to the pursuit of illusory objectives by whistles from the wings, but finding peace only when he has learned his lesson and refuses any of the material satisfactions dangled before him. The pursuit of objectives that forever recede as they are attained—inevitably so through the action of time, which changes us in the process of reaching what we crave—can find release only in the recognition of that nothingness which is the only reality. The whistle that sounds from the wings resembles the whistle

with which Hamm summons Clov to minister to his material needs. And the final, immobile position of the man in *Act Without Words* recalls the posture of the little boy in the original version of *Endgame.*

The activity of Pozzo and Lucky, the driver and the driven, always on the way from place to place; the waiting of Estragon and Vladimir, whose attention is always focused on the promise of a coming; the defensive position of Hamm, who has built himself a shelter from the world to hold on to his possessions, are all aspects of the same futile preoccupation with objectives and illusory goals. All movement is disorder. As Clov says, "I love order. It's my dream. A world where all would be silent and still and each thing in its last place, under the last dust."

Martin Esslin, "Samuel Beckett: The Search for the Self," in Twentieth Century Interpretations of 'Endgame': A Collection of Critical Essays, *Prentice-Hall, Inc., 1969, pp. 22-32.*

Antony Easthope (essay date February 1968)

[*Easthope is an English educator and critic. In the following essay originally published in* Modern Drama *in February 1968, he remarks on Hamm and Clov's relationship in* Endgame *and analyzes Beckett's dramatic method.*]

One way in which a play holds the attention of an audience for the duration of its performance is by presenting an action which may be formulated as a question: Who killed Laius? How will Hamlet revenge his father? *Endgame* has a plot at least to the extent that it holds its audience with an uncertainty, one which is continuously reiterated from the stage: Will Clov leave Hamm? At the end, when the final tableau shows Clov standing there, with umbrella, raincoat, and bag, unable to stay and unable to go, the question remains unresolved. Nevertheless, any discussion of *Endgame,* including one which proposes to consider the play's dramatic method, should begin with this question, or rather with the relationship between Hamm and Clov from which it arises. And since Clov is for the most part a passive victim, a pawn dominated by Hamm's active mastery, it is with Hamm that we should start.

In order to get even as far as the play will let us towards understanding why Hamm keeps Clov (assuming that he could in fact let him go), we must try to see what Hamm is like. He is like a king, with Clov as his servant, for he refers to "my house," "my service," and even, echoing Shakespeare's Richard III, to "my kingdom." On one occasion he uses the royal plural to Clov, "You can't leave us." In a former time he had real power, or so he claims, when Clov, as he reminds him, "inspected my paupers." Now his realm has shrunk almost to nothing and he is left with Clov, Nagg, and Nell as his courtiers. His relationship with Clov is like that between Pozzo and Lucky in *Godot,* and its quality is well conveyed by Lionel Abel's suggestion that it is an analogue of the relationship between the young Beckett and the old, blind, Joyce. Hamm treats Nagg and Nell as further objects for gratuitous affliction—"Bottle him!" Hamm seems to be a tyrant, who lives to enjoy the exercise of his power over others. But it is at this point that the difficulties begin, for to say that Hamm enjoys exercising power is to attribute a familiar form of psychological motivation to him—and it is hard to be sure he has the capacity for this. Together with its many other connotations, Hamm is the name for an actor, for one who creates an identity which has only an imaginary existence. And the tone of what Hamm says is frequently consistent with that of an assumed identity, one deliberately acted out. So he deals with the requests of his servants:

> CLOV. He wants a sugar-plum.
>
> HAMM. He'll get a sugar-plum.

Hamm's reply is such a fulsome expression of largesse and arrogant condescension that it seems merely a verbal gesture. Nagg does not get his sugarplum, but what we might take to be Hamm's intentional malice cannot properly be distinguished from a pretence of high-handed magnificence which is part of the role he plays. Hamm orders Clov to screw down the lids of the ashbins on Nagg and Nell, and then comments on himself, "My anger subsides, I'd like to pee." It is this continuous self-consciousness in Hamm's words and tone of voice which inhibits us from ascribing his cruelty to an impulse beyond the need for rhetorical coherence in the role he plays.

Hamm appears to suffer, but with this there is the same doubt as with his cruelty. While introducing himself, Hamm proclaims his agony:

> Can there be misery—(*He yawns*)—loftier than mine? No doubt. Formerly. But now?

His expression of "loftier misery" is laden with echoes of Oedipus the King and of Christ as presented in Herbert's poem, "The Sacrifice," with the famous refrain, "Was ever grief like to mine?" The salt of genuine affliction dissolves among these overtones into a self-conscious rhetoric, a heavy irony directed at the very possibility of real suffering. Hamm takes the magnitude of his "misery" as guarantee for the importance of his role. On several occasions in the play introspection leads him to talk as though he were suffering, but each time his words become a performance. When Hamm speaks of a heart dripping in his head, he is exposed immediately to the ridicule of Nagg and Nell, who react to his unhappiness as a fiction, "it's like the funny story we have heard too often." Later Hamm tells Clov that he too will go blind one day and find himself alone in "infinite emptiness"—but this again may be seen as an act, a set speech which the stage directions mark as to be performed *With prophetic relish.* Beckett has written of *Endgame* that it is "more inhuman than Godot" and Hamm's cruelty earns the play this adjective. But it may be understood in a double sense. In so far as Hamm is felt as a real character, then he is inhuman in the sense we use the word of a man whose actions are so extreme that they seem to place him beyond the pale of humanity. His boundless cynicism may be seen as a desperate attempt to anticipate the cruelty of a universe which is indifferent to his wishes, and his expressions of suffering may be symptoms of genuine agony. Thus, in his hatred of "life," Hamm becomes like King Lear, who, when stripped of all he values, can only cry, "Then kill, kill, kill,

kill, kill." To describe Hamm's putative character in such melodramatic language is an appropriate response to the play, for all this may be no more than an aspect of his deliberate playacting. Hamm may in fact be inhuman only in the strict sense of being not human, if the fiction of his role is so perfectly sustained that it excludes any capacity for genuine motive and what we take to be real humanity. Such perhaps is the implication of Hamm's admission to Clov, "I was never there," though this depends upon the stress an actor gives to the personal pronoun. So a full account of Hamm must comprehend both the surface fiction of his role and the psychological depths suggested beneath it. And the main event in *Endgame,* Hamm's story, manifests this ambiguity or doubleness with a clarity which must be considered in detail.

Hamm's story may be seen as a fictional extension of his role, demonstrating clearly how conscious he is of the part he plays. He fancies himself as a great lord, a Pharaoh or a Czar. A father comes to him, begging some corn for a starving child. With enormous complacency the master waits for the end of the plea, for the most dramatic moment, before giving his crushing reply:

> Use your head, can't you, use your head, you're on earth, there's no cure for that!

This fantasy account of the exercise of power seems no more than a perfect opportunity for Hamm to practise his histrionic talents. Yet there are many suggestions in the telling of the story which imply that Hamm is seriously involved and that his fiction reflects real anxiety and suffering. For, latent beneath the surface of his chronicle, a tenuous connection of metaphors and phrases repeated in different contexts renders Hamm's relationship with Clov as the hidden subject of his story.

Throughout the play Clov is likened to a dog. He refers to his birth as being "whelped"; he comes to Hamm when he whistles, and the master wears a whistle round his neck for this purpose. Great play is made with a stage prop, a stuffed dog, and once Clov hands this to Hamm with the revealing plural, "Your dogs are here." Clov stands continually, he cannot sit, and Hamm is concerned that the stuffed animal should be able to stand. Like Clov, the dog cannot leave, "He's not a real dog, he can't go." But, as we discover, the function of the toy dog for Hamm is to enlarge his role, bolstering his grandeur by standing there imploring him, "as if he were begging . . . for a bone." Through the figures of dog and beggar, Hamm's relationship to Clov becomes transposed into his story. So also with the reference to a child. Clov is Hamm's child, or at least, Hamm "was a father" to him. Hamm tells Clov he will give him just enough to keep him from dying, so that, like the starving boy in the story, Clov will be "hungry all the time." At the end, when Clov says he sees a small boy approaching, Hamm tells him he will need him no longer, implying that the small boy will take Clov's place. Thus Hamm's violent pronouncement to the beggar and his child is felt as though spoken to Clov. Twice elsewhere in the play Hamm says "Use your head," on both occasions while addressing Clov.

It may be that Hamm keeps coming back to his story simply in the interest of art. For the raconteur practice makes perfect, and Hamm appears to think his only concern with the anecdote is to polish its phrasing—"Technique, you know." But it is hard not to respond to the way he returns again and again to his story as symptomatic of a genuine obsession with it. If this is so, it is consistent with the character suggested behind Hamm's role. The telling of the story looks like a guilty attempt by Hamm to convince himself that nihilism justifies hardness of heart, "you're on earth, there's no cure for that!" Guilt would result if Hamm feared that his cynicism were merely a rationalization for a cruel impulse prior to it, and Clov awakens exactly this fear later in the play, the effect being to drive Hamm almost into silence:

> CLOV. (*Harshly*) When old Mother Pegg asked you for oil for her lamp and you told her to get out to hell, you knew what was happening then, no? (*Pause*) You know what she died of, Mother Pegg? Of darkness.
>
> HAMM. (*Feebly*) I hadn't any.
>
> CLOV. (*As before*) Yes, you had.

That Hamm's story disturbs him at a level which he cannot—or will not—recognize is implied by what follows it in the rest of the play. Immediately after Hamm's story the famous prayer to God takes place. Perhaps this is another facet of Hamm's role, another fiction, since it is prefaced by his remark that he may need "other characters." Or again, it may be a symptom of remorse and an authentic quest for grace, particularly if Hamm has remembered the biblical parable echoed in his story, that of Dives and Lazarus, and thought of the appalling punishment meted out to the cruel master at the end of that. Earlier Hamm had made a jocular reference to Clov's kissing him goodbye before leaving; after the story the motif recurs, but this time Hamm's phrasing sounds personally insistent:

> HAMM. Kiss me. (*Pause*) Will you not kiss me?

Is this another patronising demand for homage, dictated by the master's role? Or are we to detect in it a lurking desire for forgiveness? All through the play Hamm has nagged Clov for his painkiller; on the single occasion he repeats his request after the story, he is answered in the affirmative, and then told by Clov, "There's no more painkiller." Hamm's reaction to this seems to be the hysteria of uncontrollable agony:

> HAMM. (*Soft*) What'll I do? (*Pause. In a scream.*) What'll I do?

Yet the violence of this disappears in his next words to Clov, "What are you doing?" Anaphora smooths over the expressive intensity of Hamm's cry, making it seem less a cry of pain and more like a mere ruffle in the verbal surface. At the end of the play Clov's reported sighting of a small boy is followed by Hamm's final soliloquy, which contains a last reference to his story, "If he could have his child with him."

What this argument has tried to show is that Hamm has a double nature, existing both as consciously played role and as real character. His role as king and master seems to be unbroken and self-contained. Any subject to which he directs his attention, even his own suffering, becomes

falsified through absorption into conscious rhetoric and turned into the performance of an actor. Yet there is something more about Hamm, which escapes his attention, a network of possibilities, a string of metaphorical connections and repeated phrases, leading beyond the role he knows he is playing. This implies obliquely a psychological reality in him, one which would perhaps evaporate into fiction if Hamm were able to give it explicit articulation. And this ambivalent relationship between surface and depth in the way that Hamm is dramatised is worked out as a structural principle in the whole of *Endgame.* The depths of the play, its metaphorical and suggestive qualities, have occupied the attention of most critics of the play. Hugh Kenner in his book on Beckett and also Robert Benedetti in a recent article for the *Chicago Review* have shown how the play is aware of itself as a text performed in a theater. It is sufficient to list the technical theatrical terms used in it in order to remark the rigor with which this effect is created: "farce," "audition," "aside," "soliloquy," "dialogue," "underplot," "exit." The result of these references is that many lines come to sound as comments on the play made from the stage, "This is slow work," and so on. But if *Endgame* contains a consciousness of itself as a theatrical performance generated according to the conventions of that form, this is only part of the whole. For the verbal surface of the play is pervaded by a deliberate sense of artifice, which never allows an audience to forget they are watching a game played according to certain rules. As Hamm says, "Since that's the way we're playing it . . . let's play it that way." And a principal effect of the drama derives from the deft manner in which a consciously sustained surface, itself a meaningless exercise in various techniques, is held in tension with the expressive significance of what is suggested beneath it.

> **A principal effect of *Endgame* derives from the deft manner in which a consciously sustained surface, itself a meaningless exercise in various techniques, is held in tension with the expressive significance of what is suggested beneath it.**
>
> **—Antony Easthope**

One of the most unusual rhetorical techniques which occurs in *Endgame* is this:

> NAGG. I had it yesterday.
>
> NELL. (*Elegaic*) Ah yesterday! (*They turn painfully towards each other*)

A little later the same turn is again given to the word "yesterday" in an exchange between Nagg and Nell. A word from the first speaker's sentence is repeated with an exclamation mark in reply. The effect in both these cases is, as the stage directions make clear, to parody sentimental evocation. On another occasion the tone is marked to imply scepticism:

> CLOV. (*Dismayed*) Looks like a small boy!
>
> HAMM. (*Sarcastic*) A small . . . boy!

But when it is not discriminated by the directions the tone of the exclamation must combine contempt, scepticism and sadness. The function of the device seems to be to sterilise an emotional gesture by questioning assumptions it contains. Thus it is perfectly placed at a point when the dialogue discusses just such a movement as the turn of phrase enacts:

> HAMM. We're not beginning to . . . to . . . mean something?
>
> CLOV. Mean something! You and I, mean something! (*Brief laugh*) That's a good one!

By the end of the play the device has become a cliché, and thus when it is used twice on the mention of a heart as Hamm and Clov exchange goodbyes, the exclamation has been robbed of most of the force it had as an assertive protest:

> HAMM. A few words . . . to ponder . . . in my heart.
>
> CLOV. Your heart!

Of course what Hamm says may be a sincere plea for kindness from Clov, just as his reply may be taken to express bitter contempt for the way he has been exploited by the master. But it would be a misreading of the play to respond to the emotional significance of the exchanges without recognising that this is entirely subordinated to what is now a stock response, a merely verbal gesture. The rhythm of this rhetorical device is insidious and easily acquired by a good ear; it contributes a great deal to the unique resonance of the play.

The verbal surface of **Endgame** is aware of itself as being organized in accordance with the conventions governing conversation and stage dialogue, particularly a kind of two person dialogue not unlike that of the old music-hall tradition of the comic and the straight-man. The conversational form admits several kinds of monologue, and these are performed as such. Two anecdotes are available to eke out the entertainment, Hamm's story and Nagg's joke about the Englishman and the tailor. This he is directed to pronounce in a "(*Raconteur's voice*)." Hamm, as the best talker on the stage, has the largest repertoire of monologues. Besides anecdote he is also capable of the philosophic speculation, "Imagine if a rational being came back to earth . . . ," and, with a sense of tour de force, the prophetic admonition, "One day you'll say to yourself . . . ," which he declaims for Clov. In each case the significant undertones are ignored by the surface, so that even Hamm's frightening account of the madman who saw the beauty of the world as ashes is presented as a formal exercise, it being of course that standby of conversation, the reminiscence:

> CLOV. A madman? When was that?

> HAMM. Oh way back, way back, you weren't in the land of the living.

The language of Clov's last speech at the end of the play describes with delicate and appalling precision the feelings of a man released after a lifetime of imprisonment:

> I open the door of the cell and go. I am so bowed I only see my feet, if I open my eyes, and between my legs a little trail of black dust. I say to myself that the world is extinguished, though I never saw it lit. (*Pause*) It's easy going. (*Pause*) When I fall I'll weep for happiness.

Yet the stage directions insist that the evocative power of this language is to be deliberately suppressed: "CLOV (*fixed gaze, tonelessly, towards auditorium*)." The speech is, as Clov reminds us, the correct theatrical gesture for making an exit. For this, as for the other monologues, including Hamm's self-styled "last soliloquy," the play will accept no responsibility beyond that for applying certain theatrical and conversational conventions.

The dialogue of **Endgame** is a brilliantly contrived exercise in the art of repartee. Unfortunately, discussion of a single passage, one of the best, will have to stand for analysis of a quality of conscious formal elegance which pervades the whole:

> HAMM. Nature has forgotten us.
>
> CLOV. There's no more nature.
>
> HAMM. No more nature! You exaggerate.
>
> CLOV. In the vicinity.
>
> HAMM. But we breathe, we change! We lose our hair, our teeth! Our bloom! Our ideals!
>
> CLOV. Then she hasn't forgotten us.
>
> HAMM. But you say there is none.
>
> CLOV. (*Sadly*) No one that ever lived ever thought so crooked as we.
>
> HAMM. We do what we can.
>
> CLOV. We shouldn't.

The issue behind this exchange is clear enough—whether Nature and Nature's God have temporarily withdrawn themselves from man or have actually ceased to exist. But serious concern with this question is submerged in this sharp, witty, paradoxical dialogue, often dependent on the interplay of verbal connection and logical nonsequitur, which is of a kind that has fascinated the Irish from Swift to Shaw. Hamm's straight-man assertion provokes Clov's stock response, "There's no more Nature." His denial is categorical in form, an either/or, but Hamm impossibly calls it an exaggeration, at the same time employing a rhetorical exclamation made familiar by the rest of the play. Hamm's response, instead of collapsing the conversation, elicits an equally impossible concession from Clov, "In the vicinity," as though Nature, if it existed, could exist locally but not universally. This Hamm ignores, launching into the vigorous if paradoxical proof that universal decay is evidence for Nature's continued existence. Instead of replying to this in terms consistent with his previous denial,

Clov counters wittily by accepting the existence of human decay as evidence of Nature's benevolence, "Then she hasn't forgotten us." Hamm takes this to be Clov's admission that he was wrong, a move which Clov tries to thwart with a sententious aphorism, "No one that ever lived thought so crooked as we." Hamm pounces on this by implying that crooked thinking is all to the good. But his words are ambiguous, for "can" here means both "the best we can" and "what we have to do." Thus the Parthian shaft comes from Clov, who outwits Hamm by repeating his disapproval of crooked thinking in a way which supposes that people do by choice what Hamm has unintentionally said they do by necessity. After a pause, this vigorous little canter earns Clov his master's praise, "You're a bit of all right, aren't you?" This adapts the vulgar British phrase as admiration for Clov's high technical proficiency in playing games with a concept whose varying definitions have worried thinkers of our civilization for over two thousand years. It is because of a similar delight in technical expertise that Hamm on a later occasion cannot resist self-congratulation:

> CLOV. Do you believe in the life to come?
>
> HAMM. Mine was always that. (*Exit Clov*) Got him that time!

Once again, a serious subject, the fate of man's external soul, is used mainly as an occasion for repartee, and this juxtaposition of a formal surface with serious, often terrifying depths accounts for much of what Beckett in his correspondence with Alan Schneider referred to as "the power of the text to claw."

A word frequently applied to Beckett's work is "poetic." What the adjective really points to in Beckett's plays (a context in which it is perjorative if it replaces the honorific qualification "dramatic") is the extraordinary ability of the language and stagecraft to imply, suggest, connote, evoke, and set off expressive nuances. In this respect *Endgame* fulfills expectations which derive to us from our experience of the symbolist tradition in poetry and drama, for it was Mallarmé's principle that "to name is to destroy; to suggest is to create." It is this, and the traditional assumption that drama imitates a reality beyond itself, which Beckett has chosen to exploit. And he exploits it by providing the play with a level of action, which ignores its own significant implications. The surface of *Endgame* insists upon itself as a meaningless technical exercise of the medium in its own right and refuses to acknowledge anything beyond its own expertise. Beckett stresses this in his own comment on the play, again in a letter to Alan Schneider:

> My work is a matter of fundamental sounds (no joke intended) made as fully as possible, and I accept responsibility for nothing else. If people want to have headaches among the overtones, let them. And provide their own aspirin. Hamm as stated, and Clov as stated, together as stated, nec tecum sine te, in such a place, and in such a world, that's all I can manage, more than I could.

The life of *Endgame* is in the tension it creates by the harsh juxtaposition of the depths and the surface, the "over-

tones" and what is stated, a doubleness which is apparent in the frequent pauses in the play. On the one hand these are hushed silences in which the resonances of the text may vibrate and amplify in the mind of the audience— "God," "light," "Nature," "ended." At the same time these pauses are merely technical requirements, rests between moves in the last game which is *Endgame,* no more, no less. Thus the dramatic structure of the play enacts a dialectic which Beckett has stated elsewhere—in *Watt,* his second novel—as, "this pursuit of meaning, in this indifference to meaning." In so far as we recognise this as an insight into the conditions of human existence we will be able to respond to the full effect of *Endgame.*

Antony Easthope, "Hamm, Clov, and Dramatic Method in 'Endgame'," in Samuel Beckett's "Endgame," *edited by Harold Bloom, Chelsea House Publishers, 1988, pp. 49-58.*

Stanley Cavell   (essay date 1969)

[*Cavell is an American educator and critic. In the following excerpt from an essay originally published in 1969 as "Ending the Waiting Game: A Reading of Beckett's 'Endgame'" in his* Must We Mean What We Say, *Cavell examines Beckett's use of language in* Endgame *and interprets the play in relation to the story of Noah and to Christ's Sermon on the Mount.*]

Various keys to [*Endgame*'s] interpretation are in place: "Endgame" is a term of chess; the name Hamm is shared by Noah's cursed son, it titles a kind of actor, it starts recalling Hamlet. But no interpretation I have seen details the textual evidence for these relations nor shows how the play's meaning opens with them. Without this, we will have a general impression of the play, one something like this: Beckett's perception is of a "meaningless universe" and language in his plays "serves to express the breakdown, the disintegration of language"—by, one gathers, itself undergoing disintegration. Such descriptions are usual in the discussions of Beckett I am aware of, but are they anything more than impositions from an impression of fashionable philosophy? . . .

The first critical problem is to discover how Beckett's objects mean at all, the original source of their conviction for us, if they have conviction. My argument will be that Beckett, in *Endgame,* is not marketing subjectivity, popularizing angst, amusing and thereby excusing us with pictures of our psychopathology; he is outlining the facts—of mind, of community—which show why these have become our pastimes. The discovery of *Endgame,* both in topic and technique, is not the failure of meaning (if that means the lack of meaning) but its total, even totalitarian, success—our inability *not* to mean what we are given to mean.

Who are these people? Where are they, and how did they get there? What can illuminate their mood of bewilderment as well as their mood of appalling comprehension? What is the source of their ugly power over one another, and of their impotence? What gives to their conversation its sound, at once of madness and of plainness?

I begin with two convictions. The first is that the ground

of the play's quality is the *ordinariness* of its events. It is true that what we are given to see are two old people sticking half up out of trash cans, and an extraordinarily garbed blind paraplegic who imposes bizarre demands on the only person who can carry them out, the only inhabitant of that world who has remaining to him the power of motion. But take a step back from the bizarrerie and they are simply a family. Not just any family perhaps, but then every unhappy family is unhappy in its own way—gets in its own way in its own way. The old father and mother with no useful functions anymore are among the waste of society, dependent upon the generation they have bred, which in turn resents them for their uselessness and dependency. They do what they can best do: they bicker and reminisce about happier days. And they comfort one another as best they can, not necessarily out of love, nor even habit (this love and this habit may never have been formed) but out of the knowledge that they were both there, they have been through it together, like comrades in arms, or passengers on the same wrecked ship; and a life, like a disaster, seems to need going over and over in reminiscence, even if that is what makes it disastrous. One of their fondest memories seems to be the time their tandem bicycle crashed and they lost their legs: their past, their pain, has become their entertainment, their pastime. Comfort may seem too strong a term. One of them can, or could, scratch the other where the itch is out of reach, and Nagg will tolerate Nell's girlish rerhapsodizing the beauties of Lake Como if she will bear his telling again his favorite funny story. None of this is very *much* comfort perhaps, but then there never is very *much* comfort.

The old are also good at heaping curses on their young and at controlling them through guilt, the traditional weapons of the weak and dependent. Nagg uses the most ancient of all parental devices, claiming that something is due him from his son for the mere fact of having begot him. Why that should ever have seemed, and still seem, something in itself to be grateful for is a question of world-consuming mystery—but Hamm ought to be the least likely candidate for its effect, wanting nothing more than to wrap up and send back the gift of life. (His problem, as with any child, is to find out where it came from.) Yet he keeps his father in his house, and lays on his adopted son Clov the same claim to gratitude ("It was I was a Father to you"). Like his father, powerless to walk, needing to tell stories, he masks his dependence with bullying—the most versatile of techniques, masking also the requirements of loyalty, charity, magnanimity. All the characters are bound in the circle of tyranny, the most familiar of family circles.

Take another step back and the relationship between Hamm and his son-servant-lover Clov shows its dominance. It is, again, an ordinary neurotic relationship, in which both partners wish nothing more than to end it, but in which each is incapable of taking final steps because its end presents itself to them as the end of the world. So they remain together, each helpless in everything save to punish the other for his own helplessness, and play the consuming game of manipulation, the object of which is to convince the other that you yourself do not need to play. But any relationship of absorbing importance will form a world, as the personality does. And a critical change in ei-

ther will change the world. The world of the happy man is different from the world of the unhappy man, says Wittgenstein in the *Tractatus*. And the world of the child is different from the world of the grown-up, and that of the sick from that of the well, and the mad from the unmad. This is why a profound change of consciousness presents itself as a revelation, why it is so difficult, why its anticipation will seem the destruction of the world: even where it is a happy change, a world is always lost. I do not insist upon its appearing a homosexual relationship, although the title of the play just possibly suggests a practice typical of male homosexuality, and although homosexuality figures in the play's obsessive goal of sterility—the nonconsummation devoutly to be wished.

The language sounds as extraordinary as its people look, but it imitates, as Chekhov's does, the qualities of ordinary conversation among people whose world is shared—catching its abrupt shifts and sudden continuities; its shades of memory, regret, intimidation; its opacity to the outsider. It is an abstract imitation, where Chekhov's is objective. (I do not say "realistic," for that might describe Ibsen, or Hollywoodese, and in any case, as it is likely to be heard, would not emphasize the fact that art had gone into it.) But it is an achievement for the theater, to my mind, of the same magnitude. Not, of course, that the imitation of the ordinary is the only, or best, option for writing dialogue. Not every dramatist wants this quality; a writer like Shakespeare can get it whenever he wants it. But to insist upon the ordinary, keep its surface and its rhythm, sets a powerful device. An early movie director, René Clair I believe, remarked that if a person were shown a film of an ordinary whole day in his life, he would go mad. One thinks, perhaps, of Antonioni. At least he and Beckett have discovered new artistic resource in the fact of boredom; not as a topic ⌐erely, but as a dramatic technique. To miss the ordinariness of the lives in *Endgame* is to avoid the extraordinariness (and ordinariness) of our own.

I said there are two specific convictions from which my interpretation proceeds. The second also concerns, but more narrowly, the language Beckett has discovered or invented; not now its use in dialogue, but its grammar, its particular way of making sense, especially the quality it has of what I will call *hidden literality*. The words strew obscurities across our path and seem willfully to thwart comprehension; and then time after time we discover that their meaning has been missed only because it was so utterly bare—totally, therefore unnoticeably, in view. Such a discovery has the effect of showing us that it is *we* who had been willfully uncomprehending, misleading ourselves in demanding further, or other, meaning where the meaning was nearest. Many instances will come to light as we proceed, but an example or two may help at the outset.

At several points through the play the names God and Christ appear, typically in a form of words which conventionally expresses a curse. They are never, however, used (by the character saying them, of course) to curse, but rather in perfect literalness. Here are two instances: "What in God's name could there be on the horizon?";

"Catch him [a flea] for the love of God." In context, the first instance shows Hamm really asking whether anything on the horizon is appearing in God's name, as his sign or at his bidding; and the second instance really means that if you love God, have compassion for him, you will catch and kill the flea. Whether one will be convinced by such readings will depend upon whether one is convinced by the interpretation to be offered of the play as a whole, but they immediately suggest one motive in Beckett's uncovering of the literal: it removes curses, the curses under which the world is held. One of our special curses is that we can use the name of God naturally only to curse, take it only in vain. Beckett removes this curse by converting the rhetoric of cursing; not, as traditionally, by using the name in prayer (*that* alternative, as is shown explicitly elsewhere in the play, is obviously no longer open to us) but by turning its formulas into declarative utterances, ones of pure denotation—using the sentences "cognitively," as the logical positivists used to put it. Beckett (along with other philosophers recognizable as existentialist) shares with positivism its wish to escape connotation, rhetoric, the noncognitive, the irrationality and awkward memories of ordinary language, in favor of the directly verifiable, the isolated and perfected present. Only Beckett sees how infinitely difficult this escape will be. Positivism said that statements about God are meaningless; Beckett shows that they mean too damned much.

To undo curses is just one service of literalization; another is to unfix clichés and idioms:

HAMM. Did you ever think of one thing?

CLOV. Never.

The expected response to Hamm's question would be, "What?"; but that answer would accept the question as the cliché conversational gambit it appears to be. Clov declines the move and brings the gesture to life by taking it literally. His answer means that he has always thought only of *many* things, and in this I hear a confession of failure in following Christ's injunction to take no thought for your life, what ye shall eat, or what ye shall drink; nor yet for your body, nor for tomorrow—the moral of which is that "thine eye be single." Perhaps I hallucinate. Yet the Sermon on the Mount makes explicit appearance in the course of the play, as will emerge. Our concerns with God have now become the greatest clichés of all, and here is another curse to be undone.

CLOV. Do you believe in the life to come?

HAMM. Mine was always that.

Hamm knows he's made a joke and, I suppose, knows that the joke is on us; but at least the joke momentarily disperses the "belief" in the cliché "life to come," promised on any Sunday radio. And it is a terribly sad joke—that the life we are living is not our life, or not alive. Or perhaps it's merely that the joke is old, itself a cliché. Christ told it to us, that this life is nothing. The punch line, the knockout punch line, is that there is no other but this to come, that the life of waiting for life to come is all the life ever to come. We don't laugh; but if we could, or if we could stop finding it funny, then perhaps life would come to life, or anyway the life of life to come would end. (Clov, at one point, asks Hamm: "Don't we laugh?", not because he feels like it, but out of curiosity. In her longest speech Nell says: "Nothing is funnier than unhappiness . . . It's like the funny story we have heard too often, we still find it funny, but we don't laugh any more.") As it is, we've heard it all, seen it all too often, heard the promises, seen the suffering repeated in the same words and postures, and they are like any words which have been gone over so much that they are worn strange. We don't laugh, we don't cry; and we don't laugh that we don't cry, and we obviously can't cry about it. That's funny.

So far all that these examples have been meant to suggest is the sort of method I try to use consistently in reading the play, one in which I am always asking of a line either: What are the most ordinary circumstances under which such a line would be uttered? Or: What do the words literally say? I do not suggest that every line will yield to these questions, and I am sharply aware that I cannot provide answers to many cases for which I am convinced they are relevant. My exercise rests on the assumption that different artistic inventions demand different routes of critical discovery; and the justification for my particular procedures rests partly on an induction from the lines I feel I have understood, and partly on their faithfulness to the general direction I have found my understanding of the play as a whole to have taken. I have spoken of the effect of literalizing curses and clichés as one of "undoing" them, and this fits my sense, which I will specify as completely as I can, that the play itself is about an effort to undo, to end something by undoing it, and in particular to end a curse, and moreover the commonest, most ordinary curse of man—not so much that he was ever born and must die, but that he has to figure out the one and shape up to the other and justify what comes between, and that he is not a beast and not a god: in a word, that he is a man, and alone. All those, however, are the facts of life; the curse comes in the ways we try to deny them.

I should mention two further functions of the literal which seem to me operative in the play. It is, first, a mode which some forms of madness assume. A schizophrenic can suffer from ideas that he is literally empty or hollow or transparent or fragile or coming apart at the seams. It is also a mode in which prophecies and wishes are fulfilled, surprising all measures to avoid them. Birnam Forest coming to Dunsinane and the overthrow by a man of no woman born are textbook cases. In the *Inferno,* Lucifer is granted his wish to become the triune deity by being fixed in the center of a kingdom and outfitted with three heads. *Endgame* is a play whose mood is characteristically one of madness and in which the characters are fixed by a prophecy, one which their actions can be understood as attempting both to fulfill and to reverse.

A central controversy in contemporary analytic philosophy relates immediately to this effort at literalizing. Positivism had hoped for the construction of an ideal language (culminating the hope, since Newton and Leibniz at the birth of modern science, for a *Characteristica Universalis*) in which everything which could be said at all would be said clearly, its relations to other statements formed purely logically, its notation perspicuous—the form of the statement *looking* like what it means. (For example, in their new transcription, the statements which mean "Daddy makes money" and "Mommy makes bread" and "Mommy makes friends" and "Daddy makes jokes" will no longer look alike; interpretation will no longer be required; thought will be as reliable as calculation, and agreement will be as surely achieved.) Postpositivists (the later Wittgenstein; "ordinary language philosophy") rallied to the insistence that ordinary language—being *speech,* and speech being more than the making of statements—contains implications necessary to communication, perfectly comprehensible to anyone who can speak, but not recordable in logical systems. If, for example, in ordinary circumstances I ask "Would you like to use my scooter?", I must not simply be *inquiring* into your state of mind; I must be *implying* my willingness that you use it, offering it to you. —I *must*? Must not? But no one has been able to explain the force of this *must.* Why mustn't I just be inquiring? A positivist is likely to answer: because it would be bad manners; or, it's a joke; in any case most people wouldn't. A post-positivist is likely to feel: That isn't what I meant. Of course it *may* be bad manners (even unforgivable manners), but it *may* not even be odd (e. g., in a context in which you have asked me to guess which of my possessions you would like to use). But suppose it isn't such contexts, but one in which, normally, people *would* be offering, and suppose I keep insisting, puzzled that others are upset, that I simply want to know what's on your mind. Then aren't you going to have to say something like: You don't know what you're saying, what those words mean—a feeling that I have tuned out, become incomprehensible. Anyway, why is the result a *joke* when the normal implications of language are defeated; what kind of joke?

Hamm and Clov's conversations sometimes work by defeating the implications of ordinary language in this way.

HAMM. I've made you suffer too much.
(*Pause*)
Haven't I?

CLOV. It's not that.

HAMM. (*Shocked*) I haven't made you suffer too much?

CLOV. Yes!

HAMM. (*Relieved*) Ah you gave me a fright!
(*Pause. Coldly.*)
Forgive me.
(*Pause. Louder.*)
I said, Forgive me.

CLOV. I heard you.

Hamm's first line looks like a confession, an acknowledgment; but it is just a statement. This is shown by the question in his next speech, which is to determine whether what he said was true. His third speech looks like an appeal for forgiveness, but it turns out to be a command—a peculiar command, for it is, apparently, obeyed simply by someone's admitting that he heard it. How could a *command for forgiveness* be anything but peculiar, even preposterous? (Possibly in the way the Sermon on the Mount

is preposterous.) An ordinary circumstance for its use would be one in which someone needs forgiveness but cannot *ask* for it. Preposterous, but hardly uncommon. (One of Hamm's lines is: "It appears the case is . . . was not so . . . so unusual"; he is pretty clearly thinking of himself. He is *homme.* And "Ha-am" in Hebrew means "the people." Probably that is an accident, but I wouldn't put anything past the attentive friend and disciple of James Joyce.) In Hamm's case, moreover, it would have been trivially preposterous, and less honest, had he really been *asking* for forgiveness "for having made you suffer too much": How much is just enough? We have the need, but no way of satisfying it; as we have words, but nothing to do with them; as we have hopes, but nothing to pin them on.

Sometimes the effect of defeating ordinary language is achieved not by thwarting its "implications" but by drawing purely logical ones.

HAMM. I'll give you nothing more to eat.

CLOV. Then we'll die.

HAMM. I'll give you just enough to keep you from dying. You'll be hungry all the time.

CLOV. Then we won't die.

Clov can hardly be meaning what his words, taken together and commonly, would suggest, namely "It makes no difference whether we live or die; I couldn't care less." First, in one sense that is *so trivial* a sentiment, at their stage, that it would get a laugh—at least from clearheaded Hamm. Second, it is not true. How could it make no difference when the point of the enterprise is to die to that world? (Though of course *that* kind of living and dying, the kind that depends on literal food, may make no difference.) And he *could* care less, because he's *trying* to leave. If he were really empty of care, then maybe he could stop trying, and then maybe he could do it. The conventional reading takes Hamm's opening remark as a *threat;* but there are no more threats. It is a plain statement and Clov makes the inference; then Hamm negates the statement and Clov negates the conclusion. It is an exercise in pure logic; a spiritual exercise.

The logician's wish to translate out those messy, nonformal features of ordinary language is fully granted by Beckett, not by supposing that there is a way out of our language, but by fully accepting the fact that there is nowhere else to go. Only he is not going to call that rationality. Or perhaps he will: this is what rationality has brought us to. The strategy of literalization is: you say *only* what your words say. That's the game, and a way of winning out.

I refer to contemporary analytical philosophy, but Hamm presents a new image of what the mind, in one characteristic philosophical mood, has always felt like—crazed and paralyzed; this is part of the play's sensibility.

One thinks of Socrates' interlocutors, complaining that his questions have numbed them; of Augustine faced with his question "What is Time?" (If you do not ask me, I know; if you ask me, I do not know). Every profound philosophical vision can have the shape of madness: The world is illusion; I can doubt everything, that I am awake, that there is an external world; the mind takes isolated bits of experience and associates them into a world; each thing and each person is a metaphysical enclosure, and no two ever communicate directly, or so much as perceive one another; time, space, relations between things, are unreal. . . . It sometimes looks as if philosophy had designs on us; or as if it alone is crazy, and wants company. Then why can't it simply be ignored? But it *is* ignored; perhaps not simply, but largely so. The question remains: What makes philosophy possible? Why can't men *always* escape it? Because, evidently, men have minds, and they think. (One mad philosophical question has long been, Does the mind *always* think? Even in sleep? It is a frightening thought.) And philosophy is what thought does to itself. Kant summarized it in the opening words of the *Critique of Pure Reason*: "Human reason has this peculiar fate that in one species of its knowledge it is burdened by questions which . . . it is not able to ignore, but which . . . it is also not able to answer." And Wittgenstein, saying in his *Investigations* that his later methods (he compared them to therapies) were to bring philosophy peace at least, seemed to find opportunity, and point, within such disaster: "The philosopher is the man who has to cure himself of many sicknesses of the understanding before he can arrive at the notions of the sound human understanding" (*Remarks on the Foundations of Mathematics*)—as though there were no other philosophical path to sanity, save through madness. One will not have understood the opportunity if one is *eager* to seize it. Genuine philosophy may begin in wonder, but it continues in reluctance. . . .

Does the play take place, as is frequently suggested, after an atomic war? Are these its last survivors? Well, Beckett suggests they are, so far as they or we know, the last life. And he says twice that they are in "the shelter." Is it a bomb shelter? These considerations are doubtless resonant in the play's situation; it tells its time. But the notion leaves opaque the specific goings on in the shelter. Do these people want to survive or not? They seem as afraid of the one as of the other. Why do they wish to *insure* that nothing is surviving? Why are they *incapable* of leaving? That Hamm and Clov want (so to speak) the world to end is obvious enough, but an understanding of the way they imagine its end, the reason it must end, the terms in which it can be brought to an end, are given by placing these characters this way: The shelter they are in is the ark, the family is Noah's, and the time is sometime after the Flood.

Many surface details find a place within this picture. Most immediately there is the name of Hamm. He is, in particular, the son of Noah who saw his father naked, and like Oedipus, another son out of fortune, he is blinded by what he has seen. Because of his transgression he is cursed by his father, the particular curse being that his sons are to be the servants of men. Clov, to whom Hamm has been a father, is his servant, the general servant of all the other characters. We are told (Genesis 9:23) that Shem and Japheth, the good brothers, cover their father while carefully contriving not to look at him. I hear a reference to their action when Hamm directs Clov to "bottle him" (i.e., clamp the lid down on his father)—one of the most brutal lines in the play, as if Hamm is commenting on what has

passed for honorable conduct; he is now the good son, with a vengeance. At two points Hamm directs Clov to look out of the windows, which need to be reached by a ladder (they are situated, as it were, above the water line) and he looks out through a telescope, a very nautical instrument. (Another significant property in the shelter is a gaff.) One window looks out at the earth, the other at the ocean, which means, presumably, that they are at the edge of water, run aground perhaps. Earlier he has asked about the weather, and there was a little exchange about whether it will rain and what good that would do. Now he asks Clov to look at the earth and is told, what both knew, that all is "corpsed": Man and beast and every living thing have been destroyed from the face of the earth. Then Hamm directs Clov to look at the sea, in particular he asks whether there are gulls. Clov looks and answers, "Gulls!", perhaps with impatience (how could there be?), perhaps with longing (if only there were!), perhaps both. Hamm ought to *know* there aren't any, having looked for them until he is blind, and being told there are none day after day. And Hamm ought to ask what he really wants to know but is afraid to know, namely, whether there is a raven or a dove.

Let this suffice to establish a serious attention to the tale of Noah. Its importance starts to emerge when we notice that the entire action of the play is determined by the action of that tale. After the flood, God does two things: he establishes a covenant with Noah that the earth and men shall no more be taken from one another; and presses a characteristic commandment, to be fruitful and multiply and replenish the earth. Hamm's behavior is guided by attempts to undo or deny these specific acts of God.

Something has happened in the ark during those days and nights of world-destroying rain and the months of floating and waiting for the end, for rescue. Hamm has seen something in the ark of the covenant. I imagine it this way.

He has seen God naked. For it is, after all, the most fantastic tale. God repented, it says, that he created man. How does a God repent? How does anyone? Suppose he has a change of heart about something he has done. If this is not mere regret, then the change of heart must lead to mending one's ways or making amends. How does a God mend his ways; can he, and remain God? A further question is more pressing: How does God justify the destruction of his creation? A possible response would be: Man is sinful. But that response indicates at most that God had to do *something* about his creatures, not that he had to separate them from earth. He might have found it in himself to forgive them or to abandon them—alternatives he seems to have used, in sequence, in future millennia. Why destruction? Suppose it is said: God needs no justification. But it is not clear that God would agree; besides, all this really means is that men are God's creatures and he may do with them as he pleases. Then what did he in fact do? He did not, as he said, cause the end of flesh to come before him, for he preserved, with each species, Noah's family; enough for a new beginning. He hedged his bet. Why? And why Noah picked from all men? Those are the questions I imagine Hamm to have asked himself, and his solution is, following God, to see the end of flesh come before him. As before he imitates his good brothers, so now he imitates his God—a classical effort. Why is this his solution?

God saves enough for a new beginning because he cannot part with mankind; in the end, he cannot really end it. Perhaps this means he cannot bear not to be God. (Nietzsche said that this was true of himself, and suggested that it was true of all men. It seems true enough of Hamm. We need only add that in this matter men are being faithful to, i. e., imitating, God.) Not ending it, but with the end come before him, he cannot avoid cruelty, arbitrariness, guilt, repentance, disappointment, then back through cruelty. . . . Hamm and Clov model the relationship between God and his servants.

And if the bet must be hedged, why with Noah? The tale says, "Noah walked with God." That's all. Well, it also says that he was a just man and perfect in his generations, and that he found grace in the eyes of the Lord. Is that enough to justify marking him from all men for salvation? It is incredible. Perhaps God has his reasons, or perhaps Noah does not deserve saving, and perhaps that doesn't matter. Doesn't matter for God's purposes, that is. But how can it *not* matter to those who find themselves saved? The tale is madly silent about what Hamm saw when he saw his father naked, and why it was a transgression deserving an eternal curse. Perhaps all he saw was that his father was ordinary, undeserving of unique salvation. But he saw also that his father was untroubled by this appalling fact. Nell, at one point in her reminiscence of Lake Como, says to Nagg: "By rights we should have been drowned"—a line which both undoes a cliché ("by rights" here literally means: it would have been right if we had, and hence it is wrong that we weren't) and has the thrill of revelation I spoke of earlier (it is not Lake Como she is thinking of). But Nagg misses the boat. So blind Hamm sees both that he exists only as a product of his father ("Accursed fornicator!"), and that if either of their existences is to be provided with justification, he must be the provider; which presents itself to him as taking his father's place—the act that blinds Oedipus.

And how is one to undertake justifying his own—let alone another's—existence? One serious enough solution is to leave this business of justification to God; that is what he is for. But God has reneged this responsibility, and doubly. In meaning to destroy all flesh, he has confessed that existence cannot be justified by him. And in saving one family and commanding them to replenish the earth, there is the high hint that man is being asked to do a god's work, that he is not only abandoned to his own justification, but that he must undertake to justify God himself, to redeem God's curse and destruction. God cursed the world, and he is cursed. This seems to me to set the real problem of Theodicy, to justify God's ways to God. Its traditional question—Why did God create man and then allow him to suffer?—has a clear answer: Because it is man that God created; all men are mortal, and they suffer.

The Covenant, therefore, is a bad bargain, and the notion of replenishing the earth is a losing proposition. Promising not to destroy man *again* is hardly the point, and is not so much a promise as an apology. (As the rainbow is more a threat than a promise.) The point is to understand why it was done the first time, and what man is that he can accept such an apology. As for replenishing the earth, what will that do but create more fathers and sons, and multiply the need for justification? God was right the first time: the end of flesh is come, God's destruction is to be completed. Or rather, what must end is the mutual dependence of God and the world: *this* world, and its god, must be brought to a conclusion. Hamm's strategy is to undo all covenants and to secure fruitlessness. In a word, to disobey God perfectly, to perform man's last disobedience. No doubt Hamm acts out of compassion. ("Kill him, for the love of God.") The creation and destruction of a world of men is too great a burden of responsibility even for God. To remove that responsibility the world does not so much need to vanish as to become *uncreated*. But to accomplish that it seems that we will have to become gods. For mere men will go on hoping, go on waiting for redemption, for justification, for meaning. And these claims ineluctably retain God in creation—to his, and to our, damnation. And yet, where there is life there is hope. That is Hamm's dilemma. . . .

Hamm's problem, like Job's, is that of being singled out. Job is singled out for suffering, Hamm for rescue, and it is something of an insight to have grasped the problem still there. Job, presumably, has his answer in recognizing that there *is* no humanly recognizable reason for being singled out to suffer. That is, none having to do with *him*. Life becomes bearable when he gives up looking for such a reason. Couldn't we give up looking for a reason for being singled out for rescue? For certain spirits that is harder, for the good Christian reason that others are there, unrescued.

It is in some such way that I imagine Hamm's thoughts to have grown. It is from a mind in such straits that I can make sense (1) of his attempt to reverse creation, to empty the world of salvation, justification, meaning, testaments; and (2) of the story he tells, the composing of which is the dominant activity of his days.

He calls his story a "chronicle," suggesting that it is a record of fact. It concerns a man who had come to him for help, begging him at least to "take his child in." And we learn that this is not an isolated case, for Hamm refers to

> All those I might have helped.
> (*Pause*)
> Helped!
> (*Pause*)
> Saved.
> (*Pause*)
> Saved!
> (*Pause*)
> The place was crawling with them!

"Might have." With those words every man takes his life. Hamm is remembering something that actually happened. I imagine him to be remembering the ark being built. It would have taken a while—all those cubits to arrange, and all that food and all the paired beasts to collect. People would have got wind of it, perhaps some were hired to help in the preparations. God, the tale says, went away while it was being done, perhaps to let the family get used to the idea of their special fortune, and to get a full appreciation of God's love. Then he returned to order them into the ark, and when the family and each kind had gone in unto Noah into the ark, "the Lord shut him in" (Genesis 7:7), preserved him, bottled him. At first people would have been skeptical at Noah's folly rising there in the middle of land, but some would eventually have believed, and even if these were the gullible and lunatic who believe every announcement of doom, Noah would have known that this time they were right; but he would have had to refuse their crazed petitions to be let in. Finished, the ark stood there closed for seven days, then the rain began, and some days would have passed before it lifted off its scaffolding to be held up in the palm of God's sea. Suppose it had been built just by the family, in secret. But now the water is deep, raising the general horizon, and the ark is visible for as far as the eye can see, to anyone who is still afloat. Perhaps no one is, but Noah's family doesn't know that. Perhaps the sounds of pounding are not survivors screaming for rescue, only dead wreckage in the water. They don't know that either, but it wouldn't require much imagination to wonder whether it was. They must not imagine, or they must be mad. Imagination has to be bottled. But in Hamm it has started to leak out. He complains twice that "There's something dripping in my head"; both times his father has to suppress a laugh—how comical the young are, so serious, so pure; they'll learn. The first time is his over-hearing his parents together; he tells himself it's a heart, "A heart in my head." Something is pounding. Children will give themselves *some* explanation. The second time he thinks of it as splashing, "Splash, splash, always on the same spot." Now he tries pressing his earlier thought that it is a little vein, and now adds the idea that it is a little artery; but he gives it up and begins working on his chronicle, his story, his art-work. (His art-ery? That could mean, following Eric Partridge on the origin of the suffix "-ery," either the action [compare "drudgery"], the condition [compare "slavery"], the occupation [compare "casuistry"], the place of actions [compare "nursery"], the product of the action [compare "poetry"], or the collectivity [compare "citizenry"] of art. Each of these would fit this character and this play.) Art begins where explanations leave off, or before they start. Not everything has an explanation, and people will give themselves *some* consolation. The imagination must have something to contain it—to drip into, as it were—or we must be mad. Hamm is in both positions.

Whatever God's idea in destroying men, to have saved one family for himself puts them in the position of denying life to all other men. To be chosen, to be special, singled out, for suffering *or* for salvation, is an inescapable curse. Perhaps this was something Christ tried to show, that even to be God is to be completely unspecial, powerless to claim exemption. To deny this is to be less than a man: we are all in the same boat. But can any man, not more than a man, affirm it?

It seems possible to me that this is what **Endgame** is about, that what it envisions is the cursed world of the Old Testament ("Ah, the old questions, the old answers, there's nothing like them") and that what is to be ended is that world, followed by the new message, glad tidings brought

by a new dove of redemption, when we are ready to receive it. Without it we are paralyzed.

But I do not think this is what is seen, though it may be a permanent segment. For the new message is also present in the play, and it too is helpless. Immediately after Hamm's first full telling of the story, his telling of it to date, he wonders how he is to continue (as anyone does, artist or man, in final difficulties) and says: "Let us pray to God." There are references to food (not to loaves, but to the bribe of a sugarplum, and to calling Clov from the kitchen), and he finally persuades Clov and Nagg to join him. Nagg wants his sugarplum before he prays, but Hamm insists "God first!" —thus summarizing the First Commandment, according to Christ the first and greatest commandment. Whereupon Nagg begins to recite the Lord's Prayer, taught during the Sermon on the Mount. That occasion is alluded to further in the way Hamm immediately interrupts his father's prayer: "Silence! In silence! Where are your manners?" Christ cautions that prayer be offered "in secret" immediately before he delivers *his* Father's Prayer. If here Hamm's teaching parodies Christ's he will later imitate him more directly, as in his chronicle he presents himself as in God's position, distributing life and death to supplicants. That's the position God has put him in.

The next time he tries to finish his story, instead of praying to God he ends by calling his father. "Father, Father" he says, echoing the repeated among the seven last words, and addressed to the same old party. ("Father, Father" he says again near the end of his, and the play's, last speech.) And now it looks as if he is not only the son of the only spared man, hence has the same ancestor as all men; but the one and only son, with the father to end all fathers. No wonder he is confused about whether he is father or son.

He goes back to his chronicle, to try to end it, or make some continuation, a third time; again he gets to the point at which he is begged for salvation and again this is the stumbling block. Now he quotes the Sermon on the Mount more openly: "Get out of here and love one another! Lick your neighbor as yourself!" And now he becomes petulant: "When it wasn't bread they wanted it was crumpets." And wrathful: "Out of my sight and back to your petting parties." He can find no conclusion to the story of suffering and sin, and no answer to the prayer for salvation, no answer old or new. He has just told them again everything eternity knows: "Use your head can't you, use your head, you're on earth, there's no cure for that!" But they can't use their heads; men are enough to try the patience of a God. "How is it that ye do not understand that I spake it not to you concerning bread, that ye should beware of the leaven of the Pharisees and of the Sadducees? Then understood they how that he bade them not beware of the leaven of bread, but of the doctrine of the Pharisees and Sadduccees" (Matthew 16:11-12). Use your head, can't you? It was a parable! Get it? But he's said that before and he'll say it again, and nobody gets it. They want signs, miracles, some cure for being on earth, some way of getting over being human. Maybe that's just human; and there's no cure for that.

So Hamm renounces parable in favor of the perfectly literal. (People, he might say, have no head for figures.) Only it is just as hard to write his anti-testament that way. Maybe to receive either word one would have to have a heart in one's head. No doubt it is not very clear how that could be, but then Christ sees his disciples' lack of understanding as a lack of faith, and it has never seemed unusually clear what that would be either. ("Believe," said Augustine, "and you have eaten"; Luther thought he understood what that meant.) However it is to come, nothing less powerful than faith will be needed to remove God and his curse, the power to un-create God. Hamm, however, may believe, or half-believe—believe the way little children believe—that he really has got a blood-pumping organ upstairs. We have known for a long time that the heart has its reasons which reason knows not of. But we have come to think that reason *can* know them, that the knowing of them takes over the work of the heart, that what we require for salvation is more knowledge, knowledge of the sort we already know, that will fit the shape of our heads as they are. Hamm is half-crazy with his efforts at undoing knowledge, at not knowing. But no half-crazier than we are at our frenzy for knowledge, at knowing where we should love, meaning our lives up.

Finally, he tries to imagine that it can end without ending his story. "If I can hold my peace and sit quiet, it will be all over with sound, and motion, all over and done with." But it seems to be just the same old story. "I'll have called my father and I'll have called my . . . [he hesitates] . . . my son." He hesitates, as if not knowing whether he is the new god or the old, son or father. But at least he is putting himself into the picture; no attitude is struck now towards father or son; the son is now not another's—as if to acknowledge that all sons are his. "I'll have called . . . I'll say to myself, He'll come back. [Pause] And then? [Pause] . . . He couldn't, he has gone too far. [Pause] And then?" And then a description of confusion: "Babble, babble . . ." (Babel? If so, what does it mean? What caused Babel and its aftermath? Our presumption, in desiring God's eminence? Or our foolishness, in imagining that a tower is the way to reach heaven? In either case the confusion of tongues is God's punishment, hence proof of his existence. Or is the din rather the sound of our success, that we reached heaven and found it empty? Better to bite the tongue than admit that. Better to take over and punish ourselves than to forgo that proof.)

Here is at least one possible endgame other than the act of ending the story: I call; there is no answer. But this ending is unclear. The problem seems to be that there is no way of *knowing* there is no answer, no way of knowing the call was heard, and therefore *unanswered*. (An unconnected telephone cannot be left unanswered.)

One source of confusion seems clear enough. *Who* has gone too far to come back? The father or the son? Is it God who has gone too far, in inflicting suffering he cannot redeem? Or Christ, in really dying of suffering we cannot redeem? What does it matter? The one threatened, the other promised, the end of the world; and neither carried through. We are left holding it.

There are three other allusions to Christ which need mentioning, one at the beginning, one near the middle, and one at the end of the play. The first may seem doubtful: "Can there be misery loftier than mine?" If confirmation is wanted beyond the fact that the tone of this remark perfectly registers Hamm's aspiration (perhaps the usual tone in which Christ is imitated) there is the refrain of George Herbert's "The Sacrifice": "Was ever grief like mine?", in which the speaker is Christ. The middle allusion is the only explicit one, and it occurs with characteristic literality. After Hamm's instruction in the etiquette of prayer, the three men have a try at it, whereupon each confesses in turn that he has got nowhere. King Claudius, in a similar predicament, gives the usual honest explanation for this failure: "My words fly up, my thoughts remain below: words without thoughts never to heaven go." Hamm has a different, perhaps more honest, certainly no less responsible, explanation: "The bastard! He doesn't exist." To which Clov's response, in full, is: "Not yet," and the subject is dropped. Removing the curse, what Hamm has just said is that the bastard does not exist. That Christ was literally a bastard was among the first of the few things I was ever told about him, and I suppose other Jewish children are given comparable help to their questions. I take it this exciting gossip makes its way in other circles as an advanced joke. So it is Christ whom Clov says does not exist yet. This may mean either that we are still, in the play, in the prechristian age, with rumors, prophecies, hopes stirring; or that since we know there is a bastard, he has come, but not returned. (The French version notates the ambiguity: "Pas encore" is "Not yet." But also, I take it, "Not again.") Either way, "Not yet" is the most definite expression of hope—or, for that matter, of despair—in the play, the only expression of future which is left unchallenged, by contradiction, irony or giggles.

What weight is to be attached to this? Do those two words give *the* Endgame to this play of suffering, that with Christ's coming this will all have meaning? It seems unimaginable in this total context of run-down and the fallout of sense. Yet there is a coming at the end of the play, one which Hamm apparently takes to signal the awaited end, and upon which he dismisses Clov. Clov spies a small boy through the glass; it is a moment which is considerably longer in the French, but for some reason cut down in Beckett's English version. In the French, the boy is said to be leaning against a stone, and this seems a clear enough suggestion of the sepulchre. But even without this description, the character is sufficiently established by Hamm's response, which is to speculate about whether what Clov sees exists. (This is the only use of "exists" in the play outside the bastard remark.) The important fact for us is that after that earlier exchange between Hamm and Clov, it is Clov whose immediate response is to prepare to kill the newcomer, whereas Hamm, for the first time, prevents the destruction of a "potential procreator," saying in effect that he cannot survive anyway, that he will make no difference, present no problem. Earlier, Clov had expressed the straightest hopes for this coming, but he misses it when it comes; Hamm is now ready to admit that perhaps it has come but he sees that it is too late, that it was always too late for redemption; too late from the moment redemption became necessary. We are Christ or we are nothing—that is the position Christ has put us in. . . .

Stanley Cavell, "Ending the Waiting Game: A Reading of Beckett's 'Endgame'," in Samuel Beckett's "Endgame", *edited by Harold Bloom, Chelsea House Publishing, 1988, pp. 59-77.*

Ihab Hassan on the symbolic dramas of *Endgame*:

Endgame, I believe, may be seen as two symbolic dramas in one: an internal and an external action. The internal drama is simply that of human consciousness. The mind, the human personality, can be a closed system like chess; it can be ruled by habit and immutable laws; it may contain only one mobile impulse, Clov, ruled by a fixed authority, Hamm. And it may therefore be condemned to endless repetitions. But Clov also looks outwards, and the womb or skull-shaped room, designed originally for the play by Roger Blin, has two small windows that may be reached by a ladder—Clov has shrunk with time—and from which the emptiness of earth and sea and sky may be glimpsed. The play is therefore not entirely solipsistic. Its action may be viewed, externally, as a phase in human history, time and events preceding that phase, a slow-motion apocalypse to come after, as indeed the numerous references to the Revelation of St. John the Divine suggest. These two symbolic facets of ***Endgame*** meet: the exhaustion of history and the exhaustion of consciousness are in the end both symptoms of the exhaustion of being. This is the central intuition of the play crudely stated.

Ihab Hassan, in his The Literature of Silence: Henry Miller and Samuel Beckett, *Alfred A. Knopf, 1967.*

Jack MacGowran with Richard Toscan   (interview date July-September 1973)

[*An Irish actor, MacGowran appeared in several productions of Beckett's plays, including* Waiting for Godot, Endgame, *and* Eh Joe, *a play that Beckett wrote specifically for MacGowran. In the following excerpt from an interview first published in* Theatre Quarterly, *July-September 1973, he discusses* Endgame *and Beckett's attitude toward the play.*]

[Toscan]: *What about* **Endgame**, *in which you played Clov?*

[MacGowran]: ***Endgame*** presented different problems [from ***Waiting for Godot***]. The world upon which Clov looked, through the window, was a world devoid of anything, any human living being. So perhaps this could be taken as a futuristic play, an example of genocidal factors, of races that have been killed off. The world upon which Clov looks is more a moon-scape than an earthly vision. That's why ***Endgame*** is the harshest of the plays and the most tragic. There's less laughter to be found in ***Endgame*** than any other play—except for little moments like when Clov discovers he's got a flea or the dummy dog with the leg and sex missing.

The reason Clov doesn't leave at the end is because Hamm puts a doubt into his mind whether he does see life outside or not. If he did see life outside, Clov would escape, and Hamm wouldn't worry because he would take in the new life to help him. I have part of the original manuscript of this scene; it's much longer than the English translation and Clov talks at great length about what he's seeing outside. But Beckett wanted to leave a doubt about the existence of human life and he cut that sequence out, so as to make Clov less sure of going. Hamm says, "I don't need you any more." Clov doesn't like the fact that he's not needed—he must be needed. That is why he never leaves.

Is that Beckett's attitude toward it—that Clov will not leave?

Yes. Clov will not go because he cannot face what's outside without anybody. He's achieved one thing: He will not answer the whistle any more. But he's still dependent upon Hamm no matter what happens.

Did you discuss **Endgame** *in some detail with Beckett?*

Oh yes. Actually, the best ***Endgame*** we ever played was directed by Beckett in Paris in 1964. I got Patrick Magee to play Hamm, and I played Clov, and we got two very good character players to play the dustbin people. Beckett came over and spent six weeks directing it. He didn't go on the program as director, because there was a young director who let Beckett take over. Beckett is a marvelous director of his own work, but he's a strict disciplinarian. The play ran for nine weeks in Paris, then for two seasons at the Aldwych Theatre in London and was still playing to packed houses when we closed it.

What was Beckett's interpretation of the play as he approached it from the point of view of a director?

Interdependency—that man must depend upon his fellowman in some way no matter how awful; a love-hate relationship between Hamm and Clov that exists right through the play.

So he put the major emphasis on their relationship, rather than the "something" that's taking its course outside?

Yes. Harold Pinter came to see it one night. He dashed around afterward—he's an honest man, Pinter, and a very good playwright influenced by Beckett's work. He said to me and Pat Magee, "You know, it's not what you were saying to each other, it's what was happening in between that gave me tickles up my spine." So you see, the relationship was working. This is what Sam made sure would happen—that the relationship he wanted between Hamm and Clov was taking place. Clov takes an insane delight in saying, "There's no more painkiller," and when he wheels Hamm to the center, he *doesn't* wheel him to the center. Clov is constantly *not* doing what Hamm wants him to do. Hamm knows he's not in the center; he has a sixth sense for knowing. He places a terrible curse on Clov when he says, "One day you'll be blind like me . . . except that you won't have anyone with you." This hurts Clov; this worries him a lot. So they hurt each other mentally. They're mentally both very damaged people anyway.

Did Beckett ever talk about what it was that has decimated the population and left only Hamm and Clov?

No, never. It's some vision—there is a visionary in Beckett. The seeds of *Endgame* were in fact in Lucky's speech—"In the great deeps, the great cold on sea, on land and in the air"—referring to the return of the world to its former state of a ball of fire or the glacial age that will get rid of all the population and perhaps, by sheer luck, two people will remain. Lucky also says, "In the year of their Lord six hundred and something. . . ." Beckett can't remember the actual date, but he read it somewhere, and it was nearest to a glacial age the earth ever got in mankind's time.

Though there is the suggestion in **Endgame** *that the flea might be the first chain in the development of a new race of humans.*

That's right, and it's so awful that they want to kill it quickly before it starts, because the same thing will happen again.

In Hamm's story, he refers to the baby who was brought to him by the man who came crawling. . . .

I played it as if Clov was the person who was brought there by the man, so that the story is not really fiction at all. It's a retelling of those early years, which Clov may or may not remember because he has been there so long.

What was Beckett's attitude toward Hamm's parents, who were in the dustbins?

I think he feels that's the way most of us, in later life, treat our own parents—we put them into homes and we give them the minimum kind of treatment to keep them alive for as long as we can. The human race generally does that to an aging parent and this was his conception of how stark it could be—putting them into dustbins and giving them a biscuit or a biscuit and a half a day, anything to keep them going just for a while.

I gather then that Beckett would dismiss the critical approach to **Endgame** *that says it takes place in the mind of one man and the parents in the dustbins symbolize subconscious repression.*

He would reject that idea completely. People may think that because the play makes it possible to think that way. But I know for a fact that that's not Beckett's idea of what's happening. . . .

Many of Beckett's characters like Krapp and Vladimir have physical problems . . . .

They all have some physical problem or another. For instance, Hamm is blind and unable to move, while Clov cannot sit down. This is not just imagination. There are people in the world, Beckett has discovered, who do suffer from these kinds of things, and yet they're related, they're married to each other—in a love-hate relationship, maybe.

When Beckett gave up teaching French at Trinity College, Dublin, he left suddenly, because, as he said to me, he felt he was teaching something he knew nothing about. That decision was the birth of a writer. He came to London and took a job as an attendant in a mental home for a year. That influenced him very much—I know that *Murphy,* his first novel, came out of his experiences as a mental attendant. And, then, he has seen many people who were hand-

icapped severely in some way. When he was young, there was a war pensioners' hospital very close to where he was born. He saw them regularly every day—they were in various stages of physical disability. I am sure these experiences have influenced the fact that his characters are largely damaged people.

Beckett has said to me often, "People must think I had a very unhappy childhood, but I hadn't really. I had a very good childhood, and a very normal childhood as childhoods go. But I was more aware of unhappiness around me"—not in his own home, but just in people—"than happiness." So the sensitive chords in Beckett's nature were attuned to the unhappiness in humankind rather than the happiness.

In **Endgame** *and several of the other plays there are references to the fact that a play is going on. Does he do that deliberately as a kind of theatrical device?*

Yes, he does. Pozzo [from *Waiting for Godot*] said, "Where are we? It isn't by any chance the place known as the Board?" The "board" is the stage, so that conveys that they know it's a play that's going on. He wants to make the audience feel that it's a play that's taking place and not what really is happening.

When you work with Beckett, does he treat the plays that he has written first in French and then translated into English as equivalent plays, that is, does he make references back to the French text as being different from the English version?

Yes, he does. There was a point in *Endgame* that worried me. When Clov realizes that he's had a little victory over Hamm, he starts humming, and Hamm, if you recall, says "Don't sing," and Clov says, "One hasn't the right to sing anymore." Hamm says, "No," and Clov says, "Then how can it end?" I said to Beckett, "I'm really not quite sure what that means." He said, "Well, that was a difficulty in translation I had. When I wrote it in French, there is a French proverb which is well known, 'Everything ends with a song,' and I could not translate that proverb, which is particularly French, into English unless I did it that way." You see, it was more readily understood in French, Clov intimating that this is the end of their relationship.

Jack MacGowran and Richard Toscan, in an interview in On Beckett: Essays and Criticism, *edited by S. E. Gontarski, Grove Press, 1986, pp. 213-25.*

Richard Gilman   (essay date 1974)

[*Gilman is an American educator and critic who has written extensively on modern drama. In the following excerpt from an essay originally published in 1974 in his* The Making of Modern Drama, *he interprets* Endgame *as a play about performing.*]

If such categories as optimism and pessimism pertain at all to Beckett, then *Endgame* is much more pessimistic than *Waiting for Godot.* In its seedy room whose windows look out on empty ocean, the living world seems to have been narrowed down to four survivors: Hamm, who cannot see or stand; Clov, his servant, who cannot sit; and

Nagg and Nell, his parents, who exist throughout in ash cans. Everything is winding down to a finish, as in that ultimate phase of a chess match which gives the play its title. Humanly, it is dissolution rather than explicit death that seems to be in the offing. There are no more coffins, we are told; death as a rite, and therefore as connection to human truth, has been abrogated.

In this burned-out world, which has been compared to that of Lear at the end of his drama but perhaps more closely resembles that of Woyzeck, despair is an axiom. When at one point Clov tells Hamm that his father is weeping down in his ash can, Hamm replies, "Then he's living." He then asks Clov, "Did you ever have an instant of happiness?" to which the response is "Not to my knowledge." "You're on earth," Hamm tells him, "there's no cure for that." Only Clov seems to have any desire or capacity for a change of circumstances; he grumbles or protests bitterly throughout at his subjection to Hamm, and in fact seems in the end to have made good his repeated threats to leave, as though from a doomed house.

It is tempting to see in all this a parable of man at the end of his rope, more specifically post atomic man, and the play has indeed been staged along the lines of a vision of the world after nuclear holocaust, as well as, from a different but equally "contemporary" perspective, along Freudian and Marxist ones. But this is in a peculiar way to take the play too seriously, to give it a weight of commentary and social earnestness its imaginative structure continually subverts. We ought to know from Beckett's entire body of work that of all living writers he is the least interested in the present, in the changes time effects, and in what we might call local, temporally or spatially differentiated existence. His imagination functions almost entirely outside history: what is, has been, and what has been, will be, so that writing for him is the struggle to find new means to express this proposition of stasis. In this struggle is one source of the tension of his work.

Another related source is in the unending dialectic between what he is "expressing" on an immediate level in the words and gestures and his obsession with the literary and dramatic impulses in themselves, the human need to say and show. This is his truest subject: the illusion that our speech and movements make a *difference,* the knowledge that this is an illusion, and the tragicomic making of speech and gestures in the face of the knowledge. The materials may vary, like those of an orator on different occasions, but they remain those of a voice engaging in utterance precisely for its own sake, for the sake, that is, of meeting the obligation of making human presence known.

Such materials do not add up to a reassembling of the phenomenal world, such as we ordinarily expect from literature and drama, nor do they constitute a commentary on the present state of personality or society. "He is not writing about something, he is writing something," Beckett once said of Joyce, and it is even truer of himself. What he is writing—bringing into being—in *Endgame* is another version of his Ur-text on the human self caught between actuality and desire, the craving for justification and its objective absence; at the same time it is a drama to show the impulse of playing—by which we fill in the void—to

show it up. If it is more desperate than its predecessor, this isn't because Beckett has seen the world grow grimmer or has less hope than before (he had never had any) but because he has pushed the undertaking of artifice closer to the edge, cut down the number of possible ways out. There is not even a Godot now to provide by his felt absence a prospect of a future.

From the opening "tableau," as the stage directions call it, with Hamm sitting covered with a sheet like a piece of furniture in storage, Clov standing "motionless by the door, his eyes fixed on him," and the ash cans adding their silly, mysterious presence, the play proceeds to unfold as though it were the partly self-mocking work of a weary company of barnstormers who have set up their portable stage in some provincial town and laid out their shabby scenery and props. The text they speak has a "content" of desolation and end-of-the-world malaise, but it is interspersed with literary ironies and internal theatrical references and jokes, all of which go to sustain the thesis, most brilliantly propounded by Hugh Kenner, that *Endgame* is a play about playing, a performance "about" performing.

"What is there to keep me here?" Clov asks at one point, to which Hamm (ham actor? the reading is now a commonplace) replies, "The dialogue." "What about having

Roger Blin as Hamm in the first production of Endgame.

a good guffaw the two of us together?" Hamm says. Clov (*after reflection*): "I couldn't guffaw again today." Hamm (*after reflection*): "Nor I." "Let's stop playing!" Clov pleads near the end; Hamm calls one remark of his an "aside" and says that he's "warming up for my last soliloquy"; Clov says of his departure at the end that "this is what we call making an exit." It is all theatrical, rehearsed, in a deeply important sense *perfunctory;* the scene is not one of despair in a darkening world as much as a weary, self-conscious enactment of what such a scene is supposed to be like, of what it would be like *in literature.*

The importance of this is hard to overestimate, for it is what lifts the play wholly above the chic status of a "God-is-dead" document or an allegory of Life after the Bomb. *Endgame*'s thoroughgoing artificiality as tragedy, its self-derision—in his opening speech Hamm says, "Can there be misery—(*he yawns*)—loftier than mine?" —point directly to its imaginative purpose. As in all of Beckett's work, what is being placed on sorrowfully mocking exhibition is not the state of the world or of inner life as any philosopher or sociologist or psychiatrist could apprehend it (or as we ourselves could in our amateur practice of those roles) but the very myths of meaning, the legends of significance that go into the making of humanistic culture, providing us with a sense of purpose and validity separated by the thinnest wall from the terror of the void.

It is not that Beckett doesn't experience this emptiness—no living writer feels it more—but that he is more pertinently obsessed, as an artist, with the self-dramatizing means we take to fill it. The mockery that fills his first plays is a function of his awareness of this activity, not a repudiation of it: we can't do otherwise, *Waiting for Godot* and *Endgame* are saying; we fill the time with our comic or lugubrious or tragic dramas. Still, we have to know that they are inventions, made up in the midst of indifferent nature—stone, tree, river, muskrat, wasp—all that has no question to ask and no "role" to take on.

Thus the derision does not deny the horror or the stress on artifice annul the real. But palpable actuality isn't Beckett's subject, which is, as has been said, the relationship between actuality and our need to express it, to *express ourselves.* Such expression is always "artificial," always self-conscious (since it is consciousness of being conscious that we are impelled by), and never directly "true." "Matter has no inward," Coleridge had said, and it is this truth that we are trapped in, material beings who crave inwardness and have the capacity to imagine it. At its most formal level the expression of our inwardness becomes literature, drama, which, as Ibsen beautifully described it in *The Master Builder,* make up "castles in the air."

What *Endgame* demonstrates is how our self-dramatizing impulses, our need for building Ibsen's castles, is inseparable from the content of our experiences, how we do not in fact know our experience except in literary or histrionic terms. And this is independent of whether the experience is solemn or antic, exalted or base. We give it reality and dignity by expressing it, we validate it by finding, or rather hopelessly seeking, the "right" words and forms. This is what is going on in *Endgame* beneath the lugubriousness and anomie: "Something is taking its course," Clov says,

not their lives—they are actors, they have no "lives"—but their filling in of the emptiness with their drama.

"By his stress on the actors as professional men and so on the play as an occasion in which they operate," as Kenner has written, Beckett turns the piece from a report, however fantastic, on the state of the world to an image of the world being dramatized. In this performance the actor is not an interpreter or incarnation of surrogate emotion for the audience but simply the professional embodiment of an activity we all engage in, at every moment, to build the wall against silence and nonbeing. "Outside of here it's death," Hamm says, and what he means is not that death is closing in but that *inside,* in this stage-as-room and room-as-stage, the play goes forward to enact the human answer to it, the absurd, futile, nobly unyielding artifice of our self-expression.

If the true action and subject of the play are therefore the enactment of despair rather than despair itself, then the relationships of the characters to one another have to be seen in an untraditional light. Like Pozzo and Lucky, Hamm and Clov have been thought of as impotent master and sullenly rebellious servant (capitalism and the working class? imperialism and emerging nations?) or, more subtly, as paradigmatic of every human relation of exploitation and tyranny. But once again this is to take their connection too literally, at its verbal surface. We ought to remember that Beckett is not interested in human relations as such but in human ontology, in the status of the stripped, isolated self beneath social elaboration. It is the requirement of the stage that there be at least duality, tension demanding otherness, that turns his play away from the nearly solipsistic interior monologues of his novels.

Yet something is carried over from the fiction to the drama, and it is a central clue to Beckett's new dramaturgy. If Hamm and Clov do not represent or incarnate any types discoverable in the social world, they are not even discrete personalities, except as they possess a sort of provisional and tactical individuation as a source of dialogue and therefore of dramatic propulsion. For many things about the play suggest that there is really only one consciousness or locus of being in the room, a consciousness akin to that of the "narrator" of the novels, so that it is more than plausible to take the room or stage as the chamber of the mind and the figures in it as the mind's inventions, the cast of characters of its theater. This is almost irresistibly indicated by a passage in one of Hamm's soliloquies: "Then babble, babble, words, like the solitary child who turns himself into children, two, three, so as to be together and whisper together, in the dark."

Clov would then be an extension of Hamm, the seated, reigning, perhaps dreaming figure. Hamm has invented a servant to be his eyes and agent of mobility, as we speak of our senses and legs serving us, and he has reinvented his parents, turning them into his own grotesque children. He is now complete, the play can be staged, the desperate drama in the dark. And Beckett's play *Endgame* takes on still another implication: that it is an illusion that there are fellow actors in our dramas, we have to invent them as they invent us; we are all children in the dark, solitary, babbling, inconsolable. But we play, in this case the *end game,* the last phase of an abstract life worked out in the mind.

The recognition that there is nothing beyond this last invention except silence—the scenery trundled off, the props put away, the stage lights down—is the true source of the feeling of extremity that rises from **Endgame.** There is no doom impending from outside, no tragic or deracinated situation to live through. There is only that silence on the other side of the wall . . . and we are running out of scripts.

Richard Gilman, "Beckett," in Samuel Beckett's "Endgame", *edited by Harold Bloom, Chelsea House Publishing, 1988, pp. 79-88.*

Harold Clurman   (review date 16 February 1980)

[*Highly regarded as a director, author, and longtime drama critic for* The Nation, *Clurman was an important contributor to the development of modern American theater. In the excerpt below, he comments on the tone and humor of* Endgame.]

Samuel Beckett's **Endgame** is a Mystery of final things: as death, the end of an age. Being altogether modern, it is also a comedy. We do not weep in the theater nowadays over futility, protracted dreariness or doom: we laugh.

"Endgame" is a technical term signifying the last stage in playing a hand, the position of the important card having been generally known, and the play being determined accordingly; or the point in the game when the forces (in chess or checkers) have been greatly reduced.

The central image of the piece is that of Hamm, a blind man, paralyzed, shut off in a bare, gray room with his legless parents who remain immobilized in two dustbins. His condition does not change from first to last. Hamm has an alter ego, Clov, who might be likened to an enslaved son. There is much scurrying about on Clov's part but little action; the earth and sea outside have nothing on the horizon: all is still, inert, "corpsed." At the end of Clov's long submission to his "father" and master, Hamm, he appears to be on the verge of escape. Is there hope of resurrection in this? Probably not, but we cannot be sure. Hamm "gives up," with a weary finality: "Old endgame lost of old, play and lose and have done with losing."

I append further citations to convey the tone of what is essentially a dramatic poem. Hamm asks Clov, "Have you not had enough?" "Of what?" Clov asks. The answer is, "Of this—this—thing." He refers no doubt to the burden of life. Clov is always seen in movement, obeying Hamm's senseless orders. "I can't sit," he cries out, to which Hamm responds with, "And I can't stand. . . . Every man his specialty." "What's happening?" Hamm wants to know. Clov's reply is, "Something is taking its course." Hamm wonders, "We're not beginning to mean something?" "Mean something!" Clov mocks, "You and I mean something. . . . Oh, that's good." Hamm speculates for a moment, "Imagine if a rational being came back to earth, wouldn't he be able to get ideas into his head if he observed us long enough.. ... To think perhaps it won't all have been for nothing!" Clov asks the supreme ques-

tion, "Do you believe in the life to come?" and receives the superb answer, "Mine was always that." This is the special humor, the Beckett "joke," which makes his work seem like a scenario for a farce. Clov asks, "What is there to keep us here?" Hamm answers, "The dialogue."

The cream of the jest is the story told by the male dustbin occupant about a man who brought cloth to a tailor to have trousers made. The tailor takes an unconscionable time to finish the job. The customer, at the end of his patience, explodes, "In six days, do you hear me, six days God made the World! And you are not bloody well capable of making me a pair of trousers in three months!" The tailor retorts, "But my dear Sir, my dear Sir, look at the world and look at my trousers."

When I saw **Endgame** in Paris in 1957 I thought it "at times impressive and drab, at other times snarling through a grin. . . . Its writing has humor, tang and obliquely lyric dialogue." But I thought it lacked the tenderness which alleviated the restlessness of **Waiting for Godot.** Since then, I have seen it directed by Alan Schneider, André Greogry and now by Joseph Chaikin in the present production at M.T.C. Each of these productions had different characteristics and merits, but none of the quiet and numb ache of the first one which, though in French, had something of the wonderful lostness and melody of Jack MacGowran's eminently Irish reading of the Beckett anthology we heard some years ago at the Public Theater.

I am reminded now of what Aaron Copland once said on receiving a complete recording of Anton Webern's compositions. He admired Webern, considered him a seminal figure in modern music, a highly significant artist, but found that he had no special urge to return to repeated hearings of his work. Perhaps because I have seen **Endgame** four times I feel the same way about it. I do not feel quite this way about **Waiting for Godot.** But it may be that I have grown weary of weariness, the standstill of pained bewilderment—now become a prevalent posture—even though I cannot help being in awe of the genius of Beckett's methods of expressing it. . . .

In writing about Beckett I cannot help but contrast him in certain respects with Pinter: the first is the progenitor of the second.

The abstractions in Beckett's writing may make understanding it difficult, but its mood is always emotionally persuasive. Though Pinter may be obscure or elusive in some of his detail, his work on the whole is more "realistic": he is of his time and place and always unmistakably English. Pinter is wed to his ambiguity, as if to divulge precisely what he means would be simple-minded, almost vulgar.

Harold Clurman, in a review of "Endgame," in The Nation, *New York, Vol. 230, No. 6, February 16, 1980, pp. 187-88.*

Ruby Cohn   (essay date 1980)

[*Cohn is an American educator and critic whose writings on Beckett include* Samuel Beckett: The Comic Gamut *(1962),* Back to Beckett *(1973), and* Samuel Beckett

> [Interpretation] of *Endgame* cannot pursue the chimerical aim of expressing the play's meaning in a form mediated by philosophy. Understanding it can mean only understanding its unintelligibility, concretely reconstructing the meaning of the fact that it has no meaning.
>
> —*Theodor W. Adorno, in "Trying to Understand* Endgame," *in his* Notes to Literature, *1991.*

(1987). In the following excerpt from her Just Play: Beckett's Theater, *she compares the various drafts of* Endgame.]

A play aborted and a play jettisoned contrast with Beckett's favorite play, **Endgame,** which was worked, reworked, and translated from the French. As an approximation, Deirdre Bair is probably right [in her *Samuel Beckett,* 1978] to surmise that Beckett turned to drama when he reached a creative impasse, but drama too can be an impasse, and Beckett labored two years over **Fin de partie.** Of all his plays, it underwent most extensive revision.

Beckett wrote his friend, anglicist Jean-Jacques Mayoux:

> La rédaction définitive de Fin de partie est de 56. Mais j'avais abordé ce travail bien avant, peut-être en 54. Une première, puis une deuxième version en deux actes avait précédé celle en un acte que vous connaissez.
>
> [The final draft of Endgame dates from 56. But I had started this work much earlier, perhaps in 54. A first, then a second version in two acts had preceded the one act that you know.]

The "deuxième version en deux actes" of **Fin de partie** is in the Ohio State University Library, and the "première version" is in the Beckett collection of Reading University, England; Beckett does not mention a brief handwritten continuation of the latter, now in Trinity College Library, University of Dublin.

The twenty-one-page typescript at Reading bears no title, but Beckett's hand notes: "avant **Fin de partie.**" Another hand labels the piece "Abandoned Theatre in French," and the text does apparently abandon its two actors in the middle of their action. Bair asserts that the play was begun with specific actors in Beckett's mind—Roger Blin who played Pozzo in **Godot** and Jean Martin who played Lucky. If this is so, the new play would continue their roles of master and servant, those staples of French comedy. Designated by the letters X and F (for Factotum), the master's baptismal spoon reads Jeannot, and the servant is variously called Donald, Lucien, and, mainly, Albert. As the letter X suggests, the master is almost as unknowable as Godot, but he is distinctly visible and audible. F wants to address X as "Votre Honneur" or "Monsieur" or even "Patron," but X rejects such honorifics. F declares himself incapable of calling X "vieux con" as directed; nevertheless, he does so once, even while continuing his plea for the privilege of saying: "Votre Honneur."

X and F interact in a place undescribed in the few scenic directions, but Beckett seems to have envisioned a shelter not unlike that of **Endgame,** since F speaks of two large windows (now aveuglées), and he retires to his offstage kitchen, whereas X is confined to his wheelchair. F locates the shelter in Picardy, where destruction occurred "dans des circonstances mystérieuses" between 1914 and 1918. (In the final **Endgame** only Nell's mention of the Sedan hints at the French War, where Napoleon III was disastrously defeated in 1871.) The location may be Picardy, but the props are neutral, and X recites their inventory—a drum and stick attached to X's chair (instead of the later whistle around his neck), a superfluous syringe, a baptismal spoon, and a Bible. X does not mention his Fahrenheit thermometer, but he desires a telescope. Beckett's few scenic directions specify silence, X's drums-beating to summon F, F's entrances and exits, X's vain efforts to move his wheelchair, and F's actual movements of the chair. Beckett evidently heard the dialogue before he saw all the gestures in his mind's eye. And what he heard is an action about playing, passing time, and ending. In X's first expository monologue he says he is blind and paralyzed, then says he is pretending to be blind and paralyzed, then wonders whether he is lying or mistaken. His self-doubt is more insidious than Hamm's, as is appropriate to his name, X. Perhaps the Cartesian heritage is stronger; he doubts, therefore he is, and he doubts out loud.

Of the twenty-one typed pages at Reading University, X's opening monologue (punctuated by ten silences) takes one and a half pages, the first X-F duologue takes four and a half pages, before X recites a shorter monologue. Another five pages of duologue are followed by a shorter X monologue. Like Hamm, X tells a story, and like Hamm he comments on the interaction of master and servant. Unlike **Endgame,** however, this play ends—or breaks off—in duologue (but is carried a little further in the Trinity College manuscript). X addresses F in the *tu* form, but F shows respect for X with his *vous,* instead of the familiar equality of the final version. The pointed pointlessness of the duologues recalls **Godot** and predicts the verbal ping pong of **Endgame:**

> X: Pourquoi ne me tues-tu pas?
>
> F: (*Avec dégoût*) Je vous aime. (*Silence*)
>
> X: Pourquoi?
>
> F: Je suis malade.
>
> X: Moi aussi.
>
> F: Vous êtes malade?
>
> X: Je t'aime.
>
> F: Alors nous nous aimons.
>
>
> [X: Why don't you kill me?
>
> F: (*With disgust*) I love you. (*Silence*)

X: Why?

F: I'm sick.

X: Me too.

F: You're sick?

X: I love you.

F: Then we love one another.]

X's story and its enactment—the playing theme—gradually assume importance, but the ending theme of *Endgame* is barely seeded. F repeatedly asks if he may address X as "Your Honor," which privilege is refused. He pleads for the stability of master-servant conventions, and it early becomes evident that this pair, like Vladimir and Estragon before them, have trouble in living through endless time. Dubiously, F remarks that everything has an end, and X retorts with the stale vaudeville joke about the sausage, which has two.

The two men touch on several other subjects that will preoccupy Hamm and Clov—weather, a dog, repetition, F's departure, X's centrality, whether their activities have any meaning. More explicitly than Hamm, X sighs: "Dommage que nous soyons les derniers du genre humain." He requests F to wheel him here and there, to take him for a promenade. The connection between fact and fiction is stronger in the early version: X calls for his dog, then amends this to his wife, and finally shifts to his mother, who becomes the protagonist of his story, as enacted by F.

The mother has had a terrible accident that invalids her, but she is carefully tended: "Et hop la revoilà sur pied." ["And hup there she is on her feet again."] Three times during his narrative, X cries out disjunctively, "Cherchez-la dans le coin." ["Look for her in the corner."] After the last time, F enters disguised as the mother, but after a brief mother-son duologue, X instructs F to get rid of that putréfaction. Alone again, X broods: "Nous jouons si mal que ça n'a plus l'air d'un jeu." ["We're playing so badly that it no longer looks like a game."] Then, resolving that "Cette nuit sera comme les autres nuits" ["Tonight will be like other nights."], he corrects himself: "Nous ne jouons pas si mal que ça." ["We're not playing as badly as that."] On his drum X summons F, who informs his master: "Il s'agit de ne pas mourir." ["It's a question of not dying."] The Reading typescript breaks off after:

F: Eh bien, il y a toujours l'affaire Bom.

X: Bom . . . Ah oui, cette pauvre vieille qui réclame une goutte d'eau.

F: Non, ça c'est l'affaire Bim.

[F: Well, there's always the Bom business.

X: Bom. . . . Ah yes, that poor old woman who begs for a drop of water.

F: No, that's the Bim business.]

From the time of his collection of stories *More Pricks Than Kicks,* written over two decades earlier, Bim and Bom recur sporadically in Beckett's work. Russian clowns whose comic routines contained—and were permitted to contain—criticism of the Soviet regime, they became for Beckett emblems of human cruelty, disguised under a comic garb. In a deleted passage of *Godot* Vladimir and Estragon compare Pozzo and Lucky to Bim and Bom. In the Reading University piece Bim and Bom are transformed into parched old women, but, combined with the clown overtones of narration and disguise, their names are a not unfitting terminus for duologues at once cruel and comic.

The Trinity College manuscript continues for two handwritten pages that present a failing X informed by F that an old woman has died of thirst. Less directly reproachful than Clov, F turns a phrase that will later be modified for Hamm:

X: Et comment sais-tu qu'elle est morte?

F: Elle ne crie plus.

[X: And how do you know she's dead?

F: She's no longer crying.]

The Reading University manuscript (and its brief Trinity College continuation) do not manage to weave the several strands: the meditations of X, the master-servant duologues, the X narration that leads to an F enactment. But this abandoned piece already contains *Endgame*'s physical space, a climate of illness and disaster, the love-hate interchange of master and servant, their penchant for story and play.

There is no date on the Reading University typescript, so that we cannot know how much time elapsed before Beckett turned to a new version—still untitled but complete by April, 1956—now in Ohio State University Library. We know from Beckett's letter to Jean-Jacques Mayoux that he may have started the first draft as early as 1954, and we know from his letters to Alan Schneider that he began the two-act version in December 1955, so that at least a year separates the two stages.

In the two-act version repetitions underline the playing theme and the ending theme. To some extent Beckett divided the two themes between the two couples who people the play. Master and servant (designated as A and B) are preoccupied with playing out their daily routines. However, the servant is less servile than F, and he is a more versatile player; he appears not only as a woman, but also as a boy. Like the mother of the first draft, this boy is engendered by the master's fiction. The other couple, M and P (for Mémé and Pépé, French for Granny and Grampy) are ending their long lives in stage ashbins. The two main characters, A and B in the manuscript, address each other by Christian names; A is French Guillaume, and B English James. Lacking any other national indication, they both speak colloquial French. M once addresses P as German Walther. A little boy in A's story is French André, but in references to what will become Mother Pegg, Beckett leaves a blank space for a name.

Gone is all reference to Picardy, and the two acts of the Ohio State version take place in the unnational set of the

Endgame we know, except for the absence of the painting, and the presence of the color red—on Hamm's blanket, robe, nightcap, and handkerchief; on the faces of the three men in Act I. Nell's face is white, in premonition of her death. The "ensign crimson" versus the "pale flag," which Winnie will salvage from *Romeo and Juliet,* are already emblems of life and death. B's beret is yellow and the toy dog black, but other props are nondescript and not described—drum, Bible, and thermometer retained from the earlier draft; new additions are a gaff and an alarm-clock.

When Beckett directed *Endgame* in Berlin in 1967, he segmented the action into sixteen rehearsal scenes, which are already discernible in the two-act version, though differently proportioned. In the final play the ending action dominates the playing action after Scene 12, and Beckett emphasizes this in the English translation by borrowing Shakespeare's *Tempest* line, "Our revels now are ended"—in the original French "Finie la rigolade." The French phrase opens Act II of the earlier draft, appearing on page 35 of the sixty-five page typescript.

As in the final *Endgame,* the dialogue of the two-act version begins with an expository soliloquy by Clov-B and ends with a soliloquy of resignation by Hamm-A, but the earlier versions are longer and more repetitive. Clov's opening sentence illustrates the rhythm: "Mort lente, mort rapide, vais-je rester, vais-je le quitter, pour de bon, le quitter pour de bon, ou rester pour de bon, pour la vie, jusqu'à ce qu'il meure, ou jusqu'à ce que moi je meure?" ["Slow death, rapid death, will I stay, will I leave him, for good, leave him for good, or stay for good, for life, until he dies, or until I myself die?"] However, it is not dialogue but gesture that opens and closes the two-act play, as it does the final *Endgame.* Clov's opening mime is similar to that of *Endgame,* but at play's end Hamm-A buries his face in his hands—a less stoic gesture than curtaining his face with the "old stancher," Beckett's brilliant translation of "vieux linge."

Like his successor Hamm, A simultaneously desires an end and hesitates to end. Although the play in the theater has to end, an endless process is subliminally suggested by the repetition of phrases, gestures, pauses which do not add up to whole events. Of primary importance, therefore, is Beckett's change of Nell-M's death at the end of Act I to Clov's laconic report in revision: "Looks like it [her death]."

Death *unhappens* between the two-act and final *Endgame.* Less decrepit than Nagg, P wants to hold M's hand, and he knocks at the lid of her ashbin. Alarmed that she does not answer, P urges B to examine her bin. The servant bends over, looks in, bends still further. There is a long silence. Then B straightens up, gently covers the bin, and removes his beret. When Nagg-P asks: "Alors?" B removes the old man's skull-cap, but blind A yawns to close the act with French cliché syllables of dismay, "Oh là là."

In Act II Nell-M's ashbin is gone from the stage. Hamm-A wears a black nightcap, Clov-B a black beret, Nagg-P a black skull-cap. The faces of A, B, and P are white, like M's in Act I; are they close to death? To A's question about whether P is happy that M is dead, the old

man replies, "Très." Toward the middle of Act II, P tells B that it isn't worth the trouble to make sawdust for his bin, and B declares that these may be P's last words. They are certainly his last words in this version of the drama. Before the end of the two-act version, A speaks Hamm's final speech of *Endgame* (with a few variants); then he and B engage in a last duologue. B leaves, and A continues to speak a few feeble words. Though A has earlier told B that he has pondered about his last words, the one spoken on stage is simply "Bon."

Present from the beginning of the two-act version is the visual impression of the play we know: two ashbins and one wheelchair in a bare shelter, with two windows that B can reach only by means of a ladder. Although A asks B suspiciously whether he has shrunk (as Hamm will ask Clov), it is rather the dialogue that shrinks between Beckett's two-act and one-act versions (from sixty-five to thirty-seven typed pages). Of the four characters, only Nell-M speaks similar lines although her speeches come in a different order, and she lacks memories of Lake Como.

Beckett curtails many speeches of the three men in the final *Endgame.* Nagg-P no longer comments on Hamm-A's meditations, nor does he declare that Nell-M can crawl out of her bin; nor does he swear an oath on his honor (although Hamm does). Also excised are Clov-B's reminiscences about seaweed and seagulls, his clown business with rolling-pin and telescope, his recitation of an undesignated sonnet, his difficulties with the dative case and pronunciation of the word *Pentateuch,* and his regret that he cannot lie to Hamm-A. From the master Beckett takes away a Pascalian exclamation about infinite spaces, the measurement of temperature at 98.6 Fahrenheit, the recitation of B's basic duties, and A's ruminations about preparing his last words. Excision shortens the A-B duologues where both men struggle through time in sequences about passing the time, about the toy dog, and about tears and laughter. In one routine A and B cry in synchrony, giving a comic tone to their tears. Also deleted is B's hesitation between two commands—that of A to wheel his chair to the center of the shelter and that of P to replace the skull-cap on his head. Both commands desire a return to the *status quo ante,* delaying an end. B weighs his choice: "Mon coeur balance. (*Un temps.*) A moins d'un fait nouveau nous sommes figés pour l'éternité." ["My heart is poised between the two. (Pause.) Unless a new fact enters, we're fixed for eternity."] Eyes front, B begins to recite from Rimbaud: "O saisons, o châteaux!" The impasse passes when A commands that B serve P, and B therefore comments: "On repart. Dommage." ["We're off again. Pity."]

Beckett's most telling revision is the complete elimination of two Clov-B scenes of disguise, one in each act. Without the anticlimactic color of these scenes, the ending action becomes more continuous and relentless, apparently dating from the biblical flood. In the two-act draft, the Flood reference is specific, for B reads to A from *Genesis,* then turns to the descendants of Shem, chanting a litany of long-lived patriarchs who engendered large families. A's response is Oedipal since he asks for his mother to help him engender. When B protests that A must mean his wife, the master retorts that it's all the same to him whether it is mother, wife, sister, daughter; what counts are two breasts and a vulva. B exits, to re-enter in blonde wig, false breasts, and a skirt over his trousers. It is not clear whether A is deceived by the disguise, for B also assumes a woman's voice, and it is B who speaks what will become Nell's line in the final *Endgame*: "Alors, mon gros, c'est pour la bagatelle?" ["What is it, my pet? Time for love?" (Beckett's translation in English *Endgame*.)] Since B is both himself and the woman, there follows a comic triangular scene, but instead of two men competing for the favors of the woman, both A and B wish to foist her on the other. If a child is conceived, B's woman's voice tells A, they will drown it.

A child *is* conceived in the two-act draft. Even in the final version, Clov reports seeing a small boy through the window (a report abridged in Beckett's English translation), whereupon Hamm informs Clov that he is no longer needed. In the two-act draft, B surmises this on his own, once the boy is sighted. Soon after A calls his father the boy appears on stage, played by B in his second disguise—red cap, short trousers, and the gray smock of French schoolchildren. Changing voice with costume, B complains of hunger, and A seems to believe B's disguise. He bribes the boy with an offer of chocolate and orders him to look into an ashbin, to push his wheelchair, to bring his gaff. But when B as boy claims the chocolate, A announces that there is no more chocolate. Recalling how he desired a drum when *he* was a child, A offers his instrument to the boy and pleads: "Viens." The boy backs out of the shelter, but blind A continues to address him. He attributes to the boy the greed that Hamm will attribute to old folks. Only after a long silence does A realize that he is alone. He tries vainly to move his chair, as X tried in Beckett's Reading piece, as Hamm will try in *Endgame*. Then, throwing away the gaff, A whispers "Bon," his last word before burying his face in his hands.

In the theater B's disguises would be comic in spite of the grim overtones of Beckett's two-act play. Beckett's elimination of these comic scenes balances his decision to cut the cruellest scene from the earlier draft. In that version P is reluctant to listen to his son's story, so that A orders B to put P's head into a pillory, making him a literally captive audience. A then stages a professor-pupil scene in which he plays both professor and pupil in a lesson on madness. Not satisfied with his father as mere listener, A orders him to recite the story of his life. Canged though he is, P refuses until A, wheeled by B to P's ashbin-pillory hits him on the head with his drumstick, and then threatens him with hammer and gaff. Thus beaten into speech, the old man delivers a seriocomic life story in telegraph phrases. In Beckett's novels Molloy strikes his mother on the head, and a stranger strikes Malone, but Beckett must have decided that such physical violence is too crude for his stage, and Hamm's hostility toward his father is reduced to the verbal in the final *Endgame*. (Servant strikes master with the toy dog in both versions, but the weapon mitigates cruelty.)

In spite of the crucial concentration of two acts into one, the final *Endgame* seems more symmetrical. Hamm and Clov are more evenly balanced than are A and B. Their dialogue is more equitably shared; Clov's five laughs at the beginning are balanced by Hamm's five yawns; Hamm's wheelchair by Clov's ladder; Hamm's dark glasses by Clov's telescope, and his whistle by Clov's alarm-clock. Re-inforcing such balance is the way Hamm and Clov speak of kissing, whereas Nagg and Nell try to kiss.

Because Beckett's revision achieves balance, economy, and concentration, his few additions are noteworthy. Beckett molded *Endgame* at its beginning and end to suggest that "The end is in the beginning." Thus, only in the final version are all four characters in the same stage space at beginning and end. Only in the finished play does Hamm address his handkerchief as "old stancher" near beginning and end, and only there does he sniff for Clov near beginning and end.

Beckett supplies new binding threads in the final version. He concretizes the difficulties of ending by reference to Eleatic grains and moments, he makes the characters more aware of playing, and he underlines the ending theme by references to more phenomena running out. Dwelling on the entropic action, Beckett embellishes Hamm's wasteland prophecy and his recollection of the painter; Beckett moves the master's richest and loneliest speech to the very end of *Endgame*.

Only into the final version does Beckett introduce the old vaudeville joke about hearing that has not failed—"our what?" —and only there does he add Nagg's significant joke about the poor quality of God's created world. *Endgame* intensifies pathos as well as humor; in the final version alone we find the last moving Hamm-Clov exchange, from Hamm's "Before you go . . . say something" through Clov's most extended speech that begins: "I say to myself—sometimes. . . ." Both characters imply a link between speech and suffering, but that link is stronger in *Endgame* because Beckett's words are stronger, and they are ordered for maximum tension.

The variety of words is diminished by the increase of repetition, which was already markedly increased between the Reading and Ohio State University drafts. Several Clov threats to depart are added to the final version of *Endgame*. The most frequent scenic direction in the Reading fragment is "Silence," but "Un temps" takes the lead in the last two versions, and the final *Endgame* contains new repetitions of "Alors" and "Même jeu." As is often noted, Hamm begins his three soliloquies with the same striking phrase: "A moi de jouer," and in the final version Mother Pegg, the light, and the earth are all "éteint." Repetition itself sounds starker and more continuous in the economy of the single act.

Although the immense effort required to play, pass time, and end is common to the three versions, Beckett did not set out to compose on given themes. He probably began like other playwrights in other styles with characters in a setting—with a paralyzed master and an ailing servant in an almost hermetic room. The two-act version accommodated a second couple. With four characters confined to a single act, however, the play achieves the linear force of a tragedy by Racine, an author long appreciated by Beckett. Still, it is a circle rather than a straight line that diagrams *Endgame,* whose end echoes its beginning, whose hero orders his servant to wheel him *round* his shelter, whose dialogue is riddled by pauses and zeros, in all versions.

Along with sustained themes—playing, passing time, ending—comes a consistency of detail in the three versions. The bare set with its centered wheelchair and offcenter ashbins is the dominant image. The physical Bible of the first two drafts evaporates into words in the final version; conversely, the Reading draft merely mentions a dog, which subsequently becomes a visible toy. In the three versions the master accuses the servant of stinking, but the servant's appreciation of the master's honor undergoes a curious development. X's honor, the right to be called "Your Honor," is the most insistent phrase of the Reading draft. In the two-act Ohio State version, honor belongs to Nagg-P, or at least he mentions it when swearing an oath that he will appear when summoned. In the final play it is Hamm who promises on his honor to give Nagg a sugarplum, at which they laugh heartily. The innuendo is that Hamm has no honor, and we learn that he does indeed lack it, for "There are no more sugar-plums"—the only "no more" announced by Hamm rather than Clov. Moreover, the very coupling of honor and sugar-plums deflates honor as effectively as does Falstaff.

Few lines of dialogue survive revision into one act. However, each master—in different words—requires his servant to kiss him, and each is refused. In exactly the same words in each version, the master asks the servant why the latter doesn't kill him; in the original French the sound play mitigates the grimness: "Pourquoi ne me tues-tu pas?" In another verbal survival through only two versions, Beckett converts a question by X to a statement by Hamm. The Reading typescript has X anxiously interrogate F: "Est-ce une journée comme les autres jusqu'à présent?" pleading to be reassured about the *in*significance of this day. Early in *Endgame* Hamm asks a comparable question: "C'est une fin de journée comme les autres, n'est-ce pas, Clov?" Hamm is more or less reassured by Clov's reply: "On dirait." Later in *Endgame,* after Hamm tells Clov of the painter's catastrophic vision, master and servant agree that: "Ça a assez duré." And Hamm draws the gloomy conclusion: "Alors c'est une journée comme les autres." The English is more pointedly repetitive: "It's the end of the day like any other day, isn't it, Clov?" and "Then it's a day like any other day."

But of course Hamm is wrong. It is *not* like any other day, for only on this day are there "no more" things, from bicycle-wheels to coffins. Only on this day does Clov sight a small boy and propose to leave. It is only this unending day that Beckett stages, with the symmetries and repetitions that *seem* to support Hamm's conclusion—the old questions, the old answers, the old moves, the old pauses. This day and only this day is distinguished by its brave comic play against a background of tragic waning, but Beckett's skill—exercised in revision—leaves us with Hamm's impression. Hamm is wrong about the insignificance of the day, but he is right to worry about "beginning

to mean something." For Beckett has revised *Endgame* into its present meaningful economy.

Ruby Cohn, in her Just Play: Beckett's Theater, *Princeton University Press, 1980, 313 p.*

Kristin Morrison   (essay date 1983)

[*An American educator and critic, Morrison has written extensively on modern drama. In the following excerpt, she examines Beckett's use of narrative in* Endgame, *focusing on Hamm's chronicle and its biblical allusions.*]

After the little canters of *Waiting for Godot,* Beckett composed a substantial "chronicle" for *Endgame,* providing one of the best examples of extended narrative as an essential part of drama: the presence of story is unmistakable here, both to the audience and to characters within the play. Hamm refers by name to his "chronicle" and is self-conscious in his narration of it, aware of himself assuming the role of historian, aware of himself adopting a special voice and manner setting off these words from his other speech. His chronicle itself has to do both with origins and with ends; it "accounts for" an entire world by presenting critical events and interpreting their meaning. Hamm is the Moses of a garden desolate, the Polidore Virgile of a wrecked kingdom. He records bereft existence, a modern inversion of "providential history." The whole point of *Endgame* lies in the interrelationship between this chronicle, this value-laden record of past events, and the words and actions which make up the dramatic present of the play. The play ends when the narrative ends.

The chronicle is presented at length in two different versions at two different times. The occasions for recital of the story, the interruptions and editorial changes all suggest the extent to which this narrative is emotionally and philosophically important to Hamm, a way to give "meaning" to his life, a way to justify his behavior. First reference to the story occurs about halfway through the play, after Hamm and Clov have attempted various other diversions to make their existence bearable. Hamm's announcement "It's time for my story" is much like Winnie's in *Happy Days*; there is a sense that the best distraction has been saved till last. The story—Hamm corrects the word to "chronicle"—is one which Clov states "you've been telling yourself all your days." It has an ongoing continuity suggested by Hamm's comments "where was I?" and "No, I've done that bit." It gets Hamm through difficult moments and leads him to that final moment when "time is over, reckoning closed and story ended."

Basically, this chronicle has to do with a man and his son, the son starving, the man petitioning Hamm for aid. As is usual throughout Beckett's work, the account contains a number of clear scriptural references, three of which epitomize Christian belief: the time is Christmas Eve (when life and light are born into the world), the boon sought is bread (the divine gift that sustains life), the child has been deep in sleep for three days (prototype of death and resurrection). The bare event itself has many counterparts in Biblical stories where a parent intercedes on behalf of a dying child (or in some cases, a master tries to save a beloved servant). In most of these stories the passionate commitment of the parent is shown by his or her traveling a distance and being undeterred by difficulties (whether awe of the prophet from whom aid is sought, rebuke of his or her efforts, or the premature arrival of death itself). The story of Jairus's daughter and the story of the centurion and his servant are well known versions. In John, the event involves a solicitous father, not put off by rebuke, and a dying son:

> And there was a certain nobleman, whose son was sick at Capernaum. When he heard that Jesus was come out of Judea into Galilee, he went unto him, and besought him that he would come down, and heal his son: for he was at the point of death. Then said Jesus unto him, Except ye see signs and wonders, ye will not believe. The nobleman saith unto him, Sir, come down ere my child die. Jesus saith unto him, Go thy way; thy son liveth. And the man believed the word that Jesus had spoken unto him, and he went his way. And as he was now going down, his servants met him, and told him, saying, Thy son liveth. Then inquired he of them the hour when he began to amend. And they said unto him, Yesterday at the seventh hour the fever left him. So the father knew that it was at the same hour, in which Jesus said unto him, Thy son liveth: and himself believed, and his whole house.
>
> [John 4:46-53]

In the story of Elijah and the widow of Zarephath, there is the added element of imminent starvation, both food and life being restored to the woman and her son by the man of God in response to the widow's prayers. But as is also the case in Beckett's other work, these remote biblical allusions suggest ironic contrast: Hamm questions the suppliant father's belief that "there's manna in heaven still for imbeciles like you." There is "no cure" for being on *this* earth, no providential bread in *this* wilderness; the great faith of this father does not move Hamm's "divinity" to provide miraculous sustenance. On the contrary, Hamm tempts the man to betray his role as father, to abandon his own beneficence. Such a twist to the prototypical stories suggests what is central in Hamm's own bitter disappointment about his own existence.

One of the clues to the importance of this malevolent twist comes from the fact that Hamm interrupts his narrative before getting to his "punch line":

> Well to make it short I finally offered to take him into my service. He had touched a chord. And then I imagined already that I wasn't much longer for this world.
> (*He laughs. Pause.*)
> Well?
> (*Pause*)
> Well? Here if you were careful you might die a nice natural death, in peace and comfort.
> (*Pause*)
> Well?
> (*Pause*)
> In the end he asked me would I consent to take in the child as well—if he were still alive.
> (*Pause*)
> It was the moment I was waiting for.
> (*Pause*)

> Would I consent to take in the child . . .
> (*Pause*)
> I can see him still, down on his knees, his hands flat on the ground, glaring at me with his mad eyes, in defiance of my wishes.
> (*Pause. Normal tone.*)
> I'll soon have finished with this story.
> (*Pause*)
> Unless I bring in other characters.
> (*Pause*)
> But where would I find them?
> (*Pause*)
> Where would I look for them?
> (*Pause. He whistles. Enter Clov.*)
> Let us pray to God.

He rationalizes that he will soon have finished his story, implying that he does not want to get to the end too quickly and thus needs to stop for a while. But what he turns to when he stops reveals indirectly what there was in the narrative itself that he needed to avoid. Apparently out of the blue he says, "Let us pray" (that "oremus" of sacred liturgy which introduces commentary on the "lesson" or scriptural narrative just recited) and the prayer he gets Nagg and Clov to participate in results in an important assertion ("Our Father which art—") and an even more important judgment: "The bastard! He doesn't exist!"

Here is the source of Hamm's desolation: there is no father to care for him, no heavenly father, no earthly father to hear his cries and to provide solace. "The bastard! He doesn't exist!" serves as commentary both on traditional prayer and also on the story Hamm was just telling. The cause of all this desolation is Hamm's relationship with Nagg; the effect of it all is seen in Hamm's relationship with Clov and other "creatures." In order to understand the painful significance of the content of Hamm's chronicle, it is necessary to look carefully at both his experience as son and his experience as father.

First, Hamm's own experience as son. His hatred for Nagg ("Accursed progenitor!") is revealed early in the play and is connected with hatred for his own existence: "Why did you engender me?" is not a question so much as an expression of resentment. Hamm's lament about existence, the desire to end, has its root in his first experience of existence, his infancy and childhood. If he curses the ideal father, "that bastard" who doesn't exist, it is due to neglect from his actual father; the passage that establishes this fact comes immediately after the prayer sequence, as Nagg complains about being wakened unnecessarily:

> Whom did you call when you were a tiny boy, and were frightened, in the dark? Your mother? No. Me. We let you cry. Then we moved you out of earshot, so that we might sleep in peace.
> (*Pause*)
> I was asleep, as happy as a king, and you woke me up to have me listen to you. It wasn't indispensable, you didn't really need to have me listen to you.
> (*Pause*)
> I hope the day will come when you'll really need to have me listen to you, and need to hear my voice, any voice.
> (*Pause*)
> Yes, I hope I'll live till then, to hear you calling

me like when you were a tiny boy, and were frightened, in the dark, and I was your only hope.

This passage connects several important elements in **End-game**: Hamm's childhood fear, the dark, his father's neglect, the need to call out, the need to have a listener. The story Hamm tells now—the prayer sequence and this subsequent passage are only an interruption of that chronicle, which will eventually resume—is simply an adult version of his childhood cry. Then, and now, he *does* need someone to listen to him, and then, as now, his "only hope," his father, fails him by refusal. Later in the play, as an introduction to his final, terminal soliloquy, Hamm repeats a number of these elements in a passage similar to Nagg's. After thinking of fearful events, of being deserted by a father, "all kinds of fantasies," Hamm says: "Then babble, babble, words, like the solitary child who turns himself into children, two, three, so as to be together, and whisper together, in the dark."

The adult, as well as the child, finds remedy for desertion in storytelling: the babbles, the whispers, the pretense that others are there make the dark not so lonely, so frightening. This passage of Hamm's, like the earlier one of Nagg's, comes immediately after Hamm has speculated about the ending of the story he has been telling. If he ends his story, he will indeed be alone in the dark, a solitary child abandoned, no father to listen and comfort. And, as is the case with all of Beckett's use of narrative, it is not the mere fact of storytelling that is important, but the very content of the story itself is crucial, allowing the character simultaneously to reveal and conceal himself. Hamm's chronicle does not serve as mere distraction; it betrays his deepest fear and need, as his final brief reference to it reveals in the important last minutes of the play.

But before discussing that ending, it is necessary to examine Hamm's own experience as "father" and note how that correlates with his experience as son. Fatherhood is, in Hamm's case, a metaphor for power, a power he exercises in three ways. First, like a biological father, Hamm has given a specific son his chance in life; he says to Clov, "I was a father to you," "my house a home for you." Second, he has supplanted his own father; now he is the one to dispense pap, to promise and withhold sugarplums; now he controls Nagg, not vice versa, and in that process he duplicates Nagg's own earlier treatment of him; for example, he objects to Nagg's keeping him awake now by storytelling just as earlier Nagg had objected to having his own sleep interrupted by Hamm's infant cry. But Hamm's third and greatest assertion of power is established by his references to himself as divine, the ultimate and most powerful of fatherhoods.

Hamm is an ineffectual god of a "corpsed" world, parodying the traditional role of divinity in a number of ways. He is master-generator whose will is carried out by a servant-son. He is right at the center of his world but also, through that son, visits the perimeters, beyond which is hell, that "other hell" since as a god manqué his own paradise is itself infernal. Both he and Clov use the regal or Trinitarian plural on one occasion. Enthroned at the center of his world, he trains his blindness on the earth and "sees"—

through his son, Clov—"a multitude . . . in transports . . . of joy." [In a footnote, Morrison states: "This biblical-sounding phrase is not a direct quotation, but it has the resonance of many passages in Revelation (see, for example, 19:1-8). This association is particularly ironic since Revelation is permeated with the refrain 'behold, I come quickly.' "] Since Clov's telescope is turned toward the auditorium when he makes this grim little biblical joke, the audience, too, is included in that gray lifeless world outside of Hamm's room. That world is dead because Hamm has failed as savior: "All those I might have helped. (*Pause*) Helped! (*Pause*) Saved." Throughout the play Hamm manifests a desire to have creatures pray to him; he likes to have his dog "gazing" at him, "asking," "begging," "imploring" him. But whether it be a bone for the dog, bread and crumpets for the starving multitudes, or meaning for the audience, Hamm does not provide any manna in this wilderness, any light in this darkness. He implies, in fact, that the desolation of the earth is due to his own absence from it: "I was never there. . . . Absent, always. It all happened without me."

Thus in Hamm traditional divine attributes—benevolence, omnipotence, ubiquity, omniscience—are all inverted. Toward the end of the play Beckett introduces a biblical allusion that illustrates how deadly Hamm's pseudo-divinity is. Despite Hamm's protestation that he does not himself know what has happened or whether it matters, Clov challenges Hamm's feigned innocence: "When old Mother Pegg asked you for oil for her lamp and you told her to get out to hell, you knew what was happening then, no? (*Pause*) You know what she died of, Mother Pegg? Of darkness." This passage with its oil lamp and outer darkness contains clear reference to the New Testament parable about the wise and foolish virgins:

> Then shall the kingdom of heaven be likened unto ten virgins, which took their lamps, and went forth to meet the bridegroom. And five of them were wise, and five were foolish. They that were foolish took their lamps, and took no oil with them: but the wise took oil in their vessels with their lamps. While the bridegroom tarried, they all slumbered and slept. And at midnight there was a cry made, Behold, the bridegroom cometh; go ye out to meet him. Then all those virgins arose, and trimmed their lamps. And the foolish said unto the wise, Give us of your oil; for our lamps are gone out. But the wise answered, saying, Not so; lest there be not enough for us and you: but go ye rather to them that sell, and buy for yourselves. And while they went to buy, the bridegroom came; and they that were ready went in with him to the marriage: and the door was shut. Afterward came also the other virgins, saying, Lord, Lord, open to us. But he answered and said, Verily I say unto you, I know you not. Watch therefore; for ye know neither the day nor the hour wherein the Son of man cometh. [Matthew 25:1-13]. In a footnote, the critic suggests that the reader "see also the parable of the marriage feast, which ends with lines associating darkness and damnation; 'Then said the king to the servants, Bind him hand and foot, and take him away, and cast him into outer darkness; there shall be weeping and gnashing of

Parables are literary forms (stories) used to teach a lesson. Beckett picks up the images and basic message of this particular well-known parable and inverts it for his own purposes. Hamm is thus the god who damns by withholding or being unable to provide the means which make life possible, whether it be bread in the wilderness or light in the darkness. After facing this revelation about himself (which clearly rankles, because the phrase "Of darkness!" interrupts Hamm's speculations about his own death a few minutes later), Hamm moves on to what he calls his "last soliloquy," that moment which will end Hamm, end the play, and reveal how very significant his chronicle really is.

As son, Hamm was mistreated and abandoned, and as father, he has mistreated and failed his own creation. His chronicle is an attempt to offset the pain of these two basic related experiences.

The chronicle deals with the paternal benevolence Hamm never experienced, a father's selfless efforts to try to save a starving son. As he recounts this chronicle, Hamm uses three voices: his special narrating voice to tell the story, the father's voice as quoted by the narrating voice, and his own voice to comment on the other two. The narrating voice describes the scene and most of the action: "The man came crawling towards me, on his belly. Pale, wonderfully pale and thin, he seemed on the point of—" And then his own voice ("normal tone," Beckett calls it) comments: "No, I've done that bit." After describing at length the harshness of this Christmas day, the narrating voice gets to the main issue, narrating, commenting, and quoting:

> It was then he took the plunge. It's my little one, he said. Tsstss, a little one, that's bad. My little boy, he said, as if the sex mattered. Where did he come from? He named the hole. A good half-day, on horse. What are you insinuating? That the place is still inhabited? No no, not a soul, except himself and the child—assuming he existed. Good. I enquired about the situation at Kov, beyond the gulf. Not a sinner. Good. And you expect me to believe you have left your little one back there, all alone, and alive into the bargain? Come now!

The narration continues in this manner to recount the man's plea for bread for his child, the narrator's scorn and anger, his denial that "there's manna in heaven still" or that there is any resurrection (the earth will not awake in spring nor will one deep in sleep for three days arise), and concludes with a temptation: "I finally offered to take him into my service." At this point Hamm interrupts his narrative, worrying that his story will soon end, forcing Nagg and Clov to join in prayer, tormenting Nagg about the sugarplum, and finally talking with Clov about the dog and Clov's leaving. Then he resumes the story. This entire interruption reveals why he stops the story where he does and why he resumes it when he does. The temptation directed toward the fictional father is a crucial one: here is a man, himself starving (or so Hamm's description suggests), who seems to care more for his son than for himself.

Rather than face the pain which the spectacle of such benevolence inflicts on Hamm—he so much wishes he had had that kind of love as a child—he turns away from narration in order to berate those fathers who failed him (Our Father and Nagg) and to dominate those who stand as his "sons" (the dog and Clov). [In a footnote, the critic adds: "The similar servile role for these two is further suggested by Beckett's production notes for *Endspiel* (1967): 'Clov's pose when trying to make dog stand. Parallel backs.' "] Then, having vented his hostility in two directions, against both fathers and sons, he is able to resume narration only to break off again at the same point: "Before accepting [the proffered job] he asks if he may have his little boy with him." Hamm seems not to be able to move the narrative beyond this point. What if the man does indeed care for the child's welfare more than for his own? What if he refuses the narrator's offer of help if it does not include his son? How can Hamm face such altruism?

In both his narrative and his "normal" speculations, Hamm argues against benevolence and altruism by suggesting that earthly existence is an incurable disease. In his narrating voice he says to the suppliant father, "Use your head, can't you, use your head, you're on earth, there's no cure for that!" and repeats the line word for word later, in his "normal tone" as he speculates about all those he might have saved. But this repeated violent outburst is not followed, as it is in the chronicle, by a return to innocuous description of the weather; instead it continues, parodying the chief injunction of the New Testament: "Get out of here and love one another! Lick your neighbor as yourself!" Hamm himself has refused the starving multitude bread (and crumpets); it is a small matter for his fictive narrator to deny one small boy life.

Throughout *Endgame*, Hamm has been talking about ending, bringing all life to a halt, his own as well. In the final moments of the play there is the suggestion such a winding down to absolute zero does occur. And one of the elements that makes cessation possible is final desertion among fathers and sons: "I'll have called my father and I'll have called my . . . (he hesitates) . . . my son." If they are gone, he will again be a solitary child alone in the dark, telling himself stories. And when the story ends, Hamm will end. In the last few moments of the play, his "last soliloquy," when Nagg and Clov are silent and Hamm thinks they are both irrevocably gone, Hamm finishes his story and "gives up." The last words of his story reveal the real nature of his hatred and desolation. He picks up the narrative now at its critical point, where he had abandoned it twice before—"If he could have his child with him. . . ."—and he continues to comment:

> It was the moment I was waiting for.
> (*Pause*)
> You don't want to abandon him? You want him to bloom while you are withering? Be there to solace your last million last moments?
> (*Pause*)
> He doesn't realize, all he knows is hunger, and cold, and death to crown it all. But you! You ought to know what the earth is like, nowadays. Oh I put him before his responsibilities!
> (*Pause. Normal tone.*)
> Well, there we are, there I am, that's enough.

"That's enough" of the story because Hamm has finally stated what is particularly offensive to him in this altruistic father-son relationship. The narrator's apparent argument—life on earth is so bad that a father's real responsibility is to *avoid* sustaining his son's existence—is really only a mask for the narrator's true feelings of resentment. The words "bloom" and "wither" betray the narrator's real motive, Hamm's real feelings. The corollary of a son's life is the father's death. By the natural order of human development, as the one grows into prime, the other passes beyond it, and the only term of that beyond is death. Hamm resents the fact that he will degenerate while another flourishes; thus his determination that there be no more potential procreators in this world, no fleas nor small boys from which humanity might start all over again. His is the resentment of age toward youth, compounded by his own personal sense of never having had the solace he needed, not in childhood and not now in his old age. So he berates the father in his story, presuming to lay bare that father's true motive, to prove it not altruistic but selfish: "Be there to solace your last million last moments?" But this accusation that the father only wants to help the son so that the son will help him has no foundation in the narrative as Hamm recounts it; this is pure projection at the most critical moment of the story. Hamm is the one unsolaced.

This story has allowed Hamm to reveal his deep sense of not having been cared for (his own father moved him out of earshot and certainly did nothing so beneficent as try to save his life at the expense of his own) and his deep resentment that such care could ever exist for anyone else: the father in his story must surely be a fake altruist, as the narrator's arguments about responsibility are supposed to prove. [In a footnote, the critic adds: "In *Avant fin de partie*, there is a story about a mother and a son, in which the son expresses great care for the mother: he alone knows her well enough to realize that her disappearance is a serious matter; he alone knows where she is to be found ('Cherchez, cherchez, elle est dans le coin'); and he alone nearly perishes from shock when her battered body is finally discovered, like a sponge, every bone broken, every fracture open. Somehow, she survives and after fifteen years in casts and on a bland diet, actually recovers, nursed by her watchful son. A sense of terrible disaster and abiding loss permeates the story (years later the narrator keeps repeating not the lines about recovery but the lines 'cherchez-la dans le coin, je la connias,' as if that moment of fear were perpetually present to him). These emotional elements are much like those in Hamm's chronicle, but the reversed roles and the alternate parent are significant differences. As Beckett finally chose to formulate the play, mothers are negligible and fathers are of central importance; and the son's pain comes not from loss of the parent (by death) but from loss of the parent's *care* (which results in the *child's* death)."] At the same time, the story has allowed him to disguise this revelation as fiction: he is not saying anything about him and Nagg; he is only making up events and details to pass the time. And yet this story is also a reckoning, a way to account for his life and himself. He is able to give up, to end, to die only when "time is over, reckoning closed and story ended." These words introduce that final moment of his narrative, which

has just been discussed. He can terminate that narrative only after he has reached the stage in it when he can say, however colloquially, "there I am"; only then is the story "enough." He has recounted his deepest feelings of neglect, resentment, and hatred (felt as a child and re-enacted in reversed roles as an adult), but in doing this he has also disguised and protected himself. He has never had to say "I" except as a supposedly fictional narrator.

The final seconds of the play dramatize what the story has also revealed. Thinking he has already lost both father and son, Hamm continues to divest himself of the things that give him solace—he throws away the dog, he throws away the whistle, he repeats the announcement "Discard." Only one possession remains, his handkerchief, and his word for it betrays with concentrated irony everything that the chronicle has revealed. "Old stancher!" he says, "You . . . remain." At the beginning and at the end of the play, Hamm's first and last words contain this rather unusual term, "old stancher." Its immediate meaning is available to the audience without a dictionary, but in its etymology it carries a grim pun that establishes once more how bereft Hamm feels.

The *Oxford English Dictionary* lists several meanings of the basic term "stanch:" to stop the flow of water, the flow of blood; to stop a leak, to make something watertight; to quench, repress, extinguish (thirst, appetite, hatred, anger); to weary. And under the noun form "stancher" ("One who or that which stanches"), two examples are particularly apt: "This is the first and chiefest Bloud stencher" and "Friendship, stancher of our wounds and sorrows." The two most familiar modern uses of this word correspond to these two earlier literary examples. The audience does not need a dictionary in hand because it certainly knows the clichés "a staunch friend" and "to stanch a wound." "Friend," "wound," love and death: Beckett makes capital of these two apparently distant associations contained in Hamm's exclamation, "Old stancher! (*Pause*) You . . . remain."

Literally this stancher is the "large blood-stained handkerchief" which covers Hamm's face when the play opens and which he replaces when the play ends. It stops the flow of blood, and thus is a true and loyal friend. It literally stands by him when all else fails and must be discarded. The irony of this reference and its associations comes from the fact that "blood" itself has failed Hamm, blood relationships. Fathers and sons, sources of life and sustenance during both infancy and old age, have not been loyal and true. Fathers and sons seem, in fact, to cause "wounds and sorrows," not to bind them up. There is no young boy (as in the chronicle) to solace Hamm's "last million last moments." He is left with just a bloody rag of extinction, himself and his story ended.

In addition to this extensive use of a single narrative, *Endgame* also contains shorter narrative forms of the kind . . . seen in *Waiting for Godot*: the joke and the anecdote. When Hamm begins his brief recital "I once knew a madman," he is ostensibly recounting an event he actually experienced, as distinct from his chronicle, which is presented in its form and context as first-person narrative fiction. This anecdote is brief, moving, self-contained, re-counted once and not referred to again:

> I once knew a madman who thought the end of the world had come. He was a painter—and en-graver. I had a great fondness for him. I used to go and see him, in the asylum. I'd take him by the hand and drag him to the window. Look! There! All that rising corn! And there! Look! The sails of the herring fleet! All that loveliness! (*Pause*)
> He'd snatch away his hand and go back into his corner. Appalled. All he had seen was ashes. (*Pause*)
> He alone had been spared. (*Pause*)
> Forgotten. (*Pause*)
> It appears the case is . . . was not so . . . so un-usual.

This flash of memory into Hamm's mind makes perfect sense in context: he and Clov have been talking about the desolation all around them, the unburied dead who once were bonny "like a flower of the field"; they both are pres-ent in a room which, like that asylum, imprisons them, opening out, through windows, on the world outside. It is not unusual that the wreck of this present world should remind Hamm of that painter in the past who only per-ceived ashes and devastation. What is important about the memory in this context is that it shows the madman to have been a prophet. Even Hamm, in those days, saw the rising corn, the herring fleet, "all that loveliness" of fe-cund, nourishing nature. The painter seemed then to be insane, but he is proved, by the passage and development of time, to have been visionary—not mentally crippled, but swift. Hamm's hesitating concession, "the case is . . . was not so . . . so unusual" betrays both how pained he is by the loss of that golden world (that corn which would have fed some child, if there were beneficence) and also his awareness (kept down, like Lear's early realizations) that the madman indeed spoke true, that apparent madness was in fact real sanity.

Much critical commentary on *Endgame* has associated the play with postnuclear destruction. It is interesting in this regard to compare Hamm's anecdote of the mad painter with Alain Resnais's film *Hiroshima Mon Amour,* where scenes of lovemaking are counterpointed with memory flashes of maimed and burned bodies. Or, for that matter, to go back in time to the medieval and renaissance tradi-tion of *memento mori* with its countless woodcut emblems showing the beautiful woman (to take only one example) gazing into her mirror which reflects the skeleton she will become. This apocalyptic vision, to see the ashes of "all that loveliness" even while it still flourishes is, apparently, as Hamm reluctantly realizes, "not so unusual." His reply to Clov's observation that "There are so many terrible things" has an interesting double meaning to it: "No, no, there are not so many now" seems a denial if the focus is on "now" and also a confirmation of the devastation if the focus is on "many."

Nagg and Nell's amusement over similar devastations serves as "subplot parallel" to Hamm's anecdote and

chronicle. Nagg and Nell laugh heartily remembering "When we crashed on our tandem and lost our shanks," and Nagg's favorite joke about the tailor puts into comic relief the miserable state of that world, that botched cre-ation, in which such horrors regularly occur. This "en-gagement joke" so tickled Nell that she capsized the canoe on Lake Como where Nagg first told it to her. "By rights we should have been drowned" does not, of course, testify to an odd kindness on the part of the cosmos but rather to that continuing misfortune which has plagued Hamm's life. With no Nagg, no Nell, no marriage, no engendering, Hamm would not have found himself where he is now, surrounded by ashes and the memories and stories by which he both looks at his misery and tries to evade it.

Kristin Morrison, "Canters and Chronicles," in her Can-ters and Chronicles: The Use of Narrative in the Plays of Samuel Beckett and Harold Pinter, *The University of Chi-cago Press, 1983, pp. 9-151.*

Jean-Jacques Mayoux on "reality" in *Endgame*:

Endgame (1957), more definitely even than *Godot*, is 'in a head', and the brain-grey bare room with its two high windows is evidently a gloomy inner aspect of the micro-cosm. 'Reality' is here twice removed: it is not Beckett's but Hamm's vision, sick, subjective, severely coherent as such, yet again slyly bursting those bounds; and double-levelled since Hamm pointedly is an actor playing Hamm:

> CLOV: What is there to keep me here?

HAMM: The dialogue.

And again:

> HAMM: I'm warming up for my last soliloquy . . .

Jean-Jacques Mayoux, in his Samuel Beckett, *Longman Group, 1974.*

Scott Cutler Shershow   (essay date 1986)

[*Shershow is an American editor and critic. In the following excerpt, he remarks on comic aspects of* Endgame.]

Beckett locates his comedy precisely in the no-man's-land between the play and the world. His characters and his au-dience face the same dilemma: *they* must get through their lives and *we* must get through the play. "What's happen-ing, what's happening?" asks the main character of Beck-ett's masterpiece *Endgame.* The play's audiences may ask the same question—and receive the same answer: "Some-thing is taking its course." Stranded like us in the theatri-cal darkness, in an unspecified landscape of future time or despairing imagination, Hamm and Clove, Nagg and Neill manage to get through "this . . . this . . . thing," some-how making their dialogue a plot and themselves charac-ters. "We're getting on," Hamm periodically reassures us, enduring as we do, his boredom and frustration, his ironic but inextinguishable self-interest.

Endgame is comedy stripped to the skeleton, to the merest blueprint of familiar comic devices and conventions. A father and a son, a master and a servant, share a series of passing conflicts which are, as it were, much ado about nothingness: a few last moments of gallows humor just this side of paralysis and annihilation:

> HAMM. Sit on him!
>
> CLOVE. I can't sit.
>
> HAMM. True. And I can't stand.
>
> CLOVE. So it is.
>
> HAMM. Every man his speciality.
> (*Pause*)
> No phone calls?

This comedy goes beyond malice, beyond personality itself, to the purest incongruity of matter and spirit. There are few scenes in the history of comedy where comic derision turns so fiercely, excruciatingly, to recognition. Founded on the ironic identity between theater and life, ***Endgame*** returns again and again to that most ancient and characteristic of comic devices: the joke in which the actors "break" their characters and reveal frankly that the play is just a play:

> CLOVE. (*He gets down, picks up the telescope, turns it on auditorium*)
> I see . . . a multitude . . . in transports . . . of joy.
> (*Pause*)
> That's what I call a magnifier.
> (*He lowers the telescope, turns toward Hamm*)
> Well, don't we laugh?
>
> HAMM. (*After reflection*) I don't.
>
> CLOVE. (*After reflection*) Nor I.

Here Beckett nods to the convention, but leaves his spectators separate and distant, their laughter disconnected from its object. In the comic tradition, by contrast, when a witty servant confides his schemes to the peanut gallery, or some ironist finally tires of the contrivances of the stage—

> ORLANDO. Good day and happiness, dear Rosalind!
>
> JACQUES. Nay then God buy you, and you talk in blank verse.
>
> (*As You Like It*)

—we are *included* in the action: invited to share the comedy's magic and illusion as we will share symbolically in its concluding banquet. In Beckett, the effect of these jokes is entirely different:

> CLOVE. What is there to keep me here?
>
> HAMM. The dialogue.

Hamm and Clove admit they are part of a play *without* breaking character, because the dialogue is indeed the means and end of their shared existence. For these charac-

ters, the very last word in comic degradation, the play is, quite literally, the thing.

But even here, in this theater and this world, the show goes on: still tying the knot of complications—

> CLOVE. (*He moves the telescope*)
> Nothing . . . nothing . . . good . . . good . . . nothing . . . goo—
> (*He starts, lowers the telescope, examines it, turns it again on the without. Pause.*)
> Bad luck to it!
>
> HAMM. More complications! . . .
> Not an underplot, I trust.

—and still striving to achieve, if not a happy ending, then any kind of ending. The fragments of wit, occasional bursts of lyricism, and random literary echoes marooned among nonsense manage to get both the characters and us through this brief theatrical and historical moment before the rest is silence. Ironic comedy can go no further. The playwright is no longer godlike: he is more like the tailor in Nagg's joke:

> NAGG. . . . "God damn you to hell, Sir, no it's indecent, there are limits! In six days, do you hear me, six days, God made the world. Yes, Sir, no less, Sir, than the WORLD! And you are not bloody well capable of making me a pair of trousers in three months?"
> (*Tailor's voice, scandalized*)
> "But my dear Sir, my dear Sir, look—
> (*Disdainful gesture, disgustedly*)
> —at the world—
> (*Pause*)
> and look—
> (*Loving gesture, proudly*)
> —at my TROUSERS!"

Just so the playwright, holding up his play to the world, finds reason, one way or another, to be proud. Here, pausing at the butt end of our days and ways, comedy constricts our movement, and pinches in sensitive places: but it still fits, it still plays, and it still matters.

Scott Cutler Shershow, "The Play and the World," in his Laughing Matters: The Paradox of Comedy, *The University of Massachusetts Press, 1986, pp. 89-102.*

Richard Dutton   (essay date 1986)

[*In the excerpt below, Dutton focuses on the relationship between Hamm's and Nagg's stories and the overall setting and meaning of* Endgame.]

Endgame, [like ***Waiting for Godot***] has its echo of *The Tempest.* But where Lucky remembered divine Miranda, Hamm derisively recalls the world-weary Prospero: 'Our revels now are ended. (*He gropes for the dog.*)' The difference is of a piece with the difference between ***Waiting for Godot*** and ***Endgame.*** The latter is at once a bleaker and a more perplexing play. Vladimir and Estragon have their basic health, for all their disappointments and discomforts, whereas Hamm is confined to a wheelchair, blood intermittently flowing from his head, and Clov is stiff-limbed, unable to sit down. Pozzo and Lucky degenerate physically in the course of the earlier play, but their situation is never so extreme, so dehumanised as that of Nagg and Nell, immobile in their ash-cans. The bare stage of *Godot,* with its focal tree, is an open metaphor for anywhere, at any time, but those ash-cans and the rest of the colourless set in which they stand pose a more disturbing challenge to our understanding, to our sense of the reality of the situation. *Endgame* is chillingly fixed within a room, but one that is as difficult to account for, in conventional terms, as are the events that take place within it.

The play in effect challenges us to find a metaphor that will explain or accommodate its abnormalities. The two favourite 'solutions' have been to see it as depicting either one of the last pockets of life after a (nuclear?) holocaust or the dying moments inside the skull of someone who has suffered a cerebral haemorrhage. But neither of these is totally satisfactory: the emphasis of the play seems more on progressive degeneration than on sudden cataclysm, and anyway it refuses to succumb to a single, rational interpretation. Perhaps it is more fruitful to start from the observation that, for all the difficulties it poses, *Endgame* is an intensely self-reflexive play, endlessly commenting on its own genesis and progress. Clov's opening words, for example—'Finished, it's finished, nearly finished, it must be nearly finished'—refer as much to the play/performance as they do to anything else, while Hamm is always conscious of the theatrical context in which he exists. When Clov asks, 'What is there to keep me here?' Hamm replies, 'The dialogue'. Towards the end he becomes irate when Clov misunderstands the force of something he says, '(*angrily*). An aside, ape! Did you never hear an aside before? (*Pause.*) I'm warming up for my last soliloquy'. These moments of self-consciousness provide a running commentary on the play and its meaning, though it is one we should always treat warily:

> HAMM. We're not beginning to . . . to . . . mean something?

> CLOV. Mean something! You and I, mean something! (*Brief laugh*) Ah that's a good one!

Bearing this in mind, we may approach the bleak and perplexing nature of *Endgame* through two of its most sustained passages of self-commentary, the stories told by Nagg and Hamm. These are not overtly 'about' the play itself—though the latter, as we shall see, is intriguingly adjacent in its subject matter—but both are verbal entertainments, interrupted by their authors with observations on style and performance, and as such mirror the wider verbal entertainment of which they form a part. They are very similar, in effect, to plays-within-plays in Renaissance drama, which always mirror in some sense the plays in which they occur. Nagg's story is a well-polished produce of the raconteur's art, as carefully tailored as the trousers of which it tells, gathering in fluency and profanity until its disdainful climax. As such, it stands out markedly from the dialogue around it, with Hamm's peremptory observations and Nell's wistful reminiscences, and even more markedly from the broader context of meandering repetition, aimless conversation and staccato demands for 'pap' and painkiller. The very fact that the story has a discernible climax sets it in antithesis to the play. It tells of a time

when men had pride and a purpose in what they did, setting themselves a Renaissance goal—however difficult it might prove to achieve—of improving in their art on the nature of the world as they found it. (" 'But my dear Sir, my dear Sir, look—(*disdainful gesture, disgustedly*)—at the world—(*pause*)—and look—(*loving gesture, proudly*)—at my TROUSERS!' "). It is set ('the bluebells are blowing') against the season of spring, with all its traditional associations of vigour and aspiration. The irony, of course, is that it is the tale of a pair of trousers told by a legless man, a mocking survival of the past in every respect. It has no real validity in the present, as the indifference of the immediate audience, and Nagg's own depressed conviction that 'I never told it worse' underline. This is typical of the play's constant evocations of the past. Echoes of a time when life had a purpose, language had grace and meaning, and the arts communicated vigorously with their audiences only underline the loss of such qualities in the *Endgame* world—epitomised by the picture with its face to the wall.

This, surely, is the force of the Shakespearean echoes in the play. The revels to which Hamm alludes—the mysteries of the masque of Juno, Ceres and Iris which Prospero stages for Ferdinand and Miranda—are a long time gone in this world. It seems absurdly melodramatic, moreover, that Hamm should evoke the climax of *Richard III*—'My kingdom for a nightman!' —in his fit of exasperation with Nagg and Nell: melodramatic and in poor taste, given that a nightman is someone employed to remove night-soil—so that Shakespeare's moment of high drama has been reduced to a moment of pique and disgust. The two quotations, ironically transposed as they are, have similar effects in the broader context of the play. Both evoke masters of enterprise, politicians in their different styles—Prospero, the Renaissance mage, and Richard, the Machiavel—but focus on their moments of world-weariness and defeat. These are important moments in the Shakespearean originals, no doubt, but only moments; yet the moods they represent threaten totally to engulf the less ambitious and less articulate world of *Endgame.*

What caused the decline from Renaissance energy to *Endgame* apathy is never explained, though possibilities are obliquely suggested in other memories, particularly Nagg and Nell's recollections of a free and mobile past. Nagg's story is actually associated with their happiness, rowing on Lake Como, though also with a capsizing that almost drowned them. They also remember cycling on a tandem in the Ardennes, on the road to Sedan—a memory coloured by its association with a crash that lost them their 'shanks'. For the audience, the further association of these two places with the First World War may obliquely hint at what brought such a carefree, sugar-plum existence to an end. An even obliquer hint in the same direction may occur in the preamble to Hamm's story, where he refers to 'Something dripping in my head, ever since the fontanelles'. The latter phrase is an extremely odd one. The fontanelle is the soft, uncovered spot on a new-born baby's head, before the plates of the skull have joined together. So Hamm seems to be saying 'ever since birth'. But why be so circuitous about it, and why use the plural? It may be that Beckett is playing on the sound and shape of a relatively unfamiliar word, and so conjuring with the more familiar sound and shape of 'Dardanelles'—the scene of the disastrous Gallipoli campaign in the First World War. The phrase 'ever since the Dardanelles', in the context of a head-wound, would be much more conventional English than 'ever since the fontanelles', and perhaps the net effect of this aural pun is a running together of birth and battle which would be quite appropriate in this play.

If this punning seems a little far-fetched, it is worth noting that two lines later Hamm/Beckett again plays with the aural ambiguity of words: 'Perhaps it's a little vein. (*Pause.*) A little artery. (*Pause.*)'. Does the listener hear 'vein' or 'vain'? —particularly given that Nagg has previously mocked Hamm's self-dramatisations about the dropping in his head (including the phrase, 'Perhaps it's a little vein') as a piece of vanity. The addition of 'A little artery' seems at first to confirm that we are dealing with blood vessels, but the pause after *that* phrase allows the word 'artery' to reverberate and perhaps break down into art-ery—a product of art or affectation, chiming with vanity. No precision is possible here because the text is straining at—playing with—the limits of language itself, in typically tragicomic manner. This is the nature of language in the post-Renaissance, post-First World War of ***Endgame***—an unpredictable medium, an untrustworthy tool, a gamble. And the stories that language embodies have the same qualities.

Hamm's story is not as finished as Nagg's; it has an open-endedness which is far more in tune with the play as a whole. Indeed, it co-exists with the play, and may even overlap it, in very pointed ways. When the main telling of the story dries up, it does so with observations—'I'll soon have finished with this story. (*Pause.*) Unless I bring in other characters. (*Pause.*) But where would I find them?' —that might be those of Beckett on his play at this juncture, as much as of Hamm on his story. And in fact the story does not end here. Hamm intermittently adds details and tried new wordings for it until the dying moments of the play.

The contiguity of Hamm's story and Beckett's play is announced in the preamble, when Hamm's gloomy reflection—'It's finished, we're finished. (*Pause.*) Nearly finished.' —so closely echoes Clov's opening words to the play. Thereafter, a range of possible overlaps emerges, hinging principally on the fact that the story is a first-person narrative. Hamm never asserts that the 'I' of the story is in fact himself, and the *narrative tone* he adopts for the story-telling always preserves some distance between the two of them, but there are sufficient similarities in their manner and circumstances to suggest that it is likely. His puzzled reaction to the idea of introducing new characters into the story—'But where would I find them?' —further confirms the possibility; his powers of pure invention seem to be as diminished as any other commodity in the play, so the likelihood that his story is based on 'fact', however embroidered in the telling, is all the stronger. The most marked similarities between the character in the story and the character in the play are the histrionic, dictatorial manner and the implication that he alone can dispense food and patronage; on the other hand, the 'I' in

the story seems to be fit and mobile, busily putting up his festive decorations and only troubled by a touch of lumbago—a far cry from the haemorrhaging figure confined to his wheelchair. This is easily explained, however, if the events of the story are some time in the past, when Hamm was a younger man; this would further allow the possibility that the 'little boy' was Clov and the man his father, who (if this is 'true') must have disappeared from the scene very shortly after these events:

> HAMM. Do you remember when you came here?
>
> CLOV. No. Too small, you told me.
>
> HAMM. Do you remember your father?
>
> CLOV. (*Wearily*) Same answer.

Of course, this version of how Clov came to be with Hamm may be just as much, or as little, fiction ('you told me') as the story itself.

The timing of the story in the past, perhaps the late Victorian era, is suggested by a few incidental details. The character speaks of lighting a meerschaum pipe with 'let us say a vesta', while distance is measured by 'a good half-day, on horse'. While the timing of the 'present' in the play is never fixed, these details seem pointedly anachronistic, like the memories of Nagg and Nell. They chime, moreover, with one of the marked characteristics of the character telling the story, his obsession with a certain kind of scientific or technological factuality, constantly measuring the weather: 'zero by the thermometer'; 'fifty by the heliometer'; 'a hundred by the anemometer'; 'zero by the hygrometer'. The mixture of meerschaum and scientific data perhaps evokes the popular image of Sherlock Holmes: it certainly evokes the dispassionate, rather autocratic assumption of an absolute and verifiable physical truth which is often associated with late-Victorian science and finds its archetype in Sherlock Holmes. At its most extreme, it can be a heartless doctrine of the survival of the fittest, as in the character's contemptuous conviction of his own superiority over the man on his belly and his little boy ('as if the sex mattered')—a conviction not even shaken by the fact that this is Christmas Eve, with its message of peace on earth, good-will to all men. The outward show of decorations takes precedence over any question of human feelings or spiritual needs.

The position of the arrogant man of science is not as secure, however, as he would like to believe. For one thing, a heliometer would not give him the reading he so confidently ascribes to it; a heliometer measures the angles between the stars, or possibly the diameter of the sun, but not its brightness, for which some form of photometer would be necessary. Moreover, if all his measurements *were* correct, he would be in the midst of extreme, not to say apocalyptic weather conditions—hardly the time to be lording it over some unfortunate suppliant. This may help to explain the anticlimactic ending: just as the character relishes his triumph over the defiant suitor, Hamm's powers of invention flag and the performance ends lamely and ironically, like a sermon: 'Let us pray to God'. At least for the time being, religious faith of a sort wins out over scientific truth.

In what ways does this story mirror or comment on *Endgame* as a whole? Whether or not it literally describes Hamm's past and how Clov came into his service, it emblematically describes (as does Nagg's story) a stage in the intellectual and emotional journey to the *Endgame* world. Where Nagg's tailor had a zeal to improve on nature as he found it, the 'I' in the story is determined to dominate both it and his fellow men by force of character and by the powers of scientific reason. Both approaches fail. The myth of progress (and the art of story-telling which it in some respects resembles) evaporates in the light of human inadequacy and of the overwhelming forces both of time and of nature that oppose them. The world that is left in *Endgame* has neither zeal nor conviction, neither faith nor reason, though habits of arrogance and servitude linger on in Hamm and Clov respectively, like the memories of Nagg and Nell. The movement towards extinction seems assured. And yet it never comes: 'Finished, it's finished, nearly finished, it must be nearly finished'; 'It's finished, we're finished. (*Pause.*) Nearly finished'. Both Clov and Hamm start from the proposition that they have finished but retreat, reluctantly, to 'nearly finished'. Unlike Christ, whose final words on the Cross they are doubtless both of them echoing, they cannot achieve the satisfaction of completion. Like Hamm's story, like the play itself, they 'remain' (the play's final word) rather than end.

The speaker in Hamm's story doubted whether the little boy existed, much less could still be alive. Clov's survival into the present may just be testimony that he was wrong. By the same token, Clov's claim to see with his telescope 'a small boy' may be true, despite all the suggestions throughout the play that such development is impossible. The existence of such a 'potential procreator', as Clov calls him, might imply that life of a sort would go on, perhaps even if Clov were to leave Hamm. This is a measure of the irreducible level not so much of optimism as of pertinacity in the play. Hamm and Clov seem to form one of the sterile symbiotic relationships which are a hallmark of modern tragicomedy; each apparently needs the other to survive—Hamm chairbound, unable to reach the larder on his own, Clov mobile but not knowing the combination of the larder. They seem indispensable to each other, even though little love is lost between them: 'It's we are obliged to each other' is how Hamm Irishly puts it at the end, though Clov's version is equally valid: 'If I could kill him I'd die happy'—a sardonic summing-up of their interdependence. Yet the existence of the boy would allow the possibility of their independent survival: the boy could replace Clov with Hamm, and Clov might survive outside, since Hamm's claim that 'Outside of here it's death' would demonstrably not be true. This would be a new character for Hamm's story, just as he despaired of finding one. Life, the story and the play would go into another chapter, another act, bleaker no doubt than the present, further fallen from the glories of the past, but unquenched.

This is the real location of the play: not a particular time and space, but a place in the life-cycle, whether it be of an individual, or of a society and its civilisation, or of the human species. It represents a syndrome of moments before extinction, dragged out interminably by habit and will: finished, nearly finished is the emotional climate of the whole play, however we interpret its perplexing particularities. It is an emotional climate that virtually precludes the tragicomic hope of redemption which is so central to *Waiting for Godot.* Indeed, *Endgame* could be seen as a remorseless closing down of the possibilities both of meaning and salvation which the earlier play had grudgingly kept alive. 'We're not beginning to . . . to . . . mean something?' asks Hamm, with an incredulity that underlines just how unthinkable that is in this play. The emphasis here is not on waiting and the future, but on remembering a past to which the present seems a pointless addendum. Yet the past, as it is recalled and transmuted into 'art' by Nagg and Hamm, really has less to pride itself on than might be assumed: the trousers never achieved the desired perfection, and scientific rationalism was not the answer to everything it claimed to be. The presumption that the past was better—that life and civilisation had meaning, and so could make sense of the immense mysteries of time, age and death—is shown to be fallacious, and as that happens priorities change. The mere fact of survival into the present takes on an unlooked-for dignity, which is compounded by at least the possibility that it will go on into yet another generation. In such ironic topsyturvey-dom, the mere fact of 'remaining' becomes itself the miracle solution for which tragicomedy is always looking, and the play's 'strangeness' becomes a way of celebrating the mysterious fact that life goes on despite the odds. The mere performance or reading of so artfully self-absorbed a play becomes a proof of that fact. Every new performance or reading of *Endgame* is thus a little miracle in itself, a continuation and celebration—however weary—of the mystery of life, a tragicomedy despite itself.

Richard Dutton, in a review of "Endgame," in his Modern Tragicomedy and the British Tradition: Beckett, Pinter, Stoppard, Albee and Storey, *The Harvester Press, 1986, pp. 81-9.*

Samuel Beckett was extraordinarily well-read, and *Endgame,* like all of Beckett's drama and fiction, abounds with references to classical and biblical sources.

—*Arthur Horowitz, in his "Beckett's* Endgame *and Henley's* Invictus' " *in* Journal of Beckett Studies, *Autumn 1992.*

Paul Lawley   (essay date December 1988)

[*In the essay below, Lawley analyzes the significance of the theme of adoption in* Endgame.]

The terminal world of Beckett's *Endgame,* with its "corpsed" aspect outside the stage-refuge and its barbed play inside, sustains life solely, it seems, by reason of its ruler's procrastination. "Enough, it's time it ended, in the refuge too," proclaims Hamm at the outset. "And yet I hesitate, I hesitate to . . . to end." His hesitation is a problem not least because of "that hatred of nature as process (birth and copulation and death) which runs through the whole play" [Ronald Gaskell, *Drama and Reality,* 1972]. For if Hamm's hesitation necessitatesa prolongation of life in the refuge, the processes of nature, in one form or another, are surely unavoidable.

There is one course of action open to Hamm which offers perpetuation of life without direct involvement in the processes of nature: adoption. Indeed, this seems to be a vital means of continuation for the (now) refuge-dynasty. The legless, ashbin-bound Nagg and Nell are the biological parents of Hamm, but Hamm's central narrative, referred to by him as his "chronicle" though presented as a fiction, provides a possible version of the adoption of Clov, Hamm's present servant and "son." The crucial question towards the end of the play surrounds the possible adoption of a small boy reported by Clov to be still alive outside the refuge. In view of these instances, one is not surprised that, according to S.E. Gontarski [in *The Intent of Undoing in Samuel Beckett's Dramatic Texts,* 1985], a note written as Beckett was embarking on a two-act holograph of the play "suggests that [Hamm's] father and son are adopted; that is, Nagg too may have been someone taken into the shelter as a servant: 'A un père adoptif / un fils adoptif.' " Thus although three generations are represented on the stage, we cannot be sure, despite what is said, that the characters constitute a genetic line.

The connection between adoption and servanthood is an important one. Hamm sees all relationships, whether with his "son" or with his toy dog (these two are associated more than once), with his retainers or with his "bottled" father, in terms of dominance and servitude. Upon an adopted son he can bring to bear a pressure of obligation:

HAMM. . . . It was I was a father to you.

CLOV. Yes. (*He looks at Hamm fixedly*) You were that to me.

HAMM. My house a home for you.

CLOV. Yes. (*He looks about him*) This was that for me.

HAMM. (*Proudly*) But for me (*Gesture towards himself*) no father. But for Hamm (*Gesture towards surroundings*) no home.

The adopted child is expected to feel he owes a debt because he was *chosen.* The trouble with biological parenthood, as one of the play's funniest exchanges suggests, is that you can't choose:

HAMM. Scoundrel! Why did you engender me?

NAGG. I didn't know.

HAMM. What? What didn't you know?

NAGG. That it'd be you.

Hamm's experience in his relationship with Clov has been one of dominance and control, as much now (at least on the face of it) as in the scenario of choice so lovingly fictionalized in the chronicle. In contrast Nagg has always been a subject of his son. In his toothless second childhood, the immobile papa calls out to his own child for "me

pap!" and, having been tricked into listening to Hamm's chronicle by the promise of a non-existent sugar-plum, he presents a rich counterpoint to his current situation in his "curse." The counterpoint suggests that Hamm has retained power over his father not by growing into an independent adult but by remaining a dependent son:

> Whom did you call when you were a tiny boy, and were frightened, in the dark? Your mother? No. Me. We let you cry. Then we moved you out of earshot, so that we might sleep in peace. (*Pause*) I was asleep, as happy as a king, and you woke me up to have me listen to you. It wasn't indispensable, you didn't really need to have me listen to you. Besides I didn't listen to you. (*Pause*) I hope the day will come when you'll really need to have me listen to you, and need to hear my voice, any voice.

Hamm's *need,* both then (despite Nagg's claim) and now, is the need to exert power wilfully, even arbitrarily. As a biological son yet an adoptive father he is in an ideal position to fulfill that need.

Nagg's curse presents a scene of familial usurpation ("as happy as a king") and in doing so invites an Oedipal interpretation. Yet *Endgame* is concerned less with the dynamics of relations between father and mother and son than, as I have suggested, with the opposition of two kinds of dynastic perpetuation, biological and adoptive. In the following analysis I want to consider the significance of adoption, first in Hamm's chronicle, then in the play as a whole.

Alternating its "narrative tone" with the "normal tone" used by Hamm to comment on his own varying powers of composition, the chronicle tells of how a surviving vassal of Hamm's came begging him for bread for his child. Hamm recounts how, though doubting the very existence of the child, he proceeded to berate the man for his stupidity, optimism, and irresponsibility. The climax of the narrative, Hamm's decision about the child, is prepared with relish but never delivered:

> In the end he asked me would I consent to take in the child as well—if he were still alive. (*Pause*) It was the moment I was waiting for. (*Pause*) Would I consent to take in the child . . . (*Pause*) I can see him still, down on his knees, his hands flat on the ground, glaring at me with his mad eyes, in defiance of my wishes. (*Pause. Normal tone.*) I'll soon have finished with this story. (*Pause*) Unless I bring in other characters. (*Pause*) But where would I find them? (*Pause*) Where would I look for them? (*Pause. He whistles. Enter Clov.*) Let us pray to God.

The melodrama of the confrontation with the defiant vassal rather distracts from the decision about adoption, but it enables an effectively bathetic interruption to be made by the narrator's reflexive anxieties. The contrast is jolting, yet there is a striking similarity of phrasing which occurs across the division of "narrative" and "normal" tones: "Would I consent to *take in* the child . . ."; "Unless I *bring in* other characters." The resemblance invites us to consider the fictionali*zed* situation in terms of the fictionali*zer's* situation, the narration of situation in terms of the situation of narration—and vice-versa. The difference between the two dimensions is diminished further by Hamm's speaking of the narrator's situation ("bring in other characters") in spatial metaphors ("*where* would I *find* them? . . . *Where* would I *look for* them?") which would apply *literally* to the fictional situation (*where* was the vassal's child? —"assuming he existed,"). The aesthetic dimension of the chronicle and the experiential dimension of the chronicler move into identity through the figure of adoption: Hamm the tyrant might "take in the child" as Hamm the narrator might "bring in other characters." In each case adoption is the sole means of continuance. We can go further: in **Endgame** adoption is a figure for the fictional process itself, the only acceptable means of self-perpetuation for characters who reject the processes of nature.

A similar movement between dimensions is apparent when we consider the idea of termination in the play. "I'll soon have *finished with* this story," says Hamm. When, moments later, Clov enters in response to the whistle, he announces that there is a rat in the kitchen:

> HAMM. And you haven't exterminated him?
>
> CLOV. Half. You disturbed us.
>
> HAMM. He can't get away?
>
> CLOV. No.
>
> HAMM. You'll *finish him* later. Let us pray to God. (my emphasis)

To be finished *with* something is different from having finished it. Yet the odd thing here is that though it is the narrator Hamm who has finished *with* something, it is the rat-killer Clov whose activity is spoken of in the way one might speak of a story: the story-teller might be more frequently said to have *finished* his story than to have finished *with* it. The aesthetic connotation of "finish" (as opposed to "finish with") is strongly present—largely because of insistent repetition—in an earlier exchange:

> HAMM. Why don't you finish us? (*Pause*) I'll tell you the combination of the larder if you promise to finish me.
>
> CLOV. I couldn't finish you.
>
> HAMM. Then you shan't finish me.

The primary meaning of "finish" is clear. But, in addition, it is as though Hamm *himself* is a story that needs to be finished (off). The poise in (or of) the word is as delicate here as it is in the opening phrases of the play: "Finished, it's finished, nearly finished, it must be nearly finished." Within Clov's sentence is the feeling not just of some experience coming to an end, but (especially after the opening ritual) of a predetermined pattern about to be completed. The inflections are distinct even though combined.

The moment near the end of the play when Clov sights what looks "like a small boy!" brings together the themes of adoption (and continuance through fiction) and of termination. Having made the sighting, Clov makes for the door with the gaff:

> HAMM. No!

> (*Clov halts*)
>
> CLOV. No? A potential procreator?
>
> HAMM. If he exists he'll die there or he'll come here. And if he doesn't . . .
> (*Pause*)
>
> CLOV. You don't believe me? You think I'm inventing?
> (*Pause*)
>
> HAMM. It's the end, Clov, we've come to the end. I don't need you any more.

In this episode the adoption-decision is transferred out of the narrative dimension of the chronicle into the dimension of the action itself. Again a migration is effected: the episode from the fictional narrative is "adopted" by the actual dramatic world, or, more accurately, by Clov. But, crucially, the element of indeterminacy in the chronicle-version ("assuming he existed") has now assumed a pivotal position. Hamm's decision to end turns, it seems, not upon the decision to take in or not take in the small boy, but upon his belief that Clov is "inventing." At last Hamm too perceives adoption as the figure of fiction-as-continuance. Even though Clov intends to kill the boy, it is his *proposal* of the fiction that matters, his attempt to *bring* the boy *in* to their life-story. Hamm resists. "Not an underplot, I trust," he exclaims when Clov first registers an outside presence. He puts himself in the position of a spectator at his own endgame. "It's the end . . . we've come to the end"—not just of the experience but of the game's aesthetic pattern too: the statement is poised between the participator's (or actor's) perception of termination and the spectatorial perception of it. It is this profoundly uneasy poise which ultimately thwarts the "attempt to determine if **Endgame** imitates the act of dying or whether it imitates a game in which the players pretend to move towards death" [Charles R. Lyons, *Samuel Beckett,* 1983].

Few texts can be more explicitly structured upon binary oppositions than **Endgame.** "Outside of here it's death" announces Hamm, and in doing so he loads the onstage/offstage, inside/outside opposition with a decisive weight of signification. Upon this fundamental prescription the play's other oppositions—past/present, land/sea, nature/non-nature, light/darkness—depend. Some of the routines and jokes even underline the habit of polarization:

> (*Enter Clov holding by one of its three legs a black toy dog*)
>
> CLOV. Your dogs are here.
> (*He hands the dog to Hamm who feels it, fondles it*)
>
> HAMM. He's white, isn't he?
>
> CLOV. Nearly.
>
> HAMM. What do you mean, nearly? Is he white or isn't he?
>
> CLOV. He isn't.

And when Clov reports that the light outside is

"GRREY!", Hamm queries the information, eliciting the confirmation: "*Light black.* From pole to pole" (my emphasis).

The ubiquitous patterns of opposition form an essential context for the operation of the figure of adoption. We have seen that adoption, as presented in the play, involves a negotiation between the distinct areas or terms of an opposition, a crossing of vital boundaries for the purposes of the perpetuation of life. Yet if adoption is the agency of perpetuation, it is also an operation which cannot avoid compromising the stability of the world it is designed to maintain. In examining the climax of Hamm's chronicle, we were able to identify two distinct dimensions: that of the *narrative,* in which the fictionalized Hamm decides whether or not to take the vassal's child into the refuge, and that of the *narrator,* the actual dimension of the drama, in which the Hamm we see on the stage decides whether or not to bring other characters into his story. Although each of these dimensions insists upon a sharp inside/outside opposition, with a definite boundary, they *themselves,* despite separation by a boundary apparently no less definite (that between inset story and dramatic action, narrative of situation and situation of narrative) are blurred together by the association of the child Hamm might "take in" and the characters he might "bring in." For this is an association, a merging, of Hamm's art and his life. His life contains art, certainly, but we cannot be sure that the reverse is not also true: does art "contain" his life? Is he (self-) invented, a story? (". . . if you promise to *finish* me.")

It is at the moment Clov sights—or invents—the small boy outside the refuge that the fictional chronicle impinges most strongly upon the stage-world. The process by which action echoes—or has been pre-echoed by—fiction at this point brings the question of the ontological status of the stage-world to crisis-point—and both characters recognize this. Hamm's refusal constitutes a decision not to adopt a fresh fiction into the stage-world rather than a decision not to take in a child. Indeed, by acknowledging the possibility of fiction ("You think I'm inventing?") Hamm is uncovering the process which has enabled the game to continue. Now he can begin to renounce: "It's the end, Clov, we've come to the end . . ." And yet this renunciation of fiction can be read, and played, as a grand theatrical gesture, a richly fictional moment. As ever in Beckett, it is the imagination-dead-imagine stalemate.

In a chapter entitled "Marking and Merging Horizons" in his book *The Modern Stage and Other Worlds,* Austin E. Quigley suggests that "the glass walls marking the borders of Mrs. Alving's house in Ibsen's *Ghosts* become, in many ways, a summarizing image of the solid but permeable horizons of the modern theatre. The solid penetrability of the glass wall gradually becomes an emblem of repeatedly asserted but repeatedly undermined divisions between inner and outer, good and bad, past and present, self and other, and so on." The refuge of *Endgame* reproduces Mrs. Alving's house in a terminal phase. The divisions are more starkly asserted and the mergings correspondingly more radical, for the zone of action is now ontological and being itself is at stake. The figure of adoption is the agency through which this world of divisions is perpetuated, yet it also precipitates those mergings which compromise the divisions. In this way it simultaneously establishes and renders unstable the very ground upon which *Endgame* is played out. Adoption in *Endgame* makes, and unmakes, a world of difference.

Paul Lawley, "Adoption in 'Endgame'," in Modern Drama, *Vol. XXXI, No. 4, December, 1988, pp. 529-35.*

Shimon Levy   (essay date 1990)

[*In the excerpt below, Levy analyzes Beckett's use of space in* Endgame.]

In a play "you have definite space and people in this space. That's relaxing" [Ruby Cohn, *Back to Beckett,* 1973]. But the actual locations Beckett chooses for his characters and for the actors who play them, is anything but relaxing. In the first plays there is at least something an actor can relate to spatially—a country road and a tree; an empty room with two windows, two ashbins and a wheelchair; a mound in the middle of a "*trompe l'oeil*" desert. In later plays the actors find urns, a narrow-lit strip to pace on, a hole in the backdrop to stick a head as a mouth through. In some plays pieces of furniture are deliberately detached from the room to which they might have belonged—a bench, a table, a rocking chair. The rest of the stage space is referred to in words, lights, gestures and movement, etc. Some of the characters dwell on the very edge of the stage, suggesting that their existence is psychologically interior and real rather than exterior and fictitious.

Beckett characters are well aware of their spaces and stage locations; they go through precise routines of examining their whereabouts. In most plays they refer to their location first and foremost as a *stage* in a theatre; only then might they make other suggestions to where they are. There exists a whole range of unease between a Beckett character and his space—from slight discomfort to excruciating pain and suffering. In actually referring space to themselves, or describing it as a space of themselves, the plays manage to turn the public event of a theatre performance into a highly private matter. Lack of specificity on stage naturally avoids the realistic fallacy; rather, it calls for a process of "gap filling." Indeterminacies in the text . . . can here be seen in theatrical-performative and actual terms rather than as just "reading" into lines. In presenting a stage full with emptiness, Beckett activates the audience's imagination and involvement, and extends an invitation to make this stage space their own: a well-furnished fully decorated stage is perhaps more appealing at first sight, yet it cannot compete with the suggestiveness of an empty one. . . .

The play most concerned with space is *Endgame,* where the stage is presented as the only still barely living place on earth. The main motif of waiting in *Waiting for Godot* is here replaced with "I'll leave you—you can't," justified by the "objective" statement "there's nowhere else." Waiting is associated mainly with time; location is of lesser importance. Perhaps the meeting with Godot is to take place somewhere else on the open-ended road. Accordingly, the activity in a "waiting for . . . waiting" play is a centrifugal pressure toward the outside. With all its variations of inner and outer places, psychological spaces and many "voids in enclosure" (which serve as spatial metonyms), *Endgame* examines the confinements of a location "finished, it's finished, nearly finished, it must be nearly finished."

The characters in *Endgame* embody three stages of immobility, each governed by a corresponding limitation of space. Clov confines himself to his relatively large kitchen space (10m. X 10m.); Hamm is confined to his armchair on castors but can be moved; Nagg and Nell can only raise their heads out of the ashbins. In addition, the characters are all closed in by the stage, actors and audience are closed in by the theatre, and so on, *ad infinitum;* no one can escape.

Clov's opening moves in the play establish stage space by examining it. Stiffly staggering through the room, Clov defines the shape and size of the playing area; he moves sideways and downstage-upstage, and climbs up to the windows. His moves are related to the inside and outside worlds, and to the various "lids" and curtains that lie between them. He completes his trip in stage space by dryly commenting: "Nice dimensions, nice proportions."

The outside is said to include "earth," "sea," "hills," "nature," "flora," "pomona." Inner or closed space is represented by covers, and by closed and covered props and objects—ashbins, windows, the handkerchief on Hamm's face, the sheets over the bins—and in the dialogue: "here we're in a hole" or "put me in my coffin." Significantly, body and heart are also described in terms of closed space: "last night I saw the inside of my breast" and "the bigger a man is, the fuller he is . . . and the emptier."

It soon becomes clear that the concept of outer space and the possibility of escaping there is illusory. "Outside of here it's dead," says Hamm. Morbid imagery dominates references to the outside: "corpsed", "extinguished", "zero", "ashes" and "grey." Reversing the picture of Creation, in which Light, Earth and Water were the beginning of life, Beckett here reduces life to a blood-stained "old stancher." The room, grim as it is, remains the last source of life. In order to avoid a new beginning, a re-creation of the world, the rat will die outside and the little boy will not be allowed in. The colorful and lively scene of fishing on open seas dissipates into "there is no more nature." Nature exists, but only as a negative force: "We lose our hair, our teeth! Our bloom! Our ideals!"

Through his manipulation of space, Beckett implies that spatial relationships and structures on stage correspond to the relationship between stage and audience. The characters are provided with various "lids" which reveal or unveil: a telescope, glasses, sheets, curtains. Through the curtains, however, one sees only death, the telescope detects nothing but extinction, and the sheets, once removed, reveal the pitiful sight of Hamm. All are momentary glimpses into closed and open spaces. Inasmuch as Clov brings Hamm information from the outside, he brings the same information to the audience. Opening lids, uncovering sheets and drawing back curtains suggest a person looking inside himself, and a stage being opened and ex-

posed to the audience. The audience is drawn into the act of looking out, but the audience is on the "outside" and so ends up looking at itself. Like Clov, the audience cannot escape. Relationships among the characters mirror their spatial arrangement on stage. Clov's yearning to leave Hamm is counteracted by Hamm's paralysis and lack of will; Nagg and Nell echo this oppressive bond. The outer space for which Clov supposedly longs is suggested on stage by the two windows facing away from the audience. But the audience is also on the outside. Thus a third parallel is implied in the relationship between audience and actors, whereby the audience's yearning for freedom is counteracted by the actor's entrapment, or vice versa. Nagg and Nell, confined to their bins, often fantasize about far and open places. They speak of the Ardennes, the road to Sedan and Lake Como. Hamm, just a little more mobile than his parents, is interested in his immediate surroundings rather than in distant places. Clov, the most mobile character, is obsessed with his closed-in kitchen space. He says: "I love order. It's my dream. A world where all would be silent and still and each thing in its last place, under the last dust." Beckett thus endows his most stationary characters with memory and imagination that can compensate them for their immobility, while his more mobile characters yearn for close and closed spaces.

Ultimately, the stage in *Endgame* is a self-reflective metaphor of internal or inner space. Because Hamm is blind, his perception of space is already interior; he can indeed look only inside his breast. Throughout the play, Hamm's gaze is directed inwards, whereas Clov looks outwards—sometimes with the help of a telescope—and mutters vague remarks as to what he observes. Neither the audience nor Hamm is convinced that the objects he describes exist in reality. Does he invent them? Does he speak of them in order to aggravate Hamm, console him, or both? The audience, with Hamm, is forced to depend on Clov's eyes, on his repeated walks to the windows, and on his reports about "offstage."

In *Waiting for Godot,* Pozzo remarks, "The blind have no notion of time. The things of time are hidden from them too." But the blind do have a sense of space. By referring to its own use of space, *Endgame* brings us closer to the concept of internal or inner space.

Shimon Levy, in his Samuel Beckett's Self-Referential Drama: The Three I's, *The Macmillan Press Ltd, 1990, 137 p.*

FURTHER READING

Bibliography

Andonian, Cathleen Culotta. *Samuel Beckett: A Reference Guide.* Boston: G. K. Hall & Co., 1989, 754 p.
    Annotated bibliography of criticism on Beckett through 1984.

Biography

Bair, Deirdre. *Samuel Beckett: A Biography*. New York: Harcourt Brace Jovanovich, 1978, 736 p.

Includes a chapter that chronicles Beckett's life during the writing and early productions of *Endgame*.

Criticism

Bernstein, Jay. "Philosophy's Refuge: Adorno in Beckett." In *Philosopher's Poets*, edited by David Wood, pp. 177-91. New York: Routledge, 1990.

Analyzes Theodor Adorno's essay "Trying to Understand *Endgame*."

Chevigny, Bell Gale, ed. *Twentieth Century Interpretations of Endgame: A Collection of Critical Essays*. Englewood Cliffs, N.J.: Prentice-Hall, 1969, 120 p.

Contains essays on *Endgame* by such well known critics as Theodor Adorno, Ruby Cohn, and Richard Goldman.

Connor, Steven. "The Doubling of Presence: *Waiting for Godot, Endgame*." In his *Samuel Beckett: Repetition, Theory and Text*, pp. 118-25. New York: Basil Blackwell, 1988.

Examines meaning, repetition, and unity in *Endgame*, noting that "*Endgame* refuses the consummation of an ending which its form and title suggest."

Esslin, Martin, ed. *Samuel Beckett: A Collection of Critical Essays*. Englewood Cliffs, N.J.: Prentice-Hall, 1965, 182 p.

Collection of essays dealing with various aspects of Beckett's career and works. Several essays comment on *Endgame*.

Friedman, Melvin J., ed. *Samuel Beckett Now: Critical Approaches to His Novels, Poetry, and Plays*. Chicago: University of Chicago Press, 1970, 275 p.

Contains several essays with commentary on *Endgame* as well as a checklist of Beckett criticism.

Gassner, John. "Beckett's *Endgame* and Symbolism." In his *Theatre at the Crossroads: Plays and Playwrights of the Mid-Century American Stage*, pp. 256-61. New York: Holt, Rinehart and Winston, 1960.

Early, mixed review of *Endgame*.

Gontarski, S. E. "Sources, False Starts, and Preliminary Versions of *Fin de partie*" and "*Fin de partie* Itself." In his *The Intent of "Undoing" in Samuel Beckett's Dramatic Texts*, pp. 25-41, pp. 42-54. Bloomington: Indiana University Press, 1985.

Traces the development of *Endgame* from early drafts to the final version.

Hale, Jane Alison. "*Endgame*: 'How Are Your Eyes?'" In her *The Broken Window: Beckett's Dramatic Perspective*, pp. 45-60. West Lafayette, Ind.: Purdue University Press, 1987.

Examines Beckett's use of time and space in *Endgame*.

Lyons, Charles R. "*Endgame*." In his *Samuel Beckett*, pp. 50-74. New York: Grove Press, Inc., 1983.

Critical overview of *Endgame*, covering Beckett's treatment of such topics as character, scene, and time.

Maughlin, Susan. "Liminality: An Approach to Artistic Process in *Endgame*." In *Myth and Ritual in the Plays of Samuel Beckett*, edited by Katherine H. Burkman, pp. 86-99. Cranbury, N.J.: Associated University Presses, 1987.

Interprets *Endgame* as "the inevitable unfolding and the seemingly impossible coalescence of the creative process."

Simon, Bennett. "Beckett's *Endgame* and the Abortion of Desire." In his *Tragic Drama and the Family: Psychoanalytic Studies from Aeschylus to Beckett*, pp. 212-52. New Haven, Conn.: Yale University Press, 1988.

Focuses on the conflict between procreation and the social necessity of abortion as depicted in *Endgame*, which Simon, a medical doctor, considers to be "the archetypal modern tragedy."

Smith, Joseph H. "Notes on *Krapp, Endgame*, and 'Applied' Psychoanalysis." In *The World of Samuel Beckett*, edited by Joseph H. Smith, pp. 195-203. Baltimore, Md.: Johns Hopkins University Press, 1991.

A psychiatrist comments on Hamm, as well as questions of mental health and existence, in *Endgame*.

Additional coverage of Beckett's life and career is contained in the following sources published by Gale Research: *Concise Dictionary of British Literary Biography, 1945-1960; Contemporary Authors*, Vols. 5-8 (rev. ed.), 130 [obituary]; *Contemporary Authors New Revision Series*, Vol. 33; *Contemporary Literary Criticism*, Vols. 1, 2, 3, 4, 6, 9, 10, 11, 14, 18, 29, 57, 59; *Dictionary of Literary Biography*, Vols. 13, 15; *Dictionary of Literary Biography Yearbook: 1990; DISCovering Authors; Major 20th-Century Writers; Short Story Criticism*, Vol. 16; and *World Literature Criticism*.

Jorge Luis Borges

1899-1986

(Also wrote under pseudonym F. Bustos, and, with Adolfo Bioy Casares, under the joint pseudonyms H. Bustos Domecq, B. Lynch Davis, and B. Suarez Lynch) Argentinean short story writer, poet, essayist, translator, critic, biographer, and screenwriter.

The following entry provides an overview of Borges's career. For further information on his life and work, see *CLC*, Volumes 1, 2, 3, 4, 6, 8, 9, 10, 13, 19, 44, and 48.

INTRODUCTION

Considered among the foremost literary figures of the twentieth century, Borges is best known for his short stories which blend fantasy, realism, and his extensive knowledge of world literature, metaphysics, and mysticism. Dealing with such themes as time, memory, and the malleability of both reality and literary form, Borges combined various styles of fiction and nonfiction to create a hybrid genre that defies easy classification. Although some critics have faulted his refusal to address social and political issues in his work, Borges maintained that he was "neither a thinker nor a moralist, but simply a man of letters who turns his own perplexities and that respected system of perplexities we call philosophy into the forms of literature."

Biographical Information

Borges was born in Buenos Aires to parents of old, illustrious Argentinean families. His father, a lawyer, educator, translator, and writer, encouraged his children in their intellectual pursuits with his extensive library and broad range of interests. As a child, Borges learned Spanish and English simultaneously, and mastered French, Latin, and German during college. A family tour of Europe in 1914 was interrupted by travel restrictions necessitated by World War I, thus affording Borges time to attend the Collège Calvin in Geneva, Switzerland, from which he earned his degree in 1918. The following year he traveled in Spain where he associated with members of the literary avant-garde, particularly the Ultraists, and published his first poems, essays, and reviews. Borges returned to Buenos Aires in 1921 and, with the publication of his first books of poetry, *Fervor de Buenos Aires* (1923) and *Luna de enfrente* (1925), was recognized as one of Argentina's leading literary figures. Although primarily a poet and essayist at first, Borges began writing short stories in the 1930s, and his first collections—*Historia universal de la infamia* (1935; *A Universal History of Infamy*) and most importantly *Ficciones, 1935-1944* (1944; *Ficciones*)—confirmed him as the foremost writer in Argentina. Despite a general dislike of politics and social commentary, Borges became an outspoken critic of Juan Perón during the Argentinean dictator's reign from 1946 to 1955; in a

move to humiliate the noted writer, Perón appointed him national poultry inspector. After the return of civilian rule, however, Borges was made director of the National Library of Argentina and became a professor of English literature at the University of Buenos Aires. In the early 1960s the English translation of *Ficciones, 1935-1944* brought him international recognition and, along with many offers to teach and lecture around the world, the 1961 Prix Formentor, the International Publishers Prize, which he shared with Nobel laureate Samuel Beckett. The majority of his time from this point on was spent traveling, lecturing, and dictating new works: he had grown almost completely blind and had to rely on a secretary to read and write for him. By his own account, Borges's life was devoted almost solely to literature. As he once explained: "Few things have happened to me, and I have read a great many. Or rather, few things have happened to me more worth remembering than Schopenhauer's thought or the music of England's words."

Major Works

Borges produced major works in three genres—poetry, essays, and short fiction. His first major books of poetry,

Fervor de Buenos Aires and *Luna de enfrente*, are avant-garde collections influenced by the Ultraist movement; the poems combine urban settings and themes, metaphysical speculations, and a pronounced, often surreal, use of symbolism. His later poetry tends to be more conservative in style. The poems collected in *El hacedor* (1960; *Dreamtigers*) and *Antologia personal* (1961; *A Personal Anthology*), for example, employ rhyme and meter, ruminate on personal themes, and make reference to his own as well as other works of literature. Borges's works of fiction and nonfiction, as critics note, are often difficult to distinguish from one another. It is frequently observed that many of Borges's short stories are written in essay form; his essays often treat subject matter other authors deal with in fiction; and the very short works he called "parables" seem to defy classification, sharing the qualities of poetry, essays, and short stories. Borges's essay collections—including *Inquisiciones* (1925), *Discusión* (1932), and *Otras inquisiciones, 1937-1952* (1952; *Other Inquisitions, 1937-1952*)—address a wide variety of issues and represent many diverse styles. For example, *Discusión* collects film reviews, articles on metaphysical and aesthetic topics, and includes the essay "Narrative Art and Magic," in which Borges asserts the capacity of fantasy literature to address realistic concerns. Borges's first collection of short stories, *A Universal History of Infamy*, purports to be an encyclopedia of world criminals, containing brief, seemingly factual accounts of such real and mythical characters as "The Dread Redeemer Lazarus Morell," "The Disinterested Killer Bill Harrigan" (Billy the Kid), and "The Masked Dyer, Hakim of Merv." *Ficciones* contains many of Borges's most famous works of fiction. In "The Garden of Forking Paths" Borges combines elements of nonfiction writing—for example footnotes, references to scholarly works, and a detached, objective tone of voice—with metaphysical concepts and the structure of a detective story to show how two seemingly unrelated events—crimes committed at different points in history—intersect and resolve each other in a single moment. The enlarged English edition of *El Aleph* (1949), entitled *The Aleph, and Other Stories, 1933-1969* (1970), consists of stories and essays from various periods in Borges's career. In addition to realistic as well as metaphysical stories, the book also includes his informative "Autobiographical Essay."

Critical Reception

Although critics have praised the formal precision and contemplative tone of Borges's best poetry, and have noted the stylistic as well as thematic originality of his essays, it is for his short fiction that Borges is recognized as one of the most influential and innovative authors of the twentieth century. His experiments with the intermingling of fantasy and realistic detail presaged the "magical realist" style of fiction practiced by such major Latin American authors as Gabriel Garcia Marquez and Julio Cortazar; the latter referred to Borges as "the leading figure of our fantastic literature." His insights into the nature of literature, the creative process, and the imagination, exemplified by such works as the frequently anthologized "The Circular Ruins," have established him as one of modern literature's most philosophically accomplished authors.

Some critics have faulted Borges's writings for being esoteric, calling them little more than intellectually precious games. By exploring intellectual and philological issues, however, most commentators believe that Borges also addressed humankind's deepest concerns about the nature of existence. As critic Carter Wheelock commented: Borges "plays only one instrument—the intellectual, the epistemological—but the strumming of his cerebral guitar sets into vibration all the strings of emotion, intuition, and esthetic longing that are common to sentient humanity."

PRINCIPAL WORKS

Fervor de Buenos Aires   (poetry)   1923; revised edition, 1969

Inquisiciones   (essays)   1925

Luna de enfrente   (poetry)   1925

El tamano de mi esparanza   (essays)   1927

El idioma de los Argentinos   (essay)   1928

Cuaderno San Martin   (poetry)   1929

Evaristo Carriego   (biography)   1930
   [*Evaristo Carriego: A Book About Old-Time Buenos Aires*, 1983]

Discusión   (essays and criticism)   1932; revised edition, 1976

Historia universal de la infamia   (short stories)   1935
   [*A Universal History of Infamy*, 1972]

Historia de la eternidad   (essays)   1936; revised and enlarged edition, 1953

El jardin de senderos que se bifurcan   (short stories)   1941

Seis problemas para Don Isidro Parodi [with Adolfo Bioy Casares, as H. Bustos Domecq]   (short stories)   1942
   [*Six Problems for Don Isidro Parodi*, 1980]

Poemas, 1922-1943   (poetry)   1943; also published as *Poemas, 1923-1953* [revised and enlarged edition], 1954; also published as *Poemas, 1923-1958* [revised and enlarged edition], 1958

Ficciones, 1935-1944   (short stories)   1944
   [*Ficciones*, 1962; also published as *Fictions*, 1965]

El compardito, su destino, sus barrios, su música   (nonfiction)   1945; enlarged edition, 1968

Dos fantasías memorables [with Adolfo Bioy Casares, as H. Bustos Domecq]   (short stories)   1946

Un modelo para la muerta [with Adolfo Bioy Casares, as B. Suárez Lynch]   (short stories)   1946

El Aleph   (short stories)   1949
   [*The Aleph, and Other Stories, 1933-1969*, 1970]

Otras inquisiciones, 1937-1952   (essays)   1952
   [*Other Inquisitions, 1937-1952*, 1964]

Obras completas. 10 vols.   (essays, short stories, and poetry)   1953-67

*Días de odio [with Leopoldo Torre Nilsson]   (screenplay)   1954

Manual de zoologia fantastica [with Margarita Guerrero]   (fiction)   1957; also published as *El libro de los seres imaginarios* [revised edition], 1967

[*The Imaginary Zoo*, 1969; also published as *The Book of Imaginary Beings* (revised edition), 1969]
El hacedor (prose and poetry) 1960
[*Dreamtigers*, 1964]
Antologia personal (poetry, short stories, and essays) 1961
[*A Personal Anthology*, 1967]
Labyrinths: Selected Stories and Other Writings (short stories and essays) 1962
Obra poética, 1923-1964 (poetry) 1964; also published as *Obra poética, 1923-1966* [enlarged edition], 1966; *Obra poética, 1923-1967*, 1967; *Obra poética, 1923-1969*, 1972; *Obra poética, 1923-1976*, 1977
[*Selected Poems, 1923-1967*, 1972]
Introducción a la literatura inglesa [with María Esther Vázquez] (criticism) 1965
[*An Introduction to English Literature*, 1974]
Introducción a la literatura norteamericana [with Esther Zemborain de Torres] (criticism) 1965
[*An Introduction to American Literature*, 1973]
Crónicas de Bustos Domecq [with Adolfo Bioy Casares] (short stories) 1967
[*Chronicles of Bustos Domecq*, 1976]
Nueva antologia personal (poetry, short stories, and essays) 1968
Elogio de la sombra (poetry, short stories, and essays) 1969
[*In Praise of Darkness*, 1974]
†*Invasión* [with Hugo Santiago] (screenplay) 1969
El informe de Brodie (short stories) 1970
[*Doctor Brodie's Report*, 1972]
†*El oro de los tigres* (poetry) 1972
Borges on Writing (interviews) 1973
El libro de arena (short stories) 1975
[*The Book of Sand*, 1977]
†*La rosa profunda* (poetry) 1975
Historia de la noche (poetry) 1977
Obras completas (poetry, short stories, criticism, and essays) 1977
Obras completas en colaboracion [with Adolfo Bioy Casares, Betina Edelberg, Margarita Guerrero, Alicia Jurado, Maria Kodama, María Esther Vazquez] (short stories, essays, and criticism) 1979
Borges en/y/sobre cine (criticism) 1980
[*Borges In/And/On Film*, 1988]
Prosa completa. 2 vols. (short stories, essays, and criticism) 1980
Siete noches (lectures) 1980
[*Seven Nights*, 1984]
Antologia poetica, 1923-1977 (poetry) 1981
Borges: A Reader (poetry, short stories, criticism, and essays) 1981
Atlas [with Maria Kodama] (nonfiction) 1984
[*Atlas*, 1985]
Twenty-Four Conversations with Borges: Including a Selection of Poems (interviews and poetry) 1984

*This work is based on the short story "Emma Zunz."

†These works were translated and published as *The Gold of the Tigers: Selected Later Poems* in 1977.

CRITICISM

James E. Irby   (essay date 1962)

[*Irby has written extensively about Borges and his writings and has translated many of his works into English. In the following excerpt from his introduction to the 1964 edition of* Labyrinths, *a collection which originally appeared in 1962, he provides an overview of Borges's main themes and literary techniques.*]

Until about 1930 Borges's main creative medium was poetry: laconic free-verse poems which evoked scenes and atmospheres of old Buenos Aires or treated timeless themes of love, death and the self. He also wrote many essays on subjects of literary criticism, metaphysics and language, essays reminiscent of Chesterton's in their compactness and unexpected paradoxes. The lucidity and verbal precision of these writings belie the agitated conditions of avant-garde polemic and playfulness under which most of them were composed. During these years Borges was content to seek expression in serene lyric images perhaps too conveniently abstracted from the surrounding world and have all his speculations and creations respond primarily to the need for a new national literature as he saw it. The years from 1930 to 1940, however, brought a deep change in Borges's work. He virtually abandoned poetry and turned to the short narrative genre. Though he never lost his genuine emotion for the unique features of his native ground, he ceased to exalt them nationalistically as sole bulwarks against threatening disorder and began to rank them more humbly within a context of vast universal processes: the nightmarish city of **"Death and the Compass"** is an obvious stylization of Buenos Aires, no longer idealized as in the poems, but instead used as the dark setting for a tragedy of the human intellect. The witty and already very learned young poet who had been so active in editing such little reviews as *Martín Fierro, Prisma* and *Proa,* became a sedentary writer-scholar who spent many solitary hours in reading the most varied and unusual works of literature and philosophy and in meticulously correcting his own manuscripts, passionately but also somewhat monstrously devoted to the written word as his most vital experience, as failing eyesight and other crippling afflictions made him more and more a semi-invalid, more and more an incredible mind in an ailing and almost useless body, much like his character Ireneo Funes. Oppressed by physical reality and also by the turmoil of Europe, which had all-too-direct repercussions in Argentina, Borges sought to create a coherent fictional world of the intelligence. This world is essentially adumbrated in **"Tlön, Uqbar, Orbis Tertius."** As Borges slyly observes there, Tlön is no "irresponsible figment of the imagination"; the stimulus which prompted its formulation is stated with clarity (though not without irony) toward the end of that story's final section, projected as a kind of tentative utopia into the future beyond the grim year 1940 when it was written:

> Ten years ago any symmetry with a semblance of order—dialectical materialism, anti-Semitism, Nazism—was sufficient to charm the minds of men. How could one do other than submit to Tlön, to the minute and vast evidence of

an orderly planet? It is useless to answer that reality is also orderly. Perhaps it is, but in accordance with divine laws—I translate: inhuman laws—which we never quite grasp. Tlön is surely a labyrinth, but it is a labyrinth devised by men, a labyrinth destined to be deciphered by men.

Borges's metaphysical fictions, his finest creations, which are collected in the volumes *Ficciones* (1945) and *El Aleph* (1949), all elaborate upon the varied idealist possibilities outlined in the "article" on Tlön. In these narratives the analytical and imaginative functions previously kept separate in his essays and poems curiously fuse, producing a form expressive of all the tension and complexity of Borges's mature thought.

His fictions are always concerned with processes of striving which lead to discovery and insight; these are achieved at times gradually, at other times suddenly, but always with disconcerting and even devastating effect. They are tales of the fantastic, of the hyperbolic, but they are never content with fantasy in the simple sense of facile wish-fulfillment. The insight they provide is ironic, pathetic: a painful sense of inevitable limits that block total aspirations. Some of these narratives ("**Tlön, Uqbar, Orbis Tertius,**" "**Pierre Menard, Author of the *Quixote*,**" "**Three Versions of Judas,**" "**The Sect of the Phoenix**") might be called "pseudo essays"—mock scrutinies of authors or books or learned subjects actually of Borges's own invention—that in turning in upon themselves make the "plot" (if it can be called that) an intricate interplay of creation and critique. But all his stories, whatever their outward form, have the same self-critical dimension; in some it is revealed only in minimal aspects of tone and style (as, for example, in "**The Circular Ruins**"). Along with these "vertical" superpositions of different and mutually qualifying levels, there are also "horizontal" progressions of qualitative leaps, after the manner of tales of adventure or of crime detection (Borges's favorite types of fiction). Unexpected turns elude the predictable; hidden realities are revealed through their diverse effects and derivations. Like his beloved Chesterton, who made the Father Brown stories a vehicle for his Catholic theology, Borges uses mystery and the surprise effect in literature to achieve that sacred astonishment at the universe which is the origin of all true religion and metaphysics. However, Borges as theologian is a complete heretic, as the casuistical "**Three Versions of Judas**" more than suffices to show.

Borges once claimed that the basic devices of all fantastic literature are only four in number: the work within the work, the contamination of reality by dream, the voyage in time, and the double. These are both his essential themes—the problematical nature of the world, of knowledge, of time, of the self—and his essential techniques of construction. Indeed, in Borges's narratives the usual distinction between form and content virtually disappears, as does that between the world of literature and the world of the reader. We almost unconsciously come to accept the world of Tlön because it has been so subtly inserted into our own. In "**Theme of the Traitor and the Hero,**" Borges's discovery of his own story (which is worked up before our very eyes and has areas "not yet revealed" to him), Nolan's of Kilpatrick's treason, Ryan's of the curi-

ous martyrdom, and ours of the whole affair, are but one awareness of dark betrayal and creative deception. We are transported into a realm where fact and fiction, the real and the unreal, the whole and the part, the highest and the lowest, are complementary aspects of the same continuous being: a realm where "any man is all men," where "all men who repeat a line of Shakespeare *are* William Shakespeare." The world is a book and the book is a world, and both are labyrinthine and enclose enigmas designed to be understood and participated in by man. We should note that this all-comprising intellectual unity is achieved precisely by the sharpest and most scandalous confrontation of opposites. In "**Avatars of the Tortoise,**" the paradox of Zeno triumphantly demonstrates the unreality of the visible world, while in "**The Library of Babel**" it shows the anguishing impossibility of the narrator's ever reaching the Book of Books. And in "**The Immortal,**" possibly Borges's most complete narrative, the movements toward and from immortality become one single approximation of universal impersonality.

Borges is always quick to confess his sources and borrowings, because for him no one has claim to originality in literature; all writers are more or less faithful amanuenses of the spirit, translators and annotators of pre-existing archetypes. (Hence Tlön, the impersonal and hereditary product of a "secret society"; hence Pierre Menard, the writer as perfect reader.) By critics he has often been compared with Kafka, whom he was one of the first to translate into Spanish. Certainly, we can see the imprint of his favorite Kafka story, "The Great Wall of China," on "**The Lottery in Babylon**" and "**The Library of Babel**"; the similarity lies mainly in the narrators' pathetically inadequate examination of an impossible subject, and also in the idea of an infinite, hierarchical universe, with its corollary of infinite regression. But the differences between the two writers are perhaps more significant than their likenesses. Kafka's minutely and extensively established portrayals of degradation, his irreducible and enigmatic situations, contrast strongly with Borges's compact but vastly significant theorems, his all-dissolving ratiocination. Kafka wrote novels, but Borges has openly confessed he cannot; his miniature forms are intense realizations of Poe's famous tenets of unity of effect and brevity to the exclusion of "worldly interests." And no matter how mysterious they may seem at first glance, all Borges's works contain the keys to their own elucidation in the form of clear parallelisms with other of his writings and explicit allusions to a definite literary and philosophical context within which he has chosen to situate himself. The list of Pierre Menard's writings, as Borges has observed, is not "arbitrary," but provides a "diagram of his mental history" and already implies the nature of his "subterranean" undertaking. All the footnotes in Borges's fictions, even those marked "Editor's Note," are the author's own and form an integral part of the works as he has conceived them. Familiarity with Neo-Platonism and related doctrines will clarify Borges's preferences and intentions, just as it will, say, Yeats's or Joyce's. But, as Borges himself has remarked of the theological explications of Kafka's work, the full enjoyment of his writings precedes and in no way depends upon such interpretations. Greater and more important than his intellectual ingenuity is Borges's consummate skill as a narrator, his magic in obtaining the most powerful effects with a strict economy of means.

Borges's stories may seem mere formalist games, mathematical experiments devoid of any sense of human responsibility and unrelated even to the author's own life, but quite the opposite is true. His idealist insistence on knowledge and insight, which mean finding order and becoming part of it, has a definite moral significance, though that significance is for him inextricably dual: his traitors are always somehow heroes as well. And all his fictional situations, all his characters, are at bottom autobiographical, essential projections of his experiences as writer, reader and human being (also divided, as **"Borges and I"** tells us). He is the dreamer who learns he is the dreamed one, the detective deceived by the hidden pattern of crimes, the perplexed Averroes whose ignorance mirrors the author's own in portraying him. And yet, each of these intimate failures is turned into an artistic triumph. It could be asked what such concerns of a total man of letters have to do with our plight as ordinary, bedeviled men of our bedeviled time. Here it seems inevitable to draw a comparison with Cervantes, so apparently unlike Borges, but whose name is not invoked in vain in his stories, essays and parables. Borges's fictions, like the enormous fiction of *Don Quixote,* grow out of the deep confrontation of literature and life which is not only the central problem of all literature but also that of all human experience: the problem of illusion and reality. We are all at once writers, readers and protagonists of some eternal story; we fabricate our illusions, seek to decipher the symbols around us and see our efforts overtopped and cut short by a supreme Author; but in our defeat, as in the Mournful Knight's, there can come the glimpse of a higher understanding that prevails, at our expense. Borges's "dehumanized" exercises in *ars combinatoria* are no less human than that.

Narrative prose is usually easier to translate than verse, but Borges's prose raises difficulties not unlike those of poetry, because of its constant creative deformations and cunning artifices. Writers as diverse as George Moore and Vladimir Nabokov have argued that translations should sound like translations. Certainly, since Borges's language does not read "smoothly" in Spanish, there is no reason it should in English. Besides, as was indicated above, he considers his own style at best only a translation of others': at the end of **"Tlön, Uqbar, Orbis Tertius"** he speaks of making an "uncertain" version of Sir Thomas Browne's *Urn Burial* after the manner of the great Spanish Baroque writer Francisco de Quevedo. Borges's prose is in fact a modern adaptation of the Latinized Baroque *stil coupé.* He has a penchant for what seventeenth- and eighteenth-century rhetoricians called "hard" or "philosophic" words, and will often use them in their strict etymological sense, restoring radical meanings with an effect of metaphorical novelty. In the opening sentence of **"The Circular Ruins,"** "unanimous" means quite literally "of one mind" (*unus animus*) and thus foreshadows the magician's final discovery. Elevated terms are played off against more humble and direct ones; the image joining unlike terms is frequent; heterogeneous contacts are also created by Bor-

ges's use of colons and semicolons in place of causal connectives to give static, elliptical, overlapping effects. Somewhat like Eliot in *The Waste Land,* Borges will deliberately work quotations into the texture of his writing. The most striking example is **"The Immortal,"** which contains many more such "intrusions or thefts" than its epilogue admits. All his other stories do the same to some degree: there are echoes of Gibbon in **"The Lottery in Babylon,"** of Spengler in **"Deutsches Requiem,"** of *Borges himself* in **"The Library of Babel"** and **"Funes the Memorious,"** Borges has observed that "the Baroque is that style which deliberately exhausts (or tries to exhaust) its possibilities and borders on its own caricature." A self-parodying tone is particularly evident in **"Pierre Menard, Author of the Quixote,"** **"The Zahir,"** **"The Sect of the Phoenix."** In that sense, Borges also ironically translates himself. . . .

Borges's somewhat belated recognition as a major writer of our time has come more from Europe than from his native America. The 1961 Formentor Prize, which he shared with Samuel Beckett, is the most recent token of that recognition. In Argentina, save for the admiration of a relatively small group, he has often been criticized as non-Argentine, as an abstruse dweller in an ivory tower, though his whole work and personality could only have emerged from that peculiar crossroads of the River Plate region, and his nonpolitical opposition to Perón earned him persecutions during the years of the dictatorship. Apparently, many of his countrymen cannot pardon in him what is precisely his greatest virtue—his almost superhuman effort to transmute his circumstances into an art as universal as the finest of Europe—and expect their writers to be uncomplicated reporters of the national scene. A kind of curious inverse snobbism is evident here. As the Argentine novelist Ernesto Sábato remarked in 1945, "if Borges were French or Czech, we would all be reading him enthusiastically in bad translations."

James E. Irby, in an introduction to Labyrinths: Selected Stories & Other Writings *by Jorge Luis Borges, edited by Donald A. Yates and James E. Irby, New Directions, 1964, pp. xv-xxiii.*

"The Labyrinth"

This is the labyrinth of Crete. This is the labyrinth of Crete whose center was the Minotaur. This is the labyrinth of Crete whose center was the Minotaur that Dante imagined as a bull with a man's head in whose stone net so many generations were as lost as María Kodama and I were lost. This is the labyrinth of Crete whose center was the Minotaur that Dante imagined as a bull with a man's head in whose stone net so many generations were as lost as María Kodama and I were lost that morning, and remain lost in time, that other labyrinth.

Jorge Luis Borges, in his Atlas, *E. P. Dutton, 1985.*

Miguel Enguídanos (essay date June 1963)

[*In the following excerpt from his introduction to* Dreamtigers, *Enguídanos discusses why Borges felt this collection of story fragments, parables, and poems was the culmination of his literary career.*]

From the very first pages the English-speaking reader will discover that this [*El hacedor* translated as ***Dreamtigers***] is an intimate, personal book. . . . Borges considered *El hacedor*—I don't know whether he may have changed his mind—*his* book, the book most likely, in his opinion, to be remembered when all the rest are forgotten. And the book—Borges loved to play with this idea—that would make his earlier works unnecessary, including his two extraordinary collections of stories, ***Ficciones*** and *El Aleph.* As is so often the case, the reader, to say nothing of the critic, may not agree with the poet; they may well continue to think, and not without reason, that the great, the unique Borges is the Borges of narrative fiction. . . .

El hacedor, the original version of which appeared in Buenos Aires in 1960, is to all appearances a miscellany. In it the author is supposed to have gathered odd poems, stories, parables, sketches, fragments, and apocryphal quotations, with no other purpose than to show what time accumulates in the bottom of a writer's desk drawer. But actually this juxtaposing of fragments, bits, and snippets corresponds to a poetic criterion of an extremely high order: that of creating a book—*the* book—which is the mirror of a life. A life in which, as Borges himself confesses, "few things have happened more worth remembering than Schopenhauer's thought or the music of England's words." A life that has been, more than anything else, an internal life, a truly private life of calm self-possession and "recogimiento." [In a footnote, Enguídanos explains: "There is no choice here but to use the untranslatable Spanish word, for to live in 'recogimiento' is not simply to live in solitude; nor is it merely to live locked within oneself. A life of 'recogimiento' is the life of the solitary man who accepts and lives in perfect harmony with his solitude, nurturing himself on what the soul has within it, an unfathomable and, for many, unsuspected treasure."]

Borges has traveled a great deal. Sometimes he has made use of the customary media of transportation; but more often he has gone by way of his imagination. From his internal "recogimiento" he has ventured forth, on occasion, toward the strangest places and the remotest times. But his sallies have been only tentative explorations, amoebic assimilations of the external world. His work—and by now it can be viewed as a whole—is altogether poetic, personal, the work of a spirit so withdrawn that solitude has enlarged it and made him now see in that solitude the secret of the whole universe, now tremble before its undecipherable mysteries. Borges' "theme," then, throughout all his work—including his now famous fantasy narratives—has been simply Borges himself. It is true that, from all his excursions into nooks alien to his inner self—reading, travel, fleeting human relationships—Borges has come back burdened with every possible doubt except one. In spite of his intelligent, ironic, and painstaking defenses, each clash with external reality has reaffirmed his consciousness of self. With the world's reality in doubt, and

man's, and even God's, only one certainty remains: that of being "somebody"—a particular individual, not very easily identifiable, for he could have been named Homer, Shakespeare, or, more modestly, Jorge Luis Borges—*creating himself* from within. This *hacedor* [Enguídanos explains in a footnote that in Spanish "*Hacedor* means 'maker' but it also has the meaning of creator. Thus God is spoken of as the 'Supremo Hacedor' "] is the creator, the poet, the man capable of "singing and leaving echoing concavely in the memory of man" murmurs—in prose and in verse—of Iliads, Odysseys, lost loves, obscure gestes, impossible and desperate adventures of fantasy. Security in this "somebody," this intimate self, is not based in Borges' case on a clear consciousness of his identity or personal destiny, but rather on the certainty of the compulsive, creative, poetic force that has borne him to the final stretch of his life work without faltering. The imprecise Homer-Borges of the story **"El hacedor"** knows very well that the weapon for combating life's final disillusionment, time's inexorable weight, and the terror and anguish of darkness, is none other than his capacity to dream and to sing. Dreams and song make the world bearable, habitable; they make the dark places bright. Blindness of the soul—which is the one that counts—is the natural state of man, and woe to him who does not see in time that we live surrounded by shadows! The poet, the *hacedor,* makes this discovery one day and descends into the shadows unafraid, illumined by his creative consciousness. "In this night of his mortal eyes, into which he was now descending, love and danger were again waiting." Borges and Homer know, then, that this is where everything begins, in the bold, loving acceptance of life and in the drive that impels them to people their darkness with voices.

Dreams and song. About the whole and about the parts. About the universe and about each of its separate creatures. The creature may be a man—gaucho, hero, Irish patriot, impenitent Nazi, sacrificed Jew—any one of man's artifacts—a whole civilization, a library, a knife—or simply an animal, a tiger. "As I sleep, some dream beguiles me, and suddenly I know I am dreaming. Then I think: This is a dream, a pure diversion of my will; and now that I have unlimited power, I am going to cause a tiger."

But the *hacedor* must accept his ministry humbly. He must exercise his power, prepared, however, to recognize his ultimate impotence. For his office consists, precisely, in the will to dream very high dreams and in attempting the purest, most lasting resonances, all the while realizing and bravely accepting his incompetence. "Oh, incompetence! Never can my dreams engender the wild beast I long for. The tiger indeed appears, but stuffed or flimsy, or with impure variants of shape, or of an implausible size, or all too fleeting, or with a touch of the dog or the bird."

Dreams and song—in spite of incompetence, stumblings, and disillusionment. This is why the *hacedor* and his book are born. Their mission and message will not escape the reader who knows when a dream is a dream and who has an ear for remembering the melody of a song.

Let the reader not be confused. This book, though composed of fragments, must be appraised as if it were a multi-

---

> The brilliant insinuation, the mysterious
> or ironic reference, the small poetic
> incision, are Borges' chosen expressive
> means.
>
> —*Miguel Enguídanos*

---

ple mirror, or a mosaic of tiny mirrors. At a certain distance from its reading—once it has been digested—it will be clear that the pieces outline a whole: a self-portrait of an entire soul and body. The brilliant insinuation, the mysterious or ironic reference, the small poetic incision, are Borges' chosen expressive means. The story or short narrative, a form that made him famous, and the novel—a genre he has avoided—always seemed to him unpardonable excesses. That is why Borges feels *El hacedor* is the culmination of a literary career, a liberation from former limitations, vanities, and prejudices. That is why he feels it is *his* book. How right he is, it is still not time nor is this the place to judge; but the earnestness the poet put into the effort ought to be clearly established. In *El hacedor* stories, tales, and even poems are reduced to their minimum, almost naked expression. Everything tends toward the poetic parable: brief, but bright as a flash of lightning.

Since *El hacedor,* Borges has published an *Antología personal* in Argentina. In it he has collected, in preferential rather than chronological order, what to his mind can be submitted to the judgment of a hypothetical posterity. As the poet tells us in the prologue, the experiment has served only to prove to him his poverty, his limitations of expression, the mortality of his writings as measured by his rigorous criteria of today. But, at the same time, the task of anthologizing his own work has made him surer of himself, created a new source of vital energy, and given him a renewed illusion. "This poverty," says Borges "does not discourage me, since it gives me an illusion of continuity."

In my opinion, the several pieces that make up the present book, *El hacedor,* were also put together after Jorge Luis Borges had already begun to feel the pull of that anxiety for continuity. "For good or for ill, my readers"—Borges seems to be wanting to tell us in recent years—"these fragments piled up here by time are all that I am. The earlier work no longer matters." "The tall proud volumes casting a golden shadow in a corner were not—as his vanity had dreamed—a mirror of the world, but rather one thing more added *to* the world" ["**A Yellow Rose**"]. And this is all he as a poet feels capable of desiring: to be able to add to the world a few bits of more or less resplendent mirror yielding only an illusory reflection—ah, the timid yearning for immortality! —of what was felt, thought, and dreamed in solitude. The solitude, as we know, of one of the most solitary, intelligent, and sensitive souls of our time.

The poet is setting out, then, on his last venture. It makes one tremble to think with what assurance poets know when the final stage of a creative life begins; but at the same time it is wondrous to contemplate how the chaos that is their own life and work begins to take on meaning for them. Perhaps what is seen now will in retrospect be only another illusion, but there it is. When the uneven fragments that comprise the work are pieced together—especially the ones that appear most insignificant—they outline something the poet is consoled to behold. The parts organize themselves into a whole. "A man sets himself the task of portraying the world. Through the years he peoples a space with images of provinces, kingdoms, mountains, bays, ships, islands, fishes, rooms, tools, stars, horses, and people. Shortly before his death, he discovers that that patient labyrinth of lines traces the image of his face."

If, after all, the face is merely the mirror of the soul, it is not hard to guess the ultimate meaning of the game of illusion Jorge Luis Borges proposes to the reader in this book: the separate parts that constitute *El hacedor*—narratives, poems, parables, reflections, and interpolations—when read as a whole, trace the image of the poet's face: face-mirror-image of the soul of the creator, of the maker.

At first glance, there is nothing unusual about one poet's dedicating one of his books to another poet. That *El hacedor* should be dedicated to Leopoldo Lugones is something that need not be mentioned in this introduction if it were not that the explanation Borges gives for his dedication at the beginning of the volume requires a special imaginative effort on the part of the reader [In a footnote, Enguídanos explains that "Leopoldo Lugones (1874-1938) is the most famous of the Argentine Modernist poets. He was born in a provincial town in Córdoba and took his own life with cyanide in 1938, in Tigre, near Buenos Aires. Lugones was the most important renovating force in Argentine poetry and prose in the twentieth century. His best-known works are *Las montañas del oro* (1897), *Los crepúsculos del jardín* (1905), *Las fuerzas extrañas* (1906), *Lunario sentimental* (1909), and *La guerra gaucha* (1911)"]. Actually, without such an effort one cannot wholly enter the mysterious realm where the poet lives his dreams. The invocation of the shade of Lugones—who committed suicide in 1938—on the threshold of *El hacedor* is revealing. It is an exorcism.

The dream and the song of *El hacedor* are troubled from the start by old, malignant spirits. In conjuring his former demons—passion, intellectual pride, rebellion against the voice of the once omnipresent poet—Borges wants to be done with them. It is not merely a question of appeasing the memory of the Modernist poet, against whom Borges and his young friends in 1921 launched the most violent attacks and obstreperous jibes. Nor of recognizing, out of the creative maturity of his sixties, the right and dignity of literary prestige honorably won. Borges intends to do this, of course, but much more as well. He wants now to incorporate into his book, into his song, the feeling that in his hostility toward the great poet of the generation preceding his own there was somehow a great and heartfelt love. For without internal peace and order the poet cannot truly face the chaos of life, or manage to have his work's labyrinth of lines trace the image of his face.

There is, besides, a certain fascination in his recollection of Lugones. Borges is the present director of the National Library in Buenos Aires; in 1938, Lugones was director of the Library of the National Council of Education. In his dedication Borges deliberately fuses and confuses the two libraries and the two times, past and present: "Leaving behind the babble of the plaza, I enter the Library. I feel, almost physically, the magnetic force of the books, an ambient serenity of order, time magically desiccated and preserved." The intent is quite clear: "My vanity and nostalgia have set up an impossible scene," says Borges. The impossibility is not merely physical; it depends rather on the fact that it is a wish, a dream, too distant to be attainable; for what the poet dreams of is nothing less than a loving communion between the voices of the poets. "Perhaps so," says Borges to himself in his illusions, "but tomorrow I too will have died and our times will intermingle and chronology will be lost in a sphere of symbols. And then in some way it will be right to claim that I have brought you this book and that you, Lugones, have accepted it."

From the very first pages, therefore, the reader can discover where the poet is going in the rest of the book. Besides, without the initial exorcism of the demons of frivolity, routine reading, and pedantry, the reader might even be prevented from coming at last to trace out the portrait of his own face. And to reach this moment to which every reader—a passive poet—should be led by the hand of the *hacedor,* the active poet, there is no other way than to exorcise oneself and make ready to dream and to hear the murmurs that are heard in dreams.

Miguel Enguídanos, in an introduction to Dreamtigers *by Jorge Luis Borges, translated by Mildred Boyer and Harold Morland, University of Texas Press, 1985, pp. 9-17.*

James E. Irby   (essay date 1964)

[*In the following essay—his introduction to* Other Inquisitions—*Irby discusses the varied subjects and subtle interconnections of Borges's essays.*]

[*Otras inquisiciones* (*Other Inquisitions*)] is Borges' best collection of essays, and forms a necessary complement to the stories of *Ficciones* and *El Aleph,* which have made him famous. *Otras inquisiciones* was first published in 1952, but its pieces had appeared separately (most of them in Victoria Ocampo's review *Sur* or in the literary supplement of *La Nación*) over the preceding thirteen years. The title harks back to Borges' first volume of essays, published in 1925, when he was twenty-six. Those original *Inquisiciones* now seem to him affected and dogmatic *avant-garde* exercises; he will not have the book reprinted and buys up old copies to destroy them. The present collection's curiously ancillary title is therefore ambiguous and ironic. "Other" can mean "more of the same": more efforts doomed to eventual error, perhaps, but certainly more quests or inquiries into things, according to the etymology. But "other" is also "different," perhaps even "opposite": these essays hardly set forth inflexible dogma, with their sagacious heresies, pursuit of multiple meanings, and dubitative style. In 1925 Borges stated that his title aimed to dissociate "inquisition" once and for all

from monks' cowls and the smoke of damnation. After an inquisitorial pursuit of his own work, the effort continues.

Borges' reference to De Quincey in opening the essay on John Donne is typical in its candid confession of influence and also typical in the English and uncommon nature of that influence. For *Otras inquisiciones* will probably seem no less unusual to the English-speaking than to the Spanish-speaking reader. Traits of nineteenth-century essayists as little read today as De Quincey—whimsical bookishness, a blend of conversational discursiveness and elevated diction, informal opinion prevailing over formal analysis—combine with the many unfamiliar subjects to produce a kind of alienation effect, a somewhat archaic or even atemporal quality remote from our age of urgent involvements, as well as from current critical modes. This effect is more compounded than mitigated by a very un-nineteenth-century brevity that may seem fragmentary and, with the great heterogeneity of the subjects, make the collection appear arbitrary and without unity. But there is method here; its basic principle is already suggested by the union of diverse and opposite meanings in the title.

One of the foremost quests in *Otras inquisiciones* is for symmetries; two that are rediscovered throughout the book under various guises appear in the first two essays. In **"The Wall and the Books"** Borges evokes the Chinese emperor who both created the Great Wall and wanted all books prior to him burned. This enormous mystification inexplicably "satisfies" and, at the same time, "disturbs" Borges. His purpose then is to seek the reasons for "that emotion." (Note that the stimulus for the supposedly cerebral Borges is not an idea, that the satisfaction and disturbance are *one* feeling.) Various conjectures lead him to suggest that the aesthetic phenomenon consists in the "imminence of a revelation that is not yet produced": a kind of expanding virtuality of thought, an unresolved yet centrally focussed multiplicity of views, which the essay's form as discussion, as tacit dialogue, has already reflected. The other essays also display, centrally or laterally, paradoxes or oppositions with analogous overtones. At the end of **"Avatars of the Tortoise"** the paradoxes of Zeno and the antinomies of Kant indicate for Borges that the universe is ultimately a dream, a product of the mind, unreal because free of the apparent limits of time and space we call "real." But the paradoxical confession with which **"New Refutation of Time"** ends—"it [time] is a fire that consumes me, but I am the fire"—must conclude that "the world, alas, is real; I, alas, am Borges." Extremes of fantastic hope and skepticism paradoxically coexist in Borges' thought.

In **"Pascal's Sphere"** he examines an image which is not only paradoxical in itself—the universe as an infinite sphere, in other words, a boundless form perfectly circumscribed—but which has also served to express diametrically opposite emotions: Bruno's elation and Pascal's anguish. But the other basic symmetry to note here is Borges' history of the metaphor. Not only paradoxes are found throughout this collection, but also various listings of ideas or themes or images which though diverse in origin and detail are essentially the same. In **"The Flower of Coleridge"** the coincidence of Valéry's, Emerson's, and

Shelley's conceptions of all literature as the product of one Author seems itself to bear out that conception. At the beginning of the essay on Hawthorne, Borges again briefly traces the history of a metaphor—the likening of our dreams to a theatrical performance—and adds that true metaphors cannot be invented, since they have always existed. Such "avatars" point beyond the flux and diversity of history to a realm of eternal archetypes, which, though limited in number, "can be all things for all people, like the Apostle." While the paradox upsets our common notions of reality and suggests that irreducible elements are actually one, recurrence negates history and the separateness of individuals. Of course, this too is a paradox, as **"New Refutation of Time"** shows: time must exist in order to provide the successive identities with which it is to be "refuted." The two symmetries noted above, if we pursue their implications far enough, finally coalesce, with something of the same dizzying sense, so frequent in Borges' stories, of infinite permutations lurking at every turn. Both are uses of what he calls a pantheist extension of the principle of identity—God is all things: a suitably heterogeneous selection of these may allude to Totality—which has, as he notes in the essay on Whitman, unlimited rhetorical possibilities.

Stylistic uses of that principle are the paradoxical or near-paradoxical word pairs ("that favors or tolerates another interpretation," "our reading of Kafka refines and changes our reading of the poem") and also the ellipses and transferred epithets based on substitution of part for whole, whose possibilities for animation of the abstract and impersonal explain why Borges terms a typical example "allegorical" at the beginning of **"From Allegories to Novels."** (The classical concept of Literature's precedence over individuals, outlined in the first essay on Coleridge, is analogous to this and to the priority of archetypes. As we shall see, Borges' very personal essayistic manner actually reinforces such impersonality.) In general, the enumeration of sharply diverse yet somehow harmonizing parts that allude to some larger, static whole unnamable by any unilateral means is a common procedure underlying many features of Borges' style and form: the sentences that abruptly rotate their angular facets like cut stones, the succinct little catalogs that may comprise paragraphs and even whole essays, the allusions and generalizations that find echoes of the line of argument elsewhere and project it onto other planes, the larger confrontations of a writer with his alter ego (in himself or in another) or of the essay with its own revision or complement—all those series and inlays, in short, which are so much the curt mosaic design of this collection.

It is even possible to see the miscellaneous range of subjects taken up in *Otras inquisiciones* as yet another extension of the same "pantheist" principle, as the record of a random series of discoveries in books that variously point to one subsistent order beyond. In Borges' stories (as also in *Don Quixote*) the turning points, the crucial revelations, are very often marked by the finding of some unexpected text. *Otras inquisiciones* opens with the words "I read, not long ago . . ." and closes with the author's reflections on rereading his own essays. This ubiquitousness of books and their scrutiny is but one aspect of that ancient *topos,*

with all its Cabalist elaborations, that so fascinates Borges: the world as Book, reality transmuted into Word, into intelligible Sign. *All* reality, including the symbolic and lived aspects we normally consider separate—the translation of this unity into literary form, as **"Partial Enchantments of the *Quixote*"** points out, is the structure of work within work in Cervantes' novel, in *Hamlet,* in *Sartor Resartus,* where the boundaries between fiction and life shift and tend to disappear.

Concentric structures of this kind abound in *Ficciones* and *El Aleph,* as do direct premonitions and echoes of those stories' themes in *Otras inquisiciones.* It is easy to see, for example, that the literary games of Tlön that attribute dissimilar works to the same writer and conjecture upon the apocryphal mentality thus obtained, like Pierre Menard's art of "the deliberate anachronism and the erroneous attribution," are only somewhat more extravagant applications of the scrutinies practiced in the essays. In fact, Borges' entire work, filled with recurring variants of the same interlocking themes, is a cento of itself, a repeated approximation of archetypes like those he glimpses in others. But a more intriguing comparison between his essays and his stories can be posed in this question: what is the difference for him between one genre and the other? Are his many fictions that masquerade as essays, such as **"Tlön, Uqbar, Orbis Tertius"** or **"Pierre Menard, Author of the *Quixote,* "** distinct from the "real" essays of *Otras inquisiciones* simply because the stories have invented books and authors as their subjects? But the fiction entitled **"Story of the Warrior and the Captive"** (in *El Aleph*) contains no invented element, save the speculative elaboration upon the scant facts of its real characters' lives, and the germs of this are found also in an essay like **"The Enigma of Edward FitzGerald,"** with the same weighing of conjectures, bipartite structure, and final identity of figures greatly separate in time and place. The real difference seems to be one of emphasis or degree: fiction and fact, imagination and critique, are aspects of the same continuum throughout Borges' work, both within genres and among them. Hence, in these essays, he can use historical deeds to investigate the aesthetic phenomenon, to remark that the "inventions of philosophy are no less fantastic than those of art," to find in his own work a tendency to "evaluate religious or philosophical ideas on the basis of their aesthetic worth," and to add epilogues and afterthoughts that are the beginnings of those Chinese-box structures where literature devours and extends itself without limit.

But does Borges *believe* in his own incredible cosmologies? Clearly not: the alternative of infinite chaos is also always about to emerge. His cosmologies are like hypotheses, cherished but also incurably problematical.

—*James E. Irby*

Borges' major world-pictures have already been noted here in passing: the world as Book, the idealist and pantheist notions of the world as idea or dream, either man's or God's. (The Gnostic image suggested in the essay on John Donne—the world infinitely degraded, infinitely remote from God's perfection—is but the exact obverse of pantheism. As Borges observed in his earlier book *Discusión,* "what greater glory for a God than to be absolved of the world?") That these conceptions also coalesce is shown by the remark "we (the undivided divinity that operates within us) have dreamed the world" in **"Avatars of the Tortoise,"** by the concluding sentence of **"From Someone to Nobody,"** which suggests that all history is a dream of recurrent forms, and by the entire essay **"The Mirror of the Enigmas,"** with its "hieroglyphic" interpretation of the universe that Borges claims most befits "the intellectual God of the theologians," the infinite mind that can instantly grasp the most intricate figure in space and time (a nightmare of *ars combinatoria,* of pure chance) as a harmonious design. Borges' world-pictures all seem to join in postulating that the world is a supreme mind about to emerge from its symbols and reveal the unity of all things and beings *sub specie aeternitatis.*

But does Borges *believe* in such incredible cosmologies? Clearly not: the alternative of infinite chaos is also always about to emerge. The word "believe" here takes on the same uncertainty as "fiction" and "reality." His cosmologies are like hypotheses, cherished but also incurably problematical, as the whole tentative, self-critical cast of his style, at its most elaborate in **"New Refutation of Time,"** indicates. Such flexibility of mind he finds lacking in his former idol Quevedo, who is immune to the charm of fantastic doctrines that are "probably false," and relishes in the atheist Omar Khayyām, who could interpret the Koran with strict orthodoxy and invoke in his studies of algebra the favor of "the God Who perhaps exists," because "every cultivated man is a theologian, and faith is not a requisite." Any theme set forth by Borges will be refuted by him somewhere else: the concept of autonomous pure form espoused in **"The Wall and the Books"** and **"Quevedo"** is rejected in the first paragraphs of the essay on Bernard Shaw. Self-refutation has, besides the virtues of probity, its advantages, its "apparent desperations and secret assuagements." One could suspect that Borges' nature, like Chesterton's, is a discord, and see these essays simply as its testimony, but it seems more accurate to consider *Otras inquisiciones* as a mask, as consciously projecting the image of a "possible poet," after the manner he has noted in Whitman and Valéry, those poetic personifications of fervor and intellect, each of whom is a counterpart of Borges' creative self (the former fully as much as the latter, contrary to widespread belief).

The nature and purpose of that projection are implied in three passages from scattered essays of Borges. In 1927 he called metaphysics "the only justification and finality of any theme." In 1933 he spoke of Icelandic kennings that produce "that lucid perplexity which is the sole honor of metaphysics, its remuneration, and its source." And in 1944 he admired the "dialectical skill" of a fragment from Heraclitus, which insinuates part of its meaning and "gives us the illusion of having invented it." The themes

of *Otras inquisiciones,* as such, matter less than the state of awareness their immediacy and strangeness and scope can induce. In Borges' sense, metaphysics is not an abstruse specialty, but the quotidian acts of all our thought, pursued to their consequences and revealed as the wonders they are. All ideas are arbitrary, fantastic, and useful. They should be remembered if forgotten or obscure, subverted if sacred (another form of oblivion), made absurd if banal—all for the sake of intelligence, of perceptibility. Borges' curious erudition, plausible paradoxes, and restless scrutinies serve those functions, as does his very readable style (that worn epithet must be revived and used here). Taut and effortless, transparent and mannered, deeply true to the genius of the Spanish language yet heterodox, his rhetoric is also a silent parody and extension of itself. For even certain excesses, the abruptness of certain transitions, the dubiousness of certain obviously sentimental attachments, seem a willful demonstration of the limits of his writing and thought, as if to invite the reader, once he is sufficiently initiated (Borges' work is never hermetic and is always intended for the reader), to "improve" upon these somewhat Socratic schemes. The *activation* of thought, shared by author and reader, miraculously effected over fatal distance and time by words whose sense alters and yet lives on, is the real secret promise of the infinite dominion of mind, not its images or finalities, which are expendable. This is the "method" of Borges' essays, the process both examined and enacted in them, received and passed on, as part of a great chain of being. Hence the essay on Whitman, hence the final epigraph from the seventeenth-century German mystic Angelus Silesius:

> Freund, es ist auch genug. Im Fall du mehr willst lesen,
> So geh und werde selbst die Schrift und selbst das Wesen.
> Friend, this is enough. If you want to read more,
> Go and be yourself the letter and the spirit.

James E. Irby, in an introduction to Other Inquisitions: 1937-1952 *by Jorge Luis Borges, translated by Ruth L. C. Simms, University of Texas Press, 1964, pp. ix-xv.*

Edgardo Cozarinsky   (essay date 1980)

[*In the following essay, which originally appeared in Spanish in 1980, Cozarinsky examines Borges's narrative techniques, arguing that his style is strongly influenced by classical Hollywood film editing and the "serializing" of "significant moments."*]

Film—an *idea* of film, really—recurs in Borges's writing linked to the practice of narration, even to the possibility of attempting narration. Films also appear as reading matter, one among the countless motives for reflection lavished on us by the universe. The examples offered to Borges by films illustrate widely disparate themes: the hilarious response of a Buenos Aires audience to some scenes from *Hallelujah* and *Underworld* provoked his bitter commentary on **"Our Impossibilities"** (an article dating from 1931 and included in *Discusión* the following year but eliminated from the 1957 edition) [it was translated as **"Our Inadequacies"** in *Borges: A Reader*]; von Sternberg gave him the chance to confirm a hypothesis about the workings of all story telling (**"The Postulation of Reality"** and **"Narrative Art and Magic,"** both included in *Discusión*); Joan Crawford made an appearance in the second of these essays and Miriam Hopkins in **"History of Eternity"** from the volume of the same title; "the impetuous film *Hallelujah*" furnished one of the many results of bringing blacks to America that Borges enumerates in *Universal History of Infamy;* the modest translator Edward William Lane provided a basis for Borges's comparison with Hollywood's then rigid censorship code (**"The Translators of the 1001 Nights,"** *History of Eternity*).

During the 1920s and '30s, Borges saw the mere diffusion of images by means of film as an incalculable enrichment of life, perhaps because he knew how to recognize in those images, even though they were fictitious—or, above all, *because* they were fictitious? —signs of a broader context. In a digression, subsequently deleted when he revised *Discusión,* Borges refers in his 1929 essay **"The Other Whitman"** to the lack of communication between inhabitants of "the diverse Americas," and he proceeds to venture an opinion: it is "a lack of communication that films, with their direct presentation of destinies and their no less direct presentation of wills, tend to overcome." This catalogue of references could be extended effortlessly, but its sole importance is to establish the degree to which films were a habit for the young Borges, an accessible repertoire of allusions, which he consulted as frequently as the *Encyclopedia Britannica* or unpublished reality.

At that time, film represented to Borges the image of literature (or history or philosophy) as a single text fragmented into countless, even contradictory passages, which neither individually represented that text nor in combination exhausted it. With even greater ease than in those prestigious disciplines, this notion could come to life in the films Borges frequented and quoted from, with diminishing regularity after 1940: a cinema that in spite of Eisenstein and Welles could still seem an art unfettered by too many big names, a cinema that was, above all else, free of bibliographies and academies. Allardyce Nicoll, whose *Film and Theatre* (1936) Borges dismissed as an exercise in pedantry, seemed "well versed in libraries, erudite in card catalogues, sovereign in files," but "nearly illiterate in box-offices. . . ."

Borges felt attracted by the stylization that Josef von Sternberg imposed on his gangland characters, settings, and conventions, whose usual violence is less elliptical, less ironic than in films like *Underworld* or *TheDocks of New York*.

—*Edgardo Cozarinsky*

In this cinematic realm, many obscure narrators practiced the "differing intonation of a few metaphors" (**"The Sphere of Pascal,"** *Other Inquisitions*) whose history may be the history of the universe. "I think nowadays, while literary men seem to have neglected their epic duties, the epic has been saved for us, strangely enough, by the Westerns," Borges told Ronald Christ in an interview published in *The Paris Review* 40 (Winter/Spring 1967). "During this century," he said, "the epic tradition has been saved for the world by, of all places, Hollywood." If Hollywood really was able to compile a film-text, both craftsmanlike and collective, as well as bearing comparison to the ancient sagas, then Borges's predilection for that text is, *horribile dictu,* sophisticated. In order to belittle the films that von Sternberg composed around Marlene Dietrich, Borges repeatedly defends von Sternberg's earlier action films; and, in the interview with Christ, he recalls that "when I saw the first gangster films of von Sternberg I remember that when there was anything epic about them—I mean Chicago gangsters dying bravely—well, I felt that my eyes were full of tears." But von Sternberg was neither Wellman nor Hawks nor Walsh—figures who, with greater credibility, might embody a cinematic skald. Obviously, Borges felt attracted by the stylization that von Sternberg imposed on his gangland characters, settings, and conventions, whose usual violence is less elliptical, less ironic than in films like *Underworld* or *The Docks of New York.*

It is no accident that von Sternberg is the only film director whom Borges assiduously refers to or that those references appear in his early studies of narrative technique included in *Discusión* as well as in the 1935 prologue to the *Universal History of Infamy,* where the epic invocation turns into an exercise of verbal legerdemain. In the 1954 prologue to that book, Borges writes: "Scaffolds and pirates populate it, and the word *infamy* blares in the title; but, behind all the tumult, there is nothing. The book is nothing more than appearance, nothing more than a surface of images, and for that very reason it may prove pleasurable." Films, of course, *are* that surface of images, and nothing can be found behind the words of any literary work; but to admit and flaunt one's working against the referential function of language is as skeptical and cultivated an attitude as nostalgia for epic or disdain for romantic individualism.

Less ascetic than Valéry, Borges put his distrust of the novel into practice. His impatience with mere length is well known: "It is an impoverishing and laborious extravagance to create long books, to extend into 500 pages an idea whose perfect oral expression takes a few minutes. A better procedure is to pretend that these books already exist and to offer a summary, a commentary" (Prologue to *The Garden of the Forking Paths*). Such boldness destroys the very possibility of even approaching a genre that, in order to develop a character and to proportion its episodes, requires a necessarily unhurried orchestration of specific circumstances and trivial information. Borges has also explained that Hawthorne's talent lent itself more to the short story than to the novel because he preferred to start from situations rather than from characters: "Hawthorne first imagined a situation, perhaps involuntarily, and afterward looked for characters to embody it. I am not a novelist, but I suspect that no novelist has proceeded in that way. . . . That method may produce, or permit, admirable short stories in which, because of their brevity, the plot is more visible than the characters; but it cannot produce admirable novels, in which the overall form (if there is any) is only visible at the end and in which a single poorly imagined character may contaminate with unreality all those characters who surround him" (**"Nathaniel Hawthorne,"** *Other Inquisitions*).

So, then: distrust of the scale demanded by the novel and esteem for a format ("summary," "commentary") that makes "overall form" visible. As an expression of flexible disdain, of willingness to allow for occasional greatness in the practice of what he considers an erroneous genre, that phrase "if there is any" belongs to the same family as Valéry's most categorical observations. But the interesting thing about this apathy is that it does not suppose a rejection of narrative. In fact, a summary analysis of the most distinguishing characteristics in Borges's "fiction" reveals its undisguised narrative quality. The text may be a review of nonexistent literary works (**"The Approach to Almotasim," "An Examination of the Works of Herbert Quain"**), the exposition of apocryphal theories (**"Three Versions of Judas," "The Theologians"**), a report about an invented reality (**"The Babylonian Lottery," "The Library of Babel"**), even the connecting of probable episodes by means of a fictitious link (**"History of the Warrior and the Captive," "Averroes's Search"**). No matter. The less those texts respond to the accepted statutes of fiction, the more strongly they display the narrative process, which directs a *mise-en-scène* whose purpose is neither mimetic nor representational but intellectual: to arouse pleasure in the recognition of that "overall form," a recognition customarily postponed by the novel.

"The Wall and the Books," "Coleridge's Dream," "The Meeting in a Dream," and **"The Modesty of History"** are usually read as essays because they are included in a volume that announces itself as a collection of essays: *Other Inquisitions.* The book's real nature is a series of narrative exercises, operations that renew the workings of narrative on philosophical ideas, historical documents, and literary figures. Similarly, **"History of the Warrior and the Captive"** or **"Averroes's Search"** appear in *The Aleph* and therefore are read as "fictions." Borges's categories of narrative do not discriminate between fiction and nonfiction. The only purpose of these categories is to exhibit the inherent qualities of narrative and essayistic discourse: to unearth a design that rescues the mere telling from chaos and makes an illusion of the cosmos possible. Fiction triumphs. Tlön captures and supplants the real universe with the illusion of order: "How can one not submit to Tlön, to the minute and vast evidence of an ordered planet? It is useless to answer that reality is also ordered. Perhaps it is, but in accordance with divine laws—I translate: with inhuman laws—that we never really perceive. Tlön will be a labyrinth, but a labyrinth planned by men, a labyrinth destined to be deciphered by men" (**"Tlön, Uqbar, Orbis Tertius,"** *The Garden of the Forking Paths*).

Looking back after twenty years, Borges pronounced judgment on his first stories: "They are the irresponsible game of a timid man who did not dare to write stories and so amused himself by falsifying and betraying (sometimes without esthetic justification) other writers' stories" (Prologue to the 1954 edition of the *Universal History of Infamy*). *To falsify, to betray*—those verbs shock with their criminal connotations. Yet they apply to the transmission of every story, from the traditional tale and gossip to any projected novel being transformed into a written text. All narrative proceeds by repetitions and modifications of a *pre*-text, which it nullifies. Those "ambiguous games" that Borges mentions in his prologue quoted above are especially revealing because they reject the invention of anecdote, choosing to explore, instead, the various possibilities of narrative, even the mutually exclusive possibilities. In order to overcome his declared timidity, Borges both disguises and exhibits his own devices.

How did Borges view those games at the time he wrote them? In his prologue to the first edition, Borges says: "They derived, I believe, from my re-reading of Stevenson and Chesterton, and even from the first films of von Sternberg, and perhaps from a certain biography of Evaristo Carriego. They abuse some procedures: random enumeration, abrupt shifts in continuity, reduction of a man's entire life to two or three scenes." This enumeration of sources and methods, by contrast, is not random. In fact, examining his examples enables us to define the context Borges discovered for his idea of film.

In Stevenson, even in Chesterton, Borges admires a capacity for verbal *mise-en-scène:*

> The threads of a story come from time to time together and make a picture in the web; the characters fall from time to time into some attitude to each other or to nature, which stamps the story home like an illustration. Crusoe recoiling from the footprint, Achilles shouting over against the Trojans, Ulysses bending the great bow, Christian running with his fingers in his ears, these are each culminating moments in the legend, and each has been printed on the mind's eye forever. Other things we may forget; we may forget the words, although they are beautiful; we may forget the author's comment although perhaps it was ingenious and true; but these epoch-making scenes, which put the last mark of truth upon a story and fill up, at one blow, our capacity for sympathetic pleasure, we so adopt into the very bosom of our mind that neither time nor tide can efface or weaken the impression. This, then, is the plastic part of literature: to embody character, thought or emotion in some act or attitude that shall be remarkably striking to the mind's eye.
>
> (Stevenson, "A Gossip on Romance," *Memories and Portraits,* 1887).

Appreciation of verbal *mise-en-scène,* which Stevenson calls "the plastic part of literature," appears at a particular point in the evolution of narrative during the second half of the nineteenth century: after the inauguration of rigorous discipline by Flaubert; coincident with Henry James's early mastery in controlling points of view and alternating between "panorama" and "scene"; immediately before the consecration of these devices as technique in James's subsequent work as well as in the works of Conrad, Ford Maddox Ford, and the Joyce of "The Dead." Once systematized by Percy Lubbock in *The Craft of Fiction* and before languishing in the universities until it died out, this tradition provided the basis for the New Critics' best work in the study of fiction.

In **"The Postulation of Reality,"** which appears in *Discusión* Borges refers to these verbal, defining, and definitive images as "circumstantial invention," the third and most difficult as well as most efficient among the methods by which novelists can impose their subtle authority on the reader. He illustrates the method, magnanimously, with an example from *La gloria de Don Ramiro* [in a footnote, the translator explains that this is a "novel by the Argentine writer Enrique Larreta (1875-1961). Published in 1908, the book reflects the influence of both literary realism and naturalism, especially in its extravagant devotion to historical detail. Cozarinsky says that Borges chose his example 'magnanimously' since Borges did not ordinarily value Larreta's work] and adds:

> I have quoted a short, linear example, but I know of expanded works—Wells's rigorously imaginative novels, Defoe's exasperatingly true-to-life ones—that use no other technique than incorporating or serializing those laconic details into a lengthy development. I assert the same thing about Josef von Sternberg's cinematographic novels, which are also made up of significant moments. It is an admirable and difficult method, but its general application makes it less strictly literary than the two previous ones. (This quotation comes from the 1957 edition of *Discussion;* the original 1932 edition reads: "cinematic, ocular novels.")

What can a writer do with the novelist's tools if his own intellectual habits and work with language predispose him to writing short stories and brief, intense texts? If he is also intolerant of the novel's unavoidable long stretches? Instead of finding privileged moments in the course of narrating, is it possible for him to depart from an ordering of those "significant moments" and to omit the connective tissue that should bind them together? Or, going even further, will he be able with those isolated images—so memorable within a narrative of a certain length—to conjure up phantasmagorically the absent narration that is their "lengthy development"? *Evaristo Carriego* proposes an answer.

Comparable only to Nabokov's *Nikolai Gogol* as an example of the absorption of one literary figure by another (even though the minor stature of Carriego makes the process more obvious), Borges's 1930 book on Carriego—with its discreet "betraying" and "falsifying" of another's story that scarcely serves as a pretext—is also his first approach toward that "fiction" from which a particular timidity had held him back. At several points, Borges declares his hesitations, the obstacles he encounters in writing the book. In the first chapter—"The Palermo Section of Buenos Aires"—one reads: "The jumbled, incessant style of reality, with its punctuation of ironies, surprises, and intimations as strange as surprises, could only be recaptured by a novel, which would be out of place here." And how can he represent Palermo as it was before he knew it?

To recapture that almost static prehistory would

be to foolishly weave a chronicle of infinitesimal processes. . . . The most direct means, according to cinematographic procedure, would be to propose a continuity of discontinuous images: a yoke of wine-bearing mules, the wild ones with their eyes blindfolded; a long, still expanse of water with willow leaves floating on the surface; a vertiginous will-o'-the-wisp wading through the flooding streams on stilts; the open countryside, with nothing to do there; the tracks of a hacienda's stubbornly trampled cattle path, the route to corrals in the north; a peasant (against the dawn sky) who dismounts and slits his jaded horse's wide throat; a wisp of smoke wafting through the air.

Film suggests to Borges the possibility of connecting notable moments by means of a less discursive syntax than the verbal. Here a notion that might be termed *montage* appears. That "continuity of discontinuous images" will be the stated method in the stories of *Universal History of Infamy*.

—*Edgardo Cozarinsky*

A relationship is established among these images. In "A Gossip on Romance" Stevenson had expounded his observations as a reader and sought support from them for his method as a writer. Borges, who agrees with those observations, sees them as applicable to the films of von Sternberg; and in his early *Evaristo Carriego,* where he doubts the very fiction whose elements he invokes, he attempts the magic of conjuring up a more abundant, unlimited reality by naming some notable moments that may postulate it. Film suggests to him the possibility of connecting those moments by means of a less discursive syntax than the verbal. Here a notion that might be termed *montage* appears, operating in texts made from words. That "cinematographic procedure," that "continuity of discontinuous images" will be the stated method in the stories of *Universal History of Infamy*. One of the chapters that divide—and integrate—**"The Disinterested Killer Bill Harrigan"** opens: "History (which like a certain director, proceeds by discontinuous images) now proposes the image of a. . . ."

The stories in *Universal History of Infamy* illustrate, point by point, Chesterton's observations in his study of Stevenson: "Those flat figures could only be seen from one side. They are aspects or attitudes of men rather than men" (*R. L. Stevenson,* London, 1928). The stories also illustrate what Chesterton noted about "our modern attraction to short stories" and the "short story today" in his study of Dickens: "We get a glimpse of grey streets of London, or red plains of India, as in an opium vision; we see people, arresting people with fiery and appealing faces. But when the story is ended, the people are ended" (*Charles Dickens,* London, 1906). To the degree that they ignore what Chesterton in his book on Stevenson calls "huge hospitality for their own characters" and, like Stevenson, prefer a certain thinness in characterization, a simplification appropriate to marionette theater, the two-dimensionality of colored illustrations, Borges's early fictional essays stage a narrative mechanism more than any particular narrative itself. And they do so with the clear awareness that the mechanism is identical in written and cinematographic fiction. (A connection can be seen between this procedure and *Nabokov's Dozen,* in which the destinies of various Russian adventurers, exiled in Berlin during the 1920s and linked occasionally to movies as extras, are recapitulated in takes, sequences, lighting effects, and montage in order to establish a parodic intent.)

There was a moment, which might be situated between *Evaristo Carriego* and the writing of his first story, **"Man on the Pink Corner,"** when Stevenson and von Sternberg equally aroused Borges's attention, a moment when it seemed possible to submit Palermo's turn-of-the-century toughs as well as the neighborhood itself to a verbal treatment, the equivalent of von Sternberg's treatment of Chicago and its gangsters in *Underworld.* Impatient with the restraints that the novel seemed to impose on the exercise of fiction, Borges attempted fiction by cultivating a lucid magic. It matters little whether he was guided by the possibilities revealed to him in narratives by his favorite writers or if their writings permitted him to observe these possibilities in films.

Continuity and *discontinuity:* cinematographic language provided the point of departure for Borges's play with these concepts in his first attempts at fiction.

All narrative traditionally works by successive effects of continuity, with suspense deriving from an apparently defective continuity later restored by a postponed connection. Poetry, on the other hand, traditionally orders its emphases spatially, ignoring all requirements for connective relation other than the formal. Enumeration is one such relation, and Borges had cultivated it in his early fiction, obviously pleased with organizing his prose in a form unprecedented by the nineteenth-century novel. Every rhetorical work in the enumerative form invokes the supposed "endless variety of creation" by alluding to that creation with incongruous signs—a procedure whose illustrious, theological, and pantheistic genealogy cannot be reduced to Spitzer's "chaotic enumeration," which is linked to one notion of modernity. Nevertheless, a single characteristic is invariable: enumeration is always the double operation of naming in order to indicate the unnamed, of making the spaces between signs as denotative as the markers measuring their extension. Enumeration proposes to express the inexpressible; and, although it relies on only one scheme—enumeration—it is, like storytelling itself, syntactic by nature.

In enumeration, the discontinuity of the actual text seems to be endowed with the prestige of representing an absent, still greater text. Similarly, in *Discusión* and *Other Inquisitions,* Borges suggests that, far from denying the figure of Whitman, all the information about the poet's persona scattered throughout Whitman's work confirms his mythic stature. A comparable mechanism controls the lists of

irreconcilable or merely dissimilar unities that dizzyingly sketch the infinite in such stories as **"The Aleph," "The Zahir," "The God's Script,"** and even in the comparatively brief list of incarnations in **"The Immortal."**

By 1935, Borges's enumerations in *Universal History of Infamy* reveal how they function as concealed illusionism: they display properties of narrative usually disguised in the very act of being employed. The most famous example is the list of effects brought about by the fickle piety of Fray Bartolomé de las Casas in **"The Terrible Redeemer Lazarus Morell."** The terms in these enumerations—or the arguments united in a discourse—appear separated by what really connects them, as if by an electrical current: incongruity, paradox, simple otherness. At the same time, the enumerative combination as a whole registers the ironic richness of these minor clashes. Outside the circuit of conflict and ellipsis, these separate elements would lapse into the inertia of a historic or fictitious report uncharged by narrative.

It is no accident that, beginning with its title, an early Borges essay joins "narrative art" and "magic." His first fictions perform a kind of illusion: that *post hoc, ergo propter hoc,* an error in logic whose systematic cultivation, for Barthes, is the narrative operation par excellence, "the language of Fate." (Valéry also considered that associating the novelistic or even the fantastic world with reality was of the same order as associating trompe l'oeil with the tangible objects among which the viewer moves.) And what is that language of Fate if not an idea of montage? Cinematographic or verbal montage, which, in the chaotic archive of mankind's acts, proposes or discovers a meaning by ordering those "culminating moments" and "major scenes" in which Stevenson saw the proof and effect of the highest fiction? Stevensonsaw it as operating on different levels of fiction and nonfiction, of history and fantasy. Its name, quite simply, is narrative.

Borges on *King Kong*:

A monkey fourteen meters high (some of his fans say fifteen) is obviously charming, but perhaps that is not enough. This monkey is not full of juice; he is a dried out and dusty contraption with angular, clumsy movements. His only virtue—his height—seems not to have greatly impressed the photographer, who persists in not shooting him from below but from above, a plainly mistaken angle that invalidates and annuls his tallness. It should be added that he is hunchbacked and bowlegged, features that also shorten him. To ensure that there is nothing extraordinary about him, they make him fight monsters far stranger than he and find him lodgings in fake caverns the size of a cathedral, where his hard-won stature is lost. A carnal or romantic love for Miss Fay Wray brings to perfection the ruin of this gorilla and of the film as well.

Jorge Luis Borges, in Borges In/And/On Film, *edited by Edgardo Cozarinsky, 1988.*

Edgardo Cozarinsky, in his Borges In/and/on Film, *translated by Gloria Waldman and Ronald Christ, Lumen Books, 1988, 117 p.*

Jorge Luis Borges with Roberto Alifano (interview date 1981-1983)

[*In the following interview, Borges addresses a number of his favorite themes—labyrinths, tigers, books—and talks about his short story "Funes the Memorious."*]

[*Alifano*]: *Borges, I would like to talk with you about two images which seem to obsess you and which you repeat throughout your work. I am referring to labyrinths and to the figure of the tiger. I suggest we start with the former. How did labyrinths enter your literary work; what fascinates you about them?*

[Borges]: Well, I discovered the labyrinth in a book published in France by Garnier that my father had in his library. The book had a very odd engraving that took a whole page and showed a building that resembled an amphitheater. I remember that it had cracks and seemed tall, taller than the cypresses and the men that stood around it. My eyesight was not perfect—I was very myopic—but I thought that if I used a magnifying glass, I would be able to see a minotaur within the building. That labyrinth was, besides, a symbol of bewilderment, a symbol of being lost in life. I believe that all of us, at one time or another, have felt that we are lost, and I saw in the labyrinth the symbol of that condition. Since then, I have held that vision of the labyrinth.

Borges, what has always intrigued me about labyrinths is not that people get lost within them, but rather that they are constructions intentionally made to confound us. Don't you think that this concept is odd?

Yes, it is a very odd idea, the idea of envisioning a builder of labyrinths, the idea of an architect of labyrinths is indeed odd. It is the idea of the father of Icarus, Daedalus, who was the first builder of a labyrinth—the labyrinth of Crete. There is also Joyce's conception, if we are looking for a more literary figure. I have always been puzzled by the labyrinth. It is a very strange idea, an idea which has never left me.

Various forms of labyrinths appear in your stories. Labyrinths placed in time, like the one of **"The Garden of Forking Paths,"** *where you tell about a lost labyrinth.*

Ah, yes, I do speak of a lost labyrinth in it. Now, a lost labyrinth seems to me to be something magical, and it is because a labyrinth is a place where one loses oneself, a place (in my story) that in turn is lost in time. The idea of a labyrinth which disappears, of a lost labyrinth, is twice as magical. That story is a tale which I imagined to be multiplied or forked in various directions. In that story the reader is presented with all the events leading to the execution of a crime whose intention the reader does not understand. I dedicated that story to Victoria Ocampo . . .

Do you conceive the image of losing ourselves in a labyrinth as a pessimistic view of the future of mankind?

No, I don't. I believe that in the idea of the labyrinth there is also hope, or salvation; if we were positively sure the universe is a labyrinth, we would feel secure. But it may not be a labyrinth. In the labyrinth there is a center: that terrible center is the minotaur. However, we don't know if the universe has a center; perhaps it doesn't. Consequently, it is probable that the universe is not a labyrinth but simply chaos, and if that is so, we are indeed lost.

When I was a child I used to stop for a long time in front of the tiger's cage to see him pacing back and forth. Now that I am blind, one single color remains for me, and it is precisely the color of the tiger, the color yellow.

—Jorge Luis Borges

Yes, if it didn't have a center, it wouldn't be a cosmos but chaos. Do you believe that the universe may have a secret center?

I don't see why not. It is easy to conceive that it has a center, one that can be terrible, or demonic, or divine. I believe that if we think in those terms unconsciously we are thinking of the labyrinth. That is, if we believe there is a center, somehow we are saved. If that center exists, life is coherent. There are events which surely lead us to think that the universe is a coherent structure. Think, for example, of the rotation of the planets, the seasons of the year, the different stages in our lives. All that leads us to believe that there is a labyrinth, that there is an order, that there is a secret center of the universe, as you have suggested, that there is a great architect who conceived it. But it also leads us to think that it may be irrational, that logic cannot be applied to it, that the universe is unexplainable to us, to mankind—and *that* in itself is a terrifying idea.

All those aspects of the labyrinth fascinated you then?

Yes, all of them. But I have also been attracted by the very word *labyrinth,* which is a beautiful word. It derives from the Greek *labyrinthos,* which initially denoted the shafts and corridors of a mine and that now denotes that strange construction especially built so that people would get lost. Now the English word *maze* is not as enchanting or powerful as the Spanish word *laberinto.* Maze also denotes a dance, in which the dancers weave a sort of labyrinth in space and time. Then we find *amazement, to be amazed, to be unamazed,* but I believe that *labyrinth* is the essential word, and it is the one I am drawn to.

Let's go on to the other image: the image of the tiger. Why do you, in choosing an animal, usually choose the image of the tiger?

Chesterton said that the tiger was a symbol of terrible elegance. What a lovely phrase, don't you think so? The tiger's terrible elegance. . . . Well, when I was a child and was taken to the zoo, I used to stop for a long time in front of the tiger's cage to see him pacing back and forth. I liked his natural beauty, his black stripes and his golden stripes. And now that I am blind, one single color remains for me, and it is precisely the color of the tiger, the color yellow. For me, things may be red, they may be blue; the blues may be green, etc., but the yellow is the only color that I see. That is why, since it is the color I see most clearly, I have used it many times and I have associated it with the tiger.

You must have derived from that the title of one of your books of poems, The Gold of the Tigers. *Am I right?*

Yes, that is right. And in the last poem of that book, which has the same title as the book, I speak of the tiger and the color yellow.

> Until the hour of yellow dusk
> How often I looked
> At the mighty tiger of Bengal
> Coming and going in his set path
> Behind the iron bars,
> Unsuspecting they were his jail.
> Later, other tigers came to me,
> Blake's burning tyger;
> Then, other golds came to me,
> Zeus's golden and loving metal,
> The ring that after nine nights
> Gives birth to nine new rings and these, to nine
>   more,
> In endless repetition.
> As the years passed
> The other colors left me
> And now I am left with
> The faint light, the inextricable shadow
> And the gold of my beginnings.
> Oh dusks, tigers, radiance
> Out of myths and epics.
> Oh and even a more desired gold, your hair
> That my hands long to hold.

. . . .

Borges, I am interested to know the circumstances that led you to write that wonderful story, "Funes the Memorious." *Could we talk about that strange character who compensates for his deficiencies with his extraordinary memory. Is it true that it relates to a period of insomnia you suffered?*

Yes, it is true. And I can remember in great detail the circumstances under which I wrote that story. During a time that I had to spend in a hotel, throughout the day I feared the coming of night, because I knew that it was going to be a night of insomnia, that each time I dozed my sleep would be interrupted by atrocious nightmares. I knew that hotel very well; I had lived there as a child. The building has already disappeared; its architecture was full of all the images of the labyrinth. I remember the many patios, the corridors, the statues, the gate, the vast deserted halls, the huge main door, the other entrance doors, the carriage house, the eucalyptus trees, and even a small labyrinth built there. And I particularly remember a clock that punctuated my insomnia, for it inexorably struck every hour: the half hour, the quarter hour and the full hour. So I had no way of deceiving myself. The clock acted as a witness with its metallic ticktock.

I remember that I used to lie down and try to forget everything, and that led me, inevitably, to recall everything. I imagined the books on the shelves, the clothes on the chair, and even my own body on the bed; every detail of my body, the exact position in which my body lay. And so, since I could not erase memory, I kept thinking of those things, and also thinking: if only I could forget, I would certainly be able to sleep. Then I would recall the belief that when one sleeps, one becomes everyone, or, better said, one is no one, or if one is oneself, one sees oneself in the third person. One is, as Addison said, the actual theater, the spectators, the actors, the author of the drama, the stage—everything simultaneously.

Forgetfulness would have been a way to free yourself and to fall asleep?

Yes. But my insomnia prevented that, and I kept on thinking: continuously imagining the hotel, thinking of my body and of things beyond my body and the hotel. I would think of the adjoining streets, of the street leading to the train station, of the neighboring houses, of the tobacco shop. . . . Later I reached this conclusion: it is fortunate my memory is fallible, fortunate my memory is not infinite. How terrifying it would be if my memory were infinite! It would undoubtedly be monstrous! In that case I would remember every detail of every day of my life, which of course amounts to thousands—as Joyce showed in *Ulysses.* Each day countless things happen, but fortunately we forget them, and furthermore, many of them are repetitions. And so, from that situation I derived the notion of a person who no longer embodied the traditional definition of human faculties (that is, memory and will)— an individual who possessed only memory. Thus, I came upon the idea of that unfortunate country boy, and this was the birth of the story **"Funes the Memorious."**

One of the most admirable parables on insomnia ever written.

Well, I don't fully agree with your judgment, but there it is! Now, I will reveal something to you that perhaps would be interesting to psychologists. It is strange that after having written that story—after having described that horrible perfection of memory, which ends up destroying its possessor—the insomnia which had distressed me so much disappeared.

So that the completion of that fantastic tale had a therapeutic effect on you. There are many people who assert that that story is autobiographical; it certainly is, since it is sort of an elaboration of a mental state of yours. Do you agree?

Yes. All I did was to write down "Funes" instead of "Borges." I have omitted some aspects of myself and, obviously, I have added others that I don't possess. For example, Funes, the country boy, could not have written the story; I, on the other hand, have been able to write it and to forget Funes and also—though not always—that unpleasant insomnia. Now, I believe that that story is powerful because the reader feels that it is not simply a fantasy, but rather that I am relating something that can happen to him or her, and that happened to me when I wrote it. The entire story comes to be a sort of metaphor, or as you pointed out, a parable of insomnia.

the story of a very simple and unfortunate character killed at an early age by insomnia.

. . . . .

There is a theme I would like us to speak about: the theme of books. I know that it is one of your obsessions. I would be interested to hear your opinions on the subject.

Well, last night, in fact, I had a very strange dream. I dreamed of the burning of a great library—which I believe may have been the library of Alexandria—with its count- less volumes attacked by flames. Do you believe this dream may have some meaning?

Perhaps, Borges. Could it be that you owe your readers a book on the history of the book? Have you ever thought of writing such a book?

Dear me, no! But it is an excellent idea. It would be won- derful to write a history of the book. I'll keep it in mind; although I don't know if an eighty-three-year-old man can set such a project for himself. I don't know if I am quali- fied, and to be qualified for such a task is no easy matter; but, in any case, that work should not be approached merely as a physical labor. I, for one, am not much inter- ested in the physical nature of books; particularly in bibli- ographical books, which are generally excessively long. I am interested in the various appreciations a book has re- ceived. However, I now remember that Spengler, in his *Decline of the West*, predates my attempt, for in it he writes remarkable comments on books.

Well, you have also written some remarkable commentary on books. I remember the essay "El culto de los libros" (The Cult of Books) in your book Otras inquisiciones (Other Inquisitions), where you synthesize much of your opinions on the subject; and I also remember a poem enti- tled "Alexandria, 641 A.D.," which refers precisely to the library of Alexandria and to the caliph Omar, who burned it.

Ah, yes, in that poem I conceived the notion of having the caliph express things which most likely he never did; for he was a caliph, and a caliph would not have expressed himself thus. But, thank God, poetry (generally all litera- ture) allows such a thing, and so why couldn't we imagine the caliph speaking. He imagines that the library of Alex- andria is the memory of the world; in the vast library of Alexandria everything is found. And then Omar orders the library burned, but he thinks that is unimportant, and says: "Si de todos / No quedara uno solo, volverìan / A engendrar cada hoja y cada lìnea, / Cada trabajo y cada amor de Hércules, / Cada lección de cada manuscrito." (If of all these books / None remained, men would, once again, / Engender each page, each line, / All labor and all of Hercules's love, / Each reading of each manuscript.) In other words, if all the past is in the library, the entire past came from the imagination of men. That is why I believe that beyond its rhetorical virtue, if a work truly possesses it, each generation rewrites anew the books of earlier gen- erations. The differences are found in the cadence, in the syntax, in the form; but we are always repeating the same fables and rediscovering the same metaphors. So that, in

One notes, moreover, a definite concreteness throughout the story. That is, the character is placed in a specific location and his drama unfolds there.

I believe that I succeeded in making **"Funes the Memor- ious"** a concrete story. Yes, it does take place in a specific location; that location is Fray Bentos in Uruguay. When I was a child, I spent some time there, in the home of one of my uncles; so I do have childhood memories of the place. Then I chose a very simple character, a simple country boy. As I had to justify his condition in some way, I described a fall from a horse. Really, there are a number of little novelistic inventions that do not harm anyone. Fi- nally, I entitled the story **"Funes el memorioso"**; a title that suits the story.

Borges, in English, "Funes the Memorious" must sound odd since the word "memorious" does not exist.

True, that word does not exist in English, and it does give the story a grotesque character, an extravagant character. On the other hand, in Spanish—although I don't know if anyone has used the word *"memorioso"*—if one heard a man from the country say: *"Fulano es muy memorioso"* (that fellow is very memorious), one would certainly un- derstand him. So that, as I said, I think that the original title goes well with the story. Now, if one seeks an equiva- lent in another language, for example in French, by using the word *"memorié"* or some other similar word, the read- er is led to see it as a mental state. Thus this title evokes some respects, I concur with the caliph Omar—not the historical one, but the caliph I sketched in my poem.

Nowadays, you must have noticed it, there is a cult of books; a cult which the ancients didn't have. What are the reasons for it, Borges?

I believe there are two reasons. First, that all the great masters of mankind, curiously, have been oral; and second, that the ancients saw in the book a substitute for the oral word. I recall a phrase which is often quoted: *"Scripta manent verba volant"* (The written word stays, the spoken word flies). That phrase doesn't mean that the spoken word is ephemeral, but rather that the written word is something lasting and dead. The spoken word, it seems to me now, is somewhat winged and light—"something winged, light and sacred," Plato said in defining poetry. I think that we can apply that concept to the spoken word.

But let's recall another case. The case of Pythagoras, who never wrote so as not to tie himself to the written word, surely because he felt that writing kills and the spoken word fills with life. That is why Aristotle never speaks of Pythagoras but of the Pythagoreans. Pythagoras wished that beyond his physical death his disciples would keep his thoughts alive. Later came that often-quoted Latin phrase: *"Magister dixit"* (The master has said). Which does not mean that the Master has imposed his opinions on his disciples; it means that the disciples continue to expound on the ideas, but if someone opposes them, they invoke: "the Master has said." That phrase is a sort of formula to find reaffirmation and thus to continue professing the ideas of the Master. Speaking of the Pythagoreans, Aristotle tells us that they professed a belief in the dogma of the eternal recurrence, which, somewhat belatedly, Nietzsche would discover.

That idea of the eternal recurrence or of cyclical time was refuted by Saint Augustine in his City of God, *do you remember it?*

Yes. Saint Augustine says, in a beautiful metaphor, that the Cross of Christ saves us from the circular labyrinth of the Stoics. That idea of cyclical time was also touched upon by Hume, Blanqui and others.

In one of your essays you quote the words of Bernard Shaw. When asked if he truly believed that the Holy Spirit had written the Bible, Shaw answered: "Every book worth being reread has been written by the spirit."

Ah, yes. I completely concur with that notion, since a book goes beyond its author's intention. *Don Quixote,* for example, is more than a simple chivalric novel or the satire of a genre. It is an absolute text totally unaffected by chance. The author's intention is a meager human thing, a fallible thing. In a book—in every book—there is a need for something more, which is always mysterious. When we read an ancient book, it is as though we were reading all time that has passed from the day it was written to our present day. A book can be full of errors, we can reject its author's opinions, disagree with him or her, but the book always retains something sacred, something mortal, something magical which brings happiness. In opposition to Macedonio Fernández, who asserted that beauty was

something exclusive or given to certain chosen people, I believe that beauty can be found in all things. It would be very strange, for example, if in a book by a Thai poet (I have no knowledge of that country's literature) we could not find a line of poetry that astounds us.

Borges, you have also asserted that books grow with time, and that the readers themselves modify them and enrich them.

Certainly. Books are altered by their readers. For example, the gaucho epic, *Martín Fierro,* that we read now is not the same one written by its author, José Hernández, but rather the one read by Leopoldo Lugones, who undoubtedly enriched it. Similarly, in regard to *Don Quixote* or *Hamlet; Hamlet* is also the play that Goethe and Coleridge and Bradley read and interpreted. That is why I feel it is useful that we should maintain a cult of books, since books are a living thing in constant growth.

> I pretend that I am not blind, I still buy books. Perhaps this may seen somewhat pathetic, but it is not so. It is something genuine, something sincere and truthful. I feel the friendly gravitational force of the book.
>
> —Jorge Luis Borges

In certain ways you profess that cult of books, isn't that so, Borges?

Yes, I do. I will tell you a secret. I still continue pretending that I am not blind, I still buy books—you know that very well, I still go on filling my house with books. I feel the friendly gravitational force of the book. I don't exactly know why I believe that a book brings to us a possibility of happiness. A few months ago I was given a marvelous edition of the *Brockhaus Encyclopedia;* and the presence of twenty volumes with beautiful maps and engravings, printed in, I am sure, a no less beautiful Gothic type—that I cannot read—filled me with joy. Those books, almost sacred to me, were there, and I felt their pleasant companionship. Well, I do have a cult of books, I admit it; perhaps this may seem somewhat pathetic, but it is not so. It is something genuine, something sincere and truthful.

Borges, there are people who speak of the disappearance of books, and they assert that modern developments in communications will replace them with something more dynamic that will require less time than reading. What do you think of that?

I believe that books will never disappear. It is impossible that that will happen. Among the many inventions of man, the book, without a doubt, is the most astounding: all the others are extensions of our bodies. The telephone, for example, is the extension of our voice; the telescope and the microscope are extensions of our sight; the sword and the plow are extensions of our arms. Only the book is an extension of our imagination and memory.

What you have just said brings to mind that Bernard Shaw, in Caesar and Cleopatra, *refers to the library of Alexandria as the memory of mankind.*

Yes, I remember that also. And besides being the memory of mankind, it is also its imagination and, why not, its dreams, since it is absurd to suppose that only the waking moments of men engendered the countless pages of countless books.

Well, you state in a memorable passage that literature is a dream.

It is true. Literature is a dream, a controlled dream. Now, I believe that we owe literature almost everything we are and what we have been, also what we will be. Our past is nothing but a sequence of dreams. What difference can there be between dreaming and remembering the past? Books are the great memory of all centuries. Their function, therefore, is irreplaceable. If books disappear, surely history would disappear, and man would also disappear.

Jorge Luis Borges and Roberto Alifano, in an interview in Twenty-Four Conversations with Borges, Including a Selection of Poems: Interviews by Roberto Alifano, 1981-1983, *Lascaux Publishers, 1984, 157 p.*

James Neilson   (essay date June-July 1982)

[*In the following essay, Neilson discusses Borges's significance as an international literary figure, assessing the strengths and weaknesses of his work as well as his relationship with Argentine and Latin American culture.*]

> "*Don Quixote*", Menard told me, "was above all else an entertaining book: but now it has become an occasion for patriotic toasts, for grammatical insolence, for obscene de luxe editions. Glory is a form of incomprehension and it is perhaps the very worst."
>
> **"Pierre Menard, Author of the Quixote"**

When Jorge Luis Borges wrote that, in the early 1940s, he was already known in Argentina as a poet fond of peculiar metaphors, a fierce literary polemicist, and the author of some strange short stories that looked like essays but were, despite the academic apparatus seemingly embedded in them, exercises in fantasy. He was not considered a likely candidate for "glory." True, as early as 1933 Drieu La Rochelle had reported after a trip to Buenos Aires that *"Borges vaut le voyage."* But, this and other omens notwithstanding, Borges was still the private passion of a few, most of whom knew him personally. And even they did not, for the most part, take him very seriously. Although he was obviously, ostentatiously, clever and sensitive, he struck most of his readers then as a literary prankster whose main ambition was to concoct complicated jokes in order to discomfit Argentina's solemn academic community. He seemed too wayward to be considered a "significant" writer. The idea that he, of all the many talented individuals then writing in Argentina, would acquire worldwide fame would have seemed as absurd as any of his own metaphysical propositions.

It was not until 1961, when Borges had already written most of the books he is now so well known for (*A Universal History of Infamy,* 1935; *A History of Eternity,* 1936; *Labyrinths* 1944; *The Aleph and Other Stories,* 1949; *Other Inquisitions,* 1952; and *Dreamtigers,* 1960) that his reputation overflowed Buenos Aires and penetrated into every city in the Western world. That year Borges, who was already a sexagenarian, shared the Prix Formentor with Samuel Beckett and, with astonishing speed, became the centre of a cult whose adepts were especially numerous in the academic institutions whose practices he had gently mocked. The works that he wrote after being "discovered" are, by general agreement, inferior to those he wrote when he still belonged to Buenos Aires. But, although his powers progressively waned, his fame has not yet ceased to grow. Borgesian studies, once the preserve of a handful of devotees in communication with the master, have expanded into a sizable industry. And, inevitably, imitators soon began to appear, busying themselves with turning out enigmatic tales concerning labyrinths, mirrors, tigers, résumés of non-existent treatises, and all the other features of the Borgesian universe.

Borges himself, alarmed by this horde of intruders looting his private world, abandoned it and took refuge in Argentina's past or in Anglo-Saxon verse and Icelandic sagas, where few of his admirers have been brash enough to follow him. "I've grown so tired of labyrinths and mirrors and tigers and all that sort of thing, especially when others use them", he explained to the Argentine writer César Fernández Moreno. "That's the advantage of imitators. They cure you: so many people are doing what I did that it is no longer necessary for me to do it myself."

The enthusiasm of the world-wide Borgesian fraternity may be irksome to Borges, but its activities are unobtrusive when compared to those of his compatriots after they realised that they had an internationally acclaimed literary master in their midst. In Argentina Borges has become, like Cervantes' great *boutade* in Spain, an excuse for innumerable patriotic toasts. Last year he even suffered the indignity of being described (by a general, no less) as a "national monument"—a curious tribute to a despiser of statuary who professes to regard the nation-state as an anachronism and has fought a lifelong guerrilla campaign against nationalists. None the less, he is regularly raised aloft like a martial trophy by Argentines who rarely read any books but who are infuriated by the Swedish Academy's refusal to give their man the Nobel Prize. "Obscene de luxe editions" of his works have also appeared, as though to complete the humiliation he presaged. "Glory", in fact, has taken possession of him. His personal life today is a triumphal progress from city to city as an "ambassador of Argentine culture" on whom are bestowed a succession of literary awards (some of them enviably generous), honorary degrees, and "homages", banquets at which he is obliged to listen to well-meaning but, like the general's remark, often pompous praise.

These traditional tokens of the world's esteem for a recognised creator grown very old would, one might think, have been quite enough for a man who had spent most of his life in deliberate obscurity. But our age has devised additional indignities for men of great achievement and, in Argentina at any rate, Borges has become a media celebrity who rubs shoulders in the popular imagination with starlets, singers, soccer players and politicians. His impassive face, now and then illumined by a weary smile, gazes from television screens and the shiny pages of magazines with disconcerting frequency. Interviews with him, descriptions of him, and foreigners' articles about him—often abbreviated and sometimes oddly similar to the pastiches he once wrote—fill columns of daily, weekly, and monthly publications that range from the serious to the salaciously trivial. Some of the interviews are so extensive that they are issued as special supplements. In them are chronicled Borges's opinions about anything that may be of urgent interest to his fellow Argentines if not to Borges himself: American foreign policy, the military régime's treatment of dissidents, the state of the Argentine peso.

The creation *ex nihilo,* as it were, of a revered sage by the world's collective imagination could easily have been a story by Borges:

> I am not, either. I dreamed the world the way
> you dreamed your work, my Shakespeare: one
> of the forms of my dream was you, who, like me,
> are many and no one.
>
> ["Everything and Nothing"]

Borges is, after all, more acutely aware than most people of the whimsical relationship between a man's public reputation and his private self, or what he assumes, out of habit, is his private self. The writer, Borges believes, is created by the reader out of the materials that happen to be available, and he has always argued that reading is just as creative as writing. Many of the people who regard him with awe have not, moreover, read more than a few words of what he has written: their belief that he is important owes everything to the admiration of others who have. But in the Borgesian universe misunderstanding is an aspect of human consciousness and a basic premise of most thought. Reality is an act of faith. What better illustration of this than the metamorphosis of a secretive practitioner of minor genres into one of the best-known writers on earth, a member of that small and inscrutably selected company of men who, like Ernest Hemingway and Jean-Paul Sartre, come to mean something (although exactly what is not always easy to tell) to millions of people who usually treat literature with robust disdain?

Ever since attaining the rank of "celebrity" Borges has insisted that he is bewildered by all the attentions that are paid him. This is in part, no doubt, a calculated stance: extravagant humility about the value of his work is an important facet of his "image." Thanks to it he can enjoy, as he manifestly does enjoy, being lionised by people who often know nothing about what he has written while laughing to himself at such a preposterous situation. He is, in his way, keeping his options open, preparing himself for oblivion or glory by affecting to be indifferent to either. It is an engaging approach that has, needless to say, contributed to his fame. But it is not simply a social pose adopted for a new situation. Scepticism about the value of what he has written lies at the heart of his literary method.

Borges treats his work as though it were a long (but not very long: his *Collected Works,* published by Emecé Editores in 1974, contain little more than a thousand pages) novel. Its central character—its sole character—is Jorge Luis Borges, a figment only the innocent will confuse with the retiring, affable gentleman to be found walking along a street in Buenos Aires, delivering a lecture to furclad ladies, receiving a substantial literary prize or giving an interview. In an epilogue to this edition, Borges donned the mask of a Chilean literary historian writing a century later:

> The renown Borges enjoyed during his life, documented by a heap of monographs and controversies, can only astonish us today. It is attested that nobody was more astonished than Borges himself and that he always feared he would be declared a fraud or a botcher or a singular mixture of the two.

Borges, of course, is no fraud. How could he be? It is not as though he has ever claimed that his work had any special significance: if others choose to think it is of overwhelming importance, that is their business. If George Steiner, for example, pronounces **"Pierre Menard, Author of the Quixote"** "one of the sheer wonders of human contrivance", a "spare fable" in which "the several facets of Borges's shy genius are almost wholly crystallised", who is Borges to object? And if Vladimir Nabokov complains (about a writer called Osberg): "At first Véra and I were delighted by reading him. We felt we were on a portico, but we have learned there was no house", that is equally satisfactory. Has Borges ever pretended that there was a house attached to his finely-wrought portico?

> **Certainly, there can be few other writers
> of comparable stature who have so
> consistently excluded the principal
> preoccupations of their age from their
> work.**
>
> **—James Neilson**

Borges is no botcher, either. He has always been a most careful craftsman, making version after version of his stories, essays, and poems, and sending them to the printer with notable reluctance: he once suggested that if it were not for the importunity of publishers he would never finish anything. And when he writes he weighs the words he uses, fingering them for hours before deciding whether to use or discard them. He has always worried about form. For all his ritualistic modesty, he is a very serious and deliberate writer indeed.

His technical skill, his intelligence, his imaginativeness, cannot be doubted. His work—he characteristically refuses to call it an *oeuvre*—is all well-made. Much of it is brilliant. And it is unique: no other writer in our civilisation has ever produced anything like it. But he does present a problem. For all his ingenuity, is his work not too outlandish, too arbitrary, too narrow to bear the huge edifice of his reputation? Is he anything more than an inventor of novelties? The containers he has devised are undeniably intriguing, but are their contents worth taking seriously? They probably are, although not quite so seriously as some Borgesians would have it; but before the arguments for the defence are put forward it is useful to consider Borges's extraordinary limitations. Certainly, there can be few other writers of comparable stature who have so consistently excluded the principal preoccupations of their age from their work.

His disregard for conventional genres is striking enough: Borges has written no novels, no dramas, no "major" poems, no long biographical or critical works, no philosophical treatises. He has also, and this is even more remarkable, loftily ignored almost all the themes that, taken together, are the very stuff of modern literature. He has told us almost nothing about sexual relationships, social mores, political ideologies, or the texture of "real life." He has shown no interest in nature: his settings are as bleak and airless as a painting by de Chirico. He has also refused to recognise the individual personality: not one of his "characters", Borges apart, comes near to possessing an autonomous existence, and he has made no effort at all to satisfy this frequent demand on creative artists. Borges, in other words, seems to belong to an as yet unknown literary tradition that is quite different from the one we are familiar with and in which most of us live our intellectual lives.

This would have been easily understandable had Borges been a "primitive", driven to originality by his ignorance. But Borges is anything but a "primitive" in this sense: he is as aware of, and as knowledgeable about, a dozen literary traditions as any man of his generation. Nevertheless, he has chosen to overlook most of what has been written since his childhood in Europe or America. Although he is familiar with Joyce and Proust, Kafka and Virginia Woolf (whom he translated), he has always been most affected by the authors whose books lined the shelves of his father's substantial private library: Browne, De Quincey, Coleridge, Spencer, Shaw, Wells, Kipling, Stevenson, Chesterton, and the scholars who wrote articles for the *Encyclopaedia Britannica,* the source of much of his notorious erudition. And it is to them that he most often returns.

His father, Jorge Borges, was a professor of English, and English was the first language the young Jorge Luis learned to read. Jorge Borges was clearly an unusual paterfamilias for his time: he let his son read whatever he liked, untroubled by the thought that it might be "too old" for him. So in addition to tackling weighty tomes that would test most university graduates, young Borges was also permitted to read Sir Richard Burton's "pornographic" translation of the *Arabian Nights,* which he did with enormous pleasure, skipping over the dull and incomprehensible erotic passages to get to the magical episodes that fascinated him. These adventures apart, it was a safe, comfortable household, made disturbing only by its many mirrors. Borges looked into them with horror; could it be that only he existed? That was the origin of one of his favourite images. There, too, it occurred to him that the universe

might well be a vast library with all knowledge available to the person who knew just where to look. And he was still a small child when the tiger, leaping out at him from some volume about travels in India, became his favourite symbol for destruction, for time.

The labyrinth, perhaps the most famous of all the Borgesian metaphors, came to him much later. But perhaps it was germinating then too: certainly Buenos Aires, huge, recently contrived, and strangely repetitive with many streets almost replicas of others, seems more labyrinthine than most other cities. While still a child, moreover, he heard tales about the swaggering cut-throats, murderously and sometimes suicidally devoted to their own punctilious code, who lurked nearby. The bookish boy—and the unworldly man—rarely came into contact with them, so in his imagination they became epic heroes, elemental and wild like the heroes of the Norse sagas.

Most important of all for him, it was in his parents' house that he developed his interest in metaphysical speculation as a game, at once serious and unserious. This concern—which is as common among bright schoolboys as admiration for gangsters—was encouraged by a frequent visitor, Macedonio Fernández, a great talker whose witty paradoxes and curious fancies had a considerable influence on Argentine literature but who, unfortunately, was an indifferent writer.

It is not unusual for a writer's work to take an embryonic shape during his childhood. But few writers can have added so little afterwards as Borges. His later experiences, such as an adolescence spent in Europe (mainly Switzerland where the Borges family were trapped by the Great War, and Spain, where Borges, then a young man, found many congenial literary companions), contributed relatively little. He added two more writers, Whitman and Schopenhauer, to his mentors while in Geneva. The many others he read did not make any enduring impression. For Borges, to many the most "modern" of writers, 20th-century literature has not been very important. His intellectual background is the 19th century. This helps account for the peculiar flavour of so much of his work. In the 19th century, scholarship was less specialised and more speculative than it is today. It was closer to literature. And when it concerned the civilisations of Asia it had something of the air of a voyage of discovery through strange lands.

Borges's father was blind for some time before he died in 1938, and in several early poems Borges seems to sense that he too would go blind one day. At Christmas in the year his father died Borges struck his head on a window frame while climbing up a dark stairway. Complications ensued and he almost died. But, although he became healthy again—and he remains a remarkably healthy man—his sight began to fail, until by his sixties he was unable to read at all, even with the aid of a magnifying glass. For many decades, therefore, he has had to rely on a succession of friends and acquaintances willing to read to him and write for him. This naturally affected his work and he has written almost as much in collaboration with others, notably his lifelong friend Adolfo Bioy Casares, as he has by himself. But the effect was, in so far as can be judged, rather less than might have been expected. His blindness, the "luminous haze" in which he was condemned to live most of his life, pushed him further back into himself, away from the surrounding world, but it did not lead to any drastic change of direction. The stories he had written before 1938 were disembodied: the ones he wrote later are ethereal. His already claustrophobic universe became even more closed in. The walls surrounding him were made higher. But he had already started to build them.

Borges's fame has little to do with his verse, striking as some of it is. And it does not owe much to his stories about his martial ancestors, gauchos, and knifefighters from the less reputable suburbs of Buenos Aires. Like most of his essays, biographical or exegetical, about other writers, they are widely read because they are by Borges and not because they are irresistibly interesting themselves. His reputation rests mainly on his "fictions"—short stories, some little more than a paragraph in length, that often masquerade as scholarly essays and concern ideas rather than people—and on his genuine essays dealing with such familiar topics as Zeno's paradox of Achilles and the Tortoise; the implications of infinity (if every possible combination of letters were written down and stored in an infinite library, would not all knowledge, past, present, and future, be contained in it?) and the Eternal Recurrence; the nature of time; of death; of reality. Some of these essays, moreover, consist of quotations from other writers to which Borges has appended some cursory comments.

His preferred themes, then, are those that have troubled many thoughtful people in many places for thousands of years. They are the commonplaces of speculative philosophy. But, since the decline of religious fervour among the educated in our civilisation, most Westerners have dismissed the questions they raise—questions which have never been solved—as unanswerable, and therefore barely worth asking, by the time they reached their middle twenties, returning to them later rarely unless they were drunk, seriously ill, or overcome by a religious experience. In some Eastern societies, however, they have continued to be taken quite seriously, and respectable men can devote their lives to pondering them without fear of being regarded as excessively odd: one of the main objections to "Western materialism" in these countries is our refusal to let ultimate questions preoccupy us. It is therefore no coincidence that Borges's rise to his present position in the intellectual world has occurred at a time when many Westerners, disillusioned with their civilisation and dissatisfied with the tacit agreement to overlook the unproven nature of the axioms on which it is based, have begun to treat "the wisdom of the East" with more deference than was once the case.

Of course, Borges is not the first Western writer to decline to take anything for granted. Bishop Berkeley was as solipsistic as Borges, and Borges acknowledges his debt to him. Among the Romantics a refusal to accept without question the facile distinction habitually made between illusion and reality was something of a stock-in-trade. Western cities have always had their fringe communities of occultists, theosophists, and other students of the esoteric to whom most of Borges's assertions would have

seemed perfectly obvious, although their members would have been disconcerted by his manner of presenting them. But Borges differs from his literary predecessors, just as he differs from the intense gentlemen who think they have almost understood the inner workings of the universe as a result of their careful study of the dimensions of the Great Pyramid. He has always kept both his feet planted firmly on the safe terrain of common sense even when his mind has invaded more mystical realms. He has been able to perform this feat thanks to his famous irony, by constantly implying that he does not really believe his own heterodox conclusions: they are the fancies of the writer Borges, who is, after all, merely an invention of Borges.

Significantly, what is perhaps the most quoted paragraph in his entire work is an eloquent, although peculiar, affirmation of what he has spent so much effort rebutting:

> And yet, and yet—To deny temporal succession, to deny the ego, to deny the astronomical universe are apparent desperations and secret assuagements. . . . Time is the substance I am made of. Time is a mirror that carries me away, but I am the river; it is a tiger that tears at me, but I am the tiger; it is a fire that consumes me, but I am the fire. The world, alas, is real; I, alas, am Borges.

For the dedicated Borgesian, convinced that the master had succeeded in "refuting time" yet again, this surrender, mitigated only by "apparent", was surely distressing. But Borges the writer has, for many decades, laboured hard to dam time and thereby to win immortality, and it would not be very difficult for that Borgesian to convince himself that this unseemly dash back to orthodoxy was just an artful decoy placed to mislead pursuers: the real Borges, in so far as one can be said to exist, could make good his escape.

For American academics Borges is a copious source of thesis-fodder. For young people unafraid of literature he is a teacher and guide who takes seriously the philosophical problems they feel are more urgent than their placid elders care to appreciate.

—James Neilson

Everyone has his own Borges, taking from him what he wants for his own purposes, and discarding the rest. For most Argentines he is a totem and an entertainer. For some he is the teller of oddly abstract tales set in almost mythical periods of their national past, a celebrator of military achievements by their compatriots during and after the Wars of Independence, a poet of their streets and patios, a defender of their native idiom against the pedants who would subject them to the linguistic hegemony of Castile. What is probably his most savage essay is not directed against Adolf Hitler or his Argentine admirers, but against an unfortunate Spaniard, Dr Américo Castro, who dared to suggest that Platine Spanish had become corrupt.

For such Latin American writers as Octavio Paz and Gabriel Garcia Márquez, Borges is the genius who stripped away ornate Hispanic rhetoric from their written language, providing them with an instrument as fine as French and almost as flexible as English, and who freed them from the obligation to compile "realistic" committed novels about their own societies. Since Borges showed them that fantasy was respectable, few serious Latin American writers have looked back: for the last twenty years fantasy has been the predominant mode and it is the principal characteristic of most translated Latin American works. Here and there adherents of slightly more earthbound creeds like Marxism raise their voices in protest, deriding Borges as a cosmopolitan aesthete unconcerned with the very real sufferings of the unprivileged; but as the best-known cultivators of fantasy include such left-wing revolutionaries as Garcia Márquez and Julio Cortázar, their protests are made in vain. Another person who saw Borges as a laughing liberator was François Mauriac, who congratulated Borges for routing the naturalist rearguard in Latin America, and hoped that the same exploit would soon be repeated in France.

For American academics Borges is a copious source of thesis-fodder, the creator of texts that can be analysed in a great many rewarding ways. For young people unafraid of literature he is a teacher and guide who takes seriously, in his fashion, the philosophical problems they feel are more urgent than their placid elders, reconciled to this universe, care to appreciate. He also caters, in a very superior manner, to their appetite for "alternative realities" and unorthodox explanations of man's circumstances, a taste that is more commonly satisfied by H. Rider Haggard, Carlos Castañeda, and the producers of *Raiders of the Lost Ark*. Perhaps a thesis has already been written about the parallels between Borges's work and that of the comic-strip artists: if not, one certainly could be.

For me—and I confess that I probably have more in common with this last category of Borges's admirers than I care to admit—Borges is a writer who has effected a conjunction of Western and Eastern thought. Unlike other writers who have used Eastern settings and have even sought to describe Eastern personalities, but none the less take some basic Western assumptions for granted, Borges, no matter where he places his stories or what names he gives the insubstantial creatures that populate them, implies assumptions that would be banal enough if found in an old Chinese or Japanese tale but are astonishingly novel in a writer so knowingly aware of much Western thought.

Thus Borges's fiction, like some of his essays, has a striking similarity to the writings of Taoist monks and Zen masters. He assumes, for example, that everyday reality is not reality at all and that, at best, it may offer some clues to what lies beneath or beyond. For him, as for them, the perceptible universe is a hopelessly complex riddle, and was probably fashioned the way it is to keep men guessing and encourage some to make a futile attempt to understand it. Like them, he treats linear time as a delusion, a convenience that is a barrier to understanding rather than

a bridge: the theme of time, of the unrenounceable duty to try to foil it, is a stream that runs obsessively through his work, breaking to the surface in most of his fragments. Like the Taoists he is uneasily conscious of the transience of this dreamlike world, and he has sometimes repeated Chuang Tzu:

> I dreamed I was a butterfly flitting from flower to flower. Then I awoke. Am I now a man who dreamed he was a butterfly, or a butterfly who is now dreaming that it is a man?

This alarming possibility was made explicit in one of his best-known stories, **"The Circular Ruins"**, in which an Indian mystic who had tried to create another man "by dreaming him with meticulous integrity" discovered, "with humiliation, with terror", that he was merely the dream of another. Even the individual personality, a concept that is dear to most of us and which is fundamental to our civilisation, is treated by Borges with a disdain worthy of a Taoist monk, in flight from all earthly impediments, as a haphazard assortment of perceptions, forever changing and impossible to grasp. In accordance with this he refuses to accept responsibility for statements made many years ago: *that* Borges was another person.

Borges did not, of course, acquire his point of view after a long sojourn in the East or after any systematic study of Eastern works. He never sat at the feet of any Oriental sage. It came from promptings by such impeccably Western writers as De Quincey, Coleridge, Bishop Berkeley, and Schopenhauer, although Arthur Waley certainly made him more aware than he might have been of the close affinity between his thought and that of the Far East. In the last few years, however, his identification with the East has become increasingly explicit. He is now trying his hand at writing haiku, is working on a book of translations from the Japanese (with the help of a Japanese-speaking collaborator), and recently returned from a five-week visit to Japan. In February, moreover, Borges announced to his fellow countrymen:

> To me Japan seems a superior civilisation. I have the hope that the East will save us because the West is in decline. I am not speaking just of ourselves, but also of the United States—a country I am very fond of, as well—because I believe it is in complete decadence.

Borges's assertion, needless to say, had nothing to do with Japan's remarkable economic achievements. What most impressed him was the large number of people who wrote verse.

Borges's admiration for Japan is unlikely to bring him the trouble his earlier admirations for England and the United States provoked. Argentine self-confidence has collapsed in the last few years: praise of foreign countries, which are tacitly contrasted favourably with one's own, is not the crime it once was. In fact Borges seems, at 82, to be winning his long argument with the nationalists intent on keeping the outside world at bay. When attacked for his "cosmopolitanism", he often responded that an ability to take what is wanted from other countries without discomfort is one of the most valuable characteristics of the Argentine and that nationalism, anyway, was only a vulgar import. Certainly his origins do much to explain why he can hover above both Western and Eastern civilisations with such ease. Argentina may not be, as some would have it, a country with no culture of its own. But its culture is new and eclectic enough to force intelligent Argentines to look abroad as well.

Unlike Englishmen, Frenchmen, and Germans, they cannot immerse themselves in their own traditions entirely: apart from those of the Indians, most of these traditions came from Europe in any case. Only a minority are notably attracted by Spain rather than the other European countries. Their habitual attitude to the "mother country" differs from that of Americans for good reasons: when the Americans' forerunners won their independence from Great Britain they were, to a considerable degree, simply reasserting their inherited rights as Englishmen, and Great Britain remained one of the world's most "advanced" countries with a great deal to teach them. The fathers of Argentine independence, however, were inspired by ideas from England, France, and the United States, and saw Spain as a decayed and backward country whose legacy they should proudly reject. This feeling, only slightly modified by Spain's remarkable renaissance in the 40 years preceding the Civil War, has persisted. Interestingly, while an English accent is considered "aristocratic" by many Americans, a Spanish accent reminds Argentines of a comic immigrant grocer and some think it incongruous to hear it being employed by King Juan Carlos, for instance. For Argentines, then, it is perfectly natural to look outside the Spanish-speaking world for ideas and inspiration, and Borges is by no means the only Argentine of his class to have been as familiar with a foreign language during his childhood as with his own.

Standing on the shores of the Western world—part of it, no doubt, but not feeling themselves wholly inside it—Latin Americans can pick and choose, gathering the best the world has to offer for incorporation into the new civilisation they are trying to construct. In the past they looked chiefly to Europe: most of them to France and England; some to Germany. More recently they have tended to concentrate on the United States. Now, perhaps, they will turn to the Far East, not only to Japan but to other countries that share the same underlying tradition. It is surely not an accident that the two most distinguished Latin American writers alive today, Borges and Octavio Paz, have progressively absorbed themselves in Eastern thought over the last few decades. Some Latin Americans have always argued that they could become "universal men" more easily than any European, North American, or, for that matter, Japanese or Chinese. The development of Borges and Paz suggests that they may well have been right.

James Neilson, "In the Labyrinth: The Borges Phenomenon," in Encounter, *Vols. LVIII & LIX, Nos. 6 & 1, June-July, 1982, pp. 47-58.*

Stanton Hager (essay date 1985)

[*In the following essay, Hager examines the ways in which*

Borges's works poignantly satirize humanity's attempts to construct rational, systematic explanations of the universe.]

In the preface to Ronald Christ's *Narrow Act: Borges' Art of Allusion,* J. L. Borges wrote: "I am neither a thinker nor a moralist, but simply a man of letters who turns his own perplexities and that respected system of perplexities we call philosophy into the forms of literature." More often than not, the forms that Borges's fictions take in their investigations of philosophical perplexities are fantastic. Like the Tlönists in his story **"Tlön, Uqbar, and Orbis Tertius,"** Borges thought that "metaphysics is a branch of fantastic literature." In recalling his *Anthology of Fantastic Literature,* coedited with Silvina Ocampo and Adolfo Bioy Casares, Borges noted the "culpable omission of the unsuspected and greatest masters of the genre: Parmenides, Plato, John Scotus Erigena, Albertus Magnus, Spinoza, Leibnitz, Kant, Frances Bradley." However, what he was forced to leave out as editor he made the persistent source and subject of his own writing.

To achieve the fantastic Borges did not resort to griffins, trolls, and unicorns (he confined his interest in these creatures to his bestiary *Book of Imaginary Beings*) but turned to topoi of metaphysics such as life is a dream, the many and the One, and the world as Text. Because the fantastic nature of such topoi is not readily apparent to the metaphysicians and their believers who make them the cornerstones of rational, systematic edifices of ontological explanation, Borges's fictional strategy, to borrow Martin Heidegger's metaphor, was to "deconstruct" those edifices; or, more precisely, it was to invent and deconstruct *metaphors* of metaphysical systems. He did so for no mean or pedantic reasons—to ridicule metaphysics, to demonstrate the fallacies of particular systems, or to reconstruct his own system, for he had none—but to admire it more, to reveal philosophy's and theology's kinship with poetry, music, painting, and other constructing/deconstructing activities of the human imagination in its attempts to mirror or explain the unexplainable universe.

In a much-quoted passage from his essay **"The Wall and the Books,"** Borges wrote: "Music, states of happiness, mythology, faces molded by time, certain twilights and certain places—all these are trying to tell us something, or have told us something we should not have missed, or are about to tell us something; that imminence of a revelation that is not yet produced is, perhaps, the aesthetic reality." To feel imminently near a revelation that is never quite produced was not only the aesthetic reality for Borges, it was the central human experience. If, as Heidegger defined it, the distinguishing characteristic of humankind's *being* is its ability and need to inquire into the nature of Being, Borges would only add that it is also a part of humankind's being ultimately to recognize and reject the illusion of its "answers" to its inquiries, to return continually to a state of teasing and unsatisfied "imminence." Time and again in Borges's fictions the illusion of satisfaction is created and dissolved; closed, rational systems of explanation are elaborately constructed and as elaborately deconstructed.

The mirror and the labyrinth are Borges's chief tools of deconstruction. Borges traced his lifelong fascination with mirrors to a childhood fear. He related this fear in a number of places, including a conversation with Richard Burgin:

> [*Burgin*]: *I wonder how and when you began to use another of your favorite images, the image of the mirror.*
>
> [Borges]: Well, that, that also goes with the earliest fears of my childhood, being afraid of mirrors, being afraid of mahogany, being afraid of being repeated.

In the same conversation Borges recounted another early fear: "I don't know why, but when I first read *The Republic,* when I first read about the types, I felt a kind of fear. . . . I felt that the whole world of Plato, the world of eternal beings, was somehow uncanny and frightening." As with mirrors, Platonism and other forms of philosophical idealism became lifelong fascinations. One can easily guess that the initial fright at Platonism was the same as that caused by the reflecting surfaces of mahogany, ivory, water, and polished metal, for in Platonism reality and identity are made illusory: by duplication all substance becomes shadow. Frederick Goldin, in his book *The Mirror of Narcissus and the Courtly Love Lyric,* wrote:

> One reason for the frequency of the mirror figure is that the medieval world view was essentially Platonic: the objects of actual experience were known and judged by their resemblance to an ideal Form. Now when all existence is understood as a relation between paragon and image, between one reality and its innumerable reflections, the use of the mirror figure is inevitable.

But the use of the mirror and other figures by Plato and other idealists to argue the illusory nature of reality is not, for Borges, carried far enough. For Plato, George Berkeley, and Arthur Schopenhauer, behind illusion is truth, behind shadow is substance, behind reflection is form, God, or will. For Borges, however, behind illusion is other illusion; there is no ground of being: reality is dissolved not by one but by an infinity of mirrors. In one of Borges's most compelling fictions, **"The Circular Ruins,"** we find that behind the dream of reality is a dreaming god who in turn is dreamed by a dreaming god who is dreamed by a dreaming god ad infinitum. Likewise, in his poem **"The Game of Chess"** the unseen hand of God manipulates the players on a chessboard, but he, too, is moved by an unseen hand of a god who is moved by an unseen hand ad infinitum.

This dissolution, or deconstruction, of reality by mirror duplication is often abetted by a labyrinth. Although the labyrinth seduces with an appearance of palpable design, the mirror signals a dematerialization or distortion of reality. Often a mirror stands, like Alice's looking-glass, at the doorway of a Borges fiction, warning of things ahead turned wrong side round. Like Lewis Carroll's world, Borges's is one in which il-logic insists on its logical design. There is often, in fact, the appearance of *more* than usual design, as in the Library of **"The Library of Babel,"** with its perfectly hexagonal galleries and its identical number of books per hexagon, pages per book, lines per page, and letters per line. The pun in the title gives away the contradiction, however: the Library (system) of babble (nonsense). If we miss the pun the mirror hanging in the entranceway—which we are told causes a dispute about whether the universe, metaphorically, the Library, is or is not infinite—is a sufficient clue. It is the narrator's signal not to trust the misleading labyrinth we are about to enter. The Library, as labyrinth (other recurrent metaphors of the labyrinth in Borges's writing include palaces, gardens, and encyclopedias), is a metaphor of metaphysical system; more accurately, it comprises an infinite number of competing systems. Each book is its own system, or a clue to a larger system, and there is a quest among numberless librarians for the system of systems, the book of books, the one world that contains the universe. Inquisitors of all sorts—idealist philosophers, mystics, linguists, orthographers, cartographers, magicians—endlessly voyage up and down the infinite ladders of the Library seeking through infinite books in infinite hexagons the vindications of themselves and their systems. They start out as young men and in old age find themselves back at their natal hexagon, blind, weary, unvindicated; once dead they are hurled over the bannister into the "unfathomable air," where their bodies corrupt and dissolve in an infinite fall.

Thus deconstruction of metaphysical system in **"The Library of Babel"** is achieved by the overconstruction, proliferation, and competition of systems that collapse under the weight of their own fantastic futility. The story is Borges's most sustained parody of system. Its form is a baroque construction from which the carved cornices are constantly falling away. The reading experience is like watching a group of workers painstakingly erect a building while other workers painstakingly dismantle it.

Another fiction in which a mirror and a labyrinth conjoin to confound the systems of human reason is **"Death and the Compass,"** A rabbi, Marcel Yarmolinsky, has been murdered. Inspector Treviranus, in charge of the investigation, proposes an obvious solution to the crime: the hotel room adjacent to the victim's is occupied by a man who has in his possession the rarest sapphires in the world; meaning to rob his neighbor, a robber blunders into the victim's room instead and is forced to kill him. Private detective Erik Lönnrot, who "thought of himself as a pure thinker [that is, an idealist], an Auguste Dupin," tells the Inspector that such a solution is "possible, but not interesting." He prefers "a purely rabbinical solution." This is a classic confrontation in detective fiction: the unimaginative Inspector Lestrade jumping at the obvious explanation while the ruminating, ratiocinative Sherlock Holmes entertains a more abstruse one. Lönnrot starts on his rabbinical track by gathering together the dead rabbi's books, among which is *A Vindication of the Cabala* (the title of an actual six-page essay by Borges), and gradually he constructs a solution based on the Cabala and other esoteric Jewish lore. Thus Borges fused pure thinker (or idealist philosopher), detective, and mystic scholar. Detective-idealist-scholar Lönnrot constructs an ingenious, systematic solution to the crime—one that vindicates the Cabala, idealism, reason itself—only to find that it is the unimaginative Inspector, the empiricist who imposes no arcane and "oversubtle" systems of explanation on reality, who is vindicated: the rabbi was killed just as the Inspector proposed. Seduced by reason and metaphysics, Lönnrot is lured to the villa of Triste-le-Roy by his arch-enemy Red Scharlach (who, as Borges has pointed out elsewhere, may be Lönnrot's double) and is killed. He need not have been killed, however, if he had read enough Borges stories! When he reached the labyrinthine villa, with its uncanny, duplicating mirrors, he should have heeded his apprehensions—known that seeming design was being dissolved into nothingness; that regularity was being made irregular, logic illogical; that his elaborate construct was being parodied, deconstructed, made fantastic—and he should have turned back.

In fact, hints of this massive deconstruction were there for Lönnrot's notice throughout the story if he had not been so turned inward. As in **"The Library of Babel,"** here, too, construction and deconstruction occur simultaneously. While Lönnrot, oblivious to reality, ingeniously constructs his rational solution, readers are made aware of the chaotic, delirious manifestations of that reality. The hotel in which Yarmolinsky is murdered is described as a tower that "manifestly unites the hateful whiteness of a sanitorium, the numbered divisibility of a prison, and a general appearance of a bawdy house"; as Lönnrot drives to the remote scene of the second crime, the Rue de Toulon, readers are told that "to the left and right of the automobile, the city disintegrated"; and the Rue de Toulon itself is described as "that dirty street where cheek by jowl are the peepshow and the milk store, the bordello and the women selling Bibles." Reality is manifestly not ordered and intelligible. Moreover, and perhaps most significant, it is carnival time in the city—a time of the abandonment of reason. The reality through which "Lönnrot the reasoner" moves is a chaos, a dream, an intoxication. The carnival metaphor is reinforced by a fever metaphor that Scharlach provides at the end of the story in relating that he had received his own vision of reality as a labyrinth of mirrors during a feverish delirium and that he had decided then that it would be by means of such a labyrinth that he would entrap and kill Lönnrot.

For Borges reality is neither pure accident nor pure design but a combination of both and a worldview that is either wholly empirical or wholly metaphysical is not just inadequate; it is fantastic.

—Stanton Hager

However, although it is Treviranus the empiricist, and not Lönnrot the idealist, who is vindicated by the story's plot, and although Lönnrot suffers a fatal defeat not often suffered by the sleuths of the genre, he is by no means ridiculed by the story. His rabbinical solution, although "wrong," *remains* more interesting than the Inspector's; for Borges being interesting is more important than being correct. Besides, even though the series of crimes began accidentally, upon that accident Scharlach *did* construct

a secret design to which the Inspector, but not Lönnrot, was oblivious. The import is that reality is neither pure accident nor pure design but a combination of both and that a worldview that is either wholly empirical or wholly metaphysical is not just inadequate; it is fantastic. As the empiricist is at all times vulnerable to a dumbfounding recognition of a secret order or realm beyond his scheme (the gothic is full of such moments of fantastic revelation), so the metaphysician is vulnerable to a recognition of the limits of his scheme—of the corporeal limits of time, space, and human reason.

Borges employed construction and deconstruction not only in his fictions but in his essays. Most elaborately constructed and deconstructed of all of his essays is **"A New Refutation of Time."** The essay consists of three parts: Prologue, part A—which, as Borges explained in the Prologue, is the original article published in 1944—and part B, which is the revised article published in 1946. The argument of both articles is that time is annihilated by duplication: "[W]e can postulate two identical moments. Having postulated that identity, we must ask: Are those identical moments the same? Are the enthusiasts who devote a lifetime to a line by Shakespeare not literally Shakespeare?"

The argument is constructed upon the idealist principles of David Hume and Berkeley; or, rather, it is a deconstruction of those principles: in Borges's words at the outset of the essay, "it is the anachronous *reductio ad absurdum* of an obsolete system (Idealism) or, what is worse, the feeble machination of an Argentine adrift on the sea of metaphysics" a wry sentence in which Borges not only announces his intention to deconstruct the idealists but also deconstructs, or undermines, his deconstruction with the word *anachronous* and the whole demurring last clause—not that it is unusual to find in Borges's essays a thesis that does not believe in itself, that argues against itself while asserting itself. Deconstructing his deconstruction further, he drew attention to the "subtle joke" of the essay's title, which is a *"contradictio in adjecto,* because to say that a refutation is new (or old) is to attribute to it a predicate of a temporal nature, which restores the notion that the subject attempts to destroy." As a final stroke, Borges ended this brief five-hundred-word Prologue—dense with the rubble of a demolished argument he has not even begun to construct—with an echo of the opening. He dedicated the essay to Juan Cristósmo Lafinur, who "like all men . . . was born at the wrong time." That is, Lafinur's life, like that of all humans, is anachronous. Thus Borges was writing an anachronous argument dedicated to the anachronous lives lived by all people—anachronicity undermining both the achronicity of the idealist argument that he set forth in parts A and B *and* the sequentiality that saturates language, as that which is out of place in time is neither atemporal nor sequential.

Borges constructed his refutation of time first in part A and then again in its mirror duplication in part B. He did not choose to collapse the two articles into one, as he explained, because reading the pair of texts would make understanding the "indocile subject" easier. More wryly, more obviously, he intended the presentation of two mirrored moments—himself refuting time—in articles that must be read one after the other as both proof and disproof of his argument. But although there is a constant wryness of proof and confutation, avowal and disavowal, construction and deconstruction, that makes this essay his deftest and wittiest, poignancy is also present. Borges made metaphysics the source and subject of his writing because he was haunted by it: throughout his life he "sensed a refutation of time, which . . . comes to visit me at nights and in the weary dawns with the illusory force of an axiom." His refutation of time, although disbelieved and playfully mocked by his logical being, is deeply felt, is axiomatic for another part of his being—the being that moves through the haunting landscape of the story fragment that closes part A. In the midst of his witty *"reductio ad absurdum* of an obsolete system" is a poignant and persuasive avowal of that system, providing a temporary resolution of the essay's antinomies. Although time can be easily refuted at the level of the senses, its refutation is not so easy at the intellectual level, because the idea of succession is inseparable from the intellect. Temporality and atemporality have their separate and legitimate spheres. But having launched the argument a second time, in part B, guided it carefully with repetition and variation, persuasively drawing upon Hume, Berkeley, and Chuang Tzu, he brought part B and the essay as a whole not to another resolution but to an almost despairing disavowal:

> And yet, and yet—To deny temporal succession, to deny the ego, to deny the astronomical universe, are apparent desperations and secret assuagements. . . . Time is the substance I am made of. Time is a river that carries me away, but I am the river; it is a tiger that mangles me, but I am the tiger; it is a fire that consumes me, but I am the fire. The world, alas, is real; I, alas, am Borges.

Thus the essayist ends with a revelation suffered by so many of the characters of his fictions: having come to the limits of reason, of imagination, of metaphysical construction, he must admit the "and yet" that demolishes and makes fantastic all of his schemes. Although Borges found the blithe, fantastic denials of reality of Plato, Berkeley, Hume, and others compelling, unlike his idealist predecessors he could not escape waking from his dreams of mirrors, tigers, and labyrinths to sequential time, to Scharlach's gun, to the seeker's "fall, which is infinite."

Stanton Hager, "Palaces of the Looking Glass: Borges's Deconstruction of Metaphysics," in The Scope of the Fantastic—Theory, Technique, Major Authors: Selected Essays from the First International Conference on the Fantastic in Literature and Film, *edited by Robert A. Collins and Howard D. Pearce, Greenwood Press, 1985, pp. 231-38.*

Joseph Epstein (essay date April 1987)

[*Epstein is an American editor and essayist who has written extensively on literature, language, and American culture. In the following essay, he qualifies his enthusiasm for Borges's writings with the argument that, ultimately, Borges's work does not match the standards set by Marcel Proust, Franz Kafka, and James Joyce.*]

One of the interesting differences between high art and great science is that the former is both unique and its emergence unpredictable in a way that is not quite true of the latter. If Newton had not lived, I have seen it argued, Huygens and Leibniz would have gone on to do his principal work; Wallace was closing in on the theory of evolution for which Darwin has since been recognized as a hero of science; and Edison's work could as readily have been done by Swan (on the incandescent lamp) and Hughes (on the microphone), or so it is said. If Albert Einstein had never lived, it is possible that Ernst Mach or Max Planck or another German physicist would have set to work on the problem of relativity; but if Proust had died in his twenties, there would be no *Remembrance of Things Past,* nor, it seems safe to maintain, any other book remotely like it.

And yet there are some artists, no matter how exotic their origins or how esoteric their gifts, of whom it almost seems as if, had they not existed, they would have to have been invented. Jorge Luis Borges, the Argentine writer who was born in 1899 and who died last year at the age of eighty-seven, appears to have been such an artist. In a 1967 essay entitled "The Literature of Exhaustion," the American novelist John Barth, setting out a fairly early claim for Borges as a modern master, allowed that "someone once vexedly accused *me* of inventing" Borges. And indeed Borges was fond of speaking of himself as an invention of sorts, as if there were Borges the writer, who contrived his literary work, and Borges the man, who had gradually become lost in the writer and who was destined "to perish, definitively."

But the sense of the word "invention" I have in mind is of another, somewhat different, kind—it is the sense in which invention is spoken of as being the mother of necessity. For Jorge Luis Borges came along in time to justify the kind of writing that certain academic authors and teachers of modern literature had long been awaiting, even if, until his arrival, they themselves perhaps did not know it.

In "The Literature of Exhaustion"—the very title leaves one longing for a nap—John Barth not only asserts that Borges is one of the few writers worthy of being placed alongside such "old masters" of 20th-century fiction as Joyce and Kafka, but, of the thin line of their successors, Borges is for Barth easily the most interesting. What puts Borges in the first rank for Barth is "the combination of that intellectually profound vision with great human insight, poetic power, and consummate mastery of his means. . . ." But beyond these qualities, which define all literary artists of great power, Barth admires Borges for the way he appears to have both understood and transcended the chief aesthetic problems of the day—Barth rather bumpily calls these "the felt ultimacies of our time." In Barth's view, "it may well be that the novel's time as a major art form is up," which is to say that the day for traditional narrative, with its reliance on cause and effect, characterization, lineal anecdote, and the rest of it, is over, done, *kaput.* Barth isn't saying, or even suggesting, that the novel is dead, but instead that some of its traditionally richest possibilities may be. If this is true, the question is, where does one—if one is, as John Barth describes himself, "of the temper that chooses to 'rebel along traditional lines' "—where does one go from here? The answer, for Barth, is in the direction of Jorge Luis Borges.

Jorge Luis Borges is the answer as well for a great many other writers, critics, and teachers of literature. If the tradition of modernism in fiction is not considered at a dead end, the three writers who may be said to have carried it on with the greatest bravura have been Vladimir Nabokov, Samuel Beckett, and Jorge Luis Borges. Each in his different way is a mandarin among modern writers; each has about him the feel of an international figure. Of these three, Nabokov, despite his enormous talent, seems too much a special case—an exile and a man writing out of his own obsessions, a rare and beautiful specimen of butterfly forming a species of one; Beckett, despite his comedy of deadpan precision, is finally too dark, even for teachers and critics who do not seem to mind setting up shop right there on the rim of the abyss. But Borges—well, Borges is a different story. Borges has his obsessions, but one can separate them from his work, in a way that it is difficult to do with Nabokov; Borges has his darkness, but it is not the darkness of the inside of a shroud, as Beckett's increasingly has tended to be. Borges has the additional advantage that his work, in its various preoccupations, would seem to make striking connections with that group of writers and critics, most but not all of them university-based, who think of themselves as post-modernist. To quote a postie novelist named Ronald Sukenick on the postmodernist program in literature: "Reality doesn't exist, time doesn't exist, personality doesn't exist. . . . In view of these annihilations, it will be no surprise that literature, also, does not exist—how could it?"

Although Borges would not have put it quite so blatantly, there is evidence in his work for arguing that he, too, believed that reality, time, personality, literature itself did not quite exist. This in any case is the gravamen of those stories of Borges that are most widely admired among American academics. Ours may one day be looked back upon as a time when academics in the humanities in the United States spent themselves debating the question of whether reality truly exists: whether meaning was without meaning; whether not only beauty but ethics and morality generally were only in the eye of the beholder; and whether truth was not inseparable from political power. As Dr. Johnson refuted Bishop Berkeley's ingenious argument for the nonexistence of matter by kicking a large stone ("I refute it *thus*," said he), so today might one refute the academic contemners of reality by proposing that in an unreal world they give up their tenure ("Whaddaya, kidding me?" say they). . . .

· · · · ·

Borges's career had a most odd shape; the line describing it would run from precocity to lengthy obscurity to worldwide acclaim to the danger of academic ossification. "By the late 1920's," Monegal writes, "it was obvious in Buenos Aires that [Borges] was the most important young poet there and a leader of the avant-garde." This is all very well, but in a worldly view comparable to being the best shot-putter in the Junior League, or the winner of a na-

tional cha-cha contest for people past eighty. Borges was himself too cosmopolitan a young man not to know this. (He once jokingly proposed starting an avant-garde review to be called *Papers for the Suppression of Reality*—some joke.) By 1929, according to Monegal, Borges realized that he would never achieve his ambition of being a cosmic poet and a universally admired one. He was still chiefly living off his father, but now he turned more and more to criticism and reviewing for both obscure and popular Argentine periodicals.

Borges gives much credit during this period to the influence of a writer named Alfonso Reyes, who was the Mexican ambassador in Buenos Aires. Reyes got Borges to knock off the fine writing and the attempts to forge a style built on 17th-century models in favor of a prose that was precise, concise, and pellucid. Although at twenty-seven Borges had already had the first of the eight eye operations he would undergo before near blindness set in for good in his middle fifties, he continued to store up vast amounts of desultory reading in subjects erudite and arcane. (Borges always had scholarly tastes without any accompanying illusion that he was himself a scholar.) At this point, in his early thirties, Jorge Luis Borges was still a writer who had not found his form, a talent waiting to burst into fruition.

Curiously, Borges was never a great reader of novels, preferring instead the economy and form of the short story. "As a writer, however, I thought for years that the short story was beyond my powers," Borges writes in **"An Autobiographical Essay,"** and "it was only after a long and roundabout series of timid experiments in narration that I sat down to write real stories." At first he did stories based on incidents from the lives of legendary Buenos Aires toughs, for Borges had cultivated the acquaintance of hoodlums from the city's north side who looked back upon the days when a male virgin was someone who had not yet killed his first man. He then progressed to inventing stories or sketches around the lives of men who had in fact existed, such as Billy the Kid or the Jewish gunman Monk Eastman.

Around 1935 he began to publish tales written in the form of pseudo-essays on books or writers who never existed; these became not only Borges's trademark but the chief cause behind his eventual fame. For it is precisely this kind of thing that excites a writer and teacher like John Barth, who has noted that, instead of yet another stale narrative, Borges in these tales

> writes a remarkable and original work of literature, the implicit theme of which is the difficulty, perhaps the unnecessity, of writing original works of literature. His artistic victory, if you like, is that he confronts an intellectual dead end and employs it against itself to accomplish new human work.

In one such story, **"An Examination of the Work of Herbert Quain,"** Borges begins by announcing the death of an author who has been allotted "scarcely half a column of necrological piety" by the *Times Literary Supplement,* and whose first work, *The God of the Labyrinth,* had been obtusely compared, in the *Spectator,* with Agatha Christie, and others of whose books had been compared with Gertrude Stein. Borges then proceeds I won't say to elucidate but to elaborate upon the kind of writer Quain was. He was a writer who took special pleasure in concocting ingenious plots the purpose of which seemed to be to undermine the very notion of plot. " 'I lay claim in this novel,' I have heard [Quain] say, 'to the essential features of all games: symmetry, arbitrary rules, tedium.' " There follows some erudite chit-chat about what Quain was really up to; a few false interpretations of his work are put up and shot down; it is noted that a fallacious interpretation of one of his comedies as a Freudian work determined its success. Quain, who "was in the habit of arguing that readers were an already extinct species," produces a final book entitled *Statements* containing eight stories each of which sets out a good plot deliberately frustrated by the author. From the third of these stories, Borges tells us, he was able to extract his own story, **"The Circular Ruins,"** which actually happens to exist.

Now this may not be everybody's idea of the way to play Parcheesi. But be assured that the board, when Borges sets it up, can be very elegantly laid out, the pieces beautifully carved. One must, it is true, have a taste for puzzles and perplexities to enjoy such a story. It would be a grave mistake, however, to take Borges for a mere gamester. He is playing in earnest. Yet his position is a curious one; he is an aesthete who does not quite believe in the efficacy of art. "Music, states of happiness, mythology, faces belabored by time, certain twilights and certain places," he writes, "try to tell us something, or have said something we should not have missed, or are about to say something: this imminence of revelation which does not occur is, perhaps, the aesthetic phenomenon."

Borges's stories appear drained of all political content: He wished to entertain and move his readers toward wonder and wonderment over life's mysteries.

—Joseph Epstein

To value art above all else and yet to find art nearly valueless—this, surely, is a strange position. How did Borges come to hold it? Whence did it derive? Valéry remarks that "there is no theory that is not a fragment, carefully-prepared, of some autobiography." It is not easy, however, to discover the analogue in Borges's life for his theories about art, unless one looks to his reading, the idealism learned at his father's knee, the avant-garde atmosphere in which he came of age, his penchant for metaphysics. But it all seems somehow cerebral, not quite to touch on life, including Borges's own. Utterly skeptical though he may have been about finding meaning in life, this seems in no way to have prevented him from enjoying it thoroughly. We are used by now to our modern writers having an edge of coldness, if not outright nastiness about them—the meanness is the message—but none of this was true of

Borges, about whom Monegal has no trouble rounding up the most endearing testimonials, such as, "I believe that he is the best-humored man I ever met," and ". . . as Borges is so intelligent, when talking to him, he gives the feeling that we are also intelligent." This most modern of writers was himself a most old-fashioned gentleman.

Not that Borges's life was one of seamless serenity. Beginning in 1937, he worked for nine years in a minor position at a branch library in Buenos Aires, which he later described as "nine years of solid unhappiness." His job was to help impose a systematic organization on a collection of books so small as to require no such system. He did one hour of actual library work each day, spending the remainder reading and writing. But, now in his forties, he felt humiliated by working at so menial and dismal a job. Further humiliations were to come. During World War II, Borges was pro-British, not so easy a thing to be in preponderantly pro-German Argentina. Borges was an enemy of totalitarianism of every kind, and in his criticism and journalism attacked Hitler's anti-Semitism and his catastrophic effect on German culture. Borges was of course also a great enemy of Colonel Juan Domingo Peron, who, when he came to power, repaid the writer by keeping him under surveillance. In August 1946, Borges was notified that he had been removed from his job at the Miguel Cané branch of the municipal library and "promoted" to inspector of poultry and rabbits in the public markets of Córdoba Street—clearly a macho-style slap from, as Borges would later phrase it, "a president whose name I do not want to remember."

Yet Borges, by his own admission, was never a committed writer—never *engagé.*

> My political convictions are well known; I am a member of the Conservative party—this in itself is a form of skepticism—and no one has ever branded me a Communist, a nationalist, an anti-Semite, a follower of Billy the Kid or of the dictator Rosa. . . . I have never kept my opinions hidden, not even in trying times, but neither have I ever allowed them to find their way into my literary work, except once when I was buoyed up in exultation over the Six-Day War.

As Borges here makes plentifully clear, there was his politics and there was his writing and, insofar as he could control them, never did the twain meet. And it is true that Borges's stories do appear drained of all political content: questions of good and evil do not arise in his stories and neither can he ever be said to seek to persuade his readers to any conclusions. He wished to entertain and move them, but to move them in a particular direction—toward wonder and wonderment over life's mysteries.

While still working at the library, in 1938, the year his father died, Borges had an accident, an injury to his scalp, after which septicemia set in, causing him to fear for his sanity. As he began to recover, still uncertain of his mental abilities, he attempted a new kind of story, which turned out to be **"Pierre Menard, Author of *Don Quixote.*"** It is one of Borges's best-known stories and a work of a kind that would become characteristic of the Borges who is most revered in the academy: a narrative discourse upon an imaginary text that pretends to be an analysis of it. What in considerable part accounts for the cachet of this particular story in the university of today is that it is a story about reading. If you are going to make a major statement in the 20th century, you had better make it short: so Borges, who rarely wrote anything more than ten or twelve pages in length, appeared to believe. He also professed to believe that "the composition of vast books is a laborious and impoverishing extravagance. . . . I have preferred to write notes upon imaginary books."

A symbolist from Nîmes, a friend of Valéry, a man whose bibliography reveals him to have been devoted to the arcana of literary study at the highest level, Borges's creation Pierre Menard applies himself to "the repetition of a pre-existing book in another language"—the book in this instance being *Don Quixote* by Miguel de Cervantes. Menard, please understand, wishes to repeat Cervantes's masterpiece *literally*. The project is quite mad, of course, but then, as the narrator of the story avers, "there is no intellectual exercise which is not ultimately useless." After many drafts, which he has destroyed, Menard succeeds in reproducing a few chapters of *Don Quixote* exactly. Although both texts are verbally identical, the narrator argues for the superiority of Menard's, its greater subtlety and richness. To him, that a contemporary of Julien Benda and Bertrand Russell could turn out such a work, writing in the prose style of a 17th-century Spaniard while thinking as a 20th-century Frenchman, so that the very meanings of his words, and the meanings behind the meanings, have changed, and with it the meaning of the story—this, truly, is a remarkable accomplishment. As the narrator ends the story by noting:

> Menard (perhaps without wishing to) has enriched, by means of a new technique, the hesitant and rudimentary art of reading: the technique is one of deliberate anachronism and erroneous attributions. This technique, with its infinite applications, urges us to run through the *Odyssey* as if it were written after the *Aeneid,* and to read *Le jardin du Centaure* by Madame Henri Bachelier as if it were by Madame Henri Bachelier. This technique would fill the dullest books with adventure. Would not the attributing of *The Imitation of Christ* to Louis-Ferdinand Céline or James Joyce be a sufficient renovation of its tenuous spiritual counsels?

Although Borges began to write such stories before the new academic criticism was really under way, there is a sense in which the stories anticipate the criticism and play into it.

—*Joseph Epstein*

One could organize a whole little Franco-American school of university literary criticism around a story such as **"Pierre Menard, Author of *Don Quixote,*"** which pro-

vides maps of misreading, mines of misperception, mimes of unreality. It is very much a story for specialists, for connoisseurs ("kind of sewers," as the playful James Joyce of *Finnegans Wake* might have put it). Although Borges began to write such stories before the new academic criticism was really under way, there is a sense in which the stories anticipate the criticism and play into it. As V.S. Pritchett, who is an admirer of Borges, has written: "The risk is—and there are some signs of this already—that criticism of Borges will become an accretion that will force us to see his stories as conceits alone."

But there is more going on in Borges than the organization of conceits alone. There are stories set in the Argentine past, stories about courage, about fate, about mystery; there is also in much of his work a subtle feeling for drama, even if it is not the drama of good and evil, of men swept up by ambition, love, the ambiguities of morality. His stories are all written with a fine eye for detail, for the arresting juxtaposition of word and event, and with that precision and clarity which, combined, make for the highest literary elegance. Borges was a consummate literary artist—of that there can be no question.

The question is, to what uses did he put his artistry? How good, finally, was Borges? Opinions differ—and strongly. V.S. Pritchett, allowing that Borges can be viewed as "a learned pillager of metaphysical arguments," nonetheless maintains that he passes the test for an artist of ideas by his ability to make "an idea walk," which is to say come alive on the page. But V.S. Naipaul, allowing that Borges's puzzles and jokes can be addictive, nonetheless maintains that "they cannot always support the metaphysical interpretations they receive." Octavio Paz holds that "the great achievement of Borges was to say the most with the least," adding that he was able to combine simplicity with strangeness, "the naturalism of the uncommon, the strangeness of the familiar." This is what "gives him a unique place in the literature of the 20th century." But then there is Vladimir Nabokov, speaking perhaps with the acerbity of the rival, who once told a reporter from *Time:* "At first Vera and I were delighted by reading him. We felt we were on a portico, but we have learned that there was no house."

No one can argue that Borges made extravagant claims on his own behalf. After he achieved fame, he gave hundreds of interviews and wrote various prologues and introductions to his own books and to books about him, and in them he mastered the tone of what might be called the modest genius. "The same few plots, I am sorry to say," he wrote in the prologue to his book **Dr. Brodie's Report,** "have pursued me down through the years; I am decidedly monotonous." It is true that Borges's stories and poems and criticism seem a remarkably unified enterprise. This enterprise can, I think, be accurately described as the investigation of reality with an eye toward its destruction.

Borges is above all impressed with the mystery of life, and fascinated above all with those who set out to solve the mystery. Scholars and philosophers especially excite his aesthetic interest. "Borges," Alastair Reid once noted, "really did regard scholarship as a branch of fantastic literature." Philosophy was scarcely less fantastic to him, and he found few spectacles as risible as that of a man attempting to interpret the complexity of the world with a theory. In story after story, Borges tells of plans to find order in the world; in story after story, none is finally available. Men are swamped by infinity, chased by time, rattled by memory.

As these stories unfold—**"Tlön, Uqbar, Orbis Tertius,"** **"The Babylon Library," "The Aleph," "The Secret Miracle"**—the planes of reality and unreality intersect and blur. Labyrinths, mirrors, dreams, strange recurrences play through these works, with the effect that man's place in the world comes to seem a highly shaky proposition and human destiny, to copy a trope from Borges's story **"Averroes' Search,"** "a blind camel in the desert." Yet if man never seems so helpless or absurd as when searching for the secret meaning of life, Borges, while positing the precariousness of human existence, is also able to infuse poetry into the search, and with it emotion of the kind that results when men are shown alone and at the mercy of a universe they do not begin to understand.

But why would Borges, this gentle and altogether pleasant man, be pledged, in the words of a critic most friendly to him named Ana María Barrenechea, "to destroy reality and convert Man into a shadow"? "I am quite simply," Borges has said, "a man who uses perplexities for literary purposes." Yet can it be quite so simple? Skeptical of almost all philosophies, Borges was most partial to idealism, which posits that life does not truly exist outside the mind of the person, or divinity, who beholds it. In the idealistic view, life could well be a dream; and it was this possibility that Borges seemed to prefer to entertain. As a mere window-shopper in philosophy, I have always liked George Santayana's refutation of idealism, set out in *Egotism in German Philosophy,* which runs, "You cannot maintain that the natural world is the product of the human mind without changing the meaning of the word mind and of the word human." But why would a man of so generally skeptical a nature as Borges turn to idealism, or for that matter to playing with perplexities?

My own unfounded speculation about this has to do with the fact that for years Borges suffered from insomnia. So, too, I recently learned, did Vladimir Nabokov and the Rumanian aphorist E.M. Cioran, two other writers much given to pondering the literary uses of perplexities. So, before them, did Nietzsche, who tried to alleviate it with the use of chloral; and, before Nietzsche, so did De Quincey, who attributed to his insomnia his craving for opium. Borges spoke of "the atrocious lucidity of insomnia." There is something about this tiresome disease, to judge by the roster of writers who have suffered from it, that inflames the imagination, sending it off into dark corners and setting it intricate puzzles.

Some inkling of what a well-stocked mind suffers under insomnia is available in a brilliant Borges story entitled **"Funes the Memorius."** (Completing this story is said to have cured Borges of his own insomnia.) In it an adolescent boy, Ireneo Funes, a peasant lad who has the unusual ability to tell the precise time of the day without aid of a timepiece, is thrown from a horse and suffers what can only be described as the reverse of amnesia—henceforth,

he remembers everything. And he remembers with a vividness of detail that is not only astounding but painful:

> When he fell, he became unconscious; when he came to, the present was almost intolerable in its richness and sharpness, as were his most distant and trivial memories. Somewhat later he learned that he was paralyzed. The fact scarcely interested him. He reasoned (he felt) that his immobility was a minimum price to pay. Now his perception and his memory were infallible.

Borges goes on to report young Funes's extraordinary accomplishments: his ability to master Latin in an evening, his impatience with numbering or indeed with any system employing generalization, or even system itself, which, given his memory, he has no need of. "In the teeming world of Funes there were only details, almost immediate in their presence." To be able to forget nothing, never to turn one's mind off, is of course to live in a kind of hell. Funes's hell is also the hell of the insomniac, as well as the hell of a certain kind of writer. Ireneo Funes cannot bear it past the age of nineteen. "Ireneo Funes died in 1889," Borges concludes his story, "of congestion of the lungs," but what he really dies of is perceptual overload.

This story happens to be a little classic of modernism, in the sense in which Clement Greenberg maintained that "the essence of modernism lies in the use of the characteristic method of a discipline to criticize itself. . . ." Yet was Borges a modernist writer? He himself disdained all artistic labels, saying, "I do not profess any aesthetic. Why add to the natural limits which habit imposes on us those of some theory or other?" And yet it is difficult to disdain them when attempting to place Borges. For when one compares Borges with the modernist masters of fiction, he falls short.

As with Proust, time and memory are of paramount importance to Borges; but, unlike with Proust, in Borges they are not set in the context of love and the intricacies of social relations. Like Joyce, Borges is a master parodist and student of style; but, unlike with Joyce, style in Borges never quite achieves that density of effect that turns it into a way of viewing the world—a vision. There is a weight to Kafka that Borges does not begin to possess. Kafka's argument is with reality, which in his bureaucratic dystopias becomes a nightmare, and he is anguished at his own inability to adjust to reality of this or almost any other kind. Borges, far from arguing with reality, prefers to postulate its nonexistence. When Kafka argues with reality, one feels his very soul is at stake; when Borges plays with reality, one feels it is all in his head.

Borges had for some time been a great figure in the literary life of Argentina, but it was only in 1961, when he shared with Samuel Beckett the Formentor Prize (a $10,000 award furnished by six avant-garde publishers in Europe and the United States), that Borges's renown burst the borders of his native country. He was sixty-two years old, and the award had, in many ways, come just in time. Roughly six years before, owing to his increasing blindness, Borges had to cease writing his stories ("critical fictions," his sometime collaborator Adolfo Bioy Casares called them) and his elaborate essays. He now returned to writing poetry—metrical verse, in fact, the meter serving as an aid to the memory of a man who could no longer see his own text. He now had to be read to. Irony of ironies, he was appointed director of the National Library in Buenos Aires, causing him to remark that God had granted him "at one time 800,000 books and darkness." An all too Borgesian story, that.

"As a consequence of that prize, my books mushroomed overnight throughout the Western world," Borges noted. The first consequence was the simultaneous publication of Borges's collection of tales, *Ficciones,* in six different countries. The second consequence was the discovery of Borges by academic literary departments, who fell hungrily on the carcass of his corpus in the middle 60's and are still gnawing on the bones. Honor now followed honor. Borges was appointed to the Charles Eliot Norton Chair of Poetry at Harvard; there was a "Borges Conference" at the University of Oklahoma; magazines published special Borges issues. "An Evening with Jorge Luis Borges" became a not infrequent event on American university campuses; here Borges gave dollar value, for he was impressive on stage; besides, one could hardly watch him without recalling the blindness of Homer and Milton. In 1971 he was awarded the Jerusalem Prize. He gave more interviews than Hedda Hopper got. Monegal writes that "Borges took to fame with an almost childlike glee." One recalls the triumphal visit of Gertrude Stein to America after the publication of *The Autobiography of Alice B. Toklas.* Apparently few things excite an avant-garde writer like a crashing popular success.

In his last years, Borges with his deep-set eye sockets came, in his photographs, to resemble a wise old monkey of the kind one might see perched amid erotic sculpture on the outside wall of a temple in India. To his blindness was added loss of hearing, encasing him in a labyrinth not of his own but of nature's devising. He came to look upon death as a relief. As he wrote about the Argentine poet Leopoldo Lugones, who committed suicide on one of the islands of Tigre, "He may have felt, perhaps for the first time in his life, that he was freeing himself, at last, of the mysterious duty of searching out metaphors, adjectives, and verbs for everything in the world."

Borges's life is a fantastic, better yet a Borgesian, story, made all the richer by the fact that Borges himself enjoyed nothing quite so much as a fantastic story. As he once prophetically wrote:

> A man sets himself the task of making a plan of the universe. After many years, he fills a whole space with images of provinces, kingdoms, mountains, bays, ships, islands, fish, rooms, instruments, stars, horses, and people. On the threshold of death, he discovers that the patient labyrinth of lines has traced the likeness of his own face.

So it is with Borges, a writer without quite the power to present his readers with a new and higher organization of experience, such as only the very greatest artists can provide, but whose complexity and richness caused his art to rise above nihilism to become one of the most charming ornaments of the literature of our century.

Joseph Epstein, "Señor Borges's Portico," in Commentary, *Vol. 83, No. 4, April, 1987, pp. 55-62.*

Bella Brodzki   (essay date Summer 1990)

[*In the following essay, Brodzki analyzes Borges's representation of female characters and their role in his attempts to discuss the absolute, the "unrepresentable."*]

My concern with the relationship between woman and representation bears directly on the critical controversies raised by Borges' work, specifically the relationship between his formalism/idealism and his textual politics. I will identify (1.) the strategies by which symbols or metaphors of the feminine—as idealized or poetic objects of desire—serve his mystical and metaphysical interests, and (2.) the ways in which the presence of an apparently more localized theme in Borges' work, the machismo cult (benignly understood as the over-determined Latin American male emphasis on courage, honor, and sexual prowess) operates as the inscription of women in a variation of the classic erotic triangle, even as Borges seems to want to move beyond it. By following the gallery of portraits of women throughout his career, one can trace a change in tendency or attitude away from ideality toward corporeality, especially in his later writings. My point will be precisely that for Borges a conceptual ideal always carries an erotic component. Thus I am arguing against the view that Borges' concept of the universal by definition both eludes and excludes the feminine (despite his sentimental idealizing of women), with the ultimate hope of demonstrating that reading Borges in light of gender consideration radically extends our view of his poetics. For, the issue of gender, although perhaps a variable, cannot be read as arbitrary in narratives so engaged in the interplay of metaphor and metonymy. Indeed, the notions of sexual and textual difference are crucially tied to any reading where the claims of power and language, however ungendered (that is, metaphysical) they may appear, are at stake.

To look at how the mystical and the metaphysical converge in a symbol of the feminine in Borges' literary enterprise, it is necessary to elaborate on a poetics that strives to create cultural analogues to sacred texts, but with a twist—for, in Borges' words, "the imminence of a revelation which does not occur is perhaps the aesthetic phenomenon" (*Other Inquisitions*). Itself the manifestation of certain aesthetic and philosophical preoccupations, Borges' quest for the absolute in language at the same time represents the conceptual "impossibility of penetrating the divine scheme of the universe [and should not] dissuade us from outlining human schemes, even though we are aware that they are provisional" (*Other Inquisitions*). In place of the multiplicity of philosophical and theological systems that express a yearning for an order unattainable to human intelligence, Borges substitutes others, all testifying with ironic and paradoxical precision, to their rigorous relativity. Thus constrained only by the limits of language, he creates a form of speculative thought as ambiguous and provisional as that which we call fiction but which is no more fictional than philosophy.

We recognize this tension between the absolute and the

contingent, the universal and the perspectival, metaphor and metonymy to be oppositionally symbolized in the Zahir and the Aleph and crucially connected to two female figures, Clementina Villar and Beatriz Viterbo. As a check on the tendency toward a sacralization or teleology, the perspectival, provisional, successive configuration is necessary, but it carries its own mystique and is no less an hypostasized entity than the transcendent moment achieved, the Aleph. This is because the parabolic tactic of multiplying alternatives synoptically rather than serially does not overcome this tension but exploits it. In attempting to behold the inaccessible through language, the mode plays with the possibilities of difference (in the Derridean sense) through postponement, deferral, decentering, by forming and dissolving metaphors that hover around the absence where the unnamed, unnameable reality is inferred or intuited. It is only through the distortion of memory or supplementarity (a surplus of signification) that these metaphors are present all at once—forming the comprehensive, totalizing Aleph. In Borges' view these near-moments of self-understanding or revelation constitute the aesthetic event—its fluidity, ambiguity, heterogeneity, and open-endedness.

Haunted by "an ordinary coin worth twenty centavos" that possesses mystical attributes, the narrator of **"The Zahir"** begins his story by recounting his obsession with a model whose face had adorned posters and society magazine covers around 1930. Through a rhetorical sleight of hand whose psychoanalytical implications are not lost on the reader, the images of the coin and the face of Clementina Villar are indissoluably linked for "Borges," and threaten to drive to madness. What fascinates him about the woman is that "[s]he was in search of the Absolute, like Flaubert; only hers was an Absolute of a moment's duration" (**"The Zahir,"** *Labyrinths*), because she adhered to the capricious and shallow creed of fashion. After a decline in both family fortune and career, she dies in a modest part of town, and "Borges" goes to her wake. Viewing her, he finds her face remarkably restored to its previous youth, unaffected by the ravages of experience: "Somehow, I thought, no version of that face which has disturbed me so will stay in my memory as long as this one; it is right that it should be the last, since it might have been the first." Associated in life with free will and continual self-transformation, indeed a strange combination of self-effacement and self-absorption ("as though trying to get away from herself"), Villar is perfected, forever fixed in death. Like the Zahir from whose hold the narrator cannot escape, her omnipresent image takes on the aspects of a hypostasized entity, but whatever the metaphorical resemblance between her face and the face of the coin, hers is eventually subsumed, and lingers only as a trace, a reminder of his former obsession. By the end of the story the world is slipping away and all distinctions between thought and reality elide: "Others will dream that I am mad; I shall dream of the Zahir." The narrator waits for the inevitable effacement when the image of the coin will replace the universe itself, perhaps revealing God behind it.

In **"The Aleph,"** an ironic and poignant commentary on the nature of visionary experience, the sublime and the pa-

thetic are fused in a mystical object that is the sum of all the possible visual representations of the universe. This cosmic sphere serves as the poetic inspiration of Carlos Argentino Daneri, in whose cellar it can apparently be found. His opus is purportedly the poem of all poems, a total representation of the known world, appropriately entitled "La Tierra." It is not irrelevant that the poem is immensely dull; its epic proportions and geographic trivia, far from exhausting reality, indicate the absurdity of trying to enumerate it. Inflationary, obsessively particular, and random, the pointless variety of the poem's contents only emphasizes the poverty of the mind and method that created it.

In one of the permutations of male bonding prevalent in Borges' fiction, animosity thrives between the poet-librarian and the narrator (who calls himself "Borges"), centering around professional rivalry and a woman named Beatriz: Daneri's cousin, the narrator's love object, and dead since 1929 (it is now 1941). Her "haunting" presence is pervasive: she frames the narrative, provides the subtext. She is the unsuppressed term of the erotic triangle. Every year on her birthday the narrator pays homage "without hope but without humiliation" to her memory by visiting her house and family. She is introduced to the reader, on one of "these melancholy and vainly erotic anniversaries," by way of photographic description, in serial perspective:

> Beatriz Viterbo in profile and in full color; Beatriz wearing a mask, during the Carnival of 1921; Beatriz at her First Communion; Beatriz on the day of her wedding to Roberto Alessandri; Beatriz soon after her divorce, at a luncheon at the Turf Club; Beatriz at a seaside resort in Quilmes with Delia San Marco Porcel and Carlos Argentino; Beatriz with the Pekinese lapdog given her by Villegas Haedo; Beatriz, front and three-quarter views, smiling, on her hand chin. . . . (**"The Aleph" and Other Stories**)

There is a second "communion" with Beatriz, this time with a large, single "gaudy" portrait which provokes an intimate declaration from the narrator: "Beatriz, Beatriz Elena, Beatriz Elena Viterbo, darling Beatriz, Beatriz now gone forever, it's me, it's Borges." It is this ideal that "Borges" loves, the summation of her image, even though he knows that each particular photograph is a vapid fiction, representing an ideal never attained. Against the passage of time and the "inexorable process of endless change," idealized Beatriz both haunts and mocks him. Clearly, her name is designed to invoke Dante's beloved, Beatrice Portinari: indeed, critics have read **"The Aleph"** as a parody of Dante's masterpieces, both in the universal aspirations of the texts associated ("Borges'" narrative and Argentino's epic poem) as well as their romantic pretexts. The comparison between these elegies to lost love, however, is ironized by their divergent conclusions. Dante's quest for Beatrice ultimately leads to ascension and spiritual consummation, whereas "Borges'" underworld odyssey takes place in a rat-infested cellar in the house where Beatriz lived but which is about to be demolished to make room for an expanding bar.

And the vision of the Aleph itself, an exquisitely rendered, awesome inventory of physical, concrete, organic, sensual, immediate, simultaneous and infinite life, includes more than the narrator probably cared to see, for this point in space contains not only "the multitudes of America . . . all the mirrors on earth . . . convex equatorial deserts and each one of their grains of sand . . . tigers, pistons, bison, tides, and armies . . . the Aleph from every point and angle . . . the circulation of [the narrator's] own dark blood . . . the coupling of love and the modification of death, the reader's face," but also "the rotted dust and bones that had once deliciously been Beatriz Viterbo," as well as "unbelievable, obscene . . . letters, which Beatriz had written to Carlos Argentino."

The impossibility of putting forth in language "the ineffable core" of his story is of course part of the narrative's thematic structure, the very "despair" of the writer, the problem of representation itself:

> All language is a set of symbols whose use among its speakers assumes a shared past. How then can I translate into words the limitless Aleph, which my floundering mind can scarcely encompass? Mystics, faced with the same problem, fall back on symbols. . . . Perhaps the gods might grant me a simple metaphor, but then this account would become contaminated by literature, by fiction. . . . Really, what I want to do is impossible, for any listing of an endless series is doomed to be infinitesimal. . . . What my eyes beheld was simultaneous, but what I shall now write down will be successive, because language is successive. . . .

Then proceeding to articulate this parabolic event, "Borges" recollects the inviolate splendor of the Aleph—"all space was there, actual and undiminished." But by the end of the inventory, the reader realizes that whereas what has aroused the narrator's "infinite wonder" is the synchronic totalization of space, what has aroused his "infinite pity" is purely temporal: death, progressive decomposition, and irrevocable loss, all linked to Beatriz, whose image even the Aleph cannot preserve. Thus, however fragmented, partial, and idealized a representation, his memory of her and the multiple photographs to which he is metonymically attached serve to freeze a moment, to stop the passing of time, symbolized in a woman never won in life, now even subject to change in death. After his transcendent experience the narrator claims that he believes the Aleph to have been a false one and provides "objective" documentation to underwrite his assertion. Yet the duplicity and disappointment of which he speaks have another basis, lying in the implicit analogy between his desire for the woman never possessed and the absolute vision of the Aleph.

In both narratives, **"The Zahir"** and **"The Aleph,"** intellectual abstraction, esoteric knowledge, and the substance of material objects compete with desire—by nature elusive and ever-changing—for the imagination of a narrator who has "only" language at his disposal. That these women characters seem to lack the kind of depth that would make them worthy of such intense desire provides Borges with the opportunity to comment ironically on the fact that desire always exceeds the value of the object of desire, that

the "meaning" of the beloved herself, while subject to the limits of linguistic and visual representation, is always overdetermined and that the lover is often blind to this inherent paradox. What both complicates and simplifies Borges' use of feminine figuration to articulate the theme of longing for the Absolute is that it requires that the woman be dead as pretext. In the case of several of the poems, the death or ultimate loss of a woman serves as the occasion for writing; that the poem is actually dedicated to a particular woman or that she provides its theme is almost derivative of this first point. The issue is not that the poet or narrator only desires her now that she is dead; rather that in death she is *infinitely* desirable and infinitely open to interpretation. What remains of the face of Beatriz, the more idealized of the two women, no less appropriable than the elusive memory of a revelation whose center is absence—is the language that struggles to retrieve what visual memory cannot preserve.

Metaphysical or intellectual obsession as both theme and strategy pervades much of Borges' fiction and poetry, especially in his first-person narratives. **"The Intruder"** is yet another tale of (meta)physical obsession; it also belongs to that group of stories whose protagonists are gauchos, urban tough guys, detectives, and expresses Borges' captivation with action, physical violence, honor, treachery, and male bravado—his distinctive version of the machismo cult. This story is particularly disturbing because whereas in most of the other narratives that treat this theme women characters are "merely" absent or virtual nonentities, here a woman occupies the pivotal but silent point of an untenable erotic triangle and must serve as scapegoat in order for the primary male relationship to survive, prevail. One critic finds it "inconceivable that the same man who created **'Emma Zunz'** could also have written **'The Intruder,'**" because the former seems to affirm female empowerment and self-representation and in the latter an innocent woman is sacrificed to the frontier brutality of a fraternal bond. However, to read this story only as a celebration or glorification of misogyny is possibly to miss Borges' critical commentary and to understand its context (and content) only on the level of "naturalistic" transcription of a cultural reality.

The two almost inseparable originless brothers are described as "drovers, teamsters, horse thieves, and . . . professional gamblers . . . who have a reputation for stinginess, except when drink and cardplaying turned them into spenders" and who like "carousing with women," but whose "amorous escapades had always been carried out in darkened passageways or in whorehouses." Thus when one of the brothers, Cristián, brings Juliana Burgos to live with him as servant and concubine, a distinct departure from his previous sexual behavior is signalled. Soon after, the other brother, Eduardo, has fallen in love with her as well, and "the whole neighborhood, which may have realized it before he did, maliciously and cheerfully looked forward to the enmity about to break out between [them]." When Cristián offers Juliana to his brother in his absence ("if you want her, use her") and before departing says goodbye to him but not to her "who was no more than an object," the reader begins to sense the intimate exclusivity of the brothers' relationship and the specific na-

Borges's handwriting—a manuscript page from his essay "Kafka and his Precursors," originally written in 1951 and collected in Others Inquisitions.

ture of their rivalry. As they begin to share her body as well as benefit from her domestic service, their mutual suspicion grows, for "[i]n tough neighborhoods a man never admits to anyone—not even to himself—that a woman matters beyond lust and possession, but the two brothers were in love. This, in some way, made them feel ashamed." Soon the woman, presented as having no power and no voice, is sold to a brothel so that the brothers can rid themselves of her disruptive presence and restore their life to its previous symmetry. Yet unable to live without her conveniently near, they eventually buy her back, and the rest of the dramatic conflict is condensed into one paragraph. Cristián solves their problem by murdering her ("she won't cause us any more harm"), and the story ends with a cathartic embrace and the narrator's final comment: "One more link bound them now—the woman they had cruelly sacrificed and their common need to forget her."

René Girard's study of erotic rivalry in the novel and Eve Kosofsky Sedgwick's revision of his model of triangular desire, which elaborates a notion of the "homosocial continuum" in literature, can help us first to identify the structure of such a relationship and then analyze its sexual political implications in **"The Intruder."** Sedgwick begins with the Girardian premise that "in any erotic rivalry, the bond that links the two rivals is as intense and potent as the bond that links either of the rivals to the beloved: the bonds of 'rivalry' and 'love,' differently as they are experienced, are equally powerful and in many senses equivalent." In **"The Intruder,"** of course, as the title stresses, the fraternal bond both predates and intensifies the rivalry and is not produced by it; indeed it is the bond itself which makes the triangle possible and impossible. The woman is perceived by the men to be "other," to be an outsider who has driven a wedge between them or violated the integrity of their bond; and the narrator's words assert that the bond is strengthened by and maintained at the expense of a woman "cruelly sacrificed." Feminist extensions of this model situate such triangles within a larger symbolic and economic system, a patriarchal network that thrives on the traffic in women: that is, on the use of women as exchangeable property for the primary purpose and with the ultimate result of cementing the bonds between men. The story replicates the larger sexual organization in which woman figures as "conduit of a relationship rather than a partner to it."

The epigraph to the narrative is taken from the Biblical passage in which David laments over the dead body of his friend Jonathan: "your love to me was wonderful / passing the love of women." As a commentary on the story, it suggests the holding up of an exemplar of male bonding, one that transcends heterosexual love, one whose loss can never be superceded. But the story is framed somewhat differently, stressing the perversion of an ideal. Indeed, the narrator justifies telling the legendary story by presenting it as a kind of cultural document, a slice of less-than-desirable life: "I set down the story now because I see in it . . . a brief and tragic mirror of the character of those hard-bitten men living on the edge of Buenos Aires before the turn of the century." Had Borges, however, endowed Juliana Burgos with language to tell her side of this "mon-

strous love affair," to inscribe her own subjectivity rather than be inscribed and subsequently effaced, the narrative would gain texture and complexity, although it might lose some of its enigmatic quality. By reducing her to a mediating object within a quasi-mythic structure, Borges maintains a formal dependence on necessity, and not on contingency; yet it is precisely those aspects of contingency, differentiation, and the unexpected (Juliana was not expected to exceed her function as object of "lust and possession"), that suggest the story's real potential as "mirror" of a particular historical condition, as the narrator claims was his intention.

One could say that Borges is still too intrigued by formalism and susceptible to false nostalgia and sentimentality to develop the textual implications of sexual dehumanization for both male and female characters. Certainly this is one possible formulation for the disjunction between the narrator's rhetoric and the text's contradictory "message." But then what about **"Emma Zunz"** (*Labyrinths*)? In that narrative Borges uses a female subject, whose name serves as the title of her own story, to signify the suspension, if not the disruption, of a certain formal logic based on the politics of sexual difference, a logic that in **"The Intruder"** he certainly seems loathe to forsake. However, any attempt to compare the signifying possibilities of Emma Zunz and Juliana Burgos, respectively, must first address the difference in narrative contexts: both characters function in a linguistic and economic system where women's value is defined only through "mediation, transaction, transition, and transference" between men. And both stories are about using (carnally) violent means to achieve "pure" and abstract ends, in one case justice, in the other symmetry. But Emma Zunz is the protagonist in a clear field; the narrative begins crucially with the death of her father and then enacts through its language of figuration precisely the ways in which her subjective agency makes her unique in the Borgesian corpus while still reinscribing her in a patriarchal system she cannot transcend. The interplay of the forces of identity and sexual difference, language and power, intentionality and indeterminacy, and the critical strategies that trace them, come together in a performative moment of suspended revelation: Emma's sex/speech act. Her body/text becomes the very locus of interpretation, of self-interpretation, as Emma learns of the relationship between sex as behavior and sex as identity. The identity of Juliana Burgos *is* woman, "the intruder"; Borges situates her among men, and then proceeds to foreclose, indeed erase, whatever textual possibilities she ever presented in the narrative. Borges is willing and exquisitely able to make a woman the actor in her own drama; more difficult is conceiving of a female character on the level of, equal to male characters in the same dramatic field, a heroine whose destiny would rewrite the old script. Instead the story particularizes male violence and female victimization: one could almost imagine the savage ending giving way to the opening of a new story, one in which of course, the memory of a dead woman haunts the consciousness of two brothers locked in symbiotic conflict over her.

Because Borges notoriously privileges form over content, structure over essence, and event over character, how gender figures in his narratives is always fascinating. **"The Duel,"** a story whose title echoes other narratives about the macho code of honor, is actually, according to the narrator, about two women characters who could easily populate one of Henry James's ironic, discursive, ambiguous narratives. He alerts the reader that events are subordinate to the characters, Clara Glencairn de Figueroa and Marta Pizarro, and the relationship between them. A complex and dissimulated rivalry exists between two women active in the art world of Argentine society, whose lives draw their meaning from their all-consuming interest in each other's work "each of them was her rival's judge and only public" (**"The Duel,"** *Doctor Brodie's Report*). The intrigues of their careers are traced through a series of plot reversals and parodies of art criticism; the narrator even detects "a mutual influence" in their pictures: "Clara's sunset glows found their ways into Marta Pizarro's patios, and Marta's fondness for straight lines simplified the ornateness of Clara's final stage . . ." As he approaches the end of the story, the narrator highlights the gender-marked differences between their "intimate . . . delicate duel," in which "there were neither defeats nor victories nor even an open encounter," and those male rivalries to which Borges has devoted so much of his attention. Despite the dispassionate, ironic tone, the narrator seems genuinely to regret a cultural condition "where a woman is regarded as a member of a species, not an individual. . . ." One is nonetheless tempted to note that his own conclusion provides the best critical commentary upon the imminence of an illumination that does not occur: "The story that made its way in darkness ends in darkness."

Two stories from the collection *The Book of Sand* are significant departures from Borges' other writings in which women figure as idealized or poetic objects of desire or represent a threat or danger to men. **"Ulrike"** is a memoir of a brief love affair between a South American professor and a Norwegian woman he meets while touring England. In the longer, more diffuse narrative about a secret intellectual organization, **"The Congress,"** an amorous episode forms the centerpiece. Both, although somewhat sentimental, are positive representations of erotic fulfillment. In the story **"Ulrike"** the narrator knows almost immediately after meeting the calm, mysterious woman that he is in love: "I could never have wanted any other person by my side." She, too, seems interested in him, and because "to a bachelor getting along in years, the offer of love is a gift no longer expected," and, remembering other missed opportunities, he is willing to accept whatever conditions this ominous "miracle" imposes upon him. Abounding with references to Ibsen, Norse sagas, old conquests, and national enmities, they call each other Sigurd and Brunhilde as a sign of faith in their capacity to transcend difference. "The sword Gram" lying "naked between them," provocatively referred to in the story's epigraph, no longer separates them during their night together when "[i]n the darkness, centuries old, love flowed, and for the first and last time I possessed Ulrike's image."

Only a writer like Borges could speak of "possessing Ulrike's image" when describing a sexual union. Certainly the consummation represents the transcendence of temporal and spatial limits, but this event is not unique even if

unrepeatable; indeed its universal structure poses for Borges the same problems of representation as all other absolute moments. The question is whether his use of "image" here is a metaphor for the *totalized* experience achieved or for what always eludes a speaking subject—that is, the difference between the moment experienced and the words to translate it. To put it otherwise, which aspect or aspects of Ulrike did the narrator "possess" that night, and which eluded him? Does "image" signify for Borges the totality of the experience or the gap between the experience and its representation? Or perhaps is he alluding to a difference intrinsic to experience itself, inclusive of language, and not separable from it?

How to contend with the problem of rendering such moments is crucial to Borges' enterprise, although sometimes one wonders if the problem is merely a rhetorical one: as linguistic act it calls attention to itself but its representational status is never seriously or profoundly threatened, nor is the thematic pattern of intentionality disrupted. In **"The Congress"** the heart of the amorous episode between the narrator, Alejandro Ferri, and his new lover, Beatrice, is her response to his proposal of marriage; as "a follower of the faith" of free love, "she did not want to tie herself down to anyone." She utters the word he "never dared speak" (conspicuously absent in the text), and his words immediately follow in a torrent of poetic bliss:

> O nights, O darkness warm and shared, O love that flows in shadows like some secret river, O that instant of ecstasy when each is both, O that ecstasy's purity and innocence, O the coupling in which we became lost so as then to lose ourselves in sleep, O the first light of dawn, and I watching her.

Some time after, they part in the British Museum where they had met the winter before, and, "to avoid the anguish of waiting for letters," he does not leave her his address. Although extended over time, their erotic connection is symbolized as one ecstatic moment, one night, one dawn, a singular vision.

In the final section of **"The Congress"** we find a passage that is strikingly similar to the one earlier quoted from **"El Aleph"** when "Borges" struggles to describe his vision of the Aleph:

> All language is a set of symbols whose use among its speakers assumes a shared past. . . . How then can I translate into words the limitless Aleph, which my floundering mind can scarcely encompass? Mystics with the same problem, fall back on symbols: to signify the godhead, one Persian speaks of a bird that is somehow all birds . . . Perhaps the gods might grant me a similar metaphor. . . . (*The "Aleph" and Other Stories*)

Its analogue in **"The Congress"** comes after the episode with Beatrice and attempts to inscribe the memory of the experience Ferri had shared with the other members of the secret Congress, who have since died:

> Words are symbols that assume a shared memory. . . . The mystics invoke a rose, a kiss, a bird that is all birds, a sun that is all the stars and the

sun, a jug of wine, a garden, or the sexual act. Of these metaphors none will serve me for that long, joyous night, which left us, tired out and happy, at the borders of dawn. . . . Down through the years, without much hope, I have sought the taste of that night; a few times I thought I had recaptured it in music, in love, in untrustworthy memories, but it has never come back to me except once in a dream. (*The Book of Sand*)

Despite the literal similarity in presentation as well as the symbolic overlay of the two quintessential experiences—the problem of rendering in language that which exceeds the power of representation—there is a radical difference between the nature and content of these experiences. What marks the mystical vision of the Aleph as different from the other experiences of the infinite is that it is solitary, cerebral, and irreducible. Hence the overwhelming difficulty of recollecting and formulating a moment of pure self-containment in universal, communicable terms, that is, into language. Of course, such an understanding of language is predicated on the notion that there is potential for such communication, however ineffable the experience or imperfect the vehicle. But because the uniqueness of the thing itself cannot be grasped or articulated, to be accessible to others it must become part of a network of already constituted meanings, that is, join the cast of other already metaphorized epiphanic experiences. It is Borges' premise that these "experiences" come mediated to us by way of literature, from which we derive our "shared memory." Whether through such indirection language ever brings us any closer to the experience or whether it in fact subsumes it remains ambiguous.

In the case of the joyous nights described in **"The Congress,"** the one experience that Ferri has sought desperately to recapture in music and love, and which seems to have been retrievable only once in dream, is not mystical in the usual sense, nor sexual in any sense. His ultimate experience, identified as "the single event of [his] whole life," was the enactment of an abstract philosophical ideal, a secret organization that sought to embrace everything in "the whole world." Understood finally to be an impossibility, the Congress of the World is dissolved and "the true Congress" realized the same night: a spontaneous, organic community, without agenda, without purpose. As "the only keeper of that secret event," Ferri justifies "committing perjury" and assumes the task of narrating their story, because with the death of the only other remaining member, the community no longer exists—and will not exist in memory either when Ferri dies. The recounting of that ideal night even includes an attempt to "bring [back] Beatrice's image," but it seems to be a perfunctory gesture. What Beatrice had rejected—the notion of an exclusive human connection—Ferri ironically learns to surpass through the experience of community. Yet an irony whose effects reverberate throughout the narrative is that one of the meanings of the word "congress" is sexual union.

Many of the variations on the theme of intellectual obsession and strategies of female figuration I have attempted to trace in this essay converge in one of Borges' last poems, **"The Threatened One."** As I hope to have shown, his use

of a feminine ideal to explore metaphysical possibilities often requires the death or ultimate loss of a woman, and this absence serves as the very pretext for writing. The inevitable temporal and spatial distance between an idealized object of desire and the invoked image provides him with the symbolic means to pursue the implications of some of his favorite philosophical problems: infinite interpretation as a form of immortality, the deceptive truth of memory, life as the construction of paradoxes. I hope to have also identified some tendencies, especially in his later writings, toward a less abstract conception of woman and an attendant openness toward erotic experience, an important aspect of this process. Yet if what constitutes now the ideal seems to be as much an embodiment as an image, his quest for the Absolute has *not* attenuated; and in this perceptible movement from ideality toward corporeality, woman remains the figure of choice.

What singularly distinguishes **"The Threatened One"** from other poems and narratives in which women figure prominently is that it is situated absolutely in the present and that it is addressed to a living beloved. As in many of his other poems, Borges uses the rhetorical device of enumeration as a way to summarize his major motifs and mythologies, as a metonymy of his main subjects, a microcosm of his entire work. But here the self-contained, intimate world composed of the poet's "talismans [and] touchstones—the practice of literature, vague learning, an apprenticeship to the language used by the flinty Northland to sing of its seas and its swords, the serenity of friendship, the galleries of the Library, ordinary things, habits, the young love of my mother, the soldierly shadow cast by my dead ancestors, the timeless night, the flavor of sleep and dream" (*The Gold of the Tigers*) are cited as useless in the face of an all-consuming, threatening love. None of the familiar points of reference pertain when "[b]eing with you or without you is how I measure my time" or when a "room is unreal" because "[you] ha[ve] not seen it"; this "is love with its own mythology."

Yet images of anguish and terror of self-extinction abound: "prison walls grow larger, as in a fearful dream," and "the darkness has not brought peace" for the man who has to "hide or flee" from this love. These lines manifest a remarkable dependence upon voice or enunciation, upon the poet's own convincing unmediated confessional utterance as well as upon his beloved's voice, her sensual presence: "It is love, I know it: the anxiety and relief at hearing / your voice . . . A woman's name has me in thrall / A woman's being afflicts my whole body." What is most fascinating, perhaps, about this evocation of obsessive love is the absence of the ethereal, the abstract, the transcendent, indeed those very characteristics of romantic longing which mirror Borges' pervasive quest for the Absolute. That this movement from ideality to corporeality still revolves around woman as figure, of course, raises some new issues while masking others. The poet's dependence in **"The Threatened One"** upon the beloved's voice and physical presence is an even stronger declaration of the consumptive power of erotic desire and an admission that poesis may have its limitations. In this poetic self-portrait the repetitious effects of the conclusive words "It is love" are immediate, enduring, and absolutely corporeal—coexistent it would seem with his own being, his life. And even as this poem is addressed to, written for a specific woman, it has no meaning or value apart from her, cannot compare with her. Here there is no symbolic or metaphorical inscription of the feminine as an aspect of the quest for the Absolute, no projection backward or forward toward mystical union with a lost or deferred object, no recognition of the pleasure derived from the exercise of cerebral prowess as a means of constituting subjectivity in the world.

If the poet fears the condition of immanence in which he finds himself, it may be due precisely to love's capacity to eclipse all other things, put all else into question. If writing is predicated on loss or exile, then the entire enterprise of writing represented in the poem might now be threatened by this passion for the present, for what is none other than a competing metaphysics. To accept the performative terms of this poem, however, is not to read its ontology of female voice and body uncritically. It is to be aware that there are always at least two readers, one of whom is Borges, occupying space on both sides of the text's divide. For the "Borges" who said "I live, I allow myself to live, so that Borges may contrive his literature and that literature justifies my existence" (**"Borges and I,"** *Dreamtigers*), losing one's self in love may pose an ominous threat indeed. But only if "the other one"—the "other reader," that is—does not live to write about it. Borges' "idea of woman" ensures the vitality of each.

Bella Brodzki, "Borges and the Idea of Woman," in Modern Fiction Studies, *Vol. 36, No. 2, Summer, 1990, pp. 149-66.*

"Argumentum Ornithologicum"

I close my eyes and see a flock of birds. The vision lasts a second or perhaps less; I don't know how many birds I saw. Were they a definite or an indefinite number? This problem involves the question of the existence of God. If God exists, the number is definite, because how many birds I saw is known to God. If God does not exist, the number is indefinite, because nobody was able to take count. In this case, I saw fewer than ten birds (let's say) and more than one; but I did not see nine, eight, seven, six, five, four, three, or two birds. I saw a number between ten and one, but not nine, eight, seven, six, five, etc. That number, as a whole number, is inconceivable; *ergo,* God exists.

Jorge Luis Borges, in his Dreamtigers, *University of Texas Press, 1985.*

Edna Aizenberg   (essay date 1992)

[*In the following excerpt, Aizenberg discusses the influence Borges's work has on "postcolonial" literature and criticism.*]

1. Postmodernism holds center stage as the major critical practice of the moment. And Borges is there, of course.

Critics working in Latin American literature, however, have noted the discomforts of fitting Borges, along with other Latin American authors, into the postmodern mold; as one critic asked graphically, if with some gender bias: "Is the corset too tight for the fat lady?" One place where the corset pinches is in its elision of the Latin American condition of the texts. Typically, these are subsumed into Euro-U.S. concerns. The traits that mark their "postmodernism" are employed to illustrate trends in "late capitalist, bourgeois, informational, postindustrial society" and are said to respond to Western needs: for example, the "totalizing forces" of mass culture. What is forgotten is the peripheric, ex-centric position. The "postmodern" characteristics of Latin American and Borgesian literature enthusiastically embraced by U.S. and European critics— self-reflexivity, indeterminacy, carnivalization, decanonization, intertextuality, pastiche, hybridity, the problematizing of time and space and of historical and fictional narration—are primarily a correlative of a colonized history and an uncohered identity, of incomplete modernity and uneven cultural development, rather than postindustrialization and mass culture. Their uncritical incorporation into a metropolitan repertoire indicates that the centering impulse of a "decentered" postmodernism is far from gone.

It is at this point that postcolonialism becomes an effective heuristic tool. Like all concepts, it is a tool, and one must take care lest it too become a corset squeezing the fat lady. There are many colonialisms, diverse postcolonial situations, significant overlaps between postcolonialism and other theoretical modes, disparate and antagonistic strands of postcolonial criticism, interrogations about *post*colonialism's continuing enmeshment in the colonial gaze. Nevertheless, *grosso modo,* postcolonial theory has done much in its shift of focus from the "center" to the "margins," with the core of interest on conditions and developments at the "margins"; it has made valuable contributions to a comparative approach that contests the usual North-South perspective of literary studies and connects cultures and literatures that have infrequently, if ever, spoken to each other; and it has provided important insights for "identifying and articulating the symptomatic and distinctive features" of postcolonial texts, *from* the condition of postcoloniality.

This work is exceedingly relevant to Latin American writers, first and foremost Borges. Traits of Borges that have been understood (or misunderstood) within the two regnant contexts of study, Eurocentric or national-Latin American, acquire new sharpness when read from the perspective of postcolonialism. A postcolonial perspective brings into focus Borges's strengths and Borges's lacks. It allows for a renewed appreciation of Borges's role as a forerunner to what is significant in present literary-critical practice, particularly the writing of such "Third World" authors as Salman Rushdie, Tahar Ben Jelloun, Anton Shammas, and Sergio Chejfec, who see in the Argentine master a postcolonial precursor.

2. Postcolonial critics underscore the theoretical hegemony of Europe, a hegemony that has utilized the texts of the "margins" to construct itself—Latin American literature

and postmodernism is a case in point—yet has frequently ignored the theoretical explorations of the "margins." These explorations, in the literary texts themselves and in essays and works of criticism, more than once prefigure issues that have since become crucial to the "center," as in the case of postmodernism; and this prefiguring results precisely from the "marginal" status, with its intense sensitivity to problems of textuality and reality, to troubling epistemological questions.

Borges illustrates the elision, despite the fact that he has attained canonical rank in Euro-U.S. critical-literary discourse. Certain Borges writings are cited to buttress, say, Genette or Bloom or Foucault, whereas others are little mentioned. **"Kafka and His Precursors"** and **"Pierre Menard, Author of the *Quixote"*** fall into the first category; **"The Argentine Writer and Tradition"** into the second. Then too, what we might call the postcolonial implications of even the cited works are ignored; this is true of Borges's essays and his fictions.

Let us look at **"El escritor argentino y la tradición."** Originally delivered as a lecture in the fifties, the essay contains many of the questions that are important to postcolonial criticism and that intersect with the preoccupations of the "center." The issue of tradition itself, with the related issue of the canon, is one. Borges's purpose in the essay is to define Argentina's literary tradition in order to guide contemporary Argentine writers in their task. The title of the piece recalls Eliot's "Tradition and the Individual Talent," an essay that Borges refers to in **"Kafka and His Precursors"** to develop the now well-known idea that "every writer *creates* his own precursors." But to continue with tradition. Nowhere in his discussion does Eliot interrogate what tradition is for the English writer. He declares: the "historical sense compels a man to write . . . with a feeling that the whole of the literature of Europe from Homer and within it the literature of his own country has a simultaneous existence and composes a simultaneous order." Although Borges attempts to project an analogous sense of security and order, opening his essay by calling the problem of defining Argentine literary tradition a "pseudoproblem" and concluding with what has been read as a submission to Europe, the fact is that there is a great deal more probing of the meaning of tradition, as well as heterogeneity in describing it and subversiveness in treating it.

Borges reflects upon a number of possible traditions: the tradition of gauchesque poetry, the tradition of Spanish literature, and the Western tradition as a whole. The gauchesque receives particular attention, in large measure because it has been considered Argentina's "authentic," "native" literary tradition, and its masterwork, José Hernández's *Martín Fierro,* Argentina's canonical book. Borges's pointed analysis dwells on the primary claim to authenticity of the gauchesque, its language, supposedly derived from the spontaneous oral poetry of the gauchos. His examination in effect dismantles this claim; he indicates that the gauchesque poets, city men, cultivated a "deliberately popular language never essayed by the popular poets themselves." In the constructed idiom there was a purposeful "seeking out of native words, a profusion of local color," whereas the gaucho singers tried to express themselves in nondialectal forms and to address great abstract themes. Borges's conclusion is that gauchesque poetry, which had produced admirable books, not least Hernández's "lasting work," was nevertheless a "literary genre as artificial as any other."

The discussion is enormously suggestive. What is the relationship between orature and literature in conforming a literary tradition? Questions about the continuities and discontinuities between oral and written forms are at the heart of literary-critical discourse in Africa, for example, with the unexamined championing of the oral tradition as the model for contemporary African writing an area of debate. There is likewise the matter of an essentialized nativism as the basis of contemporary cultural tradition, what the Nigerian critic Chidi Amuta terms "raffia, calabash, and masquerade culture." The seeking out of a profusion of local color, including fixed "native" linguistic codes, is seen by Amuta and other critics as a retrograde maneuver that perpetuates the "exotic" view of the non-European and ignores the essence of postcolonial cultures and their languages as dynamic, dialectical, hybridized formations.

If a limited, conversational nativism could not form the basis for Argentine literary tradition (in the essay Borges recalls that early in his career he had been a "raffia and calabash" man), neither could the literature of the former "mother country." Borges states categorically: "Argentine history can be unmistakeably defined as a desire to become separated from Spain." Instead of positing a smooth interface between Spanish literature and Argentine literature as one grandly unbroken master narrative (a position more than once perpetuated in the teaching of Latin American literature), Borges posits rupture. For an Argentine to write like a Spaniard is testimony to "Argentine versatility" in assuming a persona rather than indication of a natural state. Of course, Borges returned again and again to the masterwork of Spanish literature, the *Quixote,* as he dialogued with Spanish writers—Quevedo, Gracián—and as he rewrote the *Martín Fierro* in his fictions; but his selective manipulation of elements of these traditions can best be explicated in the framework of the third tradition he examines, Western culture.

In their studies the Australian critics Bill Ashcroft, Gareth Griffiths, and Helen Tiffin, who are among the most prolific researchers in postcolonial theory, underscore that it "is inadequate to read" postcolonial texts "either as a reconstruction of pure traditional values or as simply foreign and intrusive." These texts are constituted in the shuttle space between the two illusory absolutes, "within and between two worlds." Postcolonial texts can further be conceived as an alternate reading practice whose aim is the revisionist appropriation and abrogation of the Western canon. These thoughts are helpful in approaching Borges's approach to the Western tradition, because his posture has been construed as nothing if not "foreign and intrusive." Borges writes: "I believe our tradition is all of Western culture," but the statement does not lead to a reiteration of the authority of the "center" to "write" Borges. Instead, Borges turns the Western tradition against itself by appropriating the right to write back to the "center." "We have a right to this tradition," he asserts, "*greater than that* which the inhabitants of one or another Western nation might have." The assertion is the takeoff point for a model of difference and a strategy of subversion.

Dialoguing with another essay, Thorstein Veblen's 1919 article "The Intellectual Pre-eminence of Jews in Modern Europe," Borges applies to the Argentine and Latin American circumstance the American thinker's notion of Jewish difference as the breeding ground for innovation. Long before Derrida's *différance,* Borges anchors his attitude toward Western discourse in "not feel[ing] tied to it by any special devotion," in "feel[ing] different," like the Jews or the Irish. Difference makes for deferral. To quote Borges again: "I believe that we . . . can handle all European themes, handle them without superstition, with an irreverence which can have, and already does have fortunate consequences."

There is in these statements of **"The Argentine Writer and Tradition"** all the creative *chutzpah* and, yes, the ambiguity—if not anxiety—of the postcolonial situation. On the one hand, the speaking back, the challenge to the metropolis, and the installation of irreverent difference as the modus operandi of fortunate literary labor; on the other the pervasive concern, common to postcolonial societies, with myths of identity and authenticity, with establishing a linguistic practice, with place and displacement, with canonicity and "uncanonicity." Borges's lifelong Hebraism, exemplified in the essay, correlates with this double movement. It was not merely the Jewish condition, traversed as it was with many similar complexities, that attracted Borges. It was also the Jewish textual tradition, some of whose views were displaced by the dominant Greek-Western logos as inauthentic—in Borges's words, "alien" to the Western mind. (What the dominant logos judged "authentic" in Jewish textuality was authenticated by its appropriation, not by its Jewish roots.)

One such view was the conception of writing as inevitably *inter*textual, constituted in the bold interaction—not decorous separation—of Torah and scholia, of canon and commentary, through an ongoing process of interpretive reconstitution. Another was the idea, carried to an extreme by the mysticism of the Kabbalah, that audacious revisionism masked as faithful reproduction formed the proper stance toward tradition. Borges's exploration and radicalization of these beliefs was clearly an attempt to find precedents, from the edge of the world, for alternative literary models: models of strategic "marginality" with the interplay of the standard and the subversive that became Borges's stance.

It is not incidental that Bloom connects Jewish hermeticism to Borges via a secularized, parodic version of the principle of "reading old texts afresh," for in his nonsuperstitious handling of Western themes the "parodic miniaturization of a vast work of art" constituted one of Borges's favorite revisionary operations. We are now so familiar with these Borgesian manipulations that we scarcely stop to consider their implications, particularly in a postcolonial context.

The biblical urtext, whose questioning "to absurdity" by the Kabbalists Borges so admired, is not the least of the vast parodied works; in Borges, Cain becomes Abel, Judas becomes Jesus, the Crucifixion of Jesus becomes the crucifixion of a medical student, Golgotha becomes an obscure Argentine ranch. The event occurs after the student "brings light" to the "heathen," in a tale audaciously entitled **"The Gospel According to Mark."** One cannot help but think here of works like Yambo Ouologuem's *Devoir de violence,* Chinua Achebe's *Things Fall Apart,* Ngũgĩ wa Thiongo's *Petals of Blood,* Timothy Findley's *Not Wanted on the Voyage,* and Gabriel Garcìa Márquez's *Cien años de soledad*—all postcolonial novels in which scripture is parodically repositioned, its orthodox presuppositions (often in the setting of the missionizing endeavor in the imperialized area) disrupted. In **"The Gospel According to Mark"** Borges gives narrative substance to the linguistic-interpretive relativization that necessarily occurs in new and hybridized settings: the student Baltasar Espinosa, whose name already bespeaks Judaic heresy and whose background and religious beliefs are already impure, cannot exert interpretive control either over the text—not accidentally an English Bible—or over events, and it is ultimately the even more mestizo Guthries/Gutres who have the last word at tale's end.

Other master myths and works, and systems of knowledge, are subjected to parallel carnivalistic-reductive techniques, frequently in an Argentine milieu: the ineffable godhead is viewed, flat on the back, in a Buenos Aires cellar; the sublime Dante Alighieri is the flatulent Carlos Argentino Danieri; Erik Lönnrot meets death in a spectral *porteño* Southside after a rigorous Spinozan quest; Qaphqa is a latrine in Babylon, synonym of Babel, synonym of Buenos Aires, as in the line from Borges where he sings to his "babelic" home city, "texted" out of cultural and linguistic fragments from the four corners of the earth. Indeed, in many of Borges's texts it is not merely the inversion of a specific writer or system that "writes back" to the "center." There is the freewheeling pastiche of authors, epochs, languages, philosophies that is equally undermining, since the very juxtaposition short-circuits metropolitan notions of linearity, epistemological security, temporal-spatial coherence, historical and fictional progression, and mimetic accuracy.

A pastiche of associations suggests itself at this point: Foucault's heterotopic reading of the signs in teacups of Western history and thought "out of a passage in Borges" from **"The Analytical Language of John Wilkins"** that contains the kind of juxtaposition just noted; a Chinese taxonomy of beasts, many fabulous (more shortly about postcolonialism and imaginary beings); or Homi Bhabha's positing of the lack of mimetic correspondence as a postcolonial strategy for shattering the mirror of Western representation, which brings to mind Borges's early championing of irrealism, a frequent recourse, he points out, of non-Western writing; or even Ngũgĩ's comment about space, time, and progress in the "Third World," in Kenya, and in Argentina:

> Skyscrapers versus mud walls and grass thatch . . . international casinos versus cattle-paths and gossip before sunset. Our erstwhile masters had left us a very unevenly cultivated land: the centre was swollen with fruit and water

sucked from the rest, while the outer parts were progressively weaker and scragglier as one moved away from the center.

In Borges one finds the "unevenness," the clashing orders, the disjunctive language of narration that results in large measure from the disorder left behind by colonialization; but it is a disorder that calls to answer established rhetorics so as to fashion novel discourses out of the challenge.

It is not for nothing that in **"Kafka and His Precursors,"** where heterogeneous pieces nudge each other, Borges fabricates a more provocative, postcolonial version of Eliot's majestic proposition that every writer's work *modifies* our conception of the past and future. According to Borges, every writer goes further: he *creates* his own forerunners. And appropriately so, for at the "periphery," where things have as yet to cohere, one must create a genealogy, an identity, and a place. Still, Borges experienced the uncoherence of the edge at a time when the Western "center" itself could not hold, as a young man beholding the spectacle of the Western order disintegrating in the trenches of the Great War, and as a writer at the height of his powers observing, from far-off Buenos Aires, the even greater falling apart of things during World War II. The postcolonial world emerged out of these conflicts; Borges, with his outsider's antennae, foresaw and registered many of the seismic shifts in the realms of thought and literature.

At the same time, however, he registered the contradictions of an intellectual caught in the divide, one whose background and formation continued to enmesh him, at many moments, in the colonial gaze. The repeated dislocations at the Casa Rosada and at the Plaza de Mayo, messy and equivocal as some might have been, were in large measure the correlatives of what Borges was chronicling in his texts; but more often than not he did not see this. At the divide, Borges was crucial in shattering time-honored, dominant codes of recognition, clearing the ground; it remained for his postcolonial ephebes to carry on the work and build in the clearing through the very process that Borges had advocated: by realizing, transforming, and transgressing the precursor.

Edna Aizenberg, "Borges, Postcolonial Precursor," in World Literature Today, *Vol. 66, No. 1, Winter, 1992, pp. 21-6.*

FURTHER READING

Biography

Monegal, Emir Rodriguez. *Jorge Luis Borges: A Literary Biography*. New York: E. P. Dutton, 1978, 502 p.

Detailed study of Borges's life and career.

Criticism

Agheana, Ion T. *The Prose of Jorge Luis Borges*. New York: Peter Lang Publishing, 1984, 320 p.

Examination of existentialist elements in Borges's fiction.

Alazraki, Jaime. *Jorge Luis Borges*. New York: Columbia University Press, 1971, 48 p.

Concise essay treating Borges's literary themes and world-view.

Bell-Villada, Gene H. *Borges and His Fiction: A Guide to His Mind and Art*. Chapel Hill: The University of North Carolina Press, 1981, 292 p.

Chronological examination of Borges's works.

Cheselka, Paul. *The Poetry and Poetics of Jorge Luis Borges*. New York: Peter Lang Publishing, 1987, 197 p.

Study of Borges's poetry "from his first ultraist poems published in Spain to the publication of *Obra poetica 1923-1964*."

Christ, Ronald J. *The Narrow Act: Borges' Art of Allusion*. New York: New York University Press, 1969, 244 p.

Analysis of the "esthetic origin, development, and masterful practice" of Borges's use of allusion.

McMurray, George R. *Jorge Luis Borges*. New York: Frederick Ungar Publishing, 1980, 255 p.

Thematic study of Borges's fiction.

Stabb, Martin S. *Jorge Luis Borges*. Boston: Twayne Publishers, 1970, 179 p.

General survey of Borges's life, career, and critical reception.

Sturrock, John. *Paper Tigers: The Ideal Fictions of Jorge Luis Borges*. Oxford: Oxford University Press, 1977, 227 p.

Examination of Borges's theory of fiction, maintaining that the Argentinean author's stories are "formal to a degree that no writer of fiction, surely, has ever surpassed."

Carolyn Forché

1950-

(Full name Carolyn Louise Forché) American poet, journalist, editor, and translator.

The following entry provides an overview of Forché's career. For further information on her life and works, see *CLC,* Volume 25.

INTRODUCTION

Chiefly regarded as a political poet, Forché is best known for *The Country between Us* (1982), which graphically documents the horrors inflicted upon the Salvadoran people during the Civil War of the late 1970s. Reacting against critics who fault her inclusion of partisan themes, Forché has asserted: "All poetry is both pure and engaged, in the sense that it is made of language, but it is also art. Any theory which takes one half of the social-esthetic dynamic and accentuates it too much results in a breakdown. Stress of purity generates a feeble estheticism that fails, in its beauty, to communicate. On the other hand, propagandistic hack-work has no independent life as poetry. What matters is not whether a poem is political, but the quality of its engagement."

Biographical Information

Born in Detroit, Michigan, Forché was raised in its neighboring suburbs and attended Catholic schools. She developed an interest in literature at age nine when her mother gave her a poetry anthology to read and suggested that she try writing a poem. Forché has commented that writing then became "an escape. Writing and daydreaming. Writing was simply the reverie that I recorded, and I wrote volumes of diaries and journals. Then, when I wasn't writing, when I was doing housework or whatever, I kept some sort of little voice running in my mind. I told myself narratives, and I made a parallel life to my own. It was completely imaginary, and most of the time everything would take place a hundred years earlier on the same spot where I was. I suspected, when I was young, that this was madness, but I couldn't give it up." Forché attended Michigan State University and later earned an M.F.A. from Bowling Green State University. After the publication of her prizewinning debut collection, *Gathering the Tribes* (1976), she traveled to Spain where she lived with exiled Salvadoran poet Claribel Alegría and, in translating Alegría's poetry into English, learned of the Salvadoran Civil War. Upon her return to the United States, she was visited by Leonel Gómez Vides, Alegría's cousin and an activist in El Salvador who encouraged Forché to witness the situation in Central America. Forché journeyed to El Salvador in 1978 in an attempt to document the war. Fearing for her life, she left the country in 1980 at the urging of her friend Archbishop Oscar Romero—two weeks before he was assassinated. A staunch critic of the United States's military

support of the Salvadoran government's repressive forces, Forché wrote of her experiences in various journals and, eventually, in *The Country between Us*. Forché continues to remain politically active: she has served on various committees studying the situation in Central America; she has worked for Amnesty International and the Western chapter of the International Association of Poets, Playwrights, Editors, Essayists and Novelists (PEN); and she has been employed as a foreign news correspondent in Beirut, Lebanon.

Major Works

The largely autobiographical *Gathering the Tribes*, which won the 1975 Yale Series of Younger Poets Award, has been praised for its focus on community, kinship, memory, ritual, and sexuality. The long poem "Burning the Tomato Worms," for example, concerns Forché's sexual awakening, her relationship with her Slovak grandmother, and her grandmother's upbringing. *The Country between Us,* for which Forché earned the 1981 Lamont Selection of the Academy of American Poets, established her reputation as a political poet. The collection is divided into three sections: "In Salvador, 1978-1980," "Reunion," and "Ourselves or Nothing." The first details the horrifying events Forché witnessed in Central America and her eventual return to the United States. In the prose poem "The Colonel," for instance, she focuses on El Salvador's totalitarian regime and the mutilation inflicted on political prisoners. The second and third sections of the book continue to emphasize the importance of memory and witness, but additionally stress the importance of interpersonal relationships as a means of achieving peace and communion. Comprised of a single poem, the third section is dedicated to Holocaust scholar Terrence des Pres and is often considered representative of Forché's poetics and political beliefs. The piece concludes: "There is a cyclone fence between / ourselves and the slaughter and behind it / we hover in a calm protected world like / netted fish, exactly like netted fish. / It is either the beginning or the end / of the world, and the choice is ourselves / or nothing." Focusing, in part, on the acts of genocide that have occurred in Latin America and the inhumanity of the Holocaust and Hiroshima, Forché's book-length poem, *The Angel of History* (1994), is similarly concerned with war, human misery, remembrance, and survival.

Critical Reception

Forché has been the recipient of numerous awards and fellowships yet her work has often been faulted for what some critics consider its overt polemics. Some scholars, however, argue that all poetry can be interpreted as a political message on some level and note that Forché's work signals the need for new schools of criticism and poetics that deliberately emphasize the political arena. Sharon Doubiago has asserted: "[This] poet, this extraordinary woman has already gone further than most ever will in trying to authenticate her voice, immersing herself and her language in the 'real' and very dangerous world. She has used her verbal training like a guerilla uses intimate knowledge of the land, taking the aesthetic jammed into her as a young working class woman gone to college and jamming it right back into the real, the political. This is a poetry of terrible witness, the strains of our villainies on the language and ethical constructs undoubtedly show. Thus the phrase 'the country between us.' "

PRINCIPAL WORKS

Gathering the Tribes (poetry) 1976
The Country between Us (poetry) 1982
Against Forgetting: Twentieth-Century Poetry of Witness [editor] (poetry) 1993
The Angel of History (poetry) 1994

CRITICISM

Larry Levis (essay date July 1981)

[*An American poet, Levis won the International Poetry Forum United States Award in 1971, the Lamont Poetry Prize in 1976, and a National Poetry Series Award in 1981. In the excerpt below, originally given as a speech in July 1981 at the Aspen Writers' Conference in Aspen, Colorado, he discusses the problems associated with attempting to convey the atrocities of war through literature and Forché's poetic treatment of the subject of violence.*]

What is it like to write about or to photograph a war that is going on now, that was going on last week, last year? In the post-Vietnam era, I believe that one of the most difficult problems is to convey, simply, information, *facts* which sound, to those who are comfortable, like "improbable tales." For any advance which might be called humane and positive, there are advances in warfare which might be called cynical and retrograde. Anyone writing about war now must bear witness to two phenomena common to any war but ostensibly more intentional and widespread now: torture and mutilation.

Item: June 20, 1981. I am staring at a photograph by Susan Meiselas which depicts a dead Nicaraguan, apparently a man and, in all probability, one who rebelled against the deposed dictator, Anastasio Samoza Debayle. I assume this because the location of the photograph, "Cuesta del Plomo," is a hillside near Managua where the National Guard carried out its assassinations. Actually, the photograph shows only half a man—the legs, clad in jeans, and, above them, a spine with all of the ribs snapped off or hacked off by some sort of macheté or tool. Some of the stubs of the stronger ribs still show in the picture. The spine resembles a delimbed tree trunk at first but soon it resembles nothing but a spine. Other bones litter the foreground. The background looks, except for a few patchy areas, as if it could be a tropical postcard with a bay, trees, and mountains in the distance. But what one notices is a spine. The rebel is not only dead, but mutilated beyond any purpose one might have who thinks of burial. There is no suggestion that his limbs were cut off and strewn in this field out of rage; it looks too much like a calculated design, a design which is, at the same time, casual. After a few moments I realize the intention of this: mutilation, too, has become a kind of art. Perverse? Nihilistic? Maybe. But art: the corpse is on display; it is meant to be seen, although it could hardly be identified by anyone looking here, for a loved one, for someone lost. The photograph by Meiselas was taken in Nicaragua, but it could just as easily have been take in Argentina, El Salvador, or Guatemala.

Item: From "Letter from El Salvador," by Tom Buckley, *The New Yorker,* June 22, 1981.

> On April 29th, the House Foreign Affairs Committee voted, 26-7, to require President Reagan to certify, as a condition for further military aid, that "indiscriminate torture and murder" by Salvadoran security forces were being brought under control. On May 11th, the Senate Foreign

Relations Committee, which is controlled by Republicans, passed a similar measure . . . It acted over the protest of Secretary Haig, who said in a letter to the committee that such a bill "would encourage left-wing insurgents and other extremists."

Item: Buckley, above.

El Salvador is receiving a hundred and forty-four million dollars in economic aid and thirty-five and a half million dollars in military aid in the fiscal year that ends on September 30th. The sums that Congress is considering for the 1982 fiscal year are ninety-one million dollars and twenty-six million dollars, respectively. No one doubts, however, that large supplemental appropriations will be sought.

And finally:

Even that sum became small change when the Reagan Administration announced on June 3rd that it had approved in principle a comprehensive program of economic and military aid for the nations of the Caribbean and Central America. Its purpose, like the old Alliance for Progress, would be to counter Communist, particularly Cuban, influence by improving the standard of living under capitalism.

Buckley ends his article with an account, published in the *Times,* of two hundred peasants who were massacred on the Honduran border as they tried to cross the Lempa River to safe territory. Witnesses said many were machine-gunned, from the air, by a helicopter, "probably one of those supplied by the United States."

Parables, like [Zbigniew] Herbert's, come into existence because they abstract their designs from experience that is already complete, and which can, therefore, become a subject of contemplation. It is experience which has ended, which has entered into, if not chronological history, at least the maker's psychic history. But how can one make a parable out of last week's massacre and preserve his or her sense of artistic integrity? Or even *sanity?* One might also ask whether the experience of contemporary warfare is fit for parable. When a situation is immense, such as Hitler's occupation of Europe, then perhaps Herbert's parables or Camus' allegory of that war, *The Plague,* can, through miniaturization, make it visible. For what Hitler did was common experience, it was *known.* The difficulty for anyone writing about El Salvador is to make known what, in fact, is happening there, to reveal a brutal, and otherwise wholly ignorable "small" war—yet one that has claimed, since January 1980, over 22,000 lives.

Lowell's lines, in such a context, begin to sound ominously prophetic: "peace to our children when they fall / in small war on the heels of small war—until the end of time." But Lowell's perspective is long. Susan Meiselas's camera is only about eight feet from that spine. And how can anyone, poet or journalist, write about torture, massacre, and mutilation without sounding hyperbolic? It is a difficult art, but one which can be done. Here is Carolyn Forché's poem, **"The Colonel":**

What you have heard is true. I was in his house. His wife carried a tray of coffee and sugar. His daughter filed her nails, his son went out for the night. There were daily papers, pet dogs, a pistol on the cushion beside him. The moon swung bare on its black cord over the house. On the television was a cop show. It was in English. Broken bottles were imbedded in the walls around the house to scoop the kneecaps from a man's legs or cut his hands to lace. On the windows there were gratings as there are in liquor stores. We had dinner, rack of lamb, good wine, a gold bell on the table for calling the maid. The maid brought green mangoes, salt, a type of bread. I was asked how I enjoyed the country. There was a brief commercial in Spanish. His wife took everything away. There was some talk then of how difficult it had become to govern. The parrot said hello on the terrace. The colonel told it to shut up, and pushed himself from the table. My friend said to me with his eyes: say nothing. The colonel returned with a sack as is used to bring groceries home. He spilled many human ears on the table. They were like dried peach halves. There is no other way to say this. He took one of them in his hands, shook it in our faces, dropped it into a water glass. It came alive there. I am tired of fooling around, he said. As for the rights of anyone, tell your people they can go fuck themselves. He swept the ears to the floor with his arm and raised the last of his wine in the air. Something for your poetry, no? he said. Some of the ears on the floor caught this scrap of his voice. Some of the ears on the floor were pressed to the ground.

El Salvador, May 1978

There are moments when life imitates art, when what appears to be on the surface a slightly surrealistic prose poem—a poem wholly imagined—is, in fact, a realistic, reportorial account of a dinner party. Had the poem been written without reference to El Salvador, its effect would be altered, changed by the fact of its being *imagined.* This is, unfortunately, not the case here. Children often ask: "Is this a *real* story?" So do adults. Carolyn Forché, who over a two-year period made several visits to El Salvador as a journalist and an observer for Amnesty International, writes the following account of the poem [in her **"El Salvador: An Aide Memoire"**]:

I was taken to the homes of landowners, with their pools set like aquamarines in the clipped grass, to the afternoon games of canasta over quaint local *pupusas* and tea, where parrots hung by their feet among the bougainvillia and nearly everything was imported, if only form Miami or New Orleans. One evening I dined with a military officer who toasted America, private enterprize, Las Vegas and the "fatherland" until his wife excused herself and in a drape of cigar smoke the events of **"The Colonel"** took place. Almost a *poème trouvé.* I had only to pare down the memory and render it whole, unlined and as precise as recollection would have it. I did not wish to endanger myself by the act of poeticizing such a necessary reportage. It became, when I wrote it, the second insistence of El Salvador to infiltrate what I so ridiculously preserved as my work's allegiance to Art. No more than in any earlier poems did I choose my subject.

What is that "allegiance to Art"? And what, given the circumstances, is sensationalism? I think, in the case of Carolyn Forché's second book, *The Country Between Us,* the poet undergoes and records a journey which reconciles the political with the artistic rather than severs that vital connection—for, finally, there is nothing sensationalistic about setting down the facts of a dinner party. If one argues that such facts remain sensationalistic in the context of poetry, it may be because readers no longer expect facts from poems, and think that all details are imagined. And if this is so, isn't one really arguing for that "inward" aesthetic which Hans Magnus Enzensberger criticizes? And isn't the result of such an aesthetic designed to limit poetry in its subjects? Therefore, isn't it, really and finally, another kind of censorship?

Unlike Herbert, Forché's position in the poems about El Salvador is admittedly partisan. She is, as are many of the people *in* El Salvador, against the military, against the government, the landowners, the mockery of "land-reform," and against U.S. aid, especially military aid. But such partisanship seems, under the conditions now apparent in that country, not Leftist so much as simply decent, and human, and discernible in many ways as a concern for the poet's friends in El Salvador. Some of them appear in **"Return":**

> for Josephine Crum
>
> Upon my return to America, Josephine:
> the iced drinks and paper umbrellas, clean
> toilets and Los Angeles palm trees moving
> like lean women, I was afraid more than
> I had been, so much so and even of motels
> that for months every tire blow-out
> was final, every strange car near the house
> kept watch and I strained even to remember
> things impossible to forget. You took
> my stories apart for hours, sitting
> on your sofa with your legs under you
> and fifty years in your face.
>   So you know
> now, you said, what kind of money
> is involved and that *campesinos* knife
> one another and you know you should
> not trust anyone and so you find a few
> people you will trust. You know the mix
> of machetés with whiskey, the slip of the
> tongue
> and that it costs hundreds of deaths.
> You've seen the pits where men and women
> are kept the few days it takes without
> food and water. You've heard the cocktail
> conversation on which depends their release.
> So you've come to understand when
> men and women of goodwill read
> torture reports with fascination.
> And such things as water pumps
> and co-op gardens are of little importance
> and takes years.
> It is not Che Guevara, this struggle.
> Camillo Torres is dead. Victor Jara
> was rounded up with the others, and Jose

> Marti is a landing strip for planes
> from Miami to Cuba. Go try on
> Americans your long, dull story
> of corruption, but better to give
> them what they want: Lil Milagro Ramirez,
> who after years of confinement did not
> know what year it was, how she walked
> with help and was forced to shit in public.
> Tell them about the razor, the live wire,
> dry ice and concrete, grey rats and above all
> who fucked her, how many times and when.
> Tell them about retaliation: Jose lying
> on the flatbed truck, waving his stumps
> in your face, his hands cut off by his
> captors and thrown to the many acres
> of cotton, lost, still and holding
> the last few lumps of leeched earth.
> Tell them Jose in his last few hours
> and later how, many months later,
> a labor leader was cut to pieces and buried.
> Tell them how his friends found
> the soldiers and made them dig him up
> and ask forgiveness of the corpse, once
> it was assembled again on the ground
> like a man. As for the cars, of course
> they watch you and for this don't flatter
> yourself. We are all watched. We are
> all assembled.
>   Josephine, I tell you
> I have not slept, not since I drove
> those streets with a gun in my lap,
> not since all manner of speaking has
> failed and the remnant of my life
> continues onward. I go mad, for example,
> in the Safeway, at the many heads
> of lettuce, papayas and sugar, pineapples
> and coffee, especially the coffee.
> And when I speak with American men,
> there is some absence of recognition:
> their constant Scotch and fine white
> hands, many hours of business, penises
> hardened to motor inns and a faint
> resemblance to their wives. I cannot
> keep going. I remember the ambassador
> from America to that country: his tanks
> of fish, his clicking pen, his rapt
> devotion to reports. His wife wrote
> his reports. She said as much as she
> gathered him each day from the embassy
> compound, that she was tired of covering
> up, sick of his drink and the failure
> of his last promotion. She was a woman
> who flew her own plane, stalling out
> after four martinis to taxi on an empty
> field in the campo and to those men
> and women announce she was there to help.
> She flew where she pleased in that country
> with her drunken kindness, while Marines
> in white gloves were assigned to protect
> her husband. It was difficult work, what
> with the suspicion on the rise in smaller
> countries that gringos die like other men.
> I cannot, Josephine, talk to them.
>
> And so you say, you've learned a little
> about starvation: a child like a supper scrap
> filling with worms, many children strung
> together, as if they were cut from paper
> and all in a delicate chain. And that people

who rescue physicists, lawyers and poets
lie in their beds at night with reports
of mice introduced into women, of men
whose testicles are crushed like eggs.
That they cup their own parts
with their bedsheets and move themselves
slowly, imagining bracelets affixing
their wrists to a wall where the naked
are pinned, where the naked are tied open
and left to the hands of those who erase
what they touch. We are all erased
by them, and no longer resemble decent
men. We no longer have the hearts,
the strength, the lives of women.
We do not hold this struggle in our hands
in the darkness but ourselves and what little
comes to the surface between our legs.
Your problem is not your life as it is
in America, not that your hands, as you
tell me, are tied to do something. It is
that you were born to an island of greed
and grace where you have this sense
of yourself as apart from others. It is
not your right to feel powerless. Better
people than you were powerless.
You have not returned to your country,
but to a life you never left.

                                                          1980

Forché can sympathize, but she refuses to falsely appropriate, for her own purposes, the consciousness of someone she is not. That is, she refuses to sentimentalize either her role or her life, and when there is an apparent impulse to do so, "I tell you / I have not slept," it is soon substantiated by the image of madness. The poem is both cunning and skeptical, even of its poet, since it is Josephine who catalogues the atrocities and tortures of El Salvador's war; just as it is Josephine who knows that distant readers are thrilled, not by political corruption, but by the facts of truly sensational tortures and massacres; and it is Josephine, sophisticated in the only worthy sense of that word, with "fifty years in her face," who knows that change might depend, unfortunately, on the possible "rescuers" hearing of such tortures, the details of such facts. For finally it is both the audience, the reader, *and* the poet who are admonished and taught by Josephine, and if the effect of torture is to disgrace the human body, and therefore the human being; in Forché's art, as in Goya's *Disasters of War,* the viewer, the reader, are made accomplices and are similarly disgraced. But art, in these poems or in Goya's etchings, is different from actual torture. In art, the effect of being disgraced is to make the viewer or the reader more conscious, more human, more capable of bearing pain and perceiving the beauty of bearing it—if only because in life, for those who are tortured, it is the opposite that happens. Such an effect is not sensationalism. Sensationalism, finally, is a lie: by overstatement, it elicits only a cheap thrill. But a poem such as **"Return"** penetrates to feelings beneath the ordinary—to a shame that makes one vulnerable and human.

The method of the poem is narrative and imagistic, and basically realistic in its presentation, its witnessing. But, as in Neruda's example, there are situations in life, in war, that defy Realism. Only the achieved image and metaphor will do: "And so you say, you've learned a little / about

starvation: a child like a supper scrap / filling with worms, many children strung / together, as if they were cut from paper / and all in a delicate chain." *A delicate chain.* The metaphor which violates all realism *returns* itself to childhood, to the image of paper dolls, which in all memory make the children who have died in El Salvador more childlike, more vulnerable, and more real even as the image becomes, in its intention, more grotesque. For finally, the situation, the witnessing, is different from Neruda's account of watching blood flow onto the street. Forché's character, Josephine, in trying to conceive of and imagine the sheer number of children who have perished is driven to create an image, a metaphor, beyond Realism, and certainly beyond the impoverishment of statistics and body counts.

Forché, in discovering another country, discovers herself—discovers, too, how American she is ("a country you never left"). Part of that discovery is the discovery of limits. It is a mature and brilliant act when Forché relinquishes her poem and allows Josephine to speak, when the poet becomes a listener as well as a speaker. For one of the ironies about the poem is the learning process, a reciprocal or dialectical process which resembles, and actualizes the paradigm of Paolo Freire's in *The Pedagogy of the Oppressed,* a book which Forché acknowledges as an influence on her work and on her life. Moreover, the irony of learning in the poem is positive: just as the poet learns to be more human from Josephine, Josephine herself, in speaking of what most torments her, becomes a poet. The poem's relationships are unshakably egalitarian. And so it is proper that Forché listens, for the duty of a poem like this is to witness and record, to detail a particular misery, to try to rescue some of the dead from an almost certain oblivion through the memorial of an elegy. Different in methods, the purpose of such art is like [Zbigniew] Herbert's, and like so many poems of war. Whether in parable or narrative, such poems oppose the frail dignity of remembering to the world . . . a world that is more likely to sleep, and forget, and enlist again.

Forché's poems detail, mostly, the progress of a human psyche learning and becoming more openly human and vulnerable in what has become a largely sinister "Vale of Soul-Making." In so far as this progress takes place at all, even if it only occurs between Forché and Josephine, such learning and transformation, though it may not end or prevent any war, is *prima facie* evidence that individuals, by changing themselves, can effect, however tenuously, the world, and can begin to change it. What we do matters, and Forché's final insistence, on "ourselves or nothing," is, especially in the light of any possible nuclear warfare, a kind of political wisdom. In essence, it extends and grimly reaffirms Auden's conclusion that "We must love one another or die." . . .

Larry Levis, "War as Parable and War as Fact: Herbert and Forché," in The American Poetry Review, *Vol. 12, No. 1, January-February, 1983, pp. 6-12.*

Carolyn Forché   (essay date July-August 1981)

[*The following is a revised version of a speech Forché origi-*

[Prior to the publication of *The Country between Us*] I had been living in El Salvador among people who would *easily* die for each other or for me even though I was a foreigner. I got used to experiencing that in El Salvador, people who felt so deeply and strongly. Something had happened to me, and I was different, and so was my work. I hadn't intended to become a "political poet." I didn't have anything against becoming one. All of a sudden, *I was.*

—Carolyn Forché, in an interview with Husayn Al-Kurdi, in The Bloomsbury Review, *July-August, 1993.*

nally gave in March 1981 at one of the first meetings of PEN West, the International Association of Poets, Playwrights, Editors, Essayists and Novelists. Here, she discusses the atrocities she saw in El Salvador, the role of the United States in the region, the relationship between poetry and politics, and her literary aims.]

The year Franco died, I spent several months on Mallorca translating the poetry of Claribel Alegria, a Salvadorean in voluntary exile. During those months the almond trees bloomed and lost flower, the olives and lemons ripened and we hauled baskets of apricots from Claribel's small *finca.* There was bathing in the *calla,* fresh squid under the palm-thatch, drunk Australian sailors to dance with at night. It was my first time in Europe and there was no better place at that time than Spain. I was there when Franco's anniversary passed for the first time in forty years without notice—and the lack of public celebration was a collective hush of relief. I travelled with Claribel's daughter, Maya Flakoll, for ten days through Andalusia by train visiting poetry shrines. The *gitanos* had finally pounded a cross into the earth to mark the grave of Federico Garcia Lorca, not where it had been presumed to be all this time, not beneath an olive tree but in a bowl of land rimmed by pines. We hiked the eleven kilometers through the Sierra Nevada foothills to *La Fuente Grande* and held a book of poems open over the silenced poet.

On Mallorca I lost interest in the *calla* sun-bathing, the parties that carried into the morning, the staggering home wine-drunk up the goat paths. I did not hike to the peak of the Teix with baskets of *entremesas* nor, despite well-intentioned urgings, could I surrender myself to the island's diversionary summer mystique.

I was busy with Claribel's poems, and with the horrific accounts of the survivors of repressive Latin American regimes. Claribel's home was frequented by these wounded, writers who had been tortured and imprisoned, who had lost husbands, wives and closest friends. In the afternoon more than once I joined Claribel in her silent vigil near the window until the mail came, her "difficult time of day,"

alone in a chair in the perfect light of thick-walled Mallorquin windows. These were her afternoons of despair, and they haunted me. In those hours I first learned of El Salvador, not from the springs of her nostalgia for "the fraternity of dipping a tortilla into a common pot of beans and meat," but from the source of its pervasive brutality. My understanding of Latin American realities was confined then to the romantic devotion to Vietnam-era revolutionary pieties, the sainthood of Ernesto Che rather than the debilitating effects of the cult of personality that arose in the collective memory of Guevara. I worked into the late hours on my poems and on translations, drinking "101" brandy and chain-smoking *Un-X-Dos.* When Cuban writer Mario Benedetti visited, I questioned him about what "an American" could do in the struggle against repression.

"As a *North*american, you might try working to influence a profound change in your country's foreign policy."

Over coffee in the mornings I studied reports from Amnesty International-London and learned of a plague on Latin exiles who had sought refuge in Spain following Franco's death: a right-wing death squad known as the "AAA"—*Anti-Communista Apostolica,* founded in Argentina and exported to assassinate influential exiles from the southern cone.

I returned to the United States and in the autumn of 1977 was invited to El Salvador by persons who knew Claribel. "How much do you know about Latin America?" I was asked. Then: "Good. At least you know that you know nothing." A young writer, politically unaffiliated, ideologically vague, I was to be blessed with the rarity of a moral and political education—what at times would seem an unbearable immersion, what eventually would become a focussed obsession. It would change my life and work, propel me toward engagement, test my endurance and find it wanting, and prevent me from ever viewing myself or my country again through precisely the same fog of unwitting connivance.

I was sent for a briefing to Dr. Thomas P. Anderson, author of *Matanza,* the definitive scholarly history of Salvador's revolution of 1932, and to Ignacio Lozano, a California newspaper editor and former ambassador (under Gerald Ford) to El Salvador. It was suggested that I visit Salvador as a journalist, a role that would of necessity become real. In January, 1978, I landed at Ilopango, the dingy center-city airport that is now Salvador's largest military base. Arriving before me were the members of a human rights investigation team headed by then Congressman John Drinan, S.J. (D-Mass.) I had been told that a black North-american, Ronald James Richardson, had been killed while in the custody of the Salvadorean government and that a Northamerican organization known as the American Institute for Free Labor Development (AIFLD, an organ of the AFL-CIO and an intelligence front) was manipulating the Salvadorean agricultural workers. Investigation of "The Richardson Case" exposed me to the *sub rosa* activities of the Salvadorean military, whose highest ranking officers and government officials were engaged in cocaine smuggling, kidnapping, extortion and terrorism; through studying AIFLD's work, I would learn of the spurious intentions of an organization destined to become the architect of the present Agrarian Reform. I was delivered the promised exposure to the stratified life of Salvador, and was welcomed "to Vietnam, circa 1959." The "Golden Triangle" had moved to the isthmus of the Americas, "rural pacification" was in embryo, the seeds of rebellion had taken root in destitution and hunger.

Later my companion and guide, "Ricardo," changed his description from Vietnam to "a Nazi forced labor camp." "It is not hyperbole," he said quietly, "you will come to see that." In those first twenty days I was taken to clinics and hospitals, villages, farms, prisons, coffee mansions and processing plants, cane mills and the elegant homes of American foreign service bureaucrats, nudged into the hillsides overlooking the capital, where I was offered cocktails and platters of ocean shrimp; it was not yet known what I would write of my impressions or where I would print them. Fortuitously, I had published nationally in my own country, and in Salvador "only poetry" did not carry the pejorative connotation I might have ascribed to it then. I knew nothing of political journalism but was willing to learn—it seemed, at the time, an acceptable way for a poet to make a living.

I lay on my belly in the *campo* and was handed a pair of field glasses. The lens sharpened on a plastic tarp tacked to four maize stalks several hundred yards away, beneath which a woman sat on the ground. She was gazing through the plastic roof of her "house" and hugging three naked, emaciated children. There was an aqua plastic dog-food bowl at her feet.

"She's watching for the plane," my friend said, "we have to get out of here now or we're going to get it too." I trained the lens on the woman's eye, gelled with disease and open to a swarm of gnats. We climbed back in the truck and rolled the windows up just as the duster plane swept back across the field, dumping a yellow cloud of pesticide over the woman and her children to protect the cotton crop around them.

At the time I was unaware of the pedagogical theories of Paulo Freire (*Pedagogy of the Oppressed*), but found myself learning *in situ* the politics of cultural immersion. It was by Ricardo's later admission "risky business," but it was thought important that a few Northamericans, particularly writers, be sensitized to Salvador prior to any military conflict. The lessons were simple and critical, the methods somewhat more difficult to detect. I was given a white lab jacket and, posing as a Northamerican physician, was asked to work in a rural hospital at the side of a Salvadorean doctor who was paid $200 a month by the Salvadorean government to care for one-hundred-thousand *campesinos*. She had no lab, no x-ray, no whole blood, plasma or antibiotics, no anesthesia or medicines, no autoclave for sterilizing surgical equipment. Her forceps were rusted, the walls of her operating room were studded with flies; beside her hospital a coffee processing plant's refuse heaps incubated the maggots, and she paid a *campesina* to swish the flies away with a newspaper while she delivered the newborn. She was forced to do caesarean sections at times without much local anesthetic.

Without supplies, she worked with only her hands and a cheap opthalmascope. In her clinic I held children in my arms who died hours later for want of a manual suction device to remove the fluid from their lungs. Their peculiar skin rashes spread to my hands, arms and belly. I dug maggots from a child's open wound with a teaspoon. I contracted four strains of dysentery and was treated by stomach antiseptics, effective and damaging enough to be banned by our own FDA. This doctor had worked in the *campo* for years, a lifetime of delivering the offspring of thirteen-year-old mothers who thought the navel marked the birth canal opening. She had worked long enough to feel that it was acceptable to ignore her own cervical cancer, and hard enough in Salvador to view her inevitable death as the least of her concerns.

I was taken to the homes of landowners, with their pools set like aquamarines in the clipped grass, to the afternoon games of canasta over quaint local *pupusas* and tea, where parrots hung by their feet among the bougainvillia and nearly everything was imported, if only from Miami or New Orleans. One evening I dined with a military officer who toasted America, private enterprise, Las Vegas, and the "fatherland" until his wife excused herself and in a drape of cigar smoke the events of **"The Colonel"** took place. Almost a *poème trouvé*, I had only to pare down the memory and render it whole, unlined and as precise as recollection would have it. I did not wish to endanger myself by the act of poeticizing such a necessary reportage. It became, when I wrote it, the second insistence of El Salvador to infiltrate what I so ridiculously preserved as my work's allegiance to Art. No more than in any earlier poems did I choose my subject.

"The Colonel"

What you have heard is true. I was in his house.
His wife carried a tray of coffee and sugar. His
daughter filed her nails, his son went out for the
night. There were daily papers, pet dogs, a pistol
on the cushion beside him. The moon swung
bare on its black cord over the house. On the
television was a cop show. It was in English.
Broken bottles were imbedded in the walls
around the house to scoop the kneecaps from a
man's legs or cut his hands to lace. . . .
                                El Salvador, May, 1978

The following day I was let into Ahuachapan prison (now an army *cuartel*). We had been driving back from a meeting with Salvadorean feminists when Ricardo swung the truck into a climb through a tube of dust toward the run-down fortification. I was thirsty, infested with intestinal parasites, fatigued from twenty days of ricocheting between extremes of poverty and wealth. I was horrified, impatient, suspicious of almost everyone, paralyzed by sympathy and revulsion. I kept thinking of the kindly, silver-haired American political officer who informed me that in Salvador, "there were always five versions of the truth." From this I was presumably to conclude that the truth could not therefore be known. Ricardo seemed by turns the Braggioni of Porter's "Flowering Judas" and a pedagogical genius of considerable vision and patience. As we walked toward the gate, he palmed the air to slow our pace.

"This is a criminal penitentiary. You will have thirty minutes inside. Realize please at all times where you are and, whatever you see here, understand that for political prisoners it is always much worse. Okay."

We shook hands with the chief guard and a few subordinates, clean-shaven youths armed with G-3s. There was first the stench: rotting blood, excrement, buckets of urine and corn-slop. A man in his thirties came toward us, dragging a swollen green leg, his pants ripped to the thigh to accommodate the swelling. He was introduced as "Miguel" and I as "a friend." The two men shook hands a long time, standing together in the filth, a firm knot of warmth between them. Miguel was asked to give me "a tour," and he agreed, first taking a coin from his pocket and slipping it into the guard station soda machine. He handed me an orange Nehi, urging me somewhat insistently to take it, and we began a slow walk into the first hall. The prison was a four-square with an open court in the center. There were bunk rooms where the cots were stacked three deep and some were hung with newsprint "for privacy." The men squatted on the ground or along the walls, some stirring small coal fires, others ducking under urine-soaked tents of newspaper. It was supper, and they were cooking their dry tortillas. I used the soda as a relief from the stench, like a hose of oxygen. There were maybe four hundred men packed into Ahuachapan, and it was an odd sight, an American woman, but there was no heckling.

"Did you hear the shots when we first pulled up?" Ricardo asked, "those were warnings—a visitor, behave."

Miguel showed me through the workrooms and latrines, finishing his sentences with his eyes; a necessary skill under repressive regimes, highly developed in Salvador. With the guards' attention diverted, he gestured toward a black open doorway and suggested that I might wander through it, stay a few moments and come back out "as if I had seen nothing."

I did as he asked, my eyes adjusting to the darkness of that shit-smeared room with its single chink of light in the concrete. There were wooden boxes stacked against one wall, each a meter by a meter with barred openings the size of a book, and within them there was breathing, raspy and half-conscious. It was a few moments before I realized that men were kept in those cages, their movement so cramped that they could neither sit, stand, nor lie down. I recall only magnified fragments of my few minutes in that room, but that I was rooted to the clay floor, unable to move either toward or away from the cages. I turned from the room toward Miguel, who pivoted on his crutch and with his eyes on the ground said in a low voice *"La Oscura,"* the dark place; "sometimes a man is kept in there a year, and cannot move when he comes out."

We caught up with Ricardo who leaned toward me and whispered, "tie your sweater sleeves around your neck. You are covered with hives."

In the cab of the truck I braced my feet against the dashboard and through the half-cracked window shook hands with the young soldiers, smiling and nodding. A hundred meters from the prison I lifted Ricardo's spare shirt in my hands and vomited. We were late for yet another meeting,

the sun had dropped behind the volcanoes, my eyes ached. When I was empty the dry heaves began, and after the sobbing a convulsive shudder. Miguel was serving his third consecutive sentence, this time for organizing a hunger strike against prison conditions. In that moment I saw him turn back to his supper, his crutch stamping circles of piss and mud beside him as he walked. I heard the screams of a woman giving birth by caesarean without anesthesia in Ana's hospital. I saw the flies fastened to the walls in her operating room, the gnats on the eyes of the starving woman, the reflection of flies on Ana's eyes in the hospital kitchen window. The shit, I imagined, was inside my nostrils and I would smell it the rest of my life, as it is for a man who in battle tastes a piece of flesh or gets the blood under his fingernails. The smell never comes out; it was something Ricardo explained once as he was falling asleep.

"Feel this," he said, maneuvering the truck down the hill road. "This is what oppression feels like. Now you have begun to learn something. When you get back to the States, what you do with this is up to you."

Between 1978 and 1981 I travelled between the United States and Salvador, writing reports on the war waiting to happen, drawing blue-prints of prisons from memory, naming the dead. I filled soup bowls with cigarette butts, grocery boxes with files on American involvement in the rural labor movement, and each week I took a stool sample to the parasite clinic. A priest I knew was gang-raped by soldiers; another was hauled off and beaten nearly to death. On one trip a woman friend and I were chased by the death squad for five minutes on the narrow backroads that circle the city—her evasive driving and considerable luck saved us. One night a year ago I was interviewing a defecting member of the Christian Democratic Party. As we started out of the drive to go back to my hotel, we encountered three plainclothesmen hunched over the roof of a taxicab, their machine guns pointed at our windshield. We escaped through a grove of avocado trees. The bodies of friends have turned up disemboweled and decapitated, their teeth punched into broken points, their faces sliced off with machetes. On the final trip to the airport we swerved to avoid a corpse, a man spread-eagled, his stomach hacked open, his entrails stretched from one side of the road to the other. We drove over them like a garden hose. My friend looked at me. *Just another dead man,* he said. And by then it had become true for me as well; the unthinkable, the sense of death within life before death.

. . . . .

"I see an injustice," wrote Czeslaw Milosz in *Native Realm;* "a Parisian does not have to bring his city out of nothingness every time he wants to describe it." So it was with Wilno, that Lithuanian/Polish/Byelorussian city of the poet's childhood, and so it has been with the task of writing about Salvador in the United States. The country called by Gabriela Mistral "the Tom Thumb of the Americas" would necessarily be described to Northamericans as "about the size of Massachusetts." As writers we could begin with its location on the Pacific south of Guatemala and west of Honduras and with Ariadne's thread of statistics: 4.5 million people, 400 per square kilometer (a country without silence or privacy), a population growth rate of 3.5% (such a population would double in two decades). But what does "90% malnutrition" mean? Or that "80% of the population has no running water, electricity or sanitary services?" I watched women push feces aside with a stick, lower their pails to the water and carry it home to wash their clothes, their spoons and plates, themselves, their infant children. The chief cause of death has been amoebic dysentery. One out of four children dies before the age of five; the average human life span is forty-six years. What does it mean when a man says "it is better to die quickly fighting than slowly of starvation"? And that such a man suffers toward that decision in what is now being called "Northamerica's backyard"? How is the language used to draw battle lines, to identify the enemy? What are the current euphemisms for empire, public defense of private wealth, extermination of human beings? If the lethal weapon is the soldier, what is meant by "nonlethal military aid?" And what determined the shift to helicopter gunships, M-16s, M-79 grenade launchers? The State Department's white paper entitled *Communist Interference in El Salvador* argues that it is a "case of indirect armed aggression against a small Third World country by Communist powers acting through Cuba." James Petras has argued that the report's "evidence is flimsy, circumstantial or nonexistent; the reasoning and logic is slipshod and internally inconsistent; it assumes what needs to be proven; and finally, what facts are presented refute the very case the State Department is attempting to demonstrate" ["White Paper on the White Paper," *The Nation* (28 March 1981)]. On the basis of this report, the popular press sounded an alarm over the "flow of arms." But from where have arms "flowed," to whom and for what? In terms of language, we could begin by asking why Northamerican arms are weighed in dollar-value and those reaching the opposition measured in tonnage. Or we could point out the nature of the international arms market, a complex global network in which it is possible to buy almost anything for the right price, no matter the country of origin or destination. The State Department conveniently ignores its own intelligence on arms flow to the civilian right, its own escalation of military assistance to the right-wing military, and even the discrepancies in its final analysis. But what does all this tell us about who is fighting whom for what? Americans have been told that there is a "fundamental difference" between "advisors" and military "trainers." Could it simply be that the euphemism for American military personnel must be changed so as not to serve as a mnemonic device for the longest war in our failing public memory? A year ago I asked the American military attaché in Salvador what would happen if one of these already proposed advisors returned to the U.S. in a flag-draped coffin. He did not argue semantics.

"That," he said smiling, "would be up to the American press, wouldn't it?"

Most of that press had held with striking fidelity to the State Department text: a vulnerable and worthy "centrist" government besieged by left and right-wing extremists, the former characterized by their unacceptable political ideology, the latter rendered non-ideologically unacceptable,

that is, only in their extremity. The familiar ring of this portrayal has not escaped U.S. apologists, who must explain why El Salvador is not "another Vietnam." Their argument hinges, it seems, on the rapidity with which the U.S. could assist the Salvadorean military in the task of "defeating the enemy." Tactically, this means sealing the country off, warning all other nations to "cease and desist" supplying arms, using violations of that warning as a pretext for blockades and interventions, but excepting ourselves in our continual armament of what we are calling "the government" of El Salvador. Ignoring the institutional self-interest of the Salvadorean army, we blame the presumably "civilian" right for the murder of thousands of *campesinos,* students, doctors, teachers, journalists, nuns, priests and children. This requires that we ignore the deposed and retired military men who command the activities of the death squads with impunity, and that the security forces responsible for the killings are under the command of the army, which is under the command of the so-called "centrist" government and is in fact the government itself.

There are other differences between the conflicts of El Salvador and Vietnam. There is no Peoples Republic of China to the north to arm and ally itself with a people engaged in a protracted war. The guerillas are not second generation Viet-minh, but young people who armed themselves after exhaustive and failed attempts at non-violent resistance and peaceful change. The popular organizations they defend were formed in the early seventies by *campesinos* who became socially conscious through the efforts of grass-roots clergymen teaching the Medellin doctrines of social justice; the precursors of these organizations were prayer and bible study groups, rural labor organizations and urban trade unions. As the military government grew increasingly repressive, the opposition widened to include all other political parties, the Catholic majority, the university and professional communities and the small business sector.

Critics of U.S. policy accurately recognize parallels between the two conflicts in terms of involvement, escalation and justification. The latter demands a vigilant "euphemology" undertaken to protect language from distortions of military expedience and political convenience. [In the 1979 *The Washington Connection and Third World Fascism*] Noam Chomsky has argued that "among the many symbols used to frighten and manipulate the populace of the democratic states, few have been more important than terror and terrorism. These terms have generally been confined to the use of violence by individuals and marginal groups. Official violence, which is far more extensive in both scale and destructiveness, is placed in a different category altogether. This usage has nothing to do with justice, causal sequence, or numbers abused." He goes on to say that "the question of proper usage is settled not merely by the official or unofficial status of the perpetrators of violence but also by their political affiliations." State violence is excused as "reactive," and the "turmoil" or "conflict" is viewed ahistorically.

It is true that there have long been voices of peaceful change and social reform in El Salvador—the so-called centrists—but the U.S. has never supported them. We backed one fraudulently elected military regime after another, giving them what they wanted and still want: a steady infusion of massive economic aid with which high ranking officers can insure their personal futures and the loyalty of their subordinates. In return we expect them to guarantee stability, which means holding power by whatever means necessary for the promotion of a favorable investment climate, even if it means exterminating the population, as it has come to mean in Salvador. The military, who always admired "*Generalissimo* Franco," and are encouraged in their anti-communist crusade, grow paranoid and genocidal. Soldiers tossed babies into the air near the Sumpul River last summer for target practice during the cattle-prod round up and massacre of six-hundred peasants. Whole families have been gunned down or hacked to pieces with machetes, including the elderly and newborn. Now that the massacre and the struggle against it have become the occasion to "test American resolve," the Salvadorean military is all too aware of the security of its position and the impugnity with which it may operate. Why would a peasant, aware of the odds, of the significance of American backing, continue to take up arms on the side of the opposition? How is it that such opposition endures, when daily men and women are doused with gasoline and burned alive in the streets as a lesson to others; when even death is not enough, and the corpses are mutilated beyond recognition? The answer to that question in El Salvador answers the same for Vietnam.

· · · · ·

We were waved past the military guard station and started down the highway, swinging into the oncoming lane to pass slow sugarcane trucks and army transports. Every few kilometers, patrols trekked the gravel roadside. It was a warm night, dry but close to the rainy season. Juan palmed the column shift, chain-smoked and motioned with his hot-boxed cigarette in the direction of San Marcos. Bonfires lit by the opposition were chewing away at the dark hillside. As we neared San Salvador, passing through the slums of Candelaria, I saw that the roads were barricaded. More than once Juan attempted a short-cut but, upon spotting military checkpoints, changed his mind. To relieve the tension he dug a handful of change from his pocket and showed me his collection of *deutschmark,* Belgian *francs,* Swedish *ore* and *kroner,* holding each to the dashboard light and naming the journalist who had given it to him, the country, the paper. His prize was a coin from the Danish reporter whose cameras had been shot away as he crouched on a rooftop to photograph an army attack on protest marchers. That was a month before, on January 22, 1980, when some hundred lost their lives; it was the beginning of a savage year of extermination. Juan rose from his seat and slipped the worthless coins back into his pocket.

Later that spring, Rene Tamsen of WHUR radio, Washington D.C., would be forced by a death squad into an unmarked car in downtown San Salvador. A Salvadorean photographer, Cesar Najarro, and his *Cronica del Pueblo* editor would be seized during a coffee break. When their mutilated bodies were discovered, it would be evident that

they had been disemboweled before death. A Mexican photojournalist, Ignacio Rodriguez, would fall in August to a military bullet. After Christmas an American freelancer, John Sullivan, would vanish from his downtown hotel room. Censorship of the press. In January, 1981, Ian Mates would hit a land mine and the South African TV cameraman would bleed to death. In a year, no one would want the Salvador assignment. In a year, journalists would appear before cameras trembling and incredulous, unable to reconcile their perceptions with those of Washington, and even established media would begin to reflect this dichotomy. Carter policy had been to downplay El Salvador in the press while providing "quiet" aid to the repressive forces. Between 1978 and 1980, investigative articles sent to national magazines mysteriously disappeared from publication mailrooms, were oddly delayed in reaching editors, or were rejected after lengthy deliberations, most often because of El Salvador's "low news value." The American inter-religious network and human rights community began to receive evidence of a conscious and concerted censorship effort in the United States. During interviews in 1978 with members of the Salvadorean right-wing business community, I was twice offered large sums of money to portray their government favorably in the American press. By early 1981, desk editors knew where El Salvador was and the playdown policy had been replaced by the Reagan administration's propaganda effort. The right-wing military cooperated in El Salvador by serving death threats on prominent journalists, while torturing and murdering others. American writers critical of U.S. policy were described by the Department of State as "the witting and unwitting dupes" of communist propagandists. Those who have continued coverage of Salvador have found that the military monitors the wire services and all telecommunications, that pseudonyms often provide no security, that no one active in the documentation of the war of extermination can afford to be traceable in the country; effectiveness becomes self-limiting. It became apparent that my education in El Salvador had prepared me to work only until March 16, 1980, when after several close calls, I was urged to leave the country. Monsignor Romero met with me, asking that I return to the U.S. and "tell the American people what is happening."

"Do you have any messages for (certain exiled friends)?"

"Yes. Tell them to come back."

"But wouldn't they be killed?"

"We are all going to be killed—you and me, all of us." he said quietly.

A week later he was shot while saying Mass in the chapel of a hospital for the incurable.

In those days [in El Salvador] I kept my work as a poet and journalist separate, of two distinct *mentalités,* but I could not keep El Salvador from my poems because it had become so much a part of my life. I was cautioned to avoid mixing art and politics, that one damages the other, and it was some time before I realized that "political poetry" often means the poetry of protest, accused of polemical didacticism, and not the poetry which implicitly celebrates politically acceptable values. I suspect that underlying this discomfort is a naive assumption: that to locate a poem in an area associated with political trouble automatically renders it political.

All poetry is both pure and engaged, in the sense that it is made of language, but it is also art. Any theory which takes one half of the social-esthetic dynamic and accentuates it too much results in a breakdown. Stress of purity generates a feeble estheticism that fails, in its beauty, to communicate. On the other hand, propagandistic hackwork has no independent life as poetry. What matters is not whether a poem is political, but the quality of its engagement.

[Hans Magnus] Enzensberger has argued the futility of locating the political aspect of poetry outside poetry itself, and that:

> Such obtuseness plays into the hands of the bourgeois esthetic which would like to deny poetry any social aspect. Too often the champions of inwardness and sensibility are reactionaries. They consider politics a special subject best left to professionals, and wish to detach it completely from all other human activity. They advise poetry to stick to such models as they have devised for it, in other words, to high aspirations and eternal values. The promised reward for this continence is timeless validity. Behind these high-sounding proclamations lurks a contempt for poetry no less profound than that of vulgar Marxism. For a political quarantine placed on poetry in the name of eternal values, itself serves political ends. [*The Consciousness Industry: On Literature, Politics and the Media*, 1974]

All language then is political; vision is always ideologically charged; perceptions are shaped *a priori* by our assumptions and sensibility formed by consciousness at once social, historical and esthetic. There is no such thing as nonpolitical poetry. The time, however, to determine what those politics will be is not the moment of taking pen to paper, but during the whole of one's life. We are responsible for the quality of our vision, we have a say in the shaping of our sensibility. In the many thousand daily choices we make, we create ourselves and the voice with which we speak and work.

From our tradition we inherit a poetic, a sense of appropriate subjects, styles, forms and levels of diction; that poetic might insist that we be attuned to the individual in isolation, to particular sensitivity in the face of "nature," to special ingenuity in inventing metaphor. It might encourage a self-regarding, inward looking poetry. Since Romanticism, didactic poetry has been presumed dead and narrative poetry has had at best a half life. Demonstration is inimical to a poetry of lyric confession and self-examination, therefore didactic poetry is seen as crude and unpoetic. To suggest a return to the formal didactic mode of Virgil's *Georgics* or Lucretius's *De Rerum Natura* would be to deny history, but what has survived of that poetic is the belief that a poet's voice must be inwardly authentic and compelling of our attention; the poet's voice must have authority.

I have been told that a poet should be of his or her time.

It is my feeling that the twentieth century human condition demands a poetry of witness. This is not accomplished without certain difficulties; the inherited poetic limits the range of our work and determines the boundaries of what might be said. There is the problem of metaphor which moved Neruda to write: "the blood of the children / flowed out onto the streets / like . . . like the blood of the children." There is the problem of poeticizing horror, resembling the problem of the photographic image which might render starvation visually appealing. There are problems of reduction and over-simplification; of our need to see the world as complex beyond our comprehension, difficult beyond our capacities for solution. If I did not wish to make poetry of what I had seen, what is it I thought poetry was?

At some point the two *mentalités* converged, and the impulse to witness confronted the prevailing poetic; at the same time it seemed clear that eulogy and censure were no longer possible and that Enzensberger is correct in stating "The poem expresses in exemplary fashion that it is not at the disposal of politics. That is its political content." I decided to follow my impulse to write narratives of witness and confrontation, to disallow obscurity and conventions which might prettify that which I wished to document. As for that wish, the poems will speak for themselves, obstinate as always. I wish also to thank my friends and *compañeros* in El Salvador for persuading me during a period of doubt that poetry could be enough.

Carolyn Forché, "El Salvador: An Aide Memoire," in The American Poetry Review, *Vol. 10, No. 4, July-August, 1981, pp. 3-8.*

> [In *The Country between Us* Forché] deals in small moments, using characteristic words like *tick, hover, cupped hands, ribbons of piss*—delicate words, even when the subject is horrific. Forché defers, letting the reader choose his or her emotion, which is far more effective than a passionate denunciation or a plea.
>
> —*Nancy L. McCann, in her review of* The Country between Us, *in* The Christian Century, *27 October 1982.*

Carolyn Forché with Jonathan Cott　(interview date 14 April 1983)

[*Cott is an American editor, producer, poet, essayist, and critic. In the following, Forché discusses her childhood, her literary influences, her travels in Central America, and her writing.*]

[*Cott*]: *Walt Whitman once wrote: "The proof of a poet is that his country absorbs him as affectionately as he has absorbed it." How do you see the state of American poetry today?*

[Forché]: I was talking to a poet the other day, and he said something very interesting. "I feel," he told me, "that I'm in exile in my own country." And it seems to me that much of the poetry written today is about this exile. In a way, there's a tendency for poets to abandon the culture at large and to write about the alienation that they feel. Throughout the Seventies, I noticed a poetry of refined and elegant language that somehow seemed to convey a sense of being detached from the culture. Many young poets who grew up in small towns were writing poetry that read as if they'd spent their childhoods in Europe, had the benefit of a classical education and had the luxury to develop a kind of distanced boredom. You get the impression that they lived very differently from the way they really did. There were exceptions, of course, but a lot of the poetry during the past decade seemed more descriptive of itself than it was of any kind of reality outside. Poets were pretty much writing for each other. And so they probably shouldn't complain today about the narrowness of their audiences, because it hasn't particularly been their concern to address a large number of readers and listeners. Of course, we've also seen a more general kind of diminishing and extreme introspection in our American culture during the past ten years—a departure from music, from art, from poetry, from political action.

Who are some of the contemporary American poets you admire?

I could name many that I admire for various reasons, though I can't give you an exhaustive list. I very much like Denise Levertov, Adrienne Rich, James Wright, and Jack Gilbert's new work. And I feel a resurgence of interest in poetry.

What do you think of the writing programs in universities today?

They've become too institutionalized, a bit too much of a club, and I think that most of the writers involved with writing programs would agree that this is the case. It's dangerous when a writing program presumes to do something that it just can't do. I mean, it does not *make* the writer; all it can do is give him or her an opportunity to write and maybe teach writing, if that's something a person wants to do for a couple of years. For me, it was an opportunity to live in a community with other young writers.

I would hope that many writers would choose *not* to train themselves in that way, however. I sort of favor the individual mentor, a writer whom one regards very highly, developing a relationship with that author's work and perhaps eventually with him or her as a teacher. I've had very good experiences as a workshop teacher, and I've had very ugly ones as well, where. . . . I don't know what to say the workshop was about, but it wasn't necessarily about poetry. And there's a tendency for a certain kind of poem to emerge that is considered acceptable, and that can be dangerous.

Yet, in another way, I want the programs to exist because they're very good for many writers at certain points in their lives. I just wish that they weren't regarded in quite the way they've been in the last decade. You see, I didn't

have any money when I went to school, and when I left the university, I had to pay off an enormous debt for my tuition. I would have had to work a nine-to-five job, and it's very difficult to write if you come home exhausted. So, working through a Master of Fine Arts program gave me the opportunity to write my first book, which then afforded me the opportunity to teach, which gave me a schedule, which enabled me to write. It helped me, and therefore I can't disparage writing programs because there will be many writers in the position I was in as well; and I would hate to see the work in this culture be produced only by those who could afford to produce it. It's a bit of snobbery just to say, "Aren't writing programs awful." I'm suspicious of that as well.

When did you first start writing poetry?

I was about nine years old—the oldest of seven children living in Farmington, Michigan. My father was at work, we were all home from school because there was a blizzard outside, and my mother said, "Why don't you write a poem?" She took out and dusted off her college poetry textbook—she had gone to college for two years before she married—and she showed me what a poem was. She explained to me what a metrical foot was, and she made the little markings and taught me the stresses. She read me some poems, and she laid them all out. I looked at these things, and right away I went and wrote a poem which, very unimaginatively, was about snow. I began to work in iambic pentameter because I didn't know there was anything else, but I was absolutely taken with writing verse.

I think I used writing as an escape. Writing and daydreaming. Writing was simply the reverie that I recorded, and I wrote volumes of diaries and journals. Then, when I wasn't writing, when I was doing housework or whatever, I kept some sort of little voice running in my mind. I told myself narratives, and I made a parallel life to my own. It was completely imaginary, and most of the time everything would take place a hundred years earlier on the same spot where I was. I suspected, when I was young, that this was madness, but I couldn't give it up. Then I lost the voice, the capacity to do this for hours and hours—I lost it when I was about seventeen. It was horrifying to realize that it was gone. For me, it was the end of my childhood. And my mind changed. But as I developed, I wrote more consciously.

So it began with my mother. She talked to me a lot when I was very young, but as the years went by, she didn't have any time. Yet what she gave me when I was nine was one of those rare, beautiful moments. And that moment was enough to last for a long time.

Your first volume of poems, **Gathering the Tribes,** *is an amazingly assured work. When did you find your own voice?*

I was twenty-four when I completed that book. It was selected when I was twenty-five and published when I was twenty-six. It represents work from age nineteen to age twenty-four, but from age nine to age nineteen, I wrote terribly.

When I was thirteen, I discovered free verse by reading e.

e. cummings, but I didn't understand free verse at all. I thought, well, it's scattered all over the page, you don't need to do it metrically, you can just use these little phrases and scatter it around . . . and you can do *whatever you want.* So I started writing nonsense, just nonsense. I was writing in lower case *i*'s all over, and it was just awful. My best work during that period was paragraphs I wrote in Catholic school, which I attended for twelve years. The nuns used to assign us to write paragraphs, and these were wonderful little passages of description, but my poetry was awful. I'm interested in prose, too; I don't make a division between poetry and prose much because I think of poetry in a broader sense.

The voice in my first book doesn't know what it thinks, it doesn't make any judgments. All it can do is perceive and describe and use language to make some sort of re-creation of moments in time. But I noticed that the person in the second book makes an utterance. And in a way, it was a little haunting to realize that some sort of maturation had occurred unconsciously.

In your early poem **"Burning the Tomato Worms,"** *you quote your Slovak grandmother, Anna, as saying:* "Mother of God / I tell you this / Dushenka / You work your life / You have nothing." *It strikes me that a lot of women you write about—the impoverished Spanish and Indian women in the American Southwest, the peasant women in El Salvador—could say this as well. There's a sense of comradeship you seem to feel with these and other women in your poetry.*

The strongest influences in my life have been women—my grandmother, my mother, many older women. With one exception, everyone who taught me in El Salvador was female—*compañeras*—It's a word in Spanish that means something more than companion.

The reality is that women are oppressed and becoming more impoverished by the year, even in *this* country. Single women with their dependent children are a sort of new, economically depressed underclass, and women of all classes and races are affected by what has been, materially, a decline in the past decade. Women of certain position and education have made great strides, but those strides, to my way of thinking, have all been at the top. In other words, you'll have women pilots and women vice-presidents of corporations, but the lot of most women has deteriorated. I've read that more than eighty percent of fathers of families, after one year of divorce, cease to contribute to child support. I've begun working with the Center for Investigative Reporting in Washington, which is now doing some work on this subject.

I feel most compelled by women; I'm more deeply affected by them. Maybe because I was raised by my mother and grandmother, and then educated by nuns—I suppose it couldn't help but happen. And I think that oppression has in many women fostered a kind of strength that is incomparable.

Your grandmother Anna seems like an incomparably strong woman.

When I first traveled to Eastern Europe, Anna was everywhere. I felt as if she had come back to me, and I felt her

in me, too. I had her until I was eighteen, and then she died. And it wasn't enough time, really—I didn't get to ask her the most important questions. And now I have to live them myself. I know the kind of life she had when she came to this country, working in the needle factory and her husband in the coke ovens and all of that. I didn't have illusions about her—she was a strong and domineering woman. She was a peasant woman, and so when I went to El Salvador and spent time with the *campesinos,* I didn't feel as uncomfortable or self-conscious as I might have without having had Anna as my grandmother.

Your epigram to the first section of your second book, **The Country between Us,** *is by the Spanish poet Antonio Machado, and it says:* "Walker, there is no road / You make your road as you walk." *Your own poems, of course, mirror your own path—one that has taken you on all kinds of open roads. You seem to be a voracious traveler.*

If I indulge myself, I could say that there's been a sort of ongoing pattern or mysterious and compelling force in my life. But when I think about the reasons for my traveling, I could also say that my grandmother Anna was a wanderer, and that my aunt once told me that in every generation in my family there's been a woman who hasn't been able to settle in one place. And they all thought I was the one; they decided that "Carolyn goes off because she's Anna, she's got that restless thing in her." Also, when I traveled to the American Southwest, I was getting over the death of a friend, and I went there to wander around and was literally taken in by an older Indian couple in a pueblo in northern New Mexico. They gave me meals, and gradually I was taught a little Tewa, and one thing led to another. And always, wherever I would go, this seemed to happen.

I had very difficult, sad times in my early adulthood, and I thought, "Well, I'm not responsible for what has happened to me, but I *am* responsible for my responses. So I have to respond well or else I'll become deranged or whatever." Then, midway through my twenties, it occurred to me that I was also responsible for what happened to me, that I had a certain amount of choice, and that the ways in which I tended could determine events. So when I first felt the urge to translate the Salvadoran poet Claribel Alegría, who lives in exile in Mallorca, I realized that I was ignorant of the reality out of which her poems were written. Going to stay with her in Mallorca was not going to Latin America, but many writers who have fled Latin America for various reasons travel to visit her. I met women there who were tortured, one in an Argentine prison. And I became very depressed. I thought maybe I had island fever. Claribel would sit with a drink every afternoon and wait for the mail to come, blank-eyed, sad, unreachable. I couldn't speak to her. She would search through the mail for news of her friends or relatives, and then an hour later she would suddenly be all cheery and dressed and ready to engage in the evening. But these moments haunted me.

I kept working on the translations, but I left very saddened. And then I came back to California and began working very intensely for Amnesty International—I was writing my letters dutifully and all that—and one day, up pulls this dusty, white jeep into my driveway, and out gets this guy with two little girls and knocks on my door. Now, I had heard about this man, Leonel Gomez Vides—I'd heard about him in Spain; there were legends about him. He introduced himself to me, but I was properly terrified about Latin American strangers who purported to be this or that. But he had the two little girls with him, so I trusted him and let him into the house. I sat him down at the kitchen table and pointed to photographs I had taken in Spain and asked him to identify various people. He was amused and said that someone was so-and-so and someone else was the husband of so-and-so, and so on. "That's very good," he told me. "Now," he said, "how would you like to do something for Central America, since you've translated these poems and obviously have an interest?" I knew that he was associated with many humanitarian projects in El Salvador, and I thought I would be the lady in white working in the orphanage for one year who pats the little bottoms! I pictured myself that way, rather heroically. I had a Guggenheim fellowship to write poetry, so I had the year free, and I said yes, I'd like to go.

So he went out to the truck, got a roll of white butcher paper and about twenty pencils, and he smoothed the paper out on the table and began to diagram and doodle and make little drawings about the Salvadoran military and the American embassy and the various components of the Salvadoran society and economic and political structures. He did this for seventy-two hours straight, with many cups of coffee, and then he would test me. He'd say, "Okay, you are this colonel and this happens and there's possibly going to be a coup, what do you do?" He made me think of every component in this scenario. And he said, "Look, you have a dead Jesuit priest and a dead parish priest, you have forty nuns and priests expelled from the country or arrested, this is the situation, and I want you to come to Salvador to learn about it, because our country is your country's next Vietnam."

Now, my ex-husband had gone to Vietnam, as had my next-door neighbor and most of my friends in school and brothers and boyfriends and husbands of friends—they all went off to the war because we were of the class that *went* to Vietnam. We used to listen to those songs in high school—about the Green Berets and about pinning silver wings on my son's chest. We literally used to cry because our friends were there and we thought they would die. But I was a *greaser,* we thought this war was right, we were very patriotic. It didn't occur *not* to be until I went to the university, and I was the only one among my circle of friends who did go. . . . So I *had* to know about El Salvador. And here this man was offering me an opportunity to understand something, and also he promised me that, in an odd way, I would be able to make a contribution. So how could I not agree? I knew that I was ignorant about the situation there, and that it would be a worse ignorance to refuse this offer. But most of my friends at the time thought I was absolutely crazy to go.

The poet Robert Bly recently spoke of our not being conscious of what we were (and are) doing in El Salvador. "We did it in Vietnam," he said, "and ever since have refused to become conscious of it. It is said that a dream will repeat itself until you understand it, until you become conscious

of what's there." And I have the sense that making things conscious is exactly what you've been trying to do in poetry.

For me, it's a process of understanding, a process that has not been completed and that probably can't be completed. But it certainly was startling for me to learn not only about Central America in a very immediate way, but also to learn about the limitations of my understanding. Because I wasn't equipped to see or analyze the world. My perceptions were very distorted—and I'm even talking about visual perception. I would notice things in very general terms, but there were certain things I would fail to see.

I would always marvel at the wealthy women in the suburbs of San Salvador—women playing canasta all day—and I spent many hours talking to them. They did not *see* poverty, it didn't exist for them. First of all, they never went outside the capital city, but even in the city, they could go through a street in a car and not see the mother who has made a nest in rubber tires for her babies. What they saw was an assembly of colors of delight, of baskets and jugs on the heads of women. Yet they were being as accurate as they could possibly be in their descriptions.

Now, as to what *I* didn't see: I was once driving past rows of cotton fields—all I could see on either side of the highway for miles was cotton fields, and it was dusty and hot, and I was rolling along thinking about something in my usual way, which is the way that has been nurtured in this country. But I didn't see *between* the rows, where there were women and children, emaciated, in a stupor, because pesticide planes had swept over and dropped chemicals all over them, and they were coughing and lethargic from those poisonous clouds . . . and also they were living in the middle of these fields because they had no place else to go, underneath sheet-plastic tarps that were no protection against the pesticides. The children had no clothing and were swollen-bellied and suffering from the second- and third-degree malnutrition that I had been taught to recognize in my work at the hospital. There they were, and I hadn't seen them. I had only seen cotton and soil between cotton plants, and a hot sky. I saw the thing endlessly and aesthetically; I saw it in a certain spatial way. So I had to be *taught* to look and to remember and to think about what I was seeing.

What you're saying reminds me of John Keats' notion that "poetry must work out its own salvation in a man: It cannot be matured by law and precept, but by sensation and watchfulness in itself. . . ."

Yes, I certainly don't mean to be programmatic in my writing, or ever to be strident or polemical. I don't want to argue a position; rather, I want to present in language the re-creation of a moment. Any judgment, any expression, even a most carefully rendered eyewitness testimony is viewed as political if you locate that testimony in an area associated with turmoil; whereas you can describe something in an area that's not so associated, and it will be considered something else. I tried not to write about El Salvador in poetry, because I thought it might be better to do so in journalistic articles. But I couldn't—the poems just came.

At the conclusion of one of your earlier poems, "What It

Cost," which is about the forced migrations in Russia and Eastern Europe of members of your grandmother's generation, one reads the words of the ghosts of the dead:

> *Haul your language south.*
> *There are knives in your pillows.*
> *The white birds fall another month.*

You've spent a lot of time in the American Southwest, and it's interesting that the first line of the first of your poems about El Salvador reads: "We have come far south." And it concludes:

> *. . . That is why we feel*
> *it is enough to listen*
> *to the wind jostling lemons,*
> *to dogs ticking across the terraces,*
> *knowing that while birds and*
> *warmer weather*
> *are forever moving north,*
> *the cries of those who vanish*
> *might take years to get here.*

As Robert Bly, again, has said, "It isn't accidental, in a way, that El Salvador is south of us, because south *in the psyche means* down." *I'm curious about your affinity with and gravitation toward the south that seems, in your case, to be physical and psychic.*

I spent my entire childhood in Michigan, and I was always compelled by the north—I happen to love the winter and the snow. I was always enamored of Russia—perhaps a sort of distorted, romantic version of Russia that comes from a twentieth-century reinterpretation of the nineteenth century. But when I got older, my inward focus was drawn less to the familiar and more to those things about which I was ignorant. And I wanted to go to the Southwest and be in the desert. I learned a lot during those weeks that I camped in the desert at different times in my twenties. I went there a lot, and that was where I became clear inside—though it does sound cliché. When I was in the Mojave Desert one time, I had this experience: I was with a friend, and we didn't speak to each other for about three or four days—I mean except for absolute necessities—but we didn't make conversation, and all of a sudden I was on this rock and I heard this *ba-bum ba-bum*. I was shocked. I realized I was hearing myself, my own life processes, and I felt a certain consciousness outside myself as well. It was quite a transfiguring experience for me. And after that I was very much drawn to the re-creation of it, by going back to the desert. One time when I was watching the sunset out there—you couldn't see any visible signs of mankind or civilization, there was no grid, and there were no wires or roads or glow of lights or anything—I realized: this is the way it was, this is the emptiness, this is the empty earth . . . but it wasn't empty, and I didn't know what was filling it. I think that I felt the need for a replacement, a spiritual palpability to replace the Catholicism that I had intellectually rejected when I was younger. And there it was again, only it wasn't with the need for a personal or an anthropomorphic conception of God.

As far as going to El Salvador is concerned, I told you what the reasons were for that. I don't know whether there's some reason *beyond* those reasons. Until you suggested this, I didn't know it was there. But I never would have thought, when I was little, that I would feel so compelled toward that particular part of the world.

In your beautiful and extraordinary long poem "Kalaloch," you describe a sexual encounter with a female stranger on a beach in the Pacific Northwest; in "For the Stranger," you present a sexual encounter with a male stranger on a train; and in your prose reverie "This Is Their Fault," you detail moments of a masochistic sexual fantasy. In all of these, there is no salaciousness, but rather a simple yet mysterious presentation of the life of desire.

One thing I try not to worry about in the poetry is how *I* appear. If you have a worry about what kind of appearance you're making, you'll censor yourself and will therefore diminish or reduce whatever it is that you've experienced. I made a rule for myself that I would have to be brave, and if something was embarrassing—and I'm very easily embarrassed—so what, it had to be put down, I had to write it.

After **"Kalaloch"** appeared, there was briefly a sort of letter-writing argument in the *American Poetry Review* about whether Carolyn Forché was gay, straight or bisexual. And I made no comment at all on it. I just thought, well, run with it, folks, you have a good time with that one because I really don't care what you think I am [*laughing*]. I thought it was a really superficial way of dealing with the poem, but it was also sort of interesting.

The way that poem came about was: There's this beach on the Olympic Peninsula where the land comes up into the water in these rock stacks and piles and formations. There's a lot of fog, and the ocean comes over the land; it's completely glazed and the land stretches out. I guess poets automatically think archetypically, and I was thinking: there're these two mothers, these two women—Earth and Water. I don't mean to make a cult of this idea, but it seemed as if it had to be that way. And they're making love. And there *was* a woman there named Jacynthe, and we *did* spend those weeks on the beach living in this little driftwood place like a couple of banshees.

Returning to the subject of masochistic fantasies, some people tend, unfortunately, to confuse sexual fantasies with the institutionalization of torture in police states.

I think many women in this culture—and I think that it's pretty well documented—imaginatively translate their experiences of childhood and develop masochism. I think most women confront that, and they are repelled by it or do battle with it. But many women whom I've spoken with do have this problem of eroticizing their oppression. Occasionally, however, there's a replay of this kind of fantasy when discussing human-rights abuses, and it has nothing to do with the reality of torture, imprisonment and assassination. It's what an inexperienced mind does with an abstraction that it has eroticized on another level in the light of its own culture. But if you're even willing to say: I had certain masochistic fantasies as a child that I later, to my own horror, saw the reality of somewhere . . . and if you're willing to acknowledge the complexity and admit that, for example, altruistic work isn't always simple, and to portray yourself as one of the people for whom it's not simple—*that*, then, is what's important. It's also important to see within ourselves first every manifestation of atrocity. The Holocaust didn't occur because only the Germans were somehow peculiar and therefore something like that couldn't happen again. We have to confront this now.

It must have been terrifying to confront the violent realities of El Salvador.

I was very close to Monsignor Oscar Romero just before he was killed. And I had a very, very close brush with death. I was with a young defecting member of the Christian Democratic party, and we confronted a death squad that had three machine guns trained on our windshield. They had enough time to kill us, but this young man had a sort of uncanny quickness of reflexes, and he managed to throw the car into reverse and floor it and get back through a walled gate. But though it was split-second, I had enough time to see the machine guns. There's no reason why I'm here. Functionally, it was a fluke.

Did you ever feel that you had come too close to the edge?

I could have, but I didn't lose my sanity even briefly. I became very lucid, but I knew what was going to happen. And I felt more and more powerless to do anything about it, because no one would listen to me. I began to realize that it wouldn't matter if they did. I had to experience the full impact of this horror, that this is indeed what happened in Vietnam . . . and that I couldn't stop it. And that I was going to have to see it almost like someone whose eyelids are held open and you can't stop lookingat something. And it was very hard to get through that period.

One of the things that's very heartening is that I met a whole network of people—many of them journalists—who never went off the path, who got involved during the Vietnam period for whatever reasons, who didn't go and climb the corporate ladder, who have maintained that their work be subservient to their conscience.

Walt Whitman wrote: "The attitude of great poets is to cheer up slaves and horrify despots."

That's an interesting view. I don't want to think of everyone who's been horrified as a despot, because a lot of people who've been horrified are very good-hearted and well-intentioned, especially the young ones. They come and they say, "What should we do?" They think that to write in an engaged way means you have to go to exotic climes. People don't want to learn about what is in their own immediate sphere. And this is understandable, isn't it, because of all the duplicity. "What should we do?" "That's not the beginning," I have to say. "Set off now and find *out* what you should do. The answer is not the beginning. The answer is maybe at the end, if you're very lucky."

Jonathan Cott, "Poetry in Motion," in Rolling Stone, *Issue 393, April 14, 1983, pp. 81, 83-7, 110-11.*

> Forché on poetry, politics, and the critical reception of *The Country between Us:*
>
> [When *The Country between Us* was published, political] poems were being criticized because of their didacticism, or because they were polemic or limited in some special poetic way. I didn't find it useful to say, "All poems are political," . . . even though I *did* say that, and of course they are. Bad poetry doesn't have to do with subject, it has to do with how much the poet interferes in the flow of consciousness to page.
>
> *Carolyn Forché, in an interview with K. K. Roeder, in* The San Francisco Review of Books, *August-October, 1993.*

Terence Diggory   (review date Fall 1983)

[*An American educator and critic, Diggory is the author of* Yeats and American Poetry: The Tradition of the Self *(1983). In the following excerpt, he provides a thematic analysis of* The Country between Us, *discussing its relationship to* Gathering the Tribes *and its focus on political concerns.*]

The honors showered upon Carolyn Forché during her brief career so far do not compensate for the misunderstanding that has accompanied them. Following her debut in the Yale Series of Younger Poets with *Gathering the Tribes* (1976), her second volume, *The Country Between Us,* was written under NEA and Guggenheim sponsorship, judged by the Poetry Society of America to be the best manuscript in progress, and awarded the Lamont Poetry Selection for 1981. A dust jacket blurb by Jacobo Timerman has Forché "replacing" Pablo Neruda as the poetic voice of South America.

Here the misunderstanding clearly surfaces. True, eight of the poems in Forché's volume deal with South America, specifically El Salvador—although, significantly, Forché takes her title from a poem about a friend from her Michigan girlhood (**"Joseph"**) in another, longer section of the volume. That section serves as a confirmation of what should be apparent even in the El Salvador poems if they are read attentively. As the Cuban writer Mario Benedetti warned Forché prior to her involvement in El Salvador, her perspective on South American experience must inevitably remain *North* American. Further, poems written from that perspective must reflect an Anglo-American literary tradition. One of the great strengths of *The Country Between Us* is that, unlike so many of her reviewers, Forché does not allow herself the illusion that a cultural perspective or a literary tradition can be, or should be, simply wished away.

The ease with which Jacobo Timerman equates Forché and Neruda is made possible only by judging the work of each writer as "political poetry," according, that is, to its subject matter rather than to those features of style through which an author creates a distinctive voice. The functioning of Carolyn Forché's voice in *The Country Be-*

tween Us has been seriously misjudged because the term "political poetry" has seemed so appropriate to that volume. Even those critics who have not been merely distracted by the content, who have directly addressed themselves to the question of voice, have been misled by the spectre of "political poetry," because for them that genre was naturally associated with certain qualities of voice that they proceeded to discover, or find lacking, in Forché. Such preconceptions account for the confusing contradictions in the critical depiction of Forché's voice, with Joyce Carol Oates, in the [4 April 1982 issue of] *New York Times Book Review,* worrying about the "impersonal and at times rhetorical poetry" produced by Forché's "self-effacing technique," while Katha Pollitt, in [the 8 May 1982 issue of] *The Nation,* laments Forché's dependence on "the misty 'poetic' language of the isolated, private self." Although appearing to differ about Forché, these critics are in fact differing about "political poetry," and are so distracted by that issue that they have neglected to read Forché.

In an attempt to read Forché on her own terms, it is useful to step back for a minute to her first volume to perceive the continuities between its poetry, political or otherwise, and the somehow specially "political" poetry of the second volume. Stanley Kunitz's Foreword to *Gathering the Tribe* defines Forché's questions—"Who am I? Why am I here? Where am I going?" —in the language of the private self that Katha Pollitt finds inhibiting in *The Country Between Us.* If Forché is inhibited in the latter volume, however, it is not merely a result of her language but of her intention, for she is still asking the same questions. Pollitt is embarrassed by **"The Island,"** for example, because she wants, but is unable, to read it as an homage to the Salvadoran poet Claribel Alegria, but Forché says explicitly, "I look for myself in her." Like the Pueblo Indians of *Gathering the Tribes* and the Slavic relatives who appear in both volumes, the Salvadorans of *The Country Between Us* serve as mirrors in which Forché seeks to define herself, a major occupation of Anglo-American poets since the Romantics. Incidentally, the "Carolina" addressed at the end of **"The Island"** is not, as Joyce Carol Oates interprets it, an example of the obscurity that "political poetry" invites through its topical allusions, but rather the poet's own first name Hispanicized. Using Claribel Alegria as her speaker, Forché quite literally is talking to herself.

With regard to image as well as voice, Forché's earlier work offers a useful corrective to the distortions required to fit her recent poems into the category of "political poetry." In **"The Memory of Elena,"** the poet and another woman, presumably the Elena of the title, lunch together in an atmosphere that, though geographically Spanish, is transformed by their awareness of South American atrocities:

> The *paella* comes, a bed of rice
> and *camarones,* fingers and shells,
> the lips of those whose lips
> have been removed, mussels
> the soft blue of a leg socket.

Katha Pollitt's comment on this passage, that "It trivial-

izes torture to present it in terms of lunch," derives from her assumption of a conflict between Forché's political intentions, to record torture, and her poetic technique, which places an undue emphasis, in Pollitt's view, on the sensibility that does the recording. What do we get, however, if we assume that intention and technique are at odds, that the poet's self enters here not as an unwanted intruder but as an intended part of the poem's subject?

We get something very much like Forché's earlier use of the image in **"Kalaloch,"** the dramatic and sexual climax of *Gathering the Tribes:*

> We went down to piles to get
> mussels, I made my shirt
> a bowl of mussel stones, carted
> them to our grate where they smoked apart.
> I pulled the mussel lip bodies out,
> chewed their squeak.

Here the image prepares for an act of oral sex between two women, described later in the poem. If we grant the author's presence its full weight in **"The Memory of Elena,"** that poem, too, depicts the communication of two women, Forché and Elena. At the most immediate level, their communion is sacramental rather than sexual, a commemoration of the dead through the communal eating of their bodies. The extremity of atrocity that is Forché's subject is thus reflected in the extremity of the response, but that is what this meal is, a response to, not an image of torture, as Pollitt would read it. The meal symbolically enacts the more literal response of the friends of a Salvadoran labor leader who "was cut to pieces and buried." As Forché recounts in **"Return":**

> his friends found
> the soldiers and made them dig him up
> and ask forgiveness of the corpse, once
> it was assembled again on the ground
> like a man.

A few lines later, Forché indicates the relevance of this image to the body politic: "We are / all assembled."

Being so much of the body, Forché's political vision is naturally sexual as well. Underlying the sacramental communion of Forché and her companion in **"The Memory of Elena"** is the companion's recollection of sexual communion with her dead husband, a victim of political oppression:

> In Buenos Aires only three
> years ago, it was the last time his hand
> slipped into her dress, with pearls
> cooling her throat and bells like
> these, chipping at the night—

Because sexual union, which joins bodies, is Forché's answer to political conflict, which tears bodies apart, the section of El Salvador poems in *The Country Between Us* is followed by a section, appropriately entitled "Reunion," of even more personal poems, many of them explicitly sexual. One of these, **"For the Stranger,"** about a brief romantic encounter on a train travelling across Europe, brings into the present the sexual invitation that is trapped in the past in **"The Memory of Elena":**

> Each time I find you

again between the cars, holding out
a scrap of bread for me, something
hot to drink, until there are
no more cities and you pull me
toward you, sliding your hands
into my coat, telling me
your name over and over, hurrying
your mouth into mine.

Here the vehicle of communion is seen in successive metamorphoses as food (including the sacramental bread that
was so important an image in *Gathering the Tribes*), as the
body, and finally as language, an obsessive naming that
gathers ritualistic force during the progress of this volume,
which seeks to rescue the dead from oblivion by remembering their names. Similarly, Forché seeks to rescue the
oppressed from silence by sharing her voice. When she
adopts the *persona* of Claribel Alegria, whose poems Forché has translated, she is "hurrying your mouth into
mine."

Clearly, Forché's purpose in entering into the lives of others is not merely selfish. She is concerned with the interaction of selves, or, to use the formulation applied by Stanley
Kunitz to *Gathering the Tribes*, her theme is kinship. If
her treatment of that theme in *The Country Between Us*
seems more mature, this growth must be partly attributed
to Forché's politicization, her greater awareness and acceptance of the conflict that exists among kin. We should
not expect Forché's political poetry to constitute a gesture
of "solidarity" any more than we should expect Robert
Lowell's "dynastic poetry" to conclude in a gesture of fil-
ial piety. Nevertheless, such expectations have misled even
Forché's most sympathetic interpreters. In an otherwise
acute discussion of Forché published in the [January-
February 1983 issue of] *American Poetry Review*, Larry
Levis equates the title phrase of Forché's concluding
poem, **"Ourselves or Nothing,"** with the famous line from
Auden's "September 1, 1939," "We must love one another
or die," a line whose simplistic assumptions later embarrassed Auden himself. To study Forché's line in its context
is to see the difference between political slogan and political poetry:

> There is a cyclone fence between
> ourselves and the slaughter and behind it
> we hover in a calm protected world like
> netted fish, exactly like netted fish.
> It is either the beginning or the end
> of the world, and the choice is ourselves
> or nothing.

How broad a scope is implied in the word "ourselves"
here? Most immediately it includes two people, Forché
and the person she is addressing, Terrence Des Pres, who
wrote in *The Survivor* about atrocities similar to those Forché witnessed in El Salvador. More broadly, the first reference to "ourselves" excludes the slaughtered Salvadorans
and embraces only those who share the *North* American
perspective of "a calm protected world." Given such restrictions, is Levis justified in taking, as he seems to do,
the second reference to "ourselves" as embracing all humanity? I think not; in fact, I think ultimately Forché
would restrict "ourselves" to the individual self that separates each of us. Such separation is what we have in com-

mon, and what we must tackle first if we are to make ad-
justments to a world that includes others. We cannot simply leap over the cyclone fence, leaving the self behind—
the gesture that proponents of "political poetry" seem to
demand. It is "ourselves or nothing" because it is only
through ourselves that we have access to others.

Despite Forché's refusal to let go of the self, there is in *The
Country Between Us* an occasional hint of the self-
effacement to which Joyce Carol Oates responded with a
slight chill. Within **"Ourselves or Nothing,"** Forché
quotes a sentence from Des Pres' book that might stand
as a statement of Forché's intention in her own: "They
turned to face the worst straight on, without sentiment or
hope, simply to keep watch over life." In the context of
the Nazi death camps that Des Pres describes, such un-
flinching confrontation can appear as heroic self-assertion,
but in the idea of simply keeping watch there is an invitation to passivity that can be heard not so much in Forché's
poems as in her own and others' comments about them.

About **"The Colonel,"** in which the title figure dumps a
sack of human ears onto the table from which he and Forché have just dined, Forché says that, "I had only to pare
down the memory and render it whole, unlined and as precise as recollection would have it. I did not wish to endanger myself by the act of poeticizing such a necessary reportage" (*American Poetry Review*, July-August 1981). If
to "poeticize" means to prettify, Forché's statement is un-
objectionable; if however, she means that **"The Colonel"**
is a "reportage" rather than poetry, Forché is disavowing
her own very significant role in giving her experience the
shape of art. That **"The Colonel"** has such shape can be
demonstrated by quoting its last two sentences, which provide perfect closure to a text in which each word is placed
with artful precision: "Some of the ears on the floor caught
this scrap of his voice. Some of the ears on the floor were
pressed to the ground." Even if we follow Forché's instructions to read **"The Colonel"** as "unlined," that is, as
prose, the repetition in these sentences produces very formal prose indeed. And if, despite Forché's temporary ban-
ishment of lineation to the composing room, we read each
sentence as a line of poetry, we discover that each is almost
perfectly anapestic, thus lending special significance to the
crucial disyllabic substitution that compresses the rhythm
at the very moment that the ears are seen to be pressed to
the ground. In the context of the volume as a whole, the
image of ears has a special resonance, for Forché is continually aware of how difficult it is for one person's voice to
reach the ears of another, spanning the distance of "the
country between us." That her voice reaches us so distinctly is a tribute to her art as well as a measure of the
horror to which her art bears witness. . . .

Terence Diggory, "Witnesses and Seers," in Salmagundi,
Vol. 61, Fall, 1983, pp. 112-24.

Michael Greer   (essay date Spring 1986)

[*In the essay below, Greer examines Forché's poetry "as a
phenomenon that is, in its very constitution and production,
social, historical, and political."*]

In the four years since their publication, the poems of Car-

Poetry makes its own demands, and Forché knows this. She has various neat and carefully crafted ways of threading sounds through a poem in order to provide the necessary momentum for what she has to say. In other words she is a poet and not a poseur.

—*John Lucas, in his "A New Daks Suit,"* in New Statesman, *1 April 1983.*

olyn Forché's *The Country Between Us* have been identified with a renewed debate concerning the claims, the merits, and the possibilities for "political poetry" in contemporary America. They have been taken as an occasion for critical pronouncements on the question of "mixing art and politics" and have been widely praised as well as strenuously criticized. The apparent plurality of critical opinion surrounding *The Country Between Us* would seem to suggest that the question of poetry's relationship to politics is once again productively open, but in fact it masks a more disturbing consensus: whatever their merit, these poems belong to a specialized genre—"political poetry." They are to be evaluated for their ability to "reconcile" or "balance" impulses generally regarded as contradictory: the personal or lyrical on the one hand, the political or engaged on the other. I see several problems with such a notion of political poetry. First, it implies that certain poems are political while others (the majority) are not, and it thus functions to marginalize those poems regarded as political without yet having explored the social and political constitution of all literary discourse. More importantly, such a notion of political poetry adopts unquestioningly an already reified conception of the social; it is incapable of helping us to think of relationships between individuals and society in terms other than those of opposition. As a result, it replicates the split in contemporary ideology between private and public. That subjects may be socially constituted is a question usually not asked. Finally, this taken-for-granted definition of political poetry is not a *historical* definition: it fails to consider the ways in which lyric poetry, since the Romantics at least, has been constituted *in opposition* or reaction to dominant modes of social and political discourse. Severed from history, the lyric poet becomes an isolated voice crying out in the empty wasteland of modernist despair: politics becomes mere psychologism and the struggle to wrest freedom from necessity is rewritten as a purely individual quest. The compulsion to read Forché's poetry as political in this narrower sense, then, has resulted in readings that distort and diminish the real accomplishments of the poems while undermining any claim they, or any contemporary poems, have to be political in any deeper sense.

In the autobiographical **"El Salvador: An Aide-Memoire,"** Forché herself has provided us with a text that asks to be read as both a preface to and a theoretical defense of the project undertaken in *The Country Between Us.* **"Aide-Memoire"** is pervaded by an uneasiness regarding the critical terms in which the poems have been received and discussed. In response to critics' classification of the poems as "political poetry," Forché writes: "I suspect that underlying this . . . is a naive assumption: that to locate a poem in an area associated with political trouble automatically renders it political." The essay, in fact, concludes with an enumeration of several of the more problematic questions concerning the theoretical status of poetry as political—suggestions, perhaps, of ways in which the political constitution of all poetry might more productively be explored. What emerges is the notion that there are really two different senses of the term "political." The first, more limited sense sees "politics" as the largely institutionalized, two-dimensional discourse of political programs and "ideologies" in the official sense; the second, invoked in response to the confinement of the first, defines politics far more broadly and flexibly as any action or discourse carried out in a social world. These two competing definitions are made dramatically clear in the juxtaposition, on the final pages of **"Aide-Memoire,"** of the following two statements. First, Forché's own allegation that "there is no such thing as nonpolitical poetry"; second, a statement from Hans Magnus Enzensberger's "Poetry and Politics": "The poem expresses in an exemplary way the fact that it is not at the disposal of politics: this is its political content" [*The Consciousness Industry,* 1974]. Where most American readers of Forché seek to reduce the political to the more limited of these two senses, Forché and Enzensberger attempt to open up the notion, to make "the political" again the site of an ongoing, daily contestation.

Enzensberger's "Poetry and Politics" effectively defines the theoretical impasse at which American practical criticism finds itself when it attempts to discuss poetry like Forché's.

> As sociology, literary criticism cannot see that language constitutes the social character of poetry, and not its entanglement in the political battle. Bourgeois literary esthetics is blind to, or else conceals, the fact that poetry is essentially social. The answers offered by the two doctrines to the question of the relationship of the poetic to the political process are correspondingly clumsy and useless: complete dependence in one case, complete independence in the other. . . . The real question remains unexamined and indeed unasked.

> This essay seeks, if not to answer, at least to ask that real question: how can we, in contemporary America, begin to think poetry as an immanently social and political act? How can poetry like Forché's help us to read other poetry in a way that avoids reproducing the bourgeois ideological separation of "the private" from "the public"? By moving between Forché's Salvadoran poems and the critical languages constructed around them, this essay seeks to begin sketching out more productive ways of thinking and talking about poetry as a phenomenon that is, in its very constitution and production, social, historical, and political.

The text in question here is "In Salvador, 1978-80," a sequence of eight poems that forms the first section of Carolyn Forché's *The Country Between Us*. It is primarily these poems that have been responsible for the association of Forché with political poetry, and more often than not they are characterized as "explicitly political" at the outset, only to be reclaimed later as successful personal lyric. [In his "War as Parable and War as Fact," *American Poetry Review* 12, No. 1 (1983)] Larry Levis, for example, begins by praising the poems for their ability to engage the political realities of Central American violence and struggle, but ends by translating the sequence into the romanticized terms of an internal struggle, "the process of a human psyche learning and becoming more openly human and vulnerable." This gesture is a common one in the criticism of American poetry: to translate external landscapes and journeys into predominantly psychological terms—but in the case of these Salvador poems this project would appear to be subverted at every turn by a poetic voice which repeatedly displaces or decenters its own subject position. The last lines of **"The Island,"** for instance, pose a question which undoes any sense we might have of a unified speaking subject, bringing vividly before us [Emile] Benveniste's fundamentally important fracturing of the subject of the enunciation from the subject of the enounced: "Carolina [Carolyn?] do you know how long it takes / any one voice to reach another?"

The epigraph to "In Salvador" is from Antonio Machado (his epitaph, in fact) and introduces one of the important structural motifs of the sequence: *"Caminante, no hay camino / se hace camino al andar."* (In English, roughly, "Walker, there is no road; the road is made by walking.") While the eight poem sequence does not explicitly comprise a coherent narrative journey, it does imply such a narrative progression, and it relies on our sense of the grouping as a whole and roughly chronological sequence. The trip is problematically framed, but remains circular and complete, the poem **"Return"** (the sixth) explicitly ending the travels and replacing the speaker in America.

The outline of this journey is as follows: **"San Onofre, California"** opens the sequence with the speaker physically—and perhaps ideologically—"at home" in the States; **"The Island"** initiates the journey to Salvador, but indirectly, through the intermediary figure of the Salvadoran poet Claribel Alegría, herself in voluntary exile on a Mallorquin island; **"The Memory of Elena"** and, especially, **"The Visitor"** and **"The Colonel"** speak from the darkest recesses of Salvador itself, the three poems together forming the sequence's literal and metaphorical center; **"Return,"** as its title suggests, expresses its speaker's moral and communicative dislocation upon her return to North America. The final two poems, **"Message"** and **"Because One Is Always Forgotten,"** complete the sequence by turning once again to the south, to face, from a now more educated—but also more unstable—North American position, those who remain in Salvador, those who will fight "for the most hopeless of revolutions."

Given this sense of a general narrative construct, it becomes important to consider how each poem undercuts or problematizes the sequence's implied linear progression: the haunting ambivalence of the first poem ("San Ono-

fre") for instance, depends on its speaker's knowing what it is she will see further south—on her having, in effect, already undertaken the journey toward which the poem gazes. A similar confusion of narrative time and tense informs **"The Island"** and **"The Colonel,"** in which the speaker's rhetorical strategies are based on a knowledge of the problem of poetic communication in a North American context, itself not explicitly encountered until later, in **"Return."** These more subtle ambivalences, of course, depend on the stability of the narrative framework from which they depart—a fact emphasized by Forché's own determination, both in public readings and in the prefatorial **"Aide-Memoire,"** to explicate and clarify the major episodes and turning points of her actual journey to Salvador.

The primary subject matter—to speak in thematic terms—of "In Salvador," that which, more than simply its setting, makes the sequence in some broad sense "political," is what Forché has called, in a provocative but largely unexamined phrase in **"Aide-Memoire,"** "the politics of cultural immersion." "It was thought important that a few North Americans, particularly writers, be sensitized to Salvador prior to any military conflict," she writes; "the lessons were simple and critical, the methods somewhat more difficult to detect." Forché herself was recruited by a group of Salvadorans to travel in and observe the Salvadoran situation *as a poet* (a fact which surprised her—"mere poetry" she says, not having in Salvador the pejorative connotations it has in an American context). Carolyn Forché, of course, is by no means the first North American writer to find herself in the role of witness and reporter: a decade earlier, for instance (in 1968) Susan Sontag undertook a similar journey into North Vietnam and chronicled her experience in her well known "Trip to Hanoi" [collected in her 1969 *Styles of Radical Will*]. And a year or so after Forché the American essayist and novelist Joan Didion traveled to El Salvador and wrote about it in her popular *Salvador*. An examination of the structural and thematic similarities among **"Aide-Memoire,"** *Salvador,* and "Trip to Hanoi" will help to define some of the key issues and problematics implied by Forché's notion of a "politics of cultural immersion."

"In the end, of course," writes Susan Sontag at the conclusion of "Trip to Hanoi," "an American has no way of incorporating Vietnam into [her] consciousness." For Sontag, a journey into North Vietnam which began as "a somewhat passive experience of historical education" became, "as it had to, an active confrontation with the limits of [her] own thinking." To immerse oneself in a revolutionary Third World culture, Sontag discovers, is to confront the profoundly ideological character of one's own vision and perception; it is to experience a dislocating alienation in which all that is real about a foreign culture seems most "unreal," and in which one's own perception is, in Russian formalist or Brechtian fashion, radically defamiliarized. As Sontag recognized early in her travels, "I had only my own culture-bound, disoriented sensibility for an instrument" with which to interpret Hanoi. Didion's *Salvador* records a similar experience of cultural dislocation: "to land at this airport [El Salvador International, outside San Salvador] . . . is to plunge directly into a state in which no ground is solid, no depth of field reliable, no perception so definite that it might not dissolve into its reverse."

If a single overriding concern unites these three writers' approaches to Salvador or Vietnam, it is a concern to respect the primacy and inescapability of cultural difference—the sense that an American writer is inhabited by America as she inhabits it, that to leave the States is far more than to simply cross a geopolitical boundary. Theirs is a project of solidarity with a foreign culture born of mutual difference, characterized by a self-conscious attention to the limits of their own perspectives, and it contrasts instructively with the anthropologist's or the ethnographer's faith in his ability to write his way into a culture. Sontag most explicitly addresses the contradictions of this felt difference when she writes: "My sense of solidarity with the Vietnamese, however genuine and felt, is a moral abstraction developed (and meant to be lived out) at a great distance from them. Since my arrival in Hanoi, I must maintain that sense of solidarity alongside new unexpected feelings which indicate that, unhappily, it will always remain a moral abstraction." Throughout these writers' descriptions of their experiences of dislocation and cultural difference, it seems, their attention to their own perceptions and interpretations, while apparently directed "inward," is also profoundly political—they seem in their own ways to have arrived at a working definition of ideology not unlike Louis Althusser's [in his 1971 *Lenin and Philosophy and Other Essays*]: "a representation of the imaginary relationships of individuals to their real conditions of existence."

If these experiences of cultural dislocation and defamiliarization form a kind of first moment in what might be called a "dynamic" of cultural immersion, a second, perhaps more unsettling moment occurs when these writers witness the economic colonization of the Third World by America firsthand and in so doing implicate themselves in the economic and political exchange systems that have, in a very real sense, produced the violence that pervades a Vietnam or a Salvador. Didion, in San Salvador's Metrocenter shopping mall, becomes fascinated with the consumer exports from the States—the Muzak and the *pâté de foie gras,* "the young matrons in tight Sergio Valente jeans, trailing maids and babies behind them and buying towels, big beach towels printed with maps of Manhattan that featured Bloomingdale's . . . the number of things that seemed to suggest a fashion for 'smart drinking,' to evoke modish cocktail hours." "This was a shopping center that embodied the future for which El Salvador was presumably being saved," she writes, with more than a touch of her characteristic irony. But a moment later the irony gives way to a painful moment of self-recognition and self-implication: "As I waited to cross back over the Boulevard de los Heroes to the Camino Real I noticed soldiers herding a young civilian into a van, their guns at the boy's back, and I walked straight ahead, not wanting to see anything at all." In this moment, Didion realizes that she, like the towels or the blue jeans, is herself an export from the capitol of consumption, is herself not only a consumer but a commodity as well. And in that moment, Didion catches herself looking the other way and confronts herself for the first time as a *norteamericana.*

A related moment of self-implication forms the climax of Forché's **"Aide-Memoire":** "On the final trip to the airport we swerved to avoid a corpse, a man spread eagled, his stomach hacked open, his entrails stretched from one side of the road to the other. We drove over them like a garden hose. My friend looked at me. *Just another dead man,* he said. And by then it had become true for me as well: the unthinkable, the sense of death within life before death." It is this sense of "death within life" that will pervade the central poems of "In Salvador" and lend to them their haunting, macabre quality, but it has more to do with than simply aesthetic tone. In this moment, Forché acknowledges and foregrounds difference at the same time that difference gives way and opens upon a larger network of political and economic exchange in which Forché, like Didion, is forced to recognize her own complicity. This dual stance—I am other and outside, but at the same time implicated—informs many of the best lines of "In Salvador" itself. It seems to reveal an interesting paradox which places Forché in the context, oddly enough perhaps, of high modernism: for her, the kind of fracturing and defamiliarizing of perception which is such a central strategy to the modernists takes on a distinctly political purpose and direction. To write about Salvador to an American audience, Forché discovers, requires one to self-consciously attend to the ideological and semiotic boundaries of one's own vision. It is in this context, too, that we may begin to see what Forché means when she describes her own poetic as a confrontation of "the impulse to witness" with the "prevailing poetic." Her own project is not to develop a political program in verse, but rather to take the American inheritance from Romanticism and modernism, which she sees as encouraging a "self-regarding, inward-looking poetry" and rewrite them in broadly political and ideological (in Althusser's sense) terms. Her project is to make a type of modernism once again historically aware of its own motivations and ideological biases. With this notion of Forché's poetics in mind, we may at last turn to some of the Salvadoran poems themselves, to follow through the implications of this confrontation of modernism and the political.

In **"San Onofre, California,"** first of the eight Salvador poems, the poet stands poised on the southern border of the United States. She lingers at the boundary, not only of a political state, but of knowledge and experience, and can conceive of Salvador only in stereotypical tourist's images. That nation before her, further south, is known to her only as images of rural poverty—and the frightening possibility of "being disappeared."

> We have come far south.
> Beyond here, the oldest women
> shelling limas into black shawls.
> Portillo scratching his name
> on the walls, the slender ribbons
> of piss, children patting the mud.
> If we go on, we might stop
> in the street in the very place
> where someone disappeared
> and the words Come with us! we might
> hear them.

The alternatives presented by the situation are not, however, as simple as they at first appear to be and the momentary acceptance of separation is not entirely motivated by selfish fear. The speaker also expresses a discretion that knows rushing south to be killed or kidnapped would stifle any hopes of extending what, from the point of view of the rest of the poems in the sequence, must be the only gesture that can help, an effort of the hands—like scratching your name into the wall. Her cultural isolation from the Central American destination of this sequence of poems is thus a knowing acceptance of distance and temporary inefficacy. The fact that is then confronted in the last lines, the knowledge that "the cries of those who vanish / might take years to get here," is not simply a signal of a refusal to accept the responsibility to act for those who have been disappeared. In a public reading, Forché has explained that this poem is in fact addressed to the people of San Onofre—some of whom were her students—and that she wanted it to make them feel their nearness to Salvador as well as their distance from it. These last lines undercut any simple geographical sense of the present, of the "here," by radically blurring the boundaries between the "here" and the "beyond here." While we are moving further south, the "birds and warmer weather / are forever moving north."

To explain what makes these last lines so haunting and successful, one needs to move to more literary and formal considerations: the poet's use of this inclusive, plural "we." When Forché writes "We feel / it is enough to listen" (rather than to act, to continue the movement southward) she does so in a voice which allows her to speak for two groups of people at once: those who know that, further south in Central America, people are vanishing every day, and those who have chosen not to accept such knowledge. She avoids a tone that would place her apart from the Californians addressed by and included in the "we," opening her voice and her poetry to the expressions of the American that she has always been and known. She speaks *to* the complacent residents of San Onofre, but at the same time she is able to speak *for* them. In the sense that we are all like the residents of San Onofre, it becomes us—the readers of the poem—who are incorporated into this poem's rationalizing logic. We become part of the poem's ambivalent collective voice; we are the ones who continue to listen placidly, knowing that as long as we may listen, the "cries of those who vanish" may never reach us. Not "here" anyway. If Salvador itself and the experience of oppression cannot be brought out of nothingness in a North American language, perhaps we can at least be made to feel our own role in the ongoing reproduction of that language. **"San Onofre"** is an effective political poem because it implicates us as readers in the production of a language for which El Salvador is little more than a distant little country "about the size of Massachusetts." We are no longer given a simple image or spatial representation of Salvador, as we are in the poem's opening lines, but are instead placed in the position of having to view our own inaction and complacency as itself part of an ongoing production of an imaginary relationship of spatial, not to mention ethical, distanciation.

Several of the poems following **"San Onofre"** engage or address the reader in a more direct, explicit fashion. In

"The Island," the poet, who has been describing what happens "in Deya when the mist / rises out of the rocks," responds to what she imagines would be an American reader's natural question: "Deya? A cluster of the teeth / the bones of the world, greener / than Corsica. In English / you have no word for this. I can't / help you." **"The Memory of Elena"** implies the presence of an imaginary listener, to whom the poem's speaker exhibits various meaningful objects: "These are the flowers we bought / this morning." And perhaps most vividly, the prose poem **"The Colonel"** begins by invoking the presence of a listener: "What you have heard is true." Only the sequence's centerpiece poem, **"The Visitor,"** is without a strong sense of implied dialogue or direct address. (It takes place in *la oscura,* the dark recesses of a Salvadoran prison, where the intolerable isolation makes all dialogue impossible.) Unlike the discourses of journalism or formalized politics, these poems do not assume a fixed or stable speaker-listener, self-other relationship. The reader is repeatedly made to feel that his or her reading of the poem is inseparable from the poem's very production and existence. In this sense, Forché's poetry may be seen as working against the ongoing commodification of poetry and of literary discourse in general, by its reinsertion of the reader at the center of textual production—as opposed to an address to an absent or distant consumer.

Here we may begin to see how Forché's poetry is ideological in Althusser's sense of ideology as an imaginary resolution of real contradictions. In contemporary America, such a gap exists between the bourgeois consumer of books of poetry (meaning all of us) and the implied reader or listener of poems like **"San Onofre"** that the former has become completely unrecognizable to the latter. Contemporary poetry has never known an environment in which the oral presentation of poems was not made a superfluous gesture by the production and distribution of books of poems, never known the reading (aloud) of a poem to be anything but a performance or spectacle. A poem like **"San Onofre"** or **"The Island"** may thus be perceived as an ideological and symbolic gesture whose purpose is to destabilize the poet-audience relationship and place the listener again—at least in the imaginary—at the center of poetic production. With this observation, we have begun to historicize Forché's poems, begun to see the objective contradictions in our own culture which make her poems possible, and necessary. By making available to us these fundamental structural contradictions of our own moment, I would argue, Forché's poetry is political in Enzensberger's second, more flexible sense.

In **"Return,"** the sixth poem of "In Salvador," the questions that have lurked behind the poet's self-consciousness about her own political role become an explicit theme. The poem is a dialogue in verse between the speaker and her friend and critic Josephine Crum, to whom the poem is dedicated, and in it the poet's doubts about her ability to communicate her experiences of immersion come to be fully expressed: "When I speak with American men / there is some absence of recognition. . . . I cannot, Josephine, talk to them." For this frustrated poet, the American attaché to Salvador is the perfect emblem of the audience she feels incapable of reaching: while his wife writes his reports and flies her plane around the country, he drinks, clicks his pen, and stares into his fish tanks, all the while surrounded by Marines in white gloves. But Josephine is a strenuous critic, and she is quick to point out that the poet's feelings of powerlessness are in themselves a retreat into self-pity and self-indulgence: "It is / not your right to feel powerless." In response to the poet's desires to retreat into a traditionally modernist stance of isolated repose and distance, the character of Josephine in this poetic drama urges the poet to assume a more collective role, to blend journalism and reportage with the "traditional" poetic mode, and thereby to reach her intended audience through a subversive infiltration of their own media discourse. Responding in her most powerful lines to the poet's sense that "I cannot keep going," Josephine challenges:

> Your problem is not your life as it is
> in America, not that your hands, as you
> tell me, are tied to do something. It is
> that you were born to an island of greed
> and grace where you have this sense
> of yourself as apart from others. It is
> not your right to feel powerless.

As a suggestion toward a possible source of rhetorical power and persuasiveness, Josephine challenges the poet to "give them what they want: Tell them about the razor, the live wire . . . tell them about retaliation." While this encouragement to adopt the strategies of sensationalism is, in the long run, not an effective characterization of Forché's poetics, it does point to the fact that torture reports, the tales of prisons told by their few survivors, and photographs of mutilated death squad victims' corpses have, since the early 1980s, become available and known by the potential readers of Forché's poems. In fact, such narratives and images have in some sense already been incorporated into the North American sociolect. Besides the popularity of books like Didion's *Salvador* here in the U.S., the popular media culture has as well begun to display its own images of Salvador. A Rolling Stones video, "Under Cover of the Night," for example, includes one scene in which a young woman searches through one of Salvador's infamous photo albums of the dead, hunting in desperation for clues about a brother, or a lover; in another scene, the character played by Mick Jagger witnesses a death squad style execution being carried out on a deserted bridge. A related confrontation with Latin American brutality is presented in the opening sequence of a September, 1985 season premiere episode of NBC's *Miami Vice:* Crockett and Tubbs, the protagonists, newly arrived in Bogata on a cocaine investigation, witness the torture and machine-gun murder of a drug trafficker. "Welcome to the Third World"—the Colombian agent tells them.

But there are clearly differences between these media representations of the Latin American Third World and Forché's imagings of Salvador. Crockett and Tubbs, for instance, never experience the sense of dislocation that characterizes Forché, Sontag and Didion as they are welcomed to the Third World—the drug agent's welcome is in fact a reassurance to the Miami pair that their position, at least, is secure, elsewhere. The shock their facial expressions is supposed to register in fact reconfirms their com-

placent superiority as Americans—they don't, as Didion does, find the need to complicate their own role in the murder. Theirs is a stable position from which to judge the Colombians, without any hint of their own implication. And the Rolling Stones video, because its narrative is controlled or recontained by the musical soundtrack, also reduces murder to a spectacle—a hollow image which assures a viewer of his own distance from the murder. (But there is one difference between these two media representations: the film technique employed in the Stones video gives the impression that the filmed murder is "real"—one is caught for a moment in a disconcerting voyeuristic position.) Raymond Williams, in his important discussion of dominant, residual, and emergent cultural forms [in his 1977 *Marxism and Literature*] describes the power of dominant cultural forms to incorporate potentially alternative or oppositional forms by rewriting them in its own terms. A project like Forché's, which wishes to produce a genuinely oppositional alternative to media and officially "political" representations of Salvador, is always susceptible to being rewritten in the terms of the dominant cultural mode. The production of oppositional forms is "usually made much more difficult," writes Williams, "by the fact that much incorporation looks like recognition, acknowledgment, and thus a form of acceptance." The television industry in the States repeatedly congratulates itself on its ability to "raise viewer consciousness" by "covering" such stories as the Ethiopian famine, or the murder of Jose Rudolfo Viera, but it is actually its frightening ability to incorporate into its own language a whole range of world events and practices—without considering its own role in their production—of which it speaks in such self-congratulatory moments. And television's own cultural dominant is, of course, the commodity, the conversion of history into a domestic spectacle.

Where television wishes to say that it "acknowledges" or "confronts" such problems as Salvadoran agrarian inequity, Williams, and, indirectly, Forché, would argue that it has instead effected its ownstyle of colonization: the representation of world as spectacle. This commodification of such images operates to effect its own kind of censorship—a censorship which it then becomes Forché's purpose to dismantle or deconstruct. Commodification, because it reinscribes these images of brutality within the familiar North American domestic context—the cop show, the music video, the evening newscast—erases all traces of those images' histories and transforms them into symbolic representations without any material referent. Cut off from their now repressed histories, these commodified images float freely among all the other "floating signifiers" produced by the technological media. In such a form, they pose no disconcerting threat to the American viewer—they are as easily absorbed as new brand names into the popular social repository.

In this context, a different strategy by which to politicize the dominant poetic comes into view. Forché's political task as a poet becomes one of reinterpreting these ungrounded images by restoring to them their repressed, obliviated histories. To politicize the modernist, or postmodernist, poetic lexicon, then, is not simply to introduce images of brutality and violence which will shock readers out

The Visitor

In Spanish you he (?) whisper
There is no time left.
It is the sound of scythes
arching in wheat,/ the ache
of some field song in Salvador./

The wind along the prison, cautious
as Francisco's hands on the inside
Touching the walls as he walks
It is his wife's breath
Slipping into his cell/ each night
as he imagines his hand/ to be hers

        It is a small country./
space → There is nothing one man
        will not do to another.

                                    Carolyn Forché

Rough draft of Forche's "The Visitor."

of their complacency (television's self-proclaimed purpose); it becomes the far more difficult task of making the material traces visible again on the surface of an already commodified, Americanized El Salvador.

Where media discourse *represents* Salvador, "pictures" it in a way that liquidates any historical traces and relegates present images to a securely bounded, formalized, and easily forgotten past, Forché's poetry makes a historical past once again available in the present. While most of the poems in the Salvador sequence effect this kind of a recuperation, **"The Memory of Elena"** most distinctively takes this movement as its formal principle. At the heart of **"The Memory of Elena"** is a macabre transformation not unlike a version of the Thyestean feast. Sitting over her lunch, the poet realizes in terror, "This is not *paella,* this is what / has become of those who remained / in Buenos Aires. This is the ring / of a rifle report on the stones." The pleasant surfaces of a cafe luncheon open onto a more terrifying memory:

> In Buenos Aires only three
> years ago, it was the last time his hand
> slipped into her dress, with pearls
> cooling her throat and bells like
> these, chipping at the night—

In **"The Memory of Elena"** the silence evoked by a description of the sounds which intrude upon it is transformed from a potentially calm and regenerative leisure into a historicized terror—the memory of a husband's murder.

> These are the flowers we bought
> this morning, the dahlias tossed
> on his grave and bells
> waiting with their tongues cut out
> for this particular silence.

In this poem, "this particular silence," this empty, quiet moment in the present, undergoes a transformation from an inert, quotidian presence and becomes the emblem of a distinct past. Onto the moment of silence between the bells is superimposed the rifle report that sounded the death of Elena's husband; the silence of the present is made to contain a three years' absence. A present and a past are seen to coexist at the very moment that the poem itself begins to dissolve into silence.

The historicizing movement of **"The Memory of Elena"** may be more fully illuminated through a consideration of the notion of history developed by a writer whose vision of the past intersects with Forché's at many points: the

German critic whose work is a dazzlingly contradictory combination of Marxism and apocalyptic gnosticism—Walter Benjamin. In his "Theses on the Philosophy of History," a text whose fragmentary, runic style has itself become an emblem of the struggle against fascism, Benjamin offers glimpses of a conception of history which sees revolution not as a struggle to liberate the future, but as a fight to redeem the past. Benjamin's Messianic version of historical materialism arises as a critique of bourgeois "universal history," or progressivism—that empirical notion of historical development which seeks to establish causal connections between successive moments, and which looks forward into a future of homogeneous, empty time. In contrast to this notion of history which "assigns to the working class the role of the redeemer of future generations," Benjamin turns his back on the future and warns: "*Even the dead* will not be safe from the enemy if he wins" [*Illuminations,* edited by Hannah Arendt, 1968].

To articulate the past historically, for Benjamin, "means to seize hold of a memory as it flashes up at a moment of danger." Radical history does not involve simply rewriting the past "the way it really was." It becomes a struggle to make available to the present images of the past which will allow "the sign of a Messianic cessation or happening . . . a revolutionary chance in the fight for the oppressed past." As I have been reading Forché here, her project seems to be just such an attempt to make these signs available to us, her North American audience. A poem like **"The Memory of Elena"** singles out and redeems a single moment of the past, makes that moment again "citable," to use Benjamin's phrase, in the very moment of the poem's reading. "Every image of the past that is not recognized by the present as one of its own concerns threatens to disappear irretrievably," writes Benjamin. In that moment of horror in which an everyday bowl of soup becomes the fingers and leg sockets of the murdered, a new relationship of present to past is established, the traces of a violent history are restored to the objects of a seemingly inert present. Forché does not allow the images of Elena's memory to disappear; she reinscribes them in our own present.

The culture of contemporary America is dominated by a discourse of forgetfulness which liquidates our history, transforming our past into a commodified image—palatable, certainly, because it no longer bears the marks of the violence and aggression that have produced our nation, our world. With our gaze turned forever forward, our faith placed in a technological progress which offers the empty hope of a utopian future, we willfully erase all records of our own history. A scant ten years later, the Vietnam war appears to have been made all but totally irretrievable; the more recent events in Salvador, the murders of Monsignor Oscar Romero, Jose Rudolfo Viera, and the thousands of other Salvadoran workers and *campesinos* have been recorded by the media and the press as if they were spectacles intended for our own momentary edification. Carolyn Forché's journey of cultural immersion in her Salvador sequence tries to combat this willful forgetfulness by politicizing our vision, making visible to us the all too immaterial traces on our own present world of America's ongoing colonization of Central America. . . . Three lines from **"Ourselves or Nothing,"** the closing poem of *The Country Between Us,* summarize what I take to be her redemptive project: "Go after that which is lost / and all the mass graves of the century's dead / will open into your early waking hours."

A single image from Benjamin's "Theses," with which this essay will end, gives us a way to imagine what a transcendent perspective on our own history might be like, were such a vision ever to be available to Benjamin, to Forché, or to ourselves. In it is pictured a fully redeemed vision of the past—glimpses of which it is Forché's purpose to evoke in poems like **"The Memory of Elena."** Benjamin's "angel of history," itself taken from Paul Klee's painting *Angelus Novus,* compresses all of our own irretrievable past into a single instant and image:

> His eyes are staring, his mouth is open, his wings are spread . . . His face is turned toward the past. Where we perceive a chain of events, he sees one single catastrophe which keeps piling wreckage upon wreckage and hurls it in front of his feet. The angel would like to stay, awaken the dead, and make whole what has been smashed. But a storm is blowing from Paradise; it has got caught in his wings with such violence that the angel can no longer close them. The storm irresistibly propels him into the future to which his back is turned, while the pile of debris before him grows skyward. This storm is what we call progress.

Michael Greer, "Politicizing the Modern: Carolyn Forché in El Salvador and America," in The Centennial Review, *Vol. XXX, No. 2, Spring, 1986, pp. 160-80.*

Carolyn Forché with Jill Taft-Kaufman (interview date January 1990)

[*Taft-Kaufman is an educator. In the following interview, Forché discusses her aims as a poet, her works-in-progress, and her experiences as a public speaker and political activist.*]

[*Taft-Kaufman*]: *Carolyn, you described your original experience in El Salvador as having created a "focused obsession" for you. Can you speak a little bit about that?*

[Forché]: Well, I've discussed elsewhere at great length the conditions under which I went to El Salvador and what happened to me there. But to address the concern about the singular focus that emerged from that experience, I think it was highly personal for me, my response to the sense of obligation that I felt toward people that I had left behind there, people who had educated me and who were in very grave danger themselves. And because of the intricate complicity of my own government in those conditions, I felt a moral obligation to respond when I returned home. And I feel that there was a period in which I believed that American public opinion influenced foreign policy decision making. And as long as I believed that there was a direct relationship between American public opinion and foreign policy decision making, I continued to believe in the validity of speaking in this country of conditions in El Salvador. So I spoke for five years in universities, and churches, and synagogues, and Kiwanis Clubs, and community centers. And finally I realized . . . it was a slow realization . . . that I had said what I could say, that I had done what I could do, and I was very tired. I reached a point where I was unable to resuscitate myself, and this coincided with the period at which I met my husband again. We had met in El Salvador earlier in a refugee camp, but we met in New York when we collaborated on photographs and text for a book, *El Salvador: work of thirty photographers,* which was a collection of photographic work of 30 journalists from Europe, Latin America, and North America, and I was engaged to do the text for the work and became very interested in the relationship between text and photographs. I believed that poetry was the wrong form for the text, and I also came to realize that discursive prose was also wrong. I was not interested in writing an extended caption for the works nor did I want the photographic work to merely illustrate what the text was talking about, so I developed for my own use a form which I felt contributed something to the work without weakening the photographic intelligence of the work. Well, not weakening, but detracting from it. It was a series of prose vignettes in various voices. Those voices were actually retrieved from memory but transformed literarily. In other words, the text was going to be written and not spoken; and so, of course, as written language differs from spoken language, it was not going to be an attempt to imitate speech. But I wanted to create a kind of symphony of voices that in juxtaposition would somehow approach for me the complexity of the situation in El Salvador at that time. Various of them were arranged sequentially within the work, with photographs appearing between these different pieces. And I did that. And I understand that the kind of work that I do as a poet, as a writer, requires a measure of tranquillity and solitude or the work simply is not done. And living on the road such as I did and speaking in public participates in another kind of life entirely, what's been called the life of applause. And I wasn't interested in public performance at that time. I began to also understand something of the nature of the function of my speaking in public. It was an unfortunate disempowerment that would occur. I would be before the audience speaking as a voice of some authority on the region, and the members of the audience would listen to this, and I watched the process by which they would internalize a kind of . . . they would internalize a feeling of general despair of sorts, an idea that there was nothing that they themselves could do. And the distance between myself and the audience and my experience of their experience maintained this, and I began to see it as a disempowering activity that I didn't want to participate in any longer. I also did not want to participate in creating the illusion that if one, say, goes to an auditorium on a Thursday evening and hears someone speak about conditions in one country or another, and then has wine and cheese afterward with the person who is speaking and goes home to the life and the life does not change at all, that there is a kind of illusion-that one has done their part. And I began to question the value of informing people, or educating them, when the experience was a kind of commodification of that . . . that the education began to be something that certain people wanted to acquire. For example, I was lecturing at a pre-

paratory school in the East, a very good preparatory school, and this school had recruited black South African students to come and had gone to some effort to bring them to the school and to provide them with a tuition-free American education of the highest quality. One of these black South African students, in particular, had been, over the Christmas break, detained and tortured. Because of the intervention of the school, he was subsequently released and permitted to return to school. The privileged students who gathered around him when they came to hear me . . . we were having a little coffee or something with the students then . . . one of the teachers mentioned to me, introducing me to the student, that he had been detained and this and that had happened, and the white students turned to him and then said, "Oh, tell us what happened to you. We want to know everything that happened to you." The black student became very shy and very afraid and ashamed, in a way, to be singled out, and didn't want to talk. And one of the white students said, "It's important for us to know." And I thought within myself, why? for what? So that this can be part of your educational experience, as much as the privilege of your very high quality education, as much as lacrosse is? In other words, that this boy's experience was viewed by the other students in a very innocent way as material for them to absorb and possess. Information that they would then have. It was a crisis for me to observe this . . . an internal crisis . . . and I began to enter a period of withdrawal, not in a sense from my own commitments, but a withdrawal into a more secluded time. I married; I became pregnant; I worked abroad. But I was very interested in entering fully into literary work again, and I had experienced a fragmentation within myself that had to do with what I believed about the authority of voice. I began reading some critical theory. . . . And I became interested in European deconstructivists. I was particularly interested in their work on holocaust testimony. That interest was lifelong for me, but was heightened by my twelve year friendship with Terrence Des Pres who died a year ago. He had written a book called *The Survivor, Anatomy of Life in the Death Camps.* And I found myself meditating on the holocaust and reading on the holocaust a great deal. I was profoundly influenced by Claude Lanzmann's work on *Shoah.* Yet when I approached the page, I found that the form that I had been writing in, which, for want of something better, I can call first-person lyric free verse narrative, was not sufficient to what I wanted to do on the page. And I had experienced something that was rather more fragmentary and something that, in a sense, was engaged constantly in an attempt to expose its own artifice and to interrogate itself. And so began the work on *The Angel of History.* And I've been working now for two years. The work is profoundly exhilarating. I'm trying to make a form which would push my work further, breaking open the forms I had been writing on before. So this work is visually very different on the page. And I've read it a few times at readings.. . . . I've performed it a few times, and I find that its effect on the audience is also very different.

Can you be more specific about the visuals and the effect?

The work is in long lines, but not even lines. The breaks or pauses are between sections of it; the breaks and pauses are horizontal; the lines are not broken. This poetry establishes a rhythmic pattern, highly varied or otherwise or not, but these lines go all the way to the margin, and certain thoughts are completed and certain are not. There are intruding voices and interrupting voices and interrogating voices, and the work seems to float on the page. It's non-linear.

No one authoritative voice, in other words.

Right. No one authoritative voice.

. . . that guides the reader.

That's correct.

No beginning, middle, and end.

No.

No closure.

It's very experimental. No closure. It began in me with a break with this idea of resolution, of closure. And I didn't know where it was going and I didn't know what it was becoming, but eventually it seemed to me that it had something to do with the 20th century and I was very influenced by Walter Benjamin, so the work begins with a Walter Benjamin quote from *Illuminations*. And that is the work from which the title derives, *The Angel of History*. So it's an exploration for me and an extension of concerns that I've probably had for a long time. I think the break, the silence. . . . I had written many, many notebooks during this silence, but I didn't want to publish poetry, and I didn't publish poetry. I haven't published a book since 1981.

The Country Between Us. . . .

Right. So, it's now eight years. I've many, many notebooks, but what I see when I examine the notebooks now are phases of development toward the work I'm doing at present. I see it in embryonic stages early on, and I begin to see what I thought were simply notes, because they didn't resemble my earlier work, were, actually in early form, the work that I have now begun to do . . . the new work, in other words. I didn't recognize it at first. I thought it was failed old work.

So, you see it now as the culmination of an implicit building process, that you were not aware was actually happening. Can you describe how your 1981 work, which was, as a lot of people would say, political . . . although I think that's an artificial distinction . . . and I know certainly you feel that all work is political. . . . Can you see a through line between what you're doing now and what you were doing then? Can you articulate that through line?

Well, you see, the way that I composed my work has changed. I still recognize and accept that work as my own, and the person who composed that work is me in another form in an earlier version of myself. But even though with **The Country Between Us** I had been radically transformed in writing that work, the form that the work took was very conventional. There was nothing particularly transformative or evolutionary about it.

Despite the fact that there was "The Colonel" and. . . .

But that's a prose poem, and it engages the imagination in a certain way. There's a single voice, and it really is not very interesting. It doesn't do anything. I began to feel that there was a certain kind of poem that I was writing, that my contemporaries were writing, and we were doing it well and less well; some of us were very good at it; some would grow fatigued and write this particular poem less well. And something that was probably very obvious to most people but wasn't obvious to me was that I began to notice that we were doing the same thing all the time. Well, . . . in other words . . . you know those little craft shops where you can learn to make figurines out of clay and paint them? . . .

Well, you get these little molds where you pour the plaster in and you peel the plaster off. And women learn that you paint the eyes a certain blue, you paint them sort of like paint-by-number figurines. And I didn't see much difference between that and what we were doing as poets. In other words, you could do that thing and you might do it very well but it still was *that* and you're not . . . there's no correspondence between the consciousness and the language. There's no pushing further; there's no exploration; there's no risk; there's no altering of possibilities; there's no extension. There's always a limit, but there's no extending of the limit. And so I began to realize that I didn't want to write that poem, necessarily. I didn't want to necessarily abandon it forever, but I wanted to see what else might happen.

And you've said that you've had different effects on your audience by performing pieces from this new work.

Well, the new work is very strange for the audience. The audience has to enter a different kind of receptivity for it. In other words, the poems that I used to write, and that many people write, are first person free verse narrative. One knows what to expect. There is a voice. There is a momentum of building of the voice. There is often an epiphany. There is usually a turn. There is a resolution. It is maybe sixteen lines or thirty-two lines or even one hundred lines, but basically the audience is led to the resolution.

And however startling or fresh the imagery, however compelling the resolution, the audience will like or not like the outcome. In other words, you can recognize a poem on the page at quite some distance, if every poem has the same presence on the page, the same arrangement, the same form. And in performing well . . . in reading the new work . . . the audience doesn't have the security of knowing how the poem is going to proceed. The audience has to become suspended because the voices intrude on one another, interrupt each other . . . the audience has to be prepared to make these leaps of interruptions continually . . . that will loop back. And they begin to get a kind of texture for what is going on . . . a feeling of the texture of the work, without the usual footholds . . . without the usual stepping stones.

. . . guidelines . . .

So my experience is that for a lot of people . . . at least they tell me . . . that they feel "suspended," or they feel like they just floated through something. The work corresponds to my own experience of consciousness at this time, and I have to trust it. It seems to have its own life, and it seems to have its own imperatives, and so I'm just following it.

People ask me "Does poetry have any effect, politically or otherwise?" Everything has an effect. Everything goes out into this web. It's like a humming web of interrelations, and it would be arrogant of us to try to suppose that we could track its activity through the web, but it will have an activity in the web, as everything does.

—*Carolyn Forché*

What kinds of performance choices has it demanded, because I would imagine that you cannot perform it the same way you could perform a conventional poem.

No. In performing the conventional poem, I always felt that one should read expressively and should project and one should at best memorize the poem so that it could be delivered without burying the face in the book. And often readings are helped by the poet telling little anecdotes or stories between the poems, sometimes having to do with the poems. And so much did this become the case that many poets would simply explain each poem before they read it, and then go on to the next one. I still, for certain audiences, such as I will have tonight, do a certain amount of that in the beginning because they are unfamiliar with some of that work, and they do want to hear it, so I will do it. With the new work, I discovered that the less I say the better. The work has to stand on its own. Sometimes I warn the audience that it will not be what they have been accustomed to hearing, and that they will have to be prepared to become lost. And I sometimes say more than that, I elaborate a little, but I found that it's best that it be done without the scaffolding of these comments. And a certain amount of it, I suppose, resembles play rather than poem. So I attempt to provide a slight alteration for the voices so that they're separated for the ear, and without engaging in very much dramatization. And the voices are figures; they're not characters; they don't develop as characters, so I don't establish a character for them in the performance. I simply pause between them and allow certain tonalities to change so that they are distinct.

What is your goal for an audience, with these performances? What would you most like an audience to come away feeling and thinking? Do you want the pieces to be . . . such as it is sometimes called with post-modern drama . . . interrogative pieces? Can you talk a little bit about that?

I don't have an objective with regard to how the work is consumed. I don't believe that that is ever in the artist's control anyway. I suppose that at best, I mean it has been a very happy situation for me when people have described how the work has affected them . . . that they were able within a certain duration to experience another consciousness or another way of being conscious. I'm not sure what happens in an audience when they hear the book. But I don't think I could be aware of that. I know the work too well to be affected the way that people who don't know it would be. So, I can't duplicate it. I can only say that either a shock of recognition that this is how the mind feels at play with the relations between things—this is how the mind receives a speech . . . that would please me . . . or someone to say that they find it very fine and strange and not at all resembling something that they would have expected or anticipated. I suppose either response is a happy one for me. But I'm not writing for a particular purpose.

Would you say that you were writing for a purpose before with your poems?

No. I would say that I was completely unaware of that issue. I think I was writing a certain way because it was how I had apprehended poetry. In other words, I grew up in a certain period, and I received a certain education, which included a Master of Fine Arts in poetry, and the particular aesthetic concerns of that institutionalized education became my own, unquestioned. I never thought about moving beyond certain conventions that I had learned. I think that I, during a period of time in my twenties, accepted on faith this idea that my work was to find my voice, and that this voice was somehow within me, that it needed only to mature, that I had to locate it, as if it was lost. And then that I had to perfect it. And then I would speak with it. And I began to see a certain artificiality in that construct, and also it seemed to me to be . . . there was a falseness to the representation of self. The voice was actually a fictional utterance. Memory was relied upon heavily in this aesthetic, without the realization that memory is fictional. There was very little understanding of what was excluded by this voice. And developing this voice in the unquestioning way that I did, what seemingly distinguished one poet from another had largely to do with either sensibility or subject matter. And slowly I came to realize that poems were not *about;* they simply *were.* I began to try other prepositions. Poems were *amid,* or *around,* or *near,* or *beyond* certain subjects. And I began to understand that language would perhaps have an apparent or initiating subject but that poems were generally "about" something else altogether. And one of the things that began to bother me was this mention of sincerity, . . . you know, that poems would be judged as good or less good depending on the degree to which this artificial, fictional constructional voice seemed sincere, whatever that means. And the dangers in this particular form were dangers of sentimentality, of memory becoming falsified into nostalgia. And, of course, if the material for one's art was to be one's life, well . . . I felt that I could not continue to . . . I did not want to appropriate experience. I was reading George Bataille's *Inner Experience,* and realizing, of course, that all project[s were] an invasion of inner experience, and I didn't want any longer to have to live in such a way as to produce in material . . . to experience so as to return to the experience in the work and I believed elitist, too, that one should not endure the experience once in life and a second time in art. In other words, this form that I had been writing on heavily depended on things that were no longer reliable for me. So, I began to see, . . . well I suppose other people see this very easily and very early in their lives, but I didn't . . . the idea of what art can do, and that I did not want any longer to make clay figures, even very good ones. I wanted to break the figures. I wanted to go out into territory that was unfamiliar to me. I wanted something that seemed more . . . that seemed to correspond . . . not to represent consciousness. . . . But I was after equivalencies; I was after explorations of language, interrogations of language, understanding, of course, that there will always be limitations. But I wanted to produce something that would move, for me, move me forward out of that reliance upon voice and representation of self in that way. It's hard because I haven't really formulated these ideas, I haven't discussed them.

Would you say that your work in some ways . . . I don't want to say "resembles" since we're trying to get away from resemblances . . . but has echoes of the kinds of work of people like. . . and these are not poets. . . like Coover and Barthelme and some of the fiction writers who are people experimenting with forms. . . .

Meta-fiction writers?

Right, meta-fiction writers. . . .

Well, you go to . . . French modernists and you find fictional attempts to work narrative in other ways. I'm very interested in them. I've returned personally to Gertrude Stein and to Joyce, and a whole seventy-year conversation in poetic form that has occurred through certain experimental artists, through American surrealists and through objectivists, and I'm very interested in that evolution. I'm now doing a load of reading of that kind. Mostly, I'm also reading the philosophy of Geary, but not because of the work that I'm doing, but because of my own interests and curiosities. I'm not sure how much influence there is there, but you see, I think it came to be a crisis for me, the crisis for this voice, that I realized that if I could write something I could just as well write its opposite. I didn't want to falsify by use of this voice, by development of this voice and how this voice would exclude any other possibility. And I also became very suspect, well . . . you know . . . the role of being a North American witness in a Latin American situation. I was uneasy with my job, my role that Monsignor Romero had wanted me to do, which was . . . they more or less said, look, an American audience will listen to a North American poet. You resemble them. If we send a Salvadoran, no one will come. And it's true, to a degree, at least it was true then, that it was much easier for me to speak. So much so was this the case, that when I was at the Human Rights Congress in Toronto in 1981, the Amnesty International meeting, I was made chairman of the Latin America and the Caribbean by the writers from the Latin America and the Caribbean because they wanted a North American spokesperson. They believed that they would be listened to, that their concerns would receive more attention, if they were voiced by a North American. I argued with them, and they said, "This is our choice. We have elected you. We have come to this

decision by consensus and we would like you to respect it." So I did, but it was very difficult. And I can't tell you, I mean there is a constellation of moving forces, of entities that have influenced this move, this decision that has evolved over a long period of time.

Does the role of metaphor change when you make such a big leap into a different area?

Metaphor for me changes in extremity. For example, I'm now interested in the idea of historical markers, of certain images, of signed languages that are . . . that signify whether or not there is an interpreter. In other words, for example, a bullet hole in a piece of cloth remains a marker of a bullet regardless of whether the apprehender knows that a bullet passed through the cloth. In other words, its nature as a sign of the bullet does not change just because the apprehender does not realize.

I think that the nature of metaphor became problematic with the historical rupture of the holocaust, because, for example, you see, the ashes of the chimneys of the extermination camps are not figurative, and they can never be. And in a certain constellation of images having to do with rail lines, ashes, chimneys, crematoria, you are not other than in the holocaust, and they have become historical markers. Now, with an historical marker what happens is that I began to perceive things in a kind of web of indeterminacy. In other words, for example, I read **"The Colonel"** poem, and these severed ears . . .

"The Colonel" poem which comes from your experience in El Salvador . . .

Right. I'm using this as an example. I read it and the severed ears, even though there is a little attempt with having the ears actually still be able to hear things, to engage them as figurative, they resist the figurative because they are actual. Now what happens when people hear the poem, if they are affected by it in a way that they enter into and accept this occurrence, they are then responsible for that information; they become witnesses as well; they are marked by the poem. If someone wants to resist the poem and question its authenticity, etc., there is an exertion of resistance, of anger, of whatever, they are also marked by their avoidance of it.

So people become historical markers as well.

Yes. And witnesses create other witnesses, and it's infinite.

And this involves what you've said in the past about the need for a poet, in the twentieth century, to be a poet of witness.

Yes. We are responsible for everything we hear and everything we see, and we in turn can make others responsible, as well. Let me give you another example. A friend of mine is working closely on some scholarship with a man whose parents survived Auschwitz. In Auschwitz it became very important for them to be punctual, to obey orders absolutely promptly. Part of the constellation of reasons why they might have survived had to do with their fear of today. They had to act always in a very quick fashion. As a result, they gave birth to a son, and in the United States, the son rebelled against this severe preoccupation and obsession with punctuality, and he became always a person who procrastinates and delays. Tony has a hard time getting his work done with this person because the person makes a religion of procrastination. When Tony understood where this tendency came from, Tony realized that the parents had been marked by the Nazis in this regard. They had, in turn marked their son, by his aversion to this punctuality. Now Tony is marked by Auschwitz because of the difficulty in their collaboration. So you see, it's an infinite kind of thing. That's one example that's experiential and not literary. But I began to see . . . for example, people ask me "Does poetry have any effect, politically or otherwise?" Everything has an effect. Everything goes out into this web. It's like a humming web of interrelations, and it would be arrogant of us to try to suppose that we could track its activity through the web, but it will have an activity in the web, as everything does. . . .

Carolyn Forché and Jill Taft-Kaufman, in an interview in Text & Performance Quarterly, *Vol. 10, No. 1, January, 1990, pp. 61-70.*

FURTHER READING

Criticism

Doubiago, Sharon. "Towards an American Criticism: A Reading of Carolyn Forché's *The Country between Us.*" *The American Poetry Review* 12, No. 1 (January-February 1983): 35-9.

Responding to negative reviews of *The Country between Us*, Doubiago lauds the volume's political content and

calls for a new school of criticism that recognizes that all writing—whether poetry or criticism—is politically motivated.

Gleason, Judith. "The Lesson of Bread." *Parnassus* 10, No. 1 (Spring-Summer 1982): 9-21.

Applauds Forché's focus on the Salvadoran Civil War and the need for community in *The Country between Us.*

Lapinski, Ann Marie. "The Education of a Poet: El Salvador Sojourn Gives Life to Her Art." *Chicago Tribune*, No. 347 (13 December 1982), 1-3.

Feature article in which Forché discusses her experiences in El Salvador and the composition, publication, and reception of the poems collected in *The Country between Us.*

Mann, John. "Carolyn Forché: Poetry and Survival." *American Poetry* 3, No. 3 (Spring 1986): 51-69.

Thematic and stylistic analysis of *The Country between Us.*

Walker, Kevin. "Inspired by War." *Detroit Free Press* (22 May 1994): 8G.

Positive review of *The Angel of History*, which Walker describes as "exquisite" and possessing "a unity that defies easy understanding."

Interview

Montenegro, David. "Carolyn Forché." *The American Poetry Review* 17, No. 6 (November-December 1988): 35-40.

Interview in which Forché discusses her new work, her experiences in El Salvador and abroad, and the thematic concerns of her work.

Additional coverage of Forché's life and career is contained in the following sources published by Gale Research: *Contemporary Authors,* Vols. 109, 117; *Contemporary Literary Criticism,* Vol. 25; and *Dictionary of Literary Biography,* Vol. 5.

Caroline Gordon

1895-1981

American novelist, short story writer, and critic.

The following entry provides an overview of Gordon's career. For further information on her life and works, see *CLC*, Volumes 6, 13, and 29.

INTRODUCTION

Often associated with the Southern Literary Renaissance and the Southern Agrarian movement, Gordon is best known for writings which synthesize elements of mythology, Southern history, and Roman Catholicism. Gordon's fiction is remarkable for its evocation of nature, its historic focus on the Western frontier and antebellum South, and its emphasis on humanity's mystical connection with the land. Preoccupied with the classical concept of the hero's journey, Gordon sought to reveal the universality of human nature throughout history: "The proper work of fiction will be both timeless and temporal, temporal in its definition of a particular society at a given moment in history, timeless in its repetition of the archetypal pattern of behavior."

Biographical Information

Gordon was born on her grandmother's farm, Meriwether, in southern Kentucky near the Tennessee border. She was educated by her father, who taught classics, and was the only female student at an all boys academy in southern Tennessee. In 1924 she married poet Allen Tate, to whom she was introduced by writer and friend William Penn Warren. In the 1920s the couple made two extended trips to Europe, and while in Paris they associated with other expatriate writers such as F. Scott and Zelda Fitzgerald, Ernest Hemingway, Gertrude Stein, and Ralph Cheever Dunning. While in Paris in 1929, Gordon worked as a secretary to her good friend and mentor Ford Madox Ford. Urging her to complete her first novel, *Penhally*, (1931), Ford typed parts of her manuscript for her, requiring that she dictate 5,000 words per day to him. During the 1930s Tate and Gordon frequently hosted such literary figures as Ford, Katherine Anne Porter, and Robert Lowell at their home, Benfolly, in southern Tennessee. During this period, Gordon struggled with her roles as wife, mother, and writer: "While I am a woman I am also a freak. The work I do is not suitable for women. It is unsexing. I speak with real conviction here. I don't write 'the womanly' novel." Gordon and her husband moved frequently as she served as teacher, lecturer, or writer-in-residence at various American universities. In 1947 Gordon converted to Roman Catholicism, which profoundly impacted her fiction. She believed that the artist had a moral obligation to serve, praise, and worship God through art. In her 1964 essay, "Letters to a Monk," published in *Ramparts*, she wrote: "I was nearly fifty year's

old before I discovered that art is the handmaiden of the Church." Gordon died in 1981 at San Cristóbal de las Casas, Chiapas, Mexico.

Major Works

Gordon's early fiction was influenced by her association with Southern Agrarianism—a literary movement, fomenting during the 1920s and 1930s, which resisted the encroaching industrialization on the South's traditional, agrarian society and emphasized the region's history. For example, the protagonist of her highly autobiographical second novel, *Aleck Maury, Sportsman* (1934), is a teacher of classical literature, a husband, and a father, who seeks refuge from the impingement of his responsibilities on his freedom through hunting, fishing, and communing with nature. This theme and character is also featured in such short stories as "Old Red," "One More Time," "To Thy Chamber Window, Sweet," "The Last Day in the Field," and "The Presence." Although she disliked the term "historical novelist," Gordon similarly focused on the South's past in such works as *None Shall Look Back* (1937), which focuses, in part, on the Civil War leader Nathan Bedford Forrest, and in *Green Centuries* (1941), which concerns the expansion of the Western frontier. Several of Gordon's works, particularly her later novels, reflect a more religious theme and her conversion to Roman Catholicism. *The Strange Children* (1951) concerns the Christian quest for salvation told from the viewpoint of a nine-year-old girl as she observes the adult world. This novel is noted for its utilization of the omniscient narrator, a literary device prominent in the works of Henry James, Anton Chekhov, and Gustave Flaubert. The theme of redemption and salvation is also present in *The Malefactors* (1956). In this work, Gordon employs the Aristotelian device of peripety, the point at which the action changes as the protagonist undergoes a spiritual, moral, or intellectual transformation. In this novel, the transformation occurs when an unfaithful husband—tormented by what he perceives as the inexorable conflict between men and women due to their disparate natures and their inability to form a lasting bond—undergoes a religious conversion. Gordon's last novel, *The Glory of Hera* (1972), is a retelling of the Greek myth of Heracles, incorporating elements of Jungian psychology and Christian concepts of salvation and grace.

Critical Reception

Early in her career, Gordon often met with critical acclaim. Ford described her first novel, *Penhally*, as "the best constructed novel in modern America," and Gordon received Guggenheim fellowships on several occasions; her "conversion" works, however, were often faulted for their didacticism, elitism, and lack of conviction. Critics note that while her fiction remains distinctively Southern in character and theme—it is often favorably compared to the works of Eudora Welty and Katherine Anne Porter—it follows, stylistically and methodologically, the European literary tradition. Scholars have additionally commented, as did Gordon in her *How to Read a Novel* (1957) and *The House of Fiction: An Anthology of the Short Story, with Commentary* (1950), that her work is informed by several philosophies and literary traditions: Aristotelian concepts of plot, classic Greek and Christian mythology, Jungian thought, and various levels of interpretation—literal, moral, anagogic, and allegorical—based upon Dante's *Convivio*.

PRINCIPAL WORKS

Penhally (novel) 1931
Aleck Maury, Sportsman (novel) 1934; also published as *The Pastimes of Aleck Maury: The Life of a True Sportsman*, 1935
The Garden of Adonis (novel) 1937
None Shall Look Back (novel) 1937; also published as *None Shall Look Back: A Story of the American Civil War*, 1937
Green Centuries (novel) 1941
The Women on the Porch (novel) 1944
The Forest of the South (short stories) 1945
The House of Fiction: An Anthology of the Short Story, with

Commentary [with Allen Tate] (anthology) 1950; revised edition, 1960
The Strange Children (novel) 1951
The Malefactors (novel) 1956
How to Read a Novel (criticism) 1957
A Good Soldier: A Key to the Novels of Ford Madox Ford (criticism) 1963
Old Red, and Other Stories (short stories) 1963
The Glory of Hera (novel) 1972
The Collected Stories of Caroline Gordon (short stories) 1981

CRITICISM

Herschel Brickell (review date 27 September 1931)

[*In the following review, Brickell praises Gordon's "polished and rhythmic" prose and thematic focus in* Penhally.]

This skilfully fictionized chapter of American cultural history [entitled ***Penhally***] deals with a theme that has a curiously ancient, almost archeological, ring, for it is concerned with the ownership of land and its influence upon the lives of people. Settlers in the colonies along the Atlantic brought with them a passion for broad acres, some of them because they or their families had owned broad acres, others no doubt, for exactly the opposite reason. With this consuming love of the land went other things, powerful family ties; the manor house a shelter for all the kin no matter how far removed, the very heart of the clan, where the young instead of moving into their own houses usually merely took over a wing of the old.

Out of this system—simplified by black slavery—complicated, too, because of the common infusion of blood from the gentry into their slaves—grew a certain type of civilization in the Southern United States. This civilization has never lacked interpreters, ranging all the way from the gushingly romantic to the Harriet Beecher Stowes, both missing the point, of course. The Southern slave-holding aristocrat did not lack his vices, but he did not manage a large plantation, taking decent care of the whites and blacks upon it, solely by drinking mint juleps before breakfast; the responsibility, the deeply rooted sense of noblesse oblige, the survival of the knightly tradition, tended to make men who were not lacking in their admirable qualities.

All this is set down because it is relevant to a discussion of Miss Gordon's novel. I have said that her theme had an ancient ring because it seems removed by a thousand years from the present American scene, not a mere hundred. Remnants of the land-loving tradition cling in the South, where the lawyer, doctor or business man will often be found working very hard to support a farm without knowing just why, when deep down he has the feeling that he is not quite a man without land. Does this not have a quaint sound when small-town populations are moving into apartment houses as fast as they can be built, and there are already almost as many tourist camps as barns, and the banks and insurance companies own all the farms, or will by January 2, 1932?

Miss Gordon has hit upon a genuinely significant theme for her excellent book. She has faced courageously, although this is her first novel, the task of telling the tale of a Kentucky estate, Penhally, from 1826 up to the present, all in the brief compass of fewer than 300 pages. This complicated story, covering a full century, and touching upon the lives of so many people in different generations, she has made into a tapestry, with the pattern always quite clear in her mind; she sends the shuttle whirling through space and time with a sure hand, and a design emerges, ready to be followed in all its richness of line and color.

It was Nicholas Llewellyn, Welsh in origin and settling in Kentucky after the family had paused for a time in Virginia—who first loved Penhally. The novel begins with a quarrel between Nicholas and his brother, Ralph, for no other reason than Ralph has suggested that a man might like to have his own house. To Nicholas, such heresy cannot be overlooked, and he invites Ralph to leave, a quarrel that is never healed. It is Nicholas who holds stubbornly to the estate during the Civil War, and whose principal concern about the conflict is that it may interfere in some way with the estate. It is after a long, long lapse of years that another Nicholas, a banker, decides to sell the place to an Eastern woman, the wife of a distant cousin, who wishes to make it into a glorified country club. The old quarrel renews itself, Nicholas's brother, who has inherited the love of the land, shooting Nicholas dead when the sale is made.

Between the first Nicholas's development of Penhally—the house grew and was beautiful in its own simple way—and the last Nicholas's willingness to part with it for money, there are many happenings. There are moving chapters on the Civil War, flashes of cavalry fighting under Morgan and others—needless to say the young men of the family go to war on horseback as naturally as if they had been Arabs; there are romances, some of which do not end at all pleasantly; there are vivid bits of characterization, such as the sketch of the head groom at Penhally; there are sly sentences here and there, of the sort that gives a book the right flavor, evidences of the author's intelligence and penetration.

Miss Gordon has written a fine novel. It will probably annoy the representatives of the Proletarian point of view, who wish the South would forget its glorious past and gaze upon its somewhat less glorious present, but this really has nothing to do with the case. Miss Gordon is quite naturally sympathetic with the people of whom she writes, since most of them are more or less her own, but she does no pleading for them, preserving her objectivity quite successfully. Her prose is polished and rhythmic, a good instrument. I wish she would give up "gotten," to voice a minor criticism, but she seldom uses grating words. *Penhally* is a notable addition to the lengthening list of recent novels about the Old South that are thoughtful and well done, and which may be read for both pleasure and profit.

Herschel Brickell, "Land and the Love of It," in New York Herald Tribune Books, *September 27, 1931, pp. 7-8.*

Edith H. Walton   (review date 21 February 1937)

[*In the following review of* None Shall Look Back, *Walton faults the novel for its failure to focus on any character, but classifies the work as a classic example of Civil War fiction.*]

By far the most ambitious of Caroline Gordon's novels, **None Shall Look Back** is a story of the Civil War which at first gives promise of outdistancing its numerous competitors. Miss Gordon, it is obvious at once, has many assets in her favor. Her style is distinguished—vastly superior, for example, to Margaret Mitchell's; in the clarity and brilliance of her battle scenes she is the equal of MacKinlay Kantor; finally, and this is perhaps most important, she is seldom unduly sentimental despite the warmth of her feeling for the South. Her pictures of plantation life at the outbreak of the war are neither cloying nor prettified.

Having said all this, it is rather difficult to explain why **None Shall Look Back** is not quite the book it should be—why it fails to move and excite one as much as one might expect. One reason, which may appear a petty one, is that Miss Gordon has neglected to focus one's interest sufficiently on any character or group of characters. Ostensibly, her story concerns the Allards of Kentucky, a proud family of tobacco planters whose lands border on the Tennessee boundary. Actually, the real hero of her book is a historical figure—the famous Nathan Bedford Forrest, major general of Confederate cavalry. Compared to Forrest, whose exploits she follows so zealously, the Allards are dim, inadequate symbols of the South's suffering and doom.

At the start of the book, however, the Allards are well in the foreground. The war, as yet, has hardly touched Kentucky, and Brackets, the home of old Fontaine Allard, is gay with gracious life and swarming with assorted relatives. It is, to be sure, their last respite from anxiety, for young Ned, a son of the household, has just enlisted in Forrest's cavalry with a number of his schoolfellows. Among them is his cousin Rives, one of the Georgia Allards, who comes thus for the first time to Brackets and for the first time meets Lucy Churchill, old Fontaine's orphan granddaughter. There are parties, balls, leave-takings before the youthful cavalcade rides off to join Forrest.

Follows, all too quickly, the struggle at Fort Donelson, where Rives and his companions have their first taste of action. The fort surrenders, but thanks to the daring initiative of Forrest, the cavalry cuts its way out. Bedraggled but free, Rives and Ned worm their way home to Brackets—arriving just in time to witness its burning by the Yankees. The family is stunned and hopeless, old Fontaine is permanently shattered, but Lucy and Rives salvage a moment of happiness from disaster. They marry at once, and Rives takes Lucy home with him to the pine woods of Georgia. His mother's household is a bleak and eccentric one, but until he is called back to service, Rives and Lucy are content.

Thereafter, and until the last bitter end, Rives serves perilously as one of Forrest's scouts. In this capacity he sees the general constantly and shares the almost fanatic devotion which Forrest inspired in his men. Bluff, shrewd, hot-tempered, incredibly courageous, Forrest was a kind of Titan who refused to admit that the South could possibly lose. Had his advice been taken after the Battle of Chickamauga, who knows, Miss Gordon implies, how history might have been changed. Chickamauga, in which Rives participates, is the high point, the climax of the novel. The rest is tragedy, with the South slowly, inexorably losing and Forrest fighting on in the face of palpable defeat.

As must be obvious, Miss Gordon has conceived her novel on a heroic scale. Theoretically it is to her credit that she has preferred to dwell on the slow collapse of the Confederacy rather than on the fortunes of private individuals. In practice, however, she sacrifices a good deal by so doing. In such a story one needs a pivot for one's sympathies and emotions, and for this neither Rives nor Lucy will serve. As the story progresses they become more and more shadowy. Rives, toward the end, is merely a convenient medium through whose eyes one sees and estimates the heroism of Forrest's achievements. Forrest himself, on the other hand, is too remote a figure. One can admire but not come close to him.

To say this may sound philistine. It is true, nevertheless, that any novel, however serious in intent, must have as its center a compelling drama of individual fortunes as well as a larger theme. Admirable, graphic, blood-chilling as they are, one could have spared some of Miss Gordon's battle scenes in favor of more arresting and more fully developed characters. A good story, after all, is essential—as the author of *Gone With the Wind* has most abundantly proved. Since, moreover, Miss Gordon has chosen to concentrate on a panoramic picture, it does seem as if she might have dealt more explicitly with the issues at stake. She shows one the suffering and the gallantry of the South, but why they fought, and for what, is a question she almost ignores.

There is always a danger of being unfair to a book of superior caliber. I hope I have made it plain that *None Shall Look Back* is such a book and that it is disappointing largely because it promises so well. On a minor scale *Aleck Maury, Sportsman* very nearly approached perfection. Though her new novel is not so well rounded, Miss Gordon has happily essayed a much more significant theme. Despite its lack of warmth and focus, *None Shall Look Back* belongs with the half-dozen really good novels of the Civil War which have appeared during the last decade. It has both distinction and dignity; I have dwelt on its defects merely because it might so easily have been the best of them all.

Edith H. Walton, "Miss Gordon's Civil War Novel," in The New York Times Book Review, *February 21, 1937, p. 6.*

Katherine Anne Porter (review date 31 March 1937)

[*Porter was an American short story writer, novelist, critic, and educator whose fiction evokes the region and culture of the American Southwest. Her popular 1962 novel,* Ship of Fools, *derived from a voyage Porter took in 1931 from Vera Cruz to Bremerhaven, is often considered an allegory relating the moral malaise of the world prior to World War II. Gordon and Porter were well-acquainted; at one point*

Porter resided at Gordon's Clarksville, Tennessee, home. In the following review, Porter provides a highly laudatory assessment of None Shall Look Back.]

Fontaine Allard, tobacco planter, slave holder full of cares and responsibilities, an old man walking in a part of his Kentucky woods, "had a strange feeling, as if a voice said to him, 'these are your father's and your fathers' before him' . . . he had actually for a moment been overcome by his attachment for that earth, those trees." This is in the beginning of *None Shall Look Back.* Toward the end, his son Ned returns from the lost war, a skeleton, a dying man. "The land's still there, I reckon," he says, and goes back to it, hoping to live, but certain at least that he shall die there, where he belongs, unchanged in his belief in the way of life he had fought for.

His brother Jim, unfit for war, had stayed at home and profited by the changing times, taking advantage of his chances with the rising merchants and industrialists. Alienated, hostile, secretly hoping that Ned may die, he watches him go, a breathing reproach, supported by two women of his family. Miss Gordon makes it quite clear, in this short bitter scene, that Jim is the truly defeated man, the lost soul who thinks nothing is worth fighting for, who sets himself to survive and profit meanly by whatever occasion offers him.

This form of opportunism is sometimes at present called "interpreting history correctly"—that is, having the foresight to get on the bandwagon and make the most of the parade. With such shabbiness Miss Gordon has nothing to do. Her story is a legend in praise of heroes, of those who fought well and lost their battle, and their lives. It seems fresh and timely at this moment when we have before our eyes the spectacle of a death-dedicated people holding out in a struggle against overwhelming odds. Of all human impulses, that of heroism changes least in its character and shape, from one epoch to another. He is forever the same, then and forever unanswerable, the man who throws his life away as if he hated living, in defense of the one thing, whatever it may be, that he cares to live for. Causes change perpetually, die, go out of fashion, are superseded according to shifting political schemes, economics, religions, but the men ready to die for them are reborn again and again, always the same men.

Miss Gordon's heart is fixed on the memory of those men who died in a single, superbly fought lost cause, in nothing diminished for being lost, and this devotion has focused her feelings and imagination to a point of fire. She states clearly in every line of her story her mystical faith that what a man lives by, he must if the time comes, die for; to live beyond or to acknowledge defeat is to die twice, and shamefully. The motive of this faith is the pride of Lucifer, and Miss Gordon makes no pretense, either for herself or for her characters, to the maudlin virtue of humility in questions of principle.

All-seeing as an ancient chronicler, she has created a panorama of a society engaged in battle for its life. The author moves about, a disembodied spectator timing her presence expertly, over her familiar territory, Kentucky, Georgia, Tennessee, Mississippi. Time, 1860 to 1864, dates which

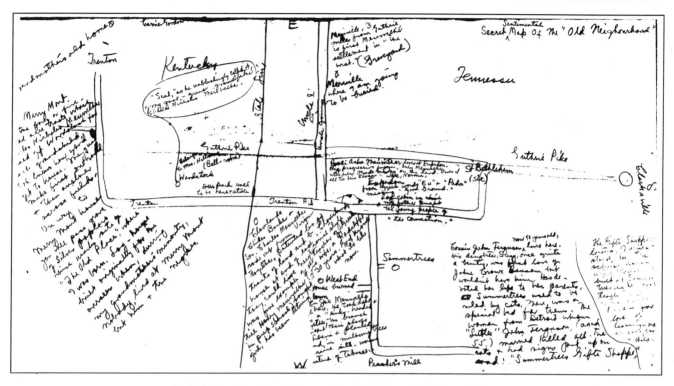

Gordon's "secret, sentimental" map of her Kentucky and Tennessee habitats.

are, after 1776, the most portentous in the history of this country. Having chosen to observe from all points of view, rather than to stand on a knoll above the battle and watch a set procession of events through a field glass, she makes her scenes move rapidly from Federal lines to Confederate, from hospitals to prisons, to the plantations; the effect could easily have become diffuse without firm handling, and the central inalterable sympathies of the chronicler herself. She might have done the neat conventional thing, and told her story through the adventures of her unlucky young pair of lovers, Lucy Churchill and her cousin, Rives Allard. But they take their proper places in the midst of a tragedy of which their own tragedy is only a part. I know of nothing more humanly touching and immediate than the story of the brief, broken marriage of Rives and Lucy; but the book is not theirs, nor was it meant to be. Rives goes to die as a scout for Nathan Bedford Forrest, that unaccountable genius of war, who remained a mystery and a figure of legend even to his own soldiers, those who knew him best. There is no accounting for Forrest and Miss Gordon does not attempt the impossible. He remains what he was, a hero and a genius.

The Allard family is a center, or rather, a point of departure and return: in the beginning they are clearly seen alive, each one a human being with his individual destiny which gradually is merged with the destiny of his time and place. Their ends are symbolically exact: the old man lapses into the escape of imbecility, the old mother into perpetual blind grief, Rives into death in battle, Jim into moral dry rot, Lucy into numbness. In the meantime, we have seen them as they were born to be, busy with the full rich occupations of family life, the work of the plantation,

the unpretentious gayety. Life for the Kentucky planters was never so grand as it was in Virginia and Louisiana or even in Mississippi, with its slightly parvenu manners, if one takes Mr. Stark Young's account at face value. The Kentucky planters were down-to-earth men, and the most tenderly bred women were not above taking a hand in the cookery. They much more resembled Madame Washington than they did Mr. Young's jewelry-conscious belles. This tone is here, properly; it pervades the book like a fresh aroma of green woods and plowed fields.

This seems to me in a great many ways a better book than **Penhally** or **Aleck Maury, Sportsman,** Miss Gordon's other two novels. The good firm style, at once homely, rhythmical and distinguished, is in all three of them, but at its best, so far, in **None Shall Look Back.** It is true I know her story by heart, but I have never heard it told better. The effect is of brilliant, instant life; there is a clear daylight over a landscape I need not close my eyes to see, peopled with figures I know well. I have always known the end, as I know the end of so many tales of love, and heroism, and death. In this retelling, it all happened only yesterday. Those men on the field are not buried yet, those women have just put on their mourning.

Katherine Anne Porter, "Dulce et Decorum Est," in The New Republic, *Vol. LXXXX, No. 1165, March 31, 1937, pp. 244-45.*

Stephen Vincent Benét   (essay date 2 November 1941)

[*Benét was an American man of letters whose poetry and fiction is often concerned with examining, understanding,*

[Caroline Gordon's] excellent, sensitive and thorough historical novel [**Green Centuries**] deals with a period that presents peculiar difficulties for the writer of fiction. We all have a sort of stereotyped idea of the bold frontiersman—clad in buckskins, adorned with a coonskin cap and armed with a long rifle that carries at least a mile, he moves through our dreams like a folk-god, the hero of a perpetual boy's story. The truth about him is a good deal harder to get at. The men he fought did not leave written records, he himself left few. That extraordinary drive which broke through the mountain wall of the Appalachians and opened our first West to settlement has not yet had its adequate historian. And yet it is one of the most colorful, interesting and vivid periods of American history.

In **Green Centuries** Miss Gordon is primarily concerned with the first wave—the first settlements on the Watauga, the Holston and the Clinch—the first Indian wars. Rion Outlaw and his younger brother Archy were living beside the Yadkin when they first heard tales of the fertile land beyond the mountains, the wonderful land of Kentuck. Rion wanted to go there with Boone, but luck was against him—it wasn't until he got mixed up with the Regulators and had to pack up and go or stay and take his chance of being hanged that he set forth. When he did so, he took black-haired Cassy Dawson with him—not to speak of Cassy's rather pathetic brother, Frank, the man who knew books and the Latin names for plants, but whose pioneering, to the end, remained amateurish. They cleared their ground on the Watauga, bred and lost their children, and suffered the tragic catastrophes that befell so many frontier families.

But the story of **Green Centuries** is not their story alone. By a perfectly plausible device Miss Gordon sends Archy Rion off to live with the Indians and to accept their way of life. So we get the whole situation from both sides—the words and the deeds of Atta Kulla Kulla and Dragging Canoe as well as the plans of Judge Henderson and the dreams of Boone—we get the Indians as human beings, not merely as painted adversaries or speechifying Noble Savages. And the novel gains greatly for it, in weight and richness.

Perhaps partly because Miss Gordon herself is a Southerner—and the South is still closer to the frontier than the North—but largely, of course, because of her imaginative talent for character, Miss Gordon has been able to get into the skin of her period to an unusual degree. I can't tell, for I don't know, how accurate in every detail is her portrayal of Indian life. But, in Atta Kulla Kulla, Dragging Canoe and the Owl, she has three characters who exist in their own right and are by no means the conventionalized redskins of fiction. No less happy is the characterization of Henry Stuart at the Indian council, self-distrustful of him-

self and his mission. The actual historical characters who enter the story—Boone, Henderson, Robertson, Sevier and the others—are naturally introduced and walk on their own feet. They are part of the warp and woof of the whole story, not separate patches of color, introduced for effect. And the story, in the end, goes back to Rion and Cassy and Archy—to the story of two ways of life, set both against a wilderness and against each other, and expressed in human terms.

Green Centuries has its high spots and its defects. The infare at Lovelattys' is an admirable and vigorous piece of description—the first journey West, Archy's capture by the Indians, the meeting of Archy and Rion at the Indian town, the fights, the councils, the curiously moving conversation between Oconostota and Atta Kulla Kulla—these are incidents that would stand out in any book. The thread of love-story between Cassy and Rion is genuine and firmly handled. Where the book is weakest, to this reviewer, is in its final section. Too many catastrophes fall upon the main characters too suddenly. They could so fall in fact; that is undisputed. But fiction has its own laws. The reader is not prepared for such comprehensive tragedy as Miss Gordon gives him in these pages and, when it comes to the almost accidental unfaithfulness of Rion and its consequences, he is bound to feel that Miss Gordon is merely putting the big pot on the little one. It is a failure of construction, not a failure of fact. It is as if Miss Gordon had suddenly decided to sweep the board of her pieces for a final effect which, when it comes, is an interesting one, but for which we have not been prepared. But it is Miss Gordon's only failure of construction and, in **Green Centuries** she has produced a distinguished, vivid and continuously readable novel which lights up an essential part of the American past.

Stephen Vincent Benét, "Land beyond the Mountains," in New York Herald Tribune Books, November 2, 1941, p. 4.

Richard Sullivan   (review date 7 October 1945)

The Forest of the South is not a haphazard collection of stories but a carefully arranged exhibit of work by a serious artist in prose. Its first virtue is an almost ponderable integrity. For a book of seventeen short pieces unlinked by plot or character it gives a remarkable impression of completeness. It seems to say, abundantly and precisely, all it means to say; it leaves no gaps.

Caroline Gordon's writing is beautifully American. It draws its substance from that part of America which may be called the near, rather than the far, South. Each of the present seventeen stories treats its own bit of that common substance in its own way; each establishes its own shape; each is peculiarly and wholly itself, without dependence on the others. Yet all together show a kind of grave, honest strength; all are wrought with the thoroughness, with what seems even the wholeheartedness, of a devoted craftsmanship.

The first piece—certainly the largest in intention as in size—is a notable story called **"The Captive."** Both as a sturdy re-creation of pioneer life, formidable in its immediacy and power, and as a swift narrative rendering of heroic human experience, this story deserves wide recognition. It is the account, told in the first person and in the gracious idiom of common speech, of a frontier woman's terrible adventure. Having seen her children brained and her cabin burned, Jinny Wiley is taken captive by a band of marauding Indians and forced to flee with them to their far-off winter camp. Shrewd, self-willed, vitally feminine despite her iron strength, she endures her slavery, not so much with hope as with a simple, instinctive fortitude. When her situation becomes finally intolerable, even for her, she breaks away in a fierce, dramatic escape which just barely gets her to the safety of a stockade. "Lord God," she says then, summing up a sequence of fantastic, nearly incredible horrors, "I was lucky to git away from them Indians!"

This writing carries the sort of conviction one might get from some unearthed old record. Its grim reality is emphasized by the paradoxical expression of violence in matter-of-fact understatement. It is charged with the certainty that here, no matter how startling to latter-day readers, is the straight and absolute reporting of truth. With the Civil War stories which follow it, and with a few others—particularly the fine **"Tom Rivers"**—which appear later in the book, **"The Captive"** represents the highest accomplishment of that specialized fiction called "historical." This is work in which human values are so strong, and human experience is so intense, that all necessary details of background and period seem by contrast to be merely random references dropped in by a narrator so fully informed as to be casual, almost indifferent, in achieving authenticity.

Conviction runs through everything in the book. All these people—Negro, Indian, white; boys, tobacco planters, elderly ladies—seem completely known. The major characters move within subtle, inclusive webs of family and community relationships, always in an atmosphere of beautifully realized natural detail. Yet despite the author's evident sensitivity to nature and the frequent loveliness with which she treats it, there is never a suggestion of any self-conscious planting of figures against a suitable lush backdrop. Rather, these people are so firmly established in whatever scene they occupy that they seem to appropriate it. And farm, plantation, forest—sky, dust and wind—are somehow energized by this complete human occupation. In that sound and excellent story, **"The Last Day in the Field"** (centering on old Aleck Maury, a character already familiar to early readers of Caroline Gordon) one gets the very radiation of the physical earth and the intimate goodness of a pair of men who walk hunting across its surface. And in **"The Brilliant Leaves"** one can hardly separate the fatal clumsiness of the young lovers from the somber poetry of the setting.

From the bloody melodrama of **"The Enemies"** to the quiet examination of character in **"Mr. Powers"**; from the misty evocation of **"Summer Dust,"** a story of childhood, to the wry and forthright passion of **"Her Quaint Honor"**; from the strange illumination of such a piece as **"The Burning Eyes"** or of the title-story, **"The Forest of the South,"** to the sharp implication of the final **"All Lovers Love the Spring,"** a wonderfully indirect handling of frustration—all through these ranges of subject and tone one knows constantly the satisfaction of reading work which, in its whole revelation, is richly informed, profoundly felt and wisely understood.

There are no standardized short story patterns in this book; there are no concessions to what less honorable writers might consider the popular taste. There is no faking, no verbal vain show, nothing tricky or pretentious or slipshod. Occasional little perversities—small digressions, concentrations on apparently unimportant details—at times thicken rather than enrich the prose; and a few minor obscurities, difficulties of identification or reference, momentarily break the flow of several stories. But these are all trivial blemishes, on the surface; the solid goodness of the work is not affected by them. That goodness goes deep.

Richard Sullivan, "Out of the 'Near South'," in The New York Times Book Review, *October 7, 1945, pp. 6, 26.*

Vivienne Koch   (essay date 1953)

[*Koch is an American critic. In the following essay, she provides an overview of Gordon's fiction through the publication of* The Strange Children.]

The work of Caroline Gordon as a writer of fiction appears to have suffered a curious lack of appreciation when compared to the lively admiration which has greeted the efforts of some other Southern women writers during the last two decades. It is my impression that of the group of talented Southern women, including Katherine Anne Porter, Carson McCullers, and Eudora Welty, whose work is widely acclaimed not only by an intellectual élite but by a popular reading audience, only Miss Welty possesses in terms of actual achievement anything like the merit attributed to her. Miss Porter has by an almost alchemical word-of-mouth campaign rolled up a reputation far out of touch with the realities of her small and precise talent for the short story. Miss McCullers' is another story and her dependence on the more decadently baroque elements in what is taken to be a Faulknerian outlook has served her, as the saying goes, only too well.

But it is not my purpose to reduce others in order to raise Miss Gordon. I wish only to place her against her contemporaries and to suggest that it is her un-modishness that is in a measure responsible for a want of wider recognition. She has not accommodated the austerities of her method to that cultivation of violence and oddity for its own sake, whether in subject-matter or style, which is one of the more distressing infantilisms of an otherwise vital and growing Southern expression in literature. And while there is nostalgia and backward glancing in her early novels of the old South, she sternly reminds herself in the title of one of them that "None shall look back." Thus she loses out, as well, at the popular romancing level of Southern fiction, for she has not gone with the wind.

Caroline Gordon, whose prose is perhaps the most unaffected and uniformly accomplished that is being written by any American woman today, should be seen as the conservator in contemporary Southern fiction of the great classical tradition of the nineteenth century novel as formulated by Stendhal, Flaubert and somewhat later, Henry James. Miss Gordon's sense of her role is inherent in the instructive critical comments on the art of fiction which she makes in her analyses of other writers' stories in her recent anthology *The House of Fiction,* co-edited with Allen Tate. While the editorial material is a joint contribution, the matter of it so faithfully reflects the principles by which Miss Gordon has won her reputation as a brilliant teacher of writing at various universities about the country that one can easily tap the author. In the Preface we are told,

> . . . James exacted of the work of fiction "a direct impression of life"; and very nearly his whole demand is in the adjective. The direct impression is the opposite of the blurred and easy impression; it creates the immediate sense of life, not the removed report. Of this school, Flaubert, Chekhov, Crane, Joyce and James were the great masters. Since Flaubert, fiction has extended or changed its subjects, but where it transcends its social or other documentary origins it is still in the Impressionist tradition; or it is sometimes called the tradition of naturalism or realism, descriptive terms with a philosophic ring, but often standing only for a sentiment about the values of life. Neither the sentiment of naturalism or realism nor any other could have, unaided, produced the art of *Madame Bovary.* A single plainly discernible principle of imaginative reality distinguished this art, by means of which it has achieved something of the self-contained objectivity of poetry. Once you get inside one of the great works of naturalism you find this principle informing with a specific actuality whatever values the author may have. This actuality reaches us as the intense *dramatic activity* of everything in the story: a snowstorm, Emma's blue eyes, the crest of a wave, an after-dinner speech. Nothing is left inert.

Miss Gordon's allegiances are clearly formulated here and in her last novel, *The Strange Children,* her fidelity to the tradition of "naturalism" as she has defined it emerges with a mature authority. It is in this finely thoughtful work that her real service to the realm of Southern letters as the conservator of the heritage of "naturalism" and thus of the mainstream of the great fiction of the western world is most powerfully demonstrated.

It would be misleading to imply that Miss Gordon has arrived at this clarity about the role of the fiction writer easily or all at once. The evidence of almost twenty-five years of writing suggests much wrestling with and re-shaping of formal intentions and means. But one can see in her first attempts at fiction, **"The Long Day"** and **"Summer Dust,"** two short stories written in 1928 and now included in *The Forest Of The South,* how firm the primary sense of lively "impression" was. The choice of the short story form indi-

cates that this sense had not yet expanded into a program confident enough for the novel. **"Summer Dust"** especially foreshadows the virtue of her later writing although it is episodic and somewhat uncertain of short-story limits. The theme is the insistent impingement of the world's evil upon a child's innocence. But what *dramatically* elucidates this problem is the fine tissue of circumstance which flows from the social and psychological structure of the South. Thus, the past and innocence is not merely Sally's preoccupation with the fairy tale of the little princess with whom, both by social credit and imagination, she has identified herself; on her peach-picking expedition with her playmates she thinks realistically with the cruel self-awareness of a child: "I'm not a nigger . . . I'm the only one who's not a nigger." The dramatic evocation of the past is in the forest in which Sally gets lost, in the sick old Negro woman endowed by local legend with mysteriouswitch-like powers, in the white tenants whose slyly just denunciation of her family suggests an opaque history of deprivation and degradation. The totality of this dramatic rendering of a limited context translates into that evil summer dust which conspires to invade the cool green herbage of Sally's innocence.

A few years later, Miss Gordon's first novel *Penhally* (1931) maps out the territory in which her naturalistic method will operate for about the first decade and a half of her work. In its first pages, the nostalgia for a lost grandeur which was the ante-bellum South is expressed obliquely through the thoughts of Nicholas Llewellyn surveying his Kentucky plantation one fine day in 1826:

> But everything was breaking up nowadays. The country was in the hands of the New England manufacturers—men who gave no thought to its true interests. The tariff of abominations, as they called it, made it almost impossible to feed and clothe your negroes . . . His people had left Virginia because everything was breaking up there. Now everything was breaking up here. The women might very well keep on crying. They would be the first to feel it if the roofs of the old places fell about their heads.

The drama of this "breaking up" is enlarged by Nicholas' memories of his boyhood, of his parents' tales, so that the perspective is pushed back some sixty years into the eighteenth century. Thus the structure of life at Penhally in the nineteenth century gains the melancholy richness of depth and distance, as if its tragic destiny were already lurking in the luxurious ambiguities of its past.

Nostalgia may be the initial impulse directing the novelist toward these materials. But even in 1931 Miss Gordon was too informed and objective toward her craft to rely naively on the sustaining power of impulse. In the fratricide committed by Nick's twentieth century descendent, Chance Llewellyn, who turns against his brother Nick, the legal heir to Penhally, for selling the estate to rich Northerners, Miss Gordon was clearly, perhaps too transparently pointing a parable. Chance (the name is useful) cannot stay the hand of time except by violence. And death to his brother is the final destruction of one link to the past he so loves. Nostalgia succumbs to the ironies of chaos.

By 1934 Miss Gordon was involved in the matrix of the Alec Maury stories. In the novel, *Alec Maury, Sportsman,* and in the shorter stories which were, no doubt, shavings from it not possible to integrate into its scheme, she found a way to present the past ironically through exploiting its rich secret life in the mind of the central figure. "**Old Red,**" one of the best short stories Miss Gordon (or, for that matter, any contemporary Southerner) has written, is a useful place to look into the more mature habits of her art as it explores the humours of nostalgia. The plot is Time; and it is a plot with which Alec Maury will have no truck:

> Time, he thought, time! They were always mouthing the word, and what did they know about it? Nothing in God's world! He saw time suddenly, a dull leaden-colored fabric depending from the old lady's hands, from the hands of all of them, a blanket pulled about between them, now here, now there, trying to cover up their nakedness . . . But time was a banner that whipped before him always in the wind! . . . Where, for instance, had this year gone? He could swear he had not wasted a minute of it, for no man living, he thought, knew better how to make each day a pleasure to him . . .

The unstated equation between Alec Maury and Old Red, the elusive fox of his hunting days, raises the memories of the old sportsman to a symbolic plane where his own evasion of those who would run him down as ruthlessly as any animal quarry takes on a heroic gallantry. But it is a gallantry tinged with pathos because we know it is time who is the real antagonist. In this story the past, as sensed through the mellow texture of Maury's sensibility (he is the kind of individualist only the old South or other societies resembling it could afford to produce), has a double function, as if cause and effect were inseparable, with protagonist and antagonist locked in a beautiful but deadly embrace.

Alec Maury, Sportsman is the extension of this atmosphere into the magical evocation of a whole vanished way of life with something of the same effect of a self-contained universe of reference as one feels in Turgenev's *Memoirs of a Sportsman* to which it bears no little resemblance. The made-upness of the world of sport, like the made-upness of "the self-contained forms of poetry," to which Miss Gordon compares the fiction she admires, is the perfect objective correlative for the kind of society old Alec stands for, and for the formal classical interests which, in the modes of rhetoric and poetry, complement in his inner life that ardent pursuit of the thing-in-itself which his fishing represents.

Miss Gordon's next three novels, *None Shall Look Back* (1937), *The Garden of Adonis* (1937), and *Green Centuries* (1941), continue the exploration of her imaginative centre, the South, at a number of levels which suggest some uncertainty of purpose. In *None Shall Look Back,* a Civil War novel with General Nathan Bedford Forrest as a more than life-sized First Cause who dominates the landscape, the level is carefully historical with a good deal of social exposition worked in. In this sense it is a *serious* historical novel (something which most novels in this

genre are not) just as the later *Green Centuries* is a serious historical study of the late eighteenth century Kentucky settlers and their battle with the new world of the frontier and the old world of the Indians.

Oddly, *The Garden of Adonis,* set squarely in modern times—the period is the depression—where for the first time in Miss Gordon's work the poor whites are of co-evalent interest with the denuded aristocrats of the land, pursues an inner theme not too remote from those of the two historical novels I have just mentioned. This theme I can only roughly delimit by calling it the theme of alienation. It is a major, a recurrent theme in Miss Gordon's writing, but it inhabits another world in the books from about 1945 on. It is often expressed in her early novels by fraternal antagonisms. Both *Green Centuries* and *Penhally* end with brother killing brother. In each case the victim is the brother who has "sold out" to the enemy—in the first instance, to the Indians; in the second, to the North.

In *The Garden of Adonis* the alienation theme is situated more complexly in the dispossession of *all* the characters from their roots in the land. Ben Allard, a descendant of the Allards in *None Shall Look Back* (it should be mentioned that Caroline Gordon has, like Faulkner, worked out a vast genealogy of over a century and a half of families in Kentucky and upper Tennessee which builds up a huge historical dossier for her to draw upon), is a landlord who really cares about the land. He is murdered by one of his most loyal tenant farmers, Ote Mortimer, a young

A family portrait of Allen, Nancy, and Caroline, painted in Paris in 1929 by Stella Bowen.

man of considerable integrity and force, displaced from his job in the auto factory, and trying a return to the land. He is a good worker but he has not the patient love which is needed to redeem the soil and when he finally kills (or appears to have killed) Allard at the end of the novel it is a symbolic act which rejects just such a love. The novel tells a parallel story of the aristocraticbut poverty-stricken Carters who marry into the Camps, a wealthy Northern industrial family whose activities have dispossessed them and thus is an attempt to handle the alienation theme from more points of view than the simpler one of historical loss which earlier satisfied Miss Gordon. It is not really successful, however, perhaps because of its attempted complexity. The Adonis symbolism, as hinted by the epigraph from Frazer's *The Golden Bough,* seems incidental rather than central to the real conflict which is social, and not sexual as the title urges. This overt reliance on myth, as we shall see in *The Women on the Porch,* fails here as there because the myth is too fragilely developed to bear the weight of the novel's meaning and so its adventitiousness to Miss Gordon's deeper interest is shown up.

Still, *The Women on the Porch* (1944) is safe to take as the initiation of Miss Gordon's most ambitious period. In this novel her absorption in Southern materials is paradoxically counterpointed by extending the frame of reference, moving from New York to Tennessee and back again. New York, as one might expect, although treated realistically enough is shadowy in comparison with Miss Gordon's South, where every aspect of setting, terrain and speech is seen with the fine clarity with which she can trace a leaf or a bug. But the novel evokes not only a rich and vaguely sinister South to which Catherine, the expatriate heroine, returns when her marriage appears threatened by her husband's infidelity, but also it introduces a kind of allegorical sociology which seems extraneous to the story.

Miss Gordon appears to be covertly arguing, as indeed she had argued more openly in *The Garden of Adonis,* that love cannot flourish without roots and that these roots lie in the land of one's birth, preferably (if this can be managed) in an ordered and predictable local society. To this end, she shows Jim Chapman, the husband, a deracinated middle-westerner teaching in New York, to have a barren emotional life of which his present affair is only a symptom. But Jim is insufficiently developed as a character for one to judge whether deracination was a cause or an effect of his problems. Jim, left by his wife, muses: "Middle-westerners, springing out of that rich, deep loam of prairie, always on their way somewhere else . . . I never felt at home but once in my life . . ." In *Green Centuries,* a few years earlier, this obsessive faith in the value of possession by the land, through a willed act of fealty to it (much as John Crowe Ransom urges this in his lovely "Antique Harvesters") was summarized by the hero, Rion, in the beautiful closing as the gazes up at the constellation for which he is named:

> But it seemed that a man had to flee further each time and leave more behind him and when he got to the new place he looked up and saw Orion fixed upon his burning wheel, always pursuing the bull, but never making the kill. Did Orion

will any longer the westward chase? No more than himself. Like the mighty hunter he had lost himself in the turning. Before him lay the empty west, behind him the loved things of which he was made . . . Were not men raised into the westward turning stars only after they had destroyed themselves? . . .

But in *The Women on the Porch,* the heroine, who in her emotional turmoil instinctively flees to the South for comfort and security, shrinks back in alarm at the static, almost paralyzed composure of her relatives at Swan Quarter. Her eventual rejection of a life as the wife of her cousin, and as the mistress of his land, a land she loves, does suggest that the claims of the South upon its lovers are crumbling under the pressures of new and inevitable alignments outsideit. But the "love" conflict then is reduced to a mere illustration of the more fundamental hostility between the two cultures symbolized by Jim, the rootless intellectual, and Catherine, the land-loving Southerner. The result is a curiously passionless love story, beautifully written and with the minor characters swiftly and memorably established, yet as a whole unsatisfying. The unstated myth which is said to inform the novel, that of Iphigenia in Aulis, another story of sacrificial flight, does not, I think, in any objective way determinable by the novel alone, enhance the meaning. But certainly with the publication of *The Strange Children* (1951) it has become plain that *The Women on the Porch* was an exploratory work, designed to accommodate Caroline Gordon's newer consciousness of naturalism as symbol (something she had evoked with exquisite precision in the death-haunted short story of that period, **"The Forest of the South"**) as well as her increasing preoccupation with the problem of the point of view.

What emerges with dazzling effect in *The Strange Children* is something that the romantic agony of the early novels only timidly hinted: Caroline Gordon's fiction is now squarely in the realm of the novel of manners, the great tradition of Flaubert and James, and like theirs her social comedy is complicated and, in the end, dominated by the perilous likeness it bears to tragedy. In this sense she connects herself with a strain abandoned in Southern fiction with the death of Ellen Glasgow, but a strain enriched both by the fuller events of her own biography as well as her more acid consciousness of what the novel, as formal means, should be doing. *The Strange Children* elegantly points the dramatic method which Miss Gordon admires as a critic and teacher of fiction. It is a novel of ideas and in it she establishes that this is her proper domain, that at last she is allowing full play to a powerful intellectual scrutiny suppressed in the earlier novels in favor of an ambivalent mystique of localism and historicism.

The Strange Children manages the seemingly impossible device of revealing a complex hierarchy of meaning through the use of a nine-year-old child as the central intelligence. As modern fiction has shown again and again, the dangers of using an immature consciousness for this task are manifold: the most obvious is the cutting down of nuance and the elimination of intellectual themes; the less obvious but the most deadly is that of the coarsely

> **What emerges with dazzling effect in *The Strange Children* is something that the romantic agony of Gordon's early novels only timidly hinted: Caroline Gordon's fiction is squarely in the realm of the novel of manners, the great tradition of Flaubert and James, and like theirs her social comedy is complicated and, in the end, dominated by the perilous likeness it bears to tragedy.**
>
> **—*Vivienne Koch***

Rousseauistic sentimentalization of childhood and adolescence which is tiresome commonplace in much contemporary writing. But the choice of Lucy Lewis, whose favorite reading is the beautifully ambiguous tale of "Undine," as central intelligence is subtly right for Miss Gordon's motive, a motive adequately laid down by her epigraph: "Rid me and deliver me from the hand of strange children whose mouth speaketh vanity . . ."

It is, of course, the ironic triumph of the novel that the strange children are the grown-ups in it and that Lucy is the wisely clairvoyant agent of judgment on them. But unlike those intolerable children of modern writing she is not all innocence and imagination; nor, as in the counter-romantic to this view of child-life, all cunning and sexuality. She is, rather, a little vessel which responds to the tremors and passions of the adult world in which she is both familiar and stranger, but always with that instinctual knowledge of good and evil which seems to be the burdensome gift of innocence.

Still, there are problems to be faced in such a choice of sensibility to reflect the complicated goings-on at Benfolly, a country house in Tennessee, where a group of neurotic and self-destructive intellectuals, both Northern and Southern, are gathered in the hectic communality of an alcoholic house party. The question of the limits of Lucy's ability to re-translate the action for us is solved by Miss Gordon's subtle modulations from the child as central intelligence to an omniscient narrator when the material becomes unmanageable for the child. This violates that strict determinism which is sometimes thought to control the point of view in the naturalistic novel, but, as even the most cursory examination of *Madame Bovary* or *Ulysses* will reveal, these small shifts of perspective are always useful when the limitations of the perceiving sensibility require them. Miss Gordon's sharp awareness of this possibility is evident in the endorsement she gives to the method of the "Roving Narrator" or the "Technique of Central Intelligence" in *The House of Fiction:*

> . . . A given technique is the result of a moral and philosophical attitude, a bias towards experience on the part of the author: and as the author begins to understand what it is in life that interests him most, he also becomes aware of the techniques which will enable him to create in

language his fullest sense of that interest. Material and technique become in the end the same thing, the one discovering the other . . . this method (the Roving Narrator) combines the advantages of the three others and involves the artist in fewer of their disadvantages than any other known technique. But it requires the greatest maturity of judgment, the greatest mastery of life and the highest technical skill to control it . . . We look at the situation by and large through the eyes of the central character or intelligence, but we stand a little above and to one side, so to speak, and actually use the eyes of the artist himself. We thus enjoy his privilege of omniscience without the dubious authority of the so-called omniscient narrator for here the artist makes his surmises, summaries and explanations in terms of what the central character sees and feels, and the usually inert masses of material are dramatized and given *authority* . . . The technique of the Central Intelligence is employed in one way or another in the greatest nineteenth century novels, from *The Idiot* and *Madame Bovary,* to the *The Ambassadors.*

Miss Gordon, then, has made it amply clear where her sights are trained and we need only look, let us say, at the moving end of *The Strange Children* to see her method in operation. We have just had the great cathartic climax of the Holy Roller meeting of the poor whites and the taking up of serpents which has resulted in near-death to one of the believers. Little Lucy, through the cruelly casual thoughtlessness of her parents, has been exposed to all this and, now, to complete her turmoil, her fall from virtue in the theft of a crucifix belonging to one of the house-guests is suddenly and humiliatingly discovered. But that is not all. Having lost the succor of the beautiful little image, whose magnetism she only half understands, she learns, along with the other grown-ups, that Uncle Tubby, her father's pyrotechnically successful poet-friend and Isabel, the wife of Kevin Reardon, have eloped. But the real horror of this is in the revelation by Kevin that Isabel is mad. It is at this point that the child, as central intelligence, delicately modulates into a more encompassing one which is that of her father's and, beyond that, through language, tone and selection of detail into that of the omniscient narrator or, more properly, the author herself:

> He [Stephen Lewis] walked to the railing and looked down at the drenched lawn. He raised his eyes to the sky. There was a rustle behind him. A slight form pressed up against his. He put his arms around the child's shoulders and drew her closer while his eyes ranged the heavens. There was his own sign, Scorpio: "The House of Death—unless a man be re-born." . . . He passed his hand over his brow. His eyes went to the house below where a single lamp glowed murkily. There a man still lay at the point of death. He told himself that it would have been no great matter if that man had died tonight, for all men, it appeared to him now, for the first time, die on the same day: the day on which their appointed task is finished. If that man had made his last journey tonight he would not have gone alone, but companioned by a larger presence, as the friend standing behind him had been com-

panioned when he, too, lay at the point of death in a strange country and in a desert. But all countries, he told himself wearily, are strange and all countries desert. He thought of another man, the friend of his youth, who only a few minutes ago had left his house without farewell . . . He saw that those days, those years had been moving toward this moment and he wondered what moment was being prepared for him and for his wife and his child and he groaned, so loud that the woman and the child stared at him wondering, too.

It is right that this concluding integration of themes should be stated through a larger vision than that of a child's. Lucy's burdens in the strange dissolution of loves and friendships that has taken place at Benfolly are profound. But it requires a more practised judgment than hers to restore the troubled movement of all the characters' lives into the universal channels of love and hate, of death and peace and rebirth. In this passage, somehow recalling in its cadences the great final lines of Joyce's "The Dead," there is no solution, only a momentary resolution into a new possibility of being.

I have scanted in this accomplished novel those elements of wit and erudition which are a new and altogether successful area of achievement for Miss Gordon, and, as a matter of fact, a province that few women writers in this country have essayed. Into this impressively knowledgable complex of reference, the issue of religion naturally enters. Miss Gordon's conversion to Catholicism has been public knowledge for some five years but there is little overt concern about religion on the part of the protagonists of the novel written concurrently with her reception into the church. Still, in the figure of Kevin Reardon, the wealthy expatriate who has become a Catholic convert, there is provided a convenient if shadowy point of reference against which to direct a subtly inferential dialectic illuminating the motives of the others: the hard-drinking mother, Sara Lewis, ambivalent in her feelings for her child and husband; Stephen Lewis, bitter and sophisticated, a historian who ridicules in his wife the mysterious inner yearning which makes her hang on Kevin's story of his "vision" with an almost physiological intensity. Oddly though, it is the child, Lucy, who in her seemingly senseless theft of Kevin's crucifix dramatically reveals the drive which they all unknowingly harbor for a saviour. The passage of Stephen's musings from which I have quoted above hints at a more open religious motive to come in Miss Gordon's writing: ". . . he would not have gone alone . . . ," thinks Lewis of the two men, the Catholic convert and the crudely believing Holy Roller lying ill in his house. Suddenly, there is a kind of incandescense and we recognize that two ways of knowing have been exhibited for us, through the dramatic mode of "naturalism," as possibilities of salvation. We have not been told; we have only, in the strict aesthetic of Miss Gordon's understanding of naturalism, been shown.

It is possible to say that *The Strange Children* which, incidentally, at one level is a fascinatingly malicious roman à clef of some pretty well-known literary figures, is the first work in which Caroline Gordon exchanges the frame of reference of a vanished hierarchy of caste and grace, repre-

sented by the old South, for the universe of order provided by the more durable scheme of Catholicism and its idea of grace. Her next work, I am willing to chance, will show this sense of possibility benefited by the full flowering of the deepened vision operative in *The Strange Children.* Alienation means no longer merely to be cast out from a social class or a local society, but a removal from God to whom we have become strange children.

Vivienne Koch, "The Conservatism of Caroline Gordon," in Southern Renascence: The Literature of the Modern South, *edited by Louis D. Rubin, Jr. and Robert D. Jacobs, The Johns Hopkins Press, 1953, pp. 325-37.*

John W. Simons   (review date 13 April 1956)

[*Simons is a Roman Catholic priest and professor of English. In the following review of* The Malefactors, *Simons lauds the book's originality and successful rendering of religious themes in vernacular terms.*]

Miss Caroline Gordon, whose novels and short stories have always been remarkable for their subtle poetic essence and vigilant craftsmanship, has never to this reviewer's knowledge attained the neon glories of best-sellerdom. It is barely possible that with the publication of her eighth novel, *The Malefactors,* she may be called upon to endure the wider success, for it deals with a theme which perversely attracts an age of almost official cynicism. It is the theme of conversion. The central figure of *The Malefactors* is a poet who, approaching middle age and seemingly forsaken by his muse, makes the discovery of Christ.

The poet, when we meet him, is forty-seven years old. For a dozen years he has written nothing of account. He is living on the income of his wealthy wife on a farm property in Pennsylvania's Bucks County—the penultimate of Eden, it would seem, of reflective or refuted artists. When the novel opens we are about to attend what the poet's wife calls a *fête,* a sort of middle-sized cattle-and-produce exhibit, of which she is patroness. The *fête* gives the novelist the opportunity to introduce the chief actors in her drama. In the meantime, through a series of deft throwbacks, we come to know the antecedent life of the protagonist, the seasons of his hopes and aridities, and something of the shape of his present disenchantment.

Tom Claiborne, a casually reared Southerner, was a highly intelligent, preternaturally gifted young man who, after he had left college and served his term in the first World War, decided on the career of poet. His early verse was enthusiastically praised by Horne Watts, an expatriate American poet of pronounced genius, who hailed the neophyte as "the new Laforgue." When circumstances arrange themselves, Claiborne accepts the invitation to join his circle in Paris. Horne the poet and Max Shull the painter are living, the newcomer discovers, in a homosexual relationship. Claiborne, though he himself is not "that way," retains the uneasy friendship of both. Later, after a period of mounting disorientation, Horne Watts, who had just completed his major poetic effort, *Pontifex,* "leaped to his death from the deck of an Atlantic steamer." Horne Watts is the literary evocation and transmutation of the actual poet Hart Crane.

Claiborne stayed on in Paris for some years editing an *avant-garde* literary journal called *Spectra*. In the meantime he had married Vera Vincent, daughter of a crazed painter, Carlo Vincent, who had, like Watts, taken his own life. Vera, deeply attached to her father, experiences a grave sense of insecurity. It becomes the more pronounced after her father's death, but she has an innocent confidence that Claiborne can redeem her from her inarticulate fears. He is incapable of meeting the exactions of her spirit, and their life together, on the surface at least, is one of sufferance rather than of love.

Tom Claiborne, accompanied by his wife, returns to New York, and for a time he continues to edit *Spectra* from that point. With the same abruptness, however, that he had quit Paris he withdraws from the journal entirely. These sudden and apparently inexplicable moves are indications of a profound *malaise*. But the move to Blencker's Brook has not solved anything, and the years pass by in idleness and sterility. The presence of Max Shull alleviates to some extent the boredom of his wife but only serves to exacerbate his own. During the time of the preparations for the *fête* Claiborne has a premonition that "something of enormous importance is about to happen." It is a premonition, none the less, which he hastens to reject.

We have arrived at the point at which the main action of the novel is set in motion. A reviewer, if he is to be sportsmanlike, must not attempt the complete—and inevitably traitorous—condensation. This is a special danger when the novel is as cunningly and curiously wrought as the one under consideration, where almost nothing fortuitous or gratuitous is allowed entrance. It is enough to say that Tom Claiborne, after a period of *longueurs,* futilities, and indirections, ultimately discovers God Himself. Or, to put it another way, he becomes the frantic victim of a Divine ambuscade, and, being caught, finds himself and his fellows. From the point of view of art, however, what matters is less what happens than the strategy by which it is accomplished—the power of poetry by which the originating vision is sustained and subdued, and through which the reader is compelled to a clear-eyed acquiescence.

Before commenting on this strategy it is only fair that the reviewer confess the difficulties he has always experienced in giving his assent to dramatizations of conversion. A conversion is admittedly a special invasion of Grace into a particular life. If the artist, in his effort to summon the mystery, gives a maximum plausibility to the motives and conditions leading up to conversion he risks an attenuation of the essentially free character of Grace. If he gives a maximum permissiveness to Grace he risks making his character seem the puppet of Grace. In this case it is the art which seems implausible, for God becomes an almost literal *deus ex machina*. Highly endowed artists from Corneille to Graham Greene have either foundered on the rock or been sucked into the whirlpool. Only Bernanos, for all his technical *gaucherie,* has come close to accomplishing the miracle.

Miss Gordon has her own resources, and they are of a quite superior order. First of all, there is the hint contained in her epigraph: "It is for Adam to interpret the voices which Eve hears." This text, taken from Maritain's essay "The Frontiers of Poetry," is to be understood as specifying the relationship between the practical or critical intelligence and poetic intuition—Claudel's *animus* and *anima*. Man's critical intelligence is situated between a lower and a higher intuition. These realms on either side of the practical reason can be mistaken for each other. The one has an obscurity "by excess of opacity"; the other, an obscurity "by excess of transparency." The poet is nourished by his intuitions, but it is the critical intelligence (Adam) which must decide on the authenticity of what the soul (Eve) experiences.

Tom Claiborne is a poet who has,—all poets have—his presences, illuminations, and voices. In his earlier life the illuminations and presences had been frequent, and his poetry thrived. In recent years they had become rarer and were of an increasingly ambiguous character. The voices, on the other hand, never entirely left him, but as his spiritual life deteriorates they become laconic, ironic, and cryptic. Claiborne's critical spirit has in the course of years gained ascendancy over the creative spirit; yet, by a strange irony, that critical spirit is powerless to probe his own *malaise*. He is congealed in his own ego and so misreads himself and those about him. He is not without his extra-rational intimations, but he has a vast amount of experience to unlearn before he can decipher them. Miss Gordon handles the voices superbly, locating each with its distinctive intonation.

Claiborne also has his memories and his dreams. Towards the end of the novel the dreams increase in number and terror, for by this time the poet is on the verge of nervous collapse. The stuff of his dreams is dredged from his past experience in life and literature, and they have a sort of higher coherence which is intractable to analysis. His father is in them. So are Carlo Vincent and Horne Watts. There are caves, corridors, cliffs, and water. The memories, too, assert themselves unsolicited. There are memories of places—Eupedon, Mio Sogno, Clermont. There are expressions—the *"Feu . . . feu"* of Pascal, the *"Tolle, lege"* of St. Augustine. There are recurrences—of the cave ("I saw it first, but George was the first to enter"); the offhand suggestion that Catherine Pollard join the Church. Things that Claiborne has done or said in one context make an uncanny reappearance in another. Once again the novelist exhibits an admirable virtuosity in the deployment of symbols and echoes.

Finally, there are people. It is they who, wittingly and unwittingly, bring Claiborne to the edge of self-realization. There are George Crenfew, his psychiatrist cousin; Catherine Pollard, whose heroic Catholicism will remind readers of a saintly woman still living; Cynthia Vail, Claiborne's ambitious paramour; Molly Archer, the lady of drunken candors; Max Shull, the painter of the St. Eustache legend (an operative symbol); Sister Immaculata, the formidable nun who is writing a *critique* of Horne Watt's poetry. And there is a host of minor figures, all of whom—even the somewhat superfluous Miss Golightly—have their function. The dead, too, possibly even more than the living, join in that skillfully discordant choir which, at one level of meaning, constitutes the Adam who interprets the voices of Eve.

When I had finished the history of Tom Claiborne—obviously and not too implausibly in the toils of Grace—I was more than ever in admiration of a novelist who had not only avoided with her usual consistency the *clichés* of her craft but had come closer than any vernacular writer to encompassing the elusive miracle.

It may be that the ghost of Hart Crane was over-intrusive. Is it the reviewer's fault if he equates *Pontifex* with *The Bridge* and finds the nun's exegesis, notmerely ingenious to excess, but unassimilable to the intent of St. Catherine's *Dialogo Divino?* Prescinding entirely from the matter of the poet's possibilities of redemption, there seems to be no way—unless, perhaps, one has a Ph. D. from Louvain—of validly interpreting the poet's bridge in the light of the saint's. Something has gone wrong in that important interview, where the hand of the artist trembled and the eyes filled with tears. But it was for the moment only. One who knows less about *The Bridge* than the novelist or the reviewer will be the safer judge.

John W. Simons, "A Cunning and Curious Dramatization," in The Commonweal, *Vol. LXIV, No. 2, April 13, 1956, pp. 54-6.*

William Van O'Connor   (essay date 1961)

[*O'Connor was an American critic, editor, and educator who was a pioneer in the development of analytical criticism, a form of critical theory which examines historical, linguistic, environmental, and cultural influences on literary works. In the following essay, which provides an overview of Gordon's fiction, he claims that Gordon is a distinctively American writer despite her allegiance to the European literary heritage.*]

Caroline Gordon belongs to the generation of writers who spent at least part of their youth in Paris. The gods of the nineteenth century had fallen, but these young people found another: Art. Like most gods, Art had many guises, and was sometimes called Poetry, sometimes The Novel, and sometimes Modernism. Art had innumerable prophets, but in its guise as The Novel the chief of these prophets were Flaubert, James, and Ford Madox Ford. Miss Gordon has expressed great reverence and respect for each of them, and was fortunate enough to be personally acquainted with Ford.

Intervening generations, younger than Miss Gordon by ten or fifteen or twenty years, have also believed in Art. Anyone who aspired to write knew that it was impious not to believe in Art. In the years between the two wars, the poets, novelists, and critics who amounted to anything in the eyes of their fellows were true believers. Art was sacred. A great many sermons or homilies were given about technique and structure and point of view.

After World War II, Art continued to be respected, but some of the young writers occasionally protested. When drunk they might even say, "Let's get off this crap about Art-ya gotta have something to say!" or, "Look, kid, if you can't invent, you can't write," or, "This technique stuff, stow it!"

The older writers, like Miss Gordon, knew the pendulum swung back and forth, toward Art, then toward Life, and they would try patiently to explain that they were not opposed to Life's getting into literature; there was no other way of serving Art. But Art had to be served. And the younger writers, rather shamefacedly, would admit, "Yeah, ya gotta serve It." Despite the seeming unanimity a schism had begun, although a rather lax theologian might say, "The differences are merely matters of emphasis. Nothing is wrong, provided each of us serves Art in his own way."

Miss Gordon, the author of many articles and books on fiction, and, like Katherine Anne Porter, a writer's writer, has served Art faithfully. She has been to school under the masters. In one of her textbooks she makes this comment on Anton Chekhov:

> Chekhov presented difficulties to his first English readers. Imaginations "conditioned" by the Victorian novelists' leisurely pace were not athletic enough for the collaboration he demanded. And, indeed, his achievements surpassed anything the Victorians had imagined. He may well be compared to the great Pointillist painter, Seurat, on whose canvas every fleck of paint, when viewed in the proper perspective, unites with a neighboring fleck of paint to make the color the artist had in mind. There are no "dead" spots on Chekhov's canvases. Each detail not only vibrates with a life of its own but "acts" upon the neighboring detail. The result is a scene of extraordinary animation. The actors' speeches and gestures are lifelike in the extreme and they move through their roles with consistent boldness, but in addition, the whole scene seems to be bathed in a living air. Reading a Chekhov story one feels often as one does on an early autumn day when fields, woods, mountains, lakes and rivers show more brilliantly for the luminous light which shimmers between us and them.

The best of Miss Gordon's stories are like that; the details are vibrant. **"The Brilliant Leaves"** is a good example. A boy watches the girl he loves fall to her death from a ledge they had been climbing. The two had arranged a tryst in the woods. She insists on climbing high into the rocks near a waterfall called Bridal Veil. She slips on a rock and falls. In the hands of certain writers the horror would be the story. Miss Gordon does much more. The woods are life and adventure, the waiting future; and the dazzlingly brilliant leaves are passion and also death. Human lives are in nature, and to live well is to live adventurously, aware of love against death, aware that death is the mother of beauty.

In the same story there is also the "death" of the women who sit gossiping, ghostlike, apart from love. They live in the little white houses that seem staid and permanent and secure. Perhaps the young man should run away with his girl—we are not told. The women on the porch have gossiped about Sally Mainwaring, now a bitter old spinster, whose young man, fearing her father, had deserted her. The boy has often heard the story, but it has not upset his sense of the equilibrium of the world. The death of his beloved shows him how precarious that equilibrium has been.

> He ran slower now, lurching sometimes from side to side, but he ran on. He ran and the brilliant, the wine-colored leaves crackled and broke under his feet. His mouth, a taut square, drew in, released whining breaths. His starting eyes fixed the ground, but he did not see the leaves that he ran over. He saw only the white houses that no matter how fast he ran kept always just ahead of him. If he did not hurry they would slide off the hill, slide off and leave him running forever through these woods, over these dead leaves.

"The Forest of the South" and **"Old Red"** also show Miss Gordon's unwillingness to describe essentially inert situations, to create what Joyce called "mere literature." She not only wants the reader to look into the eyes of the characters—she wants the characters to look back at the reader, to have a light radiating from the page.

"The Forest of the South" describes the total destruction of a Southern household, Clifton, in the Civil War. The Yankee victor, Lieutenant Munford, falls in love with the daughter, Eugenie. There is a mysterious yet beautiful light in the girl's eyes, and Munford, still loving her, realizes she is mad, and the reader realizes that her madness is the madness of the destruction itself.

Even more skillful is the whole texture of details in **"Old Red,"** undoubtedly one of the finest short stories written in our time. Its protagonist, Aleck Maury, who appears prominently in a number of Miss Gordon's stories, is a man who tries to unveil nature's secrets. He looks into the burning eyes of a possum, and he studies the soft colors in streams and lakes with the quiet intensity of a Buddhist monk. He is a scholar, and he learns to respect classic simplicity—but he loves life, not death, and hunting and fishing become the center of his pursuits. He refuses the blandishments of the ghostly ladies who sit on the porches of the white houses. In the process he alienates his wife, and she dies after having kept her illness secret from him.

The central symbol in **"Old Red"** is the fox. Mr. Maury, trying to fall asleep one night, finally realizes that he and Old Red are being pursued and will eventually be caught. But when he is caught, it will be because he can no longer run. The identification of fox and man comes gracefully and unexpectedly into the story, like an ancient tale of metamorphosis.

> If he allowed his mind to get active, really active, he would never get any sleep. He was fighting an inclination now to get up and find a cigarette. . . . The young men would hold back till Uncle James had wheeled Old Filly, then they would all be off pell-mell across the plain. He himself would be mounted on Jonesboro. Almost blind, but she would take anything you put her at. That first thicket on the edge of the woods. They would break there, one half of them going around, the other half streaking it through the woods. He was always of those going around to try to cut the fox off on the other side. No, he was down off his horse. He was

coursing with the fox through the trees. He could hear the sharp, pointed feet padding on the dead leaves, see the quick head turned now and then over the shoulder. The trees kept flashing by, one black trunk after another. And now it was a ragged mountain field and the sage grass running before them in waves to where a narrow stream curved in between the ridges. The fox's feet were light in the water. He moved forward steadily, head down. The hounds' baying grew louder. Old Mag knew the trick. She had stopped to give tongue by that big rock and now they had all leaped the gulch and were scrambling up through the pines. But the fox's feet were already hard on the mountain path. He ran slowly, past the big boulder, past the blasted pine to where the shadow of the Pinnacle Rock was black across the path. He ran on and the shadow swayed and rose to meet him. Its cool touch was on his hot tongue, his heavy flanks. He had slipped in under it. He was sinking down, panting, in black dark, on moist earth while the hounds' baying filled the valley and reverberated from the mountainside.

Miss Gordon has a fine ear for conversation, even to the shifts one hears in the speech of an educated Southerner. For example, when Aleck Maury is talking to his daughter, his language is formal. " 'Well,' he said, 'I'd better be starting.' " In the woods, thinking to himself, he says, " 'Ain't it funny now? Niggers always live in the good places.' " Miss Gordon's own prose has the simplicity of good taste. It is never pretentious. When, occasionally, it does rise toward rhetoric, the rhetoric is always justified by the action itself.

Her subject matter, too, is essentially simple. For the most part, she writes about the relationships of men and women. Ideally, she seems to say, a woman should give herself to a man, wholly and without question, and he should not betray her faith. The stories frequently have to do with betrayal, by the man, the sudden intrusion of nature (violence or death), or the breakdown of the society (the Civil War). Sometimes the failures are the woman's. By and large, Miss Gordon's subject is not a complicated one, and the grave simplicity of her style is in accord with her subject.

The Women on the Porch is in treatment and subject a fairly typical Gordon novel. A young stallion provides the central symbolism, and there is a clearly discernible pattern of imagery drawn from water and cloud and leaves. The writing, quietly beautiful, hardly calls attention to itself. Theme and subject have to do with masculine failures and women's frustrations. Because of accident, weakness of character, or possibly the period in history in which the characters find themselves, the men fail to satisfy the female need for loyal, courageous, forth-right action, for love. The novel has that firmness of surface and impersonality to which Miss Gordon's writing aspires.

The story opens:

> The sugar tree's round shadow was moving past the store. At five o'clock when the first leaves were withering on the burning macadam the storekeeper raised his eyes to the fields across the

road. The heat rose somewhere between the road and those distant woods. Always at this hour he looked, expecting to see it rise out of that far cornfield and always when he looked it was there. Only a light shimmer now above the green, but the shimmer would deepen as the field brimmed over. In a few minutes the first waves would beat against the porch. He got up and, walking to the end of the porch, lifted the lid of the red metal ice-chest.

"How about you, Ed?" he asked.

The man at the other end of the porch leaned forward, felt in his trousers pocket until he found a nickel, and pitched it to the storekeeper.

This description immediately involves the reader in the action, as though the author, Joyce-like, had dissolved into the atmosphere. It is reminiscent of the skillful opening paragraphs of *The Red Badge of Courage* and *A Farewell to Arms.* The atmosphere, of dust and heat and ennui, with occasional relief, is maintained throughout the novel.

There is lore or learning of various sorts—about flowers, mushrooms, horses, painting, local history, even architecture and literature. For the most part, all this knowledge functions unobtrusively. The story itself is about the search for love. A male reader, incidentally, might easily feel that Miss Gordon's idyll of peace deep in the forest of time, death, and danger is a woman writer's dream. She seems to ask of the male more understanding, courage, and tenacity than most mortals, male or female, possess. And the same reader, especially if he does not share Miss Gordon's respect for the "cold pastoral," for Art, might feel that something is being put over on him. The right place for cold, eternal truths is the "cold pastoral" of an inn. The poor male, with all his weaknesses, could wish that the artist had not dissolved into the atmosphere. There are a couple of questions he would like in all fairness to put to the author.

Being, for the moment, a little hard on Miss Gordon, we ought to take a look at yet another novel, *None Shall Look Back,* in which, ironically, her very artistry seems to deaden the subject. There are many beautiful, skillfully evoked scenes, but they are so numerous that one finishes the book feeling that he has seen too many pictures—of forts, cannons, gunboats, staring corpses, gutted houses, handsome young soldiers tall on their sturdy horses, and young women crying in their darkened rooms. One gives *None Shall Look Back* a sort of credence—but only the sort given to an excellent book of Civil War pictures.

Miss Gordon's Southern piety too may have interfered with the dramatic possibilities of the subject. There is not enough in the book about the human heart in conflict with itself. Faulkner quarreled with his heritage and produced *Absalom, Absalom!* Miss Gordon brought too much respect and too little skepticism to her Civil War novel.

But Miss Gordon deserves to be judged by her best work. At least two of her novels, *Penhally* and *Aleck Maury, Sportsman,* are first-rate. Ford Madox Ford said of the former that he thought it the best novel that had been produced in modern America. This may be, and probably is, too great praise. *Penhally* is, nonetheless, a very fine novel. *Aleck Maury, Sportsman* is a masterpiece.

Both novels deal with the struggle to stay the hand of time. *Penhally* has what *None Shall Look Back* lacks: an inner life growing out of two ideas in conflict. In *Penhally,* nostalgia about the old ways, the ante-bellum world, is in conflict with change, and the latter inevitably has the victory, ironic and bitter though it turns out to be.

Aleck Maury, Sportsman is about an individual man, fully aware that his enemy is time. Day after day, Maury increases his skill as a fisherman and his artfulness in dodging those who would waste *his* time. His drama is not less poignant for being quiet. For seventy years his head has been filled with the sound of clocks which are stilled only when he is standing in a stream, casting, or sitting peacefully on a smooth lake. The reader comes to share his every success, his every failure. Miss Gordon's style, touched with a detached and loving irony, has never served a happier subject. In Aleck Maury, skillful, thoughtful, and sensitive men win at least a temporary victory—all they have ever hoped to win.

Most of the critics who have written about Miss Gordon have discussed her as a Southern writer—and of course she is. Some of her characters are deracinated Southerners or Middle Westerners, usually intellectuals who have left home. They are invariably unhappy; trouble and disorder trail along their foreign paths and remain with them when they occasionally return home. Miss Gordon has also written many passages, even whole novels, about the land and its healing moral power, which gives one a sense of belonging. She especially likes land that has not given up its fruits and rewards too easily; one appreciates what one has sweated to achieve.

Is Miss Gordon's preoccupation with Art also Southern? Perhaps, but her style is closer to Willa Cather's than it is to Southern rhetoric, even the quiet rhetoric of Katherine Anne Porter. Respect for form is in part Southern—for example, in manners, which cover and control personal likes, dislikes, drives, and ambitions; possibly too in a fairly general disregard for scientific principles and a preference for the arts that bear on personal relationships; and in a more open respect and liking for "elegance." But change comes on apace, and the Southern world of Miss Gordon's youth is no longer what it was. North and South grow more, not less, alike, and at least one or two of her novels seem to acknowledge that this is so.

Miss Gordon's art, as we suggested at the beginning, is related to the nineteenth-century European heritage. In her fiction, and explicitly in her many critical discussions of the novel and short story, she has clearly identified herself with the tradition of such men as Flaubert, James, Chekhov, and Stephen Crane, and with their successors—Joyce, Ford, and Hemingway.

Did she, in choosing to be a part of this literary heritage, choose well? It is presumptuous to answer such an Olympian and possibly impertinent question. But, having posed it, we must answer. Chekhov, in one of his letters, says, "One must write about simple things: how Peter Semionovich married Maria Ivanovna. That is all." When Miss

Gordon writes about American Marias and Peters, she can be, and often is, an excellent fiction writer. She is always excellent in writing about the Aleck Maurys. She is better when the subject matter arouses her sympathy and her humor than she is when the subjects arouse her anger or lead her into large theoretical conclusions about men and women or the social order.

Miss Gordon has written enough good stories—at least two novels of a very high order and a half dozen excellent short stories—to have won a permanent place for herself in the hierarchy of American letters. Recognition has come slowly but it has come, and it continues to grow. Miss Gordon has served Art well, and, by and large, it has not betrayed her.

William Van O'Connor, "Art and Miss Gordon," in South: Modern Southern Literature in Its Cultural Setting, *edited by Louis D. Rubin, Jr. and Robert D. Jacobs, Doubleday & Company, Inc., 1961, pp. 314-22.*

Brainard Cheney   (essay date Fall 1963)

[*Cheney is an American novelist, short story writer, dramatist, and critic. In the essay below, he identifies Gordon's fiction as the artistic and personal process of "self-realization" through which she achieved her conversion to Roman Catholicism. According to Cheney, Gordon's career is "the revelation of ontological motivation" which realizes its apotheosis in* The Malefactors.]

Modernity's extended time of transition has been one which few if any seers have been able to bring into perspective. This has been peculiarly true here in the United States—for historian, philosopher, artist—all the prophets of this land, this land conceived in the delusion of escape and born to innovation. There has been no ground actually for a balanced stance between past and future here, for balancing the enduring and the changing.

Yet, even so, the modern view has not constricted all alike. There have been a few of greater perspective, a few exceptions among our poets and even among our novelists. For of all of the articulators of modern society none has kept closer to the prompter's wing than the fiction writer. The novelist in this country has remained at the elbow of the preacher and the politician and the social scientist. His myth-making, if any, has been under the Big Top and from its fabric. His prophecy has been curtain announcement.

Of that very small company who have never joined in with the circus chorus, none has been more deeply committed to her art, nor more uncompromisingly devoted to her incredible quest—nor more excluded—than Caroline Gordon.

We were still deep in the heartland of economic absolutism, when Caroline Gordon published her first story, **"Summer Dust,"** in 1929. This sensitive piece evokes girlhood at the moment the child learns what lies in wait for virginity in the deceitful world of men. It is a proper proem to her work. This virgin becomes the antagonist of Caroline Gordon's panoramic dramas of disintegration

and remains at the center of the ordeal of rediscovery as well.

The lack, not merely of popular recognition, but of critical appreciation for her work, has long been a matter of concern to the writer of this estimate. He has been inspired by her artistic commitment. The appearance of each of her stories has over the years brought him illumination. But they had not until now composed a whole, a *totum*. On re-reading the body of her fiction (eight novels and a score of short stories) he has been astonished to find, not merely dramatic sequence in her successive pieces, but the composition of an epic ordeal.

To be sure I have been aware of a relationship in her stories. And significance in it. Andrew Lytle has written [in the August 1949 issue of *Sewanee Review*] cogently about the *historic image* that informs her earlier novels to intensify the action and give it a high literary irony. And he observed that the image was dynamic, that "from novel to novel a sense of growth which distinguishes what is permanent and what there is of change" comes through. He even spoke of it as "the nearest substitute for the religious image." More recently Louise Cowan, writing on "Nature and Grace in Caroline Gordon's work," speaks of her *sacramental* attitude toward her material.

But none of all of this quite prepared me for what has finally revealed itself. What now appears to me, after re-reading her last novel, **The Malefactors,** is that it is not only the culmination of her work. It is the final flower of a quest that has ordered Caroline Gordon's whole artistic career. It is an answer to unremitting prayer. It is the revelation of ontological motivation.

If Caroline Gordon brought a longer and a deeper perspective than usual to her art, it came of no discipline of the modern day; neither sociology, nor ideology, nor politics. She has kept her distance from them. It came—in this many-voiced babbling din—of a holding onto, a sounding of the depths of her own being and nature that was not merely personal, but family and social history and tradition. It came, as Miss Cowan has remarked, of a sacramental attitude toward the world and toward the material from which she was to fashion her own imaginative microcosm. And I may add that it came, too, of her vigilant exclusion of the vulgar and the merely plausible.

When I read Caroline Gordon's first novel, **Penhally,** thirty years ago, I will confess that I thought it rather eccentric of her to take seriously (as I thought then) the principal of primogeniture. Old Nicholas Llewellyn, you will remember, is one of the few men in her fiction who will find favor with her. But I have come to a different view of her sympathy for Nicholas. **Penhally** is no apology for primogeniture. And, in the main action of the book, his successful effort to preserve the traditional order of blood relationship by preventing Alice Blair from marrying John, his chosen heir, only brought Lucy (on whom he smiled) bitterness in marriage with John and frustration to the both of them. Moreover, as an "irony within an irony" Nicholas was able to enforce this at a time when the defeat of the traditional pattern made his position meaningless for future generations. His efforts finally, in the person of Chance Llewellyn, turn out pathetically.

I see Caroline Gordon's sympathy for birthright now as merely for an institution that in its day was symbol for family and social stability. And more than stability. I see it as a manifestation of Caroline Gordon's sacramental attitude toward her material.

I have spoken of her having been engaged in a quest incredible to the modern reader, a pilgrimage—on a way unseen but felt out with her craftsman's thorn. This sword and serpent of seven wayside incantations has come to flower at last in *The Malefactors.* For I consider that work more than a triumph of art. And I think her instinct was true in selecting the only material available to her that might lead her to this goal. But perhaps I had better say this another way.

Let us recall that at this time humanism was in its phase of the Economic Man and that Marxism was the delusive social salvation of the day. The world was substantially secularized by then. They were lightless years for sanctity. In this dim hour Caroline Gordon turned to her Southern past for meaning.

Perhaps it would be relevant to recall here that this was about the time that a group of Caroline Gordon's fellow Southerners (several of whom were close to her in feeling and outlook) published that first protest against an uncritical ardor for industrialism in the United States—*I'll Take My Stand.* Though various, the essays in this symposium tended to re-examine our agrarian past sympathetically in search of *something,* something lost. It may have eluded definition at the time, but one of the group, Donald Davidson, has in retrospect suggested its metaphysical nature.

On rereading Caroline Gordon's early novels I am more convinced than ever that she turned to the society of the ante-bellum South for her material, not because of any delusion that there was life left in its wrecked and prostrate body, and not with any sentimental notion of sanctifying its memory. Indeed, it was her revulsion to sentimentality that sent her to this traditional order. Caroline Gordon carried on her long wake over the already laid out corpse of agrarian society in the South, because only there, in this whole land, remained any odor of sanctity.

If remote from the Christian Middle Ages, still agrarianism's heritage of responsibilities, of manners, morals and virtues retained more Christianity in them than all of Protestantism's pulpit splintering. A relic enhanced by the smell of distant saints.

Caroline Gordon understood that Southern society was already undone at the time of the Civil War. Recall the irresponsible commitment to the chase of Aleck Maury's Uncle James and his company in old Virginia, and the ironic figure of old Nicholas Llewellyn. Aleck Maury, himself, is a testament to a society out of balance. These were men whom the order of their day did not seriously occupy. The plantation was growing matriarchal, the men uncurious. And in *Penhally* and *None Shall Look Back,* as well as *Aleck Maury, Sportsman,* most of her men are weak, or frustrated, or spiritually exhausted. It is charac-

teristic of the decay of any masculine society that the men (its leaders) rot first.

Woman is the conservator, the vessel for the preservation of order. Thus, as we should expect, Caroline Gordon's early heroines still retain integrity, are endowed with virtue and pride. Knowing the ante-bellum South to be more Stoic than Christian, she suspected (one senses) that it was but counterfeit feudalism, too. Yet there were inviolables and an attitude of reverence toward them, there was sanctity. And the Lucys and the Charlotte Allards and the Molly Fayerlees, in their pride, preserved it. Indeed, they are women still capable of love. The complication is that they cannot find a worthy lover.

Andrew Lytle has said (in reviewing *The Forest of the South*) "As Caroline Gordon's novels show, the true antagonist is woman. Manhood best defines itself in the stress between the sexes, which is the source of physical and spiritual human intercourse."

Sex relationships, to be sure, are the stock in trade of drama and fiction. That isn't the point. Throughout Caroline Gordon's stories this dramatic conflict constitutes the axis on which her fictional world turns. It is fundamental to her understanding of human experience. It is the creative core in nature by which she intuits life's meaning. And it is the key by which she eventually unlocks a material world to the Christian spirit.

In the progression of Caroline Gordon's heroines, Mr. Lytle sees emerging as theme "What Life, the sly deceiver, does to womankind but particularly to the woman of great passion and sensibility."

I do not disagree with that finding, except as to the abstractness with which it is stated. "Life," yes, but life within the history of Southern agrarian society. (Cathy in *Green Centuries,* may seem an historical exception. But after all, the Tennessee-Kentucky frontier was proto-Southern). Life, that still breathes the values of the Southern way and burns with its pride.

And these values and that pride find their tragic immolation in Caroline Gordon's great Civil War story, *None Shall Look Back.* As Mr. Lytle has pointed out, it is a tragedy and "death becomes the Adversary"—and, among other levels of action, the Adversary in a love triangle, as the "Dark Lady" who steals Rives Allard's affections from his wife. "The moment of greatest passion," he says, "is the moment when Lucy recognizes her loss of Rives in the pre-knowledge of his death." And he concludes, "The heroine has a rival at last equal to the demands of her pride."

Pride it may be, but pride at its death. For, in Rives' dying, die the love and the virtue, and the pride as well that makes Lucy what she is, that motivate her—the intensity of meaning within a socieity that gives it sanctity.

Recall Lucy's tense terse abject moment of goodbye: "The pistols settled into their leather jackets, one on either side of his waist. His face was still bent down. She put her hands behind her to hide their trembling. She said: 'Yes.' You are going away. I may never see you again, but I will desire you all my life. 'Yes' she whispered, 'even a note.' "

When Caroline Gordon's *heroine,* in the person of Letty Allard, appears again in a novel (*The Garden of Adonis*) the Civil War is more than sixty years past and the disintegration of Southern society is far advanced. And now (the Great Depression of the 1930's) the corruption extends to Caroline Gordon's heroine, too.

Perhaps to highlight this corruption (and that of a lesser figure, Letty's counterpart, Idelle) Caroline Gordon has, so to speak, preserved two heroes in formaldehyde—Letty's father, the appealing Mister Ben and his tenant Ote Mortimer. They sparkle in colors brightened by the chemical of unreality, and move with the grace of sacrificial goats. And their hecatomb to the god of chaos is fired, each by his prostitute priestess. The faithless Idelle sends Ote to the murder of a Mister Ben, more subtly and indirectly, but no less surely drawn to the sacrifice by the adultery of his daughter. Under his nose, Letty befouls the Allard home with a casual guest—rotten scion of the old South.

It is noteworthy on the point of the appearance of Caroline Gordon's novels that *Green Centuries* should follow *The Garden of Adonis.* Having pursued the destruction of agrarian society to its end—to the consuming of even the embalmed relics of the virtues that once gave it an odor of sanctity, Caroline Gordon steps back in history, so to speak, to take a longer view of the American Experiment. But let me point out that she is still led by a metaphysical sense of smell—she is still bent on her quest. And her sensitive nose, in search of sanctity, turned up an astonishing discovery.

In *Green Centuries* Caroline Gordon's intuition succeeded in illuminating the flaw in the American myth of the frontier, which the more pedestrian historian and political philosopher have only come to perceive a quarter of a century later. And she did it, as I have intimated, by the unaccountable strategies of genius. She did it through an objective perspective on and aethetic distance from the Indians, did it at a time when the transmontane movement of English settlers to the west brought the two into fresh conflict and dramatic contrast. It was the odor of sanctity about an Indian society—far more primitive and generally reckoned recidivist, but still religious—by which she was able to render godless the smell of the sweat of the violent ever moving frontiersman.

To a little different purpose but nonetheless to my point, Mr. Lytle has analyzed the historical significance of *Green Centuries* acutely and at length. I quote here a paragraph that speaks my mind:

> Each long hunter, each frontiersman became a primitive, homespun Dr. Faustus. Having dismissed the Devil along with God (the Protestant belief in private communion with God is equivalent to Man-become-God) man no longer had any defense against his violation of the laws of nature, nor any absolute set of principles to which he might refer the processes of reason. His plight is more terrifying than that of the protagonist of Greek drama, whose fated action achieved the dignity of suffering the inscrutable will of the gods. The unbalance of a purely masculine society, sharpened by the appearance of the Indian feminine society and therefore no true opponent to the European . . . becomes the complication determining the action of *Green Centuries.*

But it is in the love relation between her man and her woman, between Rion Outlaw and Cathy that we find the core of the action that delivers Caroline Gordon's meaning. Their love has broken down under the unbearable burdens of the westward movement. At the end Rion, apostrophizing his star, reflects:

"His father had come west across the ocean, leaving all that he cared about behind. And he himself as soon as he had grown to manhood had looked at the mountains and could not rest until he knew what lay beyond them." Like Orion, "fixed upon his burning wheel . . . he had lost himself in the turning. Before him lay the empty west, behind him the loved things of which he was made." Among these last were his brother whom he murdered and his wife who has just died.

It isn't her physical death that is the measure of his loss, however. For their love has been demeaned, betrayed, wasted in the grip of the wilderness. And there is the deadening of moral sensibility and moral responsibility. Yet, we sense it is not any one of these, in itself, nor all of them. They are but the symptoms and effects of the malady.

In her next novel, *The Women on the Porch,* Caroline Gordon brings this disease to definition.

The story in its main lines of action tells about Jim and Catherine Chapman who—having lost their direction in marriage and gone on the rocks through his adultery—find their way back together in a new love. The action opens with Catherine's flight from her husband to her mother's ancestral home, from New York to rural Tennessee, from a circus to a cemetery.

Catherine is Caroline Gordon's heroine a generation away from her Southern heritage and her deepest knowledge of it comes to her, you might say, through her genes. Being an instinctual woman, though lost, she is not deeply corrupted.

As Miss Cowan has remarked, "Marriage itself—in its idea and its actuality—is the subject of this novel." And Caroline Gordon uses it as a direction-finder in a confused secular world.

Chapman, the historian, provides the enlarged (from that of *Green Centuries*) perspective to view the westward flight in its true significance. He epitomizes it in an apostrophe to the city, the brilliance and beauty of which Mr. Lytle has remarked on. I surely agree with him and I do not disagree with his interpretation of Chapman's "O City" as symbol of "the apparent triumph of the masculine impulse toward godhead." But I see another significance in the symbol and the apostrophe.

The city is symbol, too, for traditional European culture. It is from the "dead" in this civilization that the queen bee takes her wild flight westward.

Chapman, the observer, now finds himself out of moral necessity, an actor, too. He recognizes his own rootlessness in turning to his fugitive wife and her ghostly country. But he seeks more. It is only after she is gone that he sees his extra-marital sexual relation as adultery. And, as moral realization comes, he asks himself "Did the woman who once truly received a man become the repository of his real being and thenceforward, witch-like, carry it with her where ever she went?"

That is the question that takes him back to her.

In the interlude, Catherine has had an affair with her grandmother's neighbor, Tom Manigault, rich, would-be farmer. Out of the tomb, a new Eden has risen, she believes briefly. But by the time Chapman arrives she has found out that Tom is flawed by an oedipus complex.

Yet her delusion still engages her and she is hostile when Chapman, seeking forgiveness, wants to take her back. Defiantly, she confesses her adultery with Manigault.

This triggers—to use Caroline Gordon's simile—like a jack-in-the-box sprung by a careless hand, the passion that wells up in him from the depths of his nature and from the agony of a soul seeking direction and identity. He chokes her—"not to be alone in the abyss into which her words had plunged him." Her automatic digging at his hands brings him to loose her short of strangulation.

But Nature has re-established the marriage bond.

From his wife's lost *land,* Chapman views the oncoming phantoms of the westward migration now, to define the enchantment upon them, the spell of the old Gaelic goddess, Cleena, who created the delusion of a land of perpetual youth, a utopia. The flight, then, is from self, the ego from the id, from reality.

Catherine's final disillusionment comes with the unexpected death of her Cousin Willy's young stallion, symbol of her new found Eden. This makes real for her the deeper significance of her own repudiation of her affair with Manigault, when—in Miss Cowan's words—"arising from the sylvan couch she thought to call her wedding bed to find herself lost in the woods: 'I have made a mistake' " she thinks; 'I have taken the wrong road'. . . ."

So Jim's and Catherine's first step out of "the wood" comes with their discovery of the sacramental nature of marriage.

Vivienne Koch, in her essay, "The Conservatism of Caroline Gordon," speaks of *The Women on the Porch* as an "exploratory work." And Ashley Brown ("Caroline Gordon and the Impressionistic Novel") calls it "transitional." To be sure a case can be made for that view. In a sense, all of Caroline Gordon's novels before *The Malefactors* were exploratory and transitional. And a bit more than that, in this case. But in view of my thesis here, I would apply those adjectives rather to the novel that followed.

If Caroline Gordon's quest had taken her toward Christian mysticism and eventually met with personal conversion, as an artist she had still another problem. Perhaps I should say another aspect of her problem—if one looks at her fiction as self-realization. Yet the second problem, if not divorced from the first, is still very different. Within the limits of her observation and experience, she had to find the terms of moral conviction and Christian salvation in the context of contemporary life. And she had to invent a strategy and tactic to give them dramatic weight, to make the action real.

In the light of her accomplishment in *The Malefactors,* I would even call *The Strange Children* prefatory. It is, in my view, at once her cleverest (and at the time most accomplished) and slightest work. But it was necessary. It was necessary, not merely to her Christian ordeal, but to the composition of the epic *whole,* the form and unity of her *oeuvre.*

There is no central dramatic actor in *The Strange Children,* in the sense of *reversal.* No one is changed, or saved, through the action of this social comedy. The viewpoint is placed with nine-year-old Lucy, daughter of Stephan and Sarah Lewis who, if not the protagonists of, are at least the hosts to the play.

Lucy is an interesting and very much alive child and she does, perhaps, experience something like *conviction* (and unburdens her "sin") at the end. But Lucy, as an action in the play, is sacrificed to Lucy as a device for getting the story across. And the final comment on the action is in her father's voice. He seems awed by a Christian premonition, if not conviction. But here the story ends.

Regarding the novel as introductory to her next great work, it appears to me that Caroline Gordon here brings today's strange children from their cynical mirth into the light of Christian reality. And she dramatically presents the nature of conviction and the way to salvation.

I have said that all of Caroline Gordon's fiction is, in a sense, a progress toward *The Malefactors,* I have suggested that her work composes an epic quest. The pattern might be likened to that of a hunting dog, true to her scent—a cold-nosed hound on the trail of Old Red, Himself. There have been circuits, and stands, and a change of field. But in her final go, she has run Him to ground.

Categorically, *The Malefactors* is a story of Christian *conversion*—the conversion of Tom Claiborne, poet, approaching middle age, seemingly forsaken by his muse and suffering a deep malaise. But that tells little.

What is it that Caroline Gordon has done here?

One of the most lucid reviews of the novel at the time it was published in [the 13 April 1956 issue of *Commonweal*] was that of the Rev. John W. Simmons, a Catholic priest and English professor. "After a period of *longueurs,* futilities and indirections," says Father Simmons, "he becomes the frantic victim of a Divine ambuscade. . . . But from the point of view of art, what happens is less important than the strategy by which it is accomplished."

Father Simmons combines peculiar qualifications for a judgment here. He weights its difficulties:

> A conversion is admittedly a special invasion of Grace into a particular life. If the artist, in his effort to summon the mystery, gives a maximum plausibility to the motives and conditions leading up to conversion he risks an attenuation of the essentially free character of Grace. If he

Gordon, at far left, with Anne Goodwin Winslow, Andrew Lytle, Edna Lytle, Nancy Tate, Allen Tate, Robert Lowell, and Jean Stafford in Monteagle in 1942-43.

gives a maximum permissiveness to Grace he risks making his character seem the puppet of Grace. In this case it is the art which seems implausible, for God becomes an almost literal *deus ex machina.* Highly endowed artists from Corneille to Graham Greene have either foundered on the rocks or been sucked into the whirlpool. Only Bernanos, for all his *gaucherie,* has come close to accomplishing this miracle.

I have quoted Father Simmons at length, not only because of his authority, but of the discrimination with which he speaks. After surveying in considerable detail the "resources" Caroline Gordon calls into play to bring Claiborne through the hazardous *passage* for her readers, he concludes, when I had finished the history of Tom Claiborne—obviously and not too implausibly in the toils of Grace—I was more than ever in admiration of a novelist who had not only avoided with her usual consistency the clichés of her craft but had come closer than any vernacular writer to encompassing the elusive miracle.

This acknowledges a remarkable success.

Yet, I am convinced that Father Simmons fails finally to perceive Caroline Gordon's greater accomplishment. By

his own admission he does not appreciate that *Divine ambuscade* that reveals God to Tom Claiborne.

In this hour of secular man's four-dimensional uncertainty, holding his bowels in his own hands, trembling before the prospect of his blowing the earth to pieces and eyeing Venus and/or Mars in the delusion of escape, Caroline Gordon has not only made experimental for him the malaise of a fellow victim. Through analogy and paradox meaningful to him, she has revealed Grace in Action.

Or, if you prefer the Action of Grace through the effect of her dead poet, Horne Watts, on various actors in her drama, and on Claiborne in particular. Whether this unorthodox and unchurchly instrument of salvation is considered as purely fictional or as the proto-type of Hart Crane, he is appropriate to an age obsessed by licentiousness—urbane homosexuality equally with feline rut.

Father Simons says he cannot escape equating Pontifex (the name of the poem in the novel) with Crane's *The Bridge.* And I believe this is the author's intention. For thereby the action gains another dramatic dimension. But Father Simmons canfind no analogy between *The Bridge* and Saint Catherine of Sienna's *Dialogo Divino,* to identify Crane's poem with established sanctity.

He should have carried his transposition to "real life" on to identify the fictional work of Sister Immaculata with that of Sister Bernetta Quinn, who has in fact done just such an essay—the idea for which she attributes to Caroline Gordon:

> Whether consciously or not, Crane presents his Bridge as a concretization of God considered in terms of the Incarnation—an idea at least as old as the thirteenth century when Saint Catherine of Sienna used it as the focal symbol in her Dialogues.

And after developing the parallel, Sister Bernetta concludes:

> All this is not to say that in 'Proem' Crane deliberately selected Jesus Christ as the tenor of his metaphor, or (what is far less likely) that he had read Saint Catherine of Sienna, but rather that his mind, hungry for the Absolute, reached out to Roebling's triumph of engineering as one way of expressing the means to union with his Creator, so passionately and blindly desired under all his excesses.

There are many both intentional and unintentional aids to Tom Claiborne's conversion, as Father Simmons points out. There is Tom's wife, Vera, through her love and dependence on him that drove her to attempt suicide and by her being a Catholic, too. There is George Crenfew, Tom's Virgil, as Mr. Brown has pointed out. And Max Shull, with his paintings of Saint Eustace. And others.

But it is Horne Watts (in Claiborne's dream) who finally halts Tom's flight and turns him toward Grace. And it is Watts' representative in life, Catherine Pollard, in whom Claiborne first sees Christ and from whom he receives the kiss of Christ.

Watts, then, is the mysterious *way* in which God reveals Himself to this victim of a prolonged and abortive season of *humanism.* It seems to me that Horne Watts, through Hart Crane's *The Bridge* (with Sister Immaculata's recognition of the real motive of Watts' quest, supported by Sister Bernetta Quinn's essay) may have brought to the Action of Grace on Tom Claiborne something real to his secular fellow men.

Romano Guardini has said, "When a human being in the grip of divine power attempts to convey something of the holy otherness he tries one earthly simile after another. In the end he discards them all as inadequate and says apparently wild and senseless things meant to startle the heart into feeling what lies beyond the reaches of the brain." Guardini was speaking of The Beatitudes.

The truth of what Caroline Gordon has done—however she accomplishes it—lies in our realizing what Tom Claiborne finally found in Horne Watts' (or Hart Crane's) poem—that is, a recognition of man's ontological motivation—toward God, however impaled in flesh he may be.

Brainard Cheney, "Caroline Gordon's Ontological Quest," in Renascence, *Vol. XVI, No. 1, Fall, 1963, pp. 3-12.*

James E. Rocks   (essay date 1968)

[*In the essay below, Rocks discusses how* The Strange Children *exemplifies the pivotal point of Gordon's career, demonstrating the transition from the agrarian themes of her earlier fiction to her emphasis on Christian mysticism in her later works.*]

Caroline Gordon's Catholicism, as presented in her two latest novels, ***The Strange Children*** (1951), and ***The Malefactors*** (1956), is of a rather special kind, one that advocates the practice of the highest theological virtue, charity or Christian love. Eschewing pride, which negates the kind of understanding and sympathy deficient in the characters of her earlier novels, her Catholics seek selfless devotion to man and God, even if at times their means seem strangely at odds with these noble aims. Moreover, they are curious about the historical traditions, theology, and lore of their religion, and they pursue the contemplative life of service, very often and significantly in close contact with the land.

Miss Gordon's Catholicism is not easily won, however, for the struggle to find, then define and practice, this faith is not unlike the ontological search made by characters in her earlier novels. Her Catholics may not be good representatives of religion, simply because their feet are too obviously made of clay. If not idols they are complex human beings, who are—to borrow a ready example from another religious context—like Bunyan's Christian in quest of the Celestial City by way of Vanity Fair and the Slough of Despond. Her Catholics are those who experience the rigors of conversion or who strive to retain their inherited faith.

As a drama of conversion *The Strange Children* stands in an important position in Miss Gordon's intellectual growth. Although perhaps not her finest work of fiction, *The Strange Children* does mark the transition in her thinking from the agrarian myth to the Christian myth. Furthermore, this novel utilizes well those fictional techniques that are at the very center of her critical attitude. Having learned much from Flaubert, James, Conrad, Ford Madox Ford, and Joyce, Miss Gordon insists upon the informing techniques of these impressionistic novelists. Most particularly she argues for the containment of materials within the ordering principle of a consistent narrative point of view. *The Strange Children* is one of her best examples of the use of a unified post of observation, the Jamesian central intelligence, a single authority which can provide as well for tonal unity and structural coherence. Also, this novel employs the scenic techniques of drama, from which genre Miss Gordon has borrowed the concepts of complication, climax, discovery, catastrophe, and resolution. Symbol, myth, and archetypal patterns are further components of Miss Gordon's fictional creation. Her interest in myth, it might be said, follows Fugitive-Agrarian thinking: belief in a myth provides for continuity of experience and for traditional human values. *The Strange Children* is, then, a highly representative work of Caroline Gordon's intellectual and artistic maturity; an examination of it reveals the habits of her mind and the manner of her art.

A glance at Miss Gordon's growth into Roman Catholicism and her conversion in the late forties will help to explain the emergence in her art of highly structured religious themes. Each of her novels and short stories up to *The Strange Children* provides direction in the search for a stable order or morality, in short, a myth, to give coherence to the apparent flux and chaos of human existence. From the beginning of her career, when she was sympathetic to the Agrarian movement, to her conversion to Roman Catholicism, Miss Gordon examined and rejected her Southern heritage in an effort to secure a set of beliefs that would replace the traditions of her defunct antebellum morality. Those pathways on the road to Rome reveal the reasons why Miss Gordon's literary career epitomizes the artist's quest for meaning.

In all of her fiction, particularly *None Shall Look Back* (1937), Miss Gordon admits that the agrarian ethic of the South before the Civil War will no longer serve the regrettably altered world of the modern commercial South. Her first novel, *Penhally* (1931), dramatizes this painful truth. Chance Llewellyn's heroic endeavor to turn the tide of encroaching commercialism results in the catastrophic murder of his materialistic brother Nick. Representative of the schizoid nature of the modern South, Chance and Nick enact the tragic conflict of alienated brothers in a world of discord.

Penhally ends on a definite note of regret: the agrarian life, with its value derived from an intimate contact with the natural world, is still worth living. Aleck Maury, the hero of Miss Gordon's second novel, *Aleck Maury, Sportsman* (1934), and several excellent stories, "Old Red" (1933), "To thy Chamber Window, Sweet" (1934), "The Last Day in the Field" (1935), "One More Time" (1935), and "The Presence" (1948), spends his life trying to prove that man finds meaning in his natural rather than his social environment. But like Cooper's Leatherstocking or the Hemingway protagonist, with whom Maury can be compared, the hunter prototype grows old, becomes lame, and must finally confront his only significant foe, death. In "The Presence" the aged and infirm Maury turns momentarily to the religion of his beloved Aunt Victoria and senses finally that nature may be as much his antagonist as his sustainer. Death, as nature's primary agent, is man's ultimate opponent, as Maury must finally realize. But the even greater agony of death-in-life is, however, the inheritance of those modern Southerners, like the characters in *The Garden of Adonis* (1937) and *The Women on the Porch* (1944), who cannot find a morality to replace the traditions of their ancestral social order because of their determined efforts to clutch with desperation at the dead idols of their agrarian heritage.

The agrarian life and its corresponding values can serve only as a provisional or complementary ethic, or so Miss Gordon seems to be saying in *The Women on the Porch.* As the novel ends Catherine and Jim Chapman reunite, but no answer is offered for the possibility of a successful reconciliation. Human relations—most importantly, love between man and woman—require a transcendent order, some myth which, while not denying the natural or physical worlds, will provide meaning in a chaotic modern world, one in which man suffers from the so-called dissociated sensibility, a contemporary *mal du siècle.*

The critics and poets, particularly, of the Southern Renaissance originally derived much of their concern and need for just such a discipline and authority from T. S. Eliot and T. E. Hulme. Thus, for example, in appropriating a tradition of fiction the principal Fugitives and Agrarians, who became the New Critics of the forties, and their followers could readily accept the school of Flaubert and James, as did Miss Gordon, with its emphasis on the artistic ordering of materials, on certain fictional "rules," on the artist's need for self-discipline, and on the concept of tradition itself. The myth of the agrarian South provided man, in their opinion, with an ordering authority or public morality, but when the Civil War destroyed that myth the Southerner had to look in a new direction for a new authority. Miss Gordon accepts Hulme's classic position of religious orthodoxy and of man's inheritance of original sin, and thus for her—or so it would seem—the natural step from the conservative traditions and social standards of the ante-bellum South was her conversion to Roman Catholicism, a religion which encompasses both the principle of order and a belief in the gifts of grace and salvation residing in the Christian conception of God.

Particularly in the light of her Southern heritage, Miss Gordon's intellectual growth from agrarianism to religious orthodoxy represents the successful quest for a permanent morality. Only hinting in her fiction of the late forties, she bears witness fully to her conversion in *The Strange Children,* a novel which, not unlike her earlier fiction, draws extensively upon her Southern past, in fact, upon her own family experiences. Lucy Lewis, the central intelligence of the novel, is the granddaughter of sportsman Aleck Maury and the only child of Stephen and Sarah, characters who appear throughout the Maury novel and short stories and who might be said to represent the fictional transformation of Miss Gordon and Allen Tate. The setting is their former home, Benfolly, in the Tennessee town of Gloversville, the fictional name for Clarksville, where Mr. and Mrs. Tate lived for a time in the thirties. Like her outspoken grandfather Aleck and unlike her evasive parents, Lucy escapes the social world for the natural world, strongly indifferent to the sterile intellectuality which Benfolly (whose name signals, in part, Miss Gordon's judgment of it) has come to represent in this modern generation. Like Aleck in his later years, Lucy begins to reject this life more and more as she grows to understand it.

At one point Stephen says to Lucy, "You are always hanging around, listening to grown people talk." Indeed, Lucy at age nine is nosy, precocious, and very perceptive—one is rather tempted to call her a brat—but she must necessarily possess these qualities in order to serve as an effective central intelligence of the novel. The use of a child as reflector permits an ironic center, as James called his intelligence in *What Maisie Knew* (a novel that in technique is comparable to *The Strange Children,* although Miss Gordon has denied being influenced by it). James chose Maisie as his intelligence because her innocence, notwithstanding an acute response to detail and innuendo, presumably allows for a clarity of presentation and an absence of prejudice. Innocence, in other words, records with accuracy. As James said in his preface to the novel, the reader must constantly amplify and understand what Maisie observes; this is possible because the reader has a more refined insight, which interprets what the intelligence can only see. What James said of his own novel is true in large part of *The Strange Children.*

Lucy as principal reflector gives the novel a unity not unlike that achieved through a first-person narration. Furthermore, *The Strange Children* possesses a coherence unknown in Miss Gordon's other novels, engineered in part by the unities of time (the action lasts only several days), place (with one exception the scene is Benfolly), and plot (Lucy's growing realization in the context of that world). The effect of course is to qualify *The Strange Children* as Miss Gordon's most dramatic work. The preponderance of conversation, with Lucy as sole spectator, is part of the dramatic quality of the novel, as it is of *What Maisie Knew.* The conversations, moreover, replace the flashbacks, which occur in very modified form in Lucy's thoughts, and fill in the essential background information, which in the new context takes on meaning and prepares for the climax of the novel during the game of charades.

The complex symbolism in the novel establishes, furthermore, a powerful structural unity and works a coherence largely sustained by the motifs of enchantment and quest. With its obvious relevance of the Catholic theme, the quest motif merges with the medievalism of "La Belle Dame Sans Merci," "Kubla Khan," "The Lady of Shalott," *Le Morte d'Arthur* and particularly *Undine,* all of which are mentioned in the novel. *Undine,* the early nineteenth-century allegory by de la Motte-Fouqué, stimulates Lucy's vivid imagination. References to Undine, with its story of the mortal-spirit world, are relevant to both the themes and symbols of the novel.

Lucy is not unlike the water nymph Undine, who gains a soul by marrying the mortal knight Huldbrand. Lucy, too, is transformed in the course of her experiences, and although she may not acquire a soul through marriage she does undergo a kind of unrecognized conversion by realizing that her parents' world, with its meaningless exchange of liquor and sexual favors and gossip, fails to achieve the sort of grace epitomized in Kevin Reardon. Her parents' friend Tubby, remarking about the marriage of Undine and the knight, comments significantly that the nymph afterwards makes a lot of trouble for everyone. Lucy, in her own outspoken way, makes unsettling remarks to those around her, but because of their tacit indifference to her presence they fail to understand what she can see. Furthermore, water nymphs like Undine, who tantalize and enchant mortal men, are not much different from the *belles dames sans merci*—Isabel Reardon in this novel, for example—who continually delight the unsuspecting men in all of Miss Gordon's fiction. As Lucy reflects with profound insight, "The gentlemen all seemed to be afraid of these strange ladies, but they were always going around where they were." As Undine charmed Huldbrand, so does Isabel charm her husband Kevin, then their friend Tubby.

Lucy lives in an imaginative world peopled by the characters from Undine, in part because the human world of Benfolly exists as an impenetrable enigma. Lucy projects herself onto Undine, wondering what it would be like to live on the bottom of the sea. A stream flowing underground through the Lewis estate seems to Lucy like a cool flood, a kind of haven from the parched, dry earth of the farm. Suggestive both of the buried creative life (cf. "Kubla Khan") and of the corresponding waters of salvation, the stream becomes symbolic of an unknown, submerged existence—in one context (Lucy's for example), the search for a more meaningful reality than the present one, in another (Tubby's or Isabel's or the Lewises'), the inability to recognize a need to regenerate the lost soul. The water symbolism in the novel is, however, more complex because it is more varied: water often suggests a fluctuating, uncertain reality, imperceptibly distorted, as in the scene during which Tubby and Isabel go boating and swimming with Lucy, who for the first time senses that their relationship goes beyond friendship. This new reality is clear to Lucy, the water spirit—that is, within her ability to understand an affair; but Tubby does not yet know that Isabel is incurably insane. In *The Strange Children* water ranges in meaning, then, from death to salvation.

Similarly, the eye reveals the state of the inner life, either of spiritual torpor or of grace. Lucy observes the look of the eye in various individuals, comparing them in terms of deep water. Tubby's eyes, which have no vision, are black holes; to look into them is like falling into turbulent water (here the idea of water as destruction is apparent). On the other hand, Kevin's dark eyes, which are deep wells, brim over with light, the light of spiritual insight. Lucy herself, whose name means "light," has gray eyes, the indistinct color appropriate to her own uncertain spiritual condition, one which can view impartially but which, it might be said, is attracted to the brilliance of Kevin's eyes. Moreover, Lucy is drawn to the rich radiance both of Kevin's crucifix and of the altar in the nearby Catholic Church. She cannot, of course, attribute meaning to these phenomena in the larger religious context, but she is nevertheless lured toward that context through an attraction to light, the basic condition of vision, most noteworthy in terms of spiritual insight.

Further symbolism in the novel is derived from particulars out of the Southern past. Like Swan Quarter to Catherine in *The Women on the Porch* or Merry Point to Aleck Maury in *"Old Red,"* Benfolly, with its long family history, seems blank and strange to Lucy. She cannot respond to the traditions which it represents because, as a young person, she can find no reliable meaning in the past. Stephen, who concentrates his energies on the Civil War, seems removed, indifferent, and aloof to his daughter, just as he does to Maury in *"Old Red."* A portrait of Stonewall Jackson stares past her "unseeingly," with the same lack of penetrating insight as in the dull eyes of modern men like Tubby. Jackson stands in the opinion of Stephen (Tate wrote a biography of this general) for the great virtues of the ante-bellum South, but for the younger generation he represents a past which has somehow lost its relevance to the modern world. Stephen and Sarah still look back, whereas Lucy begins to look up to a higher religious reality. Curiously, in a biographical reading of the novel, Miss Gordon is dramatizing her own quest through Lucy, while at the same time presenting her earlier views through her fictional guise, Sarah; this use of a double vision provides an interesting tension in the novel and serves to indicate the transition in Miss Gordon's thought.

There is, finally, one other prominent symbol. A family of Holy Rollers, the MacDonoughs, whose religious beliefs are in contrast both to Kevin's Catholicism and the others' smug secularism, live as tenants at Benfolly. Nearby they have painted the ominous words "Prepare to Meet Thy God" on a large rock. Understandably the admonition makes Sarah and Stephen nervous, but not particularly because they see any need for redemption in their own lives. Their rather ironic view of the goings-on at the Holy Roller camp meeting obscures any understanding they might gain from applying the MacDonoughs' faith to their own lives. The fundamentalism of this group, in strong contrast to the Catholicism of Reardon, does engage his curiosity, because he can see the universal values of humility and charity that guide their lives. For a time, Lucy, too, sees the simple beliefs of these people as a substitute for the spiritual desert of Benfolly.

These symbols do, of course, contribute structural unity to the novel, but, more important, their meanings, although unclearly comprehended by young Lucy, make her sense even more conclusively her antagonism toward a world of values which she realizes are wrong but against which she can do nothing. Alienated from her father, whose retreat into the past is broken only by an occasional bow toward the present, and her mother, whose ebullience is a thin veneer covering a great but inarticulated spiritual malaise, Lucy must create her reality in the child's imaginative world of dreams and visions. When the tedium of Benfolly is broken by the arrival of Tubby, Kevin, and Isabel, who represent the eternal triangle of love, Lucy at first turns more desperately to the fiction of Undine and to the apparently humble pietism of the MacDonoughs. Finally, however, these three individuals direct her vision spiritually upward rather than selfishly inward or morally backward. With their arrival the novel moves rapidly to scenes of crisis and catastrophe, whose meaning, in the light of what is revealed about Kevin and Isabel Reardon, deserves consideration.

Kevin and Isabel initiate a change of direction in the novel; they precipitate the eventual catastrophe and dramatize before Lucy's vision the very values which emerge from the novel: damnation versus grace. Kevin's own life has been a rejection and search, an example of the Christian quest for salvation. Tubby says, in one of his moments of insight, although he means to jest, that Kevin's conversion to Catholicism illustrates a pursuit of the father image. Kevin's own mother left his father after he renounced a life of material gain for one of spiritual contemplation, the very same repudiation that Kevin would later effect. Like his father, Kevin underwent a spiritual experience (his vision after an auto accident), which caused him to evaluate his own life of riotous living and to find it wanting. Realizing that strait is the gate into heaven, he plans to give his fortune to the Trappist order and then enter a life of selfless meditation.

Such facts as these are brought out in conversations and scenes at which Lucy is conveniently present. She first meets Kevin in the darkness of night, an appropriate time for an initial confrontation with this most mysterious of men. As she is drawn to the brilliant light of his eyes, so is she attracted to his radiant crucifix, which she steals, just as Stephen had picked up his Croix de Guerre without apparent reason years before. Like her father, Lucy is subconsciously lured by the magnet of Kevin's peculiar powers and accomplishments. Lucy first sees Isabel moments after Kevin; a confusing woman to everyone except Sarah, Isabel looks into Lucy's eyes with a straight and steady regard, suggestive of possible enlightenment. Isabel wins Lucy's friendship with the gift of a small, decorated box, into which the stolen crucifix will fit. Lucy thinks that Isabel presented her with this box specifically for Kevin's crucifix, and in her confusion, therefore, she tends to think of Kevin and Isabel in the same terms. It soon becomes evident that Isabel, who escaped from her Midwest origins to the world of American expatriates and three marriages, is the typical dominating and selfish woman in Miss Gordon's fiction, demanding considerable allegiance and satisfaction from her man and accustomed to the frivolous activities that wealth and status-seeking might offer. When Kevin decided to renounce that life she broke under the strain and became emotionally unstable. Tubby, who sees the conflict only from Isabel's point of view, maintains that Kevin is confining Isabel, the victim of her eccentric husband's religious mania. But Isabel totters, nevertheless, on a thin wire of sanity, and in a very significant scene her usual balance is lost.

This scene of substantial importance occurs about midpoint in the novel and serves as a crisis. A diversion in the form of a game of charades is proposed (curiously, these people have all along been acting out their vapid lives in clever little dramas with mute histrionics). Tubby decides to enact the name of Parnell, the nineteenth-century Irish nationalist, whose marital problems might alone have shaken this particular gathering. As Tubby explains, Parnell, a name which means "a priest's mistress," is derived from St. Patronella, who before her conversion was a prostitute.

During the tableau, which Kevin calls a sacrilege, Tubby portrays a priest and Isabel, significantly, the mistress. Isabel soon begins to cry, undoubtedly because she senses that the others are aware of her affair with Tubby and, also, because the jarring overtones of the example of St. Patronella's conversion resound too clearly in the context of her own life. During the charade, Lucy holds one of the priest's garments, a costume, of course, but the imitation has a particular although unrecognized meaning for her. Lucy hears the voices of the Holy Rollers at their camp meeting mingling with Tubby's Latin intonation, different voices which Lucy must soon learn to interpret and evaluate. This juxtaposition of markedly opposite religious traditions symbolizes the conflict within Lucy between the simple, literal-minded piety of the MacDonoughs and the mysterious, almost occult, beauty of Kevin's Catholicism.

But just as she had been thrown into reality earlier in a fall from a pony, so must she now receive a rude awakening at the hands of this sect. These two incidents are important steps in Lucy's descent from innocence, a descent which is occasionally physically painful, as is the fall from the pony, a material possession which she had coveted but which she had wisely decided to relinquish. Lucy's rejection of this physical object, like the burying of the stallion in *The Women on the Porch,* and her understanding of the Holy Rollers' mindless enthusiasm and superstition are necessary before the growth of the true spiritual life can begin.

Soon after the game of charades, during a camp meeting—a catastrophe in the religious sphere, as Tubby's and Isabel's final departure together is one in the social sphere of the story—Lucy learns that a faith which negates reason and centers in a fundamentalist interpretation of the Bible leads only to disaster. In a fit of emotional frenzy MacDonough takes up a rattlesnake, which he implicitly believes will not strike him. During these moments of grotesque religiosity Tubby sneaks out to disappear with Isabel; both catastrophes, effected simultaneously, complete Lucy's initiation into moral awareness. Her renunciation of Isabel is symbolized in the act of throwing down the gold box; her final acceptance of Kevin is demonstrated through an act of penance, her return of the stolen crucifix.

It is not Lucy but rather Stephen who at last recognizes the full meaning of what has been happening at Benfolly. Stephen's epiphany, the last two paragraphs of the novel, is narrated from his point of view, with a curious omniscience intruding toward the end. This change of reflectors is detrimental to the novel, because, although Stephen is perhaps better able to formulate this revelation, Lucy is now completely aware of what Stephen meditates upon. The tone of the novel is elevated, of course, but unfortunately broken in this shift, because the story is Lucy's, only very incidentally that of Stephen, who plays one of the smallest roles in the novel. To change intelligences is to deny Lucy her final transformation from child to adult, from innocence to understanding—in fact, almost to invalidate the experiences which are at the very thematic center of the novel.

In these last moments, Stephen draws Lucy to his side and looks up at the heavens, seeing his own astrological sign, Scorpio—"The House of Death—unless a man be reborn." Feeling the wrath of the Last Judgment, for which none of them is prepared, he thinks of MacDonough, lying ill of a snake bite; of Kevin, once near death after an auto accident; and of Tubby, now facing an uncertain life blind to the truth of salvation:

> He passed his hand over his brow. His eyes went to the house below where a single lamp glowed murkily. There a man still lay at the point of death. He told himself that it would have been no great matter if that man had died tonight, for all men, it appeared to him now, for the first time, die on the same day: the day on which their appointed task is finished. If that man had made his last journey tonight he would not have gone alone, but companioned by a larger presence, as

the friend standing behind him had been companioned when he, too, lay at the point of death,

---

An excerpt from "Cock-Crow"

I am going to try to tell the stories of some heroes I have known, heroes, who, for the most part, received the kind of anonymity I have described as their reward. . . . In every case I believe that I first saw the heroes and heroines in the same attitude and in the same place. Each one of them was standing on the edge of an abyss. An abyss so deep and dark that no human eye has ever penetrated it. And each one of them had assumed the attitude that every one of us instinctively assumes when we realize that our lives are being threatened. Each one of them has just realized that he confronts a mortal enemy and that, therefore, the ensuing struggle is to the death.

I have been told ever since I can remember that this enemy does not exist and I cannot say what shape he takes for any one of them. I only know—from the look on their faces—that he inspires terror. I know, too, that some of them—it may be "the bravest and the best"— came to their dooms because they would not capitulate. Through a kind of mistaken bravery. It was the one rash step forward, the setting of the foot on what should have been solid ground but which, instead, was thin air, that sent them hurtling headlong into the abyss.

How do I know these things? I have ways of knowing. A novelist's ways of knowing are not the same as those by which we come to other forms of knowledge. A great novelist, one, who, himself, descended some distance into the abyss, describes better than any of us, I think, how he arrived at this awareness of the existence of the characters in his novels. They "appeared" before him, he said, and "solicited" his attention by arousing his curiosity as to what they were doing. I find that in my own case the characters who will be my ghostly companions for many a long day thereafter arouse my curiosity nearly always by some word or by one of those gestures that are more poignant than any spoken word. The word, I suspect, is often spoken, the hand cleaves the air again and again in the same gesture. These ghostly actors have a timeless patience. It does not seem to matter to them how long they wait in the wings. They are ready to walk on to the stage of the imagination of any one of us the moment their cue comes: that moment when the word first spoken so long ago vibrates in the air we ourselves are breathing, when the head is uplifted by the same call, the step forward or backward taken at the same challenge.

Every one of us has his ghostly company, of course. And they are all heroes. Being heroes, they all fight the same fight. They confront the powers of darkness. For that has always been the task of the hero, the confrontation of the supernatural in one or other of those forms which men of every age have labelled "monstrous."

Caroline Gordon, in her "Cock-Crow," in The Southern Review, *July 1965.*

in a strange country and in a desert. But all countries, he told himself wearily, are strange and all countries desert. He thought of another man, the friend of his youth, who only a few minutes ago had left his house without farewell. He had considered him the most gifted of all his-intimates. Always when he thought of that friend a light had seemed to play about his head. He saw him now standing at the edge of a desert that he must cross: if he turned and looked back his face would be featureless, his eye sockets blank. Stephen Lewis thought of days, or years that they had spent together. He saw that those days, those years had been moving toward this moment and he wondered what moment was being prepared for him and for his wife and his child, and he groaned, so loud that the woman and the child stared at him, wondering, too.

Everyone in the novel, except Kevin and Lucy, who are now aware of the importance of grace, is one of the strange children referred to in the title, which is drawn from the seventh and eighth verses of Psalm 144: "Rid me, and deliver me out great waters, from the hand of strange children, whose mouth speaketh vanity....." It is paradoxically the young Lucy who is closer to redemption—unlike the adults, who are strange, alien, and inexplicable, whose words and deeds are expressions of vanity not charity. Lucy has begun her conversion—whether or not to Catholicism is, in the end, irrelevant, for it is the values of the faith which matter to her at this moment in her life. For the adult, however, like Tom Claiborne in Miss Gordon's last novel, *The Malefactors,* the quest for the religious myth leads directly to Catholicism and to a mature understanding of the transcendent values of grace and salvation.

James E. Rocks, "The Christian Myth as Salvation: Caroline Gordon's 'The Strange Children'," in TSE: Tulane Studies in English, *Vol. XVI, 1968, pp. 149-60.*

Jane Gibson Brown   (essay date Spring 1977)

[*In the following essay, Brown explains the function of myth, mythical allusions, and history in Gordon's first five novels.*]

Caroline Gordon is ONE of those writers whose work has received careful attention only by a handful of perceptive critics. Yet this body of commentary, wrought by some of the best critics of modern fiction, is nonetheless inadequate for a writer of Miss Gordon's skill and scope. For, as in the best fiction of Faulkner, the levels of meaning inherent in such novels as *Penhally, Green Centuries,* and *The Women on the Porch* mark these works as the creations of a master whose craftsmanship matches her complex vision of human life and community. Lesser writers of the twentieth century have commanded greater attention, one suspects, only because Miss Gordon demands more of her readers than many are willing to give; and one must remember that the tremendous body of criticism devoted to Faulkner's work grew, like Alice, to such enormous proportions only after he had been "sanctified" by the Nobel Prize committee. Shortly before that award, all of his books were out of print. Fortunately, Miss Gordon's

earlier works—including *The Forest of the South*—have recently been reprinted by Cooper Square Press; and this event must be regarded as having major significance in restoring her art to that place in the public eye it so richly deserves. Yet critics and scholars must be apprised of the rich resources this art preserves for their discovery if they are to overcome the natural reluctance of any human being to engage in hard work.

For Miss Gordon writes in "The Great Tradition" of English fiction, a tradition whose masters are such old puzzlers as Henry James, Ford Madox Ford and James Joyce. All of these writers share in common an insistence that consciousness be fully rendered through finely wrought texture. Thus every image, every syntactical turn, indeed every word, must be weighed in terms of the overall thematic implications of the action. For to read such novels is difficult for the lazy, impossible for the dull-witted or imperceptive. These restrictions eliminate many of those scholars who might otherwise devote their attentions to Miss Gordon's work: thus the small number of articles in print and the exceptionally high caliber of her more admiring critics.

Miss Gordon has provided potential commentators with some help in their difficult task by publishing two important books on the techniques of fiction, *The House of Fiction* (with Allen Tate) and *How to Read a Novel.* The former contains a collection of short stories with commentary and an appendix which is devoted to the technical problems faced by the writer in addressing his subject matter. *How to Read a Novel* is a collection of essays on the art and craft of fiction, most of which make the point through the analysis of some specific model, in some instances held up as a negative example. Combined, these volumes provide a reader with a wide avenue of approach to Miss Gordon's own novels and short stories.

Yet she does not tell everything on the printed page. In the classroom the student can learn even more about her craft, and thus far she has kept many of her secrets to be imparted only by way of the oral tradition. As a "specialist in fictional techniques"—she refuses to be called a teacher of "creative writing"—she stresses eighteenth and nineteenth century rather than contemporary models; and her most fundamental ideas concerning plot are derived from Aristotle, with some footnoting by Flaubert and Henry James. Most important to her, in this respect, are the Aristotelian concepts of complication and resolution. In teaching the structure of action she draws on the blackboard a circle and then bisects it: all that happens on one side of the circle is complication and all that happens on the other side of the circle is resolution; the peripety, that moment in which the central character "is turned around," is a wedge which she drives into the side of the resolution with a stout piece of chalk. The peripety, she insists, is an *action* rather than an idea or insight, an event which changes the course of the main character and moves him in the direction of the resolution.

In addition to her reliance on Aristotle, she also is indebted to Dante for her view of the polysemous nature of fiction. For her there is the central action (the "literal level"), the enveloping action (akin to the "allegorical level"), and the archetypal or "mythological level" (akin, perhaps, to the "moral level"). Miss Gordon insists, in the best critical tradition, that all levels must be contained in the literal level, otherwise the work is flawed, either propagandistic or else improperly didactic. She further states that all good works of fiction have meaning on at least two of these levels and a masterpiece has meaning on all three levels.

Her reliance on Aristotle and Dante suggests the radically traditional nature of her view of art in general and of the practice of her own in particular. For Aristotle's paradigmatic plot is rooted in a view of human nature which informs all of Western civilization, a view which stresses man's finitude in the face of divine cosmic order. Complication in any action results from conflict, whether internal or external; and such conflict can only be the consequence of human flaw, a failure on the part of one or more characters to measure up to his own standards or to someone else's. Given this quality of complication, then, the action that precedes the moment in which any fictional conflict is overtly revealed is nothing more than the conditions that lead up to such a revelation and hence is a logical part of the complication. Resolution, the unraveling of the complication, involves either victory or defeat in terms of the conflict (and sometimes both). Thus what occurs on either side of the conflict grows out of the nature of the human condition as fallible and temporal.

Likewise, the existence of meanings on more than one level is a concept which grows out of the assumption that what was true of man in Aristotle's time is true in every other time, including the present. Thus when any individual is engaged in certain actions, he repeats the pattern of Aristotle's plot, whether he exists in the fictional world or the real world. These actions Miss Gordon calls "archetypal," and it is about such patterns of behavior that the master writes.

But however universal such actions may be, they always occur in a particularly social and historical context; and it is this context which Miss Gordon calls "the enveloping action." In this respect it is important to understand that the enveloping action does not alter the nature of Aristotle's structure but simply imparts to it the credibility of a particular time and place. In addition, the enveloping action performs other functions, which Andrew Lytle discusses, using the term "historic image" [in his "Caroline Gordon and the Historic Image," *Sewanee Review* LVII, (Autumn 1949)].

> This historic image of the whole allows for critical awareness of a long range of vision, by equating the given period to the past and future, sometimes explicitly, always implicitly. This makes the period at once the setting and the choral comment. Such a restriction upon the imagination adds another range of objectivity to the post of observation, another level of intensity to the action (as if the actors while performing expose to the contemporary witness, the reader, the essential meaning of their time). This is literary irony at a high level. It is the nearest substitute for the religious image. In a time of eclecticism, such as ours, while it will not directly solve the

writer's simplest technical problem, it gives him balance and lessens the risk of a faulty vision in that it keeps the scale of observation from being entirely private, or of seeming so.

Thus if the enveloping action is fully rendered, the proper work of fiction will be both timeless and temporal—timeless in its repetition of the archetypal pattern of behavior, temporal in its definition of a particular society at a given moment in history. When one understands this point, Miss Gordon's attitude, as revealed in the following exchange with Louis Rubin [in "Recent Southern Fiction: A Panel Discussion," *Bulletin of Wesleyan College* LXI (Winter, 1961)] is made clear:

> [RUBIN]: *What about you, Miss Gordon; do you have a tradition you go back to when you are writing? You told me today you are writing an historical novel.*
>
> [GORDON]: All novels are historical. I don't think I told you I was writing an historical novel; I said it went back to 1832.
>
> *Well, that sounds pretty historical.*
>
> The word has become so debased. I wrote two novels, one in Civil War times and one in pioneer times; but people didn't know how to read them. I wouldn't like to be accused of writing what is known as an historical novel.

What Miss Gordon is attempting to explain is merely her belief in the necessity for a good writer to create an enveloping action for any central action, whether it occurs in the present or in the past. A work of fiction in which the author simply attempted to re-create with character the aura of a particular time and place in the past would not, for her, exist on any level at all; for the enveloping action has no real meaning that does not grow out of the literal level. In this respect, then, *The Garden of Adonis,* where the action occurs in the same decade in which it was written, would be just as "historical" to Miss Gordon as would be *None Shall Look Back,* in which the action takes place during the Civil War and highlights such features as the career of Nathan Bedford Forrest.

To say that she is not "an historical novelist," however, is not to suggest that her fiction does not reveal a definite view of history which informs every one of her earlier novels, those set in the twentieth century as well as those set in the nineteenth and eighteenth centuries. For if individual men repeat certain archetypal actions, so do nations and even civilizations. Again Miss Gordon is consistent, for her view of American history, and more particularly the history of her own region, is essentially traditionalist, indeed understandably so for one who has always held the classical world in such high regard.

As she sees her country's (region's) history, it marks a final stage in the collapse of Western civilization and hence is a tragedy in every sense of that word. As Lytle suggests, the frontier world, rendered in *Green Centuries,* is peopled with the descendants of Europeans "released from the restraint of Christian feudal forms, . . . able now for the first time to find [their] antagonist in the absolute state of wild nature." Miss Gordon might well agree, along with such historians as Frederick Jackson Turner and Henry Nash Smith, that the frontier was the crucible of democratic sensibilities and practices, but she would not view with the same cheerful optimism this American phenomenon. For her, the freedom of the wilderness led to pride and its inevitable consequence, tragic humiliation. The loss of hierarchy she would also see as catastrophic in its implications, for in feudal society every man has his place in a social and cosmic order, always under the protection as well as the authority of someone above. In such an order, where freedom is limited by responsibility, pride is reined and human action controlled by custom and ritual. Thus in *Green Centuries* Miss Gordon tells the story of Orion Outlaw's plunge into the green wilderness of Kentucky and his ultimate realization that, in rejecting the more traditional community for a greater freedom, he has lost not only those whose love he has desired but also any sense of meaning in life.

This same story is retold in *Penhally* with a different cast of characters and with a more panoramic view of history. Here Miss Gordon confronts for the first time the Old South, as represented in the house Penhally and the succeeding generations of Llewellyns who inhabit it. Unlike Orion Outlaw, Nicholas Llewellyn, the patriarchal figure, is not a "modern" promethean but a man who understands the older hierarchical vision and therefore exhibits a traditional European sensibility. Once again, however, "democratic" ideals, as exemplified by Thomas Jefferson, begin to intrude upon Nicholas' world; and Miss Gordon traces the collapse of that world into the industrial twentieth century and through four generations of Llewellyns. Thus the tragedy of the Old South is the tragedy of Europe reenacted, the loss of a formal social structure which has existed for thousands of years, in one place or another.

In *None Shall Look Back,* Miss Gordon focuses more sharply on the Civil War, which is treated less fully in *Penhally.* Here the older order is represented most clearly by Fontaine Allard and his young kinsman Rives, while modernism, the industrial mentality so destructive to agrarian traditionalism, is best understood in the corporate person of the Yankee army, though there are "homemade" Yankees among the ranks of the Allards as well. Not as artistically satisfying as *Penhally, None Shall Look Back* nevertheless dramatizes more powerfully the conflict which Miss Gordon sees working itself out in Southern and American history.

The Garden of Adonis, set in the 1930s, depicts the plight of the Allard family as they try to remain on the land after the triumph of an industrial economy. Ben Allard, the protagonist, must struggle as surely as did his ancestors to preserve the farm he inherits. However, his enemy is not William Tecumseh Sherman or the Yankee army, but an invisible economic machine whose agent is the local bank, which renews Allard's mortgage loan each year only after placing him and his tenants under the most terrible kind of pressure. The result of that pressure is a mutual distrust leading to conflict and death. Thus again Miss Gordon finds herself revealing the breakdown of an older hierarchy, or more precisely, the ultimate consequences of that breakdown.

In *Aleck Maury, Sportsman,* the last of five novels treated in this study. Miss Gordon creates a character out of the twentieth-century hunter, a contemporary counterpart of Orion Outlaw who is saved from Orion's aimlessness by a classical education which reminds him all too painfully of what has been lost. Maury is akin to other heroes of twentieth-century fiction in that he finds a private code to give his life meaning in a society dominated by industrial "robber-barons." Forsaking family and community, the essential ingredients of a traditional order, Maury allows himself to be absorbed by hunting and fishing, cherishing the activity for its own sake rather than viewing it as a means to some economic end. Thus, though he does not live as a good man would in the Old South, he does flee from the coarse pragmatism of his age into an activity affording him a kind of dignity and discipline which his more modern friends and family lack.

In reading these novels with emphasis on their historical implications, one can see the extraordinary similarities between them: similarities which result from Miss Gordon's precise understanding of her heritage, an understanding which is most specifically defined in *I'll Take My Stand,* the controversial symposium by twelve Southerners, among them the four Fugitives for whose work as a young reporter she felt an immediate affinity. She was at the time married to Allen Tate, one of the twelve; and it was during their years together that she created this important body of fiction, which well may be the greatest literary monument of the so-called "Agrarian Movement."

Several critics—among them Andrew Lytle and Ashley Brown—have recognized and explored the relationship between Miss Gordon's historical vision and the structure of her novels. And other critics—notably Louise Cowan, Thomas Landess, and Howard Baker—have talked about her use of mythology. No one, however, has defined or discussed the manner in which she uses myth to define the archetypal nature of the central and enveloping actions in her first five novels, a set of books which form a self-contained drama of the decline of the West. One could not argue that her particular use of the classics is unique; Faulkner used mythological allusion in many of his novels. No modern writer of fiction, however, has utilized classical mythology more subtly or extensively to unite action and enveloping action into a meaningful whole.

The function of myth in these novels can be understood most readily by reference to Miss Gordon's ideas about action and the various levels on which it finds meaning. For if the same actions—whose paradigm is described by Aristotle—occur in all ages, then they have their purest and most ancient statement in myth. Myths, like fairy tales, survive and have meaning to people in a later age because these stories contain the essence of actions and experiences which are familiar and meaningful even to the illiterate. Thus when a fictional action is rendered in terms of myth, the myth serves at least two important functions, one for the writer and one for the reader. First, it tends to purify in the writer's mind the action he wishes to render, so that he can see clearly those elements which are archetypal as opposed to those which are extraneous to the true meaning of his narrative. And second, it tends to emphasize for the reader the broader implications of the narrative, lest he think that what he is reading is no more than "a slice of life" uninformed by larger significance.

In novels whose actions are set in remote times, the presence of a mythological framework further reinforces all of those functions which Lytle attributes to the "historic image." And in addition, whatever view of history pervades the narrative is further validated, since it must support the action in the mythological as well as the enveloping action. To put it another way, no view of history—including the Marxist view—can be above suspicion if it does not in some way explain the conduct of Orion, Adonis, the Trojan warriors, and the other characters who inhabit the world of mythological antiquity because that world holds up when measured against the modern, personal experiences of everyone who reads the classics, whether he lives in the North or South, America or Europe.

Miss Gordon's view of history is essentially tragic; for her, modern American experience can be viewed as having the same structure that Aristotle found in the plays of Aeschylus, Sophocles, Euripides, and in Homer's great epics. But to reinforce the archetypal nature of her historical vision, Miss Gordon renders it through allusions to myth, and more importantly, through characters who have their counterparts, whether ironic or heroic, in those classical works best known to Western man. Indeed the tissue of myth which underlies each of these five novels, uniting and elevating their central and enveloping actions, is so firm and intricate that it emerges as a major structural element.

To be sure, that tissue is more explicit in some novels than in others. In *Green Centuries,* for example, the hero's name is obviously allusory. Orion Outlaw, like his mythological namesake, is a hunter; and his brother, Archy, is an opposite in much the same way as Arion in some versions of the Greek story. Orion's last name, however, suggests the irony with which Miss Gordon invites the reader to consider her characters in terms of their classical counterparts. In making such an allusion she reveals to us the true nature of the story she is telling; but in the ironic undercutting of her characters she makes us understand more fully how much has been lost in the historical tragedy she defines in the enveloping action.

In *Penhally,* the tissue of allusion is derived from several connecting myths, including those of Orion, the Pleiades, the House of Atreus, and Aphrodite. Here the archetypal substructure is less obvious; but Orion and the Pleiades are mentioned at a crucial moment in the action so that all the complex relationships on both levels are brought together and made explicit. The reader—or scholar—must then trace the parallels between the story and the myth backward and forward in the action. When he does so, however, he will find that there is a surprising correspondence of structure in both, one which defines the relationship between the two as something more than accidental. And again, the generic nature of both the central action and mythological action is tragic, in conformity with Miss Gordon's interpretation of the South's collapse.

In *None Shall Look Back,* Miss Gordon supplies the reader with no overt references to her mythological counterpart, the Trojan War, and it is possible that she herself was only dimly aware of its existence, though too many critics and historians of the nineteenth and twentieth centuries have discussed the Civil War in this light to make such ignorance likely. In a sense the point is irrelevant, given the archetypal nature of the action. For both Homer and Miss Gordon are depicting an old and tragic story—the fall of the ancient city; and whether that city be Troy, the Old South, or Nineveh (to which her title alludes) the essential elements are the same. However, we know nothing of the dramatis personae of the Biblical city, and Homer provides prototypes for virtually all of Miss Gordon's characters, from the figure of the old patriarch to the warriors in battle, both heroic and cowardly. Thus, though never overt, the mythological tissue of *None Shall Look Back* is as pervasive as those of the other novels, and defines as tragic the enveloping action.

In *The Garden of Adonis,* Miss Gordon once again makes her use of myth overt, both in the title and in an epigraph from *The Golden Bough.* Here, as in *Green Centuries,* the use is ironic, for Ben Allard, the modern counterpart of Adonis, is cut down, never to rise again as does the god of the old fertility myth. The virgins who indulged in ritual prostitution as a sacrifice to the mythological Adonis are also ironically rendered in a number of promiscuous young women who give themselves out of lust, greed, or simple lack of concern. Thus does Miss Gordon again, by the juxtaposition of modern life against mythology, make explicit her tragic vision of history.

In *Aleck Maury, Sportsman,* the classical education of the hero, a teacher of Latin, allows Miss Gordon to introduce unobtrusive references to *The Aeneid* and therefore to give ironic form and meaning to the aimless journey of Aleck Maury through a life devoted to blood sport, a man whose renunciation of his family and community is the very antithesis of the ideals which motivated Aeneas to endure danger in order to found the New Troy. Maury, presented in a word of materialism, is a hero only by default; and his private code of conduct, so narrow when compared to the heroic vision of Rome and the Old South, is the accommodation of a good man with all that has happened to the West as Miss Gordon understands this historical catastrophe.

It is in myth, therefore, that Miss Gordon unities all the diverse elements of her fiction: the shape of the central actions, the enveloping actions, and the view of history which her enveloping actions imply. The coherent works of art which are the final product of this synthesis represent a major achievement in modern literature and define a place for Miss Gordon in the pantheon of modern writers which she does not yet occupy. For this reason, a careful examination of each of her five novels should prove useful, not only to those who would understand Miss Gordon's achievement more fully, but also to those who would understand more fully the nature of fiction itself; for as one of its greatest contemporary practioners, she has much to teach others about its techniques and mysteries.

Jane Gibson Brown, "The Early Novels of Caroline Gor-

don: Myth and History as a Fictional Technique," in The Southern Review, *Louisiana State University, Vol. XIII, No. 2, Spring, 1977, pp. 289-98.*

Veronica Makowsky (essay date Spring 1990)

[An American critic, biographer, and educator, Makowsky is the author of Caroline Gordon: A Biography *(1989). In the following essay, she explores Gordon's views about writing as a woman.]*

Caroline Gordon has been known as a "writer's writer," one who is greatly respected by her fellow artists for her craft but who has not received popular or even academic acclaim. As I became interested in Gordon's work and began to explore the possibility of a biography, I frequently wondered why Gordon was a "writer's writer," rather than a universally renowned author like Faulkner. The answer, I found, was in the way she internalized her culture's attitudes toward women and writing, both in her life and in her work.

In her later years, Gordon herself attempted to explore what she perceived as the contradictions between being a woman and being a writer. When she was about sixty years old, she offered four explanations in a letter to her friend Ward Dorrance:

> While I am a woman I am also a freak. The work I do is not suitable for a woman. It is unsexing. I speak with real conviction here. I don't write "the womanly" novel. I write the same kind of novel a man would write, only it is ten times harder for me to write it than it would be for a man who had the same degree of talent. Dr. Johnson was right: a woman at intellectual labour is always a dog walking on its hind legs. When you add to that the task of running a house, serving dinner that seems to have been prepared by an excellent cook, and all the while trying to be a good hostess—which means trying to make every man in the room have a good time—oh well, I am inclined to self-pity now and I don't deserve any pity at all, for I have a good time in this life. But I do have a lot on my hands. I bite off more than I can chew all the time.

She attributes her dilemma to biology which made woman a lower species like a dog, to society's requirement that woman be a nurturer, to literary conventions about the proper subject matter for a woman and, ultimately, to her own willfulness in biting off more than she can chew despite her knowledge of a woman's destiny. For Gordon, however, the essential enigma remains: is she a "freak" because of uncontrollable forces or because she chooses to oppose those forces?

In her unfinished and largely unpublished biography, *A Narrow Heart,* Gordon examined each of her explanations in the context of her childhood discovery of her vocation. Although young Caroline created her own creation myth, she relegated creativity to men. Gordon remembers that as a small child she concluded that "the world had been created as a plaything by a group of men, who, tired of sporting with it, had gone on to other pleasures, leaving it to roll on the way it would." In young Caroline's cos-

mology, men were by nature the creators; women, presumably, were universal housekeepers, left to make do with the world men have made and abandoned.

In accordance with this view of nature's pattern, Gordon believed that society allocated strictly determined roles for men and women. Men have not only created the world, but assigned themselves the starring roles as heroes: "A hero—any hero—spends his life in combat with the common, the only enemy, Death. When a man is faced with death, energies which he was not aware he possessed are rallied in the effort to preserve the life which, until that instant may not have seemed to him as precious as it truly is." While men are "rallied," ennobled and enlivened by their role, women's task is acquiescence to the suppression of their powers.

> The women, going to and fro in their daily work, overhear the men's talk in snatches and, acting hastily and ill-advisedly, as women always act when not restrained by the proper masculine authority, neglect their household duties and, as frenziedly as Cadmus' daughters, taking off for the mountain, set about putting . . . half-heard pernicious doctrine into effect. Cadmus' daughters and the other Maenads suckled gazelles and kids and wolves on the heights of Cithaeron.

Women who reach beyond their proper roles are associated with the bestial; they are freaks, whether they are suckling animals or are animals themselves, such as dogs walking on their hind legs.

The masculine hero, however, does need to have his exploits recorded and praised by those who "recit[e] his glorious deeds, pausing between recitals, to meditate on the mystery that set him apart from his fellows." Gordon concludes that the "novelist, like the soldier, is committed by *his* profession to a life-long study of wars and warriors" [emphasis added]. The woman who wishes to be a novelist, then, is attempting to penetrate masculine mysteries which she herself could never experience. The "womanly novel," the novel of domestic life, is therefore a second-rate subject and the woman writer faces the dilemma of trying to create art from an inferior subject or attempting a masculine subject to which her powers are ill-suited.

With such a negative attitude toward the potential of women writers, one can only wonder why Gordon wrote nine novels and many short stories. In *A Narrow Heart,* Gordon herself tries to account for this phenomenon as she presents her portrait of the artist as a young girl and attempts to absolve herself of the charge of willfulness or hubris. Gordon claims that as early as her fourth year, she felt she had a vocation, "the composing of fiction." She continues, "I did not call my work by that name in those days[.] I thought of it as 'stories' which I told myself as I went about my ordinary affairs and I cannot remember a moment of my life when the telling of those stories did not seem an obligation that had been laid upon me and one which it would be dangerous to evade."

After she has carefully established that she did not lust for her task and its potential glories, but believed that they were imposed upon her, Gordon illustrates the danger of evading her vocation with the memory of her fourth birth-

Benfolly, Allen and Caroline's home near Clarksville, Tennessee, where such writers as Katherine Anne Porter, Ford Madox Ford, and Robert Lowell visted during the 1930's.

day when she found herself alone in her grandmother's bedroom, "reflecting disconsolately that I had not done any work that day." As she stood in the chamber,

> a cry came from outside the room. A bird, per-
> haps, calling from some bough to its mate, or the
> sharp plaint that breaks from a domestic animal
> when it realizes that it is being led to slaughter
> or even the muted, soaring lament that Negro
> "hands" in those days lifted as they worked in
> the fields. . . . I remember how that hoarse
> sound speaking of some unassuageable distress,
> suddenly sounded again in the room and how
> the shadows, which up till then had lurked in the
> corners, massed themselves as if to sway for-
> ward. . . . I gave way to panic and ran across
> the room and thrust my face down into the water
> in the basin. It seemed to me deep enough to
> drown in. One of the sharpest memories of my
> life is the surprise I felt when my childish visage
> raised itself, apparently of its own accord, and
> I knew that I was still there in that room, with
> only shadows for companions.

The young Caroline feels guilty for evading her task of telling stories of the life around her, yet the nature of that life, her subject, is terrifyingly painful: the loss of the bird's mate, the slaughter of the animal, and the bondage of the black worker. Her gift or burden is so much a part of her, however, that she can only escape it by killing herself. She cannot bring herself to do so, lifts her face "apparently of its own accord," and is back to her original dilemma of confronting a subject, "shadows," for which she feels she is not suited.

Gordon's memories in *A Narrow Heart* repeatedly turn to images of various kinds of freaks who cannot reconcile their vocations with their natures or with society's expectations. Young Caroline would often play "Robin Hood" with her brothers and cousins. She was not assigned the feminine role of Maid Marian or the heroic masculine role of Robin or one of his merry men, but the more androgynous part of Allan-a-Dale, who, as her older brother points out, "was the only member of the band who could write."

Young Caroline was also fascinated by the legend of a female ghost named Tink who supposedly inhabited the woods near her grandmother's house. Tink lived in "the crotch of [a] sycamore tree" and "had her baby under one arm and her head under the other." Tink is a perfect illustration of the woman writer's dilemma. She sits at the parting of two branches or roles, that of the masculine intellect, exemplified by her head, and that of feminine nurturance, symbolized by the baby. Tink is also a freak; she cannot resolve her conflict so she can never be at rest.

Even more horrifying is Gordon's comparison of herself

as woman writer to the devil. She remembers an occasion when she believed she saw the devil in the eyes of a close friend, and she begins to muse upon the reasons for the angel's fall. In the standard version of the legend, the once perfect Lucifer has become the freak Satan because of his hubristic challenge of God's power. Gordon, though, does not dwell upon the usurpation of heaven's territory, but upon a struggle over the word. She cites various sources whom, she asserts, attribute Satan's fall to his refusal "to transmit the message" and the fact that he "wanted to be an author." As Gordon looks into the eyes of her friend, she believes Satan is vowing that "he would never leave me—until the heart which, no matter how steadfastly averted my gaze from his, beat faster at the sound of his dreadful laughter—until that heart itself, stopped beating." Once again, she sees herself as a freak, part human and part demon, with no reconciliation possible in this life.

Gordon realized that repeated images and patterns like these originate in childhood. In *A Narrow Heart,* she wrote, "Every one of us—even the foundling or 'the test tube baby'—has had a father and a mother. And therein lies the tale, the tale each one of us spends a life time spinning." Gordon's parents, James Maury Morris Gordon and Nancy Minor Meriwether, provided their only daughter with a tale rich complexity and implications, one strand of which comprises Gordon's view of the woman writer. Gordon's father was a man well educated in the classics who made his living as a teacher and preacher, but who preferred hunting and fishing to either of his livelihoods. In *Aleck Maury, Sportsman* and the Aleck Maury short stories, Gordon aligns herself with her father whom she portrays as pursuing sport with the devotion and craft of an artist.

Gordon clearly identified herself with her father, but in order to do so, she had to erase the unhappy image of her mother. Nancy Gordon was locally known as an intellectual, a "bluestocking," who could perform the Tink-like balancing act of cooking dinner with a ladle in one hand and a French novel in the other. Nancy Gordon also taught in her husband's school, but Caroline does not credit her mother with her own instruction, possibly because she more highly valued the masculine intellect. In Caroline's reminiscences, however, the learned Nancy Gordon seems to retreat from her mutually exclusive roles as intellectual and nurturer by enveloping herself in silence. In *A Narrow Heart,* Caroline Gordon remembers her as an enigmatic woman who in her last years found "there was hardly anything she cared to read. She said that she found all the imaginings of men vain." One wonders if the corollary for Nancy Gordon would be that all the imaginings of women were impossible, as they would become for her daughter.

Her education, Gordon believed, was partly responsible for her status as freak, although she was also proud of it. Rather than sending her to a girls' school, her father kept her in his own academy. Like her character Sally in **"The Petrified Woman,"** Gordon could observe that "I had to go to school with the boys. Sometimes I think that that is what makes me so peculiar," and, as this biographer

would argue, a "petrified" woman in both senses of the word.

Gordon herself remarked that "it is strange how, in this life, patterns of human conduct repeat themselves, like a recurrent *motif* in music, or a figure in a tapestry" (*Narrow Heart*). For Gordon, this pattern of conflicting roles with its consequent feeling of freakishness appears both in her life and in her writing.

In the memories of others and her own letters, Gordon often appears as a latter-day Tink, frantically attempting to keep her roles of writer and woman in equilibrium. Her friend Sally Wood recalls that when Gordon was in labor before the birth of her daughter Nancy, she "was grimly talking about her novel, her white face flinching now and then." During her father's last illness, Gordon was at the hospital, working on *The Women on the Porch* "by hand, standing at the dresser between vomitings." When Gordon and her husband Allen Tate were boarding a ship to Europe, she states that she had Nancy by one hand and a baby doll in the other while Allen carried *The Rise and Fall of the Confederacy.* Caroline, however, was not reconciled to her clearly signified role and complained when some Rhodes Scholars aboard referred to her as "the wife." During the winter in which the Tates shared a farmhouse in New York's Tory Valley with the poet Hart Crane, Caroline managed to keep writing, but her "study" was the kitchen table.

The tension from these conflicts affected Gordon's attitude toward her writing as well as her ability to write. She often said that writing was a "torment" to her, in contrast to the effortless imaginings of her childhood. In the early 1920s when she left home to become a newspaper reporter in Chattanooga, Gordon tried to write her first novel in her spare time while living in her aunt's attic. Although she had all the requisite romantic props, a garret, an autobiographical subject and a Keatsian title, *Darkling I Listen,* her novel did not pour forth with the nightingale's effortless lyricism. Instead, she said that her attempt to write led to a breakdown from which she was nursed to recovery by her aunt.

Writing was a "torment" to Gordon because she had lost her early confidence in her female imagination. Throughout her life, she needed male mentors to validate her efforts or she could not finish her work. Two of her principal mentors were Allen Tate and Ford Madox Ford. Gordon destroyed *Darkling I Listen* because as she watched Tate's face as he read it, she concluded that it wasn't any good. When she had been working on what would become her first published novel, **Penhally** (1931), for several years, Ford compelled her to finish it by dragging her to the typewriter and sometimes making her dictate to him. After her second and final divorce from Tate in 1959, she published little and left several uncompleted manuscripts.

Although her lack of confidence and her sense of herself as a freak stemmed from her status as a woman in a patriarchal world, she often deflected her hostility away from the masculine literary world and on to other women writers, particularly Katherine Anne Porter, whom she regarded as the grasshopper to her ant. Gordon envied Porter's ability to alternate her roles as woman and writer, rather than attempt Gordon's own perpetual balancing act. She wrote of one of Porter's stays at the Tates' Clarksville home, Benfolly:

> She couldn't write here—life was so distracting, what with the cats and all the fruits of the earth needing to be preserved, pickled or made into wine. She made mint liqueur, preserved peaches whole, made five gallons of elderberry wine, brandied peaches and would have brandied and preserved bushels more if I had provided her with them. All this, of course, partly out of domestic passions, partly out of charitable concern for our welfare and a good part I wickedly believe just to get out of work. She has to sever every earthly tie she has before she can do any work, go off to a hotel somewhere usually. [*The Southern Mandarins: Letters of Caroline Gordon to Sally, Wood 1924-1937*, ed. Sally Wood, 1984]

Porter could play her feminine role to the hilt with her fabled beauty and charm, and, to Caroline's chagrin, without apparent guilt over writing not accomplished. Although the anecdote is amusing, it also illustrates Gordon's need to punish herself for her hubris by attempting to maintain both roles at once and by denying herself a supportive, sympathetic identification with her fellow women writers.

Her ambivalence toward her role as a woman writer also affected the way she wrote, particularly her emphasis on factually correct settings, her stress upon technique and her tone of high seriousness. She loved to do research for her novels and zealously pursued obscure details, whether for her Civil War novel, *None Shall Look Back* (1937); her novel of Indians and pioneers, *Green Centuries* (1941); or her retelling of Greek myths, *The Glory of Hera* (1972). Not only did her pursuit of the facts sometimes become a means of procrastination, but it once even led to a charge of plagiarism when an executive from the company which published *Battles and Leaders of the Civil War* wrote to Gordon's editor, Scribner's legendary Max Perkins, to accuse Gordon of verbatim borrowings in *None Shall Look Back*. Perkins, another excellent masculine mentor, soothed the publisher's ruffled feelings, and there is no evidence that he even told Gordon of the incident. It does, however, illustrate the way Gordon, unlike her "master" Henry James, was afraid to renounce the details and trust her imagination to work upon the "germ" or essence of a situation.

Gordon's mistrust of her imagination is also indicated by her stress upon technique. She praised and thanked Ford Madox Ford for his instruction in the Flaubertian search for *le mot juste* and sometimes seemed to emulate the French master's agony over each word, sentence and paragraph. When Gordon herself became a teacher of writing in the late 1930s, she conveyed her belief in the primacy of technique to her students. In particular she emphasized the importance of point of view and concrete details through reading and analyzing the works of masters such as Ford, Flaubert, Dostoevsky, Joyce and James. In that the imaginative part of writing is a mystery and essentially unteachable, Gordon drilled her students in what they could master, technique, and most were grateful for what they had learned. In terms of her own writing, though, the privileging of technique seems an overcompensation for her ambivalence toward her female imagination and partially explains why her works are praised for their craft, not their imaginative vision.

Gordon is always remembered by others as a woman of great wit who could turn a depressing or frustrating incident into a comic anecdote with a malicious poke at herself or others. Her letters are delightful because they are full of humorous episodes such as her double-edged account of Katherine Ann Porter's "domestic passions" at Benfolly. In contrast, Gordon's fiction is characterized by solemnity and her comic genius is rarely to be found. This excision of the comic can be partially explained by Gordon's sense that real life is the tragic struggle of the hero against death, but when Gordon discusses heroes and tragedies she is referring to men while in her letters she is relating a woman's struggles against the toils and confines of domesticity. Her writing self is split into two personas, the "masculine" self who writes tragedies of mankind and his posterity and the "feminine" self who writes humorous, even grotesquely comic, accounts of domestic life in letters she considers of so little consequence that she rarely even dates them. If she had been able to unite these selves, her work may have had the universal appeal which would have carried her beyond the status of "writer's writer."

Women artists in Gordon's fiction are rarely seen, and when encountered they are presented as freaks. In *The Strange Children* (1951), the unbalanced poet Isabel Reardon is responsible for the destruction of her husband and her poet lover because she is selfish and will not efface herself as a woman supposedly should. She is associated with freaks, mermaids and sirens, to reinforce her unnatural proclivities. Cynthia in *The Malefactors* (1956) is a siren who leads the poet-protagonist Tom Claiborne away from the truth embodied in his wife Vera in order to advance her own poetic ambitions. As her name suggests, she is associated with the moon, a fickle and lesser illumination, and so is guilty of hubris in attempting to become a literary light herself.

Perhaps the most striking example of Gordon's loss of faith in her woman's imagination is her revision of her first published story "**Summer Dust.**" In the original version, the young Caroline appears as Sally, a small girl who learns the bitter lessons of sexism and racism as she encounters men and women and blacks and whites as she travels around her family's properties. Her brother tells her that "she who calleth her brother a fool is in danger of hell fire," and she herself is relieved to acknowledge that "I'm not a nigger" when she witnesses her family's attitude toward their black servants. Sally finds surcease in her imagination as she fantasizes about "a dark woman with a crimson scarf bound tightly about her head, and two round gold earrings as big as saucers, swinging out from the scarf as she walked." Like a successful woman artist, the gypsy woman is defiant, vibrant, and free in her self-expression. Gordon, though, deleted her from "**One Against Thebes,**" the version of "**Summer Dust**" she published some thirty years later, indicating that this possible role model had been similarly eradicated in Gordon during her thirty years' attempt to function as woman and artist.

If one regards the inscription Gordon chose for her tombstone as her final work, it may seem that she offers little hope that "woman writer" could become anything but a contradiction in terms. Indeed, her "final" words are not hers, but those of the male theologian Jacques Maritain, which she had already used as an epigraph for *The Malefactors:* "It is for Adam to interpret the voices which Eve hears." In one sense, this is an admission of defeat and a warning to other women: Eve had no business writing all those novels. In another sense, however, there is a faint glimmer of hope: Eve persists in writing, even to the verge of the grave, although she must use a masculine "voice" as authority and permission. However grotesque this mimicry appears, it attests to the truth Gordon felt that her life and work revealed: the female voice can be subverted and distorted into that of a freak, the male voice speaking from the female corpse, but it cannot be completely quelled or denied.

Veronica Makowsky, "Caroline Gordon on Women Writing: A Contradiction in Terms?" in The Southern Quarterly, *Vol. XXVIII, No. 3, Spring, 1990, pp. 43-52.*

Larry Allums   (essay date Spring 1990)

[*In the essay below, Allums examines Gordon's later fiction as indicative of a "distinctly Christian imagination."*]

The striking shift of artistic method at a certain point in the career of Caroline Gordon is familiar to anyone who knows her work. Also well known is the fact that the change occurs around the time of her conversion to Roman Catholicism in 1947. Generally, the novels she published before that crucial event are epic in their sweep and tragic in their movement, whereas the later novels are more restricted in terms of time and action, with one notable exception, and they move toward comic resolutions. Although this change of focus is dramatically clear, what it implies, both for her own poetics and, by extension, for the reader's understanding of the imagination itself, is still a matter of conjecture. Perhaps the change in Gordon's poetic method delineates the radical distance between the classical and Christian myths. More importantly, the later works embody the operation of a distinctly Christian imagination. Furthermore, in her final novel, a controversial retelling of the story of Heracles that seems an overly ambitious attempt to synthesize and Christianize the Greek myths, this embodiment is most clear.

Although a radical change in Gordon's work can be documented, she herself remarked in 1965 [in **"Cock-Crow"**] that her entire career was the result of a single, "lifelong study" of

> the life and times of the hero. That seems to me the proper study of every one of us all our lives through. A hero—any hero—spends his life in combat with the common, the only enemy, Death. When a man is faced with death, energies which he was not aware he possessed are rallied

in the effort to preserve the life which, until that instant, may not have seemed to him as precious as it truly is. War which, now under one disguise, now another, pits man against his arch enemy, Death, has always provided a favorable climate for the growth of the hero, as well as for the study of his ways and deeds. The novelist, like the soldier, is committed by his profession to a lifelong study of wars and warriors.

Appearances to the contrary, these remarks are consistent with Gordon's movement toward a Christian poetics. In fact, when applied to the novels, her reflections on the hero reveal more clearly the nature of her poetic metamorphosis.

When using such terms as combat, death and warriors to describe the heroic enterprise, Gordon at one extreme means them quite literally: often in the earlier novels, her protagonists find themselves in physically perilous circumstances, fighting for their lives in actual combat with an enemy. Such actions evoke the classical Greek myth, at the heart of which stands the idea of the heroic. According to the Homeric epics, virtue—*arete* or "excellence"—is closely identified with strength, skill and deeds of valor in battle, whether with men, monsters or the gods themselves. The Greek hero is consciously devoted to fulfilling the heroic ideal as if it were a calling. Indeed, it does present itself as a calling to him, a divinely proffered task that is given to him to do or not to do, as he chooses. In the *Iliad,* Achilles speaks of the dreadful choices before him:

> I carry two sorts of destiny toward the day of my death. Either, if I stay here and fight beside the city of the Trojans, my return home is gone, but my glory shall be everlasting; but if I return home to the beloved land of my fathers, the excellence of my glory is gone, but there will be a long life left for me, and my end in death will not come to me quickly.

Achilles does not speak of basing his choice on hatred for his Trojan foes. He sees that his real enemy is the common destiny of all mortals—Death—and all that remains in his power is choosing the circumstances of his ultimate defeat. Although the Homeric hero's choices have communal effects of great consequence, he knows that for him there is nothing redemptive about his life but reputation—everlasting glory. This is hardly comforting; as Achilles says while still alive, "I detest the doorways of Death," and in the *Odyssey* his shade complains in Hades that he "would rather follow the plow as thrall to another man, one with no land allotted him and not much to live on, than be a king over all the perished dead."

In many respects, Gordon's early novels are reenactments of the Homeric hero's combat with forces that would take his life. Her protagonists struggle incessantly with the fact of their mortality, spurning the love of a lady or the security of family in order to challenge that which they cannot possibly vanquish. In *None Shall Look Back,* for instance, Rives Allard compulsively seeks death on the battlefield until he finds it; in *Green Centuries,* Orion Outlaw, significantly named for the constellation of the great hunter, yields just as compulsively to the "westering" instinct and its delusive promise of boundlessness; in *Penhally,* Nicholas Llewellyn attempts to preserve his ancestral house so that its identity will survive his own dissolution in death; and in *Aleck Maury, Sportsman,* Aleck craftily tries to forestall Nature's pull toward the grave by becoming her devoted "student" and in that way learning her deadly secrets. These protagonists are essentially tragic figures, like the Greek hero himself, engaging the ultimate foe in different ways yet finally experiencing either death itself or the shock of recognizing that in the natural order, from which man cannot save himself, death reigns over life.

This tragic fact of human existence is the ontological pivot on which Gordon's poetic vision swings as she moves from her classical to her Christian phase. For the irreducible element through which the Christian myth altered Western consciousness is its revising—its re-visioning—of life and death. St. Paul wrote eloquently about the mysterious truth of the soul revealed in history as the Incarnation and called it a scandal that the Greeks could neither accept nor understand. It remains a scandal to the rational mind, yet it has transformed Western thought to such an extent that all previous myths must in some sense be measured in terms of it. Furthermore, just as Homer fully embodied the tragic vision of the classical hero in his *Iliad* and *Odyssey,* so it was another poet, Dante, who imagined the plentitude of the Christian myth in his *Commedia.*

In its magnitude and complexity, Dante's sacred poem allows us to conceive of a distinctly Christian imagination, only a potential faculty until the Incarnation, since only at that moment in history was fullness of being released into the world. As William Lynch says in *Christ and Apollo,* Christ "has subverted the whole order of the old imagination," and "the new imagination begins to assume the order of creation and to lift it into its own vitality." In a radical revision of human time and action, the Christian imagination perceives the redemptive potential not only of the present but of history as well, because it apprehends the anagogical in the light of the Incarnation and its promise.

Dante's *Commedia* simultaneously celebrates Christ's triumph over time and redefines the heroic paradigm, at the center of which still stand powerful vestiges of the classical paradigm: the ancient foe and the fact that man must struggle against it. Death remains the enemy of man, and tragedy is still a haunting possibility in spite of Christ's promise. Fearful of the journey that Virgil has outlined for him, Dante protests that he is neither Aeneas nor Paul but an ordinary mortal whose inclination is to stay in the savage wood within comforting sight of the sun rather than travel through an act of faith to the regions of the dead.

By accepting the challenge of the journey, Dante becomes the Christian Everyman and his poem that new paradigm of the soul's perilous pilgrimage through this life. It is within the trajectory of this movement that Caroline Gordon patterns her late novels and heroes. In 1944, three years before her conversion to Catholicism, she published *The Women on the Porch,* the story of a man's estrangement from and reconciliation with his wife. In it, the scope of the action is reduced and interiorized. The quest of the hero, Jim Chapman, takes him into the depths of his own soul, a journey that is, if anything, more tortuous than the

classical hero's acceptance of the battlefield challenge. Chapman himself senses this at one point as he listens to a young naval officer speak almost brightly about the prospects of war with Japan. "I was too young for the last war and am too old for this war," Chapman thinks. "But I wish I was one of them, for it is something, in this life, for a man to know where he is going, even if the appointment is with the minotaur."

[In his 1966 *The Hero with the Private Parts*] Andrew Lytle has maintained that the reconciliation at the novel's end is unconvincing: it is too sudden and unprepared. It seems instead to mark the first signs of the emergence of Gordon's Christian imagination. [In her "Nature and Grace in Caroline Gordon," *Critique* 1, no. 1 (1956)] Louise Cowan has suggested that the apparent flaw at the conclusion of *The Women on the Porch* is actually "an aperture, through which something supernatural enters into the framework of the novel." That supernatural element we may recognize as a moment of grace given to the estranged husband and wife, and it prefigures the more explicitly Christian structure of the post-conversion novels, as does the fortuitous moment, reminiscent of St. Augustine's conversion in the *Confessions,* when Chapman's eye happens to fix upon Dante's *Inferno,* which lies before him and has fallen open to the first page of the poem: *"In the middle of the journey of our life I came to myself in a dark wood where the straight way was lost."*

Jim Chapman is an intellectual, a professor of history, tormented by the agonizing uncertainties of modern life. In her next two novels, *The Strange Children* (1951) and *The Malefactors* (1956), Gordon's heroes are again writers whose muses have fallen silent and whose enemy is the death of the spirit. Both works contain an abundance of Christian elements, themes and allusions, and each ends with a moment during which, against all reason and nature, grace is offered—the grace of sudden insight. *The Strange Children* concludes with Stephen Lewis's ominous vision of the apocalypse, the event toward which, according to the Christian myth, all of history moves:

> A Perseid fell, trailing its golden dust, and then another: little meteors that had been falling through space for God knows how many years. But the other stars that shone so high and cold would fall, too, like rotten fruit—when the heavens were rolled up like a scroll and the earth reeled to and fro like a drunkard and men called upon the mountains to fall upon them and hide them from the wrath to come. This very hill upon which he stood would shake. The river which lapped it so gently might turn and, raging against it, tear it from its green base and hurl it toward the sea. But there would be no sea!

Throughout the novel Lewis has wandered through a labyrinth of hopelessness, masking his despair with a cynical cruelty that has isolated him from his family and friends, but his terrifying vision of the apocalypse awakens him to the tragic destiny that awaits him, a destiny that is at once both universal, embracing all human history, and particular, extending to him in his time and place. But he also sees the redemptive power of Christ, for the apocalypse—both as the end of history and as the death of individual men—

is a time not only of destruction but of fulfillment, the gathering together of the faithful from the four corners of the earth. Thus Lewis's vision of the end marks a new beginning; through his sudden insight—the offering of grace—he is taken, as it were, like Dante in his dream, to the gate of purgatory, and as he wonders at the necessary journey which lies before him, embracing his family for the first time in the novel, he groans "so loud that the woman and the child stared at him, wondering, too."

One need only compare this purgatorial and therefore redemptive, comic ending with the tragic conclusion of *Green Centuries,* first published in 1941, to see the radical effect of the Christian myth upon Gordon's imagination. There, Orion Outlaw sits with his dead wife and, staring out at the stars, reflects upon his past:

> When he was a boy on the Yadkin he used to like to think that he took his name from the mighty hunter, and out in the woods at night or coming home from a frolic he would look up and pick out the stars: the hunter's foot, his club, his girdle, the red eye of the bull that he pursued ever westward. . . . His father had come west across the ocean, leaving all that he cared about behind. And he himself as soon as he had grown to manhood had looked at the mountains and could not rest until he knew what lay beyond them. But it seemed that a man had to flee farther each time and leave more behind him and when he got to the new place he looked up and saw Orion fixed upon his burning wheel, always pursuing the bull but never making the kill. Did Orion will any longer the westward chase? No more than himself. Like the mighty hunter he had lost himself in the turning. Before him lay the empty west, behind him the loved things of which he was made. Those old tales of Frank's! Were not men raised into the westward turning stars only after they had destroyed themselves?

Although Orion looks into the same heavens that Stephen Lewis gazes at in *The Strange Children,* he sees only futile repetition and feels nothing but despair: nothing of his "westering" life can be redeemed, and he does not even have the luxury of a terrifying hope.

In her final novel, *The Glory of Hera,* Caroline Gordon distills her "lifelong study" of the hero, combining the divergent patterns of classical and Christian in a retelling of the life and times of Heracles. On one level a prodigious compendium of Greek myth with Heracles at its center, *The Glory of Hera* at the same time clearly issues from the Christian imagination functioning in Gordon's three previous works. A crucial distinction must be made, however, concerning this explicit treatment of Greek mythology: rather than allegorizing and thus circumscribing the classical myths neatly within the pale of the Christian myth, she appropriates them in an act of "re-reading" pagan history from her final artistic stance, that is, through the lens of Christian revelation.

In this, Gordon once again approximates the imaginative paradigm of Dante, who could not bring himself to save his beloved Virgil but could regard his mentor's great epic as being included in the transformation wrought by Christ's redemption upon all of history and even upon the act of reading itself. Thus Dante returns to the *Aeneid*—and in fact to virtually as much of pagan history as was known to him—in order to perform the "misreading" demanded by the Incarnation, a new reading which becomes possible only when the meaning of Christ fully pervades his imagination.

When using such terms as combat, death and warriors to describe the heroic enterprise, Gordon at one extreme means them quite literally: often in the earlier novels, her protagonists find themselves in physically perilous circumstances, fighting for their lives in actual combat with an enemy. Such actions evoke the classical Greek myth, at the heart of which stands the idea of the heroic.

—Larry Allums

Caroline Gordon's strategy in *The Glory of Hera* is similar; that is, she regards the Christian God's plan for mankind—the Incarnation—as the lens through which to read the Greek myths anew. Appropriating the divine mind of Zeus as a narrative post of observation, Gordon portrays the "father of gods and men" as desiring two things: to vanquish forever the dark and threatening powers that he had to defeat in order to ascend the throne and to bridge the great chasm between Olympus and earth—between the divine and the human realms. This clearly echoes the Christian myth and is a radical departure from anything we may read in handbook of mythology, yet Gordon very carefully preserves the irreconcilable gulf between the two myths: for all his power and purity of motive, Zeus cannot achieve what he desires, for he is not the God in whom, to use Dante's words from the *Inferno,* "will and power are one." The very nature of the greatest Greek god suggests the tragedy that permeates the classical world.

Thus Caroline Gordon's method in *The Glory of Hera* is not allegorical but analogical: in Zeus's scheme, Heracles's exploits and the apotheosis that finally brings peace to Olympus, we see, to use Dantean terms again, "shadowy prefaces" of Jehovah's plan for mankind, the Incarnation, and the final triumph of the resurrection. Even at the novel's comic ending, however, we recall Zeus's unfulfilled desire and the tragic residue of the partial vision of the Greeks. Heracles, the greatest of heroes, remains an incomplete image of redemption.

The Glory of Hera was to be the first of a two-part work, the second part of which Gordon did not complete before her death. Perhaps that other volume would have altered the reading of Heracles and his exploits.

As it stands, *The Glory of Hera* is a remarkable culmination of her faithfulness to a lifelong study of the hero. Steadfastly continuing the focus of her post-conversion novels, *The Glory of Hera* is the product of a distinctly

Christian imagination. It also represents Gordon's final reading of the classical Greek world that she loved so dearly.

Larry Allums, "From Classical to Christian: Versions of the Hero in the Novels of Caroline Gordon," in The Southern Quarterly, *Vol. XXVIII, No. 3, Spring, 1990, pp. 63-70.*

FURTHER READING

Bibliography

Sullivan, Mary C. "Caroline Gordon: A Reference Guide." In *Flannery O'Connor and Caroline Gordon: A Reference Guide,* edited by Robert E. Golden and Mary C. Sullivan, pp. 193-308. Boston: G. K. Hall and Co., 1977.

Annotated bibliography of Gordon's works and critical and biographical studies about her, including a chronological listing of Ph. D. dissertations.

Biography

Horsford, Howard C. "Letters of Caroline Gordon Tate to Sally Wood Kohn, 1925-1937." *The Princeton University Library Chronicle* XLIV, No. 1 (Autumn 1982): 1-24.

Relates Gordon's life between 1925 and 1937 based upon her correspondence with friend and writer Sally Wood.

Makowsky, Veronica A. "Caroline Gordon: Amateur to Professional Writer." *The Southern Review* 23, No. 4 (Autumn 1987): 778-93.

Provides excerpts from Makowsky's biography on Gordon. This essay follows the early years of Gordon's career and marriage to Allen Tate, the rigors of their life as struggling writers in the United States and Europe, and the literary personalities with whom they associated: Ford Madox Ford, Ernest Hemingway, F. Scott and Zelda Fitzgerald, Robert Lowell, and Leonie Adams.

———. *Caroline Gordon: A Biography.* New York: Oxford University Press, 1989, 260 p.

Analysis of Gordon's life and work. Discussing Gordon's Southern heritage and relating her life experiences, Makowsky asks: "What formed Caroline Gordon's imagination and the themes of her work? Who set her standards for serious art? Did male mentorship hurt or benefit her work and her reputation?"

Ross, Danforth. "Caroline Gordon, Uncle Rob and My Mother." *The Southern Quarterly* XXVII, No. 3 (Spring 1990): 9-22.

Anecdote concerning Gordon's early life on her family's farm, Meriwether, where she was born and spent her early years, and her adult years at Benfolly in Clarksville, Tennessee, where Gordon and her husband, writer Allen Tate, lived in the 1930s. The critic, a distant relative of Gordon's also chronicles her relationship with various family members.

Waldron, Ann. *Close Connections: Caroline Gordon and the Southern Renaissance.* New York: G. P. Putnam's Sons, 1987, 416 p.

A detailed account of Gordon's life and career.

Criticism

Alvis, John. "The Miltonic Argument in Caroline Gordon's *The Glory of Hera.*" *The Southern Review* 16, No. 3 (July 1980): 560-73.

Discusses the use of Christian symbolism and Greek myth in *The Glory of Hera,* focusing on interrelated themes of death, pride, saving obedience, and the journey of the hero.

Cheney, Brainard. "Caroline Gordon's *The Malefactors.*" *The Sewanee Review* LXXIX, No. 3 (Summer 1971): 360-72.

Examines the theme of conversion in *The Malefactors.* Cheney comments on the work's critical reception and argues that it represents the culmination of Gordon's personal spiritual quest.

Cowan, Bainard. "The Serpent's Coils: How to Read Caroline Gordon's Later Fiction." *The Southern Review* 16, No. 2 (April 1980): 281-98.

Stylistic analysis which attempts to explain the reoccurrence of the serpent motif and the myth of Heracles in Gordon's later fiction, particularly in the novel *The Glory of Hera,* and the transformation of the motif on four different levels: Greek religion, Jungian psychology, Augustinian Christianity, and archetypal heroic action.

Ford, Ford Madox. "A Stage in American Literature." *Bookman* LXXIV, No. 4 (December 1931): 371-76.

Essay concerning the emergence of "a formidable school of American writers" including Gordon, Ernest Hemingway, Glenway Westcott, George Davis, and Elizabeth Madox Roberts and their respective "regionalist" writings. Ford reviews Gordon's *Penhally* commending the novel as a "great literary achievement" for its accurate "chronicle of reality."

Fraistat, Rose Ann C. *Caroline Gordon as Novelist and Woman of Letters.* Baton Rouge: Louisiana State University Press, 1984, 181 p.

Describes Gordon's critical theory and categorizes her novels into two distinctive thematic periods. The early period includes Gordon's first five novels, which concern the decline of society and culture of the South and features protagonists motivated by selfish heroism, while the later novels reveal Gordon's investigation of archetypal structures in modern settings.

King, Lawrence, T. "The Novels of Caroline Gordon." *The Catholic World* 181, No. 1084 (July 1955): 274-79.

Outlines plots and themes of Gordon's first seven novels, noting the historical focus of her earlier works and the moral and philosophical themes of her later ones.

Paterson, Isabel. "Study? Family? Politics? Let's Go Fishing!: A Serene Novel About an Old-Fashioned Gentleman Who Knew How to Answer Argument." *New York Herald Tribune Book Review* 11, No. 9 (4 November 1934): 6.

Positive review of *Aleck Maury, Sportsman,* describing the work as a "serene, unpretentious, but accomplished" fictional autobiography.

Pruette, Lorine. "Shadows in Dixie." *The New York Times Book Review* (21 May 1944): 6.

Mixed review of *The Women on the Porch,* praising its stream-of-consciousness technique for its successful evocation of mood, but lamenting that the technique only serves to diffuse the reader's interest.

Rosenberger, Coleman. "Private Lives of Some Talented People." *New York Herald Tribune Book Review* 28, No. 4 (9 September 1951): 5.

    Review praising Gordon's successful creation of compelling characters in *The Strange Children*.

Interview

Baum, Catherine B., and Watkins, Floyd C. "Caroline Gordon and 'The Captive': An Interview." *The Southern Review* n. s. VII, No. 2 (April 1971): 447-62.

    Interview in which Gordon discusses the source, structure, themes, and various critical interpretations of her short story "The Captive."

Additional coverage of Gordon's life and career is contained in the following sources published by Gale Research: *Contemporary Authors,* Vols. 11-12, 103 [obituary]; *Contemporary Authors New Revision Series,* Vol. 36; *Contemporary Authors Permanent Series,* Vol. 1; *Contemporary Literary Criticism,* Vols. 6, 13, 29; *Dictionary of Literary Biography,* Vols. 4, 9, 102; *Dictionary of Literary Biography Yearbook 1981; Major 20th-Century Writers;* and *Short Story Criticism,* Vol. 15.

Joy Harjo

1951-

American poet, scriptwriter, editor, filmmaker, and musician.

The following provides an overview of Harjo's career through 1993.

INTRODUCTION

Strongly influenced by her Muscogee Creek heritage, feminist and social concerns, and her background in the arts, Harjo frequently incorporates Native American myths, symbols, and values into her writing. Her poetry emphasizes the Southwest landscape and the need for remembrance and transcendence. She asserts: "I feel strongly that I have a responsibility to all the sources that I am: to all past and future ancestors, to my home country, to all places that I touch down on and that are myself, to all voices, all women, all of my tribe, all people, all earth, and beyond that to all beginnings and endings. In a strange kind of sense [writing] frees me to believe in myself, to be able to speak, to have voice, because I have to; it is my survival."

Biographical Information

Harjo is a registered member of the Muscogee Creek tribe—her father was Creek and her mother part French and part Cherokee—and a distant cousin of Native American poet Alexander Posey. Born and raised in Oklahoma, she graduated from the Institute of American Indian Arts, a boarding school in Santa Fe, New Mexico. After graduation she joined a Native American dance troupe and worked a series of odd jobs before pursuing a college education. Intending to study medicine, Harjo attended the University of New Mexico but soon switched her major to art. She began writing poetry after hearing American poet Galway Kinnell and Native American writers Simon Ortiz and Leslie Marmon Silko read from their works. She eventually graduated with a B.A. in poetry in 1976. Attending the University of Iowa Writers' Workshop, she took classes under the direction of Silko, earning an M.F.A. in 1978. In addition to teaching at various institutions, Harjo has worked for the National Association for Third World Writers, the National Endowment for the Arts, and the National American Public Broadcasting Consortium. She has also served on the editorial boards of *Contact II, Tyuonyi*, and the *High Plains Literary Review* and has won such honors as the American Book Award from the Before Columbus Foundation, the Delmore Schwartz Memorial Poetry Award, and an NEA fellowship. Harjo is also an avid musician, frequently performing on the saxophone.

Major Works

Harjo's work is largely autobiographical, informed by her love of the natural world and preoccupation with transcendence, survival, and the limitations of language. In *The Last Song* (1975), for instance, she writes: "how can you stand it / he said / the hot oklahoma summers / where you were born / this humid thick air / is choking me /. . . . it is the only way / I know how to breathe / an ancient chant / that my mother knew / came out of a history / woven from wet tall grass / in her womb / and i know no other way / than to surround my voice / with the summer songs of crickets / in this moist south night air // oklahoma will be the last song / i'll ever sing." The search for freedom and self-actualization are considered central to her volume *She Had Some Horses* (1983), which incorporates prayer-chants and animal imagery. Nature is also a prominent theme of Harjo's prose poetry collection, *Secrets from the Center of the World* (1989), in which each poem is accompanied by a photograph of the American Southwest. Her best known and most recent volume, *In Mad Love and War* (1990), is more overtly concerned with politics, tradition, remembrance, and the transformational aspects of poetry. In the first section, which relates various acts of violence, including attempts to deny Harjo her heritage, the murder of an Indian leader, the actions of the Ku Klux Klan, and events in war-torn Nicaragua, Harjo explores the difficulties of survival in the modern world: "*. . . we have too many stories to carry on our backs like houses, we have struggled too long to let the monsters steal our sleep, sleep, go to sleep. But I never woke up. Dogs have been nipping at my heels since I learned to walk. I was taught to not dance for a rotten supper on the plates of my enemies. My mother taught me well.*" The second half of the book frequently emphasizes personal relationships and change. In the critically acclaimed "Transformations" Harjo states: "What I mean is that hatred can be turned into something else, if you have the right words, the right meanings, buried in that tender place where the most precious animals live. . . . / That's what I mean to tell you. On the other side of the place you live / stands a dark woman. She has been trying to talk to you for years. / You have called the same name in the middle of a nightmare, / from the center of miracles. She is beautiful. / This is your hatred back. She loves you."

Critical Reception

Harjo has been consistently praised for the thematic concerns of her writings, and scholars predict that she will soon become a major figure in contemporary American poetry. They note that while Harjo's work is often set in the Southwest, emphasizes the plight of the individual, and reflects Creek values, myths, and beliefs, her oeuvre has universal relevance. Dan Bellm asserts: "Harjo's work draws from the river of Native tradition, but it also swims freely in the currents of Anglo-American verse—feminist poetry of personal/political resistance, deep-image poetry of the unconscious, 'new-narrative' explorations of story and rhythm in prose-poem form."

PRINCIPAL WORKS

The Last Song (poetry) 1975
What Moon Drove Me to This? (poetry) 1979
She Had Some Horses (poetry) 1983
Origin of Apache Crown Dance (script) 1985
Furious Light (recording) 1986
*Secrets from the Center of the World [with Stephen Strom] (poetry) 1989
In Mad Love and War (poetry) 1990

---

*Strom provided the illustrations for this book.

CRITICISM

Joy Harjo with Laura Coltelli   (interview date 23 September 1985)

[*Coltelli is the author of* Winged Words: American Indian Writers Speak *(1990). In the interview below, which was originally conducted in 1985, Harjo discusses her heritage, her identity as a Native American woman, her literary interests and influences, and various aspects of her poetry.*]

[*Coltelli*]: *When did you start writing?*

[Harjo]: Not until I was about twenty-two, which I've always thought fairly late. Up to that time I was mostly interested in art, especially painting, and majored in it at the University of New Mexico until my last year, when I transferred to the English Department to graduate with a creative-writing major. I went on to get my M.F.A. in creative writing from the University of Iowa.

Why did you shift from being an art major to creative writing?

Because I found that language, through poetry, was taking on more magical qualities than my painting. I could say more when I wrote. Soon it wasn't a choice. Poetry-speaking "called me" in a sense. And I couldn't say no.

Could you speak about going back to your roots, in your poetry, of your Oklahoma land and heritage?

I just finished a poem today. It's about trying to find the way back. But it's a different place, a mythical place. It's a spiritual landscape that Oklahoma is a part of—I always see Oklahoma as my mother, my motherland. I am connected psychically; there is a birth cord that connects me. But I don't live there and don't know that I ever will. It's too familiar, and too painful. My son lives there now; he's going to Sequoyah High School, a tribal school that is now managed by the Cherokee tribe.

So my return usually takes place on a mythical level. I mean, I do travel there as often as I can. I've written a literary column for my tribal newspaper, the *Muscogee Nation News,* know my relatives, keep in touch. There are many memories there for me, it's one of my homes.

How much does your Creek heritage affect your work as a poet?

It provides the underlying psychic structure, within which is a wealth of memory. I was not brought up traditionally Creek, was raised in the north side of Tulsa in a neighborhood where there lived many other mixed-blood Indian families. My neighbors were Seminole Indian, Pawnee, other tribes, and white. I know when I write there is an old Creek within me that often participates.

You said once, memory is like "a delta in the skin," so you are "memory alive," your poetry stems from memory always at work.

It is Creek, and touches in on the larger tribal continental memory and the larger human memory, global. It's not something I consciously chose; I mean, I am not a full-blood, but it was something that chose me, that lives in me, and I cannot deny it. Sometimes I wish I could disappear into the crowds of the city and lose this responsibility, because it is a responsibility. But I can't. I also see memory as not just associated with past history, past events, past stories, but nonlinear, as in future and ongoing history, events, and stories. And it changes.

You see a very close relationship between writing poetry and "digging piles of earth with a stick: smell it, form it." So, does it mean you're still looking for your roots down there?

They're there. That's no question. When I speak of roots I often mean more than what's usually conjectured. I consider the place we all came from, since the very beginning. It's a place I don't yet have a language for. But, on the more mundane level, I did drive around the United States in my car, alone, about three or four summers ago—just to know it better, this beautiful land. And one place that was most important for me to visit was outside a little town in Alabama called Atmore. There is still a settlement of Creeks there, who hung on through the destruction set off by Andrew Jackson's greed. I went there to say hello, and they welcomed me, treated me well. There is a communication beginning between the Oklahoma Creeks and the Alabama Creeks. We [Oklahoma Creeks] still have the language, the dances, ceremonies, which they have lost much of, but then again, nothing has destroyed their memory, which is strong, and which has kept their small enclave alive through these years of the racist South. I was so proud of them, am proud that they have kept their Creekness alive when Jackson meant them to be destroyed.

My family on my father's side was originally from Alabama. They were forced to leave during the time of Removal [1832], which really wasn't that long ago. In fact, my great-great-grandfather, Menawha, led the Redstick War of the Creeks against Andrew Jackson. Of course, we know what happened, and Menawha and his family were forced into Oklahoma. Menawha said he never wanted to see a white face again; from that part of my family we were rebels, and speakers. So what I am doing makes sense in terms of a family memory.

Do you look at writing as a means of survival?

Sure. I have to. On both a personal level and a larger, communal level. I don't believe I would be alive today if it hadn't been for writing. There were times when I was conscious of holding onto a pen and letting the words flow, painful and from the gut, to keep from letting go of it all. Now, this was when I was much younger, and full of self-hatred. Writing helped me give voice to turn around a terrible silence that was killing me. And on a larger level, if we, as Indian people, Indian women, keep silent, then we will disappear, at least in this level of reality. As Audre Lorde says [in her *Sister Outsider: Essays and Speeches*], also, "Your silence will not protect you," which has been a quietly unanimous decision it seems, this last century with Indian people.

She Had Some Horses *is a kind of circular journey, walking and talking backward.* **"Call it Fear"** *is the very first poem and in the last one,* **"I Give You Back,"** *"the terrible and beautiful fear" comes to an end. Could you elaborate on that?*

"Call it Fear" was one of the earliest poems I wrote in that series, and **"I Give You Back"** one of the last. I didn't consciously set up the structure of the book that way, but maybe unconsciously I did. I want to thank Brenda Petersen, a novelist-editor friend of mine, for her arrangement. I gave her the manuscript when I couldn't get the arrangement right after many, many tries, and it is because of her that it works well. She understood that I meant a circular journey.

In the last section of the same book you see in the horses the coming of a new people. Does it also shape your identity as a woman?

I'm not sure I know what you mean. When I consider a new people, I consider a people whose spiritual selves are obvious. There are no judgments, or prejudices. Sexual identities are not cause for power plays, and we become fully who we are, whether male, female, or any combination. We need this resurrection; it's who we truly are, yet you could be deceived, especially when you look around the world and see the hatred against the female, and notice, too, that all the wars are basically race wars, white people against the darker-skinned ones. But I am especially speaking of a power that would be called woman-woman-intuitive. My work is woman-identified. One of the funniest questions I've been asked as a visitor to an Indian-culture class in a university is, by a male student, "Where are the men in your poems?" He was offended because he didn't see himself, not in the form that he looked for. I truly feel there is a new language coming about—look at the work of Meridel LeSueur, Sharon Doubiago, Linda Hogan, Alice Walker—it's coming from the women. Something has to be turned around.

The moon image is central to your poetry. Moon as wholeness, which speaks of the universe, a circular design again, which speaks also of woman's life. Is that true?

Yes, although she appears less and less in my new poems. I associate the moon with the past, evoking the past, past fears, and so on.

Your personal past?

Anyone's personal past. Now I am looking toward fire, a renewal. But still aware of the dream, in which the moon appears, a constructive kind of dreaming.

What do you mean by constructive?

I mean, consciously understanding that dreamtime is another kind of cohesive reality that we take part in.

A kind of active perception instead of a passive one.

Yes, it's much more active.

Feminism and tribal heritage—can you see any connection?

The world has changed so much. Yes, I'm sure there is a connection, but so much differs from tribe to tribe.

Because some Indian cultures are woman-oriented?

Some are woman-oriented, especially when you consider the earth as woman, like the Pueblo people of the Southwest. But all have changed over the years after much white contact. And values have changed. Many have evolved, or devolved, into male-centered, male-dominated cultures, following the pattern of the dominant Euro-culture that is American, but generally women were, are, recognized as physically, electrically, whatever, more grounded, in tune with the earth, and again, that's a generalization, because there are always exceptions. You will find "grounded" men, also. I still don't feel as if I have answered your question. I know I walk in and out of several worlds everyday. Some overlap, some never will, or at least not as harmoniously. The word "feminism" doesn't carry over to the tribal world, but a concept mirroring similar meanings would. Let's see, what would it then be called— empowerment, some kind of empowerment.

What does it mean, being an American Indian woman in the United States nowadays?

To begin, it certainly means you are a survivor. Indian people make up only about one-half of 1 percent of the total population of the United States! It means you carry with you a certain unique perception. And again you are dealing with tribal differences, personal differences, and so on. We are not all alike! Yet, I believe there is a common dream, a common thread between us, mostly unspoken.

I don't believe there are any accidents in why people were born where they were, who they were, or are. There are no accidents. So I realize that being born an American Indian woman in this time and place is with a certain reason, a certain purpose. There are seeds of dreams I hold, and responsibility, that go with being born someone, especially a woman of my tribe, who is also part of this invading other culture, and the larger globe. We in this generation, and the next generation, are dealing with a larger world than the people who went before us—that we know of, because who knows what went down many, many, many years ago that no one remembers. We are dealing with a world consciousness, and have begun to see unity, first with many tribes in the United States and North America with the Pan-Indian movement, and now with tribal people in the rest of the world, Central and South America, Africa, Australian aborigines, and so on. We are not isolated. No one is. What happens here, happens there. But it is on sometimes subtle yet disturbing levels.

Are you active in women's organizations?

Not really. Sometimes I feel I should be, but it isn't my manner. I participate by doing benefit readings, appearances, taking part when it is useful to do so. I know it is important, and groups are more powerful than one person working alone, but I guess there is no one group that I feel strong enough about to be active in, though I actively take part in many.

Are you suspicious? Of what?

I've wondered. Maybe it comes from being a mixed-blood in this world. I mean, I feel connected to others, but many women's groups have a majority of white women and I honestly can feel uncomfortable, or even voiceless some-

times. I've lived in and out of both worlds for a long time and have learned how to speak—those groups just affect others that way—with a voicelessness. It's my problem, something I've learned to get over, am learning to overcome, because I am often the only one to speak for many of us in those situations. Sometimes it gets pretty comical, bizarre. When I was on the National Endowment for the Arts literature panel I was often the spokesperson-representative for Indian people, black people, all minority people, including women's, lesbian, and gay groups. It was rather ridiculous and angering at the same time, for we were all considered outside the mainstream of American literature. And it's not true, for often we are closer to the center.

Noni Daylight appears in some of your poems, persona poems. You said, "It's like she was a good friend." Would you comment on that, on the persona in your poems?

She began quite some time ago, as a name I gave a real-life woman I couldn't name in a poem. Then she evolved into her own person, took on her own life. And then she left my poems and went into a poem by Barney Bush, a Shawnee poet, and I never saw her again. She never came back!

What about the other stories of women in your poems? Are they true stories?

Yes, always on some level. I'm a writer, I like to make up stories, to add to them, often make them larger. The "I" is not always me, but a way I chose to speak the poem. **"The Woman Hanging from the Thirteenth Floor"** is written around an imaginary woman. You could call her imaginary. But within that space she is real, also. I made a trip to Chicago, oh, about eight years ago, and one of the places I went to while I was there was the Chicago Indian Center. The center was rather bleak, as there wasn't extra money around to buy things to make the place warm, home-like; there were no curtains, nothing like that, but in one room I noticed a rocking chair. It may have been empty, or there may have been someone in it—the image stayed with me. Perhaps it was because the chair was round, and everything else, all around, was square. So, a few years after that trip, the image stayed with me, and I would see this woman, rocking and rocking, for her life, and she compelled me to write the poem. And I felt her standing behind me, urging me on as I wrote, kept looking behind me. When it first appeared, and during the first readings of the poem others would come up after the reading and say, "You know, I know that woman," or "I knew her," or "I heard the story and have a newspaper clipping of it," and the event always had occurred in a different place. And other women are composites of many women I know, or stories I've heard, probably much like a fiction writer would work.

So you became a kind of storyteller?

In a way, though I am not a good fiction writer, or should I say, have never really tried it, except in terms of screenplays.

"Language identifies the world." You said that the English language is not enough. "It is a male language, not tribal, not spiritual enough."

Yes, I said that. I have learned to love the language, or rather, what the language can express. But I have felt bound by the strictness imposed by its male-centeredness, its emphasis on nouns. So, it's also challenging, as a poet, to use it to express tribal, spiritual language, being. But maybe all poets basically are after that, and sometimes it isn't enough and that's when those boundaries become frustrating.

What do you mean by saying English is not enough, English is a male language?

Again, maybe it would be that way in any language, the sense of somehow being at a loss for words; [that] could always be the poet's dilemma. The ending of a poem, **"Bleed-Through,"** says it: "There are no words, only sounds / that lead us into the darkest nights / where stars burn into ice / where the dead arise again / to walk in shoes of fire."

Since language has an importance of its own in Indian culture, what's the contribution or influence, just in terms of language, to mainstream American literature?

What I think of immediately is the denial, the incredible denial of anything other than that based on the European soul in American literature. Anything else is seen as "foreign," or not consciously integrated into what is called American literature. It could be ethnocentrism backed by a terrible guilt about what happened in this country.

So what's the contribution, just in terms of language, to main-stream American literature?

That's a difficult question, one that will take me many months to consider, because I'm always thinking about what I can add to the language, as someone of this background—dreams, and so on. I consider first a certain lyricism, a land-based language.

The spirit of place?

Yes, the spirit of place recognized, fed, not even paved over, forgotten. Sometimes I feel like specters of forgotten ones roam the literature of some of these American writers who don't understand where they come from, who they are, where they are going. The strongest writers have always been the ones with a well-defined sense of place—I don't mean you have to be a nature writer—I'm thinking of "nonethnic" people, like Flannery O'Connor.

What about imagery?

Oh sure, imagery. That's definitely part of it.

A new feeling of landscape perhaps?

Or a knowing of the landscape, as something alive with personality, breathing. Alive with names, alive with events, nonlinear. It's not static and that's a very important point. The Western viewpoint has always been one of the land as wilderness, something to be afraid of, and conquered because of the fear.

The so-called wilderness.

Yes, it depends on your viewpoint what wilderness is. For some the city is a wilderness of concrete and steel, made within a labyrinth of mind.

You mentioned before you are not only a poet, but you're a scriptwriter for television and film. How does the process work in translating your poetical world from one medium to another?

Screenwriting is definitely related to poetry. You're dealing again with the translation of emotions into images. There's a similar kind of language involved. One goal I have, a life goal in terms of the cinema, is to create a film with a truly tribal vision, viewpoint, in terms of story, camera viewpoints, angles, everything. It hasn't been done, not on the scale I would like to do it.

What do you think of non-Indian critics of your work and of Indian literature in general?

That question could be answered many ways—I mean, there are specific non-Indian critics who get into trying to be Indian, when they don't have to. What I write, what any of us write, or are after, whether we are Indian, Chicano, Laotian, is shimmering language, poetry, the same as anyone else who is writing in whatever language; with whatever sensibilities. Or too often they won't approach the literature at all, won't read it or speak of it because, again, that guilt enters in, or that fear that keeps them from entering any place other than what is most familiar.

As far as the literature goes, I've seen much growth in these last several years, in all of us. We are setting high standards for ourselves, our own standards, mind you, in terms of what is possible with this language, and with what we have come to know as artists of this continent.

What writers are important to you?

I consider first the writers who got me turned on to writing, what writing could do. Because I was rather a late bloomer in this business, I was never turned on by conventional English-language poetry. These writers include Simon Ortiz, Leslie Silko, and many black American writers, like June Jordan, later Audre Lorde and Alice Walker. Also Pablo Neruda, James Wright, Galway Kinnell, and African writers. I love the work of Amos Tutuola, especially *The Palm Wine Drunkard*. And there are many others.

Do you see any changes in your work?

Yes, many. If I didn't see them, didn't see growth, then I wouldn't do it any more. There are leaps between **What Moon Drove Me to This?** and **She Had Some Horses,** and I expect the leap to be huge between **Horses** and this next collection I am working on. I feel like I am just now learning how to write a poem. It has taken me over ten years to get to this point of just beginning.

And what about in terms of technique?

I'm certainly much more involved with process, inner travel, when I write now than even five years ago.

Can you speak a bit more about these new poems?

For one thing they are not so personal. I am in them, for I believe poets have to be inside their poems somewhere, or the poem won't work. But they aren't so personally revealing, and the space has grown larger. The first book was definitely centered in Oklahoma, or New Mexico. Then, in *Horses,* there was much more traveling, and in the new work [*In Mad Love and War*], there is even more traveling into the inner landscape.

So, in comparison with the other books, how could you define this new book?

Oh, it's hard to say—intensity. I would hope it is more powerful, stirring. **"We Must Call a Meeting"** is one of the newest poems in it. I'll read what I have, but I might change some of it.

"We Must Call a Meeting"

I am fragile, a piece of pottery smoked from fire
                                    made of dung,
the design drawn from nightmares. I am an
    arrow, painted
                            with lightning
to seek the way to the name of the enemy,
                    but the arrow has now created
its own language.
    It is a language of lizards and storms, and we
                                    have
begun to hold conversations
        long into the night.
                        I forget to eat
I don't work. My children are hungry and the
    animals who live
in the backyard are starving.
        I begin to draw maps of stars.
The spirits of old and new ancestors perch on my
    shoulders.
I make prayers of clear stone
        of feathers from birds
            who live closest to the gods.
The voice of the stone is born
        of a meeting of yellow birds
who circle the ashes of smoldering ashes.
            The feathers sweep the prayers up
and away.
I, too, try to fly but get caught in the crossfire
                                of signals
        and my spirit drops back down to earth.
I am lost; I am looking for you
    who can help me walk this thin line between
                            the breathing
            and the dead.
You are the curled serpent in the pottery of
    nightmares.
You are the dreaming animal who paces back
    and forth in my head.
We must call a meeting.
    Give me back my language and build a house
inside it.
        A house of madness.
            A house for the dead who are not dead.
And the spiral of the sky above it.
And the sun
        and the moon.
        And the stars to guide us called promise.

Also another new poem, called **"Transformations,"** about turning someone's hatred into love. I tried to actually work that transformation in the poem.

"Transformations"

This poem is a letter to tell you that I have
smelled the hatred you have tried to find me

with; you would like to destroy me. Bone splintered in the eye of one you choose to name your enemy won't make it better for you to see. It could take a thousand years if you name it that way, but then, to see after all that time, never could anything be so clear. Memory has many forms. When I think of early winter I think of a blackbird laughing in the frozen air; guards a piece of light. I saw the whole world caught in that sound, the sun stopped for a moment because of tough belief. I don't know what that has to do with what I am trying to tell you except that I know you can turn a poem into something else. This poem could be a bear treading the far northern tundra, smelling the air for sweet alive meat. Or a piece of seaweed stumbling in the sea. Or a blackbird, laughing. What I mean is that hatred can be turned into something else, if you have the right words, the right meanings, buried in that tender place in your heart where the most precious animals live. Down the street an ambulance has come to rescue an old man who is slowly losing his life. Not many can see that he is already becoming the backyard tree he has tended for years, before he moves on. He is not sad, but compassionate for the fears moving around him.

That's what I mean to tell you. On the other side of the place you live stands a dark woman. She has been trying to talk to you for years. You have called the same name in the middle of a nightmare, from the center of miracles. She is beautiful. This is your hatred back. She loves you.

It's a kind of circular design again.

Yes.

Would you describe your writing process? I understand that you revise a lot.

I begin with the seed of an emotion, a place, and then move from there. It means hours watching the space form in the place in front of the typewriter, speaking words, listening to them, watching them form, and be crossed out, on the paper, and so on, and yes, revision. I no longer see the poem as an ending point, perhaps more the end of a journey, an often long journey that can begin years earlier, say with the blur of the memory of the sun on someone's cheek, a certain smell, an ache, and will culminate years later in a poem, sifted through a point, a lake in my heart through which language must come. That's what I work with, with my students at the university, opening that place within them of original language, which I believe must be in everyone, but not everyone can reach it.

You said before that you were speaking with your students about your work as well?

I can't separate my work, my writing, from who I am, so of course it comes into the classroom with me in one way or another.

Just a piece of paper with a new poem?

Oh no, as part of that space I teach out of, a space of intuition made up of everything I know as well as what I don't know, and I've learned in writing, and in teaching, that it is important to recognize that place, to open yourself, believing.

Joy Harjo with Laura Coltelli, in an interview in Winged Words: American Indian Writers Speak, *University of Nebraska Press, 1990, pp. 54-68.*

Harjo on language, literature, and communication:

I have a theory of communication: We're moving farther and farther away from true communication—media, you know, images, video, constant images is really where it's at right now—where you're not a participant. You watch these things happen. The next step backwards is the written language; but there's still room to lie there. Here I'm a poet, and of course I believe that incredible things can be done with the written language and that it's useful, but I also think that in developing that, we lost more than we gained. You don't have to look the person in the eyes, you don't have a voice, you don't have the atmosphere; and even though someone can read your work and participate, it's not on the level of someone being next to you. And before that, there's the oral. And there you have the eyes, you have the participation, and so on. But even then, there's a place before that in which you don't have to speak, and there is a total understanding, and no one can lie. And that's what we're going to go back to.

Joy Harjo, in an interview with John Crawford and Patricia Clark Smith, in This is about Vision: Interviews with Southwestern Writers, *edited by William Balassi, John F. Crawford, and Annie O. Eysturoy, University of New Mexico Press, 1990.*

Patricia Clark Smith and Paula Gunn Allen (essay date 1987)

[*Allen is a Laguna Pueblo novelist, poet, nonfiction writer, educator, and critic. In the following excerpt, the critics provide a thematic analysis of Harjo's poetry.*]

Joy Harjo's particular poetic turf is cities, especially from the point of view of an Indian woman traveling between them. Her poems are full of planes, cars, pick-ups, borders, and white center-lines; she writes not only of the Oklahoma of her childhood and New Mexico, where she's spent many of her adult years, but of Iowa and Kansas, Calgary and East Chicago, Anchorage and New Orleans, and corrugated tunnels in airports, "a space between leaving and staying." Her work traces the modern Pan-Indian trails criss-crossing the country, no longer trade routes in the old way, but circuits—the pow-wow circuit, the academic-feminist lecture circuit, the poetry-reading circuit. The primacy of travel in her works probably makes her . . . the most typical of contemporary American Indian writers. In and out of the Southwest, as Paula Gunn Allen remarks, wandering is an old custom among many tribes. This is perhaps especially true of Oklahoma tribal people, whose wanderings have not always been volun-

tary. In an interview, Harjo said, "maybe the people of Oklahoma always have this sense that somehow we're going to have to move again. . . . Somehow, it's not settled, even though we've all lived there since about 1830." . . .

Harjo does have a strong home-base, an acute sense of the red earth and the red people that the name Oklahoma simultaneously signifies. The literal earth is part of her early memory: "I love language, sound, how emotions, images, dreams are formed in air and on the page," she writes [in **"Bio-poetics Sketch,"** *The Greenfield Review* 9, Nos. 3-4 (Winter 1981-82)]. "When I was a little kid in Oklahoma, I would get up before everyone else and go outside to a place of rich dark earth next to the foundation of the house. I would dig piles of earth with a stick, smell it, form it. It had sound. Maybe that's when I first learned to write poetry, even though I never really wrote until I was in my early twenties."

An early poem, **"The Last Song,"** especially affirms that strong childhood bond with a particular patch of southwestern earth that "has sound," that speaks and nurtures:

> how can you stand it
> he said
> the hot oklahoma summers
> where you were born
> this humid thick air
> is choking me
> . . . . .
> it is the only way
> i know how to breathe
> an ancient chant
> that my mother knew
> came out of a history
> woven from wet tall grass
> in her womb
> and i know no other way
> than to surround my voice
> with the summer songs of crickets
> in this moist south night air
>
> oklahoma will be the last song
> i'll ever sing

Here, the land is a mother and a mother of mothers; a singer who gives human singers their songs. This is the poem of a woman who grew up not only playing in the soil, but listening to it. Most of Harjo's poetry does not center specifically on her Creek heritage—or not yet: Geary Hobson speculates [in a review of **What Moon Drove Me to This?** in *The Greenfield Review* 9, Nos. 3-4 (Winter 1981-82)] that "oklahoma will be the last song / i'll ever sing" may be a promise of the theme Harjo will turn to in time. Meanwhile, the land does not manifest itself in her poetry in spirit-figures out of her particular tribal tradition, like [Luci] Tapahonso's Snake-man or [Leslie Marmon] Silko's mountain ka'tsinas. What does pulse throughout Harjo's work is a sense that all landscape she encounters is endowed with an identity, vitality, and intelligence of its own. This sense of life and intelligence in the land is quite different from the human emotions an Anglo poet might *project* upon landscape; the life in Harjo's landscapes makes poems written out of the pathetic fallacy indeed seem pathetic by comparison.

"Kansas City" illustrates Harjo's sense of the individual identities of natural things. In that poem, Noni Daylight (a kind of alter ego who appears often in Harjo's works) elects to remain

> in Kansas City, raise the children
> she had by different men,
> all colors. Because she knew
> that each star rang with separate
> colored hue, as bands of horses,
> and wild
> like the spirit in her . . .

Her children of different colors are comparable, in their beautiful singularity, to the each-ness of stars and horses. Noni's children, Noni's men, and Noni herself are singular and vitally connected with that natural universe of stars and horses. Even though they live in Kansas City, they are not alienated from or outside of nature.

Moreover, in Harjo's poems the land acknowledges its connection to people. In **"Leaving,"** the speaker wakes as her roommate gets up to answer a late-night phone call:

> Her sister was running way from her boyfriend
>   and
> was stranded in Calgary, Alberta. Needed
>   money
> and comfort for the long return back home.
> I dreamed of a Canadian plain, and warm arms
>   around me,
> the soft skin of the body's landscape. And I
>   dreamed
> of bear, and a thousand-mile escape homeward.

Even the imagined landscape of the Canadian plain, usually considered harsh country and certainly radically different from Harjo's Oklahoma, is like the sisters and friends earlier in the poem who warm and sustain one another. Both the women and the land are soft, comforting, erotic, familiar, associated with the healing and power of the totemic bear, and with home.

Harjo turns to the theme of human erotic connections with spirit figures who embody the land in her many poems about the moon. In them, the moon appears not as symbol and certainly not as background lighting, but as a full, intelligent female person. That the moon should be so important in Harjo's work makes sense given her woman-centeredness and her representation of herself as a woman on the move. The woman-ness of the moon is in almost all cultures, and she can be there for the wanderer in Anchorage or Hong Kong; like Harjo, she is a traveler too. The moon, that medieval emblem of instability for Western Europeans, is a stable comforter for Harjo; in **"Heartbeat,"** Noni Daylight drops acid and drives through Albuquerque with a pistol cradled in her lap. In the middle of this nighttown horror, "Noni takes the hand of the moon / that she knows is in control overhead." The poem concludes, "It is not the moon, or the pistol in her lap / but a fierce anger / that will free her." Even so, given that Noni has yet to find that anger, the moon is the only entity who remains steady, who reaches out to Noni in a time when "these nights, she wants out."

And yet the comforting moon Harjo knows is also as completely herself and as mysterious as Snake-man or moun-

tain ka'tsinas. Harjo conveys this moon's wildness and independent life beautifully in **"Moonlight":** "I know when the sun is in China / because the night-shining other-light / crawls into my bed. She is moon." Harjo imagines the other side of the world,

> in Hong Kong, Where someone else has also
> awakened, the night thrown back and asked,
> "Where is the moon, my lover?"
> And from here I always answer in my dreaming,
> "The last time I saw her, she was in the arms
> of another sky."

What matters most about Harjo's moon is her ability as a living spirit to enter into the sort of dialogue with people that reassures them, no matter where they are, of their own lives and their connection with wilderness. In **"September Moon,"** as Harjo and her children try to cross Albuquerque's Central Avenue in the midst of State Fair traffic, she encounters the moon rising out of the trapped air of the urban Rio Grande Valley:

> I was fearful of traffic
> trying to keep my steps and the moon was east,
> ballooning out of the mountain ridge, out of
>   smokey clouds
> out of any skin that was covering her. Naked.
> Such beauty.
> Look.
> We are alive. The woman of the moon looking
> at us, and we are looking at her, acknowledging
> each other.

The land and the person acknowledging each other as living beings, sensate and sensual, their lives inextricably woven together in Spider Woman's web—this is what lies at the heart of American Indian ritual and southwestern American Indian women's writing.

Patricia Clark Smith and Paula Gunn Allen, "Earthy Relations, Carnal Knowledge: Southwestern American Indian Women Writers and Landscape," in The Desert Is No Lady: Southwestern Landscapes in Women's Writing and Art, *edited by Vera Norwood and Janice Monk, Yale University Press, 1987, pp. 174-96.*

Margaret Randall   (review date July 1990)

[*Randall is an American poet, editor, short story writer, and essayist. In the excerpt below, she offers a favorable assessment of* In Mad Love and War *and* Secrets from the Center of the World.]

> . . . we had nothing to lose and lost it anyway
> in the cursed country of the fox. We still talk
> about that winter, how the cold froze imaginary
> buffalo on the stuffed horizon of snow-
> banks. . . . I would like to say, with grace, we
> picked ourselves up and walked into the spring
> thaw. We didn't; the next season was
> worse. . . . I know there is something larger
> than the memory of a dispossessed people. We
> have seen it.

("Grace")

Joy Harjo's lines are a metaphor for the pain and joy of this society we inhabit together and also, more specifically, for her life as a Creek (Muscogee) woman, born in Oklahoma and raised there and in New Mexico. Her language comes from what Marge Piercy rightly calls a sacred power, and the grit and endurance of a rebellious woman struggling to survive racism, capitalism and patriarchy.

Harjo reinvents myth to fit life as she is forced, and ultimately chooses, to live it. She is never facile New Age, but deeply political, though her allegiance goes beyond party or nation. In **"Nine Below"** she writes:

> Across the frozen Bering Sea is the
> invisible border
> of two warring countries. I am loyal to
> neither,
> only to the birds who fly over, laugh at
> the ridiculous
> ways of humans, know wars destroy
> dreams, divide the
> country inside us.

This poetry is bright and courageous and well made; it speaks from a culture that is at once our history and ignored. Among the several Native American poets—especially the women—whose work has gripped us in recent years, Harjo's voice most relentlessly bridges the several worlds she inhabits. These worlds include, but are not limited to, the wisdom and warning of those who came before; a childhood ignited by oppression, alcoholism, resistance and proud memories; the young woman's cycle of hard times and early children; the poet/screenwriter/university professor who never loses her roots.

Though until very recently she had only a single book in print (*She Had Some Horses*, 1983), Harjo's unique voice is well known by most readers of contemporary American poetry. Earlier titles, *The Last Song* and *What Moon Drove Me to This?*, had long gone the way of most small-circulation collections. To a steady demand and to its credit, Thunder's Mouth has kept *She Had Some Horses* available. Harjo's poetry has begun to be anthologized, as well, in places like the new *Heath Anthology of American Literature*. Perhaps more pertinent to her broadening circle of fans, though, is that this is a poet who reads everywhere. Her passionate voice can be heard regularly in auditoriums, classrooms and bookstores, in places ranging from an Indian pow wow in New Mexico or Arizona to New York City's 92nd Street Y.

Now, in the months that bridge eighties to nineties, Harjo has two new books. *Secrets from the Center of the World* is a collaboration with photographer/astronomer Stephen Strom: 60 prose poems and 60 colored images combine to create an evocative little gem, intensely personal, hauntingly universal. And *In Mad Love and War* is the major new book those of us who love Harjo's poetry have been waiting for.

In Mad Love And War fulfills the promise. The power of *She Had Some Horses* is still there, but there is more wildness in construction and imagery. And it is a wildness that works. A collection of prose poems as well as some with a shorter breath line, the book opens with **"Grace,"** the signature poem I quote from at the beginning of this review. "Like Coyote, like Rabbit," writes Harjo, "we could

not contain our terror and clowned our way through a season of false midnights. We had to swallow that town with laughter, so it would go down easy as honey . . ."

This is what people do, when they are born of those who must fight racism, indeed genocide, to survive. They swallow towns and poverty and scorn and ecological destruction and the smallpox blanket or the bottle of cheap whiskey—"with laughter so it [will] go down easy as honey." And they remind themselves—or the poet who is sage reminds them—"there is something larger than the memory of a dispossessed people. We have seen it."

The book is divided into two sections: "The Wars" and "Mad Love." The first is a series of poems about just what its name implies, the ongoing Indian wars, inside and out of the body. The poet asks "How do I say it? In this language there are no words for how the real world collapses." But she invents them. Harjo hunts down the words, by listening to her mutable "knower" or spirit guide, and reinventing a language from the plain talk of her ancestors' stories and an always surprising almost staccato contemporary sound.

Tradition and revelation come together in her verse. In **"Deer Dancer"** there is a "brother-in-law [who] hung out with white people, went to law school with a perfect record, quit. Says you can keep your laws, your words. And practiced law on the streets with his hands . . ." It is the brother-in-law who asks *What's a girl like you doing in a place like this?* And the poet's voice responds: "That's what I'd like to know, what are we all doing in a place like this?"

The war poems are peopled with the dead who are not dead, hooded ghosts, circling panthers, the trickster, warriors all. They have come and they speak, right alongside the rioting inmates and the bootleggers. In **"Autobiography"** the mother tells her daughter about God deciding to make people: cooking the first batch too long and burning them (black people), taking the next from the oven before they were done (whites), and finally producing a perfect batch: "and these were the Indian people, just like you." Harjo internalized the fable, but pushes past it to the child's confusion: "At five I was designated to string beads in kindergarten. At seven I knew how to play chicken and win. And at fourteen I was drinking. . . ."

"Autobiography" ends:

> I have since outlived . . . my father and that
> ragged self I chased through precarious years.
> But I carry them with me the same as this body
> carries the heart as a drum. Yesterday there was
> rain traveling east to home. A hummingbird
> spoke. She was a shining piece of invisible memory, inside the raw cortex of songs. I knew then
> that this was the Muscogee season of forgiveness, time of new corn, the spiraling dance.

And, from **"Strange Fruit"**:

> . . . *we have too many stories to carry on our*
> *backs like houses, we have struggled too long to*
> *let the monsters steal our sleep, sleep, go to sleep.*
> *But I never woke up. Dogs have been nipping at*
> *my heels since I learned to walk. I was taught*

to not dance for a rotten supper on the plates of
my enemies. My mother taught me well.

A war of many layers, first autobiographical and then
about us all, at precisely those places where spirit intersects oppression on its wild flight home. **"Unmailed Letter"** is a particularly condensed example of Harjo's use of
language to translate the markings in flesh and psyche:

> Your laugh, and I considered myself
> resurrected, but then made the correction
> for time and space and it still added
> to an irrational number.
> It's elementary. You can't add
> apples and oranges. I've mixed
> faith with your distraction.
> But I was never good at math.
> Or with any test that meant jumping
> hoops
> of water. This is how it is at specifically
> noon. I am fire eaten by wind.
> I drink water for a cure
> that will teach me the fine art
> of subtraction.

One poem is a savage prayer for Anna Mae Pictou
Aquash, the Micmac American Indian Movement activist
murdered by the FBI in February of 1976. In it Harjo
could be writing about herself—or other women of
color—when she says: "You are the shimmering young
woman / who found her voice, / when you were warned
to be silent, or have your body cut away / from you like
an elegant weed." And there are two strong poems out of
Harjo's experience of the Nicaraguan revolution, **"Resurrection"** and **"The Real Revolution is Love."** Many of her
images are thunderingly precise: from **"Resurrection,"**
"Ask the women who have given away the clothes of their
dead children. Ask the frozen soul of a man who was
found in the hole left by his missing penis."

The poems in the second section all seem to drop an oc-
tave, settle in, offering up a resolution of sorts. Never less,
but certainly more comfortable. Rabbit is still with us, but
Deer has come to stay; she/he is "no imaginary tale." In
these poems the movement between inner (spirit, memory) and outer (tangible) perceptions quivers in the air,
frenzies like the long solo of a tenor sax. Take this piece
from the second movement of **"Deer Ghost"**:

> . . . I can taste you now as I squat on the earth
> floor of this home I abandoned for you. On this
> street named for a warrior people, a street
> named after bravery, I am lighting the fire that
> crawls from my spine to the gods with a coal
> from my sister's flame. This is what names me
> in the ways of my people, who have called me
> back. The deer knows what it is doing wandering
> the streets of this city . . .

Rain washes many of Harjo's images, leaving them pris-
tine, shining. In "Mad Love" as well as in "The Wars"
there are love poems that wet the tongue, connect with
every longing or satiation you've ever known. And there
are those structured on Harjo's devastating use of irony,
like **"If I Think about You Again It Will Be the Fifty-
third Monday of Next Year"**:

> And here I am stirring an imagination that has

always got me into trouble, thinking what I
could do to you. It wouldn't be pretty as the
dusk sun slipping from one bed to the next. Or
feel like a sultry fish on the dance floor with a
woman you have loved forever. Nothing like
that is what I would do to you. I could make you
into the fifth cat and turn my back. I could say
your name backward and send it to a warring
star. Or, better yet, erase it, your whole story a
sterile page, and I would rewrite it without you
in it. Yes. Let me begin with a day like this, a
musical animal like Weather Report blowing
through the black market on this snowy snowy
Monday and I can go anywhere I want, and do
without you.

Joy Harjo is the stranger who is always right next door,
the musician (yes, she does play tenor sax), religious (in
the old way), a mother, daughter, lover of women, a storyteller for whom love and memory are interchangeable
tales. . . .

[*Secrets from the Center of the World*] is a book whose
magic relies on each pairing of a startlingly beautiful landscape photo with a short prose poem written precisely to
prolong its splendor. The images pull us into themselves.
Together each set becomes much more than the sum of its
parts.

Stephen Strom is an astronomer as well as a color photographer, and his pictures are frequently like maps—of a
land as vast and rich as the star-studded heavens. The colors—muted creams, ochres, yellows, reds, browns, pur-
ples, mauves, blues, greens—might be the colors of the
sea, or the sky at sunset or dawn. Trees, specks of green
dotting undulating hills, might be planets or fish—or trees.
A lone house, one telephone pole distant from another by
who can say what emptiness, the serpentine movement of
a dry wash cutting through land that has been here forever. Suddenly, the orange fire of foliage, crease of rock, the
cool heat of violet sand. Time seems motionless; seasons
and shadows are the real agents of change.

This is how this land is, its true space and color and—most
important—light. But only those who inhabit the landscape of New Mexico, Arizona, Utah, will recognize the
simple realism of these images. Others will surely suspect
technological tampering.

There is no alteration in these photographs, nor do the
poems lack a word or possess one too many. Language and
visual image are perfectly tuned and balanced, producing
an experience in which neither illustrates the other but
each needs its counterpart. Here are some of the poems:

> If all events are related, then what story does a
> volcano erupting in Hawaii, the birth of a
> woman's second son near Gallup, and this
> shoulderbone of earth made of a mythic mon-
> ster's anger construct? Nearby a meteor crashes.
> Someone invents aerodynamics, makes wings.
> The answer is like rushing wind: simple faith.
>
> . . . .
>
> Invisible fish swim this ghost ocean now de-
> scribed by waves of sand, by water-worn rock.
> Soon the fish will learn to walk. Then humans
> will come ashore and paint dreams on the drying

stone. Then later, much later, the ocean floor will be punctuated by Chevy trucks, carrying the dreamers' descendants, who are going to the store.

. . . .

Don't bother the earth spirit who lives here. She is working on a story. It is the oldest story in the world and it is delicate, changing. If she sees you watching she will invite you in for coffee, give you warm bread, and you will be obligated to stay and listen. But this is no ordinary story. You will have to endure earthquakes, lightning, the deaths of all those you love, the most blinding beauty. It's a story so compelling you may never want to leave; this is how she traps you. See that stone finger over there? That is the only one who ever escaped.

I wish I could reproduce Strom's images as easily as I can Harjo's words. I can't, but you can get the book and see for yourself.

Margaret Randall, "Nothing to Lose," in The Women's Review of Books, *Vol. VII, Nos. 10-11, July, 1990, pp. 17-18.*

Harjo on the writing process:

There's a sort of ecstatic sadness. It's not always sadness, but there's a point of letting go at which I know I can do what I want, and it feels good, and I'm playing, I'm touching language, and I'm touching places I haven't touched before. It doesn't work if I know where I'm going and how I'm going to get there.

I think a poem has to have a huge amount of risk, and it has to have some danger, because there's danger in the universe.

Jay Harjo, in Penelope Moffet's "A Poet's Words From the Heart of Her Heritage," in the Los Angeles Times, *10 February 1989.*

Leslie Ullman   (review date Spring 1991)

[*Ullman is an American editor, poet, and educator. In the following review of* In Mad Love and War, *she states that "all these poems seem written in a moment of urgency, fed by deeply rooted memory or longing, sometimes by defiance, and always by a warriorlike compassion."*]

Joy Harjo speaks, as she has in her previous work, with great sureness of spirit and the mercurial, expansive imagination of a conjurer in this third collection, **In Mad Love and War.** Nearly all these poems seem written in a moment of urgency, fed by deeply rooted memory or longing, sometimes by defiance, and always by a warriorlike compassion that sees through the split between people and their histories, people and their hearts, people and the natural world.

These poems reflect her heritage as a Creek Indian, both

in their evocation of emblems such as deer, laughing birds, and "the language of lizards and storms," and also in their identification with people whose dreams have been thwarted by dull circumstance or outright violence: "the man from Jemez" huddled in a blanket in the snow, nearly out of his senses, who mistakes the poet for his daughter (**"Autobiography"**); civil rights activist Jacqueline Peters hanged by the Klan in an olive tree near her home in 1985 (**"Strange Fruit"**); a young Micmac woman whose remains were autopsied, buried, and then exhumed and autopsied again before her identity or the cause of her death, a bullet fired through the back of her head, was correctly identified (**"For Anna Mae Pictou Aquash, Whose Spirit Is Present Here and in the Dappled Stars . . . "**).

Harjo stands squarely in these poems as "one born of a blood who wrestled the whites for freedom" (**"Javelina"**), but her stance is not so much that of a representative of a culture as it is the more generative one of a storyteller whose stories resurrect memory, myth, and private struggles that have been overlooked, and who thus restores vitality to the culture at large. As a storyteller, Harjo steps into herself as a passionate individual living on the edge, at once goaded and strengthened by a heightened sensitivity to the natural order of things and to the ways history has violated that order. This sensitivity, a gift of her heritage, becomes her gift to the readers of her poems. The rest of the long title to her poem on Aquash reads: " . . . we remember the story and tell it again so that we may all live."

Other Harjo poems touch upon blues music and saxophones, troubled love, South American revolutionaries, figures from her childhood, weather, and landscape. These subjects become "stories" too, the way a good blues song seems to carry the whole history of an emotion, but her style finally is too fiery for blues; it is that of an alchemist who seizes and transforms images with tremendous speed. Time and again, her language enacts quicksilver darts and leaps of association, giving these poems momentum and tension that resolve finally in healing transformation. Here is an example from **"Deer Dancer,"** a narrative poem about a nude dancer in a rundown reservation bar:

> . . . She borrowed a chair for the stairway
> to heaven and stood on a table of names. And
>   danced in a room
> of children without shoes. . . .
>   . . . . .
> And then she took off her clothes. She shook
>   loose memory,
> waltzed with the empty lover we'd all become.
> She was the myth flipped down through dream-
>   time. The promise of
> feast we all knew was coming. The deer who
>   crossed through
> knots of a curse to find us. She was no slouch,
>   and neither
> were we, watching.

In **"The Fury of Rain"** Harjo takes in the full violence of a thunderstorm, letting the weather evoke a kind of ritual dance inside her:

> Thunder beings dance the flooding streets

of this city, stripped naked to their electric skele-
    tons.
I stand inside their wild and sacred ritual
on these streets of greasy rainbows
and see my own furious longing
erupt from the broken mask of change
to stone, to bear, to lightning.
Gut memory shakes this earth like a rattle. . . .

Or she exorcises the pain over a vanished lover, in **"If I Think about You Again (It Will Be the Fifty-third Monday of Next Year)"**, flinging herself into it by way of letting it go:

> . . . Hatred is a vice that
> smells like four mutilated cats smoking in a gas-
>   oline fire. And
> worse. And
> here I am stirring an imagination that has al-
>   ways got me into trouble,
> thinking what I could do to you. . . .
> I could make you the fifth cat and turn my back.
>   I could say
> your name backward and send it to a warring
>   star. Or, better yet, erase it . . .

Like a true magician, Harjo draws power from over-whelming circumstance and emotion by submitting to them, celebrating them, letting her voice and vision move in harmony with the ultimate laws of paradox and continual change. Many of her poems, such as **"We Encounter Nat King Cole as We Invent the Future,"** reach for what is healing in the forces of nature and of human imagination, for the "double rainbow / two-stepping across the valley . . . / twin gods bending over to plant something like / themselves in the wet earth, a song / larger than all our cheap hopes. . . ." And some poems, such as **"Legacy,"** reach simply for bravery and clarity, the acceptance of what is, that keep her vision honed and flashing: "I don't know the ending. / But I know the legacy of maggots is wings. / And I understand how lovers can destroy everything / together."

Leslie Ullman, "Solitaries and Storytellers, Magicians and Pagans: Five Poets in the World," in The Kenyon Review, *n.s. Vol. XIII, No. 2, Spring, 1991, pp. 179-93.*

In Mad Love and War would be my personal choice for this year's Pulitzer, its music skillful, its content inspired, often ecstatic.

—Marilyn Kallet, in "The Arrow's Own Language," in American Book Review, April-May 1991.

Dan Bellm   **(review date 2 April 1991)**

[*In the following review, Bellm offers an overview of Harjo's career.*]

In one of Joy Harjo's new poems [from ***In Mad Love and War***], a jazz musician brings trombone music home to his Papago tribe: "They had never heard anything like it," she writes, "but it was the way they had remembered." In another, a roomful of hardcore drinkers on the coldest night of the year is startled when a new stripper walks into the bar; they immediately know she is a Deer Dancer, a "myth slipped down through dreamtime," a creature of magic from "a people accustomed to hearing songs in pine trees, and making them hearts." Coming upon these poems for the first time is like walking into a new world, too—then recognizing where you are. Time isn't linear. The past and future are happening now. Many worlds exist, and can converge. Dreams carry the same weight as physical evidence, are solid as rock and bone. It becomes apparent that these things aren't just true in the world of Native American spirituality; they're simply true. An Oklahoma-born member of the Creek Nation, fully at home both in Native ways and in the more recent "main" stream of American culture, Joy Harjo is now writing a visionary poetry that is among the very best we have.

In traditional Native story and song, writes Paula Gunn Allen (Laguna Pueblo/Sioux), the aesthetics are grounded in kinship; what makes art beautiful is its communality, its expression of tribal values of proportion, harmony, and balance. The Navajo equivalent of "beautiful," Harjo writes in ***Secrets From the Center of the World*** is "an all-encompassing word, like those for land and sky, that has to do with living well, dreaming well, in a way that is complementary to all life." The poet is anonymous because poetry doesn't come from individuals; it comes from ancestor spirits and powerful dreams. Harjo's work draws from the river of Native tradition, but it also swims freely in the currents of Anglo-American verse—feminist poetry of personal/political resistance, deep-image poetry of the unconscious, "new-narrative" explorations of story and rhythm in prose-poem form. Not to mention the jazz riffs (Harjo plays the tenor sax) that swirl steadily through her latest book, ***In Mad Love and War.***

"Healing Animal" is a fine example of this way of living in a many-layered world:

> Sleep, *your back curled*
> *against my belly.*
> *I will make you something to*
> drink, / from a cup of frothy
> stars
> *from the* somewhere there is
> the perfect sound
> called up from the best-told
> stories / of benevolent gods,
> who have nothing better to
> do. / And I ask you
> what bitter words are ruining
> your soft-skinned village,
> *because I want to make a*
> *poem that will cup / the*
> *inside of your throat*
> *like the fire in the palm of a*
> *healing animal. Like*
> *the way Coltrane knew love in*
> *the fluid shape*
> *of a saxophone / that could*

change into the wings of a
blue angel. . . .

As in a shaman's ritual prayer-chant, as in jazz music, healing power in this poem is the free flight of improvisation, a way of changing one thing into another. The potion is a fluid shape in a cup, in the throat, in the palm of an animal's hand—a brew of frothy stars, perfect sound, love and fire. The body is a soft-skinned village, a community, an entire world. Many of the poems in *She Had Some Horses* (1983) use the prayer-chant tradition of healing, the original "talking cure," more explicitly. In **"The Black Room,"** the nightmare of a childhood rape is punctuated by the repeated line, "She thought she woke up." The title poem is a long litany of the "horses" inside a woman who is trying to become whole. In her new book, Harjo has moved further away from traditional song forms, and as a result, some readers will probably miss what they liked best about the earlier work. But *In Mad Love and War* is a strong leap forward; while the poems may appear less "Indian" on the surface, they have a stronger connection to tradition, which makes them freer to soar madly, risk everything, and spiral back again. The image of the spiral, "the structure of the spiraled world," recurs constantly in *Mad Love.* "Our bones are built of spirals"; stories are spirals; time is a spiral; the "Muscogee season of forgiveness, time of new corn," is marked by a spiraling dance. In **"Fury of Rain,"** she writes,

> We are all in the belly of a
> laughing god
> swimming the heavens, in
> this whirling circle.
> What we haven't imagined
> will one day
> spit us out
> magnificent and simple.

For Harjo, to live in the world is to live inside a breathing, sentient being. There are voices in the landscape; the ground speaks; things have memory. Other forms of life "have their tribes, their families, their histories, too," she says. "They are alive poems."

This doesn't mean that Harjo idealizes the natural world, or the spirit world, or Native culture; she looks and listens to know what these worlds are. The whirling circle includes murder, convulsive change, "dazzling" anger, the ravages of "the alcohol spirit." Many of Harjo's characters are "beautiful native misfits" or "broken survivors"—a woman hanging from a 13th floor window ready to jump, the Deer Dancer in the bar, a wise elder with no home who sleeps out on a sidewalk in the snow. The poems forage for sustenance in the desert, change fear to love, turn destruction into "the epic search for grace."

Inevitably, the question of physical and cultural survival is bound up with the land, which not only feeds a people but nourishes who they are. "It's true the landscape forms the mind." Harjo writes in *Secrets From the Center of the World* (1989). "If I stand here long enough I'll learn how to sing. None of that country & western heartbreak stuff, or operatic duels, but something cool as the blues, or close to the sound of a Navajo woman singing early in the morning." *Secrets* is a rather unlikely experiment that turned into a satisfying and beautiful book, a kind of trickster in the age-old tradition of Coyote, Rabbit, and Crow. On alternating pages facing Harjo's brief prose poems, Stephen Strom presents photographs of vast Navajo-country desert landscapes as 4 x 4 miniatures, tiny eye-sized windows on immense space. The one close-up looks like a panoramic view of sand dunes; the photograph before it, which looks like a close-up of a river bottom, turns out to be a distant aerial view of mud hills. As Harjo notes, the pictures "emphasize the 'not-separate' that is within and that moves harmoniously upon the landscape." The depth of field is an emblem of tribal vision.

The book's best poems enhance this play of scale and perspective, suggesting in very few words the relationship between a human life and millennial history. Next to a view of red desert, an abstract swirl of sand shaped by wind, she places this tiny but large story: "Two sisters meet on horseback. They gossip: a cousin eloped with someone's husband, twins were born to his wife. One is headed toward Tsaile, and the other to Round Rock. Their horses are rose sand, with manes of ashy rock." Another poem sketches out evolution, the synchronicity of time and the convergence of the seen and unseen, all in four sentences:

> *Invisible fish swim this ghost ocean now described*
> *by waves of sand, by water-worn rock. Soon the*
> *fish will learn to walk. Then humans will come*
> *ashore and paint dreams on the drying stone.*
> *Then later, much later, the ocean floor will be*
> *punctuated by Chevy trucks, carrying the dream-*
> *ers' descendants, who are going to the store.*

A few of the poems do seem too closely bound by what the photographs already say, or settle for a quick-and-easy poeticism that rarely appears in Harjo's other books: "Approaching in the distance is the child you were some years ago. See her laughing as she chases a white butterfly." But a more common objection to Harjo's work concerns its occasional diffuseness, a way of stating connections in a poem instead of actively reaching them.

While this is fairly true of the earlier books, it is also largely the objection of readers who stand outside the tradition of Native poetry, in which a poem is less important on its own than in its relationship to the whole body of knowledge, and in which many connections—between a cedar tree and prayer, say, or between stars and the religion of ghost dancers—can be assumed in the minds of the listeners.

In Mad Love and War is the farthest-ranging of Harjo's four books; it is both the wildest and the most disciplined. There are poems about Nicaragua and about a lynching by the Ku Klux Klan, poems about Charlie Parker and Nat King Cole, a dream song in the vision-quest tradition in which a woman warrior sics dogs on her lover across the ice of the Bering Strait. But some of my favorite poems are the quietest—like **"Crystal Lake,"** about a young girl out fishing with her grandfather and feeling "restless in adolescent heat." Or **"Summer Night"**:

> *There is an ache that begins/*
> *in the sound of an old blues*
> *song.*
> *It becomes a house where all*

*the lights have gone out/but
one.
And it burns and burns/ until
there is only the blue smoke
of dawn
and everyone is sleeping in
someone's arms/ even the
flowers
even the sound of a thousand
silences./ And the arms of
night
in the arms of day./ Everyone
except me.
But then the smell of damp
honeysuckle twisted on the
vine.
And the turn of the shoulder/
of the ordinary spirit who
keeps watch
over this ordinary street./ And
there you are, the secret
of your own flower of light/
blooming in the miraculous
dark.*

Joy Harjo's poetry continually displays this humble, startled consciousness, as in the 19th century Pawnee dream song which asks: "Let us see, is this real, / Let us see, is this real, / This life I am living? / You, Gods, who dwell everywhere, / Let us see, is this real, / This life I am living?" Sometimes youhave to stay awake all night, attuned to the ordinary spirit of the street, just listening to how the answer keeps changing.

Dan Bellm, "Ode to Joy," in The Village Voice, *Vol. XXXVI, No. 14, April 2, 1991, p. 78.*

**Harjo is angered at the apparent polarity
of life in the modern world, and her
thrust, in her work as well as in her
discussion of it, is toward reconciliation of
the polarities into an order that is
harmonious, balanced, and whole.**

**—*Paula Gunn Allen, in her* The Sacred
Hoop: Recovering the Feminine in
American Indian Traditions, *1992.***

John Scarry   (essay date Spring 1992)

[*In the essay below, Scarry provides an overview of Harjo's poetry and briefly compares her work to that of other Native American women writers.*]

Writing on Joy Harjo in 1990, [in William Balassi, et al.'s *This Is About Vision: Interviews with Southwestern Writers*], John F. Crawford referred to the poet as an artist who "resists simplicities," a particularly astute comment that could as easily allude to Harjo's approach to her work as it could to our critical reactions to that work. As a poet, Harjo has always resisted simplicities, and we must exer-

cise a similar discipline as we make judgments on her work. That work has recently taken some dramatic new directions and received important critical appreciation: her 1989 book of poems, ***Secrets from the Center of the World,*** and her 1990 volume of collected work, ***In Mad Love and War,*** have received national attention, earning the writer not only many favorable reviews but also two prestigious accolades, the William Carlos Williams Award and the Delmore Schwartz Memorial Poetry Prize. Many who saw and heard Harjo read her own poetry on the 1989 Bill Moyers PBS series "The Power of the Word" may have thought they were listening to a new poetic voice from the American Southwest, but actually they were experiencing the fruits of over two decades of poetic thinking and production. This is an appropriate juncture to review her work and try to give some indication of her place in the evolving canon of Native American literature, itself a continually growing phenomenon in the larger context of contemporary literature.

Even before we deal with Harjo's poetry, we must resist simplicities. Joy Harjo is, among other things, a painter, a filmmaker, and a musician. Until her early twenties she worked as a painter, actively seeking out one of her own family members, her great-aunt Lois Harjo Ball, for inspiration and guidance. When she found that relative, the young woman was given more than the inspiration one would find in a studio. "She was very connected to what I call the dream world," Harjo told [Susan Lepselter, in "Spinning Dreams into Words," *Tusconweekly* (27 December 1989)]. Her own poetry would provide another entrance to that world. In fact, some of the actual techniques a painter takes to a canvas have influenced Harjo's approach to the making of a poem: she has said that her whole approach to writing is similar to a painter's technique, as "images overlap until they become one piece." [quoted in John Nizalowski's "Joy Harjo: A Mystical Serse of Beauty," *Pasatiempo* (26 August 1989)]. There can also be no doubt that Harjo's extensive work in film has given her a special way of seeing, an insightful vision that leads to so many of the striking and crystalline images found throughout her poetry. It is music, however, that is an even more dominant influence on the poet. She has been described as listening to music more than reading the work of other poets, and Harjo herself has said that when she writes poetry she does not start with an image but rather with a sound. It is significant too that her favorite musical instrument is the saxophone, often described as being remarkably close to the quality of the human voice.

N. Scott Momaday has noted that Harjo's work contains the elements of "oral tradition and ancient matter," a comment that brings together two of the most important elements in her poetry, elements that have been present in her work from the beginning. One of the keys to Harjo's thinking is her firm belief—confirmed in so many of her poems—that, in her words, "in the *real* world all is in motion, in a state of change." This helps explain why it is often so difficult, if not impossible, to point to the actual moment in a Harjo poem when one world moves into the next, when one voice changes to another, or when one landscape is utterly transformed in either an evolutionary or a revolutionary way. This apparent surreality of many of Harjo's settings and situations is not really a distortion; it is simply a presentation of reality observed through the poet's prism. Her instrument is myth, which the poet uses extensively because "that's where meaning is exploded," and one is taken "into the realm where anything is possible."

It is striking how many of the poet's recurring images and lasting concerns have been present in her work from the beginning. For example, **"Are You Still There"** from her 1975 chapbook *The Last Song* contains clear indications of some of Harjo's themes and her approaches to those themes.

>   there are sixty-five miles
>   of telephone wire
>   between acoma
>   and albuquerque
>   i dial the number
>   and listen for the sound
>   of his low voice
>   on the other side
>   "hello"
>   is a gentle motion of a western wind
>   cradling tiny purple flowers
>   that grow near the road
>   towards laguna
>   i smell them
>   as i near the rio puerco bridge
>   my voice stumbles
>   returning over sandstone
>   as it passes the cănoncito exit
>   "i have missed you" he says
>   the rhythm circles the curve
>   of mesita cliffs
>   to meet me
>   but my voice is caught
>   shredded on a barbed wire fence
>   at the side of the road
>   and flutters soundless
>   in the wind

Initially one may have doubts as to the use of the telephone as a central device, and the final images may resonate with too many echoes of haiku to be completely original; but the security of the tone, along with the impressive integration of image and meaning, is remarkable in a poet writing in her early twenties. The opening lines immediately establish the exterior and interior landscapes; in fact, by the time we are shown the "tiny purple flowers / that grow near the road" we cannot be absolutely sure which landscape we are in, or if indeed it is only the speaker's own mind. Those same flowers, seen as they are in an ambiguous "cradling" by a "western wind," are filled with implications for a relationship we know is already doomed. However, the final image of the wind shows no such nurturing: barbed wire has taken over telephone wire, and conversation has become the "soundless" voice of the speaker alone. We are led, finally, back to the title and left to consider the ambiguities of "still," "you," and even the significance of the quotation marks. Does "still" mean a lack of movement, or does it mean "yet"? Is the "you" the speaker being addressed by the other person, or is it the speaker who addresses the other? The use of quotation marks around the words of the title is no help either;

we return to the title and cannot tell who is speaking, or to whom.

This poem, and several others in this first collection, show Harjo moving easily between the worlds of imagination and reality. When Dan Bellm, writing in the *Village Voice* of 2 April 1991, tells us that for this poet, "time isn't linear. The past and future are happening now. . . . Dreams carry the same weight as physical evidence, are solid as rock and bone," he could have been alluding to the poetic fluidity of Harjo's simultaneous physicality and spirituality, and her ability to combine the eternal past and the continuing present. These are among the most noteworthy of her characteristics, qualities evident in her work of nearly two decades ago.

Tracing Harjo's treatment of similar themes enables the reader to follow her thinking, noting her transformations of images and her shifts in emphasis. For example, the following poem from *The Last Song,* **"3 AM,"** is a work filled with ghosts from the Native American past, figures seen operating in an alien culture that is itself a victim of fragmentation.

>   3 AM
>   in the albuquerque airport
>   trying to find a flight
>   to old oraibi, third mesa
>   TWA
>   is the only desk open
>   bright lights outline new york
>
>   chicago
>   and the attendant doesn't know
>   that third mesa
>   is a part of the center
>   of the world
>   and who are we
>   just two indians
>   at three in the morning
>   trying to find a way back
>
>   and then i remembered
>   that time simon
>   took a yellow cab
>   out to acoma from albuquerque
>   a twenty-five dollar ride
>   to the center of himself
>
>   3 AM is not too late
>   to find the way back

Points of embarkation always carry with them haunting, romantic images for writers, and airports are redolent with meaning in more than one Harjo poem. Here the Albuquerque airport is both modern America's technology and moral nature—and both clearly have failed. Together they cannot get these Indians to their destination, a failure that stretches from our earliest history to the sleek desks of our most up-to-date airline offices. Even the airline attendant, surrounded by the triumphs of technology and framed by the glowing images of our urban culture—New York and Chicago—stands as an ineffectual center of ignorance. However, "the center / of the world" soon shifts from Indian mesas to the mind of the poetic speaker, to the landscape of memory, to the perception of self. We do not have to know who Simon was or what he found at the "center of himself"; the true journey in this poem is far beyond the failed promise of an alien culture's technology. It is significant too that the final journey in the poem—the only one truly accomplished—is the speaker's voyage back into memory. As in so many of Harjo's poems, movement and progress are only indicated or promised in the world where we expect them to happen; they really happen in the landscape of the mind, journeys made all the more vibrant and meaningful by the external paralysis we are shown only too clearly.

The same chapbook contains **"I Am a Dangerous Woman,"** a work that in many ways is a significant variation on the themes announced in **"3 AM."**

> the sharp ridges of clear blue windows
> motion to me
> from the airports second floor
> edges dance in the foothills of the sandias
> behind security guards
> who wave me into their guncatcher machine
>
> i am a dangerous woman
>
> when the machine buzzes
> they say to take off my belt
> and i remove it so easy
> that it catches the glance
> of a man standing nearby
> (maybe that is the deadly weapon
> that has the machine singing)
>
> i am a dangerous woman
> but the weapon is not visible
> security will never find it
> they can't hear the clicking
> of the gun
>   inside my head

Again, the setting is clearly the American Southwest, but the reader is immediately aware of other, overlapping settings that urge themselves upon the attention. There is the natural world and the human construction of an airport, there are men and machines, there are men and at least one woman, and, more subtly, there are cultures that encounter each other in very limited ways and only for a very limited time. In **"3 AM"** the speaker does not come forward until we are halfway through the poem; in **"I Am a Dangerous Woman"** the speaker identifies herself in the first word of the title. The tension in the latter poem is also announced early and decisively and is sustained throughout: the "sharp ridges" of the windows, the "guncatcher machine" and its buzzing, along with the most dramatic sound of all, the inaudible "clicking / of the gun" inside the speaker's mind—all combine to create a tension-filled atmosphere, one that is intensified by the strange similarity between the control imposed by the security forces and the self-control exercised by the always silent poetic speaker. Without question, **"I Am a Dangerous Woman"** is a more political, more feminist poem than **"3 AM,"** but beyond this primary distinction both works are expressions of the almost wistful determination one senses in so many of Harjo's poems. In **"3 AM"** we find ourselves huddled together in the long American night, with those in control of conquering distance no better off than the would-be passengers trying to get on a flight; this is, after all, *"Trans World* Airlines," but no airline has ever flown that will get us to the "center of the world."

Joy Harjo is clearly a highly political and feminist Native American, but she is even more the poet of myth and the subconscious; her images and landscapes owe as much to the vast stretches of our hidden mind as they do to her native Southwest. This is one reason why her **Secrets from the Center of the World** is such a continually intriguing book. Ostensibly, the setting is a landscape known to all (with the Stephen Strom photographs giving that part of the country an appropriate surreality to which all of us can truly respond), but Harjo's prose poems give us a *vision* of the land for the first time, as this seer takes us below the surface of the literal world for visions and images we recognize as simultaneously new and timeless. The following prose poem from the book gives us a fresh and arresting invitation to maintain this double vision of our world. It also contains echoes of some of her earliest images and themes.

> Near Shiprock five horses stand at the left side
> of the road, watching traffic. A pole carrying
> talk cuts through the middle of the world. They
> notice the smoking destruction from the Four
> Corners plant as it veers overhead, shake their
> heads at the ways of these thoughtless humans,
> lope toward the vortex of circling sands where
> a pattern for survival is fiercely stated.

The opening picture of the five horses is not an unexpected one—this is one of the most durable of Native American images, and certainly one of the images most associated with the poet of **She Had Some Horses**—but here the animals are seen against the ambiguous "traffic." It does not matter if we see the traffic as slow pedestrians or as roaring cars and trucks—"traffic" is an unnatural intrusion here, as is the "pole carrying talk" that cuts through the "middle of the world." The stilted phrase used to describe the telephone pole is of course an allusion to one culture's attempt to grasp the language of another, even as the technology that carries the alien language violates the land that should be sacred to all. In this context the phrase becomes a virtual parody of an entire history of an oppressed people trying to understand the oppressor. Unlike the earlier **"Are You Still There,"** this telephone pole does not show two people trying to communicate; it emphasizes the utter inability of two cultures to do so.

As the poem continues, the chasm becomes further emphasized, and the fact that, from this description of the telephone pole on, all perceptions are beyond human recognition only highlights this dismal fact. It is "they," the horses, that "notice the smoking destruction" from the nearby plant (and has that word itself been chosen for its ironic value?). By the time they shake their heads (perfectly natural for the aware human onlooker, but since none is visible here, the action takes on more significance) we are ready with the speaker to condemn the "thoughtless humans"; yet the final image is intriguing in its ambiguity. How does the "vortex of circling sands" contain "a pattern for survival"? Sand is a most natural and changeable element, but who or what will create the "fiercely stated" pattern that must be read if we are to survive?

This notion of the human connection with the land is of course a stock literary idea, but Harjo deals with it in a very different fashion throughout the book. For example, rarely has the land been treated in such a way that it has profound superiority over our human activities and aspirations: "This land is a poem of ochre and burnt sand I could never write." The land may also possess a knowledge of history that makes our libraries of written knowledge insignificant by comparison: "These smoky bluffs are old traveling companions, making their way through millenia. Ask them if you want to know about the true turning of history." The book uses the world of the American Southwest to urge us to an examination of our own. Complex reverberations of the relationships between human and other life, between past and present, and the cosmic connections between an unimaginably distant past and an equally mysterious future all come together in this deceptively simple prose poem, one that captures the essentially meditative quality of this extraordinary book: "Moencopi Rise stuns me into perfect relationship, as I feed a skinny black dog the rest of my crackers, drink coffee, contemplate the frozen memory of stones. Nearby are the footprints of dinosaurs, climbing toward the next century."

Harjo's most recent volume of poetry, *In Mad Love and War*, shows the poet becoming more personal in her concerns. These poems also bring us to and from other worlds and invite us to hear recurring echoes of Native American ways of thinking. It is this double sense of landscape, the sharp reality that is so clear to the Native American seer and the ruined earthly paradise that is such a source of pain and bewilderment to the rest of the population, that is examined so ruthlessly and lovingly in the book's first poem, **"Deer Dancer."** The opening provides a sense of in medias res tinged with a deep feeling of lassitude.

> Nearly everyone had left that bar in the middle of winter except the hardcore. It was the coldest night of the year, every place shut down, but not us. Of course we noticed when she came in. We were Indian ruins. She was the end of beauty. No one knew her, the stranger whose tribe we recognized, her family related to deer, if that's who she was, a people accustomed to hearing songs in pine trees, and making them hearts.

Significantly, the bar is nearly deserted, adding to the feeling of coldness that permeates the atmosphere. This may be a watering hole, but neither conviviality nor oblivion is achieved here. As in so much of Harjo's poetry, many of the images and settings that have become accepted as virtual Native American leitmotivs become as transformed as the landscape. Here the bar and the entire issue of alcohol become a backdrop to a much larger canvas. At the moment that the image of Beauty—clearly a visitor from another world—enters, all the "Indian ruins" recognize her for the vision she is. When a voice from the bar calls out, "What's a girl like you doing in a place like this?" the poetic speaker echoes the question for the reader's own broader ruminations: "That's what I'd like to know, what are we all doing in a place like this?"

As the vision takes off her clothes and begins to dance on a table, she is finally identified: "She was the myth slipped down through dreamtime. The promise of feast we all

knew was coming." Here also we find many of the themes we have seen in Harjo's earlier poetry. There is, first of all, the landscape that has a clearly Native American identity but that soon becomes an everywhere and anytime, with humanity thrown together in the midst of a coldness that only intensifies the need for human connection. In **"Deer Dancer"** this connection is sadly missing, and it is only when the dancer herself disrobes and moves to the music of the jukebox that "the broken survivors" who see her are stirred to a vision beyond themselves.

In terms of setting, mood, and vision, Harjo's accomplishment in this poem reminds us of no less a visionary than William Butler Yeats. **"Deer Dancer"** may be seen as something of a Native American "Second Coming." The sterility of the landscape and the objective yet involved tone of Harjo's speaker both echo the Irish poet's famous prophecy, but **"Deer Dancer"** more directly invites the reader to share in the humanity of the "Indian ruins" sitting so desolately in our native landscape. Further, what comes into that landscape is not Yeats's fear that "things fall apart" and that something terrible is threatening to be born, but rather that unity can be recovered and that a vision of Beauty can lead to a positive recapturing of something lost—and that all this can come to all of us at the most unlikely time and in the most unpromising place. This is a recurring motif in a good deal of Harjo's poetry, and, placed as it is at the beginning of *In Mad Love and War*, **"Deer Dancer"** serves as a review of these concerns and as an important announcement of the book's intentions.

Harjo's range of emotion and imagery in this volume is truly remarkable. She achieves intimacy and power in ways that send a reader to every part of the poetic spectrum for comparisons and for some frame of reference. For example, the opening of **"Summer Night"** is as filled with romantic delicacy as any sonnet from a nineteenth-century poet: "The moon is nearly full, / the humid air sweet like melon. / Flowers that have cupped the sun all day / dream of iridescent wings / under the long dark sleep." By contrast, how completely modern (and American) in tone is the exquisitely cadenced opening image of **"Bird"**: "The moon plays horn, leaning on the shoulder of the dark universe to the infinite glitter of chance." We are also struck, again in a few opening lines, by Harjo's use of her poetic voice to take one of the humblest images from her culture to discuss the steady revolution Native American art is causing in the larger culture: "I am fragile, a piece of pottery smoked from fire / made of dung, / the design drawn from nightmares. I am an arrow, painted / with lightning / to seek the way to the name of the enemy, / but the arrow has now created / its own language" (**"We Must Call a Meeting"**). As in so many of the poems in the book, these images, ideas, and intentions achieve a unity that is as effective as it is rare. The volume represents a major artistic statement and, seen in the context of Harjo's past work, indicates a remarkable new direction for the poet.

It is also instructive to place Harjo's verse and prose in the context of the work of other Native American poets. When one compares her tone to that of, say, Paula Gunn

Allen, there is a sense of greater immediacy and urgency to Harjo's voice; it grips the reader with an unmistakable intensity. If Allen can begin her "Soundings" with an almost easygoing sense of familiarity ("On such a day as this / Something unknown, familiar stirs—/ is it a thought? a breeze?"), Harjo can announce her theme in **"For Anna Mae Pictou Aquash"** by painting a scene that reveals the vibrant energy of the speaker as much as it makes us feel the underlying violence in nature.

> Beneath a sky blurred with mist and wind,
>   I am amazed as I watch the violet
> heads of crocuses erupt from the stiff earth
>   after dying for a season,
> as I have watched my own dark head
>   appear each morning after entering
> the next world
>   to come back to this one,
>   amazed.

This urgency of tone can also reach the point of near assault on the reader in its demand for attention. This raw directness is instantly apparent in the opening of **"Legacy"** from *In Mad Love and War:* "In Wheeling, West Virginia, inmates riot. / Two cut out the heart of a child rapist / and hold it steaming in a guard's face / because he will live / to tell the story."

If we consider the work of another fine poet, Wendy Rose, next to that of Joy Harjo, we also notice a distinct difference in tone. This is evident when, for example, both poets overlay monstrous urban landscapes on the spirit of ancient Native American experience. In "Leaving Port Authority for the St. Regis Rezz" Rose brings together the disparate vistas of Weehawken, New Jersey, and a distant, other setting: "I saw a mesa / between two buildings / a row of tall / thin hands on top." Harjo's opening vision in **"Climbing the Streets of Worcester, Mass.,"** though similar in conception, proceeds in a very different direction: "Houses lean forward with their hands / on thin hips. / I walk past their eyes / of pigeon grey, hear someone playing horn, and there's the wind / trying to teach some trees / to fly." Rose's imagery should not be judged in terms of Harjo's intentions, but it is noteworthy that the surreal immediacy of Harjo's lines engages the reader in a way that makes her both distinctive and compelling. However, Harjo's artistry is so secure in itself and the growth of her thinking is so impressive in itself, that one does not linger long over comparisons.

There is one other Native American poet who, if she chose to devote herself more to poetry, could produce work that would be received with the greatest attention and might well invite the closest comparisons with Harjo's work. This is Louise Erdrich. As long as Erdrich continues in the direction of commercial fiction, however, it is not an exaggeration to say that Harjo clearly remains in the very forefront of that still comparatively small group of Native American poets writing today.

Although Harjo is only approaching the most productive stage of her career, she has already been fully accepted as an important poetic voice. In a very perceptive and extremely useful review of her work, published in the *Village Voice Literary Supplement* of 2 April 1991, Dan Bellm gave this succinct appreciation of Harjo's poetry:

> Harjo's work draws from the river of Native tradition, but it also swims freely in the currents of Anglo-American verse—feminist poetry of personal/political resistance, deep-image poetry of the unconscious, "new-narrative" explorations of story and rhythm in prose-poem form.

Just as important, the poet herself is already a living resource for an entire generation of younger writers, Native American and otherwise. Although many of her literary models are firmly in her own culture, we cannot ignore some of her relatives in the craft, as distant in era and place as some of them may seem. In his introduction to *Harper's Anthology of 20th Century Native American Poetry* Brian Swann quotes Richard Hugo's 1975 comments on the then quickly emerging Native American literary movement. Hugo emphasized that Native American poets were very similar to such major twentieth-century poets as Eliot and Yeats, "who felt we inherited ruined worlds that, before they were ruined, gave man a sense of self-esteem, social unity, spiritual certainty and being at home on the earth." We have sensed, more than once, this world view in Harjo's poetry. More specifically, we have noted some similarities between **"Deer Dancer"** and "The Second Coming" of Yeats. More broadly, the cultural, artistic, and spiritual connections between Anglo-Irishman and Native American are quite striking. Both are dreamers and seekers after the visionary, and both work in cultures that often prove to be alien lands indeed. Nevertheless, Harjo, as much as Yeats, is able to survive in the larger culture while still breathing deeply of her native air. In a hostile place that has denied her dreams and often done its best to destroy the dreamer, she has responded by giving back to the larger culture values and insights it never realized it had lost.

When Yeats, at the conclusion of "The Lake Isle of Innisfree," shows his poetic self standing on a London street and thinking of his native land, the resulting image serves as a metaphor for the very isolation of the poet's insight: "I will arise and go now, for always night and day / I hear lake water lapping with low sounds by the shore; / While I stand on the roadway, or on the pavements gray, / I hear it in the deep heart's core." From her own points of exile and isolation, in bars on dusty highways or on foggy New England streets, in ancient museums or modern airports, Joy Harjo shares with us the deepest parts of her own sensibility. She also reveals those parts of the human psyche shared by us all: the deep heart's core.

John Scarry, "Representing Real Worlds: The Evolving Poetry of Joy Harjo," in World Literature Today, *Vol. 66, No. 2, Spring, 1992, pp. 286-91.*

Kathleene West   (review date Summer 1992)

[*In the following laudatory review, West discusses thematic and stylistic aspects of* In Mad Love and War.]

It is difficult not to use the word "magic" when thinking of Joy Harjo's poetry—on the page, words enter another dimension; the cadences of her stunning readings stay with the listener for days; and even the television or video screen is only a scrim easily slipped through by this poet accustomed to easing beyond the barriers of time and structured thought.

I'm not writing to the poetry mafia, or whatever you might call it. I'm writing first of all for myself. I like what I do. I want to write poems that excite me, first of all. But I also write for a larger community, with a sense of who I am and where I came from—that spirit of history.

—Joy Harjo, in an interview with Helen Jaskoski in MELUS, *Spring, 1989-1990*

In Mad Love and War continues this exploration of the *beyond:* "I know there is something larger than the memory of a dispossessed people. We have seen it," and the attempt to translate memory, time and passion into the inadequacies of first, language itself, second, into the language of the white people, a tongue already suffering the loss of much of its own integrity. "In this language there are no words for how the real world collapses." With this collection, Harjo moves ever closer to making this language expand to bear the awful burden of poetry, even while acknowledging the ultimate paradox: "All poets / understand the final uselessness of words."

But words as components of music, "chords to / other chords to other chords, if we're lucky, to melody," can be a method of understanding other worlds, if not actually entering them:

> When I am inside the Muscogee world, which is
> not a
> flip side of the Western time chain, but a form
> of
> music staggered in the ongoing event of earth
> calesthentics, the past and the future are the
> same tug-of-war.
>
> ("Original Memory")

Think how important time is to music: we keep time, mark time, beat time, measure our rhythms in three-quarter, half or full time, and the best timekeeper we have is in the beat of our heart, literally and metaphorically: "ghosts of time in tilted hats are ushered / by our heartbeats into the living room" (**"We Encounter Nat King Cole as We Invent the Future"**) and "whatever world we are entering or leaving we are still looking for love" (**"Original Memory"**).

One of the things poetry can do is to convey the power of this music:

> I know you can turn a poem into something else.
> This
> poem could be a bear treading the far northern
> tundra,
> smelling the air for sweet alive meat. Or a piece
> of

seawood stumbling in the sea. Or a blackbird, laughing. What I mean is that hatred can be turned into something else if you have the right words, the right meanings.

> ("Transformations")

When the poem/song/music coincides then one discovers, "There is more to this world that I have ever let on / to you, or anyone" (**"Deer Ghost"**).

In **"Climbing the Streets of Worcester, Mass."** the narrator hears wind, someone playing horn and

> three crows laugh
> kick up the neighbor's trash.
> Telling jokes
> they recreate the world.

Recreating the world means one has to be prepared to accept the results. In **"Song for the Deer and Myself to Return On"** the narrator sings

> the song Louis taught me:
> a song to call the deer in Creek, when hunting,
> and I am certainly hunting something as magic
> as deer
> . . . . .
> It works, of course, and deer came into this
> room
> and wondered at finding themselves
> in a house near downtown Denver.

With love and the power of music come responsibility: "I should be writing poems to change the / world. They would appear as a sacrifice of deer for the starving. Or poems / of difficulty to place my name in the Book of Poets. I should get on with it" (**"Crossing Water"**). Getting on with it means the poems of "furious love" "the dazzling whirlwind of our anger," the poems where "Nothing can be forgotten, only left behind." If there are "no damned words to make violence fit neatly," then let the poet write roughly and gasping for breath. Witness the title of a poem for a young woman murdered on the Pine Ridge Reservation: **"For Anna Mae Pictou Aquash, Whose Spirit Is Present Here and in the Dappled Stars (for we remember the story and must tell it again so we may all live)."**

Our own lives, individual, private, and small, are terribly important. In **"The Real Revolution is Love,"** men and women gather in the pre-dawn hours of Managua, Nicaragua, *"the land of revolution."* Gradually, their language alters like Pedro as he moves "to the place inside her / ear where he isn't speaking revolution." But the woman who is the object of his affection thinks instead of "a man / who keeps his political secrets to himself / in favor of love," and the narrator decides to "do what I want, and take my revolution to bed with / me, alone." Her dreams are of ancestral stories "of the very beginning" and of Columbus landing "over and over again." She knows "This is not a foreign country, but the land of our dreams."

Dreams, the ancestral past, and the power of a passionate imagination unite to create a vision of a future that is, as yet, only found in poetry:

We will make a river,
flood this city built of passion
with fire,
with a revolutionary fire.
                    ("City of Fire")

It is in Joy Harjo's poetry that the promise of poetry is
more than keen metaphor:

We are all in the belly of a laughing god
swimming the heavens, in this whirling circle.
What we haven't imagined will one day
spit us out
magnificent and simple
                    ("Fury of Rain")

In Mad Love and War has the power and beauty of prophecy and all the hope of love poised at its passionate beginning. It allows us to enter the place "we haven't imagined"
and allows us to imagine what we will do when we are
there.

*Kathleene West, in a review of "In Mad Love and War,"
in* Prairie Schooner, *Vol. 66, No. 2, Summer, 1992, pp.
128-32.*

Joy Harjo with Marilyn Kallett   (interview date
Summer 1993)

[*An American poet, educator, and translator, Kallet specializes in women's studies and English and comparative
literature. In the following, which comprises two interviews
originally conducted with Harjo in April 1991 and September 1992, Harjo discusses her literary influences and concerns, her education, the creative process, and her interest
in the arts.*]

[*Kallet*]: *What were your beginnings as a writer?*

[Harjo]: I could look at this in a couple of ways. One is
to look at the myths and stories of the people who formed
me in the place where I entered the world. . . . Another
way is to look at when I first consciously called myself a
writer. I started writing poetry when I was pretty old, actually—I was about twenty-two. I committed to poetry
the day I went in to my painting teacher who mentored
me and expected a fine career in painting for me, and told
him I was switching my major to poetry. I made the decision to learn what poetry could teach me. It was a painful
choice. I come from a family of Muscogee painters. My
grandmother and my great-aunt both got their B.F.A.'s in
Art in the early 1900s. And from the time I was very small
you could always find me drawing, whether it was in the
dirt or on paper. That was one thing that made me
happy. . . . I always said that when I grow up I am going
to be a painter, I am going to be an artist. Then I made
the decision to work with words and the power of words,
to work with language, yet I approach the art as a visual
artist. From childhood my perceptions were through the
eye of a painter. I feel any writer serves many aspects of
culture, including language, but you also serve history,
you serve the mythic structure that you're part of, the people, the earth, and so on—and none of these are separate.

*It seems like almost any question we ask about your writing,
about your cultural background, is going to lead us in the
same paths of discussion about your family life, your tribal
life, and your life as a writer.*

Well, they are not separate, really. Though the way I've
come to things is very different from say, Beth Cuthand,
who is a Cree writer from Saskatchewan, or Leslie Silko
from Laguna. There's a tendency in this country to find
one writer of a particular ethnicity and expect her to speak
for everyone and expect her experience to be representative of all Native women and all Native people. My experience is very different from Silko's and Cuthand's, although it's similar in the sense of a generational thing, of
certain influences on us and influences we have on each
other. But my experience has been predominantly urban.
I did not grow up on a reservation—we don't even have
a reservation. There are more rural areas where the people
are. I'm not a full-blood, and yet I am a full member of
my (Muscogee) tribe, and I have been a full member of my
tribe since my birth into the tribe. I find some people have
preconceived ideas—I was talking to this guy on the plane
and he says, "Well, you don't fit my idea of an Indian."
What does that mean? I think for most people in this
country, it means to be a Hollywood version of a Plains
tribe, as falsely-imagined 100 or 150 years ago. Most people in this country have learned all they know about Indian people from movies and television. . . .

Certain books have helped to popularize Plains culture.
Black Elk Speaks *is taught most often at the university. . . .*

And even then it's a perversion of what it means to be an
Indian in this country—how do you translate context?
Within my tribe you have people who are very grounded
in the traditions, and are very close to the land. Then you
have people who are heavily involved in church; some are
involved in both; some live in Tulsa, which is where I grew
up; others live all over but are still close to that place
which is home. It is more than land—but of the land—a
tradition of mythologies, of ongoing history . . . it forms
us.

*What is there specifically in the Muscogee culture that
lends itself to poetry?*

That's like asking what is it in life that lends itself to
poetry . . . it's the collective myth balanced with history.

*When you talk about particulars of individuals and tribes,
you are continually breaking down conventions and stereotypes. Does that become tiresome for you?*

Yes, it does. I find that wherever I speak I always get
asked more questions having to do with culture than with
writing.

You must feel like a cultural missionary sometimes. . . .

Right. I feel like I'm having to explain something that's
not really easily explainable.

*Among your friends, and among the other writers you men-
tioned, surely you don't have to keep explaining.*

No. There's no need. Culture just is. Certainly I'm always
asking myself questions about how we came to be, and
how we're becoming, and who we are in this world. . . .

In terms of your own background, were there people in your family who loved words? Where does your love of language come from?

Probably from both sides. I have a grandfather, my father's grandfather, who is a full-blooded Creek Baptist minister. I often feel him and I know much of what I am comes from him (including my stubbornness!) I know that he had a love for words and he spoke both Muscogee and English. My mother used to compose songs on an old typewriter. I think she loved the music more than the words, she wasn't particularly a wordsmith, but could translate heartache. From her I learned Patsy Cline, and other "heartbreak country."

Do you remember what made you write that first poetry in your twenties?

Yes, very distinctly. The urge was the same urge I had to make music. Around that time was the first time I heard music in poetry, heard Native writers like Leslie Silko, and Simon Ortiz read their work. I also heard Galway Kinnell for the first time, his was one of the first poetry readings I ever attended. I became friends with Leo Romero whose dedication to poetry impressed me. He was always writing and reading his work to me. I witnessed process and began writing my own pieces.Of course, the first attempts were rather weak. Like newborn colts trying to stand just after birth. . . .

You attended the M.F.A. Program in Creative Writing at the University of Iowa. Was that helpful to you?

Well, I have to take into consideration my age when I went—I was in my mid-twenties. I was a single mother. I arrived at this strange country with two small children—my daughter was three years old. I knew no one, did not know the place, or the people. About the university setting—I felt like I had walked into a strange land in which I had to learn another language. This comes from being of Native background, from the West, but it also comes from being a woman in that institution. I heard the Director say once to a group of possible funders—I was one of the people they chose to perform for them in the workshop—he told them that the place was actually geared for teaching male writers, which is honest; it was true, but I was shocked. I remember Jayne Ann Phillips and I looking at each other, like "can you believe this? Then why are we sitting here?" Certainly I think I learned a lot about technique. I also learned that what was most important in a poem had nothing to do in some ways with what I thought was most important. I felt like the art of poetry had broken down into sterile exercises. And yet, I know I admire some of the work of those people who taught me. But the system had separated itself from the community, from myth, from humanhood.

But you saw it through?

I did see it through. I wanted to walk away. One way I made it through was through the help of people like Sandra Cisneros—through close ties to the Indian and Chicano communities, to the African-American community, to women's groups.

Have you been able to bring back some of the technical skill you learned to what you consider fundamental?

Yes. You can have the commitment to writing, the fire, but you can write crummy poems. Certainly you need technique. I guess what I'm saying is that I felt values were out of balance.

What was missing?

Heart. And yet some of the poets who taught me there had heart in their poems. But sometimes I felt like what was more important was the facade of being a poet. It became more of an academic pursuit than a pursuit of what it means to live. Granted I was young and I had a lot of misconceptions to work through.

Could you say more about your true teachers of poetry, those who have influenced your work?

I feel like Galway Kinnell has been a teacher, even though I have never met him. I love his work. I think that what he has is a beautiful balance between technique and music. He is such a poet. He's a poet's poet with the music . . . and that's important to me. Of course James Wright. Richard Hugo. Adrienne Rich. I admire her sheer audacity. In the face of everything she learned from the fathers, given the time when she grew up and her own father's admonitions, still she became herself.

I see that in your work, too. I don't know if you are aware of how daring your work is, and how dangerous!

I'd better be! I love the work of Audre Lorde; she has also been one of my teachers.

In the dedication to **In Mad Love and War** *you affirm that "the erotic belongs in the poetry, as in the self." Can you elaborate?*

It has taken me years to divest myself of Christian guilt, the Puritan cloud that provides the base for culture in this country . . . or at least to recognize the twists and turns of that illogic in my own sensibility. In that framework the body is seen as an evil thing and is separate from spirit. The body and spirit are not separate. Nor is that construct any different in the place from which I write poetry. There is no separation. See Audre Lorde's "Uses of the Erotic: the Erotic as Power" (*Sister Outsider,* 1984) for a viable definition of the erotic. Again, there is no separation.

Feminist writings and lesbian feminist writings have been very important to you, your work?

Yes, they have.

Are there other writers who have been important to you that we should know about?

Yes. I can think of a lot of writers who are important to me—Leslie Silko, for instance, whom I met shortly after I started writing. I actually took a fiction class from her at UNM as an undergraduate. . . . I especially liked our wine breaks in our office, the stories as we listened to Fleetwood Mac, watched for rain. . . . There are a lot of people . . . Beth Brant, Louis Oliver, June Jordan. . . .

You dedicated the poem **"Hieroglyphics"** *(from* **In Mad Love and War***) to June Jordan. Why did she get that one?*

Well, it's a long story.

It's a wonderful poem. It moves across time and space, defying boundaries. Maybe June Jordan has a mythic imagination that can comprehend those leaps?

Yeah. I mean she is somebody you can talk to like that and you can't talk to everyone that way. Sometimes in a poem you assume you can.

Maybe you assume that because you need to make the poems accessible. You want people to feel like you are talking to them. **In Mad Love and War** *is a breakthrough in terms of form and content. How do you feel about being formally inventive?*

I don't know. I don't really know what I'm doing.

You lean into the unknown in those lines and see what happens?

Yes, I do. I don't analyze. I mean certainly analysis is also part of the process of writing poetry, but it's not primary. It comes later in the process.

In part it's probably discipline that lets you explore. Discipline from the habit of years of writing. Do you write daily?

I don't. I try to! (laughter) Well, do you?

No, of course not! We were talking before about having families and having lives, and here you are in Knoxville. I mean, how are you supposed to write every day? Though William Stafford writes every day, even when he's traveling.

Writing is a craft and there's something to doing it or you lose it. I used to paint and draw, and was quite a good artist, but I can't do it at the same level anymore. It's not that I've lost it but I'd have to get my chops together, so to speak, practice.

Do you regret the decision to give up painting?

I don't know that I regret it, but I certainly miss painting. That particular language was more familiar to me than the literary world. . . .

What can you do in poetry that painting could not achieve?

Speak directly in a language that was meant to destroy us.

You have focused on your writing and on your music.

Yes. If I'm not writing I'm thinking about it, or looking at things—I feel this infuses my vision. I'm listening for stories and listening to how words are put together and so on.

Living a "writer's life"?

Yes.

The theme of music gets into your poetry when you dedicate poems to Billie Holiday or make reference to Coltrane. But I also sense the influence of jazz on your forms.

Well, that wasn't conscious. I think it's coming out of playing the saxophone. I realized recently that I took it up exactly when I entered academe. I don't feel like I've become an academic but if you're going to be in that place, certainly it's going to rub off on you. (laughter)

So you needed some way back to the body?

Yes. Anyway, it was a time when I started teaching at the University of Colorado, Boulder. I had run from teaching in universities. I remember applying once years ago for the University of Texas, El Paso, and then I couldn't make it to MLA because I had no money. I preferred to keep my own hours, worked free lance, doing screenplay writing and readings and workshops—somehow the money always came in—but it's a tough existence, you have to have a lot of faith. I got a position as Assistant Professor at the University of Colorado, Boulder. I wrote **"We Must Call a Meeting"** right after I started teaching there because I was afraid that in that atmosphere, in that place, I was going to lose my poetry. That was around the time I started playing tenor sax. I play tenor and soprano now, but I realize that in a way it was a way to keep that poetry and keep that place.

Keep your sanity, keep your juice!

Yeah. I mean you pick up the saxophone again, I suppose it's like writing poetry, you are picking up the history of that. Playing saxophone is like honoring a succession of myths. . . . I never thought of this before but: the myth of saxophone and here comes Billie Holiday and there's Coltrane. I love his work dearly, especially "A Love Supreme." That song has fed me. And all of that becomes. When you play you're a part of that, you have to recognize those people.

There's a very strong sense of community in your work, community of musicians you address; community of other writers, community of women. . . . I want to ask you about your great-aunt, to whom you dedicated **She Had Some Horses.**

She's the relative I was closest to, and my life in some ways has uncannily paralleled hers. I miss her dearly. I always felt like I dropped into an alien family almost—maybe most people do—but when she and I got together, then I felt akin. She was very interested in art—she was a painter and was very supportive of the Creek Nation Museum in Okmulgee, and donated most of her paintings to them. She traveled. We followed the same routes. Like her, I left Oklahoma for New Mexico—I was sent to an Indian boarding school in Santa Fe. It was a school for the arts, very innovative in its time, sort of like an Indian *Fame* school. When I left Oklahoma to go to high school there, in a way it saved my life. . . . In my travels I often met relatives of people that she knew. I have a necklace that Maria Martinez gave her—Maria, the potter from San Ildefonso. (My great-aunt) was someone who was married for six months and didn't like it and got a divorce, and spent a lot of time driving—she liked traveling Indian country—and also opened a jewelry shop.

So there's movement, dynamism, in your family, and that restlessness. . . .

Yes. Through her and her life I understand myself more clearly, and I love her dearly and miss her.

Did she live long enough to see the book dedicated to her?

No. She died before my father . . . in '82.

But she knew you were a poet?

Oh yes. She was real proud of that.

What's new in your work that you feel comfortable talking about?

The music, what I've been actively involved in to the tune of two or three hours a night (that's a lot of time!) is working with my band *Poetic Justice*. We're working on a show, putting together performances of my poems.

Earlier you mentioned that you were frustrated about your music—why?

I want to be farther along than I am. The music is still not as far along as the poetry. I fooled around with the sax for about seven years; I've played really seriously for only two years. . . . I want to play more and spend more time with it.

What has the audience response been like?

Our first gig we played in Santa Rosa, California, as part of a show of Indian performers called Indian Airobics, and most recently in Minneapolis. There we were brought in by The Loft. The audiences loved us. We're still rather raw in actual practice, we've very recently come together, but there's something we make as a band with the music and poetry that is rather exciting.

I recently read a selection of autobiographical prose that you did, called **"Family Album"** *(The Progressive, March 1992). Are you still working on the autobiographical writing?*

I'm working on a manuscript of autobiographical writings. I call it: "A Love Supreme; Stories, Poems, and Parables." There's much interest in it.

So it's a mixture of several genres. The **"Family Album"** *piece has passages of poetry in it.*

Yes, I think it's all one. I work within that assumption.

You mentioned once before that you were putting together a book called "Reinventing the Enemy's Language." Are you still working on that?

Yes. It's an anthology of Native women's writings. The original concept was to include writings from North and South America. We have one piece from a Native woman from El Salvador. We also received some prose from Rigoberta Menchu as well as from Wilma Mankiller, Cherokee Chief. We have work in it from Canada—it's quite wideranging, and includes many genres.

What else is going on with your work? How far did you get with your essay on poetry and jazz?

Oh, it's getting there. I have rewriting, rethinking to do. Some of the pieces are meant particularly for music. We're rearranging and performing two tunes of Jim Pepper's. Jim was a friend of mine, a fine jazz saxophone player who integrated jazz and tribal forms with music. He's the same tribe, Muscogee (or Creek) as well as Kaw Indian from Oklahoma. He died recently and I wanted to play a tribute for him. So we decided on "Witchi Tia To," for which he is most famous, and "Lakota Song"—which isn't an original tune but his arrangement is unique of this Lakota woman's love song. I "sing" the women's part on tenor sax. For "Witchi Tia To" I read a poem as a tribute to him, **"The Place the Musician Became a Bear on the Streets of a City Meant to Kill Him."**

It's an intimate cosmic dance! You're doing so many things—we haven't touched on all of them—you're active in tribal life, you've been traveling to various tribal ceremonies, you teach, give workshops and readings. How do you find time to do it all? How do you make time for your writing?

I was blessed with energy. I also try to integrate each aspect of my life. The poetry I mix with the music. And so on . . . though sometimes I just lose it. Then get back up again. I get excited about the possibilities and permutations of sound, about the color blue, for instance.

I want to ask you whether there is a connection between poetry and politics, and poetry and prayer? Are these intermingled?

Of course.

In the back of **In Mad Love and War,** *there's a poem based on a Native traditional form. . . .*

Which comes out of the Beauty Way Chant. I used to speak Navajo fairly well. I know that it's influenced my writing.

I've been told that it's a very difficult language.

It's a beautiful language. I love the way that you can say things in that language. So that's been a powerful influence.

How did you learn Navajo?

When I was a student at UNM I took Navajo Language for a year and a half. I had a wonderful teacher the first year, Roseanne Willink, a Navajo from western New Mexico. We had a great time in there. I remember making up jokes and then starting dreaming in Navajo. I don't know my own language, and wish to learn.

Was your family bilingual?

No, my father's mother had died when he was young. His father married a white woman. He had a lot of difficulties as a child. He was beaten a lot by his dad, and sent to a military school in Ponca City, Oklahoma. I think being Creek—which he was proud of—became a very painful thing for him.

No wonder he had such a hard time coping. You spoke earlier about his alcoholism. He had so much to contend with as such a young person.

Yes, he did. But anyway, back to your earlier question—for me there's always a definite link between poetry and prayer. I think that you can say that a poem is always a prayer for whomever you're speaking of. **"Eagle Poem"** at the end (of **In Mad Love and War**) is most obviously a prayer. You could look at all poems as being a prayer for our continuance. I mean even the act of writing, to be creative, has everything to do with our continuance as peoples.

Joy Harjo with Marilyn Kallet, in an interview in The Kenyon Review, *n.s. Vol. XV, No. 3, Summer, 1993, pp. 57-66.*

FURTHER READING

Criticism

Berner, Robert L. Review of *In Mad Love and War*, by Joy Harjo. *World Literature Today* 65, No. 1 (Winter 1991): 167.
    Favorable assessment of *In Mad Love and War*, in which Berner praises Harjo's treatment of war, love, and transformation.

Hobson, Geary. Review of *Secrets from the Center of the World,* by Joy Harjo and Stephen Strom. *World Literature Today* 65, No. 1 (Winter 1991): 168.

Mixed assessment of *Secrets from the Center of the World.* Hobson faults Strom's illustrations but praises Harjo's stylistic and thematic focus, concluding: "Joy Harjo is indeed well on her way toward becoming a major poet."

Ruppert, Jim. "Paula Gunn Allen and Joy Harjo: Closing the Distance between Personal and Mythic Space." *American Indian Quarterly* 7, No. 1 (Spring 1983): 27-40.

Comparative analysis of Allen's and Harjo's writings. The critic states that "both writers see the importance of a vision wider than that which contemporary American society encourages. They create effective poetic structures designed to open the perceptions of readers so that the readers may be moved—through the writer's search for meaning—to significate their own lives, to perceive the mythic/spirit level of understanding inherent in Native American experience."

Additional coverage of Harjo's life and career is contained in the following sources published by Gale Research: *Contemporary Authors,* **Vol. 114;** *Contemporary Authors New Revision Series,* **Vol. 35; and** *Dictionary of Literary Biography,* **Vol. 120.**

Erica Jong

1942-

American poet, novelist, and biographer.

The following entry provides an overview of Jong's career-through 1990. For further information on her life and works, see *CLC*, Volumes 4, 6, 8, and 18.

INTRODUCTION

Best known for her novel *Fear of Flying*, Jong has received both popular and critical recognition for her frank, satirical treatment of sexuality. Her works have been interpreted both as pioneering efforts in the movement toward an authentic and free expression of female sexuality and, according to an anonymous reviewer in *Kirkus Reviews*, as "porn with a literary veneer." Some critics have noted that attention to the risque elements of Jong's fiction has eclipsed her treatment of serious social issues in her fiction and poetry.

Biographical Information

Jong grew up on the Upper West Side of New York City. Her mother, Eda Mirsky Mann, was a painter, and her father, Seymour Mann, was a musician, composer, and importer of giftware. As an adolescent, Jong wrote and illustrated numerous journals and stories. She later served as editor of the literary magazine and producer of poetry programs for campus radio at Barnard College, from which she graduated in 1963. Jong (then Erica Mann) earned an M.A. in English literature at Columbia University in 1965, and in 1966 she married Allan Jong, a Chinese-American psychiatrist. The Jongs moved to Heidelberg, Germany, where Allan served in the military until 1969, and Erica taught at the University of Maryland Overseas Division. It was in Germany that Jong departed from writing poetry in the formal style of William Butler Yeats, W. H. Auden, and Dylan Thomas, and began developing her own distinctive approach to treating the human condition in order to incorporate the sense of paranoia she experienced as a Jew living in Germany. It was with her poetry collection *Fruits and Vegetables* that Jong first gained critical attention, but it was shortly after the publication of *Fear of Flying* in 1973 that Jong received popular notice and became a famous writer. Jong's awards include *Poetry* magazine's 1971 Bess Hokin prize, the 1972 Madeline Sadin Award from *New York Quarterly*, and the 1972 Alice Faye di Castagnolia Award from the Poetry Society of America.

Major Works

In her poetry, Jong presents observations on such topics as aging, love, sex, feminism, and death, and while her treatment of these topics is often serious, her tone is largely life-affirming and humorous. Jong has asserted that the

common theme in all of her works is "the quest for self-knowledge," a theme that dominates her semi-autobiographical trilogy of novels *Fear of Flying* (1973), *How to Save Your Own Life* (1977), and *Parachutes & Kisses* (1984). These three works trace the life of Isadora Wing, a writer who travels extensively and seeks spiritual, emotional, and physical fulfillment in various relationships with men. The recipient of far more popular and critical attention than its sequels, *Fear of Flying* has been characterized as a *bildungsroman* in the tradition of Henry Miller's *Tropic of Cancer*, James Joyce's *Odyssey*, Dante's *Inferno*, and the myth of Daedalus and Icarus. In *Fanny: Being the True History of the Adventures of Fanny Hackabout-Jones* (1980) and *Serenissima: A Novel of Venice* (1987), Jong employs the settings and language of eighteenth-century England and sixteenth-century Venice, respectively. *Fanny* is Jong's version of an eighteenth-century pornographic work by John Cleland titled *Fanny Hill*, and *Serenissima* depicts Jessica Pruitt, a twentieth-century actress who falls ill and is transported in a dream to Elizabethan England, where she becomes romantically involved with William Shakespeare. In a departure from fiction, Jong has written the biography *The Devil at Large: Erica Jong on Henry Miller* (1993). Jong became close friends with Miller, who, in an early review of *Fear of Flying*, called the novel "a female *Tropic of Cancer*."

Critical Reception

Critical reaction to Jong's works has been mixed. While some critics have focused negative attention on the raw language and sexual explicitness of her works, some have lauded Jong for crossing gender barriers and paving the way for other women writers to use language previously considered the domain of male authors. Gayle Greene has asserted: "Jong confuses liberation with sexual liberation and confuses sexual liberation with the freedom to talk and act like a man, but the bold language that so impressed readers masks a conventionality, a failure to imagine otherwise." Many critics, however, have praised Jong's masterful use of humor, her ironic and honest depiction of interactions between men and women, and her insight into society as a whole. Joan Reardon has commented: "If 'woman writer' ceases to be a polite but negative label, it will be due in great measure to the efforts of Erica Jong."

PRINCIPAL WORKS

Fruits and Vegetables   (poetry)   1971
Fear of Flying   (novel)   1973
Half-Lives   (poetry)   1973
Here Comes, and Other Poems   (poetry)   1975
Loveroot   (poetry)   1975
The Poetry of Erica Jong   (poetry)   1976
How to Save Your Own Life   (novel)   1977
At the Edge of the Body   (poetry)   1979
Fanny: Being the True History of the Adventures of Fanny Hackabout-Jones   (novel)   1980
Ordinary Miracles: New Poems   (poetry)   1983
Parachutes & Kisses   (novel)   1984
Serenissima: A Novel of Venice   (novel)   1987
Any Woman's Blues   (novel)   1990
Becoming Light: Poems New and Selected   (poetry) 1991
The Devil at Large: Erica Jong on Henry Miller   (biography)   1993

CRITICISM

Harvey Shapiro   (review date 25 August 1973)

[*Shapiro is an American educator, poet, novelist, and critic who has served as editor of the* New York Times Book Review. *In the following excerpt, he provides a favorable assessment of* Half-Lives, *commenting on Jong's treatment of women's issues.*]

To write as a woman is to write from an extreme situation: the assumption behind Erica Jong's and Adrienne Rich's recent poetry. It gives energy to their lines. And I suspect, it gives them readers they might not ordinarily have. This can be a temptation (I think it is for Erica Jong) to play to that audience. But for the most part it must mean poet touching reader, reader touching poet, in a way that can make both more alive.

Erica Jong is quick, easy, raunchy (the pose is sometimes that of a female rake) and her personality so fills her poems [in *Half-Lives*] that it's difficult sometimes to see around her to her meaning. There is nothing particularly feminist or ideological in this; it's part of the personality packaging some poets fall into naturally these days. It permits the reader easy access to a book through knowing the basic plot and the main character (as, for example, Diane Wakoski: men throw me off their motorbikes).

Her free verse is held together by repetitions (a line, or phrase or syntactical unit) and it is designed to move quickly, images shifting with each line, the imagination always looking for the next turn. Given that technique, you don't stay with a line; there isn't time for that savoring of something made to last that has been one of the traditional pleasures of poetry. But then this poetry is designed to say that art isn't a refuge, that nothing lasts, that all a poet can do is to make lines out of her life to prove that life real, and when the lines stop the life has gone. (See her opening poem: "Why does life need evidence of life? / We disbelieve it / even as we live.")

Does she manipulate her audience? Maybe some of her poems use women's liberation as a piece of pop culture (to know the movement lives, take a walk down the bra-less streets of New York), as in her funny **"Seventeen Warnings in Search of a Feminist Poem."** "Beware of the man who writes flowery love letters; he is preparing for years of silence. / Beware of the man who praises liberated women; he is planning to quit his job." Some of these cartoon poems reverse Thurber's war of the sexes. The opening of her **"Anniversary"** poem, for example:

> Every night for five years
> he chewed on her
> until her fingers were red and ragged
> until blue veins hung out of her legs
> until the children tumbled
> like baby kangaroos
> out of raw crimson pouches
> in her stomach

Now it may be that in every marriage there's a victor and a victim, but is the wife always the victim (and doesn't the battle sometimes shift rapidly, to say nothing of long periods of armistice)? But wife as victim is the program. (It takes her next poem, **"Divorce,"** to reverse that.)

In general, men don't fare too well in these poems. **"How You Get Born":** "you wait in a heavy rainsoaked cloud / for your father's thunderbolt. . . . / Your mother lies in the living room dreaming your eyes. / She awakens and a shudder shakes her teeth. . . . / She slides into bed beside that gray-faced man, / your father." That's the way it used to be. In her own experience, love is better; "You on the prow / of Columbus' ship / kissing the lip / of the new world." Emily Dickinson, you've come a long way.

The manner is playful throughout but the material frequently is not. Beneath it all is her assertion in poem after poem, of the essential hard luck of being a woman poet. That's the way I read her **"Alcestis on the Poetry Circuit"** ("She must never go out of the house / unless veiled in paint. / She must wear tight shoes / so she always remembers her bondage."), which is like a verse rendition of the psychologist Matina Horner's thesis that women are conditioned by the culture to fail. And her purest Muse poem, **"Why I Died,"** is a celebration of a suicidal woman ("She is the woman I follow. / Whenever I enter a room / she has been there—") with its inevitable recall of Sylvia Plath.

Harvey Shapiro, "Two Sisters in Poetry," in The New York Times, *August 25, 1973, p. 21.*

Anatole Broyard   (review date 11 June 1975)

[*An American educator and critic, Broyard served for fifteen years as a* New York Times *book reviewer and feature writer. In the following review of* Loveroot, *he faults Jong's poetry as pretentious, commenting, "Ms. Jong is too full of herself."*]

When *Fear of Flying* ended with the runaway wife returning to scrub her infidelities in her husband's bathtub, some feminists saw Erica Jong's novel as a washout. She may have come to agree with them, for she has since divorced her second husband and written an article in *Vogue* magazine on the obsolescence of marriage. She has her own bathtub now, and her own bathos. She says, for example, that *Loveroot,* her third book of poems, was written to prove that women poets need not commit suicide.

The author leaves us in no doubt as to why some women poets did commit suicide. In a poem on Sylvia Plath and other "martyrs," she says, *Men did them in.*" They will not do her in, however, for she has seen through their "doom-saying, death-dealing" ways. She is in her own hands, her "big mouth / filled with poems," and I think it should be interesting to see what she does with her independence. History has many cunning corridors, as T. S. Eliot remarked, and in the history of the feminist movement Mrs. Jong's corridor probably has a cunning peculiar to itself.

She has come out of the bathtub to "teeter on the edge of the cosmos," to "write in neon sperm across the air." Her sisters in arms may question this reference to sperm with its suggestion of men, but it is to the author's credit that she writes as if she had generated it herself. Perhaps we have here a more modern version of Rimbaud's "alchemy" of language.

It is curious to see in how many ways women have modified Freud's famous dictum that anatomy is destiny. Recently, I suggested that, for some new women novelists, anatomy is irony. I believe Mrs. Jong would say that it is poetry. It makes up, at any rate, a good part of her own. "My breasts ache . . . my womb pulls earthward . . ." "The poems keep flowing monthly / like my blood." "I offered my belly as a bowl . . . my breasts as the chafing

dish / to keep us warm . . . I offered my navel / as a brandy snifter."

Blood recurs often enough to clot *Loveroot*'s pages. I think that, in the author's mind, blood stands for sincerity. Her poems must pass some blood test of her own devising. While only women bleed, they may soon, if I can read the signs, teach men to ejaculate blood. In spite of her proud protestations, Mrs. Jong is rather ambivalent about her body. While it is not a party to the "orgasms of gloom [that] convulse the world," it does have its burdens. It leaves her a prey to the "loneliness of pregnant whales," and it is threatened by a "blockage" which can be cured only by love, whose "first sure sign . . . is diarrhea."

In their movement toward emancipation, woman sometimes see fit to put aside coquetry, to adopt a flat-footed stance of "authenticity." "Mistakes:" the author writes, "she will make them / herself." "Life: not reasoned or easy / but at least / her own." Under the influence of this authenticity, the author tends to blunt her poems—"truth is often crude"—until the message becomes the medium. Confounding truth and poetry is one of the fond homilies of our time. I will not attempt to seduce you with poetry, Mrs. Jong implies. You must take me as I am. Sublimation is just so much hypocrisy.

Here is the cult of identity again, in one of its many manifestations. Love me, love my identity, and a militant woman's identity must be seen without bra or embellishment. She refuses any longer to be an interior decorator of the womb. Poetry is not a bauble, but a speculum.

In the "zoo-prison of marriage," the husband sleeps through his wife's "noisy nights of poetry." "The pages of your dreams," she muses in tender condescension, "are riffled by the winds of my writing." The husband dozes like a baby while the wife adventures among emergencies. The supermarket is a concentration camp where "the blue numerals" of the tally are "tattooed / on the white skins / of paper . . ." While men can "yearn / with infinite emptiness / toward the body of a woman," she "must not only inspire the poem / but also type it, / not only conceive the child," but bear it, bathe it, feed it and "carry it / everywhere, everywhere. . . ." In the author's view of marriage, there are no maids, no day camps, no anticlimaxes. The uncharitable might say that there are no children either, except for rhetorical ones.

In *Loveroot,* the drama of anatomy elbows out the drama of poetry. The blood's pulse dulls the meter. The "I" blinds the eye. The bombast drowns the music. The sincerity stifles the wit. Mrs. Jong is too full of herself. We might say of this book, as F. R. Leavis said of the Sitwells, that it belongs more to the history of publicity than to the history of poetry.

The poetry is in the pity, Wilfred Owen observed, but perhaps this sort of sympathy no longer suits our pitiless age. The poetry is in the publicity—there, isn't that more like it? Women poets need not commit suicide; Mrs. Jong is right. Still, I think she ought to be reminded that, for her, fame too may be a form of death.

Anatole Broyard, "The Poetry Is in the Publicity," in The New York Times, *June 11, 1975, p. 41.*

Jane Chance Nitzsche   (essay date Winter 1978)

[*Nitzsche is an American educator and critic. In the following essay, she delineates Jong's use of parallels to the myth of Daedalus and Icarus in* Fear of Flying.]

Although Erica Jong felt that her first novel, *Fear of Flying* (1973), was too literary for wide appeal, it rapidly became a best seller, its humor and eroticism praised on the dust jacket by John Updike and Henry Miller as well as by Hannah Greene and Elizabeth Janeway, but its literary qualities frequently ignored or even savagely castigated in reviews by such critics as Walter Clemons, Ellen Hope Meyer, Paul Theroux, Patricia S. Coyne, and Martin Amis. Characteristic of the criticisms is the following evaluation [by Hope Meyer in *The Nation,* January 12, 1974]: "literary it is not. Poorly constructed, too prone to phrases like 'our mouths melted like liquid,' it has a shapeless, self-indulgent plot and weak characterization, especially of the men." Such weaknesses supposedly exist because "There is no artistic distance between the author and her subject, and hence no objectivity."

Yet as a poet Jong received critical acclaim for *Fruits and Vegetables* (1971) and *Half-Lives* (1973), collections of poems whose colloquial diction and casual line lengths camouflage a tightly controlled form. Such control is achieved by the use of rhetorical figures and extended images, or conceits. As an example, in **"The Man Under the Bed,"** which appears in *Fear of Flying* but which was originally published in *Fruits and Vegetables,* the bogeyman of the child metamorphoses into a fantasy lover of a lonely woman lying in bed at night, in a conceit that dominates the syntax and diction of the poem through the rhetorical figure of anaphora. Jong's poetic technique has led Helen Vendler to conclude, in a review of *Half-Lives,* first that "the poems need to be seen whole" and second that "Inside her rigid frames of syntax, a playful metaphorical mind is at work, busy in powerful invention of little fables" [*The New York Times Book Review,* August 12, 1973]. These two statements might be applied equally well to Jong's very literary novel. It needs to be seen whole *because* it contains a "powerful invention of a little fable," in this case a reworking of the myth of Daedalus and Icarus, and the use of the theme and symbol of flying.

Flying as a theme both introduces and ends the novel. Isadora Wing begins her "mock memoirs" by announcing her fear of flying: after treatment by six of the 117 psychoanalysts aboard the flight to Vienna, she remains "more scared of flying than when I began my analytic adventures some thirteen years earlier." In contrast, at the end of the novel, when Isadora sits in the bathtub in her husband's hotel room admiring her body and hugging herself, she realizes "It was my fear that was missing. The cold stone I had worn inside my chest for twenty-nine years was gone. Not suddenly. And maybe not for good. But it was gone." The novel, then, traces the stages necessary to progress from a fear of "flying"—literally and apparently figuratively, judging from this last quotation—to its elimination

and subsequent replacement with a love of self. Isadora's last name, "Wing," underscores the significance of the novel's major theme and symbol.

Flying, for Jong, denotes literal flying but connotes creativity ("in the way that the word 'fire' was used by poets like Alexander Pope to mean sexual heat, creativity, inspiration, passion"), sexuality, and independence. Indeed, during the novel Isadora manifests, confronts, and rids herself of each of the three fears of flying. First, in her marriage to her second husband, Bennett, she overcomes the fear of creativity (and the habit of artistic dishonesty) so that she can fly, or explore the world of herself through poetry: "My writing is the submarine or *spaceship* which takes me to the unknown worlds within my head. And the adventure is endless and inexhaustible. If I learn to build the right vehicle, then I can discover even more territories. And each new poem is a new vehicle, designed to delve a little deeper (or *fly a little higher*) than the one before" (my italics). In her relationships with all of her men, especially with Adrian, she encounters the second fear of flying, consisting of those social or sexual inhibitions that prevent her from realizing her fantasy of the archetypal casual sexual union during which bodies flow together and zippers melt away. Only with Adrian does she overcome her fear sufficiently to brave convention, bolstered by thoughts of "D. H. Lawrence running off with his tutor's wife, of Romeo and Juliet dying for love, of Aschenbach pursuing Tadzio through plaguey Venice, of all the real and imaginary people who had picked up and burned their bridges and *taken off into the wild blue yonder.* I was one of *them!* No scared housewife, I. I was flying" (my italics). Finally, in her relationship with herself, the most important relationship of the three, she fears confronting and being herself: living independently of men, without their approval. Thus when Adrian abandons her in Paris, he forces her to survive alone, to "fly." Terrified, Isadora describes the experience as "teetering on the edge of the Grand Canyon and hoping you'd learn to fly before you hit bottom."

Jong strengthens the theme and symbol of flying by conjoining it with myth—the classical myth of flight, the myth of Daedalus and Icarus. To fly in the sexual sense, for Isadora, means adopting "borrowed wings" that belong to a man in order to fly to a heaven of ecstasy, hence to leave herself behind: "I wanted to lose myself in a man, to cease to be me, to be transported to heaven on borrowed wings." Only when Isadora, alone in her Paris hotel room at the end of the novel, realizes that overcoming her fear of sexual flying has seriously interfered with her progress toward flying independently—toward being and accepting herself—does she begin to differentiate between false and true flying. So she describes herself as "Isadora Icarus . . . And the borrowed wings never stayed on when I needed them. Maybe I really needed to grow my own." In the classical version of the myth, Icarus used his artist father's wax wings in order to escape from the labyrinth in which both he and his father had been imprisoned; although warned not to fly too close to the sun, Icarus recklessly ignored his father's advice and tumbled, his wings melted, into the sea. Clearly, Isadora Wing, assuming the role of Icarus, has also borrowed the wings of the "father"—obviously sexual, and donated by the various father figures within the novel with whom she has fallen in love, for example, Bennett *Wing,* who succeeds her first husband, the childish, insane Brian. Described as a *"good solid father figure,* a psychiatrist as an antidote to a psychotic, a good secular lay as an antidote to Brian's religious fervor," Bennett Wing appeared to Isadora *"On the wing,* you might say . . . *Wing.* I loved Bennett's name. And he was mercurial, too"—at least in his sexual acrobatics, which endow him with "wings" for Isadora (my italics). Like Icarus, however, Isadora flies too high and burns her wings, learning then how faulty this borrowed rig is: "What had love ever done for me but disappoint me? Or maybe I looked for the wrong things in love." Like many other women, Isadora has had to earn those "gossamer wings" belonging to the ideal man ("beautiful, powerful, potent, and rich") she imagines will *"fly you to the moon . . . where you would live totally satisfied forever"* (my italics). Such sexual flight leads to satisfaction with self ("the moon . . . where you would live totally satisfied forever"), but is impelled in part by a disgust with self—implied also by the need to "lose oneself " in love for a man. So Isadora decries the female body, as through advertising society programs most women to regard their bodies as too earthy and too earthly, justly requiring a narcissistic attention to "your smells, your hair, your boobs, your eyelashes, your armpits, your crotch, your stars, your scars, and your choice of Scotch in bars" in order to win those "wings" which will "fly you to the moon."

Yet the myth of the labyrinth also depicts a second means of escape. Icarus and Daedalus were imprisoned in the labyrinth by King Minos because Daedalus had previously helped Theseus to escape when he had been imprisoned. The earlier mode of escape entailed returning through the maze the same way one had entered: Theseus, with whom Minos' daughter Ariadne had recently fallen in love and for whom she had requested aid from Daedalus, was given by her a ball of string to unwind as he entered and to retrieve as he departed. This too suggests a gift, like the wax wings, of the "father" to the child, but here offered by the paternal figure Daedalus to a female child, Ariadne, and intended to effect her lover's escape, not her own. In Jong's reconstruction of the myth, the ball of string is given to the childish Isadora by Adrian, who combines both Daedalus and Ariadne, the former in his role as the second major father figure and psychiatrist in Isadora's life and the latter in his name as an anagram of Ariadne's. Specifically Isadora as Theseus must unravel the string as she explores the labyrinth of Vienna and herself by returning to the past and re-enacting troubling familial roles. Isadora explicitly refers to this part of the myth: "We quickly picked up the threads of these old patterns of behavior as we made our way through the labyrinths of Old Europe." Isadora reverts to her position as second-born in the family, Adrian reverts to his position as first-born ("Adrian, in fact, was born the same year as Randy [1937] and also had a younger brother he'd spent years learning how to bully"). Thus this relationship between Isadora and Adrian differs significantly from that between Isadora and Bennett: it depends more on unraveling the *verbal* threads of past behavior than escaping the labyrinth of the self on *sexual* wings. Of this analytic passion Isadora declares, "We talked. We talked. We talked. Psychoanalysis

on wheels. Remembrance of things past." Again and again Isadora relates her emotional and intellectual rapport with Adrian (despite his frequent sexual impotence), then contrasts it with the silence of the primarily physical relationship with Bennett. The rapport culminates—as they wander through the labyrinths of Old Europe—in the long exchange of past relationships with former lovers and spouses, of which Isadora's side is recorded in chapters twelve through fifteen ("The Madman," "The Conductor," "Arabs and Other Animals," "Travels with My Anti-Hero"). But just as the first escape from the labyrinth (the body) involved borrowing wings (wings/Bennett Wing) to fly (sexual ecstasy), so the second escape from the labyrinth (the mind) involves unraveling the ball of thread from the past (good love/Adrian Goodlove) to find the way out or to ameliorate confusion (emotional and intellectual understanding). Both escapes, however, are false. Although the dialogue of Adrian and Isadora depends on "remembrance of things past. . . . the main thing was entertainment, not *literal truth*" (my italics). Manufacturing and elaborating upon her past, Isadora tells Adrian not about herself but about her various lovers (just as Adrian's latent homosexuality led to his voyeuristic participation in Bennett and Isadora's earlier lovemaking and his caressing of Bennett's back afterwards, so this sexual aberration diagnosed by Bennett and recognized by Isadora and continues in the form of his interest in other men she has known). He requests that she find patterns ("threads") in her past by categorizing these men. When she obliges, she realizes she is escaping the labyrinth of her past—that is, fleeing from the truth of her past, her self—by following the false thread lent to her by Ariadne/Adrian.

> Oh I knew I was making my life into a song-and-dance routine, a production number, a shaggy dog story, a sick joke, a *bid*. I thought of all the longing, the pain, the letters (sent and unsent), the crying jags, the telephone monologues, the suffering, the rationalizing, the analyzing which had gone into each of these relationships, each of these relationdinghies, each of these relation-liners. I knew that the way I described them was a betrayal of their complexity, their confusion.

She flees from the complexity of the past stored in her memory—because she desperately needs to escape herself, or rather, to earn Adrian's approval of herself and thereby accept what she is.

That is, she needs to face that minotaur locked within the labyrinth. Jong's mythic parallels suggest that escaping the labyrinth of the body (through Bennett Wing, sexual love) or the labyrinth of the mind (through Adrian Goodlove, remembrance of things past) constitutes a refusal to confront oneself—envisioned in the novel not only as a labyrinth, but indeed as the minotaur within the labyrinth threatening intruders, that monster which is half beast, half human. That Jong finds the metaphor of the divided self especially relevant to twentieth-century concerns (she defines the modern as "the attempt to bring together the dissociated sensibility") has been revealed previously in her book of poems, *Half-Lives,* whose title refers to "Wholes and halves, and looking for fulfillment, at least in the 'Age of Exploration' section, and finding the separation could not be bridged." As metaphor for the divided self in *Fear of Flying,* the minotaur expresses itself chiefly through the conflict between Isadora's body and mind, or the disjunction between the woman and the artist. At fourteen, for example, Isadora saw this conflict as an either/or dilemma: *either* a woman accepts her sexuality (through intercourse with Steve, her first lover), thereby implicitly denying the artistic drive, *or* a woman denies her sexuality (through masturbation, through starvation to stop menstrual periods) to retain the option of being an artist. Later in life Isadora repeats these attempts to escape the division of self, the minotaur, by losing herself in a man ("flying"). Unfortunately, each man she chooses fulfills only one half of her divided self, either her body or her mind: Brian before his psychosis represents the intellectual who prefers a sexless relationship in marriage; Bennett, in contrast, represents the sexy psychiatrist who rarely talks to his wife about shared interests; Adrian, finally, talks incessantly but remains frequently impotent, similar then to Brian. What Isadora needs in order to fly is "a perfect man" with a mind and body equally attractive to her: "He had a face like Paul Newman and a voice like Dylan Thomas." Such a man of course does not exist, or exists only in the combined figures of Bennett and Adrian, who together mirror Isadora's divided self, her minotaur (Isadora describes Adrian as a horny minotaur): "Adrian, it seemed, wanted to teach me how to live. Bennett, it seemed, wanted to teach me how to die. And I didn't even know which I wanted. Or maybe I had pegged them wrong. Maybe Bennett was life and Adrian death. Maybe life was compromise and sadness, while ecstasy ended inevitably in death."

In the classical myth the half-beast, half-human monster was conceived by King Minos' wife Pasiphae. So the minotaur of Isadora Zelda White—her name expressing the divided self of the artist (Isadora Duncan, Zelda Fitzgerald) and the woman ("white" suggesting that purity associated with woman)—was conceived literally and figuratively by her mother. The parallel is apt: Pasiphae lusted for the bull her husband refused to sacrifice to the god Poseidon, who vengefully inhabited the bull during the begetting of the minotaur. Psychologically, then, the minotaur represents the monster (that is, the divided self) engendered by woman's intercourse with the divine (that is, begotten when woman tries to be an artist, or to aspire toward a role or an act which seems unnatural or unconventional). It is this monster a woman inherits—from her society, generally, but from her mother, specifically. Isadora reveals her heritage in chapter nine, "Pandora's Box or My Two Mothers": the bad mother or "failed artist" channels all of her creative energy into unusual clothes, decorating schemes, and vicarious plans for her daughters, all of which eschew the ordinary, whereas the good mother, a loving and sympathetic woman, adores her daughters in the most ordinary way. Clearly the bad mother resented Isadora when she interfered with her lapsed creative passion; her anger teaches her daughter the lesson of the minotaur-woman, that "being a woman meant being harried, frustrated, and always angry. It meant being split into two irreconcilable halves." The specific division of self troubling Isadora's mother occurs between her domestic and

artistic sides: "either you drowned in domesticity . . . or you longed for domesticity in all your art. You could never escape your conflict. You had conflict written in your very blood."

As the minotaur in reality, Isadora finds herself imprisoned in—or concealed by—various labyrinths of falsity throughout the novel, primarily because others—or even she herself—cannot face the monster she represents. The first labyrinth is introduced in chapter three ("Knock, Knock") when her sister Randy, representing her family, rejects the unconventional artist in her (" 'you really ought to stop writing and have a baby' ") and sends her fleeing to the closet where she mulls her feelings of being a woman trapped, a "hostage of my fantasies. The hostage of my fears. The hostage of my *false* definitions" (my italics). She knows as a woman she doesn't want to emulate Randy, bearer of children, because " 'you deny who you are' " (i. e., Randy refuses to leave the closet or labyrinth of her woman's fears created by her family and society), but she does not yet possess the courage to give birth to herself, the minotaur. Locked in this closet, hugging her knees, Isadora also becomes a fetus, eventually to be expelled from the womb of the closet: "What I really wanted was to give birth to *myself*—the little girl I might have been in a different family, a different world." The closet as both labyrinth and womb ("knock, knock") also symbolizes the role of woman as child bearer ("knocked-up"), that prison which must collapse after birth of the little girl, the true self, the minotaur ("who's there?").

The second major labyrinth is described in chapter four, "Near the Black Forest." In Heidelberg, Isadora and Bennett live in a "vast American concentration camp," a kind of ghetto or military labyrinth: "And we were living in a prison of sorts. A spiritual and intellectual ghetto which we literally could not leave without being jailed." An imprisoned Jew—that is, pretending to be an Aryan—Isadora at first dares not reveal her Jewishness, but then, lonely, bored, and trapped in her silent marriage to Bennett, she begins exploring Heidelberg, particularly for hidden signs of the Third Reich: "Only I was tracking down my past, my own Jewishness in which I had never been able to believe before." Two discoveries result from her exploration: first, as a Jew she has denied her heritage and as an artist she has covered up her inner self (minotaur) with false masks (labyrinth); second, Germany has hidden its real self, its love of Hitler, with a mask of hypocrisy. That is, as the American editor for a weekly pamphlet, *Heidelberg Alt und Neu,* she "started out being clever and superficial and dishonest. Gradually I got braver. Gradually I stopped trying to disguise myself. One by one, I peeled off the masks." Eventually her exploration of her outer prison converges with her exploration of her inner prison. Coming upon the hidden Nazi amphitheater whose pictures were concealed by little pieces of paper in old guidebooks, Isadora indignantly tells the truth about German hypocrisy in her weekly column. The symbolic meaning of the German minotaur (the hidden amphitheater paralleling the hidden love of Hitler) at the center of the external labyrinth underscores the monstrosity at the center of her internal labyrinth. Specifically, writing in early poems about romantic, unreal scenes and situations, "ruined castles" as well as "sunsets and birds and fountains" she censors her real self:

> I refused to let myself write about what really moved me: my violent feelings about Germany, the unhappiness in my marriage, my sexual fantasies, my childhood, my negative feelings about my parents. . . . Even without fascism, I had pasted imaginary oak-tag patches over certain areas of my life.

Her writing thereafter discloses the true nature of the inner monster she has previously imprisoned.

Similarly, because her husbands and lovers have related only to one half or the other of her divided self, frequently refusing to recognize the other half, they inevitably imprison the offensive half in symbolic labyrinths. First, Brian holds her hostage in their bedroom during the final period of their marriage when he becomes completely psychotic, an ironic prison given his previous neglect of her sexual needs. Second, Bennett, the Freudian psychiatrist and father figure, has imprisoned her in a motel room in San Antonio, in an Army ghetto in Heidelberg, and in their silent marriage, about which she feels ambivalent, as it expresses only one side of herself: during a Freudian lecture on the Oedipal conflicts of the artist, Bennett squeezes her hand, as if to say, "Come back home to Daddy. All is understood. How I longed to come back home to Daddy! *But how I also longed to be free!*" (my italics). She decides to leave the prison of her Freudian marriage and her Oedipal attachment to Bennett in chapter ten, appropriately entitled "Freud's House" (which they had visited before listening to the Freudian lecture). Third, Adrian, who pretends to lead her out of the labyrinth of Old Europe—and the labyrinth of her marriage—by unraveling her (false) past, merely traps her within a maze of emotional deception: the car of escape and freedom becomes itself a miniature prison from which she occasionally yearns to flee, usually when passing an airport. Eventually he abandons her in Paris, part of that European labyrinth she cannot seem to leave; *she* then promptly imprisons *herself* in a hotel room. It constitutes the most significant prison in the novel.

Isadora had erred previously in determining to escape what she regards as a labyrinth—the complexity of being herself. As Dr. Happe explains to her just before she decides to leave Bennett, " 'What makes you think your life is going to be uncomplicated? What makes you think you can avoid all conflict? What makes you think you can avoid pain? Or passion? There's something to be said for passion. Can't you ever allow yourself and forgive yourself?' " To accept the complexity of herself implies understanding the conflicting sides of herself as represented by the minotaur. And to understand herself she must confront herself by descending into the labyrinth until she reaches the center it inhabits. At first refusing to probe her true nature out of fear, Isadora huddles in the self-imposed prison of her hotel room. She remains afraid of 'flying' (connoting independence) on her own wings just as she remains afraid of the minotaur monster within her: she represents both Isadora Icarus and Theseus. To fly independently she must be whole, thus she must heal the division in her self (slay the minotaur) imprisoned by the complexi-

ty of her life. Both tasks Isadora will perform: as Isadora-Theseus she will descend into the complexity of her life in order to slay the minotaur—determine where the division of self occurs—and then as Isadora Icarus she will overcome her fear of flying by becoming independent and leaving the hotel room without the help of a father-Daedalus. Previously she has descended into herself in order to fly above the prison by writing poetry: she revealed herself honestly in her art after the Heidelberg experience. Now she must learn to reveal her self honestly in her life, without the support of a man (although Bennett guided her inadvertently to the point where she learned to write poems, just as Adrian guided her inadvertently to the point where she learns to be herself). The Theseus and Icarus portions of the myth then are clearly related.

The last four chapters of the novel detail Isadora's Theseus-like descent into her own labyrinth to face the minotaur, followed by her Icarus-like flight from the prison. At first afraid, Isadora cries like a baby, then appeals to her adult self for help. The subsequent dialogue between the two halves of her divided self, "Me" and "Me," representing this child and adult, also represent the lonely man-needing woman and the alone artist conflicting within Isadora. The confrontation with the minotaur begins. That her dilemma cannot be resolved by siding with one position or the other is reflected in the last words of the dialogue: it ends as it has begun, with the question, "Why is being alone so terrible?" Recognizing the permanent division of her self, Isadora then acquaints herself with her two sides. First, she washes her very dirty body, then she uses a mirror "to examine my physical self, to take stock so that I could remember who I was—if indeed my body could be said to be me." Her body she perceives as a cosmos or labyrinth she must explore as she has explored her feelings in her writing: "One's body is intimately related to one's writing. . . . In a sense, every poem is an attempt to extend the boundaries of one's body. One's body becomes the landscape, the sky, and finally the cosmos." During this self-scrutiny she slays the minotaur—the conflict between the two sides of herself—with the weapon of humor. Laughing at a joke she tells, she no longer remains paralyzed by fear: she can now *act*, or depart the labyrinth by retrieving the unwound thread. That is, she probes her psychological self and her past by reading the notebooks from the previous four years to determine how she has gotten here and where she is going (the true "thread" of the past leading to the reality outside the labyrinth), just as she has explored her physical self and her body. Most important, she reaches that reality when she finishes her reading: she stops blaming herself for "wanting to own your own soul. Your soul belonged to you—for better or worse." No longer fighting herself, she can begin to accept and understand herself.

That she now owns her own soul—"for better or worse"—is expressed symbolically through the chapters "Dreamwork" and "Blood-Weddings or Sic Transit," the two chapters themselves suggesting a marriage of the soul and the body respectively. The dreamwork dramatizes her mind's attempt to accept the body in that it illustrates a solution to the problem of Isadora's physical needs. The menstrual period arriving the following morning dramatizes her body's acceptance of the mind, in that it has been delayed by Isadora's worrying and exploration of her past with Adrian. Both suggest gifts she bestows upon herself (equivalent to Daedalus' gift of the string to Theseus and Ariadne and of the wings to Icarus, in that they represent the means of salvation and rescue). Her dreamwork, first, consists of two important segments. In the earlier segment, she dreams she has been awarded her college degree plus a special honor, the right to have three husbands, Bennett, Adrian, and a mysterious third. Her teacher Mrs. McIntosh, however, advises her to refuse the honor; unfortunately Isadora *wants* three husbands, thereafter because of this desire forfeiting both the degree and the honor. That is, to become a whole person (graduate with honors) by relying on (or marrying) the three males who reflect approval of aspects of Isadora's self (Bennett, her body, Adrian, her mind, and the third, everything remaining) may seem sound advice to a male and paternal Daedalus (who advocates flying on borrowed wings) but not to a female guide like Mrs. McIntosh. And Isadora seconds her: although she had viewed Adrian as a "mental double" because she wanted "a man to complete me" she subsequently realizes "People don't complete us. We complete ourselves." A better way of attaining wholeness (graduating with honors) occurs in the second important dream-segment: a book with her own name on it (that is, previous public honesty about herself in her art) must be followed by public love-making with the author Colette (that is, a public union or marriage, rather than a conflict or war, between the artist and the woman in Isadora).

Such dreamwork indicates Isadora has become her own psychiatrist. Previously she had visited six different psychiatrists, eventually marrying the Freudian analyst Bennett Wing, who counsels duty and obligation over desire and inclination and who has pinpointed her past and present problem as an Oedipal conflict. In contrast, Adrian the Laingian existentialist advises her to pursue her inclinations instead of her duties and to live *without* a past and a future. But Isadora spurns both her Daedaluses by choosing the *tertium quid* of Jung. Interestingly Jong explains of herself that "I'm really closer to being an Jungian than anything else. I believe in the communal unconscious. I really believe that what motivates human beings are their dreams, their fantasies, and their mythologies." Throughout the novel Isadora too has been motivated by fantasies—her dream of the Man-under-the-Bed (the Ideal Man), her fantasy of casual and uninhibited sexual union—so much so that she quits her marriage for the apparent embodiment of the latter in Adrian. At the end, however, signalling her independence, her dreams stress woman as rescuer—Mrs. McIntosh and Colette—both representing the woman intellectual and artist as she is; too, because these dreams dramatize her internal conflict and its resolution, they allow her to be her own rescuer, her own psychiatrist. Thus she foregoes the borrowed "wings"—borrowed advice, borrowed thread, borrowed psychiatry—of the Daedalus father (Bennett and Adrian) to grow her own wings and fly independently, thereby becoming her own mother and giving birth to herself (Anne Sexton's line, "A woman *is* her mother," precedes chapter nine, "Pandora's Box or My Two Mothers").

After this dreamwork Isadora awakens in chapter eighteen ("Blood-Weddings or Sic Transit") to discover her menstrual period has arrived. This period signals the "blood wedding," "for better or worse," between the formerly conflicting selves. Indicating wholeness, it also represents renewal, or rebirth, in three different ways. First, she is literally sure that she is not pregnant, a possibility that would have encouraged a return to Bennett: "In a sense that was sad—menstruation was always a little sad—but it was also a new beginning. I was being given another chance." Now she has the opportunity to determine whether she can live independently of male approval, indeed a new beginning. Second, more figuratively the period represents a psychological "coming of age," a transition or transit ("Sic Transit") from childhood to adulthood (hence the digression on the symbolism of menstruation in this chapter, with Isadora's remembrance of her first *menarche* "two and a half days out of Le Havre"—again, *in transit*). Third, the period provides Isadora with an opportunity to test her old "fear of flying" (independence). Beginning a period without any tampons represents every woman's fear—but Isadora copes ("flies") by first making a diaper of Bennett's old shirt, then using French toilet paper, and finally leaving the labyrinth to buy some at a drugstore. The symbolism of the diaper suggests as well that the "little girl" to whom Isadora longed to give birth, as she meditated in the closet, has indeed been born. Isadora has released herself from the prison (womb) of the labyrinth. She is now ready to fly.

Instead she returns to England via train and boat, leaving the labyrinth of Old Europe behind. (This *tertium quid* also contrasts with Bennett/Daedalus' flying and Adrian/Ariadne's automobile travel). Proof that she has finally become whole occurs when she rejects a stranger's offer of casual sex on the train to London—"The fantasy that had riveted me to the vibrating seat of the train for three years in Heidelberg and instead of turning me on, it had revolted me." She rejects "flying to the moon" on borrowed wings, not just sexual ecstasy per se but a masculine conception of female fantasy. Further, she discovers when she finds Bennett's room in England that her fear of flying (her inability to cope, her fear of independence) has disappeared, replaced by a liking for herself (an acceptance of her body as well as her mind). Her acceptance is expressed in her admiring catalogue of the erotic features of her body, thighs, belly, breasts, as she bathes in Bennett's tub. Whether Isadora returns to her husband or whether she divorces him means little because she has already "married" her selves. This reunion suggests they will live happily ever after—truly "A Nineteenth-Century Ending," as the title of this last chapter implies.

Thus the unity of the novel depends upon the mythic parallels adduced above. The myth of Icarus similarly provided a structure for James Joyce's *Portrait of the Artist as a Young Man,* in which Stephen Daedalus became an artist like the "old artificer," the father he preferred to his real one, his priestly one, his national one. But Jong interprets the myth from the woman's point of view: Isadora Icarus spurns the "old artificer"—her real father, her psychiatric fathers, her sexual and intellectual ones, refusing those borrowed wings or strings, refusing to be governed by old myths. She returns to the minotaur begotten by her two mothers and unites her divided self so that she can fly away from the labyrinth on her own wings.

Both the novel and its author have been misunderstood. Whereas Jong intended her work to "challenge the notion that intellectual women must be heads without bodies," instead her intellectual Isadora has been viewed, at least by one critic, as entirely body, "a mammoth pudenda, as roomy as the Carlsbad Caverns, luring amorous spelunkers to confusion in her plunging grottoes . . ." [Paul Theroux, *New Statesman,* April 19, 1974]. Similarly the intellectual author has herself been castigated because of Isadora's adventures. "To a lot of men," she admits, "a woman who writes about sex is basically a whore. This assumption is not made about men who write about sex." Yet Isadora has heroically reconciled her formerly divided selves of mind and body, artist and woman. So the novel itself, as this study has attempted to reveal, weds its humorous and erotic content to a carefully controlled form—achieved through the myth of Daedalus and Icarus and the theme and symbol of flying.

Jane Chance Nitzsche, " 'Isadora Icarus': The Mythic Unity of Erica Jong's 'Fear of Flying'," in Rice University Studies, *Vol. 64, No. 1, Winter, 1978, pp. 89-100.*

Joan Reardon   (essay date May-June 1978)

[*Reardon is an American educator and critic. In the following excerpt, she describes how* Fear of Flying "*demonstrates the 'coming of age' of its author, the development of her style,*" *suggesting that the novel functions as "a distinctively female idiom."*]

Initial critical reaction to Erica Jong's *Fear of Flying* sold the book but did little to establish its considerable literary value. Particularly cutting, and more often than not, hostile, were the women who linked Jong's work to the tradition of Austen, Eliot, and the Brontes in their reviews and found the novel wanting. Ironically, the feminist critics were both negative and positive. For some, the book was trivial and did not state the case; others responded like Carol Tavris who said: "Jong has captured perfectly the dilemmas of the modern woman, the ironies of liberation and independence" [*Psychology Today* 8, 1975]. And still other reviewers joined Jane Crain in an unforgiving dismissal: "Taken one by one, no feminist novel really rewards critical scrutiny—they are all too steeped in ideology to pay the elementary respect to human complexity that good fiction demands" [*Commentary,* December, 1974]. With considerably more generosity, men tended to review the book as a good popular novel, a cut above *Diary of a Mad Housewife,* with the welcome addition of considerably more humor. Though Paul Theroux [*New Statesman,* 19 April 1974] and the anonymous *TLS* reviewer [*Times Literary Supplement,* 26 July 1974] were denigrating as well as negative and Alfred Kazin disregarded the work, Henry Miller praised it as "a female *Tropic of Cancer*" [*New York Times,* 20 August 1974]. To be sure, there were references to poor characterization, lack of irony or distance in the narration, but, on balance, John Updike's ". . . feels like a winner. It has class, and sass, brightness

and bite. Containing all the cracked eggs of the feminist litany, her souffle rises with a poet's afflatus" [*The New Yorker,* 17 December 1973] seemed to be the prevailing male judgement.

Neither the reviewers nor readers read *Fear of Flying* within the context of Erica Jong's earlier statements about poetry and fiction nor did they treat the novel as a logical development of the themes and style of her poetry. More significantly, no critic pursued Christopher Lehmann-Haupt's passing observation that the novel was "sensitive to the ambiguities of growing up intelligently female these days," [*The New York Times,* 6 November 1973] or examined the novel within the literary tradition of the *bildungsroman.* Quite literally, *Fear of Flying* is the tale of Erica Jong's thinly disguised autobiographical heroine, Isadora Wing, on her journey from immaturity to maturity. As such, the plot follows the standard formula of the educational novel outlined by Jerome Buckley in *Season of Youth* in which a sequence of incidents involves a sensitive youth who leaves a provincial and constrained life in a small town, journeys to a cosmopolitan city, and begins his or her real education. After a series of initiating experiences, at least two love affairs, and a number of moral encounters, the character rearranges her/his values and pursues a career in earnest, leaving adolescence behind.

The pattern, at least in its essential aspects, parallels *Fear of Flying.* That Isadora Wing is a sensitive character is made abundantly clear in her relationships and in her engagement with literature. Her parents, especially Isadora's mother, are portrayed as understanding and curiously disapproving as they encourage and discourage their gifted daughter. Fascinated by her desire to write and simultaneously hostile because she, unlike her sisters, rejects the role of motherhood, her family becomes increasingly antagonistic. Consequently, she leaves the repressive atmosphere of home by many routes—marriage, trips to Europe, analysis by at least six different psychiatrists, and, ultimately, by an affair with Adrian. When she does at last come of age, she returns "home" to her husband Bennett on her own terms, convinced of the "wisdom of her choice" of housewife as artist.

Isadora Wing, a character who is lost both literally and psychologically throughout most of the novel, finds herself on its final page. The circuitous routes always lead back. Familiar landmarks of the past—hotels, cafes, and trains—orient her to the present. The loss of contact with actual time frees her to listen to an inner rhythm, a resolute private timing which encompasses the twenty-eight-day time sequence of the novel. She finally comes to know where she is and what time it is as she resolves her fears—of flying, of driving, of "the man under the bed," of submitting her work to a publisher—and she comes of age. "I was determined to take my fate in my own hands. I meant that I was going to stop being a schoolgirl," she says at the end of the novel. And one can assume she speaks with the authority of the author's voice.

The imagery of *Fear of Flying* supports the various stages of the heroines's coming of age and reveals the author's growing confidence in her own fictional voice. Illustrating the progress of Isadora Wing's "growing up female,"

Erica Jong uses the journey of Alice and Dante through fantasy and dream into a "wonderland" and an "inferno" from which her heroine eventually emerges with a clearer perception of herself. She refuses to be the perpetual child or the symbol of pure love. The rejection of Alice and Beatrice coincides, therefore, with Isadora's rejection of male definitions. Having exhausted the image of physical journey from place to place, Erica Jong finally employs the image of menstruation to convey the inward journey into her own womanhood.

Using Lewis Carroll and Dante to define the male image of woman as little girl and idealized lover is accomplished by Erica Jong with considerable panache. That Isadora ricochets between the two images is apparent throughout the novel. Furthermore, using the seemingly disparate authors unifies the journey motif employed extensively throughout the work—actual movement from America to Europe as well as movement in time from youth to maturity and, finally, the psychological movement toward self-understanding. Physical transport from place to place underpins the plot and supports the chapters which delineate earlier travels. Within the framework of the longer journey from New York to Vienna, and to London, another important journey is undertaken. Isadora and Adrian leave "the Congress of Dreams" together, circle through Europe, and ultimately part company in Paris. In the context of these two major journeys, Isadora relates all other past trips, excursions, and travels which have in some way or other contributed to the present, including travel from New York to California and four different journeys from New York to Europe.

The recalled journeys, which interrupt the overall movement of the plot, serve to disorientate the reader as the narrative shifts from continent to continent as well as from present to past. However, the imposing pattern is always circular. Conversation spins round and round. "We seem to be talking in circles," Isadora says to Adrian as she has said to Bennett and Brian years earlier. Words echo words as the car "goes around in circles, dodging traffic." Similarly, dreams, nightmarish or benign, repeat Isadora's endless experiences with all the analysts in her life. The same story told and retold until she finally rejects analysis in the person of Dr. Kolner:

> Why should I listen to *you* about what it means to be a woman? Are you a woman? Why shouldn't I listen to *myself* for once? And to other women? I talk to them. They tell me about themselves—and a damned lot of them feel exactly the way I do—even if it doesn't get the Good Housekeeping Seal of the American Psychoanalytic.

With this first note of freedom, struck early in the novel, Isadora moves away from the analyst's couch into the labyrinth of Europe. From the phantasmal "dream of a zipless fuck" to the "dreams of Nazis and plane crashes" entire scenes assume the "swift compression of a dream." Dreams serve to confuse reality with unreality, actual occurrences with visionary happenings.

To a heightened degree, Alice, the prototypical child, exhibits this same sense of confusion in wonderland. Within the framework of her adventures, reality and fantasy, sense and nonsense, sanity and insanity are juxtaposed to create a dream-like world. Erica Jong's repeated references to Carroll's work clearly link Alice to Isadora. Because of their repetitiousness, Isadora describes her conversations with Adrian "like quotes from *Through the Looking-Glass.*" In *Wonderland,* the Red Queen explains to Alice: "Now *here*, you see, it takes all the running *you* can do, to keep in the same place. If you want to get somewhere else, you must run at least twice as fast as that!" Similarly, in the mirrored discotheque, Isadora and Adrian find themselves "lost in a series of mirrored boxes and partitions which opened into each other . . . I felt I had been transported to some looking-glass world where, like the Red Queen, I would run and run and only wind up going backward." In addition to the patterns of vertiginous motion, and to distorted patterns of size and shape, familiar characters also transfer from *Wonderland* to *Fear of Flying.* Adrian's grin is a continual reminder of the Cheshire cat. When Alice asks the cat, "Would you tell me, please, which way I ought to walk from here?" the cat replies, "That depends a good deal on where you want to get to." Adrian, "smirking his beautiful smirk with his pipe tucked between his curling pink lips," tells Isadora, "you have to go down into yourself and salvage your own life."

Both Isadora and Alice live in a fantasy world which is more congenial to them than is reality. However, for Isadora, residence in wonderland is impossible to maintain. When the fantasy "of the zipless fuck," which Isadora pursues throughout the novel, becomes a reality, she realizes the disparity between eight-year-old naivety and twenty-nine-year-old delusion. She calls herself, "Isadora in Wonderland, the eternal naif." The fantasy "instead of turning me on, . . . revolted me! Perhaps there was no longer anything romantic about men at all?" Isadora rejects one fantasy after another as Alice, weary of the Queen's tricks, seizes the table cloth and upsets her illusory dinner party. But most importantly, Isadora outgrows the role of "Isadora Wing, clown, crybaby, fool," and opts for a life that will satisfy her rather than repeatedly seeking some fantasy lover who will disappoint her.

However, all the aspects of her journey are not as felicitous as Alice's adventures in wonderland. Isadora, because she is "bloody Jewish . . . mediocre at other things, but at suffering you're always superb," must descend to the depths of Dante's hell in order to cleanse herself of yet another illusion—another masculine image of woman. Early in the novel, she assumes the Beatrice role by idealizing her various love-relationships, "Dante and Beatrice . . . Me and Adrian?" She also links Brian and herself to the well known lovers, "What if he were Dante and I Beatrice?" She would be able to guide him through the hell of his madness. However, ultimately Isadora must identify both with the pilgrim Dante and some of the sinners he encounters on his way. She is the incontinent Francesca, "The book of my body was open and the second circle of Hell wasn't far off"; and Adrian, of course, is Paola. As the Dantean lovers are whirled and buffeted through the murky air by a great whirlwind, so Isadora and Adrian are seen in various degrees of intoxication, moving through the purple mists of the "Congress of Dreams" and motoring in endless circles through Europe. However, Isadora's journey like Dante's is ever downward. When Adrian and Isadora venture into the bizarre, mirrored, and stroboscopic world of the discotheque, Isadora renames it "The Seventh Circle." Once inside they become lost in the maze of mirrors and with mounting panic they look for familiar faces in the crowd of strangers, "all the other damned souls." Isadora's relationship with her first husband establishes still more persistent links with the damned souls in the lowest depths of hell. Brian tells her, ". . . you're in hell and I'm in hell and we're all in hell," and calls her Judas when she consents to his hospitalization. He reminds her: "Didn't I know that I would go the the Seventh Circle—the circle of the traitors? Didn't I know mine was the lowest crime in Dante's book? Didn't I know I was already in hell?" The analogy is strengthened when Isadora experiences guilt, not for betraying him, but for surviving his madness "as if I were Dante and he were Ugolino and I would return from Hell and relate his story."

To complete his arduous journey through the triple world of the *Divine Comedy* Dante required the assistance of three guides—Virgil, Statius, and finally Beatrice—symbolic representations of reason, repentance, and love. Isadora's three lovers assume comparable roles on her journey to self-understanding. Brian, whose powerful mind is condemned to madness, is the antithesis of reason, but his "verbal pyrotechnics" and his way of looking at the world "through a poet's eyes" influence Isadora's desire to write. Her second husband Bennett withdraws into his guilt and silence until "he made his life resemble death. And his death was my death too." From Bennett, Isadora learns solitude and silence and proceeds to listen to the inner voice urging her to write. The heroine's third serious lover, Adrian, becomes an "idealized lover." Like Beatrice, he is passionately loved but never possessed, "that was part of what made him so beautiful. I would write about him, talk about him, remember him, but never have him. The unattainable man." He is the guide who ultimately shows Isadora the way to self-understanding, the way to salvage her life, hit rock bottom, and climb back up again.

After Adrian leaves her in Paris, she describes the terrifying experience of being alone "like teetering on the edge of the canyon and hoping you'd learn to fly before you hit bottom." Yet, it is into this abyss that psychologically and emotionally she descends. After experiencing a period of numbness and fear, she looks into the mirror to reaffirm her physical identity. The reflection of her body assures her that she is still very much herself. She searches for her notebooks and begins to read the entries which record her past four years of married life with Bennett: "I am going to figure out how I got here . . . And where the hell was I going next?" Considering that question further, she realizes that running away from Bennett was the first step in reclaiming what she had surrendered long ago—to her parents, to Brian, to Bennett and only recently to Adrian—namely, her soul.

As Dante is instructed to wash the film of hell off his face in the morning's dew before he enters purgatory, Isadora washes herself before leaving her hotel room. She describes her trip from Paris to London as "purgatorial." The fog and cloud-cover veiling the island of England, leaving only the white cliffs of Dover visible, create the mixture of light and darkness which surrounds Dante's purgatorial mountain. Isadora enters through the custom gates like Dante passing through the gates of purgatory. The purifying bath of the last scene completes the rites of passage. Isadora has fulfilled her promise to return made earlier to Adrian. "Back where?" he questions. And she replies: "To Paradise," which, in the context of the novel, is a return to Bennett; however, now it is on her own terms.

The journeys form repetitive circular images, lending a vertiginousness and confusion appropriate to the immaturity of the heroine. Counterpointing the actual journey of Isadora—not in the traditional mode of the youthful hero from country to city but from New York to the twin capitols of the world, Paris and London—is the fantasy adventure of Alice and the pilgrimage of Dante, "mid-way this life" from sin to grace. The unusual blending of imagery from Carroll's *Alice's Adventures in Wonderland* and Dante's *Divine Comedy* reinforces the "novel of youth" and suggests as well a reappraisal of values, a purgation resulting from a process of painful soul-searching.

But these literary conventions as well as Isadora's previous twenty-eight years must be examined, evaluated, and ultimately rejected as part of what she considers the male definition. The novel of journey, the image of woman as child and icon must give way to the author's own feminine perceptions. Isadora angrily states: "I learned about women from men, I saw them through the eyes of male writers. Of course, I didn't think of them as male writers. I thought of them as writers, as authorities, as gods who knew and were to be trusted completely." Within the tradition and yet apart from it, Erica Jong uses the image of woman as child—the eternal Alice—and woman as idealized lover—the eternal Beatrice—only to reject both roles and "survive."

Indeed, the novel accomplishes more than that. It portrays not only the end of the journey but the journey itself on Erica Jong's own terms; namely, the awareness "of the fact of being female and going beyond it." In a paraphrase of her fictional heroine's words, Erica Jong has stated the case in **"The Artist as Housewife / The Housewife as Artist"**:

> The reason a woman has greater problems becoming an artist is because she has greater problems becoming a self. She can't believe in her existence past thirty. She can't believe her own voice. She can't see herself as a grown-up human being. She can't leave the room without a big wooden *pass.*
>
> [*Here Comes, and Other Poems*]

In a literary tradition where the standard of excellence is synonymous with male, the writer who is also a woman distrusts her own voice, undervalues her own experience and never really achieves a sense of self. According to Erica Jong, coming to terms with her own body, therefore, is the first corrective step for a creative woman to take, and

Fear of Flying demonstrates precisely how this is accomplished. The result boldly stated by Isadora Wing is a literary work which is the antithesis of all those books throughout all of history which "were written with sperm, not menstrual blood."

However, the precedent for a "feminist style" had been established by a number of talented women poets before Erica Jong published *Fruits and Vegetables.* Discovery of the poetry of Anne Sexton and Sylvia Plath "came as a revelation," she said, because for the first time in her reading of literature, poetry ceased to be exclusively a "masculine noun." These contemporary women poets had come to terms with themselves as women, and "wrote about their bodies and never attempted to conceal the fact that they were women." They were attuned to the special rhythm which dominated their lives from menarche to menopause, and they were fearless in tapping "a kind of hidden power." In short, they expressed themselves in their own diction. Their images and symbols were chiefly drawn from the reality of daily experience rather than from the existing literary tradition.

Sylvia Plath charted new ground as she became more and more "attuned to her body harp." The casual and continued references to the interaction of her psychological and physical states and the relationship of both to her ability to write at certain times found in both *Letters Home* and some of her early poetry clearly indicate the extent to which Plath was preoccupied with the menstrual cycle. The specific symbols which became the texture of her poetry; the ocean, the moon, pregnancy and sterility revealed her deepest feelings about life and death. More often than not these feelings were expressed in the language of blood.

In later poems like "The Munich Mannequins" menstruation becomes an image of repeated bankruptcy:

> Perfection is terrible, it cannot have children.
> Cold as snow breath, it tamps the womb
> Where the yew trees blow like hydras,
> The tree of life and the tree of life
> Unloosing their moons, month after month, to
>   no purpose.

And she concludes, "The blood flood is the flood of love. / The absolute sacrifice." Furthermore, birth, "There is no miracle more cruel than this," and the flow of blood in the afterbirth symbolized the ultimate creative act of poetry. Menstruation, signalling the failure to conceive, symbolized sterility. Because Plath was writing in her own terms about her own experiences, she opened the way for Erica Jong to explore with a surer sense the uncharted areas of female experience.

But Sylvia Plath was not alone in her efforts to create a more personal idiom in her poetry. In quite another style Anne Sexton adopts a valuable coarseness, a rude incapacity to be delicate in many of her confessional poems. Consider for a moment the titles, "In Celebration of my Uterus," and "Menstruation at Forty," poems belying their apparent flippancy and expressing, instead, a subjective and interior experience of time in relationship to the menstrual cycle, "That red disease . . . / year after year."

Rather than reject the experience of bodily pain, of hospi-

talization, of surgery and blood flow, Sexton utilizes all aspects of her physical and psychological states. In a poem on her childhood called "Those Times . . ." she contrasts the isolation of the child of six with the image of her future womanhood:

> I did not know the woman I would be
> nor that blood would bloom in me
> each month like an exotic flower.

And in the poem "The Break," the life of the roses in her hospital room is symbolically vitalized by blood:

> . . . My one dozen roses are dead.
> They have ceased to menstruate. They hang
> there like little dried up blood clots.

In "Song for a Red Nightgown" she reinforces the connection between the lunar cycle and the menses:

> surely this nightgown girl,
> this awesome flyer, has not seen
> how the moon floats through her
> and in between.

Anne Sexton is eminently qualified to draw upon personal knowledge of her physical and mental states and to translate that knowledge into viable poetry. Notwithstanding the masculine opprobrium directed toward some of her poems, she remains true to her own words, "I cannot promise very much. / I give you the images I know."

A strong case can be made for Jong's ability to crystallize the dilemma of the woman writer and communicate that anguish in a brutally forceful way.

If "woman writer" ceases to be a polite but negative label, it will be due in great measure to the efforts of Erica Jong.

—*Joan Reardon*

These are some of the women writers, therefore, who have explored "the fact of being female and go beyond it, but never deny it." Following their example, Erica Jong boldly incorporates certain private and female symbols, thought unmentionable in the past, into the artistic texture of her work. There is a noticeable evolution from the oral and sensual imagery of her first book of poems, *Fruits and Vegetables,* to the search for a genuine understanding of woman's role in the second volume, *Half-Lives.* However, the third book, *Loveroot,* states the case most explicitly. For in virtually all of these poems she is both iconoclastic about the traditional subject matter of poetry and sure about the necessity of woman's survival as both person and writer within the perimeters of feminine experience. More to the point, Erica Jong demonstrates in these poems that even the subject matter of a poem written by a woman can be, and indeed, must be different:

> I think women poets have to insist on their right

to write like women. Where their experience of the world is different, women writers ought to reflect that difference. They ought to feel a complete freedom about subject matter. But most important, our definition of femininity has to change. As long as femininity is associated with ruffles and flourishes and a lack of directness and honesty, women artists will feel a deep sense of ambivalence about their own femaleness.

[**"The Artist as Housewife / The Housewife as Artist"**]

In the volume, *Half-Lives,* Erica Jong states the dilemma of the woman poet with uncompromising severity. **"The Send-Off,"** a poem written to friends after she has sent her first book to the printer, poetically expresses the fear which was later to haunt Isadora Wing; the loneliness and half-life of the woman artist who is reminded month after month of the barrenness of her womb by the menstrual flow, the symbol of the non-event:

> The book gone to the printer to die
> and the flat-bellied author
> disguised as me
> is sick of the anger of being a woman
> and sick of the hungers
> and sick of the confessional poem of the padded
>   bra
> and the confessional poem of the tampax
> and the bad-girl poets
> who menstruate black ink.
>
> I am one!
> Born from my father's head
> disguised as a daughter
> angry at spoons and pots
> with a half-life of men behind me
> and a half-life of me ahead
> with holes in my shoes
> and holes in my husbands
> and only the monthly flow of ink to keep me sane
> and only sex to keep me pure.
>
> I want to write about something other than
>   women!
> I want to write about something other than men!
> I want stars in my open hand
> and a house round as a pumpkin
> and children's faces forming in the roots of trees.
> Instead
> I read my fortune in the bloodstains on the sheet.
>   (Singing the Monthly Blues)

The meaning is fairly obvious. The creation of the poem or novel is symbolized by the menses while the failure to conceive a child is visibly demonstrated by the discharge of the unfertilized egg, a pattern which imposes itself with idiotic, irrational punctuality on a woman's consciousness every twenty-eight days from menarche to menopause. In still another poem from the same volume, the polarity of the role of mother vs. artist is expressed in the imagery of exotic flowers:

> I imagine the inside
> of my womb to be
> the color of poppies
> and bougainvillea
> (though I've never seen it).

> But I fear the barnacle
> which might latch on
> and not let go
> and I fear the monster
> who might grow
> and bite the flowers
> and make them swell and bleed.
>
> So I keep my womb empty
> and full of possibility.
>
> Each month
> the blood sheets down
> like good red rain.
>
> I am the gardener.
> Nothing grows without me.

"Hook images," used earlier by Sylvia Plath to describe the demands of her two children on time and creative energy, appear in the poem. However, Erica Jong rejects "the barnacles which might latch on" and interprets the menstrual flow as a validation of her art and a symbol of its potency. As the last line suggests, she insists upon the right to make the final determination.

Despite the deliberateness and forcefulness of Erica Jong's poetry, it is to the novel *Fear of Flying* we must turn for a more subjective exploration of the multiple problems of "growing up female" and for more daring stylistic techniques of expressing the feminine experience. In addition to creating the sexually fanciful Isadora Wing, Erica Jong devised a subtle sequence of time to enclose the action of the novel. The Pan-Am flight to Vienna, the ten-day Congress at the Academy of Psychiatry, the two-and-a-half week motor trip through Italy, Germany and France, the climax in Paris and the short one-day trip to London is a little less than a month although the alternating chapters span the childhood, early education, university career, first marriage and almost five years of the second marriage of Isadora Wing. The elements of time present and time past merge into the climactic now by linking the climax—the end of the affair with Adrian—with the menstrual cycle.

The twenty-eight days of the novel chart the various biochemical changes, the physical experiences of ovulation and flow as well as the psychological movements of relaxation and tension which explain, at least in part, Isadora Wing's actions. In addition to the journey to a "wonderland" of sensuality and sexuality, to an "inferno" of guilt and eventual repentance, she must journey inward to define herself as a woman and to understand to what extent every woman is "tied to that body beat" month by month. Isadora's attraction to Adrian at the beginning of the Congress is directly associated with ovulation. She says:

> I seem to be involved with all the changes of my body. They never pass unnoticed. I seem to know exactly when I ovulate. In the second week of the cycle, I feel a tiny ping and then a sort of tingling ache in my lower belly. A few days later I'll often find a tiny spot of blood in the rubber yarmulke of the diaphragm. A bright red smear, the only visible trace of the egg that might have become a baby. I feel a wave of sad-

ness then which is almost indescribable. Sadness and relief.

Isadora's observation describes the emotional tension which pervades the ten-day period of the Congress. Being physically and sexually attracted to Adrian, she is also melancholy at the thought of betraying her husband Bennett. She reels emotionally from lover to husband until the last session of the Congress is over. At that point she impulsively decides to tour Europe with Adrian.

After two and a half weeks of careening through Europe in Adrian's Triumph, the beer-drinking twosome reach Paris and part because Adrian has arranged to join his wife and children in Cherbourg that very evening. Having lost a sense of time as well as her heart, Isadora describes the situation:

> The enormity of his betrayal leaves me speechless. Here I am—drunk, unwashed, not even knowing what day it is—and he's keeping track of an appointment he made over a month ago.

Alone and still dazed by his desertion, Isadora is able "to gather my terror in my two hands and possess it." Overcoming her fear of strange rooms, her fear of "the man under the bed," she finally falls asleep and awakens the next morning to discover her menstrual period has begun. In the release of tension, signalled by the physical flow, she prepares to leave the hotel. The narrative is momentarily halted by Isadora's recollection of her first period and the subsequent case of anorexia she experienced at fourteen when she almost starved herself to death and stopped menstruating for a year and a half because someone told her that "if I had babies, I'd never be an artist."

Now, twenty-nine years old and secure in the adult knowledge that menstruation cancels out the fear of pregnancy, she shampoos her hair, packs, and goes out into the sunny streets of Paris in search of a drug store and a cup of cappuccino. In her own words, she is being given another chance. Anxiety over a possible pregnancy is dispelled. While her affair with Adrian has thrown her back on her own limited resources, there have been few consequences. Isadora concludes: "In a sense it was sad—but it was also a new beginning." After the overnight journey from Paris to London, Isadora gains admission to her husband's hotel room, and the bathtub scene concludes the novel. The purification by water is certainly appropriate to the Dantean journey; however, a more subtle meaning can be attached to the bath; namely the Jewish rite of *mikvah,* the ceremonial cleansing required of all orthodox women after the menstrual period before sexual relations can be resumed. The twenty-eight days of the novel are over; a new cycle begins.

It is impossible to read *Fear of Flying* and not recognize that more than any woman writer before her, Erica Jong is fully attuned to her own body. As a result, her prose as well as her poetry is vigorous and sensual and at one with the inner rhythms which she understands so well. In the complete physicality of language and image, she insists again and again that "one's body is intimately related to one's writing."

Perceiving the coming of age of the artist in the totality of female experience, she has structured a novel on one of the most personal experiences of female physiology, the menstrual cycle, and has achieved a correlation of subject matter and form which is both artistic and universal. Indeed, Erica Jong has done more than that, she has reached the sensibilities of her reading audience with a brave and brash voice and attempted in the words of Virginia Woolf, "to measure the heat and violence of the poet's heart when caught and tangled in a woman's body." She is a writer who understands that a woman's perception of coming of age is:

> Every month,
> the reminder of emptiness
> so that you are tuned
> to your body harp,
> strung out on the harpsichord
> of all your nerves
> and hammered bloody blue
> as the crushed fingers
> of the woman pianist
> beaten by her jealous lover.
>
> Who was she?
> Someone I invented
> for this poem,
> someone I imagined . . .
>
> Never mind,
> she is me, you—
>
> Tied to that bodybeat,
> fainting on that rack of blood,
> moving to that metronome—
> empty, empty, empty.
>
> No use.
> The blood is thicker
> than the roots of trees,
> more persistent than my poetry,
> more baroque than her bruised music.
> It guilds the sky above the Virgin's head.
> It turns the lilies white.
>
> Try to run:
> the blood still follows you.
> Swear off children,
> seek a quiet room
> to practice your preludes and fugues.
> Under the piano,
> the blood accumulates:
> eventually it floats you both away.
>
> Give in.
> Babies cry and music is your life.
> Darling, you were born to bleed
> or rock.
> And the heart breaks
> either way.
>
> [*Loveroot*]

To date, *Fear of Flying* is the most compelling statement of "growing up female in America: What a liability!" In the 311 pages of Isadora's journey from youth to maturity all the old idols fall and a woman novelist has had the courage to assert her freedom and liberation from the masculine ideal on her own terms. Isadora is neither Alice nor Beatrice, inspiration nor guide. She even rejects the most irresistible myth of all—motherhood—and dares the vagaries of print. The arduous journey from childhood, re-plete with the fantasies and dreams of youth and the search for the "wrong things in love," the borrowed wings which "never stayed on when I needed them," leads ulti-mately to the conclusion, "I really needed to grow my own." Isadora Icarus:

> Isadora White Stollerman Wing . . . B.A., M.A., Phi Beta Kappa. Isadora Wing, promis-ing younger poet, Isadora Wing, promising younger sufferer. Isadora Wing, feminist and would-be liberated woman. Isadora Wing, clown, crybaby, fool. Isadora Wing, wit, scholar, ex-wife of Jesus Christ. Isadora Wing, with her fear of flying, Isadora Wing, slightly overweight sexpot with a bad case of astigmatism of the mind's eye. Isadora Wing, with her unfillable cunt and holes in her head and her heart. Isado-ra Wing of the hunger-thump. Isadora Wing whose mother wanted her to fly. Isadora Wing whose mother grounded her. Isadora Wing, pro-fessional patient, seeker of saviors, sensuality, certainty. Isadora Wing, fighter of windmills, professional mourner, failed adventuress . . .

Isadora Wing comes of age.

At this point it is difficult to assess the importance of the work of Erica Jong. Having been praised by John Updike and Henry Miller and dismissed by Alfred Kazin as a "Sexual Show-Off," she is as she has so cogently stated, "Exhibit A." However, a strong case can be made for her ability to crystallize the dilemma of the woman writer and communicate that anguish in a brutally forceful way. And an even stronger case can be made for her artistic forging of a new and bold image of the "Housewife as Artist." If "woman writer" ceases to be a polite but negative label, it will be due in great measure to the efforts of Erica Jong.

Joan Reardon, " 'Fear of Flying': Developing the Feminist Novel," in International Journal of Women's Studies, Vol. 1, No. 3, May-June, 1978, pp. 306-20.

Anne Z. Mickelson   (essay date 1979)

[*In the following excerpt from her* Reaching Out: Sensitivi-ty and Order in Recent American Fiction by Women *(1979), Mickelson provides an analysis of Jong's character-izations and use of sexual language in* Fear of Flying *and* How to Save Your Own Life, *concluding that Jong implies male dominance and female helplessness.*]

[Two] novels by Erica Jong—*Fear of Flying* and *How to Save Your Own Life*—end with a kind of symbolic ritual baptism in celebration of the female body. In the first novel, *Fear of Flying,* the heroine, Isadora Wing, returns to her patient but dull husband after an unsuccessful at-tempt to find in Adrian Goodlove the perfect combination of friend and lover. Stripping off her clothes, she climbs into the claw-footed bathtub, immerses herself in water up to her neck and contemplates her body. "A nice body," she tells us. "Mine. I decided to keep it." It's a comforting picture which leaves the reader with a sense of well-being. At the end of the second novel, *How to Save Your Own Life,* Isadora, now husbandless but firmly clasped in the arms of her young lover, Josh, finally experiences orgasm

with him. Paradoxically, she has up to this point been au-tomatically responsive to her husband's mechanical em-brace, but unable to achieve orgasm with Josh's more spontaneous and inspired lovemaking. In Joycean fashion, Isadora commemorates the momentous occasion by pass-ing water.

True, this act is involuntary and not conscious as when Leopold Bloom and Stephen Dedalus make water togeth-er in front of Bloom's house at the end of *Ulysses.* Isadora is embarrassed, demonstrating that her flaunted lack of in-hibition has not yet successfully embraced the debatable Joycean idea that the indecorous, the vulgar, the common-place reveal the higher things. She has to be assured by her lover that he loves everything about her: her "shit," her "pee," her "farts," her "tight snatch," etc. The scene re-sembles the one between Connie Chatterley and Oliver Mellors in D. H. Lawrence's *Lady Chatterley's Lover* (Jong, like Oates, has read her Lawrence) in which Mel-lors tells Connie that he is glad that she shits and pisses: "I don't want a woman as couldna shit nor piss." More will be said about Jong's language and style in the discus-sion of *How to Save Your Own Life.*

Although Jong concentrates on woman's body, its hun-gers, its drives, more centrally the novels are the story of a dying marriage and a woman's odyssey to love. Both books pose the questions: what is it to be a woman? where lies salvation? In *Fear of Flying,* the sense of crisis is com-municated by a quaking, picaresque Isadora who finally leaves her uncommunicative, joyless, psychiatrist husband for a Laingian psychologist, Adrian Goodlove. Adrian of-fers her the promise of sensual love (by squeezing her ass) and the promise of a life which he calls twentieth-century existentialism. This, he explains, means making no plans for the future, seizing the day, and feeling no guilt. As it turns out, neither promise has substance. Adrian is sensu-al in public where consummation is impossible, and impo-tent in private. He makes all the rules for the relationship while pretending there are none, and he *does* have plans of his own, which include going back to his wife and chil-dren and leaving Isadora. In one of the many good one-liner observations in the book, Isadora concludes that her fling with Adrian has been desperation masquerading as freedom.

Neither husband nor lover provides Isadora with a sense of her own identity or gives her any security. Ultimately, she has to, as all women must, try and fashion her own sense of destiny. In the course of her quest, we get good insights into how difficult this is for women in our society. Thomas Hardy observed of women in English Victorian society, "doing means marrying." Things haven't changed much since Hardy's day, according to Jong. The cruel jests aimed at unmarried women, found so frequently in fiction and comic strips, are still with us. Isadora fears being the butt of ridicule, or a "pariah," since a woman alone "is a reproach to the American way of life." Accus-tomed to being dependent first on father, then on husband, she is timid about losing dependency on some man. She dreads being alone. So she marries, and finds out that her loneliness is compounded.

In the late nineteenth-century novel and throughout twentieth-century novels, marriage is often the death of love. We are told in *Fear of Flying* that Isadora's first husband, Brian, is a good friend and lover until marriage. Then he turns into a man so completely devoted to work that he eventually breaks down. It must be said that it is difficult to be sympathetic to Isadora's early plaint about Brian's lack of virility, because of work pressures. After all, he is the one who works hard while she has time to pursue her studies and putter around the small apartment. But her confusion and unhappiness, stemming from Brian's growing madness until he is committed, are understandable. So is the story of her second marriage to a dour Chinese psychiatrist whose own life is one vast analysis, as Isadora puts it. She discovers that he punishes her with long silences which precipitate her into still greater isolation. Obstinately, despite the fact that Bennett, the husband, is no companion and insists on her dependence on him and his independence of her, Isadora clings to the idea that even a bad marriage is better than none. She demonstrates that although western woman's feet were never bound like the Chinese woman's, making the latter dependent on man for food, shelter, clothing, etc., her woman's mind has been crippled into accepting so-called inherent limitations. The author makes it clear that family, school, society have conditioned Isadora in her thinking. She is, for a while, a woman who conforms to the rigid and restraining role imposed on her, and defers to her husband's view of reality.

But despite the brain-washing, Isadora's mind persists in nagging her with questions: How can an intelligent woman fuse the physical and intellectual parts of her being into one healthy whole? How to achieve integration, exhorts Isadora? How to resolve the conflict between the creative woman and the wife? How to be feminine? What is being feminine? Is it more feminine to be a wife and mother than to be a writer?

It can be argued that some of the drama surrounding the heroine's dilemma is rubbed off by the presence of abundance: plenty of time to write, and enough money to pay analysts' fees or walk into Bloomingdale's and buy an expensive pair of shoes when she is feeling low. Certainly, there is a marked difference between Isadora and the working-class mother who is a wage earner/housewife/mother, or the artist woman who tries to paint, sculpt or write while wrestling with laundry, bills, cooking, cleaning the toilet, and checking the temperature of a sick child. There is no evidence that Isadora performs any of the chores of domesticity outside of whipping up an airy soufflé now and then. But this is irrelevant. As Virginia Woolf points out gratefully: it was the money an Aunt left her which allowed her the freedom to write. The issue which the author poses is: how can woman find self-fulfillment in some creative work without accompanying feelings of guilt? —a universal problem which is just now receiving attention.

The other problem which plagues Isadora is one which more often revolves around men, and is generally found in male writing: marriage claustrophobia, the itch to escape marriage, the desire for the mate you can't have. John Updike's stories of marriage frequently deal with this theme; for example, "Museums and Women." Isadora, in

her own words, itches for men, and particularly for some man who would be friend, lover, everything. In short, like Fellini's hero in *8 1/2*, she fantasizes about her ideal, composite mate. In the meantime, she looks with delighted longing at men; tells us how much she loves their smells, their shapes, their genitals, and is collectively in love with all men, except her husband. If there is none of the repugnance for the male body found in Oates's fiction, there is, however, a hint of female chauvinism. Isadora may revel in fantasies about the male body's perfections even when there are none, as in the case of the unappetizing would-be music conductor Charlie, but she confides that while men's bodies are beautiful, their minds are befuddled.

In between, there are comments, as in *Portnoy's Complaint,* on the problems of being Jewish and having a Jewish mother, but without the self-righteousness which mars Roth's book. Isadora's mother is an intelligent, talented woman, frustrated in her aspirations to be a painter, and anxious for her daughter to fulfill her dreams for her. It's not an uncommon wish in disappointed women, as Lawrence demonstrates with Mrs. Morel (*Sons and Lovers*) and Hardy with Mrs. Yeobright (*The Return of the Native*). Both these last-mentioned women seek self-esteem. In their particular cases, it is through their sons. Isadora's mother is not a tragic figure in the sense that Mrs. Yeobright and Mrs. Morel are. The author's observations and sentiments about family and mother are tempered with banter and humor.

Isak Dinesen once remarked that what the modern novel needs is humor, and *Fear of Flying* has that much needed ingredient. There is the funny bit about Isadora's fear on the plane: if the plane should fall how would she face God after stamping her religion Unitarian. The satire on analysts going to the Vienna convention, accompanied by scowling children and wives padding around in space shoes, is one of the best passages in the book. This high-spirited satire is not diminished by her kind words on the value of analysis. For Isadora, analysis enabled her to get some neuroses out of the way, thus permitting her to write. There is also playful wit in Isadora's sexual fantasies, for example the "zipless fuck," about which so much has been written. The departure with Adrian is truly a comedy of errors, as she describes it.

Her eye for social observation is shrewd. The scatological digression on French, German, and other nations' toilets is an incisive as Colette's observations on primitive toilet facilities provided for actresses while on tour. Good, too, are her descriptions of Beirut: veiled ladies riding in the back of a Chevrolet or a Mercedes Benz; shepherds who smoke cigarettes and carry transistors while tending flocks. There is, however, more than a hint of ethnic prejudice in her descriptions of the red-capillaried faces of German women, with their heavy bodies made still more heavy by costumes of loden cloth. But this is balanced by her honest appraisal of the former Nazi official who gives her a job (during her stay in Germany), and her self-questioning: how would she have behaved during the Hitler era?

Fear of Flying shuttles backward and forward for 311 pages, giving us a woman in Isadora Wing who is part little girl, part female rogue, part troubled artist /wife/daughter and, more specifically, a woman who gets all kinds of advice from family and the men in her life. The family wants her "to settle down" and Bennett warns her that if she leaves him, she will mess up her life. Adrian counsels her that if she is going to have something interesting to write about, she must have experience—with him. It's very much like the advice given the ladies of the Russian court by Rasputin: if you want redemption, you must sin with me. All things considered, Adrian's advice proves to be correct. Isadora fares better than the Russian ladies. If there is no salvation with him, the Adrian experience at least provides Isadora with piquant and serious material for a book (as we learn in *How to . . .*), proving the wisdom of that statement by Anaïs Nin: make literature out of misery. Isadora returns to her husband after the Adrian fiasco, convinced that no matter what her reception by Bennett will be, she will survive. "Surviving meant being born over and over. It wasn't essay, and it was always painful. But there wasn't any other choice except death."

These are brave words which promise that the woman we meet in *Fear of Flying* and who tells us: she never wants to age; wants to give birth to herself; wants a blazing sensual love and a blazing career; wants freedom and security—that this woman will find some solution to conflicting desires. To put it another way, Isadora Wing appears like some modern Persephone, who will continue to move out of the gloom of her marriage into the sunshine of a better relationship, and mature as woman and artist.

How to Save Your Own Life, sequel to *Fear of Flying,* begins with "I left my husband on Thanksgiving Day." A few pages later, Isadora confides that she had saved the thought of leaving her husband "like a sweet before bedtime, like a piece of bubble gum put on the childhood bedpost. . . ." Some 300 pages later, the reader learns that the heroine is now leaving apartment and husband. The plot is stuck, like that bubble gum on the bedpost, with repetitions of what we have already learned in *Fear of Flying.* Briefly, Bennett is dull, lacks joy and makes love mechanically, yet Isadora is afraid to leave him, clinging to the myth of husband as protector and Daddy figure. She is convinced that compromise is a way of life. The further they drift apart, the more frenetic is their lovemaking. The only new ingredient of plot is Isadora's discovery of her husband's infidelity, and her jealousy and anger that he has played the role of saint while casting her in the role of villain. However, the reader has long foreseen that Isadora, like Hemingway's Nick Adams, has concluded that "it's not fun anymore." Unlike the Hemingway hero, she is unable to make an "end to something." Maybe that's the point of the novel—the difference between the way men and women go about dissolving a relationship. Where men are active, women are passive.

Granted this, there is nothing in the characterization of the bouncing, skipping, giggling, gutsy-thinking Isadora that makes her a classic example of the intelligent but passive woman, without the self-assurance to take responsibility for her own life. She knows how to seek help from friends, analysts, lovers, and how to compensate for any failure of feminine nerve with a range of consolations that include masturbation, sniffing cocaine, smoking joints, making love with a woman, drinking six gin and tonics plus wine at one sitting, participating in a sex orgy, reading mail in the nude, and taking pot shots at critics who write nasty reviews about her work. She's about as helpless as Moll Flanders.

Nor is her jealousy of Penny, with whom Bennett has had a love affair, entirely credible since she, herself, looks upon infidelity as a diversion in an unhappy marriage. Some effort is made to enlist the reader's sympathy by noting that Penny read Isadora's short stories with Bennett during *post coitus,* but this is not too convincing. Ultimately, Isadora is redeemed for us by her honesty. She gives a belated palm to Penny for the courage to have an affair with Bennett, leave the husband who saddled her with six pregnancies, get a degree, and start a new life for herself. However, Isadora's early references to Penny as *goyish,* dumb, possessing "washed-out *shiksa* eyes" are ethnic slurs which settle like a thin layer of sludge in otherwise humorous appraisals of people. Along with certain other disclosures of malice, they detract from the picture of Isadora as a warm, Jewish girl filled with gregarious good humor, animated by kind instincts, and in love with most people and the whole universe, despite her jealousy and other problems.

The central emphasis in the novel keeps shifting to Bennett, and there are no attempts to lighten the dark strokes with which his characterization is sketched. Although Jong's men are not the unsavory characters Oates portrays so often, Bennett comes close to being the villain in this domestic drama. Isadora rationalizes that he slept with Penny in order to get back at her for her writing, while at the same time he played the role of the forgiving husband. The accusation is legitimate, for even at the end, when a childish Isadora seeks sexual revenge against Bennett by embellishing on the number of lovers she has had, he keeps intoning piously that he is prepared to forgive her. The most valuable thing to come out of this exchange, for the heroine and the reader, is Isadora's realization that during the entire marriage she has been made to feel grateful to Bennett for letting her write. Not once has she asked herself if it were all right for Bennett to practice *his* vocation of psychology. After all, that was his job. Her writing, he made her see, was a self-indulgence, toward which he was prepared to be generous. Unfortunately, the problem of writer versus woman and the guilt feelings that the conflict engenders is not satisfactorily resolved in this novel, as we see in the relationship with Isadora's next love, Josh.

Not so evident here is the humor present in the first novel, *Fear of Flying,* which keeps the details of the disintegrating marriage from falling into self-pity, and makes of Isadora a kind of Thackerayan heroine whose "one eye brims with pity while the other watches the family spoons" (for Isadora, her writing). There is one amusing description of a skiing accident, a broken leg, and a ride to the hospital in which a drugged Isadora tries to urinate into a wadded kleenex and then tosses it out of the car window, while a morose Bennett frowns over his spoiled vacation. Typically, however, where an Oates heroine traces the downward curve of her marriage by the number of miscarriages she has had, Isadora (like a Hemingway hero) sees it in terms of accidents and physical scars. And just as rain is always a presentiment of trouble in Hemingway's stories, so we read that Bennett arrives at the ski lodge bearing with him the rain.

While continuing to unravel a marriage already reduced to a limp, tangled skein, the novel retains in crumpled form many of the themes, from creativity and femininity to the hunger for love, with which the author worked in the first novel. It also contains telling observations on the drawbacks of fame; Hollywood, which is filled with divorced men with hair transplants; bachelors who give Jacuzzi parties; the loving camaraderie between intelligent, talented women; the way other women, in the scramble for success, imitate the worst of men's vices; the pressures by husband and society for a woman to use her husband's name. About the latter, Isadora is not only chagrined but feels cheated and betrayed at giving her husband—neither a reader (except for his psychology books) nor a writer—immortality by placing his name on her books.

This is a legitimate complaint. Names are important to men, as Shakespeare points out in *Othello:* "Who steals my purse steals trash;' 'tis something, nothing; / . . . But he that filches from me my good name / Robs me of that which not enriches him, / And makes me poor indeed." Of course Shakespeare is speaking of slander, but writers have always been concerned that their name "will not perish in the dust," as Southey writes. Why should women writers, or any woman, be deprived of her name, Isadora asks? Why indeed? In the case of Isadora, she is honest enough to confess that the fault lies not so much with society as with herself. She is so hungry for Bennett's approval that she gives him her work—and makes him famous.

If the heroine is chilled by her foolishness and her husband's lack of affection and care, particularly when she needs him, she is warmed by her many friendships with women. Where there are no developing and deepening relationships between women in Oates's fiction, Jong's second book emphasizes the value of women friends. The short description of the episode with Jeannie (a thinly-veiled portrait of Anne Sexton?) contains warmth and tenderness. It is Jeannie, a poet, who, at times, lives desperately on Valium and Stolichnaya vodka ("anything to oil the unconscious") who gives Isadora the push to break with husband: "Live or die . . . but for god's sake don't poison yourself with indecision." There is also lusty, 5'9" Gretchen, who points out that Bennett has treated Isadora badly until fame made her for him the goose which laid the golden egg. In reply to Isadora's wonderment that her jealousy of Penny has improved their sex life, Gretchen replies: "jealousy makes the prick grow harder. And the cunt wetter." A tough woman!

Hope, another friend, twenty-two years older than Isadora, advises her to get rid of Jewish guilt, and helps her with the publishing of her poems. Then there is Holly, a plant lover, who offers her studio, herbal tea, and sympathy. Not least among this cast of women characters is Rosanna Howard, who provides a chauffeured Rolls Royce, champagne, caviar, and her musk-scented body. Isadora, her head filled with images of Missy and Colette, Violet and Vita, Gertrude and Alice, and her blood fired by expensive wines, reels off to bed with Rosanna. She discovers that her rakish joy in breaking a taboo, and her view of her act as a punitive measure against her mother ("I felt I had gone down on my mother"), do not compensate for her aversion to vaginal taste and smell. She invokes the indulgence of "Gentle Reader" and Lesbians everywhere for her distaste: "I *tried,* I put my best tongue forward. . . ."

There are male friendships, too, but these are predominantly sexual, except for the one with eighty-seven-year-old Kurt (Henry Miller?), who is generally accompanied by his male nurse or two former Japanese wives. Isadora talks and makes love with two men, both conveniently named Jeffrey. These *Belle du Jour* diversions take place in the afternoon and Isadora is able to explain her absences to Bennett as "shopping in Bloomingdale's." Later, when she does take a token walk through the store, she notes the way some women buy, and rationalizes that the compulsive woman buyer is trying to compensate for a lack of love. It is not a very relevant or sage observation, since she herself does not look upon these afternoons of sexual love as fulfilling. Yet, obviously they give her an ego boost. Sauntering down the avenue, she is no fearful Oates heroine shrinking from the stares of men. On the contrary, she invites looks and boldly stares back with the smug assurance of sexual magnetism, and that men detect the aroma of the afternoon's lovemaking on her.

Any successful novel, as we have been told repeatedly, must deal with love in one form or another. Love must be the pervasive thread which binds the whole together in some form of tapestry. Isadora's Hollywood trip not only serves the purpose of tracing her increasing disillusionment with the unscrupulous woman producer Britt and her unhappy realization that no writer can control the quality of the movie made out of her/his work; it also brings love into her life—Josh. There is no question that describing Josh with his furry, warm, likeable face always gives Isadora pleasure. Despite the age difference of six years, which troubles Isadora only briefly, she decides to take her friend Jeannie's advice, be a fool, and give herself up to her passion for Josh.

The language of love here, as elsewhere in the author's writing, contains a sexual vocabulary in which "cunt," "cock" and "fuck" predominate, although there is also an ample sprinkling of "shit," "piss," "crap," "getting knocked up," etc. Language has always been the concern of American writers, from Hawthorne and Melville to Hemingway and to contemporary writers like Gould, Brautigan, Godwin, and Burroughs. They have attempted to find a language through which to convey the essential experience of love and of American life, while leaving the impress of personality on language. Jong chooses to write in what she feels is an earthy style. ***How to Save Your Own Life*** reveals that she is troubled by whether she has succeeded in finding the right words and voice. Through Isadora she asks: how should one write about sex? She admits that she is "plagued by the confusion between natural earthiness and licentiousness, the mistaking of openness and lack of pretense for a desire to titillate and shock."

Certainly, since women have been taught for centuries

that they are not sexual beings and that only "bad" women like sex, we need frankness on the subject. But how to write about it?

This is not a new dilemma. It faced D. H. Lawrence in *Lady Chatterley's Lover* at a time when sex was a forbidden subject both for men and women and censorship fettered all writers from treating it in an intelligent way. Lawrence, however, was determined to break through Victorian prudery. There is no doubt that he was using this last novel as a final way of ridding himself of sexual reservations resulting from the influence of early Chapel religion and a clinging to Oedipal love for his mother, which had haunted him all his life.

His purpose in *Lady Chatterley's Lover* was to structure a hero who would be earthy and, at the same time, well-read and filled with social concern. The man, Mellors, was to meet a titled lady suffering from emotional attrition; he would make her aware of the necessary value of the body's physical life. To accomplish this, Lawrence decided to have Mellors employ a special language of Midlands dialect and four-letter words during sexual scenes. At other times, Mellors would expound in perfect English on the horrors of industrialization and its effect on men and women. The shift from an educated man to one who speaks a slurring dialect interposed with "fuck," "cunt," "shit," etc. is unsuccessful. Connie's sister sums it up succinctly: "he was no simple working man, not he: he was acting! acting!"

We get the same impression of Jong's language, in which Isadora at one point is making literary references to John Keats and the next moment is sprinkling around the familiar cunts and cocks. We are to understand that education has not robbed Isadora of her essential earthiness and that she can use the language of warm, simple common woman or man, who accepts sex and the body as a natural part of life—unlike educated people who extol the mind, deny sex its rightful place in life, and are shocked by forthright language.

One serious argument against this line of reasoning is that representing the common man or woman in this way propagates a sentimental myth. Civilization long ago caught up with the simple human being who, at some time or other, expressed the physical part of his or her nature in natural, instinctive, and graceful ways. When today's dock worker, or mechanic, or farmer, or gas station attendant uses the language of "fuck," "cock," "cunt," it is as expletives or insults, regardless of their original sexual meaning. No writer to date has succeeded in semantically restoring the words. For those who grew up in poor areas, or lower middle-class neighborhoods, and heard this language every day from dull, uninteresting men and boys in their daily comments on sports, women, or the weather, it lost its shock value around the fifth grade.

I am not making the absurd claim that women don't talk this way now. I am saying that many women have utilized this means of expression as an assertion of their independence and freedom from former reticence about sex. Also, to many women writers from comfortable, middle-class

homes, it may seem like a fresh, exciting, and original approach to sexual love.

But is it? As with all patterns of language, the writer after a while is imprisoned within a rigid enclosure of words in which, as in *How to . . .*, love is reduced to cunt and cock. We don't have a man and woman experiencing a warmly human relationship in which ultimately there is a sense of rebirth and a feeling of unity with the living universe (as that post-sexual love dialogue between Isadora and Josh would have us believe). There is only an impression of disembodied genitalia in which dripping cunt meets hard cock.

Witness the following descriptions: "She wanted *this* one, this copper-colored lover, *this* pink cock. . . ." "Only his cock inside of her could give her peace." "His cock was bulging under the copper buttons of his jeans. . . ." There is a lot of copper around here and we are constantly reminded that if Josh's member is bulging, Isadora's dripping. Together with the description of the ocean thundering outside the love chamber and the water sloshing in the water bed from the exertions of the two lovers, the reader is drenched with verbal and scenic descriptions.

A more serious criticism is that what we're really looking at is genitalia parodying physical and emotional experience. If the writer is trying to tell us that for the man, his male reality is his hard, erect penis, and that for the woman, the female reality is the wetness and slipperiness of her vagina, the reader has difficulty in accepting this. In Jong's emphasis on "cock," and on "cunt" as "a dark hole," we are only too conscious of the language of pornography in which women are not women but "hot slits," "gaping holes," and "fuck tubes."

The writer attempts to cope with the sexual scenes in various ways: she avoids the greyness of clinical language; she shifts narrative voice from first to third; she gives realistic details of Isadora's various positions during intercourse. In respect to the latter, though the reader is awed by Isadora's athletic agility, the overall impression of all this rapture is of a scene straight out of *Playboy* or a Mickey Spillane novel. We have a virile, masterful Josh demanding: do you want my sperm? And Isadora, clad in a filmy, black nightgown slit up the front and with pink ribbons which push up her breasts, confiding to the reader: "She needed him. She needed this man." Instead of a woman finding her own self-worth, language and scene crystallize in the kind of male fantasy found in girlie magazines.

In using this kind of sexual vocabulary, there is a sense of the writer beggared for expression and falling back on a vocabulary of male street usage. Woman needs a sexual vocabulary of her own—not one borrowed from men's street language. Such language is always self-limiting, because it is more geared to voicing frustrations than fulfillment (God is "a shout in the street," says Stephen Dedalus). Language needs to be precise, original. It should give a sense of independent, first-hand experience as response to the encounter. It should avoid filtering the experience through terms associated with male attitudes which are demeaning to women. By adopting the male language of sexuality, Jong is also fooling herself that she is preempting man's power. All she is preempting is the pose of sexual prowess.

I said at the beginning that both works by Jong end with some sort of water ritual, which is to be interpreted as a celebration of the female body. In *Fear of Flying,* Isadora's warm, appreciative, anatomical description of her body lying in scented, soapy water helps to do just that. The water bed in *How to . . . ,* on which Isadora's love odyssey comes to a climax, is an ersatz symbol of baptism and a new life, not unlike the black nightgown that Isadora is wearing—"proof" of her womanhood. As for the question of salvation, Isadora sums it up in one phrase: "He had the cock." Freud would love it, especially since earlier Isadora has voiced the idea that women must have power.

The world of *Fear of Flying* and its sequel *How to . . .* offers us a heroine who appears to be far more intrepid and confident than any of Oates's women. Yet, ultimately, we see that Jong's Isadora Wing is as helpless as the most timid of Oates's women characters—in the common avowal that man has the power. True, Isadora's discovery comes out of sexual need and not fear, but her conclusion is basically the same as the one affirmed in book after book by Oates. Woman is helpless. Man is powerful.

Anne Z. Mickelson, "Erica Jong: Flying or Grounded," in her Reaching Out: Sensitivity and Order in Recent American Fiction by Women, *The Scarecrow Press, Inc., 1979, pp. 35-48.*

Pat Rogers   (review date 24 October 1980)

[*Rogers is an English educator, editor, and critic. In the following review, he provides a positive assessment of* Fanny.]

Have you met Miss Jones? The real Fanny Hill can at last stand up (or lie down, most of the time): it turns out that her true identity is that of Fanny Hackabout Jones, a foundling brought up in one of the stately homes of Wiltshire. Only, in the end, [of *Fanny*], it emerges that she is not who she seems. John Cleland got everything hopelessly tangled up [in his *Fanny Hill; or Memoirs of a woman of Pleasure*]: well, that's no surprise. Erica Jong relates Fanny's "True History" in three books, all but 500 pages, of pseudo-authentic language. Stylistic mannerisms by Fielding; plot rather by Smollett; research supervised by the late James Clifford and J. H. Plumb (not to mention a research trip to Bath, conducted by Russell Harty, "which was invaluable even though Bath did not finally appear in the novel"). The aim is to be true "to the spirit, if not the letter, of the eighteenth century." One has to say it: Erica Jong has succeeded remarkably well.

The most surprising thing about *Fanny* is that it really does concern the eighteenth century. Readers expecting a sequel to the adventures of Isadora Wingwill puzzle the text into convenient shapes, but they will be distorting the genuine imaginative flight-path. Sure enough, the novel has strong feminist overtones: but the sexual politics make only qualified sense in contemporary terms, and Fanny has more in common with the eighteenth-century blacks she encounters than with Isadora, "growing up female in

America" during the 1950s and 1960s. Fanny faces repression not just from cultural or socio-economic circumstances, but as a legal entity. Her mode of escape is correspondingly violent; she is on the wrong side of so many laws that a few infractions of polite *moeurs* wouldn't do much good.

Here then be ripped bodices, witchcraft, piracy, torture, murder, suicide, highway robbery, execution at the yardarm, madness, nay cruelty to horses. Fanny undergoes most of the varieties of sexual experience, without Isadora's excuse of curiosity. While she is a prostitute, she has dealings with Jonathan Swift, whose well-known obsession with horses leads him to attempt an experiment in bestiality. John Cleland exchanges clothes with her: they both enjoy this, as Fanny feels liberated in men's clothing and spends a lot of the book in drag. Later on, Fanny meets a ship's captain whose repressed homosexuality can only be sublimated by sadism, flagellation, coprophilia and bondage. (He is a slaver, and a slaverer, as one might say, to boot.)

Erica Jong has tried to give us what the blurbs used to call "the entire teeming spectacle". In *Fanny* this means ranging from country estates (Gothic piles, with formal landscaping, in the process of being Palladianized and Picturesquified) to London and the wider world. The city is lovingly evoked in all its squalor. Cries of "gardyloo" cleave the air as Fanny makes her way from whorehouse to Newgate, risking *omnia citra mortem* as she takes on a male world and a rationalist culture. For there are deists abroad (the slave-captain is that, too), apostles of optimistic Shaftesburian philosophy who turn their eyes away from the stench. Nobody could accuse the author of doing so. Along with the street cries and the Medmenham Monks, the ropedancers and the fairgrounds, there is a constant undertow of reference to biology. Fanny samples the unreliable abortive devices of the age; she witnesses mutilation and branding. No cosy Hanoverian dawn in this book.

In *How to Save Your Own Life,* Erica Jong described California as a wet dream in the mind of New York. *Fanny* is assuredly better adapted to wet-bobs than dry-bobs. As the heroine reflects:

> What a Profusion of Fluids is the Female Form! Milk, Tears, Blood—these are our Elements. We seem to be fore'er awash in Humours of divers Sorts. O we are made of Waters; we are like the Seas, teeming with Life of ev'ry Shape and Colour!

The author extracts a woozy poetry from this dampness, in which the buried equivalence seems to align reason, enlightenment and cruelty with the "dry" masculine powers. The crucial act for women is suckling, which puts them in touch with ancient instinctual forces and the radiant mysteries of being. Thus the metaphysic at the heart of the work is coherent, if not especially original.

Plainly, the only way to deal with this noisome world is through comedy. *Fanny* is not often pervaded by laughter, but there are moments of high camp: the female pirate Anne Bonny on the prow, with a cutlass in her hand and a rose in her mouth. Or the episode when Alexander Pope (sadly prone to premature ejaculation) lets slip the punchline of his still unwritten *Essay on Man* in discoursing with Fanny on sexual inequality. There are crowds of quotations in the text, knowingly dropped for fellow-buffs to pick up at the author's behest.

In *Fear of Flying* the heroine was engaged in a study of sexual slang in eighteenth-century poetry. Erica Jong's studies are displayed in lists to delight Panurge's heart, of words for the male and female pudenda, of synonyms for "whore", of fairground turns. The elaborate research seldom obtrudes distractingly, though some of the file-cards on piracy might happily have been scattered to the ocean winds.

Erica Jong states in an afterword that she has "to a large extent" confined herself to the language of the period. That is fair comment, and the intrusion of some anachronistic words (*tart; dustbin; pansy; bill* and *focus* as verbs; *sucker; to bore;* even *bluestocking*) doesn't seriously interfere with the author's purposes. Slightly more worrying is Pope's "sensitive" expression, which needs another fifty years of aesthetic development to give it the right meaning. There are a few lapses in idiom: "sheer, irrational Delight" rings false, as does theremark, "That must be quite some Letter". The most serious flaw is the repeated introduction of "Hubris" as an item of colloquial English, which is wildly out of key with the age.

The factual background is convincingly presented. There wouldn't have been many locks (just millweirs) as Fanny sailed from the Chilterns towards London: and there was no such address as 17 Hanover Square in 1724—the house later so designated had just been built, but numbering had not yet caught on. Finally, the pastoral vision of "the black and white Cows eating the beautiful moist Grass" belongs to modern Wiltshire—the meadows would then have contained not Friesians but the old longhorn breeds of cattle.

But Erica Jong does not claim absolute historical accuracy, and it is something she can afford to forgo. *Fanny* is at all events a much better book than Cleland's original *Memoirs,* with their rootless London and repetitive devices. Erica Jong has produced a richer work, with more ideas about the human condition, more tonal unity, a larger command of narrative, a deeper primal literary impulse. For this Fanny above all wants to *write*—screwing is mostly incidental—and she has an identity beyond the sexual. The book will be damned as inauthentic by people who wouldn't know 1710 from 1790, and put down by critics whose rhetoric of fiction never took them beyond chapter three of their own great opus. For readers who think that popular fiction can be entertaining without being irredeemably silly or vapid, Erica Jong has delivered a convincing piece of positive evidence.

Pat Rogers, "Blood, Milk and Tears," in The Times Literary Supplement, *No. 4047, October 24, 1980, p. 1190.*

Clive James   (review date 6 November 1980)

[*James is a well-known Australian editor, television com-* mentator, and critic. In the following negative review, he finds John Cleland's eighteenth-century work Fanny Hill superior to Jong's version of Fanny.]

Not long ago there was a popular novelist called Jeffrey Farnol, who is now entirely forgotten—which, when you think about it, is as long ago as you can get. Farnol wrote period novels in a narrative style full of e'ens, dosts, 'tises, and 'twases. Men wearing slashed doublets said things like "Gadzooks!" in order to indicate that the action was taking place in days of yore. Farnol was manifestly shaky on the subject of when yore actually was, but he had a certain naïve energy and his books were too short to bore you. His masterpiece *The Jade of Destiny,* starring a lethal swordsman called Dinwiddie, can still be consumed in a single evening by anyone who has nothing better to do.

Erica Jong knows a lot more than Farnol ever did about our literary heritage and its social background. [Her ***Fanny: Being the True History of the Adventures of Fanny Hackabout-Jones***], which purports to be the true story, told in the first person, of the girl John Cleland made famous as Fanny Hill [in his *Fanny Hill*] draws on an extensive knowledge of eighteenth-century England. This is definitely meant to be a high-class caper. Nevertheless Jeffrey Farnol would recognize a fellow practitioner. There is something Gadzooks about the whole enterprise. On top of that it is intolerably long. Where Farnol's Dinwiddie, after skewering the heavies, would have made his bow and split, Jong's Fanny hangs around for hours.

Jong's Fanny, it turns out, would have been a writer if circumstances had not dictated otherwise. Circumstances are to be congratulated. Left to herself, Jong's Fanny would have covered more paper than Ruskin. There is something self-generating about her style.

> I wrote Tragedies in Verse and Noble Epicks, Romances in the French Style and Maxims modell'd upon La Rochefoucauld's. I wrote Satyres and Sonnets, Odes and Pastorals, Eclogues and Epistles. But nothing satisfied my most exalted Standards (which had been bred upon the Classicks), and at length I committed all my Efforts to the Fire. I wrote and burnt and wrote and burnt! I would pen a Pastoral thro'out three sleepless Nights only to commit it to the Flames! And yet were my Words not wasted, for ev'ry budding Poet, I discover'd, must spend a thousand Words for ev'ry one he saves, and Words are hardly wasted if, thro' one's Profligacy with 'em, one learns true Wit and true Expression of it.

Five hundred pages of that add up to a lot of apostrophes, i'faith. But the fault lies not with the 'ties and 'twases. A historical novel can survive any amount of inept decoration if it has some architecture underneath. Take, for example, Merejkovsky's *The Romance of Leonardo da Vinci,* in the learned but stylistically frolicsome translation by Bernard Guilbert Guerney.

> "Nay, nay, God forfend, —whatever art thou saying, Lucrezia! Come out to meet her? Thou knowest not what a woman this is! Oh, Lord,' tis a fearful thing to think of the possible outcome

of all this! Why, she is pregnant! . . . But do thou hide me—hide me! . . ."

"Really, I know not where. . . ."

"'Tis all one, wherever thou wilt, —but with all speed!"

As transmitted to us by the industrious Guerney, Merejkovsky's Leonardo is every bit as noisy as Jong's Fanny. But *The Romance of Leonardo da Vinci* is a good novel in the ordinary sense and as a historical novel ranks among the greatest ever written. The characters and the action help you to penetrate history—they light up the past. Jong's Fanny makes the past darker. By the end of the book you know less about the eighteenth century than you did when you started.

Jong deserves some credit for trying to bring back yesterday, but what she is really doing, inadvertently, is helping to make you feel even worse about today. She uses pornography to preach a feminist message. This is a peculiarly modern confusion of motives. At least Cleland had the grace to leave out the philosophizing, although it should be remembered that those few general remarks which he put in were more pertinent in every way than anything which his successor has to offer. Here is Cleland's Fanny at a critical moment.

> And now! now I felt to the heart of me! I felt the prodigious keen edge with which love, presiding over this act, points the pleasure: love! that may be styled the Attic salt of enjoyment; and indeed, without it, the joy, great as it is, is still a vulgar one, whether in a king or a beggar; for it is, undoubtedly, love alone that refines, ennobles and exalts it.

Admittedly Cleland's prose has been somewhat neatened up for modern publication, but you can still see that even in its original state it must have been a less strained instrument than that wielded by Jong's Fanny. Cleland has other points of superiority too. For one thing, his pornographic scenes are actually quite effective. Indeed they are too effective, since pornography exceeds requirements if it makes you want to know the girl. Cleland's *Fanny Hill* might not strike women as a book written from the woman's viewpoint, but it can easily strike men that way. The book's concern is with women's pleasure, not men's. Cleland's Fanny does a powerfully affecting job of evoking what a woman's pleasure is like, or at any rate what a man who likes women would like to think a woman's pleasure is like. She leaves a man sorry for not having met her.

For Jong's Fanny, whose full name is Fanny Hackabout-Jones ("Fannikins to lovers besotted with her charms"), the same cannot be said. She is a bore from page one. Even in moments of alleged transport she has one eye on her literary prospects. You just know that she will one day write *Fear of Flying*. One of her early encounters is with Alexander Pope. Erica—Fanny, sorry—tries to interest Pope in her verses, but he is interested only in her breasts. Pope is but the first of several famous men who make themselves ridiculous by pursuing Jong's Fanny. (Swift involves her in a threesome with a horse.) All they see, you

see, is Fannikins's cunnikin. Passion blinds them to her attainments as a philosopher.

> And yet, clearly,' twas not the Best of all Possible Worlds for Women—unless, as Mr. Pope had argu'd, there was a hidden Justice behind this Veil of seeming Injustice. . . . Fie on't!' Twas not possible that God should approve such goings-on! A Pox on the Third Earl of Shaftesbury and his damnable Optimism!

Running away from home, Jong's Fanny falls in with a coven of witches. The witches, you will not be surprised to learn, are prototype feminists. They are given names like Isobel and Joan in order to allay your suspicions that they are really called Germaine and Kate.

> "Fanny, my Dear," says Isobel, "let me tell you my Opinion concerning Witchcraft and then Joan can tell you hers.' Tis my Belief that in Ancient Times, in the Pagan Albion of Old, Women were not as they are now, subservient to Men in ev'ry Respect. . . ."
>
> "E'en the very word 'Witch,'" Joan interrupted, "derives from our Ancestors' Word 'Wicca,' meaning only 'Wise Woman.'"
>
> Isobel lookt cross. "Are you quite finish'd, Joan?" says she. "Will you hold your Tongue now and let me speak?"

An oppressive male chauvinist society makes sure that these pioneer women's liberationists are appropriately raped and tortured, but meanwhile Jong's Fanny has become installed in a London brothel, where she shows an unusual talent for the trade. Colly Cibber's son ties her to the bed. ("Now I am truly trapp'd in my own Snares, my Arms and Legs spread wide upon the Bed so I can make no Resistance, my Ankles and Wrists chafing 'gainst the Silver Cords.") Then he enters her. (". . . Theo's Privy Member makes its Presence felt near my not quite unsullied Altar of Love.") Then he does something I can't quite figure out. ("He sinks upon me with all his Weight and wraps his bandy Legs 'round my own. . . .") How bandy can a man be?

Jong seems to take it for granted that a woman's lust can be aroused against her will, if only her assailant presses the right buttons—a very male chauvinist assumption, one would have thought. Cleland's Fanny was more discriminating. But then, Cleland's Fanny knew her own feelings. Jong makes Cleland one of her Fanny's literary lovers. Jong's Cleland is interested in role swapping and has a propensity for climbing into drag. Thus Jong lays the ghost of Cleland's commendable success in fleshing out a feminine character. She says that *he* had a feminine character. Perhaps so, but what he mainly had was imagination.

Jong's Fanny is meant to be an edifying joke, but the joke is not funny and the edification is not instructive, although it is frequently revealing. Setting out to show up Cleland, Jong unintentionally declares herself his inferior. As to the pornography, Cleland knew when to stop: his Fanny always concedes, while describing the moment of ecstasy, that beyond a certain point words fail her. Words fail

Jong's Fanny at all times, but she never stops pouring them out. Finally the sheer disproportion of the enterprise is the hardest thing to forgive.

I quite liked *Fear of Flying:* there was the promise of humor in it, if not the actuality. But in this book, which sets out to be light, comic, and picaresque, everything is undone by an utter inability to compress, allude, or elide. Is Peter de Vries to be the last author in America of short serious books that makes you laugh? Joseph Heller's *Good as Gold* is at least twice as long as it should be. By the time you get down to Erica there seems to be no awareness at all of the mark to aim at. If Max Beerbohm couldn't sustain *Zuleika Dobson,* how did Erica expect to keep Fanny going for triple the distance on a tenth the talent? I'faith,' tis a Puzzle beyond my Comprehension.

Clive James, "Fannikins's Cunnikin," in The New York Review of Books, *Vol. XXVII, No. 17, November 6, 1980, p. 25.*

C. D. B. Bryan   (review date 21 October 1984)

[*Bryan is an American novelist, editor, nonfiction writer, and critic. In the following review, he notes that* Parachutes & Kisses *lacks plot development and comments that Jong settles for "the self-aggrandizing delusions of a literary Mae West."*]

Eleven years ago in Erica Jong's best-selling *Fear of Flying,* Isadora Wing was 29 and twice married—first to a psychotic Columbia University graduate student and next to Bennett Wing, a Chinese-American Freudian child psychiatrist with whom she fearfully flew to a Psychiatric Congress in Vienna. There she met Adrian Goodlove, a British Laingian psychiatrist who spouted existentialist theory, playfully squeezed her, thought Jewish girls "bloody good in bed" and so mesmerized Isadora that she dumped Bennett in Vienna and took off with Goodlove on a haphazard trans-European motor trip, during which the main hazard turned out to be not Goodlove's losing battles with tumescence but his plan all the while to keep a scheduled appointment with his wife and children in Cherbourg. Isadora, feeling betrayed, winged back to Bennett, let herself into his empty hotel room, climbed into his tub and lay there not certain whether she had returned to soak in the hot water of his bath or their marriage.

In *How to Save Your Own Life,* Erica Jong's 1977 sequel, Isadora was 32, had divorced Bennett, with his "glum face, his nervous cough, his perpetual analyzing," and was busy dealing with the problems of having written *Candida Confesses,* an enormously successful novel whose heroine, Isadora confided, "was modelled after myself." The difficulty was "my public insisted on an exact equivalency between [Candida] and me—because my heroine, astoundingly enough, had turned out to be amanuensis to the Zeitgeist."

What *Zeitgeist?* The *Zeitgeist* of women torn between the middle-class virtues of marriage and the longing for freedom. "I suspect," Isadora had confessed in *Fear of Flying,* "I'd give [independence] up, sell my soul, my principles, my beliefs, just for a man who really loves me." She finds

that man in Miss Jong's second novel, in the writer, punster and banjo player Josh Ace, the 26-year-old son of a team of well-known Hollywood screenwriters of the 1930's. At the end of *How to Save Your Own Life,* Isadora was off to join him.

Now, with *Parachutes & Kisses,* Erica Jong's third novel in this series, Isadora is approaching 40, is separated from "cold-eyed" Josh and is "possessed of a demonical sexuality which has no need to justify itself with love." But now that "she's flush (though she never believes it) and famous (though she never believes that either) impotent men seem to be everywhere!"

Everywhere, that is, but in her bed, for in this book's opening paragraphs we learn that during her separation she has been consoling herself with a "drugged-out" disk jockey from Hartford, a "cuddly" Jewish banker from New York, a blue-eyed writer from New Orleans, a "cute" Swedish real-estate developer with Caribbean holdings, a lapsed rabbi, an antiques dealer who drives a Rolls despite being a high school dropout, a "brilliant" 26-year-old medical student with access to drugs, a plastic surgeon who's "into oral sex" and "so many others she's practically lost count." Practically.

It's hard to know what to make of this book. There are still some wonderful lines, scenes, dialogue exchanges. The *Zeitgeist* remains a woman's fear of loneliness, to which now has been added learning "how to make demonic passion jibe with domestic responsibilities, artistic responsibilities, financial responsibilities." The book speaks of Isadora's "quest for love" as being what "linked her to other women, what stirred her vitals not only to sex, but also to poetry; what made her—despite her oddness in being famous and affluent—exactly like other women, exactly like her friends, her sisters, her readers." But it is a quest centered not in her heart and mind but in her reproductive organs. There is a distressing self-serving quality to this book, an annoying arrogance, the giddy presumption that Isadora is speaking not only to women but for women, for *all* women everywhere.

In one of her chapter headings, Erica Jong quotes Muriel Rukeyser's lines "What would happen if one woman were to tell the truth about her life? The world would split open," a perfectly permissible literary hyperbole, with its promise of sensitivity, honesty and insights. But what are the truths of Isadora's life? The baby-boom generation is middle-aged; steep driveways are hell in the snow; children get hurt when parents divorce; and orgasms feel nice.

Damn it, *Fear of Flying* was fun! Isadora at 29 was fearless and vulnerable, garrulous and witty, self-mocking and guilt-ridden, tender and earthy. That book burned with a sexual and emotional energy that made one feel one might be in the presence of a young Wife of Bath. There were even moments in *How to Save Your Own Life*—a marvelously awful orgy, the impact of betrayal on a marriage—but that book contained more smoke than fire. *Parachutes & Kisses* contains no fire at all. Isadora tells us that "Life has no plot" is one of her favorite lines. Life may not have a plot, but a novel needs one. An endless recitation of sexual episodes is O.K. for the forum section of a girlie magazine, but it does not suffice for a book.

Certainly Erica Jong writes tellingly of nature's cruel paradox, which has women reaching their sexual peak just when their men are being eviscerated by midlife crises, but rather than try to deal sympathetically and insightfully with that dilemma, Isadora's solution is to avoid the problem entirely by seeking out ever younger men. Josh of the second book was six years Isadora's junior; Berkeley (Bean) Sproul III of this latest is younger than Isadora by 14 years. He is

> somebody who really loved her and would fiercely protect her no matter how quixotically. He wanted to be her Lancelot. . . . He understood that underneath her peculiar notoriety (which Josh had finally found so intimidating) there was only a woman who wanted and needed loyalty and love. He was not put off by her fame, did not see her as either a forbidding fortress or a potential acquisition. He saw her only as a person, strong, yet vulnerable.

The reader wishes him luck, for what this reviewer sees is different: Erica Jong turning her back on all that rich Chaucerian promise and settling instead for the self-aggrandizing delusions of a literary Mae West.

C. D. B. Bryan, "The Loves of Isadora, Continued," in The New York Times Book Review, October 21, 1984, p. 14.

Erica Jong has a delicious sense of humour, a greedy appetite for experience and a romantic attitude to love that combine to save her books from being either inflexibly feminist or waywardly titillating.

—*John Mellors, in* **The Listener,** *May 12, 1977.*

Rolande Diot (essay date November 1986)

[*In the following essay, Diot analyzes the role of humor in Jong's writings.*]

In *How To Save Your Own Life,* a character called Kurt Hammer is thus described by the female narrator and heroine Isadora Wing—Jong's alter ego and fantasmatic persona—in the book:

> Kurt Hammer has honed his underground reputation on tattered copies of his reputed-to-be pornographic novels, smuggled in through customs in the days where sex was considered unfit for print. Now that sex was everywhere in print, his royalties were fading. . . .

She meets him in LA, she is thirty-three and he is eighty-seven, but still full of pep and punch. Isadora calls him "her literary godfather"—or sugar daddy? Friendship, af-

fection and mutual admiration characterize their relationship: but *Fear of Flying* is not *Tropic of Cancer,* **How To Save Your Own Life** is not *Tropic of Capricorn,* nor is *Parachutes and Kisses* The Rosy Crucifixion. And yet, Jong doubtlessly attempted to write a female version of those erotic autobiographies; she tried her hand at what Miller-Hammer calls "the metaphysics of Sex", filled with delirious hysterical humor and satire. She created a woman's fantasmatic journey into sex, a marvelous "whoroscope"—Jong's own coined phrase for this Tropic of Virgo, or is it Virago? She is still an exception in the literary world: in a time of so-called women's liberation, one has still to meet the great figure of literary comedy that might reach the epic, grotesque and homeric heights of Miller's Cosmic Comedy or "cosmodemonic" trip around the tropics of Sexus, Nexus and the like. Jong's trilogy, not counting **Fanny,** is evidence of her vast talent as a pastiche writer; with Miller-Hammer in her rearview mirror—the rearview mirror of Isadora's Mercedes convertible whose license (so much so . . .) plate spells QUIM. . . . The modern broomstick of the contemporary witch/bitch embarking on her journey into the womb and the natural cavities of the female body. Riding her QUIM/QUILL, she performs her outrageous investigations into female sexuality and male idiosyncrasies and shortcomings. Her trilogy is also a marvellous empire on which the pun never sets. But Jong is not Miller. Her immense culture and gift for parody may give the illusion that her sense of comedy, her recreation of the topsy-turvy world appears like a female Rabelaisian carnival of sex and a celebration of the "cheerful body", to use Mikhail Bakhtin's words. Or is she the female schlemiel disguised as the scandalous Jewish Princess of Central Park West and Columbia? Or is she the modern embodiment of some feminine "chutzpah", the impertinent, aggressive and insolent mischievous counterpart of the schlemiel? Or would she be just the modern form of the hysterical nymphomaniac, super-woman of the best-selling type? Fraud or freak?

Jong is not Miller, nor Rabelais, nor Joyce, although she evinces reminiscences from her English lit. courses and can imitate some of the tricks, but not the greatness and vastness of vision of the creator of "chaosmos". Nobody is perfect. My contention is that she is notwithstanding the one female author that comes nearest to being one of those stars of comedy. She fails, partly, but she stands unique in the great jungle of comedy. Why so? The obvious answer is, and the feminists will not deny it—the sociocultural conditions of literary creation. It seems needless to develop this point here, since Mohadev Apte has pointed out the causes and circumstances of this situation in a remarkable chapter of his recent book *Humor and Laughter* [1985]: sexual inequality in the production of humor is responsible for the rarity of women comedians in literature and elsewhere. However, we are now witnessing a slow but undeniable progress in the liberation of women vis à vis the taboos of our judeo-christian society and its puritanical dictates. So: is it a question of time and patience? Will there eventually be a complete equality of the sexes in front of humor as in the rest of life? Or is it a question of psycho-physiology as some would have it? Should it be that humor, and the sense of it, be located in the left rather than in the right lobe of the brain, if, according to some, women are right-lobe oriented and men left-lobe dominated? This precious racist and sexist theory has its supporters in the scientific circles—vicious circles seems more adequate. An open question which it is not for me to settle at this point. What I am concerned with here is another viewpoint: that of communication. When a woman is gifted with a sense of humor and adds to it the creative talent of the satirist and humorist, like Jong, and when she is sufficiently liberated to practice self-debunking and self-disparaging humor, even sick humor; when she is bold enough to make fun of everything including death, sex, motherhood and the Virgin Mary, sickness and impotence—what next? What responses does she get from 1) her female audience 2) her male audience 3) her androgynous and/or homosexual audience—not to mention dogs and children, academics and literary critics and specialists of Humor International Incorporated. The following quotation, from *Tropic of Capricorn* will illustrate this point marvellously:

> Evelyn, on the other hand, had a laughing cunt (. . .). She was always trotting in at meal times to tell us a new joke. A comedienne of the first water, the really funny woman I ever met in my life. Everything was a joke, fuck included. She could even make a stiff prick laugh, which is saying a good deal. They say a stiff prick has no conscience, but a stiff prick that laughs too is phenomenal. (. . .) Nothing is more difficult than to make love in a circus. (. . .) She could break down the most "personal" hard-on in the world. Break it down with laughter. There was something sympathetic about this vaginal laughter. The whole world seemed to unroll like a pornographic film whose tragic theme is impotence. (. . .) The female seldom laughs, but when she does it's volcanic. When the female laughs the male had better scoot to the cyclone cellar.

This direct testimony metaphorically emphasizes the connection between sex and power, humor and impotence. Laughter is incompatible with erotic performances, a well-known physiological phenomenon, which is also attested by some aesthetic theories of modes. But if we go further in the examination of the connection between sex and power, we find that, according to Miller and males in general, humor in a woman creates sexual impotence in her male partner; and this, even when the woman is laughing, not *at* the man, nor *of* the man, but just laughing, the male experiences a great deal of tension and of subsequent frustration: he feels humiliated, reduced to the function of object, castrated. Woman is the castrating bitch again—QED. Next: sexual power and sexual domination mean control of the social and cultural scene, not to mention the political one. But it also spells the control of procreation and the creative process. The creative powers of the male are annihilated by the laughing female; Superman shrinks to the diminutive proportion of homunculus or infant. The superman of sex loses both his identity and existence, as male subject and as male organ. In *Parachutes and Kisses,* the scene with the Nobel Laureate is an example of Jong's satirical perception of a woman's power when she appropriates language—and the language and discourse of sex, a field usually reserved to men. In this hilarious scene, Isadora, the heroine and narrator, makes fun of her sexual partner during the love scene. She assumes the function of the voyeur—of herself and her partner, right in the middle of the development of the sexual act, including preliminaries and post coital communication. Isadora/Erica plays the part of the exhibitionist and rapist at the same time as she enjoys her female role. As she is unable to physically rape the man, she reduces him to impotence, symbolically, by turning him into an object: sex object and target of her sati(y)re. She grades her lovers, so to speak, by keeping an exact amount of how many orgasms she can have with them—not how many *they* can have with her. She plays the game of the multiple orgasm herself, with zest and elegance, and loses c(o)unt of them in the process; and she also evaluates, not just the quantity, but also the quality of her ecstatic moments, without losing (her) head nor control of the situation. A virtuoso performance, which elicits from the Nobel Laureate genuine admiration:

> When intellectuals copulate without love, they still must think of intellectual things to say afterward. And the Laureate was a great summerupper. 'That was a most satisfactory ejaculation', he would say, to our heroine's utter astonishment. Or on an occasion when she gave him a great blow job, he complimented her by saying, 'What a memorable arpeggio—or shall I say cadenza?' 'Why not just call it a blow job?' Isadora asked, irreverently. 'A blow job by another name is still a blow job'. Gower looked at her as if she were the crudest of vulgarians, raised his bushy eyebrows, pulled his white beard, and said: 'You certainly are an amazing woman, a woman of warmth and nuance'. Let us just say I'm a good lay'. Isadora said, 'and leave it at that'. And that, in fact, was where they left it for all time.

One word at this point about the use of the so-called 'obscene' language used by Jong and her heroine: four-letter words and the rest. There is another transgression of a taboo: that of propriety. Naming a cat a cat seems all right for a man, and a male writer: Miller always refers to women by the four-letter word and alternative to 'quim'! Feminists were enraged and protested violently, but the aggressive and disparaging vocabulary used by Miller, Mailer and others remains as part and parcel of their specific stylistic originality and flavor. It's no use trying to bowdlerise the English language, but why not turn it to our advantage and take up the glove men have dropped? says Jong, very logically and humorously. Violence and brutality and the pejorative description and evaluation of the female human being as 'bodily function' and genitals are involved in the use of obscenities; they seem normal under a man's pen. This metaphorically depicts his 'active' part, in the sexual act. Even though it may hide the anguish supposedly caused by the 'vagina dentata' ambushed in the ogress's cave. To exorcise their fright, males use obscene words as the participants in the Greek phallic processions of the ancient 'comoi' used to throw filth at the effigy of 'the Evil King', symbol of Death and Sterility. Then, when a woman appropriates this language, and discourse, what happens? The communication situation and process are different according to the sex of the woman's audience. Just like when Blacks refer to themselves as 'niggers' Jews as 'kikes' and Italians as 'wops', so does the self-disparaging pejoration of one's own self turn into a humorous operation: the symbolic destruction of one's own self-image as reviled by the enemy, but by using the enemy's weapon, thus stating one's superiority and symbolic control of the situation, and by so doing, reversing it. The power of words is thus transferred on to the *pharmakos,* and the oppressor's violence is also reversed and suffering becomes pleasure; a mixture of triumph and anguish over one's own predicament and inferiority, but at the same time an ambiguous feeling of enjoyment of this state: a kind of sado-masochistic pleasure. When Jong uses this sexual language defying taboos and propriety, an attitude which is traditionally forbidden to women, she certainly enjoys liberating her own aggressive pulses, at the expense of her own sex and kin, but at the same time, it seems to me that she rids language of its potential malignancy and hostility, its destructive quality by using it against herself, and her sisters, exactly as in the case of anti-semitic jokes told by Jews: it deflates the nasty balloons, and assumes the function of an exorcism of the evil and black magic contained in the 'rat-killing ritual' which satire is.

When Jong dares voice her body's desire and pleasure, she performs a most scandalous operation in terms of moral and aesthetic taboos: the desacralization of the so-called "mystery of the Eternal feminine" (Alas, poor Goethe . . .). Moreover, she distorts the whole narrative and offers a caricature of the real, that is, of her sexual experience. In *How To Save Your Own Life,* she depicts the various sexual idiosyncrasies of Isadora's lovers:

> An expert and diligent lover, *Roland makes love like a robot* programmed by Alex Comfort. . . .

> He returns dutifully and kisses me very wetly (as he has ever since I ran off with a man whose kisses were wetter than his). He presses his pelvis against mine with consummate technique. I feel he is using craft, *The Craft of Fucking* or *The Well-Tempered Penis* by Bennett Wing. . . .

> Jeffrey belched after eating me as if I were a mug of beer. I couldn't bring myself to touch him for another six months. . . .

As a witness of the scenes, and an actress in them, she assumes the necessary aesthetic detachment and distanciation, if not actual physical distance. If one analyzes Jong's humor in those instances from the functional point of view, it appears that the female humorist assumes the function of both object and subject of the carnival ritual: the elimination of the scapegoat in which the sacrificial victim is Woman, as sexual partner of Man, ridiculed and caricatured, made fun of as comic butt in the drama. The ritual is being performed in terms of *satire:* where both Man as male, and Woman as female are symbolically destroyed after a comic reduction. Yet, at the same time and simultaneously, the woman as humorist and puller of the strings, acts as King of Chaos, and directs the whole show. Then, the female audience laughs *at* the male victim, the poor *pharmakos,* emblem of authority, domination, exploitation and so forth—from the female standpoint. The male audience may appreciate the game, but only within the limits of *their* sense of humor.

But the operation is also pure humor, as defined by Freud: a ritual of self-debunking in which the humorist as *schlemiel* recreates and enjoys the representation of her own failures, limitations, ridicules and shortcomings—as woman, as lover, as human being, but especially as emblem of womanhood and femininity. Her body becomes the scapegoat of the ritual, and women immediately identify themselves to the victim, they laugh at themselves as objects, but rejoice at the brilliant control of the situation evinced by the subject. This temporary fit of madness and delirium, and symbolic suicide which humor is, achieves its aim: by providing both pleasure and therapy to the female audience. They purge themselves of their schizophrenia by rehearsing and exhibiting it by proxy. A very profitable deal, indeed. But how about the male audience? They laugh heartily with no hang-ups, all right. They enjoy liberating their aggressiveness at women, at the symbolic image of the neurotic, helpless and schizophrenic creature—an image which so admirably fits with their own aeon-old prejudices. MCPs, all of them, as Isadora would say. Men's pleasure is that of satire, their laughter and the catharsis it entails are different in nature from those experienced by women in the same game. But it is a perilous one: just as it is always risky for minorities, whether they be ethnic, sexual or other, to practice this kind of self-disparaging humor. In the lesbian scene of *How To Save Your Own Life,* Isadora dons the mask of the male—the butch—and tries to perform well with her female partner, Rosanna, the frigid millionaire heiress. She undergoes the agony and anxiety of the male lover trying desperately to bring his/her partner to orgasm. The narrative of the repeated failures, various grotesque devices called to assistance by Isadora, sexual aids of the most unheard-of nature—cucumbers, Coke bottles and so forth, are worth the trip. It is a kind of conjugated fiasco, whose sight and minute description is thoroughly enjoyed by both male and female members of the audience. The scene can be read as an ironic metaphor: that of the humorist as some bi-sexual 'ubermensch', who plays upon the fantasies and fantasms of both male and female readers. She resorts to such tricks as are exploited by porn-film makers: lesbian scenes are favorites, and even a serious writer, like Anais Nin, cannot resist the temptation to narrate the visit that she and Miller, our old friend Miller, made to a Paris bordello to watch two prostitutes making love, on order and for a few dollars, with the help of various sorts of dildos to the great joy of Miller, and utter puzzlement of poor humorless Anais. And this leads us to another remark about Jong's humorous techniques: she practices a carnivalisation of both male and female sexual fantasms and recreates the fantasmatic scenarios which men and women alike nourish in their erotic dreams and actual sexual games, in order to reach orgasm. What happens here is a transfer of roles: by identifying with the narrator, Isadora the butch, we assume her part and our imagination follows hers to play the impossible bi-sexual lovemaking scene which suddenly becomes real and possible: our desire receives immediate symbolical gratification. It could lead to a great oneiric recreation of the absolute act of love, where the self enjoys both its feminine and masculine half: what Diane Di Prima magnificently achieved, in her lyrical poem *Loba,* the wolf-goddess. But Jong goes one step further, it seems to me: she appropriates the dream and the impossible reconciliation of opposites and feigns to ignore the anxiety-producing otherness in the sexual relation: by pretending she is the one and the other, she suppresses the existential anguish involved, and, thanks to the momentary 'suspension of disbelief', an enormous amount of energy finds itself released and it bursts into an immense cosmic-erotic explosion of orgasm-like laughter. Anima and animus are reduced to the comic diminutive form of homunculus and homuncula, or muliercula, Don Giovanni and Donna Elvira, Quixote and Sancha, ad lib. . . .

Superwoman Jong the humorist has turned her sexual energies and formidable vitality as a woman into power: by controlling her anxiety as a female and by assuming the power of her male half, she has proved capable of turning them into the absolute power of making both men and women laugh at their libido. Creating, causing, arousing laughter is her way of bringing them to pleasure—a pleasure whose nature is so close to sexual pleasure. By mastering the taboos of sex, by exhibiting her own sexual drives, desires and perversions, in a totally unabashed manner, she has risen to the stature of the Nietzschean ubermensch of humor: beyond good and evil, beyond male and female, she has conquered absolute power and willpower. Humor is definitely connected to this notion of power: sexual power as acknowledged and exercised, freely and without shame or guilt. The only source of anguish that remains is death—non-existence. But then, both sexes are equally helpless: and there lies the real equality of sexes.

Maybe Jong has not made a giant's leap but just a small step towards this total liberation of woman regarding humor. Yet, female humor will no longer exist as such after her if women exercise their power as human beings and as producers of comedy. They will regain power through creation and recreation, but, alack poor Miller! —once they have gotten rid of procreation; which means simply the end of the human species: if humor is at this cost, who said it was a problem?

Rolande Diot, "Sexus, Nexus and Taboos Versus Female Humor: The Case of Erica Jong," in Revue Française D'Études Américaines, *No. 30, November, 1986, pp. 491-99.*

Michael Malone   (review date 19 April 1987)

[*Malone is an American novelist, editor, nonfiction writer, and critic. In the following review, he provides a mixed assessment of* Serenissima.]

Who afraid of Virginia Woolf? Not Erica Jong, who invokes Woolf's *Orlando* as an epigraph for **Serenissima,** in which Jessica Pruitt, jet-setting movie star (in Venice to judge a film festival) falls ill midway through the book (Liv Ullmann nurses her—"What are friends for?"), and travels backward in time to the 16th century. There she finds herself transformed into Shylock's daughter—the very role she's been cast to play (despite her 43 years) in "nothing less than a filmic fantasy based on *The Merchant of Venice*" conceived by a Bergmanesque Swedish genius, "undoubtedly the greatest direct of our time," as well as

her former lover. (The actor playing Shylock is also an old lover, but then presumably the honor is not a rare one.)

Nor has our heroine any fear of flying off with young William Shakespeare himself, whose first gasped words as they collide in the Ghetto Vecchio are "who ever loved, who loved not at first sight?" His next are "What's in a name? A rose by any other name would smell as sweet." He then introduces himself as "a poor player that struts and frets his hour upon the stage." Jessica's old Hollywood pals might call this Meeting Cute with a vengeance, but as Will tells her, "Marry, come up, you jest at scars that never felt a wound." The brief adventures of these time-crossed lovers lead them by foot, horse and skiff north through Italy to the Villa Montebello (Belmont in English, the bard explains), where they consummate their love, "that highest of all highs." "Who would dare describe love with the greatest poet the world has ever known? . . . Was Will Shakespeare good in bed? Let the reader judge!"

After Fanny Hackabout-Jones's willingness to kiss and tell on Pope, Hogarth and Swift, [in **Fanny**], the reader will not be surprised to hear that Jessica indeed dares describe "Will's stiff staff" in a series of tumbles, including some in which she herself is not a participant: one with his sadistic lover-patron, the Earl of Southampton, and a Venetian courtesan, making "a three-backed beast that pants and screams and begs for mercy"; one in an orgy with fantastically masked, lascivious nuns, immediately after which Will's partner, Juliet, gives birth, then chokes to death on her own vomit, leaving the poet to eulogize: "Now cracks a noble heart. Goodnight, sweet princess, and flights of angels sing thee to thy rest."

It is this nun's infant, rescued from the murderous convent, whom Jessica and Will flee Venice to save. Violence of course pursues them: Southampton wants to rape and/or kill them both; Shalach (Shylock) wants his daughter and/or his ducats back. The thuggish courtiers Bassanio and Gratiano want bloody revenge. Swords are drawn, bodices ripped and hailstorms hurled from heaven. Christian villagers rampage and slaughter the Jews of Montebello (Will hides behind a hedge ruminating on "What a piece of work is man"). Forced back to Venice by Shalach, Jessica ostensibly dies, floating out of her body to watch Southampton and Shakespeare kiss her in various places, as they "genuflect before [her] orifices." Then, alive in her coffin, like Pericles' wife, she is cast into the sea, where a storm swamps her funeral gondola. She arises, reborn into the 20th century, to discover that she has dreamed (or lived) the screenplay of **Serenissima.** As Ben Jonson might say, it's some moldy old tale.

Erica Jong has one fictional heroine, brave, bookish, beautiful and indefatigably libidinous, poet of the erogenous zone, priestess of the Great Goddess, whether that heroine is Fanny, the 18th-century whore-turned-pirate-turned-writer, or Isadora, the much married best-selling novelist of the Wing trilogy (a Jew from the West 70's), or the much-married international star Jessica Pruitt (a WASP from the East 70's, who sometimes thinks "being a Jew would be so *cozy*. They seemed to have more blood, more poetry, more sensuality than my people.") Like her predecessors, Jessica loves sex, her art, her many illustrious friends and her adorable little daughter. Like them, she is irresistibly attractive (she compares herself to a Burne-Jones angel, Botticelli's Venus and the Dark Lady).

Whether in designer clothes, or disguised as a 16th-century boy, Jessica wears—like Isadora, like Fanny—her heart on her sleeve, and thereby suffers: her "openness and trust abused," her lust for life misinterpreted, her hurts unappreciated. She fears, as they did, that she may have loved not wisely but too well (not to mention too often). "Love was my addiction." No doubt, her little body aweary of this great world, tired of the nosy *paparazzi* and the sequined glitterati (whose life style Ms. Jong captures vividly), Jessica slips into a fevered reverie of magic rings, ancient crones, mysterious potions and literary pornography.

As might be expected of a movie star who has toured *Medea* in Southern penitentiaries, who refers to her career as her "sullen craft" and "stubborn art," Jessica is perhaps a little more scholarly than the average denizen of "palmy LaLa Land." She not only knows her "Jackie O." and "Paloma P." her *carpaccio* and Pinot Grigio ("Gore V." bursts into a bedchamber where our heroine has just kneed in the groin an amorous Russian poet), she also knows her Canaletto and Miró, her Byron, Ruskin, James and Joyce. She knows the minor Elizabethan playwright Robert Greene, and the invitational policies of Manhattan PEN meetings. Her speech is sprinkled with Italian phrases; her thoughts are sprinkled with pontifical pronouncements on male domination, motherhood, culture and moral history ("That's the tragedy of our generation—we haven't even *got* a myth of good battling evil"). For Jessica, far preferable to a starring role in the miniseries "Vegas II" is a world where Will's tendency to quote his yet unwritten works on all occasions is shared by everyone: Southampton reels off sonnets, Shylock wails in passages from *Lear,* Jessica broods, "We are such stuff as dreams are made of." The odd effect is that they all sound like a mixture of Bartlett's index and Maxwell Anderson's pseudo-Elizabethan argot. The result is a slow, though short, misty dream. Shakespeare does not come to life, and Shylock we barely meet.

As she proved in **Fanny,** a picaresque of intelligence, buoyant invention and wonderful Rabelaisian energy, Erica Jong can write a historical novel that both honors its tradition with affectionate parody and creates its own full fictional reality. The Renaissance has not served her as well as did the 18th century. Perhaps had she really written the story implied by her premise, the story untold in *The Merchant of Venice* (of Shylock's daughter, who renounces her faith for a shallow suitor; who confesses, "Alack, what heinous sin is it in me! To be ashamed to be my father's child"), perhaps had she told Jessica's tale, instead of following Shakespeare and Southampton from brothel to convent, Ms. Jong would have found the plot worthy of her careful research, her rich descriptive facility and her deep love of the period. Or she might have produced the novel *Tintoretto's Daughter* that her Isadora Wing once wrote. Perhaps someday she will.

Michael Malone, "The True Adventures of Shylock's Daughter," in The New York Times Book Review, *April 19, 1987, p. 12.*

Benjamin DeMott   (review date 28 January 1990)

[*DeMott is an American novelist, short story writer, essayist, educator, and critic. Following is his mixed review of* Any Woman's Blues.]

Leila Sand, the heroine of Erica Jong's [**Any Woman's Blues**], is a mid-fortyish, compulsively fornicating artist and celebrity who, despite occasional moments of satisfaction in the natural world or in bed, is almost continuously woebegone. She's gripped by a sadomasochistic obsession (object: an obnoxiously faithless young hustler named Darton Venable Donegal IV), her muse is deserting her and her studio is in chaos. What's more, her children (twin daughters) don't need her, and wine and weed keep punching her out.

Leila fights the blues hard, to be sure, and her struggle—waged mainly in her Connecticut country house, in SoHo and in hotels and palazzi in Venice—becomes the substance of **Any Woman's Blues.** Guided by her writer pal Emmie, Leila tries Alcoholics Anonymous (and provides convincing glimpses of the comic candor and heartbreak of A.A. meetings, as well as of their democratic fellowship and quasi-religious intensity). She also battles her addiction to Dart Donegal, eventually managing to lock him out for good. And, late in the book, there's a hint of oncoming redemption through the religion of art. At one point Leila "is in a state of grace. She wants to skip, to kneel before the Madonna, to invent drawings and paintings that will communicate joy to the joyless, faith to the unbeliever, and love to the loveless. She wants everyone to savor and celebrate life because it is a feast. It is there for the taking. You have only to open your mouth, open your hand, love one another, thank God, and rejoice."

But at the end, as at the beginning, Leila's prospects inspire only wary hope. A.A. has helped, but she hasn't really kicked her habits. The young hustler is gone, but he's followed by an equally unpromising passion, a Venetian Casanova. (The pair make out on gondola rides.) Defeat sounds often in her voice: "All my life," she says, with her story winding down, "I've wanted nothing but to bring sex and friendship together—and I seem to be farther from it than ever." And the world she's made her own—overpopulated by corrupt and violent celebrities—seems doom-ridden.

Owing to the heroine's lineage, there's bounty for moralists in **Any Woman's Blues.** The preface, written by a fictional feminist literary scholar, passes the word that the book is actually the work of the sensationally uninhibited Isadora Wing, the heroine of Ms. Jong's first novel, **Fear of Flying,** which was published in 1973. (An upbeat afterword by Ms. Wing confirms the attribution.)

With this news come lessons. Famously shameless in four-letter word and deed, Isadora Wing was a creature of sexual delight, huge appetite and no guilt whatever about infidelity and promiscuity. If Leila, the first-person narrator of **Any Woman's Blues,** is Isadora 17 years later, it follows (for moralists) that sin and abomination don't pay. What happens to a female Portnoy, a supermerry, superraunchy Wife of Bath who never looks back? If she becomes Leila Sand, what happens is that she sometimes finds herself banging her frustrated head on the floor, in a pool of her own blood, wailing in wretched loneliness, no comfort left but prayer. Hedonists, attend.

For readers as opposed to moralists, though, the point about this book isn't that wanton indulgence gets its come-uppance. It's that literary self-indulgence spoils the narrative—and the central character. Isadora Wing, Leila Sand's forebear, was a figure of wit as well as appetite; her lively brain powered *Fear of Flying* with a current of shrewd, funny observation on men, women, marriage and physicality, male and female. Always she stood at a fine remove from piety and self-pity. Isadora as Leila, on the other hand, has lost several steps. She stamps and weeps and tries to "thank God for the lichen, for the raspberries, for the clouds" (the phrase "thank you" is repeated a hundred or so consecutive times on a single page). She carries on, now hysterically, now sanctimoniously, but seldom entertainingly.

At moments, Ms. Jong seems aware of the problem. When Leila's hustler tormentor walks out after a cliché-strewn, soap opera-like scene (" 'That's it!' screams Dart. 'The last straw!' "), Leila falls to the floor and weeps. Whereupon in marches Isadora Wing, in italics, as follows: *"Isadora: Couldn't she weep in a chair for once? Leila: Could you?"*

The aim of these and other tart-tongued interruptions is to lighten the proceedings, and once or twice they succeed. An occasional idiom or patch of comic invention elsewhere calls up Ms. Jong's earlier achievements. There's a "punky adorable midget" designer named "Mij Nehoc (Jim Cohen spelled backward)," and also some well-judged flame-throwing at Manhattan vanities. ("She's the charity disease queen of New York—a hotly coveted title.") Some of the chapter epigraphs, moreover—from blues lyrics by Bessie Smith, Ida Cox and others, including Piano Red ("You got the right string, baby, but the wrong yo-yo")—will make any responsible person laugh out loud.

But as a whole, *Any Woman's Blues* feels leaden. What's missing is what won the author of *Fear of Flying* a place among the true and unforgettable headliners of late-20th-century literary vaudeville: gorgeous, saving sass.

Benjamin DeMott, "The Fruits of Sin," in The New York Times Book Review, *January 28, 1990, p. 13.*

Marni Jackson   (review date 19 February 1990)

[*In the following review, Jackson characterizes* Any Woman's Blues *as "a compelling but confused novel that strains for a moral clarity beyond its grasp."*]

When Erica Jong finished writing *Any Woman's Blues,* her latest novel, she must have realized that there would be some debate over what the book was really about. Was it, as the helpful subtitle suggested, a "novel of obsession" about a successful woman, Leila Sand, in love with a hopeless cad named Dart Donegal? Was it about Leila's voyage from her addiction to love, sex and red wine to independence, sobriety and serenity? Or was the book simply a fictional veil cast over Erica Jong, famous author and bon vivant, as she tries to give up everything she urged women to pursue in her first novel, *Fear of Flying?* Only one thing is clear by the end of the novel: Alcoholics Anonymous must surely be the new church of the 1990s if even Jong's high-flying heroines are now finding their salvation in AA meetings instead of midnight trysts.

Jong's fictional alter ego is a 39-year-old painter with a weakness for too much wine and all the wrong men. "I lived for sex, for falling in love with love," confesses Leila. Her drug of choice is the fickle young Dart, who makes her life miserable: "All I can do is listen for the crushed gravel under Dart's motorcycle wheels, which seem to ride right over my heart." Dart ruins her concentration—and he does not do much for Jong's incorrigibly purple prose, either. "Love is the sweetest addiction," she writes. "Who would not sell her soul for the dream of two made one, for the sweetness of making love in the sunlight on an Adriatic beach with a young god whose armpits are lined with gold?"

When Dart disappears with a bimbo, Leila tries to make do with an impotent millionaire, followed by a corporate man more attached to his telephone than his libido. Finally, with the help of AA, she starts down the road from dependency to what the book calls "self-love, which is not to be confused with narcissism." Most of all, she wants to stop finding her reflection in the mirror of men. Leila succeeds, but true to the archetype of addiction, she suffers relapses along the way. That lets Jong do what she clearly enjoys most, which is to write about old-fashioned, reckless sex.

In fact, Leila's visit to an S-and-M brothel in New York City is the one place where the lackadaisical narrative of the novel picks up: it is a raunchy, truly shocking episode in Leila's moral education. Female masochism lurks under her obsession with Dart—who actually wears spurs—but in the brothel scene it loses its sentimental veneer. Jong should have stayed with Leila's dark side rather than swiftly repudiating it the next morning, in the interests of moral growth. The author wants to arrive at wisdom in her novel faster than her heroine deserves it. Leila's idea of convalescence is a little trip to Venice, where she has one last fling with a playboy named Renzo (is there a self-help program for authors with a weakness for bad names?). They rendezvous in a motorboat on the Venice canals. Ah, yes, recovery is a rough road. Leila's 10-year-old twin daughters are also suspiciously convenient, disappearing whenever a new lover shows up. Ever the romantic escapist, Jong seems to be running from her own thought.

Perhaps sensing that the book was skittering out of control, Jong imposes a literary device that does not work. The whole novel is presented as an "unfinished manuscript," written by Isadora Wing, Jong's heroine in her earlier novels. That coy business weakens a novel that already can barely bring itself to focus on any other character except Leila.

But Jong has an unerring instinct for what is on people's minds—in this case, the power and perils of addiction. It gives the book something of the lurid fascination of a TV movie of the week. Jong's careless, confessional style also makes the experience of reading *Any Woman's Blues* seem like leafing through a teenager's diary. "I collapse in a torrent of tears," she writes at one point. " 'No more pain! No more pain!' I mutter. But even as I imagine him waving goodbye to me, I know I am really waving goodbye to him." And so on. The novel is so at odds with itself that when Leila achieves peace of mind at the end, it simply does not ring true. It is as if Jong had invited her guests to a vegetarian banquet and then passed by with trolleys of broiled steaks. The result is a compelling but confused novel that strains for a moral clarity beyond its grasp.

Marni Jackson, "Crash Landing," in Maclean's Magazine, *Vol. 103, No. 8, February 19, 1990, p. 55.*

Gayle Greene   (essay date 1991)

[*Greene is an American educator, editor, and critic. In the following excerpt from her* Changing the Story: Feminist Fiction and the Tradition *(1991), she faults Jong for failing to challenge traditional patriarchal views of women and sexuality in* Fear of Flying.]

Accustomed as I am to having to defend my interest in *Fear of Flying,* I'll state at the outset why I find it important. Sexual liberation was an essential part of the early women's movement, and *Fear of Flying* has been taken seriously, if not as "literature," as an expression of sexual liberation—most recently, by Susan Suleiman [in *Subversive Intent: Gender, Politics, and the Avant-Garde,* 1990] who describes it as "a significant gesture, both in terms of sexual politics and in terms of . . . sexual poetics," praises its "freshness and vitality" of language, and calls it a "fictional counterpart" to such books as *Our Bodies, Our Selves* (1973) and Shere Hite's *Sexual Honesty, By Women for Women* (1974), which similarly reclaim female bodies and sexuality for females. I confess to having liked the novel when it first appeared, though it does not bear up to rereading and I don't finally share Suleiman's enthusiasm. But as the only instance of feminist metafiction I know of to sell ten million copies, it was important as a vehicle for the dissemination of feminist ideas and for the controversy it sparked, and it deserves attention as a cultural document.

Disappointed by the women of the past—in history, literature, and her family—Isadora is left to chart her own way. Turning "to our uncertain heroines for help," she encounters only "spinsters or suicides":

> Simone de Beauvoir never makes a move without wondering *what would Sartre think?* And Lillian Hellman wants to be as much of a man as Dashiell Hammett . . . . And the rest—the women writers, the women painters—most of them were shy, shrinking, schizoid. Timid in their lives and brave only in their art. Emily Dickinson, the Brontes, Virginia Woolf, Carson McCullers . . . Flannery O'Connor. .. Sylvia Plath sticking her head into an oven of myth. . . . What a group! Severe, suicidal,

strange. Where was the female Chaucer? One lusty lady who had juice and joy and love and talent too? Where could we turn for guidance?

"So the search for the impossible man went on", she laments, implying that the failure of her literary foremothers is responsible for her dependence on men. She sees an even more direct connection between the failure of her mother and her dependence on men: "So I learned about women from men". Like other contemporary women novelists, Jong writes to fill the gap between the fiction of the past and women's experience in the present.

Jong implies that she is telling "the other side of the story":

> A stiff prick, Freud said, assuming that *their* obsession was *our* obsession.

> Phallocentric, someone once said of Freud. He thought the sun revolved around the penis. And the daughter, too.

> And who could protest? Until women started writing books there was only one side of the story.

Recalling the Wife of Bath's claim that if women wrote, the stories would be different, Jong implies that she is "the female Chaucer," the "lusty lady" with "juice and love and talent too."

Like other women protagonists, Isadora seeks escape in an affair, and as in other contemporary versions of the "two-suitor convention," the husband represents the oppressive patriarchy and the lover represents liberation; for Adrian—whom she picks up at a psychiatrists' convention in Vienna, which she is attending with her husband, Bennett Wing—is Laingian, bearded, English, and sexy, and promises "spontaneity, existentialism, living in the present," against the dull security of Bennett. Adrian proposes that they have an "odyssey"—" 'you'll discover yourself' "—and urges Isadora " 'to go down into [herself] and salvage [her] own life' " to "find patterns in [her] past." As they drive through Germany and France, Isadora tells him "everything": "What was this crazy itinerary anyway if not a trip back into my past?"; "we . . . picked up the threads of these old patterns of behavior as we made our way through the labyrinth of Old Europe."

But the best Isadora can come up with is that she keeps being attracted to men who are poor risks—which is not very original but at least explains her attraction to this jerk, who is not only married but impotent; and though she senses that she is repeating this pattern with Adrian, she does not examine this too closely. Nor does she examine anything else too closely; her recounting of her past has no bearing on her present; it is merely episodic, merely there. So, too, is the structure of the novel, which, in its alternation of episodes set in the past with episodes set in the present, might provide a vehicle for plumbing the past, but does not; for Isadora's past has as little to do with her present problems—with her boredom in her marriage and fear of leaving it—as the labyrinth of old Europe has to do with the labyrinth of herself: Europe also is merely there, an exotic backdrop.

Adrian promises Isadora that she will discover her strengths and learn to "stand on [her] own two feet"; and he becomes, "perversely, an instrument of [her] freedom" when he drops her in Paris, without warning, to return to his wife. He tells Isadora he's " 'not here to rescue [her],' " and she accepts this, drawing the moral that "I wasn't Adrian's child, and it wasn't his business to rescue me. I was nobody's baby now. Liberated. Utterly free. It was the most terrifying sensation I'd ever known in my life. Like teetering on the edge of the Grand Canyon and hoping you'd learn to fly before you hit bottom."

She finds her "wings" by surviving a night alone in a hotel room in Paris. Talking herself through a panic, trying to get hold of her fear, she rehearses, again, the names of women of the past:

> Me: Think of Simone de Beauvoir!
>
> Me: I love her endurance, but her books are full of Sartre, Sartre, Sartre.
>
> Me: Think of Doris Lessing!
>
> Me: Anna Wulf can't come unless she's in love. . . .
>
> Me: Think of Sylvia Plath!
>
> Me: Dead. . . .
>
> Me: Well—think of Colette.
>
> Me: A good example. But she's one of the very few.
>
> Me: Well, why not try to be like her?
>
> Me: I'm trying. . . .
>
> Me: Then why are you so afraid of being alone?
>
> Me: We're going around in circles.

But it is her own writing, not theirs, that pulls her out of this tailspin, as she realizes, reading through her journals, how much she has changed. That night, she "assigns herself dreams as a sort of cure," and these dreams, which include "a book with her name on the cover," instruct her that she would not "be a romantic heroine" but that she would "survive": "I would go home and write about Adrian instead. I would keep him by giving him up."

The "book with her name on the cover," the book she will write, is the novel we have just read, and *Fear of Flying* ends with the protagonist ready to begin. Isadora has presumably learned "to go down into myself and salvage bits and pieces of the past," to plumb "inner space. . . . My writing is the submarine or spaceship which takes me to the unknown worlds within my head . . . a new vehicle, designed to delve a little deeper (or fly a little higher)." Whereas once she had difficulty admitting that she was "a woman writer"—

> I didn't want to risk being called all the things women writers . . . are called. . . . No "lady writer" subjects for me. . . . I languished in utter frustration, thinking that the subjects I knew about were "trivial" and "feminine"— while the subjects I knew nothing of were "profound" and "masculine". . . .

—presumably now she has the courage to tell "the other side," in authentic female voice, and *Fear of Flying* is the fruit of those lessons.

Jong confuses liberation with sexual liberation and confuses sexual liberation with the freedom to act and talk like a man, but the bold language that so impressed readers masks a conventionality, a failure to imagine otherwise.

—Gayle Greene

Isadora shows evidence of change when, at the end of the novel, on her way back to Bennett in London, she has the chance of a "zipless fuck" with a "stranger on a train"; though such a prospect once fueled her sexual fantasies, she now finds the idea "revolting." She realizes that it was wrong to want "to lose [her]self in a man, to cease to be [herself], to be transported to heaven on borrowed wings." By learning to take her writing seriously, she has, supposedly, grown wings of her own. Flight is a recurrent image in women's writing, . . . and is often a metaphor for women's writing, signifying what Grace Stewart calls the desire to escape "the polarity between woman and artist"; and since in French *voler* means not only "to fly," but "to steal," it has further associations with "stealing the language"—a connection stressed by Suleiman, who sees Jong as accomplishing both feats.

But Isadora's ending suggests that her "wings" are still Bennett's—Bennett Wing's—since she has followed her husband to London, let herself into his room, and ends up soaking in his bathtub, contemplating her options:

> Perhaps I had only come to take a bath. Perhaps I would leave before Bennett returned. Or perhaps we'd go home together and work things out. Or perhaps we'd go home together and separate. It was not clear how it would end.

At which point, the novel ends:

> But whatever happened, I knew I would survive it. I knew, above all, that I'd go on working. Surviving meant being born over and over. . . .
>
>   . . . .
>
> I hummed and rinsed my hair. As I was soaping it again, Bennett walked in.

Notwithstanding Isadora's assertion of open-ended possibilities and her insistence that she is free to leave, strong probabilities are suggested by the force of her past, which the novel does nothing to exorcise, and by her situation in the present—she is naked in her husband's bathtub. Isadora may have outgrown her desire for zipless fucks, but she has not overcome her need of Bennett. Besides, we know from the sequel, *How to Save Your Own Life* (perhaps the most embarrassing novel written in recent decades by a woman with literary pretensions), that she does not leave Bennett until she has another man lined up to take his place.

The blurb on my paperback copy of the book proclaims *Fear of Flying* "a dazzlingly uninhibited novel that exposes a woman's most intimate sexual feelings," and besides the reviewers who praised it for telling it like it is from the female sexual viewpoint, we have Jong's testimony to the numerous women readers who share her fantasy of the zipless fuck. But women's "most intimate sexual feelings" sound depressingly familiar: cunt, cock, prick, ass, tits, fuck, fuckable, blowing and being blown. These do not break new ground.

There have been various attempts to defend Jong's use of male sexual vocabulary, most notably by Suleiman, who claims that it is a way of "filching" the language from men, "a parody of language of tough-guy narrator / heroes of Miller or Mailer," a "reversal of roles *and* of language, in which the docile . . . silent, objectified woman suddenly usurps both the pornographer's language and his way of looking at the opposite sex." But even granting this as Jong's purpose, to reverse the terms is not to challenge the terms. The problem with this sexual vocabulary is that it inscribes a power struggle in which women have been "had"; to wield it is not to steal the language or demonstrate "authenticity," but to reveal a more insidious form of alienation. The challenge facing women who write about desire is to articulate new terms for sexuality that will transform the old power struggle and change "the rules of the old game"—as Drabble does in *The Waterfall.*

Jong confuses liberation with sexual liberation and confuses sexual liberation with the freedom to act and talk like a man, but the bold language that so impressed readers masks a conventionality, a failure to imagine otherwise. Isadora is right—she does "talk a good game"—and there are wonderfully quotable bits in *Fear of Flying,* which I've filched throughout chapters 1 and 2, but they are suspiciously excerptable, on the surface, as is the feminism of the novel. The novel does not, finally, challenge "the old story" at the level of plot, language, or meaning. When Isadora is falling for Adrian, she senses the presence of a "hackneyed plot," "the vocabulary of popular love songs, the cliches of the worst Hollywood movies. My heart skipped a beat. I got misty. . . . He was my sunshine"; and *Fear of Flying* is itself caught in the hackneyed, for Isadora resists one set of cliches to succumb to another and is left going "in circles," "round in circles," on a "merry-go-round," a "constant round."

Thus the ending of *How to Save Your Own Life* comes as no surprise:

> It was no good. All her feminism, all her independence, all her fame had come to this, this helplessness, this need. She needed him. She needed this man. When he entered her, when his hot cock slid into her, she was moaning something about that, about surrender.

"A stiff prick?" On the basis of Jong's fiction, "their obsession" would seem to be "our obsession."

Gayle Greene, "Old Stories," in her Changing the Story: Feminist Fiction and the Tradition, *Indiana University Press, 1991, pp. 86-102.*

Erica Jong with Lynn Spampinato   (interview date 19 April 1994)

[*In the following interview, Jong discusses her memoir* Fear of Fifty, *her views on feminism, and her goals as a writer.*]

[*Spampinato*]: *I read recently that you have two new books that are set to be published soon:* **Fear of Fifty** *and* **Twenty Forty.** *Would you like to tell me about them?*

[Jong]: *Twenty Forty* is a novel I'm still working on that is set in the future, but it is nowhere near ready for publication. *Fear of Fifty*, my mid-life memoir, will be published this August [1994], and in it I relate the events of my life, beginning on my fiftieth birthday and moving backward in time. In this process of telling my own story, I tell the story of my generation, which I refer to as "The Whiplash Generation," because we were raised to be Doris Day, grew to young womanhood wanting to be Gloria Steinem, and now we're raising our daughters in the age of Princess Diana and Madonna. So I think we've been buffeted about in our views and opinions of love, of marriage, of motherhood, of feminism, and of course, of femininity itself. I think we are really a remarkable generation. So I tell my own story (very personally and very humorously), as a way of telling the story of my generation.

What made you decide to write **Fear of Fifty** *at this point in your career?*

I think there's a sort of natural progression, which is, when you hit mid-life—we optimistically call it mid-life, it may be two-thirds of the way toward death, actually—I think that you begin to see your life in a very different perspective. If your parents are still alive, you begin to see them as human beings, rather than ogres or angels. If you have a child or children, you begin to see where you fit in on the evolutionary chain—between your parents and child. It's a moment of reappraising your life and discovering where you belong in the continuum. This is the time that people want to trace their "roots." "Where did I come from?" and "where did my family come from?" and "how did I get to be me?" become fascinating questions. Given the buffeting that my generation has experienced—with feminism going in and out of style as if it were a hemline—I was drawn to assess why I had been able to function as a creative writer in a world that is not very good to women writers. What gave me my strength, where did it come from? I discovered that it came from both my parents, in different ways. And why was I able to survive creatively when my two sisters were not as free, when my mother was not as free, when my grandmother was not as free. So it was a sort of reappraisal of my life at fifty. And I think that is very typical of the kind of changes that go on psychologically at mid-life.

You mentioned feminism going "in and out of style." Do you perceive any pervasive trends in the current state of contemporary feminist literature and publishing?

I think we went through a period when we had a tremendous split in the feminist movement, between those women who believed that feminism should reach out and embrace homemakers, women with children, women who didn't have the posture of separatists, and those feminists who were very hard line and hard core, and didn't want to open the tent to everyone. And that split I perceived to be one of the problems of the backlash era. (Not that we feminists created the backlash; it came out of the Reagan administration and the Bush administration, and a roll-back of women's rights that came along with a very reactionary trend politically.) But in a sense I think that we also *opened* ourselves to it, because as feminists we didn't spread our tent wide enough. In the 70s there was a tendency to exclude women who wanted to have children and who loved men. "Where do I fit into this movement?" they asked. Some of them felt they were treated very badly. What I see *now* is a kind of reaching out, more inclusiveness—which is good. And in the younger generation of feminists, the third-wave feminists, like Naomi Wolf, Katie Roiphe, Susie Bright, and the new people who are coming along and writing books (who are in their late twenties or early thirties) there is a much greater inclusiveness—something I have *always* been arguing for. Let's *not* have political litmus tests in order to be included in the feminist movement. You don't have to be *one* kind of feminist only to be included. And I think it's hopeful that we have more inclusiveness and a kind of "big tent" feminism now, because that gives us the hope of creating a mass movement, rather than an exclusionary movement. I'm very happy about that. The next generation, the third-wave feminists, are coming along, and they're opening the net wider. I think that's good.

How do you respond to critics, particularly feminist critics, who fault your use of sexual vocabulary in your novels? For instance, Gayle Greene, in her book Changing the Story: Feminist Fiction and the Tradition *(1991), stated: "Jong confuses liberation with sexual liberation and confuses sexual liberation with the freedom to act and talk like a man." Now she was referring specifically to* **Fear of Flying**, *but this has been a fairly consistent criticism of many of your novels. How do you respond to statements like Greene's?*

It seems to me natural that in a patriarchal society where women have been deprived of the full use of their sexuality for centuries, or where sexuality has meant a kind of terrible repression and submission for women, that many feminists will feel that the *only* way to be free is to be antisexual. Adrienne Rich has written about this; Audre Lorde has written about this. Women in sexist society frequently throw out Eros, because Eros, for women, has historically been so entrapping. But it is a *mistake* to throw out Eros, because Eros is the source of our creativity. So I understand that there are feminists who feel that I've sold out to the male principle, but they are deeply misunderstanding the thrust of my work. They themselves have bought into male dichotomies, but they don't even know it! Every creator needs to be fueled by the life-force, and the life-force is Eros. Sexuality is not a matter of bowing down to male subjugation—not at all. Sexuality can be female. I hope that women will recapture their own *pagan* sensuality, the kind of sensuality that they had thousands of years ago in a pre-patriarchal world, and I hope they

will learn to use it as a creative force. The women who criticize sexuality per se cannot even understand a female-positive Eros. They see it in terms of male pornography, which abuses women, and that's all they can *imagine*. But if you go back to an earlier tradition, if you go back to Sappho, if you go back to Nefertiti, if you go back to the Egyptian women who ruled, the Egyptian deities who inspired, you see that female sexuality does not *have* to be male dominated. The Judeo-Christian world is, in a sense, an aberration in history, in that women's sexuality has been subjugated by men. I see sexuality in a much freer sense than these feminists do. I think of the sexuality of a Sappho, a very liberating sexuality and a very pro-female sexuality. The critics to whom you refer are trapped in a kind of Judeo-Christian worldview; they think that to be pro-sex is to be pro-male-domination. They just don't understand. They are more oppressed by patriarchal thinking than I am.

In a 1987 interview with Contemporary Authors, *you stated: "I think of myself as a poet who stumbled into the habit of writing novels. But they use different muscles, really." What did you mean by using "different muscles," and do you still think of yourself as primarily a poet?*

I do apprehend the world as a poet—that is imagistically. I never outline a novel's plot first, as some thriller writers do. I always start with an image, with a sense of the language of the book, and generally with a character, and I sort of know where the arc of the story is pointing, but I never know just where it ends. I think like a poet. When I say "using different muscles," I mean that the novel can contain all kinds of things that the poem can't. The novel can be a criticism of society, the novel can include the way people cook and go to the bathroom and ride on horseback or in spaceships, and it can include all the impedimenta of the world, and you can make that part of your book's subtext. So the novel has a *reach* that the poem does not have. And that I find very beguiling—the impulse to create a world. In that sense you're using different muscles. The novel also allows for observation of character, which most modern lyric poetry does not. Speaking out of an "I" persona, which is an outgrowth of the poet's own "I," may go very close to the bone, but it doesn't paint a society as a whole. I guess those are the ways in which the two forms use different muscles. My poetry feeds my prose, and most of my books start, in some sense, through poetry. If I didn't go back and write poetry after every book of prose, I would be impoverished. Writing poems and keeping notes in notebooks restore me to myself. They are my compost heap. Through them, I get back to my center.

What would you say are your primary aims or goals as an author?

I would like to bring wholeness to contemporary women. I think that women have been deeply split—their minds have been split from their bodies, their sexuality has been split from their intelligence. I think Judeo-Christian culture has forced women into a kind of whore/madonna split and mind/body split. Each of my heroines is looking for integration. Fanny wants, as she always says, "reason and rump," Isadora is looking for sexuality and intellect both; she doesn't want to give up one for the other. To have sex but no intellect is like having breathing but not eating. So, I think the aim of my books is to accomplish a kind of integration and wholeness for modern women. My heroines begin their stories suffering from a lack of integration, and in the course of their adventures they come upon a new integration.

You seem to use a great deal of autobiographical information in your works. Would you describe your writing process? How do you incorporate your personal experience in your plots and characters?

I don't really know. I generally transform my life in the writing process. Sometimes I write books that seem more superficially autobiographical (in the sense that the heroines come from New York, are Jewish and bookish like me) and sometimes the autobiographical impulse is more hidden, as it is in **Serenissima** or **Fanny** or the future novel I'm writing now. Why I reach out and pick up certain elements of life and use them in the book, or how I transform them, I can't tell you—it's really an unconscious process. I try to make the heroines as real and visceral as I can. For example, I want them to have professions I know well. In **Any Woman's Blues**, Leila is a painter, a metier I understand very well because I come from a family of painters. In **Serenissima**, Jessica is an actress: I have many friends who are in the acting profession. I would probably not want to give a character of mine a profession that I didn't feel in my guts. But how I transform stuff that really happened to me, I really don't know—it's very intuitive.

How do you perceive yourself in relation to the larger picture of contemporary literature?

We live in a time when there has been a revolution in women's autobiographical writing. If you look at a book like Jill Ker Conway's anthology of women's autobiography [*Written by Herself: Autobiographies of American Women*, 1992], you see that this is a great age of flowering of the autobiographical impulse. Women writers have fulfilled the prophecy of Emerson ("novels will give way, by and by, to diaries or autobiographies"). Why? Because women have had to define themselves anew in this century. All the givens we were raised with have been swept away—notions of motherhood, notions of wifehood, notions of the stability of the family—everything has changed. So, we turn to autobiographical writing to help us define ourselves, and to help us define our womanhood in a time when female status is radically changing, and relations between the sexes are, too.

FURTHER READING

Criticism

Butler, Robert J. "The Woman Writer as American Picaro:

Open Journeying in Erica Jong's *Fear of Flying*." *The Centennial Review* XXXI, No. 3 (Summer 1987): 308-29.
> Discusses *Fear of Flying* as a picaresque novel, asserting that "*Fear of Flying*, like most American journey books, . . . boldly equates life with motion and stasis with death."

Ferguson, Mary Anne. "The Female Novel of Development and the Myth of Psyche." In *The Voyage In Fictions of Female Development*, edited by Elizabeth Abel, Marianne Hirsch, and Elizabeth Langland, pp. 228-43. Hanover and London: University Press of New England, 1983.
> Discusses how *Fear of Flying* and other novels "show women successfully developing, learning, growing in the world at large."

Friedman, Edward H. "The Precocious Narrator: *Fanny* and Discursive Counterpoint," in his *The Antiheroine's Voice: Narrative Discourse and Transformations of the Picaresque*, pp. 203-19. Columbia, Mo.: University of Missouri Press, 1987.
> Examines *Fanny* according to the tradition of the picaresque novel.

Guy, David. "The Devil's Inamorata." *New England Review* 15, No. 4 (Fall 1993): 184-91.
> Provides a positive assessment of Jong's discussion of Henry Miller in *The Devil at Large*.

Harder, Kelsie B. "The Masculine Imperative: Naming By Gael Greene and Erica Jong." *Literary Onomastics Studies* XI (1984): 147-63.
> Illustrates the significance of character names in Jong's works.

Johnson, Diane. "Should Novels Have a Message?: Joan Didion, Bertha Harris, and Erica Jong." In her *Terrorists and Novelists*, pp. 124-33. New York: Alfred A. Knopf, Inc., 1975.
> Discussion of the question of messages in novels, using *How to Save Your Own Life* as an example of a novel that "resembles in every way the ramblings of the deserted friend who has taken to the tape recorder and submitted the unedited transcript . . . ."

Kemp, Peter. "Moll Flounders." *The Listener* 104, No. 2685 (30 October 1980): 588-89.
> Negative assessment of *Fanny*.

Review of *At the Edge of the Body*, by Erica Jong. *Kirkus Reviews* XLVII, No. 3 (1 February 1979): 189.
> Assesses the poems in *At the Edge of the Body* as "glib, the work of an imitative, if intelligent, sensibility," and asserts that Jong "exerts her personal charm to make us accept second-rate work."

Review of *Serenissima: A Novel of Venice*, by Erica Jong. *Kirkus Reviews* LV, No. 4 (15 February 1987): 245-46.
> Responds negatively to *Serenissima*.

Kronsky, Betty. "Eat, Darling, Eat!" *The Village Voice* XVI, No. 35 (2 September 1971): 23.
> Positive assessment of *Fruits and Vegetables*.

Review of *Ordinary Miracles,* by Erica Jong. *Publisher's Weekly* 224, No. 7 (12 August 1983): 62.
    Mixed assessment of *Ordinary Miracles.*

Additional coverage of Jong's life and career is contained in the following sources published by Gale Research: *Authors in the News,* **Vol. 1;** *Contemporary Authors,* **Vols. 73-76;** *Contemporary Authors New Revision Series,* **Vol. 26;** *Contemporary Literary Criticism,* **Vols. 4, 6, 8, 18;** *Dictionary of Literary Biography,* **Vols. 2, 5, 28; and** *Major 20th-Century Writers.*

Martin Luther King, Jr.

1929-1968

American orator and essayist.

The following entry provides an overview of King's career.

INTRODUCTION

King was the leader of the civil rights movement in the United States during the 1950s and 1960s. His nonviolent approach to social reform and political activism, characterized by mass marches and large gatherings designed to demonstrate both the widespread acceptance of the tenets of civil rights and the barbarism of those who opposed them, contrasted with the confrontational methods espoused by Malcolm X and the Nation of Islam. King's *Letter from Birmingham City Jail* (1963) and the 1963 speech in which he declared "I Have a Dream" are considered the written landmarks of the movement. Today they are counted among history's great statements of human rights.

Biographical Information

King was born in Atlanta, Georgia, and was raised in a middle-class family. Following the lead of his father and grandfathers, he pursued a theological education. He studied the works of Walter Rauschenbusch, who contended that the church must work to undo social injustices, and those of Mohandas K. Gandhi, who espoused a philosophy of nonviolence. In the fall of 1951 he began his doctoral studies at Boston University and received his Ph. D. in systematic theology in 1955. That same year he rose to prominence in the civil rights movement by organizing a protest in support of Rosa Parks, a black woman who was arrested in Alabama for sitting in a "whites only" section of a public bus. Near the end of 1962 he began working to desegregate Birmingham, Alabama. His leadership produced an agreement with the Justice Department that led to the desegregation of lunch counters, restrooms, fitting rooms, and drinking fountains. In 1963 King helped plan a massive march on Washington, D.C., where an estimated 250,000 people were on hand to hear him present his famous "I Have a Dream" speech. In 1964 King received the Nobel Peace Prize. His campaign for voting rights, concentrated in Selma, Alabama, was met with violence from both police and civilians and resulted in President Lyndon Johnson signing the 1965 Voting Rights Act into law. King continued his social campaigns until April 4, 1968, when he was assassinated by James Earl Ray in Memphis, Tennessee.

Major Works

King's written works reflect his heritage in the traditions of the southern black church as well as his knowledge of

western philosophy. In *Why We Can't Wait* (1964), an account of his efforts to desegregate Birmingham, and *Where Do We Go from Here?* (1967), his response to the Black Power movement, King utilizes the Israelites' exodus from Egypt as a metaphor for the civil rights movement and suggests nonviolent solutions to the problem of social injustice. King further implements biblical theology, along with the philosophies of Gandhi and Georg Wilhelm Friedrich Hegel, in *Stride toward Freedom* (1958), a discussion of the events leading up to the Montgomery bus boycott. In his "I Have a Dream" speech, King paints a vision of a "promised land" of justice and racial equality. In the celebrated *Letter from Birmingham City Jail*, a commentary directed at his critics, King again displays his sermonic style and use of biblical allusions and rhetoric. Reminiscent of St. Paul's writings, the *Letter* has been described by Stephen Oates as "a classic in protest literature, the most elegant and learned expression of the goals and philosophy of the nonviolent movement ever written." Wesley T. Mott also commends King for harnessing "the profound emotional power of the old Negro sermon for purposes of social action."

Critical Reception

Although often praised for their emotional power and widespread appeal, King's writings have been faulted for relying too heavily on rhetorical flourishes and for not offering concrete solutions to the social, political, and economic problems they address. In a review of *Where Do We Go from Here?* Andrew Kopkind commented that although King had worthy goals, he had "no real notion of how they are to be attained, or to what they may lead." In addition, nearly twenty-five years after his death, Clayborne Carson—who had been engaged by King's widow, Coretta Scott King, to compile a collection of her husband's writings—announced that King may have plagiarized parts of his doctoral dissertation and other writings. These disclosures prompted scores of newspaper editorials and other responses arguing that the allegations had no bearing on King's contributions to the civil rights movement. In 1990 a *New York Times* editorial stated that King's "achievement glows unchallenged through the present shadow, [his] courage was not copied; and there was no plagiarism in his power."

PRINCIPAL WORKS

"A Comparison of the Conceptions of God in the Thinking of Paul Tillich and Henry Nelson Wieman" (dissertation)   1955

Stride toward Freedom: The Montgomery Story   (nonfiction)   1958

The Measure of a Man   (meditations and essays)   1959

"I Have a Dream"   (speech)   1963

Letter from Birmingham City Jail   (nonfiction)   1963; also published as *Letter from Birmingham Jail*, 1968

Strength to Love   (sermons)   1963

"Unwise and Untimely?"   (letters)   1963

A Martin Luther King Treasury   (sermons, speeches, and essays)   1964

"Nobel Prize Lecture"   (speech)   1964

Why We Can't Wait   (letter and essays)   1964

"A Time to Break the Silence"   (speech)   1967

Where Do We Go from Here: Chaos or Community?   (nonfiction)   1967

"I Have A Dream": The Quotations of Martin Luther King, Jr.   (speech excerpts)   1968

*"I See the Promised Land"   (speech)   1968

The Trumpet of Conscience   (broadcasts)   1968

We Shall Live in Peace: The Teachings of Martin Luther King, Jr.   (juvenilia and speech excerpts)   1968

The Wisdom of Martin Luther King in His Own Words   (meditations and sermons)   1968

A Martin Luther King Reader   (speeches and essays)   1969

Speeches about Vietnam   (speeches)   1969

Words and Wisdom of Martin Luther King   (meditations and speech excerpts)   1970

Speeches of Martin Luther King, Jr.   (speeches)   1972

Loving Your Enemies, Letter from Birmingham Jail, Dec-

laration of Independence from the War in Vietnam (letter and speeches)   1981

The Words of Martin Luther King, Jr.   (meditations and speeches)   1983

Testament of Hope: The Essential Writings of Martin Luther King, Jr.   (essays, speeches, sermons, and interviews)   1986

The Papers of Martin Luther King, Jr., Volume One: Called to Serve, January 1929-June 1951   (letters, student papers)   1992

*This was King's last speech, delivered on April 3, 1968—the day before his assassination.

CRITICISM

Martin Duberman   (essay date 1969)

[*Duberman is an American educator and historian. In the following essay, he praises King's* Where Do We Go from Here? *for summarizing the "conflicts within the civil rights movement" but faults King's suggested solutions as either too general or impractical.*]

In terms of character alone Martin Luther King is a phenomenon. He learned long ago that white hatred of Negroes reflects white, not Negro, deformities, and this has allowed him to feel compassion for the oppressors as well as the oppressed, to grow in strength even while surrounded by vilification. But recently the personal attacks on King have come from less traditional sources and must therefore have proved a greater challenge to his equanimity. Some of the advocates of Black Power and of black nationalism have begun to treat King's insistence on nonviolence as a prehistoric relic, and to mock King himself, with his appeals to religion, to patience and to conscience, as an irrelevancy. Their scorn has been modified in recent months by King's outspoken stand against our policy in Vietnam, but ironically that same stand has brought denunciation from a different quarter in the Negro community—from the established civil rights forces led by Roy Wilkins, Ralph Bunche and Whitney Young.

Faced with abuse on all sides, King has not only remained temperate but has continued to seek reconciliation—both within the Negro community and also interms of a larger alliance with disaffected whites. At the same time, he has continued to speak his mind, refusing to let pleas for tactical caution obscure the imperative responsibility he feels (which every citizen should feel) to apply ethical standards to international as well as domestic questions. To have managed all this in the face of heavy pressures and wounding accusations bespeaks a character of rare stability, breadth and integrity. What a pity he will never be our President.

King's new book, **Where Do We Go from Here?,** is his attempt to summarize the recent conflicts within the civil rights movement, to consider the larger context, both national and international, which helps to account for these conflicts, and finally, to suggest possible lines for action.

King is far more successful, it seems to me, in dealing with the first two of these considerations than with the third, in part because of his tendency when speaking of the future to substitute rhetoric for specificity, in part because of the difficulties of analyzing this complex, appalling moment in our nation's history. That King succeeds as well as he does is additional tribute to the unruffled intelligence of this unendingly impressive American.

The book begins with the question "Where are we?" King, in answering it, makes some subtle and needed distinctions. He rightly insists, first of all, that the disruption of the civil rights movement cannot be explained, as it so often is, by resort to pat answers. The simple equation which has the white backlash growing solely out of Watts and Black Power is inadequate. The hard truth is that the decrease in white sympathy preceded those developments. With Selma and the Voting Rights Act, one phase of the civil rights movement ended—the easy phase—where white sympathy could be readily engaged against the outright brutalities of Southern life. But as King puts it, "To stay murder is not the same thing as to ordain brotherhood." Public indignation against the Bull Connors was achieved far more easily than was the follow-up commitment to eradicate discrimination in housing, jobs and schools—in other words, to establish equal rather than improved opportunities for Negroes.

White America showed its reluctance about equality before Watts and before the emergence of Black Power, though these developments have since served as convenient excuses for still further delays. The reluctance showed in polls which indicated that 50 per cent of white Americans would object to having a Negro as a neighbor and 88 per cent to having their teenage child date a Negro. It showed in the refusal to implement vigorously civil rights legislation—a refusal which has left segregation the over-whelming pattern of our schools (84.1 per cent in the 11 Southern states), which has left Negro voter registration in Virginia, Mississippi, Louisiana and Georgia still under 50 per cent (and barely above it in four other Southern states), and which has made a mockery of open-occupancy and equal job opportunity legislation. In short, only a small minority of whites are yet authentically committed to equality, and it is this, not Negro "irresponsibility," which has prevented greater progress. The urban riots and the slogan of Black Power, as King says, "are not the causes of white resistance, they are consequences of it."

Though King's indictment of white America is as severe as it is justified, he follows it, curiously, with some optimistic predictions. The line of progress, he points out, is never straight: setbacks, disappointments, even retreats mark every movement for substantive social change. The current doldrums in which the civil rights movement finds itself were both predictable and natural, and Negroes should not, therefore, fall into pessimism or defeatism. The Negro has already won a great deal, King argues, especially in the intangible realm of heightened self-respect, and "no matter how many obstacles persist the Negro's forward march can no longer be stopped."

King bases this prediction on prescriptions which may not be filled. First, he advises black people to increase their efforts at amassing additional political and economic power. Here he agrees with the advocates of Black Power even while objecting to the way the Stokely Carmichaels have substituted for programs, slogans which imply separatism and violence.

Yet when King himself comes to spelling out a program for pooling black resources, economic and political, its stock generalities prove vulnerably close to Carmichael's sloganeering. He calls on the Negro to use his buying power to force policy changes among business concerns, but he gives no specifics as to which forms of selective buying might prove fruitful or which businesses might be the most useful targets. Likewise, when he calls on Negroes to develop "habits of thrift and techniques of wise investment," he says nothing about how these qualities may be inculcated, about where the average Negro is to find the money with which to make wise investments, or, finally, whether such middle-class "virtues" are indeed those to be highly prized and cultivated.

King does not believe that the Negro community, even if it can be brought to unified effort, will by itself have sufficient strength to achieve its goals. He understands well the bitterness and frustration out of which many Negroes, especially younger ones, have turned to black nationalism and separatism in a search for structure and purpose in their lives. But the nationalist path, King insists, can lead only to disaster; it represents what Bayard Rustin has called the "no-win" policy, the mistaken notion that there can be a separate black road to fulfillment outside the main stream of American life. What is needed instead, King argues, is a continuing (perhaps one might better say, reinvigorated) coalition between Negroes and whites, a coalition which will be strong enough to exert real pressure on the major parties to become more responsive to the needs of the poor. Only such a coalition can requisition the billions of dollars needed to correct the hard-core inequalities from which the American poor, white and black, suffer.

King's position seems to me impeccable in theory, but it suffers, as he himself must realize, from the lack of available allies for the coalition he advocates. He speaks, for example, of a large group of poor whites who in reality share common grievances with poor Negroes. But reality, as we all know, is only one, and probably one of the weaker, wellsprings of human behavior. The real question is: Can the poor whites in America be brought to recognize their common interest with poor Negroes, or will the transcending power of racism continue to prevent such a merger? Historically, the evidence is not encouraging; with the brief and limited exception of the Populist era, poor whites have put race before all other considerations—including self-interest.

And yet what other than coalition politics can King recommend? Feeling as he does that the American Negro's future rests in his own country—not in Africa, not in a union of the dark people of the world based on some mystical abstraction like *négritude*—King must then find a way to encourage American Negroes to believe that they in fact have a future (that is, an equitable one) in this country. The most hopeful path continues to be the old one of coalition politics, and it is that path to which King adheres. But at this moment in our national life the brutal fact is that coalition politics is a slim hope only.

This is a fact that King, for both tactical and temperamental reasons, cannot afford to acknowledge. Its admission is impossible tactically because it might precipitate the Negro community into the arms of black nationalism, and this, in King's view, would mean a dead end. Its admission is impossible temperamentally because King's personal optimism is deeply ingrained. He believes obstacles are always surmountable, given sufficient will and faith. He believes American racism can and will be overcome, that the goal of "genuine intergroup and interpersonal living" can be reached, though the way be difficult.

Since the grounds for such hope have in reality become tenuous and since King chooses, for reasons of tactics and temperament, not to acknowledge that fact fully, he is forced to fall back on rhetoric as a substitute for argument, to rely on eloquence to camouflage the lack of supporting data. Thus his discussion of future prospects contains more exhortation than sustained analysis: "there is nothing to keep us from remolding a recalcitrant status quo with bruised hands until we have fashioned it into a brotherhood"; "dark and demonic responses will be removed only as men are possessed by the invisible inner law which etches on their hearts the conviction that all men are brothers and that love is mankind's most potent weapon for personal and social transformation."

Exhortation, alas, even were it less pious, will not be enough to overcome the complacency and racism of the American majority or to restore the faith of the disheart-ened, alienated minority. It is far from clear what, if anything, can. The national prognosis remains poor until something—probably only an event of catastrophic proportions such as a major war or depression—plunges us to a level of despair, and thus of self-confrontation, which could, ultimately, lead to renewed health.

Martin Duberman, "Martin Luther King Jr.'s 'Where Do We Go From Here: Chaos or Community?'" in his The Uncompleted Past, *Random House, 1969, pp. 181-87.*

James H. Smylie   (essay date 1970)

[*In the following essay, Smylie examines King's use of biblical interpretation and references in his writings and sermons.*]

The purpose of the following analysis is to explore the exodus theme in King's interpretation of the New and Old Testaments. Drawing upon the religious traditions of most Americans, including those brought from Africa, King defined the chosen people, oppression under this world's pharaohs, and the promised land in the light of his interpretation and acceptance of the radical demands of Jesus Christ upon his life.

Ironically, with regard to the Negro's quest for identity in America, the theme of exodus and deliverance from bondage comes out of the Hebrew experience of slavery in Africa. Not only so, but the exodus has been a dominant theme in the way white Americans have identified themselves. For white Christians, the Bible has been the rule of faith and life. It has been natural for Americans to think of themselves as chosen people and to interpret development of the New World, apart from the political and religious degradation of the Old, in terms of a Mount Zion in the wilderness. Similarly oppressed immigrant groups in the nineteenth century looked upon America as the promised land of economic as well as political opportunity. The exodus theme has been wed to eighteenth-century conceptions of liberty and justice embedded in the Declaration of Independence. At the time of the American Revolution, patriots thought of their deliverance out of the land of Britain as out of the house of bondage, and even considered using an engraving of Moses and the children of Israel being delivered from the Pharaoh's army at the Red Sea as the Great Seal of the United States. But in the conquest for this promised land there was sin in the camp. Black slavery was America's Achan—spoil which spelled trouble as an American dilemma. The Constitutional compromises following the Revolution suggested that America might mean liberty and justice for white Americans only—not for all. For the Jew especially the exodus has been a vital part of self-understanding. Until the establishment of modern Israel, Jews thought of themselves as in exile, as wanderers over the face of the earth since the fall of Jerusalem. But in the nineteenth century, Jewish immigrants to America, under the leadership of the remarkable Isaac Meyer Wise, began to interpret diaspora in terms of challenge, not punishment. They thought of the Jewish mission as that of spreading the true knowledge and worship of God, of achieving liberty and justice for all—not as the establishment of a new Jewish state. Jewish success

---

An objective assessment of Martin Luther King, Jr.:

If the world is at all capable of candor, if the need by blacks and whites to apotheosize Martin Luther King (if for dissimilar reasons) does not exclude objective assessment, then it must surely be admitted that his nobility, his charisma, derived principally from the fact that, initially, he moralized the plight of the American black in simplistic and Manichaean terms whose veracity the enlightened Southern white was grudgingly compelled to concede and the Northern white was generally relieved, if not delighted, to champion. He was the echo chamber of the racially oppressed but an echo chamber whose reverberations were rounder, more intelligible, and much more polite than the raw cries that it transformed. Whether dreaming on the steps of the Lincoln Memorial or triumphally announcing, at the conclusion of the Selma-Montgomery march, that black people could no longer be turned around by Southern intimidation, Martin's message—in the language of the prophets and the revivalists—never directly threatened, probably never really disconcerted, and always, until near the end, evoked, in its aftermath of white guilt and black self-pity, deeply pleasurable emotions.

David L. Lewis, in his King: A Critical Biography, *Praeger Publishers, 1970.*

in America has turned the place of exile into a promised land. Instead of being Shadrachs, Meshachs, and Abednegoes, Jews have experienced a new kind of Babylonian captivity in white America's gilded ghettoes, and have become identified with America's oppressors.

There is irony in the fact that the exodus theme is about the bondage of a people under Africans. There is also irony in the fact that Martin Luther King should be so effective in dealing with the oppression of Africans in America in an idiom which has meant so much to the majority of white Americans.

King did not want to be like Moses. According to his persuasive renditions of the gospel song at Baptist conventions at the age of four or five, King wanted to be more and more like Jesus. The childlike wish was prophetic of the man. It offers a clue to understanding King's later hermeneutical principles. A descendant of slaves, reared, and educated within America's Negro community, King shared with that community its religious memories and expectations, and moved from his New Testament understanding of Jesus to an understanding of the Old Testament theme of exodus. The grandson and son of Baptist ministers, and then an ordained Baptist minister himself, King did his interpretation within the milieu of the Afro-American community. While the debate over what remained of the slave's African heritage continues, it seems clear that the shock of alienation was so great that the majority of blacks had to establish some kind of personal and corporate identity through those religious and political categories in the master's culture. While the white man taught the slave submissiveness out of the Pauline corpus, the black was learning other lessons.

This is movingly illustrated as early as 1794 in the address of Richard Allen to those who kept blacks and approved the practice of slavery in the eighteenth century. Allen, the first bishop of the African Methodist Episcopal Church, reminded Americans of a revolutionary generation that God himself was the "first pleader of the cause of slaves" ["An Address To Those Who Keep Slaves and Approve the Practice," in *The Life Experience and Gospel Labors of the Rt. Rev. Richard Allen,* 1960]. Because slavery is hateful in his sight, God, the "avenger of slaves," destroyed Pharaoh and his princes. The black preacher cautioned white Americans that they were behaving like the Pharaohs who despised the needs of feeble Israelites. But, while admitting how natural it is for slaves to hate oppressors, Allen reminded American blacks that hate was forbidden God's chosen people. "The meek and humble Jesus," he wrote, "the great pattern of humanity and every other virtue that can adorn and dignify men, hath commanded to love our enemies." Blacks were to do good to those who hated and used them spitefully. They were to give thanks to God for removing anger and bitterness from their hearts, and for delivering them from the desire to shed the blood of other men. It is not known whether King knew of Allen's combination of the exodus theme and the admonition of Jesus, but Allen's address indicates how old the approach is in the Negro community.

Obviously, the black experience in darkest America has involved considerable hatred, bitterness, and increasing hostility. From the beginning, black life was "one continual cry," to use David Walker's phrase, against American pharaohs. In the nineteenth century, Harriet Tubman was considered a Moses for her dangerous work on the underground railroad. Spirituals took on fresh cogency as blacks sang "Go down, Moses," or "Joshua fit de battle ob Jericho," or

> O Mary, doan you weep, doan you moan,
> Pharaoh's army got drownded.

They signaled one another with "Steal away to Jesus," as some of the adventuresome ones were "bound for the promised land" in Canada. When subjugation under chattel slavery was replaced with exploitation under segregation, Marcus Garvey expressed the growing frustration of Negroes in the third decade of the twentieth century. He became a Moses, with a difference. Garvey celebrated blackness in his Universal Negro Improvement Association. He wished to take blacks black to Africa, the promised land, on the Black Star Steamship Line, blessed by the Black Madonna and the Black Christ. Obviously, slave revolts and race riots in American history indicate that violence, often sublimated in spirituals, expressed the blacks' truest feelings about the dominant majority. And as frustration has grown, blacks have turned from Christianity as manifested in white and black America toward such ideologies as Communism. Langston Hughes maintained that Jesus had been sold to "Rockefeller's church" and wrote

> You ain't no good no more. . . .
> And step on the gas, Christ
> Don't be so slow about moving;
> Move.

Now King shared this legacy with the past. As a young black man himself, he felt the frustrations of blacks; but he rejected Communism as an alternative because it was a "metaphysical materialism," an "ethical relativism," and a "strangulating totalitarianism" [*Stride toward Freedom*]. His alternative was a politicizing of love, of the meekness and humility of Jesus. To be sure, it was from Gandhi's Salt March to the Sea which challenged Britain's imperial lion that King learned to appreciate the awesome power of nonviolent resistance to evil. Gandhi taught him that Christian love, part of the confessional life of his black tradition, was applicable to America and would be the instrument of his people's deliverance. But Christ, not Gandhi, supplied the spirit and motivation of his movement. King was fond of interpreting the word "love" in its biblical context. Following Anders Nygren's *Agape and Eros,* he made distinctions in the several words employed in the New Testament. *Eros* meant, in Platonic philosophy, the yearning of the soul for the divine, and in contemporary usage, a romantic love. *Philia* meant an intimate and reciprocal relation between two friends based upon mutuality. King emphasized *agape*, the "love of God operating in the human heart." This love shows that all life is interrelated. The Christian must seek the neighbor's good because of his need, and the enemy's good to restore and preserve human community. This love, King argued, involves forgiveness and reconciliation and is motivated by God's love made known on the cross: "Father, forgive them; for they know not what they do." The crucifixion represents, on the one hand, the sordid weakness of man at his worst, and on the other, the "unlimited power of God," the "magnificent symbol of love conquering hate, and of light overcoming darkness [*Strength to Love*].

Taking this imperative seriously, King was able to adopt and adapt to advantage a method of nonviolent resistance, and interpreted the biblical witness for his followers. Some admonitions of Jesus' he took quite literally. When, for example, Jesus said to Peter, "Put up thy sword," Jesus, according to King, was demanding of Peter and the other disciples a better way. It was not a cowardly command. Jesus' call was to resist evil in such a way that those resisting would *avoid internal violence of the spirit* as well as physical violence, and would suffer without retaliation. Jesus called for a resistance to the forces of evil which would not defeat or humiliate the humanity of oppressors caught in the evil. This was the pattern of God's own love, a combination of toughmindedness and tenderheartedness. He interpreted other words of Jesus in a different way. In dealing with Jesus' warning, "I have not come to bring peace, but a sword," King denied that Jesus meant a physical weapon. Rather, concentrating upon the word "peace," he suggested that Jesus intended to challenge the old shape of things with the creative demands of the Kingdom of God, to awaken a *dead passivity with living, concerned love*. For King it was only with the sword of love that the black could open the "boil" of exploitation with which America was afflicted and heal the infection. For King, love was the only pragmatic approach to black bondage in America. But the literal sword of violence was another matter. "All who take the sword will perish by the sword," he warned his hearers during the Montgomery bus boycott, in which nonviolent resistance was first employed. This was true for persons and peoples. The old law of an eye for an eye leaves everybody blind, and history is cluttered with the wreckage of nations that failed to follow Christ's command to love. It was through *agape* manifested in nonviolent resistance to evil that King hoped to cut the endless circle of bitterness, hate, and violence, counter-bitterness, counter-hate, and counter-violence.

In a remarkable paraphrase of Paul's letter to Corinth, King addressed American Christians:

> Calvary is a telescope through which we look into the long vista of eternity and see the love of God breaking into time. . . . In a world depending on force, coercive tyranny, and bloody violence, you are challenged to follow the way of love. You will then discover that unarmed love is the most powerful force in all the world [*Strength to Love*].

In this love King laid hold of one of the most important traditions of black America, turned it into an instrument of social change through nonviolent resistance, and confounded American pharaohs dependent to a large extent upon the same biblical tradition for self-identity. Moreover, King gave the basic clue for understanding his interpretation of those biblical passages which have to do with oppression and the Pharaohs, the promised land, and God's chosen people.

It is remarkable that King as a biblical interpreter alluded so infrequently in his formal writings to the Exodus narrative. In only one place did he deal with the narrative at length—and then in the most natural way—when he spoke of the dead Egyptians along the shores of the Red Sea. He was not interested, obviously, in scholarly treatments of textual variants, in the form, place, expression, and scope of texts, or, for that matter, in the differences between his world view and the world view of Hebrew people. As a matter of fact, King assumed that the exodus is an archetypal experience, and that the experience of the Hebrew people in Egypt was similar to that of blacks in America. Exodus supplied King with the metaphorical language which allowed him to interpret black experience, just as the black experience allowed him to understand something of what it must have been like in Egypt under Pharaoh. But King allowed *agape* to inform his interpretation at every point along the way.

Egypt, according to King, symbolized evil in the form of "humiliating oppression, ungodly exploitation, and crushing domination," while Pharaoh symbolized dominating oppressors and exploiters [*Strength to Love*]. King was, to be sure, preoccupied with his ministry to blacks in America. But from the very beginning of that ministry, his sympathies were as wide as humanity. The Bible, he wrote, witnesses to a thrilling story of how Moses stood in Pharaoh's court centuries ago and cried, "Let my people go." But the story of Israelites in Egypt was only the "opening chapter in a continuing story." The present struggle in the United States and throughout the world was only a "later chapter in the same story" [*Where Do We Go from Here?*]. There is, therefore, no discontinuity in the early event remembered and the existential situation from which all people in this world's Egypts seek deliverance. From the earliest days of his ministry, King's interpretation of those oppressed embraced, not only his own blacks, but all other enslaved people. Thus, those in Latin America, Asia, and Africa who had suffered from captivity were, indeed, breaking loose from the "Egypt of colonialism and imperialism." In all of these areas, some "courageous Moses" had arisen to plead for the freedom and justice of the people. Because of the liberation of people all over the world, King considered his obligations to the oppressed in America all the more urgent. The point is, however, that he interpreted Egypt as involving more people than simply those of his own minority. Moreover, his acceptance of the radical spirit and motivation of love allowed him to look with sympathy upon pharaohs and Egyptians. Oppressors are always "derivative victims" of their oppression, and King called attention to the fact that in America, the oppression of blacks had meant the financial, intellectual, and moral impoverishment of whites [*Why We Can't Wait*].

There is another continuity in addition to that which involves oppression in Egypt. Oppressed people will not put up with bondage forever. But when they seek deliverance, pharaohs and Egyptians act in a similar manner to prevent liberation. King experienced what Moses experienced in Pharaoh's court when he went before the City Commissioners of Montgomery—"pharaohs of the South," he called them—during the bus boycott. The pharaohs of this world will not give an inch. What the Exodus narrative illustrated is that evil is recalcitrant and determined, and when challenged, attempts to hold its power with fanatical resistance. When the pressure is increased, pharaohs will say, "Wait." Then pharaohs will say, "Go slower." What the pharaohs mean, according to King's interpretation of Exodus, is "Never." Pharaohs may try tokenism, but this is only a way to end pressure, not to begin the process of liberation. King was fond of developing this theme. When the demands continue, pharaohs will attempt to divide and dissolve the cohesion of the malcontents. King had to face this problem asthe Civil Rights movement began to waver with the emergence of black power advocates in the mid-nineteen-sixties. "The Pharaohs," he warned his followers, "had a favorite and effective strategy to keep their slaves in bondage: keep them fighting among themselves. The divide-and-conquer technique has been a potent weapon in the arsenal of oppression." "But," King encouraged, "when slaves unite, the Red Seas of history open and the Egypts of slavery crumble" [***Where Do We Go From Here?***]. King was especially incensed with the way in which American pharaohs attempted to force American blacks to make bricks without straw. He believed himself in a struggle for opportunity. What he was told by whites was that blacks ought to pull themselves up by their own bootstraps, following the pattern of other immigrant groups. King preached that this was a cruel jest. Blacks were not immigrants. They had been brought to America in bondage. Moreover, other minorities did not have to overcome the virus of racism which plagued American life. And the bootstrap methodology would work only if blacks had shoes. So far, the American pharaohs were satisfied to send the Negro into the wilderness without such help.

Given the mounting frustration of American blacks, King showed amazing sympathy for Pharaoh and his Egyptians. His one sermon on Exodus was on the text 14:30, "And Israel saw the Egyptians dead upon the sea shore." It is worthy of special attention because it illustrates cogently the way in which King interpreted the Old Testament with the use of the New. Pharaoh will use every means to keep Israelites in bondage. After he is forced to let them go, he will even pursue in order to enslave them again. The text describes the children of Israel looking back at the poor drowned Egyptians lying here and there upon the seashore. Pharaoh had employed legal maneuvers, economic reprisals, and even physical violence to keep Israel in bondage. Now that the ordeal was over Israelites could rejoice. For King, the point of the story was not the dead Egyptians upon the seashore. "The meaning of this story is not found in the drowning of Egyptian soldiers, for no one should rejoice at the death or defeat of a human being," he wrote. Rather, this story symbolized "the death of evil and of inhuman oppression and unjust exploitation" [***Strength to Love***]. There is something in the very nature of the universe, King held, which assists goodness in its perennial struggle with evil. "A Red Sea passage in history ultimately brings the forces of goodness to victory, and the closing of the same water marks the doom and destruction of the forces of evil" [***Strength to Love***]. This interpretation is inaccord with King's view of *agape,* and Jesus' teaching that excluded vindictiveness

King addressing a crowd at Chicago's Soldier Field.

and vengeance. After the Selma march in 1965, when the provocation had been especially great, King spoke and fell easily into the use of the exodus metaphor. "Yes," he intoned in his rich voice, "we are on the move and no wave of racism can stop us." While he accused pharaohs and Egyptians of all the stratagems of oppressors, he repeated that the purpose of the march was not to defeat or humiliate the white man. He sought, not the triumph of the black man over the white, but understanding, friendship, and the victory of "man as man."

King did not use the idiom of exodus to describe the struggle for freedom simply as a class struggle; he interpreted in theological terms the struggle of all people seeking liberation. To be sure, he referred to "something" in the very nature of the universe which champions the cause of the oppressed; but for him, God is the Lord of history and the active agent in the cause. Here the Baptist preacher faced a problem—the passivity of black Americans, particularly in black churches, used to following Jesus, "meek and humble," without asserting themselves. This was due, according to King, to a perverted interpretation of Calvinism which left all to God. Countering this enervating theological approach, King made use of the Exodus narrative. "When Moses strove to lead the Israelites to the Promised Land, God made it clear that he would not do for them what they could do for themselves," he warned. " 'And the Lord said unto Moses, Wherefore criest thou unto me? speak unto the children of israel, that they go forward' " [*Strength to Love*]. But, asserting the other side of the paradox, King confessed that all was of God. The God of the universe struggles for and with the oppressed. God remembers his people in Egypt. He gives the inner recourse to the oppressed to bear their Egypts, to break their bonds and to undertake the journey through the wilderness. He is the one who insures the victory of good over evil, truth over falsehood. Pharaoh may exploit the children of Israel—*"nevertheless afterward!"* Pilate may yield to the crowd and crucify Christ—*"nevertheless afterward!"* It is God who gives the *afterward*—the promised land.

King's interpretation of the promised land and God's chosen people is informed by his Christian humanism. As is clear from the preceding analysis, he did not see the promised land in terms of a territorial imperative. For Harriet Tubman the promised land was Canada; for Marcus Garvey it was Africa free from colonial government. For black Muslims, it has been several southern states, and morerecently, for black nationalists, it has involved political hegemony of urban ghettoes. For King the promised land was an expression of a world-wide vision. He employed it many times. In encouraging blacks during the bus boycott, he told them to walk and not get weary. They could count on a "great camp meeting in the promised land of freedom and justice" ["Out of the Long Night of Segregation," *The Presbyterian Outlook*, Feb. 10, 1958]. They were moving through the "Red Sea of injustice" [*Strength to Love*] and into the "promised land of integration and freedom" [*Why We Can't Wait*]. The peoples of the world were moving toward the "promised land of economic and cultural stability" [*Where Do We Go From Here?*]. The phrase was a metaphor which embraced all people and the whole world. King summarized this dream for the United States in his speech at the Lincoln Memorial during the Washington march, August, 1963. In an address given just before his death, he renewed and revised his dream to include the whole world. His concern for Vietnam was, therefore, not new. It should not have come as any surprise that he should have championed the antiwar cause, not only because of his nonviolent approach to life's problems, but because he attacked all racism, militarism, and materialism. King often quoted Amos. The promised land was the world in which justice would run down like waters, and righteousness like a mighty stream. America's third revolution—the Negro revolution—was to lead to such a promised land.

There is a universalism in King's conception of the promised land. There is still a particularism to his definition of God's chosen people. God calls people to serve him in the struggle against oppression, exploitation, and domination, through doing justly and seeking righteousness. Who are the chosen people? Being a member of the Christian church, King was unwilling to disregard and discard it. But he was also unwilling to identify Christian institutions with God's chosen ones. Nowhere did he express more poignantly his disappointment with the church than in his *Letter from Birmingham Jail,* answering Christian and Jewish clergymen who thought his demonstrations were "unwise and untimely." They pleaded for honest and open negotiations on racial issues in Birmingham, as though Negro rights were negotiable. To King, they were acting like Pharaoh's magicians—and were giving another indication of the churches' aiding in the maintenance of the race-caste system in American society. The church was much in evidence in Birmingham, housed in massive religious education buildings. Members of these churches had "blemished and scarred" the body of Christ through "social neglect and through fear of being nonconformists," and the judgment of God was upon the churches, as it had been upon Pharaoh. Perhaps, King mused, "I must turn my faith to the inner spiritual church, the church within the church, as the true *ekklesia* and the hope of the world." He thanked God for members of the church whose witness during the struggle for freedom was like "spiritual salt" which preserved the true meaning of the gospel of Christ in troubled times. The churches were full of "un-christian christians" and was not to be identified with the chosen people [*Why We Can't Wait*].

God's chosen people had a special responsibility to deliver the oppressed from the Egypts of oppression. King, like Richard Allen before him, maintained that the oppressed had a special place in God's economy. He believed that the black American had such a special responsibility. In his address to students in Oslo, when he was in Norway to receive the Nobel Peace Prize in 1964, he employed the biblical imagery. "We have left the dusty soils of Egypt and crossed a Red Sea whose waters had for years been hardened by a long and piercing winter of massive resistance," he said in rehearsing the history of his movement. "But before we reach the majestic shores of the promised land, there is a frustrating and bewildering wilderness ahead." Shortly thereafter when Negroes raised a cry for black power, King interpreted this in terms of the disappointments of the wilderness, and voiced a challenge to the American blacks. In *Where Do We Go from Here?*, he wrote:

> Let us therefore not think of our movement as one that seeks to integrate the Negro into all the existing values of American society. Let us be those creative dissenters who will call our beloved nation to a higher destiny, to a new plateau of compassion, to a more noble expression of humaneness.
>
> We are superbly equipped to do this. We have been seared in the flames of suffering. We have known the agony of being the underdog. We have learned from our have-not status that it profits a nation little to gain the whole world of means and lose in the end, its own soul. We must have a passion for peace formed out of wretchedness and the misery of war. Giving our ultimate allegiance to the empire of justice, we must be that colony of dissenters seeking to imbue our nation with the ideals of a higher and nobler order. So in dealing with our particular dilemma, we will challenge the nation to deal with its larger dilemma.
>
> This is the challenge. If we will dare to meet it honestly, historians in future years will have to say there lived a great people—a black people—who bore their burdens of oppression in the heat of many days and who, through tenacity and creative commitment, injected new meaning into the veins of American life.

Despite this interpretation of the special calling of the black oppressed, King was equally unwilling to identify the black community with God's chosen people. He was aware of stiff-necked Israelites. Moses soon learned that the children of Israel did not always think kindly of their deliverers and in their wilderness ordeal often yearned longingly for the fleshpots of Egypt. King knew that members of the *black bourgeoisie,* serving, as it were, in pharaoh's court, had abdicated responsibility and were as little interested in justice and nonviolent resistance to evil as were their white counterparts. All people are oppressors. Blacks are no exception.

His conception of God's chosen people was directly related to his interpretation of the radical claims of Jesus. God's chosen people are those who have been set free from the bondage of fear, black and white together, and have thus been enabled by the love of God to challenge oppression wherever it may be found. King referred to the fact that the Indians had been able to move against the British only when they had been freed from fear, and he knew that God's people must be freed from fear to march on this world's pharaohs, not away from them. Some of America's blacks were so freed. "It was Jesus of Nazareth that stirred the Negroes to protest with the creative weapon of love," King wrote of the bus boycott. They were able to use this weapon because life was centered on the will and purpose of God. According to King, it is this love for God and devotion to his will that cast out fear. The true Christian belongs to a "colony of Heaven" in which ultimate allegiance is to God. Developing this theme further, he explained how

> . . . hate is rooted in fear, and the only cure for fear-hate is love. . . . If our white brothers are to master fear they must depend not only on their commitment to Christian love but also on the Christlike love which the Negro generates toward them. Only through our adherence to love and non-violence will the fear in the white community be mitigated. A guilt-ridden white minority fears that if the Negro attains power, he will without restraint or pity act to revenge-the accumulated injustices and brutality of the years [*Stride toward Freedom*].

While it was the responsibility of the blacks to show the way, King argued that it was to be black and white together—moved by love, freed from fear, able, as were Shadrach, Meshach, and Abednego, to resist evil, and to seek after justice for all. God's chosen people know that being killed is not the ultimate evil. The ultimate evil, he said, is to be outside God's love. Those inside that love are the true people of God.

On the night before he was assassinated, King described himself as a man who wanted to do God's will. God, he maintained, had allowed him to go up into the mountain. "And I've looked over, and I've seen the Promised Land. I may not get there with you, but I want you to know tonight that we as a people will get to the Promised Land." He was engaged at the time in helping garbage workers in Memphis obtain better wages and working conditions. After King was shot, the editor of *soul force,* journal of the Southern Christian Leadership Conference, changed the allusion. Instead of using metaphors from the Exodus narrative, the editor printed words from Genesis 37:19: "Behold, this dreamer cometh . . . let us slay him. . . . And we shall see what will become of his dreams." The allusion, of course, was to Joseph, not to Moses, to the beginning of Israel's sojourn in bondage, not to the deliverance from Egypt. What comes immediately to mind is the fact that the Joseph narrative had been used in the Hebrew-Christian tradition for theodicy, to assure the faithful that God will bring good out of evil.

For the first time in American history, a President of the United States ordered flags to be flown at half-mast to honor a simple Baptist preacher and leader struck down cruelly in the prime of life. Perhaps this national action was taken as much out of fear as out of respect for the man. To be sure, King drew to himself a great many Americans, white and black, Christians and Jews, who accepted his interpretation of America's problems and his approach to their resolution. But he was despised and rejected by many others. That hostility was undoubtedly inspired and motivated in part because he employed in his rationalization biblical themes and metaphors so important to white America. This was all the more aggravating because he interpreted the Old Testament metaphorsconcerning oppression, pharaohs, and the promised land, through his understanding of the imperative placed upon him by Jesus. King was a disciplined man, but everywhere he went, violence was always a possibility, either from enraged whites or less disciplined blacks unwilling to abide by rules he established for their nonviolent resistance to evil. In the end, that violence destroyed King himself. For a black man so to live out the life of Jesus Christ by turning the other cheek, by his willingness to forgive, not seven times seven, but seventy times seven, and to love the enemy in a struggle for all exploited people, may have been the ultimate insult to whites who thought they had a corner on the favors of Jesus of Nazareth. The unforgivable sin which King committed was to expose the hypocrisy not only of Americans as Americans, but more fundamentally of Americans as Christians.

As a Christian humanist, King's approach to oppression is extremely important in a time when the tendency seems to be toward narrow tribalism on the part of whites and blacks alike, for the feeding of group-ego and group-interest. According to studies, white America, despite professions of Christian love and pledges of liberty and justice for all, moves in the direction of two separate and unequal societies based upon white supremacy and the exploitation of the blacks. The American Jews, not all of whom have been ardent supporters of the black cause, are not excluded from this judgment. Moreover, some Jews in America have grown alarmed at black anti-Semitism, and are suspicious of Americans who do not agree with them on policies having to do with the defense of Israel as a nation state. Since the Six-Day War, one American theologian has accentuated the importance of Israel as the promised land, and has suggested that now the theme of Jewish history is homecoming, not diaspora. Militant blacks, convinced by the white majority that "whitey" does not want reconciliation nor a life of reciprocity with the black, have become more revolutionary. The cry for black power has been aggravated by a "Black Manifesto." James Forman, a type of Moses perhaps more like that found in Exodus, has confronted Christian and Jewish America, beginning symbolically at Riverside Church—Rockefeller's church—and has demanded reparations, the destruction of American institutions, and a new society. Since white America understands violence, some blacks reason, it may be through violence only that they can liberate themselves from oppression and establish their identity as men. King's Christian humanism, based upon the interpretation of the Old Testament through the New, was full of expectation for all men. His dream was not marred by black nationalism or racism, for in Christ, King believed, "there is neither Jew or Greek, there is neither bond nor free, there is neither male nor female; for ye are all one in Christ Jesus. God, who made the world and all things therein . . . made of one blood all nations of men for to dwell on all the face of the earth." King, it appears from his later thought, was beginning to realize that when a people seeks liberty and justice *within* a land of bondage, they may need more than a strategy of nonviolent resistance to evil. The debate over black power forced to the front the clash between what the National Committee of Negro Clergymen call conscience-less power and powerless conscience. In this case, King, true to his interpretation of the biblical message, called for *shared* power for responsible use to meet the plight of blacks in urban slums.

When King accepted the Nobel Peace Prize, he expressed his hope in biblical terms:

> I still believe that one day mankind will bow before the altars of God and be crowned triumphant over war and bloodshed, and nonviolent

redemptive goodwill will proclaim the rule of the land. "And the lion and the lamb shall lie down together and every man shall sit under his own vine and fig tree and none shall be afraid." I still believe that we shall overcome.

He accepted the prize as a trustee on behalf of "all men who love peace and brotherhood."

James H. Smylie, "On Jesus, Pharaohs, and the Chosen People," in Interpretation: A Journal of Bible & Theology, *Vol. XXIV, No. 1, January, 1970, pp. 74-91.*

King as a preacher:

King became a great preacher, but hardly a great theologian. His gifts as a preacher appeared early, as if in the blood that coursed through generation after generation on both sides of his family. Like father, like son: his preaching resonated with an extraordinary black sermonic tradition, and careful study is beginning to suggest the significant impact of specifically Afro-American Christian thought (and not only of Afro-American Christian oratory) on the stronger features of King's own theology. But his genius as a preacher—and as a political leader—rested largely on his peerless ability to blend Euro-American and Afro-American theology and folk religion in a manner that remained firmly rooted in the particularism of his people *and* in the universality without which Christianity loses all meaning.

Eugene D. Genovese, in his "Pilgrim's Progress," The New Republic, *11 May 1992.*

Wesley T. Mott   (essay date 1975)

[*In the following excerpt, Mott assesses* Letter from Birmingham Jail *as an emotion-charged sermon in the tradition of "old-time Negro preaching."*]

[Martin Luther King, Jr.'s *Letter from Birmingham Jail*] is one of the most frequently collected items in college English anthologies and has proved the most popular reading among black and white students in basic literature courses for several years. The success of the *Letter* can be attributed, I think, to the remarkable confluence of three distinct rhetorical traits: King's heritage of the highly emotional Negro preaching tradition; his shrewd sense of political timing and polemical skill; and his conscious literary ability.

In view of King's rich legacy of sermons and speeches, it may seem inappropriate to emphasize the oral tradition behind *Letter from Birmingham Jail.* But the *Letter* has proved to be one of King's most eloquent utterances; and much of its power (and a few of its defects) arises from the same rhetorical elements that he employed in his oral addresses. His written style is only a slightly more formalized version of his platform style. In the *Letter* King retains the emotional power that is the trademark of the Negro sermon while he overcomes the flaws that hinder the utility of the sermon in the political and literary spheres.

The traditional Negro sermon derives largely from the preaching of such evangelists as Whitefield. It aims to arouse the hearer's emotions to the point where he is persuaded to turn to God or to experience God's presence. Althoughloosely based on a Biblical theme, this kind of preaching emphasizes emotional arousal to such a degree that "the theme itself is relatively unimportant" [Bruce A. Rosenberg in *The Art of the American Folk Preacher*, 1970]. Furthermore, because the preacher claims that inspiration for the sermon comes directly from God, he is not concerned with "logical organization." Rhythm and cadence almost unaided achieve the desired effect. One scholar [Rosenberg] notes that "the preacher relies upon stock phrases and passages to fill out the skel[e]ton of the sermon, and develops the message through repetition." The sermon is based, then, on a formulaic method that employs such devices as repetitive refrains, recurrent rhetorical questions, and formalized dialogue and narrative. The rhythm thus established is all-important: "The rhythm is the message; congregations have been moved to ecstasy by the rhythmic chanting of incoherencies" [Rosenberg]. The sermons of Martin Luther King, Jr., are unmistakably part of the tradition of "old-time Negro preaching." His *Letter from Birmingham Jail* draws power from this genre while avoiding its main weakness: a self-contained emotionalism that historically has encouraged the aloofness of blacks from social reform.

"Old-time preaching" is characterized by its lack of concern for logic. [William H. Pipes in *Say Amen, Brother! Old-Time Negro Preaching: A Study in American Frustration*, 1951], nevertheless, identifies a recurrent structural pattern in the sermons: (1) an introduction "to establish a common ground of religious feeling" among the audience or to establish rapport between speaker and audience; (2) a "statement of the text," which, of course, is almost always drawn from the Bible; (3) the "body of the sermon," which consists of repeated emotional climaxes; and (4) the conclusion, which resolves the emotional tension aroused by the sermon by drawing the sinners to God. Pipes's framework shows that the traditional Negro sermon, however much it derives its strength from formulaic repetition, is not mere unartistic incoherency. It justifies our treating the sermons—and, by inference, *Letter from Birmingham Jail*—as an art form.

The *Letter* is essentially a written sermon that both answers charges and exhorts to action. It is a measure of the artistic control that King exerts over the *Letter* that he creates a vivid persona aimed at arousing the sympathy of the audience. The ideal "old-time preacher" is a majestic, imposing figure; but King's projection of the image of a meek, suffering prisoner effectively strikes an appropriate rapport with his "audience." He immediately introduces himself, "confined here in the Birmingham city jail." And yet, despite adversity, he is capable of benevolence and generosity toward those eight clergymen, those "men of genuine good will" who have criticized his protest activities; he hopes his answer "will be [in] patient and reasonable terms." He is patient with the slowness the clergymen

show in coming to terms with his arguments: "I hope you are able to see the distinction I am trying to point out"; "I must honestly reiterate that I have been disappointed with the church"; "I had hoped that each of you would understand. But again I have been disappointed."

It quickly becomes clear, however, that this understatement is not the sign of an Uncle Tom cringing before his oppressors: it is a calculated rhetorical stance. The *Letter* is, of course, more than a letter to eight Birmingham clergymen: it is an open letter. King's conciliatory tone—while apparently conceding ground in its humility—is intended to reveal the inhumanity of the clergymen's position and to hold it up to the scorn of those of us who are reading over their shoulders. Against the outrages King so powerfully exposes, the recalcitrance of the eight clergymen reveals them as the true felons for their toleration of evil. *Letter from Birmingham Jail* transcends the problem of social evil in its very real Christian vision of love and brotherhood. But King's tone here is a rhetorical strategy. Its "inoffensiveness" allows an audience which might not fully sympathize with his program to participate, at least, in his argument—and perhaps unwittingly to share his lofty disdain for the kind of short-sighted criticism of which the audience itself might normally be guilty. King's stance does not hide his rage. By suppressing his personal anger and frustration, and by resisting the human impulse to bombast and diatribe, he has given structure to individual misfortune and achieved a compelling piece of polemic.

The narrator confined in the Birmingham city jail, then, is not simply the activist minister who languishes in solitary confinement, irritated by isolation from comrades, family, and the wife who had just given birth to their fourth child. The narrator is also a construction of polemical expediency and literary imagination. He is further defined in the "second stage" of the exposition of the sermon/letter, the "statement of the text." Like the traditional Negro sermon, King's *Letter* has a broad thematic unity; and like the sermon, the *Letter* draws its "text" from the Bible. King is pressed to defend his nonviolent direct action, his "meddling"; his defense is based largely upon Biblical precedent,that God commands Christians to spread the gospel and to aid their brethren regardless of where they live: "Just as the prophets of the eighth century B. C. left their villages and carried their 'thus saith the Lord' far beyond the boundaries of their home towns, and just as the Apostle Paul left his village of Tarsus and carried the gospel of Jesus Christ to the far corners of the Greco-Roman world, so am I compelled to carry the gospel of freedom beyond my own home town. Like Paul, I must constantly respond to the Macedonian call for aid." The *Letter* is both a social manifesto and a religious testament. King is arguing for a religious life that translates vision into practice and that finds the spiritual life enriched by communal efforts for justice. Although the details of King's program remain open to challenge from reactionary and radical points of view, the vision itself is virtually above criticism in the context of the letter.

Having established his text, with its justification of the active Christian life, King's persona subtly exposes the timid inaction of the eight clergymen as an ungodly denial of the necessary fruits of the religious life. To the religious man, "injustice anywhere is a threat to justice everywhere. . . . Never again can we afford to live with the narrow, provincial 'outside agitator' idea."

As we have seen in Pipes's scheme, the "third stage" of the sermon, the "body," with its repeated emotional climaxes, essentially is the sermon. Much of the raw emotional power of King's *Letter* arises simply from the increasing tempo and from the relentless force of repetition and parallelism. The first few paragraphs, which establish the speaker's personality and the text, contain relatively short sentences presented matter-of-factly; but as it proceeds, the *Letter* accelerates a strong rhythm, the sentences become longer in key emotional passages. Bruce Rosenberg has observed that many oral preachers "were unaware of creating" the moving passages of parallelism that characterize such preaching; but he suspects that "in the case of Dr. King and other preachers of comparable learning who preach spontaneously, it is hard to believe that they were not aware of the effect on the audience." King is certainly in full control of the effects produced by parallelism and repetition in the *Letter*. A few of the weaknesses of King's written style arise from the attempt to translate oral rhetoric onto paper: it is occasionally grating to hear philosophical definitions artificially confined in a paragraph structured on rigid parallelism; and repeated neatantitheses ("dark clouds of racial prejudice/radiant stars of love") are often predictable and trite. When one recalls King's ability on the platform to make clichés sound fresh and exciting, however, one is aware that these are weaknesses of adapting the message to a different medium. Even in the *Letter* he achieves great power from parallelism and repetition.

The measure of this power cannot be appreciated fully, however, by examining emotional effects apart from other rhetorical elements. Pipes notes that the Negro sermon has always contained implicitly various kinds of deductive and inductive logic, that ethics accompany emotional arousal as a secondary concern, that sources outside the Bible are sometimes cited, and that argument from authority often complements simple formulaic progression. King effectively exploits this potential in *Letter from Birmingham Jail*.

King begins his defense of the Birmingham campaign by listing the "four basic steps" of "any nonviolent campaign." One is finally less interested in the logic of his analysis than with the opportunities the "four basic steps" afford for his powerful denunciations of injustice and exhortation to action. It is the nature of men caught up in emotionally charged debate to be unimpressed by rational discourse and logical argument; certainly no one will be convinced by the logical force of King's "four basic steps" who is not already sympathetic to his nonviolent philosophy. It is not to deny the logic of King's argument, then, to say that his logical scheme is effective on a largely verbal level. Yet his logic throughout the *Letter* is unanswerable. In a brilliant paragraph he answers the charge that his actions "precipitate violence": he challenges the logic of the clergymen and in a series of increasingly dramatic,

grammatically parallel rhetorical questions, he reveals that those who make direct action necessary are guilty of precipitating violence: "Isn't this like condemning a robbed man because his possession of money precipitated the evil act of robbery? Isn't this like condemning Socrates because his unswerving commitment to truth and his philosophical inquiries precipitated the act by the misguided populace in which they made him drink hemlock? Isn't this like condemning Jesus because his unique God-consciousness and never-ceasing devotion to God's will precipitated the evil act of crucifixion?" He concludes in an eloquent understatement that resolves the tension created by the rhetorical questions: "Society must protect the robbed and punish the robber." King's devastating logic, then, exploits an untapped root ofthe traditional Negro minister's resources. It lends authority and dignity to his argument. It permits a sharp analysis that reveals unexpected and stunning truth which our comfortable commonplaces too often prevent us from seeing; it reminds us that the eight clergymen deny, in effect, the very truths their offices were created to perpetuate. But the great impact of *Letter from Birmingham Jail* does not arise from King's being a clinical logician. It is his ability to discover fundamental moral flaws in his opponents' charges that makes his argument so unanswerable. And it is his conscious literary skill with parallelism and understatement that makes his argument so emotionally convincing.

King's theme of the social and ethical implications of Christianity is reinforced by another strategy uncharacteristic of the traditional Negro sermon: reference to sources and authorities outside the Bible. The *Letter* remains, I think, an essentially Christian statement; but it gains force from King's eagerness to cite contemporary events and people and to muster authorities from Moses to Buber and Tillich, from Socrates to Jefferson and Lincoln. The references to Aquinas, Buber, and Tillich have special relevance, of course, to King's immediate audience, the clergymen. But the general effectiveness of citing authorities again lies in its impressive verbal impact. (He is not concerned here with such complex historical problems as Jefferson's keeping of slaves, or Lincoln's playing politics with the Emancipation Proclamation.) The very weight of his authorities assuages a reluctant audience's fear that his actions are frighteningly without precedent.

Herein lies King's greatest strength as a rhetorician: his ability to gently answer charges that he is impatient, radical, an "outside agitator"; to surprise the reader into an unexpected awareness of what the charges really imply; and to transform the very charges leveled against him into an occasion for exhortation and encouragement for his own camp. King has an uncanny ability to translate familiar terms into new and challenging concepts; but at the same time he convinces us that his seemingly revolutionary techniques belong to tested and revered traditions. To the assertion that negotiation would be better than the forms of direct action which produce "tension" in the community, King replies that "tension" is a necessary ingredient of any "creative" process; without continual challenge to existing conditions, opportunities for constructive change will never appear. When King says "I therefore concur with you in your call for negotiation," he has not given any ground to his accusers; on the contrary, he has usurped their ground by showing that the "negotiations" they prefer can be achieved only by his method of forcing a recalcitrant South to welcome the "tension" necessary for creative change—by nonviolent direct action. He has thus redefined a term that commonly connotes unpleasant friction into a concept that evokes promise and vitality. The dense antitheses in this paragraph depend upon rather trite metaphors ("from the bondage of myths and half-truths to the unfettered realms of creative analysis and objective appraisal"; "from the dark depths of prejudice and racism to the majestic heights of understanding and brotherhood"). But the cumulative force of King's interchangeable, formulaic metaphors carries the weight of his argument in a flight of noble emotion. Profound but elemental truth can find expression often only in language that borders on triteness.

To the charge that his actions are "illegal," King replies that "legality" and "justice" are not always compatible. Through rhetorical antitheses he demonstrates that to serve justice one must sometimes break the law: "An unjust law is a code that a numerical or power majority group compels a minority group to obey but does not make binding on itself. This is a *difference* made legal. By the same token a just law is a code that a majority compels a minority to follow and that it is willing to follow itself. This is *sameness* made legal"; "Sometimes a law is just on its face and unjust in its application"; "We should never forget that everything Adolf Hitler did in Germany was

King in Birmingham jail in 1963. While imprisoned here, he wrote his famous Letter from Birmingham Jail.

'legal' and everything the Hungarian freedom fighters did in Hungary was 'illegal.' "

By carefully establishing precedents for his nonviolent direct action, King convinces us that his program is a means of restoring what rightfully belongs to the blacks. He assures us that "there is nothing new about this kind of civil disobedience" and cites Biblical figures, Socrates, and American patriots as his predecessors. Blacks seek nothing extraordinary or alien to "the American dream." On the contrary, "our destiny is tied up with America's destiny. Before the pilgrims landed at Plymouth, we were here. Before the pen of Jefferson etched the majestic words of the Declaration of Independence across the pages of history, we were here." The very act of protest against repression, then, is not an act of arrogance but an attempt to restore and fulfill the ideals on which our nation was founded: "One day the South will know that when these disinherited children of God sat down at lunch counters, they were in reality standing up for what is best in the American dream and for the most sacred values in our Judeo-Christian heritage."

King is not simply lending "respectability" to his philosophy by citing revered precedents; he is employing sound methods of persuasive rhetoric by arguing within the frame of reference familiar to a broad audience. Again he swallows the natural impulse to assault the sacred cows of the opposition; in so doing, he has produced prose that is both inspiring and polemically effective.

King thus gives historical and philosophical justification to his movement. He proceeds to handle deftly more specific and gnawing criticism from both the clergymen and black nationalists. In one of his most brilliant passages of "redefinition," King rejects the clergymen's charge that his action is "extreme." He warns them that his "extremism" has been the last stop-gap between responsible protest and violence; for white Birmingham to ignore his movement is to invite "a frightening racial nightmare." Essentially, then, King redefines himself as a "moderate" trying to "stand in the middle of two opposing forces in the Negro community": "complacency" and black nationalism. Not to remain a sitting duck for Muslim critics, King launches into an impassioned account of the results of repression and frustration; he concludes that his philosophy of nonviolent direct action has been a "creative outlet" for these forces. That this action had been termed "extremist" King admits "initially disappointed" him. But, in another of those marvelous paragraphs that combine sophisticated technique and emotional preaching power, King decides that the charge of extremism is cause for satisfaction; for if fidelity to noble principles of love, faith, and conscience be "extreme," then extremist he admits he is. He cites towering authorities: Jesus, Amos, Paul, Luther, Bunyan, Lincoln, Jefferson—all "extremists" in the cause of truth. The relentless parallelism with which he alternates rhetorical questions with quotations from his authorities gives an air of inevitability to his self-defense.

King has here resolved attacks from white racists, white moderates, Uncle Toms, and Black Muslims. On one level, he has simply and eloquently rediscovered the kind of extremism that is always latent in social action against sharp and painful criticism from divergent groups. Surely King was especially hurt by the hostility of other blacks who felt that he had begun to drag his feet, had become ineffectual; for the moment, at least, King transcends such conflict in a vision of Christian perfection.

With authorities firmly established and the cry for freedom for blacks clearly rooted in sacred American institutions, King truly can turn the accusations of the clergymen upon their own heads. Authentic Christianity never shirks the truth. The original "God-intoxicated" Christians so faithfully followed the inner light regardless of persecution that "they brought an end to such ancient evils as infanticide and gladiatorial contests." It is the most telling blow against the clergymen that they stand accused of hypocrisy and of defending a dead institution: "Things are different now. So often the contemporary church is a weak, ineffectual voice with an uncertain sound. . . . If today's church does not recapture the sacrificial spirit of the early church, it will lose its authenticity, forfeit the loyalty of millions, and be dismissed as an irrelevant social club with no meaning for the twentieth century." King is no longer on the defensive, a man charged with "extremism"; he is now the discoverer and champion of old, cherished, and sacred values. Like the Birmingham that denies the promises of the Founding Fathers and the American dream, the eight clergymen represent a sterile convention that mocks the body of sacred truth from which it was born.

Probably the most memorable passage in *Letter from Birmingham Jail* is that in which King explores the familiar injunction to "Wait!" for civil rights rather than to provoke turmoil. Here King's greatest rhetorical assets operate simultaneously. He curtly states that "This 'Wait' has almost always meant 'Never.' " His definition is not that of a skilled grammarian: it provides an adverb as a synonym for a verb. But the meaning rings clear. In a painful, powerful paragraph, King presents the numerous abuses that black people have endured for generations. But he does more than enumerate complaints: in the merging of content and style, he also achieves great artistry. An agonizingly long series of dependent clauses establishes intellectually and sensuously the conditions that make "waiting" no longer possible ("when you have seen vicious mobs lynch your mothers and fathers at will and drown your sisters and brothers at whim; when . . . ; when . . ."). The very process of reading the series of abuses becomes so physically wearying, the cumulative impact of the grammatically parallel dependent clauses so enervating, that the long-awaited independent clause that resolves all the conditional statements deflates our expectation of a thundering protest with its eloquent understatement: "then you will understand why we find it difficult to wait." King continues: "There comes a time when the cup of endurance runs over." What better metaphor than this, not only for a recapitulation of theme, but also for what King has achieved stylistically! The torrent of adverbial clauses capturing the agony of "waiting" literally pours over the simple little cup of the main clause, moving us emotionally while convincing us intellectually that "waiting" can no longer be expected. King concludes the paragraph with another masterly stroke of understate-

ment: "I hope, sirs, you can understand our legitimate and unavoidable impatience." Controlled irony is infinitely more devastating than self-indulgent vitriol.

Pipes notes that the "fourth stage" of the Negro sermon, the conclusion, attempts to resolve the emotional intensity aroused throughout the sermon and to call the sinners to God. King releases us from the repeated emotional climaxes of *Letter from Birmingham Jail* in the final three paragraphs, a kind of apology (in the sense of "justification") for the *Letter* and a benediction urging Christian brotherhood. The next to last paragraph is an eloquent reminder that, however conciliatory and brotherly his tone has been, he has in no way conceded merit to the charges of the clergymen: "If I have said anything in this letter that overstates the truth and indicates an unreasonable impatience, I beg you to forgive me. If I have said anything that understates the truth and indicates my having a patience that allows me to settle for anything less than brotherhood, I beg God to forgive me." Most of King's rhetorical trademarks are here: the antithesis, the parallelism, the logic cloaked in strong rhythm, the understatement that cuts more deeply than overstatement. By grammatically paralleling the clergymen ("you") with God, he underlines their failure to measure their complaints against simple standards of morality; he shows that unswerving commitment to truth too often belongs to the man of God "alone in a narrow jail cell." There is release here only from the driving rhythm that marks the *Letter*; there is no escape from the quiet but profound irony of King's conclusion—only the temporary esthetic satisfaction of having comprehended anger and frustration. *Letter from Birmingham Jail* is finally more than a self-defense; it is a challenge to recognize real justice, real truth, and ultimately a challenge to act.

I have not tried to claim that King's final significance is literary rather than social and political; his lasting achievement is that he made civil rights protest a viable tactic for social change. Nor do I mean to suggest that King's vision of the struggle of blacks is more valid than that of any other faction that succeeded him; only history can determine that. What I have tried to show is that King was capable of the kind of sustained eloquence that has made Malcolm X's *Autobiography* and Eldridge Cleaver's *Soul on Ice* acknowledged masterpieces of the black experience. It is a measure of King's achievement that he pushed the traditional Negro sermon beyond its historical limitations. His *Letter* borrows the most prominent traits of this genre and successfully translates them to previously unexplored fields of polemic.

From its inception in the South in the eighteenth century, the "old-time" style of preaching was an effective tool of repression. White slavemasters actually encouraged the presence of itinerant preachers on their plantations because "they usually taught a religion of consolation rather than of revolt against their white masters" [Rosenberg]. Emotional release through religion did much "to encourage the slave along the road of mental escape from his conditions" [Pipes]. Pipes respects the "old-time" sermon as a folk-art form. But he argues that its survival continues to be an index of repression of Negroes. As Negroes have access to "new opportunities of normal expression," and educational and economic advancement, their "degree of frustration is . . . lowered." It is easy to see, then, why a new brand of black activists would be tempted to dismiss completely the politics—and indeed the style—of Martin Luther King, Jr., as outdated, irrelevant to the continuing black revolution.

Apart from its unfortunate historical connotations, the "old-time" Negro sermon has recently attained a large measure of respect for its unique artistic achievement. Bruce Rosenberg praises the old oral tradition because it "frees the minds of the audience from concern with what language, music, or story element is to come next, and so they are freer to involve themselves with the rhythm and the music and the emotion of the performance." King's achievement—as preacher, public leader, and writer—is that he harnessed the profound emotional power of the old Negro sermon for purposes of social action, thus overcoming the historical limitations of the tradition. Whether or not he had become irrelevant to the protest movement, as Cleaver has charged, King's service in transformingthe Negro sermon was crucially important. He did not abandon the genre for the sake of social engagement: he used the emotional power of the tradition to serve the protest movement. *Letter from Birmingham Jail* is convincing largely because it has an appealing emotional depth rare in argumentative writing. History will decide whether Martin Luther King, Jr. died at the peak of his effectiveness as a reform leader. *Letter from Birmingham Jail* has a timeless eloquence that finally transcends such concerns.

Wesley T. Mott, "The Rhetoric of Martin Luther King, Jr.: 'Letter From Birmingham Jail'," in PHYLON: The Atlanta University Review of Race and Culture, *Vol. XXXVI, No. 4, fourth quarter (December, 1975), pp. 411-21.*

King and the folk pulpit:

King's heritage shaped his use of sources. The mature King's fiery yet magisterial language was forged in the mighty furnace of the black folk pulpit of his father and grandfather, the highly oral tradition begun by slaves. Treating language as a communal treasure, not private property, folk preachers gained authority by identifying themselves with well-known, sanctified messages. Only in the world of print, not the folk pulpit, do words become commodities that are copyrighted, owned, packaged and sold.

King triumphed, I would argue, because he adapted the tenets, procedures and hopes of the African-American church. For him, seizing and alchemizing white sermons meant translating the black demand for equality into an idiom that white people would finally accept. In this way, he developed into something quite beyond the ken of his professors and beyond the contentions of his own student essays. He became the greatest folk preacher of all.

Keith D. Miller, in his "The Roots of the Dream," The New York Times Book Review, 15 March 1992.

Clayborne Carson, with Peter Holloran, Ralph E. Luker, and Penny Russell   (essay date 1991)

[*Carson, an American educator and historian, is the senior editor and director of the Martin Luther King, Jr. Papers project and Peter Holloran is an assistant editor on the project. Ralph E. Luker and Penny Russell are editors of volumes 1 and 2 of* The Papers of Martin Luther King, Jr. *In the following essay, they consider King's theological writings as "evidence of King's effort to construct an identity as a theologian and preacher."*]

What is the historical and biographical significance of the papers Martin Luther King, Jr. wrote as a divinity student at Crozer Theological Seminary and as a doctoral student at Boston University? Judged retroactively by the standards of academic scholarship, they are tragically flawed by numerous instances of plagiarism. Moreover, even before the Martin Luther King, Jr., Papers Project's discovery of the citation deficiencies in the papers, only a few students of King had thought them deserving of the type of careful study that would have exposed those deficiencies. Scholars, seeing the papers through the distorting prism of King's subsequent fame and martyrdom, usually considered them insignificant, except for the few clues they provide regarding the nonviolent protest strategies King later advocated. These papers disclose new meanings, however, when they are studies as evidence of King's effort to construct an identity as a theologian and preacher rather than as undistinguished scholarship or as evidence of King's adoption of ideas regarding nonviolent strategies of change.

King's appropriations of the words and ideas of others should certainly not be understood merely as violations of academic rules. They also indicate his singular ability to intertwine his words and ideas with those of others to express his beliefs persuasively and to construct a persona with broad transracial appeal. Though in large measure derivative, King's student papers document an important stage in the development of his thought and leadership qualities. As he mined theological texts for nuggets of cogency that would serve his academic ends, King resolved long-standing religious doubts and refined a method of eclectic composition that would enrich his sermons, speeches, and published writings.

King himself complicated scholarly understanding of his academic experiences through ambiguous autobiographical statements about his years at Crozer and Boston. Particularly in his first and most widely read book, *Stride toward Freedom,* King drew on various sources to strengthen his public image as a knowledgeable exponent of Christian-Gandhian strategies of nonviolent struggle. As Keith D. Miller has demonstrated, King's account, in a chapter entitled "Pilgrimage to Nonviolence," obscured the extent to which his understanding of Gandhism and other social reform strategies derived from a network of Social Gospel advocates, both black and white. Miller's work reflects a trend in King scholarship toward greater recognition of the impact of African-American religious influences on King's thought and of black religious leaders as models for his ministry. Rather than acknowledging his dependence on nonscholarly and African-American sources, however, King, in *Stride toward Freedom,* suggested that his socio-political ideas derived mainly from his readings of major theological texts. King downplayed the impact of his early experiences as the grandson of the Reverend A. D. Williams, a founder of the Atlanta chapter of the National Association for the Advancement of Colored People (NAACP); the son of the Reverend Martin Luther King, a leader of civil rights protests in the 1930s and 1940s; and an acquaintance of numerous other black proponents of the Social Gospel, including President Benjamin Mays of Morehouse College, Morehouse religion professor George D. Kelsey, and Atlanta minister William Holmes Borders. Instead, King emphasized the refinement of his ideas at predominantly white institutions. "Not until I entered Crozer Theological Seminary in 1948 . . . did I begin a serious intellectual quest for a method to eliminate social evil," he explained. While emphasizing his concern with social justice issues while a student, King also understated the importance he gave to the abstract theological issues that were actually the focus of his graduate school papers. "Although my major interest was in the fields of theology and philosophy," King remarked, "I spent a great deal of time reading the works of great social philosophers." Providing graphic descriptions of his initial encounters with the ideas of Walter Rauschenbusch, Karl Marx, and Mahatma Gandhi, King mentioned only briefly his study of systematic theology. His references to his theological readings were vague and usually in connection with their political implications. The section on his graduate school experiences includes only a brief passage describing his study of "personalistic philosophy" under Edgar S. Brightman and L. Harold DeWolf. This "personal idealism," King asserted, became his "basic philosophical position." He added that when he received his doctorate from Boston University in 1955, the "relatively divergent intellectual forces" of his academic training were "converging into a positive social philosophy" [*Stride toward Freedom*].

King's desire to stress the social and political implications of his theological training was understandable given his intended audience. As is usual for the autobiographical writing of public figures, *Stride toward Freedom* was intended to mold an image as well as to reveal personal experiences. Stressing the political uses he would make of his studies, rather than his primarily theological concerns when he wrote them, King reconstructed his past to serve his current purposes. He also overstated his familiarity with the ideas of leading intellectuals, thus underrating the importance of less prominent intellectuals and influences. The book succeeded in shaping scholarly understanding of King's intellectual development; few subsequent biographies have departed from its interpretive framework. Unfortunately, King's explanation of the development of his social and political views discouraged later researchers from giving adequate attention to either the African-American sources of his religious activism or the European-American sources of his theological perspective. Discounting the scholarly significance of his student writings

in systematic theology has led many King biographers to neglect their biographical significance. Lerone Bennett, Jr.'s generally laudatory biography, initially published during King's lifetime, set the tone for later accounts by offering faint praise for his academic achievements and concluding that King's dissertation gave him "discipline and training in the organization of ideas, if not in the creation of ideas." In the initial edition of his biography, David L. Lewis described King as lacking "the comprehensive critical apparatus and the inspired vision that bless good philosophers"; although "highly competent scholastically," King possessed an intelligence that was, in Lewis's view, "essentially derivative." James P. Hanigan, one of the few scholars to attempt a systematic study of King's ideas, similarly dismissed the notion of King as a major theologian—"a somewhat surprising assessment of a man who wrote not one word of formal theology after finishing his unpublished doctoral dissertation." This tendency to downplay King's scholarly abilities and aspirations probably accounts for the failure of previous accounts of King's student years to note the citation deficiencies of his academic writings.

King's academic papers nevertheless deserve serious study because they provide crucial evidence about his struggle to reconcile his deep feeling for African-American religious practices with his persistent theological doubts. King overcame his initial reluctance to enter the ministry only as he began to recognize his father and grandfather as appealing role models who had shown that pastoring could be combined with social activism. Like his father, grandfather, and great-grandfather before him, King came to accept the black church as an institution in which he could gain distinction and a sense of rectitude while serving the black community. As a dutiful minister's son, he felt an inalienable sense of church membership and clerical competence even while becoming a dissenter within the black Baptist tradition. King's student papers reveal both his scholarly pretensions and his honest effort to reconcile the emotional satisfactions of traditional African-American religion with the intellectual clarity he sought in theological scholarship.

In an especially revealing Crozer paper entitled **"An Autobiography of Religious Development,"** King traced this tension in his religious beliefs to his childhood, when he had felt unmoved by an evangelist visiting Ebenezer who urged his audience to join the church. King had followed his older sister in coming forward, but he realized that he "joined the church not out of any dynamic conviction, but out of a childhood desire to keep up with my sister." A "questioning and precocious type," he remembered shocking his Sunday school class at the age of thirteen "by denying the bodily resurrection of Jesus." After entering Morehouse College at the age of fifteen, he had seen "a gap between what I had learned in Sunday School and what I was learning in college." His religious doubts "began to spring forth unrelentingly" until Professor Kelsey showed him "that behind the legends and myths of the Book were many profound truths which one could not escape." Despite this religious skepticism, however, King had already decided on a ministerial career by the time he graduated from Morehouse. Theological differences did not undermine his admiration for his father's "noble example." As a student at Crozer, he still felt the effects "of the noble moral and ethical ideals I grew up under. They have been real and precious to me, and even in moments of theological doubt I could never turn away from them." Having already joined the ministry in response to "an inescapable urge to serve society," King at first accepted the Christian liberalism of his Crozer professors "with relative ease." But his theological studies focused increasingly on the metaphysics of God and religion, rather than on the social role of the Christian church. His religious upbringing had supplied satisfying answers regarding the latter; it offered him less guidance on the former.

At Crozer, King clarified his views of God and humanity and struggled to reconcile his own experience with his readings in theology. Choosing Crozer because of its reputation for liberalism and critical biblical scholarship, King initially identified with that ethos. The papers he wrote during his first-year courses on critical biblical scholarship demonstrated his appreciation of the significance of archaeological and historical evidence in the study of Scripture. Those essays satisfied the demanding standards of the distinguished biblical scholars James Bennett Pritchard and Morton Scott Enslin, but they lack self-revelatory passages and seem to have engaged King only superficially. King was more drawn to theology as taught by George Washington Davis, and he took nearly a third of his courses at Crozer with Davis. Davis exposed King to the writings of leading modern theologians, introducing him to the issues that would become the central concerns of his doctoral studies. As he became absorbed in the modern theological literature, King increasingly referred to his personal experiences to explain his gradual movement from an uncritical liberalism toward greater appreciation for traditional religious perspectives. In an essay for Davis entitled **"How Modern Christians Should Think About Man,"** he argued that liberals too "easily cast aside the term sin, failing to realize that many of our present ills result from the sins of men." King admitted that his conception of man was:

> going though a state of transition. At one time I find myself leaning toward a mild neo-orthodox view of man, and at other times I find myself leaning toward a liberal view of man. The former leaning may root back to certain experiences that I had in the south with a vicious race problem. Some of the experiences that I encountered there made it very difficult for me to believe in the essential goodness of man. On the other hand part of my liberal leaning has its source in another branch of the same root. [In] noticing the gradual improvements of this same race problem I came to see some noble possibilities in human nature. Also my liberal leaning may root back to the great imprint that many liberal theologians have left upon me and to my ever present desire to be optimistic about human nature.

In the essay King acknowledged that he had become "a victim of eclecticism," seeking to "synthesize the best in liberal theology with the best in neo-orthodox theology," particularly the writings of Karl Barth and Reinhold Nie-

buhr. Rejecting "one-sided generalizations about man," he concluded that "we shall be closest to the authentic Christian interpretation of man if we avoid both of these extremes." This statement, although largely appropriated from Walter Marshall Horton, was consistent with the views King expressed in other papers and exams; that consistency indicates how King's papers could be derivative yet reliable as expressions of his views.

King's increasing tendency to acknowledge the validity of some neoorthodox criticisms of Christian liberalism may have been related to events in his personal life that contradicted Crozer's ethos of interracial harmony. On one occasion a southern white student pulled a gun on King because he mistakenly believed that King had victimized him as a prank. During the summer after his second year at Crozer, King was involved in another incident that reminded him of his vulnerability to racial discrimination when he ventured off campus and was denied service at a New Jersey tavern.

At the heart of King's search for an intellectually and emotionally satisfying religious faith was an inquiry into the nature of divinity. Having failed to experience God's presence directly though an abrupt conversion experience, King sought a set of theological ideas that would satisfy his desire for a conception of God that was consistent with his experiences. Although King was initially convinced "that the most valid conception of God is that of theism," he had found himself during his last year at Crozer "quite confused as to which definition [of God] was the most adequate." King's intellectual search culminated in Davis's course on the Philosophy of Religion when he read Edgar S. Brightman's *A Philosophy of Religion* and adopted personalism as his theological perspective. King's essay on Brightman's book displayed the intensity of his search for religious understanding while at the same time appropriating many of Brightman's words. "How I long now for that religious experience which Dr. Brightman so cogently speaks of throughout his book," King concluded. "It seems to be an experience, the lack of which life becomes dull and meaningless." In a remarkably candid statement for a third-year seminarian he reflected on his struggle to achieve a sense of religious contentment.

> I do remember moments that I have been awe awakened; there have been times that I have been carried out of myself by something greater than myself and to that something I gave myself. Has this great something been God? Maybe after all I have been religious for a number of years, and am now only becoming aware of it.

Choosing Boston University's School of Theology because of the presence of Brightman and other leading personalists, King continued his inquiry into the nature of divinity while depending increasingly on the use of appropriated passages to formulate his synthesis of competing theological perspectives. King's Boston papers are, for the most part, competent yet routine responses to assignments, but some also include the personal digressions that enliven some of the Crozer essays. King's dissertation, **"A Comparison of the Conceptions of God in the Thinking of Paul Tillich and Henry Nelson Wieman,"** though unoriginal in its expository chapters and stylistically languid, reflected

King's religious perspective as he concluded seven years of graduate study. Cautiously critical of Wieman and Tillich, King reaffirmed his commitment to personalist theology and implicitly to conceptions of God rooted in African-American religious traditions. Setting forth a theme he would develop in many later sermons, King rejected the view that God was "supra-personal"—that is, unable to be defined by the concept of personality: "It would be better by far to admit that there are difficulties with an idea we know—such as personality—than to employ a term which is practically unknown to us in our experience." Evaluating Tillich and Wieman according to the standards of personalism and the needs of the preacher, King questioned the "positive religious value" of their conceptions of God and posited instead a God who made possible "true fellowship and communion," who was "responsive to the deepest yearnings of the human heart," a God who "both evokes and answers prayer." He concluded that Tillich's and Wieman's theologies were "lacking in positive religious value. Both concepts are too impersonal to express adequately the Christian conception of God. They provide neither the conditions of true fellowship with God nor the assurance of his goodness." King, in short, evaluated the two theologians primarily on the basis of his preconceived, experiential notion of a personal God rather than on the basis of logical shortcomings in their theological writings. Even when he applauded Tillich's and Wieman's acknowledgment of "the primacy of God over everything else in the universe," his evaluation was rooted in a priori assumptions.

> They do insist that religion begins with God and that man cannot have faith apart from him. They do proclaim that apart from God our human efforts turn to ashes and our sunrises into darkest night. They do suggest that man is not sufficient to himself for life, but is dependent upon God. All of this is good, and it may be a necessary corrective to a generation that has had all too muchfaith in man and all too little faith in God.

King's assumptions about God and humanity drew from homiletic traditions as well as from a distinctive African-American Social Gospel intellectual tradition represented in the ideas of Benjamin Mays, William Holmes Borders, Howard Thurman, and others.

King's struggle to come to terms with his African-American religious heritage expressed itself through his continuing preference for concepts of God that provided emotional as well as intellectual satisfaction and through his deepening acceptance of his calling as a preacher. During his first years of study at predominantly white institutions, King's enthusiasm for theological abstractions and interracial campus life may have contributed to occasional feelings of alienation from his cultural roots and seemingly preordained career path. A black pastor who observed King's performance as a participant in Crozer's fieldwork program found him only average in pulpit ability. Given his experience at Ebenezer, that area should have been a strength. The evaluator also asserted that King exhibited "an attitude of aloofness, disdain & possible snobbishness which prevent his coming to close grips with the rank and file of ordinary people. Also, a smugness that refuses to adapt itself to the demands of ministering effectively to the average Negro congregation." Notwithstanding this evaluation and his continuing uneasiness with the emotionalism and scriptural literalism he associated with African-American religion, King became effective as a preacher, serving as Ebenezer's assistant pastor during summer breaks and taking many homiletics courses at Crozer. Taylor Branch's account suggests that King gradually learned to combine scholarly sophistication with oratorical skill with the result that his fellow students "so admired his preaching technique that they packed the chapel whenever he delivered the regular Thursday student sermon, and kibitzers drifted into practice preaching classes when King was at the podium." Rather than allowing his theological studies to detract from his effectiveness as preacher, King filled voluminous notebooks with passages from his readings that would later embellish his sermons.

While King studied at Boston University, his preaching activities absorbed ever greater amounts of his time and became more central to his persona. King's Boston writings suggest that, rather than being driven by a need to resolve religious and career doubts, he had become content to refine the personalist perspective he had adopted at Crozer and to assimilate those aspects of scholarship that could be useful in preaching. When applying to Boston, King had insisted that "scholarship" was his goal and expressed the belief that theology "should be as scientific . . . as any other discipline," but he soon decided that he should practice his academic skills as pastor of a southern church. At Boston, while acquiring more theological erudition, King increasingly questioned the intellectual assumptions and professional values associated with academic theology. King's ardent effort to find a middle ground between academic rationalism and the comforting verities of African-American religion can be seen in his earliest recorded sermon, **"Rediscovering Lost Values,"** delivered in 1954 to a large black Baptist church in Detroit. After utilizing language that identified him as a student of systematic theology—"all reality has spiritual control" and "there is a God behind the process"—King employed language that resonated with the rhythms of the black Baptist tradition and evoked passionate responses from the congregation. King emphasized enduring religious values and advised against "little gods that are here today and gone tomorrow."

> I'm not going to put my ultimate faith in the little gods that can be destroyed in an atomic age (*Yes*), but the God who has been our help in ages past (*Come on*), and our hope for years to come (*All right*), and our shelter in the time of storm (*Oh yes*), and our eternal home (*Come on*). That's the God that I'm putting my ultimate faith in (*Oh yes, Come on now*). That's the God that I call upon you to worship this morning [**"Rediscovering Lost Values"**].

King's formal academic work at Boston was guided by DeWolf, who took over as King's adviser when Brightman died. A former minister himself, DeWolf occasionally listened to King preach and appreciated his student's preaching abilities. He later judged King as "a very good student, all business, a scholar's scholar, one digging deeply to work out and think through his philosophy of religion and life." But DeWolf was a lax mentor who did not demand of King the analytical precision that might have prepared him for a career of scholarly writing. Even if DeWolf was not consciously aware of the plagiarized passages in King's essays, his obliviousness to them suggests that he asked little more of King than accurate explication and judicious synthesis. DeWolf may have conceded more than he realized when he argued, soon after King's death, against those who questioned the originality of King's religious views. Asserting that "all modern theology which is competent is 'essentially derivative,' " DeWolf even surmised that King as a public figure had derived his "system of positive theological belief " from his mentor: "occasionally I find his language following closely the special terms of my own lectures and writings."

DeWolf recommended his student for several academic positions, and King never completely abandoned his ambition to pursue an academic career. Even after deciding to become pastor of Dexter Avenue Baptist Church, King was tempted by an offer from an Illinois college. He replied that he was not considering leaving Dexter in the immediate future but might be available in few years. Yet, despite occasional expressions of interest in academic positions, King increasingly accepted his calling as an academically educated activist minister, rather than an academic theologian. By the time he received his doctorate, King had already served almost a year as Dexter's pastor; within a year, he would begin to construct a new public identity as a sophisticated advocate of social change. His identity as a preacher remained the common element linking his years as a theological student and his years as a public figure. One of only a few black ministers with a doctorate from an accredited university, King ultimately used his scholarly credentials to supplement, rather than replace, his identity as a preacher. After leaving Boston, he displayed little interest in making an original contribution to scholarly discourse. His later writings probably reflected his recognition that preaching and political advocacy were his principal gifts.

As he entered public life, King's theological training became an asset, distinguishing him from other black leaders and providing him with intellectual resources that enhanced his ability to influence white middle-class public opinion. Even his ability to appropriate texts to express his opinions was a benefit as he drafted public statements that would not require citations. His characteristic compositional method contributed to the rhetorical skills that became widely admired when King was called unexpectedly to national leadership. His appropriations of major scholarly texts satisfied his teachers and advanced his personal ambitions; his use of politicals philosophical, and literary texts—particularly those expressing the nation's democratic ideals—inspired and mobilized many Americans, thereby advancing the cause of social justice. His use, as a student and as a leader, of hegemonic or canonized cultural materials enabled him to create a transracial identity that served his own needs and those of African Americans. Deciding against a career as a theologian, King neverthe-

less became one of the most effective popularizers of theological ideas in the twentieth century.

In his ministry and his civil rights leadership, King continued to utilize African-American and European-American cultural resources to enhance his oratory and writing. As a public figure, King gradually became more conscious of the tension between the two traditions, occasionally contrasting them and expressing his preference for black folk religion. During the early 1960s, reflecting on the changes in his religious beliefs that had resulted from years of civil rights activism (and borrowing words from his dissertation), he acknowledged that

> in the past the idea of a personal God was little more than a metaphysical category that I found theologically and philosophically satisfying. Now it is a living reality that has been validated in the experiences of everyday life. God has been profoundly real to me in recent years. . . . So in the truest sense of the Word, God is a living God. In him there is feeling and will, responsive to the deepest yearnings of the human heart; *this* God both evokes and answers prayer [*Strength to Love*].

The upsurge of racial militancy among blacks during the mid-1960s made King ever more conscious of the tension inherent in his roles as a racial leader and a racial diplomat. Although he left behind no diary or reflective journal that would allow scholars to measure the psychological costs of his effort to respond to the conflicting demands placed upon him, King's writings and oral statements hint that he struggled to maintain his core identity while sustaining his public personae. While the influence of the African-American religious tradition was immediately apparent in King's oratory, it was less evident in his theological writings, whose vocabulary contained few traces of African-American folk culture, linguistic patterns, or religious idiom. Yet, although King's literary persona remained largely that of a culturally assimilated religious leader, he occasionally noted the contrast between theological discourse and the emotionally evocative language of the black church. In a 1965 sermon, King advised his congregation that "we do not need to get philosophical about Him, because we get lost in the atmosphere of philosophy and theology sometimes." He compared Tillich's notion of God as "the new being" to the "poetic language" of black religion. "Sometimes when we've tried to see the meaning of Jesus we've said he's the lily of the valley, . . . a bright and morning star. . . . a rock in a weary land. . . . a shelter in the time of storm. . . . a mother to the motherless, and a father to the fatherless. At times we've just ended up saying he's my everything."

As a minister and protest leader, King benefited from his academic credentials and made effective use of the skills he gained as a graduate student. Notwithstanding his often-expressed desire to leave the pressing demands of movement leadership for the relative calm of academic life, however, he moved readily into the ministry and after leaving Dexter served as a pastor at Ebenezer until his death. His primary identity was clearly that of a preacher. In 1965, for example, while noting that he was "many things to many people: Civil Rights leader, agitator, trouble-maker and orator," King reaffirmed those facets of his personality that preceded his formal education, undergirded his public image, and encompassed his strengths and limitations as a student and a leader: "I am fundamentally a clergyman, a Baptist preacher. This is my being and my heritage for I am also the son of a Baptist preacher, the grandson of a Baptist preacher and the great-grandson of a Baptist preacher" ["The Un-Christian Christian," *Ebony* 20, Aug. 1965].

King's few public recollections of his graduate school experiences did not indicate conscious concern that his student compositions might have violated academic rules. Uncomfortable with his public image, even while sometimes cultivating it, he often acknowledged his limitations and insisted that he was a product of a freedom movement greater than himself. Accepting the possibility that his flaws might detract from his public image, King understood that his historical importance ultimately derived, not from his intrinsic attributes, but from the remarkable uses he made of them.

King's borrowings from European-American and African-American religious thought supplied him with a framework for understanding the flaws in his character. He may simply have concluded that his academic credentials and theological readings had served positive purposes. In one of his last sermons, King may have spoken of his own life when he addressed the Ebenezer congregation on a passage from the book of Mark. Recounting the request of James and John to sit beside Jesus, King saw the two men's desire for recognition as understandable: "Before we condemn them too quickly, let us look calmly and honestly at ourselves, and we will discover that we too have those basic desires for recognition. . . . We all want to be important, to surpass others, to achieve distinction, to lead the parade." He explained, "Somehow this warm glow we feel when we are praised, or when our name is in print, is something of the vitamin A to our ego." He warned, however, that the "drum major instinct" was dangerous if not restrained. "It causes you to lie about who you know sometimes," "to try to identify with the so-called big name people." Feelings of snobbishness could even invade the church: "The church is the one place where a Ph. D. ought to forget that he's a Ph. D." King's interpretation of the biblical story was that Jesus did not oppose the drum major instinct but instead believed that it should be put to good purposes. "If you want to be great—wonderful. But recognize that he who is greatest among you shall be your servant. You don't have to have a college degree to serve. . . . You don't have to know about Plato and Aristotle to serve." He ended the sermon by referring to his own desire for recognition, separating those aspects of his identity that were superficial from the ones that he deemed were essential. Suggesting the text for his eulogy, King advised: "Tell them not to mention that I have a Nobel Peace Prize, that isn't important. . . . Tell him not to mention where I went to school. I'd like somebody to mention that day, that Martin Luther King, Jr., tried to give his life serving others."

Clayborne Carson and others, "Martin Luther King, Jr., as Scholar: A Reexamination of His Theological Writings," in

The Journal of American History, *Vol. 78, No. 1, June, 1991, pp. 93-105.*

King and language:

In the eyes of the press and most of America, King emerged as a uniquely powerful leader. But how did this process occur? What made King a superstar?

The answer to this question can be stated in a single word: language. King's unmatched words galvanized blacks and changed the minds of moderate and uncommitted whites. Others could embrace nonviolence, get arrested, and accept martyrdom. But only King could convince middle-of-the-road whites about the meaning of the revolutionary events they were witnessing on their television screens. His persuasiveness did more than surpass that of his colleagues. It enabled him to accomplish what Frederick Douglass, Sojourner Truth, W.E.B. Du-Bois, and his own models and mentors had failed to achieve. By persuading whites to accept the principle of racial equality, he made a monumental contribution to solving the nation's most horrific problem—racial injustice.

Keith D. Miller, in his Voice of Deliverance: The Language of Martin Luther King, Jr. and Its Sources, *The Free Press, 1992.*

Keith D. Miller (essay date 1992)

[*Miller is an American educator and author. In the following essay, he examines the literary, historical, and theological influences that informed King's* Letter from a Birmingham Jail *and his famous speech "I Have a Dream," and defends King's use of "borrowed" or adapted material.*]

On August 28, 1963, one hundred fifty thousand or more demonstrators sweltered in Washington, D.C., listening to fine music from Marian Anderson, Joan Baez, and other singers. On the steps of the Lincoln Memorial an endless procession of speakers droned and droned. Despite the interruption of John Lewis's impassioned eloquence, the perspiring crowd began to wilt. Then, late in the afternoon, Mahalia Jackson revived everyone. With her hat pinned firmly to her hair, the unaccompanied Queen of Gospel swayed to a rhythm entirely her own, arousing weary listeners with the slave spiritual "I Been 'Buked and I Been Scorned":

> I been 'buked and I been scorned.
> I'm gonna tell my Lord when I get home
> Just how *long* you've been treating me wrong.

Here Jackson merged her voice with the narrator of the lyrics, identifying her experiences with those of slaves. Through this song, the slaves' indignity became her indignity and that of thousands of blacks hearing her, all of whom had been 'buked and scorned. The slaves' cry became her cry, the slaves' protest her protest.

Following this spirited performance, King stepped to the

microphone to launch the profoundly paradoxical **"I Have a Dream."** Wearing his normal funereal suit, white shirt, and black tie, he, like Jackson, evoked the woebegone past to demand a sparkling future. He cited Jefferson, alluded to Lincoln, and embraced Old Testament prophets and Christianity, presenting an entire inventory of patriotic themes and images typical of Fourth of July oratory. But, despite these nostalgic references, the first half of **"I Have a Dream"** did not celebrate a dream. It catalogued a nightmare. King damned an intolerable status quo that demeaned the Negro, who existed "on a lonely island of poverty" and was an "exile in his own land."

Then King merged his voice with others. He enlisted Amos as a spokesman for his cause:

> There are those who are asking the devotees of
> civil rights, "When
> will you be satisfied?"
> We can never be satisfied as long as the Negro
> is the victim of the
> unspeakable horrors of police brutality.
> We cannot be satisfied as long as our bodies . . .
> cannot find lodging
> in the motels of the highways or the hotels of the
> cities. . . .
> No . . . we will not be satisfied until justice rolls
> down like waters
> and righteousness like a mighty stream.

Who are the "we" of this passage? The devotees of civil rights—the disenfranchised blacks whom King represented. But the "we" of the last sentence includes more than blacks. This line harnesses a famous exclamation from an Old Testament prophet—Amos's cry "Let justice roll down like waters and righteousness like a mighty stream!" So Amos is also speaking here as King merges Amos's persona with his own. This union reflects back to the immediately preceding sentences: the "we" who cannot be satisfied until justice rolls down are the same "we" who seek lodging in the motels of the highways and the hotels of the cities. The voice of King/Amos calls for justice to run like a river and for Congress to open the dam by mandating integration. The words of Amos gave an unimpeachably authoritative tone to King's demands.

In the most famous passage of all his oratory, King again engaged in voice merging:

> I have a dream that one day this nation will rise
> up. . . .
>
> I have a dream that my four little children will
> one day . . . not be
> judged by the color of their skin but by the con-
> tent of their
> character.
> I have a dream today! . . .
> I have a dream that one day every valley shall
> be exalted and every
> hill and mountain shall be made low, the rough
> places will be
> made plain, and the crooked places will be made
> straight, and
> the glory of the Lord shall be revealed, and all
> flesh shall see it
> together.

Who is the "I" here? The "I" is surely King, the father of four young children. But who is the "I" of the last sentence? The dream is not simply King's dream. Isaiah initially sketched the scene of valleys exalted, mountains laid low, and rough places made plain—impossible geography symbolizing the coming of the kingdom of God. Jesus reaffirmed this powerful conception by quoting Isaiah's visionary language. Then Handel enshrined it in the lyrics of the *Messiah,* the most famous long piece of Christian music. Uniting his persona with those of Amos, Isaiah, Jesus, and Handel's narrator, King built his identity by evoking a sanctified past. Underlying this process of self-making is the typology of slave religion and the folk pulpit. King assumes that personality reasserts itself in readily understandable forms governing all human history. Scripture, music, and sermons describe and illuminate these patterns.

Although these forms are reliable, they can be flexible as well. Following the "I have a dream" litany, King again evoked Biblical eschatology by reworking imagery from the prophet Daniel: "With this faith we will be able to hew out of the mountain of despair a stone of hope." Interpreting a famous dream of King Nebuchadnezzar, Daniel describes a stone that smashes a figure made of precious metals, iron, and clay. Hewn from a mountain by God, the stone symbolizes God's ideal kingdom that destroys all petty, earthly kingdoms and itself endures forever. In King's speech, however, human beings extract the stone from the mountain without waiting passively for God to create the new kingdom entirely by himself. Represented by the stone from the mountain, the arrival of Daniel's ideal kingdom coincides with the arrival of Isaiah's realm of valleys upliftedand mountains levelled. King expertly merged the mountain symbols from Daniel and Isaiah into a single image of a perfected community. He also merged his dream with Nebuchadnezzar's dream.

Joining King's choir of voices was the most distinguished of all possible members: God Almighty. King orchestrated the divine voice in several ways. One was through his status as a Baptist minister. (Six years earlier he literally donned his pulpit robe to address a crowd of twenty-five thousand gathered at the same spot.) He also expressed God's Word by reiterating the vision of the prophets and Jesus, who spoke directly for God. And he used the cadences of the black pulpit to heighten his demands.

He began by invoking patriotic authority—the Declaration of Independence, the Gettysburg Address, and the Emancipation Proclamation. Religion did not enter the speech overtly until Amos spoke at the halfway point. Like other folk preachers, King here (and elsewhere) began to accentuate rhythm and vocal contrasts in the middle of his presentation. When the words of Amos emerged, so did the vocal dynamics of the folk pulpit. At exactly the same point he offered a cornucopia of rhetorical figures, packing together seven series of repeating phrases (e. g., "We are not satisfied . . ." and "I have a dream . . ."). His chockablock use of these parallelisms added another religious element, for such sequences were standard practice in the folk pulpit.

By enlisting the divine voice, King did more than create

a homiletic self. Just as C.L. Franklin assumed the mantle of a Biblical prophet, so did King in **"I Have a Dream."** His expert application of Biblical prophecy through folk preachers' techniques signified that God spoke through him.

As he catalogued an American nightmare, King essentially argued that the finest secular presences, including Jefferson and Lincoln, had failed miserably. The "architects of our republic" offered a "promissory note" that pledged liberty. But for blacks the note proved "a bad check," a check "marked insufficient funds." By introducing divine authority after secular authority, which had proven inadequate, this new Biblical prophet suggested that an impatient God would now overrule secular forces and install justice without delay. When God ordains for justice to roll down like waters, the flood must eventually cross the Mason-Dixon line. When valleys are exalted, racism will end. When the stone of hope emerges from the mountain, it will smash the flawed kingdom of segregation. Why? Because, in the holistic vision of slaves, God redeems his children in both the next world and this world, for in the end the sacred and secular worlds are inseparable.

As usual King practiced voice merging in his conclusion. The prophet adjusted and refined a passage from his acquaintance and fellow black pastor, Archibald Carey. Consider the final portion of Carey's 1952 address to the Republican National Convention:

We, Negro Americans, sing with all loyal Americans:

> My country 'tis of thee,
> Sweet land of liberty,
> Of thee I sing.
> Land where my fathers died,
> Land of the Pilgrims' pride
> From every mountainside
> Let freedom ring!

> That's exactly what we mean—from every mountain side, let freedom ring. Not only from the Green Mountains and White Mountains of Vermont and New Hampshire; not only from the Catskills of New York; but from the Ozarks in Arkansas, from the Stone Mountain in Georgia, from the Blue Ridge Mountains of Virginia—let it ring not only for the minorities of the United States, but for . . . the disinherited of all the earth—may the Republican Party, under God, from every mountainside, LET FREEDOM RING!

Here the "My" of "My country" is both the narrator of Samuel Smith's "America" and Carey and "all Negro Americans." Through voice merging, Carey enlists the first verse of "America" as an agent not for self-satisfaction but for radical political change. He unites his identity with the ultra-patriotic voice of our unofficial national anthem.

In his peroration King refined Carey's words:

> This will be the day when all of God's children will be able to sing with new meaning:

> My country 'tis of thee,
> Sweet land of liberty,

> Of thee I sing.
> Land where my fathers died,
> Land of the Pilgrim's pride,
> From every mountainside
> Let freedom ring!

> So let freedom ring from the prodigious hilltops of New Hampshire.
> Let freedom ring from the mighty mountains of New York.
> Let freedom ring from the heightening Alleghenies of Pennsylvania. . . .
> Let freedom ring from Stone Mountain of Georgia.
> Let freedom ring from Lookout Mountain of Tennessee.
> Let freedom ring from every hill and molehill in Mississippi.
> From every mountainside, let freedom ring.

This entire litany extends the lyrics of "America." King used "Let freedom ring"—the last three words from the song—to establish his concluding series. By initiating each thought, these three words organize the entire sequence. This extension is metaphorical as well as stylistic, for the narrator of "America," Carey, and King compare freedom to a mighty bell whose peal will echo across every mountain. In effect King composed another verse for the anthem as he merged his voice with "America." Surely the "My" of "My country" indicates King and "all of God's children" as well as the narrative voice of the song. He also used this sequence to apply Isaiah's dream of valleys turned upside down. In the new landscape of Isaiah/King, even the hills and molehills of Mississippi, a low-lying state, will be exalted into mountains prodigious enough to echo the peal of freedom.

Hailing Isaiah's and Carey's utopian future, King envisions a day when everyone will dismantle social barriers and merge voices by singing "America." Here he simultaneously engages in voice merging and reflects on a future of massive voice merging that will collapse all racial distinctions. He thereby takes the harmonious, heavenly vision of folk religion and sets it down squarely on earth.

In his final sentence King reinforced this entire rhetorical process by quoting yet another source:

> . . . when we allow freedom to ring . . . from every village and every hamlet, from every state and every city, we will be able to speed up that day when all of God's children—black men and white men, Jews and Gentiles, Protestants and Catholic, will be able to join hands and sing in the words of the old Negro spiritual: "Free at last! Free at last! Thank God Almighty, we're free at last!"

The "We" of "we're free at last" is not only King and his ensemble of authoritative voices. "We" are all people—blacks and whites, Jews and Christians—who experience the long-awaited coming of the kingdom of God. Reinvigorating the sacred time of folk religion, King announced that Isaiah's prophecy will finally come true: the glory of the Lord will be revealed and all flesh will see it together. All flesh, all human beings will hold hands, merge voices in song, and celebrate the fulfilled vision of slaves, Jefferson, Lincoln, Amos, Isaiah, Daniel, Jesus, Handel's narrator, Carey, and King. Through sacred time, all their hopes and longings will fuse into the same hope and the same longing, which will finally be satisfied.

Here King again simultaneously engaged in voice merging and explained his hope for massive voice merging in an eschatological future of racial justice. Through the language of his inclusive, harmonious choir, he projected the end of history, when brotherhood will triumph, identities will converge, and sacred time will reign. Justice will pour down like waters, valleys will become mountains, and the stone hewn from the mountain will smash all racist, earthly kingdoms. On this day Americans will finally create themselves and their nation.

While **"I Have a Dream"** is a great folk sermon, some of King's speeches are not folk sermons at all. In sharp contrast to this speech is a largely ghostwritten anti-war address delivered in April 1967 at Riverside Church, the institution of [Harry Emerson] Fosdick and McCracken. An important presentation, **"A Time to Break Silence"** was King's first fully publicized attack on the war in Vietnam.

Before reviving McCracken's view that only true Chris-

tianity could defeat Communism, King provided an extended political analysis of the history of Vietnam and a detailed argument about Ho Chi Minh and his followers. He then reminded listeners of the deadly effects of American firepower and argued that the majority of the enemy, the National Liberation Front, were nationalists, not Communists.

While King began by alluding to his career, he dispensed with his usual argument from authority. Apart from a brief mention of the good Samaritan, he made no significant references to the Bible. Nor did he invoke great American presidents. Refusing to argue deductively, he did not claim that all war violates Christian principles. Instead, his argument succeeded or failed on the merits of his inductive assessment of the history of Vietnam, the intentions of the Viet Cong, and the appropriateness of American intervention. Thus **"A Time to Break Silence"** clearly embodied an inductive argument replete with inductive logic. In this respect it resembles several of his other ghostwritten speeches.

By contrast **"I Have a Dream"** and virtually all of King's other memorable speeches operate by way of a deductive structure similar to that of his sermons. In **"I Have a**

At the Lincoln Memorial in Washington, D.C., King greets the 250,000 marchers who gathered to "demonstrate for freedom." Here he delivered his "I Have a Dream" speech, the most famous speech of his career.

Dream" King argues from the authority of Jefferson, Lincoln, "America," and the Bible—all of which he applies deductively to the situation of black America. According to the logic of **"I Have a Dream,"** segregation is wrong, but not for reasons unveiled in a detailed analysis, which never surfaces in the speech. Rather segregation is wrong because it eviscerates the Emancipation Proclamation, scandalizes Jefferson's vision, violates Amos's demand, stymies Isaiah's longings, and contaminates the freedom celebrated in "America." Essentially **"I Have a Dream"** contends that segregation is wrong because it prevents the highest deductive truths of the nation and the Bible from governing human relations. Enacting these deductive truths means eradicating segregation.

The deductive nature of **"I Have a Dream"** is obvious not only in contrast to **"A Time to Break Silence"** but also in the context of the other speechifying at the March on Washington. Virtually all other addresses at the March concentrated on inductive appeals. In his censored but still militant speech, John Lewis talked of a pregnant activist in Albany, Georgia, whose brutal beating took the life of her fetus. Lewis and other speakers related other recent events and complained about the congressional bottleneck preventing passage of civil rights legislation. Identifying culprits of injustice, Lewis named names and wondered aloud about creating a new political party.

By contrast, **"I Have a Dream"** alluded to no recent incidents. Unlike Lewis and the other orators, King mentioned not a single, living person by name and referred only to his four children and to one other specific, living human being—the governor of Alabama. Unlike the array of other speakers, who discussed the importance of a civil rights bill, King made no direct reference to Congress or to the pending legislation, which became the most important civil rights law in American history. Only by considering the context of **"I Have a Dream"**—not by listening to any of its lines—can anyone even tell that the speech has anything to do with John Kennedy's civil rights proposal.

Instead of talking historical particulars in the manner of **"A Time to Break Silence"** and other ghostwritten speeches, **"I Have a Dream"** and King's other sermonic speeches repeatedly enunciate overarching, deductive principles and insist that these principles demand the repeal of segregation. The argument of King's most eloquent speeches owes nothing to formal Western philosophy. The argument of his sermonic speeches—including all his spectacular oratory—is never philosophical or inductive. Rather, the argument is invariably deductive, and stands as a variation of sermonic argument.

To make such arguments King often borrowed from himself, moving material freely from speeches to sermons and sermons to speeches. The strikingly similar appeals of his memorable speeches and his sermons enabled him to interchange material through his mix-and-match method of composing. Because he generally used deductive argument in both sacred and secular orations, most of his material fit equally well into speeches and sermons, which is why his speeches seem like sermons and his sermons seem like speeches.

. . . . .

While many would rank King as the greatest American preacher of the century, one could easily wonder how he could become a stellar homilist and essayist while also directing a social revolution. He managed to become both the most accomplished preacher and the most successful reformer of the century partly because he did not begin the process of fusing the roles of preacher, theologian, and activist. Unlike white religious leaders, he preached by protesting, protested by preaching, and wrote theology by stepping into a jail cell. His successful theology consists of his sermons, speeches, civil rights essays, and political career—not his formal theological work. Had he accepted the white division of theology, homiletics, and politics, he never would have gone to jailto gain the authority to speak. By rejecting white models, he achieved the apotheosis of his own community's understanding of religious leadership, an understanding the nation came to cherish.

Nowhere is this black conception of theology more evident than in **Letter from Birmingham Jail**. Along with the Sermon on the Porch, the essay is more completely inseparable from the civil rights movement than any other example of King's discourse. Indeed a better match between words and deeds is difficult to imagine. King perfectly tailored his letter to the particulars of Birmingham in 1963, including its recent mayoral election and an unsolved rash of bombings. The principles outlined in **Letter** mandated his trip to jail, and a stay in jail mandated the explanation supplied by **Letter.** Getting arrested set the stage for **Letter**, **Letter** set the stage for future arrests.

Yet, as King masterfully performed the simultaneous roles of preacher, theologian, and activist, he wrote an essay that, unlike his other discourse, actually reflects his study of Euro-American philosophy and theology. **Letter** also manifests the powerful and more familiar influences of the black folk pulpit, *Christian Century,* Fosdick, [Harris] Wofford, and two other religious writers. All these influences converge in this extraordinary essay.

Although King's epistolary essay was inspired by Paul, his more immediate stimulant was *Christian Century*. In 1959, six months after joining the editorial staff of the journal, he informed its editor that he wanted to write "occasional articles and letters" that could reach "the Protestant leadership of our country." The editor agreed that his readership would appreciate "an occasional personal letter which you could write." Six months later the editor gave more explicit instructions, telling King and his other editors-at-large to write Christmas letters "in such a form that they can actually be sent to the people to whom they are addressed as well as appearing in the columns of the magazine." The recipients responded with a set of public letters printed in the Christmas issue of the journal. Like **Letter,** these letters ostensibly focused on their real-life addressees but actually on readers of *Christian Century.* Like **Letter,** some of them combined a cordial and respectful tone with forceful criticism of their addressees. Although King did not write a public letter on this occasion, he did so a few years later in Birmingham.

Ostensibly serving as King's response to eight moderate

clergy, *Letter* first surfaced in *Christian Century, Liberation,* and *Christianity and Crisis*—three left-of-center journals—and in pamphlets disseminated by the Fellowship of Reconciliation (FOR) and another leftist, pacifist organization, the American Friends Service Committee. Soon afterwards other readers encountered King's epistle in *The Progressive, Ebony,* and other liberal periodicals. Publication in the *New York Post* and the *San Francisco Chronicle* further expanded King's readership. (He claimed that "nearly a million copies . . . have been widely circulated in churches of most of the major denominations.") He also installed the instantly popular essay as the centerpiece for *Why We Can't Wait,* his longer account of the Birmingham movement.

Given that King wrote *Letter* for *Christian Century* and other left-of-center outlets, one can say that its original and primary audience was not the ostensible audience of eight moderate clergy. Nor was it other moderate readers. Instead, King carefully crafted a letter that could actually be mailed to its addressees while engaging the readers of *Christian Century* and other liberal Protestants. The progressive ministers and laity who raved about King's sermons at Cathedral of St. John, Riverside Church, the Chicago Sunday Evening Club, and elsewhere were the same people who subscribed to *Christian Century.* Because this journal had promulgated racial equality not merely for years, but for several decades prior to *Letter,* the vast majority of its subscribers wholeheartedly agreed with King's attack on segregation long before he wrote his essay. Had the editors of the journal failed to sympathize with King, they would not have published ["**Pilgrimage to Non-Violence**"] several years prior to *Letter.* Nor would they have welcomed him as an editor-at-large every year from 1958 until a year after the publication of *Letter.* Equally sympathetic were those who read *Letter* in other liberal forums. Although the essay eventually reached large numbers of moderates, King's main purpose was to convert the converted and reinforce their earlier support. He carefully preached to the choir, targeting an audience of liberals by asking them to invoke the role of moderates. The essay was so well written that it reached a large, spillover audience of moderates as well.

All readers perused an essay composed under trying conditions. By every account, King entered Birmingham jail with nothing to read and with no notes or examples of his own writing. However, he remembered earlier speeches and sermons and insinuated several familiar passages into his essay, including material he had originally obtained from sources. Because he relied on his memory—not directly on texts—the borrowed passages in *Letter* do not resemble his models as closely as usual. several of his sources can be clearly identified.

For his arguments about nonconformity, he recalled his own sermon **"Transformed Nonconformist,"** including passages that came from Fosdick's *Hope of the World* and from a sermon by H.H. Crane:

> FOSDICK: We Christians were intended to be that [creative] minority. We were to be the salt of the earth, said Jesus. We were to be the light of the world. We were to be the leaven in the lump of the race. . . . That is joining the real church . . . *ecclesia* . . . a minority selected from the majority . . . . There was a time . . . when Christianity was very powerful. Little groups of men and women were scattered through the Roman Empire. . . . They were far less than two per cent and the heel of persecution was often on them, but they flamed with a conviction. . . .
>
> Do you remember what Paul called them . . . "We are a colony of heaven," he said . . . [Christianity] stopped ancient curses like infanticide. It put an end to the . . . gladitorial shows.
>
> CRANE: Consider first the thermometer. Essentially, it . . . records or registers its environments. . . . Instead of being *conformed* to this world, [man] can *transform* it. . . . For when he is what his Maker obviously intended him to be, he is not a thermometer; he is a thermostat. . . . there is a thermostatic type of religion . . . and its highest expression is called vita Christianity.
>
> KING: There was a time when the church was very powerful. . . . In those days the church was not merely a thermometer that recorded the ideas and principles of popular opinion; it was a thermostat that transformed the mores of society. Whenever the early Christians entered a town, the people in power . . . immediately sought to convict the Christians for being "disturbers of the peace". . . . But the Christians pressed on in the conviction that they were a "colony of heaven". . . . Small in number, they were big in commitment. . . . By their effort and example they brought an end to such ancient evils as infanticide and gladitorial contests. Perhaps I must turn . . . to the inner spiritual church as the true *ekklesia* and hope of the world. These [ministers who support civil rights] have been the leaven in the lump of the race. Their witness has been the spiritual salt that has preserved the true meaning of the Gospel. . . .

King here eschewed the King James version of the Bible, which he normally used, and followed Fosdick in quoting from the 1922 Moffatt translation of Philippians 3:20 ("We are a colony of heaven"). Significantly, the King James translation of this verse—"For our conversation is in heaven"—fails to provide *any* Biblical support for nonconformity. Here King owes a debt not only to Fosdick's lines, but also to Fosdick's choice of a specific scripture *and* a specific translation of that scripture. This translation contrasts substantively not only with the King James edition, but with almost all other available English translations.

Turning to another familiar source, King marshalled his arguments for nonviolence and civil disobedience by refashioning ideas and language from two of Wofford's speeches. He reworded a passage from Wofford that he had used earlier in *Stride:*

> WOFFORD: . . . [*Civil* disobedience] involves the highest possible respect for the law. If we secretly violated the law, or tried to evade it, or vi-

olently tried to overthrow it, that would be undermining the idea of law, Gandhi argued. But by openly and peacefully disobeying an unjust law and asking for the penalty, we are saying that we so respect the law that when we think it is so unjust that in conscience we cannot obey, then we belong in jail until that law is changed.

> KING: In no sense do I advocate evading or defying the law. . . . One who breaks an unjust law must do so openly, lovingly, and with a willingness to accept the penalty. I submit that an individual who breaks a law that conscience tells him is unjust, and who willingly accepts the penalty of imprisonment in order to arouse the conscience of the community over its injustice, is in reality expressing the highest respect for the law.

King also paraphrased Wofford's citation of Socrates, Augustine, and Aquinas as proponents of civil disobedience and Wofford's call for nonviolent gadflies.

For part of his analysis of segregation, King turned to George Kelsey, his professor at Morehouse, whose remarks on segregation proved useful on several occasions. In *Stride*, "A Challenge to Churches and Synagogues," and *Letter*, King sometimes reiterated and sometimes adapted passages from Kelsey:

> KELSEY: . . . segregation is itself utterly un-Christian. It is established on pride, fear, and falsehood. . . . It is unbrotherly, impersonal, a complete denial of the "*I-Thou*" relationship, and a complete expression of the "*I-It*" relation. Two segregated souls never meet in God.

Compare King's statement in **"A Challenge to the Churches and Synagogues"**:

> . . . segregation is morally wrong and sinful. It is established on pride, hatred, and falsehood. It is unbrotherly and impersonal. Two segregated souls never meet in God. . . . To use the words of Martin Buber, segregation substitutes an "I-it" relationship for the "I-thou" relationship and ends up relegating persons to the status of things.

King distilled this analysis in *Letter*:

> Segregation, to use the terminology of . . . Martin Buber, substitutes an "I-it" relationship for an "I-thou" relationship and ends up relegating persons to the status of things.

For his affirmation of interdependence, King borrowed another passage from Fosdick. Fosdick's "We are intermeshed in an inescapable mutuality" became King's "We are caught in an inescapable network of mutuality."

The black church originally supplied King with ideas about nonconformity, nonviolence, segregation, interdependence, and other themes trumpeted in *Letter*. Invoking sacred time, he compared himself to the prophets and Paul and talked about Jesus, Martin Luther, John Bunyan, Lincoln, and Jefferson as though they shared his cell block in Birmingham. Wielding his customary argument from authority, he also cited Socrates, Augustine, Aquinas, Tillich, Niebuhr, T.S. Eliot, and three Old Testament heroes. He skillfully wove each of these references into the fabric of an astute analysis of segregation and civil disobedience in Birmingham.

Those who accept Martin Luther King's philosophy must believe that his death, like the deaths of countless American blacks felled by racism, will be redeemed somehow, someday.

—David L. Lewis in his King: A Critical Biography, *1970.*

While King drew on familiar sources for the content of *Letter*, the intricate structure of his argument reflects his exposure to famous Euro-American philosophers, whose works offer many precedents of fine-spun philosophical persuasion. *Christian Century* and black and white sermons provide far fewer examples of the carefully layered appeals that structure *Letter*.

King's essay can be seen as an exemplary, modern version of an oration from ancient Greece or Rome. Basically *Letter* follows the steps of a typical classical speech: introduction, proposition, division, confirmation, refutation, and peroration. His tendency to move his argument forward through skillful digressions is a standard classical strategy. Offering a modest variation of classical form, he packed the bulk of his argument into his refutation, effectively refuting both major and minor premises of the eight clergymen's implicit syllogisms. He practiced "multipremise refutation" by expressing disappointment at being labelled an extremist, then folding that argument into a vigorous defense of certain forms of extremism. His "tone of sadness and compulsion" and expert understatement (e. g., "I cannot join you in your praise of the Birmingham police department") also enjoy precedents in classical rhetoric. By registering his humility, his understatements paradoxically buttress his claims instead of undermining them.

Layered philosophical argument is just as crucial to *Letter* as the black conception of religious roles that made it possible in the first place. *Christian Century*, white sermons, and black folk religion also inform King's essay in powerful ways. *Letter* masterfully interlaces themes of Fosdick, Wofford, Crane, and Kelsey; invokes multiple authorities; reinvigorates the sacred time of the folk pulpit; and supplies rich Pauline allusions and other Biblical echoes. King carefully subsumed each of these appeals within a larger inductive argument consisting of box-within-a-box, multipremise refutation—an argument as lucid as it is intricate. His keen awareness of the readership of *Christian Century* enabled him to choose truisms from appropriate authorities (including Tillich, Niebuhr, and Martin Buber) that would fit suitably into his larger scheme.

King's study of philosophy and theology during his years at Crozer and Boston accounts for the classical argument that structures his essay. Classical rhetoric directly or indirectly influenced every masterpiece of Western philosophy and theology that King's professors assigned him to read. Though he often expressed the major themes of *Letter*—sometimes with remarkably similar wording—at no other time did he ever summon its rigorously ordered, predominantly inductive logic and controlled understatement.

The uniqueness of the essay results primarily from his decision to go to jail, which reflects Biblical and African-American precedents for combining the roles of preacher, theologian, and agitator. His isolation in Birmingham jail—an isolation he never again experienced—enabled him to translate into popular terms the kind of argument he learned in the academy.

. . . . .

Facing the task of translating black orality into print, King, like many others, began borrowing sermons early in his career. Adopting a text from nineteenth-century preacher Phillips Brooks helped him land the pulpit of one of the finest black churches in Alabama. Beginning his political career, King continued to borrow sermons. From Northern white liberals and moderates, he received nothing but accolades. When he travelled to the Cathedral of St. John, the Chicago Sunday Evening Club, Riverside Church, and the National Cathedral, congregations applauded his sermons on nonconformity, fear, and an array of other extremely familiar topics. No one groaned when he wielded quotations from Khayyam, Bowring, Shakespeare, Swinburne, Lowell, and others that many had heard before. On the contrary, white churchgoers almost invariably greeted him not merely with approbation, but with an overwhelming adulation reserved for no one else in Protestantism. African Americans also thrilled to King's addresses.

Nor did preachers complain when King borrowed their sermons. Warmly welcoming him to Riverside Church, McCracken repeatedly negotiated a spot on King's jammed schedule and always expressed exuberant pleasure at King's appearance. He did so after King borrowed his sermon about Communism and published much of it in both **"Pilgrimage"** and *Strength*. Buttrick served as an editorial associate for *Pulpit* the year before King published there a sermon based on Buttrick's explication of a parable. There is no record that Buttrick ever complained about King's sermon. Hamilton's widow, Florence Hamilton, declares that her husband "had great respect and admiration for King." Archibald Carey continued his friendship with King after King had adapted a portion of Carey's speech for **"I Have a Dream."** The nonminister Harris Wofford may speak for several of King's sources when he states that he would be "complimented" if King borrowed his lines.

King's language impressed whites not in spite of his borrowing but because of it. Much of his material resonated with white Protestants precisely because they had heard it before. Repetition aids memory: if people hear a tune often enough, they will begin humming it themselves. Listeners remember lines from folk sermons partly because preachers keep repeating their best lines. King's listeners retained his ideas and phrases more easily because the familiar strains of his sermons made them more memorable.

King also validated himself by offering forms of argument that whites had already internalized and by propounding themes that they already understood and respected. He routinely supplied surefire, doctrinally sound sermons with recipe-perfect proportions of Biblical exegesis, application, quotations, illustrations, and the like. Borrowing enabled him to foolproof his sermons against theological error, weak themes, faulty structure, and other mistakes. Had he instead supplied sermons with profoundly original content, he would never have legitimized his radical tactic of civil disobedience and his radical goals of ending racism, poverty, and war. Much too strange and much too radical to gain acceptance, he would have been dismissed as a black Eugene Debs, a black Norman Thomas, or another W.E.B. DuBois or Malcolm X.

Borrowing also let King escape the restrictions of the clock and therein become a Houdini of time. This Houdini could elude the straitjacket of twenty-four-hour days by undertaking a variety of activities at the same moment. He could simultaneously lead demonstrations; administer a large organization; raise tens of thousands of dollars; tell presidents what to do; serve time in jail; maintain a huge correspondence; and publish scores of essays as well as several books. While enchanting listeners in Cleveland, he could simultaneously direct a world famous march from Selma. He could mediate a crisis with the mayor in Chicago while confronting "Black Power" on a Mississippi highway. This ubiquitous leader could magically advise senators, write a column, publish an essay, rally voters, placate unruly staffers, preach a sermon, and comfort a church janitor—all in a single day.

Barnstorming the nation as a Houdini of time became possible only because King consulted sources and thereby foolproofed his discourse. No one can consistently compose flawless sermons without spending a gargantuan amount of time doing so. If forced to construct sermons entirely from scratch, he would have had no choice but to spend far more time writing and far less time engaged in other vital activities.

King's most grueling endeavor was a dramatic oratorical marathon that can only be compared to a non-stop, never-ending presidential campaign. Speaking on two or three hundred occasions each year, he reached hundreds of thousands of listeners in the flesh. He dedicated himself to this nostalgically old-fashioned, person-to-person communication because it was the best way to enlist support. Had he chosen not to borrow sermons, he would have communicated in person to far fewer people, seriously diluting the impact of his message.

Moreover, when King abandoned his sources, his words often fell flat. His frequently ghostwritten policy speeches—such as **"A Time to Break Silence"**—resemble the speechifying of Hubert Humphrey, George McGovern, and other liberal Democrats. Like them, he filled his policy statements with detailed political analysis, which he omitted from his sermons and sermonic speeches. Just as the oratory of Humphrey and McGovern failed to seduce voters, his policy addresses never received the enthusiasm commanded by his sermonic oratory. By contrast, his sermons always succeeded. So did almost all of his sermonic speeches, only small portions of which were ghostwritten. For that reason, he mainly cycled and recycled sermonic material—not ghostwritten language—as he conducted his marathon speaking tour over a twelve-year period.

Merging black and white homiletics, he subordinated Fosdick's entire worldview to the slaves' grand theme of deliverance. He did so by radically changing the context of borrowed themes. Unlike others, he was never content merely to preach to well-dressed Northern liberals gazing at Biblical stories frozen in sculptured stone and dazzling stained glass. Instead, he baptized the huge congregation commanded by Fosdick and [J. Wallace] Hamilton into the massive political movement imagined by W.E.B. DuBois and A. Philip Randolph. Releasing energy from the cozy, closeted sanctuaries of Northern churches, he electrified the tense streets of Alabama. Through the folk procedures of voice merging and self-making, he simultaneously propelled, intensified, and interpreted a huge national drama that Fosdick, Hamilton, and Buttrick could never have staged. Like the spirituals and gospel songs whose lyrics he wove into his oratory, he offered balm to soothe and lightning to energize both participants and spectators of that drama. No one could have predicted that a group of liberal, white sermons would help trigger a Second Reconstruction. By directing a large-scale assault on segregation, he transformed each of his sermons into a powerful political act—something that could never be said about Fosdick, Buttrick, or Hamilton. He turned their iron ore into gold.

Through skillfully choreographed political confrontations, King repeatedly tested the clichés of Jefferson ("All men are created equal"), the Bible ("You shall reap what you sow"), and progressive pulpits ("Truth crushed to earth will rise again") against the billy clubs of Southern police and the hatred of recalcitrant governors. He essentially argued that, should Bull Connor and George Wallace win, they would expose noble American truths as sheer sentimentality. In that event, the Revolution of 1776 (with its "unalienable rights"), America ("sweet land of liberty"), Christ's *agape* ("Love your enemies"), and the Christian law of history ("Unearned suffering is redemptive") would be entirely refuted, and injustice would reign forever and ever.

Similarly King tested dust and divinity, Jesus's parables, antidotes to fear, and an entire array of other orthodox and standard themes. If racists prevailed, they would disprove an entire Christian perspective, exposing a widely shared world picture as an expression of utter naïveté. By tossing boilerplate sermons into a cauldron of disruptive confrontation, King measured an entire worldview against the bomb on his porch, the hoses and dogs of Bull Connor, and the dynamite that killed four girls in Birmingham. He thereby brought to life a language that had never before spoken decisively to power brokers and presidents.

King's borrowing made it difficult for audiences to reject his leadership without also rejecting a nostalgic universe not yet shattered by Darwin, Freud, and Einstein. By trac-

ing a vision of love and justice shared by millions, he established himself as the exponent of order and stigmatized his adversaries as promoters of chaos. They had overturned God's justice by institutionalizing racial oppression. For this reason, in King's rhetorical universe, cosmic justice-necessitated disruption, and only a revolution could achieve true stability.

King adapted material in a highly creative way. No matter what he borrowed or how often, after leaving Boston University, he managed never to sound stilted or artificial. Instead, he paradoxically, but invariably, sounded exactly like himself. His long training in the folk pulpit accounts for his extraordinary ability to use others' language to become himself. This training also explains why his audiences never objected to his borrowing and why an entire generation of scholars failed to guess that he mined sources frequently. His skill in transporting procedures of folk preaching into print ensured that his borrowed lines fit his persona more closely than did the words of ghostwriters. . . .

Paradoxically King became himself by reviving and politicizing the words of others as he choreographed a grand protest against the indescribable horror, brutality, and tragedy of segregation. Borrowing beloved sermonic themes meant defining the current struggle as a drama that God would satisfactorily resolve in his reliable, beneficent universe. Borrowing also helped King emerge as an authoritative public intellectual who could simultaneously participate in the political fray and stand philosophically above it. Foolproofing his discourse enabled him to articulate the overarching principles of the movement while towering above its day-to-day frustrations. His magisterial public persona helped valorize the struggle.

Whoever would condemn King's borrowing necessarily assumes that King would have persuaded whites just as easily had he originated every word out of his mouth. But the original, sublime eloquence of Frederick Douglass, DuBois, [James] Farmer, [Fannie Lou] Hamer, and a host of other blacks long before and throughout the civil rights struggle never changed white people's minds. Had King composed original language, as they did, there is no evidence that he would have been any more persuasive than they were. Certainly he thought he had found the most persuasive words available.

Keith D. Miller, in his Voice of Deliverance: The Language of Martin Luther King, Jr. and Its Sources, *The Free Press, 1992, 282 p. [The excerpts of Martin Luther King, Jr.'s work used here were originally published in his* A Testament of Hope, HarperCollins Publishers, Inc., *1986.]*

FURTHER READING

Bosmajian, Haig A. "The Rhetoric of Martin Luther King's

Letter from Birmingham Jail." The Midwest Quarterly XXI, No. 1 (Autumn 1979): 46-62.

> Discusses structure, rhetoric, and style in *Letter from Birmingham City Jail.*

Fulkerson, Richard P. "The Public Letter as a Rhetorical Form: Structure, Logic, and Style in King's *Letter from Birmingham Jail." The Quarterly Journal of Speech* 65, No. 2 (April 1979): 121-36.

> Analysis of King's argumentative techniques in *Letter from Birmingham City Jail.*

Gasnick, Roy M. Review of *Strength to Love*, by Martin Luther King, Jr. *America* 109, No. 7 (17 August 1963): 173-74.

> Favorably reviews *Strength to Love*, concluding: "As the civil rights crisis becomes more dangerous, . . . we all need to be reminded that it *does* take strength to love. Martin Luther King, in these sermons, has pointed out the source of that strength."

The Journal of American History 78, No. 1 (June 1991).

> Issue devoted to a roundtable discussion of King's plagiarism; includes conversations with his professors from Boston University and articles by David Levering Lewis and David J. Garrow, two of King's biographers.

Klein, Mia. "The Other Beauty of Martin Luther King, Jr.'s *Letter from Birmingham Jail." College Composition and Communication* XXXII, No. 1 (February 1981): 30-7.

> Examines the emotional appeal of *Letter from Birmingham Jail*, focusing on sentence structure.

Kopkind, Andrew. "Soul Power." *The New York Review of Books* IX, No. 3 (24 August 1967): 3-4, 6.

> Review of *Where Do We Go from Here* in which Kopkind questions King's sincerity and honesty, saying "there is something disingenuous about his public voice, and about this book. He is not really telling it like it is, but as he thinks his audience wants it to be."

Oates, Stephen B. "The Intellectual Odyssey of Martin Luther King." *The Massachusetts Review* XXII, No. 2 (Summer 1981): 301-20.

Biographical sketch that traces the evolution of King's philosophy.

Pitre, Mergione. "The Economic Philosophy of Martin L. King, Jr." *The Review of Black Political Economy* 9, No. 2 (Winter 1979): 191-98.

> Describes King's plans for on-the-job training, federal housing, and a guaranteed income programs in the United States.

Scott, Robert L. "Black Power Bends Martin Luther King." In *The Rhetoric of Black Power*, edited by Robert L. Scott and Wayne Brockriede, pp. 166-77, New York: Harper & Row, 1969.

> Explains King's attitude toward the Black Power movement.

Sharma, Mohan Lal. "Martin Luther King: Modern America's Greatest Theologian of Social Action." *The Journal of Negro History* LIII, No. 3 (July 1968): 257-63.

> Discusses the intellectual movements that influenced King in his roles as theologian and activist.

Steinkraus, Warren E. "Martin Luther King's Personalism and Non-violence." *Journal of the History of Ideas* XXXIV, No. 1 (January-March 1973): 97-111.

> Analyzes King's roles as a philosopher and a public leader who advocated non-violence.

Ward, Brian. Review of *The Papers of Martin Luther King, Jr., Volume I: Called to Serve, January 1929-June 1951*, ed. by Clayborne Carson, Ralph E. Luker, and Penny Russell. *Journal of American Studies* 26, No. 3 (December 1992): 470-71.

> Provides a favorable review of *Called to Serve*, a collection of King's papers and essays delineating "the evolution of King's religious and social thought."

Willhelm, Sidney M. "Martin Luther King, Jr. and the Black Experience in America." *Journal of Black Studies* 10, No. 1 (September 1979): 3-19.

> Critiques King's analysis in *Where Do We Go from Here* of how economic factors affect African Americans.

Additional coverage of King's life and career is contained in the following sources published by Gale Research: *Black Literature Criticism*, Vol. 2; *Black Writers*; and *Contemporary Authors New Revision Series*, Vol. 27.

Marshall McLuhan

1911-1980

(Full name Herbert Marshall McLuhan) Canadian non-fiction writer, critic, and editor.

The following entry provides an overview of McLuhan's career. For further information on his life and works, see *CLC*, Volume 37.

INTRODUCTION

McLuhan gained notoriety during the 1960s for his controversial theories on communications and for the experimental literary forms in which he presented his concepts. "McLuhanism" is a term that critics apply to his theories and to the aphorisms and puns he commonly used to stimulate reader curiosity and to draw attention to his ideas. The most famous McLuhanism—"the medium is the message"—is a pivotal concept in his beliefs. McLuhan emphasized that human societies are shaped by the nature of their communications media; thus, the media through which society communicates has more impact than the content of the messages being relayed. He argued further that recently developed electronic media—particularly television, which has become the dominant form of communication in the twentieth century—are significantly altering contemporary lifestyles and initiating a new stage in human development.

Biographical Information

The son of a real estate and insurance salesman and an actress, McLuhan was born in Edmonton, Alberta, and grew up in Winnipeg, Manitoba. Though he entered the University of Manitoba as an engineering student, McLuhan switched to English, earning his M.A. degree in 1934 with a thesis on George Meredith. He spent the next two years at Cambridge University, where he attended lectures by I. A. Richards and F. R. Leavis. During his stay in England, he converted to Roman Catholicism, the beliefs of which would exert a strong influence on his later thinking. McLuhan began his teaching career in 1936 at the University of Wisconsin in Madison; he then moved in 1937 to the University of St. Louis, where he remained until 1944. After two years at Assumption University (now the University of Windsor) in Ontario, McLuhan accepted a position at St. Michael's College of the University of Toronto, where he taught for the remainder of his career.

Major Works

McLuhan's theories are elaborated in his three most important works, *The Gutenberg Galaxy: The Making of Typographic Man* (1962), *Understanding Media: The Extensions of Man* (1964), and *The Medium Is the Massage: An*

Inventory of Effects (1967). The former book presents a historical foundation for McLuhan's claims, and the latter, which became a bestseller and provoked widespread public and critical debate, examines the implications of new electronic technologies. In *The Gutenberg Galaxy*, which won the Governor General's Award for critical prose, McLuhan claims that there have been four major stages in human development, each directly related to significant changes in the means of human communication. During the first stage, preliterate humans communicated primarily by oral means and used a balance of the five senses to understand the world. McLuhan contends that preliterate societies were necessarily collective in structure and encouraged active participation among members due to their reliance on oral communication. With the creation of the alphabet, a new stage of life evolved in which humans began to use non-oral forms of communication. When printed matter had become the dominant form of mass communication after the invention of the printing press in the fifteenth century, a third stage commenced in which humans began to rely primarily on the sense of vision. "Typographic man" began to construct an understanding of life in much the same way that books convey messages—by emphasizing sequential, linear logic and rationalism. McLuhan claims that books fragmented society by promoting individualistic pursuit of knowledge. The new electronic media are initiating a fourth stage, according to McLuhan, changing human communication from the "visual-conceptual" mode of books to the "audile-tactile" mode of such media as television. Whereas print media tend to fragment society, the new electronics technology, particularly the television with its mass availability, will effect a web of interdependence that can unite humanity in a "global village." In *Understanding Media* McLuhan concentrates on the new electronics technologies and examines their effect on contemporary life. This book made McLuhan an international celebrity; he became a popular lecturer who frequently spoke on college campuses and in corporate meeting rooms. McLuhan contributed to his notoriety during the 1960s by being widely accessible and by presenting his ideas in a variety of media. According to James P. Carey, McLuhan became "a prophet, a phenomenon, a happening, a social movement." *The Medium Is the Massage*—a pun on his own most famous slogan—is the title of a book, a recording, and a television special, all of which appeared in 1967. On the television program, which aired on the National Broadcasting Company network, McLuhan explained that this title "is intended to draw attention to the fact that a medium is not something neutral—it does something to people. It takes hold of them. It rubs them off, it massages them, it bumps them around." In the book McLuhan explained the importance of examining communications media: "All media work us over completely. They are so pervasive in their personal, political, aesthetic, psychological, moral, ethical, and social consequences that they leave no part of us untouched, unaffected, unadulterated."

Critical Reception

Critics have acknowledged the important implications of McLuhan's theories and the fact that he was exploring aspects of popular culture that had been neglected by social scientists. Despite his popularity, though, critical response to *The Gutenberg Galaxy* and *Understanding Media* was largely negative. Many critics cited McLuhan's montage-like presentation of ideas as a major obstacle in conveying his ideas. McLuhan attempted to duplicate in typographic form the ways in which electronic mediums convey messages, relying on repetition, generalizations, puns, and a rapid delivery. Other commentators claimed that his facts were inaccurate, that his definitions of analytical terms lacked precision and consistency, and that his arguments were undeveloped, illogical, and obscure. McLuhan countered such criticism by maintaining that his ideas were meant to be "probes" rather than logically argued theses and that he was primarily interested in stimulating discussion of the new electronic technologies as a means toward understanding and controlling them. In retrospect, most critics view him as an important figure for having drawn attention to the relationship between communication and culture in the contemporary world.

PRINCIPAL WORKS

The Mechanical Bride: Folklore of Industrial Man (nonfiction) 1951

The Gutenberg Galaxy: The Making of Typographic Man (nonfiction) 1962

Understanding Media: The Extensions of Man (nonfiction) 1964

The Medium Is the Massage: An Inventory of Effects [with Quentin Fiore] (nonfiction) 1967

Through the Vanishing Point: Space in Poetry and Painting [with Harley Parker] (nonfiction) 1968

War and Peace in the Global Village: An Inventory of Some Current Spastic Situations That Could Be Eliminated by More Feedforward [with Quentin Fiore] (nonfiction) 1968

Counterblast (nonfiction) 1969

The Interior Landscape: The Literary Criticism of Marshall McLuhan, 1943-1962 (criticism) 1969

From Cliché to Archetype [with Wilfred Watson] (nonfiction) 1970

Letters of Marshall McLuhan (letters) 1987

Laws of Media [with Eric McLuhan] (nonfiction) 1989

CRITICISM

Marshall McLuhan with Gerald E. Stearn (interview date June 1967)

[*Stearn is an American educator, publisher, and editor. In the following excerpt from an interview originally published in* Encounter *in June 1967, McLuhan discusses some of his theories and comments on the critical reception of his work.*]

[*Stearn*]: *What originally led to your interest in media and the effect of media upon our culture?*

[McLuhan]: I was gradually made aware of these things by other people—artists, the new anthropological studies. As you become aware of the different modes of experience in other cultures—and watch them transformed by new, Western technologies—it is difficult to avoid observation. It becomes inevitable to assume that what happens to other people and cultures can happen to us. My present interest is an extension of, and derivative of, my literary work. If I could get a team of media students going, I would happily retire back into literary studies. I find media analysis very much more exciting now simply because it affects so many more people. One measure of the importance of anything is: Who is affected by it? In our time, we have devised ways of making the most trivial event affect everybody. One of the consequences of electronic environments is the total involvement of people in people. The Orientals created caste systems as an area of classified immunity.

Here perhaps my own religious faith has some bearing. I think of human charity as a total responsibility of all, for all. Therefore, my energies are directed at far more than mere political or democratic intent. Democracy as a by-product of certain technologies, like literacy and mechanical industry, is not something that I would take very seriously. But democracy as it belongs very profoundly with Christianity is something I take very seriously indeed.

There have been many more religious men than I who have not made even the most faltering steps in this direction. Once I began to move in this direction, I began to see that it had profound religious meaning. I do not think it my job to point this out. For example, the Christian concept of the mystical body—all men as members of the body of Christ—this becomes technologically a fact under electronic conditions. However, I would not try to theologize on the basis of my understanding of technology. I don't have a background in scholastic thought, never having been raised in any Catholic institution. Indeed, I have been bitterly reproached by my Catholic confrères for my lack of scholastic terminology and concepts.

When one looks back at your first book, **The Mechanical Bride,** *it appears as a strident, moral tract. What is your present attitude toward the* **Bride** *and how is it related to your more recent interests?*

Mechanical Bride is a good example of a book that was completely negated by TV. All the mechanical assumptions of American life have been shifted since TV; it's become an organic culture. Femininity has moved off the photographic, glamor cake altogether into the all-involving tactile mode. Femininity used to be a mingling of visual things. Now it's almost entirely nonvisual. I happened to observe it when it was reaching the end of its term, just before TV.

In 1936, when I arrived at Wisconsin, I confronted classes of freshmen and I suddenly realized that I was incapable of understanding them. I felt an urgent need to study their popular culture: advertising, games, movies. It was pedagogy, part of my teaching program. To meet them on their grounds was my strategy in pedagogy: the world of pop culture. Advertising was a very convenient form of approach. I used advertising in the **Bride** because of legal considerations—no permissions were needed. Otherwise I would have used picture stories of any sort from movies, magazines, anywhere. I had thirty or forty slides and gave little talks to student groups. I invited them to study these ads. In England, at Cambridge, when I arrived there, it had become popular to look at films and the popular culture around us as something to be studied and understood as a "language." Wyndham Lewis did various studies on pop culture. Leavis has a book called *Culture and Environment.* There was a similar interest in popular speech idioms, language, the *Wake. The Waste Land* is full of these pop-cult forms. Pound's *Cantos* have similar forms. Pound has a very useful guide to the *Cantos* called *Kulchur.* In doing the **Bride** I was merely trailing behind some interesting predecessors. I discovered that when you take anything out of the daily newspapers and put it on the screen, people go into a fit of laughter. Like Mort Sahl. He would take random items from the press and read them out to an audience straightforwardly. People never notice the outrageous humor until something is removed from its form. Because it's environmental and invisible. The mo-

ment you translate it into another medium it becomes visible—and hilarious.

Movies on TV are, in a sense, a parody. Just using one form over another form creates that comic effect. When movies were new it was suggested that they were a parody of life. The transcript of ordinary visual life into a new medium created hilarious comedy. The word parody means a road that goes alongside another road. A movie is a visual track that goes alongside another visual track, creating complete terror. I did take time to read the language of the form and discovered that most people couldn't read that visual language. If I merely reprinted ads, without any appended dialogue, the book would have been hilarious in any case. That kind of book ought to be an annual. When you change its environment you flash perception onto it.

In the **Bride** there is far more following of lines of force than simply moral judgments.

Wyndham Lewis was a great influence on me because of his pop-cult analysis. I found Lewis far too moralistic for my tastes. I greatly admired his *method.* Lewis looked at everything as a painter first. His moral judgments never interested me. He was horrified by Bergson and the time philosophy because it seemed to him to destroy various aspects of our Western culture. He said the whole Western culture was based on sight. But he moralized all his life about "ear people" like Bergson who were undermining the visual facets of Western culture. He attacked Spengler in the same way.

Lewis Carroll looked through the looking glass and found a kind of space-time which is the normal mode of electronic man. Before Einstein, Carroll had already entered that very sophisticated universe of Einstein. Each moment, for Carroll, had its own space and its own time. Alice makes her own space and time. Einstein, not Lewis Carroll, thought this was astonishing. . . .

Perhaps the most repeated and passionate dissents emerge from what many critics call your historicism. John Simon's charge—that you play the history of ideas game none too well—has been repeated quite often. You have said that without radio, no Hitler; that the Russians have an "ear" culture and consequently found the U-2 a sensory intruder, not merely the belligerent act of a hostile power.

The Russians find it unbearable to have "eyes" around their environment. Just as we hate the idea of having "ears" in our own—*vide*: the microphone in the embassy eagle. The Russians live much more by ear than we do. Their new high-rise apartments are at once transformed into villages. All communication between fellow apartment dwellers is like that of a village square. They must live this way. In India, for example, when they tried to put in cold running water, it pulled the village women away from the well. This destroyed community life. They had to remove the pipes. You cannot put running water into an aural community without distressful circumstances.

When you make a structural analysis, you follow lines of force and follow not just one but many, at various levels of the culture, observing patterns. All semiliterate or "backward" cultures are aural cultures, whether it's

Ghana or China. They organize space differently, at all times. The Eskimo world is an ear one. When asked to draw maps, they draw areas they've never seen. From their kyacks they've heard water lapping against shores. They map by ear and it later proves quite adequate when checked by aerial photo. Except that there is always an exaggerated area where they've camped. That part receives a stress or bulge in their map. The natural world of nonliterate man is structured by the total field of hearing. This is very difficult for literary people to grasp. The hand has no point of view. The ear has no point of view.

Years ago when I was working with Carpenter on anthropological matters, I used acoustic and auditory space frequently as a basic counterploy to visual Western man. I gave it up because I found that the literary people made desperate attempts to visualize auditory space. But you cannot visualize auditory space, that is: a total field of simultaneous relations, without center or margin. Carpenter has remarked that anthropological materials are now beginning to be made up and published by natives themselves—their own stories are being retold by natives themselves. And the results are totally different from what the anthropologists said earlier. We now realize that a nonvisual culture cannot be reported by a visual man.

A prose statement is a reduction to visual terms, like legal language—which is an extreme, unrealistic case of visual organization.

It isn't accidental that the primary arts of Russia are music and ballet. They are not a literary people at all. The world of Dostoevski is not literary. It's a newspaper world, like Edgar Allen Poe or Dickens (an Ann Landers type). This does not contradict the fact that they take literacy far more seriously (and literally) than the West does. Russians, for example, are quite agitated about the telephone.

Russia never had a Renaissance, in terms of space. Realism, perspective art, is avant-garde for them. When you have the means of realistic representation, you also have the means of mechanical production. Mechanical production comes out of visual realism in the Western world. What we think of as realism is to them (Russians) absolute fantasy.

Kafka isn't realism in our world. It's allegorical fantasy (like Bosch). Similarly, Western visual man would have great difficulty in "reading" a tactile piece of information.

To pre-literate man, space was sacred.

A lot of this aural culture is found now in the Negro world. The reason that they are so far ahead of us in the arts is, quite simply, that they haven't trained their visual sense to the point of suppressing the other senses. In music—dance and song—Negroes are ahead.

The generations gap between parents and children is quite simple—children are auditory, nonvisual in their orientation. Teen-agers are returning to a backward phase.

All literate cultures sentimentalize all primitive cultures, whether as anthropologists or new neighbors of Negroes. We sentimentalize their primitive state automatically as

superior to our own. This confuses a lot of perception, of course.

Is the Cold War then merely a sensory conflict?

We have a huge cold war going on inside our own borders concerning territorial conflicts, ambitions, jurisdictions, economic demands, etc. These are hugely exaggerated misunderstandings born of sensory divergencies. Our inability to understand them mutually exasperates our negotiations in dealing with them. This exasperation is quite independent of the actual sources of conflict. The same with Castro and dealing with Cuba, with its intensely backward, aural culture. The Cuban way of thinking and feeling about problems is quite alien to our modes of understanding. It's the same with the American Southerner, who has very backward, aural ways of thinking and feeling. It's very hard for the literate North to give him credit for being honest and sincere at all.

De Tocqueville was able to predict certain developments in American culture by contrasting the lack of auditory background in America with its ability to blueprint its development in visual, literate terms. He was making equations. He encountered a new land in which literacy had no opposition, except from Indians. Visual literacy marched unimpeded by any other sensory mode. For the first time in the history of the world, a great new technology encountered a great, new space.

De Tocqueville could not blueprint older, European cultures. But to an ear-oriented European, the American literate culture was quite visible. Mrs. Trollope spoke about auditory, nonvisual factors—which the English even in our time find impossible to deal with. They are unable to realize that they have a class struggle based upon ear culture. We accept literacy and they don't. Literacy wipes out tonality. Americans have never permitted a tone of voice to dictate a man's importance in this world. The English use that criterion entirely as a basis of judging human excellence. In highly literate, visual America it is correct spelling and grammar, not correct intonation. T. S. Eliot lacked an English voice and they did not accept him there. Pound just romped through England wearing a mask of outrageous Yankee dialect. They accepted that. The British are unaware of their auditory culture; we're quite unaware of our visual culture.

Similarly, you claim that the war in Vietnam is, more or less, a creature of television.

Without an informed public there would be no war. We live in an informational environment and war is conducted with information. TV news coverage of Vietnam has been a disaster as far as Washington is concerned because it has alienated people altogether from that war. Newspaper coverage would never alienate people from the war because it's "hot," it doesn't involve. TV does and creates absolute nausea. It's like public hangings—if there were public hangings there would be no hangings. Because public hangings would *involve* people. The distant statistical fact—"At 5:30 this morning so and so was executed"—that's hot. Washington is still fighting a "hot" war, as it were, by newspaper means and the old technologies. The effects of the new technologies on war coverage is not something Washington is prepared to cope with. In Washington people do not concede that the news on TV and news in the press are dissimilar.

TV has begun to dissolve the fabric of American life. All the assumptions—all the ground rules—based on visuality, superficiality, blueprinting, connectedness, equality, sameness—disappear with TV.

If you shut off TV, then we would end the war in Vietnam and at the same time set back the civil rights movement?

Oh yes. But there is an alternative: Put hundreds of extra lines on the TV image, step up its visual intensity to a new hot level. This might serve to reverse the whole effect of TV. It might make the TV image photographic, slick, like movies: hot and detached. Bell Telephone is now operating with eight-thousand-line TV images, not eight hundred, quite beyond the fidelity of any known photographic process.

Why hasn't this been tried?

You might well inquire. No one believes these factors have any effect whatever on our human reactions. It's like the old days when people played around with radium, painting watch dials and they licked the brushes. They didn't believe radium could affect people. . . .

When Eric Goldman asked you on "The Open Mind" if media change—the electronic revolution of our time, for example—was a "good" or "bad" thing, you replied:

> *Now, you see, you have slipped into the literary language of the classifier. The visual man is always trying to check things out by classification and matching.*
>
> *Goldman: I have set it in the language of the social commentator. You have said something is happening in our society. We now have a medium which is bombarding us, all of our senses.*
>
> *McLuhan: But when you say "good," is it good in relation to what? You know, the social scientist—*
>
> *Goldman: Is it good in relation to the established values of the West, let us say?*
>
> *McLuhan: You remember what the social scientist said to a friend of his: "How is your wife?" And the other social scientist replied, "Do you mean is she better? If so, in relation to what?"*

Classification, for the literary man, is the be-all and end-all of observations. That's why Macdonald attempts to classify me. In the medical world, classification is a form of dismissal. If the doctor says it's measles, that's it, it's over with. The rest is just routine. But classification is not the beginning of the study of a problem—it's the end. For me any of these little gestures I make are all tentative probes. That's why I feel free to make them sound as outrageous or extreme as possible. Until you make it extreme, the probe is not very efficient. Probes, to be effective, must have this edge, strength, pressure. Of course they *sound* very dogmatic. That doesn't mean you are committed to them. You may toss them away.

There is an alternative to classification and that is exploration. This doesn't easily register with nineteenth-century minds. Most nineteenth-century minds are helpless in discussing contemporary forms. They have never acquired the verbal means of grappling with a pictorial world. Macdonald has no verbal strategies for even coping with the movies, let alone more subtle or more recent forms, like radio or television.

I'm perfectly prepared to scrap any statement I ever made about any subject once I find that it isn't getting me into the problem. I have no devotion to any of my probes as if they were sacred opinions. I have no proprietary interest in my ideas and no pride of authorship as such. You have to push any idea to an extreme, you have to probe. Exaggeration, in the sense of hyperbole, is a major artistic device in all modes of art. No painter, no musician ever did anything without extreme exaggeration of a form or a mode, until he had exaggerated those qualities that interested him. Wyndham Lewis said: "Art is the expression of a colossal preference" for certain forms of rhythm, color, pigmentation, and structure. The artist exaggerates fiercely in order to register this preference in some material. You can't build a building without huge exaggeration or preference for a certain kind of space.

This question of repetition bothers them most because they are looking for values or a "point of view." Now values, insofar as they register a preference for a particular kind of effect or quality, are a highly contentious and debatable area in every field of discourse. Nobody in the twentieth century has ever come up with any meaningful definition or discussion of "value." It doesn't work any longer in economics, let alone humanist affairs. It is rather fatuous to insist upon values if you are not prepared to understand how they got there and by what they are now being undermined. The mere moralistic expression of approval or disapproval, preference or detestation, is currently being used in our world as a substitute for observation and a substitute for study. People hope that if they scream loudly enough about "values" then others will mistake them for serious, sensitive souls who have higher and nobler perceptions than ordinary people. Otherwise, why would they be screaming.

Anybody who spends his time screaming about values in our modern world is not a serious character. You might as well start screaming about a house that's burning down, shouting, "This is not the act of a serious man!" When your old world is collapsing and everything is changing at a furious pitch, to start announcing your preferences for old values is not the act of a serious person. This is frivolous, fatuous. If you were to knock on the door of one of these critics and say "Sir, there are flames leaping out of your roof, your house is burning," under these conditions he would then say to you, "That's a very interesting point of view. I personally couldn't disagree with you more." That's all these critics are saying. Their house is burning and they're saying, "Don't you have any sense of values, simply telling people about fire when you should be thinking about the serious content, the noble works of the mind?" Value is irrelevant.

But if "value is irrelevant" what about the content *of*

media? In your discussions with Eric Goldman this same point was raised:

> *Goldman: Mr. McLuhan, a number of commentators have said that as they understand your view, you really don't think that changing the contents of television would change much about this process. . . .*

> *McLuhan: No. You may have seen a* New Yorker *joke. A couple are watching TV, and one says, "When you think of the vast educational potential of TV, aren't you glad it doesn't?" This is based on the assumption, you see, that it is the content that does the educating, not the medium. Now, if it should be just the other way around— and very few people have asked themselves anything about that—then it would be understandable why these things happen involuntarily and unasked.*

> *Goldman: Take "Peyton Place." If you put on "Peyton Place" or if you put on a news documentary, the contents are radically different in that case, but still from your point of view the medium is transcending the contents in significance so far as the person out there is concerned.*

> *McLuhan: It's like changing the temperature in a room. It doesn't matter what's in the room at all, or what pictures are on the wall, or who is in the room. If the temperature drops forty degrees suddenly, the effect on our outlook, our attitude, is profound.*

> *Media are like that. They just alter the total social temperature. Since TV, the whole American political temperature has cooled down, down, down, until the political process is almost approaching* rigor mortis. *These facts of media are not the areas in which they look—after all, the medical profession was in the habit of looking in the wrong places for causes and effects for many centuries, and nobody has come up with any suggestions for how to control media or the social impact of technologies until now.*

Many people would rather be villains than nitwits. It occurs to me just now that moral vehemence may provide ersatz dignity for our normal moronic behavior. It would be possible to extend my media analysis to include the idea that the normal human condition, when faced with innovation, is that of the brainwashed idiot who tries to introduce the painfully learned responses from one situation into new situations where they apply not at all. The reason that I refrain in the book from pointing out this obvious moral is owing to the discovery, represented by the book itself, that this helpless and witless condition of persistent irrelevance of response is unnecessary at the first moment that we recognize this pattern of response and its causes. It is this discovery that fills me with optimism. The moralist has instinctively translated my forward-looking discovery into backward-looking misanthropy. Moral bitterness is a basic technique for endowing the idiot with dignity. Guilt and remorse are retrospective by definition and exempt the guilty party from any redeeming act of expiation or creative renewal. Guilt and remorse are forms of despair and sloth. Any charge of nonmoral fervor with re-

gard to my work merely points to my own effort to protect reader and critic from the rage and indignation which they have richly earned. For many years I have observed that the moralist typically substitutes anger for perception. He hopes that many people will mistake his irritation for insight. Is this not one of the great attractions of Marxism? While lacking all insight into the processes with which it is concerned, it yet provides an intensely dramatic role for the corporate expression of dissatisfactions that elude the understanding.

Do I "approve of 'Peyton Place' or of Jack Paar?" No! But they're trying to classify Paar with a good or bad "thing," not attempting to find out *what* he's doing or what effect he's having or what's really going on. They are trying to fit him into some sort of encyclopedia of culture. They find *concept* a much more convenient form of human activity than *precept*. They ask me to judge what I observe. Cocteau said: "I don't want to be famous. I just want to be believed." Any artist would say that he doesn't want people to agree or disagree with him. He just wants them to notice. I expect my audience to participate with me in a common act of exploration. I want observations, not agreement. And my own observation of our almost overwhelming cultural gradient toward the primitive—or involvement of all the senses—is attended by complete personal distaste and dissatisfaction. I have no liking for it.

Since, however, this new cultural gradient is the world, the *milieu*, in which I must live and which prepares the students I must teach, I have every motive to understand its constituents, its components, and its operations. I move around through these elements as I hope any scientist would through a world of disease and stress and misery. If a doctor, surgeon or scientist were to become personally agitated about any phenomenon whatever, he would be finished as an explorer or observer. The need to retain an attitude of complete clinical detachment is necessary for survival in this kind of work. It is not an expression of approval or a point of view or outlook. It's only a strategy of survival. Anybody who enters this kind of work with strong feelings of approval or disapproval, nineteenth-century-style point of view, fixed positions, "From where I'm sitting I would say that this is an abomination and degradation of all human values," etc.—anybody who enters any situation in our time with any such commitments has completely polished himself off the scene as an observer. He's had it. So our literary fraternities—nineteenth-century liberals if you like—are completely helpless to even approach the material of their own culture. They are so terrified, so revolted, they don't even know how to get near it and they've bothered to acquire the means of studying or of observing it.

This so-called primitivism—and it is so fatuous in our time, so uncritical—one of the more ridiculous aspects of Picasso, if you like—it's a form of surfboarding, just riding any old wave that happens to be around. On the other hand, primitivism, D. H. Lawrence style, has become in itself almost a form of *camp*. That is why we have suddenly abandoned it in favor of *camp*, which is a new artistic attitude toward our own junkyard. The sudden resolve to tackle our own junkyard as art work is a hopeful indication that we are prepared after all to look at the environment as that which is capable of formulation, patterning, shaping. It still lacks the awareness of what effects environments have upon us. They still seem to imagine that you can take it or leave it. You know the old literate attitude toward advertising in the thirties: "Personally, I can take it or leave it. I'm just not interested in it." These are the helpless victims of all advertising, these people who think that merely by subjecting themselves to it without taking an interest in it they can be immune. The idea of immunity from environments and environments created by media—so long as one concentrates upon noble content—is a cherished illusion in literary circles. I heard a Tom Swiftie the other day—" 'Don't talk to me of icebergs,' said the captain of the *Titanic* sanctimoniously." The literary professions are somewhat in that position. There are many who imagine that we can disregard these forms and their operations on human sensibilities.

Similarly, there are those who feel they can expose themselves to a hideous urban environment so long as they feel they are in a state of literary grace, as it were; that the forms of life are not in themselves communicative; that only classified data register in our apparatus. People would never dream of valuing their daily experiences in terms of what they happen to see or hear *that* day. Media like print or radio or television—which are much more environmental and pervasive forms assailing their eyes and ears all day long—these are invisible. It was only in the nineteenth century that artists, painters, and poets began to notice that it was the environmental form itself, as humanly constituted, that really provided people with the models of perception that governed their thoughts. The literary people still cherish the idea that we can fight off the sensory models imposed on our sensorium by environment, by content, by the classifiable part of the environment. It's somewhat the predicament that Malraux sees in his museum without walls. As long as you can see art inside a museum you can, as it were, protect it from all sorts of vulgarity. What happens when photo engraving and various new technologies make it possible to have far more art *outside* walls of museums than *inside*? How do you maintain taste and artistic standards when you can vulgarize the greatest art with an environment? These are the problems assailing the literary world but which have never been looked into by literary people, journalists, and reviewers.

As a person committed to literature and the literary tradition, I have studied these new environments which threaten to dissolve the whole of literary modality, the whole traditions of literary achievement, and I don't think that these are merely threats to classifiable literary values that can be fended off by staunch moralism or lively indignation. We have to discover new patterns of action, new strategies of survival.

This is where William Burroughs comes in with his *Naked Lunch*. When we invent a new technology, we become cannibals. We eat ourselves alive since these technologies are merely extensions of ourselves. The new environment shaped by electric technology is a cannibalistic one that eats people. To survive one must study the habits of cannibals.

Why are some critics so outraged by your work?

Any new demand on human perception, any new pressure to restructure the habits of perception, is the occasion for outraged response. Literary people prefer to deal with their world without disturbance to their perceptual life. In the sixteenth century, when new forms of perception came into existence with things like printing, people underwent terrified responses as recorded by Hieronymous Bosch. The world of Bosch shows space—the old familiar, comfortable, sensible space of all right-thinking people—medieval, iconic, discontinuous. Against that space he juxtaposes the new world of perspective and three-dimensional space with its strange vanishing point and continuum. By putting these two spaces together he gets the "Temptation of St. Anthony." Quite similarly, Kafka takes the plausible, reasonable, literary modes of discourse and narrative and immediately juxtaposes them with something else—creating metamorphosis, change of structure, change of perception. By putting the three-dimensional world against the metamorphic world of changed structure he gets the same degree of nightmare and terror that Bosch got by putting his two spaces together. Now Bosch was merely recording a response of his age to the experience of pictorial space. To the world of the sixteenth century, rational, three-dimensional, pictorial space was a world of absolute horror. There is no literary horror in the presence of mass culture that could match the horror which the sixteenth century felt in the presence of three-dimensional, rational space. To them it was absolute disaster, absolute spiritual disruption. In our time the plunge through the looking glass of Lewis Carroll into the discontinuous, space-time world of electric technology has created the same sense of the plunge into the abyss, the plunge into the irrational on the part of our contemporaries that we associate with existentialism. Our contemporaries are mistaken, in many ways, as to the causes of their present discontent. On the other hand, they are not mistaken about the demands on their sensibilities and on their perceptions. To shift out of a nineteenth-century, rational space into a twentieth-century space-time, noncontinuum is an experience of great discomfort because it puts one's whole sensorium under terrible pressure. . . .

Is there a real danger in the new media?

It seems to me that the great advantage in understanding the operational dynamics of various media is to quiet them down, not exploit them. If you understand these dynamics, you can control media, eliminate their effects from the environment. And this is most desirable. I think we would do ourselves a considerable kindness if we closed down TV operations for a few years. If TV was simply eliminated from the United States scene, it would be a very good thing. Just as radio has a most malignant effect in Africa or Algeria, or China—in highly auditory cultures, radio drives these people nearly mad with paranoia and tribal intensity—TV, in a highly visual culture, drives us inward in depth into a totally non-visual universe of involvement. It is destroying our entire political, educational, social, institutional life. TV will dissolve the entire fabric of society in a short time. If you understood its dynamics, you would choose to eliminate it as soon as possible. TV changes the sensory and psychic life. It is an oriental form of experience, giving people a somber, profound sense of involvement.

When an admirer called him a poet, Freud considered the judgment harmful in that it took away from his scientific intent. A Canadian writer suggests that you are not literary critic, sociologist, historian, or whatever, but, simply, a poet.

All poets have to probe to discover anything. In our world, there is so much to discover.

Can we excuse methodological lapses in the name of poetic and/or artistic license?

Our sensory modes are constituents, not classifications. I am simply identifying modes of experience. We need new perceptions to cope. Our technologies are generations ahead of our thinking. If you even begin to think about these new technologies you appear as a poet because you are dealing with the present as the future. That is my technique. Most people look back for security. Much greater perceptions and energies are needed than simply mine in the world in which we exist. Better developed talents are needed. James Joyce had these talents in a much more refined state. Joyce had a complete ecology of manmade environments which these critics should have read and studied long ago.

Will there ever be silence?

Objects are unobservable. Only relationships among objects are observable.

Are you disturbed by the sometimes harsh critical responses your work excites?

Even Hercules had to clean the Augean stables but once!

Marshall McLuhan and Gerald E. Stearn, in an interview in McLuhan: Hot and Cool, *edited by Gerald Emanuel Stearn, The Dial Press, Inc., 1967, pp. 266-302.*

George Woodcock   (essay date November 1971)

[*Woodcock is a Canadian educator, editor, and critic best known for his biographies of George Orwell and Thomas Merton. He also founded Canada's most important literary journal,* Canadian Literature, *and has written extensively on the literature of Canada. In the following essay, which was originally published in* The Nation *in November 1971, he compares McLuhan's vision of an electronic "global village" to worldviews expressed in Utopian literature.*]

It has become a commonplace in discussing the effect of the media in modern society to point to the way in which reputations can be instantly made, and lost with equal rapidity. The situation is all the more piquant when this happens to a media figure like Marshall McLuhan. Remembering his career, one is tempted to adapt the slogan of a celebrated gasoline advertisement which for some reason he overlooked in compiling *The Mechanical Bride*: "That's McLuhan—that was."

It is true that, as a disturbing sport among academics,

McLuhan has been in evidence for twenty years. But neither *The Mechanical Bride* (1951) nor *The Gutenberg Galaxy* (1962) marked the real beginning of his brief reign as a mod hero. That came with the publication of *Understanding Media* (1964), a thinly veiled celebration of the impending reign of the electronic media and the return to tribalism, now universalized. All the basic ideas of that book (and McLuhan really has few ideas, but repeats them constantly in varying forms) had in fact been sketched in *The Gutenberg Galaxy,* and the notion of swimming with the maelstrom had made its appearance in *The Mechanical Bride.* But in *Understanding Media* McLuhan translated his gospel from academic hieratic into Madison Avenue demotic, and stunned many apparently intelligent people into accepting a highly exaggerated view of the role of electronic communications in our lives.

None of the curious intermedial volumes in which, after *Understanding Media,* McLuhan tried to develop a mosaic of picture and aphorism (in a vain attempt to evade the charge that he used print to declare the end of print), made an impression like that of his earlier books, and their failure confirmed the implications of the continuing success of the paperback revolution in publishing: that under modern conditions people are in fact reading more than they did a generation ago, and that the Gutenberg dynasty remains in control of a very large territory in the Western consciousness. Since 1964, moreover, there is evidence that, like mosquitoes resisting DDT, the human mind is learning to absorb television without the extraordinary changes in consciousness McLuhan predicted. We have not yet become Global Village enough to diminish the passions of nationalism; indeed, to give an example very close to the bone when dealing with McLuhan, the spread of television in Canada, and particularly the prevalence of American shows, has been followed by an upsurge of national feeling, a strong reaction against the very influences that not long ago made it seem as though North America might become the prototype of the Global Village.

I do not know how far the evident failure of his teachings to work out in the short run has affected McLuhan's viewpoint; recently he has withdrawn into the academic fastness from which he emerged. But it is certain that during the past three or four years his influence has waned, and I doubt if there are many ardent McLuhanites left except among slightly unfashionable PR officers and belated Op artists. And now the burial beetles are at work on his reputation; interestingly, they are led by late disciples. The authors of two recent books, Jonathan Miller (*Marshall McLuhan,* 1971) and Donald F. Theall (*The Medium is the Rear View Mirror,* 1971) are former McLuhanites turning against the master, Miller in total opposition and Theall in that spirit of revisionism which to the faithful always seems worse than downright rejection.

Having held even at the height of general McLuhanacy the critical attitude of the working journalist, who knows that things are never as simple as aphorists and myth makers declare, I find it hard to resist the kind of I-told-you-so smugness which anarchists used to assume towards Trotskyists when they talked of Stalin. It is easy—all too easy—to say: How could you really believe McLuhan's nonsense about TV being *tactile?* How could you swallow those absurd assurances that an Eskimo lived in an *auditory* world when his very survival as a hunter depended on a visual sense that *reads* the landscape as accurately as any of us reads a page of print? How could you allow McLuhan the insolent claim that the front page of a newspaper, with its "instantaneous mosaic," is less rather than more visual than a page of print?

Yet McLuhan remains a phenomenon that has to be acknowledged. Even after his vogue has dissipated, some of his works will remain as curiosities in the history of Western culture. *The Gutenberg Galaxy,* for example, is likely to be read for the very feature that the later McLuhan would have dismissed as irrelevant—its content. It is, like Burton's *Anatomy of Melancholy* or Proudhon's *De la Justice,* one of those eccentric compendia of strange knowledge that omnivorous readers will find entertaining long after the argument has ceased to be topical. And even his earlier scholarly essays, recently collected in *The Interior Landscape,* plodding and murkily written though they may be, are interesting because of the traditionalist and elitist gloss which they provide on his latest work. **"The Southern Quality"** and **"Edgar Poe's Tradition,"** neither of which McLuhan has repudiated, read like parodies on the myths of gentlemanly Dixie, while an anticipation of his later excesses in relation to the media appears when he

seeks to show that the symbolist theory of analogies and correspondences originated in the front pages of newspapers, whose arbitrary juxtaposition of dissimilar incidents supposedly inspired Mallarmé and Rimbaud.

The study of this earlier McLuhan, the search for the roots of his later ideas in his Canadian origins, in his convert's Catholicism, in his admiration for Joyce, Eliot and Wyndham Lewis, provides the most interesting chapters in both Miller's *Marshall McLuhan* and Theall's *The Medium is the Rear View Mirror.*

Unfortunately Miller becomes so involved in tracing McLuhan's debt to Innis and Whorf and Giedion and the prairie Populists and the Sophist tradition that he leaves little room for what one had imagined to be the purpose of the Modern Masters series in which his book figures, the lucid exposition and criticism of the chosen writers. It seems obvious that a consciousness of space running out induced him to concentrate on the books up to *The Gutenberg Galaxy* and to say virtually nothing about *Understanding Media* or anything later. Yet it is in *Understanding Media* that McLuhan's most pernicious maxim, "The medium is the message," was worked out in such a way that the leaders of industrial and advertising corporations adopted him briefly as an instant guru. That monstrous half-truth, implying that content is irrelevant, seemed for a time to be accepted as a white flag of surrender offered

McLuhan with graduate students in his communications seminar at the University of Toronto, in the mid-1970s.

on behalf of the whole intellectual community—offered not merely because McLuhan's growing determinism made him regard the triumph of the electronic media as inevitable, but also because he seemed to desire the re-creation of a community hostile to the intellect. It is in *Understanding Media* that McLuhan finally reveals himself in all his effrontery as the know-all know-nothing, a character worthy of the imagination of his master Wyndham Lewis.

There are of course good things in Miller's little book. As a doctor knowledgeable in neurology, he is able to pick apart very effectively McLuhan's assumptions regarding the co-ordination of the senses, and as a television man he can show how McLuhan's theories fail to work out in the practice of the media. But his general hostility to his subject weakens his case. One reacts with incredulity to the dismissal of all of McLuhan as "a gigantic system of lies." It is of course something far more insidious—a gigantic chaos of half-truths.

Here—as well as in his fuller treatment of his subject—Theall is more credible than Miller. While the most Miller will allow McLuhan is that he sets us thinking, Theall does him the justice of granting that, despite his monstrous exaggerations and his pedantic ways of shocking the pedants, McLuhan has spotted some genuine trends in our society. What Theall does not develop clearly is the process by which the trend-spotter became the trend-setter. I still think the book which McLuhan has since rejected as obsolete, **The Mechanical Bride,** is his most true and useful book, since here he is merely revealing, with some acuteness, the way in which advertising both reflects and moulds the attitudes of our world. It is when in his later books he himself takes a role in moulding attitudes, and does so by intellectually dubious means, that McLuhan becomes one of the great exemplars in our generation of *la trahison des clercs.*

I am always surprised that, except for a few rather slight hints in the essays Raymond Rosenthal collected some years ago in *McLuhan: Pro and Con* (still the best book on McLuhan), nobody—and that includes Miller and Theall—has examined seriously McLuhan's role as the leading Utopian fantasist since Huxley and Orwell, or how this role is related to the fact that his transformation into a prophet took place in Canada.

Seen as a great false metaphor for the ideal society, McLuhan's vision reflects in its form the discredit that in recent years has fallen on the conventional Utopia. As a detailed model of an ideal society, Utopia began to lose its appeal as soon as the first signs of the welfare state appeared, and the failure of Utopia in time present—i. e. Communist Russia—resulted in the inversion of Utopia in the future into a negative vision, pioneered by E.M. Forster and Zamiatin, developed by Huxley and Orwell. But the desire persisted for some kind of Utopian pattern in which human alienation could be shown ending in a culture that reunited man's nature as well as his society; it persisted especially among Catholic converts who fervently believed in their own kind of vanished golden age. Man came out of a tribal world, where the unity of the group protected him psychologically as well as physically from the hostili-

ty in the darkness around the tribal fire. Let him return to a worldwide tribalism, a global village, in which a balance of all the senses and a reconciliation of intellect and emotion would at last prove itself superior to nature and transform the earth into a vast artifact.

Once one considers it in this way, McLuhan's vision is seen to have a great deal in common with many Utopian novels, and here I am not merely talking about the incidental anticipations of electronic devices which one finds in books like Bellamy's *Looking Backward.* Much more impressive is the forecast in Forster's "The Machine Stops," written about sixty years ago, of a world where man's fate is actually determined by a technological structure he himself has created and which brilliantly anticipates the type of communications network McLuhan imagines as the arterial structure of world tribalism.

Even more interesting is the anti-intellectualism, the prejudice against a literary or even a literate culture, that pervades so many Utopias. Even in *Utopia* itself there is a strong suggestion that oral is superior to written discourse, and Swift's Utopians, the Houyhnhnms, like the inhabitants of Plato's golden age, have no writing and are the wiser and more moral for the lack; the same applies to the underground people in Herbert Read's *The Green Child.* In the anti-Utopias the attack on literacy becomes an attack on thought. Anything but the most elementary intellectual activity is forbidden in the worlds of *We* and *1984* and *Brave New World,* and in the last of these, technological advances are used, as McLuhan envisages, simply to cultivate and gratify all the senses. In Huxley's novel there is also a kind of world tribalism, exemplified particularly in the ritual orgies of its people.

Though he acknowledges no debt to Huxley, what McLuhan poses as inevitable and therefore—by its Panglossian logic—desirable, is something very near to a realization of *Brave New World.* The flaw in the vision is that he does not take into account that serpent in the electronic Eden, the content in the message; man will still want to eat of the Tree of Knowledge, and from that reality McLuhan can escape no more than he now escapes the tyranny of print.

That a late-blooming Utopian vision should emerge in Canada is not surprising, particularly if one remembers the teachings of another and more reasonable Canadian guru of world fame, Northrop Frye. Writing on Canadian literature, Frye has developed the thesis that traditionally Canada was a garrison society, a society of pioneers whose situation until the recent wave of urbanization was analogous to that of a tribal people, with the northern Wilderness fulfilling the same role of circumambient enmity as the African forest. One can go beyond Frye to remark that, since a common fear creates unity in tribal and garrison communities alike, they have no need of Utopian visions. It is when human societies loosen out into civilizations, and the sense of community dissipates, that the dream of ideal worlds in past or future emerges. The Homeric Greeks, if one is to believe the epics, had no thought of either a lost golden age or an ideal Platonic republic. Similarly, one of the striking features of Canadian literature until recently was the almost complete absence of

Utopias or anti-Utopias; keeping the watch in the garrison was the important task. But now, in a mere generation, Canada has passed out of the pioneer phase, Canadian critics like Frye himself have begun to study Utopian myths, and Canadian *poètes manqués* like McLuhan have begun to create Utopian visions. The fact that what to Forster and Huxley was anti-Utopia should have become Utopia to McLuhan may be an alarming symptom of the degree of alienation in the collective Canadian psyche, struggling towards self-recognition, yet plagued by dissension. It may also be merely an externalization of McLuhan's own plight, of a longing for the return, at any cost to human dignity, to the great warm womb of the tribal unconscious.

George Woodcock, "McLuhan's Utopia," in his The World of Canadian Writing: Critiques & Recollections, *Douglas & McIntyre, 1980, pp. 235-40.*

Anthony Quinton   (essay date 1982)

[*Quinton is an English philosopher and educator. In the following essay, he maintains that McLuhan is "an academic sheep in Tom Wolfe's clothing" whose theories are neither radical nor couched in a very original manner.*]

Any effort to get a clear view of Marshall McLuhan's doctrines is seriously discouraged by his explicit and repeatedly expressed scorn for old-fashioned, print-oriented, 'linear', rationality. By rejecting as obsolete the humdrum business of setting out definite theses, assembling evidence in support of them, and undermining actual and possible objections, he opts out of the usual argumentative game of truth-seeking, rather in the style of a chess-player who kicks over the table. In this situation ordinary criticism is enfeebled by an uncomfortable suspicion that it is missing the point.

Although he writes books plentifully sprinkled with the familiar vocabulary of linear rationality ('thus', 'therefore', 'it follows', 'it is clear that'), there is, I think, no doubt of McLuhan's seriousness about this negative and seemingly self-destructive commitment. For although his books are recognisably books, for the most part full of moderately grammatical prose, they do deviate in various ways from standard forms of exposition. The two main works look ordinary enough at first. But the chapters of *The Gutenberg Galaxy* are mostly short, have no numbers, and have very long titles. What really enforces one's bewilderment are the not infrequent cases where the title-aphorism has only a very remote connection with the chapter beneath it. The thirty-three chapters of *Understanding Media* do have titles of a familiar, Vance-Packardy sort (e. g., 'Clocks: The Scent of Time' and 'Television: The Timid Giant'); seven of them are about media of communication in general, the rest about twenty-six particular media (or near-media, e. g. clothes). But the content, of the later chapters at any rate, is largely jottings, transferred, it would seem, from the notebook with a minimum of working-over. However dense and organised the prose may look, what it says is connected more by associative leaps than logical linkages. With *The Medium Is the Massage* (with Quentin Fiore, New York, 1967) a rather thin diet of prose is eked out with a great deal of typographic space-wastage and photographic interruptions, in an attempt to produce something nearer the specifications of his theory.

In varying degrees, then, his writings avoid conventional, linear logic and he instructs his readers to approach them in a non-linear way. *The Gutenberg Galaxy,* he says, is a 'mosaic image' not 'a series of views of fixed relationships in pictorial space'. You can, in effect, start anywhere and read in any direction you like. The same spirit is revealed in McLuhan's regular tactic for dealing with objectors. He sees such linear automata as bogged down in a desperate 'unawareness', so dominated by the print medium to which they are bound by habit and professional interest that they are simply not equipped to see what he is getting at.

Quite a good way of arriving at a general idea of what he is up to is provided by *McLuhan: Hot and Cool,* a collection of thirty items mostly about, but a few by, McLuhan, finished off by a thirty-six-page dialogue between McLuhan and the editor (ed. G.E. Stearn, New York 1967). The items about him vary from fairly devotional pieces, among which is a quite astounding architectural meditation in the McLuhan manner by an architect called John M. Johansen, through the slightly nervous display of interest by Tom Wolfe, to the somewhat predictable broadsides of reflex liberal ideology from Dwight Macdonald and Christopher Ricks. These are mostly rather short pieces, and even if the commentators had any inclination to give more than the most cursory survey of McLuhan's ideas (as Kenneth Boulding, a shrewd but amicable objector, clearly has), they have not had the space for it. An interesting feature of this collection is the extent to which people writing about McLuhan tend to be infected by his style, with its fusillade of scriptwriter's pleasantries, rather in the way that one's voice falls to a whisper when one is talking to a sufferer from laryngitis. What the collection lacks is any extended effort to elicit a reasonably definite structure of theory from McLuhan's writings. I should not make this complaint if I did not think the thing could be done. If McLuhan is desultory (as a matter of principle), he is also exceedingly repetitious; not only does the same quite large but wholly manageable body of leading themes recur time and time again in his writings, they are even presented in the same jocular words (he has a grandfatherly indulgence toward his own phrases). What I wish to maintain is that if we ignore his anti-linear instructions, we can easily discern beneath the thin camouflage of his expository idiosyncrasies an articulate theory of society and culture, with all the usual apparatus of first principles, explanatory supplements, and logically derived consequences. What is more, this entirely linear theoretical contraption is of a classic and familiar kind, having a very close formal analogy with the main doctrines of Marx. To speak just once in McLuhanese: he is an academic sheep in Tom Wolfe's clothing.

The fundamental principle of McLuhan's system is a theory of the main determinant of historical change in society, culture, and the human individual. Such changes according to this system are all ultimately caused by changes in the prevailing or predominating medium of human communication. McLuhan got this idea from the later works of the Canadian economic historian Harold A. Innis, but what the teacher used vertiginously enough, as an interpretative clue, the pupil asserts, with only the most occasional and perfunctory qualification, as the basic truth about causation in history. The main evidence for this proposition is provided in *The Gutenberg Galaxy* in which a vast array of disparate works is ransacked for quotations (they must make up half the book) describing the social and cultural effects of the invention of printing. Print, he tells us, *created* (that is his usual word in this connection) individualism, privacy, specialisation, detachment, mass-production, nationalism, militarism, the dissociation of sensibility, etc., etc.

The connection between cause and effect affirmed in the fundamental principle is explained by the doctrine of 'sense-ratio', which McLuhan derived, it appears, from the work of Father Walter J. Ong. McLuhan associates different historical periods or cultural situations with different balances of emphasis in the communicative and mental life of human beings as between the various senses. Tribal man, with his oral culture, was a conventional being who heard, smelt, and felt the people he was in communication with. Gutenberg man acquires information through focusing his eyes on clearly printed rows of alphabetic symbols. Tribal man brought all his senses to bear on his world in a healthy balance; Gutenberg man over-concentrates on vision and leaves his other senses numb and deprived.

The third element of McLuhan's system is a patterning or schematisation of history, which is achieved by applying the fundamental principle to raw historical fact. Broadly conceived, the schema divides human history into three parts: the remote or pre-Gutenberg past, the immediate or Gutenberg past, and the immediate or electronic future. The first and longest of these eras further subdivides, on closer inspection, into a tribal epoch of oral, face-to-face communication, an ideographic epoch, and an epoch of alphabetic handwriting (i. e., prehistory, the East, and Western civilisation from the Greeks to the Renaissance).

The final stage of this schema, the electronic future, develops into a large-scale prophecy which also implies a diagnosis of current cultural discontents. With electronic means of communication rendering printed matter more or less obsolete we are on the edge of a new type of society and a new type of man. Indeed the new men are already among us: they are our children with their sense-ratios transformed by TV-watching at an impressionable age, dedicated to 'cool', participative enjoyments like the frug, and altogether alienated from the Gutenberg assumptions of traditional instructional schooling. That is why we get on with them so badly. The coming society will be appropriate to this type of human being. It will be a 'global village', a unitary world of neo-tribesmen, sunk in their social roles and fraternally involved with one another in a way that excludes what their forebears would regard as individuality.

Faced by the inevitable we need some kind of strategy to meet it with. Here McLuhan recurs, with a frequency un-

usual even for him, to Poe's story about a sailor caught in a maelstrom who saved himself by coming to understand how it worked. As things are, ignorance about the irresistible effects of new electronic media is general and blinding. The first step, at any rate, is to understand them by directing attention away from their content to their form and its effects on sense-ratios. It is not wholly clear that there is a second step, that anything more than understanding is required.

The global village is as welcome to McLuhan as it is inevitable. In *Understanding Media* he says that the faith in which he is writing is one that 'concerns the ultimate harmony of all being'. Generally the social and cultural features of the Gutenberg era that we are about to lose are described in an unfavourable way, their connection with war, inequality, indifference, the mutilation of the self is emphasised. But on the other hand, from the time of *The Mechanical Bride* (New York, 1951) McLuhan has been insisting that he is not concerned with whether the changes he is investigating are 'a good thing', and strongly suggests that this is a crude and unenlightened sort of question to ask. Rudolph E. Morris in *McLuhan: Hot and Cool* is sufficiently impressed by these protestations of detachment to praise the book, quite wrongly, for its freedom from moral indignation (a fairly dense cloud of moral steam rises from McLuhan's collar on page thirteen of *The Mechanical Bride,* for example). Despite his insistence on detachment there is no doubt that he strongly favours the future as he describes it.

Finally McLuhan has a special intellectual technique, both of exposition and defense. His procedure is to heap evidence up in tumultuous and disparate assemblages, with little critical appraisal of his sources—unless they deviate very grossly in some way from one of his main theses—and with only the most tenuous thread of topical relevance to connect them. To justify this shapeless and enthusiastic technique of almost random accumulation he falls back on the idea that he is producing a mosaic, not a linear argument. In fact he is producing a linear argument, but one of a very fluid and unorganised kind. Objectors are discounted for benighted visuality and obsession with print. Yet McLuhan not only writes books, he is immensely bookish, in the manner of some jackdaw of a medieval compiler or of Burton in *The Anatomy of Melancholy.*

The analogy between this system and Marx's is plain enough to be set out briefly. Each system begins with a general interpretation of history, an account of the ultimate cause of historical change. Each applies this to arrive at a schematisation of the actual course of historical events. For exciting, practical purposes each schema divides history into three parts: the remote past (before print or capitalism), the immediate past (print or capitalism), and the immediate future (global village or classless society). But the remote past can be divided further, into prehistory (the oral tribe or primitive communism), the East (ideographic script or slave economy), and the early West (alphabetic script or feudalism). Both McLuhan and Marx devote their main work to the shift from the early West to the immediate past: as *The Gutenberg Galaxy* tells what print did to the scribal culture, so *Capital* describes the emergence of capitalism. Each system concludes its historical schema with a prophecy of imminent major change to a state of affairs that is nebulously described but enthusiastically welcomed. In each case the welcomed future is a reversion, in a major respect, to the initial phase of the whole historical process. McLuhan and Marx both present strategies for dealing with the inevitable. Marx calls for an activist endeavour to ease the birth-pangs of the coming order; McLuhan, less exigently, calls for an effort to understand, best pursued by reading his works. Both are strongly in favour of the future that they predict, for all its obscurity of outline. Finally both have a brisk way of disposing of hostile critics. They have a self-sealing device against any possible attempt at refutation: the theory predicts it and explains it away, what Popper calls 'reinforced dogmatism'. Objectors must be visual or bourgeois.

To point out this analogy is not to criticise McLuhan, except in so far as he maintains that his ideas cannot be set out in a conventionally systematic way. But it does put one on one's guard. A system of this form embodies two crucial elements about whose acceptability very general and very elaborately worked-out doubts have been raised: a schematisation of history which implies the inevitability of a predicted state of affairs and a strongly positive evaluation of this non-too-clearly-described inevitable future.

There is clearly something in McLuhan's fundamental principle, just as there is in Marx's. Major changes in styles of communication do have large effects. What is wrong here is the violent exaggeration with which McLuhan blows up a truth about the causal relevance of media into a full-blooded and unqualified theory of historical change. What he usually does is to argue that some change in media of communication is a necessary condition of a certain major social or cultural change, and then to represent his discovery as an account of what *created* the major change in question. Print, he says, created the large national army of modern times. Now it may be that the large national army does make a good deal of use of printed matter for such things as training manuals and quartermaster's forms. But the railway, as indispensable for rapid mobilisation of large numbers, is obviously more important. Anyway McLuhan's timing is all wrong here. The print age, for him, begins about 1500, but the type of army he has in mind first appears in the mid-nineteenth century with the American Civil War and Bismarck's wars against Austria and France, or, at the earliest, with the armies of the French Revolution and Napoleon. During the three preceding, print-dominated centuries, armies had been small bodies of mercenaries or long-service professionals.

He might, at this point, reply that the mass army of modern times was created by nationalism and that nationalism was created by print: Q.E.D. Even if we allow the questionable assumption that creation is transitive in this way, this still will not do. For how does print create nationalism? By stabilising the vernacular? But were not Elizabethan Englishmen nationalistic even though most of them were illiterate? Or is it enough that the ruling class should be literate? Then why was eighteenth-century Italy not nationalistic?

Here, right at the foundations of McLuhan's system, a persisting vagueness of terms makes it difficult beyond a certain point to see precisely what is being said. Media, he contends, are the ultimate causal factors in history. But what is a medium? Much of the time the term is taken in a fairly ordinary way to mean a technique for the communication of ideas between human beings. It is in this sense that the concept of a medium occurs in his schematisation of history. But in *Understanding Media* roads, clothes, houses, money, cars, and weapons are all included in the repertoire of media discussed, things which either do not communicate information but carry altogether heavier loads, or which communicate information only as a very minor and peripheral function (as a nun's habit says 'don't ask me to have a drink with you'). In this extended sense a medium comes to be any item of technology, and the sense in which the fundamental principle is to be taken becomes very much diluted. Nevertheless, McLuhan's fundamental principle does make a point and he has certainly assembled evidence relevant to it which is impressive in its bulk and often intellectually stimulating.

This is less true of the schematisation of history that he derives from its application, which simply draws old and familiar distinctions between historical periods in a new terminology. What everyone is used to calling modern history is renamed the Gutenberg era, ancient and medieval history is renamed the era of alphabetic script, the epoch of the oriental empires is renamed the ideographic era. This would be all right in a modest way if it served to confirm a well-known distinction and to deepen our understanding of it. But here a pedantic-looking doubt must be voiced. What does he mean when he says of some medium that it is *the* dominant medium of a given historical period? Does it mean that everyone was preoccupied with it, in which case the Gutenberg era began in Europe only a hundred years ago with a fair approximation to universal literacy? Or does it mean that *the* medium of an era is the one through which the ruling class acquires most of its information or most of its important information? In that case the beginning of the Gutenberg era is pushed back to where he wants it all right (1500 roughly), but the basis of his claim that we are on the edge of an electronic age dissolves. This serious indeterminacy is one that he generously exploits. He says that England is much less visual and print-oriented than the United States. Yet England was the first country to exhibit most of the social and cultural symptoms of Gutenbergian domination: mass-production industry, big cities, individualism, nationalism, etc. Allowing himself this degree of freedom he deprives his schematisation of any definite content.

At this point his explanation of his fundamental principle by means of sense-ratios needs to be considered. Once again a very simple point seems to have been exaggerated into confident and unqualified assertions which cry out for justification. It is reasonable and enlightening to say that tribesmen do not have a detached, impersonal point of view of a visually conceived world stretching out uniformly from them in space and time. But to talk of sense-ratios suggests a kind of mathematical precision about this kind of perception which he nowhere begins to achieve. To raise a very simple question: why does he say nothing about the blind? Plenty of blind men display all the marks of extreme visuality in his terms, are individualised, specialised, detached and so forth. But how can this be possible for people who have been blind since birth and have had to get their information either tactually through Braille or auditorily through a reader?

This becomes highly important when he arrives at the final stage of his schematisation, his prophecy about the electronic age just ahead of us, peopled with its global villagers. All the alleged products of print are declared moribund and about to disappear: the individual, privacy, specialisation, detachment, militarism, nationalism, mass-production, and so forth. In their place the world will become a unity of emotionally involved tribesmen, aware of everything that is happening everywhere. The real basis for this prediction is his account, in terms of sense-ratios, of the effect of TV on people accustomed to it from early life. TV, he says, is a cool medium, whereas print is hot. It involves the collaboration of its watcher in what it presents, for he has to fill out its low-definition picture with imaginative efforts of his own, while print, where everything is clear and determinate, imposes a passive receptiveness on the reader.

My limited observation of children's TV habits makes me doubt this. If the show interests them they watch it with passive absorption; if it does not they leave it buzzing on around them and get on with something on the floor. But I would not rest the case on such anecdotal material, particularly since the effect is alleged to take place at a fairly subconscious level, as inaccessible to naive observation as it is to modification or control. It seems reasonable, however, to argue that despite its low pictorial definition TV leaves a lot less to the supplementative imagination of its watchers than print does to its readers. But even if electronic media do decrease detachment, as they might be held to do by the very lifelikeness of their representations, why does he infer that this involvement will inevitably be fraternal and charitable? There is no necessary connection whatever between making people more emotional and excitable and making them more humane and unselfish. Words like 'sensitive' and 'involved' can be used to mean either sympathetically concerned with the welfare of others or, more neutrally, just concerned. No doubt young people at present are more given to global idealism than their elders, but then that is nearly always the case; having few other responsibilities they can afford this emotional expenditure.

Again it is not at all clear why the involving nature of exposure to electronic media should eliminate individuality. If print makes men passive it should, according to McLuhan's own argument, presumably be well equipped to stereotype them. No doubt there are many forces in the world making for Riesman's other-directedness, but TV with its rapid diffusion of advertisers' ideas of fashionable life-styles is only one of them.

McLuhan's predictions often go far beyond the global village toward the imminent formation of a kind of cosmic, preverbal consciousness. Media, like all technologies, extend or externalise our faculties. In particular media extend our senses. Electronic media, he goes on, extend or externalise the central nervous system. Here he has really taken off. Certainly tools can augment the power and precision of our muscular operations. In line with this, media strictly so called can be regarded as ways of improving the performance of our sense-organs, though this more accurately applies to things like microscopes and telescopes. Going a little further still, we can allow that computing machines can assist and improve on the thinking work of the central nervous system. But this is not to say that computers or other media detach our faculties from us altogether, that they literally externalise the human capacities they reinforce.

Perhaps a community could enslave itself to a computer by programming it to make social decisions on the basis of its inflow of information, and by linking it up with machinery designed to put the decisions into effect. Such a community would be well advised to put the main power switch in an accessible position. But since in our entropic universe destruction is easier than construction, the descendants of people clever enough to construct such an appliance ought to be clever enough to blow it up if it gets out of hand. Moreover, whatever sort of computer it is, it will not be preverbal in McLuhan's lavish sense: its tapes may have combinations of 1s and 0s on them instead of ordinary words but it will not operate with blank tape. I have almost certainly misunderstood McLuhan on this topic, probably by taking his word 'externalise' literally. If he does not mean it to be understood in that way, all he can mean is that there will be a collective consciousness—or subconsciousness—of the kind an excited patriotic crowd might have, with everybody thinking or feeling the same thing. We must try to avoid this unappetising prospect by leaving TV-watching in its current voluntary condition and keeping more than one channel going.

McLuhan describes the electronic future in reasonably attractive ways on the whole. Not least in the phrase 'global village' itself with its intimations of rusticity, friendliness, the simple life. But his neo-primitive future does seem to be without most of the things which men have laboriously struggled to achieve and in virtue of which, despite everything, they still think of themselves as superior in more than brute strength to the other animal species: freedom, individuality, foresight, even detachment, the indispensable condition of rationality itself. In so far as the outlines of the electronic future are clear they are by no means enticing, but then in so far as they are clear the arguments on which their inevitability is based are very far from persuasive. And in so far as they are not clear there is nothing to take a position for or against. But anyway taking a position about the future has little point in McLuhan's system, since it is not shown how the understanding he offers is related to any possible action. What he really offers is a kind of general relief from historical anxiety: Amazing things are going to happen but considered in themselves they are not at all bad, and the disturbance of their arrival can be brought within manageable bounds by one's being intellectually prepared for them.

Whatever else he is McLuhan is consistently interesting. His scope is unlimited and there are the added attractions of his remorseless and all-inclusive contemporaneity and his jokes. Contemporaneity is a rapidly wasting asset. *The Mechanical Bride,* which is now sixteen years old, has a largely camp interest. The jokes often seem a little automated, like those in a Bob Hope show. His technique has a Gutenbergian repeatability. 'Money,' he says, 'is the poor man's credit card.' Why not 'Gratitude is the poor man's tip' or 'Changing the furniture around is the poor man's interior decoration'. But there are so many of them that the strong can carry the weak. What he claims to offer is much more than this, a general scheme of individual and social salvation. Compared to all such schemes it perhaps makes the least exacting demands on those who would like to follow it. They do not have to mortify the flesh or hurl themselves against the armed lackeys of the bourgeoisie or undergo 500 hours of analysis. All they have to do is to read a few books, a curiously Gutenbergian device. If, as I have argued, the scheme does not stand up very well if approached with the good old linear questions, 'Just what does he mean?' 'Is there any good reason to think that it is true?' they must remember that they were offered salvation at a bargain price.

Anthony Quinton, "McLuhan," in his Thoughts and Thinkers, *Duckworth, 1982, pp. 269-76.*

Paul Levinson on McLuhan's critics and interpreters:

Given the electronic—acoustic/cyberspatial—nature of McLuhan's thinking and writing, one might ask if any [book about McLuhan] is worth reading. Why squeeze the all-at-once into the fixed sequential confines of even the most liberated hard-copy, print-on-paper book? Perhaps the prudent course would be to wait for the hypertext versions of McLuhan's work—the texts that will allow readers at the computer, coming upon McLuhan's mention of speed in a tetrad, to click a mouse that will offer them a menu of fifty other places in McLuhan's work where speed is discussed, and then to trace with equal facility the webs emanating from any of these nodes.

Paul Levinson, in his "McLuhan's Space," in Journal of Communication, *Spring, 1990.*

Arthur Kroker   (essay date 1985)

[*Kroker is a Canadian economist, educator, and critic who has written several studies on Postmodernism and popular culture. In the following excerpt, he evaluates McLuhan's contributions to the study of technology and some of his theories' shortcomings.*]

Not the least of McLuhan's contributions to the study of technology was that he transposed the literary principle of metaphor/metonymy (the play between structure and process) into a historical methodology for analysing the rise and fall of successive media of communication. In McLuhan's discourse, novels are the already obsolescent content of television; writing "turned a spotlight on the high, dim Sierras of speech"; the movie is the "mechaniza-

tion of movement and gesture"; the telegraph provides us with "diplomacy without walls"; just as "photography is the mechanization of the perspective painting and the arrested eye". To read McLuhan is to enter into a "vortex" of the critical, cultural imagination, where "fixed perspective" drops off by the way, and where everything passes over instantaneously into its opposite. Even the pages of the texts in *Explorations,* *The Medium is the Massage,* *The Vanishing Point,* or *From Cliché to Archetype* are blasted apart, counterblasted actually, in an effort to make reading itself a more subversive act of the artistic imagination. Faithful to his general intellectual project of exposing the invisible environment of the technological sensorium, McLuhan sought to make of the text itself a "counter-gradient" or "probe" for forcing to the surface of consciousness the silent structural rules, the "imposed assumptions" of the technological environment within which we are both enclosed and "processed". In *The Medium is the Massage,* McLuhan insisted that we cannot understand the technological experience from the outside. We can only comprehend how the electronic age "works us over" if we "recreate the experience" in depth and mythically, of the processed world of technology.

> All media work us over completely. They are so persuasive in their personal, political, economic, aesthetic, psychological, moral, ethical, and social consequences that they leave no part of us untouched, unaffected, unaltered. The medium is the massage. Any understanding of social and cultural change is impossible without a knowledge of the way media work as environments.

And McLuhan was adamant on the immanent relationship of technology and biology, on the fact that "the new media . . . are nature" and this for the reason that technology refers to the social and psychic "extensions" or "outerings" of the human body or senses. McLuhan could be so universal and expansive in his description of the media of communication—his studies of communication technologies range from writing and speech to the telephone, photography, television, money, comic books, chairs and wrenches—because he viewed all technology as the pushing of the "archetypal forms of the unconscious out into social consciousness." When McLuhan noted in *Counter Blast* that "environment is process, not container", he meant just this: the effect of all new technologies is to impose, silently and pervasively, their deep assumptions upon the human psyche by reworking the "ratio of the senses."

> All media are extensions of some human faculty—psychic or physical.

> Media, by altering the environment, evoke in us unique ratios of sense perceptions. The extension of any one sense alters the way we think and act—they way we perceive the world. When these ratios change, MEN CHANGE.

For McLuhan, it's a processed world now. As we enter the electronic age with its instantaneous and global movement of information, we are the first human beings to live completely within the *mediated* environment of the technostructure. The "content" of the technostructure is largely irrelevant (the "content" of a new technology is always the technique which has just been superceded: movies are the content of television; novels are the content of movies) or, in fact, a red herring distracting our attention from the essential secret of technology as the medium, or environment, within which human experience is programmed. It was McLuhan's special genius to grasp at once that the content (metonymy) of new technologies serves as a "screen", obscuring from view the disenchanted locus of the technological experience in its purely "formal" or "spatial" properties. McLuhan wished to escape the "flat earth approach" to technology, to invent a "new metaphor" by which we might "restructure our thoughts and feelings" about the subliminal, imperceptible environments of media effects.

In this understanding, technology is an "extension" of biology: the expansion of the electronic media as the "metaphor" or "environment" of twentieth-century experience implies that, for the first time, the central nervous system itself has been exteriorized. It is our plight to be processed through the technological simulacrum; to participate intensively and integrally in a "technostructure" which is nothing but a vast simulation and "amplification" of the bodily senses. Indeed, McLuhan often recurred to the "narcissus theme" in classical mythology as a way of explaining our fatal fascination with technology, viewed not as "something external" but as an extension, or projection, of the sensory faculties of the human species.

> Media tend to isolate one or another sense from the others. The result is hypnosis. The other extreme is withdrawing of sensation with resulting hallucination as in dreams or DT's, etc . . . Any medium, by dilating sense to fill the whole field, creates the necessary conditions of hypnosis in that area. This explains why at no time has any culture been aware of the effect of its media on its overall association, not even retrospectively.

All of McLuhan's writings are an attempt to break beyond the "Echo" of the narcissus myth, to show that the "technostructure" is an extension or "repetition" of ourselves. In his essay, **"The Gadget Lover"**, McLuhan noted precisely why the Greek myth of Narcissus is of such profound relevance to understanding the technological experience.

> The youth Narcissus (narcissus means *narcosis* or numbing) mistook his own reflection in the water for another person. *This extension of himself by mirror numbed his perceptions until be became the servomechanism of his own extended or repeated image.* The nymph Echo tried to win his love with fragments of his own speech, but in vain. He was numb. He had adapted to his extension of himself and had become a closed system. Now the point of this myth is the fact that men at once become fascinated by any extension of themselves in any material other than themselves. [*Understanding Media*]

Confronted with the hypnotic effect of the technological sensorium, McLuhan urged the use of any "probe"—humour, paradox, analogical juxtaposition, absurdity—as a way of making visible the "total field effect" of technology as medium. This is why, perhaps, McLuhan's intellec-

tual project actually circles back on itself, and is structured directly into the design of his texts. McLuhan makes the reader a "metonymy" to his "metaphor": he transforms the act of "reading McLuhan" into dangerous participation in a radical experiment which has, as its end, the exploration of the numbing of consciousness in the technological massage. Indeed, to read McLuhan is to pass directly into the secret locus of the "medium is the massage"; to experience anew the "media" (this time the medium of writing) as a silent gradient of ground-rules.

No less critical than Grant of the human fate in technological society, McLuhan's imagination seeks a way out of our present predicament by recovering a highly ambivalent attitude towards the *objects* of technostructure. Thus, while Grant writes in William James' sense of a "block universe" of the technological dynamo, seeing only tendencies towards domination, McLuhan privileges a historically specific study of the media of communication. In an early essay (1955), **"A Historical Approach to the Media"**, McLuhan said that if we weren't "to go on being helpless illiterates" in the new world of technology, passive victims as the "media themselves act directly toward shaping our most intimate self-consciousness", then we had to adopt the attitude of the artist. "The mind of the artist is always the point of maximal sensitivity and resourcefulness in exposing altered realities in the common culture." McLuhan would make of us "the artist, the sleuth, the detective" in gaining a critical perspective on the history of technology which "just as it began with writing ends with television." Unlike Grant's reflections on technology which are particularistic and existential, following a downward spiral (the famous Haligonian "humbug") into pure content: pure will, pure remembrance, pure duration, McLuhan's thought remains projective, metaphorical, and emancipatory. Indeed, Grant's perspective on technology is Protestant to the core in its contemplation of the nihilism of liberal society. But if Grant's tragic inquiry finds its artistic analogue in Colville's *To Prince Edward Island,* then McLuhan's discourse is more in the artistic tradition of Georges Seurat, the French painter, and particularly in one classic portrait, *A Sunday Afternoon on the Island of La Grande Jatte.* McLuhan always accorded Seurat a privileged position as the "art fulcrum between Renaissance visual and modern tactile. The coalescing of inner and outer, subject and object." McLuhan was drawn to Seurat in making painting a "light source" (a "light through situation"). Seurat did that which was most difficult and decisive: he flipped the viewer into the "vanishing point" of the painting. Or as McLuhan said, and in prophetic terms, Seurat (this "precursor of TV") presented us with a searing visual image of the age of the "anxious object."

Now, to be sure, the theme of anxiety runs deep through the liberal side of the Canadian mind. This is the world of Margaret Atwood's "intolerable anxiety" and of Northrop Frye's "anxiety structure." But McLuhan is the Canadian thinker who undertook a phenomenology of anxiety, or more precisely a historically relative study of the sources of anxiety and stress in technological society. And he did so by the simple expedient of drawing us, quickly and in depth, into Seurat's startling and menacing world of the anxious, stressful objects of technology. In his book, *Through the Vanishing Point,* McLuhan said of Seurat that "by utilizing the Newtonian analysis of the fragmentation of light, he came to the technique of divisionism, whereby each dot of paint becomes the equivalent of an actual light source, a sun, as it were. This device reversed the traditional perspective by making the viewer the vanishing point." The significance of Seurat's "reversal" of the rules of traditional perspective is that he abolished, once and for all, the medieval illusion that space is neutral, or what is the same, that we can somehow live "outside" the processed world of technology. With Seurat a great solitude and, paradoxically, a greater entanglement falls on modern being. "We are suddenly in the world of the 'Anxious Object' which is prepared to take the audience inside the painting process itself." Following C.S. Lewis in *The Discarded Image,* McLuhan noted exactly what this "flip" in spatial perspective meant. Rather than *looking in* according to the traditional spatial model of medieval discourse, modern man is suddenly *"looking out."* "Like one looking out from the saloon entrance onto the dark Atlantic, or from the lighted porch upon the dark and lonely moors." The lesson of Seurat is this: modernity is coeval with the age of the "anxious object" because we live now, fully, within the designed environment of the technological sensorium. For McLuhan, we are like astronauts in the processed world of technology. We now take our "environment" with us in the form of technical "extensions" of the human body or senses. The technostructure is both the lens through which we experience the world, and, in fact, the "anxious object" with which human experience has become imperceptibly, almost subliminally, merged.

Now, McLuhan often remarked that in pioneering the DEW [Distant Early Warning] line, Canada had also provided a working model for the artistic imagination as an "early warning system" in sensing coming shifts in the technostructure. Seurat's artistic representation of the spatial reversal at work in the electronic age, a reversal which plunges us into active participation in the "field" of technological experience, was one such early warning system. It was, in fact, to counteract our "numbing" within the age of the anxious object that McLuhan's literary and artistic imagination, indeed his whole textual strategy, ran to the baroque. As an intellectual strategy, McLuhan favoured the baroque for at least two reasons: it privileged "double perspective and contrapuntal theming"; and it sought to "capture the moment of change in order to release energy dramatically." There is, of course, a clear and decisive connection between McLuhan's attraction to Seurat as an artist who understood the spatial grammar of the electronic age and his fascination with the baroque as a method of literary imagination. If, indeed, we are now "looking out" from inside the technological sensorium; and if, in fact, in the merger of biology and technology which is the locus of the electronic age, "we" have become the vanishing points of technique, then a way had to be discovered for breaching the "invisible environment" within which we are now enclosed. For McLuhan, the use of the baroque in each of his writings, this constant resort to paradox, double perspective, to a carnival of the literary imagination in which the pages of the texts are forced to

reveal their existence also as a "medium", was also a specific strategy aimed at "recreating the experience" of technology as massage. Between Seurat (a radar for "space as process") and baroque (a "counter-gradient"): that's the artistic strategy at work in McLuhan's imagination as he confronted the subliminal, processed world of electronic technologies. . . .

McLuhan was the last and best exponent of the liberal imagination in Canadian letters. His thought brings to a new threshold of intellectual expression the fascination with the question of technology which has always, both in political and private practice, so intrigued liberal discourse in Canada. McLuhan's thought provides a new eloquence, and indeed, nobility of meaning to "creative freedom" as a worthwhile public value; and this as much as it reasserts the importance of a renewed sense of "individualism", both as the locus of a revived political community and as a creative site (the "agent intellect") for releasing, again and again, the possible "epiphanies" in technological experience. In McLuhan's writings, the traditional liberal faith in the *reason* of technological experience, a reason which could be the basis of a rational and universal political community, was all the more ennobled to the extent that the search for the "reason" in technology was combined with the Catholic quest for a new "incarnation." McLuhan's communication theory was a direct outgrowth of his Catholicism; and his religious sensibility fused perfectly with a classically liberal perspective on the question of technology and civilization. In the present orthodoxy of intellectual discourse, it is not customary to find a thinker whose inquiry is both infused by a transcendent religious sensibility and whose intellectual scholarship is motivated, not only by a desperate sense of the eclipse of reason in modern society, but by the disappearance of "civilization" itself through its own vanishing-point. As quixotic as it might be, McLuhan's intellectual project was of such an inclusive and all-embracing nature. His thought could be liberal, Catholic, and structuralist (before his time) precisely because the gravitation-point of McLuhan's thought was the preservation of the fullest degree possible of creative freedom in a modern century, which, due to the stress induced by its technology, was under a constant state of emergency. In McLuhan's discourse, individual freedom as well as civil culture itself were wagered in the contest with technology. The technological experience also made the possibility of a new "incarnation" fully ambivalent: it was also the Catholic, and by extension, liberal belief in a progressive, rational, and evolutionary history which was gambled in the discourse on technology.

But if McLuhan provides an important key to exploring the technological media, then it must also be noted that there are, at least, two major limitations in his thought which reduce his value, either as a guide to understanding technology in the Canadian circumstance or, for that matter, to a full inquiry into the meaning of the technological experience in the New World. First, McLuhan had no systematic, or even eclectic, theory of the relationship between economy and technology; and certainly no critical appreciation of the appropriation, and thus privatisation, of technology by the lead institutions, multinational corporations and the state, in advanced industrial societies. It was not, of course, that McLuhan was unaware of the relationship of corporate power and technology. One searing sub-text of *Understanding Media* and *The Mechanical Bride* had to do with the almost malignant significance of the corporate control of electronic technologies. In McLuhan's estimation, "technology is part of our bodies"; and to the extent that corporations acquire private control over the electronic media then we have, in effect, "leased out" our eyes, ears, fingers, legs, and the brain itself, to an exterior power. In the electronic age, this era of collective and integral consciousness, those with control of technological media are allowed "to play the strings of our nerves in public." The body is fully externalized, and exposed, in the interstices of the technological sensorium. For McLuhan, just like Grant, the technological dynamo breeds a new formation of power, demonic and mythic, which is capable, as one of its reflexes of vapourizing the individual subject, and of undermining all "public" communities. But if McLuhan understood the full dangers of corporate control of technological media, nowhere did he extend this insight into a reflection on the relationship of capitalism and technology. Now, it may be, as in the case of Jacques Ellul, another civil humanist, that McLuhan's intellectual preference was to privilege the question of technology over all other aspects of social experience, including the economic foundations of society. McLuhan may have been a technological determinist, or at the minimum, a "technological monist" who took *technique* to be the primary locus for the interpretation of society as a whole. If this was so, then it is particularly unfortunate since McLuhan's "blindspot" on the question of capitalism and technology undermined, in the end, his own injunction for an "historical understanding" of the evolution of technological media. In **"Catholic Humanism"** and, for that matter, in all of his writings, McLuhan urged the use of the historical imagination—an historical perspective which was to be sympathetic, realistic, and reconstructive—as our only way of understanding the great watershed in human experience precipitated by the appearance of electronic society. His was, however, a curious and somewhat constricted vision of the historical imagination: for it omitted any analysis of the precise historical conditions surrounding the development of the technological experience in North America. McLuhan was as insensitive, and indifferent, to the problem of the political economy of technology as he was to the relationship of technology and ideological hegemony in the creation of liberal society, and the liberal state, in North America. McLuhan's primary value was, of course, creative freedom, not "justice"; and his political preference was for a universal community founded on the rights of "reason", not for the "ethic of charity." This is to say, however, that McLuhan's "historical sense" already embraced, from its very beginnings, the deepest assumptions of technological society. McLuhan's mind was a magisterial account of the technological imagination itself. This was a discourse which evinced a fatal fascination with the utopian possibilities of technology. Indeed, McLuhan liked to speculate about the almost religious utopia immanent in the age of information.

> Language as the technology of human extension,
> whose powers of division and separation we

know so well, may have been the "Tower of Babel" by which men sought to scale the highest heavens. Today computers hold out the promise of a means of instant translation of any code or language into any other code or language. The computer, in short, promises by technology a Pentecostal condition of universal understanding and unity. The next logical step would seem to be, not to translate, but to by-pass languages in favour of a general cosmic consciousness which might be very like the collective unconscious dreamt by Bergson. The condition of "weightlessness" that biologists say promises a physical immortality, may be paralleled by the condition of speechlessness that could confer a perpetuity of collective harmony and peace. [*Understanding Media*]

Everything in McLuhan's thought strained towards the liberation of the "Pentecostal condition" of technology: the privileging of space over time; the fascination with the exteriorisation in electronic technology of an "inner experience" which is electric, mythic, inclusive, and configurational; the primacy of "field" over event; the vision of "processed information" as somehow consonant with the perfectibility of the human faculties. And it was this utopian, and transcendent, strain in McLuhan's thought which may, perhaps, have made it impossible for his inquiry to embrace the problematic of capitalism and technology. In McLuhan's lexicon, the privileging of the "economic" relationship belonged to an obsolete era: the now superceded age of specialism, fragmentation, and segmentation of work of the industrial revolution. McLuhan viewed himself as living on the other side, the far side, of technological history: the coming age of "cosmic man" typified by "mythic or iconic awareness" and by the substitution of the "multi-faceted for the point-of-view." What was capitalism? It was the obsolescent content of the new era of the electronic simulation of consciousness. For McLuhan, economy had also gone electronic and thus even the corporate world, with its "magic" of advertisements and its plenitude of computers, could be subsumed into the more general project of surfacing the reason in technological society. Consequently, it might be said that McLuhan's blindspot on the question of economy was due not so much to a strain of "technological determinism" in his thought, and least not in the *first* instance; but due rather to his, transparently Catholic expectation that if the electronic economy of the corporate world was not an "agent intellect" in the creation of a new technological horizon, it was, at least, a necessary catalyst in setting the conditions for "cosmic man." McLuhan was a "missionary" to the power centres of the technological experience; and he could so faithfully, and guilelessly, discuss the civilizing moment in technology because there never was any incompatibility between the Catholic foundations of his communication theory and the will to empire. If McLuhan was a deeply compromised thinker, then it was because his Catholic humanism allowed him to subordinate, and forget, the question of the private appropriation of technology. And what was, in the final instance, tragic and not comic about his intellectual fate was simply this: it was precisely the control over the speed, dissemination, and implanting of new technologies by the corporate command centres of North America which would subvert the very possibility of an age of "creative freedom".

If one limitation in McLuhan's discourse on technology was his forgetfulness of the mediation of technology by political economy, then a second limitation, or arrest, concerned McLuhan's contempt for the "national question" in Canada. It would be unfair to criticize a thinker for not violating the internal unity of his own viewpoint. McLuhan was always firm in his belief that the dawn of the "global village", this new era of "universal understanding and unity" required the by-passing of "national" political communities. The universalism of reason and the potentically new "Finn cycle" of an all-inclusive and mythic technological experience rendered obsolete *particularistic* political concerns. McLuhan's polis was the world; and his, not inaccurate, understanding of that world [in **"The Relation of Environment & Anti-Environment,"** in F. Marsen, *The Human Dialogue: Perspectives on Communications,* 1967] had it that the United States, by virtue of its leadership in electronic technologies, was the "new world environment." It was, consequently, with a noble conscience that McLuhan, like Galbraith, Easton, and Johnson before him, could turn his attention southward, passing easily and with no sign of disaffection, into the intellectual centres of the American empire. And, of course, in prophesying the end of nationalist sensibility, or the more regional sense of a "love of one's own", McLuhan was only following the flight beyond "romanticism" of the liberal political leadership of Canada, and, in particular, the "creative leadership" of Trudeau. Indeed, that Trudeau could so instantly and enthusiastically embrace McLuhan's world-sensibility was only because the latter's sense of an underlying reason in the technological order confirmed the deepest prejudices of Trudeau's own political perspective. Indeed, between Trudeau and McLuhan a parallel project was in the making: on Trudeau's part (*Federalism and the French-Canadians*) a political challenge against the "obsolete" world of ethnicity (and thus nationalism) in Québec and an invitation to Québec to join the technological (rational) society of North America; and on McLuhan's part, an epistemological and then moral decision to join in the feast of corporate advantages spread out by the masters of the empire. The common trajectories traced by Trudeau's technocratic politics and by McLuhan's sense of technological utopia reveals, powerfully so, the importance of the Catholic touch in Canadian politics and letters; just as much as it reflects, that for the empire at least, Catholicism is, indeed, intimate with the "central cultural discoveries" of the modern age. Moreover, the very existence of a "McLuhan" or a "Trudeau" as the locus of the Canadian discourse discloses the indelible character of Canada, not just as a witness to empire, but, perhaps, as a radical experiment in the working out of the intellectual and political basis of the technological imagination in North America. Canada is, and has always been, the most modern of the New World societies; because the character of its colonialism, of its domination of the land by technologies of communication, and of its imposition of an "abstract nation" upon a divergent population by a fully technological polity, has made of it a leading expression of technological liberalism in North America.

It was, consequently, the fate of McLuhan to be welcomed into the privileged circles of the corporate and intellectual elites of the United States. This was not unanticipated. The Canadian philosopher, Charles Norris Cochrane, noted [in "The Latin Spirit in Literature," *University of Toronto Quarterly* 2, No. 3 (1932-33)] that it is the peculiar feature of imperialisms that, as their energies focus, in the most mature phase of empire, on the "pragmatic will" to conquer, to expand, to live, they are often forced to seek out in the peripheral regions of the empire some new source of intellectual energy, some inspiring historical justification, which would counter the dawning sense of "intellectual futility" that so often accompanies, and undermines, the greatest successes of the will to empire. McLuhan was such an "historical energizer." His utopian vision of technological society provided the corporate leadership of the American empire with a sense of historical destiny; and, at least, with the passing illusion that their narrowminded concentration on the "business" of technology might make of them the "Atlas" of the new world of cosmic man. It was McLuhan's special ability, done, no doubt, sometimes tongue in cheek and with a proper sense of intellectual cynicism, to transfigure the grubby leadership (Grant's "creative leaders") of the American business world, and then of a good part of the new class of technocrats in the West, into the dizzying heights of a greater historical destiny, that made him such a favoured courtesan of the technological empire. Grant might say of the "creative leaders" of empire that their nihilism is such that they would always prefer to will rather than not to will, but McLuhan provided another, more radical, alternative. In the face of the incipient nihilism of the technological experience, McLuhan dangled that most precious of gifts: a sense of historical purpose (the age of communications as "cosmic consciousness"); and an intellectual justification (the technological imperative as both necessary *and* good).

While Grant's austere, and forbidding, description of technological dependency revolved around a consideration of *technique as will,* McLuhan thought of technique as possessing, at least potentially, the *poetry of consciousness.* Thus, it was not with bad faith but with the curious amorality of a thinker whose ethic, being as it was abstract freedom and reason, and who could thus screen out the barbarism of the technological dynamo, that McLuhan could associate with the leadership of technological society. And just to the extent that Grant's ruminations on technological society have led him into, almost selfimposed, solitude in Halifax (far from the "dynamic centre" of the technological dynamo in the Great Lakes region of North America), McLuhan could be a dandy of the New York intelligentsia. McLuhan's association of the values of reason and "universal unity" with the expansive momentum of the technostructure was, of course, a highly fortuitous compromise. It allowed him to serve a legitimation function for the technological dynamo, while all the while maintaining his *sang-froid* as a civil humanist who was above the fray, a Catholic intellectual among the barbarians.

McLuhan's political commitments, represented both by his rejection of the "national question" in Canada and by

McLuhan recording The Medium Is the Massage *for CBS Records. Left to right: Jerome Agel, Quentin Fiore, McLuhan, and John Simon.*

his participation, in depth, in the futurology of technological empire, are of direct consequence to his contributions to a master theory of communications. That McLuhan could find no moment of deviation between his civil humanism, founded on the defence of "civilization", and his absorption into the intellectual appendages of empire, indicates, starkly and dramatically, precisely how inert and uncritical is the supervening value of "civilization". McLuhan's lasting legacy is, perhaps, a historical one: the inherent contradiction of his discourse in remaining committed to the very technostructure which had destroyed the possibility of "civilization" indicates the ultimate failure of civil humanism in modern politics. McLuhan's humanism, and indeed his abiding Catholicism, could provide an inspiring vision of a more utopian human future; but in remaining tied to the "primacy of reason", a *reason* which was fully abstracted from history and ontology, McLuhan's discourse could always be easily turned from within. This was the comic aspect of the whole affair: the technological dynamo could also accept as its dominant value the "primacy of reason"; and, by extension, the application of technical reason, in politics, bureaucracy, science, and industry, to the proliferation of technological media. The technostructure thus absorbed McLuhan's discourse on his own terms: it transposed his search for a new, universal civilization into an historical justification of technological necessitarianism; and it showed precisely how compatible the Catholic conception of "transcendent reason" is with the rationalising impulses of the techno-

logical system. McLuhan's one possible avenue of escape: the recovery of a "grounded" and emergent cultural practice or, at least, some sense of "intimations of deprival" which had been silenced by the technological dynamo was, of course, firmly closed to him by his commitment to the universal over the local, and to the metaphorical over the historical. To dismiss McLuhan as a technological determinist is to miss entirely the point of his intellectual contribution. McLuhan's value as a theorist of culture and technology began just when he went over the hill to the side of the alien and surrealistic world of mass communications: the "real world" of technology where the nervous system is exteriorised and everyone is videoated daily like sitting screens for television. Just because McLuhan sought *to see* the real world of technology, and even to celebrate technological reason as freedom, he could provide such superb, first-hand accounts of the new society of electronic technologies. McLuhan was fated to be trapped in the deterministic world of technology, indeed to become one of the intellectual servomechanisms of the machine-world, because his Catholicism failed to provide him with an adequate cultural theory by which to escape the hegemony of the abstract media systems that he had sought to explore. Paradoxically, however, it was just when McLuhan became most cynical and most deterministic, when he became fully aware of the nightmarish quality of the "medium as massage", that his thought becomes most important as an entirely creative account of the great paradigm-shift now going on in twentieth-century experience.

McLuhan was then, in the end, trapped in the "figure" of his own making. His discourse could provide a brilliant understanding of the innerfuctioning of the technological media; but no illumination concerning how "creative freedom" might be won through in the "age of anxiety, and dread." In a fully tragic sense, McLuhan's final legacy was this: he was the playful perpetrator, and then victim, of a sign-crime.

Arthur Kroker, "Technological Humanism: The Processed World of Marshall McLuhan," in his Technology and the Canadian Mind: Innis/McLuhan/Grant, *St. Martin's Press, 1985, pp. 52-86.*

Neil Postman on revising McLuhan:

[Although] culture is a creation of speech, it is recreated anew by every medium of communication—from painting to hieroglyphs to the alphabet to television. Each medium, like language itself, makes possible a unique mode of discourse by providing a new orientation for thought, for expression, for sensibility. Which, of course, is what McLuhan meant in saying the medium is the message. His aphorism, however, is in need of amendment because, as it stands, it may lead one to confuse a message with a metaphor. A message denotes a specific, concrete statement about the world. But the forms of our media, including the symbols through which they permit conversation, do not make such statements. They are rather like metaphors, working by unobtrusive but powerful implication to enforce their special definitions of reality. Whether we are experiencing the world through the lens of speech or the printed word or the television camera, our media-metaphors classify the world for us, sequence it, frame it, enlarge it, reduce it, color it, argue a case for what the world is like.

Neil Postman, in his Amusing Ourselves to Death: Public Discourse in the Age of Show Business, *Viking Penguin, 1985.*

Brian Fawcett (review date April 1988)

[*In the following review, Fawcett offers a favorable appraisal of McLuhan's collected letters.*]

With the publication of this overdue collection [*Letters of Marshall McLuhan*], it should be clear to anyone still not convinced that Marshall McLuhan is among the small company of intellectual geniuses Canada has thus far produced. Arguably, he has been our most exciting and original thinker, and the partial eclipse of his reputation in the past decade is an indictment of our national short-sightedness and mediocrity. We seem content to lavish our "high" cultural attentions on one-eyed English walruses like Robertson Davies, while our truly public attentions go to shallow media stars like David Suzuki, Rick Hansen, and Wayne Gretzky.

Having grown up thinking that Marshall McLuhan was halfway between an idiot savant and the Devil incarnate,

I found his letters a revelation. Despite some uneven and occasionally self-serving editing, the editors of the volume have produced a book that is of international interest, one that provides major clarifications of McLuhan's extremely elliptical theoretical opus, and is a testimony to just how far ahead of his time Marshall McLuhan's thinking reached. For students of McLuhan, the book is of course compulsory. Personally, I'd venture to say that no one concerned with the structure of contemporary reality can afford not to read it.

You can skip the first 172 pages of the book, which are really little more than juvenilia. It consists chiefly of his letters to his mother, his wife-to-be, Corinne, and other family members. Towards the end, there is a rather silly correspondence with Wyndham Lewis, the English writer and portraitist, that chiefly documents McLuhan's partly successful attempts to help Lewis make money by painting portraits of the leading citizens of St. Louis, where McLuhan was teaching in a Jesuit college. It demonstrates McLuhan's generosity, but little else except that Lewis was a bit of a jerk: nothing new there.

The letters—and McLuhan's genius—really took off after 1946, reached their apex in the 1950s and continued with barely declining intensity until a stroke disabled McLuhan permanently in September 1979. Of topical interest are the extended correspondences with Ezra Pound, 1948 to 1953, and the correspondence in the 1970s with Pierre Elliott Trudeau. The meat of the volume however, is elsewhere—in the letters to people like Harold Innis, David Riesman, Walter Ong, Wilfred Watson, Peter Drucker, and then-president of the University of Toronto, Claude Bissell. In these letters, McLuhan develops, reshapes, and restates his often obscure theoretical concerns in ways that allow us to evaluate them more fully than ever before.

The letters reveal McLuhan's genius as an uneven one, created (rather than marred) by profound imbalances and idiosyncrasies. His Jesuit Christian background (and his life-long adherence to Christian intellectual habits and spiritual goals), his democratic optimism, and his almost fetishistic attachment to the Newtonian paradigm all play powerful roles in his thinking and, oddly, contribute to its originality. He was both what the editors of the volume have gone to considerable lengths to make him appear—a deeply conservative family man, a Christian and respectable University of Toronto faculty member—and the intellectual hooligan he considered himself to be. In short, though he was not a typical Canadian, he was certainly an exemplary one. He could have come from no other location and culture than ours.

Although he argued, at times vociferously, that the extrapolations he made about the consequences of mass telecommunications and other aspects of information growth were morally and politically neutral, his letters reveal him as a captive of his intellectual training and his Christian values. He didn't really see the extent to which corporate technopreneurs and political authoritarians would sequester his discoveries for their own narrow purposes. Nor did he foresee that the rapid development of mini- and microcomputers would create a whole new—and privatized—technological élite class. The global village that has resulted is a much more complex, undemocratic and potentially dangerous interdependency than he imagined, governed more by short-sighted barbarism than by visions of the universal liberation of the human mind and body. In particular, his democratic optimism blinded him—as it has George Steiner and others—to the poverty of social resources that would result from the return to tribalism in a mass and electronically manipulated form.

We do not have the luxury of assuming that the global village Marshall McLuhan imagined will be the best of all possible worlds. We're in it, and it is demonstrably not as sweet and generous as he thought it would be. We should, however, credit him for being among the first to glimpse its key components and its structure, and for having seen more of it than any single mind on the planet.

For that, he should be accorded every honour. Most of all, he should be read and thought about, so we can employ his massive insights and correct his errors.

Brian Fawcett, "Village Scribe," in Books in Canada, Vol. 17, No. 3, April, 1988, p. 31.

Michael Bliss   (essay date May 1988)

[*Bliss is a Canadian historian and educator who specializes in the history of business, economics, and modern medicine. In the following essay, he assesses McLuhan's impact on Western culture.*]

The young wonder who Marshall McLuhan was. Maybe some kind of TV commentator in the sixties? The rest of us remember "the medium is the message," and "a global village," and that McLuhan was otherwise unintelligible. He was famous for a while, and then sort of disappeared. You may have read the obituaries in 1980. Does anyone take seriously today this Canadian academic who was once billed as "the most important thinker since Newton, Darwin, Freud, Einstein, and Pavlov"?

It seems that a McLuhan revival is slowly gathering steam. Biographers and essayists are at work, the University of Toronto Press will soon publish his last manuscript, and a major collection, *Letters of Marshall McLuhan,* which was released in Canada [in November 1987], has just been published in Great Britain and the United States. The 450 letters in this volume, brilliantly annotated by William Toye, encompass McLuhan's whole career, and are offered as the "autobiography" he never bothered to write. They are an essential source for all reconsiderations of McLuhan.

He emerges from his letters as a failed metaphysician of the media. McLuhan's system and style proved ludicrously inadequate as a guide to our time, which is why he fell into comparative obscurity after about 1972. But the man and his ideas are fascinating artefacts. To a handful of true believers, McLuhan will endure as oracle. To the rest of us he is passing into history as an interesting product of a strange moment in Western culture.

Marshall McLuhan grew up in Winnipeg where his father worked as a life-insurance salesman and his mother became a professional elocutionist. The letters effectively

begin in 1934 when the twenty-three-year-old graduate of the University of Manitoba went to Cambridge on an IODE scholarship. Reacting against both his Baptist and his Canadian upbringing, he discovered culture and Roman Catholicism in England. "I simply couldn't believe that men had to live in the mean mechanical joyless rootless fashion that I saw in Winnipeg," he wrote his mother.

In 1936 McLuhan began an unremarkable apprenticeship as at teacher of literature, mostly at Saint Louis University, a Jesuit college in St. Louis, Missouri. He migrated to Assumption College in Windsor, Ontario, in 1944, largely to avoid having to serve in either country's armed forces, and in 1946 moved to St. Michael's College at the University of Toronto. He was neither prolific nor well known as a scholar, too lowbrow for most academics when he wrote about comic strips and advertising, too highbrow for many in his professorial role as an expert on difficult modernist writers such as James Joyce, T.S. Eliot, and Ezra Pound.

He got little attention for his first book, *The Mechanical Bride: Folklore of Industrial Man* (1951), or the obscure periodical, *Explorations: Studies in Culture and Communication,* that he helped edit through the 1950s. The fame began with *The Gutenberg Galaxy: The Making of Typographic Man* in 1962, followed by *Understanding Media: The Extensions of Man* in 1964. Soon it was evident that McLuhan and the media were engaged in mutual lionization: the academic preached the transcendent importance of electronic communications, the communicators heralded the visionary academic. From 1963 he presided over a special Centre for Culture and Technology at the University of Toronto, and in 1967-68 was paid the then enormous sum of $100,000 for a guest stint at Fordham University in New York. He jet-setted and hobnobbed and corresponded with prime ministers and pundits and corporation presidents; he was the subject of eight books between 1967 and 1971. McLuhan played himself in Woody Allen's film *Annie Hall.* As Tom Wolfe put it in a famous McLuhan profile, the overwhelming question was "What if he is right?"

McLuhan was much more than an intellectual gadfly or adroit self-promoter. As a literary scholar, he immersed himself in the avant-garde techniques, images, and social attitudes of modernist writers. In dozens of letters to Wyndham Lewis and Ezra Pound, both of whom he met and championed, McLuhan proved a faithful and eager disciple, mimicking even their verbal mannerisms, particularly Pound's punning wordplay. Steeped in modernism's emphasis on form over content, McLuhan latched easily and enthusiastically onto the ideas of pioneering communications theorists such as Harold Adams Innis who emphasized the primacy of the forms of media over the messages they transmit. McLuhan's synthesis, which had emerged by 1960, was based on two claims: (1) sensory perception and communications technologies are interrelated, the latter as extensions of the former; (2) new media technologies, such as the printing press, cinema, or television, change the balance of our senses, and thus create new modes of consciousness, behaviour patterns, and social forms, all of this independently of their content.

"Harry me boy, it works," McLuhan exults to another media guru in 1964. "To deal with the environment directly is my strategy Harry. . . . All that I've said about the medium is the message is sound. . . . The principle works in many ways. . . . It works also for all modes of perception. Can now put the entire *Gutenberg Galaxy* on a single page."

McLuhan was convinced that he had discovered the fundamental principles of human sensory perception and symbiosis with the environment, and began to refer to himself as a "metaphysician." As a possessor of universal insight, untempered by humility or caution, he was happy to interpret anything in literature, history, the whole universe, past, present, and future. McLuhan offered thoughts on Ovid and Aquinas and Blake and comic books, race relations and toplessness, streakers, Watergate, hippies, prayer mats, Cadillacs, corporations, Canadian culture—the works.

There were apocalyptic overtones to McLuhan's prophecies about television's destroying all established bureaucratic and political organizations. But there was also an offer of transcendence to those who believed. "I am saying it is now possible to by-pass what used to be called 'fate,' " he wrote [Pierre] Trudeau. If the prime minister would keep in touch by telephone or personal emissary, the prophet would tell him how to do it. Others could subscribe to the McLuhan *Dew-Line Newsletter,* containing the latest probes from this intellectual radar station up in barren Toronto.

Would McLuhanism supersede other views of the psyche and society? He thought comparisons between himself and Freud made sense, but only if Freud's failure was recognized: "The merely individualist psychology of Freud has flunked out in the new age of tribal and corporate identities." In fact both McLuhan and Freud were the founders of closed systems based on largely untestable hypotheses about the hidden workings of the mind. Both tried to apply their doctrines universally. Both welcomed disciples and were intolerant of critics. Both seemed, for their time, to supply dazzling insights.

But McLuhan's time was very short. He was far more shallow and reckless than Freud and far less able to handle criticism. His prophecies did not come true. Television technology did not totally tribalize today's teenagers or the rest of society. Organizations did not collapse. Content mattered. When McLuhan tried to duck his critics by labelling them mere "content men" and falling back on his Delphic, Pound-like style—as a questioner, a prober, a jester, not necessarily to be taken seriously—he stopped being taken seriously. In his later letters McLuhan seems incapable of serious dialogue about his ideas—he preaches and repeats himself—yet is pathetically eager to find intellectual support for his collapsing system. His last refuge is the arrogant elitism of modernist aesthetics—a view of the artist as prophetic outsider.

There are enough alienated intellectuals, technological determinists, Catholic neotribalists, and Cancultists to keep the McLuhanist flame flickering indefinitely. The *Letters,* a representative selection culled from the McLuhan papers in the National Archives of Canada, provide a new stock of flashing McLuhanisms. Some oracle, though. What was really in those precious letters to the prime minister's office? Nothing more concrete than a conservative Catholic's dislike of abortion and support for capital punishment. McLuhan had little more to say to the politicians and decision makers of his time than his mentors, Wyndham Lewis and Ezra Pound, had to say in theirs. He apparently did not share their flirtations with fascist ideology, but he had little more insight into political reality. The correspondence contains no anticipation of the one true global upheaval of his lifetime: "There will be no war in Europe," twenty-seven-year-old McLuhan writes in September, 1938. "The real villains in the piece are not Hitler etc. but the Comintern, the free masons and the international operators who have their headquarters in Prague." When war does come, he chooses not to serve. There are no letters printed from mid-1940 to mid-1943.

For about fifteen minutes in the 1960s there was enormous interest in the electronic media, in communications generally, and in the idea that all the old forms of behaviour were being shattered in the modern world. It was a cloistered professor of literature, an expert on the breaking of forms by Joyce, Pound, et al., who came forward with the explanations that we dutifully took seriously and then sensibly dismissed. As an intellectual, McLuhan bridged and symbolized and popularized, running a unique gamut from the modernist literary revolution of the 1890s and early 1900s to cultural theorizing in the 1960s. For that reason, and for his audacity and the fame he enjoyed, McLuhan survives.

Michael Bliss, "False Prophet," in Saturday Night, *Vol. 103, No. 5, May, 1988, pp. 59-60, 62.*

FURTHER READING

Bibliography

The Writings of Marshall McLuhan and What Has Been Written about Him. Ft. Lauderdale, Florida: Wake-Brook House, 1975, 112 p.

Lists works by and about McLuhan in chronological order from 1934 through 1975.

Biography

Marchand, Philip. *Marshall McLuhan: The Medium and the Messenger.* New York: Ticknor & Fields, 1989, 320 p.

The most comprehensive biography of McLuhan.

Wain, John. "The Incidental Thoughts of Marshall McLuhan." *Encounter* LXV, No. 1 (June 1985): 11-22.

Reminisces about his friendship with McLuhan.

Criticism

Compton, Neil. "The Paradox of Marshall McLuhan." *New American Review* 2 (1968): 77-94.

>Discusses the evolution of McLuhan's theories, noting that although his system of values has remained markedly conservative, "recent history has apparently transformed his pessimism into a kind of millennial optimism."

Duffy, Dennis. *Marshall McLuhan*. Toronto: McClelland and Stewart, 1969, 64 p.

>Basic introduction to McLuhan's theories.

Edwards, Thomas R. "McLuhan's Medium." In his *Over Here: Criticizing America, 1968-1989*, pp. 1-15. New Brunswick, N. J.: Rutgers University Press, 1991.

>Maintains that McLuhan's response to the technological advances of the 1950s and 1960s is typical of "serious, adult, bookish souls formed by the literary culture of the twenties and thirties but anxious to feel up to date and touchingly sure that an intelligent reader of Joyce and Eliot can grasp just about anything if he puts his mind to it."

Fekete, John. "Marshall McLuhan: The Critical Theory of Counterrevolution." In his *The Critical Twilight: Explorations in the Ideology of Anglo-American Literary Theory from Eliot to McLuhan*, pp. 135-189. London: Routledge & Kegan Paul, 1977.

>Examines the relationship of McLuhan's theories to a tradition of critical ideology that began with I. A. Richards and T. S. Eliot.

Finkelstein, Sidney. *Sense and Nonsense of McLuhan*. New York: International Publishers, 1968, 122 p.

>Polemical study which concludes that McLuhan's ideas are "a novel and bizarre form of obscurantism. It is that of writing a travesty on knowledge."

Kostelanetz, Richard. "Marshall McLuhan: High Priest of the Electronic Village." In his *Master Minds: Portraits of Contemporary American Artists and Intellectuals*, pp. 82-114. Toronto: Macmillan, 1967.

>Overview of McLuhan's career and major theories.

Miller, Jonathan. *Marshall McLuhan*. New York: Viking Press, 1971, 133 p.

>Unfavorably assesses the major ideas expressed in McLuhan's *Gutenberg Galaxy* and examines their precedents in the history of ideas.

Schafer, R. Murray. "McLuhan and Acoustic Space." *The Antigonish Review*, Nos. 62-63 (Summer-Fall 1985): 62-63, 105-113.

>Explains McLuhan's concept of "acoustic space."

Scholes, Robert J., and Willis, Brenda J. "Linguists, Literacy, and the Intensionality of Marshall McLuhan's Western Man." In *Literacy and Orality*, edited by David R. Olson and Nancy Torrance, pp. 215-35. Cambridge: Cambridge University Press, 1991.

>Linguistic study that identifies a fundamental flaw in McLuhan's theory of language.

Stearn, Gerald Emanuel, ed. *McLuhan: Hot & Cool*. New York: Dial Press, 1967, 312 p.

>Primarily positive essay collection that includes assessments by a variety of critics as well as essays by and an interview with McLuhan.

Theall, Donald F. *The Medium Is the Rear View Mirror: Understanding McLuhan*. Montreal: McGill-Queen's University Press, 1971, 261 p.

>Balanced examination of McLuhan's theories and the critical response to his ideas.

Additional coverage of McLuhan's life and career is contained in the following sources published by Gale Research: *Contemporary Authors*, Vols. 9-12, rev. ed., 102 [obituary]; *Contemporary Authors New Revision Series*, Vols. 12, 34; *Contemporary Literary Criticism*, Vol. 37; *Dictionary of Literary Biography*, Vol. 88; and *Major 20th-Century Writers*.

Thomas Merton

1915-1968

French-born American poet, philosopher, essayist, playwright, editor, and translator.

For further information on Merton's life and works, see *CLC*, Volumes 1, 3, 11, and 34.

INTRODUCTION

Merton was a Trappist monk who became a prolific writer and an influential social activist despite his vows of silence. His works are informed by the interplay between his contemplative life, his compassion for humanity, and his desire to work toward nonviolent solutions to world problems. A popular and critically acclaimed autobiographer, poet, and essayist, he was respected for his insight into twentieth-century social problems, his interpretations of the role of religion in modern society, and for helping to introduce Asian religions to the West.

Biographical Information

Merton was born in Prades, France, the son of two artists, both of whom died by the time Merton reached the age of sixteen. He was educated at the Lycée de Montauban in France and the Oakham School in England, and then spent a year at Clare College, Cambridge, before entering Columbia University in New York, where he studied English literature, earning a B.A. in 1938 and an M.A. in 1939. At Columbia he was strongly influenced by what became a lifelong friendship with the noted literary critic Mark Van Doren. Merton converted to Catholicism during the late 1930s, and he entered the Trappist monastery Our Lady of Gethsemani in Kentucky in 1941. Because the Trappists require their members to take a vow of silence which includes strict limitations on writing, Merton's literary output was initially severely restricted by his monastic duties. However, he was soon given numerous writing assignments by his superiors, and although he was frequently frustrated by Trappist censorship, by the 1950s he was virtually free to publish whatever he wished. At age thirty-three he published his autobiography *The Seven Storey Mountain* (1948), which became a best-seller and made him a reluctant celebrity. He continued to receive expanded responsibilities in the monastery, and in 1955 he achieved the esteemed position of Master of Novices. During the 1950s and 1960s Merton became increasingly concerned with political events occurring in the outside world, and he began advocating awareness and activism rather than isolation as the proper response to the world's problems. Along with political events, Merton became increasingly interested in the study of other religions, particularly Zen Buddhism. Merton died as a result of accidental electrocution in 1968 in Bangkok, Thailand, where he had been attending an ecumenical conference.

Major Works

Merton's oeuvre includes numerous works of autobiography, social criticism, poetry, and theology. Among his best-known works is his autobiography *The Seven Storey Mountain* which relates the events leading to his conversion to Catholicism and advocates a life of contemplation. *The Sign of Jonas* (1953) is a personal journal that vividly depicts five years of Merton's life in the monastery, focusing on his evolving understanding of the meaning of his role as a monk and his attempt to reconcile the conflict between his religious and literary aspirations. While Merton's early works largely focus on the development of a spiritual life, many of his later writings address social issues, acknowledging the need for political activism. *Seeds of Destruction* (1964), for example, examines the role and responsibility of the monastic community in relation to such social problems as racism and the threat of nuclear war. Merton's poetry also addresses both religious and secular subjects and employs a diverse range of formal and free verse techniques. Notable among his most experimental works are *Cables to the Ace; or, Familiar Liturgies of Misunderstanding* (1968) and *The Geography of Lograire* (1969), both of which combine prose with poetry.

Critical Reception

Merton's early works were praised by both readers and reviewers, in part, according to some critics, because his advocation of the need for a radically different way of life appealed to many people in the years following the chaos of World War II. Although the shift in his writings from a focus on individual spirituality to social criticism generated mixed responses, some critics feel that his later works addressing political themes have yet to be realized as his most important contributions. Assessments of Merton's poetry are varied—some critics find the majority of his verse flawed while others consider him among the most important poets of his generation. Several critics have also observed that there is much scholarship on Merton's works yet to be conducted.

PRINCIPAL WORKS

Thirty Poems (poetry) 1944

A Man in the Divided Sea (poetry) 1946

Figures for an Apocalypse (poetry) 1948

The Seven Storey Mountain (autobiography) 1948; also published as *Elected Silence: The Autobiography of Thomas Merton* [revised edition], 1949

What Is Contemplation? (essays) 1948; [revised edition], 1981

Seeds of Contemplation (essays) 1949; also published as *New Seeds of Contemplation* [revised edition], 1962

The Tears of Blind Lions (poetry) 1949

Selected Poems of Thomas Merton (poetry) 1950

The Ascent to the Truth (essays) 1951

Bread in the Wilderness (essays) 1953

The Sign of Jonas (journal) 1953

No Man Is an Island (essays) 1955

The Living Bread (essays) 1956

Praying the Psalms (essays) 1956; also published as *The Psalms Are Our Prayer*, 1957; also published as *Thomas Merton on the Psalms*, 1970

The Silent Life (essays) 1957

The Tower of Babel (drama) 1957

Thoughts in Solitude (essays) 1958

The Secular Journal of Thomas Merton (journal) 1959

Disputed Questions (essays) 1960

Spiritual Direction and Meditation (essays) 1960

The New Man (essays) 1962

Emblems of a Season of Fury (poetry) 1963

Life and Holiness (essays) 1963

Seeds of Destruction (essays) 1964; also published as *Redeeming the Time* [abridged edition], 1966

Seasons of Celebration (essays) 1965; also published as *Meditations on Liturgy*, 1976

Conjectures of a Guilty Bystander (journal) 1966

Mystics and Zen Masters (essays) 1967

Cables to the Ace; or, Familiar Liturgies of Misunderstanding (poetry) 1968

Faith and Violence: Christian Teaching and Christian Practice (essays) 1968

Landscape, Prophet and Wild-Dog (poetry) 1968

Zen and the Birds of Appetite (essays) 1968

The Climate of Monastic Prayer (essays) 1969; also published as *Contemplative Prayer*, 1969

The Geography of Lograire (poetry) 1969

Three Essays (essays) 1969

Opening the Bible (essays) 1970

Contemplation in a World of Action (essays) 1971

Thomas Merton on Peace (essays) 1971; also published as *The Nonviolent Alternative* [revised edition], 1980

The Zen Revival (essays) 1971

Early Poems: 1940-42 (poetry) 1972

The Asian Journal of Thomas Merton (journal) 1973

He Is Risen: Selections from Thomas Merton (poetry) 1975

Ishi Means Man: Essays on Native Americans (essays) 1976

Thomas Merton on Zen (essays) 1976

The Monastic Journey (essays) 1977

Love and Living (essays) 1979

Thomas Merton on St. Bernard (essays) 1980

The Literary Essays of Thomas Merton (essays) 1981

Woods, Shore, Desert: A Notebook, May, 1968 (journal) 1982

CRITICISM

Robert Lowell   (review date 22 June 1945)

[*Winner of two Pulitzer Prizes and a National Book Award, Lowell is among the most highly respected American poets of his generation as well as an acclaimed translator, playwright, and critic. Below, he presents a mixed assessment of Merton's verse.*]

Thomas Merton's career has been varied and spectacular: Cambridge University, the *New Yorker* and the Trappist monastery of Our Lady of Gethsemani. One can understand only too easily why the Protean Mr. Laughlin of the New Directions Press would be fascinated. I am sure that Catholics altogether like the idea of an "experimental" Trappist. But American Catholic culture is in a relatively receptive state of transition; in the arts, as in other things, we are taking our cue from France. Unfortunately, Merton's work has attracted almost no attentive criticism; the poet would appear to be more phenomenal than the poetry.

There is some justice in this neglect. Merton is a modest, not altogether satisfactory minor writer. But he is also, as far as my experience goes, easily the most promising of our American Catholic poets and, possibly, the most consequential Catholic poet to write in English since the death of Francis Thompson. Why the last forty years of the Catholic literary revival, which have seen the prose of Chesterton, Dawson and Waugh, have produced nothing as lasting as the light verses of Belloc is no doubt due to complex, partially intangible, causes. We must take what comes. What Merton writes is his own, subtle and intense. So small and genuine an achievement is worth consideration.

The purpose of this review is to point up what Merton has done; this involves an analysis of his limitations and faults. I shall quote to the extent of making a short anthology and hope that each quotation will be read over until it is understood. My comments are more or less footnotes.

> Through every precinct of the wintry city
> Squadroned iron resounds upon the streets;
> Herod's police
> Make shudder the dark steps of the tenements
> At the business about to be done.
>
> Neither look back upon Thy starry country
> Nor hear what rumors crowd across the dark
> While blood runs down those holy walls,
> Nor frame a childish blessing with Thy hand
> Towards that fiery spiral of exulting souls!
>
> Go, Child of God, upon the singing desert,
> Where, with eyes of flame,
> The roaming lion keeps Thy road from harm.
>   **("The Flight into Egypt")**

This is modern and traditional, graceful and quietly powerful. The first ten lines are probably the finest in the entire book. Note especially the stern imagery and rhetorical éclat of the first stanza; the subtle shift of rhythm in the second stanza, and the unity of symbol, meaning and sound in line 10. About the last three lines I am less certain. Too much depends on the word *singing* (presumably, the poet means that the desert is simple and alive, in contrast to the tortured, twisted fury of the town) which prepares for the sinless *flame* of the lion.

> Because my will is simple as a window
> And knows no pride of original earth,
> It is my life to die, like glass, by light;
> Slain in the strong rays of the bridegroom
>   son. . . .
>
> For light, my lover, steals my life in secret.
> I vanish into day, and leave no shadow
> But the geometry of my cross,
> Whose frame and structure are the strength
> By which I die. . . .
>
> Because I die by brightness and the Holy Spirit
> The Sun rejoices in your jail, my kneeling Christian. . . .
>   **("The Blessed Virgin Mary Compared to a**
>   **Window")**

At first glance this is merely a tour-de-force, in imitation of Donne's "Of My Name in the Window." Then one realizes how persistently and honestly the conceit has been elaborated, how right the tone is for Our Lady. The figure of the window-frame and its shadow is almost as good as its original. Donne's and Crashaw's contributions to the poem detract nothing from its sincerity and freshness. The extracts that I have quoted should have been the entire poem, for the rest, in spite of much incidental brilliance, is repetitive, loose, wordy.

One of Merton's faults is a contrivance that he may have learned from some of the less successful poems of Crashaw (e. g., "The Weeper"), the atomic conceit: each conceit is an entity and the whole poem is seldom much more than the sum of its parts, often it is considerably less. My quotations should have made it plain that Merton is not writing a seventeenth century pastiche; he is using the old devices as an artist, not as an antiquarian. At the same time he follows so closely on the heals of his predecessors that the capacity of his vision is narrowed. Much of the old immediacy, power and mass are lost. In fact, Merton's poems, like Christina Rosetti's, are precariously unlocated in time or place. Nor is this much helped by a trick that he may have gotten from Edith Sitwell or Cummings, that is, using a sound word where one would expect a *light* word. Occasionally this yields most effective lines, as in a Crucifixion poem which opens with: "When Romans gambled in the clash of lancelight." (*Lancelight* is an alliterative, Hopkinsian compound that works; however, the last line of the same poem is ruined by Hopkins: "Reeks of the death-thirst man-life found in the forbidden apple.") Elsewhere, as in the *singing desert* of my first quotation, a mannerism is made to bear the burden of inspiration.

"Flight Into Egypt" is in Merton's most original style; **"A Window"** is more derivative but hardly inferior. There is a third Merton who is glib, sentimental and romantic.

> When My kind Father, kinder than the sun,
> With looks and smiles bends down
> And utters my bodily life,
> My flesh obeying, praises Heaven like a smiling
>   cloud.
> Then I am the gay wheatfields, the serious hills:
> I fill the sky with words of light, and My incar-
>   nate songs
> Fly in and out the branches of My childish voice
> Like thrushes in a tree.
>   **("The Holy Child's Song")**

These lines are clearly superior to Kilmer's unwittingly obscene "Tree," but thinness is not disguised by one or two apt words and an ordered irregularity of meter. A lofty subject and enthusiastic imagery are often imaginative narcotics.

A variation on the style of **"The Flight Into Egypt"** appears in the nature poems:

> When cold November sits among the reeds like
>   an
> unlucky fisher
> And ducks drum up as sudden as the wind
> Out of the rushy river,
> We slowly come, robbed of our rod and gun,
> Walking amid the stricken cages of the trees.

This is charming and the details are solid as the details of **"The Holy Child's Song"** should have been solid. Unfortunately here, as in most of the other nature poems, the fine opening is undeveloped. Instead the cages flounder on into an impossible devotional metaphor, upholstered with *keys, jails* and *jailers.*

> Sweet brother, if I do not sleep
> My eyes are flowers for your tomb;
> And if I cannot eat my bread,
> My fasts shall live like willows where you died.
> If in the heat I find no water for my thirst,
> My thirst shall turn to springs for you, poor
>   traveller.
>
> Where, in what desolate and smoky country
> Lies your poor body, lost and dead?

And in what landscape of disaster
Has your unhappy spirit lost its road?
Come, in my labor find a resting place
And in my sorrows lay your head;
Or rather take my life and blood
And buy yourself a better bed—
Or take my breath and take my death
And buy yourself a better rest.

When all the men of war are shot
And flags are fallen into dust,
Your cross and mine shall tell men still
Christ died on each, for both of us.

For in the wreckage of your April Christ lies
     slain
And Christ weeps in the ruins of my spring:
The money of whose tears shall fall
Into your weak and friendless hand,
And buy you back to your own land:
The silence of Whose tears shall fall
Like bells upon your alien tomb.
Hear them and come: they call you home.
         **("For My Brother Reported Missing in
                    Action, 1943")**

To appreciate how this string of commonplace figures constantly keeps shifting and moving and never becomes insincere, extravagant or dead, the reader should have tried his luck with epitaphs and have failed—have failed and thought he succeeded. Comparison should be made with Crashaw's verses on "A Man and His Wife Who Were Buried Together." There the metaphors are worked out with logic and care and the meter is much firmer; but Merton's poem has its own virtues and is not overshadowed.

Robert Lowell, "The Verses of Thomas Merton," in The Commonweal, *Vol. XLII, No. 10, June 22, 1945, pp. 240-42.*

George N. Shuster   (review date 8 February 1953)

[*Shuster was an American journalist, nonfiction writer, and educator who was known by many as a modern interpreter of Roman Catholicism. In the following positive review of* The Sign of Jonas, *Shuster praises Merton's vivid and insightful depiction of life in a monastery.*]

I am quite sure there has been no book like this. [*The Sign of Jonas*] is a diary kept during five years spent in a Trappist monastery by a young monk who, as everyone doubtless knows, can write unusually well. Of course many others have described their experiences as members of religious orders, but generally they have either been too holy to tell us much of general interest, or too human to care a great deal about holiness. Thomas Merton—Father Louis of the Order of Cistercians of the Strict Observance—leaves no one in doubt that he has been earnestly trying to become a saint, and yet he has kept on being flesh and blood. He also tempts you to surmise that most of the things you have been fussing about are really not terribly important, without however creating the illusion that the peace of the cloister—in case you should be tempted to yearn for it—is devoid of a great deal of infighting with God, other people and one's self.

The book is by a man who has clung to all his five senses, which means that he is a poet. But he has acquired something more, too, and it is rare and in a way very strange. It was not yet to be found in *The Seven Storey Mountain.* One can perhaps call it the discipline of affection for other human beings—a beautiful thing to have come by and not to be had for the asking, as this diary unmistakably reveals.

Father Merton likens himself to Jonas the Prophet, who had his own ideas about the destination he wished to reach, and whom the Lord thereupon summarily clamped into the whale's belly after having suggested to that tractable beast a path to follow. As a monk he had elected to lead a life of solitude and contemplation. Soon, however, he found himself immersed in the affairs of a community which spent more time running tractors than reading *The Cloud of Unknowing.* He was virtually chained to a typewriter because his Superior decided that a few books would be helpful.

There were other chores, too. He was assigned to pump theological doctrine into the heads of novices who, one gathers, were not less immune to the disease of learning than students elsewhere normally are. He sometimes thought of going off to join a more senobitic community, or of retiring alone to a hermitage. But wise counsel succeeded in dissuading him. Father Merton relates delightfully that a fellow monk who had elected to go off into the woods by himself discovered so many people coming to him for advice that there was nothing for it but to return to the monastery for a measure of peace and quiet.

No doubt the heart of the mystery in his own case was that he, who had knocked at the gates of Gethsemani Monastery in quest of loneliness, proved to be in large measure responsible for the fact that so many human beings came rushing thither. There were those who wished to join the community, those who were seeking recollection and spiritual counsel, and of course those who suffered from that odd, insatiable curiosity for a glimpse of something unusual that had been called to their attention.

All of them, the pity, the humor, the misery and the often veiled beauty of them, are caught in the clear lens of this book. Their snores beat upon the ear of one who watches in the night, their sweat in the sticky Kentucky heat is rank in the nostrils. One has in one's mind's eye a glimpse of this young monk wrapping about his spirit the hairshirt of distaste, sometimes as barbed as loathing, so that it might become a bush of brambles wherein Saint Francis could impale himself anew in order to become Francis once again.

All is said with unforgettable definiteness (though seldom mordantly), in that mood akin to self-flagellation which all must no doubt learn to cultivate who wish to rediscover the old truth that it is beyond the shadow of any doubt easier to love the Lord God than to have affection for one's neighbor. At least, that is, when the neighbor puts up no fences.

Not that loving God is easy either. Father Merton's book is filled with gnarled and also grateful notations on the wrestling. It is likewise a report concerning victory, which one must bear in mind was not written with the idea that a vast public would read it. Some of these words about the search for insight into the Divine affection and the answers deemed to have been received are much too moving to be commented upon. They must be read, as are comparable sayings in Ramon Lull and Traherne. But there is much prose poetry in them, too, about which I shall confess that I was at first somewhat dubious, only to sense later on how fresh and clear these waters were when they welled up, and how thankful one might well be that it was so.

Though one may find it disconcerting to hear a young man tell us how keenly he has felt the joy of anticipated death, it is probably only because one has for a brief time forgotten that on this theme Plato and the Psalmist are in agreement. But it is Bonaventure, the great Franciscan, whom Father Merton most definitely echoes, even if he does not often refer to him. No doubt it is strange that the hour in which such things are written for Americans happens to be that of the triumph of their technocracy; but it is also the time of Korea and Prague.

This book is made unmistakably real and almost, at times, unbearably poignant by the fact that the exuberance of youth so often wells up through it with rapture, impatience and even bluster. Literary art has its place in the monkish scheme of things. Father Merton can dash off a note which all but sets Robert Lowell beside Milton, or strew flowers at Dylan Thomas' feet with almost bacchanalian joy. He hopes to write like Eliot, or not at all. There is a fleet but distinct echoing of Hopkins in a jagged little entry about a falcon swooping down on its prey. Nor can one think of any of our books in which so many dawn songs are sung with a sheer trembling of joy and gratitude. I fear it makes the meditations of Thoreau sitting on the edge of Walden Pond sound a little like the memoirs of a mildly intoxicated Transcendentalist greatly enjoying a fog.

Sun and forest move across Father Merton's line of vision for their own sakes as well as for whatever help religious analogy can derive from them. And when in the grip of stark tragedy (say, because a plane has carried its human cargo to swift death almost at the monastery's doorstep) this priest is not a reporter but, one might well think, the kinsman of some such painter as Georges Rouault. He can, to be sure, upon occasion be rather banal, too, as when he suddenly becomes inexplicably pious out of respect for something people are expected to be pious about.

At such moments the reader will no doubt feel that though priest may be poet and poet priest, human nature cannot always rid itself easily of the raiment which is prescribed. But one does not often feel let down with that kind of whimper. To compensate, there is the element of surprise. When Evelyn Waugh visited Gethsemani, he professed to feel that it "looked Irish." That was no doubt the sharp-tongued Englishman's way of saying that he had seen more notable scenes. At any rate, it left Father Merton with his mouth wide open in astonishment blended with a smile.

Shall one then conclude that the business of being a Trap-

pist must of necessity seem so far away from the normal concerns of men as they usually are that reading a diary devoted to it will prove a static experience at best? I believe that this book has, in spite of its implicit discontinuity, a vivid, satisfying, almost dramatic progression. In it on the one hand a monk takes on the stature of the priesthood. On the other, the conflict between elected silence and the impact of the shouting world mounts higher and higher in intensity.

If one is so minded, this struggle will seem both more exacting and more significant than are those usually waged in our world for the discovery of Achilles' heel. For here youthfully discerned time, rich and in spite of all alluring, is in a bout with Eternity, and like is constantly pitted against dislike. The chronicle is deep, beautiful and absorbing.

George N. Shuster, "Silent Searcher in a Shouting World," in The New York Times Book Review, *February 8, 1953, pp. 1, 30.*

Aelred Graham   (review date 13 May 1955)

[*Graham was an English Benedictine monk and professor of theology who studied both Western and Eastern philosophies. Below, he praises* No Man Is an Island, *discussing Merton's views on spirituality.*]

To judge from the Catholic press, the Church's activity today is as vigorous as it has ever been. The theologians, within the framework of the dogmatic formularies, continue to elucidate divine revelation; and the ecclesiastics, like good policemen, control and direct the spiritual traffic. When, however, mid-twentieth century man wishes to discover what it is all about he turns, more likely than not, to the mystics.

This is what gives to the writing of Thomas Merton its special importance. As his latest work [*No Man is an Island*] reveals signs of an all but completely achieved maturity, that importance is certain to grow. A rare and attractive combination of gifts display themselves: the readability of an accomplished writer, imaginative and intelligent, with a poet's ear for the music of words; an instinctive sense of the orthodox blended with the originality, not of one who must think differently from other people, but of one who thinks for himself. Added to these are perceptiveness, compassion, humility and an abounding common sense which relieves his uncompromising message of any suspicion of extravagance or ill-humor. The young scholastics at the Abbey of Gethsemani are fortunate in having so magnanimously sane, warmhearted and articulate a spiritual director as Father Louis.

As hitherto, he writes as the Trappist-Cistercian monk, while at the same time contriving to address himself to the world at large. The world would do well to pay heed:

> A selfish love seldom respects the rights of the beloved to be an autonomous person. . . . God is more glorified by a man who uses the good things of this life in simplicity and with gratitude than by the nervous asceticism of someone who is agitated about every detail of his self-denial.

The former uses good things and thinks of God. The latter is afraid of good things, and consequently cannot use them properly. . . . We cannot be happy if we expect to live all the time at the highest peak of intensity. Happiness is not a matter of intensity but of balance and order and rhythm and harmony. . . .

The arguments of religious men are so often insincere, and their insincerity is proportionate to their anger. Why do we get angry about what we believe? Because we do not really believe it. Or else what we pretend to be defending as the "truth" is really our own self-esteem. A man of sincerity is less interested in defending the truth than in stating it clearly, for he thinks that if the truth be clearly seen it can very well take care of itself.

How simple yet how admirably acute all this is. The book as a whole treats, as its author justly says, of "some of the basic verities on which the spiritual life depends." In a series of penetrating reflections Father Louis unfolds the theme, old yet perennially new, of man's response to reality; that is to say, how we are to bring ourselves into harmony with God and our fellow creatures. In this adjustment lies man's destiny and his sole hope of happiness. The goal ultimately to be achieved—not merely by those who live in monasteries but by all men alike—is the unitive knowledge of God in loving contemplation together with selfless good will towards the world around us.

The process of spiritual growth, as Father Louis makes clear in continuing flashes of insight, can be summed up in the Gospel paradox of surrendering self in order to gain the truer and deeper Self. "I live, now, not I, but Christ liveth in me." This "self-naughting" moves in a different dimension from that of mere virtue—hence we have to be on our guard against being righteous overmuch—even while what is involved is the totality of the "good life." Self-knowledge and an awareness of the motives for our actions are among the conditions of success. Its enemies are "fear, anxiety, greed, ambition," since by these we become preoccupied with the ego and so distort our vision of reality. "Most of the moral and mental and even religious complexities of our time go back to our desperate fear that we are not and cannot really be loved by anyone."

Father Louis, perhaps for the first time within the pages of a single book, has overlooked none of the positive elements that make for Christian holiness; both its counterfeits and the impediments to its achievement are ruthlessly exposed. Nevertheless, in the mind of one reader at least, a lingering doubt remains—more, it is true, a question of emphasis than of anything substantive. If it is here ventilated, it is in no spirit of carping criticism, but with a view either to having it dismissed or providing an occasion for one of the ablest spiritual writers of our time to clarify his thought.

Father Louis' later writings, and this book in particular, show him as aware as any man could be that Christian perfection has nothing to do with sanctified egoism. But has he been able, even here, to express that awareness in a consistently articulated doctrine? For example, the two

kinds of love, *eros* and *agape,* to which he alludes in his prologue deserve closer attention than they receive. (No one, incidentally, is better qualified than Thomas Merton to extract what is true and valuable from Nygren's great study *Agape and Eros*—a work highly relevant to his theme.) If Hope is a form of desire, as Father Louis holds with St. Thomas—in other words, Hope has the character of *eros* rather than *agape*—then how far is it spiritually profitable to develop the theme of the love of God precisely in these terms?

Hope, partaking of desire, though directed to God, is also, unlike charity (*agape*), a self-regarding virtue. We want *our* spiritual hunger satisfied. This, of course, is legitimate; but is it really what Father Louis wishes to stress so emphatically? At any rate, it would be interesting, in this connection, to have his comment on the story—a favorite of St. Francis of Sales—of the woman who carried a burning brand in one hand and a pitcher of water in the other. When asked her purpose, she replied that the brand was to burn up paradise and the water to extinguish the fires of hell. Then, she said, we shall know who are God's true lovers!

" . . . I exist in order to save my soul and give glory to God by doing so." Is not the inverse of this more in harmony with Father Louis's underlying thought? "I exist in order to give glory to God and save my soul by doing so." The difference here is worth considering. Would he agree that the most significant aspiration of the love of God ever spoken contained no element of self-regarding desire? "Not my will, but Thine be done"—a dramatic echo of the most selflessly loving prayer that we ourselves can ever say: ". . . . *Thy* kingdom come; *Thy* will be done. . . ."

Father Louis is still preoccupied with "asceticism," alive though he is to its pitfalls. Hope, he says, is asceticism's "living heart." The real danger of self-chosen austerities, or even of exceptional ascetic practices authorized for limited groups, is not so much that they can foster pharisaic pride. Though of this possibility there are abundant warnings in history, fiction and descriptive psychology. The danger is that they intensify our absorption in precisely that individual ego whose claims on our attention it is our business to ignore. How profoundly it has been remarked that humility does not consist in thinking little of self, but in not thinking of self at all. Calculated austerity not seldom merely exalts the more creditable side of the ego at the expense of the less creditable; whereas genuine holiness implies the complete self-naughting of the ego, in its creditable no less than its discreditable aspects, and the abandoning of the will to God.

Only the pure in heart can see God. For achieving such one-pointedness as is here implied a prudent disciplining of the bodily senses is indispensable. But this of itself need bring us no nearer the goal. Penintential practices can never touch the heart of the matter—which is the ordering, and very largely the elimination, of desire, the extinguishing within the human spirit of the hideous fires of lust, greed, envy, resentment and infatuation. Hence (I submit) the "heart" of asceticism is not hope or desire (even for God) but *patience*. Etymologically the Passion of Christ is simply the "patience" of Christ—in whose sufferings we ourselves similarly share, as St. Benedict observes in his Rule, "by patience."

In some later work Father Louis may perhaps consider a little more deeply the truth of man's essential passivity before God. Consciousness of our native energies and an aesthetic appreciation of the symbolism of the Liturgy, with its sacramental reenactment of Christ's sacrificial offering, should never be allowed to hide from view the existential realities of the human situation. To the question "What can I do for God?" the answer is simple enough, "Nothing at all." Our only contribution is to respond to the divine initiative and allow God to work His will in us by cooperating actively with Him from moment to moment. Radically this implies a certain desirelessness, a refusal to prefer, a non-attachment to the results of our work, what the saints call "holy indifference." If our aim, by God's grace is "to desire nothing and refuse nothing," we may safely leave asceticism to take care of itself. We shall find the duties of our state a sufficient school of selflessness. The object in view is not that by our austerities we should gain possession of God, but that by our submissiveness He should take possession of us.

Responsive to every call of duty, yet not anxiously striving, quietly alert in wise passiveness before God—*patiens divina,* in St. Thomas' phrase—we learn the deeper meaning of both contemplation and compassion. The contemplative is not one who prepares himself strenuously for some future vision; even now, if through a glass darkly, he has bridged the gap between time and eternity, and so enjoys "the sober certainty of waking bliss." To be compassionate is not to adopt an attitude, albeit a "Christlike" attitude, to the sinful and suffering; it is to recognize one's identity with them. *"That art thou"* is the basic thought of one of the world's great religions, echoing the "we are members one of another" of St. Paul. Remembering all this we shall, in our discourse, make use reluctantly of the separative "I;" just as in our prayer we shall recall, as members of the whole human family, that it was in the first person plural that we were taught to say "Our Father. . . ."

These thoughts fall obviously within the scope of a book entitled *No Man is an Island.* If their special emphasis, for what that may be worth, is not always to be found there, it must at once be said that Father Louis is having nothing pointed out to him that he has not already noted for himself. The book as it stands is the author's most valuable achievement so far; it should find its place among the enduring works of Christian spirituality.

Aelred Graham, "The Mysticism of Thomas Merton," in The Commonweal, *Vol. LXII, No. 6, May 13, 1955, pp. 155-59.*

Daniel J. Callahan (review date April 1965)

[*Callahan is an American educator and the author of numerous books addressing theological and ethical issues in contemporary life. In the following review of* Seeds of Destruction, *he faults Merton's lack of sensitivity to the complexity of modern political and moral issues but affirms the importance of Merton's extreme views on morality.*]

Thomas Merton has always occupied a special place in the American Catholic Church, though for different reasons at different times. His first acclaim came with his conversion, recorded in *The Seven Storey Mountain.* At that time, before ecumenism was much heard of, the convert was a special kind of hero, celebrated, publicized, and taken as living proof that Catholicism need not just be a matter of birth and tribal origin, but could persuade even the outsider. As a catch, Merton was something special. One had heard of the high Anglican who took the final step or of the Presbyterian who "came over," but converts from Merton's pre-Catholic world were (and still are) rare: the world of the high-level New York intellectual, the kind who went to Columbia, knew Mark Van Doren, read D. H. Lawrence and whose poetry could get published by New Directions.

Merton's second distinction lay in his acceptance of the monastic life as a Trappist monk in Gethsemani, Kentucky. After World War II, the monastic orders went through a period of sudden rejuvenation, stimulated no doubt by the horrors of that war, by the postwar chaos, and by the desire of many to find a radically different way of life. By his vast output of spiritual guidebooks, his lyrical praise of a life of prayer, and by the patently sharp contrast of his Trappist existence with his earlier student life, Merton became a symbol of the American monastic revival. At that time, too, it seemed altogether fitting that, if a monk was going to write at all, he should limit himself to the higher reaches of mysticism and the profundities of inner renewal. Poetry, though perhaps just a bit surprising, was after all known to be a mystical art.

So it went for some years and some twenty-five books, both of prose and poetry. Merton always had something of value to say, said it in a compelling way, and, no less importantly, seemed to sense well the mood of the Church. His books, to judge from the paperback reprints, the enthusiastic reviews, and the general currency of his name, sold well; there was every evidence that the Catholic public could not get enough of them.

Yet nothing goes on forever, especially revivals. The monastic boom and the thirst for the higher reaches of spiritual ardor began to show signs of waning toward the end of the 50's. They gave way to a newfound interest in social problems: race, nuclear warfare, man's life on earth among other men, poverty, the underdeveloped nations. This was the era of Pope John XXIII and the Second Vatican Council, with its stress on the Church's responsibility toward human problems, religious unity, and the needs of the secular societies of the 20th century. Oddly enough (so far as I know) Merton has not written directly of this shift in mood within the Church. But if one wants to see it exemplified, *Seeds of Destruction* is as good an indication as any. For the Merton we see here is a different, and perhaps new, Merton. There is practically no mention of the ascetical life, of prayer, or of contemplation (with the exception of one short essay dealing directly with the role of the monk in the contemporary world). Instead, there are some more characteristic notes of our day: the white liberal railing at the white liberal for being a secret enemy of the Negro (in **"Letters to a White Liberal"**); the engaged

Merton (center) with a group of fraternity brothers at Columbia University.

Christian struggling with his conscience over "the bomb"; the troubled Catholic trying to make some sense of the Church's place in a post-Christian world (in **"The Christian in the Diaspora"**); and the man of prayer giving hard-headed advice to people who live in the world (in **"Letters in a Time of Crisis"**). As these assorted subjects will suggest, *Seeds of Destruction* is not a unified book, but mainly a collection of previously published essays and unpublished letters. That does not much help the book as a whole but does at any rate give one a clue to Merton's present interests.

Merton is aware of the apparent paradox of a monk attempting to speak to problems which exist outside of the monastery walls. He does not travel; what he knows he knows only through reading, correspondence, and visitors from the outside. Yet he argues that

> No man can withdraw completely from the society of his fellow men, and the monastic community is deeply implicated, for better or for worse, in the economic, political, and social structure of the contemporary world. . . . The mere fact of "ignoring" what goes on can become a political decision.

As he points out, some contemplative communities in Europe "have officially and publicly given support to totali-

tarian movements," however much the individual members of those communities were "absorbed in otherworldly recollections." These are perceptive comments, placing monastic life in a context whose implications will seem wholly novel, even to most Catholics.

Unfortunately, what immediately follows these words is not as easy to praise. Merton speaks of the monastic life as "a definitive refusal to participate in those activities which have no other fruit than to prolong the reign of greed, cruelty and arrogance in the world of men." Just what the expression "those activities" means is not clear, but at any rate it is hard to imagine any moral, civilized person not wanting to do precisely the same thing. Heaven help us if we have to enter a monastery to prove our good intentions in this respect; yet this is what Merton comes close to saying. What does not come through is a sharp awareness that good and evil rarely come in clearly labeled packages. With the exception of genocide, arbitrary cruelty to children, and a few other textbook cases of wholly unjustifiable evil, it is extremely difficult to find activities about which one could say that they had "no fruit other than to prolong the reign of greed, cruelty and arrogance. . . ." The terrible thing about living in the world rather than in a monastery is that one can't just opt out of evil and let it go at that. Even in the case of nuclear warfare, which every sane man along with Merton will agree is wicked, there still remains the matter of weighing, as President Truman, say, had to do, the evil of destroying two cities over against the good of ending a war and thus saving many lives. I happen to think his decision was wrong, disastrously so, but that is because I think the evil far outweighed the possible good. Yet to say as much is not to deny that the situation demanded a weighing of values. Any decision would have involved some evil, and doubtless some good.

For one who lives in the world, this will seem an obvious, not to say trivial point. But calculations of this kind have an inconspicuous place in Merton's scheme of values. Though he writes movingly about the abuses of political authority, about the Negro's plight, about disarmament, he is a radically apolitical thinker, restless with the intricate subtleties of morality within a political and diplomatic context. He moves easily only in the rarefied air of ultimate goods: love, justice, perfect peace among nations. More than that, he appears to be positively skeptical of an excessive concern with anything else, especially with those worldly processes which work with material far removed from human or cosmic perfection. "Where there is no love of man," he writes, "no love of life, then make all the laws you want, all the edicts and treaties, issue all the anathemas; set up all the safeguards and inspections, fill the air with spying satellites, and land cameras on the moon. As long as you see your fellow man as a being essentially to be feared, mistrusted, hated and destroyed, there cannot be peace on earth." Perhaps Merton means the word "essentially" to be pivotal in this passage; if so, one could agree.

But what is rather frustrating about Merton's essays is that they abound in such quintessential incarnations of evil and stupidity. One can never be sure whether he thinks all men who are in some form or other suspicious and distrustful (an attitude not wholly unrealistic at times) can, ultimately, be fitted into the reprobate category, or whether he sees that even good men can on occasion possess some of the moral characteristics of the totally depraved. In his **"Letters to a White Liberal,"** he skillfully lays bare the kinds of rationalizations even a purportedly well-intentioned white can use to evade the harder demands the Negro places before him. By now, we are all fairly used to having these (our) rationalizations exposed. But Merton is not satisfied with doing that: his imagined "liberal" (each of us?), a man who would resort to repression should Negro protests get out of hand, can finally be visualized

> goose-stepping down Massachusetts Avenue in the uniform of an American Totalitarian Party in a mass rally where nothing but the most uproarious approval is manifest, except, by implication, on the part of silent and strangely scented clouds of smoke drifting over from the new "camps" where the "Negroes are living in retirement."

The picture is vivid, appalling, plausible; but is it very helpful to have such a picture painted? Does it really tell us very much about ourselves? No one could deny that resistance to the Negro is deep, nor could one deny that some people at least could be driven to seek a "final solution." But as a matter of fact, excluding a number of murders and the systematic violence in some Southern states, the remarkable thing is that whites have given way before Negro pressure: slowly, yes; reluctantly, to be sure, but still they have given way. As time goes on the Negro's problem with the white liberal is likely to be the quieter, more cutting forms of discrimination: no "final solution" but the steady heaping of indignities upon the Negro, mixed in with some genuine efforts to help him. By talking in terms of the worst possible eventualities Merton misses the gray reality, which favors neither the prophet and radical reformer nor the racist and repressive segregationist. Something similar could be said of the prospects for disarmament: neither the proponent of an aggressive nuclear weapons policy nor the proponent of unilateral disarmament will gain much of a following.

The trouble with reading prophets, and Merton seems almost consciously to adopt that stance, is that they can be both moving and irrelevant at the same time. This is Merton's problem. An articulate monk, and surely Merton is that, can recall us to those values which must sustain all we do. But then we sit down with the messy details of life, our charts, our statistics, our conflicting political demands, our social complexities, and the vision fades. But that is our problem, and it is a good thing we have the Mertons around: from time to time someone had better set squarely before us the point of what we are about. Otherwise those rich and hard details, which we who live in the world are prone to caress, will become the only values we know much about.

Daniel J. Callahan, "Unworldly Wisdom," in Commentary, *Vol. 39, No. 4, April, 1965, pp. 90, 92-4.*

Richard Kostelanetz   (review date 5 February 1978)

[*An American poet, essayist, short story writer, and novelist, Kostelanetz is noted in particular as a writer and supporter of contemporary avante-garde literature. In the following negative review of* The Collected Poems of Thomas Merton, *he faults the stylistic aspects of Merton's poems, concluding that "what remains most interesting about Merton is not his art or his thought, but his life."*]

A labor of publishing love, over a thousand pages in length, *The Collected Poems of Thomas Merton* is a disappointing volume. Bad lines abound from the book's beginning, whose opening poem, **"The Philosophers,"** begins: "As I lay sleeping in the park, / Buried in the earth, / Waiting for the Easter rains / To drench me in their mirth / And crown my seedtime with some sap and growth." A more conscientious craftsman would have cleaned such doggerel up, or out.

It was commonly joked that Merton, having taken the vow of silence, then wrote tons of garrulous prose. His poems are similarly verbose, generally more prosy than poetic, and undistinguished in both language and idea. Indicatively, Merton's poems are scarcely anthologized, and his name rarely appears in histories of American literature, his general eminence notwithstanding.

One trouble with the poems is that they are incorrigibly derivative, in a variety of styles. Little here has sufficient personal signature to be instantly attributable to Merton; even less is memorable. His religious poems, which one might expect to be extraordinary, pale beside T.S. Eliot's or those of either St. John of the Cross or, more recently, Brother Antoninus, and Merton's later poems are not much better than his earlier ones. There is nothing here as singularly inventive as, say, the "macaronic" language that enhances his novel, *My Argument With the Gestapo* (1969; written 1941).

The Collected Poems suggest to me that Merton's true medium was not poetry at all, but *prose.* The best passages here are such prose aphorisms as, "The way of man has no wisdom, but the way of God has." Or, "An age in which politicians talk about peace is an age in which everybody expects war." The best individual "poems" are those composed of curt prose paragraphs—not only the **"Original Child Bomb"** (1962), which has been widely reprinted for its political content, but my own favorites, **"Chant to Be Used in Processions Around a Site With Furnaces"** and **"Cables to the Ace."** (The latter is dedicated to his college classmate Robert Lax, whom I regard among America's greatest experimental poets, a true minimalist who can weave awesome poems from remarkably few words. Though a survivor, Lax remains the last unacknowledged—and, alas, uncollected—major poet of his post-60's generation.)

The Collected Poems also includes a section of "Humorous Verse" (which is rarely funny), **"A French Poem"** and translations, along with several "concrete poems" that Merton wrote in the final year of his life. (Only one of the last, **"Awful Music,"** is passable.) The vain attempts at "songs" particularly indicate that poetic music was not Merton's forte, and his poems suffer from both a general remoteness that perhaps reflects the monastic life and the facile indulgences that are more typical of a literary recluse immune to professional criticism.

The strongest theme of *The Collected Poems* is neither religious nor political but autobiographical, suggesting that what remains most interesting about Merton is not his art or his thought but his life. Quite simply, his example made credible an extreme religious option that would strike most of us as unthinkable. His example also earned the devotion of several loyal publishers and thousands of readers, who eagerly consumed whatever he wrote. For them too, however, the man loomed larger than his work.

Richard Kostelanetz, "The Sounds of Silence," in The New York Times Book Review, *February 5, 1978, p. 20.*

Ross Labrie   (essay date 1979)

[*In the following excerpt from his study* The Art of Thomas Merton, *Labrie discusses Merton's views on the relationship between art, society, and religion.*]

The nature of art and the relationship of the artist to society were a continuing interest of Merton's from the time of his M.A. thesis on William Blake, which turned out to be an informal and stimulating discussion of aesthetics. Antecedent to his curiosity about the nature of art was his consciousness of the artist's role in his society, a subject that he never tired of taking up. The reason was that he felt a profound intimacy between the roles of religion and art in relation to the vitality of the whole society. His notebooks reveal that he had a profound distaste for aesthetic norms that existed in a moral void. He came to feel that in a technocracy such as that evolved by twentieth century man some form of religious idealism was necessary to sustain art. He sympathized with contemporary artists who fled from the sterility and vulgarity of their civilization, but he felt that, in the absence of any alternative value systems, these artists were destined to vanish in the dead world of subjective abstraction.

In addition, in some unpublished notes on art Merton deplored the fragmentation of modern life, the "utter lack of relatedness between various phases of life and thought" and the existence of "hundreds of insignificant philosophies, each with a different set of terms." In the face of this fragmentation Merton believed that the artist reacted as he always did—"like a seismograph."

The artist registered the collapse of meaning in his culture without being able to do much about it, and his sensitivity went largely unnoticed in any case. Merton lamented the way in which, all too often, original talents went off on their own, experimenting as they pleased, with results which were often very fruitful aesthetically, but which had "little or no effect on the life or thought of the majority of men."

Merton felt that there was something vaguely pathological about modern man's obsession with creativity in an age devoted to unprecedented destructiveness, but he believed that even this condition was a sign of man's unquenchable interest in art. He saw the need for art as basic to man and argued that, if man could not have good art, he would

"jealously defend the bad." He admired the traditional Japanese concept of art in which there was no divorce between art and life, nor between art and spirituality, and he preferred this to the academic and solipsistic direction which he felt much western art had taken. Similarly, he felt closer to Latin American poets than to those in North America because in Latin America the voice of the poet had "something to do with life," whereas the North American artist appeared to be in a "spiritual torpor."

Merton believed that art did things for society that could not be done in any other way. The work of art helped to elevate and clarify the intelligence and heart both of the artist and of the spectator. In this way the art experience became "analogous to the purity of religious contemplation." He focused his attention on the experiential value of the poem or the painting: "A poem is for me," he once wrote, "the expression of an inner poetic experience, and what matters is the experience, more than the poem itself."

He saw the life of the artist as a sharing of himself with others. He expressed this vividly in a poem entitled **"The Originators:"**

> Brothers and Sisters I warn you my ideas
> Get scarlet fever every morning
> At about four and influence goes out of my windows
> Over the suburbs . . .
> And when the other's nerve ends crowed and protested
> In the tame furies of a business gospel
> His felling was my explosion.

The impact of artist on reader is symbiotically paralleled by that of the reader on the artist so that the "explosion" of the artist inside the spectator is followed by a boomerang effect in which: "I skidded off his stone head / Blind as a bullet / But found I was wearing his hat."

The reader of course had to make an effort to be intelligently receptive. The artist, Merton felt, had no obligation to make his meaning immediately clear to anyone who did not want to make an effort to discover it. On the other hand the esoteric artist who cultivated obscurity deprived not only others but himself: "If you know something and do not share it," he wrote, "you lose your knowledge of it."

Although Merton believed in the prophetic role of the artist, he stood firmly against didacticism: "The artist should preach nothing—not even his own autonomy." The contamination of art by dogma of any sort was, he felt, a matter about which the artist had to be ever vigilant. "When a Marxist-poet writes as a Marxist," he wrote to a friend, "he ceases to write as a poet," and that "goes for every other brand of dogmatism that imposes itself on art *from without.*" The most significant Catholic writers, he believed, were people who wrote as "marginal or unusual Catholics, and do not speak for the mass of our brethren." The artist could not succeed by "wearing the garments of public and collective ideas" and should do everything in his power to resist the pull of these ideas, creating his work always "outside and against the officially subsidized culture."

Merton saw the prophetic role of the artist as a natural one for the contemporary artist to assume amidst the decline in the authority of religion. At the same time there were dangers in a "myth of the genius as hero and as high priest" that took the place of religion. Certain modern writers, like Faulkner and Camus, were singled out by Merton as genuinely prophetic. He wrote to the poet Nicanor Parra in 1965 that contemporary artists tended to fulfill many of the functions that were once the monopoly of monks. He went further: "I would submit that the term 'religious' no longer conveys the idea of an imaginative awareness of basic meaning. As D. H. Lawrence asserted, 'It's not religious to be religious.'" As religion had attempted to do, the artist perceived man in terms of the wholeness of his life, a kind of vision which was uniquely valuable in a culture dominated by specialists.

A writer like Faulkner, therefore, could be profoundly biblical in his work without being a churchgoer or a conventional believer. It was the artist, "facing the problems of life without the routine consolations of conventional religion," who experienced in depth the "existential dimensions of those problems." This outlook led Merton to shift his attention from formally religious texts to literary models. He wrote to James Laughlin in 1966 that he and Jacques Maritain, who had just visited with him, both agreed that perhaps the most "living" way to approach theological and philosophical problems now that theology and philosophy were in such chaos would be in the form of "creative writing and literary criticism."

It was axiomatic for Merton that the artist had to be a spiritual man. In addition, writers like Faulkner and Camus were prophetic in the sense that in constructing myths in which they embodied their struggle with the fundamental questions of life they anticipated "in their solitude" the struggles and the general consciousness of later generations. The artist had inherited, whether he liked it or not, the combined functions of hermit, pilgrim, prophet, priest, shaman, sorcerer, soothsayer, alchemist, and bonze. The temptation for the artist who was aware of these roles to give in to posturing was obvious to Merton, and the moral solution was for the artist to concentrate on his proper "work" rather than on the role which society asked him to play.

Merton felt that the purity of the artist's vision could only be sustained through a kind of "ingrained innocence," by which he meant a freshness and seriousness of vision in the artist that could withstand the banalities of his society. Given these circumstances, the artist would prophesy, not in the sense of preaching or foretelling, but in seizing upon reality "in its moment of highest expectation and tension toward the new."

The artist as prophet would show finally "where everything connects," a reflection of Merton's own passionate role as a unifier of different kinds of experience. The artist could do all of this because in his "innocence" he perceived the paradise that had been and that was still present beneath the welter of sordid and fragmentary details that made up modern life. Merton saw the artist's creation as both analogous to the freshness of paradise and a sign of its possible recovery:

> [The] living line and the generative association, the new sound, the music, the structure, are somehow grounded, in a renewal of vision and hearing so that he who reads and understands recognizes that here is a new start, a new creation. Here the world gets another chance. Here man, here the reader discovers himself getting another start in life, in hope, in imagination.

Merton spoke of the poet as attempting to dream the world in which he lived. That dream, though intensely personal, was at once the artist's and everybody's, a paradise accessible to all, once the poet had recovered it. The freshness and power of the artist's vision in recovering the fragrance of a lost and perfect world came home to Merton in 1960 when he collaborated with the photographer Shirley Burden in a pictorial study of the Abbey of Gethsemani. When the book came out, Merton was struck with the difference between his own faded perceptions of the abbey and those which Burden manifested:

> And now a man, an artist, comes along with a camera and shows us, beyond a doubt, that the real monastery, the one that is so obvious that we no longer see it, the one that has become so familiar that we have not even looked at it for years, is not only beautiful, but romantically beautiful. It is romantic even in the ordinariness, the banality that we ourselves tend to reject.

Merton saw the artist as evoking a sense of the latent perfection of things. The business of the artist was "to reach the intimate," that is, those "ontological sources of life" that could not be clearly conceptualized, but which, once intuited, could be made "accessible to all in symbolic celebration." Good art expressed the singular. The singularity of the experience suspended within the poem or picture was paralleled by the inner principle of individuality in the form of the poem or picture. Through structure and symbol the artist wrested language from its faded and worn contexts in order to make it new. Language had to be freed from contamination by trite popular discourse and yet had also to serve its prior purpose of sharing experience with the reader.

The artist, Merton believed, went out to the object before him—a rose or a grain of sand—with complete humility, not subjecting the object to the classifying habit of the mind, but so identifying with it as to look out of it as though the artist fulfilled the role of consciousness not only for himself but for the object as well. In this way the artist became "the conscious expression, not of himself seeing and singing, but of the singing being which is his object and inspiration. He feels *'for,'* sings *'for,'* is aware *'for'* the object." This identification of natures emerged from experience rather than meditation in the same way that "a chaste man understands the nature of chastity because of the very fact that his soul is full of it." The process involved a marvellous accommodation between the artist and the world around him as well as a momentary union of the contraries within the artist—akin, Merton wrote in his notebook, to the kind of ecstacy experienced by "mystics, children, lovers."

While genuine art illuminated reality, Merton felt that little of this effect could be traced back to the artist's conscious intentions. At least 75 per cent of the process of creation, he told a group of students in the mid-1960s, was unconscious. If this were reduced to only 30 per cent, he told the class, the art would be bad. He wrote in his notebook in the same period that the creation of a work of art went far beyond the artist's understanding: "Hence to be an artist you have to be constantly ready to *mean more than you realize.* If your work corresponds only to the present level of your thought—and to the 'meaning' accessible to your environment, you are not yet an artist." In the spectator as well genuine art reached beneath the conscious mind to the darkness of the psyche in order to do its unique and necessary work.

Merton loved the mysterious way in which art drew things together. In a diary written in the last year of his life he described his pleasure in seeing a print of a photo he had taken of the northern California coast that had been developed for him by his friend John Howard Griffin. The film brought out the "sea-rock mist, diffused light and half hidden mountain . . . an interior landscape, yet there." "In other words," he wrote, "what is written within me is there." It was probably because of Merton's respect for the mystery of the artistic process that he came to place such emphasis upon spontaneity in art. His calligraphies represent the epitome of the spontaneous in his work, and his prolific output in general suggests great speed in the act of creation throughout his career—not always to the benefit of the works produced. He hoped to tap the riches of the subconscious before the conscious mind could mediate or usurp expression, and he saw this process as the secret of the Zen artist who created "without reflection." The Zen drawing, he wrote, "springs" out of emptiness, and is transferred "in a flash," by a few brush strokes, to paper. So produced, it is not a representation of anything, but is rather the subject itself, a "concretized intuition."

Merton realized that such art skirted the solipsistic, and gave only a small part of his creative time to the production of such radically spontaneous works. Even in his more representational work, however, his fondness for speed and spontaneity in creation is revealed. The emergence of a work of art from his hand always had in it something of an element of surprise for him: "We who are poets," he wrote on one occasion, "know that the reason for a poem is not discovered until the poem itself exists." For this reason, perhaps, he shied away from protracted discussions about how he put poems together.

The subjects that the contemporary artist should take up were a matter of continuing interest to Merton. His own eclecticism makes it difficult at times to think of him as pursuing any particular line, but he had established some guidelines for himself. He felt a need, for example, to purify religious verse from what he felt had become an "insatiable emotional vulgarity." Twentieth century religious verse, he believed, had for too long been singing the "same old cracked tune that the Georgians inherited from Tennyson and Swinburne." At the same time he disdained the "flood tide of spurious and pseudomodern sacred art" that had begun to show itself in religious literature, music, painting, and architecture. Churches that were constructed to resemble other undistinguished contemporary archi-

tecture—"the drive-in theater, the filling station, the motel or even the night club"—were hardly an improvement over the earlier absurdities of the pseudogothic and pseudoromanesque.

What was needed, he wrote in an unpublished manuscript entitled "The Monk and Sacred Art," was a clearing of the "confusion" surrounding religious art so that "what belongs to us and what is alien to us" can be discerned in the art of the past as well as of the present. The first requirement was for the artist to attend his craft instead of hoping that his piety would alchemically produce fine works of art. In this respect he was drawn to the Hindu tradition of art in which all artistic work became a form of yoga. In such a tradition, he observed, "there ceases to be any distinction between sacred and secular art. All art is Yoga, and even the art of making a table or a bed, or building a house, proceeds from the craftsman's Yoga and from his spiritual discipline of meditation." Religious art should emerge, he felt, only from the crucible of experience. If not, he argued in **Bread in the Wilderness**, it was third-rate, merely devotional art which, although it dealt with religious themes, was often simply the "rearrangement of well known devotional formulas, without any personal poetic assimilation."

As an artist Merton applied himself to trying to restore the face of nature and the rhythm of natural time as against the abrasive and synthetic pattern of modern life. Art should, he felt, ideally be grounded in the natural world and should represent the flowering of ordinary possibilities. Opposing himself to the artificiality of technocracy, he called on artists to refrain from trying to "make the tree bear its fruit first and the flower afterwards. We are content as artists," he wrote, "if the flower comes first and the fruit afterwards, in due time. Such is the poetic spirit."

Merton admired the traditional Japanese concept of art in which there was no divorce between art and life, nor between art and spirituality, and he preferred this to the academic and solipsistic direction which he felt much western art had taken.

—Ross Labrie

It was this instinct to conserve which attracted him to Classicism, the signs of which are everywhere in his writings. Merton came to see Classicism as the mainstream in which the values of Western civilization were kept alive, and he was grateful for this continuity in a culture in which collapse and dislocation seemed the rule. He was especially impressed by T. S. Eliot's ability to combine a sense of the past with a highly modern, experimental attitude toward form, a combination which he tried to achieve in his own writing. He liked the Classicism as well of more recent poets like Edward Dahlberg, whose work was "juiced with myth and with the lore of the fathers who know better than we."

There were Romantic elements in Merton's thought, notably in his penchant for spontaneity. The problem with Classicism was that it possessed a deliberate, static quality that seemed unexciting to him. In addition, his notebooks reveal that he was attracted to the impressionistic strain in Romanticism, its ability to "marry subject and object through the image"—as long, that is, as this marriage did not end in the closed circuit of the subjective. With his instinct for balance and unity, he gradually adjusted his outlook in order to accommodate both Classic and Romantic elements.

Seen from another vantage point, Merton affirmed the existence of a Classicism which was more dynamic than that which has been conventionally described. In a little known, privately printed note on the artist Victor Hammer he depicted Classicism not as a serene pool of light and reason but as an arena in which matter and energy with their own compelling truths were not dispelled by the light of consciousness. Thus, from the body of the "python," the "earth dragon," there would emanate a "living voice of prophecy." This prophetic voice was eloquent and significant in proportion to the force of the "darkness" which drew upon itself the "discipline of the strongest light."

Merton believed that the art object should be "organic"— that is, that it should develop the way a living organism does so that it spread outward in a "heliotropic" manner like a plant. "A tree," he wrote, "grows out into a free form, an organic form," one that is "never ideal," "never typical," and "always individual." He disliked purely naturalistic art. To copy nature, he believed, was to falsify it. The artist should not reproduce, but he should create something new. Paradoxically, the realism of the artist's creation depended upon its ability to suggest rather than to copy, since what was real in such a case was not simply the art object but the "experience of the one looking at it."

In Merton's view nothing resembled reality less than the photograph. In his own photographs—studies of roots, tree limbs, and faded barns—he concentrated on the texture of these simple things with such imagination and freedom that they resemble abstract paintings. This effect can be seen in the tree ring photograph that he provided for the dustjacket of Nicanor Parra's *Poems and Antipoems.*

Merton felt that the way out of the cul-de-sac of naturalism was through symbol, a fact which he believed even the most primitive peoples seemed to understand better than contemporary Western man. He tried to explain the transcendental effect of symbolism in describing the role of the ikon in Russian Orthodox churches. He described the ikon as more than a representation, conveying the "spiritual presence" of the figure represented, a presence that has mysteriously clothed itself in the lines and colors used by the artist. He was convinced that the search for adequate symbols should not be esoteric, contending that all things are symbolic "by their very being and nature, and all talk of something beyond themselves." Their meaning, he added, is not something we impose on them, but a

"mystery which we can discover in them, if we have the eyes to look with."

He perceived the artist's challenge as avoiding those symbols which had been debased by society and the marketplace. He wrote to a friend that he was "right to go at it with myth and symbol" since this sort of writing was the only thing conventional society could not "monkey with" even though it tried. A similar furtiveness underlay Merton's experiments in calligraphy, which he characterized as original and "nondescript" marks that stood against the mass of "practical signs and consequential digits" that were used in business, law, government, and war. His drawings were at least "new" signs, signs that could stand by themselves and exist in their own right, "transcending" all logical interpretation.

If it became evident to the artist that his society had contaminated most of the available language, he would have to resort to anti-language, as Merton chose to do in *Cables to the Ace* (1968), a poetic sequence written in what he called "antipoetry." Pushed to the wall, the artist might have no choice but to use "anti-art and non-symbol." Merton believed that twentieth century man had lost touch with the fertile mainstream of Western symbolism. By way of exception he admired T. S. Eliot's ability, especially in the *Four Quartets,* to use traditional symbols to rise above the limitations of contemporary experience in order to achieve a "deliverance from a commonplace and fictitious identity in the stream of historical continuity."

Merton saw the modern artist as frustrated in his search for the vital symbols that he believed had been buried alive amid the contemporary hunger for information and explanation. He pictured the most gifted artists of the age as driven by desperation, "running wild among the tombs in the moonlit cemeteries of surrealism." The flight from conventional symbolism became perverse and self-defeating, however, since the artist and his audience both had a basic human need for myth and symbol. In becoming instinctively suspicious of that "for which we are starved," the artist may simply aggravate his problem in communicating. Lamenting that ancient symbols had lost their meaning, the artist may become "hostile and uncommunicative, frustrating the desire for meaning by declaring that there are no meanings left and that one has to get along without them."

The corruption of cosmic symbolism led to the loss of transcendental perception. Merton illustrated this conception in terms of the passing of light through a window: "As long as it is daylight, we see through our windowpane. When night comes, we can still see through it, if there is no light inside our room. When our lights go on, then we only see ourselves and our own room reflected in the pane." The corruption of cosmic symbolism could not be blamed simply on secularism, but pointed unavoidably to a loss of vitality within the social institutions that thrived on it at one time, including Christianity.

This loss seemed both unnecessary and harmful to Merton. He revealed this conviction in a poem called **"The Lion,"** which he wrote in 1967:

> All classic shapes have vanished

From alien heavens
When there are no fabled beasts
No friendly histories
And passion has no heraldry.

Poised to write, he finds that he has "nothing left to translate / Into the figures of the night" since the traditional astronomical symbolism that had been at the heart of Western literature is no longer recognized by contemporary men. Looking up at the sky, he sees the constellation of Taurus and wonders why the image of the Lion in the night sky should ever have been put aside, observing that Gemini as well was astutely named by the ancients: "It is after all a Lion / And those two stars are permanent; / Let us agree they are twins." It was not just that these symbols had come down from the early Babylonians and that the use of them brought men of the past and present together in spirit, but that the symbols were still fresh in that they could be experienced anew by modern stargazers.

It was only through effective symbolism, Merton believed, that the deepest riches of man's unconscious life could be reached, and it was only within the dark world that there was hope of recovering an awareness of man's fundamental nature and needs. As basic archetypal forms anterior to any operation of the mind, the symbols used by the artist awakened buried feelings within the reader's unconscious and revived his strongest memories of himself as a creature. In caressing the reader's unconscious, the artist awakened the reader to the formless world of being by suggesting through symbol what could not be said. "We are children of the Unspeakable," Merton wrote, "ministers of silence."

Merton saw this underlying feeling of being, the meeting place of all life, as evoked not only through effective symbolism but through a complex interaction of speech and silence, object and emptiness. Silence, he observed paradoxically, was the "mother of speech." Life, he wrote, is not to be regarded as an uninterrupted flow of words which is finally silenced by death. Instead, its rhythm "develops in silence, comes to the surface in moments of necessary expression" and then returns to "deeper silence." He did not intend to undervalue the force of language, but rather to establish a balance between language and silence. If it was true that the reality that was inexpressible in language was found "face to face and without medium" in silence, it was also true that this reality would not ordinarily be discovered "in itself, that is to say in its own silence," unless one were first brought to it through language. In one of his taped lectures he took the view that a good poem was 50 per cent silence and that what was not said in a literary work was just as important as what was made explicit, if not more important. The silence on the page had to be attuned to the rhythms of silence and expressiveness that were rooted in experience. In introducing the Japanese edition of *Thoughts in Solitude,* he noted that the book said nothing that had not already been said better "by the wind in the pine trees. Its pages seek nothing more than to echo the silence and the peace that is 'heard' when rain wanders freely among the hills and forests."

When set within its natural context of silence, Merton felt that all language was "intrinsically poetic." At the same time, in order to offset the jadedness of conventional expression, language had to be lifted out of its conventional context and then restored to communicative power by its fresh use in a work of art. It was this sensitivity to silence—to what lay behind the word—that motivated Merton's art as well as his life as a contemplative. While differing in some other respects, the artist and the contemplative in him were in agreement on this matter.

Ross Labrie, in his The Art of Thomas Merton, *The Texas Christian University Press, 1979, 188 p.*

Sister Thérèse Lentfoehr   (essay date 1979)

[*An American poet who maintained a friendship with Merton, Lentfoehr is considered an authority on Merton's works. In the following excerpt from her study* Words and Silence: On the Poetry of Thomas Merton, *she discusses recurring social and religious themes in the poet's work.*]

After considering in some detail the several collections of poetry in the Thomas Merton canon (excepting the two last works published in his lifetime, *Cables to the Ace,* and *The Geography of Lograire*), it would seem pertinent at this point to cross chronological barriers in order to focus on poems dealing with specific subject matters that occur with a certain frequency.

It is unarguable that, whether overt or not, the ultimate referral point and matrix of all his writings—prose as well as poetry—is basically religious: the binding of man to God. Still, when considering the complete poetry canon, only about a third of the poems might be viewed as having specific religious themes. Among these a goodly number derive their inspiration from the Incarnation, with such events as proliferate from it—the Annunciation, Visitation, Nativity, Passion, and the Eucharist. In the first three the Virgin Mary's role is paramount, and since so many poems cluster around her, or are addressed to her, it seems important to isolate some of them for comment.

"The Blessed Virgin Compared to a Window" appears in Merton's first collection, *Thirty Poems* (1944), and at once conjures up Gerard Manley Hopkins's "The Blessed Virgin Compared to the Air We Breathe." Both poems elaborate a "metaphysical conceit": Merton's, the metaphor of a window representing the docile, pure soul of Mary through which God can transmit Himself unobstructedly as light through glass, and Hopkins's, the trope comparing her to air surrounding and pervading us by her influence, since she has but "one work to do / Let all God's glory through." Curiously, though Merton had read extensively in Hopkins, and while at Columbia had seriously considered writing a doctoral dissertation on his poetry, he never seems to have been influenced by Hopkins's sprung-rhythm prosody. It is also of interest to note that some ten years later, in a conference given the young monks at the abbey in his capacity of novice-master, Merton gave a careful analysis of the Hopkins poem.

The metaphor of the window is not original with Merton nor with Hopkins. The latter speaks of "glass-blue days" and of "This blue heaven" (Mary) transmitting "The hued sunbeam [Christ] perfect, not altering it." But the meta-

Merton (far left) during ordination rites.

phor had earlier sources. While Merton was still at Columbia he became familiar with the sixteenth-century Spanish mystic, St. John of the Cross, and purchased a copy of *The Ascent of Mount Carmel,* which he read assiduously in his Greenwich Village apartment. The book is an extended commentary on a poem concerning the union of the human and divine wills, in which St. John used the comparison of a ray of sunlight striking a window.

> Although obviously the nature of the window is distinct from that of the sun's ray (even if the two seem identical), we can assert that the window is the ray of light of the sun by participation.

But the metaphor was in turn borrowed by St. John of the Cross from the Pseudo Areopagite's *De Mystica Theologia* (Bk. II, Ch. 5).

Merton's poem begins:

> Because my will is simple as a window
> And knows no pride of original earth,
> It is my life to die, like glass, by light:
> Slain in the strong rays of the bridegroom sun.

The word "simple" must be taken in its scholastic preci-

sions, as having "no parts outside of parts" (St. Thomas). Merton uses it again in this same specific sense in a poem on St. Thomas Aquinas in which "the black-friar breaks the Truth, his Host, / Among his friends the simple Substances," [*A Man in the Divided Sea*]. The metaphor of the "bridegroom sun" is obviously from the Canticle of Canticles, a symbolism that appears frequently in spiritual theology. The poem continues:

> Because my love is simple as a window
> And knows no shame of original dust,
> I longed all night, (when I was visible) for dawn
>   my death:
> When I would marry day, my Holy Spirit:
> And die by transsubstantiation into light.

The reference to transsubstantiation and to the lover must again be given their full theological resonances.

Another Marian poem, and one of Merton's finest, is **"The Messenger,"** a pre-Trappist poem first published in *Spirit,* then reprinted in **Thirty Poems,** and later in the poetry column of *The New York Times Book Review.* With Ladyday in its context of spring, the "annunciation imagery" is striking, as the "tongue of March's bugle" warns of "the coming of the warrior sun."

When spring has garrisoned up her army of
    water,
A million grasses leave their tents, and stand in
    rows
To see their invincible brother.
Mending the winter's ruins with their laughter,
The flowers go out to their undestructive wars.

Then, counseling the flowers to "Walk in the woods and
be witnesses, / You, the best of these poor children," Merton moves into the final stanza, which begins the swiftness
of Gabriel's descent:

When Gabriel hit the bright shore of the world,
Yours were the eyes saw some
Star-sandalled stranger walk like lightning down
    the air,
The morning the Mother of God
Loved and dreaded the message of the angel.

In the poem **"The Oracle,"** on a quite different theme, its
final stanza alludes to Gabriel's swift movement of descent
when

. . . already, down the far, fast ladders of light
The stern, astounding angel
Starts with a truer message,
Carrying a lily.

And once again in **"Aubade—The Annunciation":**

Desires glitter in her mind
Like morning stars:

Until her name is suddenly spoken
Like a meteor falling.

A related theme is that of the visitation of Mary to Elizabeth, on which Merton wrote two poems: **"The Evening
of the Visitation"** and **"The Quickening of St. John Baptist."** In the former he asks nature to participate:

Still bend your heads like kind and humble kings
The way you did this golden morning when you
    saw
        God's Mother passing.

Manuscript versions of **"The Quickening of St. John Baptist"** present an interesting study in development: the beginnings—two columns of pencil jottings (twenty-four
lines) on a folded sheet, in which some of the key lines of
the poem already appear, as for instance:

Her salutation
Sings in the stone valley like a Charterhouse bell.

Most of the poem is a questioning of St. John Baptist, and
is couched in hermit imagery:

                        . . . small anchorite!
How did you see her in the eyeless dark?
. . . . . .
You need no eloquence, wild bairn,
Exulting in your hermitage,
Your ecstasy is your apostolate,
For whom to kick is *contemplata tradere.*

His vocation is with the Church's "hidden children":

The speechless Trappist, or the grey, granite
    Carthusian,
The quiet Carmelite, the barefoot Clare,

Planted in the night of contemplation,
Sealed in the dark and waiting to be born.
Night is our diocese and silence is our ministry
Poverty our charity and helplessness our
    tongue-tied sermon.
Beyond the scope of sight or sound we dwell
    upon the air
Seeking the world's gain in an unthinkable expe-
    rience.

In the second version of this poem (thirty-five lines), already the first line of the final version appears, "Why do
you fly from the drowned shores of Galilee?" In the manuscript of the final version (seventy-one lines) the original
title, **"A Quickening: A Song for the Visitation,"** has been
given its present title, **"The Quickening of St. John Baptist,"** and dated Feast of St. John Baptist, 1947.

Another poem in the same collection, *The Tears of the
Blind Lions,* **"To the Immaculate Virgin, on a Winter
Night,"** though written over twenty years ago, has a special contemporary significance, as Merton speaks of "a
day of blood and many beatings"—

I see the governments rise up, behind the steel
    horizon,
And take their weapons and begin to kill.

There is also an allusion to the proximity of Fort Knox:
"Out where the soldiers camp the guns begin to thump /
And another winter time comes down / To seal your years
in ice." The last lines of the poems are especially poignant:

Lady, the night has got us by the heart
And the whole world is tumbling down.
Words turn to ice in my dry throat
Praying for a land without prayer,

Walking to you on water all winter
In a year that wants more war.

Another poem, the last with the Virgin Mary as theme,
"The Annunciation," was written as a billet for the nuns
of the New York Carmel and is in Merton's new manner,
more free of elaboration, and in this instance somewhat
reminiscent of a pre-Raphaelite painting:

The girl prays by the bare wall
Between the lamp and the chair.
(Framed with an angel in our galleries
She has a richer painted room, sometimes a
    crown.
But seven pillars of obscurity
Build her to Wisdom's house, and Ark, and
    Tower.
She owns their manna in her jar.)

Fifteen years old—
The flowers printed on her dress
Cease moving in the middle of her prayer
When God, Who sends the messenger,
Meets his messenger in her heart.
Her answer, between breath and breath,
Wrings from her innocence our Sacrament!
In her white body God becomes our Bread.

These poems form an easy transition to the theme of the
Nativity, in which one is aware of the sensitivity, gentle-

ness, and joy of their author's spirit in presence of this mystery, as in **"The Holy Child's Song"**:

> When midnight occupied the porches of the
>   Poet's reason
> Sweeter than any bird
> He heard the Holy Child.

In a type of envelope style, rarely used by Merton, the above three lines are used again as a refrain at the poem's end, enclosing the child's songs as they "Fly in and out the branches of my childish voice / Like thrushes in a tree."

> And when my Mother, pretty as a church,
> Takes me upon her lap, I laugh with love,
> Loving to live in her flesh, which is my
>   house. . . .

In these poems nature is frequently used as setting—the winter season, and the animals, as the child continues his song:

> In winter when the birds put down their flutes
> And wind plays sharper than a fife upon the icy
>   rain,
> I sit in this crib,
> And laugh like fire, and clap My golden hands:
> To view my friends the timid beasts—
> Their great brown flanks, muzzles and milky
>   breath!

In the poem **"Advent,"** in metaphor we find the animals again: "minds, meek as beasts, / Stay close at home in the sweet hay; / And intellects are quieter than the flocks that feed by starlight." The moon and skies are invoked to "pour down your darkness and your brightness over all our solemn valleys." In **"Carol"**:

> God's glory, now, is kindled gentler than low
>   candlelight
> Under the rafters of a barn:
> Eternal Peace is sleeping in the hay,
> And Wisdom's born in secret in a straw-roofed
>   stable.

In **"The Fall of Night,"** the farmers coming home from the fields sing:

> We bring these heavy wagons full of hay to
>   make your bed,
> O Mercy, born between the animals.

Finally, in the poem **"A Christmas Card,"** Merton paints a winter canvas as

> . . . one by one the shepherds, with their snowy
>   feet,
> Stamp and shake out their hats upon the stable
>   dirt,
> And one by one kneel down to look upon their
>   Life.

Another frequent theme is that of children, to whom Merton often alludes, especially in his early poems. It has been said that in every poet there is a child, since in some fashion he invariably retains a child's vision. Merton is no exception, and with this vision has come an empathy with children that characterizes some of his most sensitive poems. In **"The Winter's Night,"** when "the frost cracks on the window,"

> One says the moonlight grated like a skate
> Across the freezing winter.
> Another hears the starlight breaking like a knife-
>   blade
> Upon the silent, steelbright pond. . . .
> Yet it is far from Christmas, when a star
> Sang in the pane, as brittle as their inno-
>   cence. . . .
> The moonlight rings upon the ice as sudden as
>   a footstep;
> Starlight clinks upon the dooryard stone, too
>   like a latch,
> And the children are, again, awake,
> And all call out in whispers to their guardian an-
>   gels.

In **"Aubade: Lake Erie,"** after the sun "light handed" has sown "this Indian water / With a crop of cockles," Merton calls to the children:

> Awake, in the frames of windows, innocent chil-
>   dren,
> Loving the blue, sprayed leaves of childish life,
> Applaud the bearded corn, the bleeding grape,
> And cry:
> "Here is the hay-colored sun, our marvelous
>   cousin,
> Walking in the barley."

Again in **"Evening"** is the childrens' interpretation of nature:

> They say the sky is made of glass,
> They say the smiling moon's a bride.
>   . . . .
> They name the new come planets
> With words that flower
> On little voices, light as stems of lilies.

As Merton celebrated the candor and innocence of children, so too he was most vulnerable to their suffering. In an early poem, **"Aubade: Harlem,"** "in the sterile jungles of waterpipes and ladders," he pictures a typical scene, one known to him firsthand, since before he entered the monastery he had spent many hours working in Harlem at Friendship House. The beginning and final stanza of the poem are the same, as we see.

> Across the cages of the keyless aviaries,
> The lines and wires, the gallows of the broken
>   kites,
> Crucify, against the fearful light,
> The ragged dresses of the little children.

One of the most interesting of Merton's poems on children is **"Grace's House,"** written in 1962 and inspired by a four-year-old child's pencil drawing of a house on a hill. With meticulous exactitude Merton details each object of the sketch—"No blade of grass is not counted, / No blade of grass forgotten on this hill." He details the house on the summit; a snow cloud rolling from the chimney; flowers; curtains, "Not for hiding, but for seeing out"; trees, from which animals peek out; a dog, "his foreleg curled, his eye like an aster"; a mailbox "full of Valentines for Grace".

> There is a name on the box, name of a family
> Not yet ready to be written in language.

In the second stanza appears the theme around which all

resonances cluster, as Merton fastens on an apparently in-significant detail which nonetheless provides the leitmotif of the poem, namely:

> There is no path to the summit—
> No path drawn
> To Grace's house.

—which provides the contrast between our world and hers, "our Coney Island," and her "green sun-hill",

> Between our world and hers
> Runs a sweet river
> (No, it is not the road
> It is the uncrossed crystal
> Water between our ignorance and her truth.)

The poem's last line re-introduces the theme, as Merton casually mentions "a rabbit / And two birds"—

> . . . bathing in the stream
> which is no road, because
>
> Alas, there is no road to Grace's house!

Interestingly, the German edition of Merton's *Selected Poems* is titled *Gracias Haus,* and the poem is first of the thirty-eight which comprise the selection. On sending a copy of this edition to a friend he remarked, "I think they did a very nice job. Glad my little Grace made the title!"

At about the same time **"Grace's House"** was written, a newspaper photograph of a young Chinese refugee, stopped in her flight to Hong Kong and kneeling in tears as she begged to be admitted to the city, loosed in Merton a bitterly ironic poem, **"A Picture of Lee Ying,"** written in a free, almost documentary style, as he mocks the plati-tudinal excuses offered by the authorities.

> *Point of no return* is the caption, but this is mean-
> ingless she must return that is the story
>
> She would not weep if she had reached a point
> of no return what she wants is not to return

Merton's irony cuts deep:

> When the authorities are alarmed what can you
> do
>
> You can return to China
>
> Their alarm is worse than your sorrow

But he tells her not to look at the dark side, for "You have the sympathy of millions." Then the devastatingly para-doxical conclusion:

> As a tribute to your sorrow we resolve to spend
> more money on nuclear weapons there is al-
> ways a bright side

Merton's mounting concern over the racial question found its expression in another children's poem, one of deep compassion, addressed to Carole Denise McNair, one of the children killed that tragic September of 1963 in Bir-mingham. The poem is titled **"Picture of a Black Child with a White Doll"** and is an implicit indictment of a soci-ety in which such a crime could happen.

> Your dark eyes will never need to understand
> Our sadness who see you

> Hold that plastic glass-eyed
> Merchandise as if our empty-headed race
> Worthless full of fury
> Twanging and drooling in the southern night
> With guns and phantoms
> Needed to know love.

This is in contrast to the irony that marked another poem, **"And the Children of Birmingham,"** its sharp, objective, matter-of-fact statement set in the framework of a chil-dren's story, as it parodies "Little Red Riding Hood," "Grandma's pointed teeth / ('Better to love you with')." The present poem, even as it contrasts the dark child with "That senseless platinum head / Of a hot city cupid," is pervaded by a tenderness that distinguishes its author:

> Next to your live and lovely shade
> Your smile and your person
> Yet that silly manufactured head
> Would soon kill you if it could think. . . .
> So without a thought
> Of death or fear
> Of night
> You glow full of dark red August
> Risen and Christian
> Africa purchased
> For the one lovable Father alone.

And when all was done, "They found you and made you a winner"—

> Even in most senseless cruelty
> Your darkness and childhood
> Became fortune yes became
> Irreversible luck and halo.

Not only to the suffering of children did Merton extend his concern but also to such as were caught up in some tragic circumstance or were victims of the judgment of an unhappy society. One of the most poignant poems Merton wrote, **"There Has to Be a Jail for Ladies,"** is one in which he genuinely compassionates and pleads for the "la-dies of the street," when "their beauty is taken from them, when their hearts are broken," while the government wants a jail for them "when they are ugly because they are wrong." He tells them:

> I love you, unhappy ones. . . .
> Tell me, darlings, can God be in Hell?
> You may curse; but he makes your dry voice
>   turn to
> butter. . . .
>   He will laugh at judges.
> He will laugh at the jail.
> He will make me write this song.

And the last stanza carries an unforgettable image:

> God will come to your window with skylarks
> And pluck each year like a white rose.

Like the seventeenth-century metaphysical poets whom Merton during his early student years much admired, he too wrote a number of elegies. The first, written for his brother, is well known and often quoted—**"For My Brother: Reported Missing in Action, 1943"**. A longer poem, **"The Trappist Cemetery—Gethsemani,"** is ad-dressed to his brother monks who lie in the burial ground circling the apse of the abbey church. Paradoxically, the poem is a song of joy rather than of mourning as Merton tells them not to fear that "The birds that bicker in the lonely belfry / Will ever give away your legends," but exhorts them to look and "See, the kind universe / Wheeling in love above the abbey steeple / Lights up your sleepy nursery with stars." In a somewhat effusive metaphor he recounts their lives, then asks that they teach us "how to wear / Silence, our humble armor. . . . / Because your work is not yet done," and at the last day, when "your graves, Gethsemani, give up their angels,"

> Return them to their souls to learn
> The songs and attitudes of glory.
> Then will creation rise again like gold
> Clean, from the furnace of your litanies:
> The beasts and trees shall share your resurrection,
> And a new world be born from these green tombs.

This poem was recorded for the Harvard Vocarium Series by the British playwright Robert Speaight, and also included in the *Selected Poems* edited by him in England in 1950.

For **"Elegy for the Monastery Barn,"** which first appeared in *The Strange Islands,* and later in Mark Van Doren's edition of Merton's *Selected Poems* (1959 and 1967), Merton furnished us the "poetic occasion," saying [in the preface to *The Strange Islands*] that it "was written after the cowbarn at Gethsemani burned down, one August evening in 1953, during the evening meditation. The monks left the meditation to fight a very hot fire and the poem arrived about the same time as the fire truck from the nearest town." It received comment by Mark Van Doren in his introduction to *Selected Poems,* as he had requested to include this poem about which he knew Merton to be somewhat shy. Merton remarked:

> As a matter of fact it is for me subjectively an important poem, because when I was a kid in Maryland (yes, even that, for a while) a barn burned down in the middle of the night and it is one of the earliest things I can remember. So burning barns are for me great mysteries that are important. They turn out to be the whole world, and it is the Last Judgement.

In the poem the barn is presented under the image of an old lady who, for her last hour, had dressed herself in "Too gay a dress" and calls to the countryside, "Look, how fast I dress myself in fire!" But for those who worked in her she leaves vivid memories:

> She, in whose airless heart
> We burst our veins to fill her full of hay,
> Now stands apart.
> She will not have us near her. Terribly,
> Sweet Christ, how terribly her beauty burns us now!

But as legacy she has left them her solitude, her peace, her silence. Clustered around the metaphor of the barn is the monks' ignorance of her vanity, hence their surprise at seeing her "So loved, and so attended, and so feared." The "Fifty invisible cattle" return, and the past years as well

"Assume their solemn places one by one" for this little minute of their destiny and meaning, as

> Laved in the flame as in a Sacrament
> The brilliant walls are holy
> In their first-last hour of joy.

The last two stanzas of the poem are reminiscent of the liturgy of Easter night relevant to the blessing of the new fire, Lumen Christi, which is later thrice plunged into the baptismal water. In both text and imagery the first line of the final stanza alludes to Luke 21:21, in which, foretelling the destruction of Jerusalem, Christ warns those in Judea to flee to the mountains and those in the city to depart.

> Flee from within the barn! Fly from the silence
> Of this creature sanctified by fire.

The second line touches on the petition "Sanctify this new fire," from the Exultet of the Easter night vigil. Merton continues:

> Let no man stay inside to look upon the Lord!
> Let no man wait within and see the Holy
> One sitting in the presence of disaster
> Thinking upon this barn His gentle doom!

Again there is an allusion to Luke (21:27), where "they will see the Son of Man coming in a cloud." The event of the barn fire is still kept in its spiritual dimension as it presents "the Holy / One . . . / Thinking upon this barn His gentle doom!" It is *His* barn, since all things are His and He is all things, which recalls a moving passage in William J. Lynch's *Christ and Apollo,* speaking of the Christic imagination which

> begins to assume the order of creation and to lift it into its own vitality. Thus Christ is water, gold, butter, food, a harp, a dove, the day, a house, merchant, fig, gate, stone, book, wood, light, medicine, oil, bread, arrow salt, turtle, risen sun, way, and many things besides.

With its theological resonances and significances this elegy stands out among Merton's finest, as his poetic imagination lifts a simple event—the burning barn—through the zone of the Teilhardian cosmic Christ to that of apocalyptic vision.

Emblems of a Season of Fury contains four elegies. **"Song for the Death of Averroës,"** is a simple narrative in verse-prose style, a form Merton was beginning to use in a number of poems, and is adapted from Ibn Al Arabi, after the Spanish version of Asin Palacios. The young man was sent by his father on an errand to his friend Averroës at the latter's request "to learn if it were true that God had spoken to [him] in solitude." Though at first troubled, Averroës afterward rejoiced and praised God,

> . . . who has made us live in this time when there exists one of those endowed with mystical gifts, one able to unlock His door, and praised be He for granting me, in addition, the favor of seeing one such person with my own eyes.

Ibn Al Arabi never saw Averroës again, but attended his funeral in Cordova, and saw his coffin carried on one side of the beast of burden and the books he had written on the other. To a remark of the scholar Benchobair, "No need to point it out, my son, for it is clearly evident! Blessed be thy tongue that has spoken it!" Ibn Al Arabi set the words apart for meditation:

> I planted the seed within myself thus, in two
>   verses:
>
> "On one side the Master rides: on the other side,
>   his books.
> Tell me: his desires, were they at last fulfilled?"

In the same collection there are two occasional elegies, one for Ernest Hemingway, another for James Thurber. Merton speaks affectionately of Hemingway, who passes "briefly through our midst. Your books and writings have not been consulted. Our prayers are *pro defuncto N.*"

> How slowly this bell tolls in a monastery tower
> for a whole age, and for the quick death of an un-
> ready dynasty, and for that brave illusion: the
> adventurous self!
>
> For with one shot the whole hunt is ended!

That for James Thurber is written in a tighter structure as Merton entreats him.

> Leave us, good friend, Leave our awful celebra-
>   tion
> With pity and relief.
> You are not called to solemnize with us
> Our final madness.
>
> You have not been invited to hear
> The last words of everybody.

Still another elegiac poem in the same collection, **"An Elegy for Five Old Ladies,"** had its beginning in a *New York Times* report of their deaths, "ranging in age from 80 to 96," in a driverless car which, rolling across the lawn of a rest home, plunged into a lake.

> Let the perversity of a machine become our com-
>   mon
>   study, while I name loudly five loyal
>   spouses of death!

One of Merton's late poems, **"Elegy for Father Stephen,"** first published in *Commonweal,* is for a fellow monk, one of whose duties was to tend a flower garden and prepare bouquets for the altars of the abbey church. Merton calls him "Confessor of exotic roses / Martyr of unbelievable gardens"—

> Whom we will always remember
> As a tender-hearted careworn
> Generous unsteady cliff
> Lurching in the cloister
> Like a friendly freight train
> To some uncertain station.

The metaphors are strong fibered, yet the poem carries no sadness as Merton recalls chance meetings with the monk.

> Sometimes a little dangerous at corners
> Vainly trying to smuggle
> Some enormous and perfect bouquet
> To a side altar
> In the sleeves of your cowl.

But on the day of the burial,

> A big truck with lights
> Moved like a battle cruiser
> Toward the gate
> Past your abandoned garden. . . .

The closing lines of the elegy are tender and joyous:

> As if Leviathan
> Hot on the scent of some other blood
> Had passed you by
> And never saw you hiding among the flowers.

Though at the time this poem was written, October 1966, Merton was already experimenting with surrealistic techniques, this elegy moves through clusters of simple yet strong imagery.

Another theme that runs through the fabric of much of Merton's poetry, if not explicitly then implicitly, is that of a denunciation of the so-called "world," though it is well to recall that in an entry in an early Journal, dated December 18, 1941, four days after his entering the monastery, he wrote: "I never hated less the world, scorned it less, or understood it better." Thus, he writes of the "city" because it is a symbol of much that dehumanizes man; even the titles of certain of his poems indicate this, such as the early **"Hymn of Not Much Praise for New York City":**

> . . . never let us look about us long enough to
>   wonder
> Which of the rich men, shivering in the over-
>   heated office,
> And which of the poor men, sleeping face-down
>   on
> the *Daily Mirror*
> Are still alive, and which are dead.

"In the Ruins of New York":

> This was a city
> That dressed herself in paper money.
> She lived four hundred years
> With nickels running in her veins.

"And So Goodbye to Cities":

> For cities have grown old in war and fun
> The sick idea runs riot.

And in **"How to Enter a Big City":**

> Everywhere there is optimism without love
> And pessimism without understanding.

The city as a symbol of "modern society" and the emptiness of technological man who, in conforming himself to its dictates, tends to lose all spiritual orientation was a frequent Merton theme. He had said of technology that it "alienates those who depend on it and live by it. It deadens their human qualities and their moral perceptiveness." Yet at the same time he realized that it was a fact and a necessity of modern life. Yet there is a danger—

> of technology becoming an end in itself and arro-
> gating to itself all that is best and most vital in
> human effort: thus man comes to serve his ma-
> chines instead of being served by them. This is
> completely irrational. One whom I have always
> admired as a great social critic—Charlie Chap-
> lin—made this clear long ago in "Modern
> Times" and other films.

In a poem, **"First Lesson About Man,"** he ironically describes this condition:

> Man begins in zoology
> He is the saddest animal
>
> He drives a big red car
> Called anxiety
> He dreams at night
> Of riding all the elevators
> Lost in the halls
> He never finds the right door.

In brief, flat statements Merton continues his description: "Whenever he goes to the phone / To call joy / He gets the wrong number / He knows all guns. . . . / He flies his worries / All around Venus. . . . / He drives a big white globe / Called death." The "lesson" is logically followed by an interrogation:

> Now dear children you have learned
> The first lesson about man
> Answer your text
>
> "Man is the saddest animal
> He begins in zoology
> And gets lost
> In his own bad news."

An earlier version of this last stanza read (two last lines): "And that is where he generally / Ends."

But Merton's vision of what an ideal world, an ideal city should be, he made explicit in his morality play, **The Tower of Babel.** As set in Augustinian context, he contrasts the city of man with the city of God—the former as symbol is destroyed "to give place to the light which it might have contained."

> . . . This new city will not be the tower of sin,
> but the City of God. Not the wisdom of men
> shall build this city, nor their machines, not their
> power. But the great city shall be built without
> hands, without labor, without money and with-
> out plans. It will be a perfect city, built on eter-
> nal foundations, and it shall stand forever, be-
> cause it is built by the thought and the silence
> and the wisdom and the power of God. But you,
> my brothers, and I are stones in the wall of this
> city. Let us run to find our places. Though we
> may run in the dark, our destiny is full of glory.

Sister Thérèse Lentfoehr, in her Words and Silence: On the Poetry of Thomas Merton, *New Directions, 1979, 166 p.*

D. J. R. Bruckner   (review date 23 May 1982)

[*Bruckner is an American journalist. Below, he provides a positive assessment of* The Literary Essays of Thomas Merton.]

"All innocence is a matter of belief." Thomas Merton said, "For the poet there is no magic. There is only life in all its unpredictability and freedom." Merton was the unpredictable apostle of freedom, a monk in the grand tradition who would be at home with his great medieval predecessors, men who in their time also upset prelates and officious laymen. The movement from traditional Western monasticism in his early books to the magnificent fusion

> Are monks and hippies and poets relevant?
> No, we are deliberately irrelevant. We live
> with an ingrained irrelevance which is
> proper to every human being. The
> marginal man accepts the basic irrelevance
> of the human condition, an irrelevance
> which is manifested above all by the fact
> of death.
>
> —*Thomas Merton in* The Legacy of
> Thomas Merton, *edited by Brother
> Patrick Hart, 1986.*

of Eastern and ancient Western mysticism of his last years is so impressive that his progress seems a leap. But [*The Literary Essays of Thomas Merton*], written mostly for journals and magazines, clock the movement; you can see gradual changes in language and thus realize how difficult and long his intellectual journey was.

They are not about writing but about writers, arguments about life and human understanding. For Merton cultists, every page has sacred passages. More independent readers might want to look at the introductions Merton wrote for a number of volumes of Latin American poetry and the seven essays on Albert Camus first. In these pieces can be found what the poet Jorge Carrera Andrade (as translated by Merton) called " . . . the secret country, the country that is everywhere, the country that has no map because it is within ourselves."

In the comments on Camus, written in the 60's, it is clear that Merton saw the Vatican Council's renewal efforts as the building of a new monument to a still-dead God, and he digs in the rubble of Camus's world for any bones that have life in them. He pitilessly exposes man's need for clarity. In his comparison of Camus and Teilhard de Chardin, he makes you really understand Teilhard and then back away, dismayed.

He analyzes the language of Camus's quintessential creation, Mersault, from four different viewpoints to reveal that it is understanding, not God, that is dead. What he says Camus was doing is certainly true of the French writer, but also of Merton himself: " . . . we can see what Camus is asking not only of intellectuals but also of the Church: this *purification and restitution of language so that the truth may become once again unambiguous and fully accessible to all men, especially when they need to know what to do.*"

The genius of his criticism is that his language is instinct with other tongues—French, Greek, Latin, Spanish, Arabic, Japanese, Chinese—and with values of silence too. These rich essays are no substitute for Merton's books, but they put you quickly in the company of someone who is very bright, questioning, entertaining and annoying. It is easy to forget in such sophisticated conversation the vocation of the man, so the passion of his pursuit of sanctity and his clear vision of eternity surprise the reader now and then.

D. J. R. Bruckner, in a review of "The Literary Essays of Thomas Merton," in The New York Times Book Review, *May 23, 1982, p. 15.*

Victor A. Kramer (essay date 1984)

[*Kramer is an American educator and critic. In the following excerpt from his study* Thomas Merton *he focuses on Merton's portrayal of contemporary man in* Collected Poems.]

Collected Poems, a thousand-page volume, [includes new poems that were unpublished at the time of Merton's death.] These new poems do not exhibit startling changes in technique, yet there are several points to be noted; interesting is the fact that Merton continued to experiment with various techniques. Thus, while many of his final shorter poems are conventional, others, especially the prose-poems, are unusual. Two characteristics stand out about the lyrics in this final collection. Merton includes many personal pieces in which he seems almost horrified at what he sees reflected about contemporary man, who remains unaware of his need for contemplation; but Merton is also able to attain distance, and even to laugh. This is so because he sees many connections between his life and others, while he also seems to realize that his poetry means much more to him than it ever can for others. Both **"The Originators"** and **"With the World in My Bloodstream"** bring this point home (these are the first two poems in the collection). There is a kind of lightness in many of these poems, even though Merton's view of the contemporary world (and history) is sometimes almost frightening. His title poem **"A Song: Sensation Time at the Home"** also exemplifies this. This poet certainly realizes that poetry will have little immediate effect—especially upon readers who are caught up *only* in their own sensations. This is the world of **Cables** where

> Experts control
> Spasms
> Fight ennui
> While giant smiles and minds
> Relax limits
> Save $ $ $ $ $.

It is a world which seems to be in large part lost, yet more important it is one about which the poet speaks kindly, with wit and irony, even though man seems to have given up by giving in. **"A Tune for Festive Dances in the Nineteen Sixties,"** about man's loss of identity, is a related poem. **"Man the Master"** amplifies the same themes, but again in a humorous way. Man seems so busy that he has forgotten about himself, *as self:*

> Here he comes
> Bursting with individuals
> All his beliefs fat and clean. . . .
> With innumerable wits and plans
> Nations and names problems and resolutions.

In some of these poems there exists a consistent note close to disgust. Poems such as **"Picture of a Black Child with a White Doll"** and **"Man the Master"** illustrate this. Yet it is important to realize that while there is such a somber quality, even close to bitterness, there is as well a lightness to balance it. Thus, on the one hand, Merton can provide a gaiety, yet on the other he will not bring himself to stop thinking about the distortions of contemporary man. The poet smiles, but he cannot forget his **"First Lessons About Man"** which are that

> Man begins in zoology
> He is the saddest animal
> He drives a big red car
> Called anxiety. . . .

Somewhat the same must be observed about the three prose-poems which close this collection. All treat man's misuse of language, the twisting of language to his selfish benefit, not for the benefit of others, yet all of these prose-poems are also presented with distance and humor which makes it possible for Merton's compassion to shine through. These three prose-poems which conclude **"Sensation Time"** are further indications of the writer's interests toward the very end of his career. **"Plessy vs Ferguson: Theme and Variations"** might be compared to the noise of **Cables** since in both language seems often to be used to obscure rather than to clarify. This is a study, above all, in the abuse of language. **"Rites for the Extrusion of a Leper"** implies that the Church itself can be guilty of language abuse. Merton's point is that civil government and the church continue to find ways to arrange meaning for their own benefit.

The last prose-poem, **"Ben's Last Fight"** apparently means many things. It seems to be an autobiographical poem, and it also is a statement by Merton about poetic technique. Father Louis is saying that he has learned that he can now relax. Fights with rules, with language, with the changing concerns of the world of man, are interesting, but ultimately of little lasting import; yet words can help man to remember such facts, too.

Victor A. Kramer, in his Thomas Merton, *Twayne Publishers, 1984, 164 p.*

Victor A. Kramer (essay date 1986)

[*In the following essay on* The Sign of Jonas, *originally presented in 1986 at a conference of Merton scholars, Kramer discusses Merton's struggle to reconcile the conflicts between his contemplative life and his aspirations as an artist.*]

Thomas Merton's Journal *The Sign of Jonas* is a record of his growing awareness of what it means to be a monk, yet beyond that the text suggests what it means to be so while also a writer. Merton's journal records various attempts to minimize an awareness of his incipient vocation as a man of letters, but finally the journal becomes a documentation of that very awareness. This early journal, then, might be described as the history of a man of letters *malgré lui.* Merton apparently chose the title *The Sign of Jonas* because for him it signified a generation which did not understand God, while it also was a sign of resurrection, especially the power of Christ's resurrection for

Christians. This sign also has a special application for monks who have heard the call to obey God, and specifically for Merton who found the years 1949-1952 especially difficult in terms of his vocation. Having spent a decade at Gethsemani; penned books which brought him recognition as an artist; and then finding himself ordained in 1949, yet unsure of how he would best fulfill a vocation which seemed to demand some combination of roles as monk and writer, Merton recorded in his 'journal' an answer for himself, but also paradoxically for his readers.

Another Merton book, written just before *Jonas,* is Merton's history of the Cistercians, the final section of which, 'Paradisus Claustralis', is a meditation about Cistercian common life. There Merton celebrates the life he personally felt to be intoxicating. That history, *The Waters of Siloe,* was finished just as Merton started *Jonas.* At that time, for him, monastic life seemed to be intoxicating, a life wherein love of God and others demanded self-effacement, but a life where such love brought peace unknown in other circumstances. Thus while *The Waters of Siloe* provides a sometimes romantic overview of the history and development of the Trappists, it is as well Merton's personal meditation on some of the mysteries of the contemplative life. *Siloe* also shares characteristics with other books which Merton wrote during this early period and helps us to understand why for him a monastic life made good sense. Yet for someone with a mind and heart as active as Merton such an historical method could only reveal one facet of his interests. His own inner struggles, questions about what it meant for *him* to be a monk were to be recorded in another manner. The journal *The Sign of Jonas* offers evidence of this and is perhaps the best way to understand Merton as a writer during the years immediately after *Seven Storey Mountain* was written. His title suggests the fundamental paradox which he felt about a developing career as writer and contemplative, and the writing reflects many personal doubts, questions, and investigations. In the published journal we also clearly see many of his doubts about how best he could write. The subject matter for *The Sign of Jonas,* therefore, might be described as a short history in the life of one Cistercian. It is a personal history about the difficulties and pleasures of being a writer.

In *Jonas,* dated from December of 1946 to July of 1952, Merton provides a specific record of his development as a monk, as priest *and* writer. The book is deceptively simple in appearance, but just as with *The Seven Storey Mountain,* upon examination it proves to be carefully orchestrated. The journal entries document Merton's success as a monk and show him examining issues (literary, personal, contemporary) which he finds of value in his developing spiritual life. Just like Jonas in the belly of the whale, he saw his life formed by divine providence. In this journal his job became one of organizing journal entries which were faithful to that experience, but also a book which dramatized God's providence and the mystery of that encounter with God—rather than just a particular writer-monk's actions, thoughts, and meditations.

Basic to the literary structure here is the tension which makes the writer so unhappy (as he travels toward his 'destiny in the belly of paradox') but which also allows him to produce a beautifully contrived journal. The book is arranged in six parts and also includes prologue and epilogue. In this essay I trace some of the basic literary patterns of paradox which contribute to the success of this book.

In the prologue, 'Journey to Nineveh' Merton examines the paradox, not just of his life, but of the fact that his journal records 'a rare and unusual moment in the history of one particular monastery'. What he realizes is that the phenomenon of extreme change at Gethsemani was something which suddenly occurred 'without anybody's foreseeing it and without anyone making any logical attempt to control it'. The six major units of text, arranged chronologically, are Merton's confession (and *apologia*) about how he had contrived to seek control over his life during these years, while gradually he was able to conclude that the secret both for being a successful writer, as well as a good monk, was acceptance of one's place within a particular monastery. Thus, Merton's use of his own experience (like Thoreau in *Walden* who sees such a necessity because he happens to know himself best, but also like Henry Adams whose third-person narrator envisions himself as symbol for all who have lived through similar difficulties) allows the writer to demonstrate archetypal events.

The journal *Jonas* includes eight parts. Its six major divisions are united by the prologue and epilogue. Part One begins exactly five years after Merton had come to the Abbey—toward the end of the period of simple vows, and as he 'was making up his mind to take solemn vows and stay in the monastery for good'. Subsequent sections are about steps taken toward ordination, and his first years as a priest. Merton also records facts about his personal loneliness and spiritual aridity experienced in 1949 and 1950. The final major portion of the journal covers a longer time period than any of the others. In that concluding division Merton explains how he found a new kind of spiritual peace during the Christmas season of 1950. His excerpts

Merton, shortly after he was ordained into the priesthood.

from the remaining eighteen months, or so, reflect a new found peace.

The Sign of Jonas is cumulatively a demonstration that internal observation and celebration of mystery can be built upon the simplest most ordinary kinds of circumstances; obliquely it is a demonstration that it is possible to be a man of letters even while swallowed in the belly of the whale. But the real question for Father Louis was what kind of writing to do? Merton is literally in the process of dying unto a new life, but part of that very process is in his writing, while part of the fun remains in telling about it. By giving birth unto words, the old self dies; at one point he writes:

> It is sometime in June. At a rough guess, I think it is June 13 which may or may not be the feast of Saint Anthony of Padua. In any case every day is the same for me because I have become very different from what I used to be. The man who began this journal is dead, just as the man who finished ***The Seven Storey Mountain*** when this journal began was also dead, and what is more the man who was the central figure in ***The Seven Storey Mountain*** was dead over and over. And now that all these men are dead, it is sufficient for me to say so on paper and I think I will have ended up by forgetting them.

In the prologue to his book Merton set the scene for his dying through words by insisting that these journal entries are his ideas:

> I have attempted to convey something of a monk's spiritual life and of his thoughts, not in the language of speculation but in terms of personal experience. This is always a little hazardous because it means leaving the sure, plain path of an accepted terminology and traveling in byways of poetry and intuition.

His journal succeeds as a work of art precisely because he allows the reader to glimpse the difficulties which *he* experienced; tension is usually apparent, but Merton does not linger with particulars which were disturbing. Above all, what this monk-writer has to learn is that he must accept appointed tasks as they are given. Ultimately the reader comes to perceive that maybe this writer could never fully understand why he was asked, under the special circumstances of life at Gethsemani, to be a writer. ***The Sign of Jonas*** is especially valuable therefore, because, in addition to being a record of Merton's activities during the years of preparation for the priesthood and just after, it also treats (sometimes indirectly) the question of literary vocation.

In the six major parts we would, perhaps, at first expect Merton to be concerned mostly with matters of spiritual consequence. What he cumulatively demonstrates is that the tension caused by his desire to write, and also requests by his Abbot Frederic that he write often seemed problematic. However, he learned that there is 'nothing to prevent a monk from praying even while he writes a book.'

Merton's frequent questions about what it means to be a writer are crucial; and ultimately ***Jonas*** becomes a record of his working out an accommodation with the vocation of writer. We recall, that at first Merton thought that it might have been advantageous had he not been asked to write, but ***Jonas*** demonstrates that he fast came to the realization that his earlier 'lamentations' about an obligatory writing job had been foolish. Many entries indicate that he earlier believed that he needed to cease writing for he felt he could be a better contemplative without the distractions of preparing books for the press. Yet he had been told by his superiors to go on writing and he eventually understood that he was 'to go on trying to learn to write under the strange conditions imposed by Cistercian life'. It is also clear from these journal entries that he also remained ambitious about being a good writer. Thus he indicates he was dissatisfied with a recently completed book about Mother Berkmans because it seemed too verbose and throughout ***Jonas*** it is quite clear that Merton admires other writers. Without a doubt he too wants to write well. Perhaps the fact that he included such references within this published journal indicates that he felt he had not attained the level of artistic proficiency he desired. References to T. S. Eliot, Rilke, and Dylan Thomas are typical of his self-criticism. He qualifies by adding:

> I am not talking about grammar and syntax, but about having something to say and saying it in sentences that are not half dead. Saint Paul and Saint Ignatius Martyr did not bother about grammar but they certainly knew how to write. Imperfection is the penalty of rushing into print.

What he implies is that he needs to find ways to be more concerned about good writing while less concerned about a public and literary production. He knows, as he puts it just a few pages later, 'the chief thing that has struck me today is that I still have my fingers too much in the running of my own life'. He then notes he should remember many souls are dependent upon his writing. What the writing might bring the writer should, he realizes, remain secondary.

Merton uses a journal format as a way of showing that he has finally found his vocation as contemplative, without ceasing to be concerned about his responsibilities as writer. The result is a book which documents how he found his way toward God through the writing. In his introduction to the first major section, 'Solemn Profession', he notes 'There is nothing to prevent a monk from praying, even while he writes a book'. However he adds, "This discovery did not come to me until I finally resigned myself to being a writer, and found out that the job had one big compensation: it brought me solitude." His job as a writer in this book became to show how he *gradually* came to such a realization. Throughout the journal he holds the reader's suspense. Thus early, 'February 10, Lent', he writes

> I went and talked over the whole business of my vocation again with Father Abbot and he assured me once again, patiently, that everything was quite all right and that this was where I belonged. In my bones I know that he is quite right and that I am a fool. And yet, on the surface, everything seems to be all wrong. As usual, I am making too much fuss about it.

As a strategy for the way a reader will be drawn into this

book, such expression of doubt works well. Merton will hold our subsequent attention through other reports of the *apparent* dilemma of being a writer-contemplative. Thus on March 8, he notes:

> I continue writing this journal under obedience to Dom Gildas, in spite of my personal disinclination to go on with it. It is sufficient to have the matter decided by a director. If it is tedious to keep a journal, it is still more tedious to keep wondering whether or not I ought to give the thing up. I do not know whether it will give glory to God: but my writing of it has been disinfected by obedience. I need no longer apologize either to God or to myself for keeping a journal.

But as we move with him, to, and through the text which moves toward solemn profession, the mood changes. By April 1st while the Abbot General is visiting, Merton can assure us that

> Dom Dominique said, first of all, that he was very pleased with my writing, although he did not understand the poems. He told me emphatically—in fact it was the most emphatic thing he said, and the only thing that seemed like an official pronouncement, an *ex cathedra* fulmination—that it was good and even necessary for me to go on writing. He said specialists were needed in the Order—writers, liturgists, canonists, theologians. If I had been trained in a certain profession, I should make use of my training. In any case, he concluded, it was a matter of obedience.

But, of course, this is what concerned him most. He did not want to be a 'specialist' working in what seemed like a factory which would turn out monastic literature. And a month later, more doubts. Perhaps he is writing too much:

> Today I got two new jobs. Father Abbot gave me the notes that Father Alberic was working on, for the revised edition of his history of the Order. Then I am to write a new postulant's guide. That means I now have no less than twelve jobs in various stages of completion . . . .

And there were still more temptations:

> I have also been thinking of a Spanish-English edition of the *Dark Night of the Soul,* with a preface and commentary. Somewhere I have a few notes I scraped together for a life of Father Joseph Cassant. And on top of all that Reverend Father speaks of a new critical Latin edition of Saint Bernard for 1953. That last one is definitely beyond me.

In October of 1947, he reports he has not yet resolved his dilemma. Reading other monks who have suggestions to make only makes it more difficult to know what he might do:

> When I first looked into the pages of 'The Dedicated Life and Poetry' by Patrice de la Tour du Pin and saw so many words like 'solitude' and 'virginity,' I became extremely interested. But on reading it more carefully it began to depress me a little. Clever and obscure language in a con-

text that I do not quite grasp—all the traditional formulas of the contemplative life transplanted into a garden of flowers that are no longer any fun for me . . . I am living on the inside of a wall where such metaphors have ceased to make an impression. Dedication, for us, is not romance, it is routine.

> Yet perhaps if I paid more attention to Patrice de la Tour du Pin I might discover something quite the way he does.

Merton seems to realize that he needs a method of his own, something other than routine. It is not an accident that this opening section ends with a consideration of Cistercian architecture, and question of style:

> How shall we build a beautiful monastery according to the style of some past age and according to the rules of a dead tradition? Thus we make the problem not only infinitely complicated but we make it, in fact, unsolvable. Because a dead style is dead. And the reason why it is dead is that the motives and the circumstances that once gave it life have ceased to exist.

We remember Merton wrote the same thing about his life. What we will witness in *The Sign of Jonas* is the literal building of a personal style—as the more predictable and conventional elements are eliminated.

In subsequent sections (Part two is the 'Death of an Abbot', but also the time of admitted self-satisfaction with being 'an author' after *The Seven Storey Mountain* was published) Merton structures observations around the tension of his love of God and (while he has a hard time admitting it) his pleasure in realizing he *is* 'an author'. It does not seem an accident that this part of the book begins with allusions both to T. S. Eliot and St. John of the Cross. In the second major section, 'Death of an Abbot', its arrangement is such that discussion of writing is minimized; yet the ending is especially interesting for Merton continues to wonder if his writing has any value at all:

> Sooner or later the world must burn, and all things in it—all the books, the cloister together with the brothel, Fra Angelico together with the Lucky Strike ads which I haven't seen for seven years because I don't remember seeing one in Louisville. Sooner or later it will all be consumed by fire and nobody will be left. . . .

> And here I sit writing a diary.

Nevertheless he repeats himself:

> . . . sooner or later the world must burn—and *The Seven Storey Mountain* and *Figures for an Apocalypse.*

And Merton, the journal writer, can write about what he is thinking day by day:

> And I have several times thought how at the last Day I am likely to be one of the ten most abjectly humiliated sinners in the history of the world, but it will be my joy, and it will fill me with love, and I will fly like an arrow to take a back seat very far in the back where the last shall be first. . . .

Now it is a toss-up whether I should ask Reverend Father to give me another and fatter book to fill with *Journal,* for we have been talking about my writing less. In fact, I have begun to tell him all about my temptations to become a Carthusian and he says he doesn't see why things can't be fixed up right here.

Merton leaves the reader hanging—in suspense. (Of course, we know he will ask for more blank pages, and we will be allowed to keep on reading.)

Merton uses a journal format as a way of showing that he has finally found his vocation as contemplative, without ceasing to be concerned about his responsibilities as writer. The result is a book which documents how he found his way toward God through the writing.

—Victor A. Kramer

In Parts three, four and five difficulties about writing are one of the motifs which unite Merton's journal. It is ironic that through writing he deals with the problems of writing; yet in retrospect, how could it be otherwise with visits by Evelyn Waugh, and letters from Robert Giroux, and James Laughlin and projects, projects, projects? Reading Kenneth Patchen; talking to Naomi Burton; analyzing a passage from Rilke—all these things are indications both that Merton could not deny he got his fuel from contact with things and persons literary, yet he also had to ask questions about how his own method as a writer worked. How for example, could Rilke insist that 'to people who do not know me, I cannot possibly write,' Merton wonders? 'Is this last sentence true of me? No! I write for a hundred thousand people who do not know me', says Merton. More significantly, he immediately adds 'but I am not writing for them'. This is the real paradox of a book which is first for the writer but also for a public. The journal entries of *The Sign of Jonas* are often extremely private, yet Merton also admits he realizes they will most likely be published. . . .

In the final section we see the writer moving more toward an acceptance of his role as writer while also serving as master of scholastics, and still more importantly being a monk in a particular place. Yet even then Merton was reading; making poetic observations about a Negro with his junk wagon in Louisville; working on the manuscript of *Bread in the Wilderness*; recalling Thoreau and the memories of that same junk wagon; noting Gertrude Stein. All these things conspire to give him material for his journal. All these thing are gifts. All are to be enjoyed, and that means writing.

The final section, entitled 'The Sign of Jonas', deals explicitly with Merton's realization that his 'new desert' is compassion.

What is my new desert? The name of it is *compassion.* There is no wilderness so terrible, so beautiful, so arid and so fruitful as the wilderness of compassion. It is the only desert that shall truly flourish like the lily. It shall become a pool.

Usually as the journal progresses, Merton records the fact that he knows that it will be through personal experience that he will refine his abilities as a writer; his job will be to accent *his* quiet.

The passage about Jonas and the whale prepares us for the ending of the book; it pulls many of the themes together. Merton is writing about himself and for others.

It is the whale we cherish. Jonas swims abandoned in the heart of the sea. But it is the whale that must die. Jonas is immortal. If we do not remember to distinguish between them, and if we prefer the whale and do not take Jonas out of the ocean, the inevitable will come to pass. The whale and the prophet will soon come around and meet again in their wanderings, and once again the whale will swallow the prophet. Life will be swallowed again in death and its last state will be worse than the first.

We must get Jonas out of the whale and the whale must die at a time when Jonas is in the clear, busy with his orisons, clothed and in his right mind, free, holy and walking on the shore. Such is the meaning of the desire for death that comes in the sane night, the peace that finds us for a moment in clarity, walking by the light of the stars, raised to God's connatural shore, dryshod in the heavenly country, in a rare moment of intelligence.

There are many levels of concern in *Jonas,* and Merton indicates that particular writers focus on different levels of reality; one of the most important facts of *The Sign of Jonas* is how it reveals this writer sorting out various possibilities. Sometimes this is implicit (by the materials included) and sometimes it is explicit.

The epilogue, 'Fire Watch, July 4, 1952', a long prose-poem, which grows naturally out of the preceding sections—which more and more stress the need to accept what one is given with all its particularity—is Merton's celebration of the beauty of night watch duty. It is appropriate that the end of the preceding section, six, is Merton's report of going to Louisville to become a U. S. citizen. The Independence Day song which follows is a celebration through which now as priest (yet also as an unseen man of letters always gaining more material) he can breathe life into a poem which documents the mystery of God's presence in the middle of a strange place on a hot July night. Merton walks about the place of his God-given and paradoxical literary entrapment. This place is both the ironic source of Merton's inspiration, and the documentation of the mystery of finding oneself in darkness. This is a process which Merton also gradually realized could never be completed.

Jonas ultimately focuses on what Merton calls his second level, the depth of darkness which he says is apparent when one closes one's eyes to troubles apparent on the surface. This is especially true of the conclusion of the book, 'Fire Watch, July 4, 1952', an excellent example of Merton's focus.

This concluding meditation is a lyrical description of the writer's actual movements as a night watchman when he moves from place to place within the monastery, yet on another level it is metaphor for Merton's vocation, and acceptance of that vocation. As we move with him through the various physical levels of the monastery, and finally to the spire (and his awareness of the transcendent) we come to understand that it is only through a familiarity with this world that anyone can move toward the transcendent. For this writer, then, the human element is *always* there. He stresses the fact that for him God is not easily found in abstruse theology, or by scholarly methods, but through simple living:

> Around one corner is a hole in the wall with a vat where they stew fruit. Under this vat Dom Frederic told me to burn all the letters that were in the pigeonholes of the rooms where he had been Prior. Around another corner is an old furnace where I burned the rest of the papers from the same room. . . .
>
> Then suddenly, after the old brooding catacomb, you hit something dizzy and new: the kitchen, painted by the brother novices, each wall in a different color. Some of the monks complained of the different colored walls, but a watchman has no opinions. There is tile under the shining vats and Scripture close to the ceiling: 'Little children, love one another!'

This tour through the monastery is Merton's metaphorical answer to many of the questions which he has raised throughout the entire text. All of a sudden everything seems to be falling into place—not that it is explained; rather its mystery can now be accepted. One learns to live in the present, and one stops thinking about the past. And as the tour proceeds it becomes clearer and clearer that while many questions will never be answered, one accepts one's place right now:

> With my feet on the floor I waxed when I was a postulant, I ask these useless questions. With my hand on the key by the door to the tribune, where I first heard the monks chanting the psalms, I do not wait for an answer, because I have begun to realize You never answer when I expect.
>
> The third room of the library is called hell. It is divided up by wallboard partitions into four small sections full of condemned books. The partitions are hung with American flags and pictures of Dom Edmond Obrecht. I thread my way through this unbelievable maze to the second room of the library, where the retreatants used to sit and mop their brows and listen to sermons.
>
> Questions arrive, assume their actuality, and also disappear. In this hour I shall cease to ask them, and silence shall be my answer.

As the writer continues, he speaks to his God, with whom paradoxically he knows there can be no complete dialogue:

> The marriage of souls in concepts is mostly an illusion. Thoughts which travel outward bring back reports of You from outward things: but a dialogue with You, uttered through the world, always ends by being a dialogue with my own reflection in the stream of time. With You there is no dialogue unless You choose a mountain and circle it with cloud and print Your words in fire upon the mind of Moses. What was delivered to Moses on tables of stone, as the fruit of lightning and thunder, is now more thoroughly born in our own souls as quietly as the breath of our own being.
>
> The hand lies open. The heart is dumb. The soul that held my substance together, like a hard gem in the hollow of my own power, will one day totally give in.
>
> Although I see the stars, I no longer pretend to know them. Although I have walked in those woods, how can I claim to love them? One by one I shall forget the names of individual things.

We ask, as Merton does: is one of the basic points stressed in *Jonas* that real unity with God comes only through contact with the world, and with others; is it only through such contact that one is saved? I believe Merton is coming to such a conclusion. In a passage toward the very end of this text he muses about the prayers of those who are in the world, and his relationship to them as a writer:

> I am beginning to believe that perhaps the only, or at least the quickest way, I shall become a saint is by virtue of the desires of many good people in America that I should become one. Last night I dreamt I was telling several other monks, 'I shall be a saint,' and they did not seem to question me. Furthermore, I believed it myself. If I do become one—(I shall)—it will be because of the prayers of other people who, though they are better than I am, still want me to pray for them. Perhaps I am called upon to objectify the truth that America, for all its evil, is innocent and somehow ignorantly holy.

It is ironic that Merton should have such a dream because in fact he is literally saved by his readers. In a way his journal, done in obedience—and not contemplative prayer or systematic theology—became his objectification of the truth that America is innocent and holy.

As Merton later developed as a writer, the simplicity of levels of depth, an illusion of life separated into strands, became ever more unsatisfying for him. As the literary career progressed, he assumed the responsibility of drawing more and more connections between the quiet of his monastery and the troubled surface of the world which at this particular time he chose to ignore. (What immediately sets a journal of more than a decade later, *Conjectures of a Guilty Bystander,* apart from *The Sign of Jonas* is its systematic concern with contemporary problems. In *Conjectures,* Merton makes connections between what he observes in his reading, thinking, and prayer, with the contemporary world. That is still another story.)

The Sign of Jonas is, perhaps, most importantly Merton's journal of his acceptance of a dual vocation. It is the record of someone gradually coming to the realization that not only had he not been in control of his life as he moved through Gethsemani, but ironically he would never be in control of such a deep mystery. His job as a writer was to accept what God asked him to do; and what that meant for him was that he finally wrote about the difficulty of writing and admitted he was not different than many other writers who first have to deal with themselves.

When we study the early books of Merton, it is as if there are two completely different facets to Father Louis. One is that man of "projects" who will write successful books, usually retrospective ones, such as ***The Seven Storey Mountain*** and ***The Waters of Siloe,*** or theoretical ones like ***The Ascent to Truth.*** The other facet is that much more private and imaginative Merton who will continue to look, question, and wonder—more often than not about himself. Such is the Merton who evolves in ***The Sign of Jonas.*** This does not mean that he is writing about himself as a personality; it means paradoxically that he has to learn to efface himself—at least in some ways—by writing about himself. In so doing he became a man of letters despite himself.

Victor A. Kramer, "Literary Patterns in 'The Sign of Jonas': Tension between Monk and Man of Letters," in Toward an Integrated Humanity: Thomas Merton's Journey, *edited by M. Basil Pennington, Cistercian Publications, 1988, pp. 1-23.*

William H. Shannon   (essay date 2 December 1988)

[*Shannon is a Roman Catholic priest whose writings include* The Church of Christ *(1957) and* The Response to Humanae Vitae *(1970). In the following essay, he considers the value of Merton's oeuvre and the future reputation of his works, commenting that "Merton scholarship is still in its infancy or at best in adolescence."*]

In considering the Merton literary output, one is amazed by the sheer quantity of it. That a monk, whose daily life was fairly rigorously regulated by a monastic routine that gave him only limited time for writing, should produce more than forty books and some sixty or more journals and reading notebooks, a thousand pages of poetry and upwards of 4,000 letters, boggles the mind. Of course, sheer quantity establishes no claim to lasting survival and not everything Merton wrote deserves to survive, as he himself recognized. In 1967, Merton did a self-evaluation of thirty-one of his books. Using six categories (ranging from "Best" to "Awful"), he lists fourteen as "Better," six as "Good," six as "Fair," three as "Poor." For the categories "Bad" and "Awful," he has one each. He lists none of his works as a "Best." I would venture to say that "devotional" and "inspirational" works (like ***The Living Bread,*** which Merton classifies as "Poor") are destined for literary demise. But there are other books that, while addressing the concrete circumstances of his own time with clarity and authenticity, have a quality of insight into the human condition that transcends his own generation.

My tentative list would begin with ***The Seven Storey Mountain,*** a smash hit in 1948, which sold 600,000 copies in its first year and continues year after year to attract readers. If one accepts T. S. Eliot's rather pragmatic definition of a "classic" as "a work that stays in print," The ***Mountain*** has met the test for forty years, and all the signs point to continued popularity. I would also include ***New Seeds of Contemplation*** (a far better book than its predecessor, ***Seeds of Contemplation***) and the Merton journals: ***The Sign of Jonas*** (a favorite of so many Merton readers), ***Conjectures of a Guilty Bystander*** (not actually a single journal, but made up of items from journals covering the period 1956-65), and the recently issued ***The Vow of Conversation*** (a journal of 1964-65). My list would include a fairly large sampling of Merton's letters (in which his humanity shines in both its greatness and its weakness); healthy selections from his poetry; and essays. To give one example of the latter: **"Philosophy of Solitude"** in ***Disputed Questions*** is a superb study of a fundamental need that women and men of every age and place have experienced.

Merton's works, if they survive, will do so because of their autobiographical character. In some sense practically everything he wrote is in one way or another autobiographical. Merton himself realized this aspect of his writing. As early as 1949, he recorded in his journal: "Every book I write is a mirror of my own character and conscience." I believe that it is this autobiographical strain that draws and will continue to draw people to his writings.

I stress the importance of the autobiographical thrust of Merton's writings because so many readers around the world are able to identify their story with his—a human person struggling to find meaning and to confront the absurdity that life so often appears to be. Merton knew loneliness and alienation. His clay feet are visible for us to see. Like ourselves he had attachments of which he had to rid himself and illusions he had to unmask. No wonder that, as his books mirrored his "own character and conscience," his readers found themselves mirrored as well.

But the fact that we find our stories in his does not, of itself, offer sufficient reason why his writing ought to survive. There are other people with whom we can identify in a shared humanness. What makes the difference with Thomas Merton are the special gifts he had: a deep wisdom and a marvelous facility with words. He could reach into the human heart and surface for his readers questions that, till they read him, lay hidden and unasked, struggling for expression. Though Merton was not a creative thinker, he was a creative synthesizer: he knew how to raise to a new level of understanding people's perception of God, prayer, and human life.

In short, Merton is a person who, through his writings, enters into conversation with you. He tells about himself and you see not only yourself, but every person. He writes autobiography and we find biography—our own. He digs so deeply into raw humanity that his words will reach women and men for ages to come.

It is perhaps no accident that in the last year of his life, Merton was much occupied with reflection on transculturation, whereby a person transcended a particular culture by being at home in all cultures. Thomas Merton was received into the Roman Catholic church on November 16, 1938. He became a citizen of the United States on June 22, 1951. But Merton does not belong to the Roman Catholic church. Nor does he belong to the U.S. The religious traditions of a whole humanity filtered through his fertile mind and enriched his own faith with an ever expanding catholicity. The lives and destinies of humanity touched his person and made him, as far as this is possible, a world citizen.

Besides Merton's own literary output, there are the works which his writings have inspired: books, articles and dissertations (111 of them!). Merton's classification of his own books may appropriately be applied to these. This would reveal a rather uneven picture and not an especially happy one: very few works that could be called "Better" and perhaps a reasonable number of "Good"; but all too many would qualify only as "Fair," "Poor," "Bad," or even "Awful." This may seem like a harsh evaluation, but I am convinced that Merton deserves better treatment than he has so far received. I also have the feeling that many of my colleagues would agree that Merton scholarship is still in its infancy or at best in adolescence.

What ought to be the future direction of Merton studies? The first task is the publication of what is as yet unpublished: journals, letters, and taped talks. There are four journals, 1956-68, that by Merton's will were restricted from publication for twenty-five years after his death. These can be published in 1993. There are more than sixty other journals and reading notebooks, which contain valuable material and, with careful editing ought to be published in conjunction with the restricted journals. There will be no great surprises or new revelations when the remaining journals are published. They were available to Merton's authorized biographer, Michael Mott, who gives generous excerpts from them.

In short, Merton is a person who, through his writings, enters into conversation with you. He tells about himself and you see not only yourself, but every person.

—*William H. Shannon*

Only the first of five projected volumes of letters has so far appeared. Called *The Hidden Ground of Love*, it includes more than 700 letters on religious experience and social concerns. The second volume (called *The Road to Joy*, letters to family, friends, young people, etc.) should be in print by the spring of 1989. The third volume (on monastic renewal and spiritual direction) is near completion in typescript, and the fourth (dealing with Merton's contacts with poets and other writers) is in preparation. Volume five of the letters will include correspondence that did not fit the other volumes; it will also contain a chronology of all of Merton's letters and an extensive index.

Finally, there are hundreds of taped talks. Many were intended for a limited audience within the monastery and need judicious editing. A number of such tapes, recently published, show little sign of editing and project a mediocrity onto Thomas Merton that is both misleading to readers and unfair to him.

Besides these three areas, there is a good bit of unpublished material dealing with the monastic life (for example, notes Merton used with the young monks he taught). These would have only restricted appeal and probably will not be published.

A critical study, or even a critical edition, of *The Seven Storey Mountain* is very much needed. This is the book that "launched" Merton's career as a writer. Much of what he writes later flows out of the metaphors, symbols, and reflections found in that book. It is a young monk reflecting on a young man's life and in some ways setting a future agenda: metaphors he was to live out and develop further, as well as others that later he would reject.

The Merton poetry exists in somewhat unmanageable form: a huge volume of over a thousand pages, with no introduction or notes. A fair amount of it is mediocre or just plain bad, but one will also find fine poetry there. A valuable Merton project would be to make a discriminating selection from among the eight poetry collections (1940-63). Such a selection of the best poetry, with an introduction and critical notes, would open up Merton's least-known writings. His last two volumes of poetry, *Cables to the Ace* and *The Geography of Lograire*, could receive the same treatment, but as individual works complete in themselves.

A similar selection of important essays could be made, again with proper critical notes and introduction. This would be of special value to the growing number of teachers who offer courses on Merton, or to people who would like to indulge themselves in a "home" study. Of value might be an updated revision of *The Thomas Merton Reader* or a new reader that would offer a representative selection of Merton writing, including some of the posthumously published works.

These are but a brief sampling of possible directions in which Merton scholarship and publishing might move. Thematic studies have been done, especially in dissertations, but these will best be done when all the Merton material is finally published.

An important priority for Merton scholars is to establish more contact between specialists in religious studies, theology, or spirituality and specialists in literature. Some time ago I was talking with a friend who is a teacher of literature and a highly respected scholar in the field of nineteenth-century Romantic poetry. In the course of our conversation, he said: "We people in literature do not take Thomas Merton seriously." My suggestion was that maybe they should. It is unfortunate that Merton has been seen as the almost exclusive "possession" of people in the field of religion and spirituality. Some Merton scholars are in the field of literature, but not enough. There is a need for discussions between the various disciplines. Only then can we address an important question: is Merton to be classified as a "religious" writer, with the inevitable restrictions that such a classification would impose in terms of potential readers, or is he a figure in American literature and one to be reckoned with, at that?

William H. Shannon, "The Future of Thomas Merton: Sorting Out the Legacy," in Commonweal, *Vol. CXV, No. 21, December 2, 1988, pp. 649-52.*

FURTHER READING

Bibliography

Breit, Marquita, ed. *Thomas Merton: A Bibliography.* Metuchen, NJ: The Scarecrow Press, Inc., 1974, 180 p.

> A comprehensive bibliography of primary and secondary materials on Merton's life and works.

Biographies

Furlong, Monica. *Merton: A Biography.* San Francisco: Harper & Row, Publishers, 1980, 342 p.

> Attempts to reconcile conflicting impressions of Merton's life: "[In *Merton: A Biography*] I have avoided the reverential approach, have tried to see him as the normal man he was. . . ."

Lawlor, Patrick T. "Poet to Teacher: Thomas Merton's Letters to Mark Van Doren." *Columbia Literary Columns* XXXIX, No. 1 (November 1989): 18-30.

> Discusses Merton's friendship and correspondence with Mark Van Doren.

McInerny, Dennis Q. *Thomas Merton: The Man and His Work.* Washington, D.C.: Consortium Press, 1974, 128 p.

> Biographical introduction to Merton's life and writings.

Mott, Michael. *The Seven Mountains of Thomas Merton.* Boston: Houghton Mifflin Company, 1984, 690 p.

> Widely considered one of the most complete biographies of Merton.

Wilkes, Paul. *Merton: By Those Who Knew Him Best.* San Francisco: Harper & Row, Publishers, 1984, 171 p.

> Presents biographical commentary by Merton's closest friends and acquaintances including Ernesto Cardenal, Joan Baez, and Robert Lax.

Criticism

Carruth, Hayden. Review of *The Geography of Lograire,* by Thomas Merton. *The Hudson Review* XXIII, No. 1 (Spring 1970): 187-88.

> Positive assessment of *The Geography of Lograire.*

Gregory, Horace. "Life and Poems of a Trappist Monk." *The New York Times Book Review* (3 October 1948): 4, 33.

> Positive review of *The Seven Storey Mountain* and *Figures for an Apocalypse.*

Hart, Brother Patrick, ed. *The Message of Thomas Merton.* Kalamazoo, MI: Cistercian Publications, 1981, 213 p.

> Collection of critical essays on such topics as Merton's journals, the concept of God in Merton's works, Catholic perspectives on Merton, and the place of Asian religious thought in Merton's life.

The Kentucky Review: A Thomas Merton Symposium VII, No. 2 (Summer 1987): 1-145.

> Special issue featuring biographical and critical commentary on Merton.

Kilcourse, George. "Pilgrimage to Compassion." *Commonweal* CX, No. 20 (18 November 1983): 634-37.

> Includes a positive review of *The Literary Essays of Thomas Merton.*

McSorley, Joseph. "The Cistercians." *The Catholic World* CLXX, No. 1,017 (December 1949): 198-203.

> Discusses Merton's depiction of Cistercian history in *The Waters of Siloe.*

Woodcock, George. *Thomas Merton: Monk and Poet: A Critical Study.* Vancouver: Douglas & McIntyre, 200 p.

> Examines merton's writings in the context of the diverse roles he assumed during his life.

Additional coverage of Merton's life and career is contained in the following sources published by Gale Research: *Contemporary Authors,* **Vols. 5-8, rev. ed., 25-28 (obit.);** *Contemporary Authors New Revision Series,* **Vol. 22;** *Contemporary Literary Criticism,* **Vols. 1, 3, 11, 34;** *Dictionary of Literary Biography,* **Vol. 48;** *Dictionary of Literary Biography Yearbook,* **Vol. 81; and** *Major 20th-Century Writers.*

Sabine Ulibarrí

1919-

(Full name Sabine Reyes Ulibarrí) American short story writer, poet, and critic.

The following entry presents an overview of Ulibarrí's career through 1991.

INTRODUCTION

Ulibarrí is a celebrated Chicano writer best known for short stories in the *costumbrismo* literary tradition. These works combine elements of the oral folktale and local color, depicting the history, manners, and language of the New Mexican Chicano community familiar to Ulibarrí from his childhood.

Biographical Information

Ulibarrí was born in New Mexico. He attended the University of New Mexico, Georgetown University, and the University of California at Los Angeles. He later taught Spanish at the University of New Mexico and chaired the modern and classical languages department from 1971 until 1980. He has written and spoken in support of the Chicano Movement since its inception in the 1960s, and his works display wide knowledge of and concern for the distinctive culture of New Mexico's native Spanish-speaking population.

Major Works

Ulibarrí has written poetry since childhood, and *Al cielo se sube a pie,* a collection of fifty short poems, was published in Mexico in 1961 and later in Spain. *Amor y Ecuador,* a second poetry collection, appeared in 1966. Ulibarrí is best known, however, for his short stories. The collections *Tierra Amarilla: Cuentos de Nuevo México* (1964; *Tierra Amarilla: Stories of New Mexico/Cuentos de Nuevo México*) and *Mi abuela fumaba puros y otros cuentos de Tierra Amarilla/My Grandmother Smoked Cigars, and Other Tales of Tierra Amarilla* (1977) contain some of his best-known works. Set for the most part in the Tierra Amarilla region of New Mexico where Ulibarrí was born, these stories depict the people, mores, and language of the area with insight and compassion. Although Ulibarrí's prose features realistic and naturalistic detail, particularly of landscape and behavior, commentators note that a poetic sensibility informs his fiction. In some stories that antedate these collections, such as those collected in *El Cóndor, and Other Stories* (1989), Ulibarrí combines the *costumbrismo* tradition with elements of magical realism, in which fantastic elements are presented objectively to obscure distinctions between illusion and reality. Many of his story collections, including *Primeros encuentros/First Encounters* (1982), *Gobernador Glu Glu y otros cuentos/Governor Glu Glu, and Other Stories* (1988), *Corre el*

rio/Flow of the River (1992), *El cóndor,* and *The Best of Sabine R. Ulibarrí* (1993), have been published in bilingual editions in both Spanish and English.

Critical Reception

Ulibarrí's introduction of elements of magical realism into his fiction was not enthusiastically received: Juan Bruce-Novoa proposed giving this "interesting, if not altogether successful, synthesis of New Mexican oral tradition and mainstream magical realism" the designation "magical regionalism." Ulibarrí is, however, largely commended for his facility as a *costumbrista.* The bilingual publication of much of Ulibarrí's short fiction makes him one of the most widely-read and accessible Chicano authors in the United States. Donald W. Urioste has written that Ulibarrí's stories "transcend the superficially picturesque and quaint intent of *costumbrismo* to present larger, more universal lessons about life and human conduct."

PRINCIPAL WORKS

Al cielo se sube a pie (poetry) 1961

*El mundo poético de Juán Ramón: Estudio estilístico de la
    lengua poética y de los símbolos* (criticism) 1962
Tierra Amarilla: Cuentos de Nuevo México (short sto-
    ries) 1964
*[*Tierra Amarilla: Stories of New Mexico/Cuentos de
    Nuevo México,* 1971]
Amor y Ecuador (poetry) 1966
**Mi abuela fumaba puros y otros cuentos de Tierra Amaril-
    la/My Grandma Smoked Cigars, and Other Tales of
    Tierra Amarilla* (short stories) 1977
**Primeros encuentros/First Encounters* (short stories)
    1982
Pupurupú (short stories) 1987
**Gobernador Glu Glu y otros cuentos/Governor Glu Glu,
    and Other Stories* (short stories) 1988
**El cóndor, and Other Stories* (short stories) 1989
**Corre el rio/Flow of the River* (short stories) 1992
The Best of Sabine R. Ulibarrí (short stories) 1993

*These works are published as bilingual editions in English and
Spanish.

CRITICISM

Olga Prjevalinsky Ferrer (review date Spring-Summer 1962)

[*Below, Ferrer reviews Ulibarrí's* Al cielo se sube a pie, *focusing on his use of imagery and the emergence of a personal poetic voice in the collection.*]

Fifty poems in search of heaven make up this book [*Al
cielo se sube a pie*] of heterogeneous style and tone. Unity
is achieved through the recurrence of themes.

Static poetry—this might be the definition of Sabine Ulibarrí's production. Quietude intensifies the relevance of a
moment. For Ulibarrí it is the transference of a mood
through lyric adjectivation. And this is so necessary to his
poetry that even in the use of nouns, we feel that they have
become void of essence and that it is only quality that exists and subsists. Thus, in the first poem, concerned with
the snowclad night, by means of the combination "soft-
marble" the noun has come to lose its density and consequently, one of its basic qualities and is left only with its
unuttered whiteness, which is in keeping with the reitera-
tive sequence of the concept of white in each line. Thus,
the noun has been deprived of its substantivity, remaining
with a merely adjectival purport.

Another circumstance of Sabine Ulibarrí's still, at times,
motionless poetry dwells in the lack of verbal forms. Absence of action contributes effectively to concentration on
a state of feeling, and this is what matters. The adjective
carries out the greatest poetical function in Ulibarrí's poetry.

Sabine Ulibarrí is skillful in tracing a decorative representation of the outer world, which is genuine. He may use
words borrowed from woman's environment of arts and

toils and blends them beautifully with his description. Col-
oration is also true and personal. Were he to stop there,
the poem would be perfectly achieved (**"Crepúsculo,"** for
example). However, a certain purposefulness, a self-
imposed language and a will to bring in visceral images,
divert the poem from its real meaning and its original
beauty. Probably less self-conscious motivation would free
it of what is actually alien to it, since breach of harmony
does not necessarily bring about poetical impact.

Some short compositions are written almost in the traditional "copla" form. They are acute, graceful and abundant in the natural and wise poetical figures that have been
used in Spanish folklore. The four line poem dedicated to
Mima contains simple beauty and intricate systems of correlations, parallelisms, antitheses, and designs the symmetrical pattern of a strange solitaire. In this very short
poem appears one of the fundamental themes of this book.
Its first inspiration may have been, whether conscious or
unconscious, that suggestive sentence by our very modern,
seventeenth century poet, Luis de Góngora, "pisando la
dudosa luz del día," "treading the doubtful light of day,"
but it is never said by Ulibarrí the way it had been said.
Half of this book may well be an echo of this verse. This
may be the justification for the cover's design, the contents
of the volume, and the reason, as well, for the title, *To
Heaven One Climbs On Foot.*

We referred before to some kind of visceral transference.
These anatomical allusions to blood, veins, bones, flesh,
toes, appear often in the author's poems, however, without
opening widely the door into surrealistic imagery.

Some poems, and especially **"Mujer imagen," "Vértigo,"**
have a dual and a tertiary rhythm that is extremely satisfying. These poems, like some other ones, enclose an internal
consonance and contain stanzas of an elaborate structure
of correlations, perhaps not apparent at first sight, but
very gratifying.

The play upon words of similar sound, dissimilar meaning, yields casual and curious effects that are agreeable.

The metaphor is very unusual in this book, almost absent.
There is one which has the role of a definition of the cloud:
"nube, fragante quimera del aire."

Poem XLIX, **"Dios carcelero,"** is one of the best of the
book. It could be the last and closing poem. Sabine Ulibarrí ascertains with this poem his authentic selfness. It links
him with an important line of Spanish poets. It definitely
has a "popular" inspiration, and is successful. In his wanderings along the paths, searching for heaven, this is certainly the vein that may take the poet, light-hearted and
bold, to its very threshold, and he remains very much himself, which is, I am certain, for Sabine Ulibarrí the best
way: to be, to peregrinate, to progress.

*Olga Prjevalinsky Ferrer, in a review of "Al cielo se sube a
pie," in* New Mexico Quarterly, *Vol. XXXII, Nos. 1 & 2,
Spring & Summer, 1962, pp. 238-39.*

Thelma Campbell Nason   (essay date 1971)

[*In the following excerpt from her introduction to* Tierra Amarilla, *Nason briefly describes the historical and social context of the work.*]

Tierra Amarilla. Yellow Land. The adjective evokes an erroneous concept of the small Spanish-American village whose name provides the title for [Ulibarrí's] book. Green, not yellow, is the predominant color, for the town lies in a valley cradled in the pine-haired arms of New Mexico's high northern mountains. Equally deceptive is its appearance. Somnolent, unchanging, grown shabby with the years, it impresses the casual visitor as a relic from the past, a sanctuary from modern turbulence. Yet Tierra Amarilla recently exploded into national headlines with an armed raid on the county courthouse. There are indications, too, that this glare of publicity was not merely a transient flash, that the spotlight will focus again and again on this adobe village in its stream-stitched valley.

Tierra Amarilla has never been a peaceful place. The county seat of Río Arriba County whose crowding mountains and high plateaus are snow blocked in winter and isolated in summer, it developed stalwart individualists, proud men of action who lived by struggle. Its history is interwoven with the murky complex of legal and local battles over Spanish and Mexican land grants which, since 1854, have engendered in its people a sense of injustice, envy, and sometimes hatred.

The descendants of the first colonists, who still inhabit the area, are more Spanish than American. Part of the paradox of New Mexico is the fact that the Hispanic heritage becomes more ingrown and more intense the farther it is removed from its colonial source, the "New Spain" or Mexico of three centuries ago. Spanish is the universal speech; in many mountain villages, English is seldom heard. Isolated from the normal development of the mother tongue, this speech is replete with sixteenth-century forms now obsolete in other parts of the world. Like their progenitors, the people are profoundly Catholic. Catholicism, in the words of the author of [*Tierra Amarilla*] is a religion which may be worn either as a silken cloak or as a hair shirt. Many mountain people have chosen the latter garb, with the result that religious fanaticism is characteristic of the area. It is no accident that in these mountains lies the epicenter of the mystic Penitente brotherhood whose sanguinary rituals come to light only in the observances of Holy Week. Neither is it accidental or irrelevant that barn burnings, fence cuttings, and occasional murders practiced by secret organizations preceded for many years the open violence of the Tierra Amarilla courthouse raid of June 1967.

This land and its people provide the background for both the stories in *Tierra Amarilla* and their author, Sabine Reyes Ulibarrí. . . .

Perhaps because it was so different from his adult world, the Tierra Amarilla of his childhood always remained a vibrant reality in the mind of Sabine Ulibarrí. He fascinated his friends with its stories, like that of the legendary white stallion that roamed the mountains or the good and simple priest who kept the townspeople in helpless ag-

onized laughter during his stay among them. Some of his listeners insisted that he write these stories for two reasons. In the first place, they focus on a facet of American life that is passing with no hope of return. Also, it was felt that the profound Hispanicity of this part of the country should be represented by some literary work in the language. Since the stories were written, the light of recent events has revealed a third reason—the need for developing by every means possible an understanding of the region and its problems.

Most of the stories in this small collection are golden with the light of youth. They depict customs and traditions of a bygone day. They portray foibles, injustices, and individuals from a boy's view. But underneath all of them runs a current of understanding, of empathy with the character of these strong, kindly, often violent inhabitants of the mountains of New Mexico. . . .

Welcome, then, to Tierra Amarilla. Here you will meet the descendants of men and women whose fields and houses dotted the banks of New Mexican streams before either Jamestown or Plymouth Colony was established.

Thelma Campbell Nason, in a foreword to Tierra Amarilla: Stories of New México/Cuentos de Nuevo México *by Sabine R. Ulibarrí, translated by Thelma Campbell Nason, University of New Mexico Press, 1971, pp. vii-x.*

Theodore A. Sackett   (review date December 1972)

[*In the following excerpt, Sackett commends the historical interest and poetic sensibility evident in* Tierra Amarilla.]

The new bi-lingual edition of the prose of Dr. Sabine Reyes Ulibarrí, Professor of Spanish Literature at the University of New Mexico and one of the best known American writers in the Spanish language, is a truly important book. [*Tierra Amarilla*] will be treasured by all who can appreciate the beauties of an artistic re-creation of values and a way of life which today are in a process of rapid transformation and perhaps annihilation. Those familiar with Hispanic civilization will be enchanted by Ulibarrí's work. In it they will see remembrances of life in a small village of northern New Mexico; an area which was the site of one of the earliest colonizations of what was to become these United States but which even after its forced inclusion in the Union has always managed to retain its own values and unique personality.

As Thelma Nason points out in her excellent introduction, what makes these works so unusual is the fact that Ulibarrí is above all a poet. His prose is filled with realistic details including aspects of the landscape and customs of Tierra Amarilla, but his vision is not that of a realist. Likewise, though all of the selections reflect the writer's early youth, they are written by an individual who at the time of their composition is a university student and later professor of Spanish literature. The language, form, ideas, and style of his prose spring from the rich and venerable literary tradition of Spain.

The book consists of five short stories and a *novella*. The only points of unity between these distinct art forms are the New Mexican locale and the poetic style. Besides the obvious difference in literary genre, the two kinds of literature presented here also mark distinct moments in the artistic life of the author. The stories reflect sentimental remembrances of Ulibarrí's youth in Tierra Amarilla and are fundamentally poetic in nature. The *novella*, philosophical and abstract, is the product of another side of the writer's personality, the professor and intellectual.

In conclusion, this collection of the prose writings of Sabine Ulibarrí is a unique and important literary landmark. He provides invaluable clues to the origin, identity and values of Spanish and Mexican Americans. But more important still, he does so through the eyes and with the materials of a poet. As a consequence, his writings go beyond the dimensions of the historian or the writer of fiction; they penetrate the soul of his people.

Theodore A. Sackett, in a review of "Tierra Amarilla: Stories of New Mexico-Cuentos de Nuevo México," in The Modern Language Journal, *Vol. LVI, No. 8, December, 1972, pp. 515-16.*

Rudolfo A. Anaya   (essay date 1977)

[*Anaya is a novelist, short story writer, and playwright who is considered one of the most influential authors of Chicano literature. In the following introduction to Ulibarrí's* My Grandma Smoked Cigars, *he commends the characterizations and imagery found in the stories and places them in an oral literary tradition.*]

Those of us who enjoyed the stories in *Tierra Amarilla* have eagerly awaited this new collection by Sabine Ulibarrí. And the wait was worthwhile, for in many ways *Mi Abuela Fumaba Puros* is a continuation of the former. In this bilingual edition, Ulibarrí once again combines the artistry of our oral tradition (which he knows so well) with his personal approach to the idea of story. The transformation which occurs in *Mi Abuela Fumaba Puros* is strikingly original.

Utilizing the author/child point of view, he reveals the memorable experiences of the child to the reader. The child moves through a childhood filled with baroque characters, while the author casually comments on the rites of passage. The result is an interplay and a tension of time and memory, of child and man.

Ulibarrí is a talented story teller, an expert in a tradition which the people of the Southwest have honed to perfection. In *Mi Abuela Fumaba Puros,* he addresses his readers as intimate friends, and invites us to travel with him to the world of Rìo Arriba, wherein he sketches his characters and the landscape with clear and precise images. He skillfully manipulates time, moving back and forth from the world of the narrator to the world of child, drawing us deeper into that time and universe which he recreates.

Life in rural, mountainous New Mexico is revealed in *Mi Abuela Fumaba Puros.* We rediscover the strong sense of daily life and tradition of the hardy pioneers of the land of Tierra Amarilla; we share their joys and tragedies and beliefs. Those who are sensitive to the culture of the Native American and Hispanic Southwest will experience a mild shock of recognition in the stories of doña Matilde,

the horseback ride with death, and the story of El Sanador.

These are stories we have heard before in one form or another, stories which provide intimations of a collective identity. In *My Grandma Smoked Cigars* the personal perspective of the author blends with the elements from that vast storehouse of our culture to produce the story.

Ulibarrí lays bare the emotions of the people, and yet, throughout there is a persistent vein of humor. *La gente* had an immense and ingenious repertoire of humorous stories to while away long winter evenings, and that sense of humor is reflected here. Some are ribald, paralleling the best of this form in world literature. Others are about playful jokes, given a New Mexico context. But throughout, there is the strength of love and sharing which characterizes the people of Ulibarrí's New Mexico.

His earlier book has already become a classic in its own right. Now, with its skillful characterization and artistry of story telling, *Mi Abuela Fumaba Puros—My Grandma Smoked Cigars* should join it as an equal partner.

Rudolfo A. Anaya, in an introduction to Mi Abuela Fumaba Puros y Otros Cuentos de Tierra Amarilla/My Grandma Smoked Cigars and Other Stories of Tierra Amarilla *by Sabine R. Ulibarri, Quinto Sol Publications, Inc., 1977, pp. 8-9.*

Charles M. Tatum   (review date Summer 1978)

[*In the following review, Tatum praises* My Grandma Smoked Cigars *for its sensitive character portrayal and evocatively presented memories of childhood.*]

To his published works of short stories about his native northern New Mexico, noted author and scholar Sabine Ulibarrí adds ten more sensitively rendered tales. In this attractive bilingual edition, [*Mi abuela fumaba puros y otros cuentos de Tierra Amarilla/My Grandma Smoked Cigars and Other Stories from Tierra Amarilla*], Ulibarrí presents a tapestry of childhood memories of life among the hardy and proud *hispanos* of Tierra Amarilla. His stories are a series of carefully drawn sketches of individuals—family, friends, acquaintances—who play an important role in a young boy's strides toward adulthood: the matriarchal grandmother, viewed with a combination of tenderness and fear; Uncle Cirilo, of whose size and mighty voice the child lives in awe; the legendary Negro Aguilar, whose feats as an indomitable vaquero and skilled horse-tamer are reputed in the farthest reaches of the county; the astute Elacio Sandoval, the biology teacher who talks himself out of marrying a woman he does not love; Roberto, who one day goes to town to buy nails and does not return for four years.

With obvious enthusiasm, Ulibarrí shares with us the wide range of the young boy's feelings and experiences: his terror upon finding himself face-to-face with *la llorona* herself; the profound sadness upon learning of his father's sudden death; the proud response to his much-admired childhood heroes when they deign to talk to him. The author draws on local legends and popular superstition and combines them with vivid details from his childhood to create a rich mixture of fact and fiction. His stories are tinged with hues of longing for a past that although he cannot relive, he has brought to life with deft and broad strokes of his pen. The book thus forms a composite of the memories of a writer sensitive to the child in him who looks back to a time of closeness and warmth among people who treated him with understanding and love.

Charles M. Tatum, in a review of "Mi abuela fumaba puros y otros cuentos de Tierra Amarilla/My Grandma Smoked Cigars and Other Stories from Tierra Amarilla," in World Literature Today, *Vol. 52, No. 3, Summer, 1978, p. 440.*

An excerpt from *My Grandma Smoked Cigars*

In my old age I look back on what was the life and history of Tierra Amarilla. Across so many memories, so much sympathy and a little antipathy here and there, there appears in the eyes of my affection a living mosaic, lovely in every way, pleasant in every way. In it there are beloved figures, deeply felt incidents and accidents, remembered lines and contours. Magic colors and masses. Pebbles that shine. Rocks that frighten. Changing light and shadow, sometimes revealing, sometimes concealing, according to the sun, or the moon, or the cloud, or the mist of memory. A human landscape, animated and lively. The palpitating and dramatic representation of what one day was, today is, and tomorrow ought to be.

I am surprised to see in that mosaic something I never saw before. A main theme, among others. Perhaps distance, age or tranquility are necessary in order to see the lilies of the valley. Perhaps one needs a toothache in order to remember one has teeth. If it doesn't hurt you, you don't notice, and you don't care.

Sabine R. Ulibarrí, in his Mi abuela fumaba puros y otros cuentos de Tierra Amarilla/My Grandma Smoked Cigars, and Other Stories of Tierra Amarilla, *A Quinto Sol Book, 1977.*

Francesca Miller   (essay date Winter 1983)

[*In the following excerpt, Miller explores Ulibarrí's style and themes in* First Encounters, *commending especially his portrayal of relationships between different cultural groups.*]

Tierra Amarilla, New Mexico, in which the nine short stories of *Primeros Encuentros/First Encounters* are set, is duly marked on any map of the USA, but it is a place which no longer exists, in the way that none of the places and times of our youth exist. Through the skill of the artist we can recover vanished places and peoples; such is the gift of Sabine Ulibarrí that we can know, and know intimately, a community which most of us have never visited or even imagined. The people of Tierra Amarilla are ranchers, sheep-raisers, Spanish-speaking; settlers whose heritage in this northwestern corner of New Mexico stretches back 400 years. The time of the stories is the early 20th century, a time of change, of first encounters.

Much is being written currently about the southwestern borders of the United States, about the intermingling of the cultures of hispanic and northamerican peoples. Demographers count heads, estimate "legal" and "illegal" migration patterns; public policy pundits project the political effect of an increasingly hispanic population; linguists talk about Spanglish; geographers claim that the area from 100 miles south of the United States-Mexican border to 100 miles north of it constitutes a distinct socio-economic unit, and should be recognized as such.

While not wishing to stem the flow of paperwork or of serious analysis of the border situation, I would suggest that Ulibarrí's modest work offers more enlightenment on the coming together of different culture than a statehouseful of government reports. Moreover, it is written with clarity, in a tone marked by humor and gentle irony.

Ulibarrí's style is spare and poetically evocative. He deftly conveys a sense of a character in a few lines: "Buck Armstrong was tall, strong, and robust. As taciturn as a pine log. It seemed that he went through life annoyed. He never spoke. And had he spoken, no one would have understood him." The inarticulate Buck, a pioneer Americano farmer, and his wife Abigail ("She had something of the wasp about her, something of the butterfly or the housefly."), at length win the admiration of the community for their agricultural skills:

> I don't believe that any of [the family] had ever darkened the door of either school or church. They did not know how to read or write. Their English was almost unintelligible. Their Spanish was non-existent. But they sure knew how to communicate with the earth. Their tenderness, their eloquence, was all for her. The earth understood. . . .

The quality of acceptance, which succeeds the initial scrutiny of the new arrivals, occurs throughout the book. Ulibarrí's narrators relate events as they experienced them in their youth, giving the tales an immediacy of experience, appreciated from the distance of maturity. Thus, when a stranger appears, we see him or her through young eyes which miss no detail, consumed by a curiosity far more potent than suspicion or fear. The possibility for hostility underlies the encounters, yet in most of these tales a key figure acts to deflect that potential, and to make a choice where friendship, or at least accommodation, may result. The choice is often to offer hospitality—a drink of well-water, a bed for the night, the use of a horse. The first story in the book, **"El forastero gentil/The Gallant Stranger,"** tells of an encounter loaded with the potential for hostility or even violence. The narrator is Ulibarrí's father, who was perhaps seven or eight years old at the time of the incident. The boy is standing with his older, grown brothers, and his father and uncles and the hired hands, watching a stranger approach their ranch house. Ulibarrí writes,

> As he approached on the hot and dusty road his figure became clearer. They saw he was a cowboy type . . . his high, white hat was tilted to one side, because of the sun, because of the heat. Jacket and trousers of blue wool, bleached by time and use. High-heel boots. Silver mounted spurs. The rowels left their little tracks and their

clinking on the layer of dust on the road. On his right side, in its appropriate place, he wore a frightening six-gun. He was an Americano.

This classic manifestation of the gringo desperado, even without his horse, could have been viewed with fear and hate. However, the scene is subtly altered as the young boy observes, "Sometimes he stumbled. He would twist his ankle. Those boots with high heels were not made for walking. Cowhands were not born to walk. He would straighten up and continue his way doggedly." Certainly if John Wayne or Gary Cooper had tripped on their spurs, the scene would have been re-shot.

The entrance of the cowboy, and the coming of the Americano settlers into the community of Tierra Amarilla are but the most expected of the first encounters related. In the finely-crafted **"Mónico"**, a young man, born and raised in Tierra Amarilla, has just returned from the university to take a teaching post in San Juan, an Indian town in northcentral New Mexico. He states, "I was the only non-Indian in the parish." **"Mónico"** tells us far more about initial meetings than the trials of the newly-minted teacher. The story is given an historical dimension through the legendary and recorded history of how the town was named. The pueblo had existed from times so ancient that no one could remember the Indian place name, but when the Spanish explorers came in 1598,

> The owners of the lands were so friendly and generous that the Spaniards called their pueblo 'San Juan de los Caballeros.' The concept of brotherhood was established from the very beginning of the Spanish colony in New Mexico. The Spaniards called the Indians 'hermanos' and the Indians called the Spaniards 'hermanitos'. In time 'hermanito' became 'manito'. Even today Mexicans from Mexico perjoratively call New Mexicans 'manitos', not knowing that they honor us with the word.

Mónico, an elderly Indian, helps the teacher learn the ways of San Juan. Years before, Mónico had worked on the young man's grandmother's ranch. The teacher describes the way in which the Indians would come, in his grandmother's day to Tierra Amarilla to trade their agricultural products for the ranch goods of the manitos.

> A caravan came from San Juan twice a-year. They were loaded with merchandise native to the Rio Grande and to the Indians: chile (red and green), corn meal (white and blue), clay pots, fabric, rugs, serapes, baskets, silver jewelry, fruit (fresh and dried). What I liked best were the bows and arrows, the moccasins, the chamois-skin vests embroidered with beads, the feather bonnets, the drums. All things not found in my neck of the woods.

Thus, Ulibarrí moves us over time and place and across generations, building layers of experience, of initial meetings between individuals and among groups, Indian and hispanic, gringo and nuevomexicano, Mexican and manito. And he does it all without ever saying "multiethnic" or multi-anything. Õle/Hooray! . . .

The stories are presented with the English text on the left hand page, the Spanish on the right, an arrangement which allows the reader to glance from one version to the other, comparing the texture of expression in each language. Ulibarrí does not resist bilingual plays on words; in one story, he writes of the proprietor of the general store, Don Tomás Vernes, that "he was known to his customers as 'Mr. Burns'." In another, a boy moves from the family ranch into town so that he can begin school. Though only eight, he was already able to read and write in Spanish, and through his father's reading aloud was familiar with the classics of Spanish literature. The language of the school, however, was English. One of his favorite out-of-school texts was the Denver *Mail*. In need of an English insult to hurl at his playground tormentors, he selected the phrase "Leggo, Rascal!" from the comic strip "Happy Hooligan", noting that Hooligan screamed this seeming threat at his enemies with good effect. In fact, the boy succeeded in making his version of the epithet (Rascaleggo!) sound so awful that he was reprimanded for blaspheming by one of the nuns.

The cover of **Primeros Encuentros/First Encounters** would not have caught my attention in a bookstore: it is a slim soft-covered text, with a brown-on-brown design of two men, one a manito, the other a gringo, shaking hands in front of a giant sagauro cactus. But if you find it and read it, I predict two things: a) you will want to read it aloud with someone you love; and b) you will go look for Ulibarrí's previous collections of short stories, **Tierra Amarilla** and **Mi Abuela Fumaba Puros/My Grandmother Smoked Cigars**. This was my first encounter with Sabine Ulibarrí, and I am enlightened, delighted and enriched by it.

Francesca Miller, "About Latin America: 'Primeros Encuentros/First Encounters!' " in San Francisco Review of Books, *Winter, 1983, p. 7.*

Charles Tatum   (essay date 1989)

[*Below, Tatum presents an overview of Ulibarrí's poetry and fiction, focusing on recurring themes and the author's portrayal of character.*]

Poet, essayist, and prose writer, Sabine Ulibarrí holds an important place in contemporary Chicano literature. In addition to scholarly works, textbooks and thought-provoking essays, Sabine Ulibarrí has published two books of poetry, five collections of short stories, and he has edited another collection of his students' prose and poetry. All of his creative literature was originally written in Spanish although his short stories have also appeared in bilingual editions. When compared to other Chicano writers, his literary output is significant, particularly if one takes into account that he is one of a handful of contemporary Chicano writers who is completely comfortable with written literary Spanish. This fluency with written expression is a reflection of the writer's upbringing in a completely Spanish-speaking environment where Hispanics constituted the majority culture. In addition, literary Spanish was an important part of his childhood for his father would often read Spanish literature to his family. Ulibarrí's academic training and his rigorous study of the Spanish literary masters have undoubtedly reinforced his earlier language background and contributed significantly to his mastery of the language seen in his own creative works.

His two books of poetry, *Al cielo se sube a pie* and *Amor y Eduador,* were both published in 1966 and are similar in content, language, and poetic expression although the first is perhaps broader in its subject matter. In *Al cielo se sube a pie,* using a language the Spanish poet Angel González describes as "pausado y preciso," (deliberate and precise) Ulibarrí includes poetry that deals with love, the woman, his native Tierra Amarilla, uprootedness, solitude, the tragic consequences of progress, life as a transitory state, and several other themes. His poetry is filled with color, finely rendered images, and language carefully selected and appropriate to the content. Dominant in this collection is poetry dealing with various aspects of love: the elusiveness of authentic love; the transitory nature of passion; deceit and disillusionment in the love relationship. In general, the woman/lover is idealized and exists in a more real state in his imagination than in true life. This concept seems to be in keeping with his vision of the illusory nature of love, especially physical love. The poet/male depicts himself, as, on one hand, privileged by her attention, favor, and affection yet, on the other, victimized by her distance and abandonment of him. A related love theme is his belief in the easy conquest of woman. Her willing submission is doomed not to last; only love after sacrifice and intentional effort on the part of both parties will endure. His view of woman in her role as a lover in this collection of poetry is best characterized as distrustful. She is beautiful—as he aptly describes in his series of *pie* poems—but mindless, affectionate and undependable. Her world is a limited one and her view of herself and others is shortsighted. In her relationship to the male she is the source of much of his pain and agony.

Another dominant theme in *Al cielo se sube a pie* is the poet's sense of uprootedness in an alien world in which a premium is placed on success and achievement. In the poem, **"Fuego fatuo,"** he laments having left his native rural Northern New Mexico, having paid the price of loneliness and a feeling of abandonment for less authentic and ultimately less tangible rewards. The poet describes himself as the only member of his family who has left the mountain in pursuit of an elusive star, and while he has tasted success he is still searching for the "cima errante" (wandering summit). Although he is resigned to his self-chosen fate, the poet is saddened when he lets himself remember what he has sacrificed. In **"Patria de retorno"**, ("Native Land of My Return") he recognizes the impossibility of returning to the comfort and security of his childhood home. Although he may be welcomed back by friends and family, nonetheless, he is still a "forastero en mi casa ancestral" (stranger in my ancestral home).

The poet is thus destined to wander the earth on a constant search, waiting for death, filled with hunger for permanence, plagued and saddened by his loss of roots and family. Poetry is his consolation, his vehicle to give expression to life's pain. Artistic expression provides a kind of salve for the poet's wounds and at the same time allows him to eternalize his pain.

As the title indicates, *Amor y Ecuador* has two major themes: poetry focusing on the poet's impressions and memories of Ecuador and poetry devoted to love. In the first section of the book on Ecuador, Ulibarrí shares with us the meaningfulness of his visit to the South American country in 1963. Always the keen and thoughtful observer, he records his visit in a way that allows us to share with him its personal significance. From the first poem, he draws us into the experience of passing time in the Andean country that is geographically so different from his native New Mexico yet has so much in common with it. They share a common heritage and the poet sees Albuquerque and Quito as two poles of the same Hispanic world. Ecuador in general and Quito in particular represent a positive element for the poet, something he has been out of touch with back home. He arrives in the Ecuadorian capital filled with hope and anticipation. He descends from his plane to find himself still in a world of clouds and sky and mystery. In one poem Quito is described as God's work and in another, the first line of each of a six-stanza poem devoted to Ecuador, he repeats: "Aquí todo me humaniza" (Here everything humanizes me).

The expected wonder and awe of Ecuador's rich Spanish-Indian history and its geographical splendor constitute only one aspect of his Ecuadorian poetry. In addition to this sensorial and cognitive awareness of geography and history, the poet is in touch with something deeply human that touches a sensitive chord in him. Perhaps he is at home here as he has not been since leaving his beloved mountainous Tierra Amarilla. The poet lets himself be touched by the people he passes on the streets and by the warmth and welcoming from Ecuadorian friends. He feels rejuvenated, joyful, excited and yet, profoundly saddened and angered by the misery and exploitation that surrounds him. In a poem titled **"Indosincrasia"** the poet reveals these conflicting feelings. The Indian is a reserve of dignity and strength, and at the same time the poet recognizes in his eyes the long history of frustrated hopes and suffering. The poet identifies with this experience and asks his brother, the inhabitant of the high and lonely Andes, to look into his New Mexican eyes where he will see reflected the same suffering of centuries. The poem ends on a note of solidarity and hope; together they can overcome their shared tragic history.

The poetry of the second part of *Amor y Ecuador* seems to have taken on a decidedly more melancholy tone than the love poems of *Al cielo se sube a pie*—this poetry has a bittersweet quality arising from the poet's belief that he cannot have what he wants; love, to him, is elusive, momentary, and even frightening. His own love overpowers him and he warns the beloved to flee lest she be destroyed by it. Images of abandonment, disillusionment after love making, and bitter memories of unrequited love abound. In one poem, he visits the birthplace of a past lover and is filled with the sadness of her absence. For the first time, we see references to sin and guilt associated with the poet's relationships with lovers. Tragically, the poet sees himself as destined to carry with him for life the burden of his guilt; he has altogether given up hope in salvation.

Ulibarrí's prose can best be characterized as a kind of intrahistory, a chronicling and recording of the values, sentiments, relationships, and texture of the daily lives of his friends and family, the Hispanic inhabitants of his beloved Tierra Amarilla. The writer himself has commented that with his short stories he has tried to document the history of the Hispanics of northern New Mexico, the history not yet recorded by the scholars who have written otherwise excellent studies of the region. Ulibarrí believes that these historians do not understand at a deep level the Hispanic heritage that predates by hundreds of years the arrival of the Anglo soldier and businessman in the mid-nineteenth century. He recognizes that the Hispanic world that he knew as a child is fast disappearing under the attack of the aggressive Anglo culture. His stories, then, constitute an attempt to document the *historia sentimental*, the essence of that culture before it completely disappears. In addition to this missionary zeal, his stories are just as importantly his attempt, as a personal objective, to regain his childhood experiences. As reflected in much of the poetry discussed earlier, he feels as though he has been uprooted from his culture and his family and in documenting his memories of a childhood and adolescence in Tierra Amarilla he is trying to resurrect for himself a repository of humanizing experiences. In answering the questions about his people—how they were (are); what it meant to live in an environment where Spanish was the dominant language; the significance of living daily the values and traditions of America's oldest non-Indian culture—he ultimately answers the questions about himself: Who am I? Where do I come from? What have I lost? How much of it can I regain?

Ulibarrí's short stories are more personal than documentary or social history. One looks in vain for explicitly social themes although they may be buried under a rich surface of local color, language, and family and community ties. He explains that he is different from many Chicano writers in that he was raised in a majority Hispanic culture and does not have an ax to grind in creating the world of Tierra Amarilla. This is not to say, however, that he is not socially committed—this side of him is clearly evident in his essays and in his comments made before groups such as the 1967 Cabinet hearings in El Paso.

Most of his short narrations are about individual personalities: relatives and acquaintances, those he knew well and those around whom local legends had developed; those he loved and those he feared as a child. All seem to have affected him strongly and together they make up a whole community of Hispanos from Tierra Amarilla. It is apt to compare both of his collections of short stories to Spanish and Spanish American *costumbrismo,* the literary genre that is characterized by sketches of different regional customs, language, rituals, types, and values. Local color, legends, and personalities are the stuff of his stories as he methodically sets out to recreate this world for us. His stories are not sterile reproductions but rendered so that his poetic sensibility shows through and enhances the sense of excitement and mystery he associates with those memories.

The first story of the volume *Tierra Amarilla* is an excellent example of how the author brings to bear his poetic sense upon his childhood memories. **"Mi caballo blanco"** reminds the reader of another poet, Juan Ramón Jiménez, who immortalized a little grey donkey in his memorable prose poem *Platero y yo.* Ulibarrí describes the magical qualities of a legendary horse that filled his childhood with poetry and fantasy. The young adolescent narrator tells us of the wonder with which he had heard of the marvelous feats, some real, some fictitious, of this unusual animal who roamed the high plateaus with his harem of mares. The horse symbolizes for the adolescent a world of masculine strength and sexuality, a world he is about to enter himself. He dreams of capturing this magnificent creature and parading him around the town plaza observed by lovely and awe-struck young women. He does capture the horse and goes to sleep believing that because of his feat he has finally entered the world of adulthood, yet the child in him remains; the inner excitement and laughter he feels betrays the exterior calm that for him is the proper demeanor for a real man. And when the horse escapes, not only does his fantasy world come tumbling down, but he recognizes that he's still very much a child at heart. He gratefully accepts his father's comforting words and decides that the glorious animal is better left an illusion in its freedom than being forced to enter the real world—the adult world—in captivity. Ulibarrí thus sensitively and skillfully reconstructs a pivotal moment in an adolescent's life—perhaps his own—where the battle between childhood and adulthood is fiercely waged.

The next three narrations of *Tierra Amarilla* are humorous accounts of personalities and the many stories, legends, and half-truths that developed in the community of which they were a part. The first is about Father Benito, a chubby angelic Franciscan friar who was assigned to the local parish. Although well-intentioned and loved by the parishioners he is described as somewhat naive. In addition, he was handicapped by knowing little Spanish. It was his ignorance of the language that was the source of much humor and mischief at his expense. Ulibarrí recounts that Sunday Mass was veritable torture for the parishioners who, anticipating that their dear Padre Benito was going to make a huge blunder during his sermon—he inevitably did when he gave it in his stumbling Spanish—would spend the entire mass desperately trying to keep from rolling in the aisles with laughter.

The third story of the volume is told from the perspective of a fifteen-year-old narrator who recalls how the local town drunk, Juan P., and his two spinster sisters got their name Perrodas. It seems one day many years before, the two sisters were attending a very solemn rosary for a dear friend who had passed away when one of them let pass a substantial amount of air. She fainted. The author speculates that this occurred either from embarrassment or because of the sheer amount of energy needed to contain the air. Only the dead person was not shaken by the explosion. The scandalous event was never fully discussed publicly but soon after it happened Juan and his sisters began to be called Perroda, a play on *pedorra* meaning flatulent. A more serious side of this story is the apparent delight with which the community labeled the family, thus destroying their reputation, turning Juan into a drunk, and dooming his two sisters to spinsterhood. The adolescent narrator is cognizant of this somewhat vicious side of his beloved community. The story also contains another serious sub-theme having to do with the narrator's conflict with his father who wanted him to abandon his books and his poetry to cultivate more virile and more worthwhile—in his father's view—pursuits. The narrator keenly feels this disapproval and goes to great lengths to please him by performing such manly activities as chopping wood.

"Sabélo" is a good illustration of how legends were created in Northern New Mexican communities. Once again, the story is presented by a young narrator—nine years old in this case—who filters reality through his child's imagination to give birth to another character endowed with fantastic powers. The story focuses on Don José Viejo, a sharp-tongued old man who was as ancient as hunger itself. After overcoming his fear of the old man, the young narrator develops a warm friendship with him and an almost religious respect. Don José is gifted with an innate talent for story telling, especially fantastic ones with himself as the central figure; for example, how he killed a huge bear after being badly scratched on the back. But the story that really captures the young boy's imagination has to do with Don José's ability to remove honey from a beehive without receiving so much as one sting. According to Don José, he is not bothered by the bees because, in fact, he is a bee or at least indirectly descended from bees. After swearing his young friend to secrecy, the old man tells him how this came about. His father was kind of a pied piper for bees who rescued them from captivity and liberated them in the forest. His mother was a queen bee who one day kissed her savior on the lips; he magically turned into a bee; they had a child—Don José—who was raised in the hive and then, inexplicably, took on a human form. Further, the scratches on his back are really bumblebee stripes and not wounds received at the hand of the fierce bear. The impressionable child concludes: "Yo me quedé temblando. Yo sabìa que don José Viejo no mentìa." ("I was left trembling. I knew that Don José Viego wasn't lying").

The last story of *Tierra Amarilla* differs in length, form and content from the author's other fiction. Dealing with a number of philosophical themes such as life as a dream, the father-son relationship, the development of the individual personality, the story, which is divided into six short chapters, seems to focus on the struggle of the narrator, an author of thirty years, to free himself from his dead father's image and domination to become an autonomous individual. Alejandro the narrator has returned to his birthplace, a small Hispanic town, to celebrate the completion of his biography of his father. Shortly into the visit he begins to notice that his friends and especially the family members are behaving strangely towards him, but it is not until he sees a reflection of his father's face in a raised wine glass that he is able to explain their behavior. Finally, random remarks made earlier about his resemblance to his father fall into place; somehow he has assumed his father's personality to the extent that others mistakenly are reacting as though he were him. In addition, an inner voice from his subconscious suddenly speaks to him—Alejandro believes he is hearing his own father, especially when the voice tells him, "Desde tu edad más tierna, yo te absorbì, y vivì en ti" ("From your most tender years, I absorbed you and I lived in you"). Here the confusion

between the two personalities is heightened. Are these voices real? Are they the result of the narrator's insecurity about his own identity? Is life a dream? Is he his father's dream? Is he not autonomous? What importance do his own life experiences have in defining and shaping his personality? All of these questions rush over Alejandro leaving him in a confused and vulnerable state. During the remainder of the story the narrator tries to answer these questions, all the while harrassed by what he believes to be his father's voice, which repeats that he wants to eternalize himself through his son. Alejandro falls into a troubled sleep and wakes up suffering from amnesia. He does not remember who he is or who the woman is who tenderly nurses and shows him affection. Although he does partially recover his memory, he remains at the end precariously balanced on the edge of confusion, not fully knowing who he is and not fully trusting that the woman who shows such love for him is really his wife.

With *Mi abuela fumaba puros y otros cuentos de Tierra Amarilla,* Ulibarrí adds to his published work about his native northern New Mexico ten more sensitively rendered tales. In this attractive bilingual edition, beautifully illustrated by artist Dennis Martínez, Ulibarrí presents a tapestry of childhood memories of life among the hardy and proud Hispanos of Tierra Amarilla. His stories are a series of carefully drawn sketches of individuals—family, friends, acquaintances—who play an important role in a young boy's strides towards adulthood: the matriarchal grandmother, viewed with a combination of tenderness and fear; Uncle Cirilo of whose size and mighty voice the child lives in awe; the legendary Negro Aguilar whose feats as an indomitable *vaquero* and skilled horse-tamer are reputed in the furthest reaches of the county; the astute Elacio Sandoval, the biology teacher who talks himself out of marrying the woman he does not love; Roberto, who one day goes to town to buy more nails and does not return for four years.

With obvious enthusiasm, Ulibarrí shares with us the wide range of the young boy's feelings and experiences: his terror upon finding himself face-to-face with *la llorona* herself; the profound sadness upon learning of his father's sudden death; the proud response to his much admired childhood heroes when they deign to talk to him. The author draws on local legends and popular superstition and combines them with vivid details from his childhood to create a rich mixture of fact and fiction. His stories are tinged with hues of longing for a past that although he cannot relive, he has brought to life with deft and broad strokes of his pen. The book thus forms a composite of the memories of a writer sensitive to the child in him, who looks back nostalgically to a time of closeness and warmth among people who treated him with understanding and love.

As Rudolfo Anaya points out in his introduction to this attractive volume, what emerges in all of the stories is a strong sense of daily life and tradition among the Hispanos of Northern New Mexico as well as the bonds of their loving and sharing. Another important element is humor which, while present in his earlier stories, here is more ribald.

The title story is a sensitively created and tender description of the author's grandmother, a kind of silent matriarch who sustained the family for many decades through difficult periods and tragic events. In the narrator's memory her relationship to her husband, although somewhat tumultuous, was characterized by an underlying feeling of mutual respect and fear, "somewhere between tenderness and toughness." The narrator affectionately recalls that after his grandfather died, the grandmother would absent herself to her bedroom after the evening chores were done to smoke a cigar, symbol to the child of his grandfather's power over his family and ranch business and also of his grandmother's longing for her husband. As so many of the characters of his stories, the grandmother seems to represent for the author a graphic and vital connection with his past: his Hispano community, his family, his language, and his cultural roots.

The second story, **"Brujerías o tonterías"** ("Sorcery or Foolishness") is a summary of local legends and characters (endowed with mysterious powers) who were prominent in Tierra Amarilla during the narrator's childhood: la Matilde de Ensenada who was reportedly a witch and go-between—*Trotaconventos*—between lovers; *el sanador* (the healer) another character whose knowledge of the supernatural properties of medicines and animals miraculously saves his uncle from certain death; and finally *la llorona* herself with whom the narrator has a terrifying encounter only to discover later that he had actually run into Atenencia, a mentally retarded woman who would relentlessly pursue her unfaithful husband and scare local inhabitants in the bargain.

The focus of the third story is the narrator's uncle by marriage, Cirilo, sheriff of Río Arriba County. He is described as big, fat, strong, and fearsome, especially from the point of view of the child who felt dwarfed in his presence. Not only did he capture and sometimes have to manhandle criminals, but he also kept the peace at the schoolhouse. On one occasion after the teacher could take no more harrassment from the young devils of students, Cirilo was called in. In a memorable scene, he quells the riot with merely his presence.

The next story is similar in that it also deals with another scandalously loved adventurer, who, most notably, wore no pants when he rode horseback and was punching cows. Other local characters central to other stories are: Elacio the astute biology teacher, who upon finding himself under pressure by her brothers to marry Erlinda Benavídez, arranges for his friend Jimmy Ortega to fall in love with her; Felix and Sally who found the restaurant La Casa KK—known locally as Casa CaCa—, prosper, and then split up; Mano Fashico, Don Cacahuate, Doña Cebolla, Pedro Urdemales, Bertoldo, all imaginary childhood friends from New Mexican folklore who in the words of the author "me endulzaron y enriquecieron la vida entonces y que ahora recuerdo con todo cariño" (They sweetened and enriched my life back then and I now remember them very tenderly).

In the final story of the collection, Ulibarrí describes the brotherhood of Penitentes, the secret religious organization of devout males of the community to whom, only in later years, he attributes their due and recognizes their importance in holding together the Hispano culture of northern New Mexico. It was they who filled the administrative religious and cultural vacuum of early New Mexico to give continuity and cohesiveness to the Hispano population. Ulibarrí cautions the reader not to believe all the exaggerated versions of the Penitentes' secret rituals—although in the story he does refer indirectly to some of their more extreme religious practices such as the ones that occurred during Lent.

As the title of Ulibarrí's third collection of short stories indicates, **Primeros encuentros, First Encounters** focuses on the author's early experiences with Anglos and Anglo culture. While at least one of the selections—**"Don Nicomedes"**—deals with dominant culture racism in northern New Mexico, most present a sympathetic view of the complex process of cultural melding. As in the two previous collections of short stories, the author draws heavily on his memories of growing up Hispano in Tierra Amarilla. Tinged with sadness due to the loss of childhood innocence, his young protagonists struggle to come to grips with their emergence into adulthood. Leaving the haven of the family, they venture forth to find their way in a different, but not necessarily hostile, environment.

"Un oso y un amor" ("A Bear and a Love") typifies this process. The narrator remembers tenderly the joyful and carefree times he spent as a teenager playing with his friends in the woods, his developing friendship with Shirley Cantel, an attractive Anglo girl, and then their separation as their paths divided as young adults.

Ulibarrí portrays Anglos not as flat sociological entities but as multi-dimensional characters with feelings as diverse as those of his Hispano characters. Because he remembers the two groups intermingling freely in Tierra Amarilla, their interrelationships—as in the above study—are portrayed as natural and without racial conflict. This is seen throughout the collection. In **"El forastero gentil,"** for example, an Anglo cowboy—a Texan—is welcomed by a Hispano ranch family. Knowing little about his past, but sensing that he has suffered some deep disillusionment, Don Prudencio, the father, offers him his home and his family's companionship. The author deftly contrasts the stranger's rough exterior to his gentle response to the children. The Texan and the Hispanos develop a deep mutual respect.

This same respect is a characteristic found in other stories such as **"La güera," "Adolfo Miller," "Don Nicomedes," "Don Tomás Vernes,"** and **"Mónico."** Anglos, like Hispanos, are depicted as both good and bad, energetic and lazy, brutal and gentle. Although somewhat idealized, life in Tierra Amarilla is always interesting and varied as characters from the two cultures learn more about each other.

Pupurupú, Ulibarrí's latest collection of short stories, shows two clear tendencies: a return to the nostalgic, memory-laden stories of **Tierra Amarilla** and **Mi abuela fumaba puros** and an incursion into fantasy. **Purpurupú** also contains stories that cannot neatly be classified as either predominantly nostalgic or fantastic, such as **"El juez, mi rehén,"** and **"Palomas negras."**

Stories similar to these in Ulibarrí's first two collections need only be listed here, for they are of lesser interest than those that represent the author's experimentation with fantasy. They are: **"Adios carnero,"** and **"La niña que murió de amor."**

Readers who have come to expect the simply told tales of growing up in and around Tierra Amarilla will be pleasantly surprised to find that Ulibarrí is equally comfortable exploring other literary veins. These stories are rich in tonality and psychological insight.

In **"El gobernador Glu Glu,"** the author creates a mythical land ruled by a buffoonish character, Antonio Zonto Glu Glu, who has risen to his position of power thanks to one remarkable trait: he can not utter a single word against women without biting his tongue and saying "Glu glu." These absurd syllables are somehow irresistible to women who come to adore this nondescript little man. Coached by his wife, Antonio launches his political career as a defender of women's rights, finally winning the gubernatorial election. Soon after, he dies a fulfilled and happy man. The author gently parodies the foibles of politicians and their tendency to seize upon current issues, using them for their own political gain.

"Monte Niko" is the finest example in **Pupurupú** of Ulibarrí's fantastic stories. He imbues the story's ambiance with qualities not found elsewhere in his writing. A fictitious people, the Nikoni, live harmoniously in the valley of Nikon blessed by nature and isolated from others' strife. They worship Talaniko, the god of love and peace, who has rewarded their loyalty and devotion by granting them fertile fields, spiritual tranquility, and leisure time to devote to the pursuit of art and philosophy. Niko, a young man of extraordinary sensitivity and intelligence, is chosen king to lead them. He defeats Peri Yodo, a terrible beast who is the incarnation of evil, gives his people commandments to live by, and dies soon after.

"El conejo pionero" and **"Mamá guantes"** are other stories in Ulibarrí's most recent collection that reflect the same mode as **"Monte Niko."** The first is a playful treatment of a man's friendship with a rabbit, the second is a somber consideration of interpersonal relationships.

As we have seen from the virtuosity and variety of his writings, Sabine Ulibarrí is a salient figure on the Chicano literary scene. In terms of New Mexico, he has spent a lifetime putting into words the essence of Hispano life as he lived and remembers it in Tierra Amarilla.

Charles Tatum, "Sabine Ulibarrí: Another Look at a Literary Master," in Pasó por Aquí: Critical Essays on the New Mexican Literary Tradition, 1542-1988, *edited by Erlinda Gonzales-Berry, University of New Mexico Press, 1989, pp. 231-41.*

Bruce-Novoa   (review date January-February 1990)

[*Bruce-Novoa is a distinguished Hispanic poet and critic. In the excerpt below, he offers a mixed review of* El cóndor, and Other Stories, *maintaining that Ulibarrí's blending of oral folktale elements with the techniques of magical realism is not entirely successful.*]

Ulibarrí, a native New Mexican, is no novice. When Chicano political activism was surfacing in the mid 1960s, but before any major piece of literature associated with it had been published, two books of Ulibarrí's poetry appeared, **Al cielo se sube a pie** and **Amor y Ecuador,** in Madrid in 1966. Thus, some classify him as a precursor, one of a few established writers—including José Antonio Villarreal, John Rechy, and Fray Angélico Chávez—formed before the political activism of the sixties and never associated with the activities or the ideological stance of younger Chicanos. If his poetry supported the image of aloof author in its standard Spanish, personal instead of communal topics, and somewhat international flavor, his short fiction displayed his knowledge of and concern for the communal existence of Chicanos—he would probably call them Hispanos—in his native New Mexico. **Tierra Amarilla: Stories of New Mexico/Tierra Amarilla: Cuentos de Nuevo Mexico** (1971), **Mi abuela fumaba puros y otros cuentos de Tierra Amarilla/My Grandmother Smoked Cigars and Other Stories of Tierra Amarilla** (1977), **Primeros encuentros/First Encounters** (1982) all feature regional and ethnic specificity that belie charges of cultural alienation. In those stories Ulibarrí spoke of and for the Hispano people of his region, often assuming the tone and spirit of the community "cuentero" or teller of folktales.

The new stories are a peculiar mixture of Ulibarrí's personal antecedents—a peculiar and somewhat uneasy mixture. Here, the author has selected non-ethnic topics—for example, a Russian opera singer's reincarnation for ideal love, or a German scientists' creation of a beneficent vegetable Frankenstein, or a Greek goddess-turned-statue, and others. The stories could happen anywhere, but Ulibarrí places them in New Mexico, a detail both superfluous and distracting. The New Mexican setting adds nothing to their development. Even in the story of the Greek statue, where the magical revival of the goddess through the blood of her ardent rescuer recalls the romantic bent of traditional New Mexican folktales, the story's interior logic does not incorporate the local as a necessary ingredient. The same is true of several of the stories. The result is the impression that the author tries too hard to place his region into universal literature, but only achieves it at the simplest level, loudly proclaiming that interesting things can happen in New Mexico too, believe it or not. But to achieve his goal, the author must include information and plot twists that, since they are not necessary to the story, otherwise would be eliminated. The rule of the short story is to eliminate anything not directly related to the development. When Ulibarrí takes time and space to explain the here irrelevant fact of location, he breaks that rule.

His desire to place exotic characters in New Mexico forces this strategy on him. We can ask why it matters to Ulibarrí that a Russian opera singer decide to live in Albuquerque and that her son seek love in Paris? Why must a Greek statue end up in a New Mexican museum? Why must two students study at Harvard, when that detail adds nothing to the plot? Not that these things could not happen in real life—they do and are believable—but short stories are not life, rather literary creations with generic demands. Superfluous material flaws the works. The explanation is that Ulibarrí still functions more as an oral-tradition storyteller than a literary short-story writer, despite obvious literary pretensions. One strategy of the oral-tradition performer is to relate the tale to the audience, often by placing it in their geographic or genealogic spaces. This is legitimate on Ulibarrí's part, but the stories come off as forced, too blatantly manipulated. The most disturbing flaw in the book arises, then, from the uneasy marriage of two similar, yet distinct modes of narration.

When the plot and the setting blend naturally, as in **"El cacique Cruzto,"** the story raises no such distractions. Mythical elements and strange coincidences are fully acceptable, here and in the other stories—readers are so used to what is loosely termed magical realism that Ulibarrí's fantastic plots will surprise no one at this point. When well blended, anything can go into the content; when awkwardly done, content matters little—the story rings false.

Many will consider magical realism the collection's defining mark. Ulibarrí continually mixes fantastic and realistic elements, blurring the boundary between them, a technique characteristic of this type of writing. However, once in a while Ulibarrí underestimates the reader's familiarity with the technique and explains too much. When Damian Karanova reads a letter from his deceased mother in which she speaks of people and events she could not have known, Ulibarrí adds:

> Damian remained pensive, strangely serene, thinking about the new perspectives now opening for him. What he had just read seemed perfectly logical, normal and natural to him. He did not wonder, for example, how his mother could have known twenty-five years before that there was going to be a famous singer by the name Amina Karavelha now and that she was going to give a performance on August 15th of this year. The coincidence in the names did not surprise him either.

A satire of magical realism would permit such a self-relative intervention, but nowhere does the author indicate that we are to read this as satire. The tactics of magical realism are seriously employed; no debunking is apparent, so explanation is uncalled-for and, thus, another distracting flaw.

In fact, **"Amena Karanova"** symbolizes the problems with the entire volume. Amena Karanova arrives in New Mexico by accident, decides to stay, chooses a New Mexican spouse to sire her child, and then dies, leaving the child to realize her failed dreams in a manner and in spaces that relegate the New Mexican elements to the periphery. Even the New Mexican father is a simple tool of the exotic beauty. She constructs a strange altar for her rituals, just as she builds a new room for her son to grow up in. And when the son reaches maturity, he is sent off to Europe to find a fit spouse. New Mexico is a mere setting; the New Mexican father is no more than a drone for the foreign Queen. That strangeness and estrangement permeate the text.

In the title story the contradictions of the good intentions of communal linkage and the misguided privileging of the foreign and exotic over the local come to a head. This utopian revindication of Native Americans by a non-Indian professor from the University of New Mexico could have been set in that state. Native Americans there share the necessary ingredients: an ancient tradition, the memory of independence and relative grandeur, and a condition of economic and cultural repression. Why then must Ulibarrí return to a topic of his earlier poetry, Ecuador, to find a setting? Why indulge the exoticist nostalgia for an Inca empire in South America? If readers are expected to accept the unrealistically simplistic details of a benevolent terrorism and the magical transformation of the New Mexican professor into a reincarnation of an Inca Emperor, could they not be asked to apply their imagination to a U.S. setting? Despite the apparently revolutionary plot, what is ultimately revealed here is the contradictory message of traditional U.S. mainstream imperialistic arrogance and paternalistic liberalism, both in the guise of a Latino superhero.

In **"El Condor"** the Ecuadorian underclasses, both mestizo and Native American, are pictured as unable to achieve their own liberation. Only a sensitive U.S. liberal, who has come to Ecuador for reasons far from political, can realize the extent of the oppression and create a revolution. It is he who will catalyze the native population by destroying the oppressor class, forcing a higher social consciousness among liberals, and eventually rediscovering and revitalizing native traditions. In the end, the U.S. savior becomes so steeped in the local myths and ethos that he becomes the new manifestation of a lost utopia. His physical features themselves metamorphose.

> At the same time that the color and the texture of the hair was changing, other, more radical, changes were taking place. Again the alteration was so slow that no one noticed it for a long time. Subtle deformations in the features and in the bone structure of the skull of the man who had been Dr. Garibay were taking place. The result was that the face of the old professor became the face of the posters that Ottozamìn had one day sketched [to invent the icon of the Inca hero El Condor]. He was rejuvenated entirely. He now had an athletic and heroic look. Sofía went through similar changes. She took on the appearance of an Inca princess, like the ones etched in ancient gold jewelry or painted on the ceramics of olden times. She started calling her lover 'Altor,' which in Quechua means 'king'. He called her 'Altora.'

This is all too familiar to students of Hollywood film, because it repeats one of the standard stereotypical plots about Latin America. Since *Aztec Treasure* (1914), Hollywood has filmed and refilmed avatars of "El Condor" set all over Latin America. Liberal good intentions aside, the result is usually the same: the establishment of an enlightened dictatorship by foreigners who somehow reincarnate the paternalistic dominance of ancient elitism—the Incas invoked here, after all, subjugated many tribes to create their empire. El Condor, having achieved absolute power in Ecuador, moves to a mountain palace, where he holds populist court. "Every day at six in the evening Altor came out on the balcony. The plaza was always full of Indians. He spoke to them of love, brotherhood, democracy, compassion, honesty, self-respect. He spoke to them as if they were children, his children." Latin Americans as children in need of redemption, even after they have been liberated—this is an elitist and colonialistic concept, one that all conquerors of the area have indulged in even as they presented themselves as Christian saviors and champions of democracy.

Perhaps it is too much to ask Chicanos to act outside the mainstream traditions of their country, the United States. One is what he is, and literature, no matter how much one manipulates it for personal ends, betrays underlying truths. Certainly Ulibarrí takes this venture seriously—the story contains intercalated elements from his earlier life—and we must read and criticize it with equal seriousness, and not overlook the fundamental contradictions.

Sabine Ulibarrí has produced an interesting, if not altogether successful, synthesis of New Mexican oral tradition and mainstream magical realism. Perhaps we could call it magical regionalism.

Bruce-Novoa, "Magical Regionalism," in The American Book Review, *Vol. 11, No. 6, January-February, 1990, p. 14.*

Allan Johnston   (review date Summer 1991)

[*Here, Johnston favorably reviews Ulibarrí's* El cóndor, and Other Stories.]

Sabine Ulibarri has worked much in the realm of the folktale and the oral personal anecdote. While such works are effective, they sometimes feel unfinished; the very rough-and-hewn grace that pulls them together consigns them to a specific, limited genre. In [*El Condor and Other Stories*], however, Ulibarri manages, while preserving the freshness of the anecdotal, to take us to places entirely different from those explored in a book like *My Grandmother Smoked Cigars*. Working in the realm of cultural myth, Ulibarri introduces us to a world at once homely and exotic, familiar and fantastic.

Mixing the dominant mythology of our culture with the "myths" of cultural stereotypes, Ulibarri manages to open up both realms with gentle sarcasm. For example, in **"Loripola,"** Ulibarri's send-up of Pygmalion, we find out that tacos, tamales, and burritos are actually the foods of the gods and that earthquakes, thunder, and lightning are the sounds of the gods throwing their "runny-nosed kids" around. **"Cruzto, Indian Chief"** satirizes the conversion of the Indians to Christianity, with its indigenous Christ

and series of miracles, it ultimately links all creation back to art and the artist in a masterful way.

Ulibarri's assaults on stereotypes do not stop with Chicano culture. Amarta and Amarti, sister witches, go to graduate school, become MBAs, and open a dress emporium. In **"The Man Who Didn't Eat Food,"** Helmut Heinz, a benevolent Dr. Frankenstein, makes his monster, complete with social grace and impressive sex organs, with only one glitch—this vegetal-matter man is in fact a walking, thinking potato.

I can't vouch for the Spanish renditions in this bilingual text, but the English versions of the stories offer a wry, dry, humorous mix of the folktale with high-tech kitsch. Through all its inane, insane, and mysterious elements, Ulibarri's *El Condor* offers some unusual reading.

Allan Johnston, in a review of "El Condor and Other Stories," in The Review of Contemporary Fiction, *Vol. 11, No. 2, Summer, 1991, pp. 248-49.*

FURTHER READING

Criticism

Review of *Mi abuela fumaba puros/My Grandma Smoked Cigars, y otros cuentos di Tierra Amarilla,* by Sabine R. Ulibarrí. *English Journal* 71, No. 7 (November 1982): 60.
  Favorable review noting that the stories in the collection appeal to a wide readership.

Torres, Lourdes. Review of *El cóndor, and Other Stories,* by Sabine R. Ulibarrí. *Western American Literature* XXIV, No. 3 (Fall 1989): 279-80.
  Praises Ulibarrí's effective handling of fantastic themes in *El cóndor, and Other Stories.*

Urioste, Donaldo W. "Costumbrismo in Sabine R. Ulibarrí's *Tierra Amarilla: Cuentos de Nuevo México.*" In *Missions in Conflict: Essays on U. S.-Mexican Relations and Chicano Culture,* edited by Renate von Bardeleben, pp. 169-78. Tübingen: Gunter Narr Verlag, 1986.
  Contends that *Tierra Amarilla* transcends the *costumbrista* literary tradition. Noting that the stories in the collection "focus on a facet of New Mexican life that is rapidly disappearing or is already bygone, and nostalgically depict regional customs, manners, language, types, and all the quaint local-colorist motifs that characterize this genre," Urioste maintains that they also present universal truths and themes.

Additional coverage of Ulibarrí's life and career is contained in the following sources published by Gale Research: *Contemporary Authors,* Vols. 105, 131; *Dictionary of Literary Biography,* Vol. 82; and *Hispanic Writers.*

☐ Contemporary Literary Criticism

Indexes

Literary Criticism Series
Cumulative Author Index
Cumulative Topic Index
Cumulative Nationality Index
Title Index, Volume 83

How to Use This Index

The main references

> **Calvino, Italo**
> 1923-1985.....CLC 5, 8, 11, 22, 33, 39,
> 73; SSC 3

list all author entries in the following Gale Literary Criticism series:

BLC = *Black Literature Criticism*
CLC = *Contemporary Literary Criticism*
CLR = *Children's Literature Review*
CMLC = *Classical and Medieval Literature Criticism*
DA = *DISCovering Authors*
DC = *Drama Criticism*
HLC = *Hispanic Literature Criticism*
LC = *Literature Criticism from 1400 to 1800*
NCLC = *Nineteenth-Century Literature Criticism*
PC = *Poetry Criticism*
SSC = *Short Story Criticism*
TCLC = *Twentieth-Century Literary Criticism*
WLC = *World Literature Criticism, 1500 to the Present*

The cross-references

> See also CANR 23; CA 85-88;
> obituary CA 116

list all author entries in the following Gale biographical and literary sources:

AAYA = *Authors & Artists for Young Adults*
AITN = *Authors in the News*
BEST = *Bestsellers*
BW = *Black Writers*
CA = *Contemporary Authors*
CAAS = *Contemporary Authors Autobiography Series*
CABS = *Contemporary Authors Bibliographical Series*
CANR = *Contemporary Authors New Revision Series*
CAP = *Contemporary Authors Permanent Series*
CDALB = *Concise Dictionary of American Literary Biography*
CDBLB = *Concise Dictionary of British Literary Biography*
DLB = *Dictionary of Literary Biography*
DLBD = *Dictionary of Literary Biography Documentary Series*
DLBY = *Dictionary of Literary Biography Yearbook*
HW = *Hispanic Writers*
JRDA = *Junior DISCovering Authors*
MAICYA = *Major Authors and Illustrators for Children and Young Adults*
MTCW = *Major 20th-Century Writers*
SAAS = *Something about the Author Autobiography Series*
SATA = *Something about the Author*
YABC = *Yesterday's Authors of Books for Children*

A.
See Arnold, Matthew

A. E. .... **TCLC 3, 10**
See also Russell, George William
See also DLB 19

A. M.
See Megged, Aharon

A. R. P-C
See Galsworthy, John

Abasiyanik, Sait Faik 1906-1954
See Sait Faik
See also CA 123

Abbey, Edward 1927-1989 ...... **CLC 36, 59**
See also CA 45-48; 128; CANR 2, 41

Abbott, Lee K(ittredge) 1947- ...... **CLC 48**
See also CA 124; DLB 130

Abe, Kobo 1924-1993 ..... **CLC 8, 22, 53, 81**
See also CA 65-68; 140; CANR 24; MTCW

Abelard, Peter c. 1079-c. 1142 ... **CMLC 11**
See also DLB 115

Abell, Kjeld 1901-1961 .... **CLC 15**
See also CA 111

Abish, Walter 1931- .... **CLC 22**
See also CA 101; CANR 37; DLB 130

Abrahams, Peter (Henry) 1919- ..... **CLC 4**
See also BW 1; CA 57-60; CANR 26;
DLB 117; MTCW

Abrams, M(eyer) H(oward) 1912-... **CLC 24**
See also CA 57-60; CANR 13, 33; DLB 67

Abse, Dannie 1923-............. **CLC 7, 29**
See also CA 53-56; CAAS 1; CANR 4;
DLB 27

Achebe, (Albert) Chinua(lumogu)
1930- ..... CLC 1, 3, 5, 7, 11, 26, 51, 75;
BLC; DA; WLC
See also BW 2; CA 1-4R; CANR 6, 26;
CLR 20; DLB 117; MAICYA; MTCW;
SATA 38, 40

Acker, Kathy 1948- .... **CLC 45**
See also CA 117; 122

Ackroyd, Peter 1949-.......... **CLC 34, 52**
See also CA 123; 127

Acorn, Milton 1923-.............. **CLC 15**
See also CA 103; DLB 53

Adamov, Arthur 1908-1970 ...... **CLC 4, 25**
See also CA 17-18; 25-28R; CAP 2; MTCW

Adams, Alice (Boyd) 1926- ... **CLC 6, 13, 46**
See also CA 81-84; CANR 26; DLBY 86;
MTCW

Adams, Douglas (Noel) 1952- ... **CLC 27, 60**
See also AAYA 4; BEST 89:3; CA 106;
CANR 34; DLBY 83; JRDA

Adams, Francis 1862-1893...... **NCLC 33**

Adams, Henry (Brooks)
1838-1918 .... **TCLC 4, 52; DA**
See also CA 104; 133; DLB 12, 47

Adams, Richard (George)
1920- .... **CLC 4, 5, 18**
See also AITN 1, 2; CA 49-52; CANR 3,
35; CLR 20; JRDA; MAICYA; MTCW;
SATA 7, 69

Adamson, Joy(-Friederike Victoria)
1910-1980 .... **CLC 17**
See also CA 69-72; 93-96; CANR 22;
MTCW; SATA 11, 22

Adcock, Fleur 1934-.............. **CLC 41**
See also CA 25-28R; CANR 11, 34;
DLB 40

Addams, Charles (Samuel)
1912-1988 .... **CLC 30**
See also CA 61-64; 126; CANR 12

Addison, Joseph 1672-1719 .... **LC 18**
See also CDBLB 1660-1789; DLB 101

Adler, C(arole) S(chwerdtfeger)
1932- .... **CLC 35**
See also AAYA 4; CA 89-92; CANR 19,
40; JRDA; MAICYA; SAAS 15;
SATA 26, 63

Adler, Renata 1938-............. **CLC 8, 31**
See also CA 49-52; CANR 5, 22; MTCW

Ady, Endre 1877-1919 .... **TCLC 11**
See also CA 107

Aeschylus
525B.C.-456B.C. .... **CMLC 11; DA**

Afton, Effie
See Harper, Frances Ellen Watkins

Agapida, Fray Antonio
See Irving, Washington

Agee, James (Rufus)
1909-1955 ....**TCLC 1, 19**
See also AITN 1; CA 108;
CDALB 1941-1968; DLB 2, 26

Aghill, Gordon
See Silverberg, Robert

Agnon, S(hmuel) Y(osef Halevi)
1888-1970 .... **CLC 4, 8, 14**
See also CA 17-18; 25-28R; CAP 2; MTCW

Aherne, Owen
See Cassill, R(onald) V(erlin)

Ai 1947-................... **CLC 4, 14, 69**
See also CA 85-88; CAAS 13; DLB 120

Aickman, Robert (Fordyce)
1914-1981 .... **CLC 57**
See also CA 5-8R; CANR 3

Aiken, Conrad (Potter)
1889-1973 ... **CLC 1, 3, 5, 10, 52; SSC 9**
See also CA 5-8R; 45-48; CANR 4;
CDALB 1929-1941; DLB 9, 45, 102;
MTCW; SATA 3, 30

Aiken, Joan (Delano) 1924-........ **CLC 35**
See also AAYA 1; CA 9-12R; CANR 4, 23,
34; CLR 1, 19; JRDA; MAICYA;
MTCW; SAAS 1; SATA 2, 30, 73

Ainsworth, William Harrison
1805-1882 .... **NCLC 13**
See also DLB 21; SATA 24

Aitmatov, Chingiz (Torekulovich)
1928- .... **CLC 71**
See also CA 103; CANR 38; MTCW;
SATA 56

Akers, Floyd
See Baum, L(yman) Frank

Akhmadulina, Bella Akhatovna
1937- .... **CLC 53**
See also CA 65-68

Akhmatova, Anna
1888-1966 .... **CLC 11, 25, 64; PC 2**
See also CA 19-20; 25-28R; CANR 35;
CAP 1; MTCW

Aksakov, Sergei Timofeyvich
1791-1859 .... **NCLC 2**

Aksenov, Vassily .... **CLC 22**
See also Aksyonov, Vassily (Pavlovich)

Aksyonov, Vassily (Pavlovich)
1932- .... **CLC 37**
See also Aksenov, Vassily
See also CA 53-56; CANR 12

Akutagawa Ryunosuke
1892-1927 .... **TCLC 16**
See also CA 117

Alain 1868-1951 .... **TCLC 41**

Alain-Fournier .... **TCLC 6**
See also Fournier, Henri Alban
See also DLB 65

Alarcon, Pedro Antonio de
1833-1891 .... **NCLC 1**

Alas (y Urena), Leopoldo (Enrique Garcia)
1852-1901 .... **TCLC 29**
See also CA 113; 131; HW

Albee, Edward (Franklin III)
1928- ...... CLC 1, 2, 3, 5, 9, 11, 13, 25,
53; DA; WLC
See also AITN 1; CA 5-8R; CABS 3;
CANR 8; CDALB 1941-1968; DLB 7;
MTCW

Alberti, Rafael 1902-.............. **CLC 7**
See also CA 85-88; DLB 108

Alcala-Galiano, Juan Valera y
See Valera y Alcala-Galiano, Juan

Alcott, Amos Bronson 1799-1888 .. **NCLC 1**
See also DLB 1

Alcott, Louisa May
1832-1888 .... **NCLC 6; DA; WLC**
See also CDALB 1865-1917; CLR 1;
DLB 1, 42, 79; JRDA; MAICYA;
YABC 1

Aldanov, M. A.
See Aldanov, Mark (Alexandrovich)

Aldanov, Mark (Alexandrovich)
1886(?)-1957 .... **TCLC 23**
See also CA 118

Aldington, Richard 1892-1962...... **CLC 49**
See also CA 85-88; DLB 20, 36, 100

Aldiss, Brian W(ilson)
1925-.................. **CLC 5, 14, 40**
See also CA 5-8R; CAAS 2; CANR 5, 28;
DLB 14; MTCW; SATA 34

Alegria, Claribel 1924-........... **CLC 75**
See also CA 131; CAAS 15; HW

Alegria, Fernando 1918-.......... **CLC 57**
See also CA 9-12R; CANR 5, 32; HW

Aleichem, Sholom .... **TCLC 1, 35**
See also Rabinovitch, Sholem

Aleixandre, Vicente 1898-1984 ... **CLC 9, 36**
See also CA 85-88; 114; CANR 26;
DLB 108; HW; MTCW

Alepoudelis, Odysseus
See Elytis, Odysseus

Aleshkovsky, Joseph 1929-
See Aleshkovsky, Yuz
See also CA 121; 128

Aleshkovsky, Yuz .... **CLC 44**
See also Aleshkovsky, Joseph

Alexander, Lloyd (Chudley) 1924- .. **CLC 35**
See also AAYA 1; CA 1-4R; CANR 1, 24,
38; CLR 1, 5; DLB 52; JRDA; MAICYA;
MTCW; SATA 3, 49

Alfau, Felipe 1902-.............. **CLC 66**
See also CA 137

Alger, Horatio, Jr. 1832-1899..... **NCLC 8**
See also DLB 42; SATA 16

Algren, Nelson 1909-1981 .... **CLC 4, 10, 33**
See also CA 13-16R; 103; CANR 20;
CDALB 1941-1968; DLB 9; DLBY 81,
82; MTCW

Ali, Ahmed 1910-................ **CLC 69**
See also CA 25-28R; CANR 15, 34

Alighieri, Dante 1265-1321 .... **CMLC 3**

Allan, John B.
See Westlake, Donald E(dwin)

Allen, Edward 1948-.............. **CLC 59**

Allen, Roland
See Ayckbourn, Alan

Allen, Sarah A.
See Hopkins, Pauline Elizabeth

Allen, Woody 1935-.......... **CLC 16, 52**
See also AAYA 10; CA 33-36R; CANR 27,
38; DLB 44; MTCW

Allende, Isabel 1942-.... **CLC 39, 57; HLC**
See also CA 125; 130; HW; MTCW

Alleyn, Ellen
See Rossetti, Christina (Georgina)

Allingham, Margery (Louise)
1904-1966 .... **CLC 19**
See also CA 5-8R; 25-28R; CANR 4;
DLB 77; MTCW

Allingham, William 1824-1889 ... **NCLC 25**
See also DLB 35

Allison, Dorothy E. 1949-........ **CLC 78**
See also CA 140

Allston, Washington 1779-1843.... **NCLC 2**
See also DLB 1

Almedingen, E. M. .... **CLC 12**
See also Almedingen, Martha Edith von
See also SATA 3

Almedingen, Martha Edith von 1898-1971
See Almedingen, E. M.
See also CA 1-4R; CANR 1

Almqvist, Carl Jonas Love
1793-1866 .... **NCLC 42**

Alonso, Damaso 1898-1990 .... **CLC 14**
See also CA 110; 131; 130; DLB 108; HW

Alov
See Gogol, Nikolai (Vasilyevich)

Alta 1942-...................... **CLC 19**
See also CA 57-60

Alter, Robert B(ernard) 1935-...... **CLC 34**
See also CA 49-52; CANR 1

Alther, Lisa 1944-.............. **CLC 7, 41**
See also CA 65-68; CANR 12, 30; MTCW

Altman, Robert 1925-............. **CLC 16**
See also CA 73-76; CANR 43

Alvarez, A(lfred) 1929-........... **CLC 5, 13**
See also CA 1-4R; CANR 3, 33; DLB 14,
40

Alvarez, Alejandro Rodriguez 1903-1965
See Casona, Alejandro
See also CA 131; 93-96; HW

Amado, Jorge 1912-..... **CLC 13, 40; HLC**
See also CA 77-80; CANR 35; DLB 113;
MTCW

Ambler, Eric 1909-........... **CLC 4, 6, 9**
See also CA 9-12R; CANR 7, 38; DLB 77;
MTCW

Amichai, Yehuda 1924- ...... **CLC 9, 22, 57**
See also CA 85-88; MTCW

Amiel, Henri Frederic 1821-1881 .. **NCLC 4**

Amis, Kingsley (William)
1922-.. **CLC 1, 2, 3, 5, 8, 13, 40, 44; DA**
See also AITN 2; CA 9-12R; CANR 8, 28;
CDBLB 1945-1960; DLB 15, 27, 100, 139;
MTCW

Amis, Martin (Louis)
1949-................ **CLC 4, 9, 38, 62**
See also BEST 90:3; CA 65-68; CANR 8,
27; DLB 14

Ammons, A(rchie) R(andolph)
1926-......... **CLC 2, 3, 5, 8, 9, 25, 57**
See also AITN 1; CA 9-12R; CANR 6, 36;
DLB 5; MTCW

Amo, Tauraatua i
See Adams, Henry (Brooks)

Anand, Mulk Raj 1905-........... **CLC 23**
See also CA 65-68; CANR 32; MTCW

Anatol
See Schnitzler, Arthur

Anaya, Rudolfo A(lfonso)
1937-.................. **CLC 23; HLC**
See also CA 45-48; CAAS 4; CANR 1, 32;
DLB 82; HW 1; MTCW

Andersen, Hans Christian
1805-1875 .. **NCLC 7; DA; SSC 6; WLC**
See also CLR 6; MAICYA; YABC 1

Anderson, C. Farley
See Mencken, H(enry) L(ouis); Nathan,
George Jean

Anderson, Jessica (Margaret) Queale
.... **CLC 37**
See also CA 9-12R; CANR 4

Anderson, Jon (Victor) 1940- .... **CLC 9**
See also CA 25-28R; CANR 20

Anderson, Lindsay (Gordon)
1923-..................... **CLC 20**
See also CA 125; 128

Anderson, Maxwell 1888-1959 ..... **TCLC 2**
See also CA 105; DLB 7

Anderson, Poul (William) 1926- .... **CLC 15**
See also AAYA 5; CA 1-4R; CAAS 2;
CANR 2, 15, 34; DLB 8; MTCW;
SATA 39

Anderson, Robert (Woodruff)
1917-...................... **CLC 23**
See also AITN 1; CA 21-24R; CANR 32;
DLB 7

Anderson, Sherwood
1876-1941 .... **TCLC 1, 10, 24; DA;
SSC 1; WLC**
See also CA 104; 121; CDALB 1917-1929;
DLB 4, 9, 86; DLBD 1; MTCW

Andouard
See Giraudoux, (Hippolyte) Jean

Andrade, Carlos Drummond de ...... **CLC 18**
See also Drummond de Andrade, Carlos

Andrade, Mario de 1893-1945..... **TCLC 43**

Andrewes, Lancelot 1555-1626 .... **LC 5**

Andrews, Cicily Fairfield
See West, Rebecca

Andrews, Elton V.
See Pohl, Frederik

Andreyev, Leonid (Nikolaevich)
1871-1919 .... **TCLC 3**
See also CA 104

Andric, Ivo 1892-1975 .... **CLC 8**
See also CA 81-84; 57-60; CANR 43;
MTCW

Angelique, Pierre
See Bataille, Georges

Angell, Roger 1920-.............. **CLC 26**
See also CA 57-60; CANR 13, 44

Angelou, Maya
1928-.... **CLC 12, 35, 64, 77; BLC; DA**
See also AAYA 7; BW 2; CA 65-68;
CANR 19, 42; DLB 38; MTCW;
SATA 49

Annensky, Innokenty Fyodorovich
1856-1909 .... **TCLC 14**
See also CA 110

Anon, Charles Robert
See Pessoa, Fernando (Antonio Nogueira)

Anouilh, Jean (Marie Lucien Pierre)
1910-1987 ...... **CLC 1, 3, 8, 13, 40, 50**
See also CA 17-20R; 123; CANR 32;
MTCW

Anthony, Florence
See Ai

Anthony, John
See Ciardi, John (Anthony)

Anthony, Peter
See Shaffer, Anthony (Joshua); Shaffer,
Peter (Levin)

Anthony, Piers 1934-.............. **CLC 35**
See also AAYA 11; CA 21-24R; CANR 28;
DLB 8; MTCW

Antoine, Marc
See Proust, (Valentin-Louis-George-Eugene-) Marcel

Antoninus, Brother
See Everson, William (Oliver)

Antonioni, Michelangelo 1912- ..... **CLC 20**
See also CA 73-76

Antschel, Paul 1920-1970. ...... **CLC 10, 19**
See also Celan, Paul
See also CA 85-88; CANR 33; MTCW

Anwar, Chairil 1922-1949 .... **TCLC 22**
See also CA 121

Apollinaire, Guillaume .. **TCLC 3, 8, 51; PC 7**
See also Kostrowitzki, Wilhelm Apollinaris de

Appelfeld, Aharon 1932- .... **CLC 23, 47**
See also CA 112; 133

Apple, Max (Isaac) 1941-....... **CLC 9, 33**
See also CA 81-84; CANR 19; DLB 130

Appleman, Philip (Dean) 1926- ..... **CLC 51**
See also CA 13-16R; CAAS 18; CANR 6, 29

Appleton, Lawrence
See Lovecraft, H(oward) P(hillips)

Apteryx
See Eliot, T(homas) S(tearns)

Apuleius, (Lucius Madaurensis)
125(?)-175(?) .... **CMLC 1**

Aquin, Hubert 1929-1977. .... **CLC 15**
See also CA 105; DLB 53

Aragon, Louis 1897-1982. .... **CLC 3, 22**
See also CA 69-72; 108; CANR 28; DLB 72; MTCW

Arany, Janos 1817-1882. .... **NCLC 34**

Arbuthnot, John 1667-1735. .... **LC 1**
See also DLB 101

Archer, Herbert Winslow
See Mencken, H(enry) L(ouis)

Archer, Jeffrey (Howard) 1940- .... **CLC 28**
See also BEST 89:3; CA 77-80; CANR 22

Archer, Jules 1915- .... **CLC 12**
See also CA 9-12R; CANR 6; SAAS 5; SATA 4

Archer, Lee
See Ellison, Harlan

Arden, John 1930- .... **CLC 6, 13, 15**
See also CA 13-16R; CAAS 4; CANR 31; DLB 13; MTCW

Arenas, Reinaldo
1943-1990 .... **CLC 41; HLC**
See also CA 124; 128; 133; HW

Arendt, Hannah 1906-1975 .... **CLC 66**
See also CA 17-20R; 61-64; CANR 26; MTCW

Aretino, Pietro 1492-1556 .... **LC 12**

Arghezi, Tudor. .... **CLC 80**
See also Theodorescu, Ion N.

Arguedas, Jose Maria
1911-1969 .... **CLC 10, 18**
See also CA 89-92; DLB 113; HW

Argueta, Manlio 1936-........... **CLC 31**
See also CA 131; HW

Ariosto, Ludovico 1474-1533 .... **LC 6**

Aristides
See Epstein, Joseph

Aristophanes
450B.C.-385B.C.... **CMLC 4; DA; DC 2**

Arlt, Roberto (Godofredo Christophersen)
1900-1942 .... **TCLC 29; HLC**
See also CA 123; 131; HW

Armah, Ayi Kwei 1939-.... **CLC 5, 33; BLC**
See also BW 1; CA 61-64; CANR 21; DLB 117; MTCW

Armatrading, Joan 1950-.......... **CLC 17**
See also CA 114

Arnette, Robert
See Silverberg, Robert

Arnim, Achim von (Ludwig Joachim von Arnim) 1781-1831 .... **NCLC 5**
See also DLB 90

Arnim, Bettina von 1785-1859.... **NCLC 38**
See also DLB 90

Arnold, Matthew
1822-1888 ..... **NCLC 6, 29; DA; PC 5; WLC**
See also CDBLB 1832-1890; DLB 32, 57

Arnold, Thomas 1795-1842 ...... **NCLC 18**
See also DLB 55

Arnow, Harriette (Louisa) Simpson
1908-1986 .... **CLC 2, 7, 18**
See also CA 9-12R; 118; CANR 14; DLB 6; MTCW; SATA 42, 47

Arp, Hans
See Arp, Jean

Arp, Jean 1887-1966.............. **CLC 5**
See also CA 81-84; 25-28R; CANR 42

Arrabal
See Arrabal, Fernando

Arrabal, Fernando 1932-... **CLC 2, 9, 18, 58**
See also CA 9-12R; CANR 15

Arrick, Fran. .... **CLC 30**

Artaud, Antonin 1896-1948 ..... **TCLC 3, 36**
See also CA 104

Arthur, Ruth M(abel) 1905-1979.... **CLC 12**
See also CA 9-12R; 85-88; CANR 4; SATA 7, 26

Artsybashev, Mikhail (Petrovich)
1878-1927 .... **TCLC 31**

Arundel, Honor (Morfydd)
1919-1973 .... **CLC 17**
See also CA 21-22; 41-44R; CAP 2; SATA 4, 24

Asch, Sholem 1880-1957 .... **TCLC 3**
See also CA 105

Ash, Shalom
See Asch, Sholem

Ashbery, John (Lawrence)
1927- ...... **CLC 2, 3, 4, 6, 9, 13, 15, 25, 41, 77**
See also CA 5-8R; CANR 9, 37; DLB 5; DLBY 81; MTCW

Ashdown, Clifford
See Freeman, R(ichard) Austin

Ashe, Gordon
See Creasey, John

Ashton-Warner, Sylvia (Constance)
1908-1984 .... **CLC 19**
See also CA 69-72; 112; CANR 29; MTCW

Asimov, Isaac
1920-1992 ...... **CLC 1, 3, 9, 19, 26, 76**
See also BEST 90:2; CA 1-4R; 137; CANR 2, 19, 36; CLR 12; DLB 8; DLBY 92; JRDA; MAICYA; MTCW; SATA 1, 26, 74

Astley, Thea (Beatrice May)
1925- .... **CLC 41**
See also CA 65-68; CANR 11, 43

Aston, James
See White, T(erence) H(anbury)

Asturias, Miguel Angel
1899-1974 .... **CLC 3, 8, 13; HLC**
See also CA 25-28; 49-52; CANR 32; CAP 2; DLB 113; HW; MTCW

Atares, Carlos Saura
See Saura (Atares), Carlos

Atheling, William
See Pound, Ezra (Weston Loomis)

Atheling, William, Jr.
See Blish, James (Benjamin)

Atherton, Gertrude (Franklin Horn)
1857-1948 .... **TCLC 2**
See also CA 104; DLB 9, 78

Atherton, Lucius
See Masters, Edgar Lee

Atkins, Jack
See Harris, Mark

Atticus
See Fleming, Ian (Lancaster)

Atwood, Margaret (Eleanor)
1939- ..... **CLC 2, 3, 4, 8, 13, 15, 25, 44; DA; PC 8; SSC 2; WLC**
See also AAYA 12; BEST 89:2; CA 49-52; CANR 3, 24, 33; DLB 53; MTCW; SATA 50

Aubigny, Pierre d'
See Mencken, H(enry) L(ouis)

Aubin, Penelope 1685-1731(?) .... **LC 9**
See also DLB 39

Auchincloss, Louis (Stanton)
1917- .... **CLC 4, 6, 9, 18, 45**
See also CA 1-4R; CANR 6, 29; DLB 2; DLBY 80; MTCW

Auden, W(ystan) H(ugh)
1907-1973 ...... **CLC 1, 2, 3, 4, 6, 9, 11, 14, 43; DA; PC 1; WLC**
See also CA 9-12R; 45-48; CANR 5; CDBLB 1914-1945; DLB 10, 20; MTCW

Audiberti, Jacques 1900-1965 ...... **CLC 38**
See also CA 25-28R

Auel, Jean M(arie) 1936-.......... **CLC 31**
See also AAYA 7; BEST 90:4; CA 103; CANR 21

Auerbach, Erich 1892-1957 .... **TCLC 43**
See also CA 118

Augier, Emile 1820-1889 .... **NCLC 31**

August, John
See De Voto, Bernard (Augustine)

Augustine, St. 354-430 .... **CMLC 6**

Aurelius
See Bourne, Randolph S(illiman)

Austen, Jane
1775-1817 .... NCLC 1, 13, 19, 33; DA;
WLC
See also CDBLB 1789-1832; DLB 116

Auster, Paul 1947- .... CLC 47
See also CA 69-72; CANR 23

Austin, Frank
See Faust, Frederick (Schiller)

Austin, Mary (Hunter)
1868-1934 .... TCLC 25
See also CA 109; DLB 9, 78

Autran Dourado, Waldomiro
See Dourado, (Waldomiro Freitas) Autran

Averroes 1126-1198 .... CMLC 7
See also DLB 115

Avison, Margaret 1918- .... CLC 2, 4
See also CA 17-20R; DLB 53; MTCW

Axton, David
See Koontz, Dean R(ay)

Ayckbourn, Alan
1939- .... CLC 5, 8, 18, 33, 74
See also CA 21-24R; CANR 31; DLB 13;
MTCW

Aydy, Catherine
See Tennant, Emma (Christina)

Ayme, Marcel (Andre) 1902-1967... CLC 11
See also CA 89-92; CLR 25; DLB 72

Ayrton, Michael 1921-1975 .... CLC 7
See also CA 5-8R; 61-64; CANR 9, 21

Azorin............................ CLC 11
See also Martinez Ruiz, Jose

Azuela, Mariano
1873-1952 .... TCLC 3; HLC
See also CA 104; 131; HW; MTCW

Baastad, Babbis Friis
See Friis-Baastad, Babbis Ellinor

Bab
See Gilbert, W(illiam) S(chwenck)

Babbis, Eleanor
See Friis-Baastad, Babbis Ellinor

Babel, Isaak (Emmanuilovich)
1894-1941(?) .... TCLC 2, 13
See also CA 104

Babits, Mihaly 1883-1941 .... TCLC 14
See also CA 114

Babur 1483-1530.................. LC 18

Bacchelli, Riccardo 1891-1985 ..... CLC 19
See also CA 29-32R; 117

Bach, Richard (David) 1936-....... CLC 14
See also AITN 1; BEST 89:2; CA 9-12R;
CANR 18; MTCW; SATA 13

Bachman, Richard
See King, Stephen (Edwin)

Bachmann, Ingeborg 1926-1973..... CLC 69
See also CA 93-96; 45-48; DLB 85

Bacon, Francis 1561-1626 .... LC 18
See also CDBLB Before 1660

Bacovia, George................. TCLC 24
See also Vasiliu, Gheorghe

Badanes, Jerome 1937-............ CLC 59

Bagehot, Walter 1826-1877 ...... NCLC 10
See also DLB 55

Bagnold, Enid 1889-1981 .... CLC 25
See also CA 5-8R; 103; CANR 5, 40;
DLB 13; MAICYA; SATA 1, 25

Bagrjana, Elisaveta
See Belcheva, Elisaveta

Bagryana, Elisaveta
See Belcheva, Elisaveta

Bailey, Paul 1937- .... CLC 45
See also CA 21-24R; CANR 16; DLB 14

Baillie, Joanna 1762-1851 .... NCLC 2
See also DLB 93

Bainbridge, Beryl (Margaret)
1933- .... CLC 4, 5, 8, 10, 14, 18, 22, 62
See also CA 21-24R; CANR 24; DLB 14;
MTCW

Baker, Elliott 1922- .... CLC 8
See also CA 45-48; CANR 2

Baker, Nicholson 1957- .... CLC 61
See also CA 135

Baker, Ray Stannard 1870-1946... TCLC 47
See also CA 118

Baker, Russell (Wayne) 1925-...... CLC 31
See also BEST 89:4; CA 57-60; CANR 11,
41; MTCW

Bakhtin, M.
See Bakhtin, Mikhail Mikhailovich

Bakhtin, M. M.
See Bakhtin, Mikhail Mikhailovich

Bakhtin, Mikhail
See Bakhtin, Mikhail Mikhailovich

Bakhtin, Mikhail Mikhailovich
1895-1975 .... CLC 83
See also CA 128; 113

Bakshi, Ralph 1938(?)-............ CLC 26
See also CA 112; 138

Bakunin, Mikhail (Alexandrovich)
1814-1876 .... NCLC 25

Baldwin, James (Arthur)
1924-1987 ...... CLC 1, 2, 3, 4, 5, 8, 13,
15, 17, 42, 50, 67; BLC; DA; DC 1;
SSC 10; WLC
See also AAYA 4; BW 1; CA 1-4R; 124;
CABS 1; CANR 3, 24;
CDALB 1941-1968; DLB 2, 7, 33;
DLBY 87; MTCW; SATA 9, 54

Ballard, J(ames) G(raham)
1930- .... CLC 3, 6, 14, 36; SSC 1
See also AAYA 3; CA 5-8R; CANR 15, 39;
DLB 14; MTCW

Balmont, Konstantin (Dmitriyevich)
1867-1943 .... TCLC 11
See also CA 109

Balzac, Honore de
1799-1850 .... NCLC 5, 35; DA; SSC 5;
WLC
See also DLB 119

Bambara, Toni Cade
1939- .... CLC 19; BLC; DA
See also AAYA 5; BW 2; CA 29-32R;
CANR 24; DLB 38; MTCW

Bamdad, A.
See Shamlu, Ahmad

Banat, D. R.
See Bradbury, Ray (Douglas)

Bancroft, Laura
See Baum, L(yman) Frank

Banim, John 1798-1842 .... NCLC 13
See also DLB 116

Banim, Michael 1796-1874 ...... NCLC 13

Banks, Iain
See Banks, Iain M(enzies)

Banks, Iain M(enzies) 1954- .... CLC 34
See also CA 123; 128

Banks, Lynne Reid .... CLC 23
See also Reid Banks, Lynne
See also AAYA 6

Banks, Russell 1940- .... CLC 37, 72
See also CA 65-68; CAAS 15; CANR 19;
DLB 130

Banville, John 1945-.............. CLC 46
See also CA 117; 128; DLB 14

Banville, Theodore (Faullain) de
1832-1891 .... NCLC 9

Baraka, Amiri
1934- .... CLC 1, 2, 3, 5, 10, 14, 33;
BLC; DA; PC 4
See also Jones, LeRoi
See also BW 2; CA 21-24R; CABS 3;
CANR 27, 38; CDALB 1941-1968;
DLB 5, 7, 16, 38; DLBD 8; MTCW

Barbellion, W. N. P.............. TCLC 24
See also Cummings, Bruce F(rederick)

Barbera, Jack 1945-.............. CLC 44
See also CA 110

Barbey d'Aurevilly, Jules Amedee
1808-1889 .... NCLC 1
See also DLB 119

Barbusse, Henri 1873-1935 .... TCLC 5
See also CA 105; DLB 65

Barclay, Bill
See Moorcock, Michael (John)

Barclay, William Ewert
See Moorcock, Michael (John)

Barea, Arturo 1897-1957 .... TCLC 14
See also CA 111

Barfoot, Joan 1946- .... CLC 18
See also CA 105

Baring, Maurice 1874-1945 .... TCLC 8
See also CA 105; DLB 34

Barker, Clive 1952- .... CLC 52
See also AAYA 10; BEST 90:3; CA 121;
129; MTCW

Barker, George Granville
1913-1991 .... CLC 8, 48
See also CA 9-12R; 135; CANR 7, 38;
DLB 20; MTCW

Barker, Harley Granville
See Granville-Barker, Harley
See also DLB 10

Barker, Howard 1946-............ CLC 37
See also CA 102; DLB 13

Barker, Pat 1943-................ CLC 32
See also CA 117; 122

Barlow, Joel 1754-1812 .... NCLC 23
See also DLB 37

Barnard, Mary (Ethel) 1909-....... CLC 48
See also CA 21-22; CAP 2

Barnes, Djuna
1892-1982 ... **CLC 3, 4, 8, 11, 29; SSC 3**
See also CA 9-12R; 107; CANR 16; DLB 4, 9, 45; MTCW

Barnes, Julian 1946-............. **CLC 42**
See also CA 102; CANR 19; DLBY 93

Barnes, Peter 1931- .... **CLC 5, 56**
See also CA 65-68; CAAS 12; CANR 33, 34; DLB 13; MTCW

Baroja (y Nessi), Pio
1872-1956 .... **TCLC 8; HLC**
See also CA 104

Baron, David
See Pinter, Harold

Baron Corvo
See Rolfe, Frederick (William Serafino Austin Lewis Mary)

Barondess, Sue K(aufman)
1926-1977 .... **CLC 8**
See also Kaufman, Sue
See also CA 1-4R; 69-72; CANR 1

Baron de Teive
See Pessoa, Fernando (Antonio Nogueira)

Barres, Maurice 1862-1923 .... **TCLC 47**
See also DLB 123

Barreto, Afonso Henrique de Lima
See Lima Barreto, Afonso Henrique de

Barrett, (Roger) Syd 1946- .... **CLC 35**
See also Pink Floyd

Barrett, William (Christopher)
1913-1992 .... **CLC 27**
See also CA 13-16R; 139; CANR 11

Barrie, J(ames) M(atthew)
1860-1937 .... **TCLC 2**
See also CA 104; 136; CDBLB 1890-1914; CLR 16; DLB 10, 141; MAICYA; YABC 1

Barrington, Michael
See Moorcock, Michael (John)

Barrol, Grady
See Bograd, Larry

Barry, Mike
See Malzberg, Barry N(athaniel)

Barry, Philip 1896-1949......... **TCLC 11**
See also CA 109; DLB 7

Bart, Andre Schwarz
See Schwarz-Bart, Andre

Barth, John (Simmons)
1930- ...... **CLC 1, 2, 3, 5, 7, 9, 10, 14, 27, 51; SSC 10**
See also AITN 1, 2; CA 1-4R; CABS 1; CANR 5, 23; DLB 2; MTCW

Barthelme, Donald
1931-1989 ...... **CLC 1, 2, 3, 5, 6, 8, 13, 23, 46, 59; SSC 2**
See also CA 21-24R; 129; CANR 20; DLB 2; DLBY 80, 89; MTCW; SATA 7, 62

Barthelme, Frederick 1943-........ **CLC 36**
See also CA 114; 122; DLBY 85

Barthes, Roland (Gerard)
1915-1980 .... **CLC 24, 83**
See also CA 130; 97-100; MTCW

Barzun, Jacques (Martin) 1907- .... **CLC 51**
See also CA 61-64; CANR 22

Bashevis, Isaac
See Singer, Isaac Bashevis

Bashkirtseff, Marie 1859-1884 ... **NCLC 27**

Basho
See Matsuo Basho

Bass, Kingsley B., Jr.
See Bullins, Ed

Bass, Rick 1958-................. **CLC 79**
See also CA 126

Bassani, Giorgio 1916-............. **CLC 9**
See also CA 65-68; CANR 33; DLB 128; MTCW

Bastos, Augusto (Antonio) Roa
See Roa Bastos, Augusto (Antonio)

Bataille, Georges 1897-1962 .... **CLC 29**
See also CA 101; 89-92

Bates, H(erbert) E(rnest)
1905-1974 .... **CLC 46; SSC 10**
See also CA 93-96; 45-48; CANR 34; MTCW

Bauchart
See Camus, Albert

Baudelaire, Charles
1821-1867 ..... **NCLC 6, 29; DA; PC 1; WLC**

Baudrillard, Jean 1929-........... **CLC 60**

Baum, L(yman) Frank 1856-1919 ... **TCLC 7**
See also CA 108; 133; CLR 15; DLB 22; JRDA; MAICYA; MTCW; SATA 18

Baum, Louis F.
See Baum, L(yman) Frank

Baumbach, Jonathan 1933- ...... **CLC 6, 23**
See also CA 13-16R; CAAS 5; CANR 12; DLBY 80; MTCW

Bausch, Richard (Carl) 1945- ...... **CLC 51**
See also CA 101; CAAS 14; CANR 43; DLB 130

Baxter, Charles 1947-......... **CLC 45, 78**
See also CA 57-60; CANR 40; DLB 130

Baxter, George Owen
See Faust, Frederick (Schiller)

Baxter, James K(eir) 1926-1972 .... **CLC 14**
See also CA 77-80

Baxter, John
See Hunt, E(verette) Howard, Jr.

Bayer, Sylvia
See Glassco, John

Beagle, Peter S(oyer) 1939-........ **CLC 7**
See also CA 9-12R; CANR 4; DLBY 80; SATA 60

Bean, Normal
See Burroughs, Edgar Rice

Beard, Charles A(ustin)
1874-1948 .... **TCLC 15**
See also CA 115; DLB 17; SATA 18

Beardsley, Aubrey 1872-1898 ..... **NCLC 6**

Beattie, Ann
1947- .... **CLC 8, 13, 18, 40, 63; SSC 11**
See also BEST 90:2; CA 81-84; DLBY 82; MTCW

Beattie, James 1735-1803 .... **NCLC 25**
See also DLB 109

Beauchamp, Kathleen Mansfield 1888-1923
See Mansfield, Katherine
See also CA 104; 134; DA

Beaumarchais, Pierre-Augustin Caron de
1732-1799 .... **DC 4**

Beauvoir, Simone (Lucie Ernestine Marie Bertrand) de
1908-1986 .... **CLC 1, 2, 4, 8, 14, 31, 44, 50, 71; DA; WLC**
See also CA 9-12R; 118; CANR 28; DLB 72; DLBY 86; MTCW

Becker, Jurek 1937-............ **CLC 7, 19**
See also CA 85-88; DLB 75

Becker, Walter 1950-............. **CLC 26**

Beckett, Samuel (Barclay)
1906-1989 ...... **CLC 1, 2, 3, 4, 6, 9, 10, 11, 14, 18, 29, 57, 59, 83; DA; WLC**
See also CA 5-8R; 130; CANR 33; CDBLB 1945-1960; DLB 13, 15; DLBY 90; MTCW

Beckford, William 1760-1844 .... **NCLC 16**
See also DLB 39

Beckman, Gunnel 1910-......... **CLC 26**
See also CA 33-36R; CANR 15; CLR 25; MAICYA; SAAS 9; SATA 6

Becque, Henri 1837-1899......... **NCLC 3**

Beddoes, Thomas Lovell
1803-1849 .... **NCLC 3**
See also DLB 96

Bedford, Donald F.
See Fearing, Kenneth (Flexner)

Beecher, Catharine Esther
1800-1878 .... **NCLC 30**
See also DLB 1

Beecher, John 1904-1980........... **CLC 6**
See also AITN 1; CA 5-8R; 105; CANR 8

Beer, Johann 1655-1700............. **LC 5**

Beer, Patricia 1924-............... **CLC 58**
See also CA 61-64; CANR 13; DLB 40

Beerbohm, Henry Maximilian
1872-1956 .... **TCLC 1, 24**
See also CA 104; DLB 34, 100

Begiebing, Robert J(ohn) 1946-..... **CLC 70**
See also CA 122; CANR 40

Behan, Brendan
1923-1964 .... **CLC 1, 8, 11, 15, 79**
See also CA 73-76; CANR 33; CDBLB 1945-1960; DLB 13; MTCW

Behn, Aphra
1640(?)-1689 .... **LC 1; DA; DC 4; WLC**
See also DLB 39, 80, 131

Behrman, S(amuel) N(athaniel)
1893-1973 .... **CLC 40**
See also CA 13-16; 45-48; CAP 1; DLB 7, 44

Belasco, David 1853-1931 .... **TCLC 3**
See also CA 104; DLB 7

Belcheva, Elisaveta 1893- .... **CLC 10**

Beldone, Phil "Cheech"
See Ellison, Harlan

Beleno
See Azuela, Mariano

Belinski, Vissarion Grigoryevich
1811-1848 .... **NCLC 5**

Betjeman, John
        1906-1984 . . . . **CLC 2, 6, 10, 34, 43**
        See also CA 9-12R; 112; CANR 33;
        CDBLB 1945-1960; DLB 20; DLBY 84;
        MTCW

Bettelheim, Bruno 1903-1990 . . . . . . **CLC 79**
        See also CA 81-84; 131; CANR 23; MTCW

Betti, Ugo 1892-1953 . . . . **TCLC 5**
        See also CA 104

Betts, Doris (Waugh) 1932- . . . . **CLC 3, 6, 28**
        See also CA 13-16R; CANR 9; DLBY 82

Bevan, Alistair
        See Roberts, Keith (John Kingston)

Beynon, John
        See Harris, John (Wyndham Parkes Lucas)
        Beynon

Bialik, Chaim Nachman
        1873-1934 . . . . **TCLC 25**

Bickerstaff, Isaac
        See Swift, Jonathan

Bidart, Frank 1939- . . . . **CLC 33**
        See also CA 140

Bienek, Horst 1930- . . . . **CLC 7, 11**
        See also CA 73-76; DLB 75

Bierce, Ambrose (Gwinett)
        1842-1914(?) . . . . **TCLC 1, 7, 44; DA;**
                                                SSC 9; WLC
        See also CA 104; 139; CDALB 1865-1917;
        DLB 11, 12, 23, 71, 74

Billings, Josh
        See Shaw, Henry Wheeler

Billington, (Lady) Rachel (Mary)
        1942- . . . . **CLC 43**
        See also AITN 2; CA 33-36R; CANR 44

Binyon, T(imothy) J(ohn) 1936- . . . . **CLC 34**
        See also CA 111; CANR 28

Bioy Casares, Adolfo
        1914- . . . . **CLC 4, 8, 13; HLC**
        See also CA 29-32R; CANR 19, 43;
        DLB 113; HW; MTCW

Bird, C.
        See Ellison, Harlan

Bird, Cordwainer
        See Ellison, Harlan

Bird, Robert Montgomery
        1806-1854 . . . . **NCLC 1**

Birney, (Alfred) Earle
        1904- . . . . **CLC 1, 4, 6, 11**
        See also CA 1-4R; CANR 5, 20; DLB 88;
        MTCW

Bishop, Elizabeth
        1911-1979 . . . . . . **CLC 1, 4, 9, 13, 15, 32;**
                                                DA; PC 3
        See also CA 5-8R; 89-92; CABS 2;
        CANR 26; CDALB 1968-1988; DLB 5;
        MTCW; SATA 24

Bishop, John 1935- . . . . **CLC 10**
        See also CA 105

Bissett, Bill 1939- . . . . **CLC 18**
        See also CA 69-72; CAAS 19; CANR 15;
        DLB 53; MTCW

Bitov, Andrei (Georgievich) 1937- . . . **CLC 57**
        See also CA 142

Biyidi, Alexandre 1932-
        See Beti, Mongo
        See also BW 1; CA 114; 124; MTCW

Bjarme, Brynjolf
        See Ibsen, Henrik (Johan)

Bjornson, Bjornstjerne (Martinius)
        1832-1910 . . . . **TCLC 7, 37**
        See also CA 104

Black, Robert
        See Holdstock, Robert P.

Blackburn, Paul 1926-1971 . . . . . . **CLC 9, 43**
        See also CA 81-84; 33-36R; CANR 34;
        DLB 16; DLBY 81

Black Elk 1863-1950 . . . . **TCLC 33**
        See also CA 144

Black Hobart
        See Sanders, (James) Ed(ward)

Blacklin, Malcolm
        See Chambers, Aidan

Blackmore, R(ichard) D(oddridge)
        1825-1900 . . . . **TCLC 27**
        See also CA 120; DLB 18

Blackmur, R(ichard) P(almer)
        1904-1965 . . . . **CLC 2, 24**
        See also CA 11-12; 25-28R; CAP 1; DLB 63

Black Tarantula, The
        See Acker, Kathy

Blackwood, Algernon (Henry)
        1869-1951 . . . . **TCLC 5**
        See also CA 105

Blackwood, Caroline 1931- . . . . **CLC 6, 9**
        See also CA 85-88; CANR 32; DLB 14;
        MTCW

Blade, Alexander
        See Hamilton, Edmond; Silverberg, Robert

Blaga, Lucian 1895-1961 . . . . **CLC 75**

Blair, Eric (Arthur) 1903-1950
        See Orwell, George
        See also CA 104; 132; DA; MTCW;
        SATA 29

Blais, Marie-Claire
        1939- . . . . **CLC 2, 4, 6, 13, 22**
        See also CA 21-24R; CAAS 4; CANR 38;
        DLB 53; MTCW

Blaise, Clark 1940- . . . . **CLC 29**
        See also AITN 2; CA 53-56; CAAS 3;
        CANR 5; DLB 53

Blake, Nicholas
        See Day Lewis, C(ecil)
        See also DLB 77

Blake, William
        1757-1827 . . . . . **NCLC 13, 37; DA; WLC**
        See also CDBLB 1789-1832; DLB 93;
        MAICYA; SATA 30

Blasco Ibanez, Vicente
        1867-1928 . . . . **TCLC 12**
        See also CA 110; 131; HW; MTCW

Blatty, William Peter 1928- . . . . **CLC 2**
        See also CA 5-8R; CANR 9

Bleeck, Oliver
        See Thomas, Ross (Elmore)

Blessing, Lee 1949- . . . . **CLC 54**

Blish, James (Benjamin)
        1921-1975 . . . . **CLC 14**
        See also CA 1-4R; 57-60; CANR 3; DLB 8;
        MTCW; SATA 66

Bliss, Reginald
        See Wells, H(erbert) G(eorge)

Blixen, Karen (Christentze Dinesen)
        1885-1962
        See Dinesen, Isak
        See also CA 25-28; CANR 22; CAP 2;
        MTCW; SATA 44

Bloch, Robert (Albert) 1917- . . . . **CLC 33**
        See also CA 5-8R; CANR 5; DLB 44;
        SATA 12

Blok, Alexander (Alexandrovich)
        1880-1921 . . . . **TCLC 5**
        See also CA 104

Blom, Jan
        See Breytenbach, Breyten

Bloom, Harold 1930- . . . . **CLC 24**
        See also CA 13-16R; CANR 39; DLB 67

Bloomfield, Aurelius
        See Bourne, Randolph S(illiman)

Blount, Roy (Alton), Jr. 1941- . . . . . **CLC 38**
        See also CA 53-56; CANR 10, 28; MTCW

Bloy, Leon 1846-1917 . . . . **TCLC 22**
        See also CA 121; DLB 123

Blume, Judy (Sussman) 1938- . . . **CLC 12, 30**
        See also AAYA 3; CA 29-32R; CANR 13,
        37; CLR 2, 15; DLB 52; JRDA;
        MAICYA; MTCW; SATA 2, 31

Blunden, Edmund (Charles)
        1896-1974 . . . . **CLC 2, 56**
        See also CA 17-18; 45-48; CAP 2; DLB 20,
        100; MTCW

Bly, Robert (Elwood)
        1926- . . . . **CLC 1, 2, 5, 10, 15, 38**
        See also CA 5-8R; CANR 41; DLB 5;
        MTCW

Bobette
        See Simenon, Georges (Jacques Christian)

Boccaccio, Giovanni
        1313-1375 . . . . **CMLC 13; SSC 10**

Bochco, Steven 1943- . . . . **CLC 35**
        See also AAYA 11; CA 124; 138

Bodenheim, Maxwell 1892-1954 . . . **TCLC 44**
        See also CA 110; DLB 9, 45

Bodker, Cecil 1927- . . . . **CLC 21**
        See also CA 73-76; CANR 13, 44; CLR 23;
        MAICYA; SATA 14

Boell, Heinrich (Theodor) 1917-1985
        See Boll, Heinrich (Theodor)
        See also CA 21-24R; 116; CANR 24; DA;
        DLB 69; DLBY 85; MTCW

Boerne, Alfred
        See Doeblin, Alfred

Bogan, Louise 1897-1970 . . . . . . **CLC 4, 39, 46**
        See also CA 73-76; 25-28R; CANR 33;
        DLB 45; MTCW

Bogarde, Dirk . . . . **CLC 19**
        See also Van Den Bogarde, Derek Jules
        Gaspard Ulric Niven
        See also DLB 14

Bogosian, Eric 1953- . . . . **CLC 45**
        See also CA 138

Bograd, Larry 1953-.............. **CLC 35**
See also CA 93-96; SATA 33

Boiardo, Matteo Maria 1441-1494 .... **LC 6**

Boileau-Despreaux, Nicolas
1636-1711 .... **LC 3**

Boland, Eavan (Aisling) 1944-... **CLC 40, 67**
See also CA 143; DLB 40

Boll, Heinrich (Theodor)
1917-1985 .... CLC 2, 3, 6, 9, 11, 15, 27,
39, 72; WLC
See also Boell, Heinrich (Theodor)
See also DLB 69; DLBY 85

Bolt, Lee
See Faust, Frederick (Schiller)

Bolt, Robert (Oxton) 1924-........ **CLC 14**
See also CA 17-20R; CANR 35; DLB 13;
MTCW

Bomkauf
See Kaufman, Bob (Garnell)

Bonaventura.................... **NCLC 35**
See also DLB 90

Bond, Edward 1934-...... **CLC 4, 6, 13, 23**
See also CA 25-28R; CANR 38; DLB 13;
MTCW

Bonham, Frank 1914-1989........ **CLC 12**
See also AAYA 1; CA 9-12R; CANR 4, 36;
JRDA; MAICYA; SAAS 3; SATA 1, 49,
62

Bonnefoy, Yves 1923-........ **CLC 9, 15, 58**
See also CA 85-88; CANR 33; MTCW

Bontemps, Arna(ud Wendell)
1902-1973 .... CLC 1, 18; BLC
See also BW 1; CA 1-4R; 41-44R; CANR 4,
35; CLR 6; DLB 48, 51; JRDA;
MAICYA; MTCW; SATA 2, 24, 44

Booth, Martin 1944-.............. **CLC 13**
See also CA 93-96; CAAS 2

Booth, Philip 1925-.............. **CLC 23**
See also CA 5-8R; CANR 5; DLBY 82

Booth, Wayne C(layson) 1921-..... **CLC 24**
See also CA 1-4R; CAAS 5; CANR 3, 43;
DLB 67

Borchert, Wolfgang 1921-1947 ..... **TCLC 5**
See also CA 104; DLB 69, 124

Borel, Petrus 1809-1859........ **NCLC 41**

Borges, Jorge Luis
1899-1986 ... CLC 1, 2, 3, 4, 6, 8, 9, 10,
13, 19, 44, 48, 83; DA; HLC; SSC 4;
WLC
See also CA 21-24R; CANR 19, 33;
DLB 113; DLBY 86; HW; MTCW

Borowski, Tadeusz 1922-1951..... **TCLC 9**
See also CA 106

Borrow, George (Henry)
1803-1881 .... NCLC 9
See also DLB 21, 55

Bosman, Herman Charles
1905-1951 .... TCLC 49

Bosschere, Jean de 1878(?)-1953... **TCLC 19**
See also CA 115

Boswell, James
1740-1795 .... LC 4; DA; WLC
See also CDBLB 1660-1789; DLB 104, 142

Bottoms, David 1949-............. **CLC 53**
See also CA 105; CANR 22; DLB 120;
DLBY 83

Boucicault, Dion 1820-1890...... **NCLC 41**

Boucolon, Maryse 1937-
See Conde, Maryse
See also CA 110; CANR 30

Bourget, Paul (Charles Joseph)
1852-1935 .... TCLC 12
See also CA 107; DLB 123

Bourjaily, Vance (Nye) 1922- .... **CLC 8, 62**
See also CA 1-4R; CAAS 1; CANR 2;
DLB 2

Bourne, Randolph S(illiman)
1886-1918 .... TCLC 16
See also CA 117; DLB 63

Bova, Ben(jamin William) 1932-.... **CLC 45**
See also CA 5-8R; CAAS 18; CANR 11;
CLR 3; DLBY 81; MAICYA; MTCW;
SATA 6, 68

Bowen, Elizabeth (Dorothea Cole)
1899-1973 ...... CLC 1, 3, 6, 11, 15, 22;
SSC 3
See also CA 17-18; 41-44R; CANR 35;
CAP 2; CDBLB 1945-1960; DLB 15;
MTCW

Bowering, George 1935-........ **CLC 15, 47**
See also CA 21-24R; CAAS 16; CANR 10;
DLB 53

Bowering, Marilyn R(uthe) 1949-... **CLC 32**
See also CA 101

Bowers, Edgar 1924- .... **CLC 9**
See also CA 5-8R; CANR 24; DLB 5

Bowie, David .... **CLC 17**
See also Jones, David Robert

Bowles, Jane (Sydney)
1917-1973 .... CLC 3, 68
See also CA 19-20; 41-44R; CAP 2

Bowles, Paul (Frederick)
1910- ...... CLC 1, 2, 19, 53; SSC 3
See also CA 1-4R; CAAS 1; CANR 1, 19;
DLB 5, 6; MTCW

Box, Edgar
See Vidal, Gore

Boyd, Nancy
See Millay, Edna St. Vincent

Boyd, William 1952-........ **CLC 28, 53, 70**
See also CA 114; 120

Boyle, Kay
1902-1992 ..... CLC 1, 5, 19, 58; SSC 5
See also CA 13-16R; 140; CAAS 1;
CANR 29; DLB 4, 9, 48, 86; DLBY 93;
MTCW

Boyle, Mark
See Kienzle, William X(avier)

Boyle, Patrick 1905-1982......... **CLC 19**
See also CA 127

Boyle, T. C.
See Boyle, T(homas) Coraghessan

Boyle, T(homas) Coraghessan
1948- .... CLC 36, 55
See also BEST 90:4; CA 120; CANR 44;
DLBY 86

Boz
See Dickens, Charles (John Huffam)

Brackenridge, Hugh Henry
1748-1816 .... NCLC 7
See also DLB 11, 37

Bradbury, Edward P.
See Moorcock, Michael (John)

Bradbury, Malcolm (Stanley)
1932-.................... CLC 32, 61
See also CA 1-4R; CANR 1, 33; DLB 14;
MTCW

Bradbury, Ray (Douglas)
1920- ... CLC 1, 3, 10, 15, 42; DA; WLC
See also AITN 1, 2; CA 1-4R; CANR 2, 30;
CDALB 1968-1988; DLB 2, 8; MTCW;
SATA 11, 64

Bradford, Gamaliel 1863-1932..... **TCLC 36**
See also DLB 17

Bradley, David (Henry, Jr.)
1950-.................... CLC 23; BLC
See also BW 1; CA 104; CANR 26; DLB 33

Bradley, John Ed(mund, Jr.)
1958-...................... **CLC 55**
See also CA 139

Bradley, Marion Zimmer 1930-..... **CLC 30**
See also AAYA 9; CA 57-60; CAAS 10;
CANR 7, 31; DLB 8; MTCW

Bradstreet, Anne 1612(?)-1672 ... LC 4; DA
See also CDALB 1640-1865; DLB 24

Bragg, Melvyn 1939-............. **CLC 10**
See also BEST 89:3; CA 57-60; CANR 10;
DLB 14

Braine, John (Gerard)
1922-1986 .... CLC 1, 3, 41
See also CA 1-4R; 120; CANR 1, 33;
CDBLB 1945-1960; DLB 15; DLBY 86;
MTCW

Brammer, William 1930(?)-1978 .... **CLC 31**
See also CA 77-80

Brancati, Vitaliano 1907-1954..... **TCLC 12**
See also CA 109

Brancato, Robin F(idler) 1936-..... **CLC 35**
See also AAYA 9; CA 69-72; CANR 11;
CLR 32; JRDA; SAAS 9; SATA 23

Brand, Max
See Faust, Frederick (Schiller)

Brand, Millen 1906-1980........... **CLC 7**
See also CA 21-24R; 97-100

Branden, Barbara .... **CLC 44**

Brandes, Georg (Morris Cohen)
1842-1927 .... TCLC 10
See also CA 105

Brandys, Kazimierz 1916-......... **CLC 62**

Branley, Franklyn M(ansfield)
1915-...................... **CLC 21**
See also CA 33-36R; CANR 14, 39;
CLR 13; MAICYA; SAAS 16; SATA 4,
68

Brathwaite, Edward (Kamau)
1930-...................... **CLC 11**
See also BW 2; CA 25-28R; CANR 11, 26;
DLB 125

Brautigan, Richard (Gary)
1935-1984 .... CLC 1, 3, 5, 9, 12, 34, 42
See also CA 53-56; 113; CANR 34; DLB 2,
5; DLBY 80, 84; MTCW; SATA 56

Braverman, Kate 1950- .... CLC 67
See also CA 89-92

Brecht, Bertolt
1898-1956 ...... TCLC 1, 6, 13, 35; DA;
DC 3; WLC
See also CA 104; 133; DLB 56, 124; MTCW

Brecht, Eugen Berthold Friedrich
See Brecht, Bertolt

Bremer, Fredrika 1801-1865 ..... NCLC 11

Brennan, Christopher John
1870-1932 .... TCLC 17
See also CA 117

Brennan, Maeve 1917- .... CLC 5
See also CA 81-84

Brentano, Clemens (Maria)
1778-1842 .... NCLC 1

Brent of Bin Bin
See Franklin, (Stella Maraia Sarah) Miles

Brenton, Howard 1942- .... CLC 31
See also CA 69-72; CANR 33; DLB 13;
MTCW

Breslin, James 1930-
See Breslin, Jimmy
See also CA 73-76; CANR 31; MTCW

Breslin, Jimmy .... CLC 4, 43
See also Breslin, James
See also AITN 1

Bresson, Robert 1907- .... CLC 16
See also CA 110

Breton, Andre 1896-1966... CLC 2, 9, 15, 54
See also CA 19-20; 25-28R; CANR 40;
CAP 2; DLB 65; MTCW

Breytenbach, Breyten 1939(?)- .. CLC 23, 37
See also CA 113; 129

Bridgers, Sue Ellen 1942- .... CLC 26
See also AAYA 8; CA 65-68; CANR 11,
36; CLR 18; DLB 52; JRDA; MAICYA;
SAAS 1; SATA 22

Bridges, Robert (Seymour)
1844-1930 .... TCLC 1
See also CA 104; CDBLB 1890-1914;
DLB 19, 98

Bridie, James.................. TCLC 3
See also Mavor, Osborne Henry
See also DLB 10

Brin, David 1950- .... CLC 34
See also CA 102; CANR 24; SATA 65

Brink, Andre (Philippus)
1935- .... CLC 18, 36
See also CA 104; CANR 39; MTCW

Brinsmead, H(esba) F(ay) 1922- .... CLC 21
See also CA 21-24R; CANR 10; MAICYA;
SAAS 5; SATA 18

Brittain, Vera (Mary)
1893(?)-1970 .... CLC 23
See also CA 13-16; 25-28R; CAP 1; MTCW

Broch, Hermann 1886-1951....... TCLC 20
See also CA 117; DLB 85, 124

Brock, Rose
See Hansen, Joseph

Brodkey, Harold 1930-........... CLC 56
See also CA 111; DLB 130

Brodsky, Iosif Alexandrovich 1940-
See Brodsky, Joseph
See also AITN 1; CA 41-44R; CANR 37;
MTCW

Brodsky, Joseph .. CLC 4, 6, 13, 36, 50; PC 9
See also Brodsky, Iosif Alexandrovich

Brodsky, Michael Mark 1948- ..... CLC 19
See also CA 102; CANR 18, 41

Bromell, Henry 1947-............. CLC 5
See also CA 53-56; CANR 9

Bromfield, Louis (Brucker)
1896-1956 .... TCLC 11
See also CA 107; DLB 4, 9, 86

Broner, E(sther) M(asserman)
1930- .... CLC 19
See also CA 17-20R; CANR 8, 25; DLB 28

Bronk, William 1918-............ CLC 10
See also CA 89-92; CANR 23

Bronstein, Lev Davidovich
See Trotsky, Leon

Bronte, Anne 1820-1849.......... NCLC 4
See also DLB 21

Bronte, Charlotte
1816-1855 ... NCLC 3, 8, 33; DA; WLC
See also CDBLB 1832-1890; DLB 21

Bronte, (Jane) Emily
1818-1848 .... NCLC 16, 35; DA; PC 8;
WLC
See also CDBLB 1832-1890; DLB 21, 32

Brooke, Frances 1724-1789 .... LC 6
See also DLB 39, 99

Brooke, Henry 1703(?)-1783 .... LC 1
See also DLB 39

Brooke, Rupert (Chawner)
1887-1915 .... TCLC 2, 7; DA; WLC
See also CA 104; 132; CDBLB 1914-1945;
DLB 19; MTCW

Brooke-Haven, P.
See Wodehouse, P(elham) G(renville)

Brooke-Rose, Christine 1926-...... CLC 40
See also CA 13-16R; DLB 14

Brookner, Anita 1928- ...... CLC 32, 34, 51
See also CA 114; 120; CANR 37; DLBY 87;
MTCW

Brooks, Cleanth 1906-........... CLC 24
See also CA 17-20R; CANR 33, 35;
DLB 63; MTCW

Brooks, George
See Baum, L(yman) Frank

Brooks, Gwendolyn
1917- ...... CLC 1, 2, 4, 5, 15, 49; BLC;
DA; PC 7; WLC
See also AITN 1; BW 2; CA 1-4R;
CANR 1, 27; CDALB 1941-1968;
CLR 27; DLB 5, 76; MTCW; SATA 6

Brooks, Mel..................... CLC 12
See also Kaminsky, Melvin
See also DLB 26

Brooks, Peter 1938-............. CLC 34
See also CA 45-48; CANR 1

Brooks, Van Wyck 1886-1963...... CLC 29
See also CA 1-4R; CANR 6; DLB 45, 63,
103

Brophy, Brigid (Antonia)
1929- .... CLC 6, 11, 29
See also CA 5-8R; CAAS 4; CANR 25;
DLB 14; MTCW

Brosman, Catharine Savage 1934-.... CLC 9
See also CA 61-64; CANR 21

Brother Antoninus
See Everson, William (Oliver)

Broughton, T(homas) Alan 1936- ... CLC 19
See also CA 45-48; CANR 2, 23

Broumas, Olga 1949-.......... CLC 10, 73
See also CA 85-88; CANR 20

Brown, Charles Brockden
1771-1810 .... NCLC 22
See also CDALB 1640-1865; DLB 37, 59,
73

Brown, Christy 1932-1981........ CLC 63
See also CA 105; 104; DLB 14

Brown, Claude 1937- .... CLC 30; BLC
See also AAYA 7; BW 1; CA 73-76

Brown, Dee (Alexander) 1908- .. CLC 18, 47
See also CA 13-16R; CAAS 6; CANR 11;
DLBY 80; MTCW; SATA 5

Brown, George
See Wertmueller, Lina

Brown, George Douglas
1869-1902 .... TCLC 28

Brown, George Mackay 1921-.... CLC 5, 48
See also CA 21-24R; CAAS 6; CANR 12,
37; DLB 14, 27, 139; MTCW; SATA 35

Brown, (William) Larry 1951-...... CLC 73
See also CA 130; 134

Brown, Moses
See Barrett, William (Christopher)

Brown, Rita Mae 1944-..... CLC 18, 43, 79
See also CA 45-48; CANR 2, 11, 35;
MTCW

Brown, Roderick (Langmere) Haig-
See Haig-Brown, Roderick (Langmere)

Brown, Rosellen 1939-............ CLC 32
See also CA 77-80; CAAS 10; CANR 14, 44

Brown, Sterling Allen
1901-1989 .... CLC 1, 23, 59; BLC
See also BW 1; CA 85-88; 127; CANR 26;
DLB 48, 51, 63; MTCW

Brown, Will
See Ainsworth, William Harrison

Brown, William Wells
1813-1884 .... NCLC 2; BLC; DC 1
See also DLB 3, 50

Browne, (Clyde) Jackson 1948(?)-... CLC 21
See also CA 120

Browning, Elizabeth Barrett
1806-1861 ..... NCLC 1, 16; DA; PC 6;
WLC
See also CDBLB 1832-1890; DLB 32

Browning, Robert
1812-1889 .... NCLC 19; DA; PC 2
See also CDBLB 1832-1890; DLB 32;
YABC 1

Browning, Tod 1882-1962 .... CLC 16
See also CA 141; 117

Bruccoli, Matthew J(oseph) 1931- .. CLC 34
See also CA 9-12R; CANR 7; DLB 103

Bruce, Lenny . . . . CLC 21
See also Schneider, Leonard Alfred

Bruin, John
See Brutus, Dennis

Brulls, Christian
See Simenon, Georges (Jacques Christian)

Brunner, John (Kilian Houston)
1934- . . . . CLC 8, 10
See also CA 1-4R; CAAS 8; CANR 2, 37;
MTCW

Brutus, Dennis 1924- . . . . CLC 43; BLC
See also BW 2; CA 49-52; CAAS 14;
CANR 2, 27, 42; DLB 117

Bryan, C(ourtlandt) D(ixon) B(arnes)
1936- . . . . CLC 29
See also CA 73-76; CANR 13

Bryan, Michael
See Moore, Brian

Bryant, William Cullen
1794-1878 . . . . NCLC 6; DA
See also CDALB 1640-1865; DLB 3, 43, 59

Bryusov, Valery Yakovlevich
1873-1924 . . . . TCLC 10
See also CA 107

Buchan, John 1875-1940 . . . . TCLC 41
See also CA 108; DLB 34, 70; YABC 2

Buchanan, George 1506-1582 . . . . LC 4

Buchheim, Lothar-Guenther 1918- . . . CLC 6
See also CA 85-88

Buchner, (Karl) Georg
1813-1837 . . . . NCLC 26

Buchwald, Art(hur) 1925- . . . . CLC 33
See also AITN 1; CA 5-8R; CANR 21;
MTCW; SATA 10

Buck, Pearl S(ydenstricker)
1892-1973 . . . . CLC 7, 11, 18; DA
See also AITN 1; CA 1-4R; 41-44R;
CANR 1, 34; DLB 9, 102; MTCW;
SATA 1, 25

Buckler, Ernest 1908-1984 . . . . CLC 13
See also CA 11-12; 114; CAP 1; DLB 68;
SATA 47

Buckley, Vincent (Thomas)
1925-1988 . . . . CLC 57
See also CA 101

Buckley, William F(rank), Jr.
1925- . . . . CLC 7, 18, 37
See also AITN 1; CA 1-4R; CANR 1, 24;
DLB 137; DLBY 80; MTCW

Buechner, (Carl) Frederick
1926- . . . . CLC 2, 4, 6, 9
See also CA 13-16R; CANR 11, 39;
DLBY 80; MTCW

Buell, John (Edward) 1927- . . . . CLC 10
See also CA 1-4R; DLB 53

Buero Vallejo, Antonio 1916- . . . CLC 15, 46
See also CA 106; CANR 24; HW; MTCW

Bufalino, Gesualdo 1920(?)- . . . . CLC 74

Bugayev, Boris Nikolayevich 1880-1934
See Bely, Andrey
See also CA 104

Bukowski, Charles
1920-1994 . . . . CLC 2, 5, 9, 41, 82
See also CA 17-20R; 144; CANR 40;
DLB 5, 130; MTCW

Bulgakov, Mikhail (Afanas'evich)
1891-1940 . . . . TCLC 2, 16
See also CA 105

Bulgya, Alexander Alexandrovich
1901-1956 . . . . TCLC 53
See also Fadeyev, Alexander
See also CA 117

Bullins, Ed 1935- . . . . CLC 1, 5, 7; BLC
See also BW 2; CA 49-52; CAAS 16;
CANR 24; DLB 7, 38; MTCW

Bulwer-Lytton, Edward (George Earle Lytton)
1803-1873 . . . . NCLC 1, 45
See also DLB 21

Bunin, Ivan Alexeyevich
1870-1953 . . . . TCLC 6; SSC 5
See also CA 104

Bunting, Basil 1900-1985 . . . . CLC 10, 39, 47
See also CA 53-56; 115; CANR 7; DLB 20

Bunuel, Luis 1900-1983 . . CLC 16, 80; HLC
See also CA 101; 110; CANR 32; HW

Bunyan, John 1628-1688 . . LC 4; DA; WLC
See also CDBLB 1660-1789; DLB 39

Burford, Eleanor
See Hibbert, Eleanor Alice Burford

Burgess, Anthony
CLC 1, 2, 4, 5, 8, 10, 13, 15, 22, 40, 62,
81
See also Wilson, John (Anthony) Burgess
See also AITN 1; CDBLB 1960 to Present;
DLB 14

Burke, Edmund
1729(?)-1797 . . . . LC 7; DA; WLC
See also DLB 104

Burke, Kenneth (Duva)
1897-1993 . . . . CLC 2, 24
See also CA 5-8R; 143; CANR 39; DLB 45,
63; MTCW

Burke, Leda
See Garnett, David

Burke, Ralph
See Silverberg, Robert

Burney, Fanny 1752-1840 . . . . NCLC 12
See also DLB 39

Burns, Robert
1759-1796 . . . . . . LC 3; DA; PC 6; WLC
See also CDBLB 1789-1832; DLB 109

Burns, Tex
See L'Amour, Louis (Dearborn)

Burnshaw, Stanley 1906- . . . . . CLC 3, 13, 44
See also CA 9-12R; DLB 48

Burr, Anne 1937- . . . . CLC 6
See also CA 25-28R

Burroughs, Edgar Rice
1875-1950 . . . . TCLC 2, 32
See also AAYA 11; CA 104; 132; DLB 8;
MTCW; SATA 41

Burroughs, William S(eward)
1914- . . . . CLC 1, 2, 5, 15, 22, 42, 75;
DA; WLC
See also AITN 2; CA 9-12R; CANR 20;
DLB 2, 8, 16; DLBY 81; MTCW

Burton, Richard F. 1821-1890 . . . . NCLC 42
See also DLB 55

Busch, Frederick 1941- . . . CLC 7, 10, 18, 47
See also CA 33-36R; CAAS 1; DLB 6

Bush, Ronald 1946- . . . . CLC 34
See also CA 136

Bustos, F(rancisco)
See Borges, Jorge Luis

Bustos Domecq, H(onorio)
See Bioy Casares, Adolfo; Borges, Jorge
Luis

Butler, Octavia E(stelle) 1947- . . . . . CLC 38
See also BW 2; CA 73-76; CANR 12, 24,
38; DLB 33; MTCW

Butler, Robert Olen (Jr.) 1945- . . . . . CLC 81
See also CA 112

Butler, Samuel 1612-1680 . . . . LC 16
See also DLB 101, 126

Butler, Samuel
1835-1902 . . . . . . TCLC 1, 33; DA; WLC
See also CA 104; CDBLB 1890-1914;
DLB 18, 57

Butler, Walter C.
See Faust, Frederick (Schiller)

Butor, Michel (Marie Francois)
1926- . . . . CLC 1, 3, 8, 11, 15
See also CA 9-12R; CANR 33; DLB 83;
MTCW

Buzo, Alexander (John) 1944- . . . . . . CLC 61
See also CA 97-100; CANR 17, 39

Buzzati, Dino 1906-1972 . . . . CLC 36
See also CA 33-36R

Byars, Betsy (Cromer) 1928- . . . . CLC 35
See also CA 33-36R; CANR 18, 36; CLR 1,
16; DLB 52; JRDA; MAICYA; MTCW;
SAAS 1; SATA 4, 46

Byatt, A(ntonia) S(usan Drabble)
1936- . . . . CLC 19, 65
See also CA 13-16R; CANR 13, 33;
DLB 14; MTCW

Byrne, David 1952- . . . . CLC 26
See also CA 127

Byrne, John Keyes 1926- . . . . CLC 19
See also Leonard, Hugh
See also CA 102

Byron, George Gordon (Noel)
1788-1824 . . . . . . NCLC 2, 12; DA; WLC
See also CDBLB 1789-1832; DLB 96, 110

C.3.3.
See Wilde, Oscar (Fingal O'Flahertie Wills)

Caballero, Fernan 1796-1877 . . . . . NCLC 10

Cabell, James Branch 1879-1958 . . . TCLC 6
See also CA 105; DLB 9, 78

Cable, George Washington
1844-1925 . . . . TCLC 4; SSC 4
See also CA 104; DLB 12, 74

Cabral de Melo Neto, Joao 1920- . . . CLC 76

Cabrera Infante, G(uillermo)
1929- . . . . CLC 5, 25, 45; HLC
See also CA 85-88; CANR 29; DLB 113;
HW; MTCW

Cade, Toni
See Bambara, Toni Cade

Cadmus
See Buchan, John

Caedmon fl. 658-680 . . . . CMLC 7

Caeiro, Alberto
See Pessoa, Fernando (Antonio Nogueira)

Cage, John (Milton, Jr.) 1912- ..... **CLC 41**
See also CA 13-16R; CANR 9

Cain, G.
See Cabrera Infante, G(uillermo)

Cain, Guillermo
See Cabrera Infante, G(uillermo)

Cain, James M(allahan)
1892-1977 .... **CLC 3, 11, 28**
See also AITN 1; CA 17-20R; 73-76;
CANR 8, 34; MTCW

Caine, Mark
See Raphael, Frederic (Michael)

Calasso, Roberto 1941- .... **CLC 81**
See also CA 143

Calderon de la Barca, Pedro
1600-1681 .... **LC 23; DC 3**

Caldwell, Erskine (Preston)
1903-1987 .... **CLC 1, 8, 14, 50, 60**
See also AITN 1; CA 1-4R; 121; CAAS 1;
CANR 2, 33; DLB 9, 86; MTCW

Caldwell, (Janet Miriam) Taylor (Holland)
1900-1985 .... **CLC 2, 28, 39**
See also CA 5-8R; 116; CANR 5

Calhoun, John Caldwell
1782-1850 .... **NCLC 15**
See also DLB 3

Calisher, Hortense
1911- .... **CLC 2, 4, 8, 38; SSC 15**
See also CA 1-4R; CANR 1, 22; DLB 2;
MTCW

Callaghan, Morley Edward
1903-1990 .... **CLC 3, 14, 41, 65**
See also CA 9-12R; 132; CANR 33;
DLB 68; MTCW

Calvino, Italo
1923-1985 ..... **CLC 5, 8, 11, 22, 33, 39,
73; SSC 3**
See also CA 85-88; 116; CANR 23; MTCW

Cameron, Carey 1952- .... **CLC 59**
See also CA 135

Cameron, Peter 1959- .... **CLC 44**
See also CA 125

Campana, Dino 1885-1932 .... **TCLC 20**
See also CA 117; DLB 114

Campbell, John W(ood, Jr.)
1910-1971 .... **CLC 32**
See also CA 21-22; 29-32R; CANR 34;
CAP 2; DLB 8; MTCW

Campbell, Joseph 1904-1987 .... **CLC 69**
See also AAYA 3; BEST 89:2; CA 1-4R;
124; CANR 3, 28; MTCW

Campbell, (John) Ramsey 1946- .... **CLC 42**
See also CA 57-60; CANR 7

Campbell, (Ignatius) Roy (Dunnachie)
1901-1957 .... **TCLC 5**
See also CA 104; DLB 20

Campbell, Thomas 1777-1844 .... **NCLC 19**
See also DLB 93

Campbell, Wilfred .... **TCLC 9**
See also Campbell, William

Campbell, William 1858(?)-1918
See Campbell, Wilfred
See also CA 106; DLB 92

Campos, Alvaro de
See Pessoa, Fernando (Antonio Nogueira)

Camus, Albert
1913-1960 .... **CLC 1, 2, 4, 9, 11, 14, 32,
63, 69; DA; DC 2; SSC 9; WLC**
See also CA 89-92; DLB 72; MTCW

Canby, Vincent 1924- .... **CLC 13**
See also CA 81-84

Cancale
See Desnos, Robert

Canetti, Elias 1905- ...... **CLC 3, 14, 25, 75**
See also CA 21-24R; CANR 23; DLB 85,
124; MTCW

Canin, Ethan 1960- .... **CLC 55**
See also CA 131; 135

Cannon, Curt
See Hunter, Evan

Cape, Judith
See Page, P(atricia) K(athleen)

Capek, Karel
1890-1938 ..... **TCLC 6, 37; DA; DC 1;
WLC**
See also CA 104; 140

Capote, Truman
1924-1984 ...... **CLC 1, 3, 8, 13, 19, 34,
38, 58; DA; SSC 2; WLC**
See also CA 5-8R; 113; CANR 18;
CDALB 1941-1968; DLB 2; DLBY 80,
84; MTCW

Capra, Frank 1897-1991 .... **CLC 16**
See also CA 61-64; 135

Caputo, Philip 1941- .... **CLC 32**
See also CA 73-76; CANR 40

Card, Orson Scott 1951- .... **CLC 44, 47, 50**
See also AAYA 11; CA 102; CANR 27;
MTCW

Cardenal (Martinez), Ernesto
1925- .... **CLC 31; HLC**
See also CA 49-52; CANR 2, 32; HW;
MTCW

Carducci, Giosue 1835-1907 ...... **TCLC 32**

Carew, Thomas 1595(?)-1640 .... **LC 13**
See also DLB 126

Carey, Ernestine Gilbreth 1908- .... **CLC 17**
See also CA 5-8R; SATA 2

Carey, Peter 1943- .... **CLC 40, 55**
See also CA 123; 127; MTCW

Carleton, William 1794-1869 ...... **NCLC 3**

Carlisle, Henry (Coffin) 1926- ...... **CLC 33**
See also CA 13-16R; CANR 15

Carlsen, Chris
See Holdstock, Robert P.

Carlson, Ron(ald F.) 1947- .... **CLC 54**
See also CA 105; CANR 27

Carlyle, Thomas 1795-1881 .. **NCLC 22; DA**
See also CDBLB 1789-1832; DLB 55

Carman, (William) Bliss
1861-1929 .... **TCLC 7**
See also CA 104; DLB 92

Carnegie, Dale 1888-1955 .... **TCLC 53**

Carossa, Hans 1878-1956 .... **TCLC 48**
See also DLB 66

Carpenter, Don(ald Richard)
1931- .... **CLC 41**
See also CA 45-48; CANR 1

Carpentier (y Valmont), Alejo
1904-1980 .... **CLC 8, 11, 38; HLC**
See also CA 65-68; 97-100; CANR 11;
DLB 113; HW

Carr, Emily 1871-1945 .... **TCLC 32**
See also DLB 68

Carr, John Dickson 1906-1977 ...... **CLC 3**
See also CA 49-52; 69-72; CANR 3, 33;
MTCW

Carr, Philippa
See Hibbert, Eleanor Alice Burford

Carr, Virginia Spencer 1929- .... **CLC 34**
See also CA 61-64; DLB 111

Carrier, Roch 1937- .... **CLC 13, 78**
See also CA 130; DLB 53

Carroll, James P. 1943(?)- .... **CLC 38**
See also CA 81-84

Carroll, Jim 1951- .... **CLC 35**
See also CA 45-48; CANR 42

Carroll, Lewis .... **NCLC 2; WLC**
See also Dodgson, Charles Lutwidge
See also CDBLB 1832-1890; CLR 2, 18;
DLB 18; JRDA

Carroll, Paul Vincent 1900-1968.... **CLC 10**
See also CA 9-12R; 25-28R; DLB 10

Carruth, Hayden 1921- .... **CLC 4, 7, 10, 18**
See also CA 9-12R; CANR 4, 38; DLB 5;
MTCW; SATA 47

Carson, Rachel Louise 1907-1964... **CLC 71**
See also CA 77-80; CANR 35; MTCW;
SATA 23

Carter, Angela (Olive)
1940-1992 ...... **CLC 5, 41, 76; SSC 13**
See also CA 53-56; 136; CANR 12, 36;
DLB 14; MTCW; SATA 66;
SATA-Obit 70

Carter, Nick
See Smith, Martin Cruz

Carver, Raymond
1938-1988 ... **CLC 22, 36, 53, 55; SSC 8**
See also CA 33-36R; 126; CANR 17, 34;
DLB 130; DLBY 84, 88; MTCW

Cary, (Arthur) Joyce (Lunel)
1888-1957 .... **TCLC 1, 29**
See also CA 104; CDBLB 1914-1945;
DLB 15, 100

Casanova de Seingalt, Giovanni Jacopo
1725-1798 .... **LC 13**

Casares, Adolfo Bioy
See Bioy Casares, Adolfo

Casely-Hayford, J(oseph) E(phraim)
1866-1930 .... **TCLC 24; BLC**
See also BW 2; CA 123

Casey, John (Dudley) 1939- .... **CLC 59**
See also BEST 90:2; CA 69-72; CANR 23

Casey, Michael 1947- .... **CLC 2**
See also CA 65-68; DLB 5

Casey, Patrick
See Thurman, Wallace (Henry)

Casey, Warren (Peter) 1935-1988 ... **CLC 12**
See also CA 101; 127

Casona, Alejandro .... **CLC 49**
See also Alvarez, Alejandro Rodriguez

Chernyshevsky, Nikolay Gavrilovich
    1828-1889 .... NCLC 1

Cherry, Carolyn Janice 1942-
    See Cherryh, C. J.
    See also CA 65-68; CANR 10

Cherryh, C. J. .... CLC 35
    See also Cherry, Carolyn Janice
    See also DLBY 80

Chesnutt, Charles W(addell)
    1858-1932 .... TCLC 5, 39; BLC; SSC 7
    See also BW 1; CA 106; 125; DLB 12, 50,
        78; MTCW

Chester, Alfred 1929(?)-1971 ...... CLC 49
    See also CA 33-36R; DLB 130

Chesterton, G(ilbert) K(eith)
    1874-1936 .... TCLC 1, 6; SSC 1
    See also CA 104; 132; CDBLB 1914-1945;
        DLB 10, 19, 34, 70, 98; MTCW;
        SATA 27

Chiang Pin-chin 1904-1986
    See Ding Ling
    See also CA 118

Ch'ien Chung-shu 1910- .... CLC 22
    See also CA 130; MTCW

Child, L. Maria
    See Child, Lydia Maria

Child, Lydia Maria 1802-1880 .... NCLC 6
    See also DLB 1, 74; SATA 67

Child, Mrs.
    See Child, Lydia Maria

Child, Philip 1898-1978 .... CLC 19, 68
    See also CA 13-14; CAP 1; SATA 47

Childress, Alice
    1920- .... CLC 12, 15; BLC; DC 4
    See also AAYA 8; BW 2; CA 45-48;
        CANR 3, 27; CLR 14; DLB 7, 38; JRDA;
        MAICYA; MTCW; SATA 7, 48

Chislett, (Margaret) Anne 1943-.... CLC 34

Chitty, Thomas Willes 1926-....... CLC 11
    See also Hinde, Thomas
    See also CA 5-8R

Chomette, Rene Lucien 1898-1981 .. CLC 20
    See also Clair, Rene
    See also CA 103

Chopin, Kate .... TCLC 5, 14; DA; SSC 8
    See also Chopin, Katherine
    See also CDALB 1865-1917; DLB 12, 78

Chopin, Katherine 1851-1904
    See Chopin, Kate
    See also CA 104; 122

Chretien de Troyes
    c. 12th cent. - .... CMLC 10

Christie
    See Ichikawa, Kon

Christie, Agatha (Mary Clarissa)
    1890-1976 ...... CLC 1, 6, 8, 12, 39, 48
    See also AAYA 9; AITN 1, 2; CA 17-20R;
        61-64; CANR 10, 37; CDBLB 1914-1945;
        DLB 13, 77; MTCW; SATA 36

Christie, (Ann) Philippa
    See Pearce, Philippa
    See also CA 5-8R; CANR 4

Christine de Pizan 1365(?)-1431(?) .... LC 9

Chubb, Elmer
    See Masters, Edgar Lee

Chulkov, Mikhail Dmitrievich
    1743-1792 .... LC 2

Churchill, Caryl 1938- .... CLC 31, 55
    See also CA 102; CANR 22; DLB 13;
        MTCW

Churchill, Charles 1731-1764........ LC 3
    See also DLB 109

Chute, Carolyn 1947-............. CLC 39
    See also CA 123

Ciardi, John (Anthony)
    1916-1986 .... CLC 10, 40, 44
    See also CA 5-8R; 118; CAAS 2; CANR 5,
        33; CLR 19; DLB 5; DLBY 86;
        MAICYA; MTCW; SATA 1, 46, 65

Cicero, Marcus Tullius
    106B.C.-43B.C. .... CMLC 3

Cimino, Michael 1943-............ CLC 16
    See also CA 105

Cioran, E(mil) M. 1911-.......... CLC 64
    See also CA 25-28R

Cisneros, Sandra 1954-...... CLC 69; HLC
    See also AAYA 9; CA 131; DLB 122; HW

Clair, Rene...................... CLC 20
    See also Chomette, Rene Lucien

Clampitt, Amy 1920- .... CLC 32
    See also CA 110; CANR 29; DLB 105

Clancy, Thomas L., Jr. 1947-
    See Clancy, Tom
    See also CA 125; 131; MTCW

Clancy, Tom.................... CLC 45
    See also Clancy, Thomas L., Jr.
    See also AAYA 9; BEST 89:1, 90:1

Clare, John 1793-1864 .... NCLC 9
    See also DLB 55, 96

Clarin
    See Alas (y Urena), Leopoldo (Enrique
        Garcia)

Clark, Al C.
    See Goines, Donald

Clark, (Robert) Brian 1932-........ CLC 29
    See also CA 41-44R

Clark, Curt
    See Westlake, Donald E(dwin)

Clark, Eleanor 1913- .... CLC 5, 19
    See also CA 9-12R; CANR 41; DLB 6

Clark, J. P.
    See Clark, John Pepper
    See also DLB 117

Clark, John Pepper 1935- .... CLC 38; BLC
    See also Clark, J. P.
    See also BW 1; CA 65-68; CANR 16

Clark, M. R.
    See Clark, Mavis Thorpe

Clark, Mavis Thorpe 1909- .... CLC 12
    See also CA 57-60; CANR 8, 37; CLR 30;
        MAICYA; SAAS 5; SATA 8, 74

Clark, Walter Van Tilburg
    1909-1971 .... CLC 28
    See also CA 9-12R; 33-36R; DLB 9;
        SATA 8

Clarke, Arthur C(harles)
    1917- ...... CLC 1, 4, 13, 18, 35; SSC 3
    See also AAYA 4; CA 1-4R; CANR 2, 28;
        JRDA; MAICYA; MTCW; SATA 13, 70

Clarke, Austin 1896-1974........ CLC 6, 9
    See also CA 29-32; 49-52; CAP 2; DLB 10,
        20

Clarke, Austin C(hesterfield)
    1934- .... CLC 8, 53; BLC
    See also BW 1; CA 25-28R; CAAS 16;
        CANR 14, 32; DLB 53, 125

Clarke, Gillian 1937- .... CLC 61
    See also CA 106; DLB 40

Clarke, Marcus (Andrew Hislop)
    1846-1881 .... NCLC 19

Clarke, Shirley 1925-............ CLC 16

Clash, The .... CLC 30
    See also Headon, (Nicky) Topper; Jones,
        Mick; Simonon, Paul; Strummer, Joe

Claudel, Paul (Louis Charles Marie)
    1868-1955 .... TCLC 2, 10
    See also CA 104

Clavell, James (duMaresq)
    1925-................... CLC 6, 25
    See also CA 25-28R; CANR 26; MTCW

Cleaver, (Leroy) Eldridge
    1935-................ CLC 30; BLC
    See also BW 1; CA 21-24R; CANR 16

Cleese, John (Marwood) 1939- ..... CLC 21
    See also Monty Python
    See also CA 112; 116; CANR 35; MTCW

Cleishbotham, Jebediah
    See Scott, Walter

Cleland, John 1710-1789 .... LC 2
    See also DLB 39

Clemens, Samuel Langhorne 1835-1910
    See Twain, Mark
    See also CA 104; 135; CDALB 1865-1917;
        DA; DLB 11, 12, 23, 64, 74; JRDA;
        MAICYA; YABC 2

Cleophil
    See Congreve, William

Clerihew, E.
    See Bentley, E(dmund) C(lerihew)

Clerk, N. W.
    See Lewis, C(live) S(taples)

Cliff, Jimmy.................... CLC 21
    See also Chambers, James

Clifton, (Thelma) Lucille
    1936-.............. CLC 19, 66; BLC
    See also BW 2; CA 49-52; CANR 2, 24, 42;
        CLR 5; DLB 5, 41; MAICYA; MTCW;
        SATA 20, 69

Clinton, Dirk
    See Silverberg, Robert

Clough, Arthur Hugh 1819-1861.. NCLC 27
    See also DLB 32

Clutha, Janet Paterson Frame 1924-
    See Frame, Janet
    See also CA 1-4R; CANR 2, 36; MTCW

Clyne, Terence
    See Blatty, William Peter

Cobalt, Martin
    See Mayne, William (James Carter)

Coburn, D(onald) L(ee) 1938- ...... CLC 10
    See also CA 89-92

Cocteau, Jean (Maurice Eugene Clement)
1889-1963 .... CLC 1, 8, 15, 16, 43; DA;
WLC
See also CA 25-28; CANR 40; CAP 2;
DLB 65; MTCW

Codrescu, Andrei 1946- .... CLC 46
See also CA 33-36R; CAAS 19; CANR 13,
34

Coe, Max
See Bourne, Randolph S(illiman)

Coe, Tucker
See Westlake, Donald E(dwin)

Coetzee, J(ohn) M(ichael)
1940- .... CLC 23, 33, 66
See also CA 77-80; CANR 41; MTCW

Coffey, Brian
See Koontz, Dean R(ay)

Cohen, Arthur A(llen)
1928-1986 .... CLC 7, 31
See also CA 1-4R; 120; CANR 1, 17, 42;
DLB 28

Cohen, Leonard (Norman)
1934- .... CLC 3, 38
See also CA 21-24R; CANR 14; DLB 53;
MTCW

Cohen, Matt 1942- .... CLC 19
See also CA 61-64; CAAS 18; CANR 40;
DLB 53

Cohen-Solal, Annie 19(?)- .... CLC 50

Colegate, Isabel 1931- .... CLC 36
See also CA 17-20R; CANR 8, 22; DLB 14;
MTCW

Coleman, Emmett
See Reed, Ishmael

Coleridge, Samuel Taylor
1772-1834 .... NCLC 9; DA; WLC
See also CDBLB 1789-1832; DLB 93, 107

Coleridge, Sara 1802-1852 ...... NCLC 31

Coles, Don 1928- .... CLC 46
See also CA 115; CANR 38

Colette, (Sidonie-Gabrielle)
1873-1954 ...... TCLC 1, 5, 16; SSC 10
See also CA 104; 131; DLB 65; MTCW

Collett, (Jacobine) Camilla (Wergeland)
1813-1895 .... NCLC 22

Collier, Christopher 1930- .... CLC 30
See also CA 33-36R; CANR 13, 33; JRDA;
MAICYA; SATA 16, 70

Collier, James L(incoln) 1928- ..... CLC 30
See also CA 9-12R; CANR 4, 33; JRDA;
MAICYA; SATA 8, 70

Collier, Jeremy 1650-1726 .... LC 6

Collins, Hunt
See Hunter, Evan

Collins, Linda 1931- .... CLC 44
See also CA 125

Collins, (William) Wilkie
1824-1889 .... NCLC 1, 18
See also CDBLB 1832-1890; DLB 18, 70

Collins, William 1721-1759 .... LC 4
See also DLB 109

Colman, George
See Glassco, John

Colt, Winchester Remington
See Hubbard, L(afayette) Ron(ald)

Colter, Cyrus 1910- .... CLC 58
See also BW 1; CA 65-68; CANR 10;
DLB 33

Colton, James
See Hansen, Joseph

Colum, Padraic 1881-1972........ CLC 28
See also CA 73-76; 33-36R; CANR 35;
MAICYA; MTCW; SATA 15

Colvin, James
See Moorcock, Michael (John)

Colwin, Laurie (E.)
1944-1992 .... CLC 5, 13, 23
See also CA 89-92; 139; CANR 20;
DLBY 80; MTCW

Comfort, Alex(ander) 1920-........ CLC 7
See also CA 1-4R; CANR 1

Comfort, Montgomery
See Campbell, (John) Ramsey

Compton-Burnett, I(vy)
1884(?)-1969 ...... CLC 1, 3, 10, 15, 34
See also CA 1-4R; 25-28R; CANR 4;
DLB 36; MTCW

Comstock, Anthony 1844-1915 .... TCLC 13
See also CA 110

Conan Doyle, Arthur
See Doyle, Arthur Conan

Conde, Maryse 1937-............. CLC 52
See also Boucolon, Maryse
See also BW 2

Condon, Richard (Thomas)
1915- .... CLC 4, 6, 8, 10, 45
See also BEST 90:3; CA 1-4R; CAAS 1;
CANR 2, 23; MTCW

Congreve, William
1670-1729 ... LC 5, 21; DA; DC 2; WLC
See also CDBLB 1660-1789; DLB 39, 84

Connell, Evan S(helby), Jr.
1924- .... CLC 4, 6, 45
See also AAYA 7; CA 1-4R; CAAS 2;
CANR 2, 39; DLB 2; DLBY 81; MTCW

Connelly, Marc(us Cook)
1890-1980 .... CLC 7
See also CA 85-88; 102; CANR 30; DLB 7;
DLBY 80; SATA 25

Connor, Ralph .... TCLC 31
See also Gordon, Charles William
See also DLB 92

Conrad, Joseph
1857-1924 .... TCLC 1, 6, 13, 25, 43;
DA; SSC 9; WLC
See also CA 104; 131; CDBLB 1890-1914;
DLB 10, 34, 98; MTCW; SATA 27

Conrad, Robert Arnold
See Hart, Moss

Conroy, Pat 1945-............. CLC 30, 74
See also AAYA 8; AITN 1; CA 85-88;
CANR 24; DLB 6; MTCW

Constant (de Rebecque), (Henri) Benjamin
1767-1830 .... NCLC 6
See also DLB 119

Conybeare, Charles Augustus
See Eliot, T(homas) S(tearns)

Cook, Michael 1933- .... CLC 58
See also CA 93-96; DLB 53

Cook, Robin 1940- .... CLC 14
See also BEST 90:2; CA 108; 111;
CANR 41

Cook, Roy
See Silverberg, Robert

Cooke, Elizabeth 1948- .... CLC 55
See also CA 129

Cooke, John Esten 1830-1886..... NCLC 5
See also DLB 3

Cooke, John Estes
See Baum, L(yman) Frank

Cooke, M. E.
See Creasey, John

Cooke, Margaret
See Creasey, John

Cooney, Ray .... CLC 62

Cooper, Henry St. John
See Creasey, John

Cooper, J. California............... CLC 56
See also AAYA 12; BW 1; CA 125

Cooper, James Fenimore
1789-1851 .... NCLC 1, 27
See also CDALB 1640-1865; DLB 3;
SATA 19

Coover, Robert (Lowell)
1932- ..... CLC 3, 7, 15, 32, 46; SSC 15
See also CA 45-48; CANR 3, 37; DLB 2;
DLBY 81; MTCW

Copeland, Stewart (Armstrong)
1952- .... CLC 26
See also Police, The

Coppard, A(lfred) E(dgar)
1878-1957 .... TCLC 5
See also CA 114; YABC 1

Coppee, Francois 1842-1908 ...... TCLC 25

Coppola, Francis Ford 1939-...... CLC 16
See also CA 77-80; CANR 40; DLB 44

Corbiere, Tristan 1845-1875 ..... NCLC 43

Corcoran, Barbara 1911-.......... CLC 17
See also CA 21-24R; CAAS 2; CANR 11,
28; DLB 52; JRDA; SATA 3, 77

Cordelier, Maurice
See Giraudoux, (Hippolyte) Jean

Corelli, Marie 1855-1924........ TCLC 51
See also Mackay, Mary
See also DLB 34

Corman, Cid................... CLC 9
See also Corman, Sidney
See also CAAS 2; DLB 5

Corman, Sidney 1924-
See Corman, Cid
See also CA 85-88; CANR 44

Cormier, Robert (Edmund)
1925- .... CLC 12, 30; DA
See also AAYA 3; CA 1-4R; CANR 5, 23;
CDALB 1968-1988; CLR 12; DLB 52;
JRDA; MAICYA; MTCW; SATA 10, 45

Corn, Alfred (DeWitt III) 1943-.... CLC 33
See also CA 104; DLB 120; DLBY 80

Cornwell, David (John Moore)
1931- .... CLC 9, 15
See also le Carre, John
See also CA 5-8R; CANR 13, 33; MTCW

Corrigan, Kevin................... CLC 55

Corso, (Nunzio) Gregory 1930-... CLC 1, 11
See also CA 5-8R; CANR 41; DLB 5, 16;
MTCW

Cortazar, Julio
1914-1984 ...... CLC 2, 3, 5, 10, 13, 15,
33, 34; HLC; SSC 7
See also CA 21-24R; CANR 12, 32;
DLB 113; HW; MTCW

Corwin, Cecil
See Kornbluth, C(yril) M.

Cosic, Dobrica 1921- .... CLC 14
See also CA 122; 138

Costain, Thomas B(ertram)
1885-1965 .... CLC 30
See also CA 5-8R; 25-28R; DLB 9

Costantini, Humberto
1924(?)-1987 .... CLC 49
See also CA 131; 122; HW

Costello, Elvis 1955-............. CLC 21

Cotter, Joseph Seamon Sr.
1861-1949 .... TCLC 28; BLC
See also BW 1; CA 124; DLB 50

Couch, Arthur Thomas Quiller
See Quiller-Couch, Arthur Thomas

Coulton, James
See Hansen, Joseph

Couperus, Louis (Marie Anne)
1863-1923 .... TCLC 15
See also CA 115

Court, Wesli
See Turco, Lewis (Putnam)

Courtenay, Bryce 1933-........... CLC 59
See also CA 138

Courtney, Robert
See Ellison, Harlan

Cousteau, Jacques-Yves 1910-...... CLC 30
See also CA 65-68; CANR 15; MTCW;
SATA 38

Coward, Noel (Peirce)
1899-1973 ....CLC 1, 9, 29, 51
See also AITN 1; CA 17-18; 41-44R;
CANR 35; CAP 2; CDBLB 1914-1945;
DLB 10; MTCW

Cowley, Malcolm 1898-1989 .... CLC 39
See also CA 5-8R; 128; CANR 3; DLB 4,
48; DLBY 81, 89; MTCW

Cowper, William 1731-1800....... NCLC 8
See also DLB 104, 109

Cox, William Trevor 1928- ... CLC 9, 14, 71
See also Trevor, William
See also CA 9-12R; CANR 4, 37; DLB 14;
MTCW

Cozzens, James Gould
1903-1978 .... CLC 1, 4, 11
See also CA 9-12R; 81-84; CANR 19;
CDALB 1941-1968; DLB 9; DLBD 2;
DLBY 84; MTCW

Crabbe, George 1754-1832....... NCLC 26
See also DLB 93

Craig, A. A.
See Anderson, Poul (William)

Craik, Dinah Maria (Mulock)
1826-1887 .... NCLC 38
See also DLB 35; MAICYA; SATA 34

Cram, Ralph Adams 1863-1942.... TCLC 45

Crane, (Harold) Hart
1899-1932 .... TCLC 2, 5; DA; PC 3;
WLC
See also CA 104; 127; CDALB 1917-1929;
DLB 4, 48; MTCW

Crane, R(onald) S(almon)
1886-1967 .... CLC 27
See also CA 85-88; DLB 63

Crane, Stephen (Townley)
1871-1900 ...... TCLC 11, 17, 32; DA;
SSC 7; WLC
See also CA 109; 140; CDALB 1865-1917;
DLB 12, 54, 78; YABC 2

Crase, Douglas 1944-............. CLC 58
See also CA 106

Crashaw, Richard 1612(?)-1649...... LC 24
See also DLB 126

Craven, Margaret 1901-1980....... CLC 17
See also CA 103

Crawford, F(rancis) Marion
1854-1909 .... TCLC 10
See also CA 107; DLB 71

Crawford, Isabella Valancy
1850-1887 .... NCLC 12
See also DLB 92

Crayon, Geoffrey
See Irving, Washington

Creasey, John 1908-1973.......... CLC 11
See also CA 5-8R; 41-44R; CANR 8;
DLB 77; MTCW

Crebillon, Claude Prosper Jolyot de (fils)
1707-1777 .... LC 1

Credo
See Creasey, John

Creeley, Robert (White)
1926- ..... CLC 1, 2, 4, 8, 11, 15, 36, 78
See also CA 1-4R; CAAS 10; CANR 23, 43;
DLB 5, 16; MTCW

Crews, Harry (Eugene)
1935- .... CLC 6, 23, 49
See also AITN 1; CA 25-28R; CANR 20;
DLB 6; MTCW

Crichton, (John) Michael
1942- .... CLC 2, 6, 54
See also AAYA 10; AITN 2; CA 25-28R;
CANR 13, 40; DLBY 81; JRDA;
MTCW; SATA 9

Crispin, Edmund .... CLC 22
See also Montgomery, (Robert) Bruce
See also DLB 87

Cristofer, Michael 1945(?)- .... CLC 28
See also CA 110; DLB 7

Croce, Benedetto 1866-1952 ...... TCLC 37
See also CA 120

Crockett, David 1786-1836 .... NCLC 8
See also DLB 3, 11

Crockett, Davy
See Crockett, David

Croker, John Wilson 1780-1857 .. NCLC 10
See also DLB 110

Crommelynck, Fernand 1885-1970 .. CLC 75
See also CA 89-92

Cronin, A(rchibald) J(oseph)
1896-1981 .... CLC 32
See also CA 1-4R; 102; CANR 5; SATA 25,
47

Cross, Amanda
See Heilbrun, Carolyn G(old)

Crothers, Rachel 1878(?)-1958..... TCLC 19
See also CA 113; DLB 7

Croves, Hal
See Traven, B.

Crowfield, Christopher
See Stowe, Harriet (Elizabeth) Beecher

Crowley, Aleister.................. TCLC 7
See also Crowley, Edward Alexander

Crowley, Edward Alexander 1875-1947
See Crowley, Aleister
See also CA 104

Crowley, John 1942-.............. CLC 57
See also CA 61-64; CANR 43; DLBY 82;
SATA 65

Crud
See Crumb, R(obert)

Crumarums
See Crumb, R(obert)

Crumb, R(obert) 1943-............ CLC 17
See also CA 106

Crumbum
See Crumb, R(obert)

Crumski
See Crumb, R(obert)

Crum the Bum
See Crumb, R(obert)

Crunk
See Crumb, R(obert)

Crustt
See Crumb, R(obert)

Cryer, Gretchen (Kiger) 1935-...... CLC 21
See also CA 114; 123

Csath, Geza 1887-1919........... TCLC 13
See also CA 111

Cudlip, David 1933-.............. CLC 34

Cullen, Countee
1903-1946 ...... TCLC 4, 37; BLC; DA
See also BW 1; CA 108; 124;
CDALB 1917-1929; DLB 4, 48, 51;
MTCW; SATA 18

Cum, R.
See Crumb, R(obert)

Cummings, Bruce F(rederick) 1889-1919
See Barbellion, W. N. P.
See also CA 123

Cummings, E(dward) E(stlin)
1894-1962 ...... CLC 1, 3, 8, 12, 15, 68;
DA; PC 5; WLC 2
See also CA 73-76; CANR 31;
CDALB 1929-1941; DLB 4, 48; MTCW

Cunha, Euclides (Rodrigues Pimenta) da
1866-1909 .... TCLC 24
See also CA 123

Deighton, Len . . . . **CLC 4, 7, 22, 46**
See also Deighton, Leonard Cyril
See also AAYA 6; BEST 89:2;
   CDBLB 1960 to Present; DLB 87

Deighton, Leonard Cyril 1929-
See Deighton, Len
See also CA 9-12R; CANR 19, 33; MTCW

Dekker, Thomas 1572(?)-1632 . . . . . . **LC 22**
See also CDBLB Before 1660; DLB 62

de la Mare, Walter (John)
   1873-1956 . . **TCLC 4, 53; SSC 14; WLC**
See also CDBLB 1914-1945; CLR 23;
   DLB 19; SATA 16

Delaney, Franey
See O'Hara, John (Henry)

Delaney, Shelagh 1939- . . . . **CLC 29**
See also CA 17-20R; CANR 30;
   CDBLB 1960 to Present; DLB 13;
   MTCW

Delany, Mary (Granville Pendarves)
   1700-1788 . . . . **LC 12**

Delany, Samuel R(ay, Jr.)
   1942- . . . . **CLC 8, 14, 38; BLC**
See also BW 2; CA 81-84; CANR 27, 43;
   DLB 8, 33; MTCW

De La Ramee, (Marie) Louise 1839-1908
See Ouida
See also SATA 20

de la Roche, Mazo 1879-1961 . . . . . . **CLC 14**
See also CA 85-88; CANR 30; DLB 68;
   SATA 64

Delbanco, Nicholas (Franklin)
   1942- . . . . **CLC 6, 13**
See also CA 17-20R; CAAS 2; CANR 29;
   DLB 6

del Castillo, Michel 1933- . . . . **CLC 38**
See also CA 109

Deledda, Grazia (Cosima)
   1875(?)-1936 . . . . **TCLC 23**
See also CA 123

Delibes, Miguel . . . . **CLC 8, 18**
See also Delibes Setien, Miguel

Delibes Setien, Miguel 1920-
See Delibes, Miguel
See also CA 45-48; CANR 1, 32; HW;
   MTCW

DeLillo, Don
   1936- . . . . . **CLC 8, 10, 13, 27, 39, 54, 76**
See also BEST 89:1; CA 81-84; CANR 21;
   DLB 6; MTCW

de Lisser, H. G.
See De Lisser, Herbert George
See also DLB 117

De Lisser, Herbert George
   1878-1944 . . . . **TCLC 12**
See also de Lisser, H. G.
See also BW 2; CA 109

Deloria, Vine (Victor), Jr. 1933- . . . . **CLC 21**
See also CA 53-56; CANR 5, 20; MTCW;
   SATA 21

Del Vecchio, John M(ichael)
   1947- . . . . **CLC 29**
See also CA 110; DLBD 9

de Man, Paul (Adolph Michel)
   1919-1983 . . . . **CLC 55**
See also CA 128; 111; DLB 67; MTCW

De Marinis, Rick 1934- . . . . **CLC 54**
See also CA 57-60; CANR 9, 25

Demby, William 1922- . . . . . . **CLC 53; BLC**
See also BW 1; CA 81-84; DLB 33

Demijohn, Thom
See Disch, Thomas M(ichael)

de Montherlant, Henry (Milon)
See Montherlant, Henry (Milon) de

Demosthenes 384B.C.-322B.C. . . . **CMLC 13**

de Natale, Francine
See Malzberg, Barry N(athaniel)

Denby, Edwin (Orr) 1903-1983 . . . . . **CLC 48**
See also CA 138; 110

Denis, Julio
See Cortazar, Julio

Denmark, Harrison
See Zelazny, Roger (Joseph)

Dennis, John 1658-1734 . . . . **LC 11**
See also DLB 101

Dennis, Nigel (Forbes) 1912-1989 . . . . **CLC 8**
See also CA 25-28R; 129; DLB 13, 15;
   MTCW

De Palma, Brian (Russell) 1940- . . . . **CLC 20**
See also CA 109

De Quincey, Thomas 1785-1859 . . . **NCLC 4**
See also CDBLB 1789-1832; DLB 110

Deren, Eleanora 1908(?)-1961
See Deren, Maya
See also CA 111

Deren, Maya . . . . **CLC 16**
See also Deren, Eleanora

Derleth, August (William)
   1909-1971 . . . . **CLC 31**
See also CA 1-4R; 29-32R; CANR 4;
   DLB 9; SATA 5

de Routisie, Albert
See Aragon, Louis

Derrida, Jacques 1930- . . . . **CLC 24**
See also CA 124; 127

Derry Down Derry
See Lear, Edward

Dersonnes, Jacques
See Simenon, Georges (Jacques Christian)

Desai, Anita 1937- . . . . **CLC 19, 37**
See also CA 81-84; CANR 33; MTCW;
   SATA 63

de Saint-Luc, Jean
See Glassco, John

de Saint Roman, Arnaud
See Aragon, Louis

Descartes, Rene 1596-1650 . . . . **LC 20**

De Sica, Vittorio 1901(?)-1974 . . . . . **CLC 20**
See also CA 117

Desnos, Robert 1900-1945 . . . . **TCLC 22**
See also CA 121

Destouches, Louis-Ferdinand
   1894-1961 . . . . **CLC 9, 15**
See also Celine, Louis-Ferdinand
See also CA 85-88; CANR 28; MTCW

Deutsch, Babette 1895-1982 . . . . **CLC 18**
See also CA 1-4R; 108; CANR 4; DLB 45;
   SATA 1, 33

Devenant, William 1606-1649 . . . . . . **LC 13**

Devkota, Laxmiprasad
   1909-1959 . . . . **TCLC 23**
See also CA 123

De Voto, Bernard (Augustine)
   1897-1955 . . . . **TCLC 29**
See also CA 113; DLB 9

De Vries, Peter
   1910-1993 . . . . **CLC 1, 2, 3, 7, 10, 28, 46**
See also CA 17-20R; 142; CANR 41;
   DLB 6; DLBY 82; MTCW

Dexter, Martin
See Faust, Frederick (Schiller)

Dexter, Pete 1943- . . . . **CLC 34, 55**
See also BEST 89:2; CA 127; 131; MTCW

Diamano, Silmang
See Senghor, Leopold Sedar

Diamond, Neil 1941- . . . . **CLC 30**
See also CA 108

di Bassetto, Corno
See Shaw, George Bernard

Dick, Philip K(indred)
   1928-1982 . . . . **CLC 10, 30, 72**
See also CA 49-52; 106; CANR 2, 16;
   DLB 8; MTCW

Dickens, Charles (John Huffam)
   1812-1870 . . . . . **NCLC 3, 8, 18, 26; DA;
      WLC**
See also CDBLB 1832-1890; DLB 21, 55,
   70; JRDA; MAICYA; SATA 15

Dickey, James (Lafayette)
   1923- . . . . **CLC 1, 2, 4, 7, 10, 15, 47**
See also AITN 1, 2; CA 9-12R; CABS 2;
   CANR 10; CDALB 1968-1988; DLB 5;
   DLBD 7; DLBY 82, 93; MTCW

Dickey, William 1928- . . . . **CLC 3, 28**
See also CA 9-12R; CANR 24; DLB 5

Dickinson, Charles 1951- . . . . **CLC 49**
See also CA 128

Dickinson, Emily (Elizabeth)
   1830-1886 . . **NCLC 21; DA; PC 1; WLC**
See also CDALB 1865-1917; DLB 1;
   SATA 29

Dickinson, Peter (Malcolm)
   1927- . . . . **CLC 12, 35**
See also AAYA 9; CA 41-44R; CANR 31;
   CLR 29; DLB 87; JRDA; MAICYA;
   SATA 5, 62

Dickson, Carr
See Carr, John Dickson

Dickson, Carter
See Carr, John Dickson

Didion, Joan 1934- . . . . . **CLC 1, 3, 8, 14, 32**
See also AITN 1; CA 5-8R; CANR 14;
   CDALB 1968-1988; DLB 2; DLBY 81,
   86; MTCW

Dietrich, Robert
See Hunt, E(verette) Howard, Jr.

Dillard, Annie 1945- . . . . **CLC 9, 60**
See also AAYA 6; CA 49-52; CANR 3, 43;
   DLBY 80; MTCW; SATA 10

Dillard, R(ichard) H(enry) W(ilde)
   1937- . . . . **CLC 5**
See also CA 21-24R; CAAS 7; CANR 10;
   DLB 5

Dillon, Eilis 1920-. . . . . **CLC 17**
See also CA 9-12R; CAAS 3; CANR 4, 38;
CLR 26; MAICYA; SATA 2, 74

Dimont, Penelope
See Mortimer, Penelope (Ruth)

Dinesen, Isak . . . . **CLC 10, 29; SSC 7**
See also Blixen, Karen (Christentze
Dinesen)

Ding Ling . . . . **CLC 68**
See also Chiang Pin-chin

Disch, Thomas M(ichael) 1940-. . . **CLC 7, 36**
See also CA 21-24R; CAAS 4; CANR 17,
36; CLR 18; DLB 8; MAICYA; MTCW;
SAAS 15; SATA 54

Disch, Tom
See Disch, Thomas M(ichael)

d'Isly, Georges
See Simenon, Georges (Jacques Christian)

Disraeli, Benjamin 1804-1881 . . **NCLC 2, 39**
See also DLB 21, 55

Ditcum, Steve
See Crumb, R(obert)

Dixon, Paige
See Corcoran, Barbara

Dixon, Stephen 1936-. . . . . **CLC 52**
See also CA 89-92; CANR 17, 40; DLB 130

Dobell, Sydney Thompson
1824-1874 . . . . **NCLC 43**
See also DLB 32

Doblin, Alfred . . . . **TCLC 13**
See also Doeblin, Alfred

Dobrolyubov, Nikolai Alexandrovich
1836-1861 . . . . **NCLC 5**

Dobyns, Stephen 1941-. . . . . **CLC 37**
See also CA 45-48; CANR 2, 18

Doctorow, E(dgar) L(aurence)
1931- . . . . . **CLC 6, 11, 15, 18, 37, 44, 65**
See also AITN 2; BEST 89:3; CA 45-48;
CANR 2, 33; CDALB 1968-1988; DLB 2,
28; DLBY 80; MTCW

Dodgson, Charles Lutwidge 1832-1898
See Carroll, Lewis
See also CLR 2; DA; MAICYA; YABC 2

Dodson, Owen (Vincent)
1914-1983 . . . . **CLC 79; BLC**
See also BW 1; CA 65-68; 110; CANR 24;
DLB 76

Doeblin, Alfred 1878-1957. . . . . . . **TCLC 13**
See also Doblin, Alfred
See also CA 110; 141; DLB 66

Doerr, Harriet 1910- . . . . **CLC 34**
See also CA 117; 122

Domecq, H(onorio) Bustos
See Bioy Casares, Adolfo; Borges, Jorge
Luis

Domini, Rey
See Lorde, Audre (Geraldine)

Dominique
See Proust, (Valentin-Louis-George-Eugene-)
Marcel

Don, A
See Stephen, Leslie

Donaldson, Stephen R. 1947-. . . . . . . **CLC 46**
See also CA 89-92; CANR 13

Donleavy, J(ames) P(atrick)
1926- . . . . **CLC 1, 4, 6, 10, 45**
See also AITN 2; CA 9-12R; CANR 24;
DLB 6; MTCW

Donne, John
1572-1631 . . . . **LC 10, 24; DA; PC 1**
See also CDBLB Before 1660; DLB 121

Donnell, David 1939(?)- . . . . **CLC 34**

Donoso (Yanez), Jose
1924- . . . . **CLC 4, 8, 11, 32; HLC**
See also CA 81-84; CANR 32; DLB 113;
HW; MTCW

Donovan, John 1928-1992 . . . . **CLC 35**
See also CA 97-100; 137; CLR 3;
MAICYA; SATA 29

Don Roberto
See Cunninghame Graham, R(obert)
B(ontine)

Doolittle, Hilda
1886-1961 . . . . . **CLC 3, 8, 14, 31, 34, 73;
DA; PC 5; WLC**
See also H. D.
See also CA 97-100; CANR 35; DLB 4, 45;
MTCW

Dorfman, Ariel 1942-. . . . **CLC 48, 77; HLC**
See also CA 124; 130; HW

Dorn, Edward (Merton) 1929-. . . **CLC 10, 18**
See also CA 93-96; CANR 42; DLB 5

Dorsan, Luc
See Simenon, Georges (Jacques Christian)

Dorsange, Jean
See Simenon, Georges (Jacques Christian)

Dos Passos, John (Roderigo)
1896-1970 . . . . . . **CLC 1, 4, 8, 11, 15, 25,
34, 82; DA; WLC**
See also CA 1-4R; 29-32R; CANR 3;
CDALB 1929-1941; DLB 4, 9; DLBD 1;
MTCW

Dossage, Jean
See Simenon, Georges (Jacques Christian)

Dostoevsky, Fedor Mikhailovich
1821-1881 . . . . . . **NCLC 2, 7, 21, 33, 43;
DA; SSC 2; WLC**

Doughty, Charles M(ontagu)
1843-1926 . . . . **TCLC 27**
See also CA 115; DLB 19, 57

Douglas, Ellen
See Haxton, Josephine Ayres

Douglas, Gavin 1475(?)-1522. . . . . . . **LC 20**

Douglas, Keith 1920-1944 . . . . **TCLC 40**
See also DLB 27

Douglas, Leonard
See Bradbury, Ray (Douglas)

Douglas, Michael
See Crichton, (John) Michael

Douglass, Frederick
1817(?)-1895 . . . . **NCLC 7; BLC; DA;
WLC**
See also CDALB 1640-1865; DLB 1, 43, 50,
79; SATA 29

Dourado, (Waldomiro Freitas) Autran
1926- . . . . **CLC 23, 60**
See also CA 25-28R; CANR 34

Dourado, Waldomiro Autran
See Dourado, (Waldomiro Freitas) Autran

Dove, Rita (Frances)
1952- . . . . **CLC 50, 81; PC 6**
See also BW 2; CA 109; CAAS 19;
CANR 27, 42; DLB 120

Dowell, Coleman 1925-1985. . . . . . . **CLC 60**
See also CA 25-28R; 117; CANR 10;
DLB 130

Dowson, Ernest Christopher
1867-1900 . . . . **TCLC 4**
See also CA 105; DLB 19, 135

Doyle, A. Conan
See Doyle, Arthur Conan

Doyle, Arthur Conan
1859-1930 . . . . . . **TCLC 7; DA; SSC 12;
WLC**
See also CA 104; 122; CDBLB 1890-1914;
DLB 18, 70; MTCW; SATA 24

Doyle, Conan 1859-1930
See Doyle, Arthur Conan

Doyle, John
See Graves, Robert (von Ranke)

Doyle, Roddy 1958(?)- . . . . **CLC 81**
See also CA 143

Doyle, Sir A. Conan
See Doyle, Arthur Conan

Doyle, Sir Arthur Conan
See Doyle, Arthur Conan

Dr. A
See Asimov, Isaac; Silverstein, Alvin

Drabble, Margaret
1939- . . . . **CLC 2, 3, 5, 8, 10, 22, 53**
See also CA 13-16R; CANR 18, 35;
CDBLB 1960 to Present; DLB 14;
MTCW; SATA 48

Drapier, M. B.
See Swift, Jonathan

Drayham, James
See Mencken, H(enry) L(ouis)

Drayton, Michael 1563-1631. . . . . **LC 8**

Dreadstone, Carl
See Campbell, (John) Ramsey

Dreiser, Theodore (Herman Albert)
1871-1945 . . . . **TCLC 10, 18, 35; DA;
WLC**
See also CA 106; 132; CDALB 1865-1917;
DLB 9, 12, 102, 137; DLBD 1; MTCW

Drexler, Rosalyn 1926- . . . . **CLC 2, 6**
See also CA 81-84

Dreyer, Carl Theodor 1889-1968. . . . **CLC 16**
See also CA 116

Drieu la Rochelle, Pierre(-Eugene)
1893-1945 . . . . **TCLC 21**
See also CA 117; DLB 72

Drop Shot
See Cable, George Washington

Droste-Hulshoff, Annette Freiin von
1797-1848 . . . . **NCLC 3**
See also DLB 133

Drummond, Walter
See Silverberg, Robert

Drummond, William Henry
1854-1907 . . . . **TCLC 25**
See also DLB 92

Drummond de Andrade, Carlos
1902-1987 .... CLC 18
See also Andrade, Carlos Drummond de
See also CA 132; 123

Drury, Allen (Stuart) 1918-........ CLC 37
See also CA 57-60; CANR 18

Dryden, John
1631-1700 ... LC 3, 21; DA; DC 3; WLC
See also CDBLB 1660-1789; DLB 80, 101,
131

Duberman, Martin 1930-.......... CLC 8
See also CA 1-4R; CANR 2

Dubie, Norman (Evans) 1945-...... CLC 36
See also CA 69-72; CANR 12; DLB 120

Du Bois, W(illiam) E(dward) B(urghardt)
1868-1963 ...... CLC 1, 2, 13, 64; BLC;
DA; WLC
See also BW 1; CA 85-88; CANR 34;
CDALB 1865-1917; DLB 47, 50, 91;
MTCW; SATA 42

Dubus, Andre 1936-... CLC 13, 36; SSC 15
See also CA 21-24R; CANR 17; DLB 130

Duca Minimo
See D'Annunzio, Gabriele

Ducharme, Rejean 1941-.......... CLC 74
See also DLB 60

Duclos, Charles Pinot 1704-1772 ..... LC 1

Dudek, Louis 1918- .... CLC 11, 19
See also CA 45-48; CAAS 14; CANR 1;
DLB 88

Duerrenmatt, Friedrich
.... CLC 1, 4, 8, 11, 15, 43
See also Duerrenmatt, Friedrich
See also DLB 69, 124

Duerrenmatt, Friedrich
1921-1990 ...... CLC 1, 4, 8, 11, 15, 43
See also Duerrenmatt, Friedrich
See also CA 17-20R; CANR 33; DLB 69,
124; MTCW

Duffy, Bruce (?)-................. CLC 50

Duffy, Maureen 1933- .... CLC 37
See also CA 25-28R; CANR 33; DLB 14;
MTCW

Dugan, Alan 1923- .... CLC 2, 6
See also CA 81-84; DLB 5

du Gard, Roger Martin
See Martin du Gard, Roger

Duhamel, Georges 1884-1966 .... CLC 8
See also CA 81-84; 25-28R; CANR 35;
DLB 65; MTCW

Dujardin, Edouard (Emile Louis)
1861-1949 .... TCLC 13
See also CA 109; DLB 123

Dumas, Alexandre (Davy de la Pailleterie)
1802-1870 .... NCLC 11; DA; WLC
See also DLB 119; SATA 18

Dumas, Alexandre
1824-1895 .... NCLC 9; DC 1

Dumas, Claudine
See Malzberg, Barry N(athaniel)

Dumas, Henry L. 1934-1968 ..... CLC 6, 62
See also BW 1; CA 85-88; DLB 41

du Maurier, Daphne
1907-1989 .... CLC 6, 11, 59
See also CA 5-8R; 128; CANR 6; MTCW;
SATA 27, 60

Dunbar, Paul Laurence
1872-1906 ...... TCLC 2, 12; BLC; DA;
PC 5; SSC 8; WLC
See also BW 1; CA 104; 124;
CDALB 1865-1917; DLB 50, 54, 78;
SATA 34

Dunbar, William 1460(?)-1530(?) .... LC 20

Duncan, Lois 1934-............... CLC 26
See also AAYA 4; CA 1-4R; CANR 2, 23,
36; CLR 29; JRDA; MAICYA; SAAS 2;
SATA 1, 36, 75

Duncan, Robert (Edward)
1919-1988 .... CLC 1, 2, 4, 7, 15, 41, 55;
PC 2
See also CA 9-12R; 124; CANR 28; DLB 5,
16; MTCW

Dunlap, William 1766-1839 .... NCLC 2
See also DLB 30, 37, 59

Dunn, Douglas (Eaglesham)
1942- .... CLC 6, 40
See also CA 45-48; CANR 2, 33; DLB 40;
MTCW

Dunn, Katherine (Karen) 1945-..... CLC 71
See also CA 33-36R

Dunn, Stephen 1939- .... CLC 36
See also CA 33-36R; CANR 12; DLB 105

Dunne, Finley Peter 1867-1936.... TCLC 28
See also CA 108; DLB 11, 23

Dunne, John Gregory 1932-........ CLC 28
See also CA 25-28R; CANR 14; DLBY 80

Dunsany, Edward John Moreton Drax
Plunkett 1878-1957
See Dunsany, Lord; Lord Dunsany
See also CA 104; DLB 10

Dunsany, Lord.................... TCLC 2
See also Dunsany, Edward John Moreton
Drax Plunkett
See also DLB 77

du Perry, Jean
See Simenon, Georges (Jacques Christian)

Durang, Christopher (Ferdinand)
1949- .... CLC 27, 38
See also CA 105

Duras, Marguerite
1914- ...... CLC 3, 6, 11, 20, 34, 40, 68
See also CA 25-28R; DLB 83; MTCW

Durban, (Rosa) Pam 1947-........ CLC 39
See also CA 123

Durcan, Paul 1944-........... CLC 43, 70
See also CA 134

Durrell, Lawrence (George)
1912-1990 .... CLC 1, 4, 6, 8, 13, 27, 41
See also CA 9-12R; 132; CANR 40;
CDBLB 1945-1960; DLB 15, 27;
DLBY 90; MTCW

Dutt, Toru 1856-1877.......... NCLC 29

Dwight, Timothy 1752-1817...... NCLC 13
See also DLB 37

Dworkin, Andrea 1946- .... CLC 43
See also CA 77-80; CANR 16, 39; MTCW

Dwyer, Deanna
See Koontz, Dean R(ay)

Dwyer, K. R.
See Koontz, Dean R(ay)

Dylan, Bob 1941-...... CLC 3, 4, 6, 12, 77
See also CA 41-44R; DLB 16

Eagleton, Terence (Francis) 1943-
See Eagleton, Terry
See also CA 57-60; CANR 7, 23; MTCW

Eagleton, Terry .... CLC 63
See also Eagleton, Terence (Francis)

Early, Jack
See Scoppettone, Sandra

East, Michael
See West, Morris L(anglo)

Eastaway, Edward
See Thomas, (Philip) Edward

Eastlake, William (Derry) 1917-..... CLC 8
See also CA 5-8R; CAAS 1; CANR 5;
DLB 6

Eberhart, Richard (Ghormley)
1904- .... CLC 3, 11, 19, 56
See also CA 1-4R; CANR 2;
CDALB 1941-1968; DLB 48; MTCW

Eberstadt, Fernanda 1960-........ CLC 39
See also CA 136

Echegaray (y Eizaguirre), Jose (Maria Waldo)
1832-1916 .... TCLC 4
See also CA 104; CANR 32; HW; MTCW

Echeverria, (Jose) Esteban (Antonino)
1805-1851 .... NCLC 18

Echo
See Proust, (Valentin-Louis-George-Eugene-)
Marcel

Eckert, Allan W. 1931- .... CLC 17
See also CA 13-16R; CANR 14; SATA 27,
29

Eckhart, Meister 1260(?)-1328(?) .. CMLC 9
See also DLB 115

Eckmar, F. R.
See de Hartog, Jan

Eco, Umberto 1932-........... CLC 28, 60
See also BEST 90:1; CA 77-80; CANR 12,
33; MTCW

Eddison, E(ric) R(ucker)
1882-1945 .... TCLC 15
See also CA 109

Edel, (Joseph) Leon 1907-...... CLC 29, 34
See also CA 1-4R; CANR 1, 22; DLB 103

Eden, Emily 1797-1869 .... NCLC 10

Edgar, David 1948-.............. CLC 42
See also CA 57-60; CANR 12; DLB 13;
MTCW

Edgerton, Clyde (Carlyle) 1944- .... CLC 39
See also CA 118; 134

Edgeworth, Maria 1767-1849...... NCLC 1
See also DLB 116; SATA 21

Edmonds, Paul
See Kuttner, Henry

Edmonds, Walter D(umaux) 1903- .. CLC 35
See also CA 5-8R; CANR 2; DLB 9;
MAICYA; SAAS 4; SATA 1, 27

Edmondson, Wallace
See Ellison, Harlan

Eschenbach, Wolfram von
See Wolfram von Eschenbach

Eseki, Bruno
See Mphahlele, Ezekiel

Esenin, Sergei (Alexandrovich)
1895-1925 .... **TCLC 4**
See also CA 104

Eshleman, Clayton 1935-........... **CLC 7**
See also CA 33-36R; CAAS 6; DLB 5

Espriella, Don Manuel Alvarez
See Southey, Robert

Espriu, Salvador 1913-1985........ **CLC 9**
See also CA 115; DLB 134

Espronceda, Jose de 1808-1842... **NCLC 39**

Esse, James
See Stephens, James

Esterbrook, Tom
See Hubbard, L(afayette) Ron(ald)

Estleman, Loren D. 1952-........ **CLC 48**
See also CA 85-88; CANR 27; MTCW

Eugenides, Jeffrey 1960(?)-........ **CLC 81**
See also CA 144

Euripides c. 485B.C.-406B.C. .... **DC 4**
See also DA

Evan, Evin
See Faust, Frederick (Schiller)

Evans, Evan
See Faust, Frederick (Schiller)

Evans, Marian
See Eliot, George

Evans, Mary Ann
See Eliot, George

Evarts, Esther
See Benson, Sally

Everett, Percival L. 1956-........ **CLC 57**
See also BW 2; CA 129

Everson, R(onald) G(ilmour)
1903-...................... **CLC 27**
See also CA 17-20R; DLB 88

Everson, William (Oliver)
1912-.................. **CLC 1, 5, 14**
See also CA 9-12R; CANR 20; DLB 5, 16;
MTCW

Evtushenko, Evgenii Aleksandrovich
See Yevtushenko, Yevgeny (Alexandrovich)

Ewart, Gavin (Buchanan)
1916-.................... **CLC 13, 46**
See also CA 89-92; CANR 17; DLB 40;
MTCW

Ewers, Hanns Heinz 1871-1943 ... **TCLC 12**
See also CA 109

Ewing, Frederick R.
See Sturgeon, Theodore (Hamilton)

Exley, Frederick (Earl)
1929-1992 .... **CLC 6, 11**
See also AITN 2; CA 81-84; 138; DLBY 81

Eynhardt, Guillermo
See Quiroga, Horacio (Sylvestre)

Ezekiel, Nissim 1924-............ **CLC 61**
See also CA 61-64

Ezekiel, Tish O'Dowd 1943-....... **CLC 34**
See also CA 129

Fadeyev, A.
See Bulgya, Alexander Alexandrovich

Fadeyev, Alexander.............. **TCLC 53**
See also Bulgya, Alexander Alexandrovich

Fagen, Donald 1948-.............. **CLC 26**

Fainzilberg, Ilya Arnoldovich 1897-1937
See Ilf, Ilya
See also CA 120

Fair, Ronald L. 1932-............. **CLC 18**
See also BW 1; CA 69-72; CANR 25;
DLB 33

Fairbairns, Zoe (Ann) 1948- .... **CLC 32**
See also CA 103; CANR 21

Falco, Gian
See Papini, Giovanni

Falconer, James
See Kirkup, James

Falconer, Kenneth
See Kornbluth, C(yril) M.

Falkland, Samuel
See Heijermans, Herman

Fallaci, Oriana 1930-............. **CLC 11**
See also CA 77-80; CANR 15; MTCW

Faludy, George 1913-............. **CLC 42**
See also CA 21-24R

Faludy, Gyoergy
See Faludy, George

Fanon, Frantz 1925-1961..... **CLC 74; BLC**
See also BW 1; CA 116; 89-92

Fanshawe, Ann .... **LC 11**

Fante, John (Thomas) 1911-1983 ... **CLC 60**
See also CA 69-72; 109; CANR 23;
DLB 130; DLBY 83

Farah, Nuruddin 1945-....... **CLC 53; BLC**
See also BW 2; CA 106; DLB 125

Fargue, Leon-Paul 1876(?)-1947 ... **TCLC 11**
See also CA 109

Farigoule, Louis
See Romains, Jules

Farina, Richard 1936(?)-1966 .... **CLC 9**
See also CA 81-84; 25-28R

Farley, Walter (Lorimer)
1915-1989 .... **CLC 17**
See also CA 17-20R; CANR 8, 29; DLB 22;
JRDA; MAICYA; SATA 2, 43

Farmer, Philip Jose 1918-....... **CLC 1, 19**
See also CA 1-4R; CANR 4, 35; DLB 8;
MTCW

Farquhar, George 1677-1707........ **LC 21**
See also DLB 84

Farrell, J(ames) G(ordon)
1935-1979 .... **CLC 6**
See also CA 73-76; 89-92; CANR 36;
DLB 14; MTCW

Farrell, James T(homas)
1904-1979 .... **CLC 1, 4, 8, 11, 66**
See also CA 5-8R; 89-92; CANR 9; DLB 4,
9, 86; DLBD 2; MTCW

Farren, Richard J.
See Betjeman, John

Farren, Richard M.
See Betjeman, John

Fassbinder, Rainer Werner
1946-1982 .... **CLC 20**
See also CA 93-96; 106; CANR 31

Fast, Howard (Melvin) 1914-...... **CLC 23**
See also CA 1-4R; CAAS 18; CANR 1, 33;
DLB 9; SATA 7

Faulcon, Robert
See Holdstock, Robert P.

Faulkner, William (Cuthbert)
1897-1962 ..... **CLC 1, 3, 6, 8, 9, 11, 14,**
18, 28, 52, 68; DA; SSC 1; WLC
See also AAYA 7; CA 81-84; CANR 33;
CDALB 1929-1941; DLB 9, 11, 44, 102;
DLBD 2; DLBY 86; MTCW

Fauset, Jessie Redmon
1884(?)-1961 .... **CLC 19, 54; BLC**
See also BW 1; CA 109; DLB 51

Faust, Frederick (Schiller)
1892-1944(?) .... **TCLC 49**
See also CA 108

Faust, Irvin 1924-................. **CLC 8**
See also CA 33-36R; CANR 28; DLB 2, 28;
DLBY 80

Fawkes, Guy
See Benchley, Robert (Charles)

Fearing, Kenneth (Flexner)
1902-1961 .... **CLC 51**
See also CA 93-96; DLB 9

Fecamps, Elise
See Creasey, John

Federman, Raymond 1928- ...... **CLC 6, 47**
See also CA 17-20R; CAAS 8; CANR 10,
43; DLBY 80

Federspiel, J(uerg) F. 1931-........ **CLC 42**

Feiffer, Jules (Ralph) 1929-.... **CLC 2, 8, 64**
See also AAYA 3; CA 17-20R; CANR 30;
DLB 7, 44; MTCW; SATA 8, 61

Feige, Hermann Albert Otto Maximilian
See Traven, B.

Fei-Kan, Li
See Li Fei-kan

Feinberg, David B. 1956-.......... **CLC 59**
See also CA 135

Feinstein, Elaine 1930-............ **CLC 36**
See also CA 69-72; CAAS 1; CANR 31;
DLB 14, 40; MTCW

Feldman, Irving (Mordecai) 1928-.... **CLC 7**
See also CA 1-4R; CANR 1

Fellini, Federico 1920-1993 .... **CLC 16**
See also CA 65-68; 143; CANR 33

Felsen, Henry Gregor 1916- .... **CLC 17**
See also CA 1-4R; CANR 1; SAAS 2;
SATA 1

Fenton, James Martin 1949-....... **CLC 32**
See also CA 102; DLB 40

Ferber, Edna 1887-1968........... **CLC 18**
See also AITN 1; CA 5-8R; 25-28R; DLB 9,
28, 86; MTCW; SATA 7

Ferguson, Helen
See Kavan, Anna

Ferguson, Samuel 1810-1886..... **NCLC 33**
See also DLB 32

Ferling, Lawrence
See Ferlinghetti, Lawrence (Monsanto)

Fosse, Robert Louis 1927-1987
See Fosse, Bob
See also CA 110; 123

Foster, Stephen Collins
1826-1864 .... NCLC 26

Foucault, Michel
1926-1984 .... CLC 31, 34, 69
See also CA 105; 113; CANR 34; MTCW

Fouque, Friedrich (Heinrich Karl) de la Motte
1777-1843 .... NCLC 2
See also DLB 90

Fournier, Henri Alban 1886-1914
See Alain-Fournier
See also CA 104

Fournier, Pierre 1916- .... CLC 11
See also Gascar, Pierre
See also CA 89-92; CANR 16, 40

Fowles, John
1926- .... CLC 1, 2, 3, 4, 6, 9, 10, 15, 33
See also CA 5-8R; CANR 25; CDBLB 1960
to Present; DLB 14, 139; MTCW;
SATA 22

Fox, Paula 1923- .... CLC 2, 8
See also AAYA 3; CA 73-76; CANR 20,
36; CLR 1; DLB 52; JRDA; MAICYA;
MTCW; SATA 17, 60

Fox, William Price (Jr.) 1926- ..... CLC 22
See also CA 17-20R; CAAS 19; CANR 11;
DLB 2; DLBY 81

Foxe, John 1516(?)-1587 .... LC 14

Frame, Janet .... CLC 2, 3, 6, 22, 66
See also Clutha, Janet Paterson Frame

France, Anatole .... TCLC 9
See also Thibault, Jacques Anatole Francois
See also DLB 123

Francis, Claude 19(?)- .... CLC 50

Francis, Dick 1920- .... CLC 2, 22, 42
See also AAYA 5; BEST 89:3; CA 5-8R;
CANR 9, 42; CDBLB 1960 to Present;
DLB 87; MTCW

Francis, Robert (Churchill)
1901-1987 .... CLC 15
See also CA 1-4R; 123; CANR 1

Frank, Anne(lies Marie)
1929-1945 .... TCLC 17; DA; WLC
See also AAYA 12; CA 113; 133; MTCW;
SATA 42

Frank, Elizabeth 1945- .... CLC 39
See also CA 121; 126

Franklin, Benjamin
See Hasek, Jaroslav (Matej Frantisek)

Franklin, Benjamin 1706-1790... LC 25; DA
See also CDALB 1640-1865; DLB 24, 43,
73

Franklin, (Stella Maraia Sarah) Miles
1879-1954 .... TCLC 7
See also CA 104

Fraser, (Lady) Antonia (Pakenham)
1932- .... CLC 32
See also CA 85-88; CANR 44; MTCW;
SATA 32

Fraser, George MacDonald 1925- .... CLC 7
See also CA 45-48; CANR 2

Fraser, Sylvia 1935- .... CLC 64
See also CA 45-48; CANR 1, 16

Frayn, Michael 1933- ...... CLC 3, 7, 31, 47
See also CA 5-8R; CANR 30; DLB 13, 14;
MTCW

Fraze, Candida (Merrill) 1945- ..... CLC 50
See also CA 126

Frazer, J(ames) G(eorge)
1854-1941 .... TCLC 32
See also CA 118

Frazer, Robert Caine
See Creasey, John

Frazer, Sir James George
See Frazer, J(ames) G(eorge)

Frazier, Ian 1951- .... CLC 46
See also CA 130

Frederic, Harold 1856-1898...... NCLC 10
See also DLB 12, 23

Frederick, John
See Faust, Frederick (Schiller)

Frederick the Great 1712-1786 ...... LC 14

Fredro, Aleksander 1793-1876..... NCLC 8

Freeling, Nicolas 1927- .... CLC 38
See also CA 49-52; CAAS 12; CANR 1, 17;
DLB 87

Freeman, Douglas Southall
1886-1953 .... TCLC 11
See also CA 109; DLB 17

Freeman, Judith 1946- .... CLC 55

Freeman, Mary Eleanor Wilkins
1852-1930 .... TCLC 9; SSC 1
See also CA 106; DLB 12, 78

Freeman, R(ichard) Austin
1862-1943 .... TCLC 21
See also CA 113; DLB 70

French, Marilyn 1929- ...... CLC 10, 18, 60
See also CA 69-72; CANR 3, 31; MTCW

French, Paul
See Asimov, Isaac

Freneau, Philip Morin 1752-1832.. NCLC 1
See also DLB 37, 43

Freud, Sigmund 1856-1939 .... TCLC 52
See also CA 115; 133; MTCW

Friedan, Betty (Naomi) 1921- ...... CLC 74
See also CA 65-68; CANR 18; MTCW

Friedman, B(ernard) H(arper)
1926- .... CLC 7
See also CA 1-4R; CANR 3

Friedman, Bruce Jay 1930- .... CLC 3, 5, 56
See also CA 9-12R; CANR 25; DLB 2, 28

Friel, Brian 1929- .... CLC 5, 42, 59
See also CA 21-24R; CANR 33; DLB 13;
MTCW

Friis-Baastad, Babbis Ellinor
1921-1970 .... CLC 12
See also CA 17-20R; 134; SATA 7

Frisch, Max (Rudolf)
1911-1991 ..... CLC 3, 9, 14, 18, 32, 44
See also CA 85-88; 134; CANR 32;
DLB 69, 124; MTCW

Fromentin, Eugene (Samuel Auguste)
1820-1876 .... NCLC 10
See also DLB 123

Frost, Frederick
See Faust, Frederick (Schiller)

Frost, Robert (Lee)
1874-1963 .... CLC 1, 3, 4, 9, 10, 13, 15,
26, 34, 44; DA; PC 1; WLC
See also CA 89-92; CANR 33;
CDALB 1917-1929; DLB 54; DLBD 7;
MTCW; SATA 14

Froude, James Anthony
1818-1894 .... NCLC 43
See also DLB 18, 57

Froy, Herald
See Waterhouse, Keith (Spencer)

Fry, Christopher 1907- .... CLC 2, 10, 14
See also CA 17-20R; CANR 9, 30; DLB 13;
MTCW; SATA 66

Frye, (Herman) Northrop
1912-1991 .... CLC 24, 70
See also CA 5-8R; 133; CANR 8, 37;
DLB 67, 68; MTCW

Fuchs, Daniel 1909-1993 .... CLC 8, 22
See also CA 81-84; 142; CAAS 5;
CANR 40; DLB 9, 26, 28; DLBY 93

Fuchs, Daniel 1934- .... CLC 34
See also CA 37-40R; CANR 14

Fuentes, Carlos
1928- ...... CLC 3, 8, 10, 13, 22, 41, 60;
DA; HLC; WLC
See also AAYA 4; AITN 2; CA 69-72;
CANR 10, 32; DLB 113; HW; MTCW

Fuentes, Gregorio Lopez y
See Lopez y Fuentes, Gregorio

Fugard, (Harold) Athol
1932- .... CLC 5, 9, 14, 25, 40, 80; DC 3
See also CA 85-88; CANR 32; MTCW

Fugard, Sheila 1932- .... CLC 48
See also CA 125

Fuller, Charles (H., Jr.)
1939- .... CLC 25; BLC; DC 1
See also BW 2; CA 108; 112; DLB 38;
MTCW

Fuller, John (Leopold) 1937- .... CLC 62
See also CA 21-24R; CANR 9, 44; DLB 40

Fuller, Margaret .... NCLC 5
See also Ossoli, Sarah Margaret (Fuller
marchesa d')

Fuller, Roy (Broadbent)
1912-1991 .... CLC 4, 28
See also CA 5-8R; 135; CAAS 10; DLB 15,
20

Fulton, Alice 1952- .... CLC 52
See also CA 116

Furphy, Joseph 1843-1912........ TCLC 25

Fussell, Paul 1924- .... CLC 74
See also BEST 90:1; CA 17-20R; CANR 8,
21, 35; MTCW

Futabatei, Shimei 1864-1909 ...... TCLC 44

Futrelle, Jacques 1875-1912 ...... TCLC 19
See also CA 113

G. B. S.
See Shaw, George Bernard

Gaboriau, Emile 1835-1873...... NCLC 14

Gadda, Carlo Emilio 1893-1973 .... CLC 11
See also CA 89-92

Goncourt, Edmond (Louis Antoine Huot) de
    1822-1896 .... **NCLC 7**
    See also DLB 123

Goncourt, Jules (Alfred Huot) de
    1830-1870 .... **NCLC 7**
    See also DLB 123

Gontier, Fernande 19(?)- .... **CLC 50**

Goodman, Paul 1911-1972.... **CLC 1, 2, 4, 7**
    See also CA 19-20; 37-40R; CANR 34;
    CAP 2; DLB 130; MTCW

Gordimer, Nadine
    1923- .... **CLC 3, 5, 7, 10, 18, 33, 51, 70;**
                                                    DA
    See also CA 5-8R; CANR 3, 28; MTCW

Gordon, Adam Lindsay
    1833-1870 .... **NCLC 21**

Gordon, Caroline
    1895-1981 ... **CLC 6, 13, 29, 83; SSC 15**
    See also CA 11-12; 103; CANR 36; CAP 1;
    DLB 4, 9, 102; DLBY 81; MTCW

Gordon, Charles William 1860-1937
    See Connor, Ralph
    See also CA 109

Gordon, Mary (Catherine)
    1949- .... **CLC 13, 22**
    See also CA 102; CANR 44; DLB 6;
    DLBY 81; MTCW

Gordon, Sol 1923-............... **CLC 26**
    See also CA 53-56; CANR 4; SATA 11

Gordone, Charles 1925-.......... **CLC 1, 4**
    See also BW 1; CA 93-96; DLB 7; MTCW

Gorenko, Anna Andreevna
    See Akhmatova, Anna

Gorky, Maxim.............. TCLC 8; WLC
    See also Peshkov, Alexei Maximovich

Goryan, Sirak
    See Saroyan, William

Gosse, Edmund (William)
    1849-1928 .... **TCLC 28**
    See also CA 117; DLB 57

Gotlieb, Phyllis Fay (Bloom)
    1926- .... **CLC 18**
    See also CA 13-16R; CANR 7; DLB 88

Gottesman, S. D.
    See Kornbluth, C(yril) M.; Pohl, Frederik

Gottfried von Strassburg
    fl. c. 1210- .... **CMLC 10**
    See also DLB 138

Gould, Lois .... **CLC 4, 10**
    See also CA 77-80; CANR 29; MTCW

Gourmont, Remy de 1858-1915.... **TCLC 17**
    See also CA 109

Govier, Katherine 1948-.......... **CLC 51**
    See also CA 101; CANR 18, 40

Goyen, (Charles) William
    1915-1983 .... **CLC 5, 8, 14, 40**
    See also AITN 2; CA 5-8R; 110; CANR 6;
    DLB 2; DLBY 83

Goytisolo, Juan
    1931- .... **CLC 5, 10, 23; HLC**
    See also CA 85-88; CANR 32; HW; MTCW

Gozzi, (Conte) Carlo 1720-1806 .. **NCLC 23**

Grabbe, Christian Dietrich
    1801-1836 .... **NCLC 2**
    See also DLB 133

Grace, Patricia 1937-............ **CLC 56**

Gracian y Morales, Baltasar
    1601-1658 .... **LC 15**

Gracq, Julien .... CLC 11, 48
    See also Poirier, Louis
    See also DLB 83

Grade, Chaim 1910-1982 .... **CLC 10**
    See also CA 93-96; 107

Graduate of Oxford, A
    See Ruskin, John

Graham, John
    See Phillips, David Graham

Graham, Jorie 1951-............ **CLC 48**
    See also CA 111; DLB 120

Graham, R(obert) B(ontine) Cunninghame
    See Cunninghame Graham, R(obert)
    B(ontine)
    See also DLB 98, 135

Graham, Robert
    See Haldeman, Joe (William)

Graham, Tom
    See Lewis, (Harry) Sinclair

Graham, W(illiam) S(ydney)
    1918-1986 .... **CLC 29**
    See also CA 73-76; 118; DLB 20

Graham, Winston (Mawdsley)
    1910- .... **CLC 23**
    See also CA 49-52; CANR 2, 22; DLB 77

Grant, Skeeter
    See Spiegelman, Art

Granville-Barker, Harley
    1877-1946 .... **TCLC 2**
    See also Barker, Harley Granville
    See also CA 104

Grass, Guenter (Wilhelm)
    1927- ..... **CLC 1, 2, 4, 6, 11, 15, 22, 32,**
                                        49; DA; WLC
    See also CA 13-16R; CANR 20; DLB 75,
    124; MTCW

Gratton, Thomas
    See Hulme, T(homas) E(rnest)

Grau, Shirley Ann
    1929- .... **CLC 4, 9; SSC 15**
    See also CA 89-92; CANR 22; DLB 2;
    MTCW

Gravel, Fern
    See Hall, James Norman

Graver, Elizabeth 1964-........... **CLC 70**
    See also CA 135

Graves, Richard Perceval 1945- .... **CLC 44**
    See also CA 65-68; CANR 9, 26

Graves, Robert (von Ranke)
    1895-1985 ..... **CLC 1, 2, 6, 11, 39, 44,**
                                        45; PC 6
    See also CA 5-8R; 117; CANR 5, 36;
    CDBLB 1914-1945; DLB 20, 100;
    DLBY 85; MTCW; SATA 45

Gray, Alasdair 1934- .... **CLC 41**
    See also CA 126; MTCW

Gray, Amlin 1946- .... **CLC 29**
    See also CA 138

Gray, Francine du Plessix 1930-.... **CLC 22**
    See also BEST 90:3; CA 61-64; CAAS 2;
    CANR 11, 33; MTCW

Gray, John (Henry) 1866-1934 .... **TCLC 19**
    See also CA 119

Gray, Simon (James Holliday)
    1936- .... **CLC 9, 14, 36**
    See also AITN 1; CA 21-24R; CAAS 3;
    CANR 32; DLB 13; MTCW

Gray, Spalding 1941-............. **CLC 49**
    See also CA 128

Gray, Thomas
    1716-1771 ...... **LC 4; DA; PC 2; WLC**
    See also CDBLB 1660-1789; DLB 109

Grayson, David
    See Baker, Ray Stannard

Grayson, Richard (A.) 1951-....... **CLC 38**
    See also CA 85-88; CANR 14, 31

Greeley, Andrew M(oran) 1928- .... **CLC 28**
    See also CA 5-8R; CAAS 7; CANR 7, 43;
    MTCW

Green, Brian
    See Card, Orson Scott

Green, Hannah
    See Greenberg, Joanne (Goldenberg)

Green, Hannah .... CLC 3
    See also CA 73-76

Green, Henry.................... CLC 2, 13
    See also Yorke, Henry Vincent
    See also DLB 15

Green, Julian (Hartridge) 1900-
    See Green, Julien
    See also CA 21-24R; CANR 33; DLB 4, 72;
    MTCW

Green, Julien................. CLC 3, 11, 77
    See also Green, Julian (Hartridge)

Green, Paul (Eliot) 1894-1981...... **CLC 25**
    See also AITN 1; CA 5-8R; 103; CANR 3;
    DLB 7, 9; DLBY 81

Greenberg, Ivan 1908-1973
    See Rahv, Philip
    See also CA 85-88

Greenberg, Joanne (Goldenberg)
    1932- .... **CLC 7, 30**
    See also AAYA 12; CA 5-8R; CANR 14,
    32; SATA 25

Greenberg, Richard 1959(?)- .... **CLC 57**
    See also CA 138

Greene, Bette 1934- .... **CLC 30**
    See also AAYA 7; CA 53-56; CANR 4;
    CLR 2; JRDA; MAICYA; SAAS 16;
    SATA 8

Greene, Gael .... CLC 8
    See also CA 13-16R; CANR 10

Greene, Graham
    1904-1991 .... **CLC 1, 3, 6, 9, 14, 18, 27,**
                                        37, 70, 72; DA; WLC
    See also AITN 2; CA 13-16R; 133;
    CANR 35; CDBLB 1945-1960; DLB 13,
    15, 77, 100; DLBY 91; MTCW; SATA 20

Greer, Richard
    See Silverberg, Robert

Greer, Richard
    See Silverberg, Robert

Gregor, Arthur 1923- . . . . CLC 9
See also CA 25-28R; CAAS 10; CANR 11;
SATA 36

Gregor, Lee
See Pohl, Frederik

Gregory, Isabella Augusta (Persse)
1852-1932 . . . . TCLC 1
See also CA 104; DLB 10

Gregory, J. Dennis
See Williams, John A(lfred)

Grendon, Stephen
See Derleth, August (William)

Grenville, Kate 1950- . . . . CLC 61
See also CA 118

Grenville, Pelham
See Wodehouse, P(elham) G(renville)

Greve, Felix Paul (Berthold Friedrich)
1879-1948
See Grove, Frederick Philip
See also CA 104; 141

Grey, Zane 1872-1939 . . . . TCLC 6
See also CA 104; 132; DLB 9; MTCW

Grieg, (Johan) Nordahl (Brun)
1902-1943 . . . . TCLC 10
See also CA 107

Grieve, C(hristopher) M(urray)
1892-1978 . . . . CLC 11, 19
See also MacDiarmid, Hugh
See also CA 5-8R; 85-88; CANR 33;
MTCW

Griffin, Gerald 1803-1840 . . . . NCLC 7

Griffin, John Howard 1920-1980 . . . . CLC 68
See also AITN 1; CA 1-4R; 101; CANR 2

Griffin, Peter . . . . CLC 39

Griffiths, Trevor 1935- . . . . CLC 13, 52
See also CA 97-100; DLB 13

Grigson, Geoffrey (Edward Harvey)
1905-1985 . . . . CLC 7, 39
See also CA 25-28R; 118; CANR 20, 33;
DLB 27; MTCW

Grillparzer, Franz 1791-1872 . . . . . . NCLC 1
See also DLB 133

Grimble, Reverend Charles James
See Eliot, T(homas) S(tearns)

Grimke, Charlotte L(ottie) Forten
1837(?)-1914
See Forten, Charlotte L.
See also BW 1; CA 117; 124

Grimm, Jacob Ludwig Karl
1785-1863 . . . . NCLC 3
See also DLB 90; MAICYA; SATA 22

Grimm, Wilhelm Karl 1786-1859 . . NCLC 3
See also DLB 90; MAICYA; SATA 22

Grimmelshausen, Johann Jakob Christoffel
von 1621-1676 . . . . LC 6

Grindel, Eugene 1895-1952
See Eluard, Paul
See also CA 104

Grossman, David 1954- . . . . CLC 67
See also CA 138

Grossman, Vasily (Semenovich)
1905-1964 . . . . CLC 41
See also CA 124; 130; MTCW

Grove, Frederick Philip . . . . TCLC 4
See also Greve, Felix Paul (Berthold
Friedrich)
See also DLB 92

Grubb
See Crumb, R(obert)

Grumbach, Doris (Isaac)
1918- . . . . CLC 13, 22, 64
See also CA 5-8R; CAAS 2; CANR 9, 42

Grundtvig, Nicolai Frederik Severin
1783-1872 . . . . NCLC 1

Grunge
See Crumb, R(obert)

Grunwald, Lisa 1959- . . . . CLC 44
See also CA 120

Guare, John 1938- . . . . CLC 8, 14, 29, 67
See also CA 73-76; CANR 21; DLB 7;
MTCW

Gudjonsson, Halldor Kiljan 1902-
See Laxness, Halldor
See also CA 103

Guenter, Erich
See Eich, Guenter

Guest, Barbara 1920- . . . . CLC 34
See also CA 25-28R; CANR 11, 44; DLB 5

Guest, Judith (Ann) 1936- . . . . CLC 8, 30
See also AAYA 7; CA 77-80; CANR 15;
MTCW

Guild, Nicholas M. 1944- . . . . CLC 33
See also CA 93-96

Guillemin, Jacques
See Sartre, Jean-Paul

Guillen, Jorge 1893-1984 . . . . CLC 11
See also CA 89-92; 112; DLB 108; HW

Guillen (y Batista), Nicolas (Cristobal)
1902-1989 . . . . . CLC 48, 79; BLC; HLC
See also BW 2; CA 116; 125; 129; HW

Guillevic, (Eugene) 1907- . . . . CLC 33
See also CA 93-96

Guillois
See Desnos, Robert

Guiney, Louise Imogen
1861-1920 . . . . TCLC 41
See also DLB 54

Guiraldes, Ricardo (Guillermo)
1886-1927 . . . . TCLC 39
See also CA 131; HW; MTCW

Gunn, Bill . . . . CLC 5
See also Gunn, William Harrison
See also DLB 38

Gunn, Thom(son William)
1929- . . . . CLC 3, 6, 18, 32, 81
See also CA 17-20R; CANR 9, 33;
CDBLB 1960 to Present; DLB 27;
MTCW

Gunn, William Harrison 1934(?)-1989
See Gunn, Bill
See also AITN 1; BW 1; CA 13-16R; 128;
CANR 12, 25

Gunnars, Kristjana 1948- . . . . CLC 69
See also CA 113; DLB 60

Gurganus, Allan 1947- . . . . CLC 70
See also BEST 90:1; CA 135

Gurney, A(lbert) R(amsdell), Jr.
1930- . . . . CLC 32, 50, 54
See also CA 77-80; CANR 32

Gurney, Ivor (Bertie) 1890-1937 . . . TCLC 33

Gurney, Peter
See Gurney, A(lbert) R(amsdell), Jr.

Gustafson, Ralph (Barker) 1909- . . . . CLC 36
See also CA 21-24R; CANR 8; DLB 88

Gut, Gom
See Simenon, Georges (Jacques Christian)

Guthrie, A(lfred) B(ertram), Jr.
1901-1991 . . . . CLC 23
See also CA 57-60; 134; CANR 24; DLB 6;
SATA 62; SATA-Obit 67

Guthrie, Isobel
See Grieve, C(hristopher) M(urray)

Guthrie, Woodrow Wilson 1912-1967
See Guthrie, Woody
See also CA 113; 93-96

Guthrie, Woody . . . . CLC 35
See also Guthrie, Woodrow Wilson

Guy, Rosa (Cuthbert) 1928- . . . . CLC 26
See also AAYA 4; BW 2; CA 17-20R;
CANR 14, 34; CLR 13; DLB 33; JRDA;
MAICYA; SATA 14, 62

Gwendolyn
See Bennett, (Enoch) Arnold

H. D. . . . . . . CLC 3, 8, 14, 31, 34, 73; PC 5
See also Doolittle, Hilda

Haavikko, Paavo Juhani
1931- . . . . CLC 18, 34
See also CA 106

Habbema, Koos
See Heijermans, Herman

Hacker, Marilyn 1942- . . . . CLC 5, 9, 23, 72
See also CA 77-80; DLB 120

Haggard, H(enry) Rider
1856-1925 . . . . TCLC 11
See also CA 108; DLB 70; SATA 16

Haig, Fenil
See Ford, Ford Madox

Haig-Brown, Roderick (Langmere)
1908-1976 . . . . CLC 21
See also CA 5-8R; 69-72; CANR 4, 38;
CLR 31; DLB 88; MAICYA; SATA 12

Hailey, Arthur 1920- . . . . CLC 5
See also AITN 2; BEST 90:3; CA 1-4R;
CANR 2, 36; DLB 88; DLBY 82; MTCW

Hailey, Elizabeth Forsythe 1938- . . . CLC 40
See also CA 93-96; CAAS 1; CANR 15

Haines, John (Meade) 1924- . . . . CLC 58
See also CA 17-20R; CANR 13, 34; DLB 5

Haldeman, Joe (William) 1943- . . . . . CLC 61
See also CA 53-56; CANR 6; DLB 8

Haley, Alex(ander Murray Palmer)
1921-1992 . . . . CLC 8, 12, 76; BLC; DA
See also BW 2; CA 77-80; 136; DLB 38;
MTCW

Haliburton, Thomas Chandler
1796-1865 . . . . NCLC 15
See also DLB 11, 99

Author Index

Hatteras, Amelia
See Mencken, H(enry) L(ouis)

Hatteras, Owen . . . . **TCLC 18**
See also Mencken, H(enry) L(ouis); Nathan, George Jean

Hauptmann, Gerhart (Johann Robert)
1862-1946 . . . . **TCLC 4**
See also CA 104; DLB 66, 118

Havel, Vaclav 1936- . . . . **CLC 25, 58, 65**
See also CA 104; CANR 36; MTCW

Haviaras, Stratis . . . . **CLC 33**
See also Chaviaras, Strates

Hawes, Stephen 1475(?)-1523(?) . . . . . **LC 17**

Hawkes, John (Clendennin Burne, Jr.)
1925- . . . . . . CLC 1, 2, 3, 4, 7, 9, 14, 15,
27, 49
See also CA 1-4R; CANR 2; DLB 2, 7;
DLBY 80; MTCW

Hawking, S. W.
See Hawking, Stephen W(illiam)

Hawking, Stephen W(illiam)
1942- . . . . **CLC 63**
See also BEST 89:1; CA 126; 129

Hawthorne, Julian 1846-1934 . . . . . **TCLC 25**

Hawthorne, Nathaniel
1804-1864 . . . . . . NCLC 39; DA; SSC 3;
WLC
See also CDALB 1640-1865; DLB 1, 74;
YABC 2

Haxton, Josephine Ayres 1921- . . . . **CLC 73**
See also CA 115; CANR 41

Hayaseca y Eizaguirre, Jorge
See Echegaray (y Eizaguirre), Jose (Maria Waldo)

Hayashi Fumiko 1904-1951 . . . . . . **TCLC 27**

Haycraft, Anna
See Ellis, Alice Thomas
See also CA 122

Hayden, Robert E(arl)
1913-1980 . . . . . . CLC 5, 9, 14, 37; BLC;
DA; PC 6
See also BW 1; CA 69-72; 97-100; CABS 2;
CANR 24; CDALB 1941-1968; DLB 5,
76; MTCW; SATA 19, 26

Hayford, J(oseph) E(phraim) Casely
See Casely-Hayford, J(oseph) E(phraim)

Hayman, Ronald 1932- . . . . **CLC 44**
See also CA 25-28R; CANR 18

Haywood, Eliza (Fowler)
1693(?)-1756 . . . . **LC 1**

Hazlitt, William 1778-1830 . . . . . . **NCLC 29**
See also DLB 110

Hazzard, Shirley 1931- . . . . **CLC 18**
See also CA 9-12R; CANR 4; DLBY 82;
MTCW

Head, Bessie 1937-1986 . . . **CLC 25, 67; BLC**
See also BW 2; CA 29-32R; 119; CANR 25;
DLB 117; MTCW

Headon, (Nicky) Topper 1956(?)- . . . **CLC 30**
See also Clash, The

Heaney, Seamus (Justin)
1939- . . . . CLC 5, 7, 14, 25, 37, 74
See also CA 85-88; CANR 25;
CDBLB 1960 to Present; DLB 40;
MTCW

Hearn, (Patricio) Lafcadio (Tessima Carlos)
1850-1904 . . . . **TCLC 9**
See also CA 105; DLB 12, 78

Hearne, Vicki 1946- . . . . **CLC 56**
See also CA 139

Hearon, Shelby 1931- . . . . **CLC 63**
See also AITN 2; CA 25-28R; CANR 18

Heat-Moon, William Least . . . . **CLC 29**
See also Trogdon, William (Lewis)
See also AAYA 9

Hebbel, Friedrich 1813-1863 . . . . . **NCLC 43**
See also DLB 129

Hebert, Anne 1916- . . . . **CLC 4, 13, 29**
See also CA 85-88; DLB 68; MTCW

Hecht, Anthony (Evan)
1923- . . . . **CLC 8, 13, 19**
See also CA 9-12R; CANR 6; DLB 5

Hecht, Ben 1894-1964 . . . . **CLC 8**
See also CA 85-88; DLB 7, 9, 25, 26, 28, 86

Hedayat, Sadeq 1903-1951 . . . . **TCLC 21**
See also CA 120

Heidegger, Martin 1889-1976 . . . . . . **CLC 24**
See also CA 81-84; 65-68; CANR 34;
MTCW

Heidenstam, (Carl Gustaf) Verner von
1859-1940 . . . . **TCLC 5**
See also CA 104

Heifner, Jack 1946- . . . . **CLC 11**
See also CA 105

Heijermans, Herman 1864-1924 . . . **TCLC 24**
See also CA 123

Heilbrun, Carolyn G(old) 1926- . . . . . **CLC 25**
See also CA 45-48; CANR 1, 28

Heine, Heinrich 1797-1856 . . . . **NCLC 4**
See also DLB 90

Heinemann, Larry (Curtiss) 1944- . . **CLC 50**
See also CA 110; CANR 31; DLBD 9

Heiney, Donald (William)
1921-1993 . . . . **CLC 9**
See also CA 1-4R; 142; CANR 3

Heinlein, Robert A(nson)
1907-1988 . . . . . . CLC 1, 3, 8, 14, 26, 55
See also CA 1-4R; 125; CANR 1, 20;
DLB 8; JRDA; MAICYA; MTCW;
SATA 9, 56, 69

Helforth, John
See Doolittle, Hilda

Hellenhofferu, Vojtech Kapristian z
See Hasek, Jaroslav (Matej Frantisek)

Heller, Joseph
1923- . . . . CLC 1, 3, 5, 8, 11, 36, 63; DA;
WLC
See also AITN 1; CA 5-8R; CABS 1;
CANR 8, 42; DLB 2, 28; DLBY 80;
MTCW

Hellman, Lillian (Florence)
1906-1984 . . . . . . CLC 2, 4, 8, 14, 18, 34,
44, 52; DC 1
See also AITN 1, 2; CA 13-16R; 112;
CANR 33; DLB 7; DLBY 84; MTCW

Helprin, Mark 1947- . . . . . CLC 7, 10, 22, 32
See also CA 81-84; DLBY 85; MTCW

Helyar, Jane Penelope Josephine 1933-
See Poole, Josephine
See also CA 21-24R; CANR 10, 26

Hemans, Felicia 1793-1835 . . . . . . **NCLC 29**
See also DLB 96

Hemingway, Ernest (Miller)
1899-1961 . . . . CLC 1, 3, 6, 8, 10, 13, 19,
30, 34, 39, 41, 44, 50, 61, 80; DA; SSC 1;
WLC
See also CA 77-80; CANR 34;
CDALB 1917-1929; DLB 4, 9, 102;
DLBD 1; DLBY 81, 87; MTCW

Hempel, Amy 1951- . . . . **CLC 39**
See also CA 118; 137

Henderson, F. C.
See Mencken, H(enry) L(ouis)

Henderson, Sylvia
See Ashton-Warner, Sylvia (Constance)

Henley, Beth . . . . **CLC 23**
See also Henley, Elizabeth Becker
See also CABS 3; DLBY 86

Henley, Elizabeth Becker 1952-
See Henley, Beth
See also CA 107; CANR 32; MTCW

Henley, William Ernest
1849-1903 . . . . **TCLC 8**
See also CA 105; DLB 19

Hennissart, Martha
See Lathen, Emma
See also CA 85-88

Henry, O. . . . . TCLC 1, 19; SSC 5; WLC
See also Porter, William Sydney

Henry, Patrick 1736-1799 . . . . **LC 25**

Henryson, Robert 1430(?)-1506(?) . . . . **LC 20**

Henry VIII 1491-1547 . . . . **LC 10**

Henschke, Alfred
See Klabund

Hentoff, Nat(han Irving) 1925- . . . . . **CLC 26**
See also AAYA 4; CA 1-4R; CAAS 6;
CANR 5, 25; CLR 1; JRDA; MAICYA;
SATA 27, 42, 69

Heppenstall, (John) Rayner
1911-1981 . . . . **CLC 10**
See also CA 1-4R; 103; CANR 29

Herbert, Frank (Patrick)
1920-1986 . . . . **CLC 12, 23, 35, 44**
See also CA 53-56; 118; CANR 5, 43;
DLB 8; MTCW; SATA 9, 37, 47

Herbert, George 1593-1633 . . . . **LC 24; PC 4**
See also CDBLB Before 1660; DLB 126

Herbert, Zbigniew 1924- . . . . **CLC 9, 43**
See also CA 89-92; CANR 36; MTCW

Herbst, Josephine (Frey)
1897-1969 . . . . **CLC 34**
See also CA 5-8R; 25-28R; DLB 9

Hergesheimer, Joseph
1880-1954 . . . . **TCLC 11**
See also CA 109; DLB 102, 9

Herlihy, James Leo 1927-1993 . . . . . . **CLC 6**
See also CA 1-4R; 143; CANR 2

Hermogenes fl. c. 175- . . . . **CMLC 6**

Hernandez, Jose 1834-1886 . . . . . . **NCLC 17**

Herrick, Robert
1591-1674 . . . . **LC 13; DA; PC 9**
See also DLB 126

Herring, Guilles
See Somerville, Edith

Herriot, James 1916- . . . . CLC 12
    See also Wight, James Alfred
    See also AAYA 1; CANR 40

Herrmann, Dorothy 1941- . . . . CLC 44
    See also CA 107

Herrmann, Taffy
    See Herrmann, Dorothy

Hersey, John (Richard)
    1914-1993 . . . . . . CLC 1, 2, 7, 9, 40, 81
    See also CA 17-20R; 140; CANR 33;
    DLB 6; MTCW; SATA 25;
    SATA-Obit 76

Herzen, Aleksandr Ivanovich
    1812-1870 . . . . NCLC 10

Herzl, Theodor 1860-1904 . . . . TCLC 36

Herzog, Werner 1942- . . . . CLC 16
    See also CA 89-92

Hesiod c. 8th cent. B.C.- . . . . CMLC 5

Hesse, Hermann
    1877-1962 . . . . CLC 1, 2, 3, 6, 11, 17, 25,
                        69; DA; SSC 9; WLC
    See also CA 17-18; CAP 2; DLB 66;
    MTCW; SATA 50

Hewes, Cady
    See De Voto, Bernard (Augustine)

Heyen, William 1940- . . . . CLC 13, 18
    See also CA 33-36R; CAAS 9; DLB 5

Heyerdahl, Thor 1914- . . . . CLC 26
    See also CA 5-8R; CANR 5, 22; MTCW;
    SATA 2, 52

Heym, Georg (Theodor Franz Arthur)
    1887-1912 . . . . TCLC 9
    See also CA 106

Heym, Stefan 1913- . . . . CLC 41
    See also CA 9-12R; CANR 4; DLB 69

Heyse, Paul (Johann Ludwig von)
    1830-1914 . . . . TCLC 8
    See also CA 104; DLB 129

Hibbert, Eleanor Alice Burford
    1906-1993 . . . . CLC 7
    See also BEST 90:4; CA 17-20R; 140;
    CANR 9, 28; SATA 2; SATA-Obit 74

Higgins, George V(incent)
    1939- . . . . CLC 4, 7, 10, 18
    See also CA 77-80; CAAS 5; CANR 17;
    DLB 2; DLBY 81; MTCW

Higginson, Thomas Wentworth
    1823-1911 . . . . TCLC 36
    See also DLB 1, 64

Highet, Helen
    See MacInnes, Helen (Clark)

Highsmith, (Mary) Patricia
    1921- . . . . CLC 2, 4, 14, 42
    See also CA 1-4R; CANR 1, 20; MTCW

Highwater, Jamake (Mamake)
    1942(?)- . . . . CLC 12
    See also AAYA 7; CA 65-68; CAAS 7;
    CANR 10, 34; CLR 17; DLB 52;
    DLBY 85; JRDA; MAICYA; SATA 30,
    32, 69

Hijuelos, Oscar 1951- . . . . . . CLC 65; HLC
    See also BEST 90:1; CA 123; HW

Hikmet, Nazim 1902(?)-1963 . . . . CLC 40
    See also CA 141; 93-96

Hildesheimer, Wolfgang
    1916-1991 . . . . CLC 49
    See also CA 101; 135; DLB 69, 124

Hill, Geoffrey (William)
    1932- . . . . CLC 5, 8, 18, 45
    See also CA 81-84; CANR 21;
    CDBLB 1960 to Present; DLB 40;
    MTCW

Hill, George Roy 1921- . . . . CLC 26
    See also CA 110; 122

Hill, John
    See Koontz, Dean R(ay)

Hill, Susan (Elizabeth) 1942- . . . . . . CLC 4
    See also CA 33-36R; CANR 29; DLB 14,
    139; MTCW

Hillerman, Tony 1925- . . . . CLC 62
    See also AAYA 6; BEST 89:1; CA 29-32R;
    CANR 21, 42; SATA 6

Hillesum, Etty 1914-1943 . . . . TCLC 49
    See also CA 137

Hilliard, Noel (Harvey) 1929- . . . . . . CLC 15
    See also CA 9-12R; CANR 7

Hillis, Rick 1956- . . . . CLC 66
    See also CA 134

Hilton, James 1900-1954 . . . . TCLC 21
    See also CA 108; DLB 34, 77; SATA 34

Himes, Chester (Bomar)
    1909-1984 . . . . CLC 2, 4, 7, 18, 58; BLC
    See also BW 2; CA 25-28R; 114; CANR 22;
    DLB 2, 76; MTCW

Hinde, Thomas . . . . CLC 6, 11
    See also Chitty, Thomas Willes

Hindin, Nathan
    See Bloch, Robert (Albert)

Hine, (William) Daryl 1936- . . . . CLC 15
    See also CA 1-4R; CAAS 15; CANR 1, 20;
    DLB 60

Hinkson, Katharine Tynan
    See Tynan, Katharine

Hinton, S(usan) E(loise)
    1950- . . . . CLC 30; DA
    See also AAYA 2; CA 81-84; CANR 32;
    CLR 3, 23; JRDA; MAICYA; MTCW;
    SATA 19, 58

Hippius, Zinaida . . . . TCLC 9
    See also Gippius, Zinaida (Nikolayevna)

Hiraoka, Kimitake 1925-1970
    See Mishima, Yukio
    See also CA 97-100; 29-32R; MTCW

Hirsch, E(ric) D(onald), Jr. 1928- . . . CLC 79
    See also CA 25-28R; CANR 27; DLB 67;
    MTCW

Hirsch, Edward 1950- . . . . CLC 31, 50
    See also CA 104; CANR 20, 42; DLB 120

Hitchcock, Alfred (Joseph)
    1899-1980 . . . . CLC 16
    See also CA 97-100; SATA 24, 27

Hitler, Adolf 1889-1945 . . . . TCLC 53
    See also CA 117

Hoagland, Edward 1932- . . . . CLC 28
    See also CA 1-4R; CANR 2, 31; DLB 6;
    SATA 51

Hoban, Russell (Conwell) 1925- . . CLC 7, 25
    See also CA 5-8R; CANR 23, 37; CLR 3;
    DLB 52; MAICYA; MTCW; SATA 1, 40

Hobbs, Perry
    See Blackmur, R(ichard) P(almer)

Hobson, Laura Z(ametkin)
    1900-1986 . . . . CLC 7, 25
    See also CA 17-20R; 118; DLB 28;
    SATA 52

Hochhuth, Rolf 1931- . . . . CLC 4, 11, 18
    See also CA 5-8R; CANR 33; DLB 124;
    MTCW

Hochman, Sandra 1936- . . . . CLC 3, 8
    See also CA 5-8R; DLB 5

Hochwaelder, Fritz 1911-1986 . . . . . . CLC 36
    See also CA 29-32R; 120; CANR 42;
    MTCW

Hochwalder, Fritz
    See Hochwaelder, Fritz

Hocking, Mary (Eunice) 1921- . . . . . CLC 13
    See also CA 101; CANR 18, 40

Hodgins, Jack 1938- . . . . CLC 23
    See also CA 93-96; DLB 60

Hodgson, William Hope
    1877(?)-1918 . . . . TCLC 13
    See also CA 111; DLB 70

Hoffman, Alice 1952- . . . . CLC 51
    See also CA 77-80; CANR 34; MTCW

Hoffman, Daniel (Gerard)
    1923- . . . . CLC 6, 13, 23
    See also CA 1-4R; CANR 4; DLB 5

Hoffman, Stanley 1944- . . . . CLC 5
    See also CA 77-80

Hoffman, William M(oses) 1939- . . . CLC 40
    See also CA 57-60; CANR 11

Hoffmann, E(rnst) T(heodor) A(madeus)
    1776-1822 . . . . NCLC 2; SSC 13
    See also DLB 90; SATA 27

Hofmann, Gert 1931- . . . . CLC 54
    See also CA 128

Hofmannsthal, Hugo von
    1874-1929 . . . . TCLC 11; DC 4
    See also CA 106; DLB 81, 118

Hogan, Linda 1947- . . . . CLC 73
    See also CA 120

Hogarth, Charles
    See Creasey, John

Hogg, James 1770-1835 . . . . NCLC 4
    See also DLB 93, 116

Holbach, Paul Henri Thiry Baron
    1723-1789 . . . . LC 14

Holberg, Ludvig 1684-1754 . . . . LC 6

Holden, Ursula 1921- . . . . CLC 18
    See also CA 101; CAAS 8; CANR 22

Holderlin, (Johann Christian) Friedrich
    1770-1843 . . . . NCLC 16; PC 4

Holdstock, Robert
    See Holdstock, Robert P.

Holdstock, Robert P. 1948- . . . . CLC 39
    See also CA 131

Holland, Isabelle 1920- . . . . CLC 21
    See also AAYA 11; CA 21-24R; CANR 10,
    25; JRDA; MAICYA; SATA 8, 70

Holland, Marcus
    See Caldwell, (Janet Miriam) Taylor
    (Holland)

Hollander, John   1929-...... **CLC 2, 5, 8, 14**
See also CA 1-4R; CANR 1; DLB 5;
SATA 13

Hollander, Paul
See Silverberg, Robert

Holleran, Andrew   1943(?)-........ **CLC 38**
See also CA 144

Hollinghurst, Alan   1954-......... **CLC 55**
See also CA 114

Hollis, Jim
See Summers, Hollis (Spurgeon, Jr.)

Holmes, John
See Souster, (Holmes) Raymond

Holmes, John Clellon   1926-1988.... **CLC 56**
See also CA 9-12R; 125; CANR 4; DLB 16

Holmes, Oliver Wendell
1809-1894 .... **NCLC 14**
See also CDALB 1640-1865; DLB 1;
SATA 34

Holmes, Raymond
See Souster, (Holmes) Raymond

Holt, Victoria
See Hibbert, Eleanor Alice Burford

Holub, Miroslav   1923-............. **CLC 4**
See also CA 21-24R; CANR 10

Homer   c. 8th cent. B.C.-..... **CMLC 1; DA**

Honig, Edwin   1919-............. **CLC 33**
See also CA 5-8R; CAAS 8; CANR 4;
DLB 5

Hood, Hugh (John Blagdon)
1928-..................... **CLC 15, 28**
See also CA 49-52; CAAS 17; CANR 1, 33;
DLB 53

Hood, Thomas   1799-1845....... **NCLC 16**
See also DLB 96

Hooker, (Peter) Jeremy   1941-...... **CLC 43**
See also CA 77-80; CANR 22; DLB 40

Hope, A(lec) D(erwent)   1907-.... **CLC 3, 51**
See also CA 21-24R; CANR 33; MTCW

Hope, Brian
See Creasey, John

Hope, Christopher (David Tully)
1944-....................... **CLC 52**
See also CA 106; SATA 62

Hopkins, Gerard Manley
1844-1889 .... **NCLC 17; DA; WLC**
See also CDBLB 1890-1914; DLB 35, 57

Hopkins, John (Richard)   1931-...... **CLC 4**
See also CA 85-88

Hopkins, Pauline Elizabeth
1859-1930 .... **TCLC 28; BLC**
See also BW 2; CA 141; DLB 50

Hopkinson, Francis   1737-1791 ...... **LC 25**
See also DLB 31

Hopley-Woolrich, Cornell George   1903-1968
See Woolrich, Cornell
See also CA 13-14; CAP 1

Horatio
See Proust, (Valentin-Louis-George-Eugene-)
Marcel

Horgan, Paul   1903-............. **CLC 9, 53**
See also CA 13-16R; CANR 9, 35;
DLB 102; DLBY 85; MTCW; SATA 13

Horn, Peter
See Kuttner, Henry

Hornem, Horace Esq.
See Byron, George Gordon (Noel)

Horovitz, Israel   1939-............. **CLC 56**
See also CA 33-36R; DLB 7

Horvath, Odon von
See Horvath, Oedoen von
See also DLB 85, 124

Horvath, Oedoen von   1901-1938... **TCLC 45**
See also Horvath, Odon von
See also CA 118

Horwitz, Julius   1920-1986........ **CLC 14**
See also CA 9-12R; 119; CANR 12

Hospital, Janette Turner   1942-..... **CLC 42**
See also CA 108

Hostos, E. M. de
See Hostos (y Bonilla), Eugenio Maria de

Hostos, Eugenio M. de
See Hostos (y Bonilla), Eugenio Maria de

Hostos, Eugenio Maria
See Hostos (y Bonilla), Eugenio Maria de

Hostos (y Bonilla), Eugenio Maria de
1839-1903 .... **TCLC 24**
See also CA 123; 131; HW

Houdini
See Lovecraft, H(oward) P(hillips)

Hougan, Carolyn   1943-........... **CLC 34**
See also CA 139

Household, Geoffrey (Edward West)
1900-1988 .... **CLC 11**
See also CA 77-80; 126; DLB 87; SATA 14,
59

Housman, A(lfred) E(dward)
1859-1936 ...... **TCLC 1, 10; DA; PC 2**
See also CA 104; 125; DLB 19; MTCW

Housman, Laurence   1865-1959 ..... **TCLC 7**
See also CA 106; DLB 10; SATA 25

Howard, Elizabeth Jane   1923- ... **CLC 7, 29**
See also CA 5-8R; CANR 8

Howard, Maureen   1930- ..... **CLC 5, 14, 46**
See also CA 53-56; CANR 31; DLBY 83;
MTCW

Howard, Richard   1929-...... **CLC 7, 10, 47**
See also AITN 1; CA 85-88; CANR 25;
DLB 5

Howard, Robert Ervin   1906-1936... **TCLC 8**
See also CA 105

Howard, Warren F.
See Pohl, Frederik

Howe, Fanny   1940-............. **CLC 47**
See also CA 117; SATA 52

Howe, Julia Ward   1819-1910 ..... **TCLC 21**
See also CA 117; DLB 1

Howe, Susan   1937-................. **CLC 72**
See also DLB 120

Howe, Tina   1937-................ **CLC 48**
See also CA 109

Howell, James   1594(?)-1666 .... **LC 13**

Howells, W. D.
See Howells, William Dean

Howells, William D.
See Howells, William Dean

Howells, William Dean
1837-1920 .... **TCLC 7, 17, 41**
See also CA 104; 134; CDALB 1865-1917;
DLB 12, 64, 74, 79

Howes, Barbara   1914-............. **CLC 15**
See also CA 9-12R; CAAS 3; SATA 5

Hrabal, Bohumil   1914-........ **CLC 13, 67**
See also CA 106; CAAS 12

Hsun, Lu .... **TCLC 3**
See also Shu-Jen, Chou

Hubbard, L(afayette) Ron(ald)
1911-1986 .... **CLC 43**
See also CA 77-80; 118; CANR 22

Huch, Ricarda (Octavia)
1864-1947 .... **TCLC 13**
See also CA 111; DLB 66

Huddle, David   1942- .... **CLC 49**
See also CA 57-60; DLB 130

Hudson, Jeffrey
See Crichton, (John) Michael

Hudson, W(illiam) H(enry)
1841-1922 .... **TCLC 29**
See also CA 115; DLB 98; SATA 35

Hueffer, Ford Madox
See Ford, Ford Madox

Hughart, Barry   1934-............. **CLC 39**
See also CA 137

Hughes, Colin
See Creasey, John

Hughes, David (John)   1930- .... **CLC 48**
See also CA 116; 129; DLB 14

Hughes, (James) Langston
1902-1967 ..... **CLC 1, 5, 10, 15, 35, 44;**
BLC; DA; DC 3; PC 1; SSC 6; WLC
See also AAYA 12; BW 1; CA 1-4R;
25-28R; CANR 1, 34; CDALB 1929-1941;
CLR 17; DLB 4, 7, 48, 51, 86; JRDA;
MAICYA; MTCW; SATA 4, 33

Hughes, Richard (Arthur Warren)
1900-1976 .... **CLC 1, 11**
See also CA 5-8R; 65-68; CANR 4;
DLB 15; MTCW; SATA 8, 25

Hughes, Ted
1930- .... **CLC 2, 4, 9, 14, 37; PC 7**
See also CA 1-4R; CANR 1, 33; CLR 3;
DLB 40; MAICYA; MTCW; SATA 27,
49

Hugo, Richard F(ranklin)
1923-1982 .... **CLC 6, 18, 32**
See also CA 49-52; 108; CANR 3; DLB 5

Hugo, Victor (Marie)
1802-1885 .. **NCLC 3, 10, 21; DA; WLC**
See also DLB 119; SATA 47

Huidobro, Vicente
See Huidobro Fernandez, Vicente Garcia

Huidobro Fernandez, Vicente Garcia
1893-1948 .... **TCLC 31**
See also CA 131; HW

Hulme, Keri   1947- .... **CLC 39**
See also CA 125

Hulme, T(homas) E(rnest)
1883-1917 .... **TCLC 21**
See also CA 117; DLB 19

Hume, David   1711-1776............. **LC 7**
See also DLB 104

James, Andrew
See Kirkup, James

James, C(yril) L(ionel) R(obert)
1901-1989 .... **CLC 33**
See also BW 2; CA 117; 125; 128; DLB 125;
MTCW

James, Daniel (Lewis) 1911-1988
See Santiago, Danny
See also CA 125

James, Dynely
See Mayne, William (James Carter)

James, Henry
1843-1916 ...... **TCLC 2, 11, 24, 40, 47;**
DA; SSC 8; WLC
See also CA 104; 132; CDALB 1865-1917;
DLB 12, 71, 74; MTCW

James, Montague (Rhodes)
1862-1936 .... **TCLC 6**
See also CA 104

James, P. D. .... **CLC 18, 46**
See also White, Phyllis Dorothy James
See also BEST 90:2; CDBLB 1960 to
Present; DLB 87

James, Philip
See Moorcock, Michael (John)

James, William 1842-1910..... **TCLC 15, 32**
See also CA 109

James I 1394-1437 .... **LC 20**

Jameson, Anna 1794-1860 .... **NCLC 43**
See also DLB 99

Jami, Nur al-Din 'Abd al-Rahman
1414-1492 .... **LC 9**

Jandl, Ernst 1925- .... **CLC 34**

Janowitz, Tama 1957- .... **CLC 43**
See also CA 106

Jarrell, Randall
1914-1965 .... **CLC 1, 2, 6, 9, 13, 49**
See also CA 5-8R; 25-28R; CABS 2;
CANR 6, 34; CDALB 1941-1968; CLR 6;
DLB 48, 52; MAICYA; MTCW; SATA 7

Jarry, Alfred 1873-1907....... **TCLC 2, 14**
See also CA 104

Jarvis, E. K.
See Bloch, Robert (Albert); Ellison, Harlan;
Silverberg, Robert

Jeake, Samuel, Jr.
See Aiken, Conrad (Potter)

Jean Paul 1763-1825 .... **NCLC 7**

Jeffers, (John) Robinson
1887-1962 .... **CLC 2, 3, 11, 15, 54; DA;**
WLC
See also CA 85-88; CANR 35;
CDALB 1917-1929; DLB 45; MTCW

Jefferson, Janet
See Mencken, H(enry) L(ouis)

Jefferson, Thomas 1743-1826 .... **NCLC 11**
See also CDALB 1640-1865; DLB 31

Jeffrey, Francis 1773-1850....... **NCLC 33**
See also DLB 107

Jelakowitch, Ivan
See Heijermans, Herman

Jellicoe, (Patricia) Ann 1927- ...... **CLC 27**
See also CA 85-88; DLB 13

Jen, Gish .... **CLC 70**
See also Jen, Lillian

Jen, Lillian 1956(?)-
See Jen, Gish
See also CA 135

Jenkins, (John) Robin 1912- .... **CLC 52**
See also CA 1-4R; CANR 1; DLB 14

Jennings, Elizabeth (Joan)
1926- .... **CLC 5, 14**
See also CA 61-64; CAAS 5; CANR 8, 39;
DLB 27; MTCW; SATA 66

Jennings, Waylon 1937-.......... **CLC 21**

Jensen, Johannes V. 1873-1950.... **TCLC 41**

Jensen, Laura (Linnea) 1948- ...... **CLC 37**
See also CA 103

Jerome, Jerome K(lapka)
1859-1927 .... **TCLC 23**
See also CA 119; DLB 10, 34, 135

Jerrold, Douglas William
1803-1857 .... **NCLC 2**

Jewett, (Theodora) Sarah Orne
1849-1909 .... **TCLC 1, 22; SSC 6**
See also CA 108; 127; DLB 12, 74;
SATA 15

Jewsbury, Geraldine (Endsor)
1812-1880 .... **NCLC 22**
See also DLB 21

Jhabvala, Ruth Prawer
1927- .... **CLC 4, 8, 29**
See also CA 1-4R; CANR 2, 29; DLB 139;
MTCW

Jiles, Paulette 1943-........... **CLC 13, 58**
See also CA 101

Jimenez (Mantecon), Juan Ramon
1881-1958 .... **TCLC 4; HLC; PC 7**
See also CA 104; 131; DLB 134; HW;
MTCW

Jimenez, Ramon
See Jimenez (Mantecon), Juan Ramon

Jimenez Mantecon, Juan
See Jimenez (Mantecon), Juan Ramon

Joel, Billy .... **CLC 26**
See also Joel, William Martin

Joel, William Martin 1949-
See Joel, Billy
See also CA 108

John of the Cross, St. 1542-1591 .... **LC 18**

Johnson, B(ryan) S(tanley William)
1933-1973 .... **CLC 6, 9**
See also CA 9-12R; 53-56; CANR 9;
DLB 14, 40

Johnson, Benj. F. of Boo
See Riley, James Whitcomb

Johnson, Benjamin F. of Boo
See Riley, James Whitcomb

Johnson, Charles (Richard)
1948- .... **CLC 7, 51, 65; BLC**
See also BW 2; CA 116; CAAS 18;
CANR 42; DLB 33

Johnson, Denis 1949-............. **CLC 52**
See also CA 117; 121; DLB 120

Johnson, Diane 1934-........ **CLC 5, 13, 48**
See also CA 41-44R; CANR 17, 40;
DLBY 80; MTCW

Johnson, Eyvind (Olof Verner)
1900-1976 .... **CLC 14**
See also CA 73-76; 69-72; CANR 34

Johnson, J. R.
See James, C(yril) L(ionel) R(obert)

Johnson, James Weldon
1871-1938 .... **TCLC 3, 19; BLC**
See also BW 1; CA 104; 125;
CDALB 1917-1929; CLR 32; DLB 51;
MTCW; SATA 31

Johnson, Joyce 1935-............. **CLC 58**
See also CA 125; 129

Johnson, Lionel (Pigot)
1867-1902 .... **TCLC 19**
See also CA 117; DLB 19

Johnson, Mel
See Malzberg, Barry N(athaniel)

Johnson, Pamela Hansford
1912-1981 .... **CLC 1, 7, 27**
See also CA 1-4R; 104; CANR 2, 28;
DLB 15; MTCW

Johnson, Samuel
1709-1784 .... **LC 15; DA; WLC**
See also CDBLB 1660-1789; DLB 39, 95,
104, 142

Johnson, Uwe
1934-1984 .... **CLC 5, 10, 15, 40**
See also CA 1-4R; 112; CANR 1, 39;
DLB 75; MTCW

Johnston, George (Benson) 1913- ... **CLC 51**
See also CA 1-4R; CANR 5, 20; DLB 88

Johnston, Jennifer 1930-.......... **CLC 7**
See also CA 85-88; DLB 14

Jolley, (Monica) Elizabeth 1923- ... **CLC 46**
See also CA 127; CAAS 13

Jones, Arthur Llewellyn 1863-1947
See Machen, Arthur
See also CA 104

Jones, D(ouglas) G(ordon) 1929-.... **CLC 10**
See also CA 29-32R; CANR 13; DLB 53

Jones, David (Michael)
1895-1974 .... **CLC 2, 4, 7, 13, 42**
See also CA 9-12R; 53-56; CANR 28;
CDBLB 1945-1960; DLB 20, 100; MTCW

Jones, David Robert 1947-
See Bowie, David
See also CA 103

Jones, Diana Wynne 1934- .... **CLC 26**
See also AAYA 12; CA 49-52; CANR 4,
26; CLR 23; JRDA; MAICYA; SAAS 7;
SATA 9, 70

Jones, Edward P. 1950-........... **CLC 76**
See also BW 2; CA 142

Jones, Gayl 1949-.......... **CLC 6, 9; BLC**
See also BW 2; CA 77-80; CANR 27;
DLB 33; MTCW

Jones, James 1921-1977.... **CLC 1, 3, 10, 39**
See also AITN 1, 2; CA 1-4R; 69-72;
CANR 6; DLB 2; MTCW

Jones, John J.
See Lovecraft, H(oward) P(hillips)

Jones, LeRoi .... **CLC 1, 2, 3, 5, 10, 14**
See also Baraka, Amiri

Jones, Louis B. .... **CLC 65**
See also CA 141

Jones, Madison (Percy, Jr.) 1925- . . . **CLC 4**
See also CA 13-16R; CAAS 11; CANR 7

Jones, Mervyn 1922- . . . . **CLC 10, 52**
See also CA 45-48; CAAS 5; CANR 1;
MTCW

Jones, Mick 1956(?)- . . . . **CLC 30**
See also Clash, The

Jones, Nettie (Pearl) 1941- . . . . **CLC 34**
See also BW 2; CA 137

Jones, Preston 1936-1979 . . . . **CLC 10**
See also CA 73-76; 89-92; DLB 7

Jones, Robert F(rancis) 1934- . . . . **CLC 7**
See also CA 49-52; CANR 2

Jones, Rod 1953- . . . . **CLC 50**
See also CA 128

Jones, Terence Graham Parry
1942- . . . . **CLC 21**
See also Jones, Terry; Monty Python
See also CA 112; 116; CANR 35; SATA 51

Jones, Terry
See Jones, Terence Graham Parry
See also SATA 67

Jones, Thom 1945(?)- . . . . **CLC 81**

Jong, Erica 1942- . . . . . . **CLC 4, 6, 8, 18, 83**
See also AITN 1; BEST 90:2; CA 73-76;
CANR 26; DLB 2, 5, 28; MTCW

Jonson, Ben(jamin)
1572(?)-1637 . . . . **LC 6; DA; DC 4; WLC**
See also CDBLB Before 1660; DLB 62, 121

Jordan, June 1936- . . . . **CLC 5, 11, 23**
See also AAYA 2; BW 2; CA 33-36R;
CANR 25; CLR 10; DLB 38; MAICYA;
MTCW; SATA 4

Jordan, Pat(rick M.) 1941- . . . . **CLC 37**
See also CA 33-36R

Jorgensen, Ivar
See Ellison, Harlan

Jorgenson, Ivar
See Silverberg, Robert

Josephus, Flavius c. 37-100 . . . . . **CMLC 13**

Josipovici, Gabriel 1940- . . . . **CLC 6, 43**
See also CA 37-40R; CAAS 8; DLB 14

Joubert, Joseph 1754-1824 . . . . **NCLC 9**

Jouve, Pierre Jean 1887-1976 . . . . . . **CLC 47**
See also CA 65-68

Joyce, James (Augustine Aloysius)
1882-1941 . . . . . . **TCLC 3, 8, 16, 35; DA;**
SSC 3; WLC
See also CA 104; 126; CDBLB 1914-1945;
DLB 10, 19, 36; MTCW

Jozsef, Attila 1905-1937 . . . . **TCLC 22**
See also CA 116

Juana Ines de la Cruz 1651(?)-1695 . . . **LC 5**

Judd, Cyril
See Kornbluth, C(yril) M.; Pohl, Frederik

Julian of Norwich 1342(?)-1416(?) . . . . **LC 6**

Just, Ward (Swift) 1935- . . . . **CLC 4, 27**
See also CA 25-28R; CANR 32

Justice, Donald (Rodney) 1925- . . **CLC 6, 19**
See also CA 5-8R; CANR 26; DLBY 83

Juvenal c. 55-c. 127 . . . . **CMLC 8**

Juvenis
See Bourne, Randolph S(illiman)

Kacew, Romain 1914-1980
See Gary, Romain
See also CA 108; 102

Kadare, Ismail 1936- . . . . **CLC 52**

Kadohata, Cynthia . . . . **CLC 59**
See also CA 140

Kafka, Franz
1883-1924 . . . . **TCLC 2, 6, 13, 29, 47, 53;**
DA; SSC 5; WLC
See also CA 105; 126; DLB 81; MTCW

Kahn, Roger 1927- . . . . **CLC 30**
See also CA 25-28R; CANR 44; SATA 37

Kain, Saul
See Sassoon, Siegfried (Lorraine)

Kaiser, Georg 1878-1945 . . . . **TCLC 9**
See also CA 106; DLB 124

Kaletski, Alexander 1946- . . . . **CLC 39**
See also CA 118; 143

Kalidasa fl. c. 400- . . . . **CMLC 9**

Kallman, Chester (Simon)
1921-1975 . . . . **CLC 2**
See also CA 45-48; 53-56; CANR 3

Kaminsky, Melvin 1926-
See Brooks, Mel
See also CA 65-68; CANR 16

Kaminsky, Stuart M(elvin) 1934- . . . **CLC 59**
See also CA 73-76; CANR 29

Kane, Paul
See Simon, Paul

Kane, Wilson
See Bloch, Robert (Albert)

Kanin, Garson 1912- . . . . **CLC 22**
See also AITN 1; CA 5-8R; CANR 7;
DLB 7

Kaniuk, Yoram 1930- . . . . **CLC 19**
See also CA 134

Kant, Immanuel 1724-1804 . . . . . . **NCLC 27**
See also DLB 94

Kantor, MacKinlay 1904-1977 . . . . . . **CLC 7**
See also CA 61-64; 73-76; DLB 9, 102

Kaplan, David Michael 1946- . . . . . . **CLC 50**

Kaplan, James 1951- . . . . **CLC 59**
See also CA 135

Karageorge, Michael
See Anderson, Poul (William)

Karamzin, Nikolai Mikhailovich
1766-1826 . . . . **NCLC 3**

Karapanou, Margarita 1946- . . . . **CLC 13**
See also CA 101

Karinthy, Frigyes 1887-1938 . . . . . . **TCLC 47**

Karl, Frederick R(obert) 1927- . . . . . **CLC 34**
See also CA 5-8R; CANR 3, 44

Kastel, Warren
See Silverberg, Robert

Kataev, Evgeny Petrovich 1903-1942
See Petrov, Evgeny
See also CA 120

Kataphusin
See Ruskin, John

Katz, Steve 1935- . . . . **CLC 47**
See also CA 25-28R; CAAS 14; CANR 12;
DLBY 83

Kauffman, Janet 1945- . . . . **CLC 42**
See also CA 117; CANR 43; DLBY 86

Kaufman, Bob (Garnell)
1925-1986 . . . . **CLC 49**
See also BW 1; CA 41-44R; 118; CANR 22;
DLB 16, 41

Kaufman, George S. 1889-1961 . . . . . **CLC 38**
See also CA 108; 93-96; DLB 7

Kaufman, Sue . . . . **CLC 3, 8**
See also Barondess, Sue K(aufman)

Kavafis, Konstantinos Petrou 1863-1933
See Cavafy, C(onstantine) P(eter)
See also CA 104

Kavan, Anna 1901-1968 . . . . . . **CLC 5, 13, 82**
See also CA 5-8R; CANR 6; MTCW

Kavanagh, Dan
See Barnes, Julian

Kavanagh, Patrick (Joseph)
1904-1967 . . . . **CLC 22**
See also CA 123; 25-28R; DLB 15, 20;
MTCW

Kawabata, Yasunari
1899-1972 . . . . **CLC 2, 5, 9, 18**
See also CA 93-96; 33-36R

Kaye, M(ary) M(argaret) 1909- . . . . . **CLC 28**
See also CA 89-92; CANR 24; MTCW;
SATA 62

Kaye, Mollie
See Kaye, M(ary) M(argaret)

Kaye-Smith, Sheila 1887-1956 . . . . . **TCLC 20**
See also CA 118; DLB 36

Kaymor, Patrice Maguilene
See Senghor, Leopold Sedar

Kazan, Elia 1909- . . . . **CLC 6, 16, 63**
See also CA 21-24R; CANR 32

Kazantzakis, Nikos
1883(?)-1957 . . . . **TCLC 2, 5, 33**
See also CA 105; 132; MTCW

Kazin, Alfred 1915- . . . . **CLC 34, 38**
See also CA 1-4R; CAAS 7; CANR 1;
DLB 67

Keane, Mary Nesta (Skrine) 1904-
See Keane, Molly
See also CA 108; 114

Keane, Molly . . . . **CLC 31**
See also Keane, Mary Nesta (Skrine)

Keates, Jonathan 19(?)- . . . . **CLC 34**

Keaton, Buster 1895-1966 . . . . **CLC 20**

Keats, John
1795-1821 . . . **NCLC 8; DA; PC 1; WLC**
See also CDBLB 1789-1832; DLB 96, 110

Keene, Donald 1922- . . . . **CLC 34**
See also CA 1-4R; CANR 5

Keillor, Garrison . . . . **CLC 40**
See also Keillor, Gary (Edward)
See also AAYA 2; BEST 89:3; DLBY 87;
SATA 58

Keillor, Gary (Edward) 1942-
See Keillor, Garrison
See also CA 111; 117; CANR 36; MTCW

Keith, Michael
See Hubbard, L(afayette) Ron(ald)

Keller, Gottfried 1819-1890 . . . . **NCLC 2**
See also DLB 129

Kellerman, Jonathan 1949- .... **CLC 44**
See also BEST 90:1; CA 106; CANR 29

Kelley, William Melvin 1937- ...... **CLC 22**
See also BW 1; CA 77-80; CANR 27;
DLB 33

Kellogg, Marjorie 1922- .... **CLC 2**
See also CA 81-84

Kellow, Kathleen
See Hibbert, Eleanor Alice Burford

Kelly, M(ilton) T(erry) 1947- .... **CLC 55**
See also CA 97-100; CANR 19, 43

Kelman, James 1946- .... **CLC 58**

Kemal, Yashar 1923- .... **CLC 14, 29**
See also CA 89-92; CANR 44

Kemble, Fanny 1809-1893 .... **NCLC 18**
See also DLB 32

Kemelman, Harry 1908- .... **CLC 2**
See also AITN 1; CA 9-12R; CANR 6;
DLB 28

Kempe, Margery 1373(?)-1440(?) ..... **LC 6**

Kempis, Thomas a 1380-1471 .... **LC 11**

Kendall, Henry 1839-1882 .... **NCLC 12**

Keneally, Thomas (Michael)
1935- ...... **CLC 5, 8, 10, 14, 19, 27, 43**
See also CA 85-88; CANR 10; MTCW

Kennedy, Adrienne (Lita)
1931- .... **CLC 66; BLC**
See also BW 2; CA 103; CABS 3;
CANR 26; DLB 38

Kennedy, John Pendleton
1795-1870 .... **NCLC 2**
See also DLB 3

Kennedy, Joseph Charles 1929- ...... **CLC 8**
See also Kennedy, X. J.
See also CA 1-4R; CANR 4, 30, 40;
SATA 14

Kennedy, William 1928- ... **CLC 6, 28, 34, 53**
See also AAYA 1; CA 85-88; CANR 14,
31; DLBY 85; MTCW; SATA 57

Kennedy, X. J. .... **CLC 42**
See also Kennedy, Joseph Charles
See also CAAS 9; CLR 27; DLB 5

Kent, Kelvin
See Kuttner, Henry

Kenton, Maxwell
See Southern, Terry

Kenyon, Robert O.
See Kuttner, Henry

Kerouac, Jack ..... **CLC 1, 2, 3, 5, 14, 29, 61**
See also Kerouac, Jean-Louis Lebris de
See also CDALB 1941-1968; DLB 2, 16;
DLBD 3

Kerouac, Jean-Louis Lebris de 1922-1969
See Kerouac, Jack
See also AITN 1; CA 5-8R; 25-28R;
CANR 26; DA; MTCW; WLC

Kerr, Jean 1923- .... **CLC 22**
See also CA 5-8R; CANR 7

Kerr, M. E. .... **CLC 12, 35**
See also Meaker, Marijane (Agnes)
See also AAYA 2; CLR 29; SAAS 1

Kerr, Robert .... **CLC 55**

Kerrigan, (Thomas) Anthony
1918- .... **CLC 4, 6**
See also CA 49-52; CAAS 11; CANR 4

Kerry, Lois
See Duncan, Lois

Kesey, Ken (Elton)
1935- ...... **CLC 1, 3, 6, 11, 46, 64; DA;
WLC**
See also CA 1-4R; CANR 22, 38;
CDALB 1968-1988; DLB 2, 16; MTCW;
SATA 66

Kesselring, Joseph (Otto)
1902-1967 .... **CLC 45**

Kessler, Jascha (Frederick) 1929- .... **CLC 4**
See also CA 17-20R; CANR 8

Kettelkamp, Larry (Dale) 1933- .... **CLC 12**
See also CA 29-32R; CANR 16; SAAS 3;
SATA 2

Keyber, Conny
See Fielding, Henry

Keyes, Daniel 1927- .... **CLC 80; DA**
See also CA 17-20R; CANR 10, 26;
SATA 37

Khayyam, Omar
1048-1131 .... **CMLC 11; PC 8**

Kherdian, David 1931- .... **CLC 6, 9**
See also CA 21-24R; CAAS 2; CANR 39;
CLR 24; JRDA; MAICYA; SATA 16, 74

Khlebnikov, Velimir .... **TCLC 20**
See also Khlebnikov, Viktor Vladimirovich

Khlebnikov, Viktor Vladimirovich 1885-1922
See Khlebnikov, Velimir
See also CA 117

Khodasevich, Vladislav (Felitsianovich)
1886-1939 .... **TCLC 15**
See also CA 115

Kielland, Alexander Lange
1849-1906 .... **TCLC 5**
See also CA 104

Kiely, Benedict 1919- .... **CLC 23, 43**
See also CA 1-4R; CANR 2; DLB 15

Kienzle, William X(avier) 1928- .... **CLC 25**
See also CA 93-96; CAAS 1; CANR 9, 31;
MTCW

Kierkegaard, Soren 1813-1855 .... **NCLC 34**

Killens, John Oliver 1916-1987 ..... **CLC 10**
See also BW 2; CA 77-80; 123; CAAS 2;
CANR 26; DLB 33

Killigrew, Anne 1660-1685 .... **LC 4**
See also DLB 131

Kim
See Simenon, Georges (Jacques Christian)

Kincaid, Jamaica 1949- ... **CLC 43, 68; BLC**
See also BW 2; CA 125

King, Francis (Henry) 1923- ..... **CLC 8, 53**
See also CA 1-4R; CANR 1, 33; DLB 15,
139; MTCW

King, Martin Luther, Jr.
1929-1968 .... **CLC 83; BLC; DA**
See also BW 2; CA 25-28; CANR 27, 44;
CAP 2; MTCW; SATA 14

King, Stephen (Edwin)
1947- .... **CLC 12, 26, 37, 61**
See also AAYA 1; BEST 90:1; CA 61-64;
CANR 1, 30; DLBY 80; JRDA; MTCW;
SATA 9, 55

King, Steve
See King, Stephen (Edwin)

Kingman, Lee.................... **CLC 17**
See also Natti, (Mary) Lee
See also SAAS 3; SATA 1, 67

Kingsley, Charles 1819-1875 ..... **NCLC 35**
See also DLB 21, 32; YABC 2

Kingsley, Sidney 1906- .... **CLC 44**
See also CA 85-88; DLB 7

Kingsolver, Barbara 1955- ...... **CLC 55, 81**
See also CA 129; 134

Kingston, Maxine (Ting Ting) Hong
1940- .... **CLC 12, 19, 58**
See also AAYA 8; CA 69-72; CANR 13,
38; DLBY 80; MTCW; SATA 53

Kinnell, Galway
1927- .... **CLC 1, 2, 3, 5, 13, 29**
See also CA 9-12R; CANR 10, 34; DLB 5;
DLBY 87; MTCW

Kinsella, Thomas 1928- .... **CLC 4, 19**
See also CA 17-20R; CANR 15; DLB 27;
MTCW

Kinsella, W(illiam) P(atrick)
1935- .... **CLC 27, 43**
See also AAYA 7; CA 97-100; CAAS 7;
CANR 21, 35; MTCW

Kipling, (Joseph) Rudyard
1865-1936 ...... **TCLC 8, 17; DA; PC 3;
SSC 5; WLC**
See also CA 105; 120; CANR 33;
CDBLB 1890-1914; DLB 19, 34, 141;
MAICYA; MTCW; YABC 2

Kirkup, James 1918- .... **CLC 1**
See also CA 1-4R; CAAS 4; CANR 2;
DLB 27; SATA 12

Kirkwood, James 1930(?)-1989 ...... **CLC 9**
See also AITN 2; CA 1-4R; 128; CANR 6,
40

Kis, Danilo 1935-1989 .... **CLC 57**
See also CA 109; 118; 129; MTCW

Kivi, Aleksis 1834-1872 .... **NCLC 30**

Kizer, Carolyn (Ashley)
1925- .... **CLC 15, 39, 80**
See also CA 65-68; CAAS 5; CANR 24;
DLB 5

Klabund 1890-1928 .... **TCLC 44**
See also DLB 66

Klappert, Peter 1942- .... **CLC 57**
See also CA 33-36R; DLB 5

Klein, A(braham) M(oses)
1909-1972 .... **CLC 19**
See also CA 101; 37-40R; DLB 68

Klein, Norma 1938-1989 .... **CLC 30**
See also AAYA 2; CA 41-44R; 128;
CANR 15, 37; CLR 2, 19; JRDA;
MAICYA; SAAS 1; SATA 7, 57

Klein, T(heodore) E(ibon) D(onald)
1947- .... **CLC 34**
See also CA 119; CANR 44

Kleist, Heinrich von
1777-1811 .... **NCLC 2, 37**
See also DLB 90

Klima, Ivan 1931- .... **CLC 56**
See also CA 25-28R; CANR 17

Klimentov, Andrei Platonovich 1899-1951
See Platonov, Andrei
See also CA 108

Klinger, Friedrich Maximilian von
1752-1831 .... **NCLC 1**
See also DLB 94

Klopstock, Friedrich Gottlieb
1724-1803 .... **NCLC 11**
See also DLB 97

Knebel, Fletcher 1911-1993 .... **CLC 14**
See also AITN 1; CA 1-4R; 140; CAAS 3;
CANR 1, 36; SATA 36; SATA-Obit 75

Knickerbocker, Diedrich
See Irving, Washington

Knight, Etheridge
1931-1991 .... **CLC 40; BLC**
See also BW 1; CA 21-24R; 133; CANR 23;
DLB 41

Knight, Sarah Kemble 1666-1727 ..... **LC 7**
See also DLB 24

Knowles, John
1926- .... **CLC 1, 4, 10, 26; DA**
See also AAYA 10; CA 17-20R; CANR 40;
CDALB 1968-1988; DLB 6; MTCW;
SATA 8

Knox, Calvin M.
See Silverberg, Robert

Knye, Cassandra
See Disch, Thomas M(ichael)

Koch, C(hristopher) J(ohn) 1932- ... **CLC 42**
See also CA 127

Koch, Christopher
See Koch, C(hristopher) J(ohn)

Koch, Kenneth 1925- .... **CLC 5, 8, 44**
See also CA 1-4R; CANR 6, 36; DLB 5;
SATA 65

Kochanowski, Jan 1530-1584 .... **LC 10**

Kock, Charles Paul de
1794-1871 .... **NCLC 16**

Koda Shigeyuki 1867-1947
See Rohan, Koda
See also CA 121

Koestler, Arthur
1905-1983 .... **CLC 1, 3, 6, 8, 15, 33**
See also CA 1-4R; 109; CANR 1, 33;
CDBLB 1945-1960; DLBY 83; MTCW

Kogawa, Joy Nozomi 1935- .... **CLC 78**
See also CA 101; CANR 19

Kohout, Pavel 1928- .... **CLC 13**
See also CA 45-48; CANR 3

Koizumi, Yakumo
See Hearn, (Patricio) Lafcadio (Tessima
Carlos)

Kolmar, Gertrud 1894-1943 .... **TCLC 40**

Konrad, George
See Konrad, Gyoergy

Konrad, Gyoergy 1933- ...... **CLC 4, 10, 73**
See also CA 85-88

Konwicki, Tadeusz 1926- ..... **CLC 8, 28, 54**
See also CA 101; CAAS 9; CANR 39;
MTCW

Koontz, Dean R(ay) 1945- .... **CLC 78**
See also AAYA 9; BEST 89:3, 90:2;
CA 108; CANR 19, 36; MTCW

Kopit, Arthur (Lee) 1937- .... **CLC 1, 18, 33**
See also AITN 1; CA 81-84; CABS 3;
DLB 7; MTCW

Kops, Bernard 1926- .... **CLC 4**
See also CA 5-8R; DLB 13

Kornbluth, C(yril) M. 1923-1958 .... **TCLC 8**
See also CA 105; DLB 8

Korolenko, V. G.
See Korolenko, Vladimir Galaktionovich

Korolenko, Vladimir
See Korolenko, Vladimir Galaktionovich

Korolenko, Vladimir G.
See Korolenko, Vladimir Galaktionovich

Korolenko, Vladimir Galaktionovich
1853-1921 .... **TCLC 22**
See also CA 121

Kosinski, Jerzy (Nikodem)
1933-1991 .... **CLC 1, 2, 3, 6, 10, 15, 53,
70**
See also CA 17-20R; 134; CANR 9; DLB 2;
DLBY 82; MTCW

Kostelanetz, Richard (Cory) 1940- .. **CLC 28**
See also CA 13-16R; CAAS 8; CANR 38

Kostrowitzki, Wilhelm Apollinaris de
1880-1918
See Apollinaire, Guillaume
See also CA 104

Kotlowitz, Robert 1924- .... **CLC 4**
See also CA 33-36R; CANR 36

Kotzebue, August (Friedrich Ferdinand) von
1761-1819 .... **NCLC 25**
See also DLB 94

Kotzwinkle, William 1938- ... **CLC 5, 14, 35**
See also CA 45-48; CANR 3, 44; CLR 6;
MAICYA; SATA 24, 70

Kozol, Jonathan 1936- .... **CLC 17**
See also CA 61-64; CANR 16

Kozoll, Michael 1940(?)- .... **CLC 35**

Kramer, Kathryn 19(?)- .... **CLC 34**

Kramer, Larry 1935- .... **CLC 42**
See also CA 124; 126

Krasicki, Ignacy 1735-1801 .... **NCLC 8**

Krasinski, Zygmunt 1812-1859 .... **NCLC 4**

Kraus, Karl 1874-1936 .... **TCLC 5**
See also CA 104; DLB 118

Kreve (Mickevicius), Vincas
1882-1954 .... **TCLC 27**

Kristeva, Julia 1941- .... **CLC 77**

Kristofferson, Kris 1936- .... **CLC 26**
See also CA 104

Krizanc, John 1956- .... **CLC 57**

Krleza, Miroslav 1893-1981 .... **CLC 8**
See also CA 97-100; 105

Kroetsch, Robert 1927- ...... **CLC 5, 23, 57**
See also CA 17-20R; CANR 8, 38; DLB 53;
MTCW

Kroetz, Franz
See Kroetz, Franz Xaver

Kroetz, Franz Xaver 1946- .... **CLC 41**
See also CA 130

Kroker, Arthur 1945- .... **CLC 77**

Kropotkin, Peter (Aleksieevich)
1842-1921 .... **TCLC 36**
See also CA 119

Krotkov, Yuri 1917- .... **CLC 19**
See also CA 102

Krumb
See Crumb, R(obert)

Krumgold, Joseph (Quincy)
1908-1980 .... **CLC 12**
See also CA 9-12R; 101; CANR 7;
MAICYA; SATA 1, 23, 48

Krumwitz
See Crumb, R(obert)

Krutch, Joseph Wood 1893-1970 .... **CLC 24**
See also CA 1-4R; 25-28R; CANR 4;
DLB 63

Krutzch, Gus
See Eliot, T(homas) S(tearns)

Krylov, Ivan Andreevich
1768(?)-1844 .... **NCLC 1**

Kubin, Alfred 1877-1959 .... **TCLC 23**
See also CA 112; DLB 81

Kubrick, Stanley 1928- .... **CLC 16**
See also CA 81-84; CANR 33; DLB 26

Kumin, Maxine (Winokur)
1925- .... **CLC 5, 13, 28**
See also AITN 2; CA 1-4R; CAAS 8;
CANR 1, 21; DLB 5; MTCW; SATA 12

Kundera, Milan
1929- .... **CLC 4, 9, 19, 32, 68**
See also AAYA 2; CA 85-88; CANR 19;
MTCW

Kunitz, Stanley (Jasspon)
1905- .... **CLC 6, 11, 14**
See also CA 41-44R; CANR 26; DLB 48;
MTCW

Kunze, Reiner 1933- .... **CLC 10**
See also CA 93-96; DLB 75

Kuprin, Aleksandr Ivanovich
1870-1938 .... **TCLC 5**
See also CA 104

Kureishi, Hanif 1954(?)- .... **CLC 64**
See also CA 139

Kurosawa, Akira 1910- .... **CLC 16**
See also AAYA 11; CA 101

Kushner, Tony 1957(?)- .... **CLC 81**
See also CA 144

Kuttner, Henry 1915-1958 .... **TCLC 10**
See also CA 107; DLB 8

Kuzma, Greg 1944- .... **CLC 7**
See also CA 33-36R

Kuzmin, Mikhail 1872(?)-1936 .... **TCLC 40**

Kyd, Thomas 1558-1594 ...... **LC 22; DC 3**
See also DLB 62

Kyprianos, Iossif
See Samarakis, Antonis

La Bruyere, Jean de 1645-1696 ...... **LC 17**

Lacan, Jacques (Marie Emile)
1901-1981 . . . . CLC 75
See also CA 121; 104

Laclos, Pierre Ambroise Francois Choderlos
de 1741-1803 . . . . NCLC 4

Lacolere, Francois
See Aragon, Louis

La Colere, Francois
See Aragon, Louis

La Deshabilleuse
See Simenon, Georges (Jacques Christian)

Lady Gregory
See Gregory, Isabella Augusta (Persse)

Lady of Quality, A
See Bagnold, Enid

La Fayette, Marie (Madelaine Pioche de la
Vergne Comtes 1634-1693 . . . . . . LC 2

Lafayette, Rene
See Hubbard, L(afayette) Ron(ald)

Laforgue, Jules 1860-1887 . . . . NCLC 5

Lagerkvist, Paer (Fabian)
1891-1974 . . . . CLC 7, 10, 13, 54
See also Lagerkvist, Par
See also CA 85-88; 49-52; MTCW

Lagerkvist, Par
See Lagerkvist, Paer (Fabian)
See also SSC 12

Lagerloef, Selma (Ottiliana Lovisa)
1858-1940 . . . . TCLC 4, 36
See also Lagerlof, Selma (Ottiliana Lovisa)
See also CA 108; CLR 7; SATA 15

Lagerlof, Selma (Ottiliana Lovisa)
See Lagerloef, Selma (Ottiliana Lovisa)
See also CLR 7; SATA 15

La Guma, (Justin) Alex(ander)
1925-1985 . . . . CLC 19
See also BW 1; CA 49-52; 118; CANR 25;
DLB 117; MTCW

Laidlaw, A. K.
See Grieve, C(hristopher) M(urray)

Lainez, Manuel Mujica
See Mujica Lainez, Manuel
See also HW

Lamartine, Alphonse (Marie Louis Prat) de
1790-1869 . . . . NCLC 11

Lamb, Charles
1775-1834 . . . . NCLC 10; DA; WLC
See also CDBLB 1789-1832; DLB 93, 107;
SATA 17

Lamb, Lady Caroline 1785-1828 . . NCLC 38
See also DLB 116

Lamming, George (William)
1927- . . . . CLC 2, 4, 66; BLC
See also BW 2; CA 85-88; CANR 26;
DLB 125; MTCW

L'Amour, Louis (Dearborn)
1908-1988 . . . . CLC 25, 55
See also AITN 2; BEST 89:2; CA 1-4R;
125; CANR 3, 25, 40; DLBY 80; MTCW

Lampedusa, Giuseppe (Tomasi) di . . . TCLC 13
See also Tomasi di Lampedusa, Giuseppe

Lampman, Archibald 1861-1899 . . NCLC 25
See also DLB 92

Lancaster, Bruce 1896-1963 . . . . CLC 36
See also CA 9-10; CAP 1; SATA 9

Landau, Mark Alexandrovich
See Aldanov, Mark (Alexandrovich)

Landau-Aldanov, Mark Alexandrovich
See Aldanov, Mark (Alexandrovich)

Landis, John 1950- . . . . CLC 26
See also CA 112; 122

Landolfi, Tommaso 1908-1979 . . . CLC 11, 49
See also CA 127; 117

Landon, Letitia Elizabeth
1802-1838 . . . . NCLC 15
See also DLB 96

Landor, Walter Savage
1775-1864 . . . . NCLC 14
See also DLB 93, 107

Landwirth, Heinz 1927-
See Lind, Jakov
See also CA 9-12R; CANR 7

Lane, Patrick 1939- . . . . CLC 25
See also CA 97-100; DLB 53

Lang, Andrew 1844-1912 . . . . TCLC 16
See also CA 114; 137; DLB 98, 141;
MAICYA; SATA 16

Lang, Fritz 1890-1976 . . . . CLC 20
See also CA 77-80; 69-72; CANR 30

Lange, John
See Crichton, (John) Michael

Langer, Elinor 1939- . . . . CLC 34
See also CA 121

Langland, William
1330(?)-1400(?) . . . . LC 19; DA

Langstaff, Launcelot
See Irving, Washington

Lanier, Sidney 1842-1881 . . . . NCLC 6
See also DLB 64; MAICYA; SATA 18

Lanyer, Aemilia 1569-1645 . . . . LC 10

Lao Tzu . . . . CMLC 7

Lapine, James (Elliot) 1949- . . . . . . CLC 39
See also CA 123; 130

Larbaud, Valery (Nicolas)
1881-1957 . . . . TCLC 9
See also CA 106

Lardner, Ring
See Lardner, Ring(gold) W(ilmer)

Lardner, Ring W., Jr.
See Lardner, Ring(gold) W(ilmer)

Lardner, Ring(gold) W(ilmer)
1885-1933 . . . . TCLC 2, 14
See also CA 104; 131; CDALB 1917-1929;
DLB 11, 25, 86; MTCW

Laredo, Betty
See Codrescu, Andrei

Larkin, Maia
See Wojciechowska, Maia (Teresa)

Larkin, Philip (Arthur)
1922-1985 . . . . CLC 3, 5, 8, 9, 13, 18, 33,
39, 64
See also CA 5-8R; 117; CANR 24;
CDBLB 1960 to Present; DLB 27;
MTCW

Larra (y Sanchez de Castro), Mariano Jose de
1809-1837 . . . . NCLC 17

Larsen, Eric 1941- . . . . CLC 55
See also CA 132

Larsen, Nella 1891-1964 . . . . . CLC 37; BLC
See also BW 1; CA 125; DLB 51

Larson, Charles R(aymond) 1938- . . . CLC 31
See also CA 53-56; CANR 4

Latham, Jean Lee 1902- . . . . CLC 12
See also AITN 1; CA 5-8R; CANR 7;
MAICYA; SATA 2, 68

Latham, Mavis
See Clark, Mavis Thorpe

Lathen, Emma . . . . CLC 2
See also Hennissart, Martha; Latsis, Mary
J(ane)

Lathrop, Francis
See Leiber, Fritz (Reuter, Jr.)

Latsis, Mary J(ane)
See Lathen, Emma
See also CA 85-88

Lattimore, Richmond (Alexander)
1906-1984 . . . . CLC 3
See also CA 1-4R; 112; CANR 1

Laughlin, James 1914- . . . . CLC 49
See also CA 21-24R; CANR 9; DLB 48

Laurence, (Jean) Margaret (Wemyss)
1926-1987 . . CLC 3, 6, 13, 50, 62; SSC 7
See also CA 5-8R; 121; CANR 33; DLB 53;
MTCW; SATA 50

Laurent, Antoine 1952- . . . . CLC 50

Lauscher, Hermann
See Hesse, Hermann

Lautreamont, Comte de
1846-1870 . . . . NCLC 12; SSC 14

Laverty, Donald
See Blish, James (Benjamin)

Lavin, Mary 1912- . . . . . . CLC 4, 18; SSC 4
See also CA 9-12R; CANR 33; DLB 15;
MTCW

Lavond, Paul Dennis
See Kornbluth, C(yril) M.; Pohl, Frederik

Lawler, Raymond Evenor 1922- . . . . CLC 58
See also CA 103

Lawrence, D(avid) H(erbert Richards)
1885-1930 . . . . . . TCLC 2, 9, 16, 33, 48;
DA; SSC 4; WLC
See also CA 104; 121; CDBLB 1914-1945;
DLB 10, 19, 36, 98; MTCW

Lawrence, T(homas) E(dward)
1888-1935 . . . . TCLC 18
See also Dale, Colin
See also CA 115

Lawrence of Arabia
See Lawrence, T(homas) E(dward)

Lawson, Henry (Archibald Hertzberg)
1867-1922 . . . . TCLC 27
See also CA 120

Lawton, Dennis
See Faust, Frederick (Schiller)

Laxness, Halldor . . . . CLC 25
See also Gudjonsson, Halldor Kiljan

Layamon fl. c. 1200- . . . . CMLC 10

Laye, Camara 1928-1980 . . . CLC 4, 38; BLC
See also BW 1; CA 85-88; 97-100;
CANR 25; MTCW

Leverson, Ada 1865(?)-1936(?) .... **TCLC 18**
See also Elaine
See also CA 117

Levertov, Denise
1923- ...... **CLC 1, 2, 3, 5, 8, 15, 28, 66**
See also CA 1-4R; CAAS 19; CANR 3, 29;
DLB 5; MTCW

Levi, Jonathan.................... **CLC 76**

Levi, Peter (Chad Tigar) 1931- ..... **CLC 41**
See also CA 5-8R; CANR 34; DLB 40

Levi, Primo
1919-1987 .... **CLC 37, 50; SSC 12**
See also CA 13-16R; 122; CANR 12, 33;
MTCW

Levin, Ira 1929- .... **CLC 3, 6**
See also CA 21-24R; CANR 17, 44;
MTCW; SATA 66

Levin, Meyer 1905-1981 .... **CLC 7**
See also AITN 1; CA 9-12R; 104;
CANR 15; DLB 9, 28; DLBY 81;
SATA 21, 27

Levine, Norman 1924- .... **CLC 54**
See also CA 73-76; CANR 14; DLB 88

Levine, Philip 1928- .. **CLC 2, 4, 5, 9, 14, 33**
See also CA 9-12R; CANR 9, 37; DLB 5

Levinson, Deirdre 1931- .... **CLC 49**
See also CA 73-76

Levi-Strauss, Claude 1908- .... **CLC 38**
See also CA 1-4R; CANR 6, 32; MTCW

Levitin, Sonia (Wolff) 1934- .... **CLC 17**
See also CA 29-32R; CANR 14, 32; JRDA;
MAICYA; SAAS 2; SATA 4, 68

Levon, O. U.
See Kesey, Ken (Elton)

Lewes, George Henry
1817-1878 .... **NCLC 25**
See also DLB 55

Lewis, Alun 1915-1944........... **TCLC 3**
See also CA 104; DLB 20

Lewis, C. Day
See Day Lewis, C(ecil)

Lewis, C(live) S(taples)
1898-1963 ..... **CLC 1, 3, 6, 14, 27; DA;**
                                       WLC
See also AAYA 3; CA 81-84; CANR 33;
CDBLB 1945-1960; CLR 3, 27; DLB 15,
100; JRDA; MAICYA; MTCW;
SATA 13

Lewis, Janet 1899- .... **CLC 41**
See also Winters, Janet Lewis
See also CA 9-12R; CANR 29; CAP 1;
DLBY 87

Lewis, Matthew Gregory
1775-1818 .... **NCLC 11**
See also DLB 39

Lewis, (Harry) Sinclair
1885-1951 ..... **TCLC 4, 13, 23, 39; DA;**
                                       WLC
See also CA 104; 133; CDALB 1917-1929;
DLB 9, 102; DLBD 1; MTCW

Lewis, (Percy) Wyndham
1884(?)-1957 .... **TCLC 2, 9**
See also CA 104; DLB 15

Lewisohn, Ludwig 1883-1955...... **TCLC 19**
See also CA 107; DLB 4, 9, 28, 102

Lezama Lima, Jose 1910-1976 ... **CLC 4, 10**
See also CA 77-80; DLB 113; HW

L'Heureux, John (Clarke) 1934- .... **CLC 52**
See also CA 13-16R; CANR 23

Liddell, C. H.
See Kuttner, Henry

Lie, Jonas (Lauritz Idemil)
1833-1908(?) .... **TCLC 5**
See also CA 115

Lieber, Joel 1937-1971............. **CLC 6**
See also CA 73-76; 29-32R

Lieber, Stanley Martin
See Lee, Stan

Lieberman, Laurence (James)
1935- .... **CLC 4, 36**
See also CA 17-20R; CANR 8, 36

Lieksman, Anders
See Haavikko, Paavo Juhani

Li Fei-kan 1904-................. **CLC 18**
See also CA 105

Lifton, Robert Jay 1926-......... **CLC 67**
See also CA 17-20R; CANR 27; SATA 66

Lightfoot, Gordon 1938-.......... **CLC 26**
See also CA 109

Lightman, Alan P. 1948- .... **CLC 81**
See also CA 141

Ligotti, Thomas 1953- .... **CLC 44**
See also CA 123

Liliencron, (Friedrich Adolf Axel) Detlev von
1844-1909 .... **TCLC 18**
See also CA 117

Lima, Jose Lezama
See Lezama Lima, Jose

Lima Barreto, Afonso Henrique de
1881-1922 .... **TCLC 23**
See also CA 117

Limonov, Eduard................. **CLC 67**

Lin, Frank
See Atherton, Gertrude (Franklin Horn)

Lincoln, Abraham 1809-1865..... **NCLC 18**

Lind, Jakov .... **CLC 1, 2, 4, 27, 82**
See also Landwirth, Heinz
See also CAAS 4

Lindbergh, Anne (Spencer) Morrow
1906- .... **CLC 82**
See also CA 17-20R; CANR 16; MTCW;
SATA 33

Lindsay, David 1878-1945 .... **TCLC 15**
See also CA 113

Lindsay, (Nicholas) Vachel
1879-1931 .... **TCLC 17; DA; WLC**
See also CA 114; 135; CDALB 1865-1917;
DLB 54; SATA 40

Linke-Poot
See Doeblin, Alfred

Linney, Romulus 1930- .... **CLC 51**
See also CA 1-4R; CANR 40, 44

Linton, Eliza Lynn 1822-1898.... **NCLC 41**
See also DLB 18

Li Po 701-763 .... **CMLC 2**

Lipsius, Justus 1547-1606 .... **LC 16**

Lipsyte, Robert (Michael)
1938- .... **CLC 21; DA**
See also AAYA 7; CA 17-20R; CANR 8;
CLR 23; JRDA; MAICYA; SATA 5, 68

Lish, Gordon (Jay) 1934-.......... **CLC 45**
See also CA 113; 117; DLB 130

Lispector, Clarice 1925-1977....... **CLC 43**
See also CA 139; 116; DLB 113

Littell, Robert 1935(?)- .... **CLC 42**
See also CA 109; 112

Little, Malcolm 1925-1965
See Malcolm X
See also BW 1; CA 125; 111; DA; MTCW

Littlewit, Humphrey Gent.
See Lovecraft, H(oward) P(hillips)

Litwos
See Sienkiewicz, Henryk (Adam Alexander
Pius)

Liu E 1857-1909............... **TCLC 15**
See also CA 115

Lively, Penelope (Margaret)
1933- .... **CLC 32, 50**
See also CA 41-44R; CANR 29; CLR 7;
DLB 14; JRDA; MAICYA; MTCW;
SATA 7, 60

Livesay, Dorothy (Kathleen)
1909- .... **CLC 4, 15, 79**
See also AITN 2; CA 25-28R; CAAS 8;
CANR 36; DLB 68; MTCW

Livy c. 59B.C.-c. 17 .... **CMLC 11**

Lizardi, Jose Joaquin Fernandez de
1776-1827 .... **NCLC 30**

Llewellyn, Richard .... **CLC 7**
See also Llewellyn Lloyd, Richard Dafydd
Vivian
See also DLB 15

Llewellyn Lloyd, Richard Dafydd Vivian
1906-1983 .... **CLC 80**
See also Llewellyn, Richard
See also CA 53-56; 111; CANR 7;
SATA 11, 37

Llosa, (Jorge) Mario (Pedro) Vargas
See Vargas Llosa, (Jorge) Mario (Pedro)

Lloyd Webber, Andrew 1948-
See Webber, Andrew Lloyd
See also AAYA 1; CA 116; SATA 56

Llull, Ramon c. 1235-c. 1316..... **CMLC 12**

Locke, Alain (Le Roy)
1886-1954 .... **TCLC 43**
See also BW 1; CA 106; 124; DLB 51

Locke, John 1632-1704 .... **LC 7**
See also DLB 101

Locke-Elliott, Sumner
See Elliott, Sumner Locke

Lockhart, John Gibson
1794-1854 .... **NCLC 6**
See also DLB 110, 116

Lodge, David (John) 1935-........ **CLC 36**
See also BEST 90:1; CA 17-20R; CANR 19;
DLB 14; MTCW

Loennbohm, Armas Eino Leopold 1878-1926
See Leino, Eino
See also CA 123

Loewinsohn, Ron(ald William)
  1937- .... **CLC 52**
  See also CA 25-28R

Logan, Jake
  See Smith, Martin Cruz

Logan, John (Burton) 1923-1987..... **CLC 5**
  See also CA 77-80; 124; DLB 5

Lo Kuan-chung 1330(?)-1400(?)...... **LC 12**

Lombard, Nap
  See Johnson, Pamela Hansford

London, Jack.. **TCLC 9, 15, 39; SSC 4; WLC**
  See also London, John Griffith
  See also AITN 2; CDALB 1865-1917;
  DLB 8, 12, 78; SATA 18

London, John Griffith 1876-1916
  See London, Jack
  See also CA 110; 119; DA; JRDA;
  MAICYA; MTCW

Long, Emmett
  See Leonard, Elmore (John, Jr.)

Longbaugh, Harry
  See Goldman, William (W.)

Longfellow, Henry Wadsworth
  1807-1882 .... **NCLC 2, 45; DA**
  See also CDALB 1640-1865; DLB 1, 59;
  SATA 19

Longley, Michael 1939-.......... **CLC 29**
  See also CA 102; DLB 40

Longus fl. c. 2nd cent. - .... **CMLC 7**

Longway, A. Hugh
  See Lang, Andrew

Lopate, Phillip 1943- .... **CLC 29**
  See also CA 97-100; DLBY 80

Lopez Portillo (y Pacheco), Jose
  1920- .... **CLC 46**
  See also CA 129; HW

Lopez y Fuentes, Gregorio
  1897(?)-1966 .... **CLC 32**
  See also CA 131; HW

Lorca, Federico Garcia
  See Garcia Lorca, Federico

Lord, Bette Bao 1938-............ **CLC 23**
  See also BEST 90:3; CA 107; CANR 41;
  SATA 58

Lord Auch
  See Bataille, Georges

Lord Byron
  See Byron, George Gordon (Noel)

Lord Dunsany .... **TCLC 2**
  See also Dunsany, Edward John Moreton
  Drax Plunkett

Lorde, Audre (Geraldine)
  1934-1992 .... **CLC 18, 71; BLC**
  See also BW 1; CA 25-28R; 142; CANR 16,
  26; DLB 41; MTCW

Lord Jeffrey
  See Jeffrey, Francis

Lorenzo, Heberto Padilla
  See Padilla (Lorenzo), Heberto

Loris
  See Hofmannsthal, Hugo von

Loti, Pierre .... **TCLC 11**
  See also Viaud, (Louis Marie) Julien
  See also DLB 123

Louie, David Wong 1954- .... **CLC 70**
  See also CA 139

Louis, Father M.
  See Merton, Thomas

Lovecraft, H(oward) P(hillips)
  1890-1937 .... **TCLC 4, 22; SSC 3**
  See also CA 104; 133; MTCW

Lovelace, Earl 1935-.............. **CLC 51**
  See also BW 2; CA 77-80; CANR 41;
  DLB 125; MTCW

Lovelace, Richard 1618-1657....... **LC 24**
  See also DLB 131

Lowell, Amy 1874-1925 .... **TCLC 1, 8**
  See also CA 104; DLB 54, 140

Lowell, James Russell 1819-1891 .. **NCLC 2**
  See also CDALB 1640-1865; DLB 1, 11, 64,
  79

Lowell, Robert (Traill Spence, Jr.)
  1917-1977 ... **CLC 1, 2, 3, 4, 5, 8, 9, 11,
                     15, 37; DA; PC 3; WLC**
  See also CA 9-12R; 73-76; CABS 2;
  CANR 26; DLB 5; MTCW

Lowndes, Marie Adelaide (Belloc)
  1868-1947 .... **TCLC 12**
  See also CA 107; DLB 70

Lowry, (Clarence) Malcolm
  1909-1957 ....**TCLC 6, 40**
  See also CA 105; 131; CDBLB 1945-1960;
  DLB 15; MTCW

Lowry, Mina Gertrude 1882-1966
  See Loy, Mina
  See also CA 113

Loxsmith, John
  See Brunner, John (Kilian Houston)

Loy, Mina .... **CLC 28**
  See also Lowry, Mina Gertrude
  See also DLB 4, 54

Loyson-Bridet
  See Schwob, (Mayer Andre) Marcel

Lucas, Craig 1951- .... **CLC 64**
  See also CA 137

Lucas, George 1944-.............. **CLC 16**
  See also AAYA 1; CA 77-80; CANR 30;
  SATA 56

Lucas, Hans
  See Godard, Jean-Luc

Lucas, Victoria
  See Plath, Sylvia

Ludlam, Charles 1943-1987 ..... **CLC 46, 50**
  See also CA 85-88; 122

Ludlum, Robert 1927- .... **CLC 22, 43**
  See also AAYA 10; BEST 89:1, 90:3;
  CA 33-36R; CANR 25, 41; DLBY 82;
  MTCW

Ludwig, Ken..................... **CLC 60**

Ludwig, Otto 1813-1865.......... **NCLC 4**
  See also DLB 129

Lugones, Leopoldo 1874-1938 ..... **TCLC 15**
  See also CA 116; 131; HW

Lu Hsun 1881-1936 .... **TCLC 3**

Lukacs, George .... **CLC 24**
  See also Lukacs, Gyorgy (Szegeny von)

Lukacs, Gyorgy (Szegeny von) 1885-1971
  See Lukacs, George
  See also CA 101; 29-32R

Luke, Peter (Ambrose Cyprian)
  1919- .... **CLC 38**
  See also CA 81-84; DLB 13

Lunar, Dennis
  See Mungo, Raymond

Lurie, Alison 1926-........ **CLC 4, 5, 18, 39**
  See also CA 1-4R; CANR 2, 17; DLB 2;
  MTCW; SATA 46

Lustig, Arnost 1926-.............. **CLC 56**
  See also AAYA 3; CA 69-72; SATA 56

Luther, Martin 1483-1546.......... **LC 9**

Luzi, Mario 1914-................. **CLC 13**
  See also CA 61-64; CANR 9; DLB 128

Lynch, B. Suarez
  See Bioy Casares, Adolfo; Borges, Jorge
  Luis

Lynch, David (K.) 1946-........... **CLC 66**
  See also CA 124; 129

Lynch, James
  See Andreyev, Leonid (Nikolaevich)

Lynch Davis, B.
  See Bioy Casares, Adolfo; Borges, Jorge
  Luis

Lyndsay, Sir David 1490-1555 ...... **LC 20**

Lynn, Kenneth S(chuyler) 1923-.... **CLC 50**
  See also CA 1-4R; CANR 3, 27

Lynx
  See West, Rebecca

Lyons, Marcus
  See Blish, James (Benjamin)

Lyre, Pinchbeck
  See Sassoon, Siegfried (Lorraine)

Lytle, Andrew (Nelson) 1902-...... **CLC 22**
  See also CA 9-12R; DLB 6

Lyttelton, George 1709-1773....... **LC 10**

Maas, Peter 1929- .... **CLC 29**
  See also CA 93-96

Macaulay, Rose 1881-1958 ..... **TCLC 7, 44**
  See also CA 104; DLB 36

Macaulay, Thomas Babington
  1800-1859 .... **NCLC 42**
  See also CDBLB 1832-1890; DLB 32, 55

MacBeth, George (Mann)
  1932-1992 .... **CLC 2, 5, 9**
  See also CA 25-28R; 136; DLB 40; MTCW;
  SATA 4; SATA-Obit 70

MacCaig, Norman (Alexander)
  1910- .... **CLC 36**
  See also CA 9-12R; CANR 3, 34; DLB 27

MacCarthy, (Sir Charles Otto) Desmond
  1877-1952 .... **TCLC 36**

MacDiarmid, Hugh
  .... **CLC 2, 4, 11, 19, 63; PC 9**
  See also Grieve, C(hristopher) M(urray)
  See also CDBLB 1945-1960; DLB 20

MacDonald, Anson
  See Heinlein, Robert A(nson)

Macdonald, Cynthia 1928-...... **CLC 13, 19**
  See also CA 49-52; CANR 4, 44; DLB 105

MacDonald, George 1824-1905 . . . . . **TCLC 9**
See also CA 106; 137; DLB 18; MAICYA;
SATA 33

Macdonald, John
See Millar, Kenneth

MacDonald, John D(ann)
1916-1986 . . . . **CLC 3, 27, 44**
See also CA 1-4R; 121; CANR 1, 19;
DLB 8; DLBY 86; MTCW

Macdonald, John Ross
See Millar, Kenneth

Macdonald, Ross . . . . **CLC 1, 2, 3, 14, 34, 41**
See also Millar, Kenneth
See also DLBD 6

MacDougal, John
See Blish, James (Benjamin)

MacEwen, Gwendolyn (Margaret)
1941-1987 . . . . **CLC 13, 55**
See also CA 9-12R; 124; CANR 7, 22;
DLB 53; SATA 50, 55

Machado (y Ruiz), Antonio
1875-1939 . . . . **TCLC 3**
See also CA 104; DLB 108

Machado de Assis, Joaquim Maria
1839-1908 . . . . **TCLC 10; BLC**
See also CA 107

Machen, Arthur . . . . **TCLC 4**
See also Jones, Arthur Llewellyn
See also DLB 36

Machiavelli, Niccolo 1469-1527 . . **LC 8; DA**

MacInnes, Colin 1914-1976 . . . . . . **CLC 4, 23**
See also CA 69-72; 65-68; CANR 21;
DLB 14; MTCW

MacInnes, Helen (Clark)
1907-1985 . . . . **CLC 27, 39**
See also CA 1-4R; 117; CANR 1, 28;
DLB 87; MTCW; SATA 22, 44

Mackay, Mary 1855-1924
See Corelli, Marie
See also CA 118

Mackenzie, Compton (Edward Montague)
1883-1972 . . . . **CLC 18**
See also CA 21-22; 37-40R; CAP 2;
DLB 34, 100

Mackenzie, Henry 1745-1831 . . . . **NCLC 41**
See also DLB 39

Mackintosh, Elizabeth 1896(?)-1952
See Tey, Josephine
See also CA 110

MacLaren, James
See Grieve, C(hristopher) M(urray)

Mac Laverty, Bernard 1942- . . . . **CLC 31**
See also CA 116; 118; CANR 43

MacLean, Alistair (Stuart)
1922-1987 . . . . **CLC 3, 13, 50, 63**
See also CA 57-60; 121; CANR 28; MTCW;
SATA 23, 50

Maclean, Norman (Fitzroy)
1902-1990 . . . . **CLC 78; SSC 13**
See also CA 102; 132

MacLeish, Archibald
1892-1982 . . . . **CLC 3, 8, 14, 68**
See also CA 9-12R; 106; CANR 33; DLB 4,
7, 45; DLBY 82; MTCW

MacLennan, (John) Hugh
1907-1990 . . . . **CLC 2, 14**
See also CA 5-8R; 142; CANR 33; DLB 68;
MTCW

MacLeod, Alistair 1936- . . . . **CLC 56**
See also CA 123; DLB 60

MacNeice, (Frederick) Louis
1907-1963 . . . . **CLC 1, 4, 10, 53**
See also CA 85-88; DLB 10, 20; MTCW

MacNeill, Dand
See Fraser, George MacDonald

Macpherson, (Jean) Jay 1931- . . . . . . **CLC 14**
See also CA 5-8R; DLB 53

MacShane, Frank 1927- . . . . **CLC 39**
See also CA 9-12R; CANR 3, 33; DLB 111

Macumber, Mari
See Sandoz, Mari(e Susette)

Madach, Imre 1823-1864 . . . . **NCLC 19**

Madden, (Jerry) David 1933- . . . . **CLC 5, 15**
See also CA 1-4R; CAAS 3; CANR 4;
DLB 6; MTCW

Maddern, Al(an)
See Ellison, Harlan

Madhubuti, Haki R.
1942- . . . . **CLC 6, 73; BLC; PC 5**
See also Lee, Don L.
See also BW 2; CA 73-76; CANR 24;
DLB 5, 41; DLBD 8

Madow, Pauline (Reichberg) . . . . **CLC 1**
See also CA 9-12R

Maepenn, Hugh
See Kuttner, Henry

Maepenn, K. H.
See Kuttner, Henry

Maeterlinck, Maurice 1862-1949 . . . **TCLC 3**
See also CA 104; 136; SATA 66

Maginn, William 1794-1842 . . . . . . **NCLC 8**
See also DLB 110

Mahapatra, Jayanta 1928- . . . . **CLC 33**
See also CA 73-76; CAAS 9; CANR 15, 33

Mahfouz, Naguib (Abdel Aziz Al-Sabilgi)
1911(?)-
See Mahfuz, Najib
See also BEST 89:2; CA 128; MTCW

Mahfuz, Najib . . . . **CLC 52, 55**
See also Mahfouz, Naguib (Abdel Aziz
Al-Sabilgi)
See also DLBY 88

Mahon, Derek 1941- . . . . **CLC 27**
See also CA 113; 128; DLB 40

Mailer, Norman
1923- . . . . . . **CLC 1, 2, 3, 4, 5, 8, 11, 14,
28, 39, 74; DA**
See also AITN 2; CA 9-12R; CABS 1;
CANR 28; CDALB 1968-1988; DLB 2,
16, 28; DLBD 3; DLBY 80, 83; MTCW

Maillet, Antonine 1929- . . . . **CLC 54**
See also CA 115; 120; DLB 60

Mais, Roger 1905-1955 . . . . **TCLC 8**
See also BW 1; CA 105; 124; DLB 125;
MTCW

Maistre, Joseph de 1753-1821 . . . . **NCLC 37**

Maitland, Sara (Louise) 1950- . . . . . . **CLC 49**
See also CA 69-72; CANR 13

Major, Clarence
1936- . . . . **CLC 3, 19, 48; BLC**
See also BW 2; CA 21-24R; CAAS 6;
CANR 13, 25; DLB 33

Major, Kevin (Gerald) 1949- . . . . **CLC 26**
See also CA 97-100; CANR 21, 38;
CLR 11; DLB 60; JRDA; MAICYA;
SATA 32

Maki, James
See Ozu, Yasujiro

Malabaila, Damiano
See Levi, Primo

Malamud, Bernard
1914-1986 . . . . . . **CLC 1, 2, 3, 5, 8, 9, 11,
18, 27, 44, 78; DA; SSC 15; WLC**
See also CA 5-8R; 118; CABS 1; CANR 28;
CDALB 1941-1968; DLB 2, 28;
DLBY 80, 86; MTCW

Malaparte, Curzio 1898-1957 . . . . . **TCLC 52**

Malcolm, Dan
See Silverberg, Robert

Malcolm X . . . . **CLC 82; BLC**
See also Little, Malcolm

Malherbe, Francois de 1555-1628 . . . . . **LC 5**

Mallarme, Stephane
1842-1898 . . . . **NCLC 4, 41; PC 4**

Mallet-Joris, Francoise 1930- . . . . . . **CLC 11**
See also CA 65-68; CANR 17; DLB 83

Malley, Ern
See McAuley, James Phillip

Mallowan, Agatha Christie
See Christie, Agatha (Mary Clarissa)

Maloff, Saul 1922- . . . . **CLC 5**
See also CA 33-36R

Malone, Louis
See MacNeice, (Frederick) Louis

Malone, Michael (Christopher)
1942- . . . . **CLC 43**
See also CA 77-80; CANR 14, 32

Malory, (Sir) Thomas
1410(?)-1471(?) . . . . **LC 11; DA**
See also CDBLB Before 1660; SATA 33, 59

Malouf, (George Joseph) David
1934- . . . . **CLC 28**
See also CA 124

Malraux, (Georges-)Andre
1901-1976 . . . . . . **CLC 1, 4, 9, 13, 15, 57**
See also CA 21-22; 69-72; CANR 34;
CAP 2; DLB 72; MTCW

Malzberg, Barry N(athaniel) 1939- . . . **CLC 7**
See also CA 61-64; CAAS 4; CANR 16;
DLB 8

Mamet, David (Alan)
1947- . . . . **CLC 9, 15, 34, 46; DC 4**
See also AAYA 3; CA 81-84; CABS 3;
CANR 15, 41; DLB 7; MTCW

Mamoulian, Rouben (Zachary)
1897-1987 . . . . **CLC 16**
See also CA 25-28R; 124

Mandelstam, Osip (Emilievich)
1891(?)-1938(?) . . . . **TCLC 2, 6**
See also CA 104

Mander, (Mary) Jane 1877-1949 . . . **TCLC 31**

Mandiargues, Andre Pieyre de ...... **CLC 41**
See also Pieyre de Mandiargues, Andre
See also DLB 83

Mandrake, Ethel Belle
See Thurman, Wallace (Henry)

Mangan, James Clarence
1803-1849 .... **NCLC 27**

Maniere, J.-E.
See Giraudoux, (Hippolyte) Jean

Manley, (Mary) Delariviere
1672(?)-1724 .... **LC 1**
See also DLB 39, 80

Mann, Abel
See Creasey, John

Mann, (Luiz) Heinrich 1871-1950 ... **TCLC 9**
See also CA 106; DLB 66

Mann, (Paul) Thomas
1875-1955 .... **TCLC 2, 8, 14, 21, 35, 44;**
DA; SSC 5; WLC
See also CA 104; 128; DLB 66; MTCW

Manning, David
See Faust, Frederick (Schiller)

Manning, Frederic 1887(?)-1935 ... **TCLC 25**
See also CA 124

Manning, Olivia 1915-1980 ...... **CLC 5, 19**
See also CA 5-8R; 101; CANR 29; MTCW

Mano, D. Keith 1942- .... **CLC 2, 10**
See also CA 25-28R; CAAS 6; CANR 26;
DLB 6

Mansfield, Katherine
.... **TCLC 2, 8, 39; SSC 9; WLC**
See also Beauchamp, Kathleen Mansfield

Manso, Peter 1940- .... **CLC 39**
See also CA 29-32R; CANR 44

Mantecon, Juan Jimenez
See Jimenez (Mantecon), Juan Ramon

Manton, Peter
See Creasey, John

Man Without a Spleen, A
See Chekhov, Anton (Pavlovich)

Manzoni, Alessandro 1785-1873 .. **NCLC 29**

Mapu, Abraham (ben Jekutiel)
1808-1867 .... **NCLC 18**

Mara, Sally
See Queneau, Raymond

Marat, Jean Paul 1743-1793 .... **LC 10**

Marcel, Gabriel Honore
1889-1973 .... **CLC 15**
See also CA 102; 45-48; MTCW

Marchbanks, Samuel
See Davies, (William) Robertson

Marchi, Giacomo
See Bassani, Giorgio

Margulies, Donald .... **CLC 76**

Marie de France c. 12th cent. - .... **CMLC 8**

Marie de l'Incarnation 1599-1672 .... **LC 10**

Mariner, Scott
See Pohl, Frederik

Marinetti, Filippo Tommaso
1876-1944 .... **TCLC 10**
See also CA 107; DLB 114

Marivaux, Pierre Carlet de Chamblain de
1688-1763 .... **LC 4**

Markandaya, Kamala .... **CLC 8, 38**
See also Taylor, Kamala (Purnaiya)

Markfield, Wallace 1926- .... **CLC 8**
See also CA 69-72; CAAS 3; DLB 2, 28

Markham, Edwin 1852-1940 ..... **TCLC 47**
See also DLB 54

Markham, Robert
See Amis, Kingsley (William)

Marks, J
See Highwater, Jamake (Mamake)

Marks-Highwater, J
See Highwater, Jamake (Mamake)

Markson, David M(errill) 1927- .... **CLC 67**
See also CA 49-52; CANR 1

Marley, Bob .... **CLC 17**
See also Marley, Robert Nesta

Marley, Robert Nesta 1945-1981
See Marley, Bob
See also CA 107; 103

Marlowe, Christopher
1564-1593 ..... **LC 22; DA; DC 1; WLC**
See also CDBLB Before 1660; DLB 62

Marmontel, Jean-Francois
1723-1799 .... **LC 2**

Marquand, John P(hillips)
1893-1960 .... **CLC 2, 10**
See also CA 85-88; DLB 9, 102

Marquez, Gabriel (Jose) Garcia ...... **CLC 68**
See also Garcia Marquez, Gabriel (Jose)

Marquis, Don(ald Robert Perry)
1878-1937 .... **TCLC 7**
See also CA 104; DLB 11, 25

Marric, J. J.
See Creasey, John

Marrow, Bernard
See Moore, Brian

Marryat, Frederick 1792-1848 .... **NCLC 3**
See also DLB 21

Marsden, James
See Creasey, John

Marsh, (Edith) Ngaio
1899-1982 .... **CLC 7, 53**
See also CA 9-12R; CANR 6; DLB 77;
MTCW

Marshall, Garry 1934- .... **CLC 17**
See also AAYA 3; CA 111; SATA 60

Marshall, Paule
1929- .... **CLC 27, 72; BLC; SSC 3**
See also BW 2; CA 77-80; CANR 25;
DLB 33; MTCW

Marsten, Richard
See Hunter, Evan

Martha, Henry
See Harris, Mark

Martin, Ken
See Hubbard, L(afayette) Ron(ald)

Martin, Richard
See Creasey, John

Martin, Steve 1945- .... **CLC 30**
See also CA 97-100; CANR 30; MTCW

Martin, Violet Florence
1862-1915 .... **TCLC 51**

Martin, Webber
See Silverberg, Robert

Martindale, Patrick Victor
See White, Patrick (Victor Martindale)

Martin du Gard, Roger
1881-1958 .... **TCLC 24**
See also CA 118; DLB 65

Martineau, Harriet 1802-1876 .... **NCLC 26**
See also DLB 21, 55; YABC 2

Martines, Julia
See O'Faolain, Julia

Martinez, Jacinto Benavente y
See Benavente (y Martinez), Jacinto

Martinez Ruiz, Jose 1873-1967
See Azorin; Ruiz, Jose Martinez
See also CA 93-96; HW

Martinez Sierra, Gregorio
1881-1947 .... **TCLC 6**
See also CA 115

Martinez Sierra, Maria (de la O'LeJarraga)
1874-1974 .... **TCLC 6**
See also CA 115

Martinsen, Martin
See Follett, Ken(neth Martin)

Martinson, Harry (Edmund)
1904-1978 .... **CLC 14**
See also CA 77-80; CANR 34

Marut, Ret
See Traven, B.

Marut, Robert
See Traven, B.

Marvell, Andrew
1621-1678 .... **LC 4; DA; WLC**
See also CDBLB 1660-1789; DLB 131

Marx, Karl (Heinrich)
1818-1883 .... **NCLC 17**
See also DLB 129

Masaoka Shiki .... **TCLC 18**
See also Masaoka Tsunenori

Masaoka Tsunenori 1867-1902
See Masaoka Shiki
See also CA 117

Masefield, John (Edward)
1878-1967 .... **CLC 11, 47**
See also CA 19-20; 25-28R; CANR 33;
CAP 2; CDBLB 1890-1914; DLB 10;
MTCW; SATA 19

Maso, Carole 19(?)- .... **CLC 44**

Mason, Bobbie Ann
1940- .... **CLC 28, 43, 82; SSC 4**
See also AAYA 5; CA 53-56; CANR 11,
31; DLBY 87; MTCW

Mason, Ernst
See Pohl, Frederik

Mason, Lee W.
See Malzberg, Barry N(athaniel)

Mason, Nick 1945- .... **CLC 35**
See also Pink Floyd

Mason, Tally
See Derleth, August (William)

Mass, William
See Gibson, William

Masters, Edgar Lee
1868-1950 . . . . . . TCLC **2, 25**; DA; PC **1**
See also CA 104; 133; CDALB 1865-1917;
DLB 54; MTCW

Masters, Hilary 1928- . . . . CLC **48**
See also CA 25-28R; CANR 13

Mastrosimone, William 19(?)- . . . . . . CLC **36**

Mathe, Albert
See Camus, Albert

Matheson, Richard Burton 1926- . . . CLC **37**
See also CA 97-100; DLB 8, 44

Mathews, Harry 1930- . . . . CLC **6, 52**
See also CA 21-24R; CAAS 6; CANR 18,
40

Mathias, Roland (Glyn) 1915- . . . . . . CLC **45**
See also CA 97-100; CANR 19, 41; DLB 27

Matsuo Basho 1644-1694 . . . . PC **3**

Mattheson, Rodney
See Creasey, John

Matthews, Greg 1949- . . . . CLC **45**
See also CA 135

Matthews, William 1942- . . . . CLC **40**
See also CA 29-32R; CAAS 18; CANR 12;
DLB 5

Matthias, John (Edward) 1941- . . . . . . CLC **9**
See also CA 33-36R

Matthiessen, Peter
1927- . . . . CLC **5, 7, 11, 32, 64**
See also AAYA 6; BEST 90:4; CA 9-12R;
CANR 21; DLB 6; MTCW; SATA 27

Maturin, Charles Robert
1780(?)-1824 . . . . NCLC **6**

Matute (Ausejo), Ana Maria
1925- . . . . CLC **11**
See also CA 89-92; MTCW

Maugham, W. S.
See Maugham, W(illiam) Somerset

Maugham, W(illiam) Somerset
1874-1965 . . . . . . CLC **1, 11, 15, 67**; DA;
SSC **8**; WLC
See also CA 5-8R; 25-28R; CANR 40;
CDBLB 1914-1945; DLB 10, 36, 77, 100;
MTCW; SATA 54

Maugham, William Somerset
See Maugham, W(illiam) Somerset

Maupassant, (Henri Rene Albert) Guy de
1850-1893 . . . . NCLC **1, 42**; DA; SSC **1**;
WLC
See also DLB 123

Maurhut, Richard
See Traven, B.

Mauriac, Claude 1914- . . . . CLC **9**
See also CA 89-92; DLB 83

Mauriac, Francois (Charles)
1885-1970 . . . . CLC **4, 9, 56**
See also CA 25-28; CAP 2; DLB 65;
MTCW

Mavor, Osborne Henry 1888-1951
See Bridie, James
See also CA 104

Maxwell, William (Keepers, Jr.)
1908- . . . . CLC **19**
See also CA 93-96; DLBY 80

May, Elaine 1932- . . . . CLC **16**
See also CA 124; 142; DLB 44

Mayakovski, Vladimir (Vladimirovich)
1893-1930 . . . . TCLC **4, 18**
See also CA 104

Mayhew, Henry 1812-1887 . . . . . . NCLC **31**
See also DLB 18, 55

Maynard, Joyce 1953- . . . . CLC **23**
See also CA 111; 129

Mayne, William (James Carter)
1928- . . . . CLC **12**
See also CA 9-12R; CANR 37; CLR 25;
JRDA; MAICYA; SAAS 11; SATA 6, 68

Mayo, Jim
See L'Amour, Louis (Dearborn)

Maysles, Albert 1926- . . . . CLC **16**
See also CA 29-32R

Maysles, David 1932- . . . . CLC **16**

Mazer, Norma Fox 1931- . . . . CLC **26**
See also AAYA 5; CA 69-72; CANR 12,
32; CLR 23; JRDA; MAICYA; SAAS 1;
SATA 24, 67

Mazzini, Guiseppe 1805-1872 . . . . NCLC **34**

McAuley, James Phillip
1917-1976 . . . . CLC **45**
See also CA 97-100

McBain, Ed
See Hunter, Evan

McBrien, William Augustine
1930- . . . . CLC **44**
See also CA 107

McCaffrey, Anne (Inez) 1926- . . . . . . CLC **17**
See also AAYA 6; AITN 2; BEST 89:2;
CA 25-28R; CANR 15, 35; DLB 8;
JRDA; MAICYA; MTCW; SAAS 11;
SATA 8, 70

McCann, Arthur
See Campbell, John W(ood, Jr.)

McCann, Edson
See Pohl, Frederik

McCarthy, Charles, Jr. 1933-
See McCarthy, Cormac
See also CANR 42

McCarthy, Cormac . . . . CLC **4, 57**
See also McCarthy, Charles, Jr.
See also DLB 6

McCarthy, Mary (Therese)
1912-1989 . . . CLC **1, 3, 5, 14, 24, 39, 59**
See also CA 5-8R; 129; CANR 16; DLB 2;
DLBY 81; MTCW

McCartney, (James) Paul
1942- . . . . CLC **12, 35**

McCauley, Stephen (D.) 1955- . . . . . CLC **50**
See also CA 141

McClure, Michael (Thomas)
1932- . . . . CLC **6, 10**
See also CA 21-24R; CANR 17; DLB 16

McCorkle, Jill (Collins) 1958- . . . . . . CLC **51**
See also CA 121; DLBY 87

McCourt, James 1941- . . . . CLC **5**
See also CA 57-60

McCoy, Horace (Stanley)
1897-1955 . . . . TCLC **28**
See also CA 108; DLB 9

McCrae, John 1872-1918 . . . . TCLC **12**
See also CA 109; DLB 92

McCreigh, James
See Pohl, Frederik

McCullers, (Lula) Carson (Smith)
1917-1967 . . . . CLC **1, 4, 10, 12, 48**; DA;
SSC **9**; WLC
See also CA 5-8R; 25-28R; CABS 1, 3;
CANR 18; CDALB 1941-1968; DLB 2, 7;
MTCW; SATA 27

McCulloch, John Tyler
See Burroughs, Edgar Rice

McCullough, Colleen 1938(?)- . . . . . . CLC **27**
See also CA 81-84; CANR 17; MTCW

McElroy, Joseph 1930- . . . . CLC **5, 47**
See also CA 17-20R

McEwan, Ian (Russell) 1948- . . . CLC **13, 66**
See also BEST 90:4; CA 61-64; CANR 14,
41; DLB 14; MTCW

McFadden, David 1940- . . . . CLC **48**
See also CA 104; DLB 60

McFarland, Dennis 1950- . . . . CLC **65**

McGahern, John 1934- . . . . CLC **5, 9, 48**
See also CA 17-20R; CANR 29; DLB 14;
MTCW

McGinley, Patrick (Anthony)
1937- . . . . CLC **41**
See also CA 120; 127

McGinley, Phyllis 1905-1978 . . . . . . CLC **14**
See also CA 9-12R; 77-80; CANR 19;
DLB 11, 48; SATA 2, 24, 44

McGinniss, Joe 1942- . . . . CLC **32**
See also AITN 2; BEST 89:2; CA 25-28R;
CANR 26

McGivern, Maureen Daly
See Daly, Maureen

McGrath, Patrick 1950- . . . . CLC **55**
See also CA 136

McGrath, Thomas (Matthew)
1916-1990 . . . . CLC **28, 59**
See also CA 9-12R; 132; CANR 6, 33;
MTCW; SATA 41; SATA-Obit 66

McGuane, Thomas (Francis III)
1939- . . . . CLC **3, 7, 18, 45**
See also AITN 2; CA 49-52; CANR 5, 24;
DLB 2; DLBY 80; MTCW

McGuckian, Medbh 1950- . . . . CLC **48**
See also CA 143; DLB 40

McHale, Tom 1942(?)-1982 . . . . CLC **3, 5**
See also AITN 1; CA 77-80; 106

McIlvanney, William 1936- . . . . CLC **42**
See also CA 25-28R; DLB 14

McIlwraith, Maureen Mollie Hunter
See Hunter, Mollie
See also SATA 2

McInerney, Jay 1955- . . . . CLC **34**
See also CA 116; 123

McIntyre, Vonda N(eel) 1948- . . . . . CLC **18**
See also CA 81-84; CANR 17, 34; MTCW

McKay, Claude . . . . . TCLC **7, 41**; BLC; PC **2**
See also McKay, Festus Claudius
See also DLB 4, 45, 51, 117

McKay, Festus Claudius   1889-1948
    See McKay, Claude
    See also BW 1; CA 104; 124; DA; MTCW;
    WLC

McKuen, Rod   1933-.............. **CLC 1, 3**
    See also AITN 1; CA 41-44R; CANR 40

McLoughlin, R. B.
    See Mencken, H(enry) L(ouis)

McLuhan, (Herbert) Marshall
    1911-1980 .... **CLC 37, 83**
    See also CA 9-12R; 102; CANR 12, 34;
    DLB 88; MTCW

McMillan, Terry (L.)   1951-..... **CLC 50, 61**
    See also CA 140

McMurtry, Larry (Jeff)
    1936- .... **CLC 2, 3, 7, 11, 27, 44**
    See also AITN 2; BEST 89:2; CA 5-8R;
    CANR 19, 43; CDALB 1968-1988;
    DLB 2; DLBY 80, 87; MTCW

McNally, T. M.   1961- .... **CLC 82**

McNally, Terrence   1939-...... **CLC 4, 7, 41**
    See also CA 45-48; CANR 2; DLB 7

McNamer, Deirdre   1950-.......... **CLC 70**

McNeile, Herman Cyril   1888-1937
    See Sapper
    See also DLB 77

McPhee, John (Angus)   1931- ...... **CLC 36**
    See also BEST 90:1; CA 65-68; CANR 20;
    MTCW

McPherson, James Alan
    1943-..................... **CLC 19, 77**
    See also BW; CA 25-28R; CAAS 17;
    CANR 24; DLB 38; MTCW

McPherson, William (Alexander)
    1933-...................... **CLC 34**
    See also CA 69-72; CANR 28

McSweeney, Kerry .... **CLC 34**

Mead, Margaret   1901-1978........ **CLC 37**
    See also AITN 1; CA 1-4R; 81-84;
    CANR 4; MTCW; SATA 20

Meaker, Marijane (Agnes)   1927-
    See Kerr, M. E.
    See also CA 107; CANR 37; JRDA;
    MAICYA; MTCW; SATA 20, 61

Medoff, Mark (Howard)   1940-... **CLC 6, 23**
    See also AITN 1; CA 53-56; CANR 5;
    DLB 7

Medvedev, P. N.
    See Bakhtin, Mikhail Mikhailovich

Meged, Aharon
    See Megged, Aharon

Meged, Aron
    See Megged, Aharon

Megged, Aharon   1920-............ **CLC 9**
    See also CA 49-52; CAAS 13; CANR 1

Mehta, Ved (Parkash)   1934-....... **CLC 37**
    See also CA 1-4R; CANR 2, 23; MTCW

Melanter
    See Blackmore, R(ichard) D(oddridge)

Melikow, Loris
    See Hofmannsthal, Hugo von

Melmoth, Sebastian
    See Wilde, Oscar (Fingal O'Flahertie Wills)

Meltzer, Milton   1915-............ **CLC 26**
    See also AAYA 8; CA 13-16R; CANR 38;
    CLR 13; DLB 61; JRDA; MAICYA;
    SAAS 1; SATA 1, 50

Melville, Herman
    1819-1891 .... **NCLC 3, 12, 29, 45; DA;
                                SSC 1; WLC**
    See also CDALB 1640-1865; DLB 3, 74;
    SATA 59

Menander
    c. 342B.C.-c. 292B.C.... **CMLC 9; DC 3**

Mencken, H(enry) L(ouis)
    1880-1956 .... **TCLC 13**
    See also Hatteras, Owen
    See also CA 105; 125; CDALB 1917-1929;
    DLB 11, 29, 63, 137; MTCW

Mercer, David   1928-1980.......... **CLC 5**
    See also CA 9-12R; 102; CANR 23;
    DLB 13; MTCW

Merchant, Paul
    See Ellison, Harlan

Meredith, George   1828-1909... **TCLC 17, 43**
    See also CA 117; CDBLB 1832-1890;
    DLB 18, 35, 57

Meredith, William (Morris)
    1919-............... **CLC 4, 13, 22, 55**
    See also CA 9-12R; CAAS 14; CANR 6, 40;
    DLB 5

Merezhkovsky, Dmitry Sergeyevich
    1865-1941 .... **TCLC 29**

Merimee, Prosper
    1803-1870 .... **NCLC 6; SSC 7**
    See also DLB 119

Merkin, Daphne   1954-............ **CLC 44**
    See also CA 123

Merlin, Arthur
    See Blish, James (Benjamin)

Merrill, James (Ingram)
    1926- .... **CLC 2, 3, 6, 8, 13, 18, 34**
    See also CA 13-16R; CANR 10; DLB 5;
    DLBY 85; MTCW

Merriman, Alex
    See Silverberg, Robert

Merritt, E. B.
    See Waddington, Miriam

Merton, Thomas
    1915-1968 .... **CLC 1, 3, 11, 34, 83**
    See also CA 5-8R; 25-28R; CANR 22;
    DLB 48; DLBY 81; MTCW

Merwin, W(illiam) S(tanley)
    1927- ...... **CLC 1, 2, 3, 5, 8, 13, 18, 45**
    See also CA 13-16R; CANR 15; DLB 5;
    MTCW

Metcalf, John   1938-.............. **CLC 37**
    See also CA 113; DLB 60

Metcalf, Suzanne
    See Baum, L(yman) Frank

Mew, Charlotte (Mary)
    1870-1928 .... **TCLC 8**
    See also CA 105; DLB 19, 135

Mewshaw, Michael   1943-........... **CLC 9**
    See also CA 53-56; CANR 7; DLBY 80

Meyer, June
    See Jordan, June

Meyer, Lynn
    See Slavitt, David R(ytman)

Meyer-Meyrink, Gustav   1868-1932
    See Meyrink, Gustav
    See also CA 117

Meyers, Jeffrey   1939-............ **CLC 39**
    See also CA 73-76; DLB 111

Meynell, Alice (Christina Gertrude Thompson)
    1847-1922 .... **TCLC 6**
    See also CA 104; DLB 19, 98

Meyrink, Gustav .... **TCLC 21**
    See also Meyer-Meyrink, Gustav
    See also DLB 81

Michaels, Leonard   1933-........ **CLC 6, 25**
    See also CA 61-64; CANR 21; DLB 130;
    MTCW

Michaux, Henri   1899-1984 ...... **CLC 8, 19**
    See also CA 85-88; 114

Michelangelo   1475-1564............ **LC 12**

Michelet, Jules   1798-1874....... **NCLC 31**

Michener, James A(lbert)
    1907(?)-.......... **CLC 1, 5, 11, 29, 60**
    See also AITN 1; BEST 90:1; CA 5-8R;
    CANR 21; DLB 6; MTCW

Mickiewicz, Adam   1798-1855 ..... **NCLC 3**

Middleton, Christopher   1926-...... **CLC 13**
    See also CA 13-16R; CANR 29; DLB 40

Middleton, Stanley   1919-........ **CLC 7, 38**
    See also CA 25-28R; CANR 21; DLB 14

Migueis, Jose Rodrigues   1901-..... **CLC 10**

Mikszath, Kalman   1847-1910 ..... **TCLC 31**

Miles, Josephine
    1911-1985 .... **CLC 1, 2, 14, 34, 39**
    See also CA 1-4R; 116; CANR 2; DLB 48

Militant
    See Sandburg, Carl (August)

Mill, John Stuart   1806-1873..... **NCLC 11**
    See also CDBLB 1832-1890; DLB 55

Millar, Kenneth   1915-1983 .... **CLC 14**
    See also Macdonald, Ross
    See also CA 9-12R; 110; CANR 16; DLB 2;
    DLBD 6; DLBY 83; MTCW

Millay, E. Vincent
    See Millay, Edna St. Vincent

Millay, Edna St. Vincent
    1892-1950 ...... **TCLC 4, 49; DA; PC 6**
    See also CA 104; 130; CDALB 1917-1929;
    DLB 45; MTCW

Miller, Arthur
    1915- .... **CLC 1, 2, 6, 10, 15, 26, 47, 78;
                                DA; DC 1; WLC**
    See also AITN 1; CA 1-4R; CABS 3;
    CANR 2, 30; CDALB 1941-1968; DLB 7;
    MTCW

Miller, Henry (Valentine)
    1891-1980 .... **CLC 1, 2, 4, 9, 14, 43;
                                DA; WLC**
    See also CA 9-12R; 97-100; CANR 33;
    CDALB 1929-1941; DLB 4, 9; DLBY 80;
    MTCW

Miller, Jason   1939(?)- .... **CLC 2**
    See also AITN 1; CA 73-76; DLB 7

Miller, Sue   1943-................ **CLC 44**
    See also BEST 90:3; CA 139

Miller, Walter M(ichael, Jr.)
1923- . . . . **CLC 4, 30**
See also CA 85-88; DLB 8

Millett, Kate 1934- . . . . **CLC 67**
See also AITN 1; CA 73-76; CANR 32;
MTCW

Millhauser, Steven 1943- . . . . **CLC 21, 54**
See also CA 110; 111; DLB 2

Millin, Sarah Gertrude 1889-1968 . . **CLC 49**
See also CA 102; 93-96

Milne, A(lan) A(lexander)
1882-1956 . . . . **TCLC 6**
See also CA 104; 133; CLR 1, 26; DLB 10,
77, 100; MAICYA; MTCW; YABC 1

Milner, Ron(ald) 1938- . . . . **CLC 56; BLC**
See also AITN 1; BW; CA 73-76;
CANR 24; DLB 38; MTCW

Milosz, Czeslaw
1911- . . . **CLC 5, 11, 22, 31, 56, 82; PC 8**
See also CA 81-84; CANR 23; MTCW

Milton, John 1608-1674 . . . **LC 9; DA; WLC**
See also CDBLB 1660-1789; DLB 131

Minehaha, Cornelius
See Wedekind, (Benjamin) Frank(lin)

Miner, Valerie 1947- . . . . **CLC 40**
See also CA 97-100

Minimo, Duca
See D'Annunzio, Gabriele

Minot, Susan 1956- . . . . **CLC 44**
See also CA 134

Minus, Ed 1938- . . . . **CLC 39**

Miranda, Javier
See Bioy Casares, Adolfo

Miro (Ferrer), Gabriel (Francisco Victor)
1879-1930 . . . . **TCLC 5**
See also CA 104

Mishima, Yukio
. . . . **CLC 2, 4, 6, 9, 27; DC 1; SSC 4**
See also Hiraoka, Kimitake

Mistral, Frederic 1830-1914 . . . . . **TCLC 51**
See also CA 122

Mistral, Gabriela . . . . **TCLC 2; HLC**
See also Godoy Alcayaga, Lucila

Mistry, Rohinton 1952- . . . . **CLC 71**
See also CA 141

Mitchell, Clyde
See Ellison, Harlan; Silverberg, Robert

Mitchell, James Leslie 1901-1935
See Gibbon, Lewis Grassic
See also CA 104; DLB 15

Mitchell, Joni 1943- . . . . **CLC 12**
See also CA 112

Mitchell, Margaret (Munnerlyn)
1900-1949 . . . . **TCLC 11**
See also CA 109; 125; DLB 9; MTCW

Mitchell, Peggy
See Mitchell, Margaret (Munnerlyn)

Mitchell, S(ilas) Weir 1829-1914 . . **TCLC 36**

Mitchell, W(illiam) O(rmond)
1914- . . . . **CLC 25**
See also CA 77-80; CANR 15, 43; DLB 88

Mitford, Mary Russell 1787-1855 . . **NCLC 4**
See also DLB 110, 116

Mitford, Nancy 1904-1973 . . . . **CLC 44**
See also CA 9-12R

Miyamoto, Yuriko 1899-1951 . . . . . **TCLC 37**

Mo, Timothy (Peter) 1950(?)- . . . . . . **CLC 46**
See also CA 117; MTCW

Modarressi, Taghi (M.) 1931- . . . . . . **CLC 44**
See also CA 121; 134

Modiano, Patrick (Jean) 1945- . . . . . **CLC 18**
See also CA 85-88; CANR 17, 40; DLB 83

Moerck, Paal
See Roelvaag, O(le) E(dvart)

Mofolo, Thomas (Mokopu)
1875(?)-1948 . . . . **TCLC 22; BLC**
See also CA 121

Mohr, Nicholasa 1935- . . . . . . **CLC 12; HLC**
See also AAYA 8; CA 49-52; CANR 1, 32;
CLR 22; HW; JRDA; SAAS 8; SATA 8

Mojtabai, A(nn) G(race)
1938- . . . . **CLC 5, 9, 15, 29**
See also CA 85-88

Moliere 1622-1673 . . . . **LC 10; DA; WLC**

Molin, Charles
See Mayne, William (James Carter)

Molnar, Ferenc 1878-1952 . . . . **TCLC 20**
See also CA 109

Momaday, N(avarre) Scott
1934- . . . . **CLC 2, 19; DA**
See also AAYA 11; CA 25-28R; CANR 14,
34; MTCW; SATA 30, 48

Monette, Paul 1945- . . . . **CLC 82**
See also CA 139

Monroe, Harriet 1860-1936 . . . . . . **TCLC 12**
See also CA 109; DLB 54, 91

Monroe, Lyle
See Heinlein, Robert A(nson)

Montagu, Elizabeth 1917- . . . . **NCLC 7**
See also CA 9-12R

Montagu, Mary (Pierrepont) Wortley
1689-1762 . . . . **LC 9**
See also DLB 95, 101

Montagu, W. H.
See Coleridge, Samuel Taylor

Montague, John (Patrick)
1929- . . . . **CLC 13, 46**
See also CA 9-12R; CANR 9; DLB 40;
MTCW

Montaigne, Michel (Eyquem) de
1533-1592 . . . . **LC 8; DA; WLC**

Montale, Eugenio 1896-1981 . . . **CLC 7, 9, 18**
See also CA 17-20R; 104; CANR 30;
DLB 114; MTCW

Montesquieu, Charles-Louis de Secondat
1689-1755 . . . . **LC 7**

Montgomery, (Robert) Bruce 1921-1978
See Crispin, Edmund
See also CA 104

Montgomery, L(ucy) M(aud)
1874-1942 . . . . **TCLC 51**
See also AAYA 12; CA 108; 137; CLR 8;
DLB 92; JRDA; MAICYA; YABC 1

Montgomery, Marion H., Jr. 1925- . . **CLC 7**
See also AITN 1; CA 1-4R; CANR 3;
DLB 6

Montgomery, Max
See Davenport, Guy (Mattison, Jr.)

Montherlant, Henry (Milon) de
1896-1972 . . . . **CLC 8, 19**
See also CA 85-88; 37-40R; DLB 72;
MTCW

Monty Python . . . . **CLC 21**
See also Chapman, Graham; Cleese, John
(Marwood); Gilliam, Terry (Vance); Idle,
Eric; Jones, Terence Graham Parry; Palin,
Michael (Edward)
See also AAYA 7

Moodie, Susanna (Strickland)
1803-1885 . . . . **NCLC 14**
See also DLB 99

Mooney, Edward 1951- . . . . **CLC 25**
See also CA 130

Mooney, Ted
See Mooney, Edward

Moorcock, Michael (John)
1939- . . . . **CLC 5, 27, 58**
See also CA 45-48; CAAS 5; CANR 2, 17,
38; DLB 14; MTCW

Moore, Brian
1921- . . . . **CLC 1, 3, 5, 7, 8, 19, 32**
See also CA 1-4R; CANR 1, 25, 42; MTCW

Moore, Edward
See Muir, Edwin

Moore, George Augustus
1852-1933 . . . . **TCLC 7**
See also CA 104; DLB 10, 18, 57, 135

Moore, Lorrie . . . . **CLC 39, 45, 68**
See also Moore, Marie Lorena

Moore, Marianne (Craig)
1887-1972 . . . . **CLC 1, 2, 4, 8, 10, 13, 19,**
                                          47; DA; PC 4
See also CA 1-4R; 33-36R; CANR 3;
CDALB 1929-1941; DLB 45; DLBD 7;
MTCW; SATA 20

Moore, Marie Lorena 1957-
See Moore, Lorrie
See also CA 116; CANR 39

Moore, Thomas 1779-1852 . . . . **NCLC 6**
See also DLB 96

Morand, Paul 1888-1976 . . . . **CLC 41**
See also CA 69-72; DLB 65

Morante, Elsa 1918-1985 . . . . **CLC 8, 47**
See also CA 85-88; 117; CANR 35; MTCW

Moravia, Alberto . . . . **CLC 2, 7, 11, 27, 46**
See also Pincherle, Alberto

More, Hannah 1745-1833 . . . . **NCLC 27**
See also DLB 107, 109, 116

More, Henry 1614-1687 . . . . **LC 9**
See also DLB 126

More, Sir Thomas 1478-1535 . . . . **LC 10**

Moreas, Jean . . . . **TCLC 18**
See also Papadiamantopoulos, Johannes

Morgan, Berry 1919- . . . . **CLC 6**
See also CA 49-52; DLB 6

Morgan, Claire
See Highsmith, (Mary) Patricia

Morgan, Edwin (George) 1920- . . . . . **CLC 31**
See also CA 5-8R; CANR 3, 43; DLB 27

Morgan, (George) Frederick
1922- .... **CLC 23**
See also CA 17-20R; CANR 21

Morgan, Harriet
See Mencken, H(enry) L(ouis)

Morgan, Jane
See Cooper, James Fenimore

Morgan, Janet 1945- .... **CLC 39**
See also CA 65-68

Morgan, Lady 1776(?)-1859...... **NCLC 29**
See also DLB 116

Morgan, Robin 1941-.............. **CLC 2**
See also CA 69-72; CANR 29; MTCW

Morgan, Scott
See Kuttner, Henry

Morgan, Seth 1949(?)-1990 .... **CLC 65**
See also CA 132

Morgenstern, Christian
1871-1914 .... **TCLC 8**
See also CA 105

Morgenstern, S.
See Goldman, William (W.)

Moricz, Zsigmond 1879-1942 ..... **TCLC 33**

Morike, Eduard (Friedrich)
1804-1875 .... **NCLC 10**
See also DLB 133

Mori Ogai .... **TCLC 14**
See also Mori Rintaro

Mori Rintaro 1862-1922
See Mori Ogai
See also CA 110

Moritz, Karl Philipp 1756-1793 ...... **LC 2**
See also DLB 94

Morland, Peter Henry
See Faust, Frederick (Schiller)

Morren, Theophil
See Hofmannsthal, Hugo von

Morris, Bill 1952-................ **CLC 76**

Morris, Julian
See West, Morris L(anglo)

Morris, Steveland Judkins 1950(?)-
See Wonder, Stevie
See also CA 111

Morris, William 1834-1896 .... **NCLC 4**
See also CDBLB 1832-1890; DLB 18, 35, 57

Morris, Wright 1910-... **CLC 1, 3, 7, 18, 37**
See also CA 9-12R; CANR 21; DLB 2;
DLBY 81; MTCW

Morrison, Chloe Anthony Wofford
See Morrison, Toni

Morrison, James Douglas 1943-1971
See Morrison, Jim
See also CA 73-76; CANR 40

Morrison, Jim .... **CLC 17**
See also Morrison, James Douglas

Morrison, Toni
1931-.. **CLC 4, 10, 22, 55, 81; BLC; DA**
See also AAYA 1; BW; CA 29-32R;
CANR 27, 42; CDALB 1968-1988;
DLB 6, 33; DLBY 81; MTCW; SATA 57

Morrison, Van 1945- .... **CLC 21**
See also CA 116

Mortimer, John (Clifford)
1923- .... **CLC 28, 43**
See also CA 13-16R; CANR 21;
CDBLB 1960 to Present; DLB 13;
MTCW

Mortimer, Penelope (Ruth) 1918-.... **CLC 5**
See also CA 57-60

Morton, Anthony
See Creasey, John

Mosher, Howard Frank 1943-...... **CLC 62**
See also CA 139

Mosley, Nicholas 1923-........ **CLC 43, 70**
See also CA 69-72; CANR 41; DLB 14

Moss, Howard
1922-1987 .... **CLC 7, 14, 45, 50**
See also CA 1-4R; 123; CANR 1, 44;
DLB 5

Mossgiel, Rab
See Burns, Robert

Motion, Andrew 1952-............ **CLC 47**
See also DLB 40

Motley, Willard (Francis)
1912-1965 .... **CLC 18**
See also BW; CA 117; 106; DLB 76

Motoori, Norinaga 1730-1801 .... **NCLC 45**

Mott, Michael (Charles Alston)
1930- .... **CLC 15, 34**
See also CA 5-8R; CAAS 7; CANR 7, 29

Mowat, Farley (McGill) 1921- ..... **CLC 26**
See also AAYA 1; CA 1-4R; CANR 4, 24,
42; CLR 20; DLB 68; JRDA; MAICYA;
MTCW; SATA 3, 55

Moyers, Bill 1934- .... **CLC 74**
See also AITN 2; CA 61-64; CANR 31

Mphahlele, Es'kia
See Mphahlele, Ezekiel
See also DLB 125

Mphahlele, Ezekiel 1919-..... **CLC 25; BLC**
See also Mphahlele, Es'kia
See also BW; CA 81-84; CANR 26

Mqhayi, S(amuel) E(dward) K(rune Loliwe)
1875-1945 .... **TCLC 25; BLC**

Mr. Martin
See Burroughs, William S(eward)

Mrozek, Slawomir 1930-........ **CLC 3, 13**
See also CA 13-16R; CAAS 10; CANR 29;
MTCW

Mrs. Belloc-Lowndes
See Lowndes, Marie Adelaide (Belloc)

Mtwa, Percy (?)-................. **CLC 47**

Mueller, Lisel 1924-........... **CLC 13, 51**
See also CA 93-96; DLB 105

Muir, Edwin 1887-1959 .... **TCLC 2**
See also CA 104; DLB 20, 100

Muir, John 1838-1914 .... **TCLC 28**

Mujica Lainez, Manuel
1910-1984 .... **CLC 31**
See also Lainez, Manuel Mujica
See also CA 81-84; 112; CANR 32; HW

Mukherjee, Bharati 1940-......... **CLC 53**
See also BEST 89:2; CA 107; DLB 60;
MTCW

Muldoon, Paul 1951-......... **CLC 32, 72**
See also CA 113; 129; DLB 40

Mulisch, Harry 1927-............ **CLC 42**
See also CA 9-12R; CANR 6, 26

Mull, Martin 1943-.............. **CLC 17**
See also CA 105

Mulock, Dinah Maria
See Craik, Dinah Maria (Mulock)

Munford, Robert 1737(?)-1783 .... **LC 5**
See also DLB 31

Mungo, Raymond 1946-........... **CLC 72**
See also CA 49-52; CANR 2

Munro, Alice
1931- .... **CLC 6, 10, 19, 50; SSC 3**
See also AITN 2; CA 33-36R; CANR 33;
DLB 53; MTCW; SATA 29

Munro, H(ector) H(ugh) 1870-1916
See Saki
See also CA 104; 130; CDBLB 1890-1914;
DA; DLB 34; MTCW; WLC

Murasaki, Lady................. **CMLC 1**

Murdoch, (Jean) Iris
1919- ...... **CLC 1, 2, 3, 4, 6, 8, 11, 15,
22, 31, 51**
See also CA 13-16R; CANR 8, 43;
CDBLB 1960 to Present; DLB 14;
MTCW

Murnau, Friedrich Wilhelm
See Plumpe, Friedrich Wilhelm

Murphy, Richard 1927-........... **CLC 41**
See also CA 29-32R; DLB 40

Murphy, Sylvia 1937-............. **CLC 34**
See also CA 121

Murphy, Thomas (Bernard) 1935-... **CLC 51**
See also CA 101

Murray, Albert L. 1916- .... **CLC 73**
See also BW; CA 49-52; CANR 26; DLB 38

Murray, Les(lie) A(llan) 1938- ..... **CLC 40**
See also CA 21-24R; CANR 11, 27

Murry, J. Middleton
See Murry, John Middleton

Murry, John Middleton
1889-1957 .... **TCLC 16**
See also CA 118

Musgrave, Susan 1951- .... **CLC 13, 54**
See also CA 69-72

Musil, Robert (Edler von)
1880-1942 .... **TCLC 12**
See also CA 109; DLB 81, 124

Musset, (Louis Charles) Alfred de
1810-1857 .... **NCLC 7**

My Brother's Brother
See Chekhov, Anton (Pavlovich)

Myers, Walter Dean 1937- ... **CLC 35; BLC**
See also AAYA 4; BW; CA 33-36R;
CANR 20, 42; CLR 4, 16; DLB 33;
JRDA; MAICYA; SAAS 2; SATA 27, 41,
71

Myers, Walter M.
See Myers, Walter Dean

Myles, Symon
See Follett, Ken(neth Martin)

Orton, Joe . . . . **CLC 4, 13, 43; DC 3**
  See also Orton, John Kingsley
  See also CDBLB 1960 to Present; DLB 13

Orton, John Kingsley 1933-1967
  See Orton, Joe
  See also CA 85-88; CANR 35; MTCW

Orwell, George
  . . . . **TCLC 2, 6, 15, 31, 51; WLC**
  See also Blair, Eric (Arthur)
  See also CDBLB 1945-1960; DLB 15, 98

Osborne, David
  See Silverberg, Robert

Osborne, George
  See Silverberg, Robert

Osborne, John (James)
  1929- . . . . CLC 1, 2, 5, 11, 45; DA; WLC
  See also CA 13-16R; CANR 21;
    CDBLB 1945-1960; DLB 13; MTCW

Osborne, Lawrence 1958- . . . . **CLC 50**

Oshima, Nagisa 1932- . . . . **CLC 20**
  See also CA 116; 121

Oskison, John Milton
  1874-1947 . . . . **TCLC 35**
  See also CA 144

Ossoli, Sarah Margaret (Fuller marchesa d')
  1810-1850
  See Fuller, Margaret
  See also SATA 25

Ostrovsky, Alexander
  1823-1886 . . . . **NCLC 30**

Otero, Blas de 1916-1979 . . . . **CLC 11**
  See also CA 89-92; DLB 134

Otto, Whitney 1955- . . . . **CLC 70**
  See also CA 140

Ouida . . . . **TCLC 43**
  See also De La Ramee, (Marie) Louise
  See also DLB 18

Ousmane, Sembene 1923- . . . . **CLC 66; BLC**
  See also BW; CA 117; 125; MTCW

Ovid 43B.C.-18th cent. (?) . . . **CMLC 7; PC 2**

Owen, Hugh
  See Faust, Frederick (Schiller)

Owen, Wilfred (Edward Salter)
  1893-1918 . . . . . . **TCLC 5, 27; DA; WLC**
  See also CA 104; 141; CDBLB 1914-1945;
    DLB 20

Owens, Rochelle 1936- . . . . **CLC 8**
  See also CA 17-20R; CAAS 2; CANR 39

Oz, Amos 1939- . . . **CLC 5, 8, 11, 27, 33, 54**
  See also CA 53-56; CANR 27; MTCW

Ozick, Cynthia
  1928- . . . . **CLC 3, 7, 28, 62; SSC 15**
  See also BEST 90:1; CA 17-20R; CANR 23;
    DLB 28; DLBY 82; MTCW

Ozu, Yasujiro 1903-1963 . . . . **CLC 16**
  See also CA 112

Pacheco, C.
  See Pessoa, Fernando (Antonio Nogueira)

Pa Chin
  See Li Fei-kan

Pack, Robert 1929- . . . . **CLC 13**
  See also CA 1-4R; CANR 3, 44; DLB 5

Padgett, Lewis
  See Kuttner, Henry

Padilla (Lorenzo), Heberto 1932- . . . **CLC 38**
  See also AITN 1; CA 123; 131; HW

Page, Jimmy 1944- . . . . **CLC 12**

Page, Louise 1955- . . . . **CLC 40**
  See also CA 140

Page, P(atricia) K(athleen)
  1916- . . . . **CLC 7, 18**
  See also CA 53-56; CANR 4, 22; DLB 68;
    MTCW

Paget, Violet 1856-1935
  See Lee, Vernon
  See also CA 104

Paget-Lowe, Henry
  See Lovecraft, H(oward) P(hillips)

Paglia, Camille (Anna) 1947- . . . . . . **CLC 68**
  See also CA 140

Paige, Richard
  See Koontz, Dean R(ay)

Pakenham, Antonia
  See Fraser, (Lady) Antonia (Pakenham)

Palamas, Kostes 1859-1943 . . . . **TCLC 5**
  See also CA 105

Palazzeschi, Aldo 1885-1974 . . . . . . **CLC 11**
  See also CA 89-92; 53-56; DLB 114

Paley, Grace 1922- . . . . **CLC 4, 6, 37; SSC 8**
  See also CA 25-28R; CANR 13; DLB 28;
    MTCW

Palin, Michael (Edward) 1943- . . . . . **CLC 21**
  See also Monty Python
  See also CA 107; CANR 35; SATA 67

Palliser, Charles 1947- . . . . **CLC 65**
  See also CA 136

Palma, Ricardo 1833-1919 . . . . **TCLC 29**

Pancake, Breece Dexter 1952-1979
  See Pancake, Breece D'J
  See also CA 123; 109

Pancake, Breece D'J . . . . **CLC 29**
  See also Pancake, Breece Dexter
  See also DLB 130

Panko, Rudy
  See Gogol, Nikolai (Vasilyevich)

Papadiamantis, Alexandros
  1851-1911 . . . . **TCLC 29**

Papadiamantopoulos, Johannes 1856-1910
  See Moreas, Jean
  See also CA 117

Papini, Giovanni 1881-1956 . . . . **TCLC 22**
  See also CA 121

Paracelsus 1493-1541 . . . . **LC 14**

Parasol, Peter
  See Stevens, Wallace

Parfenie, Maria
  See Codrescu, Andrei

Parini, Jay (Lee) 1948- . . . . **CLC 54**
  See also CA 97-100; CAAS 16; CANR 32

Park, Jordan
  See Kornbluth, C(yril) M.; Pohl, Frederik

Parker, Bert
  See Ellison, Harlan

Parker, Dorothy (Rothschild)
  1893-1967 . . . . **CLC 15, 68; SSC 2**
  See also CA 19-20; 25-28R; CAP 2;
    DLB 11, 45, 86; MTCW

Parker, Robert B(rown) 1932- . . . . . . **CLC 27**
  See also BEST 89:4; CA 49-52; CANR 1,
    26; MTCW

Parkes, Lucas
  See Harris, John (Wyndham Parkes Lucas)
    Beynon

Parkin, Frank 1940- . . . . **CLC 43**

Parkman, Francis, Jr.
  1823-1893 . . . . **NCLC 12**
  See also DLB 1, 30

Parks, Gordon (Alexander Buchanan)
  1912- . . . . **CLC 1, 16; BLC**
  See also AITN 2; BW; CA 41-44R;
    CANR 26; DLB 33; SATA 8

Parnell, Thomas 1679-1718 . . . . **LC 3**
  See also DLB 94

Parra, Nicanor 1914- . . . . **CLC 2; HLC**
  See also CA 85-88; CANR 32; HW; MTCW

Parrish, Mary Frances
  See Fisher, M(ary) F(rances) K(ennedy)

Parson
  See Coleridge, Samuel Taylor

Parson Lot
  See Kingsley, Charles

Partridge, Anthony
  See Oppenheim, E(dward) Phillips

Pascoli, Giovanni 1855-1912 . . . . . . **TCLC 45**

Pasolini, Pier Paolo
  1922-1975 . . . . **CLC 20, 37**
  See also CA 93-96; 61-64; DLB 128;
    MTCW

Pasquini
  See Silone, Ignazio

Pastan, Linda (Olenik) 1932- . . . . . . **CLC 27**
  See also CA 61-64; CANR 18, 40; DLB 5

Pasternak, Boris (Leonidovich)
  1890-1960 . . . . . . **CLC 7, 10, 18, 63; DA;**
                                              PC 6; WLC
  See also CA 127; 116; MTCW

Patchen, Kenneth 1911-1972 . . . **CLC 1, 2, 18**
  See also CA 1-4R; 33-36R; CANR 3, 35;
    DLB 16, 48; MTCW

Pater, Walter (Horatio)
  1839-1894 . . . . **NCLC 7**
  See also CDBLB 1832-1890; DLB 57

Paterson, A(ndrew) B(arton)
  1864-1941 . . . . **TCLC 32**

Paterson, Katherine (Womeldorf)
  1932- . . . . **CLC 12, 30**
  See also AAYA 1; CA 21-24R; CANR 28;
    CLR 7; DLB 52; JRDA; MAICYA;
    MTCW; SATA 13, 53

Patmore, Coventry Kersey Dighton
  1823-1896 . . . . **NCLC 9**
  See also DLB 35, 98

Paton, Alan (Stewart)
  1903-1988 . . . . . . **CLC 4, 10, 25, 55; DA;**
                                                       WLC
  See also CA 13-16; 125; CANR 22; CAP 1;
    MTCW; SATA 11, 56

Paton Walsh, Gillian 1937-
  See Walsh, Jill Paton
  See also CANR 38; JRDA; MAICYA;
    SAAS 3; SATA 4, 72

Pinkwater, Manus
See Pinkwater, Daniel Manus
See also SATA 8

Pinsky, Robert 1940- . . . . **CLC 9, 19, 38**
See also CA 29-32R; CAAS 4; DLBY 82

Pinta, Harold
See Pinter, Harold

Pinter, Harold
1930- . . . . . **CLC 1, 3, 6, 9, 11, 15, 27, 58,**
73; DA; WLC
See also CA 5-8R; CANR 33; CDBLB 1960
to Present; DLB 13; MTCW

Pirandello, Luigi
1867-1936 . . . . . . **TCLC 4, 29; DA; WLC**
See also CA 104

Pirsig, Robert M(aynard)
1928- . . . . **CLC 4, 6, 73**
See also CA 53-56; CANR 42; MTCW;
SATA 39

Pisarev, Dmitry Ivanovich
1840-1868 . . . . **NCLC 25**

Pix, Mary (Griffith) 1666-1709 . . . . . . **LC 8**
See also DLB 80

Pixerecourt, Guilbert de
1773-1844 . . . . **NCLC 39**

Plaidy, Jean
See Hibbert, Eleanor Alice Burford

Planche, James Robinson
1796-1880 . . . . **NCLC 42**

Plant, Robert 1948- . . . . **CLC 12**

Plante, David (Robert)
1940- . . . . **CLC 7, 23, 38**
See also CA 37-40R; CANR 12, 36;
DLBY 83; MTCW

Plath, Sylvia
1932-1963 . . . . . **CLC 1, 2, 3, 5, 9, 11, 14,**
17, 50, 51, 62; DA; PC 1; WLC
See also CA 19-20; CANR 34; CAP 2;
CDALB 1941-1968; DLB 5, 6; MTCW

Plato 428(?)B.C.-348(?)B.C. . . . . **CMLC 8; DA**

Platonov, Andrei . . . . **TCLC 14**
See also Klimentov, Andrei Platonovich

Platt, Kin 1911- . . . . **CLC 26**
See also AAYA 11; CA 17-20R; CANR 11;
JRDA; SAAS 17; SATA 21

Plick et Plock
See Simenon, Georges (Jacques Christian)

Plimpton, George (Ames) 1927- . . . . . **CLC 36**
See also AITN 1; CA 21-24R; CANR 32;
MTCW; SATA 10

Plomer, William Charles Franklin
1903-1973 . . . . **CLC 4, 8**
See also CA 21-22; CANR 34; CAP 2;
DLB 20; MTCW; SATA 24

Plowman, Piers
See Kavanagh, Patrick (Joseph)

Plum, J.
See Wodehouse, P(elham) G(renville)

Plumly, Stanley (Ross) 1939- . . . . . . **CLC 33**
See also CA 108; 110; DLB 5

Plumpe, Friedrich Wilhelm
1888-1931 . . . . **TCLC 53**
See also CA 112

Poe, Edgar Allan
1809-1849 . . . . . **NCLC 1, 16; DA; PC 1;**
SSC 1; WLC
See also CDALB 1640-1865; DLB 3, 59, 73,
74; SATA 23

Poet of Titchfield Street, The
See Pound, Ezra (Weston Loomis)

Pohl, Frederik 1919- . . . . **CLC 18**
See also CA 61-64; CAAS 1; CANR 11, 37;
DLB 8; MTCW; SATA 24

Poirier, Louis 1910-
See Gracq, Julien
See also CA 122; 126

Poitier, Sidney 1927- . . . . **CLC 26**
See also BW; CA 117

Polanski, Roman 1933- . . . . **CLC 16**
See also CA 77-80

Poliakoff, Stephen 1952- . . . . **CLC 38**
See also CA 106; DLB 13

Police, The . . . . **CLC 26**
See also Copeland, Stewart (Armstrong);
Summers, Andrew James; Sumner,
Gordon Matthew

Pollitt, Katha 1949- . . . . **CLC 28**
See also CA 120; 122; MTCW

Pollock, (Mary) Sharon 1936- . . . . . **CLC 50**
See also CA 141; DLB 60

Pomerance, Bernard 1940- . . . . **CLC 13**
See also CA 101

Ponge, Francis (Jean Gaston Alfred)
1899-1988 . . . . **CLC 6, 18**
See also CA 85-88; 126; CANR 40

Pontoppidan, Henrik 1857-1943 . . . **TCLC 29**

Poole, Josephine . . . . **CLC 17**
See also Helyar, Jane Penelope Josephine
See also SAAS 2; SATA 5

Popa, Vasko 1922- . . . . **CLC 19**
See also CA 112

Pope, Alexander
1688-1744 . . . . **LC 3; DA; WLC**
See also CDBLB 1660-1789; DLB 95, 101

Porter, Connie (Rose) 1959(?)- . . . . . **CLC 70**
See also CA 142

Porter, Gene(va Grace) Stratton
1863(?)-1924 . . . . **TCLC 21**
See also CA 112

Porter, Katherine Anne
1890-1980 . . . . . . **CLC 1, 3, 7, 10, 13, 15,**
27; DA; SSC 4
See also AITN 2; CA 1-4R; 101; CANR 1;
DLB 4, 9, 102; DLBY 80; MTCW;
SATA 23, 39

Porter, Peter (Neville Frederick)
1929- . . . . **CLC 5, 13, 33**
See also CA 85-88; DLB 40

Porter, William Sydney 1862-1910
See Henry, O.
See also CA 104; 131; CDALB 1865-1917;
DA; DLB 12, 78, 79; MTCW; YABC 2

Portillo (y Pacheco), Jose Lopez
See Lopez Portillo (y Pacheco), Jose

Post, Melville Davisson
1869-1930 . . . . **TCLC 39**
See also CA 110

Potok, Chaim 1929- . . . . **CLC 2, 7, 14, 26**
See also AITN 1, 2; CA 17-20R; CANR 19,
35; DLB 28; MTCW; SATA 33

Potter, Beatrice
See Webb, (Martha) Beatrice (Potter)
See also MAICYA

Potter, Dennis (Christopher George)
1935- . . . . **CLC 58**
See also CA 107; CANR 33; MTCW

Pound, Ezra (Weston Loomis)
1885-1972 . . . . . . **CLC 1, 2, 3, 4, 5, 7, 10,**
13, 18, 34, 48, 50; DA; PC 4; WLC
See also CA 5-8R; 37-40R; CANR 40;
CDALB 1917-1929; DLB 4, 45, 63;
MTCW

Povod, Reinaldo 1959- . . . . **CLC 44**
See also CA 136

Powell, Anthony (Dymoke)
1905- . . . . **CLC 1, 3, 7, 9, 10, 31**
See also CA 1-4R; CANR 1, 32;
CDBLB 1945-1960; DLB 15; MTCW

Powell, Dawn 1897-1965 . . . . **CLC 66**
See also CA 5-8R

Powell, Padgett 1952- . . . . **CLC 34**
See also CA 126

Powers, J(ames) F(arl)
1917- . . . . **CLC 1, 4, 8, 57; SSC 4**
See also CA 1-4R; CANR 2; DLB 130;
MTCW

Powers, John J(ames) 1945-
See Powers, John R.
See also CA 69-72

Powers, John R. . . . . **CLC 66**
See also Powers, John J(ames)

Pownall, David 1938- . . . . **CLC 10**
See also CA 89-92; CAAS 18; DLB 14

Powys, John Cowper
1872-1963 . . . . **CLC 7, 9, 15, 46**
See also CA 85-88; DLB 15; MTCW

Powys, T(heodore) F(rancis)
1875-1953 . . . . **TCLC 9**
See also CA 106; DLB 36

Prager, Emily 1952- . . . . **CLC 56**

Pratt, E(dwin) J(ohn)
1883(?)-1964 . . . . **CLC 19**
See also CA 141; 93-96; DLB 92

Premchand . . . . **TCLC 21**
See also Srivastava, Dhanpat Rai

Preussler, Otfried 1923- . . . . **CLC 17**
See also CA 77-80; SATA 24

Prevert, Jacques (Henri Marie)
1900-1977 . . . . **CLC 15**
See also CA 77-80; 69-72; CANR 29;
MTCW; SATA 30

Prevost, Abbe (Antoine Francois)
1697-1763 . . . . **LC 1**

Price, (Edward) Reynolds
1933- . . . . **CLC 3, 6, 13, 43, 50, 63**
See also CA 1-4R; CANR 1, 37; DLB 2

Price, Richard 1949- . . . . **CLC 6, 12**
See also CA 49-52; CANR 3; DLBY 81

Prichard, Katharine Susannah
1883-1969 . . . . **CLC 46**
See also CA 11-12; CANR 33; CAP 1;
MTCW; SATA 66

Priestley, J(ohn) B(oynton)
1894-1984 . . . . **CLC 2, 5, 9, 34**
See also CA 9-12R; 113; CANR 33;
CDBLB 1914-1945; DLB 10, 34, 77, 100,
139; DLBY 84; MTCW

Prince 1958(?)- . . . . **CLC 35**

Prince, F(rank) T(empleton) 1912- . . **CLC 22**
See also CA 101; CANR 43; DLB 20

Prince Kropotkin
See Kropotkin, Peter (Aleksieevich)

Prior, Matthew 1664-1721 . . . . **LC 4**
See also DLB 95

Pritchard, William H(arrison)
1932- . . . . **CLC 34**
See also CA 65-68; CANR 23; DLB 111

Pritchett, V(ictor) S(awdon)
1900- . . . . **CLC 5, 13, 15, 41; SSC 14**
See also CA 61-64; CANR 31; DLB 15,
139; MTCW

Private 19022
See Manning, Frederic

Probst, Mark 1925- . . . . **CLC 59**
See also CA 130

Prokosch, Frederic 1908-1989 . . . . **CLC 4, 48**
See also CA 73-76; 128; DLB 48

Prophet, The
See Dreiser, Theodore (Herman Albert)

Prose, Francine 1947- . . . . **CLC 45**
See also CA 109; 112

Proudhon
See Cunha, Euclides (Rodrigues Pimenta) da

Proulx, E. Annie 1935- . . . . **CLC 81**

Proust, (Valentin-Louis-George-Eugene-)
Marcel
1871-1922 . . . **TCLC 7, 13, 33; DA; WLC**
See also CA 104; 120; DLB 65; MTCW

Prowler, Harley
See Masters, Edgar Lee

Prus, Boleslaw . . . . **TCLC 48**
See also Glowacki, Aleksander

Pryor, Richard (Franklin Lenox Thomas)
1940- . . . . **CLC 26**
See also CA 122

Przybyszewski, Stanislaw
1868-1927 . . . . **TCLC 36**
See also DLB 66

Pteleon
See Grieve, C(hristopher) M(urray)

Puckett, Lute
See Masters, Edgar Lee

Puig, Manuel
1932-1990 . . . **CLC 3, 5, 10, 28, 65; HLC**
See also CA 45-48; CANR 2, 32; DLB 113;
HW; MTCW

Purdy, Al(fred Wellington)
1918- . . . . **CLC 3, 6, 14, 50**
See also CA 81-84; CAAS 17; CANR 42;
DLB 88

Purdy, James (Amos)
1923- . . . . **CLC 2, 4, 10, 28, 52**
See also CA 33-36R; CAAS 1; CANR 19;
DLB 2; MTCW

Pure, Simon
See Swinnerton, Frank Arthur

Pushkin, Alexander (Sergeyevich)
1799-1837 . . . . . . **NCLC 3, 27; DA; WLC**
See also SATA 61

P'u Sung-ling 1640-1715 . . . . **LC 3**

Putnam, Arthur Lee
See Alger, Horatio, Jr.

Puzo, Mario 1920- . . . . **CLC 1, 2, 6, 36**
See also CA 65-68; CANR 4, 42; DLB 6;
MTCW

Pym, Barbara (Mary Crampton)
1913-1980 . . . . **CLC 13, 19, 37**
See also CA 13-14; 97-100; CANR 13, 34;
CAP 1; DLB 14; DLBY 87; MTCW

Pynchon, Thomas (Ruggles, Jr.)
1937- . . . . . **CLC 2, 3, 6, 9, 11, 18, 33, 62,
72; DA; SSC 14; WLC**
See also BEST 90:2; CA 17-20R; CANR 22;
DLB 2; MTCW

Q
See Quiller-Couch, Arthur Thomas

Qian Zhongshu
See Ch'ien Chung-shu

Qroll
See Dagerman, Stig (Halvard)

Quarrington, Paul (Lewis) 1953- . . . . **CLC 65**
See also CA 129

Quasimodo, Salvatore 1901-1968 . . . **CLC 10**
See also CA 13-16; 25-28R; CAP 1;
DLB 114; MTCW

Queen, Ellery . . . . **CLC 3, 11**
See also Dannay, Frederic; Davidson,
Avram; Lee, Manfred B(ennington);
Sturgeon, Theodore (Hamilton); Vance,
John Holbrook

Queen, Ellery, Jr.
See Dannay, Frederic; Lee, Manfred
B(ennington)

Queneau, Raymond
1903-1976 . . . . **CLC 2, 5, 10, 42**
See also CA 77-80; 69-72; CANR 32;
DLB 72; MTCW

Quevedo, Francisco de 1580-1645 . . . . **LC 23**

Quiller-Couch, Arthur Thomas
1863-1944 . . . . **TCLC 53**
See also CA 118; DLB 135

Quin, Ann (Marie) 1936-1973 . . . . . . **CLC 6**
See also CA 9-12R; 45-48; DLB 14

Quinn, Martin
See Smith, Martin Cruz

Quinn, Simon
See Smith, Martin Cruz

Quiroga, Horacio (Sylvestre)
1878-1937 . . . . **TCLC 20; HLC**
See also CA 117; 131; HW; MTCW

Quoirez, Francoise 1935- . . . . **CLC 9**
See also Sagan, Francoise
See also CA 49-52; CANR 6, 39; MTCW

Raabe, Wilhelm 1831-1910 . . . . **TCLC 45**
See also DLB 129

Rabe, David (William) 1940- . . . **CLC 4, 8, 33**
See also CA 85-88; CABS 3; DLB 7

Rabelais, Francois
1483-1553 . . . . **LC 5; DA; WLC**

Rabinovitch, Sholem 1859-1916
See Aleichem, Sholom
See also CA 104

Radcliffe, Ann (Ward) 1764-1823 . . **NCLC 6**
See also DLB 39

Radiguet, Raymond 1903-1923 . . . . **TCLC 29**
See also DLB 65

Radnoti, Miklos 1909-1944 . . . . **TCLC 16**
See also CA 118

Rado, James 1939- . . . . **CLC 17**
See also CA 105

Radvanyi, Netty 1900-1983
See Seghers, Anna
See also CA 85-88; 110

Raeburn, John (Hay) 1941- . . . . **CLC 34**
See also CA 57-60

Ragni, Gerome 1942-1991 . . . . **CLC 17**
See also CA 105; 134

Rahv, Philip 1908-1973 . . . . **CLC 24**
See also Greenberg, Ivan
See also DLB 137

Raine, Craig 1944- . . . . **CLC 32**
See also CA 108; CANR 29; DLB 40

Raine, Kathleen (Jessie) 1908- . . . **CLC 7, 45**
See also CA 85-88; DLB 20; MTCW

Rainis, Janis 1865-1929 . . . . **TCLC 29**

Rakosi, Carl . . . . **CLC 47**
See also Rawley, Callman
See also CAAS 5

Raleigh, Richard
See Lovecraft, H(oward) P(hillips)

Rallentando, H. P.
See Sayers, Dorothy L(eigh)

Ramal, Walter
See de la Mare, Walter (John)

Ramon, Juan
See Jimenez (Mantecon), Juan Ramon

Ramos, Graciliano 1892-1953 . . . . . **TCLC 32**

Rampersad, Arnold 1941- . . . . **CLC 44**
See also CA 127; 133; DLB 111

Rampling, Anne
See Rice, Anne

Ramuz, Charles-Ferdinand
1878-1947 . . . . **TCLC 33**

Rand, Ayn
1905-1982 . . . . . . **CLC 3, 30, 44, 79; DA;
WLC**
See also AAYA 10; CA 13-16R; 105;
CANR 27; MTCW

Randall, Dudley (Felker)
1914- . . . . **CLC 1; BLC**
See also BW; CA 25-28R; CANR 23;
DLB 41

Randall, Robert
See Silverberg, Robert

Ranger, Ken
See Creasey, John

Ransom, John Crowe
1888-1974 . . . . **CLC 2, 4, 5, 11, 24**
See also CA 5-8R; 49-52; CANR 6, 34;
DLB 45, 63; MTCW

Rao, Raja 1909- . . . . **CLC 25, 56**
See also CA 73-76; MTCW

Rosenfeld, Samuel 1896-1963
See Tzara, Tristan
See also CA 89-92

Rosenthal, M(acha) L(ouis) 1917-... **CLC 28**
See also CA 1-4R; CAAS 6; CANR 4;
DLB 5; SATA 59

Ross, Barnaby
See Dannay, Frederic

Ross, Bernard L.
See Follett, Ken(neth Martin)

Ross, J. H.
See Lawrence, T(homas) E(dward)

Ross, Martin
See Martin, Violet Florence
See also DLB 135

Ross, (James) Sinclair 1908-....... **CLC 13**
See also CA 73-76; DLB 88

Rossetti, Christina (Georgina)
1830-1894 ... **NCLC 2; DA; PC 7; WLC**
See also DLB 35; MAICYA; SATA 20

Rossetti, Dante Gabriel
1828-1882 .... **NCLC 4; DA; WLC**
See also CDBLB 1832-1890; DLB 35

Rossner, Judith (Perelman)
1935- .... **CLC 6, 9, 29**
See also AITN 2; BEST 90:3; CA 17-20R;
CANR 18; DLB 6; MTCW

Rostand, Edmond (Eugene Alexis)
1868-1918 .... **TCLC 6, 37; DA**
See also CA 104; 126; MTCW

Roth, Henry 1906-.......... **CLC 2, 6, 11**
See also CA 11-12; CANR 38; CAP 1;
DLB 28; MTCW

Roth, Joseph 1894-1939......... **TCLC 33**
See also DLB 85

Roth, Philip (Milton)
1933- ...... **CLC 1, 2, 3, 4, 6, 9, 15, 22,
31, 47, 66; DA; WLC**
See also BEST 90:3; CA 1-4R; CANR 1, 22,
36; CDALB 1968-1988; DLB 2, 28;
DLBY 82; MTCW

Rothenberg, Jerome 1931-....... **CLC 6, 57**
See also CA 45-48; CANR 1; DLB 5

Roumain, Jacques (Jean Baptiste)
1907-1944 .... **TCLC 19; BLC**
See also BW; CA 117; 125

Rourke, Constance (Mayfield)
1885-1941 .... **TCLC 12**
See also CA 107; YABC 1

Rousseau, Jean-Baptiste 1671-1741 ... **LC 9**

Rousseau, Jean-Jacques
1712-1778 .... **LC 14; DA; WLC**

Roussel, Raymond 1877-1933 ..... **TCLC 20**
See also CA 117

Rovit, Earl (Herbert) 1927-........ **CLC 7**
See also CA 5-8R; CANR 12

Rowe, Nicholas 1674-1718.......... **LC 8**
See also DLB 84

Rowley, Ames Dorrance
See Lovecraft, H(oward) P(hillips)

Rowson, Susanna Haswell
1762(?)-1824 .... **NCLC 5**
See also DLB 37

Roy, Gabrielle 1909-1983....... **CLC 10, 14**
See also CA 53-56; 110; CANR 5; DLB 68;
MTCW

Rozewicz, Tadeusz 1921-........ **CLC 9, 23**
See also CA 108; CANR 36; MTCW

Ruark, Gibbons 1941- .... **CLC 3**
See also CA 33-36R; CANR 14, 31;
DLB 120

Rubens, Bernice (Ruth) 1923-... **CLC 19, 31**
See also CA 25-28R; CANR 33; DLB 14;
MTCW

Rudkin, (James) David 1936- ...... **CLC 14**
See also CA 89-92; DLB 13

Rudnik, Raphael 1933-............. **CLC 7**
See also CA 29-32R

Ruffian, M.
See Hasek, Jaroslav (Matej Frantisek)

Ruiz, Jose Martinez .... **CLC 11**
See also Martinez Ruiz, Jose

Rukeyser, Muriel
1913-1980 .... **CLC 6, 10, 15, 27**
See also CA 5-8R; 93-96; CANR 26;
DLB 48; MTCW; SATA 22

Rule, Jane (Vance) 1931-.......... **CLC 27**
See also CA 25-28R; CAAS 18; CANR 12;
DLB 60

Rulfo, Juan 1918-1986.... **CLC 8, 80; HLC**
See also CA 85-88; 118; CANR 26;
DLB 113; HW; MTCW

Runeberg, Johan 1804-1877...... **NCLC 41**

Runyon, (Alfred) Damon
1884(?)-1946 .... **TCLC 10**
See also CA 107; DLB 11, 86

Rush, Norman 1933-............. **CLC 44**
See also CA 121; 126

Rushdie, (Ahmed) Salman
1947- .... **CLC 23, 31, 55**
See also BEST 89:3; CA 108; 111;
CANR 33; MTCW

Rushforth, Peter (Scott) 1945- ..... **CLC 19**
See also CA 101

Ruskin, John 1819-1900......... **TCLC 20**
See also CA 114; 129; CDBLB 1832-1890;
DLB 55; SATA 24

Russ, Joanna 1937-............... **CLC 15**
See also CA 25-28R; CANR 11, 31; DLB 8;
MTCW

Russell, George William 1867-1935
See A. E.
See also CA 104; CDBLB 1890-1914

Russell, (Henry) Ken(neth Alfred)
1927- .... **CLC 16**
See also CA 105

Russell, Willy 1947-............. **CLC 60**

Rutherford, Mark .... **TCLC 25**
See also White, William Hale
See also DLB 18

Ruyslinck, Ward
See Belser, Reimond Karel Maria de

Ryan, Cornelius (John) 1920-1974 ... **CLC 7**
See also CA 69-72; 53-56; CANR 38

Ryan, Michael 1946- .... **CLC 65**
See also CA 49-52; DLBY 82

Rybakov, Anatoli (Naumovich)
1911- .... **CLC 23, 53**
See also CA 126; 135

Ryder, Jonathan
See Ludlum, Robert

Ryga, George 1932-1987 .... **CLC 14**
See also CA 101; 124; CANR 43; DLB 60

S. S.
See Sassoon, Siegfried (Lorraine)

Saba, Umberto 1883-1957 .... **TCLC 33**
See also CA 144; DLB 114

Sabatini, Rafael 1875-1950 .... **TCLC 47**

Sabato, Ernesto (R.)
1911- .... **CLC 10, 23; HLC**
See also CA 97-100; CANR 32; HW;
MTCW

Sacastru, Martin
See Bioy Casares, Adolfo

Sacher-Masoch, Leopold von
1836(?)-1895 .... **NCLC 31**

Sachs, Marilyn (Stickle) 1927- ..... **CLC 35**
See also AAYA 2; CA 17-20R; CANR 13;
CLR 2; JRDA; MAICYA; SAAS 2;
SATA 3, 68

Sachs, Nelly 1891-1970 .... **CLC 14**
See also CA 17-18; 25-28R; CAP 2

Sackler, Howard (Oliver)
1929-1982 .... **CLC 14**
See also CA 61-64; 108; CANR 30; DLB 7

Sacks, Oliver (Wolf) 1933- .... **CLC 67**
See also CA 53-56; CANR 28; MTCW

Sade, Donatien Alphonse Francois Comte
1740-1814 .... **NCLC 3**

Sadoff, Ira 1945-.................. **CLC 9**
See also CA 53-56; CANR 5, 21; DLB 120

Saetone
See Camus, Albert

Safire, William 1929-............. **CLC 10**
See also CA 17-20R; CANR 31

Sagan, Carl (Edward) 1934-........ **CLC 30**
See also AAYA 2; CA 25-28R; CANR 11,
36; MTCW; SATA 58

Sagan, Francoise .... **CLC 3, 6, 9, 17, 36**
See also Quoirez, Francoise
See also DLB 83

Sahgal, Nayantara (Pandit) 1927-... **CLC 41**
See also CA 9-12R; CANR 11

Saint, H(arry) F. 1941- .... **CLC 50**
See also CA 127

St. Aubin de Teran, Lisa 1953-
See Teran, Lisa St. Aubin de
See also CA 118; 126

Sainte-Beuve, Charles Augustin
1804-1869 .... **NCLC 5**

**Saint-Exupery, Antoine (Jean Baptiste Marie
Roger) de** 1900-1944 ... **TCLC 2; WLC**
See also CA 108; 132; CLR 10; DLB 72;
MAICYA; MTCW; SATA 20

St. John, David
See Hunt, E(verette) Howard, Jr.

Saint-John Perse
See Leger, (Marie-Rene Auguste) Alexis
Saint-Leger

Saintsbury, George (Edward Bateman)
1845-1933 .... **TCLC 31**
See also DLB 57

Sait Faik .... **TCLC 23**
See also Abasiyanik, Sait Faik

Saki .... **TCLC 3; SSC 12**
See also Munro, H(ector) H(ugh)

Salama, Hannu 1936-............. **CLC 18**

Salamanca, J(ack) R(ichard)
1922- .... **CLC 4, 15**
See also CA 25-28R

Sale, J. Kirkpatrick
See Sale, Kirkpatrick

Sale, Kirkpatrick 1937- .... **CLC 68**
See also CA 13-16R; CANR 10

Salinas (y Serrano), Pedro
1891(?)-1951 .... **TCLC 17**
See also CA 117; DLB 134

Salinger, J(erome) D(avid)
1919- ...... **CLC 1, 3, 8, 12, 55, 56; DA;**
SSC 2; WLC
See also AAYA 2; CA 5-8R; CANR 39;
CDALB 1941-1968; CLR 18; DLB 2, 102;
MAICYA; MTCW; SATA 67

Salisbury, John
See Caute, David

Salter, James 1925- .... **CLC 7, 52, 59**
See also CA 73-76; DLB 130

Saltus, Edgar (Everton)
1855-1921 .... **TCLC 8**
See also CA 105

Saltykov, Mikhail Evgrafovich
1826-1889 .... **NCLC 16**

Samarakis, Antonis 1919- .... **CLC 5**
See also CA 25-28R; CAAS 16; CANR 36

Sanchez, Florencio 1875-1910 ..... **TCLC 37**
See also HW

Sanchez, Luis Rafael 1936-........ **CLC 23**
See also CA 128; HW

Sanchez, Sonia 1934-... **CLC 5; BLC; PC 9**
See also BW; CA 33-36R; CANR 24;
CLR 18; DLB 41; DLBD 8; MAICYA;
MTCW; SATA 22

Sand, George
1804-1876 ...... **NCLC 2, 42; DA; WLC**
See also DLB 119

Sandburg, Carl (August)
1878-1967 .... **CLC 1, 4, 10, 15, 35; DA;**
PC 2; WLC
See also CA 5-8R; 25-28R; CANR 35;
CDALB 1865-1917; DLB 17, 54;
MAICYA; MTCW; SATA 8

Sandburg, Charles
See Sandburg, Carl (August)

Sandburg, Charles A.
See Sandburg, Carl (August)

Sanders, (James) Ed(ward) 1939- ... **CLC 53**
See also CA 13-16R; CANR 13, 44;
DLB 16

Sanders, Lawrence 1920-.......... **CLC 41**
See also BEST 89:4; CA 81-84; CANR 33;
MTCW

Sanders, Noah
See Blount, Roy (Alton), Jr.

Sanders, Winston P.
See Anderson, Poul (William)

Sandoz, Mari(e Susette)
1896-1966 .... **CLC 28**
See also CA 1-4R; 25-28R; CANR 17;
DLB 9; MTCW; SATA 5

Saner, Reg(inald Anthony) 1931- .... **CLC 9**
See also CA 65-68

Sannazaro, Jacopo 1456(?)-1530 ...... **LC 8**

Sansom, William 1912-1976....... **CLC 2, 6**
See also CA 5-8R; 65-68; CANR 42;
DLB 139; MTCW

Santayana, George 1863-1952 ..... **TCLC 40**
See also CA 115; DLB 54, 71

Santiago, Danny .... **CLC 33**
See also James, Daniel (Lewis); James,
Daniel (Lewis)
See also DLB 122

Santmyer, Helen Hoover
1895-1986 .... **CLC 33**
See also CA 1-4R; 118; CANR 15, 33;
DLBY 84; MTCW

Santos, Bienvenido N(uqui) 1911-... **CLC 22**
See also CA 101; CANR 19

Sapper .... **TCLC 44**
See also McNeile, Herman Cyril

Sappho fl. 6th cent. B.C.-.... **CMLC 3; PC 5**

Sarduy, Severo 1937-1993 .... **CLC 6**
See also CA 89-92; 142; DLB 113; HW

Sargeson, Frank 1903-1982 .... **CLC 31**
See also CA 25-28R; 106; CANR 38

Sarmiento, Felix Ruben Garcia
See Dario, Ruben

Saroyan, William
1908-1981 ..... **CLC 1, 8, 10, 29, 34, 56;**
DA; WLC
See also CA 5-8R; 103; CANR 30; DLB 7,
9, 86; DLBY 81; MTCW; SATA 23, 24

Sarraute, Nathalie
1900- .... **CLC 1, 2, 4, 8, 10, 31, 80**
See also CA 9-12R; CANR 23; DLB 83;
MTCW

Sarton, (Eleanor) May
1912- .... **CLC 4, 14, 49**
See also CA 1-4R; CANR 1, 34; DLB 48;
DLBY 81; MTCW; SATA 36

Sartre, Jean-Paul
1905-1980 .... **CLC 1, 4, 7, 9, 13, 18, 24,**
44, 50, 52; DA; DC 3; WLC
See also CA 9-12R; 97-100; CANR 21;
DLB 72; MTCW

Sassoon, Siegfried (Lorraine)
1886-1967 .... **CLC 36**
See also CA 104; 25-28R; CANR 36;
DLB 20; MTCW

Satterfield, Charles
See Pohl, Frederik

Saul, John (W. III) 1942- .... **CLC 46**
See also AAYA 10; BEST 90:4; CA 81-84;
CANR 16, 40

Saunders, Caleb
See Heinlein, Robert A(nson)

Saura (Atares), Carlos 1932-....... **CLC 20**
See also CA 114; 131; HW

Sauser-Hall, Frederic 1887-1961.... **CLC 18**
See also CA 102; 93-96; CANR 36; MTCW

Saussure, Ferdinand de
1857-1913 .... **TCLC 49**

Savage, Catharine
See Brosman, Catharine Savage

Savage, Thomas 1915- .... **CLC 40**
See also CA 126; 132; CAAS 15

Savan, Glenn .... **CLC 50**

Saven, Glenn 19(?)- .... **CLC 50**

Sayers, Dorothy L(eigh)
1893-1957 .... **TCLC 2, 15**
See also CA 104; 119; CDBLB 1914-1945;
DLB 10, 36, 77, 100; MTCW

Sayers, Valerie 1952-............. **CLC 50**
See also CA 134

Sayles, John (Thomas)
1950- .... **CLC 7, 10, 14**
See also CA 57-60; CANR 41; DLB 44

Scammell, Michael .... **CLC 34**

Scannell, Vernon 1922- .... **CLC 49**
See also CA 5-8R; CANR 8, 24; DLB 27;
SATA 59

Scarlett, Susan
See Streatfeild, (Mary) Noel

Schaeffer, Susan Fromberg
1941- .... **CLC 6, 11, 22**
See also CA 49-52; CANR 18; DLB 28;
MTCW; SATA 22

Schary, Jill
See Robinson, Jill

Schell, Jonathan 1943-............ **CLC 35**
See also CA 73-76; CANR 12

Schelling, Friedrich Wilhelm Joseph von
1775-1854 .... **NCLC 30**
See also DLB 90

Scherer, Jean-Marie Maurice 1920-
See Rohmer, Eric
See also CA 110

Schevill, James (Erwin) 1920-....... **CLC 7**
See also CA 5-8R; CAAS 12

Schiller, Friedrich 1759-1805 .... **NCLC 39**
See also DLB 94

Schisgal, Murray (Joseph) 1926-..... **CLC 6**
See also CA 21-24R

Schlee, Ann 1934-............... **CLC 35**
See also CA 101; CANR 29; SATA 36, 44

Schlegel, August Wilhelm von
1767-1845 .... **NCLC 15**
See also DLB 94

Schlegel, Friedrich 1772-1829 .... **NCLC 45**
See also DLB 90

Schlegel, Johann Elias (von)
1719(?)-1749 .... **LC 5**

Schmidt, Arno (Otto) 1914-1979.... **CLC 56**
See also CA 128; 109; DLB 69

Schmitz, Aron Hector 1861-1928
See Svevo, Italo
See also CA 104; 122; MTCW

Schnackenberg, Gjertrud 1953-..... **CLC 40**
See also CA 116; DLB 120

Schneider, Leonard Alfred 1925-1966
See Bruce, Lenny
See also CA 89-92

Schnitzler, Arthur
1862-1931 . . . . **TCLC 4; SSC 15**
See also CA 104; DLB 81, 118

Schor, Sandra (M.) 1932(?)-1990 . . . **CLC 65**
See also CA 132

Schorer, Mark 1908-1977 . . . . **CLC 9**
See also CA 5-8R; 73-76; CANR 7;
DLB 103

Schrader, Paul (Joseph) 1946- . . . . . . **CLC 26**
See also CA 37-40R; CANR 41; DLB 44

Schreiner, Olive (Emilie Albertina)
1855-1920 . . . . **TCLC 9**
See also CA 105; DLB 18

Schulberg, Budd (Wilson)
1914- . . . . **CLC 7, 48**
See also CA 25-28R; CANR 19; DLB 6, 26,
28; DLBY 81

Schulz, Bruno
1892-1942 . . . . **TCLC 5, 51; SSC 13**
See also CA 115; 123

Schulz, Charles M(onroe) 1922- . . . . **CLC 12**
See also CA 9-12R; CANR 6; SATA 10

Schumacher, E(rnst) F(riedrich)
1911-1977 . . . . **CLC 80**
See also CA 81-84; 73-76; CANR 34

Schuyler, James Marcus
1923-1991 . . . . **CLC 5, 23**
See also CA 101; 134; DLB 5

Schwartz, Delmore (David)
1913-1966 . . . . . . **CLC 2, 4, 10, 45; PC 8**
See also CA 17-18; 25-28R; CANR 35;
CAP 2; DLB 28, 48; MTCW

Schwartz, Ernst
See Ozu, Yasujiro

Schwartz, John Burnham 1965- . . . . **CLC 59**
See also CA 132

Schwartz, Lynne Sharon 1939- . . . . . **CLC 31**
See also CA 103; CANR 44

Schwartz, Muriel A.
See Eliot, T(homas) S(tearns)

Schwarz-Bart, Andre 1928- . . . . **CLC 2, 4**
See also CA 89-92

Schwarz-Bart, Simone 1938- . . . . **CLC 7**
See also CA 97-100

Schwob, (Mayer Andre) Marcel
1867-1905 . . . . **TCLC 20**
See also CA 117; DLB 123

Sciascia, Leonardo
1921-1989 . . . . **CLC 8, 9, 41**
See also CA 85-88; 130; CANR 35; MTCW

Scoppettone, Sandra 1936- . . . . **CLC 26**
See also AAYA 11; CA 5-8R; CANR 41;
SATA 9

Scorsese, Martin 1942- . . . . **CLC 20**
See also CA 110; 114

Scotland, Jay
See Jakes, John (William)

Scott, Duncan Campbell
1862-1947 . . . . **TCLC 6**
See also CA 104; DLB 92

Scott, Evelyn 1893-1963 . . . . **CLC 43**
See also CA 104; 112; DLB 9, 48

Scott, F(rancis) R(eginald)
1899-1985 . . . . **CLC 22**
See also CA 101; 114; DLB 88

Scott, Frank
See Scott, F(rancis) R(eginald)

Scott, Joanna 1960- . . . . **CLC 50**
See also CA 126

Scott, Paul (Mark) 1920-1978 . . . . **CLC 9, 60**
See also CA 81-84; 77-80; CANR 33;
DLB 14; MTCW

Scott, Walter
1771-1832 . . . . **NCLC 15; DA; WLC**
See also CDBLB 1789-1832; DLB 93, 107,
116; YABC 2

Scribe, (Augustin) Eugene
1791-1861 . . . . **NCLC 16**

Scrum, R.
See Crumb, R(obert)

Scudery, Madeleine de 1607-1701 . . . . . **LC 2**

Scum
See Crumb, R(obert)

Scumbag, Little Bobby
See Crumb, R(obert)

Seabrook, John
See Hubbard, L(afayette) Ron(ald)

Sealy, I. Allan 1951- . . . . **CLC 55**

Search, Alexander
See Pessoa, Fernando (Antonio Nogueira)

Sebastian, Lee
See Silverberg, Robert

Sebastian Owl
See Thompson, Hunter S(tockton)

Sebestyen, Ouida 1924- . . . . **CLC 30**
See also AAYA 8; CA 107; CANR 40;
CLR 17; JRDA; MAICYA; SAAS 10;
SATA 39

Secundus, H. Scriblerus
See Fielding, Henry

Sedges, John
See Buck, Pearl S(ydenstricker)

Sedgwick, Catharine Maria
1789-1867 . . . . **NCLC 19**
See also DLB 1, 74

Seelye, John 1931- . . . . **CLC 7**

Seferiades, Giorgos Stylianou 1900-1971
See Seferis, George
See also CA 5-8R; 33-36R; CANR 5, 36;
MTCW

Seferis, George . . . . **CLC 5, 11**
See also Seferiades, Giorgos Stylianou

Segal, Erich (Wolf) 1937- . . . . **CLC 3, 10**
See also BEST 89:1; CA 25-28R; CANR 20,
36; DLBY 86; MTCW

Seger, Bob 1945- . . . . **CLC 35**

Seghers, Anna . . . . **CLC 7**
See also Radvanyi, Netty
See also DLB 69

Seidel, Frederick (Lewis) 1936- . . . . . **CLC 18**
See also CA 13-16R; CANR 8; DLBY 84

Seifert, Jaroslav 1901-1986 . . . . . **CLC 34, 44**
See also CA 127; MTCW

Sei Shonagon c. 966-1017(?) . . . . . . **CMLC 6**

Selby, Hubert, Jr. 1928- . . . . . **CLC 1, 2, 4, 8**
See also CA 13-16R; CANR 33; DLB 2

Selzer, Richard 1928- . . . . **CLC 74**
See also CA 65-68; CANR 14

Sembene, Ousmane
See Ousmane, Sembene

Senancour, Etienne Pivert de
1770-1846 . . . . **NCLC 16**
See also DLB 119

Sender, Ramon (Jose)
1902-1982 . . . . **CLC 8; HLC**
See also CA 5-8R; 105; CANR 8; HW;
MTCW

Seneca, Lucius Annaeus
4B.C.-65. . . . . **CMLC 6**

Senghor, Leopold Sedar
1906- . . . . **CLC 54; BLC**
See also BW; CA 116; 125; MTCW

Serling, (Edward) Rod(man)
1924-1975 . . . . **CLC 30**
See also AITN 1; CA 65-68; 57-60; DLB 26

Serna, Ramon Gomez de la
See Gomez de la Serna, Ramon

Serpieres
See Guillevic, (Eugene)

Service, Robert
See Service, Robert W(illiam)
See also DLB 92

Service, Robert W(illiam)
1874(?)-1958 . . . . . . **TCLC 15; DA; WLC**
See also Service, Robert
See also CA 115; 140; SATA 20

Seth, Vikram 1952- . . . . **CLC 43**
See also CA 121; 127; DLB 120

Seton, Cynthia Propper
1926-1982 . . . . **CLC 27**
See also CA 5-8R; 108; CANR 7

Seton, Ernest (Evan) Thompson
1860-1946 . . . . **TCLC 31**
See also CA 109; DLB 92; JRDA; SATA 18

Seton-Thompson, Ernest
See Seton, Ernest (Evan) Thompson

Settle, Mary Lee 1918- . . . . **CLC 19, 61**
See also CA 89-92; CAAS 1; CANR 44;
DLB 6

Seuphor, Michel
See Arp, Jean

**Sevigne, Marie (de Rabutin-Chantal) Marquise
de** 1626-1696 . . . . **LC 11**

Sexton, Anne (Harvey)
1928-1974 . . . . **CLC 2, 4, 6, 8, 10, 15, 53;
DA; PC 2; WLC**
See also CA 1-4R; 53-56; CABS 2;
CANR 3, 36; CDALB 1941-1968; DLB 5;
MTCW; SATA 10

Shaara, Michael (Joseph Jr.)
1929-1988 . . . . **CLC 15**
See also AITN 1; CA 102; DLBY 83

Shackleton, C. C.
See Aldiss, Brian W(ilson)

Shacochis, Bob . . . . **CLC 39**
See also Shacochis, Robert G.

Author Index

Simak, Clifford D(onald)
1904-1988 .... CLC **1, 55**
See also CA 1-4R; 125; CANR 1, 35;
DLB 8; MTCW; SATA 56

Simenon, Georges (Jacques Christian)
1903-1989 .... CLC **1, 2, 3, 8, 18, 47**
See also CA 85-88; 129; CANR 35;
DLB 72; DLBY 89; MTCW

Simic, Charles 1938- ... CLC **6, 9, 22, 49, 68**
See also CA 29-32R; CAAS 4; CANR 12,
33; DLB 105

Simmons, Charles (Paul) 1924- ..... CLC **57**
See also CA 89-92

Simmons, Dan 1948- .... CLC **44**
See also CA 138

Simmons, James (Stewart Alexander)
1933- .... CLC **43**
See also CA 105; DLB 40

Simms, William Gilmore
1806-1870 .... NCLC **3**
See also DLB 3, 30, 59, 73

Simon, Carly 1945- .... CLC **26**
See also CA 105

Simon, Claude 1913- .... CLC **4, 9, 15, 39**
See also CA 89-92; CANR 33; DLB 83;
MTCW

Simon, (Marvin) Neil
1927- .... CLC **6, 11, 31, 39, 70**
See also AITN 1; CA 21-24R; CANR 26;
DLB 7; MTCW

Simon, Paul 1942(?)- .... CLC **17**
See also CA 116

Simonon, Paul 1956(?)- .... CLC **30**
See also Clash, The

Simpson, Harriette
See Arnow, Harriette (Louisa) Simpson

Simpson, Louis (Aston Marantz)
1923- .... CLC **4, 7, 9, 32**
See also CA 1-4R; CAAS 4; CANR 1;
DLB 5; MTCW

Simpson, Mona (Elizabeth) 1957- ... CLC **44**
See also CA 122; 135

Simpson, N(orman) F(rederick)
1919- .... CLC **29**
See also CA 13-16R; DLB 13

Sinclair, Andrew (Annandale)
1935- .... CLC **2, 14**
See also CA 9-12R; CAAS 5; CANR 14, 38;
DLB 14; MTCW

Sinclair, Emil
See Hesse, Hermann

Sinclair, Iain 1943- .... CLC **76**
See also CA 132

Sinclair, Iain MacGregor
See Sinclair, Iain

Sinclair, Mary Amelia St. Clair 1865(?)-1946
See Sinclair, May
See also CA 104

Sinclair, May .... TCLC **3, 11**
See also Sinclair, Mary Amelia St. Clair
See also DLB 36, 135

Sinclair, Upton (Beall)
1878-1968 ...... CLC **1, 11, 15, 63; DA;
WLC**
See also CA 5-8R; 25-28R; CANR 7;
CDALB 1929-1941; DLB 9; MTCW;
SATA 9

Singer, Isaac
See Singer, Isaac Bashevis

Singer, Isaac Bashevis
1904-1991 .... CLC **1, 3, 6, 9, 11, 15, 23,
38, 69; DA; SSC 3; WLC**
See also AITN 1, 2; CA 1-4R; 134;
CANR 1, 39; CDALB 1941-1968; CLR 1;
DLB 6, 28, 52; DLBY 91; JRDA;
MAICYA; MTCW; SATA 3, 27;
SATA-Obit 68

Singer, Israel Joshua 1893-1944 ... TCLC **33**

Singh, Khushwant 1915- .... CLC **11**
See also CA 9-12R; CAAS 9; CANR 6

Sinjohn, John
See Galsworthy, John

Sinyavsky, Andrei (Donatevich)
1925- .... CLC **8**
See also CA 85-88

Sirin, V.
See Nabokov, Vladimir (Vladimirovich)

Sissman, L(ouis) E(dward)
1928-1976 .... CLC **9, 18**
See also CA 21-24R; 65-68; CANR 13;
DLB 5

Sisson, C(harles) H(ubert) 1914- ..... CLC **8**
See also CA 1-4R; CAAS 3; CANR 3;
DLB 27

Sitwell, Dame Edith
1887-1964 .... CLC **2, 9, 67; PC 3**
See also CA 9-12R; CANR 35;
CDBLB 1945-1960; DLB 20; MTCW

Sjoewall, Maj 1935- .... CLC **7**
See also CA 65-68

Sjowall, Maj
See Sjoewall, Maj

Skelton, Robin 1925- .... CLC **13**
See also AITN 2; CA 5-8R; CAAS 5;
CANR 28; DLB 27, 53

Skolimowski, Jerzy 1938- .... CLC **20**
See also CA 128

Skram, Amalie (Bertha)
1847-1905 .... TCLC **25**

Skvorecky, Josef (Vaclav)
1924- .... CLC **15, 39, 69**
See also CA 61-64; CAAS 1; CANR 10, 34;
MTCW

Slade, Bernard .... CLC **11, 46**
See also Newbound, Bernard Slade
See also CAAS 9; DLB 53

Slaughter, Carolyn 1946- .... CLC **56**
See also CA 85-88

Slaughter, Frank G(ill) 1908- ...... CLC **29**
See also AITN 2; CA 5-8R; CANR 5

Slavitt, David R(ytman) 1935- .... CLC **5, 14**
See also CA 21-24R; CAAS 3; CANR 41;
DLB 5, 6

Slesinger, Tess 1905-1945 .... TCLC **10**
See also CA 107; DLB 102

Slessor, Kenneth 1901-1971 .... CLC **14**
See also CA 102; 89-92

Slowacki, Juliusz 1809-1849 ..... NCLC **15**

Smart, Christopher 1722-1771 .... LC **3**
See also DLB 109

Smart, Elizabeth 1913-1986 .... CLC **54**
See also CA 81-84; 118; DLB 88

Smiley, Jane (Graves) 1949- ... CLC **53, 76**
See also CA 104; CANR 30

Smith, A(rthur) J(ames) M(arshall)
1902-1980 .... CLC **15**
See also CA 1-4R; 102; CANR 4; DLB 88

Smith, Betty (Wehner) 1896-1972 ... CLC **19**
See also CA 5-8R; 33-36R; DLBY 82;
SATA 6

Smith, Charlotte (Turner)
1749-1806 .... NCLC **23**
See also DLB 39, 109

Smith, Clark Ashton 1893-1961 .... CLC **43**
See also CA 143

Smith, Dave .... CLC **22, 42**
See also Smith, David (Jeddie)
See also CAAS 7; DLB 5

Smith, David (Jeddie) 1942-
See Smith, Dave
See also CA 49-52; CANR 1

Smith, Florence Margaret
1902-1971 .... CLC **8**
See also Smith, Stevie
See also CA 17-18; 29-32R; CANR 35;
CAP 2; MTCW

Smith, Iain Crichton 1928- .... CLC **64**
See also CA 21-24R; DLB 40, 139

Smith, John 1580(?)-1631 .... LC **9**

Smith, Johnston
See Crane, Stephen (Townley)

Smith, Lee 1944- .... CLC **25, 73**
See also CA 114; 119; DLBY 83

Smith, Martin
See Smith, Martin Cruz

Smith, Martin Cruz 1942- .... CLC **25**
See also BEST 89:4; CA 85-88; CANR 6,
23, 43

Smith, Mary-Ann Tirone 1944- ..... CLC **39**
See also CA 118; 136

Smith, Patti 1946- .... CLC **12**
See also CA 93-96

Smith, Pauline (Urmson)
1882-1959 .... TCLC **25**

Smith, Rosamond
See Oates, Joyce Carol

Smith, Sheila Kaye
See Kaye-Smith, Sheila

Smith, Stevie .... CLC **3, 8, 25, 44**
See also Smith, Florence Margaret
See also DLB 20

Smith, Wilbur A(ddison) 1933- ..... CLC **33**
See also CA 13-16R; CANR 7; MTCW

Smith, William Jay 1918- .... CLC **6**
See also CA 5-8R; CANR 44; DLB 5;
MAICYA; SATA 2, 68

Smith, Woodrow Wilson
See Kuttner, Henry

Stanton, Schuyler
See Baum, L(yman) Frank

Stapledon, (William) Olaf
1886-1950 . . . . TCLC 22
See also CA 111; DLB 15

Starbuck, George (Edwin)   1931- . . . . CLC 53
See also CA 21-24R; CANR 23

Stark, Richard
See Westlake, Donald E(dwin)

Staunton, Schuyler
See Baum, L(yman) Frank

Stead, Christina (Ellen)
1902-1983 . . . . CLC 2, 5, 8, 32, 80
See also CA 13-16R; 109; CANR 33, 40;
MTCW

Stead, William Thomas
1849-1912 . . . . TCLC 48

Steele, Richard   1672-1729 . . . . LC 18
See also CDBLB 1660-1789; DLB 84, 101

Steele, Timothy (Reid)   1948- . . . . CLC 45
See also CA 93-96; CANR 16; DLB 120

Steffens, (Joseph) Lincoln
1866-1936 . . . . TCLC 20
See also CA 117

Stegner, Wallace (Earle)
1909-1993 . . . . CLC 9, 49, 81
See also AITN 1; BEST 90:3; CA 1-4R;
141; CAAS 9; CANR 1, 21; DLB 9;
DLBY 93; MTCW

Stein, Gertrude
1874-1946 . . . . . . TCLC 1, 6, 28, 48; DA;
WLC
See also CA 104; 132; CDALB 1917-1929;
DLB 4, 54, 86; MTCW

Steinbeck, John (Ernst)
1902-1968 . . . . . . CLC 1, 5, 9, 13, 21, 34,
45, 75; DA; SSC 11; WLC
See also AAYA 12; CA 1-4R; 25-28R;
CANR 1, 35; CDALB 1929-1941; DLB 7,
9; DLBD 2; MTCW; SATA 9

Steinem, Gloria   1934- . . . . CLC 63
See also CA 53-56; CANR 28; MTCW

Steiner, George   1929- . . . . CLC 24
See also CA 73-76; CANR 31; DLB 67;
MTCW; SATA 62

Steiner, K. Leslie
See Delany, Samuel R(ay, Jr.)

Steiner, Rudolf   1861-1925 . . . . TCLC 13
See also CA 107

Stendhal   1783-1842 . . . . NCLC 23; DA; WLC
See also DLB 119

Stephen, Leslie   1832-1904 . . . . TCLC 23
See also CA 123; DLB 57

Stephen, Sir Leslie
See Stephen, Leslie

Stephen, Virginia
See Woolf, (Adeline) Virginia

Stephens, James   1882(?)-1950 . . . . . . TCLC 4
See also CA 104; DLB 19

Stephens, Reed
See Donaldson, Stephen R.

Steptoe, Lydia
See Barnes, Djuna

Sterchi, Beat   1949- . . . . CLC 65

Sterling, Brett
See Bradbury, Ray (Douglas); Hamilton,
Edmond

Sterling, Bruce   1954- . . . . CLC 72
See also CA 119; CANR 44

Sterling, George   1869-1926 . . . . TCLC 20
See also CA 117; DLB 54

Stern, Gerald   1925- . . . . CLC 40
See also CA 81-84; CANR 28; DLB 105

Stern, Richard (Gustave)   1928- . . . CLC 4, 39
See also CA 1-4R; CANR 1, 25; DLBY 87

Sternberg, Josef von   1894-1969 . . . . . CLC 20
See also CA 81-84

Sterne, Laurence
1713-1768 . . . . LC 2; DA; WLC
See also CDBLB 1660-1789; DLB 39

Sternheim, (William Adolf) Carl
1878-1942 . . . . TCLC 8
See also CA 105; DLB 56, 118

Stevens, Mark   1951- . . . . CLC 34
See also CA 122

Stevens, Wallace
1879-1955 . . . . TCLC 3, 12, 45; DA;
PC 6; WLC
See also CA 104; 124; CDALB 1929-1941;
DLB 54; MTCW

Stevenson, Anne (Katharine)
1933- . . . . CLC 7, 33
See also CA 17-20R; CAAS 9; CANR 9, 33;
DLB 40; MTCW

Stevenson, Robert Louis (Balfour)
1850-1894 . . . . NCLC 5, 14; DA;
SSC 11; WLC
See also CDBLB 1890-1914; CLR 10, 11;
DLB 18, 57, 141; JRDA; MAICYA;
YABC 2

Stewart, J(ohn) I(nnes) M(ackintosh)
1906- . . . . CLC 7, 14, 32
See also CA 85-88; CAAS 3; MTCW

Stewart, Mary (Florence Elinor)
1916- . . . . CLC 7, 35
See also CA 1-4R; CANR 1; SATA 12

Stewart, Mary Rainbow
See Stewart, Mary (Florence Elinor)

Stifter, Adalbert   1805-1868 . . . . . . NCLC 41
See also DLB 133

Still, James   1906- . . . . CLC 49
See also CA 65-68; CAAS 17; CANR 10,
26; DLB 9; SATA 29

Sting
See Sumner, Gordon Matthew

Stirling, Arthur
See Sinclair, Upton (Beall)

Stitt, Milan   1941- . . . . CLC 29
See also CA 69-72

Stockton, Francis Richard   1834-1902
See Stockton, Frank R.
See also CA 108; 137; MAICYA; SATA 44

Stockton, Frank R. . . . . TCLC 47
See also Stockton, Francis Richard
See also DLB 42, 74; SATA 32

Stoddard, Charles
See Kuttner, Henry

Stoker, Abraham   1847-1912
See Stoker, Bram
See also CA 105; DA; SATA 29

Stoker, Bram . . . . TCLC 8; WLC
See also Stoker, Abraham
See also CDBLB 1890-1914; DLB 36, 70

Stolz, Mary (Slattery)   1920- . . . . CLC 12
See also AAYA 8; AITN 1; CA 5-8R;
CANR 13, 41; JRDA; MAICYA;
SAAS 3; SATA 10, 71

Stone, Irving   1903-1989 . . . . CLC 7
See also AITN 1; CA 1-4R; 129; CAAS 3;
CANR 1, 23; MTCW; SATA 3;
SATA-Obit 64

Stone, Oliver   1946- . . . . CLC 73
See also CA 110

Stone, Robert (Anthony)
1937- . . . . CLC 5, 23, 42
See also CA 85-88; CANR 23; MTCW

Stone, Zachary
See Follett, Ken(neth Martin)

Stoppard, Tom
1937- . . . . . . CLC 1, 3, 4, 5, 8, 15, 29, 34,
63; DA; WLC
See also CA 81-84; CANR 39;
CDBLB 1960 to Present; DLB 13;
DLBY 85; MTCW

Storey, David (Malcolm)
1933- . . . . CLC 2, 4, 5, 8
See also CA 81-84; CANR 36; DLB 13, 14;
MTCW

Storm, Hyemeyohsts   1935- . . . . CLC 3
See also CA 81-84

Storm, (Hans) Theodor (Woldsen)
1817-1888 . . . . NCLC 1

Storni, Alfonsina
1892-1938 . . . . TCLC 5; HLC
See also CA 104; 131; HW

Stout, Rex (Todhunter)   1886-1975 . . . CLC 3
See also AITN 2; CA 61-64

Stow, (Julian) Randolph   1935- . . CLC 23, 48
See also CA 13-16R; CANR 33; MTCW

Stowe, Harriet (Elizabeth) Beecher
1811-1896 . . . . NCLC 3; DA; WLC
See also CDALB 1865-1917; DLB 1, 12, 42,
74; JRDA; MAICYA; YABC 1

Strachey, (Giles) Lytton
1880-1932 . . . . TCLC 12
See also CA 110; DLBD 10

Strand, Mark   1934- . . . . . . CLC 6, 18, 41, 71
See also CA 21-24R; CANR 40; DLB 5;
SATA 41

Straub, Peter (Francis)   1943- . . . . . . CLC 28
See also BEST 89:1; CA 85-88; CANR 28;
DLBY 84; MTCW

Strauss, Botho   1944- . . . . CLC 22
See also DLB 124

Streatfeild, (Mary) Noel
1895(?)-1986 . . . . CLC 21
See also CA 81-84; 120; CANR 31;
CLR 17; MAICYA; SATA 20, 48

Stribling, T(homas) S(igismund)
1881-1965 . . . . CLC 23
See also CA 107; DLB 9

Tate, (John Orley) Allen
　　1899-1979 .... **CLC 2, 4, 6, 9, 11, 14, 24**
　　See also CA 5-8R; 85-88; CANR 32;
　　DLB 4, 45, 63; MTCW

Tate, Ellalice
　　See Hibbert, Eleanor Alice Burford

Tate, James (Vincent) 1943- . . **CLC 2, 6, 25**
　　See also CA 21-24R; CANR 29; DLB 5

Tavel, Ronald 1940- . . . . **CLC 6**
　　See also CA 21-24R; CANR 33

Taylor, Cecil Philip 1929-1981 . . . . . **CLC 27**
　　See also CA 25-28R; 105

Taylor, Edward 1642(?)-1729. . . . **LC 11; DA**
　　See also DLB 24

Taylor, Eleanor Ross 1920- . . . . **CLC 5**
　　See also CA 81-84

Taylor, Elizabeth 1912-1975 . . . **CLC 2, 4, 29**
　　See also CA 13-16R; CANR 9; DLB 139;
　　MTCW; SATA 13

Taylor, Henry (Splawn) 1942- . . . . . **CLC 44**
　　See also CA 33-36R; CAAS 7; CANR 31;
　　DLB 5

Taylor, Kamala (Purnaiya) 1924-
　　See Markandaya, Kamala
　　See also CA 77-80

Taylor, Mildred D. . . . . **CLC 21**
　　See also AAYA 10; BW; CA 85-88;
　　CANR 25; CLR 9; DLB 52; JRDA;
　　MAICYA; SAAS 5; SATA 15, 70

Taylor, Peter (Hillsman)
　　1917- . . . . . . **CLC 1, 4, 18, 37, 44, 50, 71;**
　　　　　　　　　　　　　　　　　　　　　　　SSC 10
　　See also CA 13-16R; CANR 9; DLBY 81;
　　MTCW

Taylor, Robert Lewis 1912- . . . . **CLC 14**
　　See also CA 1-4R; CANR 3; SATA 10

Tchekhov, Anton
　　See Chekhov, Anton (Pavlovich)

Teasdale, Sara 1884-1933. . . . . **TCLC 4**
　　See also CA 104; DLB 45; SATA 32

Tegner, Esaias 1782-1846. . . . . **NCLC 2**

Teilhard de Chardin, (Marie Joseph) Pierre
　　1881-1955 . . . . **TCLC 9**
　　See also CA 105

Temple, Ann
　　See Mortimer, Penelope (Ruth)

Tennant, Emma (Christina)
　　1937- . . . . **CLC 13, 52**
　　See also CA 65-68; CAAS 9; CANR 10, 38;
　　DLB 14

Tenneshaw, S. M.
　　See Silverberg, Robert

Tennyson, Alfred
　　1809-1892 . . **NCLC 30; DA; PC 6; WLC**
　　See also CDBLB 1832-1890; DLB 32

Teran, Lisa St. Aubin de . . . . **CLC 36**
　　See also St. Aubin de Teran, Lisa

Teresa de Jesus, St. 1515-1582 . . . . . . **LC 18**

Terkel, Louis 1912-
　　See Terkel, Studs
　　See also CA 57-60; CANR 18; MTCW

Terkel, Studs . . . . **CLC 38**
　　See also Terkel, Louis
　　See also AITN 1

Terry, C. V.
　　See Slaughter, Frank G(ill)

Terry, Megan 1932- . . . . **CLC 19**
　　See also CA 77-80; CABS 3; CANR 43;
　　DLB 7

Tertz, Abram
　　See Sinyavsky, Andrei (Donatevich)

Tesich, Steve 1943(?)- . . . . **CLC 40, 69**
　　See also CA 105; DLBY 83

Teternikov, Fyodor Kuzmich 1863-1927
　　See Sologub, Fyodor
　　See also CA 104

Tevis, Walter 1928-1984 . . . . **CLC 42**
　　See also CA 113

Tey, Josephine. . . . . **TCLC 14**
　　See also Mackintosh, Elizabeth
　　See also DLB 77

Thackeray, William Makepeace
　　1811-1863 .... **NCLC 5, 14, 22, 43; DA;**
　　　　　　　　　　　　　　　　　　　　　　　WLC
　　See also CDBLB 1832-1890; DLB 21, 55;
　　SATA 23

Thakura, Ravindranatha
　　See Tagore, Rabindranath

Tharoor, Shashi 1956- . . . . **CLC 70**
　　See also CA 141

Thelwell, Michael Miles 1939- . . . . . **CLC 22**
　　See also CA 101

Theobald, Lewis, Jr.
　　See Lovecraft, H(oward) P(hillips)

Theodorescu, Ion N. 1880-1967
　　See Arghezi, Tudor
　　See also CA 116

Theriault, Yves 1915-1983. . . . . **CLC 79**
　　See also CA 102; DLB 88

Theroux, Alexander (Louis)
　　1939- . . . . **CLC 2, 25**
　　See also CA 85-88; CANR 20

Theroux, Paul (Edward)
　　1941- . . . . **CLC 5, 8, 11, 15, 28, 46**
　　See also BEST 89:4; CA 33-36R; CANR 20;
　　DLB 2; MTCW; SATA 44

Thesen, Sharon 1946- . . . . **CLC 56**

Thevenin, Denis
　　See Duhamel, Georges

Thibault, Jacques Anatole Francois
　　1844-1924
　　See France, Anatole
　　See also CA 106; 127; MTCW

Thiele, Colin (Milton) 1920- . . . . **CLC 17**
　　See also CA 29-32R; CANR 12, 28;
　　CLR 27; MAICYA; SAAS 2; SATA 14,
　　72

Thomas, Audrey (Callahan)
　　1935- . . . . **CLC 7, 13, 37**
　　See also AITN 2; CA 21-24R; CAAS 19;
　　CANR 36; DLB 60; MTCW

Thomas, D(onald) M(ichael)
　　1935- . . . . **CLC 13, 22, 31**
　　See also CA 61-64; CAAS 11; CANR 17;
　　CDBLB 1960 to Present; DLB 40;
　　MTCW

Thomas, Dylan (Marlais)
　　1914-1953 . . . **TCLC 1, 8, 45; DA; PC 2;**
　　　　　　　　　　　　　　　　　　　　　SSC 3; WLC
　　See also CA 104; 120; CDBLB 1945-1960;
　　DLB 13, 20, 139; MTCW; SATA 60

Thomas, (Philip) Edward
　　1878-1917 . . . . **TCLC 10**
　　See also CA 106; DLB 19

Thomas, Joyce Carol 1938- . . . . **CLC 35**
　　See also AAYA 12; BW; CA 113; 116;
　　CLR 19; DLB 33; JRDA; MAICYA;
　　MTCW; SAAS 7; SATA 40

Thomas, Lewis 1913-1993 . . . . **CLC 35**
　　See also CA 85-88; 143; CANR 38; MTCW

Thomas, Paul
　　See Mann, (Paul) Thomas

Thomas, Piri 1928- . . . . **CLC 17**
　　See also CA 73-76; HW

Thomas, R(onald) S(tuart)
　　1913- . . . . **CLC 6, 13, 48**
　　See also CA 89-92; CAAS 4; CANR 30;
　　CDBLB 1960 to Present; DLB 27;
　　MTCW

Thomas, Ross (Elmore) 1926- . . . . . . **CLC 39**
　　See also CA 33-36R; CANR 22

Thompson, Francis Clegg
　　See Mencken, H(enry) L(ouis)

Thompson, Francis Joseph
　　1859-1907 . . . . **TCLC 4**
　　See also CA 104; CDBLB 1890-1914;
　　DLB 19

Thompson, Hunter S(tockton)
　　1939- . . . . **CLC 9, 17, 40**
　　See also BEST 89:1; CA 17-20R; CANR 23;
　　MTCW

Thompson, James Myers
　　See Thompson, Jim (Myers)

Thompson, Jim (Myers)
　　1906-1977(?) . . . . **CLC 69**
　　See also CA 140

Thompson, Judith . . . . **CLC 39**

Thomson, James 1700-1748. . . . . **LC 16**

Thomson, James 1834-1882 . . . . . . **NCLC 18**

Thoreau, Henry David
　　1817-1862 . . . . . . **NCLC 7, 21; DA; WLC**
　　See also CDALB 1640-1865; DLB 1

Thornton, Hall
　　See Silverberg, Robert

Thurber, James (Grover)
　　1894-1961 . . . **CLC 5, 11, 25; DA; SSC 1**
　　See also CA 73-76; CANR 17, 39;
　　CDALB 1929-1941; DLB 4, 11, 22, 102;
　　MAICYA; MTCW; SATA 13

Thurman, Wallace (Henry)
　　1902-1934 . . . . **TCLC 6; BLC**
　　See also BW; CA 104; 124; DLB 51

Ticheburn, Cheviot
　　See Ainsworth, William Harrison

Tieck, (Johann) Ludwig
　　1773-1853 . . . . **NCLC 5**
　　See also DLB 90

Tiger, Derry
　　See Ellison, Harlan

Tilghman, Christopher 1948(?)- . . . . . **CLC 65**

Tillinghast, Richard (Williford)
1940- .... CLC 29
See also CA 29-32R; CANR 26

Timrod, Henry 1828-1867 .... NCLC 25
See also DLB 3

Tindall, Gillian 1938- .... CLC 7
See also CA 21-24R; CANR 11

Tiptree, James, Jr. .... CLC 48, 50
See also Sheldon, Alice Hastings Bradley
See also DLB 8

Titmarsh, Michael Angelo
See Thackeray, William Makepeace

Tocqueville, Alexis (Charles Henri Maurice
Clerel Comte) 1805-1859..... NCLC 7

Tolkien, J(ohn) R(onald) R(euel)
1892-1973 .... CLC 1, 2, 3, 8, 12, 38;
DA; WLC
See also AAYA 10; AITN 1; CA 17-18;
45-48; CAP 2;
CDBLB 1914-1945; DLB 15; JRDA;
MAICYA; MTCW; SATA 2, 24, 32

Toller, Ernst 1893-1939 .... TCLC 10
See also CA 107; DLB 124

Tolson, M. B.
See Tolson, Melvin B(eaunorus)

Tolson, Melvin B(eaunorus)
1898(?)-1966 .... CLC 36; BLC
See also BW; CA 124; 89-92; DLB 48, 76

Tolstoi, Aleksei Nikolaevich
See Tolstoy, Alexey Nikolaevich

Tolstoy, Alexey Nikolaevich
1882-1945 .... TCLC 18
See also CA 107

Tolstoy, Count Leo
See Tolstoy, Leo (Nikolaevich)

Tolstoy, Leo (Nikolaevich)
1828-1910 ...... TCLC 4, 11, 17, 28, 44;
DA; SSC 9; WLC
See also CA 104; 123; SATA 26

Tomasi di Lampedusa, Giuseppe 1896-1957
See Lampedusa, Giuseppe (Tomasi) di
See also CA 111

Tomlin, Lily..................... CLC 17
See also Tomlin, Mary Jean

Tomlin, Mary Jean 1939(?)-
See Tomlin, Lily
See also CA 117

Tomlinson, (Alfred) Charles
1927- .... CLC 2, 4, 6, 13, 45
See also CA 5-8R; CANR 33; DLB 40

Tonson, Jacob
See Bennett, (Enoch) Arnold

Toole, John Kennedy
1937-1969 .... CLC 19, 64
See also CA 104; DLBY 81

Toomer, Jean
1894-1967 ...... CLC 1, 4, 13, 22; BLC;
PC 7; SSC 1
See also BW; CA 85-88;
CDALB 1917-1929; DLB 45, 51; MTCW

Torley, Luke
See Blish, James (Benjamin)

Tornimparte, Alessandra
See Ginzburg, Natalia

Torre, Raoul della
See Mencken, H(enry) L(ouis)

Torrey, E(dwin) Fuller 1937- .... CLC 34
See also CA 119

Torsvan, Ben Traven
See Traven, B.

Torsvan, Benno Traven
See Traven, B.

Torsvan, Berick Traven
See Traven, B.

Torsvan, Berwick Traven
See Traven, B.

Torsvan, Bruno Traven
See Traven, B.

Torsvan, Traven
See Traven, B.

Tournier, Michel (Edouard)
1924- .... CLC 6, 23, 36
See also CA 49-52; CANR 3, 36; DLB 83;
MTCW; SATA 23

Tournimparte, Alessandra
See Ginzburg, Natalia

Towers, Ivar
See Kornbluth, C(yril) M.

Townsend, Sue 1946- .... CLC 61
See also CA 119; 127; MTCW; SATA 48,
55

Townshend, Peter (Dennis Blandford)
1945- .... CLC 17, 42
See also CA 107

Tozzi, Federigo 1883-1920....... TCLC 31

Traill, Catharine Parr
1802-1899 .... NCLC 31
See also DLB 99

Trakl, Georg 1887-1914.......... TCLC 5
See also CA 104

Transtroemer, Tomas (Goesta)
1931- .... CLC 52, 65
See also CA 117; 129; CAAS 17

Transtromer, Tomas Gosta
See Transtroemer, Tomas (Goesta)

Traven, B. (?)-1969............ CLC 8, 11
See also CA 19-20; 25-28R; CAP 2; DLB 9,
56; MTCW

Treitel, Jonathan 1959- .... CLC 70

Tremain, Rose 1943-............. CLC 42
See also CA 97-100; CANR 44; DLB 14

Tremblay, Michel 1942-.......... CLC 29
See also CA 116; 128; DLB 60; MTCW

Trevanian (a pseudonym) 1930(?)-... CLC 29
See also CA 108

Trevor, Glen
See Hilton, James

Trevor, William
1928- .... CLC 7, 9, 14, 25, 71
See also Cox, William Trevor
See also DLB 14, 139

Trifonov, Yuri (Valentinovich)
1925-1981 .... CLC 45
See also CA 126; 103; MTCW

Trilling, Lionel 1905-1975 .... CLC 9, 11, 24
See also CA 9-12R; 61-64; CANR 10;
DLB 28, 63; MTCW

Trimball, W. H.
See Mencken, H(enry) L(ouis)

Tristan
See Gomez de la Serna, Ramon

Tristram
See Housman, A(lfred) E(dward)

Trogdon, William (Lewis) 1939-
See Heat-Moon, William Least
See also CA 115; 119

Trollope, Anthony
1815-1882 ...... NCLC 6, 33; DA; WLC
See also CDBLB 1832-1890; DLB 21, 57;
SATA 22

Trollope, Frances 1779-1863 ..... NCLC 30
See also DLB 21

Trotsky, Leon 1879-1940........ TCLC 22
See also CA 118

Trotter (Cockburn), Catharine
1679-1749 .... LC 8
See also DLB 84

Trout, Kilgore
See Farmer, Philip Jose

Trow, George W. S. 1943-......... CLC 52
See also CA 126

Troyat, Henri 1911-............. CLC 23
See also CA 45-48; CANR 2, 33; MTCW

Trudeau, G(arretson) B(eekman) 1948-
See Trudeau, Garry B.
See also CA 81-84; CANR 31; SATA 35

Trudeau, Garry B................ CLC 12
See also Trudeau, G(arretson) B(eekman)
See also AAYA 10; AITN 2

Truffaut, Francois 1932-1984....... CLC 20
See also CA 81-84; 113; CANR 34

Trumbo, Dalton 1905-1976 .... CLC 19
See also CA 21-24R; 69-72; CANR 10;
DLB 26

Trumbull, John 1750-1831....... NCLC 30
See also DLB 31

Trundlett, Helen B.
See Eliot, T(homas) S(tearns)

Tryon, Thomas 1926-1991 .... CLC 3, 11
See also AITN 1; CA 29-32R; 135;
CANR 32; MTCW

Tryon, Tom
See Tryon, Thomas

Ts'ao Hsueh-ch'in 1715(?)-1763....... LC 1

Tsushima, Shuji 1909-1948
See Dazai, Osamu
See also CA 107

Tsvetaeva (Efron), Marina (Ivanovna)
1892-1941 ....TCLC 7, 35
See also CA 104; 128; MTCW

Tuck, Lily 1938-................. CLC 70
See also CA 139

Tu Fu 712-770.................... PC 9

Tunis, John R(oberts) 1889-1975 ... CLC 12
See also CA 61-64; DLB 22; JRDA;
MAICYA; SATA 30, 37

Tuohy, Frank.................... CLC 37
See also Tuohy, John Francis
See also DLB 14, 139

Tuohy, John Francis 1925-
See Tuohy, Frank
See also CA 5-8R; CANR 3

Turco, Lewis (Putnam) 1934- ... **CLC 11, 63**
See also CA 13-16R; CANR 24; DLBY 84

Turgenev, Ivan
1818-1883 ...... **NCLC 21; DA; SSC 7; WLC**

Turner, Frederick 1943- .... **CLC 48**
See also CA 73-76; CAAS 10; CANR 12, 30; DLB 40

Tusan, Stan 1936- .... **CLC 22**
See also CA 105

Tutu, Desmond M(pilo)
1931- .... **CLC 80; BLC**
See also BW; CA 125

Tutuola, Amos 1920- ... **CLC 5, 14, 29; BLC**
See also BW; CA 9-12R; CANR 27; DLB 125; MTCW

Twain, Mark
... **TCLC 6, 12, 19, 36, 48; SSC 6; WLC**
See also Clemens, Samuel Langhorne
See also DLB 11, 12, 23, 64, 74

Tyler, Anne
1941- .... **CLC 7, 11, 18, 28, 44, 59**
See also BEST 89:1; CA 9-12R; CANR 11, 33; DLB 6; DLBY 82; MTCW; SATA 7

Tyler, Royall 1757-1826. .... **NCLC 3**
See also DLB 37

Tynan, Katharine 1861-1931 ...... **TCLC 3**
See also CA 104

Tytell, John 1939- .... **CLC 50**
See also CA 29-32R

Tyutchev, Fyodor 1803-1873 ..... **NCLC 34**

Tzara, Tristan .... **CLC 47**
See also Rosenfeld, Samuel

Uhry, Alfred 1936- .... **CLC 55**
See also CA 127; 133

Ulf, Haerved
See Strindberg, (Johan) August

Ulf, Harved
See Strindberg, (Johan) August

Ulibarri, Sabine R(eyes) 1919- ..... **CLC 83**
See also CA 131; DLB 82; HW

Unamuno (y Jugo), Miguel de
1864-1936 .... **TCLC 2, 9; HLC; SSC 11**
See also CA 104; 131; DLB 108; HW; MTCW

Undercliffe, Errol
See Campbell, (John) Ramsey

Underwood, Miles
See Glassco, John

Undset, Sigrid
1882-1949 .... **TCLC 3; DA; WLC**
See also CA 104; 129; MTCW

Ungaretti, Giuseppe
1888-1970 .... **CLC 7, 11, 15**
See also CA 19-20; 25-28R; CAP 2; DLB 114

Unger, Douglas 1952- .... **CLC 34**
See also CA 130

Unsworth, Barry (Forster) 1930- .... **CLC 76**
See also CA 25-28R; CANR 30

Updike, John (Hoyer)
1932- ...... **CLC 1, 2, 3, 5, 7, 9, 13, 15, 23, 34, 43, 70; DA; SSC 13; WLC**
See also CA 1-4R; CABS 1; CANR 4, 33; CDALB 1968-1988; DLB 2, 5; DLBD 3; DLBY 80, 82; MTCW

Upshaw, Margaret Mitchell
See Mitchell, Margaret (Munnerlyn)

Upton, Mark
See Sanders, Lawrence

Urdang, Constance (Henriette)
1922- .... **CLC 47**
See also CA 21-24R; CANR 9, 24

Uriel, Henry
See Faust, Frederick (Schiller)

Uris, Leon (Marcus) 1924- ...... **CLC 7, 32**
See also AITN 1, 2; BEST 89:2; CA 1-4R; CANR 1, 40; MTCW; SATA 49

Urmuz
See Codrescu, Andrei

Ustinov, Peter (Alexander) 1921- .... **CLC 1**
See also AITN 1; CA 13-16R; CANR 25; DLB 13

V
See Chekhov, Anton (Pavlovich)

Vaculik, Ludvik 1926- .... **CLC 7**
See also CA 53-56

Valenzuela, Luisa 1938- ... **CLC 31; SSC 14**
See also CA 101; CANR 32; DLB 113; HW

Valera y Alcala-Galiano, Juan
1824-1905 .... **TCLC 10**
See also CA 106

Valery, (Ambroise) Paul (Toussaint Jules)
1871-1945 .... **TCLC 4, 15; PC 9**
See also CA 104; 122; MTCW

Valle-Inclan, Ramon (Maria) del
1866-1936 .... **TCLC 5; HLC**
See also CA 106; DLB 134

Vallejo, Antonio Buero
See Buero Vallejo, Antonio

Vallejo, Cesar (Abraham)
1892-1938 .... **TCLC 3; HLC**
See also CA 105; HW

Valle Y Pena, Ramon del
See Valle-Inclan, Ramon (Maria) del

Van Ash, Cay 1918- .... **CLC 34**

Vanbrugh, Sir John 1664-1726 ...... **LC 21**
See also DLB 80

Van Campen, Karl
See Campbell, John W(ood, Jr.)

Vance, Gerald
See Silverberg, Robert

Vance, Jack .... **CLC 35**
See also Vance, John Holbrook
See also DLB 8

Vance, John Holbrook 1916-
See Queen, Ellery; Vance, Jack
See also CA 29-32R; CANR 17; MTCW

Van Den Bogarde, Derek Jules Gaspard Ulric Niven 1921-
See Bogarde, Dirk
See also CA 77-80

Vandenburgh, Jane .... **CLC 59**

Vanderhaeghe, Guy 1951- .... **CLC 41**
See also CA 113

van der Post, Laurens (Jan) 1906- ... **CLC 5**
See also CA 5-8R; CANR 35

van de Wetering, Janwillem 1931- .. **CLC 47**
See also CA 49-52; CANR 4

Van Dine, S. S. .... **TCLC 23**
See also Wright, Willard Huntington

Van Doren, Carl (Clinton)
1885-1950 .... **TCLC 18**
See also CA 111

Van Doren, Mark 1894-1972 ..... **CLC 6, 10**
See also CA 1-4R; 37-40R; CANR 3; DLB 45; MTCW

Van Druten, John (William)
1901-1957 .... **TCLC 2**
See also CA 104; DLB 10

Van Duyn, Mona (Jane)
1921- .... **CLC 3, 7, 63**
See also CA 9-12R; CANR 7, 38; DLB 5

Van Dyne, Edith
See Baum, L(yman) Frank

van Itallie, Jean-Claude 1936- .... **CLC 3**
See also CA 45-48; CAAS 2; CANR 1; DLB 7

van Ostaijen, Paul 1896-1928 ..... **TCLC 33**

Van Peebles, Melvin 1932- ...... **CLC 2, 20**
See also BW; CA 85-88; CANR 27

Vansittart, Peter 1920- .... **CLC 42**
See also CA 1-4R; CANR 3

Van Vechten, Carl 1880-1964 ...... **CLC 33**
See also CA 89-92; DLB 4, 9, 51

Van Vogt, A(lfred) E(lton) 1912- ..... **CLC 1**
See also CA 21-24R; CANR 28; DLB 8; SATA 14

Varda, Agnes 1928- .... **CLC 16**
See also CA 116; 122

Vargas Llosa, (Jorge) Mario (Pedro)
1936- .... **CLC 3, 6, 9, 10, 15, 31, 42; DA; HLC**
See also CA 73-76; CANR 18, 32, 42; HW; MTCW

Vasiliu, Gheorghe 1881-1957
See Bacovia, George
See also CA 123

Vassa, Gustavus
See Equiano, Olaudah

Vassilikos, Vassilis 1933- .... **CLC 4, 8**
See also CA 81-84

Vaughn, Stephanie .... **CLC 62**

Vazov, Ivan (Minchov)
1850-1921 .... **TCLC 25**
See also CA 121

Veblen, Thorstein (Bunde)
1857-1929 .... **TCLC 31**
See also CA 115

Vega, Lope de 1562-1635. .... **LC 23**

Venison, Alfred
See Pound, Ezra (Weston Loomis)

Verdi, Marie de
See Mencken, H(enry) L(ouis)

Verdu, Matilde
See Cela, Camilo Jose

Verga, Giovanni (Carmelo)
1840-1922 .... TCLC 3
See also CA 104; 123

Vergil 70B.C.-19B.C. .... CMLC 9; DA

Verhaeren, Emile (Adolphe Gustave)
1855-1916 .... TCLC 12
See also CA 109

Verlaine, Paul (Marie)
1844-1896 .... NCLC 2; PC 2

Verne, Jules (Gabriel)
1828-1905 .... TCLC 6, 52
See also CA 110; 131; DLB 123; JRDA;
MAICYA; SATA 21

Very, Jones 1813-1880........... NCLC 9
See also DLB 1

Vesaas, Tarjei 1897-1970 .... CLC 48
See also CA 29-32R

Vialis, Gaston
See Simenon, Georges (Jacques Christian)

Vian, Boris 1920-1959 .... TCLC 9
See also CA 106; DLB 72

Viaud, (Louis Marie) Julien 1850-1923
See Loti, Pierre
See also CA 107

Vicar, Henry
See Felsen, Henry Gregor

Vicker, Angus
See Felsen, Henry Gregor

Vidal, Gore
1925- ..... CLC 2, 4, 6, 8, 10, 22, 33, 72
See also AITN 1; BEST 90:2; CA 5-8R;
CANR 13; DLB 6; MTCW

Viereck, Peter (Robert Edwin)
1916- .... CLC 4
See also CA 1-4R; CANR 1; DLB 5

Vigny, Alfred (Victor) de
1797-1863 .... NCLC 7
See also DLB 119

Vilakazi, Benedict Wallet
1906-1947 .... TCLC 37

Villiers de l'Isle Adam, Jean Marie Mathias
Philippe Auguste Comte
1838-1889 .... NCLC 3; SSC 14
See also DLB 123

Vincent, Gabrielle a pseudonym...... CLC 13
See also CA 126; CLR 13; MAICYA;
SATA 61

Vinci, Leonardo da 1452-1519....... LC 12

Vine, Barbara .... CLC 50
See also Rendell, Ruth (Barbara)
See also BEST 90:4

Vinge, Joan D(ennison) 1948- ...... CLC 30
See also CA 93-96; SATA 36

Violis, G.
See Simenon, Georges (Jacques Christian)

Visconti, Luchino 1906-1976....... CLC 16
See also CA 81-84; 65-68; CANR 39

Vittorini, Elio 1908-1966...... CLC 6, 9, 14
See also CA 133; 25-28R

Vizinczey, Stephen 1933-.......... CLC 40
See also CA 128

Vliet, R(ussell) G(ordon)
1929-1984 .... CLC 22
See also CA 37-40R; 112; CANR 18

Vogau, Boris Andreyevich 1894-1937(?)
See Pilnyak, Boris
See also CA 123

Vogel, Paula A(nne) 1951-........ CLC 76
See also CA 108

Voight, Ellen Bryant 1943- .... CLC 54
See also CA 69-72; CANR 11, 29; DLB 120

Voigt, Cynthia 1942- .... CLC 30
See also AAYA 3; CA 106; CANR 18, 37,
40; CLR 13; JRDA; MAICYA;
SATA 33, 48

Voinovich, Vladimir (Nikolaevich)
1932-.................... CLC 10, 49
See also CA 81-84; CAAS 12; CANR 33;
MTCW

Voloshinov, V. N.
See Bakhtin, Mikhail Mikhailovich

Voltaire
1694-1778 ... LC 14; DA; SSC 12; WLC

von Daeniken, Erich 1935- .... CLC 30
See also von Daniken, Erich
See also AITN 1; CA 37-40R; CANR 17,
44

von Daniken, Erich .... CLC 30
See also von Daeniken, Erich

von Heidenstam, (Carl Gustaf) Verner
See Heidenstam, (Carl Gustaf) Verner von

von Heyse, Paul (Johann Ludwig)
See Heyse, Paul (Johann Ludwig von)

von Hofmannsthal, Hugo
See Hofmannsthal, Hugo von

von Horvath, Odon
See Horvath, Oedoen von

von Horvath, Oedoen
See Horvath, Oedoen von

von Liliencron, (Friedrich Adolf Axel) Detlev
See Liliencron, (Friedrich Adolf Axel)
Detlev von

Vonnegut, Kurt, Jr.
1922-...... CLC 1, 2, 3, 4, 5, 8, 12, 22,
40, 60; DA; SSC 8; WLC
See also AAYA 6; AITN 1; BEST 90:4;
CA 1-4R; CANR 1, 25;
CDALB 1968-1988; DLB 2, 8; DLBD 3;
DLBY 80; MTCW

Von Rachen, Kurt
See Hubbard, L(afayette) Ron(ald)

von Rezzori (d'Arezzo), Gregor
See Rezzori (d'Arezzo), Gregor von

von Sternberg, Josef
See Sternberg, Josef von

Vorster, Gordon 1924-............ CLC 34
See also CA 133

Vosce, Trudie
See Ozick, Cynthia

Voznesensky, Andrei (Andreievich)
1933-.................... CLC 1, 15, 57
See also CA 89-92; CANR 37; MTCW

Waddington, Miriam 1917- .... CLC 28
See also CA 21-24R; CANR 12, 30;
DLB 68

Wagman, Fredrica 1937-.......... CLC 7
See also CA 97-100

Wagner, Richard 1813-1883....... NCLC 9
See also DLB 129

Wagner-Martin, Linda 1936-....... CLC 50

Wagoner, David (Russell)
1926- .... CLC 3, 5, 15
See also CA 1-4R; CAAS 3; CANR 2;
DLB 5; SATA 14

Wah, Fred(erick James) 1939-...... CLC 44
See also CA 107; 141; DLB 60

Wahloo, Per 1926-1975 .... CLC 7
See also CA 61-64

Wahloo, Peter
See Wahloo, Per

Wain, John (Barrington)
1925-.............. CLC 2, 11, 15, 46
See also CA 5-8R; CAAS 4; CANR 23;
CDBLB 1960 to Present; DLB 15, 27,
139; MTCW

Wajda, Andrzej 1926-............. CLC 16
See also CA 102

Wakefield, Dan 1932-.............. CLC 7
See also CA 21-24R; CAAS 7

Wakoski, Diane
1937-.......... CLC 2, 4, 7, 9, 11, 40
See also CA 13-16R; CAAS 1; CANR 9;
DLB 5

Wakoski-Sherbell, Diane
See Wakoski, Diane

Walcott, Derek (Alton)
1930- .... CLC 2, 4, 9, 14, 25, 42, 67, 76;
BLC
See also BW; CA 89-92; CANR 26;
DLB 117; DLBY 81; MTCW

Waldman, Anne 1945- .... CLC 7
See also CA 37-40R; CAAS 17; CANR 34;
DLB 16

Waldo, E. Hunter
See Sturgeon, Theodore (Hamilton)

Waldo, Edward Hamilton
See Sturgeon, Theodore (Hamilton)

Walker, Alice (Malsenior)
1944- .... CLC 5, 6, 9, 19, 27, 46, 58;
BLC; DA; SSC 5
See also AAYA 3; BEST 89:4; BW;
CA 37-40R; CANR 9, 27;
CDALB 1968-1988; DLB 6, 33; MTCW;
SATA 31

Walker, David Harry 1911-1992.... CLC 14
See also CA 1-4R; 137; CANR 1; SATA 8;
SATA-Obit 71

Walker, Edward Joseph 1934-
See Walker, Ted
See also CA 21-24R; CANR 12, 28

Walker, George F. 1947-....... CLC 44, 61
See also CA 103; CANR 21, 43; DLB 60

Walker, Joseph A. 1935-.......... CLC 19
See also BW; CA 89-92; CANR 26; DLB 38

Walker, Margaret (Abigail)
1915- .... CLC 1, 6; BLC
See also BW; CA 73-76; CANR 26;
DLB 76; MTCW

Walker, Ted .... CLC 13
See also Walker, Edward Joseph
See also DLB 40

Author Index

Wallace, David Foster 1962- .... **CLC 50**
See also CA 132

Wallace, Dexter
See Masters, Edgar Lee

Wallace, Irving 1916-1990 ...... **CLC 7, 13**
See also AITN 1; CA 1-4R; 132; CAAS 1;
CANR 1, 27; MTCW

Wallant, Edward Lewis
1926-1962 .... **CLC 5, 10**
See also CA 1-4R; CANR 22; DLB 2, 28;
MTCW

Walpole, Horace 1717-1797 .... **LC 2**
See also DLB 39, 104

Walpole, Hugh (Seymour)
1884-1941 .... **TCLC 5**
See also CA 104; DLB 34

Walser, Martin 1927- .... **CLC 27**
See also CA 57-60; CANR 8; DLB 75, 124

Walser, Robert 1878-1956 .... **TCLC 18**
See also CA 118; DLB 66

Walsh, Jill Paton .... **CLC 35**
See also Paton Walsh, Gillian
See also AAYA 11; CLR 2; SAAS 3

Walter, Villiam Christian
See Andersen, Hans Christian

Wambaugh, Joseph (Aloysius, Jr.)
1937- .... **CLC 3, 18**
See also AITN 1; BEST 89:3; CA 33-36R;
CANR 42; DLB 6; DLBY 83; MTCW

Ward, Arthur Henry Sarsfield 1883-1959
See Rohmer, Sax
See also CA 108

Ward, Douglas Turner 1930- ...... **CLC 19**
See also BW; CA 81-84; CANR 27; DLB 7,
38

Ward, Peter
See Faust, Frederick (Schiller)

Warhol, Andy 1928(?)-1987 .... **CLC 20**
See also AAYA 12; BEST 89:4; CA 89-92;
121; CANR 34

Warner, Francis (Robert le Plastrier)
1937- .... **CLC 14**
See also CA 53-56; CANR 11

Warner, Marina 1946- .... **CLC 59**
See also CA 65-68; CANR 21

Warner, Rex (Ernest) 1905-1986 .... **CLC 45**
See also CA 89-92; 119; DLB 15

Warner, Susan (Bogert)
1819-1885 .... **NCLC 31**
See also DLB 3, 42

Warner, Sylvia (Constance) Ashton
See Ashton-Warner, Sylvia (Constance)

Warner, Sylvia Townsend
1893-1978 .... **CLC 7, 19**
See also CA 61-64; 77-80; CANR 16;
DLB 34, 139; MTCW

Warren, Mercy Otis 1728-1814... **NCLC 13**
See also DLB 31

Warren, Robert Penn
1905-1989 .... **CLC 1, 4, 6, 8, 10, 13, 18,
39, 53, 59; SSC 4; WLC**
See also AITN 1; CA 13-16R; 129;
CANR 10; CDALB 1968-1988; DLB 2,
48; DLBY 80, 89; MTCW; SATA 46, 63

Warshofsky, Isaac
See Singer, Isaac Bashevis

Warton, Thomas 1728-1790 .... **LC 15**
See also DLB 104, 109

Waruk, Kona
See Harris, (Theodore) Wilson

Warung, Price 1855-1911 .... **TCLC 45**

Warwick, Jarvis
See Garner, Hugh

Washington, Alex
See Harris, Mark

Washington, Booker T(aliaferro)
1856-1915 .... **TCLC 10; BLC**
See also BW; CA 114; 125; SATA 28

Washington, George 1732-1799 ...... **LC 25**
See also DLB 31

Wassermann, (Karl) Jakob
1873-1934 .... **TCLC 6**
See also CA 104; DLB 66

Wasserstein, Wendy
1950- .... **CLC 32, 59; DC 4**
See also CA 121; 129; CABS 3

Waterhouse, Keith (Spencer)
1929- .... **CLC 47**
See also CA 5-8R; CANR 38; DLB 13, 15;
MTCW

Waters, Roger 1944- .... **CLC 35**
See also Pink Floyd

Watkins, Frances Ellen
See Harper, Frances Ellen Watkins

Watkins, Gerrold
See Malzberg, Barry N(athaniel)

Watkins, Paul 1964- .... **CLC 55**
See also CA 132

Watkins, Vernon Phillips
1906-1967 .... **CLC 43**
See also CA 9-10; 25-28R; CAP 1; DLB 20

Watson, Irving S.
See Mencken, H(enry) L(ouis)

Watson, John H.
See Farmer, Philip Jose

Watson, Richard F.
See Silverberg, Robert

Waugh, Auberon (Alexander) 1939- .. **CLC 7**
See also CA 45-48; CANR 6, 22; DLB 14

Waugh, Evelyn (Arthur St. John)
1903-1966 ...... **CLC 1, 3, 8, 13, 19, 27,
44; DA; WLC**
See also CA 85-88; 25-28R; CANR 22;
CDBLB 1914-1945; DLB 15; MTCW

Waugh, Harriet 1944- .... **CLC 6**
See also CA 85-88; CANR 22

Ways, C. R.
See Blount, Roy (Alton), Jr.

Waystaff, Simon
See Swift, Jonathan

Webb, (Martha) Beatrice (Potter)
1858-1943 .... **TCLC 22**
See also Potter, Beatrice
See also CA 117

Webb, Charles (Richard) 1939- ...... **CLC 7**
See also CA 25-28R

Webb, James H(enry), Jr. 1946- .... **CLC 22**
See also CA 81-84

Webb, Mary (Gladys Meredith)
1881-1927 .... **TCLC 24**
See also CA 123; DLB 34

Webb, Mrs. Sidney
See Webb, (Martha) Beatrice (Potter)

Webb, Phyllis 1927- .... **CLC 18**
See also CA 104; CANR 23; DLB 53

Webb, Sidney (James)
1859-1947 .... **TCLC 22**
See also CA 117

Webber, Andrew Lloyd .... **CLC 21**
See also Lloyd Webber, Andrew

Weber, Lenora Mattingly
1895-1971 .... **CLC 12**
See also CA 19-20; 29-32R; CAP 1;
SATA 2, 26

Webster, John 1579(?)-1634(?) .... **DC 2**
See also CDBLB Before 1660; DA; DLB 58;
WLC

Webster, Noah 1758-1843 .... **NCLC 30**

Wedekind, (Benjamin) Frank(lin)
1864-1918 .... **TCLC 7**
See also CA 104; DLB 118

Weidman, Jerome 1913- .... **CLC 7**
See also AITN 2; CA 1-4R; CANR 1;
DLB 28

Weil, Simone (Adolphine)
1909-1943 .... **TCLC 23**
See also CA 117

Weinstein, Nathan
See West, Nathanael

Weinstein, Nathan von Wallenstein
See West, Nathanael

Weir, Peter (Lindsay) 1944- .... **CLC 20**
See also CA 113; 123

Weiss, Peter (Ulrich)
1916-1982 .... **CLC 3, 15, 51**
See also CA 45-48; 106; CANR 3; DLB 69,
124

Weiss, Theodore (Russell)
1916- .... **CLC 3, 8, 14**
See also CA 9-12R; CAAS 2; DLB 5

Welch, (Maurice) Denton
1915-1948 .... **TCLC 22**
See also CA 121

Welch, James 1940- .... **CLC 6, 14, 52**
See also CA 85-88; CANR 42

Weldon, Fay
1933(?)- .... **CLC 6, 9, 11, 19, 36, 59**
See also CA 21-24R; CANR 16;
CDBLB 1960 to Present; DLB 14;
MTCW

Wellek, Rene 1903- .... **CLC 28**
See also CA 5-8R; CAAS 7; CANR 8;
DLB 63

Weller, Michael 1942- .... **CLC 10, 53**
See also CA 85-88

Weller, Paul 1958- .... **CLC 26**

Wellershoff, Dieter 1925- .... **CLC 46**
See also CA 89-92; CANR 16, 37

Welles, (George) Orson
1915-1985 .... **CLC 20, 80**
See also CA 93-96; 117

Wellman, Mac 1945- .... **CLC 65**

Wellman, Manly Wade 1903-1986 .. **CLC 49**
See also CA 1-4R; 118; CANR 6, 16, 44;
SATA 6, 47

Wells, Carolyn 1869(?)-1942 ...... **TCLC 35**
See also CA 113; DLB 11

Wells, H(erbert) G(eorge)
1866-1946 .... **TCLC 6, 12, 19; DA;
SSC 6; WLC**
See also CA 110; 121; CDBLB 1914-1945;
DLB 34, 70; MTCW; SATA 20

Wells, Rosemary 1943-............ **CLC 12**
See also CA 85-88; CLR 16; MAICYA;
SAAS 1; SATA 18, 69

Welty, Eudora
1909- ...... **CLC 1, 2, 5, 14, 22, 33; DA;
SSC 1; WLC**
See also CA 9-12R; CABS 1; CANR 32;
CDALB 1941-1968; DLB 2, 102;
DLBY 87; MTCW

Wen I-to 1899-1946 .... **TCLC 28**

Wentworth, Robert
See Hamilton, Edmond

Werfel, Franz (V.) 1890-1945 ...... **TCLC 8**
See also CA 104; DLB 81, 124

Wergeland, Henrik Arnold
1808-1845 .... **NCLC 5**

Wersba, Barbara 1932-............ **CLC 30**
See also AAYA 2; CA 29-32R; CANR 16,
38; CLR 3; DLB 52; JRDA; MAICYA;
SAAS 2; SATA 1, 58

Wertmueller, Lina 1928- .... **CLC 16**
See also CA 97-100; CANR 39

Wescott, Glenway 1901-1987....... **CLC 13**
See also CA 13-16R; 121; CANR 23;
DLB 4, 9, 102

Wesker, Arnold 1932- .... **CLC 3, 5, 42**
See also CA 1-4R; CAAS 7; CANR 1, 33;
CDBLB 1960 to Present; DLB 13;
MTCW

Wesley, Richard (Errol) 1945-....... **CLC 7**
See also BW; CA 57-60; CANR 27; DLB 38

Wessel, Johan Herman 1742-1785 .... **LC 7**

West, Anthony (Panther)
1914-1987 .... **CLC 50**
See also CA 45-48; 124; CANR 3, 19;
DLB 15

West, C. P.
See Wodehouse, P(elham) G(renville)

West, (Mary) Jessamyn
1902-1984 .... **CLC 7, 17**
See also CA 9-12R; 112; CANR 27; DLB 6;
DLBY 84; MTCW; SATA 37

West, Morris L(anglo) 1916-..... **CLC 6, 33**
See also CA 5-8R; CANR 24; MTCW

West, Nathanael
1903-1940 .... **TCLC 1, 14, 44**
See also CA 104; 125; CDALB 1929-1941;
DLB 4, 9, 28; MTCW

West, Owen
See Koontz, Dean R(ay)

West, Paul 1930- .... **CLC 7, 14**
See also CA 13-16R; CAAS 7; CANR 22;
DLB 14

West, Rebecca 1892-1983 .. **CLC 7, 9, 31, 50**
See also CA 5-8R; 109; CANR 19; DLB 36;
DLBY 83; MTCW

Westall, Robert (Atkinson)
1929-1993 .... **CLC 17**
See also AAYA 12; CA 69-72; 141;
CANR 18; CLR 13; JRDA; MAICYA;
SAAS 2; SATA 23, 69; SATA-Obit 75

Westlake, Donald E(dwin)
1933- .... **CLC 7, 33**
See also CA 17-20R; CAAS 13; CANR 16,
44

Westmacott, Mary
See Christie, Agatha (Mary Clarissa)

Weston, Allen
See Norton, Andre

Wetcheek, J. L.
See Feuchtwanger, Lion

Wetering, Janwillem van de
See van de Wetering, Janwillem

Wetherell, Elizabeth
See Warner, Susan (Bogert)

Whalen, Philip 1923- .... **CLC 6, 29**
See also CA 9-12R; CANR 5, 39; DLB 16

Wharton, Edith (Newbold Jones)
1862-1937 ...... **TCLC 3, 9, 27, 53; DA;
SSC 6; WLC**
See also CA 104; 132; CDALB 1865-1917;
DLB 4, 9, 12, 78; MTCW

Wharton, James
See Mencken, H(enry) L(ouis)

Wharton, William (a pseudonym)
.... **CLC 18, 37**
See also CA 93-96; DLBY 80

Wheatley (Peters), Phillis
1754(?)-1784 .... **LC 3; BLC; DA; PC 3;
WLC**
See also CDALB 1640-1865; DLB 31, 50

Wheelock, John Hall 1886-1978.... **CLC 14**
See also CA 13-16R; 77-80; CANR 14;
DLB 45

White, E(lwyn) B(rooks)
1899-1985 .... **CLC 10, 34, 39**
See also AITN 2; CA 13-16R; 116;
CANR 16, 37; CLR 1, 21; DLB 11, 22;
MAICYA; MTCW; SATA 2, 29, 44

White, Edmund (Valentine III)
1940- .... **CLC 27**
See also AAYA 7; CA 45-48; CANR 3, 19,
36; MTCW

White, Patrick (Victor Martindale)
1912-1990 .. **CLC 3, 4, 5, 7, 9, 18, 65, 69**
See also CA 81-84; 132; CANR 43; MTCW

White, Phyllis Dorothy James 1920-
See James, P. D.
See also CA 21-24R; CANR 17, 43; MTCW

White, T(erence) H(anbury)
1906-1964 .... **CLC 30**
See also CA 73-76; CANR 37; JRDA;
MAICYA; SATA 12

White, Terence de Vere 1912-...... **CLC 49**
See also CA 49-52; CANR 3

White, Walter F(rancis)
1893-1955 .... **TCLC 15**
See also White, Walter
See also CA 115; 124; DLB 51

White, William Hale 1831-1913
See Rutherford, Mark
See also CA 121

Whitehead, E(dward) A(nthony)
1933- .... **CLC 5**
See also CA 65-68

Whitemore, Hugh (John) 1936-..... **CLC 37**
See also CA 132

Whitman, Sarah Helen (Power)
1803-1878 .... **NCLC 19**
See also DLB 1

Whitman, Walt(er)
1819-1892 ..... **NCLC 4, 31; DA; PC 3;
WLC**
See also CDALB 1640-1865; DLB 3, 64;
SATA 20

Whitney, Phyllis A(yame) 1903-.... **CLC 42**
See also AITN 2; BEST 90:3; CA 1-4R;
CANR 3, 25, 38; JRDA; MAICYA;
SATA 1, 30

Whittemore, (Edward) Reed (Jr.)
1919- .... **CLC 4**
See also CA 9-12R; CAAS 8; CANR 4;
DLB 5

Whittier, John Greenleaf
1807-1892 .... **NCLC 8**
See also CDALB 1640-1865; DLB 1

Whittlebot, Hernia
See Coward, Noel (Peirce)

Wicker, Thomas Grey 1926-
See Wicker, Tom
See also CA 65-68; CANR 21

Wicker, Tom .... **CLC 7**
See also Wicker, Thomas Grey

Wideman, John Edgar
1941- .... **CLC 5, 34, 36, 67; BLC**
See also BW; CA 85-88; CANR 14, 42;
DLB 33

Wiebe, Rudy (Henry) 1934-... **CLC 6, 11, 14**
See also CA 37-40R; CANR 42; DLB 60

Wieland, Christoph Martin
1733-1813 .... **NCLC 17**
See also DLB 97

Wieners, John 1934-............... **CLC 7**
See also CA 13-16R; DLB 16

Wiesel, Elie(zer)
1928- .... **CLC 3, 5, 11, 37; DA**
See also AAYA 7; AITN 1; CA 5-8R;
CAAS 4; CANR 8, 40; DLB 83;
DLBY 87; MTCW; SATA 56

Wiggins, Marianne 1947-.......... **CLC 57**
See also BEST 89:3; CA 130

Wight, James Alfred 1916-
See Herriot, James
See also CA 77-80; SATA 44, 55

Wilbur, Richard (Purdy)
1921- .... **CLC 3, 6, 9, 14, 53; DA**
See also CA 1-4R; CABS 2; CANR 2, 29;
DLB 5; MTCW; SATA 9

Wild, Peter 1940-................. **CLC 14**
See also CA 37-40R; DLB 5

Wilde, Oscar (Fingal O'Flahertie Wills)
1854(?)-1900 .... **TCLC 1, 8, 23, 41; DA;
SSC 11; WLC**
See also CA 104; 119; CDBLB 1890-1914;
DLB 10, 19, 34, 57, 141; SATA 24

Wolff, Sonia
See Levitin, Sonia (Wolff)

Wolff, Tobias (Jonathan Ansell)
1945- . . . . **CLC 39, 64**
See also BEST 90:2; CA 114; 117; DLB 130

Wolfram von Eschenbach
c. 1170-c. 1220 . . . . **CMLC 5**
See also DLB 138

Wolitzer, Hilma 1930- . . . . **CLC 17**
See also CA 65-68; CANR 18, 40; SATA 31

Wollstonecraft, Mary 1759-1797 . . . . . . **LC 5**
See also CDBLB 1789-1832; DLB 39, 104

Wonder, Stevie . . . . **CLC 12**
See also Morris, Steveland Judkins

Wong, Jade Snow 1922- . . . . **CLC 17**
See also CA 109

Woodcott, Keith
See Brunner, John (Kilian Houston)

Woodruff, Robert W.
See Mencken, H(enry) L(ouis)

Woolf, (Adeline) Virginia
1882-1941 . . . . . . **TCLC 1, 5, 20, 43; DA;**
SSC 7; WLC
See also CA 104; 130; CDBLB 1914-1945;
DLB 36, 100; DLBD 10; MTCW

Woollcott, Alexander (Humphreys)
1887-1943 . . . . **TCLC 5**
See also CA 105; DLB 29

Woolrich, Cornell 1903-1968 . . . . **CLC 77**
See also Hopley-Woolrich, Cornell George

Wordsworth, Dorothy
1771-1855 . . . . **NCLC 25**
See also DLB 107

Wordsworth, William
1770-1850 . . . . **NCLC 12, 38; DA; PC 4;**
WLC
See also CDBLB 1789-1832; DLB 93, 107

Wouk, Herman 1915- . . . . **CLC 1, 9, 38**
See also CA 5-8R; CANR 6, 33; DLBY 82;
MTCW

Wright, Charles (Penzel, Jr.)
1935- . . . . **CLC 6, 13, 28**
See also CA 29-32R; CAAS 7; CANR 23,
36; DLBY 82; MTCW

Wright, Charles Stevenson
1932- . . . . **CLC 49; BLC 3**
See also BW; CA 9-12R; CANR 26;
DLB 33

Wright, Jack R.
See Harris, Mark

Wright, James (Arlington)
1927-1980 . . . . **CLC 3, 5, 10, 28**
See also AITN 2; CA 49-52; 97-100;
CANR 4, 34; DLB 5; MTCW

Wright, Judith (Arandell)
1915- . . . . **CLC 11, 53**
See also CA 13-16R; CANR 31; MTCW;
SATA 14

Wright, L(aurali) R. 1939- . . . . **CLC 44**
See also CA 138

Wright, Richard (Nathaniel)
1908-1960 . . . . **CLC 1, 3, 4, 9, 14, 21, 48,**
74; BLC; DA; SSC 2; WLC
See also AAYA 5; BW; CA 108;
CDALB 1929-1941; DLB 76, 102;
DLBD 2; MTCW

Wright, Richard B(ruce) 1937- . . . . . . **CLC 6**
See also CA 85-88; DLB 53

Wright, Rick 1945- . . . . **CLC 35**
See also Pink Floyd

Wright, Rowland
See Wells, Carolyn

Wright, Stephen 1946- . . . . **CLC 33**

Wright, Willard Huntington 1888-1939
See Van Dine, S. S.
See also CA 115

Wright, William 1930- . . . . **CLC 44**
See also CA 53-56; CANR 7, 23

Wu Ch'eng-en 1500(?)-1582(?) . . . . **LC 7**

Wu Ching-tzu 1701-1754 . . . . **LC 2**

Wurlitzer, Rudolph 1938(?)- . . . **CLC 2, 4, 15**
See also CA 85-88

Wycherley, William 1641-1715 . . . . **LC 8, 21**
See also CDBLB 1660-1789; DLB 80

Wylie, Elinor (Morton Hoyt)
1885-1928 . . . . **TCLC 8**
See also CA 105; DLB 9, 45

Wylie, Philip (Gordon) 1902-1971 . . . **CLC 43**
See also CA 21-22; 33-36R; CAP 2; DLB 9

Wyndham, John
See Harris, John (Wyndham Parkes Lucas)
Beynon

Wyss, Johann David Von
1743-1818 . . . . **NCLC 10**
See also JRDA; MAICYA; SATA 27, 29

Yakumo Koizumi
See Hearn, (Patricio) Lafcadio (Tessima
Carlos)

Yanez, Jose Donoso
See Donoso (Yanez), Jose

Yanovsky, Basile S.
See Yanovsky, V(assily) S(emenovich)

Yanovsky, V(assily) S(emenovich)
1906-1989 . . . . **CLC 2, 18**
See also CA 97-100; 129

Yates, Richard 1926-1992 . . . . . **CLC 7, 8, 23**
See also CA 5-8R; 139; CANR 10, 43;
DLB 2; DLBY 81, 92

Yeats, W. B.
See Yeats, William Butler

Yeats, William Butler
1865-1939 . . . . . **TCLC 1, 11, 18, 31; DA;**
WLC
See also CA 104; 127; CDBLB 1890-1914;
DLB 10, 19, 98; MTCW

Yehoshua, A(braham) B.
1936- . . . . **CLC 13, 31**
See also CA 33-36R; CANR 43

Yep, Laurence Michael 1948- . . . . . . **CLC 35**
See also AAYA 5; CA 49-52; CANR 1;
CLR 3, 17; DLB 52; JRDA; MAICYA;
SATA 7, 69

Yerby, Frank G(arvin)
1916-1991 . . . . **CLC 1, 7, 22; BLC**
See also BW; CA 9-12R; 136; CANR 16;
DLB 76; MTCW

Yesenin, Sergei Alexandrovich
See Esenin, Sergei (Alexandrovich)

Yevtushenko, Yevgeny (Alexandrovich)
1933- . . . . **CLC 1, 3, 13, 26, 51**
See also CA 81-84; CANR 33; MTCW

Yezierska, Anzia 1885(?)-1970 . . . . . **CLC 46**
See also CA 126; 89-92; DLB 28; MTCW

Yglesias, Helen 1915- . . . . **CLC 7, 22**
See also CA 37-40R; CANR 15; MTCW

Yokomitsu Riichi 1898-1947 . . . . . . **TCLC 47**

Yonge, Charlotte (Mary)
1823-1901 . . . . **TCLC 48**
See also CA 109; DLB 18; SATA 17

York, Jeremy
See Creasey, John

York, Simon
See Heinlein, Robert A(nson)

Yorke, Henry Vincent 1905-1974 . . . **CLC 13**
See also Green, Henry
See also CA 85-88; 49-52

Young, Al(bert James)
1939- . . . . **CLC 19; BLC**
See also BW; CA 29-32R; CANR 26;
DLB 33

Young, Andrew (John) 1885-1971 . . . . **CLC 5**
See also CA 5-8R; CANR 7, 29

Young, Collier
See Bloch, Robert (Albert)

Young, Edward 1683-1765 . . . . **LC 3**
See also DLB 95

Young, Marguerite 1909- . . . . **CLC 82**
See also CA 13-16; CAP 1

Young, Neil 1945- . . . . **CLC 17**
See also CA 110

Yourcenar, Marguerite
1903-1987 . . . . **CLC 19, 38, 50**
See also CA 69-72; CANR 23; DLB 72;
DLBY 88; MTCW

Yurick, Sol 1925- . . . . **CLC 6**
See also CA 13-16R; CANR 25

Zabolotskii, Nikolai Alekseevich
1903-1958 . . . . **TCLC 52**
See also CA 116

Zamiatin, Yevgenii
See Zamyatin, Evgeny Ivanovich

Zamyatin, Evgeny Ivanovich
1884-1937 . . . . **TCLC 8, 37**
See also CA 105

Zangwill, Israel 1864-1926 . . . . **TCLC 16**
See also CA 109; DLB 10, 135

Zappa, Francis Vincent, Jr. 1940-1993
See Zappa, Frank
See also CA 108; 143

Zappa, Frank . . . . **CLC 17**
See also Zappa, Francis Vincent, Jr.

Zaturenska, Marya 1902-1982 . . . . **CLC 6, 11**
See also CA 13-16R; 105; CANR 22

Zelazny, Roger (Joseph) 1937- . . . . . **CLC 21**
See also AAYA 7; CA 21-24R; CANR 26;
DLB 8; MTCW; SATA 39, 57

Zhdanov, Andrei A(lexandrovich)
1896-1948 .... **TCLC 18**
See also CA 117

Zhukovsky, Vasily 1783-1852 .... **NCLC 35**

Ziegenhagen, Eric .... **CLC 55**

Zimmer, Jill Schary
See Robinson, Jill

Zimmerman, Robert
See Dylan, Bob

Zindel, Paul 1936- .... **CLC 6, 26; DA**
See also AAYA 2; CA 73-76; CANR 31;
CLR 3; DLB 7, 52; JRDA; MAICYA;
MTCW; SATA 16, 58

Zinov'Ev, A. A.
See Zinoviev, Alexander (Aleksandrovich)

Zinoviev, Alexander (Aleksandrovich)
1922- .... **CLC 19**
See also CA 116; 133; CAAS 10

Zoilus
See Lovecraft, H(oward) P(hillips)

Zola, Emile (Edouard Charles Antoine)
1840-1902 ...... **TCLC 1, 6, 21, 41; DA;**
WLC
See also CA 104; 138; DLB 123

Zoline, Pamela 1941- .... **CLC 62**

Zorrilla y Moral, Jose 1817-1893 .. **NCLC 6**

Zoshchenko, Mikhail (Mikhailovich)
1895-1958 .... **TCLC 15; SSC 15**
See also CA 115

Zuckmayer, Carl 1896-1977 .... **CLC 18**
See also CA 69-72; DLB 56, 124

Zuk, Georges
See Skelton, Robin

Zukofsky, Louis
1904-1978 .... **CLC 1, 2, 4, 7, 11, 18**
See also CA 9-12R; 77-80; CANR 39;
DLB 5; MTCW

Zweig, Paul 1935-1984 .... **CLC 34, 42**
See also CA 85-88; 113

Zweig, Stefan 1881-1942 .... **TCLC 17**
See also CA 112; DLB 81, 118

Literary Criticism Series
Cumulative Topic Index

This index lists all topic entries in the Gale Literary Criticism Series *Classical and Medieval Literature Criticism, Contemporary Literary Criticism, Literature Criticism from 1400 to 1800, Nineteenth-Century Literature Criticism,* and *Twentieth-Century Literary Criticism.*

Topic Index

Young Playwrights Festival
    1988—CLC 55: 376-81
    1989—CLC 59: 398-403
    1990—CLC 65: 444-48

CLC Cumulative Nationality Index

Nationality Index

Nationality Index

Nationality Index

Nationality Index

CLC-83 Title Index

Title Index

ISBN 0-8103-4991-4

90000

9 780810 349919